REPRESENTATIVE ENGLISH PLAYS

REPRESENTATIVE ENGLISH PLAYS

FROM THE MIRACLE PLAYS TO PINERO

EDITED WITH INTRODUCTIONS AND NOTES

BY

J. S. P. TATLOCK

AND THE LATE

R. G. MARTIN

SECOND EDITION

REVISED AND ENLARGED

APPLETON-CENTURY-CROFTS, INC.

New York

695-22

PRINTED IN U. S. A.

E–86718

D. M.

M. F. T.

J. W. T.

Vide quattro stelle
Non viste mai fuor che alla prima gente

PREFACE

In the present collection, for the first time, representative English plays from the earliest period almost to the present day have been included in one volume. In a single volume of readable form it is obviously impossible to include all celebrated or influential plays, or plays of all types. Some long periods, such as the nineteenth century, with relatively few plays of high excellence, are difficult to represent adequately in so small a collection. As to principles of choice, a collection merely of the best or at present most attractive plays would lack balance and meaning for the student; one merely of typical plays would lack interest for the reader. Choice must be made on practical and not purely theoretical grounds, by a series of checks and balances; now one consideration will prevail, now another. Probably no two editors would independently agree, and it is impossible to content every reader. In the present work the principal considerations have been excellence, influence and historical importance, representative and typical character (for a body of drama or for an age), and the importance of the type. Occasionally the mere celebrity of a play or its author has been allowed to turn the scale. Lyly's *Mother Bombie* was chosen, rather than one of his other plays, as exemplifying the strong Latin influence which helped to transform the medieval into the modern drama; Marlowe's *Edward II* as one of his best plays and as exemplifying the plays on English history written by so many besides Shakespeare; Dryden's *Conquest of Granada* rather than *All for Love* as being more influential, original and characteristic; Bulwer's *Lady of Lyons* as extremely popular in its day, and as characteristic of a long and barren period which it would be unsatisfying to leave almost unrepresented. It is unnecessary to explain the omission of the everywhere-accessible Shakespeare; in so small a collection it was the only way to do him full justice and honor.

The editorial matter is meant to be, as Bacon said of his Essays, "certain brief notes, set down rather significantly than curiously." The introductions, while giving the necessary facts, are devoted rather to criticism and interpretation of the plays in themselves and in reference to their time. The foot-notes are meant simply to answer tersely questions which any attentive reader not familiar with a play or with the language of its time is likely to ask. The brief bibliography mentions general works, important or convenient editions, some historical and critical studies, and biographies. Here is recorded the source for the text of the several plays, and also, for supplementary reading, other plays of like character, and a few of types unrepresented in the collection. All pains have been taken to make the texts both accurate and readable; in no case have careless and popular modern editions been followed, yet in general textual problems and apparatus have been disregarded. Even in the medieval texts no changes have been made, except as consistently as possible to modernize the spelling (even at the cost of slightly increasing the original roughness of verse and rime); the reader may rest assured that he is getting, as the modern reader very properly wishes, that which the author wrote and that only. Elsewhere also the spelling, punctuation and capitalizing have been modernized, and some latitude has been allowed as to stage-directions. It should be added that Mr. Martin was mainly responsible for the editing of the medieval and Elizabethan plays, except for the introductions to Jonson and Webster; and Mr. Tatlock is responsible for those and for the remainder of the volume.

It is a pleasure to thank those who have lightened and otherwise assisted the editors' work. President W. A. Neilson generously allowed them to make use of certain of his texts;[1] and Marjorie Fenton Tatlock gave frequent assistance and advice. Professors J. M. Manly, R. W. Bond, and G. R. Noyes, C. F. McClumpha Esqre., G. A. Aitken Esqre., M. V. O., and Professor Dr. F. Lindner granted permission to use texts of the miracle plays and Lyly, of Dryden, Otway, Steele, and Fielding; and Messrs. D. C. Heath and Co., to use texts of Lillo and Robertson. Professor Jane J. Swenarton of Vassar College has given well-informed and judicious help in revising for this second edition.

J. S. P. T.

1 In *The Chief Elizabethan Dramatists* (Houghton, Mifflin and Co., 1911).

TABLE OF CONTENTS

REPRESENTATIVE ENGLISH PLAYS

REPRESENTATIVE ENGLISH PLAYS

I. THE MIDDLE AGES

MIRACLE PLAYS

Pope Urban IV, when he instituted in 1264 the church festival of Corpus Christi, became a real though unwitting patron of the drama. On the continent, Corpus Christi Day, the Thursday after Trinity Sunday, was soon established as an occasion for presenting religious plays. In England especially was the day notable, for the trade guilds, the associations of craftsmen roughly corresponding to the trade unions of our day, adopted it as their chief holiday, and assisted the church in its celebration with a procession through the town. In another way also they came to the aid of the church by taking over a form of activity which had for some time been growing in disfavor with the church authorities; namely, the performance of the liturgical plays. Originally introduced at Christmas and Easter for the edification of ignorant audiences, these became so popular that their primary didactic purpose was in danger of being forgotten. From motives in which religion and business — for the church feast brought visitors and trade to town — were oddly mixed, the guilds added pageantry to their procession, and were soon giving performances on a scale more sumptuous than the church had ever reached.

By the time that the miracle, or, as they are sometimes called, mystery, plays passed from the hands of Mother Church into the care of the guilds, they had already developed into a great drama of many acts, covering scriptural and apocryphal history from the Fall of the Angels to the Last Judgment. They were, therefore, well adapted for guild performance. Each guild took one section of the Bible story and tried to outdo its rivals in effectiveness of presentation. A quaint humor often marked the distribution of the separate plays among the various guilds. It is not difficult to see why, in the York plays, the Shipwrights undertook the Building of the Ark, and the Fishmongers the Flood; nor why in the same cycle the Goldsmiths selected the story of the Three Kings, with their offerings of gold and spices; the Vintners, the Miracle at Cana; the Bakers, the Last Supper. To the Tanners was assigned the Fall of Lucifer and the torments of the fallen angels in hell, where the tanning process was likely to be thorough; while the Cooks, well trained in taking things from the fire, could present, more fittingly than any other craft, the Harrying of Hell.

The performances took place upon pageant wagons, which could be drawn from place to place through the town. At street corners or open squares stations were assigned for the acting of the plays. When the play of the creation had been acted at the first station the pageant wagon moved on to the second station, while the story of the fall of Adam and Eve took its place at the first station, and so on. This method made possible the simultaneous production of many plays, each little audience, of course, seeing the entire sequence in the proper order. The wagons seem usually to have been built with two platforms, the lower curtained in and serving as a dressing room for the actors, the upper as the stage. Costumes and properties were sometimes handsome and costly, but in general scenery and properties were of the simplest. Among the most prominent was Hell mouth, a great gaping pair of jaws at one side of the stage, painted flame color and belching forth the smoke of the torment, from which leaped forth the Devil with his boisterous "Ho! Ho!" and into which he pitched the lost souls with his wooden pitchfork and himself plunged at the end of the play. Some attempt was made at appropriateness of costume: God appeared in white leather, with gilded face and hair, the Devil in black leather, with full equipment of horns, hoofs, and a tail. But Herod boasted the full panoply of a knight of chivalry, and in general anachronism of attire as well as of speech was rampant.

We have records of such dramatic activity lasting from the thirteenth until far into the sixteenth century, all over England, as well as in Scotland, Wales, and Ireland. Not only the cathedral towns but market towns and even villages had their collective or individual miracle plays. The greatest activity, however, seems to have been localized in certain places. There are extant manuscripts, the earliest belonging to the fifteenth century, for four great cycles of miracle plays: the York, Chester, Towneley or Wakefield, and Coventry cycles. While each has its individual characteristics, all cover about the same ground and influences of one cycle upon another are evident. Of the authors practically nothing is known, but we infer that they were churchmen. What we know of the history of the miracles makes it seem improbable that any one man should have created all the plays of a cycle. As they come down to us they may rather represent the bringing together and amplification of the work of many hands, and such a cycle as that of York, with its forty-eight episodes, may have been in process of development for decades before its text was reduced to the comparative orderliness of our manuscript version. Occasionally, as in some plays of the Towneley cycle, there are manifest excellences in the handling of situation, the characterization, and the quality of the verse, which lead us to infer composition by a hand more competent than that of the average clerical playwright.

A modern reader is likely to underestimate the dramatic effectiveness of the miracle plays. Their writers had, of course, little or no apprehension of the niceties of technique — they were concerned chiefly with making the teaching of the play so plain that the most ignorant spectator must understand; hence the wearisome repetitions, the expounding of Christian doctrines in long didactic passages which sadly interrupt the action, the introduction of Doctor or Expositor to drive the moral home. The literary value is mostly not great. But the plays possess the virtues of strength and sincerity and human interest. With no finesse but sometimes with power they present some of the great episodes in the Bible story, in particular those of Christ's life and passion. By frequent bits of homely realism they made their audiences realize the humanness of the Bible figures, and that was a useful service. The occasional coarseness of language and situation should not blind us to the simple reverence of purpose and treatment. The impressiveness of the Passion Play at Oberammergau is sufficient evidence that the theory of the miracle play is sound.

The three plays which follow fairly represent the miracle at its best. Though the long didactic beginning of the Towneley *Noah's Flood* is characteristic in its dullness, the play brightens up at once when Noah returns to the bosom of his family. From the rank and file of miracle personages a few stand out with special clearness, usually because the spirit of comedy has touched them into life. Of these Noah's wife seems to have been a particular favorite, for in the York and Chester cycles she plays the shrew as she does here, and in them also the taming of the shrew is done in the same rough-and-tumble fashion. One of the unintentionally amusing things about the play is the naïveté with which the passage of time is recorded, (e. g., on p. 11). The local allusion of Noah's wife ("Stafford blue," p. 8), and the oaths by *Peter* (p. 10), *Mary* (p. 8), and "God's pain" (i.e., Christ's sufferings on the cross, p. 8), illustrate the lack of historical sense.

The Brome play is so called because the manuscript was found in Brome Hall, Suffolk. *Abraham and Isaac* is the most truly pathetic of all the miracle plays. The scene is pathetic rather than tragic because, since Abraham is from the first determined to obey the will of God, his natural revulsion against killing his son never reaches the intensity of the struggle with fate, involved in true tragedy. But this is as close an approach to tragedy as we find at this stage of the drama. Despite the ineptitude and slowness of the beginning, the playwright really understands how to handle his material in such a way as to produce on the audience the effect he desires. A briefer treatment would have been better — to hold the situation merely to the point of maximum emotional response, but the tension of suspense is undeniable. The characterization is not quite individual; we feel about Abraham and Isaac that they are rather types of parenthood and childhood than an individual father and an individual son. The child's actual physical terror at the bright sword and his messages to his mother are notable as showing how the miracle authors sometimes visualized and humanized their material.

The Towneley *Second Shepherds' Play* (*Second* because the Towneley cycle contains two versions of the announcement to the shepherds) is the flower of the miracle plays. Here is an admirable acting play, with plot, characterization, atmosphere. The exposition is clear and reasonably rapid, providing a neat differentiation of the three shepherds as they make their appearance one after another. Mak and Gill are masterpieces in miniature of comic characterization, done with deftness and gusto. The action mounts steadily to the climax; the understanding of the value of suspense at the climactic point, when the discomfited shepherds actually leave the house, only to return in response to the youngest shepherd's kindly thought of a gift to the child is proof enough that the man who made this play was a real dramatist. After the punishment of Mak there is an artless transition to the angels' song and the traditional bit of the gifts to the Christ child. The blending of Yorkshire setting and figures with the Bible story is naïve and delightful. This episode of Mak is true farce comedy, comedy better than anything else England was to produce till the middle of the sixteenth century.

MIRACLE PLAYS

NOAH'S FLOOD

NAMES OF THE CHARACTERS

GOD.	FIRST SON.	FIRST WIFE.
NOAH.	SECOND SON.	SECOND WIFE.
NOAH'S WIFE.	THIRD SON.	THIRD WIFE.

Noah. Mightful God very, maker of all that is,
Three persons without nay,[1] one God in endless bliss,
Thou made both night and day, beast, fowl, and fish;
All creatures that live may, wrought thou at thy wish,
As thou well might;
The sun, the moon, verament,[2]
Thou made, the firmament,
The stars also, full fervent,
To shine thou made full bright.

Angels thou made full even, all orders that is,
To have the bliss in heaven: this did thou more and less,
Full marvelous to neven;[3] yet was there unkindness
More by folds seven than I can well express.
For why?
Of all angels in brightness
God gave Lucifer most lightness;
Yet proudly he flitted[4] his dais,
And set him even him by.

He thought himself as worthy as him that him made
In brightness, in beauty; therefore he him degraded,
Put him in a low degree soon after, in a braid,[5]
Him and all his meinie,[6] where he may be unglad
For ever.
Shall they never win away
Hence unto doomsday,
But burn in bale[7] for ay;
Shall they never dissever.

Soon after that gracious lord to his likeness made man,
That place to be restored even as he began,
Of the Trinity by accord, Adam, and Eve, that woman.
To multiply without discord in paradise put he them,
And sithen[8] to both
Gave in commandment
On the tree of life to lay no hand.
But yet the false fiend
Made him with man wroth,

Enticed man to gluttony, stirred him to sin in pride.
But in paradise securely[9] might no sin abide,
And therefore man full hastily was put out in that tide,
In woe and wandreth[10] for to be, pains[11] full unrid[12]
To know,
First in earth, sithen in hell
With fiends for to dwell,
But[13] he his mercy mell[14]
To those that will him trow.[15]

Oil of mercy he us hight,[16] as I have heard rede,[17]
To every living wight that would love him and dread;
But now before his sight every living lede,[18]
Most part day and night, sin in word and deed,
Full bold;

1 denial.
2 truly.
3 name.
4 forsook.
5 moment.
6 company.
7 torment.
8 afterward.
9 certainly.
10 wretchedness.
11 MS. *in pains*.
12 cruel.
13 unless.
14 interpose.
15 believe.
16 promised.
17 say.
18 people.

Some in pride, ire, and envy,
Some in covetyse [19] and gluttony,
Some in sloth and lechery,
And otherwise many fold.

Therefore I dread lest God on us will take vengeance,
For sin is now allowed without any repentance;
Six hundred years and odd have I, without distance,[20]
On earth, as any sod, lived with great grievance
Alway;
And now I wax old,
Sick, sorry, and cold,
As muck upon mould
I wither away.

But yet will I cry for mercy and call:
Noah thy servant am I, Lord over all!
Therefore me and my fry,[21] shall with me fall,
Save from villainy, and bring to thy hall
In heaven,
And keep me from sin
This world within;
Comely King of mankind,
I pray thee hear my steven! [22]

God. Since I have made all-thing that is living,
Duke, emperor, and king, with mine own hand,
For to have their liking by sea and by sand,
Every man to my bidding should be bowing
Full fervent,
That made man such a creature,
Fairest of favor;
Man must love me paramour,[23]
By reason, and repent.

Methought I showed man love when I made him to be
All angels above, like to the Trinity;
And now in great reproof full low lies he
On earth, himself to stuff with sin that displeases me
Most of all;
Vengeance will I take
On earth for sin's sake,
My grame [24] thus will I wake,
Both of [25] great and small.

I repent full sore that ever made I man;
By me he sets no store, and I am his sovereign.
I will destroy therefore both beast, man, and woman;
All shall perish, less and more; that bargain may they ban,[26]
That ill has done.
On earth I see right nought
But sin that is unsought; [27]
Of those that well has wrought
Find I but a few.

Therefore shall I fordo [28] all this middle-earth [29]
With floods that shall flow, and run with hideous rerd; [30]
I have good cause thereto: for me no man is afeared.
As I say shall I do: of vengeance draw my sword,
And make end
Of all that bears life,
Save Noah and his wife,
For they would never strive
With me nor me offend.

[To] him to mickle win [31] hastily will I go,
To Noah my servant. ere I blin,[32] to warn him of his woe.
On earth I see but sin running to and fro,
Among both more and min,[33] each one other's foe
With all their intent;
All shall I fordo
With floods that shall flow,
Work shall I them woe,
That will not repent.

Noah, my friend, I thee command, from cares thee to keel,[34]
A ship that thou ordain [35] of nail and board full well.
Thou was alway well working, to me true as steel,
To my bidding obedient; friendship shall thou feel
To meed.[36]
Of length thy ship be
Three hundred cubits, warn I thee,
Of height even thirty,
Of fifty also in breadth.

19 covetousness; the seven deadly sins are here listed.
20 without dispute, beyond doubt.
21 offspring; understand *who* before *shall*.
22 voice.
23 as a lover
24 anger.
25 against.
26 rue.
27 unatoned.
28 destroy.
29 world.
30 uproar.
31 joy.
32 cease.
33 less.
34 cool, assuage.
35 make.
36 reward.

Anoint thy ship with pitch and tar without and also within,
The water out to spar:[37] this is a noble gin;[38]
Look no man thee mar. Three chess[39] chambers begin;
Thou must spend many a spar this work ere thou win
To end fully.
Make in thy ship also
Parlors one or two,
And houses of office mo,[40]
For beasts that there must be.

One cubit in height a window shall thou make;
On the side a door with sleight[41] beneath shall thou take;
With thee shall no man fight, nor do thee no kind wrake.[42]
When all is done thus right, thy wife, that is thy make,[43]
Take in to thee;
Thy sons of good fame,
Shem, Japhet, and Ham,
Take in also them,
Their wives also three.

For all shall be fordone that live on land but ye,
With floods that from above shall fall, and that plenty;
It shall begin full soon to rain incessantly,
After days seven be done, and endure days forty,
Without fail.
Take to thy ship also,
Of each kind, beasts two,
Male and female, but no mo,
Ere thou pull up thy sail.

For they may thee avail when all this thing is wrought;
Stuff thy ship with victual, for hunger that ye perish not.
Of beasts, fowl, and cattle, for them have thou in thought;
For them is my counsel, that some succor be sought
In haste;
They must have corn and hay,
And other meat alway.
Do now as I thee say,
In the name of the Holy Ghost.

Noah. Ah, benedicite![44] What art thou that thus
Tells afore that shall be? Thou art full marvelous!
Tell me, for charity, thy name so gracious.

God. My name is of dignity, and also full glorious
To know.
I am God most mighty,
One God in Trinity,
Made thee and each man to be;
To love me well thou ought.

Noah. I thank thee, Lord so dear, that would vouchsafe
Thus low to appear to a simple knave;
Bless us, Lord, here, for charity I it crave;
The better may we steer the ship that we shall have,
Certain.

God. Noah, to thee and to thy fry
My blessing grant I:
Ye shall wax and multiply,
And fill the earth again,

When all these floods are past and fully gone away.

Noah. Lord, homeward will I haste as fast as that I may.
My [wife][45] will I fraist[46] what she will say,
And I am aghast that we get some fray
Betwixt us both;
For she is full teethy,[47]
For little oft angry,
If anything wrong be,
Soon is she wroth.

Then he goes to his wife.

God speed, dear wife; how fare ye?

Wife. Now, as ever might I thrive, the worse I thee see!
Do tell me belive,[48] where has thou thus long been?
To death may we drive, or life for thee,[49]
For want.
When we sweat or swink,[50]
Thou does what thou think,
Yet of meat and of drink
Have we very scant.

Noah. Wife, we are hard stead with tidings new.

37 shut.
38 device.
39 tiers of.
40 more.
41 skill.
42 kind of wrong.
43 mate.
44 bless me!
45 missing in MS.
46 ask.
47 testy.
48 quickly.
49 for all you care
50 work.

Wife. But thou were worthy be clad in Stafford blue,[51]
For thou art alway adread, be it false or true.
But God knows I am led, and that may I rue,
Full ill;
For I dare be thy borrow,[52]
From even unto morrow
Thou speaks ever of sorrow;
God send thee once thy fill!

We women may wary [53] all ill husbands;
I have one, by Mary! that loosed me of my bands!
If he teen [54] I must tarry, howsoever it stands,
With semblance full sorry, wringing both my hands
For dread.
But yet other while,
What with game and with guile,
I shall smite and smile,
And quit him his meed.[55]

Noah. We! hold thy tongue, ramskyt, or I shall thee still!
Wife. By my thrift, if thou smite, I shall turn thee until!
Noah. We shall assay as tight. Have at thee, Gill!
Upon the bone shall it bite.
Wife. Ah, so! Marry, thou smites ill!
But I suppose
I shall not in thy debt
Flit of this flet! [56]
Take thee there a languet [57]
To tie up thy hose!

Noah. Ah! wilt thou so? Marry, that is mine!
Wife. Thou shall [58] three for two, I swear by God's pain!
Noah. And I shall quit thee then, in faith, ere syne.[59]
Wife. Out upon thee, ho!
Noah. Thou can both bite and whine
With a rerd! [60]
For all if she strike
Yet fast will she screech;
In faith, I hold none [such]
In all middle-earth.

But I will keep charity, for I have at do.[61]
Wife. Here shall no man tarry thee; I pray thee, go to!
Full well may we miss thee, as ever have I ro.[62]
To spin will I dress [63] me.
Noah. We! farewell, lo!
But, wife,
Pray for me busily
Till eft [64] I come unto thee.
Wife. Even as thou prays for me,
As ever might I thrive.

Noah. I tarry full long from my work, I trow;
Now my gear will I fang,[65] and thitherward draw.
I may full ill go, the sooth for to know;
But if [66] God help among, I may sit down daw [67]
To ken.
Now assay will I
How I can of wrightry; [68]
In nomine Patris, et Filii,
Et Spiritus Sancti, Amen.

To begin of this tree my bones will I bend;
I trow from the Trinity succor will be sent.
It fares full fair, methinks, this work to my hand;
Now blessed be he that this can amend.
Lo, here the length,
Three hundred cubits evenly;
Of breadth, lo, is it fifty;
The height is even thirty
Cubits full strength.[69]

Now my gown will I cast, and work in my coat;
Make will I the mast, ere I flit one foot.
Ah, my back, I trow, will burst! this is a sorry note!
It is wonder that I last, such an old dote,[70]
All dold,[71]
To begin such a work,
My bones are so stark,
No wonder if they wark,[72]
For I am full old.

51 beaten black and blue.
52 pledge.
53 curse.
54 grieve.
55 give him his deserts.
56 flee from this dwelling.
57 thong.
58 understand *have*.
59 long.
60 cf. n. 30.
61 work to do.
62 rest.
63 prepare.
64 again.
65 take.
66 unless.
67 a sluggard.
68 carpentry.
69 Qy. *streght?*
70 dotard.
71 stupid. stiff.
72 ache.

The top and the sail both will I make,
The helm and the castle [73] also will I take;
To drive each nail will I not forsake;
This gear may never fail, that dare I undertake
Anon.
This is a noble gin:
These nails so they run
Through more and min,
These boards each one;

Window and door, even as he said,
Three chess [74] chambers, they are well made,
Pitch and tar full sure thereupon laid.
This will ever endure, therefore am I paid;
For why?
It is better wrought
Than I could have thought;
Him that made all of nought
I thank only.

Now will I hie me and nothing be lither,[75]
My wife and my meinie to bring even hither.
Tent [76] hither tidily, wife, and consider;
Hence must us flee, all sam [77] together
In haste.
Wife. Why, sir, what ails you?
Who is that assails you?
To flee it avails you
And [78] ye be aghast.

Noah. There is yarn on the reel other, my dame.
Wife. Tell me that each a deal,[79] else get ye blame.
Noah. He that cares may keel, blessed be his name!
He has [spoken] [80] for our sele [81] to shield us from shame,
And said,
All this world about
With floods so stout,
That shall run in a rout,
Shall be overlaid.

He said all shall be slain but only we,
Our bairns that are bain,[82] and their wives three;
A ship he bade me ordain to save us and our fee; [83]
Therefore with all our main thank we that free
Beeter of bale.[84]
Hie us fast, go we thither.
Wife. I wot never whither;
I daze and I didder [85]
For fear of that tale.

Noah. Be not afeared; have done. Truss sam our gear,
That we be there ere noon without more dere.[86]
1 Son. It shall be done full soon. Brothers, help to bear.
2 Son. Full long shall I not hone [87] to do my dever,[88]
Brother Shem.
3 Son. Without any yelp,[89]
At my might shall I help.
Wife. Yet for dread of a skelp,[90]
Help well thy dam.

Noah. Now are we there as we should be;
Do get in our gear, our cattle and fee,
Into this vessel here, my children free.
Wife. I was never barred ere, as ever might I thee,[91]
In such an hostry [92] as this.
In faith, I can not find
Which is before, which is behind.
But shall we here be pinned,
Noah, as have thou bliss?

Noah. Dame, as it is skill,[93] here must us abide grace;
Therefore, wife, with good will come into this place.
Wife. Sir, for Jack nor for Jill will I turn my face,
Till I have on this hill spun a space
On my rock.[94]
Well were he might get me!
Now will I down set me;
Yet rede [95] I no man let [96] me,
For dread of a knock.

Noah. Behold to the heaven the cataracts all,
That are open full even, great and small,
And the planets seven left has their stall;
These thunders and levin [97] down gar [98] fall,
Full stout,
Both halls and bowers,

73 poop.
74 cf. n. 39 above.
75 lazy.
76 take heed.
77 together.
78 if.
79 every bit.
80 suggested by Manly.
81 happiness.
82 obedient.
83 property.
84 helper of misery.
85 tremble.
86 harm, hindrance.
87 delay.
88 duty (*devoir*).
89 boasting.
90 blow.
91 thrive.
92 hostelry, inn.
93 reason.
94 distaff.
95 advice
96 hinder.
97 lightning
98 make.

Castles and towers,
Full sharp are these showers
That runs about.

Therefore, wife, have done; come into ship fast.
Wife. Yea, Noah, go clout thy shoon;[99] the better will they last.
1 Wife. Good mother, come in soon, for all is overcast,
Both the sun and the moon.
2 Wife. And many a wind blast[1]
Full sharp;
These floods so they run;
Therefore, mother, come in.
Wife. In faith, yet will I spin;
All in vain ye carp.

3 Wife. If ye like, ye may spin, mother, in the ship.
Noah. Now is this twice; come in, dame, on my friendship.
Wife. Whether I lose or win, in faith, thy fellowship
Set I not at a pin. This spindle will I slip
Upon this hill,
Ere I stir one foot.
Noah. Peter! I trow we dote.
Without any more note,
Come in if ye will.

Wife. Yea, water nighs so near that I sit not dry;
Into ship with a birr[2] therefore will I hie,
For dread that I drown here.
Noah. Dame, securely,
It is bought full dear, ye abode so long by
Out of ship.
Wife. I will not for thy bidding
Go from door to midden.[3]
Noah. In faith, and for your long tarrying
Ye shall lick on the whip.

Wife. Spare me not, I pray thee, but even as thou think,
These great words shall not flay[4] me.
Noah. Abide, dame, and drink,
For beaten shall thou be with this staff till thou stink.
Are strokes good? Say me!
Wife. What say ye, Wat Wink?
Noah. Speak!
Cry me mercy, I say!
Wife. Thereto say I nay.
Noah. But thou do, by this day,
Thy head shall I break.

Wife. Lord, I were at ease and heartily full whole,
Might I once have a mess of widow's cole[5];
For thy soul, without lese,[6] should I deal penny dole.[7]
So would more, no frese,[8] that I see on this sole[9]
Of wives that are here;
For the life that they lead,
Would their husbands were dead!
For, as ever eat I bread,
So would I our sire[10] were.

Noah. Ye men that has wives, while they are young,
If ye love your lives, chastise their tongue.
Methinks my heart rives, both liver and lung,
To see such strifes wedmen[11] among.
But I,
As have I bliss,
Shall chastise this.
Wife. Yet may ye miss,
Nicol Needy!

Noah. I shall make thee still as stone, beginner of blunder!
I shall beat thee, back and bone, and break all in sunder.
Wife. Out, alas, I am gone! out upon thee, man's wonder!
Noah. See how she can groan, and I lie under!
But, wife,
In this haste let us ho,[12]
For my back is near in two.
Wife. And I am beaten so blue
That I may not thrive.

1 Son. Ah, why fare ye thus, father and mother both?
2 Son. Ye should not be so spitous,[13] standing in such a woth.[14]
3 Son. These[15] are so hideous, with many a cold cothe.[16]

99 patch thy shoes.
1 probably a verb; blows.
2 rush.
3 dunghill; the whole phrase means "do any slightest thing."
4 put to flight.
5 broth. fare; MS. *coyll*, Scotch *kail.*
6 lying.
7 alms (in memory of the dead).
8 doubt.
9 place; Noah's wife is here speaking directly to the audience, as does Noah in the next stanza.
10 i.e. Noah.
11 married people
12 stop.
13 malicious.
14 peril.
15 Manly suggests *These* [*strifes*].
16 disease.

Noah. We will do as ye bid us; we will no more be wroth,
Dear bairns.
Now to the helm will I hent,[17]
And to my ship tent.[18]
Wife. I see in the firmament,
Methinks, the seven stars.

Noah. This is a great flood, wife, take heed.
Wife. So methought, as I stood; we are in great dread,
These waves are so wood.[19]
Noah. Help, God, in this need!
As thou art steersman good, and best, as I rede,
Of all,
Thou rule in this race,[20]
As thou me behight[21] has.
Wife. This is a parlous case;
Help, God, when we call!

Noah. Wife, tent the steer-tree,[22] and I shall assay
The deepness of the sea that we bear,[23] if I may.
Wife. That shall I do full wisely. Now go thy way,
For upon this flood have we floated many a day
With pain.
Noah. Now the water will I sound.
Ah! it is far to the ground;
This travail, I expound,
Had I to tine.[24]

Above all hills bedene[25] the flood is risen late
Cubits fifteen; but in a higher state
It may not be, I ween, for this well I wit,
This forty days has rain been; it will therefore abate
Full leal.[26]
This water in haste
Eft will I test;
Now am I aghast:
It is waned a great deal.

Now are the weathers[27] ceased and cataracts knit,[28]
Both the most and the least.
Wife. Methinks, by my wit,
The sun shines in the east; lo, is not yond it?
We should have a good feast were these floods flitted,[29]
So spitous.
Noah. We have been here, all we,
Three hundred days and fifty.
Wife. Yea, now wanes the sea;
Lord, well is us!

Noah. The third time will I prove what deepness we bear.
Wife. How long shall thou hove?[30]
Lay[31] in thy line there.
Noah. I may touch with my loof[32] the ground even here.
Wife. Then begins to grow to us merry cheer.
But, husband,
What ground may this be?
Noah. The hills of Armenia.
Wife. Now blessed be he
That thus for us can ordain!

Noah. I see the tops of hills high, many at a sight;
Nothing to let[33] me, the weather is so bright.
Wife. These are of mercy tokens full right.
Noah. Dame, thou counsel me what fowl best might
And could,
With flight of wing,
Bring, without tarrying,
Of mercy some tokening,
Either by north or south,

For this is the first day of the tenth month.
Wife. The raven, durst I lay,[34] will come again soon;
As fast as thou may, cast him forth; have done.
He may happen today come again, ere noon,
With graith.[35]
Noah. I will cast out also
Doves one or two.
Go your way, go,
God send you some wathe![36]

Now are these fowls flown into sere[37] countries;
Pray we fast each one, kneeling on our knee,

17 seize.
18 cf. n. 76 above.
19 wild.
20 difficulty.
21 promised.
22 helm.
23 have.
24 This work (i.e. the sounding). I perceive, I have had in vain.
25 completely.
26 thoroughly.
27 tempests.
28 restrained.
29 gone.
30 tarry.
31 cast.
32 hand.
33 hinder.
34 wager.
35 without delay.
36 hunting.
37 several.

To him that is alone worthiest of degree,
That he would send anon our fowls some fee
To glad us.
Wife. They may not fail of land,
The water is so waning.
Noah. Thank we God all-wielding,
That lord that made us.

It is a wonder thing, methinks soothly,
They are so long tarrying, the fowls that we
Cast out in the morning.
Wife. Sir, it may be
They tarry till they bring.[38]
Noah. The raven is a-hungry
Alway;
He is without any reason;
And [39] he find any carrion,
As peradventure may [befall,] [40]
He will not away.

The dove is more gentle, her trust I unto,
Like unto the turtle,[41] for she is ay true.
Wife. Hence but a little she comes. Lo, lo!
She brings in her bill some novels [42] new.
Behold!
It is of an olive tree
A branch, thinks me.
Noah. It is sooth; perdy,
Right so is it called.

Dove, bird full blest, fair might thee befall!
Thou art true for to trust, as stone in the wall.
Full well I it wist thou would come to thy hall.
Wife. A true token is't we shall be saved all;
For why?
The water, since she came
Of deepness plumb,
Is fallen a fathom
And more, hardily.[43]

1 Son. These floods are gone, father, behold!
2 Son. There is left right none, and [for] that be ye bold.
3 Son. As still as a stone our ship is stalled.
Noah. Upon land here anon that we were, fain I would.
My children dear,
Shem, Japhet, and Ham,
With glee and with game,
Come, go we all sam;
We will no longer abide here.

Wife. Here have we been, Noah, long enough,
With tray [44] and with teen,[45] and dreed [46] mickle woe.
Noah. Behold, on this green neither cart nor plough
Is left, as I ween, neither tree nor bough,
Nor other thing,
But all is away;
Many castles, I say,
Great towns of array,
Flitted has this flowing.[47]

Wife. These floods not afright all this world so wide
Has moved with might, on sea and by side.
Noah. To death are they dight,[48] proudest of pride,
Every wight that ever was spied
With sin;
All are they slain,
And put unto pain.
Wife. From thence again
May they never win.

Noah. Win? No, iwis,[49] but [50] he that might has
Would mind of [51] their miss, and admit them to grace.
As he in bale is bliss, I pray him in this space,
In heaven high with his to purvey us a place,
That we
With his saints in sight,
And his angels bright,
May come to his light.
Amen, for charity.

38 i.e. some booty.
39 if.
40 MS. *befon.*
41 turtle-dove.
42 tidings.
43 certainly.
44 affliction.
45 grief.
46 endured.
47 this flood has removed.
48 delivered.
49 certainly.
50 unless.
51 remember.

ABRAHAM AND ISAAC

NAMES OF THE CHARACTERS

ABRAHAM.
ISAAC.
GOD.
AN ANGEL.
DOCTOR.

[*Enter Abraham and Isaac.*]

Ab. Father of Heaven, omnipotent,
With all my heart to thee I call;
Thou hast given me both land and rent,
And my livelihood thou hast me sent;
I thank thee highly evermore for all.

First of the earth thou madest Adam,
And Eve also to be his wife;
All other creatures of them two came;
And now thou hast granted to me, Abraham,
Here in this land to lead my life.

In mine age thou hast granted me this,
That this young child with me shall won;[1]
I love nothing so much, iwis,[2]
Except thine own self, dear Father of bliss,
As Isaac here, my own sweet son.

I have divers children mo,
The which I love not half so well;
This fair sweet child he cheers me so,
In every place where that I go,
That no disease[3] here may I feel.

And therefore, Father of Heaven, I thee pray
For his health and also for his grace;
Now, Lord, keep him both night and day,
That never disease nor no fray
Come to my child in no place.

Now come on, Isaac, my own sweet child,
Go we home and take our rest.

Isaac. Abraham, mine own father so mild,
To follow you I am full prest,[4]
Both early and late.

Ab. Come on, sweet child, I love thee best
Of all the children that ever I begat.

[*God speaks from above.*]

Deus. Mine angel, fast hie thee thy way,
And unto middle-earth[5] anon thou go.
Abraham's heart now will I assay,
Whether that he be steadfast or no.

Say I commanded him for to take
Isaac, his young son, that he loves so well,
And with his blood sacrifice he make,
If any of my friendship he will feel.

Show him the way unto the hill
Where that his sacrifice shall be.
I shall assay now his good will,
Whether he loveth better his child or me.
All men shall take example by him
My commandments how they shall keep.

Ab. Now, Father of Heaven, that formed all things,
My prayers I make to thee again,
For this day my tender offering
Here must I give to thee, certain.
Ah, Lord God, Almighty King,
What manner[6] best will make thee most fain?
If I had thereof very knowing,
It should be done with all my main
Full soon anon.
To do thy pleasure on a hill,
Verily, it is my will,
Dear Father, God in Trinity!

[*Enter Angel.*]

Angel. Abraham, Abraham, will thou rest!
Our Lord commandeth thee for to take
Isaac, thy young son, that thou lovest best,
And with his blood sacrifice that thou make.

Into the land of Vision thou go,
And offer thy child unto thy Lord;

1 dwell.
2 certainly.
3 dis-ease, trouble; so hereafter.
4 ready.
5 the world.
6 i.e. of offering.

I shall thee lead and show also.
Unto God's hest,[7] Abraham, accord,

And follow me upon this green!
Ab. Welcome to me be my Lord's sand,[8]
And his hest I will not withstand;
Yet Isaac, my young son in land,
A full dear child to me hath been!

I had liefer, if God had been pleased,
For to have forborne all the good that I have,
Than [that] Isaac, my son, should have been diseased,
So God in heaven my soul may save!

I loved never thing so much on earth,
And now I must the child go kill!
Ah, Lord God, my conscience is strongly stirred,
And yet, my dear Lord, I am sore afeared
To grutch [9] anything against your will.

I love my child as my life,
But yet I love my God much more;
For though my heart would make any strife,
Yet will I not spare for child nor wife,
But do after my Lord's lore.[10]

Though I love my son never so well,
Yet smite off his head soon I shall.
Ah, Father of Heaven, to thee I kneel,
A hard death my son shall feel,
For to honor thee, Lord, withal!

Angel. Abraham, Abraham, this is well said,
And all these commandments look that thou keep;
But in thy heart be nothing dismayed.
Ab. Nay, nay, forsooth! I hold me well pleased
To please my God to the best that I have.

For though my heart be heavily set
To see the blood of my own dear son,
Yet for all this I will not let.
But Isaac, my son, I will go fet,[11]
And come as fast as ever we can.

[*Exit Angel.*]

Now, Isaac, my own son dear,
Where art thou, child? Speak to me.

Is. My fair sweet father, I am here,
And make my prayers to the Trinity.

Ab. Rise up, my child, and fast come hither,
My gentle bairn that art so wise,
For we two, child, must go together,
And unto my Lord make sacrifice.

Is. I am full ready, my father, lo!
Given to your hands, I stand right here,
And whatsoever ye bid me do,
It shall be done with glad cheer,
Full well and fine.
Ab. Ah, Isaac, my own son so dear,
God's blessing I give thee, and mine.

Hold this fagot upon thy back,
And here myself fire shall bring.
Is. Father, all this here will I pack,
I am full fain to do your bidding.
Ab. Ah, Lord of Heaven, my hands I wring,
This child's words all to-wound [12] my heart!

Now, Isaac, son, go we our way
Unto yon mount, with all our main.
Is. Go we, my dear father, as fast as I may;
To follow you I am full fain,
Although I be slender.
Ab. Ah, Lord, my heart breaketh in twain,
This child's words, they be so tender!

Ah, Isaac son, anon lay it down,
No longer upon thy back it hold,
For I must make ready boon [13]
To honor my Lord God as I should.

Is. Lo, my dear father, where it is!
To cheer you, alway I draw me near.
But, father, I marvel sore at this,
Why that ye make this heavy cheer;

And also, father, ever more dread I:
Where is your quick [14] beast that ye should kill?
Both fire and wood we have ready,
But quick beast have we none on this hill.

A quick beast, I wot well, must be dead,
Your sacrifice for to make.

7 command.
8 sending, message.
9 begrudge.
10 bidding.
11 fetch.
12 *to* has an intensive force; wound sorely.
13 prayer.
14 live.

Ab. Dread thee nought, my child, I thee rede;[15]
Our Lord will send me unto this stead[16]
Some manner of beast for to take,
Through his sweet sand.
Is. Yea, father, but my heart beginneth to quake
To see that sharp sword in your hand.

Why bear ye your sword drawn so?
Of your countenance I have much wonder.
Ab. Ah, Father of Heaven, so I am woe!
This child here breaks my heart in sunder.

Is. Tell me, my dear father, ere that ye cease,
Bear ye your sword drawn for me?
Ab. Ah, Isaac, sweet son, peace, peace!
For, iwis, thou break my heart in three!

Is. Now truly, somewhat, father, ye think,
That ye mourn thus more and more.
Ab. Ah. Lord of Heaven, thy grace let sink,
For my heart was never half so sore!

Is. I pray you, father, that ye will let me that wit,[17]
Whether shall I have any harm or no.
Ab. Iwis, sweet son, I may not tell thee yet,
My heart is now so full of woe.

Is. Dear father, I pray you, hide it not from me,
But some of your thought that ye tell me.
Ab. Ah, Isaac, Isaac, I must kill thee!
Is. Kill me, father? Alas, what have I done?

If I have trespassed against you aught,
With a yard[18] ye may make me full mild,
And with your sharp sword kill me not,
For iwis, father, I am but a child.

Ab. I am full sorry, son, thy blood for to spill,
But truly, my child, I may not choose.
Is. Now I would to God my mother were here on this hill!

She would kneel for me on both her knees
To save my life.
And sithen[19] that my mother is not here,
I pray you, father, change your cheer,
And kill me not with your knife.

Ab. Forsooth, son, but if[20] I thee kill,
I should grieve God right sore, I dread;
It is his commandment and also his will
That I should do this same deed.

He commanded me, son, for certain,
To make my sacrifice with thy blood.
Is. And is it God's will that I should be slain?
Ab. Yea, truly, Isaac, my son so good,
And therefore my hands I wring!

Is. Now, father, against my Lord's will
I will never grutch, loud nor still.
He might have sent me a better destiny,
If it had been his will.[21]

Ab. Forsooth, son, but if I did this deed,
Grievously displeased our Lord will be.
Is. Nay, nay, father, God forbid
That ever ye should grieve him for me!

Ye have other children, one or two,
The which ye should love well by kind.[22]
I pray you, father, make ye no woe,
For be I once dead and from you gone,
I shall be soon out of your mind.

Therefore do our Lord's bidding,
And when I am dead, then pray for me.
But, good father, tell ye my mother nothing,
Say that I am in another country dwelling.
Ab. Ah, Isaac, Isaac, blessed may thou be!

My heart beginneth strongly to rise
To see the blood of thy blessed body!
Is. Father, since it may be no other wise,
Let it pass over, as well as I.

But, father, ere I go unto my death,
I pray you bless me with your hand.
Ab. Now, Isaac, with all my breath,

15 counsel.
16 place.
17 know.
18 rod.
19 since.
20 unless.
21 *will* is Manly's emendation; MS *pleer*.
22 nature.

My blessing I give thee upon this land,
And, God's also thereto, iwis.
Isaac, Isaac, son, up thou stand,
Thy fair sweet mouth that I may kiss.

Is. Now farewell, my own father so fine,
And greet well my mother on earth.
But I pray you, father, to hide my eyne,[23]
That I see not the stroke of your sharp sword
That my flesh shall defile.
Ab. Son, thy words make me to weep full sore—
Now, my dear son Isaac, speak no more.
Is. Ah, my own dear father, wherefore?
We shall speak together here but a while.

And sithen that I must needs be dead,
Yet, my dear father, to you I pray,
Smite but few strokes at my head,
And make an end as soon as ye may,
And tarry not too long.
Ab. Thy meek words, child, make me afraid;
So "welawey!" [24] may be my song,

Except alone God's will.
Ah, Isaac, my own sweet child,
Yet kiss me again upon this hill!
In all this world is none so mild.

Is. Now truly, father, all this tarrying,
It doth my heart but harm;
I pray you, father, make an ending.
Ab. Come up, sweet son, into my arm.

I must bind thy hands two,
Although thou be never so mild.
Is. Ah, mercy, father! Why should ye do so?
Ab. That thou should'st not let,[25] my child.

Is. Nay, iwis, father, I will not let you;
Do on, for me, your will,
And on the purpose that ye have set you,
For God's love, keep it forth still.

I am full sorry this day to die,
But yet I keep [26] not my God to grieve.
Do on your list [27] for me hardily,
My fair sweet father, I give you leave.

But, father, I pray you evermore,
Tell ye my mother no deal;[28]
If she wist it, she would weep full sore,
For iwis, father, she loveth me full well;
God's blessing may she have!

Now farewell, my mother so sweet,
We two be like no more to meet.
Ab. Ah, Isaac, Isaac, son, thou makest me to greet,[29]
And with thy words thou distemperest me.

Is. Iwis, sweet father, I am sorry to grieve you;
I cry you mercy for that I have done,
And for all trespass that ever I did move you;
Now, dear father, forgive me that I have done.
God of Heaven be with me!

Ab. Ah, dear child, leave off thy moans,
In all thy life thou grieved me never once;
Now blessed be thou, body and bones,
That ever thou were bred and born!
Thou hast been to me child full good.
But iwis, child, though I mourn never so fast,
Yet must I needs here at the last
In this place shed all thy blood.

Therefore, my dear son, here shall thou lie.
Unto my work I must me stead;[30]
Iwis, I had as lief myself to die—
If God will be pleased with my deed—
And mine own body for to offer!
Is. Ah, mercy, father! mourn ye no more.
Your weeping maketh my heart sore
As my own death that I shall suffer.

Your kerchief, father, about my eyes ye wind.
Ab. So I shall, my sweetest child on earth.
Is. Now yet, good father, have this in mind,
And smite me not often with your sharp sword,
But hastily that it be sped.

Here Abraham laid a cloth on Isaac's face, thus saying:

23 eyes. 24 an exclamation of grief. 25 hinder. 26 wish. 27 pleasure. 28 nothing. 29 weep. 30 address.

Ab. Now farewell, my child, so full of grace.
Is. Ah, father, father, turn downward my face!
For of your sharp sword I am ever adread.

Ab. To do this deed I am full sorry,
But, Lord, thine hest I will not withstand.
Is. Ah, Father of Heaven, to thee I cry;
Lord, receive me into thy hand!

Ab. Lo, now is the time come certain
That my sword in his neck shall bite.
Ah, Lord, my heart riseth there-against,
I may not find it in my heart to smite!
My heart will not now thereto!
Yet fain I would work my Lord's will,
But this young innocent lieth so still,
I may not find it in my heart him to kill—
O Father of Heaven, what shall I do!

Is. Ah, mercy, father, why tarry ye so,
And let me lie thus long on this heath?
Now I would to God the stroke were done!
Father, I pray you heartily, short me of my woe,
And let me not look thus after my death.

Ab. Now, heart, why wouldst not thou break in three?
Yet shall thou not make me to my God unmild.
I will no longer let for thee,
For that my God aggrieved would be.
Now hold the stroke, my own dear child.

Here Abraham drew his stroke, and the Angel took the sword in his hand suddenly.

Ang. I am an angel, thou mayest see blithe,
That from heaven to thee is sent.
Our Lord thanketh thee a hundred sithes [31]
For the keeping of his commandment.

He knoweth thy will and also thy heart,
That thou dreadest him above all thing,
And some of thy heaviness for to depart,[32]
A fair ram yonder I gan [33] bring;

He standeth tied, lo, among the briars.
Now, Abraham, amend thy mood,
For Isaac, thy young son, that here is,
This day shall not shed his blood.

Go, make thy sacrifice with yon ram.
Now farewell, blessed Abraham,
For unto heaven I go now home:
The way is full gain.[34]
Take up thy son so free!
[*Exit Angel.*]

Ab. Ah, Lord, I thank thee for thy great grace,
Now am I eased [35] in divers wise.
Arise up, Isaac, my dear son, arise,
Arise up, sweet child, and come to me!

Is. Ah, mercy, father, why smite ye not?
Ah, smite on, father, once with your knife!
Ab. Peace, my sweet son, and take no thought,
For our Lord of Heaven hath granted thy life
By his angel now,

That thou shalt not die this day, son, truly.
Is. Ah, father, full glad then were I,
Iwis, father, I say, iwis,
If this tale were true!
Ab. A hundred times, my son fair of hue,
For joy thy mouth now will I kiss.

Is. Ah, my dear father Abraham,
Will not God be wroth that we do thus?
Ab. No, no, hardily, my sweet son! for yon same ram
He hath sent hither down to us.[36]

Yon beast shall die here in thy stead,
In the worship of our Lord alone;
Go fet him hither, my child, indeed.
Is. Father, I will go hent [37] him by the head,
And bring yon beast with me anon.

Ah, sheep, sheep, blessed may thou be,
That ever thou were sent down hither!

31 times.
32 remove.
33 did.
34 straight.
35 Manly's emendation; MS. *yeyed.*
36 Line arrangement according to Manly.
37 seize.

Thou shall this day die for me,
In the worship of the Holy Trinity.
Now come fast and go we together,
To my father of Heaven.
Though thou be never so gentle and good,
Yet had I liefer thou sheddest thy blood,
Iwis, sheep, than I!

Lo, father, I have brought here, full smart,
This gentle sheep, and him to you I give,
But, Lord God, I thank thee with all my heart,
For I am glad that I shall live,
And kiss once my dear mother.
Ab. Now be right merry, my sweet child,
For this quick beast that is so mild
Here I shall present before all other.

Is. And I will fast begin to blow,
This fire shall burn a full good speed,
But, father, will I stoop down low,
Ye will not kill me with your sword, I trow?
Ab. No, hardily, sweet son, have no dread,
My mourning is past.
Is. Yea, but I would that sword were in a gleed,[38]
For, iwis, father, it makes me full ill aghast.

Here Abraham made his offering, kneeling and saying thus:

Ab. Now, Lord God of Heaven in Trinity,
Almighty God omnipotent,
My offering I make in the worship of thee,
And with this quick beast I thee present.
Lord, receive thou mine intent,
As [thou] art God and ground of our grace.

Deus. Abraham, Abraham, well may thou speed,
And Isaac, thy young son, thee by!
Truly, Abraham, for this deed,
I shall multiply both your seed,
As thick as stars be in the sky,
Both more and less,
And as thick as gravel in the sea,
So thick multiplied your seed shall be:
This grant I you for your goodness.
Of you shall come fruit great,
And ever be in bliss without end,
For ye dread me, as God alone,
And keep my commandments every one;
My blessing I give, wheresoever ye wend!

Ab. Lo, Isaac, my son, how think ye
Of this work that we have wrought?
Full glad and blithe we may be,
Against the will of God that we grutched not,
Upon this fair heath.
Is. Ah, father, I thank our Lord every deal,
That my wit served me so well
For to dread God more than my death.

Ab. Why, dearworthy son, were thou adread?
Hardily, child, tell me thy lore.
Is. Yea, by my faith, father, now have I rede,[39]
I was never so afraid before,
As I have been on yon hill.
But, by my faith, father, I swear
I will nevermore come there,
But it be against my will!

Ab. Yea, come on with me, my own sweet son,
And homeward fast now let us go.
Is. By my faith, father, thereto I grant;
I had never so good will to go home,
And to speak with my dear mother!
Ab. Ah, Lord of Heaven, I thank thee!
For now may I lead home with me
Isaac, my young son so free,
The gentlest child above all other,
This may I well avow.

Now, go we forth, my blessed son.
Is. I grant, father, and let us go,
For, by my troth, were I at home,
I would never go out under that form.[40]
I pray God give us grace evermo,
And all those that we be holden to.

[*Exeunt. Enter Doctor.*]

Doctor.[41] Lo, sovereigns and sirs, now have we showed
This solemn story to great and small;
It is good learning to learned and lewd,[42]

38 five.
39 judgment.
40 in that manner, for that purpose.
41 A Doctor, or Expositor, frequently accompanied the miracle and morality plays to expound the moral teaching.
42 ignorant.

And the wisest of us all,
Without any berrying.[43]
For this story showeth you [here].
How we should keep, to our power,
God's commandments without grutching.

Trow ye, sirs, and [44] God sent an angel,
And commanded you your child to slay,
By your troth, is there any of you
That either would grutch or strive there-against?
How think ye now, sirs, thereby?
I trow there be three or four or more.
And these women that weep so sorrowfully
When that their children die them from,
As nature will and kind,
It is but folly, I may well avow,
To grutch against God or to grieve you,
For ye shall never see him mischiefed, well I know,
By land or water, have this in mind.

And grutch not against our Lord God,
In wealth or woe, whether [45] that he you send,
Though ye be never so hard bestead,
For when he will, he may it amend.
His commandments truly if ye keep with good heart,
As this story hath now showed you before,
And faithfully serve him while ye be quart,[46]
That ye may please God both even and morn.
Now Jesu, that wore the crown of thorn,
Bring us all to heaven's bliss!

THE SECOND SHEPHERDS' PLAY

NAMES OF THE CHARACTERS

FIRST SHEPHERD.
SECOND SHEPHERD.
THIRD SHEPHERD.
MAK.
GILL, *Mak's wife.*
AN ANGEL.
MARY.

Scene: Bethlehem, and the open country near it.

[SCENE I

Enter First Shepherd.]

1 Shep. Lord! what, these weathers are cold! and I am ill happed; [1]
I am near-hand [2] dold,[3] so long have I napped;
My legs they fold, my fingers are chapped;
It is not as I would, for I am all lapped
In sorrow.
In storms and tempest,
Now in the east, now in the west,
Woe is him has never rest,
Mid-day nor morrow!
But we seely [4] shepherds, that walk on the moor,
In faith, we are near-hands out of the door;
No wonder, as it stands, if we be poor,
For the tilth of our lands lies fallow as the floor,
As ye ken.
We are so lamed,[5]
For-taxed [6] and shamed,[7]
We are made hand-tamed
With these gentlery men.

Thus they reave [8] us our rest, Our Lady them wary! [9]
These men that are lord-fast,[10] they cause the plough tarry.

43 threshing: "the teaching of this story comes out without any threshing" (L. Toulmin Smith).
44 if.
45 whichever.
46 in health.
1 clothed.
2 almost.
3 numb.
4 poor.
5 MS. *hamyd*, crippled.
6 overtaxed.
7 MS. *ramyd*, oppressed (?).
8 rob of.
9 curse.
10 bound to the service of lords.

That [11] men say is for the best, we find
 it contrary;
Thus are husbands [12] opprest, in point to
 miscarry
 In life.
Thus hold they us under,
Thus they bring us in blunder;
It were great wonder,
 And [13] ever should we thrive.

For may he get a painted sleeve, or a
 brooch nowadays,
Woe is him that him grieves, or once
 again-says! [14]
Dare no man him reprieve,[15] what mas-
 tery he makes; [16]
And yet may no man believe one word
 that he says,
 No letter.
He can make purveyance,[17]
With boast and bragance,[18]
And all is through maintenance
 Of men that are greater.

There shall come a swain, as proud as a
 po,[19]
He must borrow my wain, my plough
 also;
Then I am full fain to grant ere he go.
Thus live we in pain, anger, and woe,
 By night and day.
He must have if he longed,
If I should forego it;
I were better be hanged
 Than once say him nay.

It does me good, as I walk thus by mine
 own,[20]
Of this world for to talk in manner of
 moan.[21]
To my sheep will I stalk and hearken
 anon,
There abide on a balk,[22] or sit on a stone
 Full soon,
For I trow, pardie,[23]
True men if they be,
We get more company
 Ere it be noon.

[*Enter Second Shepherd.*]

2 Shep. Benste [24] and Dominus! what
 may this bemean? [25]
Why fares this world thus? Oft have
 we not seen!
Lord, these weathers are spitous,[26] and
 the weathers full keen;
And the frosts so hideous they water
 mine een,[27]
 No lie.
Now in dry, now in wet,
Now in snow, now in sleet,
When my shoon freeze to my feet
 It is not all easy.

But as far as I ken, or yet as I go,
We seely wed-men dree mickle woe; [28]
We have sorrow then and then, it falls
 oft so.
Seely Capel, our hen, both to and fro
 She cackles;
But begin she to croak,
To groan or to cluck,
Woe is him, our cock,
 For he is in the shackles.

These men that are wed have not all their
 will;
When they are full hard stead,[29] they
 sigh full still;
God wot they are led full hard and full
 ill,
In bower nor in bed they say nought
 theretill,[30]
 This tide.
My part have I found,
I know my lesson:
Woe is him that is bound,
 For he must abide.

But now late in our lives—a marvel to
 me,
That I think my heart rives such wonders
 to see,
What that destiny drives, it should so
 be!—
Some men will have two wives, and some
 men three,
 In store.
Some are woe that have any;
But so far can [31] I,
Woe is him that has many,
 For he feels sore.

But young men of wooing, for God that
 you bought,

11 that which.
12 husbandmen.
13 if.
14 speaks against him
15 reprove.
16 however masterfully he acts.
17 the right to buy provisions for the royal household at a fixed price, irrespective of the market price.
18 bragging.
19 peacock.
20 by myself.
21 in a complaining way.
22 ridge.
23 *par Dieu.*
24 shortened from *Benedicite!* bless me!
25 mean.
26 spiteful.
27 eyes.
28 we poor married men endure much woe.
29 bestead.
30 thereto.
31 know.

Be well ware of wedding, and think in your thought:
"Had I wist" is a thing it serves of nought;
Mickle still mourning has wedding home brought,
And griefs,
With many a sharp shower,
For thou may catch in an hour
That shall [savor] full sour
As long as thou lives.

For, as ever read I epistle, I have one to my fere [32]
As sharp as a thistle, as rough as a briar;
She is browed like a bristle, with a sour [looking] [33] cheer;
Had she once wet her whistle she could sing full clear
Her pater-noster.
She is as great as a whale,
She has a gallon of gall;
By him that died for us all,
I would I had run till I had lost her!

1 Shep. God look over the row! full deafly ye stand.
2 Shep. Yea, the devil in thy maw, so tarrying!
Saw thou anywhere of Daw?
1 Shep. Yea, on a lea [34] land
Heard I him blow; he comes here at hand,
Not far;
Stand still.
2 Shep. Why?
1 Shep. For he comes, hope I.
2 Shep. He will make us both a lie,
But if [35] we beware.

[*Enter Third Shepherd.*]

3 Shep. Christ's cross me speed, and Saint Nicholas!
Thereof had I need, it is worse than it was.
Whoso could, take heed, and let the world pass:
It is ever in dread and brittle as glass,
And slithers. [36]
This world fared never so,
With marvels mo and mo,
Now in weal, now in woe,
And all-thing writhes. [37]

Was never since Noah's flood such floods seen,
Winds and rains so rude, and storms so keen;
Some stammered, some stood in doubt, as I ween;
Now God turn all to good! I say as I mean.
For ponder:
These floods so they drown
Both in fields and in town,
And bear all down,
And that is a wonder.

We that walk in the nights, our cattle to keep,
We see sudden sights, when other men sleep.
Yet methink my heart lights—I see shrews [38] peep.
Ye are two tall wights: [39] I will give my sheep
A turn.
But full ill have I meant,
As I walk on this bent, [40]
I may lightly repent,
My toes if I spurn. [41]

Ah, sir, God you save, and master mine!
A drink fain would I have, and somewhat to dine.
1 Shep. Christ's curse, my knave, thou art a lither hind! [42]
2 Shep. What, the boy list [43] rave!
Abide unto syne; [44]
We have made it. [45]
Ill thrift on thy pate!
Through the shrew came late,
Yet is he in state
To dine, if he had it.

3 Shep. Such servants as I, that sweats and swinks, [46]
Eats our bread full dry, and that me forthinks; [47]
We are oft wet and weary when master-men winks, [48]
Yet comes full lately both dinners and drinks.
But naitly [49]
Both our dame and our sire,
When we have run in the mire,
They can nip at our hire, [50]
And pay us full lately.

32 mate.
33 MS. *loten*.
34 fallow.
35 unless.
36 is slippery, unreliable.
37 is awry.
38 knaves.
39 stout fellows.
40 heath.
41 if I stumble.
42 lazy servant.
43 pleases to.
44 wait till later.
45 i.e. our meal.
46 work.
47 repents.
48 sleep.
49 thoroughly.
50 take a bit off our wages.

But hear my truth, master, for the fare that ye make,
I shall do thereafter work as I take;[51]
I shall do a little, sir, and among[52] ever lake,[53]
For yet lay my supper never on my stomach
In fields.
Whereto should I threap?[54]
With my staff can I leap,
And men say "light cheap
Litherly foryields."[55]

1 Shep. Thou were an ill lad to ride a-wooing
With a man that had but little of spending.
2 Shep. Peace, boy, I bade; no more jangling,
Or I shall make thee full rad,[56] by the heaven's king,
With thy gauds![57]
Where are our sheep, boy, we scorn?
3 Shep. Sir, this same day at morn
I them left in the corn,
When they rang Lauds;[58]

They have pasture good, they can not go wrong.
1 Shep. That is right. By the rood, these nights are long!
Yet I would, ere we yode,[59] one gave us a song.
2 Shep. So I thought as I stood, to mirth us among.[60]
3 Shep. I grant.
1 Shep. Let me sing the tenory.
2 Shep. And I the treble so high.
3 Shep. Then the mean falls to me;
Let see how ye chant.[61]

Enter Mak, with a cloak thrown over his smock.

Mak. Now, Lord, for thy names seven,[62] that made both moon and stars,
Well more than I can neven,[63] thy will, Lord, of me tharns;[64]
I am all uneven,[65] that moves oft my harns;[66]
Now would God I were in heaven, for there weep no bairns
So still!

1 Shep. Who is that pipes so poor?
Mak. Would God ye wist how I fared!
Lo, a man that walks on the moor,
And has not all his will!

2 Shep. Mak, where has thou gone? Tell us tidings.
3 Shep. Is he come? Then each one take heed to his thing.
(*Takes his cloak from him.*)
Mak. What! I be a yeoman, I tell you, of the king;
The self and the same, sent[67] from a great lording,
And such.
Fie on you! Go hence
Out of my presence!
I must have reverence.
Why, who be I?

1 Shep. Why make ye it so quaint? Mak, ye do wrong.
2 Shep. But, Mak, list ye saint?[68] I trow that ye long.
3 Shep. I trow the shrew can paint, the devil might him hang!
Mak. I shall make complaint, and make you all to thwang.[69]
At a word,
And tell even how ye doth.
1 Shep. But, Mak, is that sooth?
Now take out that southern tooth,[70]
And set in a turd!

2 Shep. Mak, the devil in your eye! a stroke would I lend you.
3 Shep. Mak, know ye not me? By God, I could teen[71] you.
Mak. God look you all three! methought I had seen you.
Ye are a fair company.
1 Shep. Can ye now mean you?[72]
2 Shep. Shrew, jape![73]
Thus late as thou goes,
What will men suppose?
And thou has an ill noise[74]
Of stealing of sheep.

Mak. And I am true as steel, all men wit!
But a sickness I feel, that holds me full hot,
My belly fares not well, it is out of estate.

51 i.e. I 'll work as I 'm paid.
52 now and then.
53 play.
54 argue.
55 a cheap bargain yields poorly.
56 afraid.
57 tricks.
58 an early morning service of the church.
59 went.
60 for mirth among us.
61 (The song is wanting.)
62 The seven sacred names of God in rabbinical literature.
63 name.
64 lacks; i.e. thy will toward me leaves something to be desired.
65 upset.
66 brains.
67 lit. messenger; MS. *sond.*
68 play the saint.
69 be flogged.
70 i.e. which makes you talk like a south of England man, deceitfully.
71 hurt, beat.
72 remember.
73 joke on.
74 reputation.

3 Shep. Seldom lies the devil dead by the gate.[75]
Mak. Therefore
Full sore am I and ill,
If I stand stone still;
I eat not a needle
This month and more.

1 Shep. How fares thy wife? By my hood, how fares she?
Mak. Lies weltering,[76] by the rood, by the fire, lo!
And a house full of brewed[77] she drinks well too;
Ill speed other good that she will do
But so!
Eats as fast as she can,
And each year that comes to man,
She brings forth a lakin,[78]
And some years two.

But were I not more gracious, and richer by far,
I were eaten out of house and of harbor;
Yet is she a foul dowse,[79] if ye come near.
There is none that trows nor knows a worse
Than ken I.
Now will ye see what I proffer?
To give all in my coffer
To-morn[80] next to offer[81]
Her head-mass penny.

2 Shep. I wot so forwaked[82] is none in this shire:
I would sleep if I took less to my hire.
3 Shep. I am cold and naked, and would have a fire.
1 Shep. I am weary, for-raked,[83] and run in the mire.
Wake thou!
2 Shep. Nay, I will lie down-by,
For I must sleep, truly.
3 Shep. As good a man's son was I
As any of you.

But, Mak, come hither! between shall thou lie down.
Mak. Then might I let[84] you bedene[85] of that ye would round,[86]
No dread.
From my top to my toe
Manus tuas commendo,
Pontio Pilato!
Christ's cross me speed!

Then he rises, while the shepherds are asleep, and says:
Now were time for a man that lacks what he would,
To stalk privily then unto a fold,
And nimbly to work then, and be not too bold,
For he might aby[87] the bargain, if it were told,
At the ending.
Now were time for to reel;[88]
But he needs good counsel
That fain would fare well,
And has but little spending.

But about you a circle as round as a moon,
Till I have done that I will, till that it be noon,
That ye lie stone-still, till that I have done,
And I shall say there-till of good words a few
On height;[89]
Over your heads my hand I lift,
Out go your eyes, fordo your sight![90]
But yet I must make better shift,
And it be right.

Lord, what, they sleep hard! that may ye all hear.
Was I never a shepherd, but now will I lere.[91]
If the flock be scared, yet shall I nip near.
How! Draw hitherward! now mends our cheer
From sorrow.
A fat sheep, I dare say,
A good fleece, dare I lay.
Eft quite[92] when I may,
But this will I borrow.
[*Exit, with sheep.*]

[SCENE 2. *Mak at the door of his house.*]

Mak. How, Gill, art thou in? Get u[s]
some light.
Wife. Who makes such din this time o[f]
the night?

75 a proverb, implying suspicion of Mak: it's not safe to trust appearances.
76 lounging.
77 i.e. ale.
78 plaything, i.e. baby.
79 dear. *douce;* ironical.
80 tomorrow; MS. inserts *at* before *next.*
81 to pay for her funeral service.
82 worn out with watching.
83 worn out with walking.
84 hinder.
85 altogether.
86 whisper; two lines seem to be missing here.
87 pay dearly for.
88 set about the business.
89 aloud.
90 This is excell[ent] fooling: Mak p[re]tends to cast [a] charm over [the] sleeping s[hep]herds.
91 learn.
92 repay.

I am set for to spin; I hope not I might
Rise a penny to win. I shrew them on
height
So fares!
A housewife that has been
To be raced thus between!
Here may no note [93] be seen
For such small chares.[94]

Mak. Good wife, open the heck! [95] Sees
thou not what I bring?
Wife. I may thole [96] thee draw the sneck.[97]
Ah, come in, my sweeting!
Mak. Yea, thou there not reck of my long
standing.
Wife. By the naked neck art thou like for
to hang!
Mak. Do way!
I am worthy my meat,
For in a strait can I get
More than they that swink and sweat
All the long day.

Thus it fell to my lot, Gill, I had such
grace.
Wife. It were a foul blot to be hanged
for the case.
Mak. I have scaped, Gillot, oft as hard a
glace.[98]
Wife. But so long goes the pot to the
water, men says,
At last
Comes it home broken.
Mak. Well know I the token,
But let it never be spoken.
But come and help fast.

I would he were slain, I list well eat:
This twelvemonth was I not so fain of
one sheep-meat.
Wife. Come they ere he be slain, and hear
the sheep bleat —
Mak. Then might I be ta'en: that were a
cold sweat!
Go spar [99]
The gate door.
Wife. Yes, Mak,
For and they come at thy back —
Mak. Then might I aby, for all the pack,
The devil of the worse! [1]

Wife. A good bourd [2] have I spied, since
thou can none:
Here shall we him hide till they be gone,
In my cradle abide—let me alone—
And I shall lie beside in childbed and
groan.
Mak. Thou rede! [3]
And I shall say thou was lighted [4]
Of a knave child this night.
Wife. Now, well is me! Day bright,
That ever I was bred!

This is a good guise and a far cast;
Yet a woman's advice helps at the last!
I wot never who spies; again go thou
fast!
Mak. But I come ere they rise, else blows
a cold blast!
I will go sleep.

[Scene 3. *Mak returns to the Shepherds.*]

Yet sleeps all this meinie,[5]
And I shall go stalk privily,
As it had never been I
That carried their sheep.

1 Shep. *Resurrex a mortruis!* [6] have hold
my hand!
Judas carnas dominus! I may not well
stand.
My foot sleeps, by Jesus! and I water
fasting.
I thought that we laid us full near Eng-
land.
2 Shep. Ah, yea!
Lord, what, I have slept well!
As fresh as an eel,
As light I me feel
As leaf on a tree.

3 Shep. Benste [7] be herein! So my
[body] quakes,
My heart is out of skin, what-so it makes.
Who makes all this din? So my brows
black!
To the door will I win. Hark, fellows,
wake!
We were four:
See ye anywhere of Mak now?
1 Shep. We were up ere thou.
2 Shep. Man, I give God a vow,
Yet yede [8] he nowhere.

3 Shep. Methought he was lapt in a wolf-
skin.
1 Shep. So are many happed now:
namely, within.

93 work.
94 jobs.
95 door.
96 allow.
97 latch.
98 blow.
99 shut.
1 then might I have a devil of a time from the whole pack (roughly).
2 trick.
3 advise well.
4 delivered.
5 company.
6 Mock Latin here and in following line.
7 God's blessing.
8 went.

3 Shep. When we had long napped, methought with a gin [9]
A fat sheep he trapped, but he made no din.
2 Shep. Be still!
Thy dream makes thee wood,[10]
It is but phantom, by the rood.
1 Shep. Now God turn all to good,
If it be his will!

2 Shep. Rise, Mak, for shame! thou lies right long.
Mak. Now Christ's holy name be us among!
What is this? For Saint James, I may not well go!
I trow I be the same. Ah, my neck has lain wrong
Enough,
Mickle thank, since yester-even!
Now, by Saint Stephen,
I was flayed [11] with a sweven! [12]
My heart out of-slough [13]

I thought Gill began to croak, and travail full sad,
Well near at the first cock, of a young lad
For to mend our flock. Then be I never glad;
I have tow on my rock,[14] more than ever I had.
Ah, my head!
A house full of young tharms,[15]
The devil knock out their harns! [16]
Woe is him has many bairns,
And thereto little bread!

I must go home, by your leave, to Gill, as I thought.
I pray you look my sleeve, that I steal nought:
I am loth you to grieve, or from you take aught.
[*Exit Mak.*]
3 Shep. Go forth, ill might thou cheve! [17]
Now would I we sought,
This morn,
That we had all our store.
1 Shep. But I will go before.
Let us meet.
2 Shep. Where?
3 Shep. At the crooked thorn.

[SCENE 4. *Mak's house.*]

Mak. (*Knocking.*) Undo this door! who is here? How long shall I stand?
Wife. Who makes such a bere? [18]—Now walk in the waniand! [19]
Mak. Ah, Gill, what cheer?—It is I, Mak, your husband.
Wife. Then may we see here the devil in a band,
Sir Guile! [20]
Lo, he comes with a late,[21]
As he were holden in the throat.
I may not sit at my note [22]
A hand-long while.

Mak. Will ye hear what fare she makes to get her a gloze? [23]
And does nought but lakes,[24] and claws her toes.
Wife. Why, who wanders, who wakes, who comes, who goes?
Who brews, who bakes? What makes me thus hose?
And then
It is ruth [25] to behold,
Now in hot, now in cold;
Full woful is the household
That wants a woman.

But what end hast thou made with the herds,[26] Mak?
Mak. The last word that they said when I turned my back,
They would look that they had their sheep, all the pack.
I hope they will not be well paid when they their sheep lack,
Pardie!
But howso the game goes,
To me they will suppose,[27]
And make a foul noise,
And cry out upon me.

But thou must do as thou hight,[28]
Wife. I accord me thereto:
I shall swaddle him right in my cradle.
If it were a greater sleight, yet could I help till.[29]
I will lie down straight; come hap [30] me.
Mak. I will.

9 trick.
10 mad.
11 frightened.
12 dream.
13 jumped out of my breast (?).
14 distaff; more to provide for.
15 bellies, i.e. children.
16 brains.
17 thrive.
18 noise.
19 waning of the moon—an unlucky season.
20 The meaning of these two lines is not clear; apparently something uncomplimentary.
21 noise.
22 work.
23 excuse.
24 plays.
25 pity.
26 shepherds.
27 suspect.
28 promised.
29 toward our purpose.
30 wrap up.

Wife. Behind!
Come Coll and his marrow,[31]
They will nip us full narrow.
Mak. But I may cry out "Harrow!" [32]
The sheep if they find.

Wife. Hearken ay when they call: they will come anon.
Come and make ready all, and sing by thine own;
Sing "Lullay!" thou shall, for I must groan,
And cry out by the wall on Mary and John,
[Full] [33] sore.
Sing "Lullay" on fast
When thou hears at the last;
And but I play a false cast,
Trust me no more.

[Scene 5. *The fields.*]

3 Shep. Ah, Coll, good morn! Why sleeps thou not?
1 Shep. Alas, that ever was I born! We have a foul blot!
A fat wether have we lorn.[34]
3 Shep. Marry, Gods forbid!
2 Shep. Who should do us that scorn?
That were a foul spot.
1 Shep. Some shrew.[35]
I have sought with my dogs,
All Horbury Shrogs,[36]
And of fifteen hogs
Found I but one ewe.

3 Shep. Now trow me if ye will: by Saint Thomas of Kent,[37]
Either Mak or Gill was at that assent!
1 Shep. Peace, man, be still! I saw when he went.
Thou slanders him ill; thou ought to repent,
Good speed.
2 Shep. Now as ever might I thee,[38]
If I should even here die,
I would say it were he
That did that same deed.

3 Shep. Go we thither, I rede, and run on our feet.
Shall I never eat bread, the sooth till I wit.
1 Shep. Nor drink in my head with him till I meet.
2 Shep. I will rest in no stead [39] till that I him greet,
My brother.
One I will hight: [40]
Till I see him in sight
Shall I never sleep one night
There [41] I do another.

[Scene 6. *The Shepherds come to Mak's house.*]

3 Shep. Will ye hear how they hack! [42] our sire [43] list croon.
1 Shep. Heard I never none crack so clear out of tune.
Call on him.
2 Shep. Mak! undo your door soon.
Mak. Who is it that spake, as it were noon,
On loft? [44]
Who is that, I say?
3 Shep. Good fellows, were it day!
Mak. As far as ye may,
Good, speak soft,

Over a sick woman's head that is at malease; [45]
I had liefer be dead or she had any disease.
Wife. Go to another stead; I may not well quease.[46]
Each foot that ye tread goes through my nose,
So high!
1 Shep. Tell us, Mak, if ye may,
How fare ye, I say?
Mak. But are ye in this town to-day?
Now how fare ye?

Ye have run in the mire, and are wet yet;
I shall make you a fire, if ye will sit.
A nurse would I hire; think ye one yet.[47]
Well quit is my hire—[48] my dream, this is it—[49]
A season.
I have bairns, if ye knew,
Well more than enow;
But we must drink as we brew,
And that is but reason.

I would ye dined ere ye yode; methink that ye sweat.

31 mate.
32 a call for help.
33 Ms. *for*.
34 lost.
35 knave.
36 Horbury Thickets; Horbury is a village near Wakefield. The reference helps to localize the Towneley plays at Wakefield.
37 Thomas à Becket, buried in Canterbury Cathedral, in Kent.
38 thrive.
39 place.
40 one thing I promise.
41 where.
42 sing; the shepherds hear Mak and Gill singing their pretended lullaby.
43 i.e. Mak.
44 loudly.
45 in distress.
46 meaning unknown (N. E. D.); perhaps wheeze, breathe?
47 i.e. tell me of one if you can.
48 I am well paid.
49 i.e., this is just what I dreamed.

2 Shep. Nay, neither mends our mood,[50]
drink nor meat.
Mak. Why, sir, ails you aught but good?
3 Shep. Yea, our sheep that we get,
Are stolen as they yode; our loss is
great.
Mak. Sirs, drink!
Had I been there,
Some should have bought it full sore.
1 Shep. Marry, some men trows that ye
were,
And that us forthinks.[51]

2 Shep. Mak, some men trows that it
should be ye.
3 Shep. Either ye or your spouse; so say
we.
Mak. Now if ye have suspicion to Gill or
to me,
Come and rip our house, and then may
ye see
Who had her,
If I any sheep fot,[52]
Either cow or stot,[53]
And Gill, my wife, rose not
Here since she laid her.

As I am both true and leal, to God here
I pray,
That this be the first meal that I shall
eat this day.
1 Shep. Mak, as I have seel,[54] advise thee,
I say;
He learned timely to steal, that could
not say nay.
Wife. I swelt![55]
Out, thieves, from my won![56]
Ye come to rob us, for the nonce.
Mak. Hear ye not how she groans?
Your hearts should melt.

Wife. Out, thieves, from my bairn! Nigh
him not there!
Mak. Wist ye how she had fared, your
hearts would be sore.
Ye do wrong, I you warn, that thus
comes before
To a woman that has fared—but I say
no more!
Wife. Ah, my middle!
I pray to God so mild,
If ever I you beguiled,
That I eat this child
That lies in this cradle.

Mak. Peace, woman, for God's pain, and
cry not so:
Thou spills thy brain, and makes me full
woe.
2 Shep. I trow our sheep be slain. What
find ye two?
3 Shep. All work we in vain; as well may
we go.
But, hatters,[57]
I can find no flesh,
Hard nor nesh,[58]
Salt nor fresh,
But two toom[59] platters:

Quick[60] cattle but this, tame nor wild,
None, as have I bliss, as loud as he
smiled.
Wife. No, so God me bless, and give me
joy of my child!
1 Shep. We have marked amiss; I hold
us beguiled.
2 Shep. Sir, done!
Sir, Our Lady him save!
Is your child a knave?[61]
Mak. Any lord might him have,
This child to his son.

When he wakens he kips,[62] that joy is to
see.
3 Shep. In good time to his hips, and in
seel![63]
But who were his gossips,[64] so soon
ready?
Mak. So fair fall their lips!
1 Shep. Hark now, a lie!
Mak. So God them thank,
Parkin, and Gibbon Waller, I say,
And gentle John Horne, in good fay,[65]
He made all the garray,[66]
With the great shank.[67]

2 Shep. Mak, friends will we be, for we
are all one.
Mak. We![68] now I hold for me, for
amends get I none.
Farewell all three! all glad were ye gone.
[*They leave the house.*]
3 Shep. Fair words may there be, but
love is there none
This year.
1 Shep. Gave ye the child anything?
2 Shep. I trow, not one farthing.
3 Shep. Fast again will I fling,
Abide ye me there.
[*He returns to the house.*]

50 helps our case.
51 makes us repent.
52 fetched.
53 steer.
54 bliss.
55 faint.
56 house (pl. in text).
57 an exclamation.
58 soft.
59 empty.
60 living.
61 boy.
62 snatches.
63 good luck to him!
64 godparents.
65 faith.
66 commotion.
67 long legs.
68 an exclamation.

Mak, take it to no grief, if I come to thy bairn.
Mak. Nay, thou does me great reprief,[69] and foul has thou fared.
3 Shep. The child will it not grieve, that little day-star.
Mak, with your leave, let me give your bairn
But sixpence.
Mak. Nay, do way: [70] he sleeps.
3 Shep. Methink he peeps.
Mak. When he wakens he weeps.
I pray you go hence.

[*First and Second Shepherds return.*]
3 Shep. Give me leave him to kiss, and lift up the clout.
What the devil is this? He has a long snout!
1 Shep. He is marked amiss. We wait ill about.
2 Shep. Ill spun weft, I wis, ay comes foul out.
Aye, so?
He is like to our sheep!
3 Shep. How, Gib, may I peep?
1 Shep. I trow, kind [71] will creep
Where it may not go.[72]

2 Shep. This was a quaint gaud,[73] and a far cast;
It was a high fraud.
3 Shep. Yea, sirs, was 't.
Let burn this bawd, and bind her fast.
A false scold hangs at the last;
So shall thou.
Will ye see how they swaddle
His four feet in the middle?
Saw I never in a cradle
A horned lad ere now.

Mak. Peace, bid I! What, let be your fare!
I am he that him gat, and yond woman him bare.
1 Shep. What devil shall he hight,[74] Mak? Lo, God, Mak's heir!
2 Shep. Let be all that. Now God give him care,
I say.
Wife. A pretty child is he,
As sits on a woman's knee;
A dilly-down, pardie,
To gar [75] a man laugh.

3 Shep. I know him by the ear-mark—that is a good token.
Mak. I tell you, sirs, hark, his nose was broken.
Sithen [76] told me a clerk that he was forspoken.[77]
1 Shep. This is a false work—I would fain be wroken: [78]
Get a weapon!
Wife. He was taken by an elf,[79]
I saw it myself;
When the clock struck twelve,
Was he forshapen.[80]

2 Shep. Ye two are well feoffed sam [81] in a stead.
1 Shep. Since they maintain their theft, let do them to dead.[82]
Mak. If I trespass eft, gird [83] off my head!
With you will I be left.[84]
1 Shep. Sirs, do my rede:
For this trespass,
We will neither ban nor flyte [85]
Fight nor chide,
But have done as tight,
And cast him in canvas.
[*They toss Mak in a sheet.*]

[Scene 7. *The fields.*]

1 Shep. Lord, what! I am sore, in point for to burst;
In faith, I may no more; therefore will I rest.
2 Shep. As a sheep of seven score he weighed in my fist.
For to sleep anywhere, methink that I list.
3 Shep. Now I pray you,
Lie down on this green.
1 Shep. On these thieves yet I mean.[86]
3 Shep. Whereto should ye tene? [87]
Do as I say you.

An Angel sings "Gloria in Excelsis"; then let him say:
Rise, herdmen hend,[88] for now is he born
That shall take from the fiend that [89] Adam had lorn:
That warlock [90] to shend,[91] this night is he born.

69 injury.
70 have done, quit.
71 nature.
72 walk; this was a common proverb, here signifying that nature will show itself in its true colors.
73 trick.
74 be named.
75 make.
76 afterwards.
77 bewitched.
78 revenged.
79 i.e. by the fairies, and a changeling substituted.
80 changed in shape.
81 agreed together.
82 have them put to death.
83 strike.
84 I shall be in your power.
85 curse nor wrangle.
86 consider.
87 grieve.
88 gracious.
89 that which.
90 fiend.
91 overthrow.

God is made your friend now at this morn.
He behests [92]
To Bedlem [93] go see,
There lies that free [94]
In a crib full poorly,
Betwixt two beasts.

1 Shep. This was a quaint steven [95] that ever yet I heard.
It is a marvel to neven,[96] thus to be scared.
2 Shep. Of God's son of heaven, he spake upward.
All the wood in a levin,[97] methought that he gard [98]
Appear.
3 Shep. He spake of a bairn
In Bedlem, I you warn.
1 Shep. That betokens yond star;
Let us seek him there.

2 Shep. Say, what was his song? Heard ye not how he cracked it,
Three breves to a long? [99]
3 Shep. Yea, marry, he hacked [1] it.
Was no crochet wrong, nor nothing that lacked it.
1 Shep. For to sing us among, right as he knacked [2] it,
I can.
2 Shep. Let see how ye croon.
Can ye bark at the moon?
3 Shep. Hold your tongues, have done!
1 Shep. Hark after, then.

2 Shep. To Bedlem he bade that we should gang; [3]
I am full feared that we tarry too long.
3 Shep. Be merry and not sad; of mirth is our song,
Everlasting glad to meed may we fang [4]
Without noise.
1 Shep. Hie we thither forthy,[5]
If we be wet and weary,
To that child and that lady:
We have it not to lose.

2 Shep. We find by the prophecy—let be your din!—
Of David and Isaiah, and more than I mind,
They prophesied by clergy, that in a virgin
Should he light and lie, to slocken [6] our sin
And slake it,
Our kind from woe;
For Isaiah said so,
Ecce virgo
Concipiet a child that is naked.

3 Shep. Full glad may we be and abide that day,
That lovely to see that all mights may.[7]
Lord, well were me for once and for ay,
Might I kneel on my knee some word for to say
To that child.
But the angel said
In a crib was he laid,
He was poorly arrayed,
Both meek [8] and mild.

1 Shep. Patriarchs that have been, and prophets before,
They desired to have seen this child that is born.
They are gone full clean; that have they lorn.
We shall see him, I ween, ere it be morn,
To token.[9]
When I see him and feel,
Then wot I full well
It is true as steel
That prophets have spoken:

To so poor as we are that he would appear,
First find, and declare by his messenger.
2 Shep. Go we now, let us fare; the place is us near.
3 Shep. I am ready and yare,[10] go we in fere [11]
To that bright.[12]
Lord, if thy will it be,
We are lewd,[13] all three;
Thou grant us somekind glee,
To comfort thy wight.

[Scene 8. *The stable in Bethlehem.*]

1 Shep. Hail, comely and clean! hail, young child!
Hail, Maker, as I mean, of a maiden so mild!
Thou hast waried,[14] I ween, the warlock so wild,
so wild,

92 commands.
93 Bethlehem.
94 noble (child).
95 voice.
96 name
97 in a flash of lightning.
98 made.
99 three short notes to one long note.
1 sang.
2 trilled.
3 go.
4 everlasting gladness may we take as our reward.
5 therefore.
6 do away with.
7 to see that lovely one that shall have all power.
8 Ms. *mener;* Kittredge's emendation.
9 for evidence.
10 prepared.
11 together.
12 supply "one" or "child."
13 ignorant.
14 banned.

The false guiler of teen,[15] now goes he beguiled.
Lo, he merries![16]
Lo, he laughs, my sweeting!
A welfare[17] meeting!
I have holden my highting.[18]
Have a bob of cherries!

2 Shep. Hail, sovereign savior, for thou has us sought!
Hail, freely[19] food[20] and flower, that all-thing has wrought!
Hail, full of favor, that made all of nought!
Hail! I kneel and I cower. A bird have I brought
To my bairn.
Hail, little tiny mop,[21]
Of our creed thou art crop![22]
I would drink in thy cup,
Little day-star!

3 Shep. Hail, darling dear, full of godhead!
I pray thee be near, when that I have need.
Hail! sweet is thy cheer! My heart would bleed
To see thee sit here in so poor weed,
With no pennies.
Hail! put forth thy dall![23]
I bring thee but a ball;
Have and play thee with all,
And go to the tennis.

Mary. The Father of Heaven, God omnipotent,
That set all on seven,[24] his son has he sent.
My name could he neven,[25] and alighted ere he went.
I conceived him full even, through might, as he meant;
And now he is born.
He keep you from woe!
I shall pray him so;
Tell forth as ye go,
And mind on this morn.

1 Shep. Farewell, lady, so fair to behold,
With thy child on thy knee.
2 Shep. But he lies full cold.
Lord, well is me! now we go, thou behold.
3 Shep. Forsooth, already it seems to be told
Full oft.
1 Shep. What grace we have found!
2 Shep. Come forth, now are we won.[26]
3 Shep. To sing are we bound:
Let take on loft.[27]

[*Exeunt.*]

15 woe.
16 is merry.
17 happy.
18 kept my promise.
19 noble.
20 child (that which is fed).
21 moppet, darling.
22 flower.
23 hand.
24 completed the work of creation in seven days.
25 did he name.
26 successful in our quest.
27 let it ring on high.

THE MORALITY

EVERYMAN

The morality is, by the most recent and most exact definition (W. R. Mackenzie in *The English Moralities*) "a play allegorical in structure, which has for its main object the teaching of some lesson for the guidance of life, and in which the principal characters are personified abstractions or highly universalized types." It will be readily seen that the morality differs from the miracle in several important respects. Whereas in the typical miracle the writer found his material arranged to his hand and took his plot, his chief characters, and sometimes the basis for his dialogue, from the Bible narrative, the author of the morality, though he frequently had recourse for plot to the moral allegories of which the Middle Ages were so fond, was compelled to rely more upon his own invention. The purpose of the miracle was to familiarize the audience with Bible history and the doctrines of the church; the morality was equally didactic but its teaching was more abstract. The people of the miracle were historical and real, in the sense that they stepped straight out of the Bible to the stage, where, to be sure, they were sometimes joined by such thoroughly English figures as those of the *Second Shepherds' Play*; the personages of the morality were virtues and vices acting in accordance with their names, or types of humanity in general, and thus by nature had somewhat less of individuality and human appeal. In one respect, however, the conception of character in the morality is stronger than that in the miracle. The morality is based on the idea that character is not static, but subject to change and development; the element of conflict between vice and virtue, wisdom and folly, at the heart of the morality, is of the very essence of drama.

Though the morality may be called younger than the miracle, it must not be thought of as an evolution from the older didactic drama. It was in all probability of independent origin, springing up apparently near the very end of the fourteenth century. The oldest surviving example is *The Castle of Perseverance*, dating from about 1400. Four other moralities are assigned to the fifteenth century; during the sixteenth the type attained considerable popularity, and the middle fifty years of that century may be called the morality's heyday.

The morality plays may be classified in several groups on the basis of allegorical structure, as follows (the classification is Mackenzie's): 1, those which depict a conflict between virtues and vices for supremacy, or for the possession of man; 2, those which illustrate a special text; 3, those which give warning of the summons of death; 4, those which take one side of a religious or political controversy. Of the first and largest class, *The Castle of Perseverance* is a good example: the seven cardinal virtues defend the castle and its lord Mankind against the attack of the seven deadly sins. Not all the warfare of the morality stage symbolized the struggle everlasting of man's spiritual nature; John Redford's excellent *Wit and Science*, wherein Science (Learning) and Idleness are at odds over the young gallant Wit, is one of several plays in which the strife is intellectual rather than spiritual. Such plays, in their purpose to popularize secular learning, show the spirit of the Renascence; advocates and opponents of the Reformation also discovered that the stage could be made to serve for propaganda, and there result such moralities, in the fourth of our classes, as Lyndsay's political *Satire of the Three Estates* and Bishop Bale's violently anti-papal *Kyng Johan*. The second class, (which may be typified by *All for Money*, illustrating the text "The love of money is the root of all evil"), is small and unimportant; the third is even smaller, comprising but two plays, but of these one is the finest of all the moralities, *Everyman*, which is probably from the Dutch.

To revert to our definition, it is evident that *Everyman* is "allegorical in structure," and that it teaches a lesson for the guidance of life. Apart from the general didacticism, there are passages upholding specific doctrines and practices of the church — e.g., Everyman's confession and penance (pp. 40–1), the enumeration of the seven sacraments, the praise of the priesthood immediately following. These passages, which convey the specific ecclesiastical moral of the efficacy of the sacraments, doubtless point to clerical composition. Of the characters, God is humanized, with little of the typical or abstract about him, Everyman is a highly universalized type, Friendship, Kindred and Cousin are also types, while the others are abstractions. Only Everyman himself possesses much vitality, but the development of his character is done with force and skill. The way in which his first gay nonchalance shades into a dawning comprehension of his danger as he comes to understand the seriousness of Death's summons, his increasing panic as one after another of his false friends deserts him, until he breaks out in an appeal of genuine terror —

> Good Deeds, I pray you, help me in this need,
> Or else I am for ever damned indeed, —

his relief when Knowledge promises to stand by him, his pious assurance of well-being after he has received the sacraments, and the fresh access of fear when his bodily faculties leave him fainting on the brink of the grave — this true picture of human life is presented with grim earnestness, yet with a sympathy which grips the heart. The real power of *Everyman* lies in its universal appeal — it comes home to men's business and bosoms. The modern revival of the play gave convincing proof that the morality was not the lifeless shell it has often been made out, and rendered quite intelligible the hold it had upon sixteenth-century audiences.

THE MORAL PLAY OF EVERYMAN

NAMES OF THE CHARACTERS

God.	Goods.	Discretion.
Death.	Good Deeds.	Five-Wits.
Everyman.	Knowledge.	Angel.
Fellowship.	Confession.	Messenger.
Kindred.	Beauty.	Doctor.
Cousin.	Strength.	

Here beginneth a treatise how the High Father of Heaven sendeth Death to summon every creature to come and give account of their lives in this world and is in manner of a moral play.

Messenger. I pray you all give your audience,
And hear this matter with reverence,
By figure [1] a moral play:
The *Summoning of Everyman* called it is,
That of our lives and ending shows
How transitory we be all day.
This matter is wondrous precious,
But the intent of it is more gracious,
And sweet to bear away.
The story saith:—Man, in the beginning,
Look well, and take good heed to the ending,
Be you never so gay;
Ye think sin in the beginning full sweet,
Which in the end causeth the soul to weep,
When the body lieth in clay.
Here shall you see how Fellowship and Jollity,
Both Strength, Pleasure, and Beauty,
Will fade from thee as flower in May.
For ye shall hear, how our heaven king
Calleth Everyman to a general reckoning:
Give audience, and hear what he doth say.

God speaketh.

God. I perceive here in my majesty,
How that all creatures be to me unkind,
Living without dread in worldly prosperity;
Of ghostly [2] sight the people be so blind,
Drowned in sin, they know me not for their God;
In worldly riches is all their mind.
They fear not my righteousness, the sharp rod;
My law that I showed, when I for them died,
They forget clean, and shedding of my blood red;
I hanged between two, it cannot be denied;
To get them life I suffered to be dead;
I healed their feet, with thorns hurt was my head;
I could do no more than I did truly.
And now I see the people do clean forsake me:
They use the seven deadly sins damnable,

1 in form.

2 spiritual.

As pride, covetise, wrath, and lechery,
Now in the world be made commendable,
And thus they leave of angels the heavenly company;
Every man liveth so after his own pleasure,
And yet of their life they be nothing sure.
I see the more that I them forbear
The worse they be from year to year;
All that liveth appaireth[3] fast;
Therefore I will in all the haste
Have a reckoning of every man's person.
For and[4] I leave the people thus alone
In their life and wicked tempests,
Verily they will become much worse than beasts,
For now one would by envy another up eat;
Charity they all do clean forget.
I hoped well that every man
In my glory should make his mansion,
And thereto I had them all elect;
But now I see, like traitors deject,
They thank me not for the pleasure that I to them meant,
Nor yet for their being that I them have lent.
I proffered the people great multitude of mercy,
And few there be that ask it heartily;
They be so cumbered with worldly riches,
That needs on them I must do justice,
On every man living without fear.
Where art thou, Death, thou mighty messenger?

Death. Almighty God, I am here at your will,
Your commandment to fulfil.

God. Go thou to Everyman,
And show him in my name
A pilgrimage he must on him take,
Which he in no wise may escape;
And that he bring with him a sure reckoning
Without delay or any tarrying.

Death. Lord, I will in the world go run over all,
And cruelly out search both great and small.
Every man will I beset that liveth beastly
Out of God's laws, and dreadeth not folly.
He that loveth riches I will strike with my dart,
His sight to blind, and from heaven to depart,[5]
Except that alms be his good friend,
In hell for to dwell, world without end.
Lo, yonder I see Everyman walking;
Full little he thinketh on my coming;
His mind is on fleshly lusts and his treasure,
And great pain it shall cause him to endure
Before the Lord, Heaven King.

Enter Everyman.

Everyman, stand still! Whither art thou going
Thus gaily? Hast thou thy Maker forgot?

Everyman. Why askest thou?
Wouldest thou wit?[6]

Death. Yea, sir, I will show you;
In great haste I am sent to thee
From God, out of his majesty.

Every. What, sent to me?

Death. Yea, certainly.
Though thou have forgot him here,
He thinketh on thee in the heavenly sphere,
As, ere we depart, thou shalt know.

Every. What desireth God of me?

Death. That shall I show thee:
A reckoning he will needs have,
Without any longer respite.

Every. To give a reckoning longer leisure I crave;
This blind matter troubleth my wit.

Death. On thee thou must take a long journey;
Therefore thy book of count with thee thou bring,
For turn again thou can not by no way;
And look thou be sure of thy reckoning,
For before God thou shalt answer, and show
Thy many bad deeds and good but a few,
How thou hast spent thy life, and in what wise,
Before the chief lord of paradise.
Have ado that we were in that way,
For, wit thou well, thou shalt make none attorney.[7]

Every. Full unready I am such reckoning to give.
I know thee not; what messenger art thou?

Death. I am Death, that no man dreadeth.
For every man I rest,[8] and no man spare;

3 decays. 4 if. 5 separate. 6 know. 7 advocate. 8 arrest.

For it is God's commandment
That all to me should be obedient.
Every. O Death, thou comest when I had thee least in mind!
In thy power it lieth me to save;
Yet of my good [9] will I give thee, if thou will be kind,
Yea, a thousand pound shalt thou have,
And defer this matter till another day.
Death. Everyman, it may not be by no way.
I set not by gold, silver, nor riches,
Nor by pope, emperor, king, duke, nor princes;
For and I would receive gifts great,
All the world I might get,
But my custom is clean contrary.
I give thee no respite; come hence, and not tarry.
Every. Alas, shall I have no longer respite?
I may say Death giveth no warning.
To think on thee, it maketh my heart sick,
For all unready is my book of reckoning,
But twelve year and I might have abiding,
My counting book I would make so clear,
That my reckoning I should not need to fear.
Wherefore, Death, I pray thee, for God's mercy,
Spare me till I be provided of remedy.
Death. Thee availeth not to cry, weep, and pray,
But haste thee lightly that thou were gone that journey,
And prove thy friends if thou can.
For, wit thou well, the tide abideth no man,
And in the world each living creature
For Adam's sin must die of nature.
Every. Death, if I should this pilgrimage take,
And my reckoning surely make,
Show me, for saint [10] charity,
Should I not come again shortly?
Death. No, Everyman; and thou be once there,
Thou mayst never more come here,
Trust me verily.
Every. O gracious God, in the high seat celestial,
Have mercy on me in this most need!
Shall I have no company from this vale terrestrial
Of mine acquaintance that way me to lead?
Death. Yea, if any be so hardy,
That would go with thee and bear thee company.
Hie thee that thou were gone to God's magnificence,
Thy reckoning to give before his presence.
What, weenest thou thy life is given thee,
And thy worldly goods also?
Every. I had wend [11] so, verily.
Death. Nay, nay; it was but lent thee;
For as soon as thou art gone,
Another a while shall have it, and then go therefrom,
Even as thou hast done.
Everyman, thou art mad! Thou hast thy wits five,
And here on earth will not amend thy life!
For suddenly I do come.
Every. O wretched caitiff, whither shall I flee,
That I might scape this endless sorrow?
Now, gentle Death, spare me till to-morrow,
That I may amend me
With good advisement.
Death. Nay, thereto I will not consent,
Nor no man will I respite;
But to the heart suddenly I shall smite
Without any advisement.
And now out of thy sight I will me hie;
See thou make thee ready shortly,
For thou mayst say this is the day
That no man living may scape away.
Every. Alas! I may well weep with sighs deep;
Now have I no manner of company
To help me in my journey, and me to keep;
And also my writing is full unready.
How shall I do now for to excuse me?
I would to God I had never been gotten!
To my soul a full great profit it had been,
For now I fear pains huge and great.
The time passeth; Lord, help, that all wrought!
For though I mourn it availeth nought.
The day passeth, and is almost agone;
I wot not well what for to do.
To whom were I best my complaint to make?
What and I to Fellowship thereof spake,
And showed him of this sudden chance?
For in him is all mine affiance; [12]

9 property. 10 holy. 11 thought. 12 confidence.

We have in the world so many a day
Been good friends in sport and play.
I see him yonder, certainly;
I trust that he will bear me company;
Therefore to him will I speak to ease my sorrow.
Well met, good Fellowship, and good morrow!

Fellowship speaketh. Everyman, good morrow! By this day,
Sir, why lookest thou so piteously?
If any thing be amiss, I pray thee me say,
That I may help to remedy.

Every. Yea, good Fellowship, yea,
I am in great jeopardy.

Fellow. My true friend, show to me your mind;
I will not forsake thee, to my life's end,
In the way of good company.

Every. That was well spoken, and lovingly.

Fellow. Sir, I must needs know your heaviness;
I have pity to see you in any distress.
If any have you wronged ye shall revenged be,
Though I on the ground be slain for thee,
Though that I know before that I should die.

Every. Verily, Fellowship, gramercy.[13]

Fellow. Tush! by thy thanks I set not a straw.
Show me your grief, and say no more.

Every. If I my heart should to you break,
And then you to turn your mind from me,
And would not me comfort. when ye hear me speak,
Then should I ten times sorrier be.

Fellow. Sir, I say as I will do indeed.

Every. Then be you a good friend at need.
I have found you true here before.

Fellow. And so ye shall evermore;
For, in faith, and thou go to hell,
I will not forsake thee by the way.

Every. Ye speak like a good friend, I believe you well;
I shall deserve it, and I may.

Fellow. I speak of no deserving, by this day.
For he that will say and nothing do
Is not worthy with good company to go.
Therefore show me the grief of your mind,
As to your friend most loving and kind.

Every. I shall show you how it is:
Commanded I am to go a journey,
A long way, hard and dangerous,
And give a strait count without delay
Before the high judge Adonai.[14]
Wherefore I pray you, bear me company,
As ye have promised, in this journey.

Fellow. That is matter indeed! Promise is duty,
But and I should take such a voyage on me,
I know it well, it should be to my pain;
Also it makes me afeard, certain.
But let us take counsel here as well as we can,
For your words would fear[15] a strong man.

Every. Why, ye said, if I had need,
Ye would me never forsake, quick[16] nor dead,
Though it were to hell, truly.

Fellow. So I said, certainly.
But such pleasures be set aside, the sooth to say;
And also, if we took such a journey,
When should we come again?

Every. Nay, never again till the day of doom.

Fellow. In faith, then will not I come there!
Who hath you these tidings brought?

Every. Indeed, Death was with me here.

Fellow. Now, by God that all hath bought,
If Death were the messenger,
For no man that is living to-day
I will not go that loath[17] journey—
Not for the father that begat me!

Every. Ye promised other wise, pardie![18]

Fellow. I wot well I say so, truly;
And yet if thou wilt eat, and drink, and make good cheer,
Or haunt to women the lusty company,
I would not forsake you while the day is clear,
Trust me verily!

Every. Yea, thereto ye would be ready;
To go to mirth, solace, and play,
Your mind will sooner apply,
Than to bear me company in my long journey.

Fellow. Now, in good faith, I will not[19] that way.
But and thou will murder, or any man kill,

13 thanks.
14 God.
15 frighten.
16 living.
17 loathsome.
18 *par Dieu.*
19 have no desire.

In that I will help thee with a good will!
Every. Oh, that is a simple advice indeed!
Gentle Fellow, help me in my necessity;
We have loved long, and now I need;
And now, gentle Fellowship, remember me.
Fellow. Whether ye have loved me or no,
By Saint John, I will not with thee go!
Every. Yet I pray thee, take the labor and do so much for me
To bring me forward, for saint charity,
And comfort me till I come without the town.
Fellow. Nay, and thou would give me a new gown,
I will not a foot with thee go;
But and thou had tarried, I would not have left thee so.
And as now, God speed thee in thy journey!
For from thee I will depart as fast as I may.
Every. Whither away, Fellowship? will thou forsake me?
Fellow. Yea, by my fay![20] To God I betake[21] thee.
Every. Farewell, good Fellowship; for thee my heart is sore.
Adieu for ever, I shall see thee no more.
Fellow. In faith, Everyman, farewell now at the end;
For you I will remember that parting is mourning.
Every. Alack! shall we thus depart indeed?
Ah, Lady, help! without any more comfort,
Lo, Fellowship forsaketh me in my most need.
For help in this world whither shall I resort?
Fellowship herebefore with me would merry make,
And now little sorrow for me doth he take.
It is said, in prosperity men friends may find,
Which in adversity be full unkind.
Now whither for succor shall I flee,
Sith[22] that Fellowship hath forsaken me?
To my kinsmen I will truly,
Praying them to help me in my necessity;
I believe that they will do so,
For kind[23] will creep where it may not go.[24]
I will go say,[25] for yonder I see them go.
Where be ye now, my friends and kinsmen?
Kindred. Here be we now at your commandment.
Cousin, I pray you show us your intent
In any wise, and not spare.
Cousin. Yea, Everyman, and to us declare
If ye be disposed to go any whither,
For wit you well, [we] will live and die together.
Kin. In wealth and woe we will with you hold,
For over his kin a man may be bold.
Every. Gramercy, my friends and kinsmen kind;
Now shall I show you the grief of my mind.
I was commanded by a messenger,
That is an high king's chief officer:
He bade me go a pilgrimage to my pain,
And I know well I shall never come again;
Also I must give a reckoning strait,
For I have a great enemy that hath me in wait,[26]
Which intendeth me for to hinder.
Kin. What account is that which ye must render?
That would I know.
Every. Of all my works I must show
How I have lived and my days spent;
Also of ill deeds, that I have used
In my time, sith life was me lent;
And of all virtues that I have refused.
Therefore I pray you go thither with me,
To help to make mine account, for saint charity.
Cous. What, to go thither? Is that the matter?
Nay, Everyman, I had liefer fast bread and water
All this five year and more.
Every. Alas, that ever I was born!
For now shall I never be merry
If that you forsake me.
Kin. Ah, sir, what, ye be a merry man!
Take good heart to you, and make no moan.
But one thing I warn you, by Saint Anne,

20 faith.
21 commend.
22 since.
23 kinship.
24 walk: the line is a proverbial expression of the idea that blood-relationship will compel assistance, even though the latter be given unwillingly. Cf. *Second Shepherds' Play*, p. 28.
25 assay, try.
26 lies in wait for me.

As for me, ye shall go alone.
Every. My Cousin, will you not with me go?
Cous. No, by our Lady! I have the cramp in my toe.
Trust not to me, for, so God me speed,
I will deceive you in your most need.
Kin. It availeth not us to tice.[27]
Ye shall have my maid with all my heart;
She loveth to go to feasts, there to be nice,[28]
And to dance, and abroad to start:
I will give her leave to help you in that journey,
If that you and she may agree.
Every. Now show me the very effect of your mind;
Will you go with me, or abide behind?
Kin. Abide behind? yea, that will I and I may!
Therefore farewell till another day.
Every. How should I be merry or glad?
For fair promises men to me make,
But when I have most need, they me forsake.
I am deceived; that maketh me sad.
Cous. Cousin Everyman, farewell now,
For verily I will not go with you.
Also of mine own an unready reckoning
I have to account; therefore I make tarrying.
Now, God keep thee, for now I go.
Every. Ah, Jesus, is all come hereto?
Lo, fair words make fools fain;
They promise, and nothing will do certain.
My kinsmen promised me faithfully
For to abide with me steadfastly,
And now fast away do they flee:
Even so Fellowship promised me.
What friend were best me of to provide?
I lose my time here longer to abide.
Yet in my mind a thing there is—
All my life I have loved riches;
If that my Good now help me might,
He would make my heart full light.
I will speak to him in this distress.—
Where art thou, my Goods and Riches?
Goods. Who calleth me? Everyman? what hast thou haste?
I lie here in corners, trussed and piled so high,
And in chests I am locked so fast,
Also sacked in bags, thou mayst see with thine eye,
I cannot stir; in packs low I lie.
What would ye have, lightly me say.
Every. Come hither, Good, in all the haste thou may,
For of counsel I must desire thee.
Goods. Sir, and ye in the world have sorrow or adversity,
That can I help you to remedy shortly.
Every. It is another disease that grieveth me;
In this world it is not, I tell thee so.
I am sent for another way to go,
To give a strait count general
Before the highest Jupiter [29] of all.
And all my life I have had joy and pleasure in thee,
Therefore I pray thee go with me;
For, peradventure, thou mayst before God Almighty
My reckoning help to clean and purify,
For it is said ever among,
That money maketh all right that is wrong.
Goods. Nay, Everyman, I sing another song,
I follow no man in such voyages;
For and I went with thee,
Thou shouldst fare much the worse for me;
For because on me thou did set thy mind,
Thy reckoning I have made blotted and blind,
That thine account thou can not make truly;
And that hast thou for the love of me.
Every. That would grieve me full sore,
When I should come to that fearful answer.
Up, let us go thither together!
Goods. Nay, not so; I am too brittle, I may not endure;
I will follow [no] man one foot, be ye sure.
Every. Alas, I have thee loved, and had great pleasure
All my life-days in good and treasure.
Goods. That is to thy damnation without lesing,[30]
For my love is contrary to the love everlasting.
But if thou had me loved moderately during,[31]
As [32] to the poor give part of me,
Then shouldst thou not in this dolor be,
Nor in this great sorrow and care.

27 entice.
28 wanton.
29 A curious intrusion of the name of the pagan deity.
30 lying.
31 for a while.
32 in such a way as.

Every. Lo, now was I deceived ere I was ware,
And all I may wite[33] my spending of time.
Goods. What, weenest thou that I am thine?
Every. I had wend so.
Goods. Nay, Everyman, I say no;
As for a while I was lent thee,
A season thou hast had me in prosperity.
My condition is man's soul to kill;
If I save one, a thousand I do spill,[34]
Weenest thou that I will follow thee?
Nay, from this world not verily.
Every. I had wend otherwise.
Goods. Therefore to thy soul Good is a thief;
For when thou art dead, this is my guise[35]—
Another to deceive in the same wise
As I have done thee, and all to his soul's reprief.[36]
Every. O false Good, cursed thou be!
Thou traitor to God, that hast deceived me,
And caught me in thy snare.
Goods. Marry, thou brought thyself in care,
Whereof I am glad,
I must needs laugh, I cannot be sad.
Every. Ah, Good, thou hast had long my heartly love;
I gave thee that which should be the Lord's above.
But wilt thou not go with me in deed?
I pray thee truth to say.
Goods. No, so God me speed,
Therefore farewell, and have good day.
Every. Oh, to whom shall I make my moan
For to go with me in that heavy journey?
First Fellowship said he would with me go;
His words were very pleasant and gay,
But afterward he left me alone.
Then spake I to my kinsmen all in despair,
And also they gave me words fair,
They lacked no fair speaking,
But all forsake me in the ending.
Then went I to my Goods, that I loved best,
In hope to have comfort, but there had I least;
For my Goods sharply did me tell
That he bringeth many into hell.
Then of myself I was ashamed,
And so I am worthy to be blamed;
Thus may I well myself hate.
Of whom shall I now counsel take?
I think that I shall never speed
Till that I go to my Good-Deed.
But alas, she is so weak,
That she can neither go nor speak;
Yet will I venture on her now.—
My Good-Deeds, where be you?
Good-Deeds. Here I lie, cold in the ground;
Thy sins have me sore bound,
That I cannot stir.
Every. O Good-Deeds, I stand in fear;
I must you pray of counsel,
For help now should come right well.
Good-D. Everyman, I have understanding
That ye be summoned account to make
Before Messias, of Jerusalem King;
And you do by me[37] that journey with you will I take.
Every. Therefore I come to you, my moan to make;
I pray you that ye will go with me.
Good-D. I would full fain, but I cannot stand, verily.
Every. Why, is there anything on you fallen?
Good-D. Yea, sir, I may thank you of all;[38]
If ye had perfectly cheered[39] me,
Your book of count now full ready had been.
Look, the books of your works and deeds eke—
Ah, see how they lie under the feet,
To your soul's heaviness.
Every. Our Lord Jesus, help me!
For one letter here I can not see.
Good-D. There is a blind reckoning in time of distress!
Every. Good-Deeds, I pray you, help me in this need,
Or else I am for ever damned indeed.
Therefore help me to make reckoning
Before the redeemer of all thing,
That king is, and was, and ever shall.
Good-D. Everyman, I am sorry of your fall,
And fain would I help you, and I were able.
Every. Good-Deeds, your counsel I pray you give me.
Good-D. That shall I do verily;

[33] blame to. [34] destroy. [35] practice. [36] reproof, shame. [37] by my advice. [38] for everything. [39] cherished.

Though that on my feet I may not go,
I have a sister, that shall with you also,
Called Knowledge, which shall with you abide,
To help you to make that dreadful reckoning.

Knowledge. Everyman, I will go with thee, and be thy guide,
In thy most need to go by thy side.

Every. In good condition I am now in every thing,
And am wholly content with this good thing;
Thanked be God my Creator!

Good-D. And when he hath brought you there,
Where thou shalt heal thee of thy smart,
Then go you with your reckoning and your Good-Deeds together,
For to make you joyful at heart
Before the blessed Trinity.

Every. My Good-Deeds, gramercy;
I am well content, certainly,
With your words sweet.

Know. Now go we together lovingly,
To Confession, that cleansing river.

Every. For joy I weep; I would we were there.
But, I pray you, give me cognition [40]
Where dwelleth that holy man, Confession.

Know. In the house of salvation:
We shall find him in that place,
That shall us comfort by God's grace.—

Enter Confession.

Lo, this is Confession. Kneel down and ask mercy,
For he is in good conceit [41] with God almighty.

Every. O glorious fountain that all uncleanness doth clarify,
Wash me from the spots of vice unclean,
That on me no sin may be seen.
I come with Knowledge for my redemption,
Redempt with hearty and full contrition;
For I am commanded a pilgrimage to take,
And great accounts before God to make.
Now, I pray you, Shrift,[42] mother of salvation,
Help my good deeds for my piteous exclamation.

Confession. I know your sorrow well, Everyman;
Because with Knowledge ye come to me,
I will you comfort as well as I can,
And a precious jewel I will give thee,
Called penance, voider [43] of adversity;
Therewith shall your body chastised be,
With abstinence and perseverance in God's service:
Here shall you receive that scourge of me,
Which is penance strong, that ye must endure,
To remember thy Savior was scourged for thee
With sharp scourges, and suffered it patiently;
So must thou, ere thou scape that painful pilgrimage.
Knowledge, keep him in this voyage,
And by that time Good-Deeds will be with thee.
But in any wise, be sicker [44] of mercy,
For your time draweth fast; and ye will saved be,
Ask God mercy, and He will grant truly.
When with the scourge of penance man doth him bind,
The oil of forgiveness then shall he find.

Every. Thanked be God for his gracious work,
For now I will my penance begin;
This hath rejoiced and lighted my heart,
Though the knots be painful and hard within.

Know. Everyman, look your penance that ye fulfil,
What pain that ever it to you be,
And Knowledge shall give you counsel at will,
How your account ye shall make clearly.

Every. O eternal God, O heavenly figure,
O way of righteousness, O goodly vision,
Which descended down in a virgin pure
Because he would Everyman redeem,
Which Adam forfeited by his disobedience,
O blessed Godhead, elect and high-divine,
Forgive my grievous offence;
Here I cry thee mercy in this presence.
O ghostly treasure, O ransomer and redeemer,
Of all the world hope and conductor,
Mirror of joy, founder of mercy,
Which illumineth heaven and earth thereby,
Hear my clamorous complaint, though it late be!

40 knowledge.
41 favor.
42 absolution.
43 MS. *voice voider;* probably a scribal error.
44 sure.

Receive my prayers; unworthy in this heavy life
Though I be, a sinner most abominable,
Yet let my name be written in Moses' table.
O Mary, pray to the Maker of all thing,
Me for to help at my ending,
And save me from the power of my enemy,
For Death assaileth me strongly;
And, Lady, that I may by means of thy prayer
Of your Son's glory to be partner,
By the means of his passion I it crave,
I beseech you, help my soul to save!—
Knowledge, give me the scourge of penance,
My flesh therewith shall give acquaintance.
I will now begin, if God give me grace.

Know. Everyman, God give you time and space:
Thus I bequeath you in the hands of our Savior,
Now may you make your reckoning sure.

Every. In the name of the Holy Trinity,
My body sore punished shall be:
(*Scourges himself.*)
Take this, body, for the sin of the flesh;
Also thou delightest to go gay and fresh,
And in the way of damnation thou did me bring;
Therefore suffer now strokes of punishing.
Now of penance I will wade the water clear,
To save me from purgatory, that sharp fire.

Good-D. I thank God, now I can walk and go,
And am delivered of my sickness and woe.
Therefore with Everyman I will go, and not spare;
His good works I will help him to declare.

Know. Now, Everyman, be merry and glad;
Your Good-Deeds cometh now, ye may not be sad;
Now is your Good-Deeds whole and sound,
Going upright upon the ground.

Every. My heart is light, and shall be evermore;
Now will I smite faster than I did before.

Good-D. Everyman, pilgrim, my special friend,
Blessed be thou without end;
For thee is prepared the eternal glory.
Ye have me made whole and sound,
Therefore I will bide by thee in every stound.[45]

Every. Welcome, my Good-Deeds! Now I hear thy voice,
I weep for very sweetness of love.

Know. Be no more sad, but ever rejoice:
God seeth thy living in his throne above.
Put on this garment to thy behoof,[46]
Which is wet with your tears,
Or else before God you may it miss,
When ye to your journey's end come shall.

Every. Gentle Knowledge, what do ye it call?

Know. It is a garment of sorrow,
From pain it will you borrow;[47]
Contrition it is,
That getteth forgiveness;
It pleaseth God passing well.

Good-D. Everyman, will you wear it for your heal?
(*Everyman puts on robe of contrition.*)

Every. Now blessed be Jesu, Mary's Son,
For now have I on true contrition.
And let us go now without tarrying.
Good-Deeds, have we clear our reckoning?

Good-D. Yea, indeed I have [it] here.

Every. Then I trust we need not fear.
Now, friends, let us not part in twain.

Know. Nay, Everyman, that will we not, certain.

Good-D. Yet must thou lead with thee
Three persons of great might.

Every. Who should they be?

Good-D. Discretion and Strength they hight,[48]
And thy Beauty may not abide behind.

Know. Also ye must call to mind
Your Five-wits as for your counsellors.

Good-D. You must have them ready at all hours.

Every. How shall I get them hither?

Know. You must call them all together,
And they will hear you incontinent.

Every. My friends, come hither and be present,
Discretion, Strength, my Five-wits, and Beauty.

Beauty. Here at your will we be all ready.
What will ye that we should do?

45 hour. 46 benefit. 47 redeem. 48 are called.

Good-D. That ye would with Everyman go,
And help him in his pilgrimage.
Advise you, will ye with him or not in that voyage?
Strength. We will bring him all thither,
To his help and comfort, ye may believe me.
Discretion. So will we go with him all together.
Every. Almighty God, loved might thou be,
I give thee laud that I have hither brought
Strength, Discretion, Beauty, and Five-wits; lack I nought;
And my Good-Deeds, with Knowledge clear,
All be in my company at my will here;
I desire no more to my business.
Stren. And I, Strength, will by you stand in distress,
Though thou would in battle fight on the ground.
Five-Wits. And though it were through the world round,
We will not depart for sweet nor sour.
Beau. No more will I unto death's hour,
Whatsoever thereof befall.
Discr. Everyman, advise you first of all,
Go with a good advisement and deliberation.
We all give you virtuous monition
That all shall be well.
Every. My friends, hearken what I will tell:
I pray God reward you in his heavenly sphere.
Now hearken, all that be here,
For I will make my testament
Here before you all present.
In alms half my good I will give with my hands twain
In the way of charity, with good intent,
And the other half still shall remain
In quethe [49] to be returned there it ought to be.
This I do in despite of the fiend of hell,
To go quite out of his peril
Ever after and this day.
Know. Everyman, hearken what I say;
Go to Priesthood, I you advise,
And receive of him in any wise
The holy sacrament and ointment together,
Then shortly see ye turn again hither;
We will all abide you here.

Five-W. Yea, Everyman, hie you that ye ready were.
There is no emperor, king, duke, nor baron,
That of God hath commission,
As hath the least priest in the world being; [50]
For of the blessed sacraments pure and benign
He beareth the keys, and thereof hath the cure
For man's redemption, it is ever sure,
Which God for our soul's medicine
Gave us out of his heart with great pain.
Here in this transitory life, for thee and me
The blessed sacraments seven there be:
Baptism, confirmation, with priesthood good,
And the sacrament of God's precious flesh and blood,
Marriage, the holy extreme unction, and penance;
These seven be good to have in remembrance,
Gracious sacraments of high divinity.
Every. Fain would I receive that holy body,
And meekly to my ghostly [51] father I will go.

Exit Everyman.

Five-W. Everyman, that is the best that ye can do.
God will you to salvation bring,
For priesthood exceedeth all other thing;
To us Holy Scripture they do teach,
And convert man from sin, heaven to reach.
God hath to them more power given,
Than to any angel that is in heaven:
With five words he may consecrate
God's body in flesh and blood to make,
And handleth his Maker between his hands.
The priest bindeth and unbindeth all bands,
Both in earth and in heaven.
Thou ministers all the sacraments seven.
Though we kiss thy feet thou were worthy.
Thou art surgeon that cureth sin deadly:
No remedy we find under God
But all only priesthood.
Everyman, God gave priests that dignity,
And setteth them in his stead among us to be;

9 bequest. 50 living. 51 spiritual.

Thus be they above angels in degree.
Know. If priests be good, it is so surely.
But when Jesus hanged on the cross with great smart,
There he gave, out of his blessed heart,
The same sacrament in great torment;
He sold them not to us, that Lord omnipotent.
Therefore Saint Peter the apostle doth say
That Jesus' curse have all they
Which God their Savior do buy or sell,
Or they for any money do take or tell.[52]
Sinful priests give the sinners example bad,
Their children sit by other men's fires, I have heard,
And some haunt women's company,
With unclean life, as lusts of lechery;
These be with sin made blind.
Five-W. I trust to God no such may we find.
Therefore let us priesthood honor,
And follow their doctrine for our souls' succor;
We be their sheep, and they shepherds be,
By whom we all be kept in surety.
Peace, for yonder I see Everyman come,
Which hath made true satisfaction.

Re-enter Everyman.

Good-D. Methink it is he indeed.
Every. Now Jesu be your alder speed.[53]
I have received the sacrament for my redemption,
And then mine extreme unction:
Blessed be all they that counselled me to take it!
And now, friends, let us go without longer respite;
I thank God that ye have tarried so long.
Now set each of you on this rod[54] your hand,
And shortly follow me.
I go before, there I would be; God be your guide.
Stren. Everyman, we will not from you go,
Till ye have done this voyage long.
Discr. I, Discretion, will bide by you also.
Know. And though this pilgrimage be never so strong,[55]
I will never part you from.
Everyman, I will be as sure by thee
As ever I did by Judas Maccabee.
Every. Alas, I am so faint I may not stand,
My limbs under me do fold.
Friends, let us not turn again to this land,
Not for all the world's gold,
For into this cave must I creep,
And turn to earth and there to sleep.
Beau. What, into this grave? alas!
Every. Yea, there shall ye consume more and less.
Beau. And what, should I smother here?
Every. Yea, by my faith, and never more appear.
In this world live no more we shall,
But in heaven before the highest Lord of all.
Beau. I cross out all this! Adieu, by Saint John!
I take my tap in my lap and am gone.[56]
Every. What, Beauty, whither will ye?
Beau. Peace! I am deaf, I look not behind me,
Not and thou wouldest give me all the gold in thy chest.
Every. Alas, whereto may I trust?
Beauty goeth fast away from me,
She promised with me to live and die.
Stren. Everyman, I will thee also forsake and deny;
Thy game liketh[57] me not at all.
Every. Why, then ye will forsake me all!
Sweet Strength, tarry a little space.
Stren. Nay, sir, by the rood of grace,
I will hie me from thee fast,
Though thou weep to[58] thy heart tobrast.[59]
Every. Ye would ever bide by me, ye said.
Stren. Yea, I have you far enough conveyed;
Ye be old enough, I understand,
Your pilgrimage to take on hand.
I repent me that I hither came.
Every. Strength, you to displease I am to blame;
Will you break promise that is debt?
Stren. In faith, I care not;
Thou art but a fool to complain,
You spend your speech and waste your brain;
Go, thrust thee into the ground!
Every. I had wend surer I should you have found.
He that trusteth in his Strength,

52 count.
53 the help of you all.
54 rood, cross.
55 hard.
56 proverbial expression for a hasty departure; literally *tap* is a bunch of tow for spinning.
57 pleaseth.
58 till.
59 break in pieces.

She him deceiveth at the length.
Both Strength and Beauty forsake me,
Yet they promised me fair and lovingly.
Discr. Everyman, I will after Strength be gone,
As for me I will leave you alone.
Every. Why, Discretion, will ye forsake me?
Discr. Yea, in faith, I will go from thee,
For when Strength goeth before
I follow after evermore.
Every. Yet, I pray thee, for the love of the Trinity,
Look in my grave once piteously.
Discr. Nay, so nigh will I not come.
Farewell, every one!
Every. Oh, all thing faileth, save God alone,
Beauty, Strength, and Discretion;
For when Death bloweth his blast,
They all run from me full fast.
Five-W. Everyman, my leave now of thee I take;
I will follow the other, for here I thee forsake.
Every. Alas! then may I wail and weep,
For I took you for my best friend.
Five-W. I will no longer thee keep;
Now farewell, and there an end.
Every. O Jesu, help! all have forsaken me!
Good-D. Nay, Everyman, I will bide with thee,
I will not forsake thee indeed;
Thou shalt find me a good friend at need.
Every. Gramercy, Good-Deeds, now may I true friends see;
They have forsaken me every one,
I loved them better than my Good-Deeds alone.
Knowledge, will ye forsake me also?
Know. Yea, Everyman, when ye to death shall go;
But not yet for no manner of danger.
Every. Gramercy, Knowledge, with all my heart.
Know. Nay, yet I will not from hence depart,
Till I see where ye shall be come.
Every. Methink, alas, that I must be gone,
To make my reckoning and my debts pay,
For I see my time is nigh spent away.
Take example, all ye that this do hear or see,
How they that I love best do forsake me,
Except my Good-Deeds that bideth truly.
Good-D. All earthly things is but vanity:
Beauty, Strength, and Discretion, do man forsake,
Foolish friends and kinsmen that fair spake,
All flee save Good-Deeds, and that am I.
Every. Have mercy on me, God most mighty,
And stand by me, thou Mother and Maid, holy Mary.
Good-D. Fear not, I will speak for thee.
Every. Here I cry God mercy.
Good-D. Short our end, and minish our pain;
Let us go and never come again.
Every. Into thy hands, Lord, my soul I commend,
Receive it, Lord, that it be not lost!
As thou me boughtest, so me defend,
And save me from the fiend's boast,
That I may appear with that blessed host
That shall be saved at the day of doom.
In manus tuas—of mights most
For ever—*commendo spiritum meum*
(*Dies.*)
Know. Now hath he suffered that we all shall endure;
The Good-Deeds shall make all sure.
Now hath he made ending;
Methinketh that I hear angels sing
And make great joy and melody,
Where Everyman's soul received shall be.
Angel. Come, excellent elect spouse to Jesu;
Here above thou shalt go,
Because of thy singular virtue.
Now the soul is taken the body from
Thy reckoning is crystal-clear.
Now shalt thou into the heavenly sphere,
Unto the which all ye shall come
That live well before the day of doom.
Doctor.[60] This moral men may have in mind;
Ye hearers, take it of worth, old and young,
And forsake Pride, for he deceiveth you in the end,
And remember Beauty, Five-wits, Strength, and Discretion,
They all at the last do Everyman forsake,
Save his Good-Deeds, there doth he take.
But beware, and they be small
Before God, he hath no help at all.
None excuse may be there for Everyman.

60 cf. note on Doctor at end of *Abraham and Isaac.*

Alas, how shall he do then?
For after death amends may no man make,
For then mercy and pity do him forsake.
If his reckoning be not clear when he doth come,
God will say—*Ite maledicti in ignem æternum.*
And he that hath his account whole and sound,
High in heaven he shall be crowned;
Unto which place God bring us all thither,
That we may live body and soul together.
Thereto help the Trinity!
Amen, say ye, for saint charity.

FINIS

THUS ENDETH THIS MORAL PLAY OF EVERYMAN.

II. THE ELIZABETHAN PERIOD

JOHN LYLY

MOTHER BOMBIE

John Lyly (c. 1554–1606), a Kentishman, educated at Oxford (B.A. 1573; M.A. 1575), made a great reputation with his didactic romance *Euphues: the Anatomy of Wit*, 1578, and its sequel *Euphues and his England*, 1580, which established in popular favor the artificial prose style called Euphuism. In 1584 was acted his first play, *Alexander and Campaspe*, and he continued to write for the stage for some fifteen years. He applied for the Mastership of the Revels, but failed to win the post. Between 1589 and 1601 he was a member of four parliaments. His importance in English literature lies in his contributions to the development of prose style and of refined comedy.

By the time that he inaugurated the great period of Elizabethan drama, the leaven of the Renascence had been at work in England for three quarters of a century. Although the miracle play reached its full development quite unaffected by the new learning, the morality and the secular interlude (the latter as practised by John Heywood between 1520 and 1540), however vernacular they may be in form and spirit, show that the English drama was responding to influences from abroad. Both at court, where humanism took hold early and where translations of Latin comedy were actually performed before 1525, and in the schools and colleges, where the plays of Plautus and Terence were studied, acted, and used for models, the popularized classics inspired court entertainers and pedagogues to adaptation and imitation. To Nicholas Udall belongs the honor of writing, probably during his term of mastership at Eton, 1534–41, the first regular English comedy, *Ralph Roister Doister*. In this play Udall, adapting the *Miles Gloriosus* of Plautus to English life, brings to comedy a sense of form lacking in miracle, morality, and interlude. Even so native a product as *Gammer Gurton's Needle*, 1550–60, a farce comedy of village life straight from the soil, was written by a fellow of Christ's College, Cambridge, and exhibits in its division into acts and scenes the tendency to regularization. Tragedy, likewise, felt the classic influence: *Gorboduc*, 1562, is our first regular tragedy, British in subject-matter, but in manner patterned on the tragedies of Seneca. The writers of the old didactic drama had vigor and sincerity and strong emotional appeal, but had no model except experience, no critical faculty, low artistic standards. To give it a permanent value the English drama needed conscious artists with professional pride and technical training. After some decades of experimental work like that named above, such an artist appeared in the person of Lyly.

Lyly's university education and his connection with the court determined the style of his work. All but one of his eight plays employ classical material, and that one is done in the manner of Latin comedy. They are the work of a clever young college man, fired with enthusiasm by his reading of classical myth and Latin comedy, delighting in his already established reputation as a witty master of prose, and ambitious to gain court favor. Edward Blount, who published six of Lyly's plays in 1632, called them "Court Comedies," and the term was well chosen. They were well adapted to appeal to Elizabeth, learned, pleasure-loving, avid of flattery, and to her brilliant group of courtiers. Three of them deal in thinly veiled allusion with matters of court gossip: *Endimion* with the relations of Elizabeth with Mary, Queen of Scots, and her son James; *Sapho and Phao* with the Duc d'Alençon's vain effort to win Elizabeth's hand in marriage; *Midas* with Philip of Spain and his ambition to win back England for Catholicism. Three others are pastoral comedies, using mythological story and figures, and adroitly flattering the Queen. *Alexander and Campaspe*, presenting a romantic, pseudo-historical episode in the life of Alexander the Great, is seemingly without ulterior purpose, as is the rustic farce-comedy, *Mother Bombie*. Allusive, witty, reflecting in tone the politeness of court manners, these plays were admirably adapted for their time and audience, and justify Lyly's reputation as our first dramatist to write plays of real artistic value.

The play which follows is unique in Lyly's work in that it presents English life and English people unhampered by mythological accessories. The scene is laid in Rochester, in Lyly's own county of Kent. The occasional local allusions and the introduction of homely figures like the village wise-woman, the hackneyman, and the fiddlers, add a pleasant touch of realism. In structure, however, the play is obviously modeled upon the Terentian comedy. Though no direct source has been found, names, material, love-plots of children against their parents, aided by roguish servants, and the solution, by revelation of a long-concealed substitution of one pair of children for another, are reminiscent of Latin comedy. Then, too, in its approximation to the unities of time, place, and action, the play shows Lyly's classical training; although the theory of the unities was first formulated by the Italian critic Castelvetro in 1570, it is based on the usual practice of the Greek and Roman dramatists. The time is limited to two days in all, a reasonably close approach to the norm of Latin comedy. Unity of place is strictly observed, all the action occurring in an open square, about which are located the dwellings of the chief characters and the tavern. The only episode which can be objected to as in any way extraneous is the comic business of the hackneyman's suit against Dromio, surely no very serious interruption of the main action. As an early example, then, of classical method applied to English stuff, the play is historically important.

Mother Bombie is the most complicated in structure of Lyly's plays. There are three main lines of action — the love-affair of Candius and Livia, opposed by their parents and forwarded by the pages; the proposed matches between Candius and Silena on the one hand, and Accius and Livia on the other, furthered by the parents, real or supposed, thwarted by the pages, and nearly resulting in the betrothal of Accius and Silena; the love-story of Mæstius and Serena, apparently hopeless of fulfilment, but ending happily in the revelation that they are not brother and sister, a discovery which legitimizes their union and renders impossible that of the foolish children. The tangling of these threads is done with no small skill, but the complication would be difficult for an audience to follow were it not for the constant comments on the situation of the moment that Lyly puts into the mouths of the actors. Soliloquy and aside are used to their full capacity. The plotting is mechanical even to the paralleling of one scene by another in a manner recalling the use of balance and antithesis in one of Lyly's Euphuistic sentences. The first five scenes will serve for illustration. In scene one Memphio informs his servant Dromio of his desire to match his foolish son Accius to the daughter of his neighbor Stellio, and bids Dromio set about the matter. In scene two Stellio informs his servant Riscio of his desire to match his foolish daughter Silena to the son of his neighbor Memphio, and entrusts the management of the affair to Riscio. In scene three Prisius and Sperantus agree that their children must not marry, and the plan of Sperantus to marry his son Candius to Stellio's daughter finds correspondence in the plan of Prisius to marry his daughter Livia to Memphio's son. The love-scene between Candius and Livia is witnessed by the fathers, who cap the lovers' speeches with antiphonal comments, and each of whom, after disclosing himself, dismisses his offspring with a long reproof. In the first scene of act two Dromio and Riscio echo each other's very words as they reveal the parts they are to play, while Halfpenny and Lucio are no sooner desired then they appear, and the four depart into the tavern to lay out their campaign of cozenage. The scene following presents the four scheming fathers entering severally in search of their respective servants, and, after soliloquies of one pattern, disappearing into the tavern door which has already welcomed the boys. Like the Euphuistic sentence, nothing could be more polished in its way, or more artificial.

The double disguising in act four Lyly brings off with fair success. The approval of the betrothal of Candius and Livia by their fathers, the latter under the impression that they are witnessing the plighting of Accius and Silena, is truly comic and well managed. The corresponding situation, which brings the climax of the complication in the unmasking of Accius and Silena by their fathers is almost too intricate to be quite effective; Lyly evades rather than solves his difficulty by huddling his main group off the stage before he has begun to get out of the situation all the fun there is in it. The *dénouement* is brought about, as usual with Lyly, in brusque and mechanical fashion; here the confession of Vicinia corresponds to the oracle which brings the solution in the three allegorical plays, and to the *deus ex machina* of the pastoral comedies.

Lyly's curious method of group rather than individual characterization is well exemplified in *Mother Bombie*. Here we have four old men, four knavish pages, three young couples, three fiddlers, three village types, two old women. The groups are somewhat distinguished one from another, but inside the group distinction is almost lacking. Memphio and Stellio are rich, Prisius and Sperantus are poor; their occupations vary; but beyond these trivial differences they all act and speak alike. The same is true of the pages, except that, as is customary in plays written for boys to perform, the sharpest wit is given to the smallest boy, in this case Halfpenny. Such lack of individuality makes us feel about Lyly's people that they are puppets cleverly manipulated, not well rounded human beings. Candius and Livia,

Mæstius and Serena, are unsatisfactory lovers, because the artificiality of their handling and their speech forbids real passion. As for Accius and Silena, idiocy seems to us scarcely to furnish material for real comedy, but fools and madmen were regarded as legitimate game in an age when people of fashion found amusement in visiting the inmates of Bedlam. Mother Bombie is interesting as a type of the wise-woman, who appears in later Elizabethan plays, but, except in so far as her oracular utterance urges Vicinia to confession, she has no influence on the action.

Curious to a modern reader are the parade of schoolboy learning in the Latin quotations and the intolerable punning, more often simulating than attaining wit. Here again we must remember that taste changes and make allowance for the author, a product of Renascence culture, and a conscious stylist, delighting in the use of language for its own sake, and writing for an audience which enjoyed hearing him "torture one poor word ten thousand ways." In general, the style of the play is less Euphuistic than that of its predecessors. Lyly tended more and more in his play-writing to abandon the niceties of Euphuism for a more natural style, and *Mother Bombie*, written about 1594, belongs to his later work. Moreover, *Mother Bombie* seems not to have been performed at court, as the earlier plays had been, and the delicate sentence structure of *Endimion* was perhaps not altogether suited for a popular audience.

MOTHER BOMBIE

By JOHN LYLY

NAMES OF THE CHARACTERS

MEMPHIO, *an avaricious old man.*
STELLIO, *a wealthy husbandman.*
PRISIUS, *a fuller.*
SPERANTUS, *a farmer.*
CANDIUS, *son to Sperantus.*
MÆSTIUS, *son to Memphio; supposed son to Vicinia.*
ACCIUS, *supposed son to Memphio.*
DROMIO, *a boy, servant to Memphio.*
RISCIO, *a boy, servant to Stellio.*
HALFPENNY, *a boy, servant to Sperantus.*
LUCIO, *a boy, servant to Prisius.*
SYNIS, NASUTUS, BEDUNENUS, *three fiddlers.*
HACKNEYMAN.
SERGEANT.
SCRIVENER.
LIVIA, *daughter to Prisius.*
SERENA, *daughter to Stellio; supposed daughter to Vicinia.*
SILENA, *supposed daughter to Stellio.*
VICINIA, *a nurse, mother to Accius and Silena.*
MOTHER BOMBIE, *a fortune-teller.*
RIXULA, *a girl servant to Prisius.*

Scene—Rochester: an open square or street.

ACT I.

SCENE 1.

Enter Memphio and Dromio.

Mem. Boy, there are three things that make my life miserable: a threadbare purse, a curst[1] wife, and a fool to my heir.

Dro. Why then, sir, there are three medicines for these three maladies: a pikestaff to take a purse on the highway, a holly wand to brush choler from my mistress' tongue, and a young wench for my young master; so that as your worship being wise begot a fool, so he, being a fool, may tread out a wise man.

Mem. Aye; but, Dromio, these medicines bite hot on[2] great mischiefs; for so might I have a rope about my neck, horns upon my head, and in my house a litter of fools.

Dro. Then, sir, you had best let some wise man sit on your son, to hatch him a good wit; they say if ravens sit on hens' eggs, the chickens will be black, and so forth.

Mem. Why, boy, my son is out of the shell, and is grown a pretty cock.

Dro. Carve him, master, and make him a capon, else all your breed will prove coxcombs.

Mem. I marvel he is such an ass; he takes it not of his father.

Dro. He may for any thing you know.

Mem. Why, villain, dost thou think me a fool?

Dro. O no, sir; neither are you sure that you are his father.

1 shrewish.

2 are closely akin to.

Mem. Rascal, dost thou imagine thy mistress naught of her body? [3]

Dro. No, but fantastical of her mind; and it may be when this boy was begotten she thought of a fool, and so conceived a fool, yourself being very wise, and she surpassing honest.

Mem. It may be; for I have heard of an Ethiopian, that thinking of a fair picture, brought forth a fair lady, and yet no bastard.

Dro. You are well read, sir; your son may be a bastard, and yet legitimate; yourself a cuckold, and yet my mistress virtuous; all this in conceit.

Mem. Come, Dromio, it is my grief to have such a son that must inherit my lands.

Dro. He needs not, sir; I'll beg him for a fool.[4]

Mem. Vile boy! thy young master?

Dro. Let me have in [5] a device.

Mem. I'll have thy advice, and if it fadge,[6] thou shalt eat till thou sweat, play till thou sleep, and sleep till thy bones ache.

Dro. Aye, marry, now you tickle me, I am both hungry, gamesome, and sleepy, and all at once. I'll break this head against the wall, but I'll make it bleed good matter.

Mem. Then this it is; thou knowest I have but one son, and he is a fool.

Dro. A monstrous fool!

Mem. A wife, and she an arrant scold.

Dro. Ah, master, I smell your device; it will be excellent!

Mem. Thou canst not know it till I tell it.

Dro. I see it through your brains. Your hair is so thin, and your skull so transparent, I may sooner see it than hear it.

Mem. Then, boy, hast thou a quick wit, and I a slow tongue. But what is't?

Dro. Marry, either you would have your wife's tongue in your son's head, that he might be a prating fool; or his brains in her brain pan, that she might be a foolish scold.

Mem. Thou dreamest, Dromio; there is no such matter. Thou knowest I have kept him close, so that my neighbors think him to be wise, and her to be temperate, because they never heard them speak.

Dro. Well?

Mem. Thou knowest that Stellio hath a good farm and a fair daughter; yea, so fair that she is mewed up,[7] and only looketh out at the windows, lest she should by some roisting courtier be stolen away.

Dro. So, sir.

Mem. Now if I could compass a match between my son and Stellio's daughter, by conference of us parents, and without theirs, I should be blessed, he cozened,[8] and thou forever set at liberty.

Dro. A singular conceit.

Mem. Thus much for my son. Now for my wife: I would have this kept from her, else shall I not be able to keep my house from smoke; for let it come to one of her ears, and then woe to both mine! I would have her go to my house into the country whilst we conclude this, and this once done, I care not if her tongue never have done. These if thou canst effect, thou shalt make thy master happy.

Dro. Think it done; this noddle shall coin such new device as you shall have your son married by to-morrow.

Mem. But take heed that neither the father nor the maid speak to my son, for then his folly will mar all.

Dro. Lay all the care on me. *Sublevabo te onere:* I will rid you of a fool.

Mem. Wilt thou rid me for a fool?

Dro. Tush! quarrel not.

Mem. Then for the dowry, let it be at least two hundred ducats, and after his death the farm.

Dro. What else?

Mem. Then let us in, that I may furnish thee with some better counsel, and my son with better apparel.

Dro. Let me alone.— (*Aside.*) I lack but a wag more to make of my counsel, and then you shall see an exquisite cozenage, and the father more fool than the son.— But hear you, sir; I forgot one thing.

Mem. What's that?

Dro. Nay; *Expellas furca licet, usque recurret.*[9]

Mem. What's the meaning?

Dro. Why, though your son's folly be thrust up with a pair of horns on a fork, yet being natural, it will have his [10] course.

Mem. I pray thee, no more, but about it.

Exeunt.

3 unchaste.
4 beg to be appointed his guardian (so that I can get the profit from managing his property).
5 suggest.
6 succeed.
7 confined; hawks were kept in a *mews.*
8 cheated.
9 From Horace (*Ep.* I. x. 24): "You may drive nature from its course, but it will always return."
10 its.

SCENE 2.

Enter Stellio and Riscio.

Stel. Riscio, my daughter is passing amiable, but very simple.

Ris. You mean a fool, sir.

Stel. Faith, I imply so much.

Ris. Then I apply it fit: the one she takes of her father, the other of her mother; now you may be sure she is your own.

Stel. I have penned her up in a chamber, having only a window to look out, that youths, seeing her fair cheeks, may be enamored before they hear her fond [11] speech. How likest thou this head? [12]

Ris. There is very good workmanship in it, but the matter is but base; if the stuff had been as good as the mold, your daughter had been as wise as she is beautiful.

Stel. Dost thou think she took her foolishness of me?

Ris. Aye, and so cunningly that she took it not from you.

Stel. Well, *Quod natura dedit, tollere nemo potest.*[13]

Ris. A good evidence to prove the fee-simple [14] of your daughter's folly.

Stel. Why?

Ris. It came by nature, and if none can take it away, it is perpetual.

Stel. Nay, Riscio, she is no natural fool, but in this consisteth her simplicity, that she thinketh herself subtle; in this her rudeness, that she imagines she is courtly; in this the overshooting of herself, that she overweeneth of herself.

Ris. Well, what follows?

Stel. Riscio, this is my plot. Memphio hath a pretty stripling to his son, whom with cockering [15] he hath made wanton: his girdle must be warmed, the air must not breathe on him, he must lie abed till noon, and yet in his bed break his fast; that which I do to conceal the folly of my daughter, that doth he in too much cockering of his son. Now, Riscio, how shall I compass a match between my girl and his boy?

Ris. Why, with a pair of compasses; and bring them both into the circle, I'll warrant they'll match themselves.

Stel. Tush! plot it for me that never speaking to one another, they be in love one with another. I like not solemn wooing, it is for courtiers; let country folks believe others' reports as much as their own opinions.

Ris. O then, so it be a match you care not.

Stel. Not I, nor for a match neither, were it not I thirst after my neighbor's farm.

Ris. (*Aside.*) A very good nature.—Well, if by flat wit I bring this to pass, what's my reward?

Stel. Whatsoever thou wilt ask.

Ris. I'll ask no more than by my wit I can get in the bargain.

Stel. Then about it.

Exit.

Ris. If I come not about [16] you, never trust me. I'll seek out Dromio, the counsellor of my conceit. *Exit.*

SCENE 3.

Enter Prisius and Sperantus.

Pris. It is unneighborly done to suffer your son since he came from school to spend his time in love; and unwisely done to let him hover over my daughter, who hath nothing to her dowry but her needle, and must prove a sempster; nor he anything to take to but a grammar, and cannot at the best be but a schoolmaster.

Sper. Prisius, you bite and whine, wring me on the withers, and yet wince yourself; it is you that go about to match your girl with my boy, she being more fit for seams than for marriage, and he for a rod than a wife.

Pris. Her birth requires a better bridegroom than such a groom.

Sper. And his bringing up another-gate [17] marriage than such a minion.

Pris. Marry, gup! [18] I am sure he hath no better bread than is made of wheat, nor worn finer cloth than is made of wool, nor learned better manners than are taught in schools.

Sper. Nor your minx had no better grandfather than a tailor, who (as I have heard) was poor and proud; nor a better father than yourself, unless your wife borrowed a better, to make her daughter a gentlewoman.

Pris. Twit not me with my ancestors, nor my wife's honesty; if thou dost—

(*Threatening him.*)

11 foolish.
12 Possibly Stellio shows Riscio a portrait of his daughter.
13 "What nature has given, no one can take away."
14 title.
15 petting.
16 get the better of.
17 another kind of.
18 go up, hold on!

Sper. Hold thy hands still, thou hadst best; and yet it is impossible, now I remember, for thou hast the palsy.

Pris. My hands shake so that wert thou in place where,[19] I would teach thee to cog.[20]

Sper. Nay, if thou shake thy hands, I warrant thou canst not teach any to cog. But, neighbor, let not two old fools fall out for two young wantons.

Pris. Indeed, it becometh men of our experience to reason, not rail; to debate the matter, not to combat it.

Sper. Well, then, this I'll tell thee friendly. I have almost these two years cast in my head how I might match my princox[21] with Stellio's daughter, whom I have heard to be very fair, and know shall be very rich: she is his heir; he dotes, he is stooping old, and shortly must die. Yet by no means, either by blessing or cursing, can I win my son to be a wooer, which I know proceeds not of bashfulness but stubbornness, for he knows his good; though I say it, he hath wit at will; as for his personage, I care not who sees him; I can tell you he is able to make a lady's mouth water if she wink not.

Pris. Stay, Sperantus, this is like my case, for I have been tampering as long to have a marriage committed between my wench and Memphio's only son: they say he is as goodly a youth as one shall see in a summer's day, and as neat a stripling as ever went on neat's leather; his father will not let him be forth of his sight, he is so tender over him; he yet lies with his mother for[22] catching cold. Now my pretty elf, as proud as the day is long, she will none of him; she forsooth will choose her own husband: made marriages prove mad marriages; she will choose with her eye, and like with her heart, before she consent with her tongue; neither father nor mother, kith nor kin, shall be her carver in[23] a husband, she will fall to where she likes best; and thus the chick scarce out of her shell cackles as though she had been trodden with an hundred cocks, and mother of a thousand eggs.

Sper. Well then, this is our best, seeing we know each other's mind, to devise to govern our own children; for my boy, I'll keep him to his books, and study shall make him leave to love; I'll break him of his will, or his bones with a cudgel.

Pris. And I'll no more dandle my daughter; she shall prick on a clout[24] till her fingers ache, or I'll cause her leave to make my heart ache. But in good time, though with ill luck, behold if they be not both together; let us stand close and hear all, so shall we prevent all.

(*They stand aside.*)

Enter Candius and Livia.

Sper. (*Aside.*) This happens pat; take heed you cough not, Prisius.

Pris. (*Aside.*) Tush! spit not you; and I'll warrant, I, my beard is as good as a handkerchief.

Liv. Sweet Candius, if thy father should see us alone, would he not fret? The old man methinks should be full of fumes.

Can. Tush! let him fret one heart-string against another, he shall never trouble the least vein of my little finger. The old churl thinks none wise unless he have a beard hang dangling to his waist. When my face is bedaubed with hair as his, then perchance my conceit may stumble on his staidness.

Pris. (*Aside.*) Aye? In what book read you that lesson?

Sper. (*Aside.*) I know not in what book he read it, but I am sure he was a knave to learn it.

Can. I believe, fair Livia, if your sour sire should see you with your sweetheart he would not be very patient.

Liv. The care is taken. I'll ask him blessing as a father, but never take counsel for an husband; there is as much odds between my golden thoughts and his leaden advice, as between his silver hairs and my amber locks. I know he will cough for anger that I yield not, but he shall cough me a fool for his labor.[25]

Sper. (*Aside to Pris.*) Where picked your daughter that work, out of broad-stitch?

Pris. (*Aside.*) Out of a flirt's sampler. But let us stay the end; this is but the beginning; you shall hear two children well brought up!

Can. Parents in these days are grown peevish: they rock their children in their cradles till they sleep, and cross them about their bridals till their hearts ache. Marriage among them is become a mar-

19 a more fitting place.
20 lie; *cog* is punningly used just below in its first sense of cheating at dice, for which a steady hand would be needed.
21 pert boy.
22 for fear of.
23 provider of.
24 sew cloth.
25 be only a fool for his pains.

ket. What will you give with your daughter? What jointure will you make for your son? And many a match is broken off for a penny more or less, as though they could not afford their children at such a price, when none should cheapen such ware but affection, and none buy it but love.

Sper. (*Aside.*) Learnedly and scholar-like.

Liv. Indeed our parents take great care to make us ask blessing and say grace when we are little ones, and growing to years of judgment, they deprive us of the greatest blessing and the most gracious things to our minds, the liberty of our minds; they give us pap with a spoon before we can speak, and when we speak for that we love, pap with a hatchet;[26] because their fancies being grown musty with hoary age, therefore nothing can relish in their thoughts that savors of sweet youth; they study twenty years together to make us grow as straight as a wand, and in the end by bowing us, make us crooked as a cammock.[27] For mine own part, sweet Candius, they shall pardon me, for I will measure my love by mine own judgment, not my father's purse or peevishness. Nature hath made me his child, not his slave; I hate Memphio and his son deadly, if I wist he would place his affection by his father's appointment.

Pris. (*Aside.*) Wittily but uncivilly!

Can. Be of that mind still, my fair Livia; let our fathers lay their purses together, we our hearts: I will never woo where I cannot love. Let Stellio enjoy his daughter. But what have you wrought here?

Liv. Flowers, fowls, beasts, fishes, trees, plants, stones, and what not. Among flowers, cowslips and lilies, for our names Candius and Livia. Among fowls, turtles[28] and sparrows, for our truth and desires. Among beasts, the fox and the ermine, for beauty and policy. And among fishes, the cockle and the tortoise, because of Venus. Among trees, the vine wreathing about the elm, for our embracings. Among stones, Asbeston, which being hot, will never be cold,[29] for our constancies. Among plants, thyme and heartsease, to note that if we take time we shall ease our hearts.

Pris. (*Aside.*) There's a girl that knows her liripoop.[30]

Sper. (*Aside.*) Listen, and you shall hear my son's learning.

Liv. What book is that?

Can. A fine pleasant poet, who entreateth of the art of love, and of the remedy.

Liv. Is there art in love?

Can. A short art and a certain: three rules in three lines.

Liv. I pray thee, repeat them.

Can. *Principio quod amare velis reperire labora,*
Proximus huic labor est placidam exorare puellam,
Tertius ut longo tempore duret amor.[31]

Liv. I am no Latinist, Candius; you must construe it.

Can. So I will, and pace[32] it too; thou shalt be acquainted with case, gender and number. First, one must find out a mistress whom before all others he voweth to serve. Secondly, that he use all the means that he may to obtain her. And the last, with deserts, faith, and secrecy, to study to keep her.

Liv. What's the remedy?

Can. Death.

Liv. What of all the book is the conclusion?

Can. This one verse: *Non caret effectu quod voluere duo.*

Liv. What's that?

Can. Where two are agreed, it is impossible but they must speed.

Liv. Then cannot we miss; therefore give me thy hand, Candius.

Pris. (*Advancing.*) Soft, Livia, take me with you;[33] it is not good in law without witness.

Sper. And as I remember, there must be two witnesses. God give you joy, Candius; I was worth the bidding to dinner, though not worthy to be of the counsel.

Pris. I think this hot love hath provided but cold cheer.

Sper. Tush! in love is no lack. But blush not, Candius, you need not be ashamed of your cunning; you have made love a book-case, and spent your time well at school learning to love by art and hate

26 A proverbial expression for the rough performance of necessary service, such as the feeding of children; Lyly so entitled one of his pamphlets, an attack on a political opponent.

27 a crooked stick.

28 turtle-doves, taken as types of constancy, as sparrows were of lasciviousness.

29 A bit of Lyly's pseudo-science.

30 "Properly the degree of knowledge that would qualify one to wear a liripoop (*liripipium*) or scarf as doctor." (Bond).

31 Ovid, *Ars Amat.* i. 35–38.

32 parse.

33 let me understand you.

against nature. But I perceive the worser child the better lover.

Pris. And my minion hath wrought well, where every stitch in her sampler is a pricking stitch at my heart. You take your pleasure on parents: they are peevish, fools, churls, overgrown with ignorance, because overworn with age; little shalt thou know the case of a father before thyself be a mother, when thou shalt breed thy child with continual pains, and bringing it forth with deadly pangs, nurse it with thine own paps, and nourish it up with motherly tenderness; and then find them to curse thee with their hearts, when they should ask blessing on their knees, and the collop [34] of thine own bowels to be the torture of thine own soul; with tears trickling down thy cheeks, and drops of blood falling from thy heart, thou wilt in uttering of thy mind wish them rather unborn than unnatural, and to have had their cradles their graves rather than thy death their bridals. But I will not dispute what thou shouldst have done, but correct what thou hast done; I perceive sewing is an idle exercise, and that every day there come more thoughts into thine head than stitches into thy work; I'll see whether you can spin a better mind than you have stitched, and if I coop you not up, then let me be the capon.

Sper. As for you, sir boy, instead of poring on a book, you shall hold the plough; I'll make repentance reap what wantonness hath sown. But we are both well served: the sons must be masters,[35] the fathers gaffers;[35] what we get together with a rake, they cast abroad with a fork, and we must weary our legs to purchase our children arms.[36] Well, seeing that booking is but idleness, I'll see whether threshing be any occupation; thy mind shall stoop to my fortune or mine shall break the laws of nature. How like a micher [37] he stands, as though he had truanted from honesty! Get thee in, and for the rest let me alone. In, villain!

Pris. And you, pretty minx, that must be fed with love upon sops,[38] I'll take an order to cram you with sorrows. Get you in, without look or reply.

Exeunt Candius and Livia.

Sper. Let us follow, and deal as rigorously with yours as I will with mine, and you shall see that hot love will soon wax cold. I'll tame the proud boy, and send him as far from his love as he is from his duty.

Pris. Let us about it, and also go on with matching them to our minds; it was happy that we prevented that by chance which we could never yet suspect by circumstance. *Exeunt.*

ACT II.

Scene 1.

Enter at opposite sides Dromio and Riscio.

Dro. Now if I could meet with Riscio it were a world of waggery.

Ris. Oh, that it were my chance, *Obviam dare Dromio,* to stumble upon Dromio, on whom I do nothing but dream.

Dro. His knavery and my wit should make our masters, that are wise, fools; their children, that are fools, beggars; and us two, that are bond, free.

Ris. He to cozen and I to conjure would make such alterations that our masters should serve themselves; the idiots, their children, serve us; and we to wake our wits between them all.

Dro. *Hem quam opportune:* look if he drop not full in my dish!

Ris. *Lupus in fabula!* Dromio, embrace me! hug me! kiss my hand! I must make thee fortunate.

Dro. Riscio, honor me! kneel down to me! kiss my feet! I must make thee blessed.

Ris. My master, old Stellio, hath a fool to his daughter.

Dro. Nay; my master, old Memphio, hath a fool to his son.

Ris. I must convey [39] a contract.

Dro. And I must convey a contract.

Ris. Between her and Memphio's son, without speaking one to another.

Dro. Between him and Stellio's daughter, without one speaking to the other.

Ris. Dost thou mock me, Dromio?

Dro. Thou dost me else.

Ris. Not I; for all this is true.

Dro. And all this.

Ris. Then are we both driven to our wits' ends, for if either of them had been wise

34 piece.
35 gentlemen . . . commoners.
36 coats of arms, token of gentility.
37 truant.
38 sops, sweet cakes dipped in wine, was a luxurious dish.
39 arrange secretly.

we might have tempered; if no marriage, yet a close [40] marriage.

Dro. Well, let us sharpen our accounts; there 's no better grindstone for a young man's head than to have it whet upon an old man's purse. Oh, thou shalt see my knavery shave like a razor!

Ris. Thou for the edge, and I the point, will make the fool bestride our mistress' backs, and then have at the bag with the dudgeon haft,[41] that is, at the dudgeon dagger, by which hangs his tantony [42] pouch.

Dro. These old huddles have such strong purses with locks, when they shut them they go off like a snaphance.[43]

Ris. The old fashion is best: a purse with a ring round about it, as a circle to curse a knave's hand from it. But, Dromio, two they say may keep counsel if one be away; but to convey knavery, two are too few and four too many.

Dro. And in good time, look where Halfpenny, Sperantus' boy, cometh; though bound up in *decimo sexto* [44] for carriage, yet a wit in *folio* for cozenage.

Enter Halfpenny.

Single Halfpenny, what news are now current?

Half. Nothing but that such double coistrels [45] as you be are counterfeit.

Ris. Are you so dapper? We 'll send you for an halfpenny loaf.

Half. I shall go for silver though, when you shall be nailed up for slips.[46]

Dro. Thou art a slipstring,[47] I 'll warrant.

Half. I hope you shall never slip string, but hang steady.

Ris. Dromio, look here; now is my hand on my halfpenny.

Half. Thou liest; thou hast not a farthing to lay thy hands on: I am none of thine. But let me be wagging; my head is full of hammers,[48] and they have so malletted my wit that I am almost a malcontent.

Dro. Why, what 's the matter?

Half. My master hath a fine scholar to his son, Prisius a fair lass to his daughter.

Dro. Well!

Half. They two love one another deadly.

Ris. In good time!

Half. The fathers have put them up,[49] utterly disliking the match, and have appointed the one shall have Memphio's son, the other Stellio's daughter; this works like wax, but how it will fadge in the end, the hen that sits next the cock cannot tell.

Ris. If thou have but any spice of knavery we 'll make thee happy.

Half. Tush! doubt not of mine; I am as full for my pitch [50] as you are for yours; a wren's egg is as full of meat as a goose egg, though there be not so much in it; you shall find this head well stuffed, though there went little stuff to it.

Dro. *Laudo ingenium,* I like thy sconce; [51] then hearken. Memphio made me of his counsel about marriage of his son to Stellio's daughter; Stellio made Riscio acquainted to plot a match with Memphio's son. To be short, they be both fools.

Half. But they are not fools that be short; if I thought thou meantest so, *Senties qui vir sim,* thou shouldst have a crow to pull.[52]

Ris. Be not angry, Halfpenny; for fellowship we will be all fools, and for gain all knaves. But why dost thou laugh?

Half. At mine own conceit and quick censure.

Ris. What 's the matter?

Half. Suddenly methought you two were asses, and that the least ass was the more ass.

Ris. Thou art a fool; that cannot be.

Half. Yea, my young master taught me to prove it by learning, and so I can out of Ovid by a verse.

Ris. Prithee, how?

Half. You must first for fashion's sake confess yourselves to be asses.

Dro. Well!

Half. Then stand you here, and you there.

Ris. Go to!

Half. Then this is the verse as I point it: *Cum mala per longas invaluere moras.*[53] So you see the least ass is the more ass.

Ris. We 'll bite thee for an ape if thou bob us like asses. But to end all, if thou wilt join with us we will make a match between the two fools, for that must be our task; and thou shalt devise to couple

40 secret.

41 A purse was carried hanging from the girdle, and sometimes a dagger was thrust through the straps.

42 short for St. Anthony; meaning obscure.

43 firelock musket.

44 Halfpenny was evidently a very small boy.

45 knaves.

46 counterfeits.

47 one who deserves to be hanged.

48 I 'm hammering out a device.

49 confined them.

50 degree.

51 headpiece, i.e. wit.

52 a bone to pick with me.

53 Ovid *Rem. Am.* 92. The only excuse for a poor pun consists in Halfpenny's pointing at his fellows as he pronounces ***long-as*** and ***mor-as.***

Candius and Livia by overreaching their fathers.

Half. Let me alone, *Non enim mea pigra juventus:* there 's matter in this noddle.

Enter Lucio.

But look where Prisius' boy comes, as fit as a pudding for a dog's mouth.

Luc. Pop three knaves in a sheath, I 'll make it a right Tunbridge case and be the bodkin.

Ris. Nay, the bodkin is here already; you must be the knife.

Half. I am the bodkin; look well to your ears, I must bore them.

Dro. Mew [54] thy tongue or we 'll cut it out; this I speak representing the person of a knife, as thou didst that in shadow of a bodkin.

Luc. I must be gone. *Taedet,* it irketh; *Oportet,* it behoveth. My wits work like barm, alias yeast, alias sizing, alias rising, alias God's good.

Half. The new wine is in thine head, yet was he fain to take this metaphor from ale; and now you talk of ale, let us all to the wine.

Dro. Four makes a mess, and we have a mess of masters that must be cozened; let us lay our heads together, they are married and cannot.

Half. Let us consult at the tavern, where, after to the health of Memphio, drink we to the life of Stellio; I carouse to Prisius, and brinch [55] you Mas.[56] Sperantus; we shall cast up our accounts and discharge our stomachs, like men that can digest anything.

Luc. I see not yet what you go about.

Dro. Lucio, that can pierce a mud wall of twenty foot thick, would make us believe he cannot see a candle through a paper lanthorn; his knavery is beyond *Ela,* and yet he says he knows not *Gam ut.*[57]

Luc. I am ready; if any cozenage be ripe, I 'll shake the tree.

Half. Nay, I hope to see thee so strong to shake three trees [58] at once.

Dro. We burn time, for I must give a reckoning of my day's work; let us close to the bush [59] *ad deliberandum.*

Half. Indeed, *Inter pocula philosophandum:* it is good to plea among pots.

Ris. Thine will be the worst; I fear we shall leave a halfpenny in hand.

Half. Why sayest thou that? Thou hast left a print deeper in thy hand [60] already than a halfpenny can leave, unless it should sing worse than an hot iron.

Luc. All friends, and so let us sing; 'tis a pleasant thing to go into the tavern clearing the throat.

Song.

Omnes. *Io Bacchus!* To thy table
Thou call'st every drunken rabble;
We already are stiff drinkers,
Then seal us for thy jolly skinkers.[61]
Dro. Wine, O Wine!
O juice divine!
How dost thou the nowl [62] refine!
Ris. Plump thou mak'st men's ruby faces,
And from girls canst fetch embraces.
Half. By thee our noses swell
With sparkling carbuncle.
Luc. O the dear blood of grapes
Turns us to antic shapes,
Now to show tricks like apes;
Dro. Now lion-like to roar;
Ris. Now goatishly to whore;
Half. Now hoggishly i' th' mire;
Luc. Now flinging hats i' th' fire.
Omnes. *Io Bacchus!* At thy table
Make us of thy reeling rabble.

Exeunt into tavern.

Scene 2.

Enter Memphio.

Mem. I marvel I hear no news of Dromio; either he slacks the matter or betrays his master. I dare not motion anything to Stellio till I know what my boy hath done; I 'll hunt him out; if the loiter-sack [63] be gone springing into a tavern I 'll fetch him reeling out.

Exit into tavern.

Enter Stellio.

Stel. Without doubt Riscio hath gone beyond himself in casting beyond the moon.[64] I fear the boy be run mad with studying, for I know he loved me so well that for my favor he will venture to run out of his wits; and, it may be, to quicken his invention, he is gone into this Ivy-

54 hold.
55 pledge.
56 master.
57 "*Ut* and *la* were respectively the lowest and highest in the Hexachord, or scale of six notes, whose names were derived from the initial syllables in the lines of a Latin hymn to St. John." (Bond.) The implication is that Lucio, though a past master of knavery, does not admit knowing anything of it.
58 i. e. the gallows.
59 An ivy bush was the sign of a tavern.
60 Felony was punished by branding in the hand.
61 drawers of wine; hence topers.
62 head.
63 loiterer.
64 proverbial for an impossible design.

bush, a notable nest for a grape owl. I'll ferret him out, yet in the end use him friendly; I cannot be merry till I hear what's done in the marriages.

Exit into tavern.

Enter Prisius.

Pris. I think Lucio be gone a-squirreling, but I'll squirrel him for it; I sent him on my errand, but I must go for an answer myself. I have tied up the loving worm my daughter, and will see whether fancy can worm fancy out of her head. This green nosegay [65] I fear my boy hath smelt to, for if he get but a penny in his purse he turns it suddenly into *argentum potabile;* [66] I must search every place for him, for I stand on thorns till I hear what he hath done.

Exit into tavern.

Enter Sperantus.

Sper. Well, be as may be is no banning. I think I have charmed my young master: a hungry meal, a ragged coat, and a dry cudgel have put him quite beside his love and his logic too. Besides his pigsnie [67] is put up, and therefore now I'll let him take the air and follow Stellio's daughter with all his learning, if he mean to be my heir. The boy hath wit sans measure, more than needs; cat's meat and dog's meat enough for the vantage. Well, without Halfpenny all my wit is not worth a dodkin; [68] that mite is miching [69] in this grove, for as long as his name is Halfpenny he will be banqueting for the other halfpenny.

Exit into tavern.

SCENE 3.

Enter Candius.

Can. He must needs go that the devil drives! A father? A fiend! that seeks to place affection by appointment, and to force love by compulsion. I have sworn to woo Silena, but it shall be so coldly that she shall take as small delight in my words as I do contentment in his commandment. I'll teach him one school trick in love. But behold! who is that cometh out of Stellio's house? It should seem to be Silena by her attire.

Enter Silena.

By her face I am sure it is she. O fair face! O lovely countenance! How now, Candius, if thou begin to slip at beauty on a sudden, thou wilt surfeit with carousing it at the last. Remember that Livia is faithful; aye, and let thine eyes witness Silena is amiable. Here shall I please my father and myself: I will learn to be obedient, and come what will, I'll make a way; if she seem coy I'll practise all the art of love; if I find her coming, [70] all the pleasures of love.

Sil. My name is Silena; I care not who know it, so I do not. My father keeps me close, so he does; and now I have stolen out, so I have, to go to old Mother Bombie to know my fortune, so I will; for I have as fair a face as ever trod on shoe sole, and as free a foot as ever looked with two eyes.

Can. (*Aside.*) What? I think she is lunatic or foolish. Thou art a fool, Candius: so fair a face cannot be the scabbard of a foolish mind; mad she may be, for commonly in beauty so rare there falls passion's extreme. Love and beauty disdain a mean, not therefore because beauty is no virtue, but because it is happiness; and we scholars know that virtue is not to be praised, but honored. I will put on my best grace.—(*To Silena.*) Sweet wench, thy face is lovely, thy body comely, and all that the eyes can see, enchanting. You see how, unacquainted, I am bold to board [71] you.

Sil. My father boards me already; therefore I care not if your name were Geoffrey.

Can. She raves, or overreaches.— I am one, sweet soul, that loves you, brought hither by report of your beauty, and here languisheth with your rareness.

Sil. I thank you that you would call.

Can. I will always call on such a saint that hath power to release my sorrows; yield, fair creature, to love.

Sil. I am none of that sect.

Can. The loving sect is an ancient sect, and an honorable, and therefore love should be in a person so perfect.

Sil. Much! [72]

Can. I love thee much; give me one word of comfort.

Sil. I' faith, sir, no! and so tell your master.

65 i. e. the ivy bush.
66 *aurum potabile,* gold liquefied in oil, was much esteemed as a cordial in the old alchemical pharmacopœia.
67 pig's eye, a term of endearment.
68 a small Dutch coin.
69 loitering.
70 responsive.
71 accost.
72 an exclamation of contempt.

Can. I have no master, but come to make choice of a mistress.
Sil. Ah ha! are you there with your bears?[73]
Can. (*Aside.*) Doubtless she is an idiot of the newest cut. I'll once more try her.— I have loved thee long, Silena.
Sil. In your tother hose.
Can. (*Aside.*) Too simple to be natural, too senseless to be artificial.— You said you went to know your fortune: I am a scholar, and am cunning in palmistry.
Sil. The better for you, sir. Here's my hand; what's o'clock?
Can. The line of life is good, Venus' mount very perfect: you shall have a scholar to your first husband.
Sil. You are well seen[74] in crane's dirt, your father was a poulter. Ha, ha, ha!
Can. Why laugh you?
Sil. Because you should see my teeth.
Can. (*Aside.*) Alas, poor wench, I see now also thy folly; a fair fool is like a fresh weed, pleasing leaves and sour juice. I will not yet leave her; she may dissemble.— I cannot choose but love thee.
Sil. I had thought to ask you.
Can. Nay then, farewell; either too proud to accept, or too simple to understand.
Sil. You need not be so crusty, you are not so hard baked.
Can. Now I perceive thy folly, who hath raked together all the odd blind phrases that help them that know not how to discourse; but when they cannot answer wisely, either with gibing cover their rudeness, or by some new-coined byword bewray their peevishness. I am glad of this; now shall I have color to refuse the match, and my father reason to accept of Livia. I will home and repeat to my father our wise encounter, and he shall perceive there is nothing so fulsome as a she fool.

Exit.

Sil. Good God! I think gentlemen had never less wit in a year. We maids are mad wenches; we gird them and flout them out of all scotch and notch,[75] and they cannot see it. I will know of the old woman whether I be a maid or no, and then if I be not I must needs be a man. (*Knocks at Mother Bombie's door.*) God be here!

Enter Mother Bombie.

Bom. Who's there?
Sil. One that would be a maid.
Bom. If thou be not, it is impossible thou shouldst be, and a shame thou art not.
Sil. They say you are a witch.
Bom. They lie; I am a cunning woman.
Sil. Then tell me something.
Bom. Hold up thy hand; not so high.—

Thy father knows thee not;
Thy mother bare thee not;
Falsely bred, truly begot;
Choice of two husbands, but never
tied in bands,
Because of love and natural bonds.

Sil. I thank you for nothing, because I understand nothing: though you be as old as you are, yet am I as young as I am, and because that I am so fair, therefore are you so foul; and so farewell, frost, my fortune naught me cost.

Exit.

Bom. If thou be not, it is impossible thou know thy hard fortune, but in the end thou shalt, and that must bewray what none can discover. In the mean season I will profess cunning for all comers.

Exit.

Scene 4.

Enter Dromio, Riscio, Lucio, Halfpenny.

Dro. We were all taken tardy.
Ris. Our masters will be overtaken[76] if they tarry.
Half. Now must every one by wit make an excuse, and every excuse must be cozenage.
Luc. Let us remember our complot.
Dro. We will all plod on that; oh, the wine hath turned my wit to vinegar.
Ris. You mean 't is sharp.
Half. Sharp? I'll warrant 't will serve for as good sauce to knavery as—
Luc. As what?
Half. As thy knavery meat for his wit.
Dro. We must all give a reckoning for our day's travel.
Ris. Tush! I am glad we scaped the reckoning for our liquor. If you be examined how we met, swear by chance, for so they met and therefore will believe it; if how much we drunk, let them answer themselves: they know best because they paid it.

73 is that what you are after? 74 skilled. 75 beyond measure. 76 i. e. by drink.

Half. We must not tarry: *abeundum est mihi;* I must go and cast this matter in a corner.

Dro. *I prae, sequar;* a bowl, and I 'll come after with a broom. Every one remember his cue.

Ris. Aye, and his k,[77] or else we shall thrive ill.

Half. When shall we meet?

Ris. Tomorrow, fresh and fasting.

Dro. Fast eating our meat, for we have drunk for tomorrow, and tomorrow we must eat for today.

Half. Away, away; if our masters take us here, the matter is marred.

Luc. Let us every one to his task.

Exeunt.

SCENE 5.

Enter Memphio, Stellio, Prisius, Sperantus.

Mem. How luckily we met on a sudden in a tavern, that drunk not together almost these thirty years.

Stel. A tavern is the rendezvous, the exchange, the staple[78] for good fellows; I have heard my great-grandfather tell how his great-grandfather should say that it was an old proverb when his great-grandfather was a child that it was a good wind that blew a man to the wine.

Pris. The old time was a good time! Ale was an ancient drink, and accounted of our ancestors authentical; Gascon wine was liquor for a lord, sack a medicine for the sick, and I may tell you, he that had a cup of red wine to his oysters was hoisted in the Queen's subsidy book.[79]

Sper. Aye, but now you see to what looseness this age is grown: our boys carouse sack like double beer, and say that which doth an old man good can do a young man no harm; old men, say they, eat pap, why should not children drink sack? Their white heads have cozened time out of mind our young years.

Mem. Well, the world is wanton since I knew it first: our boys put as much now in their bellies in an hour as would clothe their whole bodies in a year; we have paid for their tippling eight shillings, and as I have heard, it was as much as bought Rufus, sometime king of this land, a pair of hose.

Pris. Is 't possible?

Stel. Nay, 't is true; they say ale is out of request, 't is hogs' porridge, broth for beggars, a caudle for constables, watchmen's mouth glue; the better it is, the more like bird lime it is, and never makes one staid but in the stocks.

Mem. I'll teach my wag-halter to know grapes from barley.

Pris. And I mine to discern a spigot from a faucet.

Sper. And I mine to judge the difference between a black bowl and a silver goblet.

Stel. And mine shall learn the odds between a stand[80] and a hogshead; yet I cannot choose but laugh to see how my wag answered me when I struck him for drinking sack.

Pris. Why, what said he?

Stel. "Master, it is the sovereignest drink in the world, and the safest for all times and weathers; if it thunder, though all the ale and beer in the town turn, it will be constant; if it lighten, and that any fire come to it, it is the aptest wine to burn, and the most wholesomest when it is burnt.[81] So much for summer. If it freeze, why, it is so hot in operation that no ice can congeal it; if it rain, why, then he that cannot abide the heat of it, may put in water. So much for winter." And so ran his way, but I'll overtake him.

Sper. Who would think that my hop on my thumb, Halfpenny, scarce so high as a pint pot, would reason the matter? But he learned his lear[82] of my son, his young master, whom I have brought up at Oxford, and I think must learn here in Kent at Ashford.

Mem. Why, what said he?

Sper. He boldly rapped it out, *Sine Cerere et Baccho friget Venus:*[83] without wine and sugar his veins would wax cold.

Mem. They were all in a pleasant vein! But I must be gone, and take account of my boy's business; farewell, neighbors, God knows when we shall meet again.— (*Aside.*) Yet I have discovered[84] nothing: my wine hath been my wit's friend. I long to hear what Dromio hath done.

Exit.

Stel. I cannot stay, but this good fellowship shall cost me the setting on at our next meeting.— (*Aside.*) I am glad I blabbed nothing of the marriage; now I

77 punningly on *cue*,
78 meeting place.
79 "hoisted into the list of wealthy persons who might be called on for a royal loan." (Bond.)
80 cask.
81 heated.
82 learning.
83 a Latin proverb.
84 revealed.

hope to compass it. I know my boy hath been bungling about it.

Exit.

Pris. Let us all go, for I must to my clothes that hang on the tenters.[85] (*Aside.*) My boy shall hang with them, if he answer me not his day's work.

Exit.

Sper. If all be gone, I 'll not stay. Halfpenny, I am sure, hath done me a pennyworth of good, else I 'll spend his body in buying a rod.

Exit.

ACT III.

Scene 1.

Enter Mæstius and Serena.

Mæs. Sweet sister, I know not how it cometh to pass, but I find in myself passions more than brotherly.

Ser. And I, dear brother, find my thoughts entangled with affections beyond nature, which so flame into my distempered head that I can neither without danger smother the fire, nor without modesty [86] disclose my fury.

Mæs. Our parents are poor, our love unnatural; what then can happen to make us happy?

Ser. Only to be content with our father's mean estate, to combat against our own intemperate desires, and yield to the success of fortune, who, though she hath framed us miserable, cannot make us monstrous.

Mæs. It is good counsel, fair sister, if the necessity of love could be relieved by counsel. Yet this is our comfort, that these unnatural heats have stretched themselves no further than thoughts. Unhappy me, that they should stretch so!

Ser. That which nature warranteth laws forbid. Strange it seemeth in sense that because thou art mine, therefore thou must not be mine.

Mæs. So it is, Serena; the nearer we are in blood, the further we must be from love, and the greater the kindred, the less the kindness must be; so that between brothers and sisters superstition hath made affection cold, between strangers custom hath bred love exquisite.

Ser. They say there is hard by an old cunning woman who can tell fortunes, expound dreams, tell of things that be lost, and divine of accidents to come; she is called the good woman, who yet never did hurt.

Mæs. Nor any good, I think, Serena. Yet to satisfy thy mind we will see what she can say.

Ser. Good brother, let us.

Mæs. Who is within?

Enter Mother Bombie.

Bom. The dame of the house.

Mæs. She might have said the beldam, for her face and years and attire.

Ser. Good mother, tell us, if by your cunning you can, what shall become of my brother and me.

Bom. Let me see your hands, and look on me steadfastly with your eyes.

You shall be married tomorow hand in hand,
By the laws of God, nature, and the land;
Your parents shall be glad, and give you their land.
You shall each of you displace a fool,
And both together must relieve a fool.
If this be not true, call me old fool.

Mæs. This is my sister, marry we cannot; our parents are poor and have no land to give us; each of us is a fool to come for counsel to such an old fool.

Ser. These doggerel rhymes and obscure words coming out of the mouth of such a weather-beaten witch are thought divinations of some holy spirit, being but dreams of decayed brains; for mine own part, I would thou mightest sit on that stool till he and I marry by law.

Bom. I say Mother Bombie never speaks but once, and yet never spake untruth once.

Ser. Come, brother, let us to our poor home; this is our comfort, to bewray our passions since we cannot enjoy our love.

Mæs. Content, sweet sister, and learn of me hereafter that these old saws of such old hags are but false fires to lead one out of a plain path into a deep pit.

Exeunt.

Scene 2.

Enter Dromio and Riscio.

Dro. *Ingenium quondam fuerat pretiosus auro:* the time was when wit would work like wax and crock up [87] gold like honey.

85 frames for stretching cloth. 86 shamefacedness. (Bond.) 87 collect.

Ris. *At nunc barbaries grandis habere nihil:* but now wit and honesty buy nothing in the market.

Dro. What, Riscio, how sped'st thou after thy potting?

Ris. Nay, my master rung all in the tavern, and thrust all out in the house. But how sped'st thou?

Dro. I? It were a day's work to discourse it. He spake nothing but sentences,[88] but they were vengible long ones, for when one word was out he made pause of a quarter long till he spake another.

Ris. Why, what did he in all that time?

Dro. Break interjections like wind, as *eho! ho! to!*

Ris. And what thou?

Dro. Answer him in his own language, as *evax! vah! hui!*

Ris. These were conjunctions rather than interjections. But what of the plot?

Dro. As we concluded, I told him that I understood that Silena was very wise and could sing exceedingly; that my device was, seeing Accius his son a proper youth and could also sing sweetly, that he should come in the nick when she was singing, and answer her.

Ris. Excellent!

Dro. Then he asked how it should be devised that she might come abroad; I told him that was cast [89] already by my means: then the song being ended, and they seeing one another, noting the apparel, and marking the personages, he should call in his son for fear he should overreach his speech.

Ris. Very good!

Dro. Then that I had gotten a young gentleman that resembled his son in years and favor, that having Accius' apparel should court Silena; whom she, finding wise, would after that by small entreaty be won without more words, and so the marriage clapped up by this cozenage, and his son never speak word for himself.

Ris. Thou boy! So have I done in every point, for the song, the calling her in, and the hoping that another shall woo Accius, and his daughter wed him. I told him this wooing should be tonight, and they early married in the morning, without any words saving to say after the priest.

Dro. All this fadges well; now if Halfpenny and Lucio have played their parts we shall have excellent sport—and here they come. How wrought the wine, my lads?

Enter Halfpenny and Lucio.

Half. How? Like wine, for my body being the rundlet [90] and my mouth the vent, it wrought two days over, till I had thought the hoops of my head would have flown asunder.

Luc. The best was our masters were as well whittled as we, for yet they lie by it.

Ris. The better for us! We did but a little parboil our livers; they have sod [91] theirs in sack these forty years.

Half. That makes them spit white broth as they do. But to the purpose: Candius and Livia will send their attires, you must send the apparel of Accius and Silena; they wonder wherefore, but commit the matter to our quadrupartite wit.

Luc. If you keep promise to marry them by your device, and their parents consent, you shall have ten pounds apiece for your pains.

Dro. If we do it not we are undone, for we have broached a cozenage already, and my master hath the tap in his hand that it must needs run out. Let them be ruled and bring hither their apparel, and we will determine; the rest commit to our intricate considerations. Depart.

Exeunt Halfpenny and Lucio.

Enter Accius and Silena.

Dro. Here comes Accius tuning his pipes. I perceive my master keeps touch.[92]

Ris. And here comes Silena with her wit of proof; [93] marry, it will scarce hold out question shot. Let us in to instruct our masters in the cue.

Dro. Come, let us be jogging. But wer 't not a world to hear them woo one another?

Ris. That shall be hereafter to make us sport, but our masters shall never know it.

Exeunt.

Scene 3.

Enter Accius and Silena singing.

Sil.
O Cupid, monarch over kings,
Wherefore hast thou feet and wings?
It is to show how swift thou art,
When thou wound'st a tender heart;

88 maxims.
89 planned.
90 keg.
91 soaked.
92 keeps his promise.
93 proof armor.

Thy wings being clipped, and feet held still,
Thy bow could not so many kill.

Ac. It is all one in Venus' wanton school
Who highest sits, the wise man or the fool;
Fools in love's college
Have far more knowledge
To read a woman over,
Than a neat prating lover.
Nay, 't is confest
That fools please women best.

Enter Memphio and Stellio.

Mem. Accius, come in, and that quickly! What! Walking without leave?

Stel. Silena, I pray you look homeward; it is a cold air, and you want your muffler.

Exeunt Accius and Silena.

Mem. (*Aside.*) This is pat! If the rest proceed, Stellio is like to marry his daughter to a fool; but a bargain is a bargain.

Stel. (*Aside.*) This frames to my wish! Memphio is like to marry a fool to his son; Accius' tongue shall tie all Memphio's land to Silena's dowry, let his father's teeth undo them if he can. But here I see Memphio; I must seem kind, for in kindness lies cozenage.

Mem. (*Aside.*) Well, here is Stellio. I 'll talk of other matters, and fly from the mark I shoot at, lapwing-like flying far from the place where I nestle.—Stellio, what make you abroad? I heard you were sick since our last drinking.

Stel. You see reports are no truths; I heard the like of you, and we are both well. I perceive sober men tell most lies, for *in vino veritas;* if they had drunk wine they would have told the truth.

Mem. Our boys will be sure then never to lie, for they are ever swilling of wine. But, Stellio, I must strain courtesy with you; I have business, I cannot stay.

Stel. In good time, Memphio, for I was about to crave your patience to depart; it stands me upon.— (*Aside.*) Perhaps I may move his patience ere it be long.

Mem. (*Aside.*) Good silly Stellio; we must buckle shortly.

Exeunt.

SCENE 4.

Enter Halfpenny, Lucio, Rixula, with clothes belonging to Candius and Livia.

Luc. Come, Rixula, we have made thee privy to the whole pack;[94] there lay down the pack.

Rix. I believe unless it be better handled we shall out of doors.

Half. I care not. *Omnem solum forti patria:* I can live in Christendom as well as in Kent.

Luc. And I 'll sing *Patria ubicunque bene:* every house is my home where I may staunch hunger.

Rix. Nay, if you set all on hazard, though I be a poor wench I am as hardy as you both. I cannot speak Latin, but in plain English, if anything fall out cross, I 'll run away.

Half. He loves thee well that would run after.

Rix. Why, Halfpenny, there 's no goose so gray in the lake that cannot find a gander for her make.[95]

Luc. I love a nut-brown lass: 't is good to recreate.

Half. Thou meanest a brown nut is good to crack.

Luc. Why, would it not do thee good to crack such a nut?

Half. I fear she is worm-eaten within, she is so moth-eaten without.

Rix. If you take your pleasure of me, I 'll in and tell your practices against your masters.

Half. In faith, sour heart, he that takes his pleasure on thee is very pleasurable.

Rix. You mean knavishly, and yet I hope foul water will quench hot fire as soon as fair.

Half. Well then, let fair words cool that choler which foul speeches hath kindled; and because we are all in this case, and hope all to have good fortune, sing a roundelay, and we 'll help,—such as thou wast wont when thou beatedst hemp.[96]

Luc. It was crabs she stamped,[97] and stole one away to make her a face.

Rix. I agree, in hope that the hemp shall come to your wearing; a halfpenny halter may hang you both, that is, Halfpenny and you may hang in a halter.

Half. Well brought about.

Rix. 'T will when 't is about your neck.

Luc. Nay, now she 's in, she will never out.

Rix. Nor when your heads are in, as it is likely, they should not come out. But hearken to my song.

They sing.

94 plot.
95 mate.
96 Beating hemp was the occupation of those confined in houses of correction.
97 crab-apples she pounded.

Song.

Rix. Full hard did I sweat
When hemp I did beat,
Then thought I of nothing but hanging;
The hemp being spun,
My beating was done;
Then I wished for a noise [98]
Of crack-halter boys,
On those hempen strings to be twanging.
Long looked I about,
The city throughout—

Boys. And found no such fiddling varlets.
Rix. Yes, at last coming hither,
I saw four together.
Boys. May thy hemp choke such singing harlots.
Rix. To whit, to whoo, the owl does cry;
Phip, phip, the sparrows as they fly;
The goose does hiss, the duck cries quack,
A rope the parrot, that holds tack.[99]
Boys. The parrot and the rope be thine.
Rix. The hanging yours, but the hemp mine.

Enter Dromio and Riscio, with clothes belonging to Accius and Silena.

Dro. Yonder stand the wags; I am come in good time.

Ris. All here before me! You make haste!

Rix. I believe to hanging, for I think you have all robbed your masters; here 's every man his baggage.

Half. That is, we are all with thee, for thou art a very baggage.

Rix. Hold thy peace, or of mine honesty I 'll buy a halfpenny purse with thee.

Dro. Indeed, that 's big enough to put thy honesty in. But come, shall we go about the matter?

Luc. Now it is come to the pinch, my heart pants.

Half. I for my part am resolute, *in utrumque paratus,* ready to die or to run away.

Luc. But hear me. I was troubled with a vile dream, and therefore it is little time spent to let Mother Bombie expound it; she is cunning in all things.

Dro. Then will I know my fortune.

Rix. And I 'll ask for a silver spoon which was lost last day, which I must pay for.

Ris. And I 'll know what will become of our devices.

Half. And I.

Dro. Then let us all go quickly; we must not sleep in this business, our masters are so watchful about it.

They knock at Mother Bombie's door. Enter Mother Bombie.

Bom. Why do you rap so hard at the door?

Dro. Because we would come in.

Bom. Nay, my house is no inn.

Half. Cross yourselves, how she looks!

Dro. Mark her not; she 'll turn us all to apes.

Bom. What would you with me?

Ris. They say you are cunning, and are called the good woman of Rochester.

Bom. If never to do harm be to do good, I dare say I am not ill. But what 's the matter?

Luc. I had an ill dream, and desire to know the signification.

Bom. Dreams, my son, have their weight; though they be of a troubled mind, yet are they signs of fortune. Say on.

Luc. In the dawning of the day, for about that time by my starting out of sleep I found it to be, methought I saw a stately piece of beef, with a cape cloak of cabbage, embroidered with pepper; having two honorable pages with hats of mustard on their heads; himself in great pomp sitting upon a cushion of white brewis [1] lined with brown bread. Methought being powdered,[2] he was much troubled with the salt rheum; and therefore there stood by him two great flagons of sack and beer, the one to dry up his rheum, the other to quench his choler. I, as one envying his ambition, hungering and thirsting after his honor, began to pull his cushion from under him, hoping by that means to give him a fall; and with putting out my hand awaked, and found nothing in all this dream about me but the salt rheum.

Dro. A dream for a butcher.

Luc. Soft, let me end it. Then I slumbered again, and methought there came in a leg of mutton.

Dro. What! All gross [3] meat? A rack [4] had been dainty.

Luc. Thou fool, how could it come in, unless it had been a leg? Methought his hose were cut and drawn out with parsley. I thrust my hand into my pocket for a knife, thinking to hox [5] him, and so awaked.

Bom. Belike thou went supperless to bed.

98 band of musicians. 99 is appropriate. 1 meat broth, with bread soaked in it. 2 salted. 3 common. 4 neck of mutton. 5 hamstring.

Luc. So I do every night but Sundays. Prisius hath a weak stomach, and therefore we must starve.

Bom. Well, take this for answer, though the dream be fantastical:

They that in the morning sleep dream of eating
Are in danger of sickness or of beating,
Or shall hear of a wedding fresh a-beating.[6]

Luc. This may be true.

Half. Nay then, let me come in with a dream, short but sweet, that my mouth waters ever since I waked. Methought there sat upon a shelf three damask prunes in velvet caps and pressed satin gowns, like judges; and that there were a whole handful of currants to be arraigned of a riot, because they clung together in such clusters; twelve raisins of the sun[7] were empaneled in a jury; and as a leaf of whole mace, which was bailiff, was carrying the quest[8] to consult, methought there came an angry cook and gelded the jury of their stones, and swept both judges, jurors, rebels, and bailiff into a porridge pot. Whereat I, being melancholy, fetched a deep sigh that waked myself and my bedfellow.

Dro. This was devised, not dreamt; and the more foolish, being no dream, for that dreams excuse the fantasticalness.

Half. Then ask my bedfellow—you know him—who dreamt that night that the king of diamonds was sick.

Bom. But thy years and humors, pretty child, are subject to such fancies, which the more unsensible they seem, the more fantastical they are; therefore this dream is easy.

To children this is given from the gods:
To dream of milk, fruit, babies, and rods;
They betoken nothing but that wantons must have rods.

Dro. Ten to one thy dream is true; thou wilt be swinged.

Rix. Nay, Gammer, I pray you tell me who stole my spoon out of the buttery.

Bom. Thy spoon is not stolen, but mislaid;
Thou art an ill housewife, though a good maid.
Look for thy spoon where thou hadst like to be no maid.

Rix. Body of me! let me fetch the spoon! I remember the place!

Luc. Soft, swift; the place, if it be there now, will be there tomorrow.

Rix. Aye, but perchance the spoon will not.

Half. Wert thou once put to it?

Rix. No, sir boy, it was put to me.

Luc. How was it missed?

Dro. I 'll warrant for want of a mist. But what 's my fortune, mother?

Bom. Thy father doth live because he doth dye;
Thou hast spent all thy thrift with a die,
And so like a beggar thou shalt die.

Ris. I would have liked well if all the gerunds had been there, *di, do,* and *dum;* but all in *die,* that 's too deadly.

Dro. My father indeed is a dyer, and I have been a dicer; but to die a beggar, give me leave not to believe, Mother Bombie. And yet it may be: I have nothing to live by but knavery, and if the world grow honest, welcome beggary. But what hast thou to say, Riscio?

Ris. Nothing till I see whether all this be true that she hath said.

Half. Aye, Riscio would fain see thee beg.

Ris. Nay, mother, tell us this: what is all our fortunes? We are about a matter of ledgermain—how will it fadge?

Bom. You shall all thrive like cozeners,
That is, to be cozened by cozeners;
All shall end well, and you be found cozeners.

Dro. Gramercy, Mother Bombie; we are all pleased, if you were for your pains.
(*Offers her money.*)

Bom. I take no money but good words. Rail not if I tell true; if I do not, revenge. Farewell.

Exit.

Dro. Now have we nothing to do but to go about this business. Accius' apparel let Candius put on, and I will array Accius with Candius' clothes.

Ris. Here is Silena's attire; Lucio, put it upon Livia, and give me Livia's for Silena. This done, let Candius and Livia come forth, and let Dromio and me alone for the rest.

Half. What shall become of Accius and Silena?

Dro. Tush! their turn shall be next, all must be done orderly. Let 's to it, for now it works.

Exeunt.

6 under way. 7 sun-dried. 8 jury.

ACT IV.

Scene 1.

Enter Candius and Livia in the clothes of Accius and Silena.

Liv. This attire is very fit. But how if this make me a fool and Silena wise? You will then woo me and wed her.

Can. Thou knowest that Accius is also a fool, and his raiment fits me, so that if apparel be infectious, I am also like to be a fool, and he wise. What would be the conclusion, I marvel.

Enter Dromio and Riscio.

Liv. Here comes our counsellors.

Dro. Well said; I perceive turtles fly in couples.

Ris. Else how should they couple?

Liv. So do knaves go double, else how should they be so cunning in doubling?

Can. *Bona verba,* Livia.

Dro. I understand Latin; that is, Livia is a good word.

Can. No, I bid her use good words.

Ris. And what deeds?

Can. None but a deed of gift.

Ris. What gift?

Can. Her heart.

Dro. Give me leave to pose you, though you be a graduate; for I tell you we in Rochester spur so many hackneys that we must needs spur scholars, for we take them for hackneys.

Liv. Why so, sir boy?

Dro. Because I knew two hired for ten groats apiece to say service on Sunday, and that 's no more than a post-horse from hence to Canterbury.

Ris. He knows what he says, for he once served the post-master.

Can. Indeed, I think he served some post to his master. But come, Dromio, post [9] me.

Dro. You say you would have her heart for a deed.

Can. Well?

Dro. If you take her heart for *cor,* that heart in her body, then know this: *Molle eius levibus, cor enim violabile telis;* a woman's heart is thrust through with a feather. If you mean she should give a heart named *cervus,* then are you worse, for *cornua cervus habet;* that is to have one's heart grow out at his head, which will make one ache at the heart in their body.

Enter Prisius and Sperantus.

Liv. I beshrew your hearts, I hear one coming; I know it is my father by his coming.

Can. What must we do?

Dro. Why, as I told you, and let me alone with the old men. Fall you to your bridal.

Pris. Come, neighbor, I perceive the love of our children waxeth key-cold.

Sper. I think it was never but lukewarm.

Pris. Bavins [10] will have their flashes and youth their fancies, the one as soon quenched as the other burnt. But who be these?

Can. Here do I plight my faith, taking thee for the staff of my age, and of my youth the solace.

Liv. And I vow to thee affection which nothing can dissolve, neither the length of time, nor malice of fortune, nor distance of place.

Can. But when shall we be married?

Liv. A good question, for that one delay in wedding brings an hundred dangers in the church: we will not be asked,[11] and a license is too chargeable, and to tarry till tomorrow too tedious.

Dro. There 's a girl stands on pricks till she be married.

Can. To avoid danger, charge, and tediousness, let us now conclude it in the next church.

Liv. Agreed.

Pris. What be these that hasten so to marry?

Dro. Marry, sir, Accius, son to Memphio, and Silena, Stellio's daughter.

Sper. I am sorry, neighbor, for our purposes are disappointed.

Pris. You see marriage is destiny; made in heaven, though consummated on earth.

Ris. How like you them? Be they not a pretty couple?

Pris. Yes; God give them joy, seeing in spite of our hearts they must join.

Dro. I am sure you are not angry, seeing things past cannot be recalled; and being witnesses to their contract, will be also well-willers to the match.

Sper. For my part, I wish them well.

Pris. And I; and since there is no remedy, I am glad of it.

9 pun on Dromio's *pose* above.

10 fagots.

11 the banns will not be asked.

Ris. But will you never hereafter take it in dudgeon,[12] but use them as well as though yourselves had made the marriage?

Pris. Not I.

Sper. Nor I.

Dro. Sir, here 's two old men are glad that your loves, so long continued, is so happily concluded.

Can. We thank them; and if they will come to Memphio's house, they shall take part of a bad dinner.—(*Aside.*) This cottons,[13] and works like wax in a sow's ear.

Exeunt Candius and Livia.

Pris. Well, seeing our purposes are prevented, we must lay other plots, for Livia must not have Candius.

Sper. Fear not, for I have sworn that Candius shall not have Livia. But let us not fall out because our children fall in.

Pris. Wilt thou go soon to Memphio's house?

Sper. Aye, and if you will, let us, that we may see how the young couple bride it, and so we may teach our own.

Exeunt.

Scene 2.

Enter Lucio and Halfpenny.

Luc. By this time I am sure the wags have played their parts; there rests nothing now for us but to match Accius and Silena.

Half. It was too good to be true, for we should laugh heartily, and without laughing my spleen would split. But whist! here comes the man,—

Enter Accius in Candius' clothes.

and yonder the maid. Let us stand aside.

Enter Silena in Livia's clothes.

Ac. What means my father to thrust me forth in another boy's coat. I 'll warrant 't is to as much purpose as a hem in the forehead.[14]

Half. There was an ancient proverb knocked in the head.

Ac. I am almost come into my nonage, and yet I never was so far as the proverbs of this city.

Luc. There 's a quip for the suburbs of Rochester.

Half. Excellently applied.

Sil. Well, though this furniture [15] make me a sullen dame, yet I hope in mine own I am no saint.

Half. A brave fight is like to be between a cock with a long comb and a hen with a long leg.

Luc. Nay, her wits are shorter than her legs.

Half. And his comb longer than his wit.

Ac. I have yonder uncovered a fair girl; I 'll be so bold as spur [16] her what might a body call her name.

Sil. I cannot help you at this time; I pray you come again tomorrow.

Half. Aye, marry, sir!

Ac. You need not be so lusty, you are not so honest.

Sil. I cry you mercy, I took you for a joint stool.[17]

Luc. Here 's courting for a conduit or a bakehouse.

Sil. But what are you for a man? Methinks you look as pleaseth God.

Ac. What, do you give me the boots? [18]

Half. Whither will they? Here be right cobbler's cuts!

Ac. I am taken with a fit of love; have you any mind of marriage?

Sil. I had thought to have asked you.

Ac. Upon what acquaintance?

Sil. Who would have thought it?

Ac. Much in my gascoigns, more in my round hose; [19] all my father's are as white as daisies, as an egg full of meat.

Sil. And all my father's plate is made of crimson velvet.

Ac. That 's brave with bread!

Half. These two had wise men to their fathers.

Luc. Why?

Half. Because when their bodies were at work about household stuff their minds were busied about commonwealth matters.

Ac. This is pure lawn; what call you this, a pretty face to your hair?

Sil. Wisely! You have picked a raisin out of a frail [20] of figs.

Ac. Take it as you list; you are in your own clothes.

12 be offended.
13 succeeds.
14 Accius and Silena are made to talk almost pure nonsense through the scene.
15 clothing.
16 ask.
17 a proverbial expression of scorn.
18 mock me.
19 "Gaskins were loose, wide breeches; the round hose fitted the leg closely. The latter would therefore indicate a closer degree of acquaintance or favor." (Bond.)
20 wicker basket.

Sil. Saving a reverence,[21] that 's a lie! My clothes are better—my father borrowed these.

Ac. Long may he so do. I could tell that these are not mine, if I would blab it like a woman.

Sil. I had as lief you should tell them it snowed.

Luc. Come, let us take them off, for we have had the cream of them.

Half. I warrant if this be the cream, the milk is very flat. Let us join issue with them.

Luc. To have such issue of our bodies, is worse than have an issue in the body. (*To Silena.*) God save you, pretty mouse.

Sil. You may command and go without.

Half. There 's a gleek[22] for you; let me have my gird.[23]—(*To Silena.*) On thy conscience, tell me what 't is o'clock?

Sil. I cry you mercy, I have killed your cushion.

Half. I am paid,[24] and struck dead in the nest. I am sure this soft youth, who is not half so wise as you are fair, nor you altogether so fair as he is foolish, will not be so captious.

Ac. Your eloquence passes my recognoscence.

Enter Memphio and Stellio, behind.

Luc. I never heard that before; but shall we two make a match between you?

Sil. I 'll know first who was his father.

Ac. My father? What need you to care? I hope he was none of yours!

Half. A hard question, for it is odds but one begat them both; he that cut out the upper leather, cut out the inner, and so with one awl stitched two soles together.

Stel. (*Aside to Luc.*) What is she?

Luc. 'T is Prisius' daughter.

Stel. In good time; it fadges.

Mem. (*Aside to Half.*) What is he?

Half. Sperantus' son.

Mem. So? 'T will cotton.

Ac. Damsel, I pray you, how old are you?

Mem. (*Aside.*) My son would scarce have asked such a foolish question.

Sil. I shall be eighteen next bear-baiting.

Stel. (*Aside.*) My daughter would have made a wiser answer.

Half. (*To Luc.*) O how fitly this comes off!

Ac. My father is a scold; what 's yours?

Mem. My heart throbs,—I 'll look him in the face; and yonder I espy Stellio.

Stel. My mind misgives me,—but whist! yonder is Memphio.

Ac. (*To Mem.*) In faith, I perceive an old saw and a rusty: no fool to the old fool. I pray you, wherefore was I thrust out like a scarecrow in this similitude?

Mem. My son! And I ashamed! Dromio shall die!

Sil. Father, are you sneaking behind? I pray you, what must I do next?

Stel. My daughter! Riscio, thou hast cozened me!

Luc. Now begins the game.

Mem. How came you hither?

Ac. Marry, by the way from your house hither.

Mem. How chance in this attire?

Ac. How chance Dromio bid me?

Mem. Ah, thy son will be begged for a concealed fool![25]

Ac. Will I? I' faith, sir, no.

Stel. Wherefore came you hither, Silena, without leave?

Sil. Because I did, and I am here because I am.

Stel. Poor wench, thy wit is improved[26] to the uttermost.

Half. Aye, 't is an hard matter to have a wit of the old rent, every one racks[27] his commons so high.

Mem. (*Aside.*) Dromio told me that one should meet Stellio's daughter and court her in person of my son.

Stel. (*Aside.*) Riscio told me one should meet Memphio's son, and plead in place of my daughter.

Mem. (*Aside.*) But alas! I see that my son hath met with Silena himself, and bewrayed his folly.

Stel. (*Aside.*) But I see my daughter hath prattled with Accius, and discovered[28] her simplicity.

Luc. A brave cry to hear the two old mules weep over the two young fools.

Mem. Accius, how likest thou Silena?

Ac. I take her to be pregnant.

Sil. Truly, his talk is very personable.

Stel. Come in, girl; this gear must be fetched about.[29]

Mem. Come, Accius, let us go in.

Luc. (*To Stel.*) Nay, sir, there is no harm done; they have neither bought nor

21 begging your pardon; from the Latin *salva reverentia*, and used apologetically before strong or indecent language.
22 scoff.
23 taunt.
24 paid in full, discomfited.
25 cf. p. 48, n. 4.
26 a secondary meaning, to raise the rent of, is punningly referred to in the next speech.
27 charges exorbitant rent for.
28 revealed.
29 this matter must be handled in a roundabout fashion.

sold; they may be twins for their wits and years.

Mem. (*To Half.*) But why diddest thou tell me it was Sperantus' son?

Half. Because I thought thee a fool to ask who thine own son was.

Luc. (*To Stel.*) And so, sir, for your daughter education hath done much; otherwise by nature they are soft-witted enough.

Mem. Alas, their joints are not yet tied;[30] they are not yet come to years and discretion.

Ac. Father, if my hands be tied shall I grow wise?

Half. Aye, and Silena too, if you tie them fast to your tongues.

Sil. You may take your pleasure of my tongue, for it is no man's wife.

Mem. Come in, Accius.

Stel. Come in, Silena. I will talk with Memphio's son, but as for Riscio—!

Mem. As for Dromio—!

Exeunt Memphio, Accius, Stellio, Silena.

Half. Ass for you all four!

Enter Dromio and Riscio.

Dro. How goes the world now? We have made all sure; Candius and Livia are married, their fathers consenting, yet not knowing.

Luc. We have flat marred all! Accius and Silena courted one another; their fathers took them napping, both are ashamed, and you both shall be swinged.

Ris. Tush! let us alone; we will persuade them that all falls out for the best, for if underhand this match had been concluded, they both had been cozened, and now, seeing they find both to be fools, they may be both better advised. But why is Halfpenny so sad?

Enter Hackneyman and Sergeant.

Half. Because I am sure I shall never be a penny.

Ris. Rather pray there be no fall of money, for thou wilt then go for a *q*.[31]

Dro. But did not the two fools currently[32] court one another?

Luc. Very good words, fitly applied, brought in the nick.

Serg. (*Seizing Dro.*) I arrest you.

Dro. Me, sir? Why then didst not bring a stool with thee that I might sit down?

Hack. He arrests you at my suit for a horse.

Ris. The more ass he! If he had arrested a mare instead of an horse it had been but a slight oversight; but to arrest a man that hath no likeness of a horse is flat lunacy or alecy.[33]

Hack. Tush! I hired him a horse.

Dro. I swear then he was well ridden.

Hack. I think in two days he was never baited.

Half. Why, was it a bear thou rid'st on?

Hack. I mean he never gave him bait.

Luc. Why, he took him for no fish.

Hack. I mistake none of you when I take you for fools! I say thou never gavest my horse meat.

Dro. Yes, in four and forty hours I am sure he had a bottle[34] of hay as big as his belly.

Serg. Nothing else? Thou shouldst have given him provender.

Ris. Why, he never asked for any.

Hack. Why, dost thou think a horse can speak?

Dro. No, for I spurred[35] him till my heels ached and he said never a word.

Hack. Well, thou shalt pay sweetly for spoiling him! It was as lusty a nag as any in Rochester, and one that would stand upon no ground.

Dro. Then is he as good as ever he was. I'll warrant he'll do nothing but lie down.

Hack. I lent him thee gently.[36]

Dro. And I restored him so gently that he neither would cry *wyhie*,[37] nor wag the tail.

Hack. But why didst thou bore him through the ears?

Luc. It may be he was set on the pillory[38] because he had not a true pace.

Half. No, it was for tiring.[39]

Hack. He would never tire; it may be he would be so weary he would go no further or so.

Dro. Yes, he was a notable horse for service; he would tire and retire.

Hack. Do you think I'll be jested out of my horse? Sergeant, wreak thy office on him.

Ris. Nay, stay, let him be bailed.

Hack. So he shall when I make him a bargain.

Dro. It was a very good horse. I must

30 their bones are not yet set.
31 the abbreviation for farthing.
32 readily.
33 a coinage of Halfpenny's: drunkenness.
34 bale.
35 pun on *spur*—ask.
36 as to a gentleman; or cheap.
37 whinny.
38 The ears of those condemned to the pillory were frequently cropped or bored as an additional punishment.
39 adorning.

needs confess; and now hearken to his qualities, and have patience to hear them, since I must pay for him. He would stumble three hours in one mile: I had thought I had rode upon addices[40] between this and Canterbury. If one gave him water, why, he would lie down and bathe himself like a hawk. If one ran him, he would simper and mump[41] as though he had gone a-wooing to a malt-mare[42] at Rochester; he trotted before and ambled behind, and was so obedient that he would do duty every minute on his knees, as though every stone had been his father.

Hack. I am sure he had no diseases.

Dro. A little rheum or pose;[43] he lacked nothing but an handkercher.

Serg. Come, what a tale of a horse have we here! I cannot stay; thou must with me to prison.

Ris. If thou be a good fellow, hackneyman, take all our four bonds for the payment; thou knowest we are town-born children, and will not shrink[44] the city for a pelting[45] jade.

Half. I'll enter into a statute merchant[46] to see it answered. But if thou wilt have bonds thou shalt have a bushel full.

Hack. Alas, poor ant! Thou bound in a statute merchant? A brown thread will bind thee fast enough. But if you will be content all four jointly to enter into a bond, I will withdraw the action.

Dro. Yes, I'll warrant they will. How say you?

Half. I yield.

Ris. And I.

Luc. And I.

Hack. Well, call the scrivener.

Serg. Here's one hard by; I'll call him. (*Knocks at Scrivener's door.*)

Ris. A scrivener's shop hangs to a sergeant's mace like a burr to a frieze coat.

Scriv. (*Within.*) What's the matter?

Hack. You must take a note of a bond.

Dro. Nay, a pint of courtesy pulls on a pot of wine. In this tavern we'll dispatch.

Hack. Agreed.

Exeunt all but Riscio.

Ris. Now if our wits be not in the wane, our knavery shall be at the full. They will ride them worse than Dromio rid his horse, for if the wine master their wits, you shall see them bleed their follies.

Exit.

ACT V.

Scene 1.

Enter Dromio, Riscio, Lucio, and Halfpenny.

Dro. Every fox to his hole, the hounds are at hand.

Ris. The sergeant's mace lies at pawn for the reckoning, and he under the board to cast it up.

Luc. The scrivener cannot keep his pen out of the pot; every goblet is an inkhorn.

Half. The hackneyman he whisks with his wand as if the tavern were his stable and all the servants his horses: "Jost there up, bay Richard!"—and white loaves are horsebread in his eyes.

Dro. It is well I have my acquittance, and he such a bond as shall do him no more good than the bond of a fagot. Our knaveries are now come to the push, and we must cunningly dispatch all. We two will go see how we may appease our masters, you two how you may couceal the late marriage; if all fall out amiss, the worst is beating, if to the best, the worst is liberty.

Ris. Then let's about it speedily, for so many irons in the fire together require a diligent plumber.

Exeunt.

Scene 2.

Enter Vicinia.

Vic. My heart throbs, my ears tingle, my mind misgives me, since I hear such muttering of marriages in Rochester. My conscience, which these eighteen years hath been frozen with concealed[47] guiltiness, begins now to thaw in open grief. But I will not accuse myself till I see more danger; the good old woman Mother Bombie shall try her cunning upon me, and if I perceive my case is desperate by her, then will I rather prevent, although with shame, than report too late and be inexcusable.

Knocks. Enter Mother Bombie.

God speed, good mother.

Bom. Welcome, sister.

Vic. I am troubled in the night with

40 adzes.
41 grimace.
42 brewer's mare.
43 cold.
44 quit.
45 paltry.
46 a bond, acknowledged before the chief magistrate of a trading town, giving to the obligee power of seizure of the land of the obligor if he forfeited. (N. E. D.)
47 Qq. *coniealed.*

dreams, and in the day with fears; mine estate bare, which I cannot well bear, but my practices devilish, which I cannot recall. If therefore in these same years there be any deep skill, tell what my fortune shall be, and what my fault is.

Bom. In studying to be over-natural
Thou art like to be unnatural,
And all about a natural,[48]
Thou shalt be eased of a charge,
If thou thy conscience discharge.
And this I commit to thy charge.

Vic. Thou hast touched me to the quick, mother; I understand thy meaning, and thou well knowest my practice. I will follow thy counsel. But what will be the end?

Bom. Thou shalt know before this day end. Farewell.

Exit.

Vic. Now I perceive I must either bewray a mischief or suffer a continual inconvenience. I must haste homewards, and resolve to make all whole; better a little shame than an infinite grief. The strangeness will abate the fault, and the bewraying wipe it clean away.

Exit.

Scene 3.

Enter Synis, Nasutus, and Bedunenus.

Syn. Come, fellows, 't is almost day; let us have a fit of mirth at Sperantus' door, and give a song to the bride.

Nas. I believe they are asleep; it were pity to awake them.

Bed. 'T were a shame they should sleep the first night.

Syn. But who can tell at which house they lie? At Prisius', it may be. We'll try both.

Nas. Come, let's draw like men.

Syn. Now tune, tune, I say! That boy, I think, will never profit in his faculty:[49] he loses his rosin that his fiddle goes "cush! cush!" like as one should go wet-shod; and his mouth so dry that he hath not spittle for his pin[50] as I have.

Bed. Marry, sir, you see I go wet-shod and dry-mouthed, for yet could I never get new shoes or good drink; rather than I'll lead this life, I'll throw my fiddle into the leads for a hobbler.[51]

Syn. Boy, no more words! There's a time for all things. Though I say it that should not, I have been a minstrel these thirty years, and tickled more strings than thou hast hairs, but yet was never so misused.

Nas. Let us not brabble,[52] but play; tomorrow is a new day.

Bed. I am sorry I speak in your cast.[53] What shall we sing?

Syn. "The Love-Knot," for that's best for a bridal.

(*They sing.*)

Good morrow, fair bride, and send you joy of your bridal.

(*Sperantus looks out.*)

Sper. What a mischief make the twanglers here? We have no trenchers to scrape. It makes my teeth on edge to hear such grating. Get you packing, or I'll make you wear double stocks,[54] and yet you shall be never the warmer.

Syn. We come for good will, to bid the bride and bridegroom God give them joy.

Sper. Here's no wedding.

Syn. Yes, your son and Prisius' daughter were married; though you seem strange, yet they repent it not, I am sure.

Sper. My son, villain! I had rather he were fairly hanged.

Nas. So he is, sir; you have your wish.

Enter Candius.

Can. Here, fiddlers, take this, and not a word. Here is no wedding, it was at Memphio's house. Yet gramercy; your music, though it missed the house, hit the mind; we were a-preparing our wedding gear.

Syn. I cry you mercy, sir; I think it was Memphio's son that was married.

Exit Candius.

Sper. O ho, the case is altered! Go thither then, and be haltered for me.

Nas. What's the alms?

Syn. An angel.

Bed. I'll warrant there's some work towards; ten shillings is money in master Mayor's purse.[55]

Syn. Let us to Memphio's, and share equally; when we have done all, thou shalt have new shoes.

Bed. Aye, such as they cry at the 'sizes: "a mark in issues![56] and mark in is-

48 idiot.
49 improve in his profession.
50 to make the pegs of his instrument hold fast.
51 into the gutter for a mark to throw at.
52 wrangle.
53 *cast* was an actor's part in a play; hence, *to speak in one's cast* is to interrupt.
54 pun on *stocks*—stockings.
55 i.e. even to a rich man.
56 thirteen shillings four pence (a mark) in fines; there is probably, as Bond suggests, a bad pun on *issues*—his shoes.

sues!"—and yet I never saw so much leather as would piece one's shoes.

Syn. No more; there 's the money.

Bed. A good handsel,[57] and I think the maidenhead of your liberality.

Nas. Come, here 's the house; what shall we sing?

Syn. You know Memphio is very rich and wise, and therefore let us strike the gentle stroke, and sing a catch.

Song.

All. The bride this night can catch no cold;
No cold; the bridegroom 's young, not old;
Like ivy he her fast does hold,
Syn. And clips her,
Nas. And lips her,
Bed. And flips her too.
All. Then let them alone: they know what they do.
Syn. At laugh and lie down if they play,
Nas. What ass against the sport can bray?
Bed. Such tick-tack has held many a day,
Syn. And longer,
Nas. And stronger;
Bed. It still holds, too.
All. Then let them alone; they know what they do.
This night
In delight
Does thump away sorrow.
Of billing
Take your filling;
So good morrow, good morrow.

Nas. Good morrow, mistress bride, and send you a huddle.[58]

Mem. (*Above.*) What crowding [59] knaves have we there? Case up your fiddles, or the constable shall cage you up! What bride talk you of?

Syn. Here 's a wedding in Rochester, and 't was told me first that Sperantus' son had married Prisius' daughter. We were there, and they sent us to your worship, saying your son was matched with Stellio's daughter.

Mem. Hath Sperantus that churl nothing to do but mock his neighbors? I 'll be even with him! And get you gone, or I swear by the rood's body,[60] I 'll lay you by the heels!

Nas. Sing a catch! Here 's a fair catch indeed! Sing till we catch cold on our feet, and be called knave till our ears glow on our heads! Your worship is wise, sir!

Mem. Dromio, shake off a whole kennel of officers to punish these jarring rogues. I 'll teach them to stretch their dried sheeps' guts at my door, and to mock one that stands to be mayor.

Dro. (*Above.*) I had thought they had been sticking of pigs, I heard such a squeaking. I go, sir.

Syn. Let us be packing.

Nas. Where is my scabbard? Every one sheathe his science.

Bed. A bots on the shoemaker that made this boot for my fiddle; 't is too strait.

Syn. No more words; 't will be thought they were the four waits,[61] and let them wring.[62] As for the wags that set us on work, we 'll talk with them.

Exeunt.

Enter Memphio and Dromio.

Dro. They be gone, sir.

Mem. If they had stayed, the stocks should have stayed them. But, sirrah, what shall we now do?

Dro. As I advised you, make a match, for better one house be cumbered with two fools than two.

Mem. 'T is true; for it being bruited that each of us have a fool, who will tender marriage to any of them, that is wise? Besides, fools are fortunate, fools are fair, fools are honest.

Dro. Aye, sir, and more than that, fools are not wise; a wise man is melancholy for moonshine in the water, careful, building castles in the air, and commonly hath a fool to his heir.

Mem. But what sayest thou to thy dame's chafing?

Dro. Nothing, but all her dishes are chafing dishes.

Mem. I would her tongue were in thy belly!

Dro. I had as lief have a raw neat's tongue in my stomach.

Mem. Why?

Dro. Marry, if the clapper hang within an inch of my heart, that [63] makes mine ears burn a quarter of a mile off, do you not think it would beat my heart black and blue?

Mem. Well, patience is a virtue, but pinching is worse than any vice! I will break this matter to Stellio, and if he be willing this day shall be their wedding.

Dro. Then this day shall be my liberty.

Mem. Aye, if Stellio's daughter had been

57 earnest money.
58 embrace.
59 fiddling.
60 the body of Christ on the cross.
61 singers.
62 take the onus of it.
63 i. e. clapper.

wise, and by thy means cozened of a fool.

Dro. Then, sir, I 'll revolt, and dash out the brains of your devices.

Mem. Rather thou shalt be free.

Exeunt.

Enter Sperantus, Halfpenny, Prisius, and Lucio.

Sper. Boy, this smoke is a token of some fire; I like not the look of it. Wherefore should these minstrels dream of a marriage?

Half. Alas, sir, they rustle into every place. Give credit to no such words.

Sper. I will to Prisius; I cannot be quiet —and in good time I meet him. Good morrow, neighbor.

Pris. I cast the morrow in thy face, and bid good night to all neighborhood.

Sper. This is your old trick, to pick one's purse and then to pick quarrels. I tell thee, I had rather thou shouldest rob my chest than embezzle my son.

Pris. Thy son! My daughter is seduced! For I hear say she is married, and our boys can tell. (*To Luc.*) How sayest thou? Tell the truth, or I 'll grind thee to powder in my mill. Be they married?

Luc. True it is they were both in a church.

Pris. That 's no fault; the place is holy.

Half. And there was with them a priest.

Sper. Why, what place fitter for a priest than a church?

Luc. And they took one another by the hand.

Pris. Tush! that 's but common courtesy.

Half. And the priest spake many kind words.

Sper. That showed he was no dumb minister. But what said they? Diddest thou hear any words between them?

Luc. Faith, there was a bargain during life, and the clock cried, "God give them joy!"

Pris. Villain, they be married!

Half. Nay, I think not so.

Sper. Yes, yes! "God give you joy!" is a binder. I 'll quickly be resolved. Candius, come forth.

Re-enter Candius.

Pris. And I 'll be put out of doubt. Livia, come forth.

Enter Livia.

Sper. The micher hangs down his head!

Pris. The baggage begins to blush!

Half. Now begins the game!

Luc. I believe it will be no game for us.

Sper. Are you married, young master?

Can. I cannot deny it, it was done so lately.

Sper. But thou shalt repent it was done so soon.

Pris. Then 't is bootless to ask you, Livia.

Liv. Aye, and needless to be angry.

Pris. It shall pass anger; thou shalt find it rage.

Liv. You gave your consent.

Pris. Impudent giglot,[64] was it not enough to abuse me, but also to belie me?

Can. You, sir, agreed to this match.

Sper. Thou brazen-face boy, thinkest thou by learning to persuade me to that which thou speakest? Where did I consent, when, what witness?

Can. In this place yesterday before Dromio and Riscio.

Pris. I remember we heard a contract between Memphio's son and Stellio's daughter; and that our good wills being asked, which needed not, we gave them, which booted not.

Can. 'T was but the apparel of Accius and Silena; we were the persons.

Pris. O villainy not to be borne! (*To Luc.*) Wast thou privy to this practice?

Luc. In a manner.

Pris. I 'll pay thee after a manner!

Sper. And you, oatmeal groat! you were acquainted with this plot?

Half. Accessory, as it were.

Sper. Thou shalt be punished as principal. Here comes Memphio and Stellio; they belike were privy, and all their heads were laid together to grieve our hearts.

Enter Memphio, Stellio, Dromio, and Riscio.

Mem. Come, Stellio, the assurance may be made tomorrow, and our children assured today.

Stel. Let the conveyance run as we agreed.

Pris. You convey[65] cleanly indeed, if cozenage be clean dealing, for in the apparel of your children you have conveyed a match between ours which grieves us not a little.

Mem. Nay, in the apparel of your children you have discovered the folly of ours, which shames us overmuch.

Stel. But 't is no matter; though they be fools they are no beggars.

64 wanton.

65 steal.

Sper. And though ours be disobedient, they be no fools.

Dro. So now they tune their pipes.

Ris. You shall hear sweet music between a hoarse raven and a screech owl.

Mem. Neighbors, let us not vary; our boys have played their cheating parts. I suspected no less at the tavern, where our four knaves met together.

Ris. If it were knavery for four to meet in a tavern, your worships wot well there were other four.

Stel. This villain calls us knaves by craft.

Luc. Nay, truly, I dare swear he used no craft, but means plainly.

Sper. This is worse! Come, Halfpenny, tell the truth, and scape the rod.

Half. As good confess here, being trussed,[66] as at home with my hose about my heels.

Dro. Nay, I'll tell thee, for 't will never become thee to utter it.

Mem. Well, out with it!

Dro. Memphio had a fool to his son, which Stellio knew not; Stellio a fool to his daughter, unknown to Memphio: to cozen each other, they dealt with their boys for a match; we met with Lucio and Halfpenny, who told the love between their masters' children—the youth deeply in love, the fathers unwilling to consent.

Ris. I'll take the tale by the end. Then we four met, which argued we were no mountains; and in a tavern we met, which argued we were mortal; and every one in his wine told his day's work, which was a sign we forgot not our business; and seeing all our masters troubled with devices, we determined a little to trouble the water before they drank: so that in the attire of your children our masters' wise children bewrayed their good natures, and in the garments of our masters' children yours made a marriage. This all stood upon us poor children and your young children, to show that old folks may be overtaken by children.

Pris. Here's a children indeed! I'll never forget it.

Mem. I will! Accius, come forth.

Stel. I forgive all. Silena, come forth.

Enter Accius and Silena.

Sper. Neighbor, these things cannot be recalled, therefore as good consent; seeing in all our purposes also we missed the mark, for they two will match their children.

Pris. Well, of that more anon; not so suddenly, lest our ungracious youths think we dare do no other. But in truth, their love stirs up nature in me.

Mem. Come, Accius, thou must be married to Silena. How art thou minded?

Ac. What, for ever and ever?

Mem. Aye, Accius, what else?

Ac. I shall never be able to abide it, it will be so tedious.

Stel. Silena, thou must be betrothed to Accius, and love him for thy husband.

Sil. I had as lief have one of clouts.

Stel. Why, Silena?

Sil. Why, look how he looks!

Ac. If you will not, another will.

Sil. I thank you for mine old cap.

Ac. And if you be so lusty, lend me two shillings.

Pris. (*To Sper.*) We are happy we missed the foolish match.

Mem. Come, you shall presently be contracted.

Dro. Contract their wits no more; they be shrunk close already.

Ac. Well, father, here's my hand; strike the bargain.

Sil. Must he lie with me?

Stel. No, Silena, lie by thee.

Ac. I shall give her the humble-bee's kiss.

Enter Vicinia, Mæstius, and Serena.

Vic. I forbid the banns.

Ris. What, dost thou think them rats, and fearest they shall be poisoned?

Mem. You, Vicinia? Wherefore?

Vic. Hearken! About eighteen years ago I nursed thee a son, Memphio, and thee a daughter, Stellio.

Stel. True.

Mem. True.

Vic. I had at that time two children of mine own, and being poor, thought it better to change them than kill them. I imagined if by device I could thrust my children into your houses, they should be well brought up in their youth and wisely provided for in their age. Nature wrought with me, and when they were weaned I sent home mine instead of yours, which hitherto you have kept tenderly as yours. Growing in years, I found the children I kept at home to love dearly, at first like brother and sister, which I rejoiced at; but at length

66 i.e. before my breeches are taken down and I'm spanked.

too forward in affection, which, although inwardly I could not mislike, yet openly I seemed to disallow. They increased in their loving humors; I ceased not to chastise them for their loose demeanors. At last it came to my ears that my son that was out with Memphio was a fool, that my daughter with Stellio was also unwise, and yet, being brother and sister, there was a match in hammering betwixt them.

Mem. What monstrous tale is this?

Stel. And I am sure incredible.

Sper. Let her end her discourse.

Ac. I'll never believe it.

Mem. Hold thy peace!

Vic. My very bowels yearned within me that I should be author of such vile incest, an hindrance to lawful love. I went to the good old woman, Mother Bombie, to know the event of this practice; who told me this day I might prevent the danger, and upon submission escape the punishment. Hither am I come to claim my children, though both fools, and to deliver yours, both loving.

Mem. Is this possible? How shall we believe it?

Stel. It cannot sink into my head.

Vic. This trial cannot fail. Your son, Memphio, had a mole under his ear; I framed one under my child's ear by art; you shall see it taken away with the juice of mandrage.[67] Behold now for your son's! No herb can undo that nature hath done. Your daughter, Stellio, hath on her wrist a mole, which I counterfeited on my daughter's arm, and that shall you see taken away as the other. Thus you see I do not dissemble, hoping you will pardon me, as I have pitied them.

Mem. This is my son! O fortunate Memphio!

Stel. This is my daughter! More than thrice happy Stellio!

Mæst. How happy is Mæstius, how blessed Serena, that being neither children to poor parents, nor brother and sister by nature, may enjoy their love by consent of parents and nature.

Ac. Soft! I'll not swap my father for all this.

Sil. What, do you think I'll be cozened of my father? Methinks I should not. Mother Bombie told me my father knew me not, my mother bore me not, falsely bred, truly begot. A bots on Mother Bombie!

Dro. Mother Bombie told us we should be found cozeners, and in the end be cozened by cozeners; well fare Mother Bombie!

Ris. I heard Mother Bombie say that thou shalt die a beggar; beware of Mother Bombie!

Pris. Why, have you all been with Mother Bombie?

Luc. All, and as far as I can see, she foretold all.

Mem. Indeed she is cunning and wise, never doing harm, but still practising good. Seeing these things fall out thus, are you content, Stellio, the match go forward?

Stel. Aye, with double joy, having found for a fool a wise maid, and finding between them both exceeding love.

Pris. Then to end all jars, our children's matches shall stand with our good liking. Livia, enjoy Candius.

Sper. Candius, enjoy Livia.

Can. How shall we recompense fortune, that to our loves hath added our parents' good wills?

Mæst. How shall we requite fortune, that to our loves hath added lawfulness, and to our poor estate competent living?

Mem. Vicinia, thy fact[68] is pardoned, though the law would see it punished. We be content to keep Silena in the house with the new married couple.

Stel. And I do maintain Accius in our house.

Vic. Come, my children, though fortune hath not provided you lands, yet you see you are not destitute of friends. I shall be eased of a charge both in purse and conscience: in conscience, having revealed my lewd practice; in purse, having you kept of alms.

Ac. Come, if you be my sister it's the better for you.

Sil. Come, brother, methinks it's better than it was; I should have been but a bald bride. I'll eat as much pie as if I had been married.

Mem. Let's also forgive the knavery of our boys, since all turns to our good haps.

Stel. Agreed; all are pleased now the boys are unpunished.

Enter Hackneyman, Sergeant, and Scrivener.

Hack. Nay, soft, take us with you, and seek redress for our wrongs, or we'll complain to the mayor.

Pris. What's the matter?

67 mandragora.

68 crime.

Hack. I arrested Memphio's boy for an horse. After much mocking, at the request of his fellow wags I was content to take a bond jointly of them all; they had me into a tavern; there they made me, the scrivener, and the sergeant drunk, pawned his mace for the wine, and sealed me an obligation nothing to the purpose. I pray you, read it.

Mem. What wags be these! Why, by this bond you can demand nothing, and things done in drink may be repented in soberness, but not remedied.

Dro. Sir, I have his acquittance; let him sue his bond.

Hack. I'll cry quittance with thee!

Serg. And I, or it shall cost me the laying on freely of my mace.

Scriv. And I'll give thee such a dash with a pen as shall cost thee many a pound, with such a *Noverint*[69] as Cheapside[70] can show none such.

Half. Do your worst; our knaveries will revenge it upon your children's children.

Mem. Thou boy! (*To Hack.*) We will pay the hire of the horse, be not angry. The boys have been in a merry cozening vein, for they have served their masters of the same sort; but all must be forgotten. Now all are content but the poor fiddlers; they shall be sent for to the marriage, and have double fees.

Dro. You need no more send for a fiddler to a feast than a beggar to a fair.

Stel. This day we will feast at my house.

Mem. Tomorrow at mine.

Pris. The next day at mine.

Sper. Then at mine the last day, and even so spend this week in good cheer.

Dro. Then we were best be going whilst every one is pleased. And yet these couples are not fully pleased till the priest have done his worst.

Ris. Come, Sergeant, we'll toss it[71] this week, and make thy mace arrest a boiled capon.

Serg. No more words at the wedding; if the mayor should know it, I were in danger of mine office.

Ris. Then take heed how, on such as we are, you show a cast[72] of your office.

Half. If you mace us, we'll pepper you.

Ac. Come, sister, the best is, we shall have good cheer these four days.

Luc. And be fools for ever.

Sil. That's none of our upseekings.

Exeunt.

69 the first word of the phrase with which deeds began: "Know all men by these presents."
70 the ecclesiastical court of appeal for the province of Canterbury was held in Bow Church, Cheapside.
71 toss cups, drink.
72 specimen.

CHRISTOPHER MARLOWE

THE TROUBLESOME REIGN AND LAMENTABLE DEATH OF EDWARD THE SECOND

Christopher Marlowe (1564–1593) was the son of a shoemaker of Canterbury, and went to the old King's School of that town. Thence in 1579 he went up to Cambridge on a scholarship which he held all during his residence at the university, where he took a bachelor's degree in 1584, a master's in 1587. Between 1587, when *Tamburlaine* was acted, and 1593 he produced at least six plays, as well as the unfinished narrative poem, *Hero and Leander*. All that is certainly known of his death is that he was killed in a brawl, due to reasons unknown.

The feeling of national unity which had been growing in England under the Tudor sovereigns, especially during the reign of the great Maiden Queen, received a tremendous impulse from the defeat of the Armada in 1588. The mistrust of Spain, shown in the popular discontent with Mary Tudor's marriage to Philip, accentuated by the resentment of Spanish oppression of the Netherlands, and fanned into a white heat of hatred by Philip's ambitious project of regaining England for the Pope, probably did more to make England a united nation than any other one cause. The fears of a Catholic uprising were dissipated by the staunch loyalty of the English Catholics, and the jubilation over a great crisis safely passed found one means of expression in the glorious flood of Elizabethan literature. To this national inspiration the drama, just finding itself in the decade from 1580 to 1590, responded with extraordinary vigor. The twenty years following the Armada saw the rise and full development of a new and quite native form of drama, taking its subject-matter from the history, authentic or legendary, of Britain, the chronicle-history play. It has been estimated that such plays during the period of their popularity constituted more than a fifth of the contemporary drama. Of the thirty-seven plays in the Shakespeare canon ten (counting parts of plays individually) are of this type, while *Cymbeline*, *Lear*, and *Macbeth* are from much the same sources. It was natural that during a period of strong national feeling Englishmen should take interest in the history of their country. What numerous historical works in prose and verse did for readers, the chronicle plays did for spectators, and their actual educative function must not be overlooked. Forerunners of the type may be found in such a play as Bale's *Kyng Johan* (1538) and a few Senecan tragedies like *Gorboduc* (1562), but it was not till 1586–7 in *The Famous Victories of Henry V* that we get our first example. To raise the chronicle-history play to the plane of artistic drama was the work of two men, Marlowe and Shakespeare.

Edward II is generally accepted as being the latest of Marlowe's plays, written probably about 1592. Not so rich in poetry as *Tamburlaine* or *Dr. Faustus*, nor so theatrically effective as the melodramatic *Jew of Malta*, in technique it is Marlowe's best work. The material is taken from the source that supplied Shakespeare with his knowledge of English history, Holinshed's *Chronicles of England, Scotland, and Ireland*, with occasional borrowings from the older chronicles of Fabyan (e.g., the song on Bannockburn, II. ii) and Stow. The play is, however, so much more than a mere transference to the stage of Holinshed's narrative that a comparison of the play with the historical account reveals, as can nothing else, Marlowe's methods as a playmaker.

The action covers a period of twenty years, from 1307, when Gaveston was recalled, to the death of Edward in 1327. Marlowe's treatment of the story shows a selection and transposing of events in order to bring out the one essential fact of the King's utter incompetence and subjection to unworthy favorites. Gaveston was executed in 1312, and the troubles in Ireland (II. ii) and in Scotland (II. ii) occurred after his death, but Marlowe shifts both forward in point of time in order to connect them with Gaveston's baleful influence. Warwick died in his bed in 1315, seven years before the battle of Boroughbridge, but Marlowe keeps him alive to have him captured and ordered to execution in retaliation for his killing of Gaveston. At the time the play opens the Earl of Kent was six years old, but Marlowe, needing a counsellor and supporter of the King, used Kent for the purpose. In the play young Spencer immediately succeeds Gaveston as the King's favorite; really the younger Hugh le Despenser, who had been an enemy of Gaveston, remained an opponent of Edward's for some six years after Gaveston's death. Historically the Mortimers belong with the Spencers, i.e., to the later part of the reign, but in order to motivate the affair between the Queen and young Mortimer Marlowe transfers them to the beginning of the play and makes them leaders in the barons' councils.

What does all this rearrangement mean? It means that Marlowe was working with a definite dramatic end in view, with all his faculties alert to make the play a single, logical portrayal of the King's fatal weakness and its consequences to him and to the realm. In the first place he had to show in action the evil influence of Gaveston over Edward. This he does by showing the King's unkingly infatuation with an arrogant favorite who holds his position only by flattering the royal vanity, an infatuation so complete that it leads to the insulting and final alienation of a faithful and loving Queen. The practical effects of Gaveston's pandering to the King's love of pleasure are seen in the hostility of the great barons and the affronts to English honor in Scotland and Ireland. With Gaveston out of the way (III. ii), Marlowe is faced by the difficulty of avoiding in the Spencer story a mere repetition of that of Gaveston. He had already, by introducing young Spencer in II. i as a dependent of Gaveston's, and thus preparing for Spencer's promotion to Gaveston's shoes, prevented his play from breaking in two on Gaveston's disappearance. Now he solves his fresh problem by shifting the interest from the affairs of the kingdom to the more familiar situation of the eternal triangle — husband, offended wife, lover. From the first Mortimer has been the main reliance of the Queen in her effort to maintain her position with the King; when the King himself impugns her honor by flinging Mortimer's name in her face we are fully prepared for her soliloquy at the end of the scene (II. iv), and the understanding between her and Mortimer in IV. iv and v. The development of their love affair, merely hinted at in Holinshed, is rather left for the actors to bring out than explained in the text, but Marlowe makes the situation clear. Mortimer's relations with the Queen place him definitely at the head of the revolting barons, and he is thus ready to play his part as chief actor in Edward's deposition and murder, and as virtual ruler of the realm until the young King asserts himself at the end of the play.

Detailed analysis of this sort is useful not only for showing how Marlowe met the problem of making a play out of unpromising material, but also how, in the process of making the story truly dramatic, his method tends to break away from the chronicle-history form and approaches tragedy. In early crude examples of the type — plays like *The Famous Victories of Henry V*, *Jack Straw*, Peele's *Edward I*, *Henry VI* — the emphasis is frankly on circumstance, what happened during the reign of a certain king. Events are set down in chronological order, and the writer is more concerned with the effect of the immediate situation than with the coherent development of a logical story. Characters are presented in a purely superficial way, and the unity of the play is secured only by the presence in the chief scenes of the same leading figures. The progress of the play is, therefore, clumsy and jerky. Is the chief interest in *Edward II* in event or in character? Clearly what interests Marlowe most is the character of Edward himself; by centering attention on the petulant king, powerless to command even his own desires, and by careful analysis of Edward's weakness, Marlowe shifts the emphasis from event to character, and in so doing almost writes tragedy. The method of securing dramatic unity by focusing attention on a central character Marlowe had employed in his previous plays; but there is this fundamental difference between *Edward II* and its predecessors, that while in *Tamburlaine*, *Faustus*, and *The Jew* all the other characters are completely subordinated to the one commanding figure, are satellites shining only by light reflected from their sun, in *Edward II* Marlowe develops four characters with distinct personalities of their own — Edward, Gaveston, Mortimer, and the Queen. Of these Isabella is the least satisfactory, probably because, although her abandonment of the King for Mortimer is well enough motivated, Marlowe does not give us a chance to see the development of her passion. One genuine love-scene between her and Mortimer would have helped us to a sympathetic understanding of the Queen, and done away with the apparent abruptness of her change of heart. Marlowe's was an essentially masculine intellect, and his inability to portray women with success is as striking as Byron's. Gaveston, in his combination of arrogance and sycophancy, stands out as a clear study of the royal favorite. Mortimer's most prominent trait is a headstrong resolve to rule or be ruined, to be all or nothing; his last words have the true Marlowe ring of towering ambition and undaunted defiance in the face of defeat.

Upon Edward the poet lavishes all his power. Edward has the fatal flaw in character which brings tragedy upon its possessor, a flaw which at the same time unites him with Marlowe's other heroes in their *Amour de l'Impossible*, to use Symonds's often-quoted phrase. The lust for power seen in varying manifestations in Tamburlaine, Faustus, and Barabas the Jew, in Edward is replaced by an inordinate desire for affection, to love and to be loved by the one object of his affection. Since this is not a case of one of those deathless passions between man and woman which make the world seem well lost for love, Marlowe has the difficult task of gaining sympathy for an unsympathetic figure without palliating its weakness. That he has done so must be the verdict of the reader upon finishing the long and pathetic presentation of Edward's humiliation and death. As Schelling puts it: "Contemptible in his unkingliness up to the moment of the turning of the tide against him, the royal sorrows and the unregal inflictions put upon him arouse our sympathies until, when the pitiful catastrophe which overtakes him is reached, contempt is transmuted into sympathetic grief that any king could so fall."

More than any other of Marlowe's plays *Edward II* exhibits a restraint, a conscious attempt to place dramatic truth before poetic imagination. As a result the verse is inferior as poetry to that of the others. We catch echoes of "Marlowe's mighty line" in passages like Gaveston's soliloquies in the first scene, in Edward's speeches in the deposition scene where he gives up "the sweet fruition of an earthly crown," in the scene where he is murdered, in Mortimer's last speech. It may be questioned, indeed, whether the glorious sweep and daring of *Tamburlaine* and *Dr. Faustus* might not have been out of place in this study of English history. And this may certainly be said, that while in the preceding plays we feel Marlowe's failure to make his finest lyrical passages dramatically appropriate, *Edward II* shows him on his way to accomplishment. He had already settled one thing: that blank verse was to be the medium of Elizabethan drama.

It is a truism that on the serious side Shakespeare was deeply indebted to Marlowe. Marlowe was Shakespeare's master in chronicle-history: the two may have worked together on *Henry VI*, *Richard III* is the application to chronicle-history of Marlowe's centralizing method, and *Richard II* shows at every turn the influence of *Edward II*. Had Marlowe been permitted to live and work his way to true tragedy as did Shakespeare, *Edward II* might have proved the transitional stage that *Richard II* was for Shakespeare. But "cut was the branch that might have grown full straight," and Marlowe's *Lear* and *Hamlet* were never written.

THE TROUBLESOME REIGN AND LAMENTABLE DEATH OF EDWARD THE SECOND

BY CHRISTOPHER MARLOWE

NAMES OF THE CHARACTERS

KING EDWARD THE SECOND.
PRINCE EDWARD, *his Son, afterwards King Edward the Third.*
EARL OF KENT, *Brother to King Edward the Second.*
GAVESTON.
ARCHBISHOP OF CANTERBURY.
BISHOP OF COVENTRY.
BISHOP OF WINCHESTER.
WARWICK.
LANCASTER.
PEMBROKE.
ARUNDEL.
LEICESTER.
BERKELEY.
MORTIMER, *the elder.*
MORTIMER, *the younger, his Nephew.*
SPENCER, *the elder.*
SPENCER, *the younger, his Son.*
BALDOCK.
BEAUMONT.
TRUSSEL.
GURNEY.
MATREVIS.
LIGHTBORN.
SIR JOHN OF HAINAULT.
LEVUNE.
RICE AP HOWELL.
Abbot, Monks, Herald, Lords, Poor Men, JAMES, *Mower, Champion, Messengers, Soldiers, and Attendants.*
QUEEN ISABELLA, *Wife to King Edward the Second.*
Niece to King Edward the Second, Daughter to the Duke of Gloucester.
Ladies.

ACT I.

SCENE 1. *A street in London.*

Enter Gaveston, reading on a letter that was brought him from the King.

Gaveston. "My father is deceas'd! Come, Gaveston,
And share the kingdom with thy dearest friend."
Ah! words that make me surfeit with delight!
What greater bliss can hap to Gaveston
Than live and be the favorite of a king!
Sweet prince, I come; these, these thy amorous lines

Might have enforc'd me to have swum from France,
And, like Leander, gasp'd upon the sand,
So thou would'st smile, and take me in thine arms.
The sight of London to my exil'd eyes
Is as Elysium to a new-come soul;
Not that I love the city, or the men,
But that it harbors him I hold so dear—
The king, upon whose bosom let me die,
And with the world be still at enmity.
What need the arctic people love star-light,
To whom the sun shines both by day and night?
Farewell base stooping to the lordly peers!
My knee shall bow to none but to the king.
As for the multitude, that are but sparks
Rak'd up in embers of their poverty;—
Tanti.[1] I'll fawn first on the wind
That glanceth at my lips, and flieth away.

Enter three Poor Men.

But how now, what are these?

Poor Men. Such as desire your worship's service.

Gav. What canst thou do?

1 P. Man. I can ride.

Gav. But I have no horses.—What art thou?

2 P. Man. A traveler.

Gav. Let me see: thou would'st do well
To wait at my trencher and tell me lies at dinner time;
And as I like your discoursing, I'll have you.—
And what art thou?

3 P. Man. A soldier, that hath serv'd against the Scot.

Gav. Why, there are hospitals for such as you.
I have no war, and therefore, sir, begone.

3 P. Man. Farewell, and perish by a soldier's hand,
That would'st reward them with an hospital.

Gav. (*Aside.*) Aye, aye, these words of his move me as much
As if a goose should play the porpentine,
And dart her plumes, thinking to pierce my breast.
But yet it is no pain to speak men fair;
I'll flatter these, and make them live in hope.—
You know that I came lately out of France,
And yet I have not view'd my lord the king;
If I speed well, I'll entertain you all.

All. We thank your worship.

Gav. I have some business: leave me to myself.

All. We will wait here about the court.

Exeunt.

Gav. Do.—These are not men for me:
I must have wanton poets, pleasant wits,
Musicians, that with touching of a string
May draw the pliant king which way I please.
Music and poetry is his delight;
Therefore I'll have Italian masks by night,
Sweet speeches, comedies, and pleasing shows;
And in the day, when he shall walk abroad,
Like sylvan nymphs my pages shall be clad;
My men, like satyrs grazing on the lawns,
Shall with their goat-feet dance an antic hay.[2]
Sometime a lovely boy in Dian's shape,
With hair that gilds the water as it glides,
Crownets of pearl about his naked arms,
And in his sportful hands an olive tree,
To hide those parts which men delight to see,
Shall bathe him in a spring; and there hard by,
One like Actæon peeping through the grove
Shall by the angry goddess be transform'd,
And running in the likeness of an hart
By yelping hounds pull'd down, and seem to die;—
Such things as these best please his majesty,
My lord.—Here comes the king, and the nobles
From the parliament. I'll stand aside.

Retires.

Enter King Edward, Lancaster, the Elder Mortimer, Young Mortimer, Kent, Warwick, and Attendants.

K. Edw. Lancaster!

Lan. My lord.

Gav. (*Aside.*) That Earl of Lancaster do I abhor.

K. Edw. Will you not grant me this?—(*Aside.*) In spite of them

1 "so much for them."

2 a rustic dance.

I'll have my will; and these two Mortimers,
That cross me thus, shall know I am displeas'd.
E. Mor. If you love us, my lord, hate Gaveston.
Gav. (*Aside.*) That villain Mortimer! I'll be his death.
Y. Mor. Mine uncle here, this earl, and I myself
Were sworn to your father at his death,
That he should ne'er return into the realm;
And know, my lord, ere I will break my oath,
This sword of mine, that should offend your foes,
Shall sleep within the scabbard at thy need,
And underneath thy banners march who will,
For Mortimer will hang his armor up.
Gav. (*Aside.*) *Mort Dieu!*
K. Edw. Well, Mortimer, I'll make thee rue these words.
Beseems it thee to contradict thy king?
Frown'st thou thereat, aspiring Lancaster?
The sword shall plane the furrows of thy brows,
And hew these knees that now are grown so stiff.
I will have Gaveston; and you shall know
What danger 't is to stand against your king.
Gav. (*Aside.*) Well done, Ned!
Lan. My lord, why do you thus incense your peers,
That naturally would love and honor you
But for that base and obscure Gaveston?
Four earldoms have I, besides Lancaster—
Derby, Salisbury, Lincoln, Leicester,—
These will I sell, to give my soldiers pay,
Ere Gaveston shall stay within the realm;
Therefore, if he be come, expel him straight.
Kent. Barons and earls, your pride hath made me mute;
But now I'll speak, and to the proof, I hope.
I do remember, in my father's days,
Lord Percy of the north, being highly mov'd,
Braved Moubery [3] in presence of the king;
For which, had not his highness lov'd him well,
He should have lost his head; but with his look
The undaunted spirit of Percy was appeas'd,
And Moubery and he were reconcil'd:
Yet dare you brave the king unto his face?—
Brother, revenge it, and let these their heads
Preach upon poles, for trespass of their tongues.
War. O, our heads!
K. Edw. Aye, yours; and therefore I would wish you grant—
War. Bridle thy anger, gentle Mortimer.
Y. Mor. I cannot, nor I will not; I must speak.—
Cousin, our hands I hope shall fence our heads,
And strike off his that makes you threaten us.
Come, uncle, let us leave the brain-sick king,
And henceforth parley [4] with our naked swords.
E. Mor. Wiltshire hath men enough to save our heads.
War. All Warwickshire will love him for my sake.
Lan. And northward Gaveston hath many friends.—
Adieu, my lord; and either change your mind,
Or look to see the throne, where you should sit,
To float in blood; and at thy wanton head,
The glozing [5] head of thy base minion thrown.
Exeunt all except King Edward, Kent, Gaveston, and Attendants.
K. Edw. I cannot brook these haughty menaces.
Am I a king, and must be overrul'd?—
Brother, display my ensigns in the field;
I'll bandy [6] with the barons and the earls,
And either die or live with Gaveston.
Gav. I can no longer keep me from my lord.
(*Comes forward.*)
K. Edw. What, Gaveston! welcome!—Kiss not my hand—
Embrace me, Gaveston, as I do thee.

3 Mowbray; the spelling shows the old pronunciation.
4 Q. *parle.*
5 flattering.
6 dispute.

Why should'st thou kneel? Know'st thou not who I am?
Thy friend, thyself, another Gaveston!
Not Hylas was more mourn'd of Hercules,
Than thou hast been of me since thy exile.

Gav. And since I went from hence, no soul in hell
Hath felt more torment than poor Gaveston.

K. Edw. I know it.—Brother, welcome home my friend.
Now let the treacherous Mortimers conspire,
And that high-minded Earl of Lancaster:
I have my wish, in that I joy thy sight;
And sooner shall the sea o'erwhelm my land,
Than bear the ship that shall transport thee hence.
I here create thee Lord High Chamberlain,
Chief Secretary to the state and me,
Earl of Cornwall, King and Lord of Man.

Gav. My lord, these titles far exceed my worth.

Kent. Brother, the least of these may well suffice
For one of greater birth than Gaveston.

K. Edw. Cease, brother, for I cannot brook these words.
Thy worth, sweet friend, is far above my gifts.
Therefore, to equal it, receive my heart.
If for these dignities thou be envíed,
I'll give thee more; for, but to honor thee,
Is Edward pleas'd with kingly regiment.[7]
Fear'st[8] thou thy person? Thou shalt have a guard.
Wantest thou gold? Go to my treasury.
Would'st thou be lov'd and fear'd? Receive my seal;
Save or condemn, and in our name command
Whatso thy mind affects, or fancy likes.

Gav. It shall suffice me to enjoy your love,
Which whiles I have, I think myself as great
As Cæsar riding in the Roman street,
With captive kings at his triumphant car.

Enter the Bishop of Coventry.

K. Edw. Whither goes my lord of Coventry so fast?

B. of Cov. To celebrate your father's exequies.
But is that wicked Gaveston return'd?

K. Edw. Aye, priest, and lives to be reveng'd on thee,
That wert the only cause of his exile.

Gav. 'T is true; and but for reverence of these robes,
Thou should'st not plod one foot beyond this place.

B. of Cov. I did no more than I was bound to do;
And, Gaveston, unless thou be reclaim'd,
As then I did incense the parliament,
So will I now, and thou shalt back to France.

Gav. Saving your reverence, you must pardon me.

K. Edw. Throw off his golden mitre, rend his stole,
And in the channel[9] christen him anew.

Kent. Ah, brother, lay not violent hands on him!
For he'll complain unto the see of Rome.

Gav. Let him complain unto the see of hell!
I'll be reveng'd on him for my exile.

K. Edw. No, spare his life, but seize upon his goods.
Be thou lord bishop and receive his rents,
And make him serve thee as thy chaplain.
I give him thee—here, use him as thou wilt.

Gav. He shall to prison, and there die in bolts.

K. Edw. Aye, to the Tower, the Fleet,[10] or where thou wilt.

B. of Cov. For this offense, be thou accurst of God!

K. Edw. Who's there? Convey this priest to the Tower.

B. of Cov. True, true.

K. Edw. But in the meantime, Gaveston, away,
And take possession of his house and goods.
Come, follow me, and thou shalt have my guard
To see it done, and bring thee safe again.

Gav. What should a priest do with so fair a house?
A prison may best beseem his holiness.

Exeunt.

7 rule. 8 fearest for. 9 gutter. 10 a prison in London.

SCENE 2. *Westminster.*

Enter on one side both the Mortimers; on the other, Warwick and Lancaster.

War. 'T is true; the bishop is in the Tower,
And goods and body given to Gaveston.
Lan. What! will they tyrannize upon the church?
Ah, wicked king! accursed Gaveston!
This ground, which is corrupted with their steps,
Shall be their timeless [11] sepulchre or mine.
Y. Mor. Well, let that peevish Frenchman guard him sure;
Unless his breast be sword-proof he shall die.
E. Mor. How now! why droops the Earl of Lancaster?
Y. Mor. Wherefore is Guy of Warwick discontent?
Lan. That villain Gaveston is made an earl.
E. Mor. An earl!
War. Aye, and besides Lord Chamberlain of the realm,
And Secretary too, and Lord of Man.
E. Mor. We may not, nor we will not suffer this.
Y. Mor. Why post we not from hence to levy men?
Lan. "My Lord of Cornwall" now at every word!
And happy is the man whom he vouchsafes,
For vailing of [12] his bonnet, one good look.
Thus, arm in arm, the king and he doth march:
Nay, more, the guard upon his lordship waits;
And all the court begins to flatter him.
War. Thus leaning on the shoulder of the king,
He nods and scorns and smiles at those that pass.
E. Mor. Doth no man take exceptions at the slave?
Lan. All stomach [13] him, but none dare speak a word.
Y. Mor. Ah, that bewrays their baseness, Lancaster!
Were all the earls and barons of my mind,
We'd hale him from the bosom of the king,
And at the court-gate hang the peasant up,
Who, swoln with venom of ambitious pride,
Will be the ruin of the realm and us.

Enter the Archbishop of Canterbury and an Attendant.

War. Here comes my lord of Canterbury's grace.
Lan. His countenance bewrays he is displeas'd.
A. of Cant. First were his sacred garments rent and torn,
Then laid they violent hands upon him; next
Himself imprisoned, and his goods asseiz'd;
This certify the Pope;—away, take horse.
Exit Attend.
Lan. My lord, will you take arms against the king?
A. of Cant. What need I? God himself is up in arms,
When violence is offered to the church.
Y. Mor. Then will you join with us that be his peers,
To banish or behead that Gaveston?
A. of Cant. What else, my lords? for it concerns me near;
The bishopric of Coventry is his.

Enter Queen Isabella.

Y. Mor. Madam, whither walks your majesty so fast?
Q. Isab. Unto the forest, gentle Mortimer,
To live in grief and baleful discontent;
For now my lord the king regards me not,
But dotes upon the love of Gaveston.
He claps his cheeks, and hangs about his neck,
Smiles in his face, and whispers in his ears;
And when I come he frowns, as who should say,
"Go whither thou wilt, seeing I have Gaveston."
E. Mor. Is it not strange that he is thus bewitch'd?
Y. Mor. Madam, return unto the court again.
That sly inveigling Frenchman we'll exile,
Or lose our lives; and yet, ere that day come,

11 untimely. 12 doffing. 13 are angered at.

The king shall lose his crown; for we have power,
And courage too, to be reveng'd at full.
Q. Isab. But yet lift not your swords against the king.
Lan. No; but we'll lift Gaveston from hence.
War. And war must be the means, or he'll stay still.
Q. Isab. Then let him stay; for rather than my lord
Shall be oppress'd by civil mutinies,
I will endure a melancholy life,
And let him frolic with his minion.
A. of Cant. My lords, to ease all this, but hear me speak:—
We and the rest, that are his counsellors,
Will meet, and with a general consent
Confirm his banishment with our hands and seals.
Lan. What we confirm the king will frustrate.
Y. Mor. Then may we lawfully revolt from him.
War. But say, my lord, where shall this meeting be?
A. of Cant. At the New Temple.
Y. Mor. Content.
A. of Cant. And, in the meantime, I'll entreat you all
To cross to Lambeth, and there stay with me.
Lan. Come then, let's away.
Y. Mor. Madam, farewell!
Q. Isab. Farewell, sweet Mortimer, and, for my sake,
Forbear to levy arms against the king.
Y. Mor. Aye, if words will serve; if not, I must.

Exeunt.

SCENE 3. *A street in London.*

Enter Gaveston and Kent.

Gav. Edmund, the mighty Prince of Lancaster,
That hath more earldoms than an ass can bear,
And both the Mortimers, two goodly men,
With Guy of Warwick, that redoubted knight,
Are gone toward Lambeth—there let them remain!

Exeunt.

SCENE 4. *The New Temple.*

Enter Nobles.

Lan. Here is the form of Gaveston's exile:
May it please your lordship to subscribe your name.
A. of Cant. Give me the paper.
(*He subscribes, as do the others after him.*)
Lan. Quick, quick, my lord; I long to write my name.
War. But I long more to see him banish'd hence.
Y. Mor. The name of Mortimer shall fright the king,
Unless he be declin'd from that base peasant.

Enter King Edward, Gaveston, and Kent.

K. Edw. What, are you mov'd that Gaveston sits here?
It is our pleasure; we will have it so.
Lan. Your grace doth well to place him by your side,
For nowhere else the new earl is so safe.
E. Mor. What man of noble birth can brook this sight?
Quam male conveniunt! [14]
See what a scornful look the peasant casts!
Pem. Can kingly lions fawn on creeping ants?
War. Ignoble vassal, that like Phaeton
Aspir'st unto the guidance of the sun!
Y. Mor. Their downfall is at hand, their forces down;
We will not thus be fac'd and overpeer'd.
K. Edw. Lay hands on that traitor Mortimer!
E. Mor. Lay hands on that traitor Gaveston!
Kent. Is this the duty that you owe your king?
War. We know our duties—let him know his peers.
K. Edw. Whither will you bear him? Stay, or ye shall die.
E. Mor. We are no traitors; therefore threaten not.
Gav. No, threaten not, my lord, but pay them home!
Were I a king——
Y. Mor. Thou villain, wherefore talk'st thou of a king,
That hardly art a gentleman by birth?

[14] how ill they agree!

K. Edw. Were he a peasant, being my minion,
I'll make the proudest of you stoop to him.
Lan. My lord, you may not thus disparage us.—
Away, I say, with hateful Gaveston!
E. Mor. And with the Earl of Kent that favors him.
(*Attendants remove Kent and Gaveston.*)
K. Edw. Nay, then, lay violent hands upon your king.
Here, Mortimer, sit thou in Edward's throne;
Warwick and Lancaster, wear you my crown.
Was ever king thus over-rul'd as I?
Lan. Learn then to rule us better, and the realm.
Y. Mor. What we have done, our heart-blood shall maintain.
War. Think you that we can brook this upstart pride?
K. Edw. Anger and wrathful fury stops my speech.
A. of Cant. Why are you mov'd? Be patient, my lord,
And see what we your counsellors have done.
Y. Mor. My lords, now let us all be resolute,
And either have our wills, or lose our lives.
K. Edw. Meet you for this, proud over-daring peers?
Ere my sweet Gaveston shall part from me,
This isle shall fleet [15] upon the ocean,
And wander to the unfrequented Inde.
A. of Cant. You know that I am legate to the Pope.
On your allegiance to the see of Rome,
Subscribe, as we have done, to his exile.
Y. Mor. Curse him, if he refuse; and then may we
Depose him and elect another king.
K. Edw. Aye, there it goes! but yet I will not yield.
Curse me, depose me, do the worst you can.
Lan. Then linger not, my lord, but do it straight.
A. of Cant. Remember how the bishop was abus'd!
Either banish him that was the cause thereof,
Or I will presently discharge these lords
Of duty and allegiance due to thee.

K. Edw. (*Aside.*) It boots me not to threat; I must speak fair.—
The legate of the Pope will be obey'd.
My lord, you shall be Chancellor of the realm;
Thou, Lancaster, High Admiral of our fleet;
Young Mortimer and his uncle shall be earls;
And you, Lord Warwick, President of the North;
And thou, of Wales. If this content you not,
Make several kingdoms of this monarchy,
And share it equally amongst you all,
So I may have some nook or corner left,
To frolic with my dearest Gaveston.
A. of Cant. Nothing shall alter us, we are resolv'd.
Lan. Come, come, subscribe.
Y. Mor. Why should you love him whom the world hates so?
K. Edw. Because he loves me more than all the world.
Ah, none but rude and savage-minded men
Would seek the ruin of my Gaveston;
You that be noble-born should pity him.
War. You that are princely-born should shake him off.
For shame subscribe, and let the lown [16] depart.
E. Mor. Urge him, my lord.
A. of Cant. Are you content to banish him the realm?
K. Edw. I see I must, and therefore am content.
Instead of ink, I'll write it with my tears.
(*Subscribes.*)
Y. Mor. The king is love-sick for his minion.
K. Edw. 'T is done; and now, accursed hand, fall off!
Lan. Give it me; I'll have it publish'd in the streets.
Y. Mor. I'll see him presently despatch'd away.
A. of Cant. Now is my heart at ease.
War. And so is mine.
Pem. This will be good news to the common sort.
E. Mor. Be it or no, he shall not linger here.
Exeunt all except King Edward.
K. Edw. How fast they run to banish him I love!

[15] float.

[16] loon, base fellow.

They would not stir, were it to do me good.
Why should a king be subject to a priest?
Proud Rome! that hatchest such imperial grooms,
For these thy superstitious taper-lights,
Wherewith thy antichristian churches blaze,
I'll fire thy crazed buildings, and enforce
The papal towers to kiss the lowly ground!
With slaughtered priests make Tiber's channel swell,
And banks rais'd higher with their sepulchres!
As for the peers, that back the clergy thus,
If I be king, not one of them shall live.

Re-enter Gaveston.

Gav. My lord, I hear it whispered everywhere,
That I am banish'd, and must fly the land.
K. Edw. 'T is true, sweet Gaveston—O! were it false!
The legate of the Pope will have it so,
And thou must hence, or I shall be depos'd.
But I will reign to be reveng'd of them;
And therefore, sweet friend, take it patiently.
Live where thou wilt, I'll send thee gold enough;
And long thou shalt not stay, or if thou dost,
I'll come to thee; my love shall ne'er decline.
Gav. Is all my hope turn'd to this hell of grief?
K. Edw. Rend not my heart with thy too piercing words:
Thou from this land, I from myself am banish'd.
Gav. To go from hence grieves not poor Gaveston;
But to forsake you, in whose gracious looks
The blessedness of Gaveston remains,
For nowhere else seeks he felicity.
K. Edw. And only this torments my wretched soul
That, whether I will or no, thou must depart.
Be governor of Ireland in my stead,
And there abide till fortune call thee home.
Here take my picture, and let me wear thine;
(*They exchange pictures.*)
O, might I keep thee here as I do this,
Happy were I! but now most miserable!
Gav. 'T is something to be pitied of a king.
K. Edw. Thou shalt not hence—I'll hide thee, Gaveston.
Gav. I shall be found, and then 't will grieve me more.
K. Edw. Kind words and mutual talk makes our grief greater;
Therefore, with dumb embracement, let us part.—
Stay, Gaveston, I cannot leave thee thus.
Gav. For every look, my lord drops down a tear.
Seeing I must go, do not renew my sorrow.
K. Edw. The time is little that thou hast to stay,
And, therefore, give me leave to look my fill.
But come, sweet friend, I'll bear thee on thy way.
Gav. The peers will frown.
K. Edw. I pass [17] not for their anger—Come let's go;
O that we might as well return as go!

Enter Edmund and Queen Isabella.

Q. Isab. Whither goes my lord?
K. Edw. Fawn not on me, French strumpet! Get thee gone!
Q. Isab. On whom but on my husband should I fawn?
Gav. On Mortimer! with whom, ungentle queen—
I say no more. Judge you the rest, my lord.
Q. Isab. In saying this, thou wrong'st me, Gaveston.
Is't not enough that thou corrupt'st my lord,
And art a bawd to his affections,
But thou must call mine honor thus in question?
Gav. I mean not so; your grace must pardon me.
K. Edw. Thou art too familiar with that Mortimer.
And by thy means is Gaveston exil'd;
But I would wish thee reconcile the lords,
Or thou shalt ne'er be reconcil'd to me.
Q. Isab. Your highness knows it lies not in my power.

17 care.

K. Edw. Away then! touch me not.—
Come, Gaveston.
Q. Isab. Villain! 't is thou that robb'st me of my lord.
Gav. Madam, 't is you that rob me of my lord.
K. Edw. Speak not unto her; let her droop and pine.
Q. Isab. Wherein, my lord, have I deserv'd these words?
Witness the tears that Isabella sheds,
Witness this heart, that, sighing for thee, breaks,
How dear my lord is to poor Isabel.
K. Edw. And witness Heaven how dear thou art to me!
There weep; for till my Gaveston be repeal'd,
Assure thyself thou com'st not in my sight.

Exeunt Edward and Gaveston.

Q. Isab. O miserable and distressed queen!
Would, when I left sweet France and was embark'd,
That charming Circe, walking on the waves,
Had chang'd my shape, or at the marriage-day
The cup of Hymen had been full of poison,
Or with those arms that twin'd about my neck
I had been stifled, and not liv'd to see
The king my lord thus to abandon me!
Like frantic Juno will I fill the earth
With ghastly murmur of my sighs and cries;
For never doted Jove on Ganymede
So much as he on cursed Gaveston.
But that will more exasperate his wrath;
I must entreat him, I must speak him fair.
And be a means to call home Gaveston.
And yet he 'll ever dote on Gaveston;
And so am I for ever miserable.

Re-enter Nobles to the Queen.

Lan. Look where the sister of the King of France
Sits wringing of her hands, and beats her breast!
War. The king, I fear, hath ill-entreated her.
Pem. Hard is the heart that injures such a saint.
Y. Mor. I know 't is 'long of Gaveston she weeps.
E. Mor. Why? He is gone.
Y. Mor. Madam, how fares your grace?
Q. Isab. Ah, Mortimer! now breaks the king's hate forth,
And he confesseth that he loves me not.
Y. Mor. Cry quittance, madam, then; and love not him.
Q. Isab. No, rather will I die a thousand deaths!
And yet I love in vain;—he 'll ne'er love me.
Lan. Fear ye not, madam; now his minion 's gone,
His wanton humor will be quickly left.
Q. Isab. O never, Lancaster! I am enjoin'd
To sue upon you all for his repeal;
This wills my lord, and this must I perform,
Or else be banish'd from his highness' presence.
Lan. For his repeal? Madam, he comes not back,
Unless the sea cast up his shipwrack'd body.
War. And to behold so sweet a sight as that,
There 's none here but would run his horse to death.
Y. Mor. But, madam, would you have us call him home?
Q. Isab. Aye, Mortimer, for till he be restor'd,
The angry king hath banish'd me the court;
And, therefore, as thou lov'st and tend'rest me,
Be thou my advocate unto these peers.
Y. Mor. What! would you have me plead for Gaveston?
E. Mor. Plead for him he that will, I am resolv'd.
Lan. And so am I, my lord. Dissuade the queen.
Q. Isab. O Lancaster! let him dissuade the king,
For 't is against my will he should return.
War. Then speak not for him, let the peasant go.
Q. Isab. 'T is for myself I speak, and not for him.
Pem. No speaking will prevail, and therefore cease.
Y. Mor. Fair queen, forbear to angle for the fish
Which, being caught, strikes him that takes it dead;
I mean that vile torpedo, Gaveston,
That now, I hope, floats on the Irish seas.

Q. Isab. Sweet Mortimer, sit down by me a while,
And I will tell thee reasons of such weight
As thou wilt soon subscribe to his repeal.
Y. Mor. It is impossible; but speak your mind.
Q. Isab. Then thus,—but none shall hear it but ourselves.
(*Talks to Young Mortimer apart.*)
Lan. My lords, albeit the queen win Mortimer,
Will you be resolute, and hold with me?
E. Mor. Not I, against my nephew.
Pem. Fear not, the queen's words cannot alter him.
War. No? Do but mark how earnestly she pleads!
Lan. And see how coldly his looks make denial!
War. She smiles; now for my life his mind is chang'd.
Lan. I 'll rather lose his friendship, I, than grant.
Y. Mor. Well, of necessity it must be so.
My lords, that I abhor base Gaveston,
I hope your honors make no question,
And therefore, though I plead for his repeal,
'T is not for his sake, but for our avail;
Nay, for the realm's behoof, and for the king's.
Lan. Fie, Mortimer, dishonor not thyself!
Can this be true, 't was good to banish him?
And is this true, to call him home again?
Such reasons make white black, and dark night day.
Y. Mor. My lord of Lancaster, mark the respect.[18]
Lan. In no respect can contraries be true.
Q. Isab. Yet, good my lord, hear what he can allege.
War. All that he speaks is nothing; we are resolv'd.
Y. Mor. Do you not wish that Gaveston were dead?
Pem. I would he were!
Y. Mor. Why, then, my lord, give me but leave to speak.
E. Mor. But, nephew, do not play the sophister.
Y. Mor. This which I urge is of a burning zeal
To mend the king, and do our country good.
Know you not Gaveston hath store of gold,
Which may in Ireland purchase him such friends
As he will front the mightiest of us all?
And whereas he shall live and be belov'd,
'T is hard for us to work his overthrow.
War. Mark you but that, my lord of Lancaster.
Y. Mor. But were he here, detested as he is,
How easily might some base slave be suborn'd
To greet his lordship with a poniard,
And none so much as blame the murderer,
But rather praise him for that brave attempt,
And in the chronicle enrol his name
For purging of the realm of such a plague!
Pem. He saith true.
Lan. Aye, but how chance this was not done before?
Y. Mor. Because, my lords, it was not thought upon.
Nay, more, when he shall know it lies in us
To banish him, and then to call him home,
'T will make him vail[19] the top-flag of his pride,
And fear to offend the meanest nobleman.
E. Mor. But how if he do not, nephew?
Y. Mor. Then may we with some color[20] rise in arms;
For howsoever we have borne it out,
'T is treason to be up against the king.
So we shall have the people of our side,
Which for his father's sake lean to the king,
But cannot brook a night-grown mushroom,
Such a one as my lord of Cornwall is,
Should bear us down of the nobility.
And when the commons and the nobles join,
'T is not the king can buckler Gaveston;
We 'll pull him from the strongest hold he hath.
My lords, if to perform this I be slack,
Think me as base a groom as Gaveston.
Lan. On that condition, Lancaster will grant.
War. And so will Pembroke and I.
E. Mor. And I.

18 consideration. 19 lower. 20 pretext.

Y. Mor. In this I count me highly gratified,
And Mortimer will rest at your command.
Q. Isab. And when this favor Isabel forgets,
Then let her live abandon'd and forlorn.—
But see, in happy time, my lord the king,
Having brought the Earl of Cornwall on his way,
Is new return'd. This news will glad him much,
Yet not so much as me. I love him more
Than he can Gaveston; would he lov'd me
But half so much, then were I treble-blest.

Re-enter King Edward, mourning.

K. Edw. He 's gone, and for his absence thus I mourn.
Did never sorrow go so near my heart
As doth the want of my sweet Gaveston;
And could my crown's revenue bring him back,
I would freely give it to his enemies,
And think I gain'd, having bought so dear a friend.
Q. Isab. Hark! how he harps upon his minion.
K. Edw. My heart is as an anvil unto sorrow,
Which beats upon it like the Cyclops' hammers,
And with the noise turns up my giddy brain,
And makes me frantic for my Gaveston.
Ah! had some bloodless Fury rose from hell,
And with my kingly scepter struck me dead,
When I was forc'd to leave my Gaveston!
Lan. *Diablo!* What passions call you these?
Q. Isab. My gracious lord, I come to bring you news.
K. Edw. That you have parley'd with your Mortimer!
Q. Isab. That Gaveston, my lord, shall be repeal'd.
K. Edw. Repeal'd! The news is too sweet to be true?
Q. Isab. But will you love me, if you find it so?
K. Edw. If it be so, what will not Edward do?
Q. Isab. For Gaveston, but not for Isabel.
K. Edw. For thee, fair queen, if thou lov'st Gaveston.
I'll hang a golden tongue about thy neck,
Seeing thou hast pleaded with so good success.
Q. Isab. No other jewels hang about my neck
Than these, my lord; nor let me have more wealth
Than I may fetch from this rich treasury.
O how a kiss revives poor Isabel!
K. Edw. Once more receive my hand; and let this be
A second marriage 'twixt thyself and me.
Q. Isab. And may it prove more happy than the first!
My gentle lord, bespeak these nobles fair,
That wait attendance for a gracious look,
And on their knees salute your majesty.
K. Edw. Courageous Lancaster, embrace thy king!
And, as gross vapors perish by the sun,
Even so let hatred with thy sovereign's smile.
Live thou with me as my companion.
Lan. This salutation overjoys my heart.
K. Edw. Warwick shall be my chiefest counsellor:
These silver hairs will more adorn my court
Than gaudy silks, or rich embroidery.
Chide me, sweet Warwick, if I go astray.
War. Slay me, my lord, when I offend your grace.
K. Edw. In solemn triumphs, and in public shows,
Pembroke shall bear the sword before the king.
Pem. And with this sword Pembroke will fight for you.
K. Edw. But wherefore walks young Mortimer aside?
Be thou commander of our royal fleet;
Or, if that lofty office like thee not,
I make thee here Lord Marshal of the realm.
Y. Mor. My lord, I'll marshal so your enemies,
As England shall be quiet, and you safe.
K. Edw. And as for you, Lord Mortimer of Chirke,
Whose great achievements in our foreign war
Deserves no common place nor mean reward,

Be you the general of the levied troops,
That now are ready to assail the Scots.

E. Mor. In this your grace hath highly honored me,
For with my nature war doth best agree.

Q. Isab. Now is the King of England rich and strong,
Having the love of his renowned peers.

K. Edw. Aye, Isabel, ne'er was my heart so light.
Clerk of the crown, direct our warrant forth
For Gaveston to Ireland:

Enter Beaumont with warrant.

Beaumont, fly
As fast as Iris or Jove's Mercury.

Beau. It shall be done, my gracious lord. *Exit.*

K. Edw. Lord Mortimer, we leave you to your charge.
Now let us in, and feast it royally.
Against our friend the Earl of Cornwall comes,
We'll have a general tilt and tournament;
And then his marriage shall be solemniz'd.
For wot you not that I have made him sure [21]
Unto our cousin, the Earl of Gloucester's heir?

Lan. Such news we hear, my lord.

K. Edw. That day, if not for him, yet for my sake,
Who in the triumph will be challenger,
Spare for no cost; we will requite your love.

War. In this, or aught, yonr highness shall command us.

K. Edw. Thanks, gentle Warwick: come, let's in and revel.

Exeunt all except the Mortimers.

E. Mor. Nephew, I must to Scotland; thou stayest here.
Leave now to oppose thyself against the king.
Thou seest by nature he is mild and calm,
And seeing his mind so dotes on Gaveston,
Let him without controlment have his will.
The mightiest kings have had their minions:
Great Alexander loved Hephestion;
The conquering Hercules [22] for Hylas wept;
And for Patroclus stern Achilles droop'd:
And not kings only, but the wisest men:
The Roman Tully lov'd Octavius;
Grave Socrates, wild Alcibiades.
Then let his grace, whose youth is flexible,
And promiseth as much as we can wish,
Freely enjoy that vain, light-headed earl;
For riper years will wean him from such toys.

Y. Mor. Uncle, his wanton humor grieves not me;
But this I scorn, that one so basely born
Should by his sovereign's favor grow so pert,
And riot it with the treasure of the realm.
While soldiers mutiny for want of pay,
He wears a lord's revenue on his back,
And Midas-like, he jets [23] it in the court,
With base outlandish cullions [24] at his heels,
Whose proud fantastic liveries make such show
As if that Proteus, god of shapes, appear'd.
I have not seen a dapper Jack so brisk;
He wears a short Italian hooded cloak
Larded with pearl, and, in his Tuscan cap,
A jewel of more value than the crown.
While others walk below, the king and he
From out a window laugh at such as we,
And flout our train, and jest at our attire.
Uncle, 't is this that makes me impatient.

E. Mor. But, nephew, now you see the king is chang'd.

Y. Mor. Then so am I, and live to do him service:
But whiles I have a sword, a hand, a heart,
I will not yield to any such upstart.
You know my mind; come, uncle, let's away.

Exeunt

ACT II.

Scene 1. *Gloucester's house.*

Enter Young Spencer and Baldock.

Bald. Spencer, seeing that our lord th' Earl of Gloucester's dead,

21 betrothed him. 22 Qq. *Hector.* 23 swaggers. 24 scoundrels.

Which of the nobles dost thou mean to serve?

Y. Spen. Not Mortimer, nor any of his side,
Because the king and he are enemies.
Baldock, learn this of me, a factious lord
Shall hardly do himself good, much less us;
But he that hath the favor of a king,
May with one word advance us while we live.
The liberal Earl of Cornwall is the man
On whose good fortune Spencer's hope depends.

Bald. What, mean you then to be his follower?

Y. Spen. No, his companion; for he loves me well,
And would have once preferr'd[25] me to the king.

Bald. But he is banish'd; there's small hope of him

Y. Spen. Aye, for a while; but, Baldock, mark the end.
A friend of mine told me in secrecy
That he's repeal'd, and sent for back again;
And even now a post came from the court
With letters to our lady from the king;
And as she read she smil'd, which makes me think
It is about her lover Gaveston.

Bald. 'T is like enough; for since he was exil'd
She neither walks abroad, nor comes in sight.
But I had thought the match had been broke off,
And that his banishment had chang'd her mind.

Y. Spen. Our lady's first love is not wavering;
My life for thine, she will have Gaveston.

Bald. Then hope I by her means to be preferr'd,
Having read unto her since she was a child.

Y. Spen. Then, Baldock, you must cast the scholar off,
And learn to court it like a gentleman.
'T is not a black coat and a little band,
A velvet-cap'd cloak, fac'd before with serge,
And smelling to a nosegay all the day,
Or holding of a napkin in your hand,
Or saying a long grace at a table's end,
Or making low legs[26] to a nobleman,
Or looking downward with your eyelids close,
And saying, "Truly, an 't may please your honor,"
Can get you any favor with great men;
You must be proud, bold, pleasant, resolute,
And now and then stab, as occasion serves.

Bald. Spencer, thou know'st I hate such formal toys,
And use them but of mere hypocrisy.
Mine old lord whiles he liv'd was so precise,
That he would take exceptions at my buttons,
And being like pin's heads, blame me for the bigness;
Which made me curate-like in mine attire,
Though inwardly licentious enough
And apt for any kind of villainy.
I am none of these common pedants, I,
That cannot speak without *propterea quod.*

Y. Spen. But one of those that saith *quando-quidem,*
And hath a special gift to form a verb.

Bald. Leave off this jesting, here my lady comes.

Enter King Edward's Niece.

Niece. The grief for his exile was not so much
As is the joy of his returning home.
This letter came from my sweet Gaveston:—
What need'st thou, love, thus to excuse thyself?
I know thou couldst not come and visit me.
(*Reads.*) "I will not long be from thee, though I die."
This argues the entire love of my lord;
(*Reads.*) "When I forsake thee, death seize on my heart:"
But stay thee here where Gaveston shall sleep.
(*Puts the letter into her bosom.*)
Now to the letter of my lord the king.—
He wills me to repair unto the court,
And meet my Gaveston. Why do I stay,
Seeing that he talks thus of my marriage-day?
Who 's there? Baldock!
See that my coach be ready, I must hence.

25 recommended.

26 bows.

Bald. It shall be done, madam.
Niece. And meet me at the park-pale presently.
Exit Baldock.
Spencer, stay you and bear me company,
For I have joyful news to tell thee of.
My lord of Cornwall is a-coming over,
And will be at the court as soon as we.
Y. Spen. I knew the king would have him home again.
Niece. If all things sort[27] out as I hope they will,
Thy service, Spencer, shall be thought upon.
Y. Spen. I humbly thank your ladyship.
Niece. Come, lead the way; I long till I am there.
Exeunt.

SCENE 2. *Before Tynemouth Castle.*

Enter King Edward, Queen Isabella, Kent, Lancaster, Young Mortimer, Warwick, Pembroke, and Attendants.

K. Edw. The wind is good, I wonder why he stays;
I fear me he is wrack'd upon the sea.
Q. Isab. Look, Lancaster, how passionate he is,
And still his mind runs on his minion!
Lan. My lord,—
K. Edw. How now! what news? Is Gaveston arriv'd?
Y. Mor. Nothing but Gaveston!—What means your grace?
You have matters of more weight to think upon;
The King of France sets foot in Normandy.
K. Edw. A trifle! we'll expel him when we please.
But tell me, Mortimer, what's thy device
Against the stately triumph we decreed?
Y. Mor. A homely one, my lord, not worth the telling.
K. Edw. Pray thee let me know it.
Y. Mor. But, seeing you are so desirous, thus it is:
A lofty cedar-tree, fair flourishing,
On whose top-branches kingly eagles perch,
And by the bark a canker[28] creeps me up,
And gets into the highest bough of all:
The motto, *Aeque tandem.*[29]
K. Edw. And what is yours, my lord of Lancaster?
Lan. My lord, mine's more obscure than Mortimer's.
Pliny reports there is a flying fish
Which all the other fishes deadly hate,
And therefore, being pursued, it takes the air:
No sooner is it up, but there's a fowl
That seizeth it; this fish, my lord, I bear:
The motto this: *Undique mors est.*[30]
K. Edw. Proud Mortimer! ungentle Lancaster!
Is this the love you bear your sovereign?
Is this the fruit your reconcilement bears?
Can you in words make show of amity,
And in your shields display your rancorous minds!
What call you this but private libelling
Against the Earl of Cornwall and my brother?
Q. Isab. Sweet husband, be content; they all love you.
K. Edw. They love me not that hate my Gaveston.
I am that cedar, shake me not too much;
And you the eagles; soar ye ne'er so high,
I have the jesses[31] that will pull you down;
And *Aeque tandem* shall that canker cry
Unto the proudest peer of Britainy.
Though thou compar'st him to a flying fish,
And threatenest death whether he rise or fall,
'T is not the hugest monster of the sea,
Nor foulest harpy that shall swallow him.
Y. Mor. If in his absence thus he favors him,
What will he do whenas he shall be present?
Lan. That shall we see; look where his lordship comes.
Enter Gaveston.
K. Edw. My Gaveston!
Welcome to Tynemouth! Welcome to thy friend!
Thy absence made me droop and pine away;
For, as the lovers of fair Danaë,
When she was lock'd up in a brazen tower,

27 fall.
28 canker-worm.
29 "Justly at length."
30 "On every side is death."
31 straps round a hawk's legs, to which the leash was fastened.

Desir'd her more, and wax'd outrageous,
So did it fare with me; and now thy sight
Is sweeter far than was thy parting hence
Bitter and irksome to my sobbing heart.

Gav. Sweet lord and king, your speech preventeth [32] mine;
Yet have I words left to express my joy:
The shepherd nipt with biting winter's rage
Frolics not more to see the painted spring,
Than I do to behold your majesty.

K. Edw. Will none of you salute my Gaveston?

Lan. Salute him? yes. Welcome, Lord Chamberlain!

Y. Mor. Welcome is the good Earl of Cornwall!

War. Welcome, Lord Governor of the Isle of Man!

Pem. Welcome, Master Secretary!

Kent. Brother, do you hear them?

K. Edw. Still will these earls and barons use me thus?

Gav. My lord, I cannot brook these injuries.

Q. Isab. (*Aside.*) Ay me, poor soul, when these begin to jar.

K. Edw. Return it to their throats, I'll be thy warrant.

Gav. Base, leaden earls, that glory in your birth,
Go sit at home and eat your tenants' beef;
And come not here to scoff at Gaveston,
Whose mounting thoughts did never creep so low
As to bestow a look on such as you.

Lan. Yet I disdain not to do this for you.
(*Draws his sword and offers to stab Gaveston.*)

K. Edw. Treason! treason! where's the traitor?

Pem. Here! here!

K. Edw. Convey hence Gaveston; they'll murder him.

Gav. The life of thee shall salve this foul disgrace.

Y. Mor. Villain! thy life, unless I miss mine aim.
(*Wounds Gaveston.*)

Q. Isab. Ah! furious Mortimer, what hast thou done?

Y. Mor. No more than I would answer, were he slain.
Exit Gaveston with Attendants.

K. Edw. Yes, more than thou canst answer, though he live.
Dear shall you both abye [33] this riotous deed.
Out of my presence! Come not near the court!

Y. Mor. I'll not be barr'd the court for Gaveston.

Lan. We'll hale him by the ears unto the block.

K. Edw. Look to your own heads; his is sure enough.

War. Look to your own crown, if you back him thus.

Kent. Warwick, these words do ill beseem thy years.

K. Edw. Nay, all of them conspire to cross me thus;
But if I live, I'll tread upon their heads
That think with high looks thus to tread me down.
Come, Edmund, let's away and levy men,
'T is war that must abate these barons' pride.
Exeunt King Edward, Queen Isabella and Kent.

War. Let's to our castles, for the king is mov'd.

Y. Mor. Mov'd may he be, and perish in his wrath!

Lan. Cousin, it is no dealing with him now,
He means to make us stoop by force of arms;
And therefore let us jointly here protest [34]
To persecute that Gaveston to the death.

Y. Mor. By heaven, the abject villain shall not live!

War. I'll have his blood, or die in seeking it.

Pem. The like oath Pembroke takes.

Lan. And so doth Lancaster.
Now send our heralds to defy the king;
And make the people swear to put him down.

Enter a Post.

Y. Mor. Letters! From whence?

Mess. From Scotland, my lord.
(*Giving letters to Mortimer.*)

Lan. Why, how now, cousin, how fares all our friends?

Y. Mor. My uncle's taken prisoner by the Scots.

32 anticipates. 33 pay for. 34 vow.

Lan. We'll have him ransom'd, man; be of good cheer.
Y. Mor. They rate his ransom at five thousand pound.
Who should defray the money but the king,
Seeing he is taken prisoner in his wars?
I'll to the king.
Lan. Do, cousin, and I'll bear thee company.
War. Meantime, my lord of Pembroke and myself
Will to Newcastle here, and gather head.[35]
Y. Mor. About it then, and we will follow you.
Lan. Be resolute and full of secrecy.
War. I warrant you.
Exit with Pembroke.
Y. Mor. Cousin, and if he will not ransom him,
I'll thunder such a peal into his ears,
As never subject did unto his king.
Lan. Content, I'll bear my part—Holla! who's there?

Enter Guard.

Y. Mor. Aye, marry, such a guard as this doth well.
Lan. Lead on the way.
Guard. Whither will your lordships?
Y. Mor. Whither else but to the king.
Guard. His highness is dispos'd to be alone.
Lan. Why, so he may, but we will speak to him.
Guard. You may not in, my lord.
Y. Mor. May we not?

Enter King Edward and Kent.

K. Edw. How now!
What noise is this? Who have we there? Is't you? (*Going.*)
Y. Mor. Nay, stay, my lord, I come to bring you news;
Mine uncle's taken prisoner by the Scots.
K. Edw. Then ransom him.
Lan. 'Twas in your wars; you should ransom him.
Y. Mor. And you shall ransom him, or else——
Kent. What, Mortimer, you will not threaten him!
K. Edw. Quiet yourself, you shall have the broad seal,[36]
To gather for him thoroughout the realm.
Lan. Your minion Gaveston hath taught you this.
Y. Mor. My lord, the family of the Mortimers
Are not so poor, but, would they sell their land,
'T would levy men enough to anger you.
We never beg, but use such prayers as these.
K. Edw. Shall I still be haunted thus?
Y. Mor. Nay, now you are here alone, I'll speak my mind.
Lan. And so will I, and then, my lord, farewell.
Y. Mor. The idle triumphs, masques, lascivious shows,
And prodigal gifts bestow'd on Gaveston,
Have drawn thy treasury dry, and made thee weak;
The murmuring commons, overstretched, [break.][37]
Lan. Look for rebellion, look to be depos'd.
Thy garrisons are beaten out of France,
And, lame and poor, lie groaning at the gates;
The wild O'Neill, with swarms of Irish kerns,[38]
Lives uncontroll'd within the English pale;
Unto the walls of York the Scots made road,
And unresisted drave away rich spoils.
Y. Mor. The haughty Dane commands the narrow seas,[39]
While in the harbor ride thy ships unrigg'd.
Lan. What foreign prince sends thee ambassadors?
Y. Mor. Who loves thee, but a sort[40] of flatterers?
Lan. Thy gentle queen, sole sister to Valois,
Complains that thou hast left her all forlorn.
Y. Mor. Thy court is naked, being bereft of those
That make a king seem glorious to the world;
I mean the peers, whom thou should'st dearly love.
Libels are cast against thee in the street;
Ballads and rhymes made of thy overthrow.

35 forces.
36 the state seal, as warrant for the levying of taxes.
37. Qq. *hath.*
38 light armed, irregular foot soldiers.
39 the English Channel.
40 crowd.

Lan. The northern borderers seeing their houses burnt,
Their wives and children slain, run up and down,
Cursing the name of thee and Gaveston.
Y. Mor. When wert thou in the field with banner spread,
But once? and then thy soldiers march'd like players,
With garish robes, not armor; and thyself,
Bedaub'd with gold, rode laughing at the rest,
Nodding and shaking of thy spangled crest,
Where women's favors hung like labels down.
Lan. And therefore came it, that the fleering[41] Scots,
To England's high disgrace, have made this jig;
Maids of England, sore may you mourn,—
For your lemans[42] you have lost at Bannocksbourn,—[43]
With a heave and a ho!
What weeneth[44] the King of England,
So soon to have won Scotland?—
With a rombelow!
Y. Mor. Wigmore[45] shall fly, to set my uncle free.
Lan. And when 't is gone, our swords shall purchase more.
If ye be mov'd, revenge it as you can;
Look next to see us with our ensigns spread.
Exit with Young Mortimer.
K. Edw. My swelling heart for very anger breaks!
How oft have I been baited by these peers,
And dare not be reveng'd, for their power is great!
Yet, shall the crowing of these cockerels
Affright a lion? Edward, unfold thy paws,
And let their lives' blood slake thy fury's hunger.
If I be cruel and grow tyrannous,
Now let them thank themselves, and rue too late.
Kent. My lord, I see your love to Gaveston
Will be the ruin of the realm and you,
For now the wrathful nobles threaten wars,
And therefore, brother, banish him for ever.
K. Edw. Art thou an enemy to my Gaveston?
Kent. Aye, and it grieves me that I favored him.
K. Edw. Traitor, begone! whine thou with Mortimer.
Kent. So will I, rather than with Gaveston.
K. Edw. Out of my sight, and trouble me no more!
Kent. No marvel though thou scorn thy noble peers,
When I thy brother am rejected thus.
Exit.
K. Edw. Away!
Poor Gaveston, thou[46] hast no friend but me!
Do what they can, we'll live in Tynemouth here,
And, so I walk with him about the walls,
What care I though the earls begirt us round?—
Here comes she that's cause of all these jars.

Enter Queen Isabella, King Edward's Niece, two Ladies, Gaveston, Baldock and Young Spencer.

Q. Isab. My lord, 't is thought the earls are up in arms.
K. Edw. Aye, and 't is likewise thought you favor 'em.
Q. Isab. Thus do you still suspect me without cause?
Niece. Sweet uncle, speak more kindly to the queen.
Gav. My lord, dissemble with her, speak her fair.
K. Edw. Pardon me, sweet, I forgot myself.
Q. Isab. Your pardon is quickly got of Isabel.
K. Edw. The younger Mortimer is grown so brave,
That to my face he threatens civil wars.
Gav. Why do you not commit him to the Tower?
K. Edw. I dare not, for the people love him well.
Gav. Why, then we'll have him privily made away.
K. Edw. Would Lancaster and he had both carous'd
A bowl of poison to each other's health?

[41] jeering.
[42] lovers.
[43] Bannockburn was not fought until 1314, some years after the events of this scene; Marlowe took the song from Fabyan's *Chronicle*.
[44] thinketh.
[45] Young Mortimer's estate.
[46] Qq. *that*.

But let them go, and tell me what are these.
Niece. Two of my father's servants whilst he liv'd,—
May 't please your grace to entertain them now.
K. Edw. Tell me, where wast thou born? What is thine arms?
Bald. My name is Baldock, and my gentry
I fetcht from Oxford, not from heraldry.
K. Edw. The fitter art thou, Baldock, for my turn.
Wait on me, and I 'll see thou shalt not want.
Bald. I humbly thank your majesty.
K. Edw. Knowest thou him, Gaveston?
Gav. Aye, my lord;
His name is Spencer, he is well allied;
For my sake, let him wait upon your grace;
Scarce shall you find a man of more desert.
K. Edw. Then, Spencer, wait upon me; for his sake
I 'll grace thee with a higher style ere long.
Y. Spen. No greater titles happen unto me,
Than to be favored of your majesty!
K. Edw. Cousin, this day shall be your marriage-feast.
And, Gaveston, think that I love thee well
To wed thee to our niece, the only heir
Unto the Earl of Gloucester late deceas'd.
Gav. I know, my lord, many will stomach [47] me,
But I respect neither their love nor hate.
K. Edw. The headstrong barons shall not limit me;
He that I list to favor shall be great.
Come, let 's away; and when the marriage ends,
Have at the rebels, and their 'complices!
Exeunt.

Scene 3. *Near Tynemouth Castle.*

Enter Kent, Lancaster, Young Mortimer, Warwick, and Pembroke.

Kent. My lords, of love to this our native land
I come to join with you and leave the king;
And in your quarrel and the realm's behoof
Will be the first that shall adventure life.
Lan. I fear me, you are sent of policy,
To undermine us with a show of love.
War. He is your brother; therefore have we cause
To cast [48] the worst, and doubt of your revolt.
Kent. Mine honor shall be hostage of my truth;
If that will not suffice, farewell, my lords.
Y. Mor. Stay, Edmund; never was Plantagenet
False to his word, and therefore trust we thee.
Pem. But what 's the reason you should leave him now?
Kent. I have inform'd the Earl of Lancaster.
Lan. And it sufficeth. Now, my lords, know this,
That Gaveston is secretly arriv'd,
And here in Tynemouth frolics with the king.
Let us with these our followers scale the walls,
And suddenly surprise them unawares.
Y. Mor. I 'll give the onset.
War. And I 'll follow thee.
Y. Mor. This tattered ensign of my ancestors,
Which swept the desert shore of that dead sea
Whereof we got the name of Mortimer,[49]
Will I advance upon these castle-walls.
Drums, strike alarum! raise them from their sport,
And ring aloud the knell of Gaveston!
Lan. None be so hardy as to touch the king;
But neither spare you Gaveston nor his friends.
Exeunt.

Scene 4. *Tynemouth Castle.*

Enter King Edward and Young Spencer.

K. Edw. O tell me, Spencer, where is Gaveston?
Spen. I fear me he is slain, my gracious lord.
K. Edw. No, here he comes; now let them spoil and kill.

Enter Queen Isabella, King Edward's Niece, Gaveston, and Nobles.

47 regard with resentment. 48 suspect. 49 a false etymology, tracing the name *Mortimer* to *Mortuum Mare*.

Fly, fly, my lords, the earls have got the hold;
Take shipping and away to Scarborough;
Spencer and I will post away by land.

Gav. O stay, my lord, they will not injure you.

K. Edw. I will not trust them; Gaveston, away!

Gav. Farewell, my lord.

K. Edw. Lady, farewell.

Niece. Farewell, sweet uncle, till we meet again.

K. Edw. Farewell, sweet Gaveston; and farewell, niece.

Q. Isab. No farewell to poor Isabel thy queen?

K. Edw. Yes, yes, for Mortimer, your lover's sake.

Exeunt all but Queen Isabella.

Q. Isab. Heavens can witness I love none but you!
From my embracements thus he breaks away.
O that mine arms could close this isle about,
That I might pull him to me where I would!
Or that these tears that drizzle from mine eyes
Had power to mollify his stony heart,
That when I had him we might never part.

Enter Lancaster, Warwick, Young Mortimer, and others. Alarums.

Lan. I wonder how he scap'd!

Y. Mor. Who 's this? The queen!

Q. Isab. Aye, Mortimer, the miserable queen,
Whose pining heart her inward sighs have blasted,
And body with continual mourning wasted.
These hands are tir'd with haling of my lord
From Gaveston, from wicked Gaveston,
And all in vain; for, when I speak him fair,
He turns away, and smiles upon his minion.

Y. Mor. Cease to lament, and tell us where 's the king?

Q. Isab. What would you with the king? Is 't him you seek?

Lan. No, madam, but that cursed Gaveston.
Far be it from the thought of Lancaster
To offer violence to his sovereign.
We would but rid the realm of Gaveston:
Tell us where he remains, and he shall die.

Q. Isab. He 's gone by water unto Scarborough;
Pursue him quickly, and he cannot scape;
The king hath left him, and his train is small.

War. Forslow[50] no time, sweet Lancaster; let 's march.

Y. Mor. How comes it that the king and he is parted?

Q. Isab. That thus your army, going several ways,
Might be of lesser force; and with the power
That he intendeth presently to raise,
Be easily suppress'd; therefore be gone.

Y. Mor. Here in the river rides a Flemish hoy;[51]
Let 's all aboard, and follow him amain.

Lan. The wind that bears him hence will fill our sails.
Come, come aboard, 't is but an hour's sailing.

Y. Mor. Madam, stay you within this castle here.

Q. Isab. No, Mortimer, I 'll to my lord the king.

Y. Mor. Nay, rather sail with us to Scarborough.

Q. Isab. You know the king is so suspicious,
As if he hear I have but talk'd with you,
Mine honor will be call'd in question;
And therefore, gentle Mortimer, be gone.

Y. Mor. Madam, I cannot stay to answer you,
But think of Mortimer as he deserves.

Exeunt all except Queen Isabella.

Q. Isab. So well hast thou deserv'd, sweet Mortimer,
As Isabel could live with thee for ever!
In vain I look for love at Edward's hand,
Whose eyes are fix'd on none but Gaveston;
Yet once more I 'll importune him with prayers.
If he be strange and not regard my words,
My son and I will over into France,
And to the king my brother there complain,
How Gaveston hath robb'd me of his love:
But yet I hope my sorrows will have end,
And Gaveston this blessed day be slain.

Exit.

50 delay.

51 a small sloop.

SCENE 5. *The open country.*

Enter Gaveston, pursued.

Gav. Yet, lusty lords, I have escap'd your hands,
Your threats, your 'larums, and your hot pursuits;
And though divorced from King Edward's eyes,
Yet liveth Pierce of Gaveston unsurpris'd,[52]
Breathing, in hope (*malgrado* [53] all your beards,
That muster rebels thus against your king),
To see his royal sovereign once again.

Enter Warwick, Lancaster, Pembroke, Young Mortimer, Soldiers, James, and other Attendants of Pembroke.

War. Upon him, soldiers, take away his weapons.
Y. Mor. Thou proud disturber of thy country's peace,
Corrupter of thy king, cause of these broils,
Base flatterer, yield! and were it not for shame,
Shame and dishonor to a soldier's name,
Upon my weapon's point here shouldst thou fall,
And welter in thy gore.
Lan. Monster of men!
That, like the Greekish strumpet,[54] train'd [55] to arms
And bloody wars so many valiant knights;
Look for no other fortune, wretch, than death!
King Edward is not here to buckler thee.
War. Lancaster, why talk'st thou to the slave?
Go, soldiers, take him hence, for, by my sword,
His head shall off. Gaveston, short warning
Shall serve thy turn; it is our country's cause
That here severely we will execute
Upon thy person. Hang him at a bough.
Gav. My lord!—
War. Soldiers, have him away;—
But for thou wert the favorite of a king,
Thou shalt have so much honor at our hands—
Gav. I thank you all, my lords: then I perceive
That heading is one, and hanging is the other,
And death is all.

Enter Earl of Arundel.

Lan. How now, my lord of Arundel?
Arun. My lords, King Edward greets you all by me.
War. Arundel, say your message.
Arun. His majesty,
Hearing that you had taken Gaveston,
Entreateth you by me, yet but he may
See him before he dies; for why, he says,
And sends you word, he knows that die he shall;
And if you gratify his grace so far,
He will be mindful of the courtesy.
War. How now!
Gav. Renowned Edward, how thy name
Revives poor Gaveston!
War. No, it needeth not;
Arundel, we will gratify the king
In other matters; he must pardon us in this.
Soldiers, away with him!
Gav. Why, my lord of Warwick,
Will not these delays beget my hopes?
I know it, lords, it is this life you aim at,
Yet grant King Edward this.
Y. Mor. Shalt thou appoint
What we shall grant? Soldiers, away with him!
Thus we'll gratify the king:
We'll send his head by thee; let him bestow
His tears on that, for that is all he gets
Of Gaveston, or else his senseless trunk.
Lan. Not so, my lords, lest he bestow more cost
In burying him than he hath ever earn'd.
Arun. My lords, it is his majesty's request,
And in the honor of a king he swears
He will but talk with him, and send him back.
War. When, can you tell? Arundel, no; we wot
He that the care of realm remits,
And drives his nobles to these exigents [56]
For Gaveston, will, if he sees him once,
Violate any promise to possess him.
Arun. Then if you will not trust his grace in keep,
My lords, I will be pledge for his return.
Y. Mor. 'T is honorable in thee to offer this;
But for we know thou art a noble gentleman,

[52] uncaptured. [53] "in spite of." [54] Helen of Troy. [55] lured. [56] extremities.

We will not wrong thee so, to make away
A true man for a thief.
Gav. How mean'st thou, Mortimer? That is over-base.
Y. Mor. Away, base groom, robber of king's renown!
Question with thy companions and thy mates.
Pem. My Lord Mortimer, and you, my lords, each one,
To gratify the king's request therein,
Touching the sending of this Gaveston,
Because his majesty so earnestly
Desires to see the man before his death,
I will upon mine honor undertake
To carry him, and bring him back again;
Provided this, that you, my lord of Arundel,
Will join with me.
War. Pembroke, what wilt thou do?
Cause yet more bloodshed? Is it not enough
That we have taken him, but must we now
Leave him on "had I wist," and let him go?
Pem. My lords, I will not over-woo your honors,
But if you dare trust Pembroke with the prisoner,
Upon mine oath, I will return him back.
Arun. My lord of Lancaster, what say you in this?
Lan. Why, I say, let him go on Pembroke's word.
Pem. And you, Lord Mortimer?
Y. Mor. How say you, my lord of Warwick?
War. Nay, do your pleasures, I know how 't will prove.
Pem. Then give him me.
Gav. Sweet sovereign, yet I come
To see thee ere I die.
War. (*Aside.*) Yet not perhaps,
If Warwick's wit and policy prevail.
Y. Mor. My lord of Pembroke, we deliver him you;
Return him on your honor. Sound, away!

Exeunt all except Pembroke, Arundel, Gaveston, James, and other Attendants of Pembroke.

Pem. My lord [Arundel,] you shall go with me.
My house is not far hence; out of the way
A little, but our men shall go along.
We that have pretty wenches to our wives,
Sir, must not come so near and baulk their lips.
Arun. 'T is very kindly spoke, my lord of Pembroke;
Your honor hath an adamant of power
To draw a prince.
Pem. So, my lord. Come hither, James:
I do commit this Gaveston to thee,
Be thou this night his keeper; in the morning
We will discharge thee of thy charge. Be gone.
Gav. Unhappy Gaveston, whither goest thou now?

Exit with James and the other Attendants.

Horse-boy. My lord, we'll quickly be at Cobham.

Exeunt.

ACT III.

SCENE 1. *The open country near Warwick.*

Enter Gaveston mourning, James, and other Attendants of Pembroke.

Gav. O treacherous Warwick, thus to wrong thy friend!
James. I see it is your life these arms pursue.
Gav. Weaponless must I fall, and die in bands?
O must this day be period [57] of my life?
Center of all my bliss! An [58] ye be men,
Speed to the king.

Enter Warwick and his company.

War. My lord of Pembroke's men,
Strive you no longer—I will have that Gaveston.
James. Your lordship doth dishonor to yourself,
And wrong our lord, your honorable friend.
War. No, James, it is my country's cause I follow.
Go, take the villain; soldiers, come away.
We'll make quick work. Commend me to your master,
My friend, and tell him that I watch'd it well.
Come, let thy shadow [59] parley with King Edward.

57 end. 58 if. 59 ghost.

Gav. Treacherous earl, shall I not see the king?
War. The king of Heaven, perhaps no other king.
Away!
Exeunt Warwick and his men with Gaveston.
James. Come, fellows, it booted not for us to strive,
We will in haste go certify our lord.
Exeunt.

SCENE 2. *Near Boroughbridge, in Yorkshire.*

Enter King Edward and Young Spencer, Baldock, and Nobles of the King's side, and Soldiers with drums and fifes.

K. Edw. I long to hear an answer from the barons
Touching my friend, my dearest Gaveston.
Ah! Spencer, not the riches of my realm
Can ransom him! Ah, he is mark'd to die!
I know the malice of the younger Mortimer,
Warwick I know is rough, and Lancaster
Inexorable, and I shall never see
My lovely Pierce, my Gaveston again!
The barons overbear me with their pride.
Y. Spen. Were I King Edward, England's sovereign,
Son to the lovely Eleanor of Spain,
Great Edward Longshanks' issue, would I bear
These braves, this rage, and suffer uncontroll'd
These barons thus to beard me in my land,
In mine own realm? My lord, pardon my speech:
Did you retain your father's magnanimity,
Did you regard the honor of your name,
You would not suffer thus your majesty
Be counterbuff'd of [60] your nobility.
Strike off their heads, and let them preach on poles!
No doubt, such lessons they will teach the rest,
As by their preachments they will profit much,
And learn obedience to their lawful king.
K. Edw. Yea, gentle Spencer, we have been too mild,
Too kind to them; but now have drawn our sword,
And if they send me not my Gaveston,
We 'll steel it [61] on their crest, and poll [62] their tops.
Bald. This haught [63] resolve becomes your majesty,
Not to be tied to their affection,
As though your highness were a schoolboy still,
And must be aw'd and govern'd like a child.

Enter the Elder Spencer, with his truncheon and Soldiers.

E. Spen. Long live my sovereign, the noble Edward,
In peace triumphant, fortunate in wars!
K. Edw. Welcome, old man, com'st thou in Edward's aid?
Then tell thy prince of whence, and what thou art.
E. Spen. Lo, with a band of bowmen and of pikes,
Brown bills and targeteers, four hundred strong,
Sworn to defend King Edward's royal right,
I come in person to your majesty,
Spencer, the father of Hugh Spencer there,
Bound to your highness everlastingly,
For favor done, in him, unto us all.
K. Edw. Thy father, Spencer?
Y. Spen. True, an it like your grace,
That pours, in lieu of all your goodness shown,
His life, my lord, before your princely feet.
K. Edw. Welcome ten thousand times, old man, again.
Spencer, this love, this kindness to thy king,
Argues thy noble mind and disposition.
Spencer, I here create thee Earl of Wiltshire,
And daily will enrich thee with our favor,
That, as the sunshine, shall reflect o'er thee.
Beside, the more to manifest our love,
Because we hear Lord Bruce doth sell his land,
And that the Mortimers are in hand [64] withal,
Thou shalt have crowns of us t' outbid the barons:

60 affronted by. 61 use our steel. 62 lop off. 63 lofty. 64 negotiating.

And, Spencer, spare them not, but lay it on.
Soldiers, a largess, and thrice welcome all!

Y. Spen. My lord, here comes the queen.

Enter Queen Isabella, her son Prince Edward, and Levune, a Frenchman.

K. Edw. Madam, what news?

Q. Isab. News of dishonor, lord, and discontent.
Our friend Levune, faithful and full of trust,
Informeth us, by letters and by words,
That Lord Valois our brother, King of France,
Because your highness hath been slack in homage,
Hath seized Normandy into his hands.
These be the letters, this the messenger.

K. Edw. Welcome, Levune. Tush, Sib, if this be all
Valois and I will soon be friends again.—
But to my Gaveston; shall I never see,
Never behold thee now?—Madam, in this matter,
We will employ you and your little son;
You shall go parley with the king of France.—
Boy, see you bear you bravely to the king,
And do your message with a majesty.

P. Edw. Commit not to my youth things of more weight
Than fits a prince so young as I to bear,
And fear not, lord and father, Heaven's great beams
On Atlas' shoulder shall not lie more safe,
Than shall your charge committed to my trust.

Q. Isab. Ah, boy, this towardness makes thy mother fear
Thou art not mark'd to many days on earth.

K. Edw. Madam, we will that you with speed be shipp'd,
And this our son; Levune shall follow you
With all the haste we can despatch him hence.
Choose of our lords to bear you company,
And go in peace; leave us in wars at home.

Q. Isab. Unnatural wars, where subjects brave their king;
God end them once! My lord, I take my leave,
To make my preparation for France.

Exit with Prince Edward.

Enter Arundel.

K. Edw. What, Lord Arundel, dost thou come alone?

Arun. Yea, my good lord, for Gaveston is dead.

K. Edw. Ah, traitors! have they put my friend to death?
Tell me, Arundel, died he ere thou cam'st,
Or didst thou see my friend to take his death?

Arun. Neither, my lord; for as he was surpris'd,
Begirt with weapons and with enemies round,
I did your highness' message to them all;
Demanding him of them, entreating rather,
And said, upon the honor of my name,
That I would undertake to carry him
Unto your highness, and to bring him back.

K. Edw. And tell me, would the rebels deny me that?

Y. Spen. Proud recreants!

K. Edw. Yea, Spencer, traitors all.

Arun. I found them at the first inexorable;
The Earl of Warwick would not bide the hearing,
Mortimer hardly; Pembroke and Lancaster
Spake least: and when they flatly had denied,
Refusing to receive me pledge for him,
The Earl of Pembroke mildly thus bespake;
"My lords, because our sovereign sends for him,
And promiseth he shall be safe return'd,
I will this undertake, to have him hence,
And see him re-delivered to your hands."

K. Edw. Well, and how fortunes [it] that he came not?

Y. Spen. Some treason or some villainy was cause.

Arun. The Earl of Warwick seiz'd him on his way;
For being delivered unto Pembroke's men,
Their lord rode home, thinking his prisoner safe;
But ere he came, Warwick in ambush lay,
And bare him to his death; and in a trench
Strake off his head, and march'd unto the camp.

Y. Spen. A bloody part, flatly against law of arms!
K. Edw. O shall I speak, or shall I sigh and die!
Y. Spen. My lord, refer your vengeance to the sword
Upon these barons; hearten up your men;
Let them not unreveng'd murder your friends!
Advance your standard, Edward, in the field,
And march to fire them from their starting holes.
K. Edw. (*Kneeling.*) By earth, the common mother of us all,
By Heaven, and all the moving orbs thereof,
By this right hand, and by my father's sword,
And all the honors 'longing to my crown,
I will have heads and lives for him, as many
As I have manors, castles, towns, and towers!—
(*Rises.*)
Treacherous Warwick! traitorous Mortimer!
If I be England's king, in lakes of gore
Your headless trunks, your bodies will I trail,
That you may drink your fill, and quaff in blood,
And stain my royal standard with the same,
That so my bloody colors may suggest
Remembrance of revenge immortally
On your accursed traitorous progeny,
You villains, that have slain my Gaveston!
And in this place of honor and of trust,
Spencer, sweet Spencer, I adopt thee here:
And merely of our love we do create thee
Earl of Gloucester, and Lord Chamberlain,
Despite of times, despite of enemies.
Y. Spen. My lord, here 's a messenger from the barons.
Desires access unto your majesty.
K. Edw. Admit him near.

Enter the Herald from the Barons with his coat of arms.

Her. Long live King Edward, England's lawful lord!
K. Edw. So wish not they, I wis, that sent thee hither.
Thou com'st from Mortimer and his 'complices,
A ranker rout of rebels never was.
Well, say thy message.
Her. The barons up in arms, by me salute
Your highness with long life and happiness;
And bid me say, as plainer to your grace,
That if without effusion of blood
You will this grief have ease and remedy,
That from your princely person you remove
This Spencer, as a putrifying branch,
That deads the royal vine, whose golden leaves
Empale your princely head, your diadem,
Whose brightness such pernicious upstarts dim,
Say they; and lovingly advise your grace,
To cherish virtue and nobility,
And have old servitors in high esteem,
And shake off smooth dissembling flatterers.
This granted, they, their honors, and their lives,
Are to your highness vow'd and consecrate.
Y. Spen. Ah, traitors! will they still display their pride?
K. Edw. Away, tarry no answer, but be gone!
Rebels, will they appoint their sovereign
His sports, his pleasures, and his company?
Yet, ere thou go, see how I do divorce
(*Embraces Spencer.*)
Spencer from me.—Now get thee to thy lords,
And tell them I will come to chastise them
For murdering Gaveston; hie thee, get thee gone!
Edward with fire and sword follows at thy heels.
Exit Herald.
My lords, perceive you how these rebels swell?
Soldiers, good hearts, defend your sovereign's right,
For now, even now, we march to make them stoop.
Away!
Exeunt. Alarums, excursions, a great fight, and a retreat (sounded within.)

SCENE 3. *Battle-field at Boroughbridge, in Yorkshire.*

Enter King Edward, the Elder Spencer, Young Spencer, and Noblemen of the King's side.

K. Edw. Why do we sound retreat? Upon them, lords!
This day I shall pour vengeance with my sword
On those proud rebels that are up in arms
And do confront and countermand their king.
Y. Spen. I doubt it not, my lord, right will prevail.
E. Spen. 'T is not amiss, my liege, for either part
To breathe awhile; our men, with sweat and dust
All chok'd well near, begin to faint for heat;
And this retire refresheth horse and man.
Y. Spen. Here come the rebels.

Enter the Barons, Young Mortimer, Lancaster, Warwick, Pembroke, and others.

Y. Mor. Look, Lancaster, yonder is Edward
Among his flatterers.
Lan. And there let him be
Till he pay dearly for their company.
War. And shall, or Warwick's sword shall smite in vain.
K. Edw. What, rebels, do you shrink and sound retreat?
Y. Mor. No, Edward, no; thy flatterers faint and fly.
Lan. Thou'd best betimes forsake them and their trains,[65]
For they'll betray thee, traitors as they are.
Y. Spen. Traitor on thy face, rebellious Lancaster!
Pem. Away, base upstart, brav'st thou nobles thus?
E. Spen. A noble attempt and honorable deed,
Is it not, trow ye, to assemble aid,
And levy arms against your lawful king!
K. Edw. For which ere long their heads shall satisfy,
T' appease the wrath of their offended king.
Y. Mor. Then, Edward, thou wilt fight it to the last,
And rather bathe thy sword in subjects' blood,
Than banish that pernicious company?
K. Edw. Aye, traitors all, rather than thus be brav'd,
Make England's civil towns huge heaps of stones,
And ploughs to go about our palace-gates.
War. A desperate and unnatural resolution!
Alarum! to the fight!
St. George for England, and the barons' right!
K. Edw. Saint George for England, and King Edward's right!
Alarums. Exeunt the two parties severally.

SCENE 4. *The same.*

Enter King Edward and his followers, with the Barons and Kent, captives.

K. Edw. Now, lusty lords, now, not by chance of war,
But justice of the quarrel and the cause,
Vail'd[66] is your pride; methinks you hang the heads,
But we'll advance[67] them, traitors. Now 't is time
To be aveng'd on you for all your braves,
And for the murder of my dearest friend,
To whom right well you knew our soul was knit,
Good Pierce of Gaveston, my sweet favorite.
Ah, rebels, recreants, you made him away!
Kent. Brother, in regard of thee, and of thy land,
Did they remove that flatterer from thy throne.
K. Edw. So, sir, you have spoke; away, avoid our presence!
Exit Kent.
Accursed wretches, was 't in regard of us,
When we had sent our messenger to request
He might be spar'd to come to speak with us,
And Pembroke undertook for his return
That thou, proud Warwick, watch'd the prisoner,
Poor Pierce, and headed him 'gainst law of arms?
For which thy head shall overlook the rest,

65 plots. 66 humbled. 67 raise.

As much as thou in rage outwent'st the rest.

War. Tyrant, I scorn thy threats and menaces;
It is but temporal that thou canst inflict.

Lan. The worst is death, and better die to live
Than live in infamy under such a king.

K. Edw. Away with them, my lord of Winchester!
These lusty leaders, Warwick and Lancaster,
I charge you roundly—off with both their heads!
Away!

War. Farewell, vain world!

Lan. Sweet Mortimer, farewell.

Y. Mor. England, unkind to thy nobility,
Groan for this grief, behold how thou art maim'd!

K. Edw. Go take that haughty Mortimer to the Tower,
There see him safe bestow'd; and for the rest,
Do speedy execution on them all.
Begone!

Y. Mor. What, Mortimer! can ragged stony walls
Immure thy virtue that aspires to Heaven?
No, Edward, England's scourge, it may not be;
Mortimer's hope surmounts his fortune far.

(*The captive Barons are led off.*)

K. Edw. Sound drums and trumpets! March with me, my friends,
Edward this day hath crown'd him king anew.

Exeunt all except Young Spencer, Levune, and Baldock.

Y. Spen. Levune, the trust that we repose in thee,
Begets the quiet of King Edward's land.
Therefore begone in haste, and with advice
Bestow that treasure on the lords of France,
That, therewith all enchanted, like the guard
That suffered Jove to pass in showers of gold
To Danaë, all aid may be denied
To Isabel, the queen, that now in France
Makes friends, to cross the seas with her young son,
And step into his father's regiment.[68]

Levune. That 's it these barons and the subtle queen
Long levell'd at.

Bal. Yea, but, Levune, thou seest
These barons lay their heads on blocks together;
What they intend, the hangman frustrates clean.

Levune. Have you no doubt, my lords, I'll clap so close
Among the lords of France with England's gold,
That Isabel shall make her plaints in vain,
And France shall be obdurate with her tears.

Y. Spen. Then make for France amain; Levune, away!
Proclaim King Edward's wars and victories.

Exeunt.

ACT IV.

SCENE 1. *Near the Tower of London.*

Enter Kent.

Kent. Fair blows the wind for France; blow gentle gale,
Till Edmund be arriv'd for England's good!
Nature, yield to my country's cause in this.
A brother? No, a butcher of thy friends!
Proud Edward, dost thou banish me thy presence?
But I'll to France, and cheer the wronged queen,
And certify what Edward's looseness is.
Unnatural king! to slaughter noblemen
And cherish flatterers! Mortimer, I stay
Thy sweet escape: stand gracious, gloomy night,
To his device.

Enter Young Mortimer, disguised.

Y. Mor. Holla! who walketh there?
Is 't you, my lord?

Kent. Mortimer, 't is I;
But hath thy potion wrought so happily?

Y. Mor. It hath, my lord; the warders all asleep,

68 rule.

I thank them, gave me leave to pass in peace.
But hath your grace got shipping unto France?
Kent. Fear it not.
Exeunt.

SCENE 2. *Paris.*

Enter Queen Isabella and her son, Prince Edward.

Q. Isab. Ah, boy! our friends do fail us all in France.
The lords are cruel, and the king unkind;
What shall we do?
P. Edw. Madam, return to England,
And please my father well, and then a fig
For all my uncle's friendship here in France.
I warrant you, I'll win his highness quickly;
'A loves me better than a thousand Spencers.
Q. Isab. Ah, boy, thou art deceiv'd, at least in this,
To think that we can yet be tun'd together;
No, no, we jar too far. Unkind Valois!
Unhappy Isabel! when France rejects,
Whither, oh! whither dost thou bend thy steps?

Enter Sir John of Hainault.

Sir J. Madam, what cheer?
Q. Isab. Ah! good Sir John of Hainault,
Never so cheerless, nor so far distrest.
Sir J. I hear, sweet lady, of the king's unkindness;
But droop not, madam; noble minds contemn
Despair. Will your grace with me to Hainault,
And there stay time's advantage with your son?
How say you, my lord, will you go with your friends,
And share of [69] all our fortunes equally?
P. Edw. So pleaseth the queen, my mother, me it likes.
The King of England, nor the court of France,
Shall have me from my gracious mother's side,
Till I be strong enough to break a staff;
And then have at the proudest Spencer's head.
Sir J. Well said, my lord.
Q. Isab. O, my sweet heart, how do I moan thy wrongs,
Yet triumph in the hope of thee, my joy!
Ah, sweet Sir John! even to the utmost verge
Of Europe, or the shore of Tanais,
Will we with thee to Hainault—so we will:—
The marquis is a noble gentleman;
His grace, I dare presume, will welcome me.
But who are these?

Enter Kent and Young Mortimer.

Kent. Madam, long may you live,
Much happier than your friends in England do!
Q. Isab. Lord Edmund and Lord Mortimer alive!
Welcome to France! The news was here, my lord,
That you were dead, or very near your death.
Y. Mor. Lady, the last was truest of the twain;
But Mortimer, reserv'd for better hap,
Hath shaken off the thraldom of the Tower,
And lives t' advance your standard, good my lord.
P. Edw. How mean you? An [70] the king, my father, lives?
No, my Lord Mortimer, not I, I trow.
Q. Isab. Not, son! why not? I would it were no worse.
But, gentle lords, friendless we are in France.
Y. Mor. Monsieur le Grand, a noble friend of yours,
Told us, at our arrival, all the news:
How hard the nobles, how unkind the king
Hath show'd himself; but, madam, right makes room
Where weapons want; and, though a many friends
Are made away, as Warwick, Lancaster,
And others of our party and faction;
Yet have we friends, assure your grace, in England
Would cast up caps, and clap their hands for joy,
To see us there, appointed for [71] our foes.

69 Qq. *shake off.* 70 if. 71 equipped to meet.

Kent. Would all were well, and Edward well reclaim'd,
For Engand's honor, peace, and quietness.
Y. Mor. But by the sword, my lord 't must be deserv'd;
The king will ne'er forsake his flatterers.
Sir J. My lord of England, sith the ungentle king
Of France refuseth to give aid of arms
To this distressed queen his sister here,
Go you with her to Hainault. Doubt ye not,
We will find comfort, money, men, and friends
Ere long, to bid the English king a base.[72]
How say, young prince? What think you of the match?
P. Edw. I think King Edward will outrun us all.
Q. Isab. Nay, son, not so; and you must not discourage
Your friends, that are so forward in your aid.
Kent. Sir John of Hainault, pardon us, I pray;
These comforts that you give our woful queen
Bind us in kindness all at your command.
Q. Isab. Yea, gentle brother; and the God of heaven
Prosper your happy motion, good Sir John.
Y. Mor. This noble gentleman, forward in arms,
Was born, I see, to be our anchor-hold.
Sir John of Hainault, be it thy renown,
That England's queen and nobles in distress,
Have been by thee restor'd and comforted.
Sir J. Madam, along, and you my lords, with me,
That England's peers may Hainault's welcome see.
Exeunt.

SCENE 3. *The King's Palace, London.*

Enter King Edward, Arundel, the Elder and Younger Spencer, with others.

K. Edw. Thus after many threats of wrathful war,
Triumpheth England's Edward with his friends;
And triumph, Edward, with his friends uncontroll'd!
My lord of Gloucester, do you hear the news?
Y. Spen. What news, my lord?
K. Edw. Why, man, they say there is great execution
Done through the realm; my lord of Arundel,
You have the note, have you not?
Arun. From the Lieutenant of the Tower, my lord.
K. Edw. I pray let us see it. (*Takes the note.*) What have we there?
Read it, Spencer.
(*Young Spencer reads the names.*)
Why, so; they bark'd apace a month ago:
Now, on my life, they 'll neither bark nor bite.
Now, sirs, the news from France? Gloucester, I trow
The lords of France love England's gold so well
As Isabella gets no aid from thence.
What now remains? Have you proclaim'd, my lord,
Reward for them can bring in Mortimer?
Y. Spen. My lord, we have; and if he be in England,
'A will be had ere long, I doubt it not.
K. Edw. If, dost thou say? Spencer, as true as death,
He is in England's ground; our portmasters
Are not so careless of their king's command.

Enter a Post.

How now, what news with thee? From whence come these?
Post. Letters, my lord, and tidings forth of France;—
To you, my lord of Gloucester, from Levune.
(*Gives letters to Young Spencer.*)
K. Edw. Read.
Y. Spen. (*Reads.*)
"My duty to your honor premised, &c., I have, according to instructions in that behalf, dealt with the King of France his lords, and effected that the queen, all discontented and discomforted, is gone: whither, if you ask, with Sir John of Hainault, brother to the marquis, into Flanders. With them are gone Lord Edmund, and the Lord Mortimer, having in their company divers of your nation, and

72 challenge; a reference to the game of prisoner's base.

others; and, as constant report goeth, they intend to give King Edward battle in England, sooner than he can look for them. This is all the news of import.
Your honor's in all service, LEVUNE."

K. Edw. Ah, villains! hath that Mortimer escap'd?
With him is Edmund gone associate?
And will Sir John of Hainault lead the round?
Welcome, a' God's name, madam, and your son;
England shall welcome you and all your rout.
Gallop apace, bright Phœbus, through the sky,
And dusky night, in rusty iron car,
Between you both shorten the time, I pray,
That I may see that most desired day
When we may meet these traitors in the field.
Ah, nothing grieves me but my little boy
Is thus misled to countenance their ills.
Come, friends, to Bristow,[73] there to make us strong;
And, winds, as equal be to bring them in,
As you injurious were to bear them forth! *Exeunt.*

SCENE 4. *Near Harwich.*

Enter Queen Isabella, her son, Prince Edward, Kent, Young Mortimer, and Sir John of Hainault.

Q. Isab. Now, lords, our loving friends and countrymen,
Welcome to England all, with prosperous winds!
Our kindest friends in Belgia have we left,
To cope with friends at home; a heavy case
When force to force is knit, and sword and glaive[74]
In civil broils make kin and countrymen
Slaughter themselves in others, and their sides
With their own weapons gor'd! But what 's the help?
Misgovern'd kings are cause of all this wrack;
And, Edward, thou art one among them all,
Whose looseness hath betray'd thy land to spoil,
Who made the channels overflow with blood.
Of thine own people patron shouldst thou be,
But thou——

Y. Mor. Nay, madam, if you be a warrior,
You must not grow so passionate in speeches.
Lords,
Sith that we are by sufferance of Heaven
Arriv'd and armed in this prince's right,
Here for our country's cause swear we to him
All homage, fealty, and forwardness;
And for the open wrongs and injuries
Edward hath done to us, his queen and land,
We come in arms to wreak it with the sword;
That England's queen in peace may repossess
Her dignities and honors; and withal
We may remove these flatterers from the king,
That havocs England's wealth and treasury.

Sir J. Sound trumpets, my lord, and forward let us march.
Edward will think we come to flatter him.

Kent. I would he never had been flattered more.
Exeunt.

SCENE 5. *Near Bristol.*

Enter King Edward, Baldock, and Young Spencer, flying about the stage.

Y. Spen. Fly, fly, my lord! the queen is over-strong;
Her friends do multiply, and yours do fail.
Shape we our course to Ireland, there to breathe.

K. Edw. What! was I born to fly and run away,
And leave the Mortimers conquerors behind?
Give me my horse, and let 's reinforce our troops:
And in this bed of honor die with fame.

73 Bristol.

74 spear.

Bald. O no, my lord, this princely resolution
Fits not the time; away! we are pursu'd.
Exeunt.

Enter Kent, with sword and target.

Kent. This way he fled, but I am come too late.
Edward, alas! my heart relents for thee.
Proud traitor, Mortimer, why dost thou chase
Thy lawful king, thy sovereign, with thy sword?
Vile wretch! and why hast thou, of all unkind,[75]
Borne arms against thy brother and thy king?
Rain showers of vengeance on my cursed head,
Thou God, to whom in justice it belongs
To punish this unnatural revolt!
Edward, this Mortimer aims at thy life!
O fly him, then! But, Edmund, calm this rage,
Dissemble, or thou diest; for Mortimer
And Isabel do kiss, while they conspire;
And yet she bears a face of love forsooth.
Fie on that love that hatcheth death and hate!
Edmund, away! Bristow to Longshanks' blood
Is false. Be not found single for suspect:[76]
Proud Mortimer pries near into thy walks.

Enter Queen Isabella, Prince Edward, Young Mortimer, and Sir John of Hainault.

Q. Isab. Successful battle gives the God of kings
To them that fight in right and fear his wrath.
Since then successfully we have prevailed,
Thanked be Heaven's great architect, and you.
Ere farther we proceed, my noble lords,
We here create our well-beloved son,
Of love and care unto his royal person,
Lord Warden of the realm, and sith the fates
Have made his father so unfortunate,
Deal you, my lords, in this, my loving lords,
As to your wisdoms fittest seems in all.

Kent. Madam, without offense, if I may ask,
How will you deal with Edward in his fall?

P. Edw. Tell me, good uncle, what Edward do you mean?

Kent. Nephew, your father; I dare not call him king.

Y. Mor. My lord of Kent, what needs these questions?
'T is not in her controlment, nor in ours,
But as the realm and parliament shall please;
So shall your brother be disposed of.—
(*Aside to the Queen.*) I like not this relenting mood in Edmund.
Madam, 't is good to look to him betimes.

Q. Isab. My lord, the Mayor of Bristow knows our mind.

Y. Mor. Yea, madam, and they scape not easily
That fled the field.

Q. Isab. Baldock is with the king,
A goodly chancellor, is he not, my lord?

Sir J. So are the Spencers, the father and the son.

Kent. This Edward is the ruin of the realm.

Enter Rice ap Howell and the Mayor of Bristol, with the Elder Spencer prisoner, and Attendants.

Rice. God save Queen Isabel, and her princely son!
Madam, the mayor and citizens of Bristow,
In sign of love and duty to this presence,
Present by me this traitor to the state,
Spencer, the father to that wanton Spencer,
That, like the lawless Catiline of Rome,
Reveled in England's wealth and treasury.

Q. Isab. We thank you all.

Y. Mor. Your loving care in this
Deserveth princely favors and rewards.
But where 's the king and the other Spencer fled?

Rice. Spencer the son, created Earl of Gloucester,
Is with that smooth-tongu'd scholar Baldock gone
And shipt but late for Ireland with the king.

Y. Mor. (*Aside.*) Some whirlwind fetch them back or sink them all!—
They shall be started thence, I doubt it not.

75 most unnatural of all.

76 be not found walking alone lest you be suspected.

P. Edw. Shall I not see the king my father yet?
Kent. (*Aside.*) Unhappy 's Edward, chas'd from England's bounds.
Sir J. Madam, what resteth, why stand you in a muse?
Q. Isab. I rue my lord's ill-fortune; but alas!
Care of my country call'd me to this war.
Y. Mor. Madam, have done with care and sad complaint;
Your king hath wrong'd your country and himself,
And we must seek to right it as we may.
Meanwhile, have hence this rebel to the block.
Your lordship cannot privilege your head.
E. Spen. Rebel is he that fights against his prince;
So fought not they that fought in Edward's right.
Y. Mor. Take him away, he prates.
Exeunt Attendants with the Elder Spencer.
You, Rice ap Howell,
Shall do good service to her majesty,
Being of countenance in your country here,
To follow these rebellious runagates.
We in meanwhile, madam, must take advice
How Baldock, Spencer, and their 'complices
May in their fall be followed to their end.
Exeunt.

SCENE 6. *The Abbey of Neath.*

Enter the Abbot, Monks, King Edward, Young Spencer, and Baldock, the three latter disguised.

Abbot. Have you no doubt, my lord; have you no fear;
As silent and as careful we will be,
To keep your royal person safe with us,
Free from suspect and fell invasion
Of such as have your majesty in chase,
Yourself, and those your chosen company,
As danger of this stormy time requires.
K. Edw. Father, thy face should harbor no deceit.
O! hadst thou ever been a king, thy heart,
Pierced deeply with sense of my distress,
Could not but take compassion of my state.
Stately and proud, in riches and in train,
Whilom I was, powerful, and full of pomp:
But what is he whom rule and empery
Have not in life or death made miserable?
Come, Spencer; come, Baldock, come, sit down by me;
Make trial now of that philosophy,
That in our famous nurseries of arts
Thou suck'dst from Plato and from Aristotle.
Father, this life contemplative is Heaven.
O that I might this life in quiet lead!
But we, alas! are chas'd; and you, my friends,
Your lives and my dishonor they pursue.
Yet, gentle monks, for treasure, gold, nor fee,
Do you betray us and our company.
Monks. Your grace may sit secure, if none but we
Do wot of your abode.
Y. Spen. Not one alive; but shrewdly I suspect
A gloomy fellow in a mead below.
'A gave a long look after us, my lord;
And all the land I know is up in arms,
Arms that pursue our lives with deadly hate.
Bald. We were embark'd for Ireland, wretched we!
With awkward winds and [with] sore tempests driven
To fall on shore, and here to pine in fear
Of Mortimer and his confederates.
K. Edw. Mortimer! who talks of Mortimer?
Who wounds me with the name of Mortimer,
That bloody man? Good father, on thy lap
Lay I this head, laden with mickle care.
O might I never open these eyes again!
Never again lift up this drooping head!
O never more lift up this dying heart!
Y. Spen. Look up, my lord.—Baldock, this drowsiness
Betides no good; here even we are betray'd.

Enter, with Welsh hooks, Rice ap Howell, a Mower, and Leicester.

Mow. Upon my life, these be the men ye seek.
Rice. Fellow, enough.—My lord, I pray be short,
A fair commission warrants what we do.
Leices. The queen's commission, urg'd by Mortimer;
What cannot gallant Mortimer with the queen?
Alas! see where he sits, and hopes unseen
T' escape their hands that seek to reave his life.
Too true it is, *Quem dies vidit veniens superbum,*
Hunc dies vidit fugiens jacentem.[77]
But, Leicester, leave to grow so passionate.
Spencer and Baldock, by no other names,
I do arrest you of high treason here.
Stand not on titles, but obey th' arrest;
'T is in the name of Isabel the queen.
My lord, why droop you thus?
K. Edw. O day, the last of all my bliss on earth!
Center of all misfortune! O my stars,
Why do you lour unkindly on a king?
Comes Leicester, then, in Isabella's name
To take my life, my company from me?
Here, man, rip up this panting breast of mine,
And take my heart in rescue of my friends!
Rice. Away with them!
Y. Spen. It may become thee yet
To let us take our farewell of his grace.
Abbot. (*Aside.*) My heart with pity earns[78] to see this sight,
A king to bear these words and proud commands.
K. Edw. Spencer, ah, sweet Spencer, thus then must we part?
Y. Spen. We must, my lord, so will the angry Heavens.
K. Edw. Nay, so will hell and cruel Mortimer;
The gentle Heavens have not to do in this.
Bald. My lord, it is in vain to grieve or storm.
Here humbly of your grace we take our leaves;
Our lots are cast; I fear me, so is thine.
K. Edw. In Heaven we may, in earth ne'er shall we meet:
And, Leicester, say, what shall become of us?
Leices. Your majesty must go to Killingworth.[79]
K. Edw. Must! it is somewhat hard, when kings *must* go.
Leices. Here is a litter ready for your grace,
That waits your pleasure, and the day grows old.
Rice. As good be gone, as stay and be benighted.
K. Edw. A litter hast thou? Lay me in a hearse,
And to the gates of hell convey me hence;
Let Pluto's bells ring out my fatal knell,
And hags howl for my death at Charon's shore,
For friends hath Edward none but these and these,
And these must die under a tyrant's sword.
Rice. My lord, be going; care not for these,
For we shall see them shorter by the heads.
K. Edw. Well, that shall be, shall be: part we must!
Sweet Spencer, gentle Baldock, part we must!
Hence feigned weeds! unfeigned are my woes;
(*Throws off his disguise.*)
Father, farewell! Leicester, thou stay'st for me,
And go I must. Life, farewell, with my friends.
Exeunt Edward and Leicester.
Y. Spen. O! is he gone? Is noble Edward gone?
Parted from hence, never to see us more?
Rend, sphere of Heaven! and, fire, forsake thy orb!
Earth, melt to air! gone is my sovereign,
Gone, gone, alas! never to make return.
Bald. Spencer, I see our souls are fleeted hence;
We are depriv'd the sunshine of our life:
Make for a new life, man; throw up thy eyes,
And heart, and hand to Heaven's immortal throne;
Pay nature's debt with cheerful countenance;
Reduce we all our lessons unto this:
To die, sweet Spencer, therefore live we all;
Spencer, all live to die, and rise to fall.

77 "Whom the dawn sees proud, evening sees prostrate." (Seneca, *Thyestes*, 613.) 78 yearns. 79 Kenilworth.

Rice. Come, come, keep these preachments till you come to the place appointed. You, and such as you are, have made wise work in England. Will your lordships away?

Mow. Your lordship, I trust, will remember me?

Rice. Remember thee, fellow! what else? Follow me to the town.

Exeunt.

ACT V.

SCENE 1. *A room in Kenilworth Castle.*

Enter King Edward, Leicester, the Bishop of Winchester for the crown, and Trussel.

Leices. Be patient, good my lord, cease to lament,
Imagine Killingworth Castle were your court,
And that you lay for pleasure here a space,
Not of compulsion or necessity.

K. Edw. Leicester, if gentle words might comfort me,
Thy speeches long ago had eas'd my sorrows;
For kind and loving hast thou always been.
The griefs of private men are soon allay'd,
But not of kings. The forest deer, being struck,
Runs to an herb that closeth up the wounds;
But, when the imperial lion's flesh is gor'd,
He rends and tears it with his wrathful paw,
[And] highly scorning that the lowly earth
Should drink his blood, mounts up into the air.
And so it fares with me, whose dauntless mind
The ambitious Mortimer would seek to curb,
And that unnatural queen, false Isabel,
That thus hath pent and mew'd me in a prison;
For such outrageous passions cloy my soul,
As with the wings of rancor and disdain
Full often am I soaring up to Heaven,
To plain [80] me to the gods against them both.
But when I call to mind I am a king,
Methinks I should revenge me of my wrongs,
That Mortimer and Isabel have done.
But what are kings, when regiment [81] is gone,
But perfect shadows in a sunshine day?
My nobles rule, I bear the name of king;
I wear the crown, but am controll'd by them,
By Mortimer, and my unconstant queen,
Who spots my nuptial bed with infamy;
Whilst I am lodg'd within this cave of care,
Where sorrow at my elbow still attends,
To company my heart with sad laments,
That bleeds within me for this strange exchange.
But tell me, must I now resign my crown,
To make usurping Mortimer a king?

B. of Win. Your grace mistakes; it is for England's good,
And princely Edward's right we crave the crown.

K. Edw. No, 't is for Mortimer, not Edward's head;
For he 's a lamb, encompassed by wolves,
Which in a moment will abridge his life.
But if proud Mortimer do wear this crown,
Heavens turn it to a blaze of quenchless fire!
Or like the snaky wreath of Tisiphon,
Engirt the temples of his hateful head;
So shall not England's vine be perished,
But Edward's name survives, though Edward dies.

Leices. My lord, why waste you thus the time away?
They stay your answer; will you yield your crown?

K. Edw. Ah, Leicester, weigh how hardly I can brook
To lose my crown and kingdom without cause;
To give ambitious Mortimer my right,
That like a mountain overwhelms my bliss,
In which extreme my mind here murdered is.
But what the heavens appoint, I must obey!
Here, take my crown; the life of Edward too;
(*Taking off the crown.*)

80 complain.

81 sovereignty.

Two kings in England cannot reign at once.
But stay awhile, let me be king till night,
That I may gaze upon this glittering crown;
So shall my eyes receive their last content,
My head, the latest honor due to it,
And jointly both yield up their wished right.
Continue ever, thou celestial sun;
Let never silent night possess this clime:
Stand still, you watches of the element;
All times and seasons, rest you at a stay,
That Edward may be still fair England's king!
But day's bright beam doth vanish fast away,
And needs I must resign my wished crown.
Inhuman creatures! nurs'd with tiger's milk!
Why gape you for your sovereign's overthrow!
My diadem I mean, and guiltless life.
See, monsters, see, I'll wear my crown again!
(*He puts on the crown.*)
What, fear you not the fury of your king?
But, hapless Edward, thou art fondly[82] led;
They pass[83] not for thy frowns as late they did,
But seek to make a new-elected king;
Which fills my mind with strange despairing thoughts,
Which thoughts are martyred with endless torments,
And in this torment comfort find I none,
But that I feel the crown upon my head;
And therefore let me wear it yet awhile.

Trus. My lord, the parliament must have present news,
And therefore say, will you resign or no?
(*The King rageth.*)

K. Edw. I'll not resign, but whilst I live [be king.][84]
Traitors, be gone and join with Mortimer!
Elect, conspire, install, do what you will:—
Their blood and yours shall seal these treacheries!

B. of Win. This answer we'll return, and so farewell.
(*Going with Trussel.*)

Leices. Call them again, my lord, and speak them fair;
For if they go, the prince shall lose his right.

K. Edw. Call thou them back, I have no power to speak.

Leices. My lord, the king is willing to resign.

B. of Win. If he be not, let him choose.

K. Edw. O would I might, but heavens and earth conspire
To make me miserable! Here receive my crown;
Receive it? No, these innocent hands of mine
Shall not be guilty of so foul a crime.
He of you all that most desires my blood,
And will be call'd the murderer of a king,
Take it. What, are you mov'd? Pity you me?
Then send for unrelenting Mortimer,
And Isabel, whose eyes, being turn'd to steel,
Will sooner sparkle fire than shed a tear.
Yet stay, for rather than I'll look on them,
Here, here!
(*Gives the crown.*)
Now, sweet God of Heaven,
Make me despise this transitory pomp,
And sit for ay enthronized in Heaven!
Come, death, and with thy fingers close my eyes,
Or if I live, let me forget myself.

B. of Win. My lord—

K. Edw. Call me not lord; away—out of my sight!
Ah, pardon me: grief makes me lunatic!
Let not that Mortimer protect my son;
More safety is there in a tiger's jaws,
Than his embracements. Bear this to the queen,
Wet with my tears, and dried again with sighs;
(*Gives a handkerchief.*)
If with the sight thereof she be not mov'd,
Return it back and dip it in my blood.
Commend me to my son, and bid him rule
Better than I. Yet how have I transgress'd,
Unless it be with too much clemency?

Trus. And thus most humbly do we take our leave.

K. Edw. Farewell;

82 foolishly. 83 care. 84 Qq. omit.

Exeunt the Bishop of Winchester and Trussel.

I know the next news that they bring
Will be my death; and welcome shall it be;
To wretched men, death is felicity.

Enter Berkeley,[85] *who gives a paper to Leicester.*

Leices. Another post! what news brings he?
K. Edw. Such news as I expect—come, Berkeley, come,
And tell thy message to my naked breast.
Berk. My lord, think not a thought so villainous
Can harbor in a man of noble birth.
To do your highness service and devoir,
And save you from your foes, Berkeley would die.
Leices. My lord, the council of the queen commands
That I resign my charge.
K. Edw. And who must keep me now? Must you, my lord?
Berk. Aye, my most gracious lord; so 't is decreed.
K. Edw. (*Taking the paper.*) By Mortimer, whose name is written here!
Well may I rend his name that rends my heart!
(*Tears it.*)
This poor revenge has something eas'd my mind.
So may his limbs be torn, as is this paper!
Hear me, immortal Jove, and grant it too!
Berk. Your grace must hence with me to Berkeley straight.
K. Edw. Whither you will; all places are alike,
And every earth is fit for burial.
Leices. Favor him, my lord, as much as lieth in you.
Berk. Even so betide my soul as I use him.
K. Edw. Mine enemy hath pitied my estate,
And that 's the cause that I am now remov'd.
Berk. And thinks your grace that Berkeley will be cruel?
K. Edw. I know not; but of this am I assured,
That death ends all, and I can die but once.
Leicester, farewell!

85 Qq. *Bartley*, showing pronunciation.

Leices. Not yet, my lord; I 'll bear you on your way.
Exeunt.

SCENE 2. *The Palace, London.*

Enter Queen Isabella and Young Mortimer.

Y. Mor. Fair Isabel, now have we our desire;
The proud corrupters of the light-brain'd king
Have done their homage to the lofty gallows,
And he himself lies in captivity.
Be rul'd by me, and we will rule the realm.
In any case take heed of childish fear,
For now we hold an old wolf by the ears,
That, if he slip, will seize upon us both,
And gripe the sorer, being gript himself.
Think therefore, madam, that imports us much
To erect [86] your son with all the speed we may,
And that I be protector over him;
For our behoof will bear the greater sway
Whenas a king's name shall be under writ.
Q. Isab. Sweet Mortimer, the life of Isabel,
Be thou persuaded that I love thee well,
And therefore, so the prince my son be safe,
Whom I esteem as dear as these mine eyes,
Conclude against his father what thou wilt,
And I myself will willingly subscribe.
Y. Mor. First would I hear news that he were depos'd,
And then let me alone to handle him.

Enter Messenger.

Letters! from whence?
Mess. From Killingworth, my lord.
Q. Isab. How fares my lord the king?
Mess. In health, madam, but full of pensiveness.
Q. Isab. Alas, poor soul, would I could ease his grief!

Enter the Bishop of Winchester with the crown.

Thanks, gentle Winchester. (*To the Messenger.*) Sirrah, be gone.
Exit Messenger.

86 make king.

B. of Win. The king hath willingly resign'd his crown.
Q. Isab. O happy news! send for the prince, my son.
B. of Win. Further, or [87] this letter was seal'd, Lord Berkeley came,
So that he now is gone from Killingworth;
And we have heard that Edmund laid a plot
To set his brother free; no more but so.
The lord of Berkeley is so pitiful
As Leicester that had charge of him before.
Q. Isab. Then let some other be his guardian.
Y. Mor. Let me alone, here is the privy seal.
Exit the Bishop of Winchester.
Who 's there?—Call hither Gurney and Matrevis.
To dash the heavy-headed Edmund's drift,
Berkeley shall be discharg'd, the king remov'd,
And none but we shall know where he lieth.
Q. Isab. But, Mortimer, as long as he survives,
What safety rests for us, or for my son?
Y. Mor. Speak, shall he presently be despatch'd and die?
Q. Isab. I would he were, so 't were not by my means.

Enter Matrevis and Gurney.

Y. Mor. Enough.—
Matrevis, write a letter presently
Unto the lord of Berkeley from ourself
That he resign the king to thee and Gurney;
And when 't is done, we will subscribe our name.
Mat. It shall be done, my lord.
Y. Mor. Gurney.
Gur. My lord.
Y. Mor. As thou intend'st to rise by Mortimer,
Who now makes Fortune's wheel turn as he please,
Seek all the means thou canst to make him droop,
And neither give him kind word nor good look.
Gur. I warrant you, my lord.
Y. Mor. And this above the rest: because we hear
That Edmund casts [88] to work his liberty,
Remove him still from place to place by night,
Till at the last he come to Killingworth,
And then from thence to Berkeley back again;
And by the way, to make him fret the more,
Speak curstly to him, and in any case
Let no man comfort him; if he chance to weep,
But amplify his grief with bitter words.
Mat. Fear not, my lord, we 'll do as you command.
Y. Mor. So now away; post thitherwards amain.
Q. Isab. Whither goes this letter? To my lord the king?
Commend me humbly to his majesty,
And tell him that I labor all in vain
To ease his grief, and work his liberty;
And bear him this as witness of my love.
(*Gives a ring.*)
Mat. I will, madam.
Exit with Gurney.
Enter Prince Edward, and Kent talking with him.

Y. Mor. Finely dissembled. Do so still, sweet queen.
Here comes the young prince with the Earl of Kent.
Q. Isab. Something he whispers in his childish ears.
Y. Mor. If he have such access unto the prince,
Our plots and stratagems will soon be dash'd.
Q. Isab. Use Edmund friendly, as if all were well.
Y. Mor. How fares my honorable lord of Kent?
Kent. In health, sweet Mortimer. How fares your grace?
Q. Isab. Well, if my lord your brother were enlarg'd.
Kent. I hear of late he hath depos'd himself.
Q. Isab. The more my grief.
Y. Mor. And mine.
Kent. (*Aside.*) Ah, they do dissemble!
Q. Isab. Sweet son, come hither, I must talk with thee.
Y. Mor. Thou being his uncle, and the next of blood,
Do look to be protector o'er the prince.

[87] ere.

[88] plots.

Kent. Not I, my lord; who should protect the son,
But she that gave him life? I mean the queen.
P. Edw. Mother, persuade me not to wear the crown:
Let him be king—I am too young to reign.
Q. Isab. But be content, seeing 't is his highness' pleasure.
P. Edw. Let me but see him first, and then I will.
Kent. Aye, do, sweet nephew.
Q. Isab. Brother, you know it is impossible.
P. Edw. Why, is he dead?
Q. Isab. No, God forbid!
Kent. I would those words proceeded from your heart.
Y. Mor. Inconstant Edmund, dost thou favor him,
That wast the cause of his imprisonment?
Kent. The more cause have I now to make amends.
Y. Mor. (*Aside to Q. Isab.*) I tell thee, 't is not meet that one so false
Should come about the person of a prince.—
My lord, he hath betray'd the king his brother,
And therefore trust him not.
P. Edw. But he repents, and sorrows for it now.
Q. Isab. Come, son, and go with this gentle lord and me.
P. Edw. With you I will, but not with Mortimer.
Y. Mor. Why, youngling, 'sdain'st thou so of Mortimer?
Then I will carry thee by force away.
P. Edw. Help, uncle Kent! Mortimer will wrong me.
Q. Isab. Brother Edmund, strive not; we are his friends;
Isabel is nearer than the Earl of Kent.
Kent. Sister, Edward is my charge, redeem him.
Q. Isab. Edward is my son, and I will keep him.
Kent. Mortimer shall know that he hath wrong'd me!—
(*Aside.*) Hence will I haste to Killingworth Castle,
And rescue aged Edward from his foes.
To be reveng'd on Mortimer and thee.
Exeunt on one side Queen Isabella, Prince Edward, and Young Mortimer; on the other Kent.

SCENE 3. *Kenilworth Castle.*

Enter Matrevis and Gurney, and Soldiers, with King Edward.

Mat. My lord, be not pensive, we are your friends;
Men are ordain'd to live in misery,
Therefore come,—dalliance dangereth our lives.
K. Edw. Friends, whither must unhappy Edward go?
Will hateful Mortimer appoint no rest?
Must I be vexed like the nightly bird,
Whose sight is loathsome to all winged fowls?
When will the fury of his mind assuage?
When will his heart be satisfied with blood?
If mine will serve, unbowel straight this breast,
And give my heart to Isabel and him;
It is the chiefest mark they level at.
Gur. Not so, my liege, the queen hath given this charge
To keep your grace in safety;
Your passions make your dolors to increase.
K. Edw. This usage makes my misery to increase.
But can my air of life continue long
When all my senses are annoy'd with stench?
Within a dungeon England's king is kept,
Where I am starv'd for want of sustenance.
My daily diet is heart-breaking sobs,
That almost rends the closet of my heart.
Thus lives old Edward not reliev'd by any,
And so must die, though pitied by many.
O, water, gentle friends, to cool my thirst,
And clear my body from foul excrements!
Mat. Here's channel[89] water, as our charge is given.
Sit down, for we'll be barbers to your grace.
K. Edw. Traitors, away! What, will you murder me,
Or choke your sovereign with puddle water?
Gur. No; but wash your face, and shave away your beard,
Lest you be known and so be rescued.
Mat. Why strive you thus? Your labor is in vain.

89 gutter.

K. Edw. The wren may strive against the lion's strength,
But all in vain: so vainly do I strive
To seek for mercy at a tyrant's hand.
(*They wash him with puddle water, and shave his beard away.*)
Immortal powers that knows the painful cares
That wait upon my poor distressed soul,
O level all your looks upon these daring men,
That wrongs their liege and sovereign, England's king!
O Gaveston, 't is for thee that I am wrong'd,
For me, both thou and both the Spencers died!
And for your sakes a thousand wrongs I'll take.
The Spencers' ghosts, wherever they remain,
Wish well to mine; then tush, for them I'll die!

Mat. 'Twixt theirs and yours shall be no enmity.
Come, come away; now put the torches out;
We'll enter in by darkness to Killingworth.

Enter Kent.

Gur. How now, who comes there?

Mat. Guard the king sure: it is the Earl of Kent.

K. Edw. O gentle brother, help to rescue me!

Mat. Keep them asunder; thrust in the king.

Kent. Soldiers, let me but talk to him one word.

Gur. Lay hands upon the earl for this assault.

Kent. Lay down your weapons, traitors! Yield the king!

Mat. Edmund, yield thou thyself, or thou shalt die.

Kent. Base villains, wherefore do you gripe me thus?

Gur. Bind him and so convey him to the court.

Kent. Where is the court but here? Here is the king,
And I will visit him; why stay you me?

Mat. The court is where Lord Mortimer remains;
Thither shall your honor go; and so farewell.

Exeunt Matrevis and Gurney, with King Edward.

Kent. O miserable is that commonweal,
Where lords keep courts, and kings are lock'd in prison!

Sol. Wherefore stay we? On, sirs, to the court!

Kent. Aye, lead me whither you will, even to my death.
Seeing that my brother cannot be releas'd.

Exeunt.

SCENE 4. *The Palace, London.*

Enter Young Mortimer, alone.

Y. Mor. The king must die, or Mortimer goes down;
The commons now begin to pity him.
Yet he that is the cause of Edward's death,
Is sure to pay for it when his son's of age;
And therefore will I do it cunningly.
This letter, written by a friend of ours,
Contains his death, yet bids them save his life.
(*Reads.*)
"Edwardum occidere nolite timere—bonum est:
Fear not to kill the king, 't is good he die."
But read it thus, and that's another sense:
"Edwardum occidere nolite—timere bonum est:
Kill not the king, 't is good to fear the worst."
Unpointed [90] as it is, thus shall it go,
That, being dead, if it chance to be found,
Matrevis and the rest may bear the blame,
And we be quit that caus'd it to be done.
Within this room is lock'd the messenger
That shall convey it, and perform the rest;
And by a secret token that he bears,
Shall he be murdered when the deed is done.—
Lightborn, come forth!

Enter Lightborn.

Art thou as resolute as thou wast?

Light. What else, my lord? And far more resolute.

Y. Mor. And hast thou cast how to accomplish it?

90 unpunctuated.

Light. Aye, aye, and none shall know which way he died.
Y. Mor. But at his looks, Lightborn, thou wilt relent.
Light. Relent! ha, ha! I use much to relent.
Y. Mor. Well, do it bravely, and be secret.
Light. You shall not need to give instructions;
'T is not the first time I have kill'd a man.
I learn'd in Naples how to poison flowers;
To strangle with a lawn[91] thrust through the throat;
To pierce the windpipe with a needle's point;
Or whilst one is asleep, to take a quill
And blow a little powder in his ears;
Or open his mouth and pour quicksilver down.
And yet I have a braver way than these.
Y. Mor. What 's that?
Light. Nay, you shall pardon me; none shall know my tricks.
Y. Mor. I care not how it is, so it be not spied.
Deliver this to Gurney and Matrevis.
(*Gives letter.*)
At every ten mile's end thou hast a horse.
Take this (*Gives money*); away! and never see me more.
Light. No?
Y. Mor. No;
Unless thou bring me news of Edward's death.
Light. That will I quickly do. Farewell, my lord.
Exit.
Y. Mor. The prince I rule, the queen do I command,
And with a lowly congee[92] to the ground,
The proudest lords salute me as I pass;
I seal, I cancel, I do what I will.
Fear'd am I more than lov'd;—let me be fear'd,
And when I frown, make all the court look pale.
I view the prince with Aristarchus' eyes,
Whose looks were as a breeching[93] to a boy.
They thrust upon me the protectorship,
And sue to me for that that I desire.
While at the council-table, grave enough,
And not unlike a bashful puritan,
First I complain of imbecility,
Saying it is *onus quam gravissimum*,[94]
Till being interrupted by my friends,
Suscepi that *provinciam*[95] as they term it;
And to conclude, I am Protector now.
Now is all sure: the queen and Mortimer
Shall rule the realm, the king, and none rule us.
Mine enemies will I plague, my friends advance;
And what I list command who dare control?
Major sum quam cui possit fortuna nocere.[96]
And that this be the coronation-day,
It pleaseth me, and Isabel the queen.
(*Trumpets within.*)
The trumpets sound, I must go take my place.

Enter the young King, Queen Isabella, the Archbishop of Canterbury, Champion and Nobles.

A. of Cant. Long live King Edward, by the grace of God
King of England and Lord of Ireland!
Cham. If any Christian, Heathen, Turk, or Jew,
Dares but affirm that Edward 's not true king,
And will avouch his saying with the sword,
I am the champion that will combat him.
Y. Mor. None comes; sound trumpets!
(*Trumpets sound.*)
K. Edw. Third. Champion, here 's to thee.
(*Gives a purse.*)
Q. Isab. Lord Mortimer, now take him to your charge.

Enter Soldiers, with Kent prisoner.

Y. Mor. What traitor have we there with blades and bills?
Sol. Edmund, the Earl of Kent.
K. Edw. Third. What hath he done?
Sol. 'A would have taken the king away perforce,
As we were bringing him to Killingworth.
Y. Mor. Did you attempt this rescue, Edmund? Speak.
Kent. Mortimer, I did; he is our king,
And thou compell'st this prince to wear the crown.

91 a small roll of fine linen.
92 bow.
93 whipping.
94 "the heaviest burden possible."
95 "I have undertaken that office."
96 "I am too great for fortune to injure." (Ovid, *Metamorphoses*, vi. 195.)

Y. Mor. Strike off his head! he shall have martial law.
Kent. Strike off my head! Base traitor, I defy thee!
K. Edw. Third. My lord, he is my uncle, and shall live.
Y. Mor. My lord, he is your enemy, and shall die.
Kent. Stay, villains!
K. Edw. Third. Sweet mother, if I cannot pardon him,
Entreat my Lord Protector for his life.
Q. Isab. Son, be content; I dare not speak a word.
K. Edw. Third. Nor I, and yet methinks I should command;
But, seeing I cannot, I'll entreat for him—
My lord, if you will let my uncle live,
I will requite it when I come to age.
Y. Mor. 'T is for your highness' good, and for the realm's.—
How often shall I bid you bear him hence?
Kent. Art thou king? Must I die at thy command?
Y. Mor. At our command—Once more, away with him!
Kent. Let me but stay and speak; I will not go.
Either my brother or his son is king,
And none of both them thirst for Edmund's blood:
And therefore, soldiers, whither will you hale me?

Soldiers hale Kent away, and carry him to be beheaded.

K. Edw. Third. What safety may I look for at his hands,
If that my uncle shall be murdered thus?
Q. Isab. Fear not, sweet boy, I'll guard thee from thy foes;
Had Edmund liv'd, he would have sought thy death.
Come, son, we'll ride a-hunting in the park.
K. Edw. Third. And shall my uncle Edmund ride with us?
Q. Isab. He is a traitor; think not on him. Come.

Exeunt.

SCENE 5. *Berkeley Castle.*

Enter Matrevis and Gurney.

Mat. Gurney, I wonder the king dies not,
Being in a vault up to the knees in water,
To which the channels of the castle run,
From whence a damp continually ariseth,
That were enough to poison any man,
Much more a king brought up so tenderly.
Gur. And so do I, Matrevis: yesternight
I opened but the door to throw him meat,
And I was almost stifled with the savor.
Mat. He hath a body able to endure
More than we can inflict: and therefore now
Let us assail his mind another while.
Gur. Send for him out thence, and I will anger him.
Mat. But stay, who 's this?

Enter Lightborn.

Light. My Lord Protector greets you.
(*Gives letter.*)
Gur. What 's here? I know not how to construe it.
Mat. Gurney, it was left unpointed for the nonce;[97]
"Edwardum occidere nolite timere:"
That 's his meaning.
Light. Know ye this token? I must have the king.
(*Gives token.*)
Mat. Aye, stay awhile, thou shalt have answer straight.—
(*Aside.*) This villain 's sent to make away the king.
Gur. (*Aside.*) I thought as much.
Mat. (*Aside.*) And when the murder 's done,
See how he must be handled for his labor.
Pereat iste![98] Let him have the king.—
What else? Here is the keys, this is the lock;[99]
Do as you are commanded by my lord.
Light. I know what I must do; get you away;
Yet be not far off, I shall need your help.
See that in the next room I have a fire;
And get me a spit, and let it be red-hot.
Mat. Very well.
Gur. Need you anything besides?
Light. What else? A table and a featherbed.
Gur. That 's all?
Light. Aye, aye; so, when I call you bring it in.
Mat. Fear not thou that.
Gur. Here 's a light, to go into the dungeon.
(*Gives a light, and exit with Matrevis.*)
Light. So now

97 purposely. 98 "let this man die." 99 Qq. *lake*.

Must I about this gear;[1] ne'er was there any
So finely handled as this king shall be.
For here 's a place indeed, with all my heart!
K. Edw. Who 's there? What light is that?
Wherefore com'st thou?
Light. To comfort you, and bring you joyful news.
K. Edw. Small comfort finds poor Edward in thy looks.
Villain, I know thou com'st to murder me.
Light. To murder you, my most gracious lord!
Far is it from my heart to do you harm.
The queen sent me to see how you were used,
For she relents at this your misery:
And what eyes can refrain from shedding tears,
To see a king in this most piteous state?
K. Edw. Weep'st thou already? List awhile to me
And then thy heart, were it as Gurney's is,
Or as Matrevis', hewn from the Caucasus,
Yet will it melt, ere I have done my tale.
This dungeon where they keep me is the sink
Wherein the filth of all the castle falls.
Light. O villains!
K. Edw. And there in mire and puddle have I stood
This ten days' space; and, lest that I should sleep,
One plays continually upon a drum.
They give me bread and water, being a king;
So that, for want of sleep and sustenance,
My mind 's distempered, and my body 's numb'd,
And whether I have limbs or no I know not.
O, would my blood dropp'd out from every vein,
As doth this water from my tattered robes!
Tell Isabel, the queen, I look'd not thus,
When for her sake I ran at tilt in France,
And there unhors'd the Duke of Cleremont.
Light. O speak no more, my lord! this breaks my heart.
Lie on this bed, and rest yourself awhile.
K. Edw. These looks of thine can harbor nought but death:
I see my tragedy written in thy brows.
Yet stay awhile; forbear thy bloody hand,
And let me see the stroke before it comes,
That even then when I shall lose my life,
My mind may be more steadfast on my God.
Light. What means your highness to mistrust me thus?
K. Edw. What mean'st thou to dissemble with me thus?
Light. These hands were never stain'd with innocent blood,
Nor shall they now be tainted with a king's.
K. Edw. Forgive my thought for having such a thought.
One jewel have I left; receive thou this.
(*Giving jewel.*)
Still fear I, and I know that what 's the cause,
But every joint shakes as I give it thee.
O, if thou harbor'st murder in thy heart,
Let this gift change thy mind, and save thy soul!
Know that I am a king: O at that name
I feel a hell of grief! Where is my crown?
Gone, gone! and do I remain alive?
Light. You 're overwatched,[2] my lord; lie down and rest.
K. Edw. But that grief keeps me waking, I should sleep;
For not these ten days have these eyelids clos'd.
Now as I speak they fall, and yet with fear
Open again. O wherefore sitt'st thou here?
Light. If you mistrust me, I 'll begone, my lord.
K. Edw. No, no, for if thou mean'st to murder me,
Thou wilt return again, and therefore stay.
Light. He sleeps.
K. Edw. (*Waking.*) O let me not die yet! Stay, O stay a while!
Light. How now, my lord?
K. Edw. Something still buzzeth in mine ears,
And tells me if I sleep I never wake;
This fear is that which makes me tremble thus.

[1] business.

[2] worn out with waking.

And therefore tell me, wherefore art thou come?
Light. To rid thee of thy life.—Matrevis, come!

Enter Matrevis and Gurney.

K. Edw. I am too weak and feeble to resist:—
Assist me, sweet God, and receive my soul!
Light. Run for the table.
K. Edw. O spare me, or despatch me in a trice.
(*Matrevis brings in a table.*)
Light. So, lay the table down, and stamp on it,
But not too hard, lest that you bruise his body.
(*King Edward is murdered.*)
Mat. I fear me that this cry will raise the town,
And therefore, let us take horse and away.
Light. Tell me, sirs, was it not bravely done?
Gur. Excellent well; take this for thy reward.
(*Gurney stabs Lightborn.*)
Come, let us cast the body in the moat,
And bear the king's to Mortimer our lord:
Away!

Exeunt with the bodies.

SCENE 6. *The Palace, London.*

Enter Young Mortimer and Matrevis.

Y. Mor. Is't done, Matrevis, and the murderer dead?
Mat. Aye, my good lord; I would it were undone!
Y. Mor. Matrevis, if thou now growest penitent
I'll be thy ghostly father; therefore choose,
Whether thou wilt be secret in this,
Or else die by the hand of Mortimer.
Mat. Gurney, my lord, is fled, and will, I fear,
Betray us both; therefore let me fly.
Y. Mor. Fly to the savages!
Mat. I humbly thank your honor.

Exit.

Y. Mor. As for myself, I stand as Jove's huge tree,
And others are but shrubs compar'd to me.
All tremble at my name, and I fear none;
Let's see who dare impeach me for his death!

Enter Queen Isabella.

Q. Isab. Ah, Mortimer, the king my son hath news
His father's dead, and we have murdered him!
Y. Mor. What if he have? The king is yet a child.
Q. Isab. Aye, but he tears his hair, and wrings his hands,
And vows to be reveng'd upon us both.
Into the council-chamber he is gone,
To crave the aid and succor of his peers.
Ay me! see here he comes, and they with him.
Now, Mortimer, begins our tragedy.

Enter King Edward the Third, Lords and Attendants.

1 Lord. Fear not, my lord, know that you are a king.
K. Edw. Third. Villain!—
Y. Mor. How now, my lord!
K. Edw. Third. Think not that I am frighted with thy words!
My father's murdered through thy treachery;
And thou shalt die, and on his mournful hearse
Thy hateful and accursed head shall lie,
To witness to the world, that by thy means
His kingly body was too soon interr'd.
Q. Isab. Weep not, sweet son!
K. Edw. Third. Forbid me not to weep, he was my father;
And, had you lov'd him half so well as I,
You could not bear his death thus patiently.
But you, I fear, conspir'd with Mortimer.
1 Lord. Why speak you not unto my lord the king?
Y. Mor. Because I think scorn to be accus'd.
Who is the man dares say I murdered him?
K. Edw. Third. Traitor! in me my loving father speaks,
And plainly saith, 't was thou that murd'redst him.
Y. Mor. But has your grace no other proof than this?

K. Edw Third. Yes, if this be the hand of Mortimer.
(*Showing letter.*)
Y. Mor. (*Aside.*) False Gurney hath betray'd me and himself.
Q. Isab. (*Aside.*) I fear'd as much; murder cannot be hid.
Y. Mor. It is my hand; what gather you by this?
K. Edw. Third. That thither thou didst send a murderer.
Y. Mor. What murderer? Bring forth the man I sent.
K. Edw. Third. Ah, Mortimer, thou knowest that he is slain;
And so shalt thou be too.—Why stays he here?
Bring him unto a hurdle, drag him forth;
Hang him, I say, and set his quarters up,
But bring his head back presently[3] to me.
Q. Isab. For my sake, sweet son, pity Mortimer!
Y. Mor. Madam, entreat not; I will rather die,
Than sue for life unto a paltry boy.
K. Edw. Third. Hence with the traitor! with the murderer!
Y. Mor. Base Fortune, now I see that in thy wheel
There is a point, to which when men aspire,
They tumble headlong down: that point I touch'd,
And, seeing there was no place to mount up higher,
Why should I grieve at my declining fall?—
Farewell, fair queen; weep not for Mortimer,
That scorns the world, and, as a traveller,
Goes to discover countries yet unknown.
K. Edw. Third. What! suffer you the traitor to delay?
(*Young Mortimer is taken away.*)
Q. Isab. As thou receivedst thy life from me,
Spill not the blood of gentle Mortimer!
K. Edw. Third. This argues that you spilt my father's blood,
Else would you not entreat for Mortimer.
Q. Isab. I spill his blood? No!
K. Edw. Third. Aye, madam, you; for so the rumor runs.
Q. Isab. That rumor is untrue; for loving thee,
Is this report rais'd on poor Isabel.
K. Edw. Third. I do not think her so unnatural.
2 Lord. My lord, I fear me it will prove too true.
K. Edw. Third. Mother, you are suspected for his death,
And therefore we commit you to the Tower
Till further trial may be made thereof;
If you be guilty, though I be your son,
Think not to find me slack or pitiful.
Q. Isab. Nay, to my death, for too long have I liv'd
Whenas my son thinks to abridge my days.
K. Edw. Third. Away with her! her words enforce these tears,
And I shall pity her if she speak again.
Q. Isab. Shall I not mourn for my beloved lord,
And with the rest accompany him to his grave?
2 Lord. Thus, madam, 't is the king's will you shall hence.
Q. Isab. He hath forgotten me; stay, I am his mother.
2 Lord. That boots not; therefore, gentle madam, go.
Q. Isab. Then come, sweet death, and rid me of this grief.
Exit.

Re-enter 1 Lord, with the head of Young Mortimer.

1 Lord. My lord, here is the head of Mortimer.
K. Edw. Third. Go fetch my father's hearse, where it shall lie;
And bring my funeral robes.
Exeunt Attendants.
Accursed head,
Could I have rul'd thee then, as I do now,
Thou had'st not hatched this monstrous treachery!—
Here comes the hearse; help me to mourn, my lords.

Re-enter Attendants with the hearse and funeral robes.

Sweet father, here unto thy murdered ghost
I offer up this wicked traitor's head;
And let these tears, distilling from mine eyes,
Be witness of my grief and innocency.
Exeunt.

[3] immediately.

THOMAS DEKKER

THE SHOEMAKERS' HOLIDAY

Thomas Dekker (c. 1572–1632 or later) was a Londoner, possibly of Dutch descent. His name first appears early in 1598 in the diary of Philip Henslowe, proprietor of the Rose and Fortune theaters. Dekker was one of the most prolific of Henslowe's play-carpenters, for he is mentioned as sole author or collaborator in connection with forty-one plays in the five years 1598–1602. The diary also throws a sad light on Dekker's hand-to-mouth existence, by its records of loans made by Henslowe, sometimes to rescue him from the debtors' prison; there is reason to believe that he was once confined for debt for three years together. From 1603 to 1613 he turned out a series of prose pamphlets, chiefly on London life, vividly informing and forceful in style. He drops out of sight early in the thirties.

The Shoemakers' Holiday is the merriest example of a sort of play very popular with London playgoers of Elizabethan days, the *bourgeois* comedy of London life, — citizens' comedy, it has been called, to distinguish it from the romantic comedy of Shakespeare, the satirical humor-comedy of Ben Jonson, and the tragicomedy of Beaumont and Fletcher. Such plays were written for the most part by dramatists not so fortunate as these men, who had established positions as writers for the high-class theaters such as the Globe and the Blackfriars, and for a better class of auditors than those which filled the more popular houses like the Rose and the Fortune. Dekker, Heywood, and, less representatively, Middleton, are the best known members of a large group of playwrights who thus catered to the theatrical wants of the common people, giving them in large measure pictures of the life which they lived.

The Shoemakers' Holiday was finished by July 15, 1599, when Henslowe enters a payment for it of three pounds — so munificently were his fortunate authors rewarded! It may have been written in the six weeks immediately preceding, for on May 30, Dekker had received payment for *Agamemnon;* the enormous difference in subject-matter between two consecutive plays is suggestive of the versatility of the popular playwright, as the short interim is of the forced draught under which he worked. The play was performed by the Admiral's Men at the Rose; its success we may infer from the fact that on New Year's Day of 1600 it was acted at court, a distinction which had been granted on December 27, 1599, to another of Dekker's plays, the masque-like *Old Fortunatus.* Thus even the playwrights of the people had their occasional social triumphs. Dekker took his story from a collection of three prose tales on shoemakers, *The Gentle Craft* (1598), by Thomas Deloney, whose position in the narrative-fiction of the day as a purveyor of romantically rose-colored, pseudo-realistic tales for the consumption of middle-class readers somewhat corresponds to that of Dekker in the drama. From the second of these stories, that of the two royal shoemakers Crispine and Crispinianus, Dekker obtained the background of war, the motive of the Lacy-Rose story, the shoe-fitting episode, Rose's flight to the Lord Mayor's, and the final royal sanction of their marriage. From Deloney's account of Simon Eyre, the madcap shoemaker of Tower Street, come practically all the figures and details of the Eyre story, as well as the suggestion for the Ralph-Jane story, although Dekker reverses Deloney's situation of the lost wife returning from France to prevent her husband from marrying again. There are in the play three threads of incident — a romantic love-story, a *bourgeois* love-story, and a picture of London life and manners supplying the background. The binding of the three Dekker accomplishes skilfully enough according to Elizabethan standards. The relations of Lacy and Ralph, first as soldiers enlisted for the French war, second as employees of Eyre, unite the first two. Hammon, appearing first as the suitor of Rose, later as the lover of Jane, furnishes another bond. It is Lacy, as Hans, who is responsible for Eyre's first commercial success, which leads to Eyre's election as sheriff. The Lord Mayor's entertainment of the new sheriff and his apprentices at Old Ford brings Lacy and Rose together again, and prepares for Rose's escape to Eyre's protection at the end of act four. The two love-threads are firmly knotted by Firk's tricks for the weddings, and the complications of the last act are extensive and yet natural. In other words, the play holds together well — it is Dekker's most coherent piece of plotting. The weakest link in the chain, the point where credulity is subjected to the severest strain, is the opportune removal by death of several aldermen who stood between Eyre and the Lord Mayoralty (IV. iv), but it would be captious to inquire too closely into the ways of Providence when it comes to the aid of a hard-pressed dramatist.

The romantic plot has been criticised as

thin. True, of incident it contains not much. Right here, however, is shown Dekker's dramatic instinct. The really notable part of the play, what every reader remembers, is not the story of Lacy and Rose, pretty though it be, but the scenes of London life. Now by itself the story of Simon Eyre's rise to fame and fortune is not dramatic at all, consisting simply of a fortunate investment, a consequent election as sheriff, a rapid promotion to the Lord Mayoralty. The people of this group are thoroughly well done. Eyre, Margery, Firk, Hodge, have vitality enough to carry three or four plots, but by themselves they furnish only characterization. The wittiest comedy of manners grows tedious if its people do nothing but talk — as may be learned from no less a person than Ben Jonson. Dekker accordingly gets all the fun he can out of the personalities and mannerisms of his trades-people, and uses the people of the love-stories for incident. As far as character-drawing goes, on the other hand, Lacy and Rose are not much more than sketched in comparison with the robust modeling of the comic group. They are sufficiently developed to make their actions seem natural and that is all that we require. Then, for the purpose of strengthening plot, of adding complication, Dekker introduces the *bourgeois* love-story, with its sentimental rather than romantic tinge. Is not this proportioned use of incident and character much the same sort of work that Shakespeare does in his best chronicle-histories, *Henry IV*, let us say? Taken by itself the story of the Percys' rebellion in *1 Henry IV*, although it contains the essential contrast between Prince Hal and Hotspur, is neither rich in incident nor particularly interesting. Shakespeare therefore adds the comic group of Falstaff and his associates, with little story of their own, but firmly characterized, helping to characterize the prince, and supplying with their bustling comedy an illusion of action to fill the gaps in the main plot. The whole thing is a matter of proportion, and Dekker's play stands the test of analysis pretty well.

It is for its rollicking presentation of London life that we chiefly value *The Shoemakers' Holiday*. The picture it gives of the comfortable position of middle-class trades-people, the pride in honest labor and the possibilities of reward, the pleasant relations between master and men, the friendly intercourse between court and city, between blue blood and red — making due allowances for the dramatist's privilege of selection — somehow impresses us as being essentially true. The hearty feeling of national well-being is that of the years after the Armada, for, though the action is ostensibly set in the time of Henry V, it is the life of his own day that Dekker reflects. For his intimate acquaintance with city customs and manners Dekker needed no information from Deloney. He was a Londoner born and bred, a citizen of no mean city, and proud of his heritage. The author of books like *The Gull's Hornbook* (that inimitable series of directions to the country youth how to conduct himself in tavern, play house, the aisles of Paul's Cathedral), *The Bellman of London* and *Lanthorn and Candlelight*, with their exposures of rascality of every sort, and *The Wonderful Year*, with its memorable pictures of the plague of 1603, knew only too well the seamy side of city life. But in our play he writes only for the glory of the city and its craftsmen. He is in his happiest mood and the warm human sympathy evident in nearly all his work finds expression in the gusto with which he portrays the shoemaker and his group.

The genial humor of the play, its warm friendliness, distinguishes it from the realistic work of Jonson and Middleton. Eyre, in his mannerisms, reminds us somewhat of Jonson's humor comedy, but assuredly he is no humor type. His manner of speech represents merely the ebullient vitality of the man; it is not a temperamental crotchet, a genuine warp of character setting him apart from his fellows, like Morose's aversion to noise in *The Silent Woman*, or Kitely's jealousy in *Every Man in His Humor*. He is, therefore, not one-sided, as Jonson's people so frequently are, but is well-rounded and true to human nature. Nor has Dekker's work the satirical undertone of Jonson's. Jonson, like the classic authors, writes with the moral end of teaching virtue by making folly ridiculous. Sometimes, in deed, as in *Volpone*, the depiction of folly is so searching that it becomes downright castigation of vice, and the play almost loses the feeling of comedy. Dekker, except in his allegorical *Old Fortunatus*, is nothing of the reformer or conscious moralist. Jonson, on the whole, does not approve of his fellow-men; Dekker loves them, and smiles at their foibles with the large tolerance of the true humorist. So sure is Jonson of his moral rectitude, so confident of his superior taste, that his attitude toward his audience is usually contemptuous; Dekker sets out with no other purpose than to entertain, and is frankly pleased in giving pleasure. With Middleton, Dekker has more in common. Though Middleton deals with the same sort of material as does Jonson, he comes to his work with no moral preoccupation, but purely as the artist. He sets life before us as he sees it, without telling us what to think of it, and is for that reason the greater realist of the two. More of a realist, indeed, than Dekker, who is a good deal of a romanticist in his confidence in the fundamental goodness of human nature. Almost always there is in Dekker a touch of romance and of honest sentiment which the comedies of Middleton, brilliant but hard, lack. Less skilful than Middleton in plot-construction, as a creator of character he is, in comedy at least, Middleton's superior.

What we remember from Middleton is the story, the ingenious intrigue, and the social background; he created no characters so sympathetic or of such enduring vitality as Eyre, Friscobaldo in *The Honest Whore*, and the heroine in *Patient Grissil.* Middleton and Dekker part company most widely in this matter of sympathy with the life about them, and the sympathetic display of the author's personality in his work; where Middleton completely effaces himself, always in Dekker's plays we feel the man himself, cheery, friendly, lovable.

THE SHOEMAKERS' HOLIDAY, OR THE GENTLE CRAFT

BY THOMAS DEKKER

NAMES OF THE CHARACTERS

THE KING.
THE EARL OF CORNWALL.
SIR HUGH LACY, *Earl of Lincoln.*
ROWLAND LACY, *alias* HANS, } *his Nephews.*
ASKEW, } *his Nephews.*
SIR ROGER OATELY, *Lord Mayor of London.*
Master HAMMON, } *Citizens of London.*
Master WARNER, } *Citizens of London.*
Master SCOTT, } *Citizens of London.*
SIMON EYRE, *the Shoemaker.*
ROGER, *called* HODGE, } EYRE'S *Journeymen.*
FIRK, } EYRE'S *Journeymen.*
RALPH, } EYRE'S *Journeymen.*
LOVELL, *a Courtier.*
DODGER, *a Servant to the* EARL OF LINCOLN.
A Dutch Skipper.
A Boy.
ROSE, *Daughter of* SIR ROGER.
SYBIL, *her Maid.*
MARGERY, *Wife of* SIMON EYRE.
JANE, *Wife of* RALPH.
Courtiers Attendants, Officers, Soldiers, Hunters, Shoemakers, Apprentices, Servants.

Scene.—London and Old Ford.

THE PROLOGUE

As it was pronounced before the Queen's Majesty

As wretches in a storm, expecting day,
With trembling hands and eyes cast up to heaven,
Make prayers the anchor of their conquer'd hopes,
So we, dear goddess, wonder of all eyes,
Your meanest vassals, through mistrust and fear
To sink into the bottom of disgrace
By our imperfect pastimes, prostrate thus
On bended knees, our sails of hope do strike,
Dreading the bitter storms of your dislike.
Since then, unhappy men, our hap is such
That to ourselves ourselves no help can bring,
But needs must perish, if your saint-like ears,
Locking the temple where all mercy sits,
Refuse the tribute of our begging tongues;
Oh, grant, bright mirror of true chastity,
From those life-breathing stars, your sun-like eyes,
One gracious smile; for your celestial breath
Must send us life, or sentence us to death.

ACT I.

SCENE 1. *A street in London.*

Enter the Lord Mayor and the Earl of Lincoln.

Linc. My lord mayor, you have sundry times
Feasted myself and many courtiers more;
Seldom or never can we be so kind
To make requital of your courtesy.
But leaving this, I hear my cousin Lacy
Is much affected to [1] your daughter Rose.

L. Mayor. True, my good lord, and she loves him so well
That I mislike her boldness in the chase.

Linc. Why, my lord mayor, think you it then a shame,
To join a Lacy with an Oateley's name?

L. Mayor. Too mean is my poor girl for his high birth;
Poor citizens must not with courtiers wed,

[1] inclined to.

Who will in silks and gay apparel spend
More in one year than I am worth, by far:
Therefore your honor need not doubt[2] my girl.

Linc. Take heed, my lord, advise you what you do!
A verier unthrift lives not in the world,
Than is my cousin;[3] for I'll tell you what:
'T is now almost a year since he requested
To travel countries for experience.
I furnisht him with coin, bills of exchange,
Letters of credit, men to wait on him,
Solicited my friends in Italy
Well to respect him. But, to see the end,
Scant had he journey'd through half Germany,
But all his coin was spent, his men cast off,
His bills embezzl'd,[4] and my jolly coz,[5]
Asham'd to show his bankrupt presence here,
Became a shoemaker in Wittenberg,
A goodly science for a gentleman
Of such descent! Now judge the rest by this:
Suppose your daughter have a thousand pound,
He did consume me more in one half year:
And make him heir to all the wealth you have
One twelvemonth's rioting will waste it all.
Then seek, my lord, some honest citizen
To wed your daughter to.

L. Mayor. I thank your lordship.
(*Aside.*) Well, fox, I understand your subtilty.—
As for your nephew, let your lordship's eye
But watch his actions, and you need not fear,
For I have seen my daughter far enough.
And yet your cousin Rowland might do well,
Now he hath learn'd an occupation:
And yet I scorn to call him son-in-law.

Linc. Aye, but I have a better trade for him.
I thank his grace, he hath appointed him
Chief colonel of all those companies
Must'red in London and the shires about,
To serve his highness in those wars of France.
See where he comes!—

Enter Lovell, Lacy, and Askew.

Lovell, what news with you?

Lovell. My Lord of Lincoln, 't is his highness' will,
That presently[6] your cousin ship for France
With all his powers; he would not for a million,
But they should land at Dieppe within four days.

Linc. Go certify his grace, it shall be done.

Exit Lovell.

Now, cousin Lacy, in what forwardness
Are all your companies?

Lacy. All well prepar'd.
The men of Hertfordshire lie at Mile-end,
Suffolk and Essex train in Tothill-fields,
The Londoners and those of Middlesex,
All gallantly prepar'd in Finsbury,
With frolic spirits long for their parting hour.

L. Mayor. They have their imprest,[7] coats, and furniture;[8]
And, if it please your cousin Lacy come
To the Guildhall, he shall receive his pay;
And twenty pounds besides my brethren
Will freely give him, to approve our loves
We bear unto my lord, your uncle here.

Lacy. I thank your honor.

Linc. Thanks, my good lord mayor.

L. Mayor. At the Guildhall we will expect your coming.

Exit.

Linc. To approve your loves to me? No, subtilty.
Nephew, that twenty pound he doth bestow
For joy to rid you from his daughter Rose.
But, cousins both, now here are none but friends,
I would not have you cast an amorous eye
Upon so mean a project as the love
Of a gay, wanton, painted citizen.
I know, this churl even in the height of scorn

2 suspect.
3 *Cousin* was used of any relative outside the immediate family.
4 wasted.
5 cousin.
6 at once.
7 advance-pay.
8 equipment.

Doth hate the mixture of his blood with thine.
I pray thee, do thou so! Remember, coz,
What honorable fortunes wait on thee.
Increase the king's love, which so brightly shines,
And gilds thy hopes. I have no heir but thee,—
And yet not thee, if with a wayward spirit
Thou start from the true bias[9] of my love.

Lacy. My lord, I will for honor, not desire
Of land or livings, or to be your heir,
So guide my actions in pursuit of France,
As shall add glory to the Lacies' name.

Linc. Coz, for those words here 's thirty portagues,[10]
And, nephew Askew, there 's a few for you.
Fair Honor, in her loftiest eminence,
Stays in France for you, till you fetch her thence.
Then, nephews, clap swift wings on your designs.
Begone, begone, make haste to the Guildhall;
There presently I 'll meet you. Do not stay:
Where honor beckons[11] shame attends delay.

Exit.

Askew. How gladly would your uncle have you gone!

Lacy. True, coz, but I 'll o'erreach his policies.
I have some serious business for three days,
Which nothing but my presence can dispatch.
You, therefore, cousin, with the companies,
Shall haste to Dover; there I 'll meet with you:
Or, if I stay past my prefixed time,
Away for France; we 'll meet in Normandy.
The twenty pounds my lord mayor gives to me
You shall receive, and these ten portagues,
Part of mine uncle's thirty. Gentle coz,
Have care to our great charge; I know, your wisdom
Hath tried itself in higher consequence.

Askew. Coz, all myself am yours: yet have this care,
To lodge in London with all secrecy;
Our uncle Lincoln hath, besides his own,
Many a jealous eye, that in your face
Stares only to watch means for your disgrace.

Lacy. Stay, cousin, who be these?

Enter Simon Eyre, Margery, his wife, Hodge, Firk, Jane, and Ralph with a piece [of leather].

Eyre. Leave whining, leave whining! Away with this whimp'ring, this puling, these blubb'ring tears, and these wet eyes! I 'll get thy husband discharg'd, I warrant thee, sweet Jane; go to!

Hodge. Master, here be the captains.

Eyre. Peace, Hodge; husht, ye knave, husht!

Firk. Here be the cavaliers and the colonels, master.

Eyre. Peace, Firk; peace, my fine Firk! Stand by with your pishery-pashery, away! I am a man of the best presence; I 'll speak to them, an[12] they were Popes. —Gentlemen, captains, colonels, commanders! Brave men, brave leaders, may it please you to give me audience. I am Simon Eyre, the mad shoemaker of Tower Street; this wench with the mealy mouth that will never tire, is my wife, I can tell you; here 's Hodge, my man and my foreman; here 's Firk, my fine firking[13] journeyman, and this is blubbered Jane. All we come to be suitors for this honest Ralph. Keep him at home, and as I am a true shoemaker and a gentleman of the gentle craft, buy spurs yourself, and I 'll find ye boots these seven years.

Marg. Seven years, husband?

Eyre. Peace, midriff, peace! I know what I do. Peace!

Firk. Truly, master cormorant,[14] you shall do God good service to let Ralph and his wife stay together. She 's a young new-married woman; if you take her husband away from her a-night, you undo her; she may beg in the daytime; for he 's as good a workman at a prick and an awl as any is in our trade.

Jane. O let him stay, else I shall be undone!

Firk. Aye, truly, she shall be laid at one side like a pair of old shoes else, and be occupied for no use.

---

9 inclination.
10 a gold coin of Portugal, worth about four pounds.
11 Qq. *become.*
12 if.
13 frisky.
14 quibble on *colonel.*

Lacy. Truly, my friends, it lies not in my power:
The Londoners are press'd,[15] paid, and set forth
By the lord mayor; I cannot change a man.

Hodge. Why, then you were as good be a corporal as a colonel, if you cannot discharge one good fellow; and I tell you true, I think you do more than you can answer, to press a man within a year and a day of his marriage.

Eyre. Well said, melancholy Hodge; gramercy, my fine foreman.

Marg. Truly, gentlemen, it were ill done for such as you, to stand so stiffly against a poor young wife, considering her case: she is new-married, but let that pass. I pray, deal not roughly with her: her husband is a young man, and but newly ent'red; but let that pass.

Eyre. Away with your pishery-pashery, your pols and your edipols![16] Peace, midriff; silence, Cicely Bumtrinket! Let your head[17] speak.

Firk. Yea, and the horns too, master.

Eyre. Too soon, my fine Firk, too soon! Peace, scoundrels! See you this man? Captains, you will not release him? Well, let him go; he 's a proper shot; let him vanish! Peace, Jane, dry up thy tears, they 'll make his powder dankish.[18] Take him, brave men; Hector of Troy was an hackney to him, Hercules and Termagant[19] scoundrels. Prince Arthur's Round-table—by the lord of Ludgate!—ne'er fed such a tall,[20] such a dapper swordsman; by the life of Pharaoh, a brave, resolute swordman! Peace, Jane! I say no more, mad knaves.

Firk. See, see, Hodge, how my master raves in commendation of Ralph!

Hodge. Ralph, th' art a gull[21] by this hand, an thou goest not.

Askew. I am glad, good Master Eyre, it is my hap
To meet so resolute a soldier.
Trust me, for your report and love to him,
A common slight regard shall not respect him.

Lacy. Is thy name Ralph?

Ralph. Yes, sir.

Lacy. Give me thine hand;
Thou shalt not want, as I am a gentleman.
Woman, be patient; God, no doubt, will send
Thy husband safe again; but he must go,
His country's quarrel says it shall be so.

Hodge. Th' art a gull, by my stirrup, if thou dost not go. I will not have thee strike thy gimlet into these weak vessels; prick thine enemies, Ralph.

Enter Dodger.

Dodger. My lord, your uncle on the Tower-hill
Stays with the lord-mayor and the aldermen,
And doth request you, with all speed you may,
To hasten thither.

Askew. Cousin, let 's go.

Lacy. Dodger, run you before, tell them we come.—

Exit Dodger.

This Dodger is mine uncle's parasite,
The arrant'st varlet that e'er breath'd on earth;
He sets more discord in a noble house
By one day's broaching of his pickthank tales,[22]
Than can be salv'd again in twenty years,
And he, I fear, shall go with us to France,
To pry into our actions.

Askew. Therefore, coz,
It shall behove you to be circumspect.

Lacy. Fear not, good cousin.—Ralph, hie to your colors.

Exeunt Lacy and Askew.

Ralph. I must, because there 's no remedy;
But, gentle master and my loving dame,
As you have always been a friend to me,
So in mine absence think upon my wife.

Jane. Alas, my Ralph.

Marg. She cannot speak for weeping.

Eyre. Peace, you crack'd[23] groats, you mustard tokens,[24] disquiet not the brave soldier. Go thy ways, Ralph!

Jane. Aye, aye, you bid him go; what shall I do
When he is gone?

Firk. Why, be doing with me or my fellow Hodge; be not idle.

Eyre. Let me see thy hand, Jane. This

15 impressed into service.
16 Classical oaths by Pollux; applied by Eyre to Margery's repetitions.
17 i.e. master.
18 damp.
19 supposed to be a god of the Saracens.
20 brave.
21 fool.
22 tales told to curry favor.
23 spoiled.
24 Tokens given to purchasers of mustard, entitling them to a small repayment when a certain number had been accumulated; transferred, a term of contempt. (N. E. D.)

fine hand, this white hand, these pretty fingers must spin, must card, must work; work, you bombast cotton-candle-quean;[25] work for your living, with a pox to you. —Hold thee, Ralph, here's five sixpences for thee; fight for the honor of the gentle craft, for the gentlemen shoemakers, the courageous cordwainers, the flower of St. Martin's, the mad knaves of Bedlam, Fleet Street, Tower Street and Whitechapel; crack me the crowns of the French knaves; a pox on them, crack them; fight, by the lord of Ludgate; fight, my fine boy!

Firk. Here, Ralph, here's three twopences; two carry into France, the third shall wash our souls at parting, for sorrow is dry. For my sake, firk the *Basa mon cues.*[26]

Hodge. Ralph, I am heavy at parting; but here's a shilling for thee. God send[27] thee to cram thy slops[28] with French crowns, and thy enemies' bellies with bullets.

Ralph. I thank you, master, and I thank you all.
Now, gentle wife, my loving, lovely Jane,
Rich men, at parting, give their wives rich gifts,
Jewels and rings to grace their lily hands.
Thou know'st our trade makes rings for women's heels:
Here take this pair of shoes, cut out by Hodge,
Stitch'd by my fellow Firk, seam'd by myself,
Made up and pink'd[29] with letters for thy name.
Wear them, my dear Jane, for thy husband's sake,
And every morning when thou pull'st them on,
Remember me, and pray for my return.
Make much of them; for I have made them so
That I can know them from a thousand mo.

Drum sounds. Enter the Lord Mayor, the Earl of Lincoln, Lacy, Askew, Dodger, and Soldiers. They pass over the stage; Ralph falls in amongst them; Firk and the rest cry "Farewell," etc., and so exeunt.

ACT II.

Scene 1. *A garden at Old Ford.*[30]

Enter Rose, alone, making a garland.

Rose. Here sit thou down upon this flow'ry bank
And make a garland for thy Lacy's head.
These pinks, these roses, and these violets,
These blushing gilliflowers, these marigolds,
The fair embroidery of his coronet,
Carry not half such beauty in their cheeks,
As the sweet count'nance of my Lacy doth.
O my most unkind father! O my stars,
Why lower'd you so at my nativity,
To make me love, yet live robb'd of my love?
Here as a thief am I imprisoned
For my dear Lacy's sake within those walls,
Which by my father's cost were builded up
For better purposes. Here must I languish
For him that doth as much lament, I know,
Mine absence, as for him I pine in woe.

Enter Sybil.

Sybil. Good morrow, young mistress. I am sure you make that garland for me, against[31] I shall be Lady of the Harvest.

Rose. Sybil, what news at London?

Sybil. None but good; my lord mayor, your father, and master Philpot, your uncle, and Master Scot, your cousin, and Mistress Frigbottom by Doctors' Commons, do all, by my troth, send you most hearty commendations.

Rose. Did Lacy send kind greetings to his love?

Sybil. O yes, out of cry,[32] by my troth. I scant knew him; here 'a wore a scarf; and here a scarf, here a bunch of feathers, and here precious stones and jewels, and a pair of garters,—O, monstrous! like one of our yellow silk curtains at home here in Old Ford House here, in Master Bellymount's chamber. I stood at our door in Cornhill, look'd

25 delicate, pampered creature.
26 uncomplimentary term for the French.
27 grant.
28 loose breeches.
29 pricked.
30 The lord-mayor's country house was in Old Ford, then a suburb, now a part of London.
31 in anticipation of the time when.
32 beyond measure.

at him, he at me indeed, spake to him, but he not to me, not a word; marry go-up, thought I, with a wanion![33] He pass'd by me as proud—Marry foh! are you grown humorous,[34] thought I; and so shut the door, and in I came.

Rose. O Sybil, how dost thou my Lacy wrong!
My Rowland is as gentle as a lamb,
No dove was ever half so mild as he.

Sybil. Mild? yea, as a bushel of stampt crabs.[35] He lookt upon me as sour as verjuice.[36] Go thy ways, thought I, thou may'st be much in my gaskins,[37] but nothing in my nether-stocks.[38] This is your fault, mistress, to love him that loves not you; he thinks scorn to do as he's done to; but if I were as you, I'd cry, "Go by, Jeronimo, go by!"[39]
I'd set mine old debts against my new driblets,
And the hare's foot against the goose giblets,[40]
For if ever I sigh, when sleep I should take,
Pray God I may lose my maidenhead when I wake.

Rose. Will my love leave me then, and go to France?

Sybil. I know not that, but I am sure I see him stalk before the soldiers. By my troth, he is a proper[41] man; but he is proper that proper doth. Let him go snick-up,[42] young mistress.

Rose. Get thee to London, and learn perfectly
Whether my Lacy go to France, or no.
Do this, and I will give thee for thy pains
My cambric apron and my Romish gloves,
My purple stockings and a stomacher.
Say, wilt thou do this, Sybil, for my sake?

Sybil. Will I, quoth'a? At whose suit? By my troth, yes, I'll go. A cambric apron, gloves, a pair of purple stockings, and a stomacher! I'll sweat in purple, mistress, for you; I'll take anything that comes, a' God's name. O rich! a cambric apron! Faith, then have at "up tails all."[43] I'll go jiggy-joggy to London, and be here in a trice, young mistress.
Exit.

Rose. Do so, good Sybil. Meantime wretched I
Will sit and sigh for his lost company.
Exit.

SCENE 2. *A street in London.*

Enter Lacy, like a Dutch Shoemaker.

Lacy. How many shapes have gods and kings devis'd,
Thereby to compass their desired loves!
It is no shame for Rowland Lacy, then,
To clothe his cunning with the gentle craft,
That, thus disguis'd, I may unknown possess
The only happy presence of my Rose.
For her have I forsook my charge in France,
Incurr'd the king's displeasure, and stirr'd up
Rough hatred in mine uncle Lincoln's breast.
O love, how powerful art thou, that canst change
High birth to baseness, and a noble mind
To the mean semblance of a shoemaker!
But thus it must be; for her cruel father,
Hating the single union of our souls,
Has secretly convey'd my Rose from London,
To bar me of her presence; but I trust,
Fortune and this disguise will further me
Once more to view her beauty, gain her sight.
Here in Tower Street with Eyre the shoemaker
Mean I a while to work; I know the trade,
I learnt it when I was in Wittenberg.
Then cheer thy hoping spirits, be not dismay'd,
Thou canst not want: do Fortune what she can,
The gentle craft is living for a man.
Exit.

SCENE 3. *Before Eyre's house.*

Enter Eyre, making himself ready.[44]

Eyre. Where be these boys, these girls,

33 with a vengeance.
34 capricious.
35 crushed crab apples.
36 juice of green fruits.
whole phrase cf.
37 loose breeches.
38 stockings; for the whole phrase cf. *Mother Bombie,* p. 65, n. 19.
39 A line from Kyd's *Spanish Tragedy* which passed into common use.
40 i.e. I'd get a new lover.
41 handsome.
42 go and be hanged!
43 The name of a popular rollicking tune.
44 dressing.

these drabs, these scoundrels? They wallow in the fat brewis [45] of my bounty, and lick up the crumbs of my table, yet will not rise to see my walks cleansed. Come out, you powder-beef [46] queans! What, Nan! what, Madge Mumble-crust! Come out, you fat midriff-swag-belly-whores, and sweep me these kennels [47] that the noisome stench offend not the noses of my neighbors. What, Firk, I say! What, Hodge! Open my shop windows! What, Firk, I say!

Enter Firk.

Firk. O master, is 't you that speak bandog [48] and Bedlam [49] this morning? I was in a dream, and mused what madman was got into the street so early. Have you drunk this morning that your throat is so clear?

Eyre. Ah, well said, Firk; well said, Firk. To work, my fine knave, to work! Wash thy face, and thou 't be more blest.

Firk. Let them wash my face that will eat it. Good master, send for a souse-wife,[50] if you 'll have my face cleaner.

Enter Hodge.

Eyre. Away, sloven! avaunt, scoundrel!—Good-morrow, Hodge; good-morrow, my fine foreman.

Hodge. O master, good-morrow; y' are an early stirrer. Here 's a fair morning.—Good-morrow, Firk, I could have slept this hour. Here 's a brave day towards.[51]

Eyre. Oh, haste to work, my fine foreman, haste to work.

Firk. Master, I am dry as dust to hear my fellow Roger talk of fair weather; let us pray for good leather, and let clowns and ploughboys and those that work in the fields pray for brave days. We work in a dry shop; what care I if it rain?

Enter Margery.

Eyre. How now, Dame Margery, can you see to rise? Trip and go, call up the drabs, your maids.

Marg. See to rise? I hope 't is time enough, 't is early enough for any woman to be seen abroad. I marvel how many wives in Tower Street are up so soon. Gods me, 't is not noon,—here 's a yawling! [52]

Eyre. Peace, Margery, peace! Where 's Cicely Bumtrinket, your maid? She has a privy fault, she farts in her sleep. Call the quean up; if my men want shoe-thread, I 'll swinge her in a stirrup.

Firk. Yet that 's but a dry beating; here 's still a sign of drought.

Enter Lacy, disguised, singing.

Lacy. *Der was een bore van Gelderland,*
Frolick sie byen;
He was als dronck he cold nyet stand,
Upsolce sie byen.
Tap eens de canneken,
Drincke, schone mannekin.[53]

Firk. Master, for my life, yonder 's a brother of the gentle craft; if he bear not Saint Hugh's bones,[54] I 'll forfeit my bones; he 's some uplandish [55] workman: hire him, good master, that I may learn some gibble-gabble; 't will make us work the faster.

Eyre. Peace, Firk! A hard world! Let him pass, let him vanish; we have journeymen enow. Peace, my fine Firk!

Marg. Nay, nay, y' are best follow your man's counsel; you shall see what will come on 't. We have not men enow, but we must entertain every butter-box; [56] but let that pass.

Hodge. Dame, 'fore God, if my master follow your counsel, he 'll consume little beef. He shall be glad of men an he can catch them.

Firk. Aye, that he shall.

Hodge. 'Fore God, a proper man, and I warrant, a fine workman. Master, farewell; dame, adieu; if such a man as he cannot find work, Hodge is not for you. (*Offers to go.*)

Eyre. Stay, my fine Hodge.

Firk. Faith, an your foreman go, dame, you must take a journey to seek a new journeyman; if Roger remove, Firk follows. If Saint Hugh's bones shall not be set a-work, I may prick mine awl in the walls, and go play. Fare ye well, master; good-bye, dame.

Eyre. Tarry, my fine Hodge, my brisk

45 beef broth.
46 salted beef.
47 gutters.
48 watch dog.
49 madman; is it you that is growling like a madman here?
50 a woman who sold pickled pigs' feet and ears.
51 in prospect.
52 bawling.
53 Hans speaks a pseudo-Dutch.
There was a boor from Gelderland,
Jolly they be;
He was so drunk he could not stand,
Drunken (?) they be:
Clink then the cannikin,
Drink, pretty mannikin!
(Neilson.)
54 St. Hugh was the patron saint of shoemakers; his bones were said to have been made into shoemaker's tools.
55 from the country.
56 Dutchman.

foreman! Stay, Firk! Peace, pudding-broth! By the lord of Ludgate, I love my men as my life. Peace, you gallimaufry![57] Hodge, if he want work, I 'll hire him. One of you to him; stay,—he comes to us.

Lacy. *Goeden dach, meester, ende, u, vro, oak.*[58]

Firk. Nails,[59] if I should speak after him without drinking, I should choke. And you, friend Oake, are you of the gentle craft?

Lacy. *Yaw, yaw, ik bin den skomawker.*[60]

Firk. *Den skomaker,* quoth'a! And hark you, *skomaker,* have you all your tools, a good rubbing-pin, a good stopper, a good dresser, your four sorts of awls, and your two balls of wax, your paring knife, your hand-and-thumb-leathers, and good St. Hugh's bones to smooth up your work?

Lacy. *Yaw, yaw; be niet vorveard. Ik hab all de dingen voour mack skooes groot and cleane.*[61]

Firk. Ha, ha! Good master, hire him; he 'll make me laugh so that I shall work more in mirth than I can in earnest.

Eyre. Hear ye, friend, have ye any skill in the mystery[62] of cordwainers?

Lacy. *Ik weet niet wat yow seg; ich verstaw you niet.*[63]

Firk. Why, thus, man: (*Imitating by gesture a shoemaker at work.*) *Ich verste u niet,* quoth 'a.

Lacy. *Yaw, yaw, yaw; ick can dat wel doen.*[64]

Firk. *Yaw, yaw!* He speaks yawing like a jackdaw that gapes to be fed with cheese-curds. Oh, he 'll give a villanous pull at a can of double-beer; but Hodge and I have the vantage, we must drink first, because we are the eldest journeymen.

Eyre. What is thy name?

Lacy. Hans—Hans Meulter.

Eyre. Give me thy hand; th' art welcome. —Hodge, entertain him; Firk, bid him welcome; come, Hans. Run, wife, bid your maids, your trullibubs,[65] make ready my fine men's breakfasts. To him, Hodge!

Hodge. Hans, th' art welcome; use thyself friendly, for we are good fellows; if not, thou shalt be fought with, wert thou bigger than a giant.

Firk. Yea, and drunk with, wert thou Gargantua.[66] My master keeps no cowards, I tell thee.—Ho, boy, bring him an heel-block, here 's a new journeyman.

Enter Boy.

Lacy. *O, ich wersto you; ich moet een halve dossen cans betaelen; here, boy, nempt dis skilling, tap eens freelicke.*[67]

Exit Boy.

Eyre. Quick, snipper-snapper, away! Firk, scour thy throat; thou shalt wash it with Castilian liquor.

Enter Boy.

Come, my last of the fives,[68] give me a can. Have to thee, Hans; here, Hodge; here, Firk; drink, you mad Greeks, and work like true Trojans, and pray for Simon Eyre, the shoemaker.—Here, Hans, and th' art welcome.

Firk. Lo, dame, you would have lost a good fellow that will teach us to laugh. This beer came hopping in well.

Marg. Simon, it is almost seven.

Eyre. Is 't so, Dame Clapper-dudgeon?[69] Is 't seven a clock, and my men 's breakfast not ready? Trip and go, you sous'd conger,[70] away! Come, you mad hyperboreans; follow me, Hodge; follow me, Hans, come after, my fine Firk; to work a while, and then to breakfast.

Exit.

Firk. Soft! *Yaw, yaw,* good Hans, though my master have no more wit but to call you afore me, I am not so foolish to go behind you, I being the elder journeyman.

Exeunt.

SCENE 4. *A field near Old Ford.*

Halloaing within. Enter Warner and Hammon, like Hunters.

Ham. Cousin, beat every brake, the game's not far;
This way with winged feet he fled from death,

---

57 a dish of hashed meats.
58 *Good-day, master, and you, goodwife, too.*
59 God's nails; an oath.
60 *Yes, yes, I am a shoemaker.*
61 *Yes, yes; be not afraid. I have everything to make boots big and little.*
62 trade.
63 *I don't know what you say; I don't understand you.*
64 *Yes, yes; I can do that well.*
65 slatterns.
66 A gluttonous giant in Rabelais' satire of that name.
67 *O, I understand you; I must pay for half-a-dozen cans; here, boy, take this shilling, tap once freely.*
68 my number five last, a small size.
69 Margery's tongue makes as much noise as a beggar's clap-dish.
70 conger-eel.

Whilst the pursuing hounds, scenting his steps,
Find out his highway to destruction.
Besides, the miller's boy told me even now,
He saw him take soil,[71] and he halloaed him,
Affirming him to have been so embost [72]
That long he could not hold.

Warn. If it be so,
'T is best we trace these meadows by Old Ford.

A noise of Hunters within. Enter a Boy.

Ham. How now, boy? Where's the deer? Speak, saw'st thou him?

Boy. O yea; I saw him leap through a hedge, and then over a ditch, then at my lord mayor's pale, over he skipt me, and in he went me, and "holla" the hunters cried, and "there, boy; there, boy!" But there he is, a' mine honesty.

Ham. Boy, Godamercy. Cousin, let's away; I hope we shall find better sport to-day.

Exeunt.

SCENE 5. *The garden at Old Ford.*

Sounds of hunting within. Enter Rose and Sybil.

Rose. Why, Sybil, wilt thou prove a forester?

Sybil. Upon some, no. Forester? Go by; no, faith, mistress. The deer came running into the barn through the orchard and over the pale; I wot well, I lookt as pale as a new cheese to see him. But whip, says Goodman Pinclose, up with his flail, and our Nick with a prong, and down he fell, and they upon him, and I upon them. By my troth, we had such sport; and in the end we ended him; his throat we cut, flay'd him, unhorn'd him, and my lord mayor shall eat of him anon, when he comes.

(*Horns sound within.*)

Rose. Hark, hark, the hunters come; y' are best take heed,
They'll have a saying to you for this deed.

Enter Hammon, Warner, Huntsmen, and Boy.

Ham. God save you, fair ladies.

Sybil. Ladies! O gross! [73]

Warn. Came not a buck this way?

Rose. No, but two does.

Ham. And which way went they? Faith, we'll hunt at those.

Sybil. At those? Upon some, no. When, can you tell?

Warn. Upon some, aye.

Sybil. Good Lord!

Warn. Wounds! [74] Then farewell!

Ham. Boy, which way went he?

Boy. This way, sir, he ran.

Ham. This way he ran indeed, fair Mistress Rose;
Our game was lately in your orchard seen.

Warn. Can you advise, which way he took his flight?

Sybil. Follow your nose; his horns will guide you right.

Warn. T' art a mad wench.

Sybil. O, rich!

Rose. Trust me, not I.
It is not like that the wild forest-deer
Would come so near to places of resort;
You are deceiv'd, he fled some other way.

Warn. Which way, my sugar-candy, can you show?

Sybil. Come up, good honeysops, upon some, no.

Rose. Why do you stay, and not pursue your game?

Sybil. I'll hold my life, their hunting-nags be lame.

Ham. A deer more dear is found within this place.

Rose. But not the deer, sir, which you had in chase.

Ham. I chas'd the deer, but this dear chaseth me.

Rose. The strangest hunting that ever I see.
But where's your park?

(*She offers to go away.*)

Ham. 'T is here: O stay!

Rose. Impale me, and then I will not stray.

Warn. They wrangle, wench; we are more kind than they.

Sybil What kind of hart is that dear heart you seek?

Warn. A hart, dear heart.

Sybil. Who ever saw the like?

Rose. To lose your heart, is't possible you can?

Ham. My heart is lost.

Rose. Alack, good gentleman!

71 cover. 72 exhausted. 73 stupid. 74 God's wounds; an oath.

Ham. This poor lost heart would I wish you might find.

Rose. You, by such luck, might prove your hart a hind.

Ham. Why, Luck had horns, so have I heard some say.

Rose. Now, God, an 't be his will, send Luck into your way.

Enter the Lord Mayor and Servants.

L. Mayor. What, Master Hammon? Welcome to Old Ford!

Sybil. Gods pittikins,[75] hands off, sir! Here 's my lord.

L. Mayor. I hear you had ill-luck, and lost your game.

Ham. 'T is true, my lord.

L. Mayor. I am sorry for the same. What gentleman is this?

Ham. My brother-in-law.

L. Mayor. Y' are welcome both; sith Fortune offers you
Into my hands, you shall not part from hence,
Until you have refresht your wearied limbs.
Go, Sybil, cover the board! You shall be guest
To no good cheer, but even a hunter's feast.

Ham. I thank your lordship.—Cousin, on my life,
For our lost venison I shall find a wife.

Exeunt all but Mayor.

L. Mayor. In, gentlemen; I'll not be absent long.—
This Hammon is a proper gentleman,
A citizen by birth, fairly allied;
How fit an husband were he for my girl!
Well, I will in, and do the best I can,
To match my daughter to this gentleman.

Exit.

ACT III.

Scene 1. *A room in Eyre's house.*

Enter Lacy as Hans, Skipper, Hodge, and Firk.

Skip. *Ick sal yow wat seggen, Hans; dis skip dat comen from Candy, is all vol, by Got's sacrament, van sugar, civet, almonds, cambrick, end alle dingen, towsand towsand ding. Nempt it, Hans, nempt it vor u meester. Daer be de bils van laden. Your meester Simon Eyre sal hae good copen. Wat seggen yow, Hans?* [76]

Firk. *Wat seggen de reggen de copen, slopen*—laugh, Hodge, laugh!

Hans. *Mine liever broder Firk, bringt Meester Eyre tot det signe un Swannekin; daer sal yow finde dis skipper end me. Wat seggen yow, broder Firk? Doot it, Hodge.*[77] *Come, Skipper.*

Exeunt.

Firk. Bring him, quoth you? Here 's no knavery, to bring my master to buy a ship worth the lading of two or three hundred thousand pounds. Alas, that 's nothing; a trifle, a bauble, Hodge.

Hodge. The truth is, Firk, that the merchant owner of the ship dares not show his head, and therefore this skipper that deals for him, for the love he bears to Hans, offers my master Eyre a bargain in the commodities. He shall have a reasonable day of payment; he may sell the wares by that time, and be an huge gainer himself.

Firk. Yea, but can my fellow Hans lend my master twenty porpentines as an earnest penny?

Hodge. Portagues, thou wouldst say; here they be, Firk; hark, they jingle in my pocket like St. Mary Overy's bells.[78]

Enter Eyre and Margery.

Firk. Mum, here comes my dame and my master. She 'll scold, on my life, for loitering this Monday; but all 's one, let them all say what they can, Monday 's our holiday.

Marg. You sing, Sir Sauce, but I beshrew your heart.
I fear, for this your singing we shall smart.

Firk. Smart for me, dame; why, dame, why?

Hodge. Master, I hope you 'll not suffer my dame to take down your journeymen.

Firk. If she take me down, I 'll take her

75 by God's pity.

76 *I'll tell you what, Hans; this ship that is come from Candia, is quite full, by God's sacrament, of sugar, civet, almonds, cambric, and all things; a thousand thousand things. Take it, Hans, take it for your master. There are the bills of lading. Your master, Simon Eyre, shall have a good bargain. What say you, Hans?*

77 *My dear brother Firk, bring Master Eyre to the sign of the Swan; there shall you find the skipper and me. What say you, brother Firk? Do it, Hodge.*

78 The Church of St. Mary Overy was at the Borough end of London Bridge.

up; yea, and take her down too, a button-hole lower.

Eyre. Peace, Firk; not I, Hodge; by the life of Pharaoh, by the lord of Ludgate, by this beard, every hair whereof I value at a king's ransom, she shall not meddle with you.—Peace, you bombast-cotton-candle-quean; away, queen of clubs; quarrel not with me and my men, with me and my fine Firk; I'll firk you, if you do.

Marg. Yea, yea, man, you may use me as you please; but let that pass.

Eyre. Let it pass, let it vanish away; peace! Am I not Simon Eyre? Are not these my brave men, brave shoemakers, all gentlemen of the gentle craft? Prince am I none, yet am I nobly born, as being the sole son of a shoemaker. Away, rubbish! vanish, melt! melt, like kitchen-stuff!

Marg. Yea, yea, 't is well; I must be call'd rubbish, kitchen-stuff, for a sort [79] of knaves.

Firk. Nay, dame, you shall not weep and wail in woe for me. Master, I'll stay no longer; here's an inventory of my shop-tools. Adieu, master; Hodge, farewell.

Hodge. Nay, stay, Firk; thou shalt not go alone.

Marg. I pray, let them go; there be moe maids than Mawkin, more men than Hodge, and more fools than Firk.

Firk. Fools? Nails! if I tarry now, I would my guts might be turn'd to shoe-thread.

Hodge. And if I stay, I pray God I may be turn'd to a Turk, and set in Finsbury [80] for boys to shoot at.—Come, Firk.

Eyre. Stay, my fine knaves, you arms of my trade, you pillars of my profession. What, shall a tittle-tattle's words make you forsake Simon Eyre?—Avaunt, kitchen-stuff! Rip, you brown-bread Tannikin; [81] out of my sight! Move me not! Have not I ta'en you from selling tripes in Eastcheap, and set you in my shop, and made you hail-fellow with Simon Eyre, the shoemaker? And now do you deal thus with my journeymen? Look, you powder-beef-quean, on the face of Hodge; here's a face for a lord.

Firk. And here's a face for any lady in Christendom.

Eyre. Rip, you chitterling,[82] avaunt! Boy, bid the tapster of the Boar's Head fill me a dozen cans of beer for my journeymen.

Firk. A dozen cans? O, brave! Hodge, now I'll stay.

Eyre. (*In a low voice to the Boy.*) An the knave fills any more than two, he pays for them. (*Exit Boy.*) —A dozen cans of beer for my journeymen. (*Re-enter Boy.*) Here, you mad Mesopotamians, wash your livers with this liquor. Where be the odd ten?—No more, Madge, no more.—Well said.[83] Drink and to work!—What work dost thou, Hodge? What work?

Hodge. I am a making a pair of shoes for my lord mayor's daughter, Mistress Rose.

Firk. And I a pair of shoes for Sybil, my lord's maid. I deal with her.

Eyre. Sybil? Fie, defile not thy fine workmanly fingers with the feet of kitchenstuff and basting-ladles. Ladies of the court, fine ladies, my lads, commit their feet to our apparelling; put gross work to Hans. Yark [84] and seam, yark and seam!

Firk. For yarking and seaming let me alone, an I come to 't.

Hodge. Well, master, all this is from the bias.[85] Do you remember the ship my fellow Hans told you of? The skipper and he are both drinking at the Swan. Here be the portagues to give earnest. If you go through with it, you cannot choose but be a lord at least.

Firk. Nay, dame, if my master prove not a lord, and you a lady, hang me.

Marg. Yea, like enough, if you may loiter and tipple thus.

Firk. Tipple, dame? No, we have been bargaining with Skellum Skanderbag: [86] can you Dutch spreaken for a ship of silk Cyprus, laden with sugar-candy?

Enter Boy with a velvet coat and an Alderman's gown. Eyre puts them on.

Eyre. Peace, Firk; silence, Tittle-tattle! Hodge, I'll go through with it. Here's a seal-ring, and I have sent for a guarded gown [87] and a damask cassock. See

79 pack.
80 Finsbury was a practice ground for archery.
81 Dutchwoman.
82 sausage; addressed to Margery.
83 well done.
84 jerk.
85 beside the point.
86 German: *Schelm*, a scoundrel. Skanderbag, or Scander Beg (i.e. Lord Alexander), a Turkish name for John Kastriota, the Albanian hero, who freed his country from the yoke of the Turks (1443–1467). (Neilson.)
87 a robe ornamented with guards or facings.

where it comes; look here, Maggy; help me, Firk; apparel me, Hodge; silk and satin, you mad Philistines, silk and satin.

Firk. Ha, ha, my master will be as proud as a dog in a doublet, all in beaten[88] damask and velvet.

Eyre. Softly, Firk, for rearing[89] of the nap, and wearing threadbare my garments. How dost thou like me, Firk? How do I look, my fine Hodge?

Hodge. Why, now you look like yourself, master. I warrant you, there 's few in the city but will give you the wall,[90] and come upon you with[91] the right worshipful.

Firk. Nails, my master looks like a threadbare cloak new turn'd and drest. Lord, Lord, to see what good raiment doth! Dame, dame, are you not enamored?

Eyre. How say'st thou, Maggy, am I not brisk? Am I not fine?

Marg. Fine? By my troth, sweetheart, very fine! By my troth, I never likt thee so well in my life, sweetheart; but let that pass. I warrant, there be many women in the city have not such handsome husbands, but only for their apparel; but let that pass too.

Re-enter Hans and Skipper.

Hans. *Godden day, mester. Dis be de skipper dat heb de skip van marchandice; de commodity ben good; nempt it, master, nempt it.*[92].

Eyre. Godamercy, Hans; welcome, skipper. Where lies this ship of merchandise?

Skip. *De skip ben in revere; dor be van sugar, civet, almonds, cambrick, and a towsand towsand tings, gotz sacrament; nempt it, mester: ye sal heb good copen.*[93]

Firk. To him, master! O sweet master! O sweet wares! Prunes, almonds, sugar-candy, carrot-roots, turnips, O brave fatting meat! Let not a man buy a nutmeg but yourself.

Eyre. Peace, Firk! Come, skipper, I 'll go aboard with you.—Hans, have you made him drink?

Skip. *Yaw, yaw, ic heb veale gedrunck.*[94]

Eyre. Come, Hans, follow me. Skipper, thou shalt have my countenance in the city.

Exeunt.

Firk. *Yaw heb veale gedrunck,* quoth 'a. They may well be called butter-boxes, when they drink fat veal and thick beer too. But come, dame, I hope you 'll chide us no more.

Marg. No, faith, Firk; no, perdy,[95] Hodge. I do feel honor creep upon me, and which is more, a certain rising in my flesh; but let that pass.

Firk. Rising in your flesh do you feel, say you? Aye, you may be with child, but why should not my master feel a rising in his flesh, having a gown and a gold ring on? But you are such a shrew, you 'll soon pull him down.

Marg. Ha, ha! prithee, peace! Thou mak'st my worship laugh; but let that pass. Come, I 'll go in; Hodge, prithee, go before me; Firk, follow me.

Firk. Firk doth follow: Hodge, pass out in state.

Exeunt

SCENE 2. *London: a room in Lincoln's house.*

Enter the Earl of Lincoln and Dodger.

Linc. How now, good Dodger, what 's the news in France?

Dodger. My lord, upon the eighteenth day of May
The French and English were prepar'd to fight;
Each side with eager fury gave the sign
Of a most hot encounter. Five long hours
Both armies fought together; at the length
The lot of victory fell on our side.
Twelve thousand of the Frenchmen that day died,
Four thousand English, and no man of name
But Captain Hyam and young Ardington,
Two gallant gentlemen, I knew them well.

Linc. But Dodger, prithee, tell me, in this fight
How did my cousin Lacy bear himself?

88 stamped.
89 ruffling.
90 yield precedence.
91 salute.
92 *Good day, master. This is the skipper that has the ship of merchandise; the commodity is good; take it, master, take it.*
93 *The ship lies in the river; there are sugar, civet, almonds, cambric, and a thousand thousand things. By God's sacrament, take it, master; you shall have a good bargain.*
94 *Yes, yes, I have drunk well.*
95 Fr. *Par Dieu.*

Dodger. My lord, your cousin Lacy was not there.
Linc. Not there?
Dodger. No, my good lord.
Linc. Sure, thou mistakest.
I saw him shipp'd, and a thousand eyes beside
Were witnesses of the farewells which he gave,
When I, with weeping eyes, bid him adieu.
Dodger, take heed.
Dodger. My lord, I am advis'd
That what I spake is true: to prove it so,
His cousin Askew, that supplied his place,
Sent me for him from France, that secretly
He might convey himself thither.
Linc. Is 't even so?
Dares he so carelessly venture his life
Upon the indignation of a king?
Has he despis'd my love, and spurn'd those favors
Which I with prodigal hand pour'd on his head?
He shall repent his rashness with his soul;
Since of my love he makes no estimate,
I 'll make him wish he had not known my hate.
Thou hast no other news?
Dodger. None else, my lord.
Linc. None worse I know thou hast.—Procure the king
To crown his giddy brows with ample honors,
Send him chief colonel, and all my hope
Thus to be dash'd! But 't is in vain to grieve,
One evil cannot a worse relieve.
Upon my life, I have found out his plot;
That old dog, Love, that fawn'd upon him so,
Love to that puling girl, his fair-cheek'd Rose,
The lord mayor's daughter, hath distracted him,
And in the fire of that love's lunacy
Hath he burnt up himself, consum'd his credit,
Lost the king's love, yea, and I fear, his life,
Only to get a wanton to his wife,
Dodger, it is so.
Dodger. I fear so, my good lord.
Linc. It is so—nay, sure it cannot be!
I am at my wits' end. Dodger!
Dodger. Yea, my lord.
Linc. Thou art acquainted with my nephew's haunts,
Spend this gold for thy pains; go seek him out.
Watch at my lord mayor's—there if he live,
Dodger, thou shalt be sure to meet with him.
Prithee, be diligent.—Lacy, thy name
Liv'd once in honor, now 't is dead in shame.—
Be circumspect.
Dodger. I warrant you, my lord.
Exeunt.

SCENE 3. *London: a room in the Lord Mayor's house.*

Enter the Lord Mayor and Master Scott.

L. Mayor. Good Master Scott, I have been bold with you,
To be a witness to a wedding-knot
Betwixt young Master Hammon and my daughter.
O, stand aside; see where the lovers come.

Enter Master Hammon and Rose.

Rose. Can it be possible you love me so?
No, no, within those eyeballs I espy
Apparent likelihoods of flattery.
Pray now, let go my hand.
Ham. Sweet Mistress Rose,
Misconstrue not my words, nor misconceive
Of my affection, whose devoted soul
Swears that I love thee dearer than my heart.
Rose. As dear as your own heart? I judge it right,
Men love their hearts best when they 're out of sight.
Ham. I love you, by this hand.
Rose. Yet hands off now!
If flesh be frail, how weak and frail 's your vow!
Ham. Then by my life I swear.
Rose. Then do not brawl;
One quarrel loseth wife and life and all.
Is not your meaning thus?
Ham. In faith, you jest.
Rose. Love loves to sport; therefore leave love, y' are best.

L. Mayor. What? square [96] they, Master Scott?
Scott. Sir, never doubt,
Lovers are quickly in, and quickly out.
Ham. Sweet Rose, be not so strange in fancying me.
Nay, never turn aside, shun not my sight:
I am not grown so fond, to fond [97] my love
On any that shall quit it with disdain;
If you will love me, so;—if not, farewell.
L. Mayor. Why, how now, lovers, are you both agreed?
Ham. Yes, faith, my lord.
L. Mayor. 'T is well, give me your hand,
Give me yours, daughter.—How now, both pull back!
What means this, girl?
Rose. I mean to live a maid.
Ham. (*Aside.*) But not to die one; pause, ere that be said.
L. Mayor. Will you still cross me, still be obstinate?
Ham. Nay, chide her not, my lord, for doing well;
If she can live an happy virgin's life,
'T is far more blessed than to be a wife.
Rose. Say, sir, I cannot: I have made a vow,
Whoever be my husband, 't is not you.
L. Mayor. Your tongue is quick; but Master Hammon, know,
I bade you welcome to another end.
Ham. What, would you have me pule and pine and pray,
With "lovely lady," "mistress of my heart,"
"Pardon your servant," and the rhymer play,
Railing on Cupid and his tyrant's-dart;
Or shall I undertake some martial spoil,
Wearing your glove at tourney and at tilt,
And tell how many gallants I unhors'd—
Sweet, will this pleasure you?
Rose. Yea, when wilt begin?
What, love rhymes, man? Fie on that deadly sin!
L. Mayor. If you wilt have her, I'll make her agree.
Ham. Enforced love is worse than hate to me.
(*Aside.*) There is a wench keeps shop in the Old Change,
To her will I—it is not wealth I seek.
I have enough—and will prefer her love
Before the world.—My good lord mayor, adieu.
Old love for me, I have no luck with new.
Exit.
L. Mayor. Now, mammet,[98] you have well behav'd yourself,
But you shall curse your coyness if I live.—
Who 's within there? See you convey your mistress
Straight to th' Old Ford! I'll keep you straight enough,
Fore God, I would have sworn the puling girl
Would willingly accepted Hammon's love;
But banish him, my thoughts!—Go, minion, in!
Exit Rose.
Now tell me, Master Scott, would you have thought
That Master Simon Eyre, the shoemaker,
Had been of wealth to buy such merchandise?
Scott. 'T was well, my lord, your honor and myself
Grew partners with him; for your bills of lading
Show that Eyre's gains in one commodity
Rise at the least to full three thousand pound,
Besides like gain in other merchandise.
L. Mayor. Well, he shall spend some of his thousands now,
For I have sent for him to the Guildhall.

Enter Eyre.

See, where he comes.—Good morrow, Master Eyre.
Eyre. Poor Simon Eyre, my lord, your shoemaker.
L. Mayor. Well, well, it likes [99] yourself to term you so.

Enter Dodger.

Now Master Dodger, what 's the news with you?
Dodger. I'd gladly speak in private to your honor.
L. Mayor. You shall, you shall.—Master Eyre and Master Scott,
I have some business with this gentleman;
I pray, let me entreat you to walk before

96 quarrel. 97 found; a pun upon *fond*. 98 puppet. 99 pleases.

To the Guildhall; I'll follow presently.
Master Eyre, I hope ere noon to call you sheriff.

Eyre. I would not care, my lord, if you might call me
King of Spain.—Come, Master Scott.

Exeunt Eyre and Scott.

L. Mayor. Now, Master Dodger, what 's the news you bring?

Dodger. The Earl of Lincoln by me greets your lordship,
And earnestly requests you, if you can,
Inform him where his nephew Lacy keeps.

L. Mayor. Is not his nephew Lacy now in France?

Dodger. No, I assure your Lordship, but disguis'd
Lurks here in London.

L. Mayor. London? Is 't even so?
It may be; but upon my faith and soul,
I know not where he lives, or whether he lives:
So tell my Lord of Lincoln. Lurk in London?
Well, Master Dodger, you perhaps may start him;
Be but the means to rid him into France,
I'll give you a dozen angels[1] for your pains:
So much I love his honor, hate his nephew.
And, prithee, so inform thy lord from me.

Dodger. I take my leave.

Exit Dodger.

L. Mayor. Farewell, good Master Dodger.
Lacy in London? I dare pawn my life,
My daughter knows thereof, and for that cause
Deni'd young Master Hammon in his love.
Well, I am glad I sent her to Old Ford.
Gods Lord, 't is late! to Guildhall I must hie;
I know my brethren stay[2] my company.

Exit.

SCENE 4. *London: a room in Eyre's house.*

Enter Firk, Margery, Lacy as Hans, and Roger.

Marg. Thou goest too fast for me, Roger. O, Firk!

Firk. Aye, forsooth.

Marg. I pray thee, run—do you hear?—run to Guildhall, and learn if my husband, Master Eyre, will take that worshipful vocation of Master Sheriff upon him. Hie thee, good Firk.

Firk. Take it? Well, I go; an he should not take it, Firk swears to forswear him. Yes, forsooth, I go to Guildhall.

Marg. Nay, when? Thou art too compendious and tedious.

Firk. O rare, your excellence is full of eloquence; how like a new cart-wheel my dame speaks, and she looks like an old musty ale-bottle[3] going to scalding.

Marg. Nay, when? Thou wilt make me melancholy.

Firk. God forbid your worship should fall into that humor;—I run.

Exit.

Marg. Let me see now, Roger and Hans.

Hodge. Aye, forsooth, dame—mistress, I should say, but the old term so sticks to the roof of my mouth, I can hardly lick it off.

Marg. Even what thou wilt, good Roger; dame is a fair name for any honest Christian; but let that pass. How dost thou, Hans?

Hans. *Mee tanck you, vro.*[4]

Marg. Well, Hans and Roger, you see, God hath blest your master, and, perdy, if ever he comes to be Master Sheriff of London—as we are all mortal—you shall see, I will have some odd thing or other in a corner for your: I will not be your back-friend;[5] but let that pass. Hans, pray thee, tie my shoe.

Hans. *Yaw, ic sal, vro.*[6]

Marg. Roger, thou know'st the length of my foot; as it is none of the biggest, so I thank God, it is handsome enough; prithee, let me have a pair of shoes made, cork, good Roger, wooden heel too.

Hodge. You shall.

Marg. Art thou acquainted with never a farthingale-maker, nor a French hood-maker? I must enlarge my bum, ha, ha! How shall I look in a hood, I wonder! Perdy, oddly, I think.

Hodge. (*Aside.*) As a cat out of a pillory.—Very well, I warrant you, mistress.

Marg. Indeed, all flesh is grass; and, Roger, canst thou tell where I may buy a good hair?

Hodge. Yes, forsooth, at the poulterer's in Gracious Street.

1 coins worth ten shillings.
2 wait for.
3 leather bottle.
4 *I thank you, mistress!*
5 false friend.
6 *Yes I shall, mistress.*

Marg. Thou art an ungracious wag: perdy, I mean a false hair for my periwig.

Hodge. Why, mistress, the next time I cut my beard, you shall have the shavings of it; but they are all true hairs.

Marg. It is very hot, I must get me a fan or else a mask.

Hodge. (*Aside.*) So you had need, to hide your wicked face.

Marg. Fie, upon it, how costly this world's calling is; perdy, but that it is one of the wonderful works of God, I would not deal with it.—Is not Firk come yet? Hans, be not so sad, let it pass and vanish, as my husband's worship says.

Hans. *Ick bin vrolicke, lot see yow soo.*[7]

Hodge. Mistress, will you drink[8] a pipe of tobacco?

Marg. Oh, fie upon it, Roger, perdy! These filthy tobacco-pipes are the most idle slavering baubles that ever I felt. Out upon it! God bless us, men look not like men that use them.

Enter Ralph, being lame.

Hodge. What, fellow Ralph? Mistress, look here, Jane's husband! Why, how now, lame? Hans, make much of him, he 's a brother of our trade, a good workman, and a tall[9] soldier.

Hans. You be welcome, broder.

Marg. Perdy, I knew him not. How dost thou, good Ralph? I am glad to see thee well.

Ralph. I would to God you saw me, dame, as well
As when I went from London into France.

Marg. Trust me, I am sorry, Ralph, to see thee impotent. Lord, how the wars have made him sunburnt! The left leg is not well; 't was a fair gift of God the infirmity took not hold a little higher, considering thou camest from France; but let that pass.

Ralph. I am glad to see you well, and I rejoice
To hear that God hath blest my master so
Since my departure.

Marg. Yea, truly, Ralph, I thank my Maker; but let that pass.

Hodge. And, sirrah Ralph, what news, what news in France?

Ralph. Tell me, good Roger, first, what news in England?
How does my Jane? When didst thou see my wife?
Where lives my poor heart? She 'll be poor indeed,
Now I want limbs to get whereon to feed.

Hodge. Limbs? Hast thou not hands, man? Thou shalt never see a shoemaker want bread, though he have but three fingers on a hand.

Ralph. Yet all this while I hear not of my Jane.

Marg. O Ralph, your wife,—perdy, we know not what 's become of her. She was here a while, and because she was married, grew more stately than became her; I check'd her, and so forth; away she flung, never returned, nor said bye nor bah; and, Ralph, you know, "ka me, ka thee."[10] And, so as I tell ye—— Roger, is not Firk come yet?

Hodge. No, forsooth.

Marg. And so, indeed, we heard not of her, but I hear she lives in London; but let that pass. If she had wanted, she might have opened her case to me or my husband, or to any of my men; I am sure, there 's not any of them, perdy, but would have done her good to his power. Hans, look if Firk be come.

Hans. *Yaw, ik sal, vro.*[11]

Exit Hans.

Marg. And so, as I said—but, Ralph, why dost thou weep? Thou knowest that naked we came out of our mother's womb, and naked we must return; and, therefore, thank God for all things.

Hodge. No, faith, Jane is a stranger here; but, Ralph, pull up a good heart, I know thou hast one. Thy wife, man, is in London; one told me, he saw her a while ago very brave[12] and neat; we 'll ferret her out, an London hold her.

Marg. Alas, poor soul, he 's overcome with sorrow; he does but as I do, weep for the loss of any good thing. But, Ralph, get thee in, call for some meat and drink, thou shalt find me worshipful towards thee.

Ralph. I thank you, dame; since I want limbs and lands,
I 'll trust to God, my good friends, and my hands.

Enter Hans and Firk running.

7 *I am merry; let 's see you so.*
8 smoke.
9 brave
10 scratch me, and I 'll scratch thee.
11 *Yes, I shall, mistress.*
12 fine.

Firk. Run, good Hans! O Hodge, O mistress! Hodge, heave up thine ears; mistress, smug up your looks; on with your best apparel; my master is chosen, my master is called, nay, condemn'd by the cry of the country to be sheriff of the city for this famous year now to come. And, time now being, a great many men in black gowns were askt for their voices and their hands, and my master had all their fists about his ears presently, and they cried "Aye, aye, aye, aye"—and so I came away—

Wherefore without all other grieve
I do salute you, Mistress Shrieve.[13]

Hans. Yaw, my mester is de groot man, de shrieve.

Hodge. Did I not tell you, mistress? Now I may boldly say: Good-morrow to your worship.

Marg. Good-morrow, good Roger. I thank you, my good people all.—Firk, hold up thy hand: here 's a three-penny piece for thy tidings.

Firk. 'T is but three-half-pence, I think. Yes, 't is three-pence, I smell the rose.[14]

Hodge. But, mistress, be rul'd by me, and do not speak so pulingly.

Firk. 'T is her worship speaks so, and not she. No, faith, mistress, speak me in the old key: "To it, Firk"; "there, good Firk"; "ply your business, Hodge"; "Hodge, with a full mouth"; "I 'll fill your bellies with good cheer, till they cry twang."

Enter Eyre wearing a gold chain.

Hans. See, myn liever broder, heer compt my meester.[15]

Marg. Welcome home, Master Shrieve; I pray God continue you in health and wealth.

Eyre. See here, my Maggy, a chain, a gold chain for Simon Eyre. I shall make thee a lady; here 's a French hood for thee; on with it, on with it! dress thy brows with this flap of a shoulder of mutton,[16] to make thee look lovely. Where be my fine men? Roger, I 'll make over my shop and tools to thee; Firk, thou shalt be the foreman; Hans, thou shalt have an hundred for twenty.[17] Be as mad knaves as your master Sim Eyre hath been, and you shall live to be sheriffs of London.—How dost thou like me, Margery? Prince am I none, yet am I princely born. Firk, Hodge, and Hans!

All Three. Aye, forsooth, what says your worship, Master Sheriff?

Eyre. Worship and honor, you Babylonian knaves, for the gentle craft. But I forgot myself, I am bidden by my lord mayor to dinner to Old Ford; he 's gone before, I must after. Come, Madge, on with your trinkets! Now, my true Trojans, my fine Firk, my dapper Hodge, my honest Hans, some device, some odd crotchets, some morris, or such like, for the honor of the gentlemen shoemakers. Meet me at Old Ford, you know my mind. Come, Madge, away. Shut up the shops, knaves, and make holiday.

Exeunt.

Firk. O rare! O brave! Come, Hodge; follow me, Hans;
We 'll be with them for a morris-dance.

Exeunt.

SCENE 5. *A room at Old Ford.*

Enter the Lord Mayor, Rose, Eyre, Margery in a French hood, Sybil, and other Servants.

L. Mayor. Trust me, you are as welcome to Old Ford
As I myself.

Marg. Truly, I thank your lordship

L. Mayor. Would our bad cheer were worth the thanks you give.

Eyre. Good cheer, my lord mayor, fine cheer! A fine house, fine walls, all fine and neat.

L. Mayor. Now, by my troth, I 'll tell thee, Master Eyre,
It does me good, and all my brethren,
That such a madcap fellow as thyself
Is ent'red into our society.

Marg. Aye, but, my lord, he must learn now to put on gravity.

Eyre. Peace, Maggy, a fig for gravity! When I go to Guildhall in my scarlet gown, I 'll look as demurely as a saint, and speak as gravely as a justice of peace; but now I am here at Old Ford, at my good lord mayor's house, let it go by, vanish, Maggy, I 'll be merry; away with flip-flap, these fooleries, these gulleries. What, honey? Prince am I none, yet am I princely born. What says my lord mayor?

13 sheriff.

14 The three-penny silver pieces of Queen Elizabeth had a rose on the obverse side.

15 *See, my dear brothers, here comes my master.*

16 a hood trimmed with fur or sheep's wool.

17 i e. for the twenty portagues lent by Hans.

L. Mayor. Ha, ha, ha! I had rather than a thousand pound, I had an heart but half so light as yours.

Eyre. Why, what should I do, my lord? A pound of care pays not a dram of debt. Hum, let's be merry, whiles we are young; old age, sack and sugar will steal upon us, ere we be aware.

THE FIRST THREE MEN'S SONG [18]

O the month of May, the merry month of May,
So frolic, so gay, and so green, so green, so green!
O, and then did I unto my true love say:
"Sweet Peg, thou shalt be my summer's queen!

"Now the nightingale, the pretty nightingale,
The sweetest singer in all the forest's choir,
Entreats thee, sweet Peggy, to hear thy true love's tale;
Lo, yonder she sitteth, her breast against a briar.

"But O, I spy the cuckoo, the cuckoo, the cuckoo;
See where she sitteth: come away, my joy;
Come away, I prithee: I do not like the cuckoo
Should sing where my Peggy and I kiss and toy."

O the month of May, the merry month of May,
So frolic, so gay, and so green, so green, so green!
And then did I unto my true love say:
"Sweet Peg, thou shalt be my summer's queen!"

L. Mayor. It's well done. Mistress Eyre, pray, give good counsel
To my daughter.

Marg. I hope, Mistress Rose will have the grace to take nothing that's bad.

L. Mayor. Pray God she do; for i' faith, Mistress Eyre,
I would bestow upon that peevish girl
A thousand marks more than I mean to give her
Upon condition she'd be rul'd by me.
The ape still crosseth me. There came of late
A proper gentleman of fair revenues,
Whom gladly I would call son-in-law:
But my fine cockney would have none of him.
You'll prove a coxcomb for it, ere you die:
A courtier, or no man, must please your eye.

Eyre. Be rul'd, sweet Rose: th' art ripe for a man. Marry not with a boy that has no more hair on his face than thou hast on thy cheeks. A courtier, wash, go by, stand not upon pishery-pashery: those silken fellows are but painted images, outsides, outsides, Rose; their inner linings are torn. No, my fine mouse, marry me with a gentleman grocer like my lord mayor, your father; a grocer is a sweet trade: plums, plums. Had I a son or daughter should marry out of the generation and blood of the shoemakers, he should pack. What, the gentle trade is a living for a man through Europe, through the world.

(*A noise within of a tabor and a pipe.*)

L. Mayor. What noise is this?

Eyre. O my lord mayor, a crew of good fellows that for love to your honor are come hither with a morris-dance. Come in, my Mesopotamians, cheerily!

Enter Hodge, Hans, Ralph, Firk, and other Shoemakers, in a morris; after a little dancing, the Lord Mayor speaks.

L. Mayor. Master Eyre, are all these shoemakers?

Eyre. All cordwainers, my good lord mayor.

Rose. (*Aside.*) How like my Lacy looks yond shoemaker!

Hans. (*Aside.*) O that I durst but speak unto my love!

L. Mayor. Sybil, go fetch some wine to make these drink. You are all welcome.

All. We thank your lordship.

(*Rose takes a cup of wine and goes to Hans.*)

Rose. For his sake whose fair shape thou represent'st,
Good friend, I drink to thee.

Hans. *Ic bedancke, good frister.* [19]

Marg. I see, Mistress Rose, you do not want judgment; you have drunk to the properest man I keep.

Firk. Here be some have done their parts to be as proper as he.

L. Mayor. Well, urgent business calls me back to London.
Good fellows, first go in and taste our cheer;

[18] A catch for three voices. The quartos do not indicate the places for the songs.

[19] *I thank you, good maid!*

And to make merry as you homeward go,
Spend these two angels in beer at Stratford-Bow.

Eyre. To these two, my mad lads, Sim Eyre adds another; then cheerily, Firk; tickle it, Hans, and all for the honor of shoemakers.

All go dancing out.

L. Mayor. Come, Master Eyre, let 's have your company.

Exeunt.

Rose. Sybil, what shall I do?

Sybil. Why, what 's the matter?

Rose. That Hans the shoemaker is my love Lacy,
Disguis'd in that attire to find me out.
How should I find the means to speak with him?

Sybil. What, mistress, never fear; I dare venture my maidenhead to nothing, and that 's great odds, that Hans the Dutchman, when we come to London, shall not only see and speak with you, but in spite of all your father's policies steal you away and marry you. Will not this please you?

Rose. Do this, and ever be assured of my love.

Sybil. Away, then, and follow your father to London, lest your absence cause him to suspect something:
To-morrow, if my counsel be obey'd,
I 'll bind you prentice to the gentle trade.

Exeunt.

ACT IV.

Scene 1. *A street in London.*

Jane in a Seamster's shop, working; enter Master Hammon, muffled: he stands aloof.

Ham. Yonder 's the shop, and there my fair love sits.
She 's fair and lovely, but she is not mine.
O, would she were! Thrice have I courted her,
Thrice hath my hand been moist'ned with her hand,
Whilst my poor famisht eyes do feed on that
Which made them famish. I am unfortunate:
I still love one, yet nobody loves me.
I muse in other men what women see
That I so want! Fine Mistress Rose was coy,
And this too curious![20] Oh, no, she is chaste,
And for she thinks me wanton, she denies
To cheer my cold heart with her sunny eyes.
How prettily she works! Oh pretty hand!
Oh happy work! It doth me good to stand
Unseen to see her. Thus I oft have stood
In frosty evenings, a light burning by her,
Enduring biting cold, only to eye her.
One only look hath seem'd as rich to me
As a king's crown; such is love's lunacy.
Muffled I 'll pass along, and by that try
Whether she know me.

Jane. Sir, what is 't you buy?
What is 't you lack, sir, calico, or lawn,
Fine cambric shirts, or bands, what will you buy?

Ham. (*Aside.*) That which thou wilt not sell. Faith, yet I 'll try:—
How do you sell this handkerchief?

Jane. Good cheap.

Ham. And how these ruffs?

Jane. Cheap too.

Ham. And how this band?

Jane. Cheap too.

Ham. All cheap; how sell you then this hand?

Jane. My hands are not to be sold.

Ham. To be given then!
Nay, faith, I come to buy.

Jane. But none knows when.

Ham. Good sweet, leave work a little while; let 's play.

Jane. I cannot live by keeping holiday.

Ham. I 'll pay you for the time which shall be lost.

Jane. With me you shall not be at so much cost.

Ham. Look, how you wound this cloth, so you wound me.

Jane. It may be so.

Ham. 'T is so.

Jane. What remedy?

Ham. Nay, faith, you are too coy.

Jane. Let go my hand.

Ham. I will do any task at your command,
I would let go this beauty, were I not
In mind to disobey you by a power

20 capricious.

That controls kings: I love you!
Jane. So, now part.
Ham. With hands I may, but never with my heart.
In faith, I love you.
Jane. I believe you do.
Ham. Shall a true love in me breed hate in you?
Jane. I hate you not.
Ham. Then you must love.
Jane. I do.
What are you better now? I love not you.
Ham. All this, I hope, is but a woman's fray,
That means, "Come to me," when she cries, "Away!"
In earnest, mistress, I do not jest,
A true chaste love hath ent'red in my breast.
I love you dearly, as I love my life,
I love you as a husband loves a wife;
That, and no other love, my love requires.
Thy wealth, I know, is little; my desires
Thirst not for gold. Sweet, beauteous Jane, what 's mine
Shall, if thou make myself thine, all be thine.
Say, judge, what is thy sentence, life or death?
Mercy or cruelty lies in thy breath.
Jane. Good sir, I do believe you love me well;
For 't is a silly conquest, silly pride
For one like you—I mean a gentleman—
To boast that by his love-tricks he hath brought
Such and such women to his amorous lure;
I think you do not so, yet many do,
And make it even a very trade to woo.
I could be coy, as many women be,
Feed you with sunshine smiles and wanton looks,
But I detest witchcraft; say that I
Do constantly believe you constant have——
Ham. Why dost thou not believe me?
Jane. I believe you;
But yet, good sir, because I will not grieve you
With hopes to taste fruit which will never fall,
In simple truth this is the sum of all:
My husband lives, at least, I hope he lives.
Prest was he to these bitter wars in France;
Bitter they are to me by wanting him.
I have but one heart, and that heart 's his due.
How can I then bestow the same on you?
Whilst he lives, his I live, be it ne'er so poor,
And rather be his wife than a king's whore.
Ham. Chaste and dear woman, I will not abuse thee,
Although it cost my life, if thou refuse me.
Thy husband, prest for France, what was his name?
Jane. Ralph Damport.
Ham. Damport?—Here 's a letter sent
From France to me, from a dear friend of mine,
A gentleman of place; here he doth write
Their names that have been slain in every fight.
Jane. I hope death's scroll contains not my love's name.
Ham. Cannot you read?
Jane. I can.
Ham. Peruse the same.
To my remembrance such a name I read
Amongst the rest. See here.
Jane. Ay me, he 's dead!
He 's dead! If this be true, my dear heart 's slain!
Ham. Have patience, dear love.
Jane. Hence, hence!
Ham. Nay, sweet Jane,
Make not poor sorrow proud with these rich tears.
I mourn thy husband's death, because thou mourn'st.
Jane. That bill is forg'd; 't is sign'd by forgery.
Ham. I 'll bring thee letters sent besides to many,
Carrying the like report: Jane, 't is too true.
Come, weep not: mourning, though it rise from love,
Helps not the mourned, yet hurts them that mourn.
Jane. For God's sake, leave me.
Ham. Whither dost thou turn?
Forget the dead, love them that are alive;
His love is faded, try how mine will thrive.
Jane. 'T is now no time for me to think on love.
Ham. 'T is now best time for you to think on love,
Because your love lives not.
Jane. Though he be dead,
My love to him shall not be buried;

For God's sake, leave me to myself alone.
Ham. 'T would kill my soul, to leave thee drown'd in moan.
Answer me to my suit, and I am gone;
Say to me yea or no.
Jane. No.
Ham. Then farewell!
One farewell will not serve, I come again;
Come, dry these wet cheeks; tell me, faith, sweet Jane,
Yea or no, once more.
Jane. Once more I say no;
Once more be gone, I pray; else will I go.
Ham. Nay, then I will grow rude, by this white hand,
Until you change that cold "no"; here I'll stand
Till by your hard heart——
Jane. Nay, for God's love, peace!
My sorrows by your presence more increase.
Not that you thus are present, but all grief
Desires to be alone; therefore in brief
Thus much I say, and saying bid adieu:
If ever I wed man, it shall be you.
Ham. O blessed voice! Dear Jane, I'll urge no more,
Thy breath hath made me rich.
Jane. Death makes me poor.
Exeunt.

SCENE 2. *London: a street before Hodge's shop.*

Hodge, at his shop-board, Ralph, Firk, Hans, and a Boy at work.

All. Hey, down a down, down derry.
Hodge. Well said, my hearts; ply your work to-day, we loit'red yesterday; to it pell-mell, that we may live to be lord mayors, or aldermen at least.
Firk. Hey, down a down, derry.
Hodge. Well said, i' faith! How say'st thou, Hans, doth not Firk tickle it?
Hans. *Yaw, mester.*
Firk. Not so neither, my organ-pipe squeaks this morning for want of liquoring. Hey, down a down, derry!
Hans. *Forward, Firk, tow best un jolly youngster. Hort, I, mester, ic bid yo, cut me un pair vampres vor Mester Jeffre's boots.*[21]
Hodge. Thou shalt, Hans.
Firk. Master!
Hodge. How now, boy?
Firk. Pray, now you are in the cutting vein, cut me out a pair of counterfeits,[22] or else my work will not pass current; hey, down a down!
Hodge. Tell me, sirs, are my cousin Mistress Priscilla's shoes done?
Firk. Your cousin? No, master; one of your aunts, hang her; let them alone.
Ralph. I am in hand with them; she gave charge that none but I should do them for her.
Firk. Thou do for her? Then 't will be a lame doing, and that she loves not. Ralph, thou might'st have sent her to me, in faith, I would have yarked and firked your Priscilla. Hey, down a down, derry. This gear will not hold.
Hodge. How say'st thou, Firk, were we not merry at Old Ford?
Firk. How, merry! Why, our buttocks went jiggy-joggy like a quagmire. Well, Sir Roger Oatmeal, if I thought all meal of that nature, I would eat nothing but bagpuddings.
Ralph. Of all good fortunes my fellow Hans had the best.
Firk. 'T is true, because Mistress Rose drank to him.
Hodge. Well, well, work apace. They say, seven of the aldermen be dead, or very sick.
Firk. I care not, I'll be none.
Ralph. No, nor I; but then my Master Eyre will come quickly to be lord mayor.
Enter Sybil.
Firk. Whoop, yonder comes Sybil.
Hodge. Sybil, welcome, i' faith; and how dost thou, mad wench?
Firk. Sib-whore, welcome to London.
Sybil. Godamercy, sweet Firk; good lord, Hodge, what a delicious shop you have got! You tickle it, i' faith.
Ralph. Godamercy, Sybil, for our good cheer at Old Ford.
Sybil. That you shall have, Ralph.
Firk. Nay, by the mass, we had tickling cheer, Sybil; and how the plague dost thou and Mistress Rose and my lord mayor? I put the women in first.
Sybil. Well, Godamercy; but God's me, I forget myself, where's Hans the Fleming?

21 *Forward, Firk, thou art a jolly youngster. Hark, ay, master, I pray you cut me a pair of vamps for Master Jeffrey's boots.*

22 vamps: used here for the sake of the pun in *pass current.*

Firk. Hark, butter-box, now you must yelp out some *spreken.*

Hans. *Vat begaie you? Vat vod you, Frister?* [23]

Sybil. Marry, you must come to my young mistress, to pull on her shoes you made last.

Hans. *Vare ben your edle fro, vare ben your mistris?* [24]

Sybil. Marry, here at our London house in Cornhill.

Firk. Will nobody serve her turn but Hans?

Sybil. No, sir. Come, Hans, I stand upon needles.

Hodge. Why then, Sybil, take heed of pricking.

Sybil. For that let me alone. I have a trick in my budget. Come, Hans.

Hans. *Yaw, yaw, ic sall meete yo gane.*[25]

Exeunt Hans and Sybil.

Hodge. Go, Hans, make haste again. Come, who lacks work?

Firk. I, master, for I lack my breakfast; 't is munching-time, and past.

Hodge. Is 't so? Why, then leave work, Ralph. To breakfast! Boy, look to the tools. Come, Ralph; come, Firk.

Exeunt.

Scene 3. *The same.*

Enter a Serving-man.

Serv. Let me see now, the sign of the Last in Tower Street. Mass, yonder 's the house. What, haw! Who 's within?

Enter Ralph.

Ralph. Who calls there? What want you, sir?

Serv. Marry, I would have a pair of shoes made for a gentlewoman against to-morrow morning. What, can you do them?

Ralph. Yes, sir, you shall have them. But what length 's her foot?

Serv. Why, you must make them in all parts like this shoe; but, at any hand, fail not to do them, for the gentlewoman is to be married very early in the morning.

Ralph. How? by this shoe must it be made? By this? Are you sure, sir, by this?

Serv. How, by this? Am I sure, by this? Art thou in thy wits? I tell thee, I must have a pair of shoes, dost thou mark me? A pair of shoes, two shoes, made by this very shoe, this same shoe, against to-morrow morning by four o'clock. Dost understand me? Canst thou do 't?

Ralph. Yes, sir, yes—I—I—I can do 't. By this shoe, you say? I should know this shoe. Yes, sir, yes, by this shoe, I can do 't. Four o'clock, well. Whither shall I bring them?

Serv. To the sign of the Golden Ball in Watling Street; inquire for one Master Hammon, a gentleman, my master.

Ralph. Yea, sir; by this shoe, you say?

Serv. I say, Master Hammon at the Golden Ball; he 's the bridegroom, and those shoes are for his bride.

Ralph. They shall be done by this shoe. Well, well, Master Hammon at the Golden Shoe—I would say, the Golden Ball; very well, very well. But I pray you, sir, where must Master Hammon be married?

Serv. At Saint Faith's Church, under Paul's. But what 's that to thee? Prithee, dispatch those shoes, and so farewell.

Exit.

Ralph. By this shoe, said he. How am I amaz'd
At this strange accident! Upon my life,
This was the very shoe I gave my wife,
When I was prest for France; since when, alas!
I never could hear of her. It is the same,
And Hammon's bride no other but my Jane.

Enter Firk.

Firk. 'Snails,[26] Ralph, thou hast lost thy part of three pots, a countryman of mine gave me to breakfast.

Ralph. I care not; I have found a better thing.

Firk. A thing? Away! Is it a man's thing, or a woman's thing?

Ralph. Firk, dost thou know this shoe?

Firk. No, by my troth; neither doth that know me! I have no acquaintance with it, 't is a mere stranger to me.

Ralph. Why, then I do; this shoe, I durst be sworn,
Once covered the instep of my Jane.
This is her size, her breadth, thus trod my love;

23 *What do you want, what would you, girl?*
24 *Where is your noble lady, where is your mistress?*
25 *Yes, yes, I shall go with you.*
26 God's nails.

These true-love knots I prickt. I hold my life,
By this old shoe I shall find out my wife.

Firk. Ha, ha! Old shoe, that wert new! How a murrain came this ague-fit of foolishness upon thee?

Ralph. Thus, Firk: even now here came a serving-man;
By this shoe would he have a new pair made
Against to-morrow morning for his mistress,
That 's to be married to a gentleman.
And why may not this be my sweet Jane?

Firk. And why may'st not thou be my sweet ass? Ha, ha!

Ralph. Well, laugh and spare not! But the truth is this:
Against to-morrow morning I'll provide
A lusty crew of honest shoemakers,
To watch the going of the bride to church.
If she prove Jane, I'll take her in despite
From Hammon and the devil, were he by.
If it be not my Jane, what remedy?
Hereof I am sure, I shall live till I die,
Although I never with a woman lie.
Exit.

Firk. Thou lie with a woman to build nothing but Cripplegates! Well, God sends fools fortune, and it may be, he may light upon his matrimony by such a device; for wedding and hanging goes by destiny.
Exit.

SCENE 4. *London: a room in the Lord Mayor's house.*

Enter Lacy as Hans and Rose, arm in arm.

Hans. How happy am I by embracing thee!
Oh, I did fear such cross mishaps did reign
That I should never see my Rose again.

Rose. Sweet Lacy, since fair opportunity
Offers herself to further our escape,
Let not too over-fond esteem of me
Hinder that happy hour. Invent the means,
And Rose will follow thee through all the world.

Hans. Oh, how I surfeit with excess of joy,
Made happy by thy rich perfection!
But since thou pay'st sweet interest to my hopes,
Redoubling love on love, let me once more
Like to a bold-fac'd debtor crave of thee
This night to steal abroad, and at Eyre's house,
Who now by death of certain aldermen
Is mayor of London, and my master once,
Meet thou thy Lacy, where in spite of change,
Your father's anger, and mine uncle's hate,
Our happy nuptials will we consummate.

Enter Sybil.

Sybil. Oh God, what will you do, mistress? Shift for yourself, your father is at hand! He 's coming, he 's coming! Master Lacy, hide yourself in my mistress! For God's sake, shift for yourselves!

Hans. Your father come! Sweet Rose, what shall I do?
Where shall I hide me? How shall I escape?

Rose. A man, and want wit in extremity?
Come, come, be Hans still, play the shoemaker,
Pull on my shoe.

Enter the Lord Mayor.

Hans. Mass, and that 's well rememb'red.

Sybil. Here comes your father.

Hans. *Forware, metresse, 't is un good skow, it sal vel dute, or ye sal neit betallen.*[27]

Rose. Oh God, it pincheth me; what will you do?

Hans. (*Aside.*) Your father's presence pincheth, not the shoe.

L. Mayor. Well done; fit my daughter well, and she shall please thee well.

Hans. *Yaw, yaw, ick weit dat well; forware, 't is un good skoo, 't is gimait van neitz leither: se ever, mine here.*[28]

Enter a Prentice.

L. Mayor. I do believe it.—What 's the news with you?

Prentice. Please you, the Earl of Lincoln at the gate
Is newly lighted, and would speak with you.

27 *Indeed, mistress, 't is a good shoe, it shall fit well, or you shall not pay.*

28 *Yes, yes, I know that well; indeed, 't is a good shoe, 't is made of neat's leather; see here, sir!*

L. Mayor. The Earl of Lincoln come to speak with me?
Well, well, I know his errand. Daughter Rose,
Send hence your shoemaker, dispatch, have done!
Syb, make things handsome! Sir boy, follow me.

Exit.

Hans. Mine uncle come! Oh, what may this portend?
Sweet Rose, this of our love threatens an end.

Rose. Be not dismay'd at this; whate'er befall,
Rose is thine own. To witness I speak truth,
Where thou appoint'st the place, I'll meet with thee.
I will not fix a day to follow thee,
But presently [29] steal hence. Do not reply:
Love which gave strength to bear my father's hate,
Shall now add wings to further our escape.

Exeunt.

SCENE 5. *Another room in the same house.*

Enter the Lord Mayor and the Earl of Lincoln.

L. Mayor. Believe me, on my credit, I speak truth:
Since first your nephew Lacy went to France
I have not seen him. It seem'd strange to me,
When Dodger told me that he stay'd behind,
Neglecting the high charge the king imposed.

Lincoln. Trust me, Sir Roger Oateley, I did think
Your counsel had given head to this attempt,
Drawn to it by the love he bears your child.
Here I did hope to find him in your house;
But now I see mine error, and confess,
My judgment wrong'd you by conceiving so.

L. Mayor. Lodge in my house, say you? Trust me, my lord,
I love your nephew Lacy too too dearly,
So much to wrong his honor; and he hath done so,
That first gave him advice to stay from France.
To witness I speak truth, I let you know
How careful I have been to keep my daughter
Free from all conference or speech of him;
Not that I scorn your nephew, but in love
I bear your honor, lest your noble blood
Should by my mean worth be dishonored.

Lincoln. (*Aside.*) How far the churl's tongue wanders from his heart!—
Well, well, Sir Roger Oateley, I believe you,
With more than many thanks for the kind love
So much you seem to bear me. But, my lord,
Let me request your help to seek my nephew,
Whom if I find, I'll straight embark for France.
So shall your Rose be free, my thoughts at rest,
And much care die which now lies in my breast.

Enter Sybil.

Sybil. Oh Lord! Help, for God's sake! My mistress; oh, my young mistress!

L. Mayor. Where is thy mistress? What's become of her?

Sybil. She's gone, she's fled!

L. Mayor. Gone! Whither is she fled?

Sybil. I know not, forsooth; she's fled out of doors with Hans the shoemaker; I saw them scud, scud, scud, apace, apace!

L. Mayor. Which way? What, John! Where be my men? Which way?

Sybil. I know not, an it please your worship.

L. Mayor. Fled with a shoemaker? Can this be true?

Sybil. Oh Lord, sir, as true as God's in Heaven.

Lincoln. Her love turn'd shoemaker? I am glad of this.

L. Mayor. A Fleming butter-box, a shoemaker!
Will she forget her birth, requite my care
With such ingratitude? Scorn'd she young Hammon
To love a honniken,[30] a needy knave?
Well, let her fly, I'll not fly after her.

[29] at once.

[30] Meaning not known.

Let her starve, if she will: she 's none of mine.

Lincoln. Be not so cruel, sir.

Enter Firk with shoes.

Sybil. I am glad she 's scapt.

L. Mayor. I 'll not account of her as of my child.
Was there no better object for her eyes,
But a foul drunken lubber, swill-belly,
A shoemaker? That 's brave!

Firk. Yea, forsooth; 't is a very brave shoe, and as fit as a pudding.

L. Mayor. How now, what knave is this? From whence comest thou?

Firk. No knave, sir. I am Firk the shoemaker, lusty Roger's chief lusty journeyman, and I have come hither to take up the pretty leg of sweet Mistress Rose, and thus hoping your worship is in as good health, as I was at the making hereof, I bid you farewell, yours, Firk.

L. Mayor. Stay, stay, Sir Knave!

Lincoln. Come hither, shoemaker!

Firk. 'T is happy the knave is put before the shoemaker, or else I would not have vouchsafed to come back to you. I am moved, for I stir.

L. Mayor. My lord, this villain calls us knaves by craft.

Firk. Then 't is by the gentle craft, and to call one knave gently, is no harm. Sit your worship merry! Syb, your young mistress—I 'll so bob[31] them, now my Master Eyre is lord mayor of London.

L. Mayor. Tell me, sirrah, whose man are you?

Firk. I am glad to see your worship so merry. I have no maw to this gear, no stomach as yet to a red petticoat. (*Pointing to Sybil.*)

Lincoln. He means not, sir, to woo you to his maid,
But only doth demand whose man you are.

Firk. I sing now to the tune of Rogero.[32] Roger, my fellow, is now my master.

Lincoln. Sirrah, know'st thou one Hans, a shoemaker?

Firk. Hans, shoemaker? Oh yes, stay, yes, I have him. I tell you what, I speak it in secret: Mistress Rose and he are by this time—no, not so, but shortly are to come over one another with "Can you dance the shaking of the sheets?" It is that Hans—(*Aside.*) I 'll so gull[33] these diggers![34]

L. Mayor. Know'st thou, then, where he is?

Firk. Yes, forsooth; yea, marry!

Lincoln. Canst thou, in sadness[35]——

Firk. No, forsooth, no, marry!

L. Mayor. Tell me, good honest fellow, where he is,
And thou shalt see what I 'll bestow on thee.

Firk. Honest fellow? No, sir; not so, sir; my profession is the gentle craft; I care not for seeing, I love feeling; let me feel it here; *aurium tenus,* ten pieces of gold; *genuum tenus,* ten pieces of silver; and then Firk is your man—(*Aside.*) in a new pair of stretchers.[36]

L. Mayor. Here is an angel, part of thy reward,
Which I will give thee; tell me where he is.

Firk. No point.[37] Shall I betray my brother? No! Shall I prove Judas to Hans? No! Shall I cry treason to my corporation? No, I shall be firkt and yerkt then. But give me your angel; your angel shall tell you.

Lincoln. Do so, good fellow; 't is no hurt to thee.

Firk. Send simpering Syb away.

L. Mayor. Huswife, get you in.

Exit Sybil.

Firk. Pitchers have ears, and maids have wide mouths; but for Hans Prauns, upon my word, to-morrow morning he and young Mistress Rose go to this gear, they shall be married together, by this rush, or else turn Firk to a firkin of butter, to tan leather withal.

L. Mayor. But art thou sure of this?

Firk. Am I sure that Paul's steeple is a handful higher than London Stone,[38] or that the Pissing-Conduit[39] leaks nothing but pure Mother Bunch?[40] Am I sure I am lusty Firk? God's nails, do you think I am so base to gull you?

Lincoln. Where are they married? Dost thou know the church?

Firk. I never go to church, but I know the name of it; it is a swearing church—stay a while, 't is—aye, by the mass, no,

31 flout.
32 This, and the "Shaking of the Sheets" (below) were popular dance tunes, to which also ballads were set.
33 fool.
34 *i.e.* diggers for information.
35 seriously.
36 lies.
37 not at all; Fr. *ne point.*
38 A stone which marked the center from which the old Roman roads radiated.
39 a small conduit in Cornhill.
40 Mother Bunch was a well-known ale-wife.

no,—'t is—aye, by my troth, no, nor that; 't is—aye, by my faith, that, that, 't is, aye, by my Faith's Church under Paul's Cross. There they shall be knit like a pair of stockings in matrimony; there they 'll be incony.[41]

Lincoln. Upon my life, my nephew Lacy walks
In the disguise of this Dutch shoemaker.

Firk. Yes, forsooth.

Lincoln. Doth he not, honest fellow?

Firk. No, forsooth; I think Hans is nobody but Hans, no spirit.

L. Mayor. My mind misgives me now, 't is so, indeed.

Lincoln. My cousin speaks the language, knows the trade.

L. Mayor. Let me request your company, my lord;
Your honorable presence may, no doubt,
Refrain their headstrong rashness, when myself
Going alone perchance may be o'erborne.
Shall I request this favor?

Lincoln. This, or what else.

Firk. Then you must rise betimes, for they mean to fall to their hey-pass and repass,[42] pindy-pandy, which hand will you have, very early.

L. Mayor. My care shall every way equal their haste.
This night accept your lodging in my house,
The earlier shall we stir, and at Saint Faith's
Prevent this giddy hare-brain'd nuptial.
This traffic of hot love shall yield cold gains:
They ban [43] our loves, and we 'll forbid their banns.

Exit.

Lincoln. At Saint Faith's Church thou say'st?

Firk. Yes, by their troth.

Lincoln. Be secret, on thy life.

Exit.

Firk. Yes, when I kiss your wife! Ha, ha, here 's no craft in the gentle craft. I came hither of purpose with shoes to Sir Roger's worship, whilst Rose, his daughter, be cony-catcht [44] by Hans. Soft now; these two gulls will be at Saint Faith's Church to-morrow morning, to take Master Bridegroom and Mistress Bride napping, and they, in the mean time, shall chop up the matter at the Savoy.[45] But the best sport is, Sir Roger Oateley will find my fellow lame Ralph's wife going to marry a gentleman, and then he 'll stop her instead of his daughter. Oh brave! there will be fine tickling sport. Soft now, what have I to do? Oh, I know; now a mess of shoemakers meet at the Woolsack in Ivy Lane, to cozen [46] my gentleman of lame Ralph's wife, that 's true.

Alack, alack!
Girls, hold out tack! [47]
For now smocks for this jumbling
Shall go to wrack.

Exit.

ACT V.

SCENE 1. *A room in Eyre's house.*

Enter Eyre, Margery, Hans, and Rose.

Eyre. This is the morning, then; stay, my bully, my honest Hans, is it not?

Hans. This is the morning that must make us two happy or miserable; therefore, if you——

Eyre. Away with these ifs and ans, Hans, and these et caeteras! By mine honor, Rowland Lacy, none but the king shall wrong thee. Come, fear nothing, am not I Sim Eyre? Is not Sim Eyre lord mayor of London? Fear nothing, Rose: let them all say what they can; dainty, come thou to me—laughest thou?

Marg. Good my lord, stand her friend in what thing you may.

Eyre. Why, my sweet Lady Madgy, think you Simon Eyre can forget his fine Dutch journeyman? No, vah! Fie, I scorn it, it shall never be cast in my teeth, that I was unthankful. Lady Madgy, thou had'st never cover'd thy Saracen's head with this French flap, nor loaden thy bum with this farthingale ('t is trash, trumpery, vanity); Simon Eyre had never walk'd in a red petticoat, nor wore a chain of gold, but for my fine journeyman's portagues.—And shall I leave him? No! Prince am I none, yet bear a princely mind.

Hans. My lord, 't is time for us to part from hence.

Eyre. Lady Madgy, Lady Madgy, take

41 snug.
42 conjuring terms.
43 curse.
44 spirited away.
45 A chapel in London, formerly connected with the Savoy palace.
46 cheat.
47 stoutly.

two or three of my pie-crust-eaters, my buff-jerkin varlets, that do walk in black gowns at Simon Eyre's heels; take them, good Lady Madgy; trip and go, my brown queen of periwigs, with my delicate Rose and my jolly Rowland to the Savoy; see them linkt, countenance the marriage; and when it is done, cling, cling together, you Hamborow turtle-doves. I'll bear you out, come to Simon Eyre; come, dwell with me, Hans, thou shalt eat minc'd-pies and marchpane.[48] Rose, away, cricket; trip and go, my Lady Madgy, to the Savoy; Hans, wed, and to bed; kiss, and away! Go, vanish!

Marg. Farewell, my lord.

Rose. Make haste, sweet love.

Marg. She'd fain the deed were done.

Hans. Come, my sweet Rose; faster than deer we'll run.

Exeunt Hans, Rose, and Margery.

Eyre. Go, vanish, vanish! Avaunt, I say! By the lord of Ludgate, it's a mad life to be a lord mayor; it's a stirring life, a fine life, a velvet life, a careful life. Well, Simon Eyre, yet set a good face on it, in the honor of Saint Hugh. Soft, the king this day comes to dine with me, to see my new buildings; his majesty is welcome, he shall have good cheer, delicate cheer, princely cheer. This day, my fellow prentices of London come to dine with me too, they shall have fine cheer, gentlemanlike cheer. I promised the mad Cappadocians, when we all served at the Conduit together,[49] that if ever I came to be mayor of London, I would feast them all, and I'll do't, I'll do't, by the life of Pharaoh; by this beard, Sim Eyre will be no flincher. Besides, I have procur'd that upon every Shrove Tuesday, at the sound of the pancake bell, my fine dapper Assyrian lads shall clap up their shop windows, and away. This is the day, and this day they shall do't, they shall do't.

Boys, that day are you free, let masters care,
And prentices shall pray for Simon Eyre.

Exit.

Scene 2. *A street near St. Faith's Church.*

Enter Hodge, Firk, Ralph, and five or six Shoemakers, all with cudgels or such weapons.

Hodge. Come, Ralph; stand to it, Firk. My masters, as we are the brave bloods of the shoemakers, heirs apparent to Saint Hugh, and perpetual benefactors to all good fellows, thou shalt have no wrong: were Hammon a king of spades, he should not delve in thy close without thy sufferance. But tell me, Ralph, art thou sure 'tis thy wife?

Ralph. Am I sure this is Firk? This morning, when I strokt on[50] her shoes, I lookt upon her, and she upon me, and sighed, askt me if ever I knew one Ralph. Yes, said I. For his sake, said she—tears standing in her eyes—and for thou art somewhat like him, spend this piece of gold. I took it; my lame leg and my travel beyond sea made me unknown. All is one for that: I know she's mine.

Firk. Did she give thee this gold? O glorious glittering gold! She's thine own, 'tis thy wife, and she loves thee; for I'll stand to't, there's no woman will give gold to any man, but she thinks better of him than she thinks of them she gives silver to. And for Hammon, neither Hammon nor hangman shall wrong thee in London. Is not our old master Eyre lord mayor? Speak, my hearts.

All. Yes, and Hammon shall know it to his cost.

Enter Hammon, his man, Jane, and others.

Hodge. Peace, my bullies; yonder they come.

Ralph. Stand to't, my hearts. Firk, let me speak first.

Hodge. No, Ralph, let me.—Hammon, whither away so early?

Ham. Unmannerly, rude slave, what's that to thee?

Firk. To him, sir? Yes, sir, and to me, and others. Good-morrow, Jane, how dost thou? Good Lord, how the world is changed with you! God be thanked!

Ham. Villains, hands off! How dare you touch my love?

All. Villains? Down with them! Cry clubs for prentices![51]

Hodge. Hold, my hearts! Touch her, Hammon? Yea, and more than that: we'll carry her away with us. My masters and gentlemen, never draw your bird-spits; shoemakers are steel to the

48 A sweetmeat made of sugar and almonds.

49 Apprentices carried water from the conduits to their masters' homes.

50 fitted.

51 "Clubs" was the rallying cry of the London apprentices.

back, men every inch of them, all spirit.

All of Hammon's side. Well, and what of all this?

Hodge. I'll show you.—Jane, dost thou know this man? 'T is Ralph, I can tell thee; nay, 't is he in faith, though he be lam'd by the wars. Yet look not strange, but run to him, fold him about the neck and kiss him.

Jane. Lives then my husband? Oh, God, let me go!
Let me embrace my Ralph.

Ham. What means my Jane?

Jane. Nay, what meant you, to tell me he was slain?

Ham. Pardon me, dear love, for being misled.
(*To Ralph.*) 'T was rumor'd here in London thou wert dead.

Firk. Thou seest he lives. Lass, go, pack home with him.
Now, Master Hammon, where 's your mistress, your wife?

Serv. 'Swounds, master, fight for her! Will you thus lose her?

All. Down with that creature! Clubs! Down with him!

Hodge. Hold, hold!

Ham. Hold, fool! Sirs, he shall do no wrong.
Will my Jane leave me thus, and break her faith?

Firk. Yea, sir! She must, sir! She shall, sir! What then? Mend it!

Hodge. Hark, fellow Ralph, follow my counsel: set the wench in the midst, and let her choose her man, and let her be his woman.

Jane. Whom shall I choose? Whom should my thoughts affect
But him whom Heaven hath made to be my love?
Thou art my husband, and these humble weeds
Make thee more beautiful than all his wealth.
Therefore, I will but put off this attire,
Returning it into the owner's hand,
And after ever be thy constant wife.

Hodge. Not a rag, Jane! The law 's on our side: he that sows in another man's ground, forfeits his harvest. Get thee home, Ralph; follow him, Jane; he shall not have so much as a busk-point [52] from thee.

Firk. Stand to that, Ralph; the appurtenances are thine own. Hammon, look not at her!

Serv. O, swounds, no!

Firk. Blue coat, be quiet, we'll give you a new livery else; we'll make Shrove Tuesday Saint George's Day [53] for you. Look not, Hammon, leer not! I'll firk you! For thy head now, one glance, one sheep's eye, anything, at her! Touch not a rag, lest I and my brethren beat you to clouts.

Serv. Come, Master Hammon, there's no striving here.

Ham. Good fellows, hear me speak; and, honest Ralph,
Whom I have injured most by loving Jane,
Mark what I offer thee: here in fair gold
Is twenty pound, I'll give it for thy Jane;
If this content thee not, thou shalt have more.

Hodge. Sell not thy wife, Ralph; make her not a whore.

Ham. Say, wilt thou freely cease thy claim in her,
And let her be my wife?

All. No, do not, Ralph.

Ralph. Sirrah Hammon, Hammon, dost thou think a shoemaker is so base to be a bawd to his own wife for commodity? Take thy gold, choke with it! Were I not lame, I would make thee eat thy words.

Firk. A shoemaker sell his flesh and blood? O indignity!

Hodge. Sirrah, take up your pelf, and be packing.

Ham. I will not touch one penny, but in lieu
Of that great wrong I offered thy Jane,
To Jane and thee I give that twenty pound.
Since I have fail'd of her, during my life,
I vow, no woman else shall be my wife.
Farewell, good fellows of the gentle trade:
Your morning mirth my mourning day hath made.

Exit.

Firk. (*To the Serving-man.*) Touch the gold, creature, if you dare! Y' are best be trudging. Here, Jane, take thou it. Now let's home, my hearts.

Hodge. Stay! Who comes here? Jane, on again with thy mask!

52 A lace with a tag, which fastened the busk, or piece of wood or whalebone used to stiffen a corset.

53 It was a fashionable custom to wear blue coats on St. George's day.

Enter the Earl of Lincoln, the Lord Mayor, and Servants.

Lincoln. Yonder 's the lying varlet mockt us so.
L. Mayor. Come hither, sirrah!
Firk. I, sir? I am sirrah? You mean me, do you not?
Lincoln. Where is my nephew married?
Firk. Is he married? God give him joy, I am glad of it. They have a fair day, and the sign is in a good planet, Mars in Venus.
L. Mayor. Villain, thou toldst me that my daughter Rose
This morning should be married at Saint Faith's;
We have watch'd there these three hours at the least,
Yet see we no such thing.
Firk. Truly, I am sorry for 't; a bride 's a pretty thing.
Hodge. Come to the purpose. Yonder 's the bride and bridegroom you look for, I hope. Though you be lords, you are not to bar by your authority men from women, are you?
L. Mayor. See, see, my daughter 's maskt.
Lincoln. True, and my nephew,
To hide his guilt, counterfeits him lame.
Firk. Yea, truly; God help the poor couple, they are lame and blind.
L. Mayor. I 'll ease her blindness.
Lincoln. I 'll his lameness cure.
Firk. Lie down, sirs, and laugh! My fellow Ralph is taken for Rowland Lacy, and Jane for Mistress Damask Rose. This is all my knavery.
L. Mayor. What, have I found you, minion?
Lincoln. O base wretch!
Nay, hide thy face, the horror of thy guilt
Can hardly be washt off. Where are thy powers?
What battles have you made? O yes, I see,
Thou fought'st with Shame, and Shame hath conquer'd thee.
This lameness will not serve.
L. Mayor. Unmask yourself.
Lincoln. Lead home your daughter.
L. Mayor. Take your nephew hence.
Ralph. Hence! Swounds, what mean you? Are you mad? I hope you cannot enforce my wife from me. Where 's Hammon?
L. Mayor. Your wife?
Lincoln. What, Hammon?
Ralph. Yea, my wife; and, therefore, the proudest of you that lays hands on her first, I 'll lay my crutch 'cross his pate.
Firk. To him, lame Ralph! Here 's brave sport!
Ralph. Rose call you her? Why, her name is Jane. Look here else; do you know her now?
(*Unmasking Jane.*)
Lincoln. Is this your daughter?
L. Mayor. No, nor this your nephew.
My Lord of Lincoln, we are both abus'd
By this base, crafty varlet.
Firk. Yea, forsooth, no varlet; forsooth, no base; forsooth, I am but mean; no crafty neither, but of the gentle craft.
L. Mayor. Where is my daughter Rose?
Where is my child?
Lincoln. Where is my nephew Lacy married?
Firk. Why, here is good lac'd mutton,[54] as I promist you.
Lincoln. Villain, I 'll have thee punisht for this wrong.
Firk. Punish the journeyman villain, but not the journeyman shoemaker.

Enter Dodger.

Dodger. My lord, I come to bring unwelcome news.
Your nephew Lacy and your daughter Rose
Early this morning wedded at the Savoy,
None being present but the lady mayoress.
Besides, I learnt among the officers,
The lord mayor vows to stand in their defense
'Gainst any that shall seek to cross the match.
Lincoln. Dares Eyre the shoemaker uphold the deed?
Firk. Yes, sir, shoemakers dare stand in a woman's quarrel, I warrant you, as deep as another, and deeper too.
Dodger. Besides, his grace to-day dines with the mayor;
Who on his knees humbly intends to fall
And beg a pardon for your nephew's fault.
Lincoln. But I 'll prevent him! Come, Sir Roger Oateley;
The king will do us justice in this cause.
Howe'er their hands have made them man and wife,
I will disjoin the match, or lose my life.
Exeunt.

54 a slang term for a woman.

Firk. Adieu, Monsieur Dodger! Farewell, fools! Ha, ha! Oh, if they had stay'd, I would have so lam'd them with flouts! O heart, my codpiece-point is ready to fly in pieces every time I think upon Mistress Rose. But let that pass, as my lady mayoress says.

Hodge. This matter is answer'd. Come, Ralph; home with thy wife. Come, my fine shoemakers, let 's to our master's the new lord mayor, and there swagger this Shrove Tuesday. I 'll promise you wine enough, for Madge keeps the cellar.

All. O rare! Madge is a good wench.

Firk. And I 'll promise you meat enough, for simp'ring Susan keeps the larder. I 'll lead you to victuals, my brave soldiers; follow your captain. O brave! Hark, hark!

(*Bell rings.*)

All. The pancake-bell [55] rings, the pancake-bell! Trilill, my hearts!

Firk. O brave! O sweet bell! O delicate pancakes! Open the doors, my hearts, and shut up the windows! keep in the house, let out the pancakes! O rare, my hearts! Let 's march together for the honor of Saint Hugh to the great new hall [56] in Gracious Street corner, which our master, the new lord mayor, hath built.

Ralph. O the crew of good fellows that will dine at my lord mayor's cost to-day!

Hodge. By the Lord, my lord mayor is a most brave man. How shall prentices be bound to pray for him and the honor of the gentlemen shoemakers! Let 's feed and be fat with my lord's bounty.

Firk. O musical bell, still! O Hodge, O my brethren! There 's cheer for the heavens: venison-pasties walk up and down piping hot, like sergeants; beef and brewis [57] comes marching in dry-vats,[58] fritters and pancakes comes trowling in in wheel-barrows; hens and oranges hopping in porters'-baskets, collops [59] and eggs in scuttles, and tarts and custards comes quavering in in malt-shovels.

Enter more Prentices.

All. Whoop, look here, look here!

Hodge. How now, mad lads, whither away so fast?

1 Prentice. Whither? Why, to the great new hall, know you not why? The lord mayor hath bidden all the prentices in London to breakfast this morning.

All. O brave shoemakers, O brave lord of incomprehensible good-fellowship! Whoo! Hark you! The pancake-bell rings.

(*Cast up caps.*)

Firk. Nay, more, my hearts! Every Shrove Tuesday is our year of jubilee; and when the pancake-bell rings, we are as free as my lord mayor; we may shut up our shops, and make holiday; I 'll have it call'd Saint Hugh's Holiday.

All. Agreed, agreed! Saint Hugh's Holiday.

Hodge. And this shall continue for ever.

All. O brave! Come, come, my hearts! Away, away!

Firk. O eternal credit to us of the gentle craft! March fair, my hearts! O rare!

Exeunt.

SCENE 3. *A street in London.*

Enter the King and his Train over the stage.

King. Is our lord mayor of London such a gallant?

Nobleman. One of the merriest madcaps in your land.
Your grace will think, when you behold the man,
He 's rather a wild ruffian than a mayor.
Yet thus much I 'll ensure your majesty,
In all his actions that concern his state
He is as serious, provident, and wise,
As full of gravity amongst the grave,
As any mayor hath been these many years.

King. I am with child [60] till I behold this huffcap.[61]
But all my doubt is, when we come in presence,
His madness will be dasht clean out of countenance.

Nobleman. It may be so, my liege.

King. Which to prevent,
Let some one give him notice, 't is our pleasure
That he put on his wonted merriment.
Set forward!

All. On afore!

Exeunt.

55 Pancakes were a feature of the Shrove Tuesday menu; hence the bell which rang for Shrove Tuesday services was called the pancake bell.
56 Leadenhall.
57 beef broth.
58 barrels.
59 bacon.
60 in suspense.
61 swaggerer.

SCENE 4. *A great hall.*

Enter Eyre, Hodge, Firk, Ralph, and other Shoemakers, all with napkins on their shoulders.

Eyre. Come, my fine Hodge, my jolly gentlemen shoemakers; soft, where be these cannibals, these varlets, my officers? Let them all walk and wait upon my brethren; for my meaning is, that none but shoemakers, none but the livery of my company shall in their satin hoods wait upon the trencher of my sovereign.

Firk. O my lord, it will be rare!

Eyre. No more, Firk; come, lively! Let your fellow-prentices want no cheer; let wine be plentiful as beer, and beer as water. Hang these penny-pinching fathers, that cram wealth in innocent lambskins. Rip, knaves, avaunt! Look to my guests!

Hodge. My lord, we are at our wits' end for room; those hundred tables will not feast the fourth part of them.

Eyre. Then cover me those hundred tables again, and again, till all my jolly prentices be feasted. Avoid, Hodge! Run, Ralph! Frisk about, my nimble Firk! Carouse me fathom-healths to the honor of the shoemakers. Do they drink lively, Hodge? Do they tickle it, Firk?

Firk. Tickle it? Some of them have taken their liquor standing so long that they can stand no longer; but for meat, they would eat it an they had it.

Eyre. Want they meat? Where 's this swag-belly, this greasy kitchen-stuff cook? Call the varlet to me! Want meat? Firk, Hodge, lame Ralph, run, my tall men, beleaguer the shambles, beggar all Eastcheap, serve me whole oxen in chargers, and let sheep whine upon the tables like pigs for want of good fellows to eat them. Want meat? Vanish, Firk! Avaunt, Hodge!

Hodge. Your lordship mistakes my man Firk; he means, their bellies want meat, not the boards; for they have drunk so much, they can eat nothing.

The Second Three Men's Song

Cold 's the wind, and wet 's the rain,
  Saint Hugh be our good speed:
Ill is the weather that bringeth no gain,
  Nor helps good hearts in need.

Trowl[62] the bowl, the jolly nut-brown bowl,
  And here, kind mate, to thee:
Let 's sing a dirge for Saint Hugh's soul,
  And down it merrily.

Down a down hey down a down,
  (*Close with the tenor boy.*)
  Hey derry derry, down a down!
Ho, well done; to me let come!
  Ring compass,[63] gentle joy.

Trowl the bowl, the nut-brown bowl,
  And here, kind mate, to thee: etc.
(*Repeat as often as there be men to drink; and at last when all have drunk, this verse:*)
Cold's the wind, and wet's the rain,
  Saint Hugh be our good speed:
Ill is the weather that bringeth no gain,
Nor helps good hearts in need.

Enter Hans, Rose, and Margery.

Marg. Where is my lord?

Eyre. How now, Lady Madgy?

Marg. The king's most excellent majesty is new come; he sends me for thy honor; one of his most worshipful peers bade me tell thou must be merry, and so forth; but let that pass.

Eyre. Is my sovereign come? Vanish, my tall shoemakers, my nimble brethren; look to my guests, the prentices. Yet stay a little! How now, Hans? How looks my little Rose?

Hans. Let me request you to remember me.
I know, your honor easily may obtain
Free pardon of the king for me and Rose,
And reconcile me to my uncle's grace.

Eyre. Have done, my good Hans, my honest journeyman; look cheerily! I 'll fall upon both my knees, till they be as hard as horn, but I 'll get thy pardon.

Marg. Good my lord, have a care what you speak to his grace.

Eyre. Away, you Islington whitepot![64] hence, you hopper-arse! you barley-pudding, full of maggots! you broiled carbonado![65] avaunt, avaunt, avoid, Mephistophiles! Shall Sim Eyre learn to speak of you, Lady Madgy? Vanish, Mother Miniver[66]-cap; vanish, go, trip and go; meddle with your partlets[67] and your pishery-pashery, your flews[68] and your whirligigs; go, rub,[69] out of mine alley! Sim Eyre knows how to speak to a Pope,

32 pass.
63 sound the whole range of notes.
64 "A dish, made of milk, eggs, and sugar, baked in a pot." (Webster.)
65 a steak cut crossways.
66 fur.
67 ruffs for the neck.
68 flaps; as resembling the hanging chaps of a hound.
69 obstruction, a term in bowling; hence the point of "alley."

to Sultan Soliman, to Tamburlaine, an he were here, and shall I melt, shall I droop before my sovereign? No, come, my Lady Madgy! Follow me, Hans! About your business, my frolic free-booters! Firk, frisk about, and about, and about, for the honor of mad Simon Eyre, lord mayor of London.

Firk. Hey, for the honor of the shoemakers!

Exeunt.

SCENE 5. *An open yard before the hall.*

A long flourish, or two. Enter the King, Nobles, Eyre, Margery, Lacy, Rose. Lacy and Rose kneel.

King. Well, Lacy, though the fact was very foul
Of your revolting from our kingly love
And your own duty, yet we pardon you.
Rise both, and, Mistress Lacy, thank my lord mayor
For your young bridegroom here.

Eyre. So, my dear liege, Sim Eyre and my brethren, the gentlemen shoemakers, shall set your sweet majesty's image cheek by jowl by Saint Hugh for this honor you have done poor Simon Eyre. I beseech your grace, pardon my rude behavior; I am a handicraftsman, yet my heart is without craft; I would be sorry at my soul, that my boldness should offend my king.

King. Nay, I pray thee, good lord mayor, be even as merry
As if thou wert among thy shoemakers;
It does me good to see thee in this humor.

Eyre. Say'st thou me so, my sweet Dioclesian? Then, hump! Prince am I none, yet am I princely born. By the lord of Ludgate, my liege, I'll be as merry as a pie.[70]

King. Tell me, in faith, mad Eyre, how old thou art.

Eyre. My liege, a very boy, a stripling, a younker; you see not a white hair on my head, not a gray in this beard. Every hair, I assure thy majesty, that sticks in this beard, Sim Eyre values at the King of Babylon's ransom; Tamar Cham's beard was a rubbing brush to 't: yet I'll shave it off, and stuff tennis-balls[71] with it, to please my bully king.

King. But all this while I do not know your age.

Eyre. My liege, I am six and fifty year old, yet I can cry hump! with a sound heart for the honor of Saint Hugh. Mark this old wench, my king: I danc'd the shaking of the sheets with her six and thirty years ago, and yet I hope to get two or three young lord mayors, ere I die. I am lusty still, Sim Eyre still. Care and cold lodging brings white hairs. My sweet Majesty, let care vanish, cast it upon thy nobles, it will make thee look always young like Apollo, and cry hump! Prince am I none, yet am I princely born.

King. Ha, ha!
Say, Cornwall, didst thou ever see his like?

Nobleman. Not I, my lord.

Enter the Earl of Lincoln and the Lord Mayor.

King. Lincoln, what news with you?

Lincoln. My gracious lord, have care unto yourself,
For there are traitors here.

All. Traitors? Where? Who?

Eyre. Traitors in my house? God forbid! Where be my officers? I'll spend my soul, ere my king feel harm.

King. Where is the traitor, Lincoln?

Lincoln. Here he stands.

King. Cornwall, lay hold on Lacy!—Lincoln, speak,
What canst thou lay unto thy nephew's charge?

Lincoln. This, my dear liege: your Grace, to do me honor,
Heapt on the head of this degenerate boy
Desertless favors; you made choice of him
To be commander over powers in France.
But he——

King. Good Lincoln, prithee, pause a while!
Even in thine eyes I read what thou wouldst speak.
I know how Lacy did neglect our love,
Ran himself deeply, in the highest degree,
Into vile treason——

Lincoln. Is he not a traitor?

King. Lincoln, he was; now have we pard'ned him.
'T was not a base want of true valor's fire.
That held him out of France, but love's desire.

70 magpie.

71 The tennis-balls of the time were stuffed with hair

Lincoln. I will not bear his shame upon my back.
King. Nor shalt thou, Lincoln; I forgive you both.
Lincoln. Then, good my liege, forbid the boy to wed
One whose mean birth will much disgrace his bed.
King. Are they not married?
Lincoln. No, my liege.
Both. We are.
King. Shall I divorce them then? O be it far
That any hand on earth should dare untie
The sacred knot, knit by God's majesty;
I would not for my crown disjoin their hands
That are conjoin'd in holy nuptial bands.
How say'st thou, Lacy, wouldst thou lose thy Rose?
Lacy. Not for all India's wealth, my sovereign.
King. But Rose, I am sure, her Lacy would forego?
Rose. If Rose were askt that question, she 'd say no.
King. You hear them, Lincoln?
Lincoln. Yea, my liege, I do.
King. Yet canst thou find i' th' heart to part these two?
Who seeks, besides you, to divorce these lovers?
L. Mayor. I do, my gracious lord, I am her father.
King. Sir Roger Oateley, our last mayor, I think?
Nobleman. The same, my liege.
King. Would you offend Love's laws?
Well, you shall have your wills, you sue to me,
To prohibit the match. Soft, let me see—
You both are married, Lacy, art thou not?
Lacy. I am, dread sovereign.
King. Then, upon thy life,
I charge thee, not to call this woman wife.
L. Mayor. I thank your grace.
Rose. O my most gracious lord! (*Kneels.*)
King. Nay, Rose, never woo me; I tell you true,
Although as yet I am a bachelor,
Yet I believe I shall not marry you.
Rose. Can you divide the body from the soul,
Yet make the body live?
King. Yea, so profound?
I cannot, Rose, but you I must divide.
This fair maid, bridegroom, cannot be your bride.
Are you pleas'd, Lincoln? Oateley, are you pleas'd?
Both. Yes, my lord.
King. Then must my heart be eas'd;
For, credit me, my conscience lives in pain,
Till these whom I divorc'd, be join'd again.
Lacy, give me thy hand; Rose, lend me thine!
Be what you would be! Kiss now! So, that 's fine.
At night, lovers, to bed!—Now, let me see,
Which of you all mislikes this harmony.
L. Mayor. Will you then take from me my child perforce?
King. Why tell me, Oateley: shines not Lacy's name
As bright in the world's eye as the gay beams
Of any citizen?
Lincoln. Yea, but, my gracious lord,
I do mislike the match far more than he;
Her blood is too too base.
King. Lincoln, no more.
Dost thou not know that love respects no blood,
Cares not for difference of birth or state?
The maid is young, well born, fair, virtuous,
A worthy bride for any gentleman.
Besides, your nephew for her sake did stoop
To bear necessity, and, as I hear,
Forgetting honors and all courtly pleasures,
To gain her love, became a shoemaker.
As for the honor which he lost in France,
Thus I redeem it: Lacy, kneel thee down!—
Arise, Sir Rowland Lacy! Tell me now,
Tell me in earnest, Oateley, canst thou chide,
Seeing thy Rose a lady and a bride?
L. Mayor. I am content with what your grace hath done.
Lincoln. And I, my liege, since there 's no remedy.
King. Come on, then, all shake hands: I'll have you friends;
Where there is much love, all discord ends.
What says my mad lord mayor to all this love?
Eyre. O my liege, this honor you have done to my fine journeyman here, Row-

land Lacy, and all these favors which you have shown to me this day in my poor house, will make Simon Eyre live longer by one dozen of warm summers more than he should.

King. Nay, my mad lord mayor, that shall be thy name;
If any grace of mine can length thy life,
One honor more I'll do thee: that new building,
Which at thy cost in Cornhill is erected,
Shall take a name from us; we'll have it call'd
The Leadenhall, because in digging it
You found the lead that covereth the same.

Eyre. I thank your majesty.

Marg. God bless your grace!

King. Lincoln, a word with you!

Enter Hodge, Firk, Ralph, and more Shoemakers.

Eyre. How now, my mad knaves? Peace, speak softly, yonder is the king.

King. With the old troop which there we keep in pay,
We will incorporate a new supply.
Before one summer more pass o'er my head,
France shall repent, England was injured.
What are all these?

Lacy. All shoemakers, my liege,
Sometime my fellows; in their companies
I liv'd as merry as an emperor.

King. My mad lord mayor, are all these shoemakers?

Eyre. All shoemakers, my liege; all gentlemen of the gentle craft, true Trojans, courageous cordwainers; they all kneel to the shrine of holy Saint Hugh.

All the Shoemakers. God save your majesty!

King. Mad Simon, would they anything with us?

Eyre. Mum, mad knaves! Not a word! I'll do 't, I warrant you. They are all beggars, my liege; all for themselves, and I for them all on both my knees do entreat, that for the honor of poor Simon Eyre and the good of his brethren, these mad knaves, your grace would vouchsafe some privilege to my new Leadenhall, that it may be lawful for us to buy and sell leather there two days a week.

King. Mad Sim, I grant your suit, you shall have patent
To hold two market-days in Leadenhall,
Mondays and Fridays, those shall be the times.
Will this content you?

All. Jesus bless your grace!

Eyre. In the name of these my poor brethren shoemakers, I most humbly thank your grace. But before I rise, seeing you are in the giving vein and we in the begging, grant Sim Eyre one boon more.

King. What is it, my lord mayor?

Eyre. Vouchsafe to taste of a poor banquet that stands sweetly waiting for your sweet presence.

King. I shall undo thee, Eyre, only with feasts;
Already have I been too troublesome;
Say, have I not?

Eyre. O my dear king, Sim Eyre was taken unawares upon a day of shroving,[72] which I promist long ago to the prentices of London.
For, an 't please your highness, in time past,
I bare the water-tankard,[73] and my coat
Sits not a whit the worse upon my back;
And then, upon a morning, some mad boys,
It was Shrove Tuesday, even as 't is now,
gave me my breakfast, and I swore then by the stopple of my tankard, if ever I came to be lord mayor of London, I would feast all the prentices. This day, my liege, I did it, and the slaves had an hundred tables five times covered; they are gone home and vanisht;
Yet add more honor to the gentle trade,
Taste of Eyre's banquet, Simon 's happy made.

King. Eyre, I will taste of thy banquet, and will say,
I have not met more pleasure on a day.
Friends of the gentle craft, thanks to you all,
Thanks, my kind lady mayoress, for our cheer.—
Come, lords, a while let 's revel it at home!
When all our sports and banquetings are done,
Wars must right wrongs which Frenchmen have begun.

Exeunt.

72 merry-making.

73 cf. p. 150, n. 49.

THOMAS HEYWOOD

A WOMAN KILLED WITH KINDNESS

Thomas Heywood (c. 1574–1641) was of a Lincolnshire family, and may have been a member of the college of Peterhouse, Cambridge. We get our first definite information about him from Henslowe's Diary in 1596. He seems to have begun writing for the stage about 1594, and continued active until within a few years of his death, thus almost spanning the greatest years of the Elizabethan drama. His productivity was amazing: he himself tells us that he had a hand or "a main finger" in two hundred and twenty plays, of which only nineteen (four in two parts) survive. Meanwhile he was acting, perhaps till 1620 or so. He did also a considerable amount of miscellaneous writing in prose and loose, easy-running verse.

As *The Shoemakers' Holiday* represents domestic, or *bourgeois*, drama on the side of comedy, so *A Woman Killed with Kindness* is an example, and the best example, of domestic, or *bourgeois*, tragedy. The two plays spring from the same environment, and were written for identical audiences, by men who had a good deal in common. Both Dekker and Heywood were of the middle class themselves, and reflect in their work the temper and moral soundness of the solid citizenry of London. Like the earlier play, *A Woman Killed with Kindness* was written for Henslowe, and brought the same price of three pounds; as an interesting illustration of the comparative value of plays and costumes in the manager's eyes, we may note that on March 7, 1603, the day after he paid for the play, he spent ten shillings on a black satin dress for Mrs. Frankford.

No other piece of dramatic criticism has had the influence of Aristotle's attempt in his *Poetics* to formulate, from the practice of the Athenian dramatists, the laws or practice of tragedy. One of Aristotle's conclusions was that tragedy was concerned with the fate of persons of high rank, or at least illustrious above their fellows. This limitation was accepted by Renascence scholars, and in general governed the practice of Elizabethan, Restoration, and eighteenth-century writers of tragedy. It is, for instance, true of Shakespeare's tragedy, for even in *Romeo and Juliet*, though the personages may not be called illustrious in a strict sense, yet we think of the Capulets and Montagues as of the aristocracy of Verona, and the star-crossed lovers themselves are by their passion and unhappy fate sensibly, if not actually, raised above ordinary citizens. There were, however, in the Elizabethan period men who realized that tragic feeling was not necessarily confined to the palace; that circumstance might lift to tragic dignity the lives of obscure people. One of the most powerful of pre-Shakesperean plays, so grim and stark in its realism, so impressive in the portrayal of the murderess its heroine, that conjecture as to its authorship has even been busy with Shakespeare's name, is *Arden of Feversham*, written about 1590. This dramatization of Holinshed's account of a murder of a husband by a wife and her paramour, is the first extant example, though we hear of such plays earlier, of a group of murder plays, domestic tragedies, frequently taken from real life. For a number of years about the turn of the century, under the influence of a general swing toward realism manifest also in comedy, where Ben Jonson led a revolt against romantic comedy and chronicle-history, plays of this sort were especially popular. Henslowe's Diary gives us the names of several no longer extant, and surviving plays such as *A Warning for Fair Women* (1599), *Two Lamentable Tragedies* (1599), and *The Yorkshire Tragedy* (1605), are home-bred tragedies dealing in rather artless fashion with family strife and bloodshed. Another kind of domestic drama, also popular in the same period, was that which showed the trials of a virtuous wife at the hands of a prodigal and unfaithful husband; such plays, though full of pathos, usually stopped short of tragedy, and ended in the reform of the erring husband and his reconciliation with his patient wife. *The Shoemakers' Holiday*, in the episode of Jane, has a hint of the motive, and, in *Patient Grissil*, Dekker deals with the subject more at large. *How a Man May Choose a Good Wife from a Bad* (1602), *The London Prodigal* (1605), and Marston's *The Dutch Courtesan* (1605) are representative of the type.

A Woman Killed with Kindness, belonging specifically to the first of the above-mentioned groups, is thus related to a considerable body of plays of its own day. Heywood may fairly be called the most important of writers of domestic drama, not alone because of the number of examples he has given us, but from his sincere and affecting handling of his material. Once he treats the wronged-wife motive, in his comedy *The Wise Woman of Hogsdon* (printed 1638). Usually, however, he deals seriously with domestic infelicity, and always from the point of view of a husband whose wife has transgressed. The story of Jane Shore in the two-part chronicle play *Edward IV* (1598), although involving two kings, is in effect a domestic tragedy; "the whole treatment of that delicate subject, the relation of a true and honorable man to the wife who has wronged him, but whom he continues to love in a spirit chastened by his wrongs, is handled with the same delicacy, the same wide tolerance and sympathy, and yet with the ethical soundness, which Heywood displays with so much effect in *A Woman Killed with Kindness*" (Schelling, *Elizabethan Drama,* I. 283). Heywood returned to the theme in *The English Traveller* (1633), a very fine play, and in *The Late Lancashire Witches* (1634,) where the wife, having fallen from grace by indulging in witchcraft, is handed over to justice by her husband. What chiefly distinguishes Heywood's domestic tragedies in which an adulterous wife figures from those by other men is the wife's treatment at the hands of her husband. The Elizabethan code of morals justified summary and bloody vengeance. Such a punishment, indeed, Mrs. Frankford expects:

> ". . . Mark not my face,
> Nor hack me with your sword; but let me go
> Perfect and undeformed to my tomb.
> I am not worthy that I should prevail
> In the least suit; no, not to speak to you,
> Nor look on you, nor to be in your presence;
> Yet, as an abject, this one suit I crave;
> This granted, I am ready for my grave."

Heywood's delicacy of feeling and perception of true honor in such circumstances win our admiration, as he shows the husband remembering that vengeance is God's and leaving the wife to the torture of her guilty conscience. So, in *The English Traveller,* young Geraldine, discovering the adultery of Mrs. Wincot, with whom he has exchanged vows of fidelity, forbears punishment more severe than a passionate upbraiding of her crime, and allows her to die of a broken heart. It is no easy matter for a dramatist to handle a situation of this sort in such a way as to preserve our sympathy and respect for the injured husband. It would have been far easier, as well as more theatrically effective, for Heywood to have had Frankford take refuge behind "the unwritten law," and satisfy the natural expectation of his audience with a scene of bloody retribution. Heywood makes his solution possible and sympathetic by a thorough characterization of Frankford as a Christian gentleman, and by a masterly depiction of the man's emotion at the crisis. He prays for patience before he disturbs the guilty pair, his first natural impulse toward immediate revenge displays itself when he pursues Wendoll with drawn sword, and he has to struggle in private with his anger before he can pronounce the lenient sentence on his wife. We see in action his better nature contending with his worse, and the struggle humanizes as the victory ennobles him. Heywood commands our admiration, moreover, by the fine restraint with which he handles the story. Neither in the climactic scenes, nor in the equally difficult scenes of Mrs. Frankford's repentance and death in act five, does he allow intrusion of sentimentality. Frankford indulges in no false heroics, Mrs. Frankford in no mawkish agonizings. No better illustration could be found of the difference between true sentiment and false sentimentality; the sentimental dramatists of the eighteenth century could have studied this play with profit. The only speeches which do not ring true are those of Wendoll in V. iii, but from him we should not expect honest penitence.

It must be admitted that the play, considering it as a whole, is not a model structurally. It is typical of one method of Elizabethan construction, which violates unity of action by a combination of two plots essentially unconnected. Heywood was a frequent offender in this respect: *The English Traveller* and *The Captives* are flagrant examples. In this case the sub-plot does not, as sometimes, offer so violent a contrast in feeling with the main plot that the dignity of the play is practically destroyed. Here the sub-plot, dealing as it does with a question of personal and family honor, in a way supports the more serious ethical problem of the main plot. There is also this to be said for the sub-plot, that by the rapidity of its development it helps to conceal the bareness of the main plot, whose exposition is very leisurely. But the actual binding of the plots is of the flimsiest: the two groups of people are brought together in the opening scene, Wendoll and Cranwell are transferred from one group to the other, the people of the sub-plot are present at Mrs. Frankford's death, but of interaction between the groups there is none. As for the main plot itself, barring the slowness of the exposition, it is well done, with one important exception. The climactic upbuilding to the scene of the discovery is strong; devices like Frankford's unwillingness to believe Nicholas's story, the card game, and the feigned letter are effectively used. The climax is stirring, the pathos of the situation enhanced by the skilful introduction of the children, and the last act avoids anticlimax; the business of the lute is particularly effective. The use of suspense is notable, in Frankford's hesitation before entering the house and at the door of the chamber, and in the pause before Mrs. Frankford's fate is made known. The one great flaw in the play is the ease with which Mrs. Frankford falls. This is altogether a matter of characterization. Nothing in the exposition of the woman's character prepares us for the abruptness of her yielding, nor is Wendoll presented as so attractive as to make it credible. Heywood was a master in portraying a gentleman — he was no hand at a villain. Wendoll is throughout stiff, stagy, impossible.

Bourgeois tragedy seems to have lost popular favor not long after 1605. Save for two or three plays of Heywood's, and fine single examples in Middleton's and Rowley's *The Fair Quarrel* (printed 1617) and *The Witch of Edmonton* (1621), assigned to Dekker, Rowley and Ford, domestic drama of a serious sort was practically abandoned during the rest of the Elizabethan period. The sentimental drama of the eighteenth century revived interest in domestic problems from a moral point of view, but it was not until Lillo wrote *George Barnwell* in 1731 that bourgeois tragedy appeared again upon the London stage. By that time the sentimentalizing and moralizing tendency had become so strong that *Barnwell* is as strenuously didactic as a Morality. Not until we come to the modern realistic drama do we find any achievement in domestic tragedy so appealing as *A Woman Killed with Kindness.* The simplicity of method, the sanity, the sound ethics, the freedom from preaching, of this, the flower of Elizabethan domestic tragedies, are enough to insure for Heywood an honorable place in the history of the drama.

A WOMAN KILLED WITH KINDNESS

By THOMAS HEYWOOD.

NAMES OF THE CHARACTERS

Sir Francis Acton, *Brother to Mistress Frankford.*
Sir Charles Mountford.
Master John Frankford.
Master Malby, *friend to Sir Francis.*
Master Wendoll, *friend to Frankford.*
Master Cranwell.
Master Shafton, *false friend to Sir Charles.*
Old Mountford, *Uncle to Sir Charles.*
Master Sandy.
Master Roder.
Master Tidy, *Cousin to Sir Charles.*
Nicholas, Jenkin, Roger Brickbat, Jack Slime, Spigot, Butler, — *Household Servants to Frankford.*
Sheriff.
Keeper of Prison.
Sheriff's Officers, Sergeant, Huntsmen, Falconers, Coachmen, Carters, Servants, Musicians.
Mistress Anne Frankford.
Susan, *Sister to Sir Charles Mountford.*
Cicely, *Maid to Mistress Frankford.*
Women Servants in Frankford's household.

Scene.—Yorkshire.

PROLOGUE.

I come but like a harbinger, being sent
To tell you what these preparations mean.
Look for no glorious state; our Muse is bent
Upon a barren subject, a bare scene.
We could afford this twig a timber-tree,
Whose strength might boldly on your favors build;
Our russet, tissue; drone, a honey-bee;
Our barren plot, a large and spacious field;
Our coarse fare, banquets; our thin water, wine;
Our brook, a sea; our bat's eyes, eagle's sight;
Our poet's dull and earthy Muse, divine;
Our ravens, doves; our crow's black feathers, white.
But gentle thoughts, when they may give the foil,[1]
Save them that yield, and spare where they may spoil.

[1] defeat.

ACT I.

Scene 1. *Room in Frankford's house.*

Enter Master Frankford, Mistress Frankford, Sir Francis Acton, Sir Charles Mountford, Master Malby, Master Wendoll, and Master Cranwell.

Sir F. Some music, there! None lead the bride a dance?
Sir C. Yes, would she dance *The Shaking of the Sheets;* [2]
But that 's the dance her husband means to lead her.
Wen. That 's not the dance that every man must dance,
According to the ballad.
Sir F. Music, ho!
By your leave, sister,—by your husband's leave,
I should have said,—the hand that but this day

[2] A well-known ballad and dance tune.

Was given you in the church I'll borrow.— Sound!
This marriage music hoists me from the ground.
Frank. Aye, you may caper; you are light and free!
Marriage hath yok'd my heels; pray, then, pardon me.
Sir F. I'll have you dance too, brother!
Sir C. Master Frankford,
You are a happy man, sir, and much joy
Succeed your marriage mirth: you have a wife
So qualified, and with such ornaments
Both of the mind and body. First, her birth
Is noble, and her education such
As might become the daughter of a prince;
Her own tongue speaks all tongues, and her own hand
Can teach all strings to speak in their best grace,
From the shrill'st treble to the hoarsest base.
To end her many praises in one word,
She's Beauty and Perfection's eldest daughter,
Only found by yours, though many a heart hath sought her.
Frank. But that I know your virtues and chaste thoughts,
I should be jealous of your praise, Sir Charles.
Cran. He speaks no more than you approve.
Mal. Nor flatters he that gives to her her due.
Mrs. F. I would your praise could find a fitter theme
Than my imperfect beauties to speak on!
Such as they be, if they my husband please,
They suffice me now I am marrièd.
His sweet content is like a flattering glass,
To make my face seem fairer to mine eye;
But the least wrinkle from his stormy brow
Will blast the roses in my cheeks that grow.
Sir F. A perfect wife already, meek and patient!
How strangely the word husband fits your mouth,
Not married three hours since! Sister, 't is good;
You that begin betimes thus must needs prove
Pliant and duteous in your husband's love.—
Gramercies, brother! Wrought her to 't already,—
"Sweet husband," and a curtsey, the first day?
Mark this, mark this, you that are bachelors,
And never took the grace [3] of honest man;
Mark this, against [4] you marry, this one phrase:
In a good time that man both wins and woos
That takes his wife down [5] in her wedding shoes.
Frank. Your sister takes not after you, Sir Francis,
All his wild blood your father spent on you;
He got her in his age, when he grew civil.
All his mad tricks were to his land entail'd,
And you are heir to all; your sister, she
Hath to her dower her mother's modesty.
Sir C. Lord, sir, in what a happy state live you!
This morning, which to many seems a burden,
Too heavy to bear, is unto you a pleasure.
This lady is no clog, as many are;
She doth become you like a well-made suit,
In which the tailor hath us'd all his art;
Not like a thick coat of unseason'd frieze,
Forc'd on your back in summer. She's no chain
To tie your neck, and curb you to the yoke;
But she's a chain of gold to adorn your neck.
You both adorn each other, and your hands,
Methinks, are matches. There's equality
In this fair combination; you are both
Scholars, both young, both being descended nobly.
There's music in this sympathy; it carries
Consort [6] and expectation of much joy,

3 attained the honor. 4 in anticipation of the time when. 5 reduces her to submission. 6 harmony.

Which God bestow on you from this first day
Until your dissolution,—that 's for ay!

Sir F. We keep you here too long, good brother Frankford.
Into the hall; away! Go cheer your guests.
What! Bride and bridegroom both withdrawn at once?
If you be miss'd, the guests will doubt their welcome,
And charge you with unkindness.

Frank. To prevent it,
I 'll leave you here, to see the dance within.

Mrs. F. And so will I.

Exeunt Master and Mistress Frankford.

Sir F. To part you it were sin.—
Now, gallants, while the town musicians
Finger their frets within, and the mad lads
And country lasses, every mother's child,
With nosegays and bride-laces [7] in their hats,
Dance all their country measures, rounds, and jigs,
What shall we do? Hark! They 're all on the hoigh; [8]
They toil like mill-horses, and turn as round,—
Marry, not on the toe! Aye, and they caper,
Not without cutting; you shall see, to-morrow,
The hall-floor peckt and dinted like a mill-stone,
Made with their high shoes. Though their skill be small,
Yet they tread heavy where their hob-nails fall.

Sir C. Well, leave them to their sports!—Sir Francis Acton,
I 'll make a match with you! Meet me to-morrow
At Chevy Chase; I 'll fly my hawk with yours.

Sir F. For what? For what?

Sir C. Why, for a hundred pound.

Sir F. Pawn me some gold of that!

Sir C. Here are ten angels; [9]
I 'll make them good a hundred pound to-morrow
Upon my hawk's wing.

Sir F. 'T is a match; 't is done.
Another hundred pounds upon your dogs;—
Dare ye, Sir Charles?

Sir C. I dare; were I sure to lose,
I durst do more than that; here is my hand,
The first course for a hundred pound!

Sir F. A match.

Wen. Ten angels on Sir Francis Acton's hawk;
As much upon his dogs!

Cran. I 'm for Sir Charles Mountford: I have seen
His hawk and dog both tried. What! Clap you hands,[10]
Or is 't no bargain?

Wen. Yes, and stake them down.
Were they five hundred, they were all my own.

Sir F. Be stirring early with the lark to-morrow;
I 'll rise into my saddle ere the sun
Rise from his bed.

Sir C. If there you miss me, say
I am no gentleman! I 'll hold my day.

Sir F. It holds on all sides.—Come, to-night let 's dance;
Early to-morrow let 's prepare to ride:
We 'd need be three hours up before the bride. *Exeunt.*

Scene 2. *Yard of the same.*

Enter Nicholas and Jenkin, Jack Slime, Roger Brickbat, with Country Wenches, and two or three Musicians.

Jen. Come, Nick, take you Joan Miniver, to trace withal; Jack Slime, traverse you with Cicely Milkpail; I will take Jane Trubkin, and Roger Brickbat shall have Isabel Motley. And now that they are busy in the parlor, come, strike up; we 'll have a crash [11] here in the yard.

Nich. My humor is not compendious: dancing I possess not, though I can foot it; yet, since I am fallen into the hands of Cicely Milkpail, I consent.

Slime. Truly, Nick, though we were never brought up like serving courtiers, yet we have been brought up with serving creatures,—aye, and God's creatures, too; for we have been brought up to serve sheep, oxen, horses, hogs, and such like; and, though we be but country fellows, it may be in the way of dancing we can do the horse-trick as well as the serving-men.

Brick. Aye, and the cross-point too.

Jen. O Slime! O Brickbat! Do not you know that comparisons are odious?

7 streamers. 8 excited. 9 gold coins worth ten shillings. 10 shake hands on it. 11 revel.

Now we are odious ourselves, too; therefore there are no comparisons to be made betwixt us.

Nich. I am sudden, and not superfluous; I am quarrelsome, and not seditious; I am peaceable, and not contentious; I am brief, and not compendious.

Slime. Foot it quickly! If the music overcome not my melancholy, I shall quarrel; and if they suddenly do not strike up, I shall presently strike thee down.

Jen. No quarreling, for God's sake! Truly, if you do, I shall set a knave between ye.

Slime. I come to dance, not to quarrel. Come, what shall it be? *Rogero?*

Jen. *Rogero?* No; we will dance *The Beginning of the World.*

Cicely. I love no dance so well as *John come kiss me now.*

Nich. I that have ere now deserv'd a cushion, call for the *Cushion-dance.*

Brick. For my part, I like nothing so well as *Tom Tyler.*

Jen. No; we'll have *The Hunting of the Fox.*

Slime. *The Hay, The Hay!* There's nothing like *The Hay.*[12]

Nich. I have said, I do say, and I will say again——

Jen. Every man agree to have it as Nick says!

All. Content.

Nich. It hath been, it now is, and it shall be——

Cicely. What, Master Nicholas? What?

Nich. *Put on your Smock a' Monday.*

Jen. So the dance will come cleanly off! Come, for God's sake, agree of something: if you like not that, put it to the musicians; or let me speak for all, and we'll have *Sellenger's Round.*

All. That, that, that!

Nich. No, I am resolv'd thus it shall be; first take hands, then take ye to your heels.

Jen. Why, would you have us run away?

Nich. No; but I would have you shake your heels.—Music, strike up!

They dance; Nick dancing, speaks stately and scurvily, the rest after the country fashion.

Jen. Hey! Lively, my lasses! Here's a turn for thee!

Exeunt.

SCENE 3. *Chevy Chase.*

Wind horns. Enter Sir Charles Mountford, Sir Francis Acton, Malby, Cranwell, Wendoll, Falconers, and Huntsmen.

Sir C. So; well cast off! Aloft, aloft! Well flown!
Oh, now she takes her at the souse,[13] and strikes her
Down to the earth, like a swift thunder-clap.

Wen. She hath struck ten angels out of my way.

Sir F. A hundred pound from me.

Sir C. What, falconer!

Falc. At hand, sir!

Sir C. Now she hath seiz'd the fowl and 'gins to plume[14] her,
Rebeck[15] her not; rather stand still and check her!
So, seize her gets,[16] her jesses, and her bells!
Away!

Sir F. My hawk kill'd, too.

Sir C. Aye, but 't was at the querre,[17]
Not at the mount like mine.

Sir F. Judgment, my masters!

Cran. Yours miss'd her at the ferre.[18]

Wen. Aye, but our merlin first had plum'd the fowl,
And twice renew'd[19] her from the river too.
Her bells, Sir Francis, had not both one weight,
Nor was one semi-tune above the other.
Methinks, these Milan bells do sound too full,
And spoil the mounting of your hawk.

Sir C. 'T is lost.

Sir F. I grant it not. Mine likewise seiz'd a fowl
Within her talons, and you saw her paws
Full of the feathers; both her petty singles[20]
And her long singles gripp'd her more than other;
The terrials[21] of her legs were stain'd with blood,
Not of the fowl only; she did discomfit

12 All these were well-known dance tunes.
13 while the victim was rising from the ground.
14 pluck.
15 recall.
16 same as *jesses*; straps on a hawk's legs, to which the leash was attached.
17 swoop.
18 unexplained.
19 renewed the attack upon.
20 the outer claws of a hawk's feet; the *long singles* were the middle claws.
21 unexplained.

Some of her feathers; but she brake away.
Come, come; your hawk is but a rifler.[22]

Sir C. How!

Sir F. Aye, and your dogs are trindle-tails [23] and curs.

Sir C. You stir my blood.
You keep not one good hound in all your kennel,
Nor one good hawk upon your perch.

Sir F. How, knight!

Sir C. So, knight. You will not swagger, sir?

Sir F. Why, say I did?

Sir C. Why, sir,
I say you would gain as much by swagg'ring
As you have got by wagers on your dogs.
You will come short in all things.

Sir F. Not in this!
Now I'll strike home.
(*Strikes Sir Charles.*)

Sir C. Thou shalt to thy long home,
Or I will want my will.

Sir F. All they that love Sir Francis, follow me!

Sir C. All that affect Sir Charles, draw on my part!

Cran. On this side heaves my hand.

Wen. Here goes my heart.

They divide themselves. Sir Charles Mountford, Cranwell, Falconer, and Huntsman, fight against Sir Francis Acton, Wendoll, his Falconer and Huntsman; and Sir Charles hath the better, and beats them away, killing both of Sir Francis's men. Exeunt all but Sir Charles Mountford.

Sir C. My God, what have I done! What have I done!
My rage hath plung'd into a sea of blood,
In which my soul lies drown'd. Poor innocents,
For whom we are to answer! Well, 't is done,
And I remain the victor. A great conquest,
When I would give this right hand, nay, this head,
To breathe in them new life whom I have slain!—
Forgive me, God! 'T was in the heat of blood,
And anger quite removes me from myself.
It was not I, but rage, did this vile murder;
Yet I, and not my rage, must answer it.
Sir Francis Acton, he is fled the field;
With him all those that did partake his quarrel;
And I am left alone with sorrow dumb,
And in my height of conquest overcome.

Enter Susan.

Susan. O God! My brother wounded 'mong the dead!
Unhappy jest, that in such earnest ends!
The rumor of this fear stretcht to my ears,
And I am come to know if you be wounded.

Sir C. Oh, sister, sister! Wounded at the heart.

Susan. My God forbid!

Sir C. In doing that thing which he forbade,
I am wounded, sister.

Susan. I hope, not at the heart.

Sir C. Yes, at the heart.

Susan. O God! A surgeon, there.

Sir C. Call me a surgeon, sister, for my soul!
The sin of murder, it hath pierc'd my heart
And made a wide wound there; but for these scratches,
They are nothing, nothing.

Susan. Charles, what have you done?
Sir Francis hath great friends, and will pursue you
Unto the utmost danger [24] of the law.

Sir C. My conscience is become mine enemy,
And will pursue me more than Acton can.

Susan. Oh, fly, sweet brother!

Sir C. Shall I fly from thee?
Why, Sue, art weary of my company?

Susan. Fly from your foe!

Sir C. You, sister, are my friend,
And flying you, I shall pursue my end.

Susan. Your company is as my eyeball dear;
Being far from you, no comfort can be near.
Yet fly to save your life! What would I care
To spend my future age in black despair,
So you were safe? And yet to live one week
Without my brother Charles, through every cheek
My streaming tears would downwards run so rank,[25]

22 bungler. 23 curly-tailed, low-bred. 24 power. 25 copiously.

Till they could set on either side a bank,
And in the midst a channel; so my face
For two salt-water brooks shall still find place.

Sir C. Thou shalt not weep so much; for I will stay,
In spite of danger's teeth. I'll live with thee,
Or I'll not live at all. I will not sell
My country and my father's patrimony,
Nor thy sweet sight, for a vain hope of life.

Enter Sheriff, with Officers.

Sher. Sir Charles, I am made the unwilling instrument
Of your attach [26] and apprehension.
I'm sorry that the blood of innocent men
Should be of you exacted. It was told me
That you were guarded with a troop of friends,
And therefore I come thus arm'd.

Sir C. Oh, Master Sheriff!
I came into the field with many friends,
But see, they all have left me; only one
Clings to my sad misfortune, my dear sister.
I know you for an honest gentleman;
I yield my weapons, and submit to you.
Convey me where you please!

Sher. To prison, then,
To answer for the lives of these dead men.

Susan. O God! O God!

Sir C. Sweet sister, every strain
Of sorrow from your heart augments my pain;
Your grief abounds, and hits against my breast.

Sher. Sir, will you go?

Sir C. Even where it likes you best.
Exeunt.

ACT II.

Scene 1. *Frankford's study.*

Enter Master Frankford.

Frank. How happy am I amongst other men,
That in my mean estate embrace content!
I am a gentleman, and by my birth
Companion with a king; a king's no more.
I am possess'd of many fair revenues,
Sufficient to maintain a gentleman;
Touching my mind, I am studied in all arts,
The riches of my thoughts; and of my time
Have been a good proficient; [27] but, the chief
Of all the sweet felicities on earth,
I have a fair, a chaste, and loving wife,—
Perfection all, all truth, all ornament.
If man on earth may truly happy be,
Of these at once possest, sure, I am he.

Enter Nicholas.

Nich. Sir, there's a gentleman attends without
To speak with you.

Frank. On horseback?

Nich. Yes, on horseback.

Frank. Entreat him to alight, I will attend him.
Know'st thou him, Nick?

Nich. Know him? Yes; his name's Wendoll.
It seems, he comes in haste: his horse is booted
Up to the flank in mire, himself all spotted
And stain'd with plashing. Sure, he rid in fear,
Or for a wager. Horse and man both sweat;
I ne'er saw two in such a smoking heat.

Frank. Entreat him in: about it instantly!
Exit Nicholas.
This Wendoll I have noted, and his carriage
Hath pleas'd me much; by observation
I have noted many good deserts in him.
He's affable, and seen [28] in many things;
Discourses well; a good companion;
And though of small means, yet a gentleman
Of a good house, though somewhat prest by want.
I have preferr'd him to a second place
In my opinion and my best regard.

Enter Wendoll, Mistress Frankford, and Nicholas.

Mrs. F. Oh, Master Frankford! Master Wendoll here
Brings you the strangest news that e'er you heard.

Frank. What news, sweet wife? What news, good Master Wendoll?

Wen. You knew the match made 'twixt Sir Francis Acton

26 arrest. 27 have made good use of. 28 accomplished.

And Sir Charles Mountford?

Frank. True; with their hounds and hawks.

Wen. The matches were both play'd.

Frank. Ha? And which won?

Wen. Sir Francis, your wife's brother, had the worst,
And lost the wager.

Frank. Why, the worse his chance;
Perhaps the fortune of some other day
Will change his luck.

Mrs. F. Oh, but you hear not all.
Sir Francis lost, and yet was loth to yield.
At length the two knights grew to difference,
From words to blows, and so to banding sides;
Where valorous Sir Charles slew, in his spleen,
Two of your brother's men,—his falconer,
And his good huntsman, whom he lov'd so well.
More men were wounded, no more slain outright.

Frank. Now, trust me, I am sorry for the knight.
But is my brother safe?

Wen. All whole and sound,
His body not being blemish'd with one wound.
But poor Sir Charles is to the prison led,
To answer at th' assize for them that 's dead.

Frank. I thank your pains, sir. Had the news been better,
Your will was to have brought it, Master Wendoll.
Sir Charles will find hard friends; his case is heinous
And will be most severely censur'd on.[29]
I 'm sorry for him. Sir, a word with you!
I know you, sir, to be a gentleman
In all things; your possibilities [30] but mean:
Please you to use my table and my purse;
They 're yours.

Wen. O Lord, sir! I shall ne'er deserve it.

Frank. O sir, disparage not your worth too much:
You are full of quality [31] and fair desert.
Choose of my men which shall attend on you,
And he is yours. I will allow you, sir,
Your man, your gelding, and your table, all
At my own charge; be my companion!

Wen. Master Frankford, I have oft been bound to you
By many favors; this exceeds them all,
That I shall never merit your least favor;
But when your last remembrance I forget,
Heaven at my soul exact that weighty debt!

Frank. There needs no protestation; for I know you
Virtuous, and therefore grateful.—Prithee, Nan,
Use him with all thy loving'st courtesy!

Mrs. F. As far as modesty may well extend,
It is my duty to receive your friend.

Frank. To dinner! Come, sir, from this present day,
Welcome to me for ever! Come, away!
Exeunt Frankford, Mistress Frankford, and Wendoll.

Nich. I do not like this fellow by no means:
I never see him but my heart still yearns.[32]
Zounds! I could fight with him, yet know not why;
The devil and he are all one in mine eye.

Enter Jenkin.

Jen. O Nick! What gentleman is that comes to lie at our house? My master allows him one to wait on him, and I believe it will fall to thy lot.

Nich. I love my master; by these hilts, I do;
But rather than I 'll ever come to serve him,
I 'll turn away my master.

Enter Cicely.

Cic. Nich'las! where are you, Nich'las? You must come in, Nich'las, and help the young gentleman off with his boots.

Nich. If I pluck off his boots, I 'll eat the spurs,
And they shall stick fast in my throat like burrs.

Cic. Then, Jenkin, come you!

Jen. Nay, 't is no boot [33] for me to deny it. My master hath given me a coat here, but he takes pains himself to brush it once or twice a day with a holly wand.

Cic. Come, come, make haste, that you

29 judged. 30 resources. 31 natural gifts. 32 grieves. 33 use.

may wash your hands again, and help to serve in dinner!

Jen. You may see, my masters, though it be afternoon with you, 't is yet but early days with us, for we have not din'd yet. Stay but a little; I 'll but go in and help to bear up the first course, and come to you again presently.

Exeunt.

SCENE 2. *The Jail.*

Enter Malby and Cranwell.

Mal. This is the sessions-day; pray can you tell me
How young Sir Charles hath sped? Is he acquit,
Or must he try the laws' strict penalty?

Cran. He 's clear'd of all, spite of his enemies,
Whose earnest labor was to take his life.
But in this suit of pardon he hath spent
All the revenues that his father left him;
And he is now turn'd a plain countryman,
Reform'd in all things. See, sir, here he comes.

Enter Sir Charles and his Keeper.

Keep. Discharge your fees, and you are then at freedom.

Sir C. Here, Master Keeper, take the poor remainder
Of all the wealth I have! My heavy foes
Have made my purse light; but, alas! to me
'T is wealth enough that you have set me free.

Mal. God give you joy of your delivery!
I am glad to see you abroad, Sir Charles.

Sir C. The poorest knight in England, Master Malby.
My life has cost me all my patrimony
My father left his son. Well, God forgive them
That are the authors of my penury!

Enter Shafton.

Shaft. Sir Charles! A hand, a hand! At liberty?
Now, by the faith I owe, I am glad to see it.
What want you? Wherein may I pleasure you?

Sir C. Oh me! Oh, most unhappy gentleman!
I am not worthy to have friends stirr'd up,
Whose hands may help me in this plunge of want.
I would I were in Heaven, to inherit there
Th' immortal birthright which my Savior keeps,
And by no unthrift can be bought and sold;
For here on earth what pleasures should we trust!

Shaft. To rid you from these contemplations,
Three hundred pounds you shall receive of me;
Nay, five for fail.[34] Come, sir, the sight of gold
Is the most sweet receipt for melancholy,
And will revive your spirits. You shall hold law
With your proud adversaries. Tush! let Frank Acton
Wage, with his knighthood, like expense with me,
And he will sink, he will.—Nay, good Sir Charles,
Applaud your fortune and your fair escape
From all these perils.

Sir C. Oh, sir! they have undone me.
Two thousand and five hundred pound a year
My father at his death possest me of;
All which the envious Acton made me spend;
And, notwithstanding all this large expense,
I had much ado to gain my liberty;
And I have only now a house of pleasure,
With some five hundred pounds reserv'd,
Both to maintain me and my loving sister.

Shaft. (*Aside.*) That must I have, it lies convenient for me.
If I can fasten but one finger on him,
With my full hand I 'll gripe him to the heart.
'T is not for love I proffer'd him this coin,
But for my gain and pleasure.—Come, Sir Charles,
I know you have need of money; take my offer.

Sir C. Sir, I accept it, and remain indebted
Even to the best of my unable[35] power.

[34] to prevent failure.

[35] feeble.

Come, gentlemen, and see it tend'red down!
Exeunt.

SCENE 3. *Frankford's house.*

Enter Wendoll, melancholy.

Wen. I am a villain, if I apprehend[36]
But such a thought! Then, to attempt the deed,
Slave, thou art damn'd without redemption.—
I'll drive away this passion with a song.
A song! Ha, ha! A song! As if, fond[37] man,
Thy eyes could swim in laughter, when thy soul
Lies drench'd and drowned in red tears of blood!
I'll pray, and see if God within my heart
Plant better thoughts. Why, prayers are meditations,
And when I meditate (oh, God forgive me!)
It is on her divine perfections.
I will forget her; I will arm myself
Not t' entertain a thought of love to her;
And, when I come by chance into her presence,
I'll hale these balls until my eye-strings crack,
From being pull'd and drawn to look that way.

Enter, over the Stage, Frankford, his Wife, and Nicholas, and exeunt.

O God, O God! With what a violence
I'm hurried to mine own destruction!
There goest thou, the most perfectest man
That ever England bred a gentleman,
And shall I wrong his bed?—Thou God of thunder!
Stay, in Thy thoughts of vengeance and of wrath,
Thy great, almighty, and all-judging hand
From speedy execution on a villain,—
A villain and a traitor to his friend.

Enter Jenkin.

Jen. Did your worship call?
Wen. He doth maintain me; he allows me largely
Money to spend.
Jen. By my faith, so do not you me: I cannot get a cross[38] of you.
Wen. My gelding, and my man.
Jen. That's Sorrel and I.
Wen. This kindness grows of no alliance[39] 'twixt us.
Jen. Nor is my service of any great acquaintance.
Wen. I never bound him to me by desert.
Of a mere stranger, a poor gentleman,
A man by whom in no kind he could gain,
He hath plac'd me in the height of all his thoughts,
Made me companion with the best and chiefest
In Yorkshire. He cannot eat without me,
Nor laugh without me; I am to his body
As necessary as his digestion,
And equally do make him whole or sick.
And shall I wrong this man? Base man! Ingrate!
Hast thou the power, straight with thy gory hands,
To rip thy image from his bleeding heart,
To scratch thy name from out the holy book
Of his remembrance, and to wound his name
That holds thy name so dear? Or rend his heart
To whom thy heart was knit and join'd together?—
And yet I must. Then Wendoll, be content!
Thus villains, when they would, cannot repent.
Jen. What a strange humor is my new master in! Pray God he be not mad; if he should be so, I should never have any mind to serve him in Bedlam.[40] It may be he's mad for missing of me.
Wen. What, Jenkin! Where's your mistress?
Jen. Is your worship married?
Wen. Why dost thou ask?
Jen. Because you are my master; and if I have a mistress, I would be glad, like a good servant, to do my duty to her.
Wen. I mean Mistress Frankford.
Jen. Marry, sir, her husband is riding out of town, and she went very lovingly to bring him on his way to horse. Do you

36 conceive. 37 foolish. 38 a coin with a cross on one side 39 kinship. 40 lunatic asylum.

see, sir? Here she comes, and here I go.
Wen. Vanish!

Exit Jenkin.

Enter Mistress Frankford.

Mrs. F. You are well met, sir; now, in troth, my husband
Before he took horse, had a great desire
To speak with you; we sought about the house,
Halloo'd into the fields, sent every way,
But could not meet you. Therefore, he enjoin'd me
To do unto you his most kind commends,—
Nay, more: he wills you, as you prize his love,
Or hold in estimation his kind friendship,
To make bold in his absence, and command
Even as himself were present in the house;
For you must keep his table, use his servants,
And be a present Frankford in his absence.
Wen. I thank him for his love.—
(*Aside.*) Give me a name, you, whose infectious tongues
Are tipt with gall and poison: as you would
Think on a man that had your father slain,
Murd'red your children, made your wives base strumpets,
So call me, call me so; print in my face
The most stigmatic title of a villain,
For hatching treason to so true a friend!
Mrs. F. Sir, you are much beholding to my husband;
You are a man most dear in his regard.
Wen. I am bound unto your husband, and you too.
(*Aside.*) I will not speak to wrong a gentleman
Of that good estimation, my kind friend.
I will not; zounds! I will not. I may choose,
And I will choose. Shall I be so misled,
Or shall I purchase to my father's crest
The motto of a villain? If I say
I will not do it, what thing can enforce me?
What can compel me? What sad destiny
Hath such command upon my yielding thoughts?
I will not;—ha! Some fury pricks me on;
The swift fates drag me at their chariot wheel,
And hurry me to mischief. Speak I must:
Injure myself, wrong her, deceive his trust!
Mrs. F. Are you not well, sir, that you seem thus troubled?
There is sedition in your countenance.
Wen. And in my heart, fair angel, chaste and wise.
I love you! Start not, speak not, answer not;
I love you,—nay, let me speak the rest;
Bid me to swear, and I will call to record
The host of Heaven.
Mrs. F. The host of Heaven forbid
Wendoll should hatch such a disloyal thought?
Wen. Such is my fate; to this suit was I born,
To wear rich pleasure's crown, or fortune's scorn.
Mrs. F. My husband loves you.
Wen. I know it.
Mrs. F. He esteems you,
Even as his brain, his eye-ball, or his heart.
Wen. I have tried it.
Mrs. F. His purse is your exchequer, and his table
Doth freely serve you.
Wen. So I have found it.
Mrs. F. Oh, with what face of brass, what brow of steel,
Can you, unblushing, speak this to the face
Of the espous'd wife of so dear a friend?
It is my husband that maintains your state.—
Will you dishonor him that in your power
Hath left his whole affairs? I am his wife,
It is to me you speak.
Wen. O speak no more;
For more than this I know, and have recorded
Within the red-leav'd table of my heart.
Fair, and of all belov'd, I was not fearful
Bluntly to give my life into your hand,
And at one hazard all my earthly means.
Go, tell your husband; he will turn me off,
And I am then undone. I care not, I;

'T was for your sake. Perchance, in rage he 'll kill me;
I care not, 't was for you. Say I incur
The general name of villain through the world,
Of traitor to my friend; I care not, I.
Beggary, shame, death, scandal, and reproach,—
For you I 'll hazard all. Why, what care I?
For you I 'll live, and in your love I 'll die.

Mrs. F. You move me, sir, to passion and to pity.
The love I bear my husband is as precious
As my soul's health.

Wen. I love your husband too,
And for his love I will engage my life.
Mistake me not; the augmentation
Of my sincere affection borne to you
Doth no whit lessen my regard to him.
I will be secret, lady, close as night;
And not the light of one small glorious star
Shall shine here in my forehead, to bewray
That act of night.

Mrs. F. What shall I say?
My soul is wandering, and hath lost her way.
Oh, Master Wendoll! Oh!

Wen. Sigh not, sweet saint;
For every sigh you breathe draws from my heart
A drop of blood.

Mrs. F. I ne'er offended yet:
My fault, I fear, will in my brow be writ.
Women that fall, not quite bereft of grace,
Have their offenses noted in their face.
I blush, and am asham'd. Oh, Master Wendoll,
Pray God I be not born to curse your tongue,
That hath enchanted me! This maze I am in
I fear will prove the labyrinth of sin.

Enter Nicholas behind.

Wen. The path of pleasure and the gate to bliss,
Which on your lips I knock at with a kiss!

Nich. I 'll kill the rogue.

Wen. Your husband is from home, your bed 's no blab.
Nay, look not down and blush!

Exeunt Wendoll and Mistress Frankford.

Nich. Zounds! I 'll stab.
Aye, Nick, was it thy chance to come just in the nick?
I love my master, and I hate that slave;
I love my mistress, but these tricks I like not.
My master shall not pocket up this wrong;
I 'll eat my fingers first. What say'st thou, metal?
Does not the rascal Wendoll go on legs
That thou must cut off? Hath he not ham-strings
That thou must hough? Nay, metal, thou shalt stand
To all I say. I 'll henceforth turn a spy,
And watch them in their close conveyances.[41]
I never look'd for better of that rascal,
Since he came miching[42] first into our house.
It is that Satan hath corrupted her;
For she was fair and chaste. I 'll have an eye
In all their gestures. Thus I think of them:
If they proceed as they have done before,
Wendoll 's a knave, my mistress is a——

Exit.

ACT III.

SCENE 1. *Sir Charles Mountford's house.*

Enter Sir Charles Mountford and Susan.

Sir C. Sister, you see we are driven to hard shift,
To keep this poor house we have left unsold.
I 'm now enforc'd to follow husbandry,
And you to milk; and do we not live well?
Well, I thank God.

Susan. O brother! here 's a change,
Since old Sir Charles died, in our father's house.

Sir C. All things on earth thus change, some up, some down;
Content 's a kingdom, and I wear that crown.

Enter Shafton, with a Sergeant.

41 secret practices.

42 sneaking.

Shaft. Good morrow, morrow, Sir Charles! What! With your sister,
Plying your husbandry?—Sergeant, stand off!—
You have a pretty house here, and a garden,
And goodly ground about it. Since it lies
So near a lordship that I lately bought,
I would fain buy it of you. I will give you——

Sir C. Oh, pardon me; this house successively
Hath long'd to me and my progenitors
Three hundred years. My great-great-grandfather,
He in whom first our gentle style[43] began,
Dwelt here, and in this ground increast this mole-hill
Unto that mountain which my father left me.
Where he the first of all our house began,
I now the last will end, and keep this house,—
This virgin title, never yet deflower'd
By any unthrift of the Mountfords' line.
In brief, I will not sell it for more gold
Than you could hide or pave the ground withal.

Shaft. Ha, ha! a proud mind and a beggar's purse!
Where 's my three hundred pounds, besides the use?[44]
I have brought it to an execution
By course of law. What! Is my money ready?

Sir C. An execution, sir, and never tell me
You put my bond in suit? You deal extremely.

Shaft. Sell me the land, and I'll acquit you straight.

Sir C. Alas, alas! 'T is all trouble hath left me
To cherish me and my poor sister's life.
If this were sold, our names should then be quite
Raz'd from the bead-roll[45] of gentility.
You see what hard shift we have made to keep it
Allied still to our name. This palm you see,
Labor hath glow'd within; her silver brow,
That never tasted a rough winter's blast
Without a mask or fan, doth with a grace
Defy cold winter, and his storms outface.

Susan. Sir, we feed sparing, and we labor hard,
We lie uneasy, to reserve to us
And our succession this small spot of ground.

Sir C. I have so bent my thoughts to husbandry,[46]
That I protest I scarcely can remember
What a new fashion is; how silk or satin
Feels in my hand. Why, pride is grown to us
A mere, mere stranger. I have quite forgot
The names of all that ever waited on me.
I cannot name ye any of my hounds,
Once from whose echoing mouths I heard all music
That e'er my heart desir'd. What should I say?
To keep this place, I have chang'd myself away.

Shaft. Arrest him at my suit!—Actions and actions
Shall keep thee in perpetual bondage fast;
Nay, more, I 'll sue thee by a late appeal,
And call thy former life in question.
The keeper is my friend; thou shalt have irons,
And usage such as I 'll deny to dogs.—
Away with him.

Sir C. You are too timorous.[47]
But trouble is my master,
And I will serve him truly.—My kind sister,
Thy tears are of no use to mollify
The flinty man. Go to my father's brother,
My kinsmen, and allies; entreat them for me,
To ransom me from this injurious man
That seeks my ruin.

Shaft. Come, irons! Come away;
I 'll see thee lodg'd far from the sight of day.

Exeunt, except Susan.

Susan. My heart 's so hard'ned with the frost of grief,
Death cannot pierce it through.—Tyrant too fell!
So lead the fiends condemned souls to hell.

43 rank as gentry.
44 interest.
45 list; properly a list of names to be prayed for.
46 economy.
47 Neilson suggests *tyrannous*.

Enter Sir Francis Acton and Malby.

Sir F. Again to prison! Malby, hast thou seen
A poor slave better tortur'd? Shall we hear
The music of his voice cry from the grate,[48]
Meat, for the Lord's sake? No, no; yet I am not
Throughly reveng'd. They say, he hath a pretty wench
Unto his sister; shall I, in mercy-sake
To him and to his kindred, bribe the fool
To shame herself by lewd, dishonest lust?
I'll proffer largely; but, the deed being done,
I'll smile to see her base confusion.

Mal. Methinks, Sir Francis, you are full reveng'd
For greater wrongs than he can proffer you.
See where the poor sad gentlewoman stands!

Sir F. Ha, ha! Now will I flout her poverty,
Deride her fortunes, scoff her base estate;
My very soul the name of Mountford hates.
But stay, my heart! Oh, what a look did fly
To strike my soul through with thy piercing eye!
I am enchanted; all my spirits are fled,
And with one glance my envious spleen struck dead.

Susan. Acton! That seeks our blood! *Runs away.*

Sir F. O chaste and fair!

Mal. Sir Francis! Why, Sir Francis! Zounds, in a trance?
Sir Francis! What cheer, man? Come, come, how is't?

Sir F. Was she not fair? Or else this judging eye
Cannot distinguish beauty.

Mal. She was fair.

Sir F. She was an angel in a mortal's shape,
And ne'er descended from old Mountford's line.
But soft, soft, let me call my wits together!
A poor, poor wench, to my great adversary
Sister, whose very souls denounce stern war
One against other! How now, Frank, turn'd fool
Or madman, whether? But no! Master of
My perfect senses and directest wits.
Then why should I be in this violent humor
Of passion and of love? And with a person
So different every way, and so oppos'd
In all contractions[49] and still-warring actions?
Fie, fie! How I dispute against my soul!
Come, come; I'll gain her, or in her fair quest
Purchase my soul free and immortal rest. *Exeunt.*

SCENE 2. *Frankford's house.*

Enter three or four Serving-men, one with a voider[50] and a wooden knife, to take away all; another the salt and bread; another with the table-cloth and napkins; another the carpet;[51] Jenkin with two lights after them.

Jen. So; march in order, and retire in battle array! My master and the guests have supp'd already; all's taken away. Here, now spread for the serving-men in the hall!—Butler, it belongs to your office.

But. I know it, Jenkin. What d' ye call the gentleman that supp'd there to-night?

Jen. Who? My master?

But. No, no; Master Wendoll, he's a daily guest. I mean the gentleman that came but this afternoon.

Jen. His name's Master Cranwell. God's light! Hark, within there; my master calls to lay more billets[52] upon the fire. Come, come! Lord, how we that are in office here in the house are troubled! One spread the carpet in the parlor, and stand ready to snuff the lights; the rest be ready to prepare their stomachs! More lights in the hall, there! Come, Nicholas.

Exeunt all but Nicholas.

Nich. I cannot eat; but had I Wendoll's heart,
I would eat that. The rogue grows impudent,

48 grated window of the debtor's prison.
49 dealings.
50 crumb-tray.
51 table-cloth.
52 logs.

Oh! I have seen such vile, notorious tricks,
Ready to make my eyes dart from my head.
I'll tell my master; by this air, I will;
Fall what may fall, I'll tell him. Here he comes.

Enter Master Frankford, as it were brushing the crumbs from his clothes with a napkin, as newly risen from supper.

Frank. Nicholas, what make you here? Why are not you
At supper in the hall, among your fellows?
Nich. Master, I stay'd your rising from the board,
To speak with you.
Frank. Be brief then, gentle Nicholas;
My wife and guests attend [53] me in the parlor.
Why dost thou pause? Now, Nicholas, you want money,
And, unthrift-like, would eat into your wages
Ere you had earn'd it. Here, sir, 's half-a-crown;
Play the good husband,[54]—and away to supper!
Nich. By this hand, an honorable gentleman! I will not see him wrong'd.
Sir, I have serv'd you long; you entertain'd me
Seven years before your beard; you knew me, sir,
Before you knew my mistress.
Frank. What of this, good Nicholas?
Nich. I never was a make-bate [55] or a knave;
I have no fault but one—I'm given to quarrel,
But not with women. I will tell you, master,
That which will make your heart leap from your breast,
Your hair to startle from your head, your ears to tingle.
Frank. What preparation 's this to dismal news?
Nich. 'Sblood! sir, I love you better than your wife.
I'll make it good.
Frank. You are a knave, and I have much ado
With wonted patience to contain my rage,
And not to break thy pate. Thou art a knave.
I'll turn you, with your base comparisons,
Out of my doors.
Nich. Do, do.
There is not room for Wendoll and me too,
Both in one house. O master, master,
That Wendoll is a villain!
Frank. Aye, saucy?
Nich. Strike, strike, do strike; yet hear me! I am no fool;
I know a villain, when I see him act
Deeds of a villain. Master, master, the base slave
Enjoys my mistress, and dishonors you.
Frank. Thou hast kill'd me with a weapon, whose sharp point
Hath prick'd quite through and through my shiv'ring heart.
Drops of cold sweat sit dangling on my hairs,
Like morning's dew upon the golden flowers,
And I am plung'd into strange agonies.
What did'st thou say? If any word that toucht
His credit, or her reputation,
It is as hard to enter my belief,
As Dives into heaven.
Nich. I can gain nothing:
They are two that never wrong'd me. I knew before
'T was but a thankless office, and perhaps
As much as is my service, or my life
Is worth. All this I know; but this, and more,
More by a thousand dangers, could not hire me
To smother such a heinous wrong from you.
I saw, and I have said.
Frank. (*Aside.*) 'T is probable. Though blunt, yet he is honest.
Though I durst pawn my life, and on their faith
Hazard the dear salvation of my soul,
Yet in my trust I may be too secure.
May this be true? Oh, may it? Can it be?
Is it by any wonder possible?
Man, woman, what thing mortal can we trust,
When friends and bosom wives prove so unjust?—
What instance [56] hast thou of this strange report?
Nich. Eyes, eyes.

[53] await. [54] thrifty man. [55] breeder of quarrels. [56] evidence.

Frank. Thy eyes may be deceiv'd, I tell thee;
For should an angel from the heavens drop down,
And preach this to me that thyself hast told,
He should have much ado to win belief;
In both their loves I am so confident.

Nich. Shall I discourse the same by circumstance?

Frank. No more! To supper, and command your fellows
To attend us and the strangers! Not a word,
I charge thee, on thy life! Be secret then;
For I know nothing.

Nich. I am dumb; and, now that I have eas'd my stomach,[57]
I will go fill my stomach. *Exit.*

Frank. Away! Begone!—
She is well born, descended nobly;
Virtuous her education; her repute
Is in the general voice of all the country
Honest and fair; her carriage, her demeanor,
In all her actions that concern the love
To me her husband, modest, chaste, and godly.
Is all this seeming gold plain copper?
But he, that Judas that hath borne my purse,
Hath sold me for a sin. O God! O God!
Shall I put up these wrongs? No! Shall I trust
The bare report of this suspicious groom,
Before the double-gilt, the well-hatch'd[58] ore
Of their two hearts? No, I will lose these thoughts;
Distraction I will banish from my brow,
And from my looks exile sad discontent,
Their wonted favors in my tongue shall flow;
Till I know all, I'll nothing seem to know.—
Lights and a table there! Wife, Master Wendoll,
And gentle Master Cranwell!

Enter Mistress Frankford, Master Wendoll, Master Cranwell, Nicholas, and Jenkin with cards, carpets, stools, and other necessaries.

Frank. O! Master Cranwell, you are a stranger here,
And often balk[59] my house; faith, y' are a churl!—
Now we have supp'd, a table, and to cards!

Jen. A pair[60] of cards, Nicholas, and a carpet to cover the table! Where's Cicely, with her counters and her box? Candles and candlesticks, there! Fie! We have such a household of serving-creatures! Unless it be Nick and I, there's not one amongst them all that can say bo to a goose.—Well said,[61] Nick!

(*They spread a carpet: set down lights and cards.*)

Mrs. F. Come, Mr. Frankford, who shall take my part?[62]

Frank. Marry, that will I, sweet wife.

Wen. No, by my faith, when you are together, I sit out. It must be Mistress Frankford and I, or else it is no match.

Frank. I do not like that match.

Nich. (*Aside.*) You have no reason, marry, knowing all.

Frank. 'T is no great matter, neither.—Come, Master Cranwell, shall you and I take them up?

Cran. At your pleasure, sir.

Frank. I must look to you, Master Wendoll, for you'll be playing false. Nay, so will my wife, too.

Nich. (*Aside.*) Aye, I will be sworn she will.

Mrs. F. Let them that are taken playing false, forfeit the set!

Frank. Content; it shall go hard but I'll take you.

Cran. Gentlemen, what shall our game be?

Wen. Master Frankford, you play best at noddy.[63]

Frank. You shall not find it so; indeed, you shall not.

Mrs. F. I can play at nothing so well as double-ruff.

Frank. If Master Wendoll and my wife be together, there's no playing against them at double-hand.

Nich. I can tell you, sir, the game that Master Wendoll is best at.

Wen. What game is that, Nick?

57 anger.
58 of noble origin.
59 shun.
60 pack.
61 well done.
62 be my partner.
63 This, and the other games mentioned, were all popular at the time. The *doubles entendres* throughout the scene should be noted; such scenes, punning on the terms employed in various games, occur in several Elizabethan plays.

Nich. Marry, sir, knave out of doors.
Wen. She and I will take you at lodam.
Mrs. F. Husband, shall we play at saint?
Frank. (*Aside.*) My saint 's turn'd devil. —No, we 'll none of saint:
You are best at new-cut, wife, you 'll play at that.
Wen. If you play at new-cut, I 'm soonest hitter of any here, for a wager.
Frank. (*Aside.*) 'T is me they play on.— Well, you may draw out;
For all your cunning, 't will be to your shame;
I 'll teach you, at your new-cut, a new game.
Come, come!
Cran. If you cannot agree upon the game,
To post and pair!
Wen. We shall be soonest pairs; and my good host,
When he comes late home, he must kiss the post.[64]
Frank. Whoever wins, it shall be to thy cost.
Cran. Faith, let it be vide-ruff, and let 's make honors!
Frank. If you make honors, one thing let me crave:
Honor the king and queen, except the knave.
Wen. Well, as you please for that.— Lift [65] who shall deal?
Mrs. F. The least in sight. What are you, Master Wendoll?
Wen. I am a knave.
Nich. (*Aside.*) I 'll swear it.
Mrs. F. I a queen.
Frank. (*Aside.*) A quean,[66] thou should'st say.—Well, the cards are mine:
They are the grossest pair [67] that e'er I felt.
Mrs. F. Shuffle, I 'll cut: would I had never dealt!
Frank. I have lost my dealing.
Wen. Sir, the fault 's in me;
This queen I have more than mine own, you see.
Give me the stock! [67]
Frank. My mind 's not on my game.
Many a deal I 've lost; the more 's your shame.
You have serv'd me a bad trick, Master Wendoll.
Wen. Sir, you must take your lot. To end this strife,
I know I have dealt better with your wife.
Frank. Thou hast dealt falsely, then.
Mrs. F. What 's trumps?
Wen. Hearts. Partner, I rub.[68]
Frank. (*Aside.*) Thou robb'st me of my soul, of her chaste love;
In thy false dealing thou hast robb'd my heart.—
Booty you play; [69] I like a loser stand,
Having no heart, or here or in my hand.
I will give o'er the set, I am not well.
Come, who will hold my cards?
Mrs. F. Not well, sweet Master Frankford?
Alas, what ails you? 'T is some sudden qualm.
Wen. How long have you been so, Master Frankford?
Frank. Sir, I was lusty, and I had my health,
But I grew ill when you began to deal.—
Take hence this table!—Gentle Master Cranwell,
Y' are welcome; see your chamber at your pleasure!
I am sorry that this megrim [70] takes me so,
I cannot sit and bear you company.—
Jenkin, some lights, and show him to his chamber!
Exeunt Cranwell and Jenkin.
Mrs. F. A nightgown for my husband; quickly, there!
It is some rheum or cold.
Wen. Now, in good faith,
This illness you have got by sitting late
Without your gown.
Frank. I know it, Master Wendoll.
Go, go to bed, lest you complain like me!—
Wife, prithee, wife, into my bed-chamber!
The night is raw and cold, and rheumatic.
Leave me my gown and light; I 'll walk away my fit.
Wen. Sweet sir, good night!
Frank. Myself, good night!
Exit Wendoll.
Mrs. F. Shall I attend you, husband?
Frank. No, gentle wife, thou 'lt catch cold in thy head.
Prithee, begone, sweet; I 'll make haste to bed.

64 be shut out.
65 cut.
66 strumpet.
67 pack.
68 take all the cards of the suit.
69 "To play booty was to join with confederates to victimize another player." (N. E. D.)
70 headache.

Mrs. F. No sleep will fasten on mine eyes, you know,
Until you come.
Exit Mrs. Frankford.

Frank. Sweet Nan, I prithee, go!—
I have bethought me; get me by degrees
The keys of all my doors, which I will mould
In wax, and take their fair impression,
To have by them new keys. This being compast,
At a set hour a letter shall be brought me,
And when they think they may securely play,
They nearest are to danger.—Nick, I must rely
Upon thy trust and faithful secrecy.

Nich. Build on my faith!

Frank. To bed, then, not to rest!
Care lodges in my brain, grief in my breast.
Exeunt.

SCENE 3. *Old Mountford's house.*

Enter Susan, Old Mountford, Sandy, Roder, and Tidy.

Old Mount. You say my nephew is in great distress;
Who brought it to him but his own lewd life?
I cannot spare a cross. I must confess,
He was my brother's son; why, niece, what then?
This is no world in which to pity men.

Susan. I was not born a beggar, though his extremes
Enforce this language from me. I protest
No fortune of mine own could lead my tongue
To this base key. I do beseech you, uncle,
For the name's sake, for Christianity,
Nay, for God's sake, to pity his distress.
He is denied the freedom of the prison,
And in the hole is laid with men condemn'd;
Plenty he hath of nothing but of irons,
And it remains in you to free him thence.

Old Mount. Money I cannot spare; men should take heed.
He lost my kindred when he fell to need.
Exit.

Susan. Gold is but earth; thou earth enough shalt have,
When thou hast once took measure of thy grave.
You know me, Master Sandy, and my suit.

Sandy. I knew you, lady, when the old man liv'd;
I knew you ere your brother sold his land.
Then you were Mistress Sue, trick'd up in jewels;
Then you sung well, play'd sweetly on the lute;
But now I neither know you nor your suit.
Exit.

Susan. You, Master Roder, was my brother's tenant;
Rent-free he plac'd you in that wealthy farm,
Of which you are possest.

Roder. True, he did;
And have I not there dwelt still for his sake?
I have some business now; but, without doubt,
They that have hurl'd him in, will help him out.
Exit.

Susan. Cold comfort still. What say you, cousin Tidy?

Tidy. I say this comes of roysting,[71] swaggering.
Call me not cousin; each man for himself!
Some men are born to mirth, and some to sorrow:
I am no cousin unto them that borrow.
Exit.

Susan. O Charity, why art thou fled to heaven,
And left all things upon this earth uneven?
Their scoffing answers I will ne'er return,
But to myself his grief in silence mourn.

Enter Sir Francis and Malby.

Sir F. She is poor, I'll therefore tempt her with this gold.
Go, Malby, in my name deliver it,
And I will stay thy answer.

Mal. Fair mistress, as I understand your grief
Doth grow from want, so I have here in store
A means to furnish you, a bag of gold,

[71] roistering.

Which to your hands I freely tender you.
Susan. I thank you, Heavens! I thank you, gentle sir:
God make me able to requite this favor!
Mal. This gold Sir Francis Acton sends by me,
And prays you—
Susan. Acton? O God! That name I'm born to curse.
Hence, bawd; hence, broker! See, I spurn his gold.
My honor never shall for gain be sold.
Sir F. Stay, lady, stay!
Susan. From you I'll posting hie,
Even as the doves from feather'd eagles fly.
Exit.
Sir F. She hates my name, my face; how should I woo?
I am disgrac'd in every thing I do.
The more she hates me, and disdains my love,
The more I am rapt in admiration
Of her divine and chaste perfections.
Woo her with gifts I cannot, for all gifts
Sent in my name she spurns; with looks I cannot,
For she abhors my sight; nor yet with letters,
For none she will receive. How then? how then?
Well, I will fasten such a kindness on her,
As shall o'ercome her hate and conquer it.
Sir Charles, her brother, lies in execution
For a great sum of money; and, besides,
The appeal is sued still for my huntsmen's death,
Which only I have power to reverse.
In her I'll bury all my hate of him.—
Go seek the keeper, Malby, bring him to me!
To save his body, I his debts will pay;
To save his life, I his appeal will stay.
Exeunt.

ACT IV.

Scene 1. *A prison cell.*

Enter Sir Charles Mountford, with irons, his feet bare, his garments all ragged and torn.

Sir C. Of all on the earth's face most miserable,
Breathe in this hellish dungeon thy laments!
Thus like a slave ragg'd, like a felon gyv'd,—
That hurls thee headlong to this base estate.
Oh, unkind uncle! Oh, my friends ingrate!
Unthankful kinsmen! Mountford's all too base,
To let thy name be fetter'd in disgrace.
A thousand deaths here in this grave I die;
Fear, hunger, sorrow, cold, all threat my death,
And join together to deprive my breath.
But that which most torments me, my dear sister
Hath left[72] to visit me, and from my friends
Hath brought no hopeful answer; therefore, I
Divine they will not help my misery.
If it be so, shame, scandal, and contempt
Attend their covetous thoughts; need make their graves!
Usurers they live, and may they die like slaves!

Enter Keeper.

Keep. Knight, be of comfort, for I bring thee freedom
From all thy troubles.
Sir C. Then, I am doom'd to die:
Death is the end of all calamity.
Keep. Live! Your appeal is stay'd; the execution
Of all your debts discharg'd; your creditors
Even to the utmost penny satisfied.
In sign whereof your shackles I knock off.
You are not left so much indebted to us
As for your fees; all is discharg'd; all paid.
Go freely to your house, or where you please;
After long miseries, embrace your ease.
Sir C. Thou grumblest out the sweetest music to me
That ever organ play'd.—Is this a dream?
Or do my waking senses apprehend
The pleasing taste of these applausive[73] news?
Slave that I was, to wrong such honest friends.

72 ceased.

73 ioyful.

My loving kinsman, and my near allies!
Tongue, I will bite thee for the scandal breath'd
Against such faithful kinsmen; they are all
Compos'd of pity and compassion,
Of melting charity and of moving ruth.
That which I spoke before was in my rage;
They are my friends, the mirrors of this age;
Bounteous and free. The noble Mountford's race
Ne'er bred a covetous thought, or humor base.

Enter Susan.

Susan. I cannot longer stay from visiting
My woful brother. While I could, I kept
My hapless tidings from his hopeful ear.
Sir C. Sister, how much am I indebted to thee
And to thy travail!
Susan. What, at liberty?
Sir C. Thou seest I am, thanks to thy industry.
Oh! Unto which of all my courteous friends
Am I thus bound? My uncle Mountford, he
Even of an infant lov'd me; was it he?
So did my cousin Tidy; was it he?
So Master Roder, Master Sandy, too.
Which of all these did this high kindness do?
Susan. Charles, can you mock me in your poverty,
Knowing your friends deride your misery?
Now, I protest I stand so much amaz'd,
To see your bonds free, and your irons knock'd off,
That I am rapt into a maze of wonder;
The rather for I know not by what means
This happiness hath chanc'd.
Sir C. Why, by my uncle,
My cousins, and my friends; who else, I pray,
Would take upon them all my debts to pay?
Susan. Oh, brother! they are men all of flint,
Pictures of marble, and as void of pity
As chased bears. I begg'd, I sued, I kneel'd,
Laid open all your griefs and miseries,
Which they derided; more than that, denied us
A part in their alliance; but, in pride,
Said that our kindred with our plenty died.
Sir C. Drudges too much,[74]—what did they? Oh, known evil!
Rich fly the poor, as good men shun the devil.
Whence should my freedom come? Of whom alive,
Saving of those, have I deserv'd so well?
Guess, sister, call to mind, remember[75] me!
These have I rais'd, they follow the world's guise,
Whom rich in honor, they in woe despise.
Susan. My wits have lost themselves; let 's ask the keeper!
Sir C. Gaoler!
Keep. At hand, sir.
Sir C. Of courtesy resolve me one demand!
What was he took the burden of my debts
From off my back, stayed my appeal to death,
Discharg'd my fees, and brought me liberty?
Keep. A courteous knight, one call'd Sir Francis Acton.
Sir C. Ha! Acton! Oh me! More distress'd in this
Than all my troubles! Hale me back,
Double my irons, and my sparing meals
Put into halves, and lodge me in a dungeon
More deep, more dark, more cold, more comfortless!
By Acton freed! Not all thy manacles
Could fetter so my heels, as this one word
Hath thrall'd my heart; and it must now lie bound
In more strict prison than thy stony gaol.
I am not free, I go but under bail.
Keep. My charge is done, sir, now I have my fees.
As we get little, we will nothing leese.[76]
Sir C. By Acton freed, my dangerous opposite!
Why, to what end? On what occasion? Ha!
Let me forget the name of enemy,
And with indifference balance[77] this high favor!

[74] too base in their conduct. (Ward.) [75] remind. [76] lose. [77] weigh impartially.

Susan. (*Aside.*) His love to me, upon my soul, 't is so!
That is the root from whence these strange things grow.

Sir C. Had this proceeded from my father, he
That by the law of Nature is most bound
In offices of love, it had deserv'd
My best employment to requite that grace.
Had it proceeded from my friends, or him,
From them this action had deserv'd my life,—
And from a stranger more, because from such
There is less execution of good deeds.
But he, nor father, nor ally, nor friend,
More than a stranger, both remote in blood,
And in his heart oppos'd my enemy,
That this high bounty should proceed from him,—
Oh! there I lose myself. What should I say,
What think, what do, his bounty to repay?

Susan. You wonder, I am sure, whence this strange kindness
Proceeds in Acton; I will tell you, brother.
He dotes on me, and oft hath sent me gifts,
Letters, and tokens; I refus'd them all.

Sir C. I have enough, though poor: my heart is set,
In one rich gift to pay back all my debt.
Exeunt.

SCENE 2. *Frankford's house.*

Enter Frankford and Nicholas, with keys.

Frank. This is the night that I must play my part,
To try two seeming angels.—Where 's my keys?

Nich. They are made according to your mould in wax.
I bade the smith be secret, gave him money,
And here they are. The letter, sir!
(*Gives Nicholas letter.*)

Frank. True, take it, there it is;
And when thou seest me in my pleasant'st vein,
Ready to sit to supper, bring it me!

Nich. I 'll do 't; make no more question but I 'll do it.
Exit.

Enter Mistress Frankford, Cranwell, Wendoll, and Jenkin.

Mrs. F. Sirrah, 't is six o'clock already struck;
Go bid them spread the cloth, and serve in supper!

Jen. It shall be done, forsooth, mistress. Where 's Spigot, the butler, to give us out salt and trenchers?
Exit.

Wen. We that have been a hunting all the day,
Come with prepared stomachs.—Master Frankford,
We wish'd you at our sport.

Frank. My heart was with you, and my mind was on you.—
Fie, Master Cranwell! You are still thus sad.—
A stool, a stool! Where 's Jenkin, and where 's Nick?
'T is supper time at least an hour ago.
What 's the best news abroad?

Wen. I know none good.

Frank. (*Aside.*) But I know too much bad.

Enter Butler and Jenkin, with a tablecloth, bread, trenchers, and salt; then exeunt.

Cran. Methinks, sir, you might have that interest [78]
In your wife's brother, to be more remiss [79]
In his hard dealing against poor Sir Charles,
Who, as I hear, lies in York Castle, needy
And in great want.

Frank. Did not more weighty business of mine own
Hold me away, I would have labor'd peace
Betwixt them with all care; indeed I would, sir.

Mrs. F. I 'll write unto my brother earnestly
In that behalf.

Wen. A charitable deed,
And will beget the good opinion
Of all your friends that love you, Mistress Frankford.

[78] influence with.

[79] lenient.

Frank. That 's you, for one; I know you love Sir Charles,
(*Aside.*) And my wife too, well.
Wen. He deserves the love
Of all true gentlemen; be yourselves judge!
Frank. But supper, ho!—Now, as thou lov'st me, Wendoll,
Which I am sure thou dost, be merry, pleasant,
And frolic it to-night!—Sweet Mr. Cranwell,
Do you the like!—Wife, I protest, my heart
Was ne'er more bent on sweet alacrity.
Where be those lazy knaves to serve in supper?

Enter Nicholas.

Nich. Here 's a letter, sir.
Frank. Whence comes it, and who brought it?
Nich. A stripling that below attends your answer,
And, as he tells me, it is sent from York.
Frank. Have him into the cellar, let him taste
A cup of our March beer; go, make him drink!
Nich. I'll make him drunk, if he be a Trojan.[80]
Frank. (*After reading the letter.*) My boots and spurs! Where 's Jenkin? God forgive me,
How I neglect my business!—Wife, look here!
I have a matter to be tried to-morrow
By eight o'clock; and my attorney writes me,
I must be there betimes with evidence,
Or it will go against me. Where 's my boots?

Re-enter Jenkin, with boots and spurs.

Mrs. F. I hope your business craves no such despatch,
That you must ride to-night?
Wen. (*Aside.*) I hope it doth.
Frank. God's me! No such despatch?
Jenkin, my boots! Where 's Nick? Saddle my roan,
And the gray dapple for himself!—Content ye,
It much concerns me.—Gentle Master Cranwell,
And Master Wendoll, in my absence use
The very ripest pleasure of my house!
Wen. Lord! Master Frankford, will you ride to-night?
The ways are dangerous.
Frank. Therefore will I ride
Appointed[81] well; and so shall Nick, my man.
Mrs. F. I'll call you up by five o'clock to-morrow.
Frank. No, by my faith, wife, I'll not trust to that:
'T is not such easy rising in a morning
From one I love so dearly. No, by my faith,
I shall not leave so sweet a bedfellow,
But with much pain. You have made me a sluggard
Since I first knew you.
Mrs. F. Then, if you needs will go
This dangerous evening, Master Wendoll,
Let me entreat you bear him company.
Wen. With all my heart, sweet mistress.—My boots, there!
Frank. Fie, fie, that for my private business
I should disease[82] a friend, and be a trouble
To the whole house!—Nick!
Nich. Anon, sir!
Frank. Bring forth my gelding!—As you love me, sir,
Use no more words: a hand, good Master Cranwell!
Cran. Sir, God be your good speed!
Frank. Good night, sweet Nan; nay, nay, a kiss, and part!
(*Aside.*) Dissembling lips, you suit[83] not with my heart.
Exeunt Frankford and Nicholas.
Wen. (*Aside.*) How business, time, and hours, all gracious prove,
And are the furtherers to my new-born love!
I am husband now in Master Frankford's place,
And must command the house.—My pleasure is
We will not sup abroad so publicly,
But in your private chamber, Mistress Frankford.
Mrs. F. Oh, sir! you are too public in your love,
And Master Frankford's wife——
Cran. Might I crave favor,
I would entreat you I might see my chamber.
I am on the sudden grown exceeding ill,
And would be spar'd from supper.

80 good fellow. 81 armed. 82 inconvenience. 83 agree.

Wen. Light there, ho!—
See you want nothing, sir, for if you do,
You injure that good man, and wrong me too.

Cran. I will make bold; good night!
Exit.

Wen. How all conspire
To make our bosom[84] sweet, and full entire!
Come, Nan, I prithee, let us sup within!

Mrs. F. Oh! what a clog unto the soul is sin!
We pale offenders are still full of fear;
Every suspicious eye brings danger near;
When they, whose clear hearts from offense are free,
Despise report, base scandals do outface,
And stand at mere defiance with disgrace.

Wen. Fie, fie! You talk too like a puritan.

Mrs. F. You have tempted me to mischief, Master Wendoll:
I have done I know not what. Well, you plead custom;
That which for want of wit I granted erst,
I now must yield through fear. Come, come, let's in;
Once over shoes, we are straight o'er head in sin.

Wen. My jocund soul is joyful beyond measure;
I'll be profuse in Frankford's richest treasure.
Exeunt.

SCENE 3. *Another part of the house.*

Enter Cicely, Jenkin, Butler, and other Serving-men.

Jen. My mistress and Master Wendoll, my master, sup in her chamber to-night. Cicely, you are preferr'd, from being the cook, to be chambermaid. Of all the loves betwixt thee and me, tell me what thou think'st of this?

Cic. Mum; there's an old proverb,—when the cat's away, the mouse may play.

Jen. Now you talk of a cat, Cicely, I smell a rat.

Cic. Good words, Jenkin, lest you be call'd to answer them!

Jen. Why, God made my mistress an honest woman! Are not these good words? Pray God my new master play not the knave with my old master! Is there any hurt in this? God send no villainy intended; and if they do sup together, pray God they do not lie together! God make my mistress chaste, and make us all His servants! What harm is there in all this? Nay, more; here in my hand, thou shalt never have my heart, unless thou say, Amen.

Cic. Amen; I pray God, I say.

Enter Serving-man.

Serving-man. My mistress sends that you should make less noise, to lock up the doors, and see the household all got to bed. You, Jenkin, for this night are made the porter, to see the gates shut in.

Jen. Thus by little and little I creep into office. Come, to kennel, my masters, to kennel; 't is eleven o'clock already.

Serving-man. When you have lock'd the gates in, you must send up the keys to my mistress.

Cic. Quickly, for God's sake, Jenkin; for I must carry them. I am neither pillow nor bolster, but I know more than both.

Jen. To bed, good Spigot; to bed, good honest serving-creatures; and let us sleep as snug as pigs in pease-straw!
Exeunt.

SCENE 4. *Outside the house.*

Enter Frankford and Nicholas.

Frank. Soft, soft! We've tied our geldings to a tree,
Two flight-shot[85] off, lest by their thundering hoofs
They blab our coming back. Hear'st thou no noise?

Nich. Hear? I hear nothing but the owl and you.

Frank. So; now my watch's hand points upon twelve,
And it is dead midnight. Where are my keys?

Nich. Here, sir.

Frank. This is the key that opes my outward gate;
This, the hall-door; this, the withdrawing-chamber;
But this, that door that's bawd unto my shame,

84 intimacy.

85 bow-shots.

Fountain and spring of all my bleeding thoughts,
Where the most hallowed order and true knot
Of nuptial sanctity hath been profan'd.
It leads to my polluted bed-chamber,
Once my terrestrial heaven, now my earth's hell,
The place where sins in all their ripeness dwell.—
But I forget myself; now to my gate!

Nich. It must ope with far less noise
Than Cripplegate,[86] or your plot 's dash'd.

Frank. So; reach me my dark lantern to the rest!
Tread softly, softly!

Nich. I will walk on eggs this pace.

Frank. A general silence hath surpris'd the house,
And this is the last door. Astonishment,
Fear, and amazement, beat upon my heart,
Even as a madman beats upon a drum.
Oh, keep my eyes, you Heavens, before I enter,
From any sight that may transfix my soul;
Or, if there be so black a spectacle,
Oh, strike mine eyes stark blind; or, if not so,
Lend me such patience to digest my grief,
That I may keep this white and virgin hand
From any violent outrage, or red murder!—
And with that prayer I enter.

Exeunt into the house.

SCENE 5. *The hall of the house.*

Enter Nicholas.

Nich. Here 's a circumstance![87]
A man may be made cuckold in the time
That he 's about it. An[88] the case were mine,
As 't it my master's, 'sblood! (that he makes me swear!)
I would have plac'd his action,[89] enter'd there;
I would, I would!

Enter Frankford.

Frank. Oh! oh!

Nich. Master! 'Sblood! Master, master!

Frank. Oh me unhappy! I have found them lying
Close in each other's arms, and fast asleep.
But that I would not damn two precious souls,
Bought with my Savior's blood, and send them, laden
With all their scarlet sins upon their backs,
Unto a fearful judgment, their two lives
Had met upon my rapier.

Nich. Master, what, have you left them sleeping still?
Let me go wake 'em!

Frank. Stay, let me pause awhile!—
Oh, God! Oh, God! That it were possible
To undo things done; to call back yesterday;
That Time could turn up his swift sandy glass,
To untell[90] the days, and to redeem these hours!
Or that the sun
Could, rising from the west, draw his coach backward;
Take from th' account of time so many minutes,
Till he had all these seasons call'd again,
Those minutes, and those actions done in them,
Even from her first offense; that I might take her
As spotless as an angel in my arms!
But, oh! I talk of things impossible,
And cast beyond the moon.[91] God give me patience;
For I will in, and wake them.

Exit.

Nich. Here 's patience perforce!
He needs must trot afoot that tires his horse.

Enter Wendoll running over the stage in a night-gown,[92] Frankford after him with his sword drawn; a maid in her smock stays his hand, and clasps hold on him. He pauses for a while.

Frank. I thank thee, maid; thou, like the angel's hand,
Hast stay'd me from a bloody sacrifice.—
Go, villain; and my wrongs sit on thy soul
As heavy as this grief doth upon mine!

86 One of the old gates of London.
87 formality.
88 if.
89 established his case. (Ward.)
90 count backwards.
91 proverbial for any impossible wish.
92 dressing-gown.

When thou record'st my many courtesies,
And shalt compare them with thy treacherous heart,
Lay them together, weigh them equally,—
'T will be revenge enough. Go, to thy friend
A Judas; pray, pray, lest I live to see
Thee, Judas-like, hang'd on an elder-tree!

Enter Mistress Frankford in her smock, night-gown, and night-attire.

Mrs. F. Oh, by what word, what title, or what name,
Shall I entreat your pardon? Pardon! Oh!
I am as far from hoping such sweet grace,
As Lucifer from Heaven. To call you husband,—
Oh me, most wretched! I have lost that name;
I am no more your wife.
Nich. 'Sblood, sir, she swoons.
Frank. Spare thou thy tears, for I will weep for thee;
And keep thy count'nance, for I'll blush for thee.
Now, I protest, I think 't is I am tainted,
For I am most asham'd; and 't is more hard
For me to look upon thy guilty face
Than on the sun's clear brow. What would'st thou speak?
Mrs. F. I would I had no tongue, no ears, no eyes,
No apprehension, no capacity.
When do you spurn me like a dog? When tread me
Under feet? When drag me by the hair?
Though I deserve a thousand thousand fold,
More than you can inflict—yet, once my husband,
For womanhood, to which I am a shame,
Though once an ornament—even for His sake,
That hath redeem'd our souls, mark not my face,
Nor hack me with your sword; but let me go
Perfect and undeformed to my tomb!
I am not worthy that I should prevail
In the least suit; no, not to speak to you,
Nor look on you, nor to be in your presence;
Yet, as an abject, this one suit I crave;
This granted, I am ready for my grave.
Frank. My God, with patience arm me!—Rise, nay, rise,
And I'll debate with thee. Was it for want
Thou play'dst the strumpet? Wast thou not supplied
With every pleasure, fashion, and new toy,—
Nay, even beyond my calling?[93]
Mrs. F. I was.
Frank. Was it, then, disability in me;
Or in thine eye seem'd he a properer man?
Mrs. F. Oh, no!
Frank. Did I not lodge thee in my bosom?
Wear thee here in my heart?
Mrs. F. You did.
Frank. I did, indeed; witness my tears, I did—
Go, bring my infants hither!—
(*Two Children are brought in.*)
Oh, Nan! Oh, Nan!
If neither fear of shame, regard of honor,
The blemish of my house, nor my dear love,
Could have withheld thee from so lewd a fact,[94]
Yet for these infants, these young, harmless souls,
On whose white brows thy shame is character'd,
And grows in greatness as they wax in years,—
Look but on them, and melt away in tears!—
Away with them; lest, as her spotted body
Hath stain'd their names with stripe of bastardy,
So her adulterous breath may blast their spirits
With her infectious thoughts! Away with them!
Exeunt Children.
Mrs. F. In this one life, I die ten thousand deaths.
Frank. Stand up, stand up! I will do nothing rashly.
I will retire awhile into my study,
And thou shalt hear thy sentence presently.
Exit.
Mrs. F. 'T is welcome, be it death. Oh me, base strumpet,
That, having such a husband, such sweet children,

93 rank.

94 crime.

Must enjoy neither! Oh, to redeem my honor,
I'd have this hand cut off, these my breasts sear'd;
Be rack'd, strappado'd, put to any torment:
Nay, to whip but this scandal out, I'd hazard
The rich and dear redemption of my soul!
He cannot be so base as to forgive me,
Nor I so shameless to accept his pardon.
Oh, women, women, you that yet have kept
Your holy matrimonial vow unstain'd,
Make me your instance; when you tread awry,
Your sins, like mine, will on your conscience lie.

Enter Cicely, Spigot, all the Serving-men, and Jenkin, as newly come out of bed.

All. Oh, mistress, mistress! What have you done, mistress?
Nich. 'Sblood, what a caterwauling keep you here!
Jen. O Lord, mistress, how comes this to pass? My master is run away in his shirt, and never so much as call'd me to bring his clothes after him.
Mrs. F. See what guilt is! Here stand I in this place,
Asham'd to look my servants in the face.

Enter Frankford and Cranwell; whom seeing, she falls on her knees.

Frank. My words are regist'red in Heaven already.
With patience hear me! I'll not martyr thee,
Nor mark thee for a strumpet; but with usage
Of more humility torment thy soul,
And kill thee even with kindness.
Cran. Master Frankford—
Frank. Good Master Cranwell!—Woman, hear thy judgment!
Go make thee ready in thy best attire;
Take with thee all thy gowns, all thy apparel;
Leave nothing that did ever call thee mistress,
Or by whose sight, being left here in the house,
I may remember such a woman by.
Choose thee a bed and hangings for thy chamber;
Take with thee every thing which hath thy mark,
And get thee to my manor seven mile off,
Where live;—'t is thine; I freely give it thee.
My tenants by [95] shall furnish thee with wains
To carry all thy stuff within two hours;
No longer will I limit [96] thee my sight.
Choose which of all my servants thou lik'st best,
And they are thine to attend thee.
Mrs. F. A mild sentence.
Frank. But, as thou hop'st for Heaven, as thou believ'st
Thy name's recorded in the book of life,
I charge thee never after this sad day
To see me, or to meet me; or to send,
By word or writing, gift or otherwise,
To move me, by thyself, or by thy friends;
Nor challenge any part in my two children.
So farewell, Nan; for we will henceforth be
As we had never seen, ne'er more shall see.
Mrs. F. How full my heart is, in mine eyes appears;
What wants in words, I will supply in tears.
Frank. Come, take your coach, your stuff; all must along.
Servants and all make ready; all begone!
It was thy hand cut two hearts out of one.

Exeunt.

ACT V.

SCENE 1. *Before Sir Francis Acton's house.*

Enter Sir Charles Mountford, gentleman-like, and Susan, gentlewoman-like.

Susan. Brother, why have you trick'd [97] me like a bride,
Bought me this gay attire, these ornaments?
Forget you our estate, our poverty?
Sir C. Call me not brother, but imagine me
Some barbarous outlaw, or uncivil kern; [98]

95 nearby. 96 allow. 97 adorned. 98 Irish irregular foot-soldier.

For if thou shutt'st thine eye, and only hear'st
The words that I shall utter, thou shalt judge me
Some staring ruffian, not thy brother Charles.
Oh, sister!——

Susan. Oh, brother! what doth this strange language mean?

Sir C. Dost love me, sister? Would'st thou see me live
A bankrupt beggar in the world's disgrace,
And die indebted to mine enemies?
Wouldst thou behold me stand like a huge beam
In the world's eye, a by-word and a scorn?
It lies in thee of these to acquit me free,
And all my debt I may outstrip by thee.

Susan. By me? Why, I have nothing, nothing left;
I owe even for the clothes upon my back;
I am not worth——

Sir C. O sister, say not so!
It lies in you my downcast state to raise;
To make me stand on even points with the world.
Come, sister, you are rich; indeed, you are,
And in your power you have, without delay
Acton's five hundred pounds back to repay.

Susan. Till now I had thought you lov'd me. By my honor
(Which I have kept as spotless as the moon),
I ne'er was mistress of that single doit[99]
Which I reserv'd not to supply your wants;
And do you think that I would hoard from you?
Now, by my hopes of Heaven, knew I the means
To buy you from the slavery of your debts
(Especially from Acton, whom I hate),
I would redeem it with my life or blood!

Sir C. I challenge it, and, kindred set apart,
Thus, ruffian-like, I lay siege to your heart.
What do I owe to Acton?

Susan. Why, some five hundred pounds; towards which, I swear,
In all the world I have not one denier.[1]

Sir C. It will not prove so. Sister, now resolve[2] me:
What do you think (and speak your conscience)
Would Acton give, might he enjoy your bed?

Susan. He would not shrink to spend a thousand pound
To give the Mountfords' name so deep a wound.

Sir C. A thousand pound! I but five hundred owe:
Grant him your bed; he 's paid with interest so.

Susan. Oh, brother!

Sir C. Oh, sister! only this one way,
With that rich jewel you my debts may pay.
In speaking this my cold heart shakes with shame;
Nor do I woo you in a brother's name,
But in a stranger's. Shall I die in debt
To Acton, my grand foe, and you still wear
The precious jewel that he holds so dear?

Susan. My honor I esteem as dear and precious
As my redemption.

Sir C. I esteem you, sister,
As dear, for so dear prizing it.

Susan. Will Charles
Have me cut off my hands, and send them Acton?
Rip up my breast, and with my bleeding heart
Present him as a token?

Sir C. Neither, sister;
But hear me in my strange assertion!
Thy honor and my soul are equal in my regard;
Nor will thy brother Charles survive thy shame.
His kindness, like a burden, hath surcharg'd me,
And under his good deeds I stooping go,
Not with an upright soul. Had I remain'd
In prison still, there doubtless I had died.
Then, unto him that freed me from that prison,
Still do I owe this life. What mov'd my foe
To enfranchise me? 'T was, sister, for your love;
With full five hundred pounds he bought your love;—
And shall he not enjoy it? Shall the weight

99 any small coin. 1 penny. 2 assure.

Of all this heavy burden lean on me,
And will not you bear part? You did partake
The joy of my release; will you not stand
In joint-bond bound to satisfy the debt?
Shall I be only charg'd?

Susan. But that I know
These arguments come from an honor'd mind,
As in your most extremity of need
Scorning to stand in debt to one you hate,—
Nay, rather would engage your unstain'd honor,
Than to be held ingrate,—I should condemn you.
I see your resolution, and assent;
So Charles will have me, and I am content.

Sir C. For this I trick'd you up.

Susan. But here 's a knife.
To save mine honor, shall slice out my life.

Sir C. I know thou pleasest me a thousand times
More in that resolution than thy grant.—
Observe her love; to soothe it to my suit,
Her honor she will hazard, though not lose;
To bring me out of debt, her rigorous hand
Will pierce her heart,—O wonder!—that will choose,
Rather than stain her blood, her life to lose.
Come, you sad sister to a woful brother,
This is the gate. I'll bear him such a present,
Such an acquittance for the knight to seal,
As will amaze his senses, and surprise
With admiration all his fantasies.

Enter Sir Francis Acton and Malby.

Susan. Before his unchaste thoughts shall seize on me,
'T is here shall my imprison'd soul set free.

Sir F. How! Mountford with his sister, hand in hand!
What miracle 's afoot?

Mal. It is a sight
Begets in me much admiration.[3]

Sir C. Stand not amaz'd to see me thus attended!
Acton, I owe thee money, and, being unable
To bring thee the full sum in ready coin,
Lo! for thy more assurance, here 's a pawn,—
My sister, my dear sister, whose chaste honor
I prize above a million. Here! Nay, take her;
She 's worth your money, man; do not forsake her.

Sir F. I would he were in earnest!

Susan. Impute it not to my immodesty.
My brother, being rich in nothing else
But in his interest that he hath in me,
According to his poverty hath brought you
Me, all his store; whom, howsoe'er you prize,
As forfeit to your hand, he values highly,
And would not sell, but to acquit your debt,
For any emperor's ransom.

Sir F. Stern heart, relent,
Thy former cruelty at length repent!
Was ever known, in any former age,
Such honorable, wrested[4] courtesy?
Lands, honors, life, and all the world forego,
Rather than stand engag'd to such a foe!

Sir C. Acton, she is too poor to be thy bride,
And I too much oppos'd to be thy brother.
There, take her to thee; if thou hast the heart
To seize her as a rape, or lustful prey;
To blur our house, that never yet was stain'd;
To murder her that never meant thee harm;
To kill me now, whom once thou sav'dst from death:—
Do them at once; on her all these rely,
And perish with her spotless chastity.

Sir F. You overcome me in your love, Sir Charles.
I cannot be so cruel to a lady
I love so dearly. Since you have not spar'd
To engage your reputation to the world,
Your sister's honor, which you prize so dear,
Nay, all the comforts which you hold on earth,
To grow out of my debt, being your foe,—
Your honor'd thoughts, lo! thus I recompense.

3 wonder.

4 over-wrought.

Your metamorphos'd foe receives your gift
In satisfaction of all former wrongs.
This jewel I will wear here in my heart;
And where before I thought her, for her wants,
Too base to be my bride, to end all strife,
I seal you my dear brother, her my wife.

Susan. You still exceed us. I will yield to fate,
And learn to love, where I till now did hate.

Sir C. With that enchantment you have charm'd my soul
And made me rich even in those very words!
I pay no debt, but am indebted more;
Rich in your love, I never can be poor.

Sir F. All 's mine is yours; we are alike in state;
Let 's knit in love what was oppos'd in hate!
Come, for our nuptials we will straight provide,
Blest only in our brother and fair bride.

Exeunt.

SCENE 2. *Frankford's house.*

Enter Cranwell, Frankford, and Nicholas.

Cran. Why do you search each room about your house,
Now that you have despatch'd your wife away?

Frank. Oh, sir, to see that nothing may be left
That ever was my wife's. I lov'd her dearly;
And when I do but think of her unkindness,
My thoughts are all in hell; to avoid which torment,
I would not have a bodkin or a cuff,
A bracelet, necklace, or rebato wire,[5]
Nor anything that ever was call'd hers,
Left me, by which I might remember her.—
Seek round about.

Nich. 'Sblood! master, here 's her lute flung in a corner.

Frank. Her lute! O God! Upon this instrument
Her fingers have run quick division,[6]
Sweeter than that which now divides our hearts.
These frets have made me pleasant, that have now
Frets of my heart-strings made. O Master Cranwell!
Oft hath she made this melancholy wood,
Now mute and dumb for her disastrous chance,
Speak sweetly many a note, sound many a strain
To her own ravishing voice; which being well strung,
What pleasant strange airs have they jointly sung!—
Post with it after her!—Now nothing 's left;
Of her and hers I am at once bereft.

Nich. I 'll ride and overtake her; do my message,
And come back again.

Exit.

Cran. Meantime, sir, if you please,
I 'll to Sir Francis Acton, and inform him
Of what hath past betwixt you and his sister.

Frank. Do as you please.—How ill am I bested,
To be a widower ere my wife be dead!

Exeunt.

SCENE 3. *A country road.*

Enter Mistress Frankford, with Jenkin, her maid Cicely, her Coachmen, and three Carters.

Mrs. F. Bid my coach stay! Why should I ride in state,
Being hurl'd so low down by the hand of fate?
A seat like to my fortunes let me have,—
Earth for my chair, and for my bed a grave!

Jen. Comfort, good mistress; you have watered your coach with tears already. You have but two miles now to go to your manor. A man cannot say by my old master Frankford as he may say by me, that he wants manors; for he hath three or four, of which this is one that we are going to now.

Cic. Good mistress, be of good cheer! Sorrow, you see, hurts you, but helps you not; we all mourn to see you so sad.

Carter. Mistress, I spy one of my landlord's men
Come riding post: 't is like he brings some news.

5 wire used to support a ruff.

6 variation.

Mrs. F. Comes he from Master Frankford, he is welcome;
So are his news, because they come from him.

Enter Nicholas.

Nich. There!
Mrs. F. I know the lute. Oft have I sung to thee;
We both are out of tune, both out of time.

Nich. Would that had been the worst instrument that e'er you played on! My master commends him to ye; there 's all he can find that was ever yours; he hath nothing left that ever you could lay claim to but his own heart, and he could afford you that! All that I have to deliver you is this: he prays you to forget him; and so he bids you farewell.

Mrs. F. I thank him; he is kind, and ever was.
All you that have true feeling of my grief,
That know my loss, and have relenting hearts,
Gird me about, and help me with your tears
To wash my spotted sins! My lute shall groan;
It cannot weep, but shall lament my moan.

Enter Wendoll behind.

Wen. Pursu'd with horror of a guilty soul,
And with the sharp scourge of repentance lash'd,
I fly from mine own shadow. O my stars!
What have my parents in their lives deserv'd,
That you should lay this penance on their son?
When I but think of Master Frankford's love,
And lay it to my treason, or compare
My murdering him for his relieving me,
It strikes a terror like a lightning's flash,
To scorch my blood up. Thus I, like the owl,
Asham'd of day, live in these shadowy woods,
Afraid of every leaf or murmuring blast,
Yet longing to receive some perfect knowledge
How he hath dealt with her. (*Seeing Mistress Frankford.*) O my sad fate!
Here, and so far from home, and thus attended!
O God! I have divorc'd the truest turtles [7]
That ever liv'd together, and, being divided,
In several places make their several moan;
She in the fields laments, and he at home;
So poets write that Orpheus made the trees
And stones to dance to his melodious harp,
Meaning the rustic and the barbarous hinds,
That had no understanding part in them:
So she from these rude carters tears extracts,
Making their flinty hearts with grief to rise,
And draw down rivers from their rocky eyes.

Mrs. F. (*To Nicholas.*) If you return unto my master, say
(Though not from me, for I am all unworthy
To blast his name so with a strumpet's tongue)
That you have seen me weep, wish myself dead!
Nay, you may say, too, for my vow is pass'd,
Last night you saw me eat and drink my last.
This to your master you may say and swear;
For it is writ in heaven, and decreed here.

Nich. I'll say you wept; I'll swear you made me sad.
Why, how now, eyes? What now? What 's here to do?
I'm gone, or I shall straight turn baby too.

Wen. (*Aside.*) I cannot weep, my heart is all on fire.
Curs'd be the fruits of my unchaste desire!

Mrs. F. Go, break this lute upon my coach's wheel,
As the last music that I e'er shall make,—
Not as my husband's gift, but my farewell

[7] turtle doves.

To all earth's joy; and so your master tell!
Nich. If I can for crying.
Wen. (*Aside.*) Grief, have done,
Or, like a madman, I shall frantic run.
Mrs. F. You have beheld the wofull'st wretch on earth,—
A woman made of tears; would you had words
To express but what you see! My inward grief
No tongue can utter; yet unto your power
You may describe my sorrow, and disclose
To thy sad master my abundant woes.
Nich. I'll do your commendations.[8]
Mrs. F. Oh, no!
I dare not so presume; nor to my children;
I am disclaim'd in both; alas! I am.
Oh, never teach them, when they come to speak,
To name the name of mother: chide their tongue,
If they by chance light on that hated word;
Tell them 't is naught; for when that word they name,
Poor, pretty souls! they harp on their own shame.
Wen. (*Aside.*) To recompense their wrongs, what canst thou do?
Thou hast made her husbandless, and childless too.
Mrs. F. I have no more to say.—Speak not for me;
Yet you may tell your master what you see.
Nich. I'll do 't.

Exit.

Wen. (*Aside.*) I'll speak to her, and comfort her in grief.
Oh, but her wound cannot be cur'd with words!
No matter, though; I'll do my best good will
To work a cure on her whom I did kill.
Mrs. F. So, now unto my coach, then to my home,
So to my death-bed; for from this sad hour,
I never will nor eat, nor drink, nor taste
Of any cates[9] that may preserve my life.
I never will nor smile, nor sleep, nor rest;
But when my tears have wash'd my black soul white,
Sweet Savior, to thy hands I yield my sprite.
Wen. (*Coming forward.*) O Mistress Frankford!
Mrs. F. Oh, for God's sake, fly!
The devil doth come to tempt me, ere I die.
My coach!—This sin, that with an angel's face
Conjur'd[10] mine honor, till he sought my wrack,
In my repentant eye seems ugly, black.

Exeunt all except Wendoll and Jenkin; the Carters whistling.

Jen. What, my young master, that fled in his shirt! How come you by your clothes again? You have made our house in a sweet pickle, ha' ye not, think you? What, shall I serve you still, or cleave to the old house?
Wen. Hence, slave! Away, with thy unseason'd mirth!
Unless thou canst shed tears, and sigh, and howl,
Curse thy sad fortunes, and exclaim on fate,
Thou art not for my turn.
Jen. Marry, an you will not, another will; farewell, and be hang'd! Would you had never come to have kept this coil[11] within our doors! We shall ha' you run away like a sprite again.

Exit.

Wen. She 's gone to death; I live to want and woe,
Her life, her sins, and all upon my head.
And I must now go wander, like a Cain,
In foreign countries and remoted climes,
Where the report of my ingratitude
Cannot be heard. I'll over first to France,
And so to Germany and Italy;
Where, when I have recover'd, and by travel
Gotten those perfect tongues,[12] and that these rumors
May in their height abate, I will return:
And I divine (however now dejected),
My worth and parts being by some great man prais'd,
At my return I may in court be rais'd.

Exit.

8 present your respects.
9 food.
10 seduced by his charm.
11 made this trouble.
12 those languages perfectly.

SCENE 4. *Before the Manor House.*

Enter Sir Francis Acton, Sir Charles Mountford, Cranwell, Malby, and Susan.

Sir. F. Brother, and now my wife, I think these troubles,
Fall on my head by justice of the heavens,
For being so strict to you in your extremities;
But we are now aton'd.[13] I would my sister
Could with like happiness o'ercome her griefs
As we have ours.

Susan. You tell us, Master Cranwell, wondrous things
Touching the patience of that gentleman,
With what strange virtue he demeans[14] his grief.

Cran. I told you what I was a witness of;
It was my fortune to lodge there that night.

Sir F. Oh, that same villain, Wendoll! 'T was his tongue
That did corrupt her; she was of herself
Chaste and devoted well. Is this the house?

Cran. Yes, sir; I take it, here your sister lies.

Sir F. My brother Frankford show'd too mild a spirit
In the revenge of such a loathed crime.
Less than he did, no man of spirit could do.
I am so far from blaming his revenge,
That I commend it. Had it been my case,
Their souls at once had from their breasts been freed;
Death to such deeds of shame is the due meed.

Enter Jenkin and Cicely.

Jen. Oh, my mistress, my mistress! my poor mistress!

Cicely. Alas! that ever I was born; what shall I do for my poor mistress?

Sir C. Why, what of her?

Jen. Oh, Lord, sir! she no sooner heard that her brother and her friends had come to see how she did, but she, for very shame of her guilty conscience, fell into such a swoon, that we had much ado to get life into her.

Susan. Alas, that she should bear so hard a fate!
Pity it is repentance comes too late.

Sir F. Is she so weak in body?

Jen. O sir, I can assure you there's no hope of life in her; for she will take no sust'nance: she hath plainly starv'd herself, and now she is as lean as a lath. She ever looks for the good hour. Many gentlemen and gentlewomen of the country are come to comfort her.

Exeunt.

SCENE 5. *Mistress Frankford's Bedchamber.*

Mistress Frankford in bed; enter Sir Charles Mountford, Sir Francis Acton, Malby, and Susan.

Mal. How fare you, Mistress Frankford?

Mrs. F. Sick, sick, oh, sick! Give me some air, I pray you!
Tell me, oh, tell me, where is Master Frankford?
Will not he deign to see me ere I die?

Mal. Yes, Mistress Frankford; divers gentlemen,
Your loving neighbors, with that just request
Have mov'd, and told him of your weak estate:
Who, though with much ado to get belief,
Examining of the general circumstance,
Seeing your sorrow and your penitence,
And hearing therewithal the great desire
You have to see him, ere you left the world,
He gave to us his faith to follow us,
And sure he will be here immediately.

Mrs. F. You have half reviv'd me with the pleasing news,
Raise me a little higher in my bed.
Blush I not, brother Acton? Blush I not, Sir Charles?
Can you not read my fault writ in my cheek?
Is not my crime there? Tell me, gentlemen.

Sir C. Alas, good mistress, sickness hath not left you
Blood in your face enough to make you blush.

13 reconciled.

14 exercises.

Mrs. F. Then, sickness, like a friend, my fault would hide.—
Is my husband come? My soul but tarries
His arrive; then I am fit for heaven.
Sir F. I came to chide you, but my words of hate
Are turn'd to pity and compassionate grief.
I came to rate [15] you, but my brawls, you see,
Melt into tears, and I must weep by thee.—
Here 's Master Frankford now.

Enter Frankford.

Frank. Good morrow, brother; morrow, gentlemen!
God, that hath laid his cross upon our heads,
Might (had He pleas'd) have made our cause of meeting
On a more fair and more contented ground;
But He that made us made us to this woe.
Mrs. F. And is he come? Methinks that voice I know.
Frank. How do you, woman?
Mrs. F. Well, Master Frankford, well; but shall be better,
I hope within this hour. Will you vouchsafe,
Out of your grace and your humanity,
To take a spotted strumpet by the hand?
Frank. This hand once held my heart in faster bonds,
Than now 't is gripp'd by me. God pardon them
That made us first break hold!
Mrs. F. Amen, amen!
Out of my zeal to Heaven, whither I 'm now bound,
I was so impudent to wish you here;
And once more beg your pardon. O good man,
And father to my children, pardon me.
Pardon, oh, pardon me: my fault so heinous is,
That if you in this world forgive it not,
Heaven will not clear it in the world to come.
Faintness hath so usurp'd upon my knees,
That kneel I cannot; but on my heart's knees
My prostrate soul lies thrown down at your feet,
To beg your gracious pardon. Pardon, oh, pardon me!
Frank. As freely, from the low depth of my soul,
As my Redeemer hath forgiven His death,
I pardon thee. I will shed tears for thee; pray with thee;
And, in mere pity of thy weak estate,
I 'll wish to die with thee.
All. So do we all.
Nich. So will not I;
I 'll sigh and sob, but, by my faith, not die.
Sir F. Oh, Master Frankford, all the near alliance
I lose by her, shall be supplied in thee.
You are my brother by the nearest way;
Her kindred hath fall'n off, but yours doth stay.
Frank. Even as I hope for pardon, at that day
When the Great Judge of Heaven in scarlet sits,
So be thou pardon'd! Though thy rash offence
Divorc'd our bodies, thy repentant tears
Unite our souls.
Sir C. Then comfort, Mistress Frankford!
You see your husband hath forgiven your fall;
Then rouse your spirits, and cheer your fainting soul!
Susan. How is it with you?
Sir F. How do you feel yourself?
Mrs. F. Not of this world.
Frank. I see you are not, and I weep to see it.
My wife, the mother to my pretty babes!
Both those lost names I do restore thee back,
And with this kiss I wed thee once again.
Though thou art wounded in thy honor'd name,
And with that grief upon thy death-bed liest,
Honest in heart, upon my soul, thou diest.
Mrs. F. Pardon'd on earth, soul, thou in heaven art free;
Once more thy wife, dies thus embracing thee.[16]

(*Dies.*)

15 upbraid.

16 Verity suggests, *Once more* (*i. e.* Kiss me once more); *thy wife dies, etc.*

Frank. New-married, and new-widow'd.—Oh! she 's dead,
And a cold grave must be her nuptial bed.
Sir C. Sir, be of good comfort, and your heavy sorrow
Part equally amongst us; storms divided
Abate their force, and with less rage are guided.
Cran. Do, Master Frankford; he that hath least part,
Will find enough to drown one troubled heart.
Sir F. Peace with thee, Nan!—Brothers and gentlemen,
All we that can plead interest in her grief,
Bestow upon her body funeral tears!
Brother, had you with threats and usage bad
Punish'd her sin, the grief of her offense
Had not with such true sorrow touch'd her heart.
Frank. I see it had not; therefore, on her grave
Will I bestow this funeral epitaph,
Which on her marble tomb shall be engrav'd.
In golden letters shall these words be fill'd:[17]
Here lies she whom her husband's kindness kill'd.

THE EPILOGUE.

An honest crew, disposed to be merry,
Came to a tavern by, and call'd for wine.
The drawer brought it, smiling like a cherry,
And told them it was pleasant, neat[18] and fine.
"Taste it," quoth one. He did so. "Fie!" quoth he;
"This wine was good; now 't runs too near the lee."

Another sipp'd, to give the wine his due,
And said unto the rest it drunk too flat;
The third said it was old; the fourth, too new;
"Nay," quoth the fifth, "the sharpness likes[19] me not."
Thus, gentlemen, you see how, in one hour,
The wine was new, old, flat, sharp, sweet, and sour.

Unto this wine we do allude[20] our play,
Which some will judge too trivial, some too grave:
You as our guests we entertain this day,
And bid you welcome to the best we have.
Excuse us, then; good wine may be disgrac'd,
When every several mouth hath sundry taste.

17 cut and filled in with gold. (N.)
18 pure.
19 pleases.
20 compare.

BEAUMONT AND FLETCHER

PHILASTER

Francis Beaumont (c. 1584–1616) came of an old Leicestershire family, his father being a Justice of Common Pleas. He entered Oxford in 1597, and the Middle Temple as a law student in 1600. He may have been writing for the stage as early as 1605, and was soon working in collaboration with Fletcher. He cannot be traced on the stage after 1612. He died a month before Shakespeare, and was buried in Westminster Abbey.

John Fletcher (1579–1625) was the son of a clergyman who rose to be Bishop of London. From the time that he entered Cambridge in 1591 we lose sight of him until he appears in 1607 as a dramatist. He continued active as a playwright till his death of the plague; collaborating at first with Beaumont, afterward with Shakespeare, Massinger, Field, and others. Tradition has it that Beaumont and Fletcher lived together in terms of closest intimacy on the Bankside. In the share which each contributed to the work going under their names there has been great interest from their own day to ours, but only six or seven plays are now believed to be of their joint authorship.

To Beaumont and Fletcher is usually ascribed the honor of introducing to the English stage a new type of play, the tragicomedy, or, as it has sometimes been loosely called, the romance. *Philaster* was staged somewhere between 1608 and 1610. By that time Shakespeare had perfected romantic love-comedy, introduced by Lyly, chronicle-history, and tragedy; Ben Jonson had introduced the comedy of humors, Jonson and Middleton had established realistic comedy, and the vogue of domestic drama was practically over. Realism, owing largely to Jonson's influence, had been the prevailing force for a number of years, and the time was ripe for a swing of the pendulum of popular taste back toward romanticism. Into the vexed question of priority between Shakespeare and Beaumont and Fletcher, specifically between the dates of production of *Cymbeline* and *Philaster*, it is not profitable here to venture. The more generally accepted opinion is to the effect that the younger dramatists were the innovators; certain it is that to them we owe the popularization and fixing of the chief features of the new type.

In order to account for the wide difference in spirit and manner between this tragicomedy and earlier work it is necessary to understand certain social changes which had been taking place. The drama of 1580–1600 is marked by a very healthy tone; during the next ten years an element of decadence crept in, and, broadly speaking, the drama degenerated steadily until the closing of the theaters in 1642. Times had changed since the brave days of Queen Bess. As G. C. Macaulay says (*Camb. Hist. Engl. Lit.*, VI. 121): "The genuinely national interest in the drama which especially characterized the last fifteen years of Elizabeth had, to a great extent, passed away, and the taste of the court had become gradually more and more the prevailing influence." Now the court of James was morally much less sound than that of Elizabeth. Corruption, political and social, was rife, and as the drama increasingly came to be the plaything of the court it reflected with increasing faithfulness the moral tone of the court. The immediate effect was a stimulation to greater brilliance, but at the expense of depth and a true interpretation of national life. "Closely connected with the want of moral earnestness was the demand for theatrical entertainments which did not make any serious appeal to the intellect; and hence, on the one hand, the exaggerated love of pageantry, which was gratified by the magnificence of the masques presented at court, and, on the other, the growing preference . . . for plots full of interesting events and surprising turns of fortune, rather than such as were developed naturally from situation and characters: the result being a comparative neglect of character interest, and a disregard for the principle of artistic unity" (*Camb. Hist.*, VI. 122). To be purveyors of entertainment of this new sort for court audiences Beaumont and Fletcher were by birth and breeding well fitted. We get with them for the first time men of good family writing for the stage and it is not surprising that they should have been leaders in a new court drama.

Philaster is so thoroughly typical an example of Beaumont and Fletcher's tragicomedy that an analysis of it along the lines suggested by Professor Thorndike's study will serve to characterize the *genre*. The scene of the play is Sicily, but so far as realism of setting is concerned it might be anywhere else in the world; the locality of these plays is perfectly immaterial — the action always occurs in a No-man's Land of romance. As usual however, in Elizabethan drama, the speech and manner of the inhabitants even of No-man's Land occasionally bear a strange resemblance to those of the citizens of a more familiar city on the banks of the Thames; the captain's oration to the mob might be delivered by Simon Eyre to a band of shoemaker apprentices, and it is with a right London swagger that the scene goes. The plot, probably invented, is highly ingenious, very complicated, and utterly improbable. With a story of pure sentimental love is contrasted one of base sensual passion; from the conflict of the two sorts of love arise the complications, for upon the discovery of Megra's intrigue with Pharamond hangs her spiteful accusation regarding Arethusa and the supposed Bellario, the working out of which fills the rest of the play. The action is developed by a series of striking situations, each of which is carefully planned to secure the greatest degree of theatrical effectiveness, regardless of its probability or improbability. The play begins on a note of excitement in Philaster's almost hysterical defiance of Pharamond, capped by an obviously feigned submission, followed by a surprise as Arethusa woos Philaster and the rivals are again brought into conflict. Between two scenes of lust is laid the strongly contrasting, sentimental conversation of Arethusa and Bellario. The fourth scene of act II is a good illustration of a situation developed for its own sake. With its cleverly arranged exits and entrances, its working up to the unexpected appearance of Megra on the balcony, and her sensational charge, it is most skilfully handled; but we should note that the revelation of the intrigue, out of which all possible effect is obtained, has no permanent interest of its own, and that the one point in which the scene advances plot is in the rousing of suspicion about Arethusa, which could have been done far more simply. The appeal of the third act is mainly through impassioned rhetoric. Replete with sensation are the wood scenes of act IV, with turn and counterturn, surprising meetings and equally surprising exits, culminating in the amazing episodes where Philaster wounds Arethusa and the sleeping Bellario. Probability would suggest that in the third scene Bellario, who could not very well help seeing that Arethusa's life was endangered, might easily have prevented bloodshed by revealing his identity, but in that event, of course, the play would have ended then and there; Bellario, therefore, keeps silence and meekly disappears at Philaster's command. The conduct of the rest of the scene is highly ingenious as Bellario takes on himself the crime of wounding Arethusa, while Philaster, not to be outdone in generosity, crawls out from under his bush to confess his guilt. The union of Philaster and Arethusa in act V seems to clear her honor, though the charge against her has never been refuted, but we are in difficulties once more when the king pronounces his sentence of death on the lovers. At this critical juncture the mob constitutes itself a *deus ex machina*, and Philaster's quelling of the riot seems to establish him in favor. Here Megra, who has almost been forgotten, reiterates her charge, and Philaster is on the point of killing himself when Bellario makes his confession. The skill with which this *dénouement* is secured is undeniable, as is also the artificiality of structure which makes it possible. No better example could be found of the use of surprise in tragicomedy, for the audience is as much astounded as are the persons of the play by Bellario's metamorphosis. Coleridge has called attention to Shakespeare's preference for the "expectation method" of *dénouement* as contrasted with the "surprise method." Shakespeare uses the former consistently; with him, as, for instance, in the church scene in *Much Ado About Nothing*, no character assumes disguise without informing the audience of the fact and its purpose. The audience is therefore at all times more cognizant of the true situation than are the persons of the play — is sure that the truth will be revealed in time to avert a tragic conclusion, and the play is kept in the realm of comedy. The sole intention of Beaumont and Fletcher, on the contrary, is to provide as sensational an ending as possible, and they delight in harrowing the feelings of the audience till the last moment. Where in Shakespeare the spectators think of the characters, their emotions, and their behavior in the situation, in tragicomedy their attention is directed to the event itself. The violent contrast of tragic and comic feeling involved in the surprise method is an essential characteristic of tragicomedy. The gist of the complications in *Philaster* is expressed in Philaster's reproach to Bellario in the last scene:

> "All these jealousies
> Had flown to nothing, if thou hadst discovered
> What now we know."

Such stressing of plot, or, more accurately, of situation, is practically certain to result in a slurring of characterization. Anything like psychological analysis or logical development of character is sacrificed to immediate theatrical effectiveness. The behavior of Philaster is a case in point. When viewed coolly he stands forth a cad of deepest dye. His readiness to believe the worst of Arethusa in the face of her own and Bellario's protestations of innocence shakes our confidence in him, and when this egregious hero attempts to kill first his mistress and later a sleeping boy all semblance of consistency and lifelikeness is destroyed. Most of the characters are exaggerated or intensified on some one side; they are too indubitably bad or too angelically good. Euphrasia's sentimental devotion, Megra's lustfulness, Pharamond's poltroonery, Philaster's sensibility, are emphasized to the point of impossibility. Essentially they are not much more than types, which appear again and again in tragicomedy and the later Fletcherian romantic tragedy. As always, the chief figures are of high rank, and make no impression of reality. Lamb's well-known apology for the behavior of the people in Restoration comedy on the ground that they live in a world of their own, like fairies, might be applied to Philaster, Bellario, Megra, and the rest.

Whatever criticism may be passed upon plotting and characterization, no dissent is possible from the unanimous opinion as to the dramatic propriety and poetic beauty of Beaumont and Fletcher's verse. Smooth, easy-running, adapting itself with perfect facility to the action, as adequate for the expression of frantic passion or heart-broken pathos as for the badinage of courtiers, ever without strain or visible effort, it is the perfection of dramatic blank verse. Nothing quite like it had been heard on the Elizabethan stage before; small wonder that it delighted the auditors and readers of its own day, and that it was regarded by the Restoration as the perfect model of dramatic dialogue. At its best it has a haunting beauty, especially when Arethusa or Bellario is speaking. Bellario's reply to Philaster's

> "Oh, but thou dost not know
> What 't is to die"—
> "Yes, I do know, my lord:
> 'T is less than to be born; a lasting sleep,
> A quiet resting from all jealousy,
> A thing we all pursue; I know, besides,
> It is but giving over of a game
> That must be lost";

and Bellario's speech in V. ii:

> "Alas, my lord, my life is not a thing
> Worthy your noble thoughts; 't is not a life,
> 'T is but a piece of childhood thrown away"—

the exquisite tenderness of these is beyond praise.

On the basis of stylistic differences attempts have been made to assign various parts of the play to one or the other of the joint authors, and while such identifications are always dangerous, it may be well to summarize the conclusions reached by Thorndike and Gayley, two of the most careful and recent of investigators. To Beaumont are assigned I. i (to entrance of King), ii; II. i, ii (to entrance of Megra, Gayley), iii, iv (to re-entrance of Dion); III. i, ii (in part); IV. i, ii, iii, iv; V. i, ii, v. To Fletcher: I. i (from entrance of King); II. ii (only from entrance of Megra, Gayley), iv. (from re-entrance of Dion); III. ii (in part); V. iii, iv. This gives to Beaumont much the greater share in the composition, and most of the finest poetry of the play, like Philaster's description of Bellario in I. ii, and all the wood scenes.

Philaster was popular in its own day, held the stage up to the closing of the theaters, was put on as soon as they reopened (Pepys saw it in 1661 and 1668), and had several revivals in the eighteenth century. Its theatrical effectiveness and the astonishing brilliance of the verse are quite sufficient to account for its longevity, and its importance in the history of the drama is enhanced by the fact that in tragicomedy may be partly found the roots of the heroic drama of the Restoration.

PHILASTER, OR LOVE LIES A-BLEEDING

By FRANCIS BEAUMONT AND JOHN FLETCHER.

NAMES OF THE CHARACTERS

The King of Sicily.
Philaster, *Heir to the Crown.*
Pharamond, *Prince of Spain.*
Dion, a Lord.
Cleremont, Thrasiline, } *Noble Gentlemen, his associates.*
An Old Captain.
Five Citizens.
A Country Fellow.
Two Woodmen.
The King's Guard and Train.
Arethusa, *Daughter of the King.*
Euphrasia, *Daughter of Dion, but disguised like a Page and called* Bellario.
Megra, *a lascivious Lady.*
Galatea, *a wise, modest Lady attending the Princess.*
Two other Ladies.

Scene.—Sicily.

ACT I.

Scene 1. *The presence chamber in the palace.*

Enter Dion, Cleremont, and Thrasiline.

Cle. Here's nor lords nor ladies.

Dion. Credit me, gentlemen, I wonder at it. They receiv'd strict charge from the King to attend here; besides, it was boldly published that no officer should forbid any gentleman that desired to attend and hear.

Cle. Can you guess the cause?

Dion. Sir, it is plain, about the Spanish

Prince that 's come to marry our kingdom's heir and be our sovereign.

Thra. Many that will seem to know much say she looks not on him like a maid in love.

Dion. Faith, sir, the multitude, that seldom know any thing but their own opinions, speak that they would have; but the prince, before his own approach, receiv'd so many confident messages from the state, that I think she 's resolv'd to be rul'd.

Cle. Sir, it is thought, with her he shall enjoy both these kingdoms of Sicily and Calabria.

Dion. Sir, it is without controversy so meant. But 't will be a troublesome labor for him to enjoy both these kingdoms with safety, the right heir to one of them living, and living so virtuously: especially, the people admiring the bravery of his mind and lamenting his injuries.

Cle. Who? Philaster?

Dion. Yes; whose father, we all know, was by our late King of Calabria unrighteously deposed from his fruitful Sicily. Myself drew some blood in those wars, which I would give my hand to be washed from.

Cle. Sir, my ignorance in state-policy will not let me know why, Philaster being heir to one of these kingdoms, the King should suffer him to walk abroad with such free liberty.

Dion. Sir, it seems your nature is more constant than to inquire after state-news. But the King, of late, made a hazard of both the kingdoms, of Sicily and his own, with offering but to imprison Philaster; at which the city was in arms, not to be charm'd down by any state-order or proclamation, till they saw Philaster ride through the streets pleas'd and without a guard: at which they threw their hats and their arms from them; some to make bonfires, some to drink, all for his deliverance: which wise men say is the cause the King labors to bring in the power of a foreign nation to awe his own with.

Enter Galatea, a Lady, and Megra.

Thra. See, the ladies! What 's the first?

Dion. A wise and modest gentlewoman that attends the princess.

Cle. The second?

Dion. She is one that may stand still discreetly enough and ill-favor'dly dance her measure; simper when she is courted by her friend, and slight her husband.

Cle. The last?

Dion. Faith, I think she is one whom the state keeps for the agents of our confederate princes; she 'll cog[1] and lie with a whole army, before the league shall break. Her name is common through the kingdom, and the trophies of her dishonor advanced beyond Hercules' Pillars.[2] She loves to try the several constitutions of men's bodies; and, indeed, has destroyed the worth of her own body by making experiment upon it for the good of the commonwealth.

Cle. She 's a profitable member.

Meg. Peace, if you love me! You shall see these gentlemen stand their ground and not court us.

Gal. What if they should?

La. What if they should!

Meg. Nay, let her alone.—What if they should? Why, if they should, I say they were never abroad. What foreigner would do so? It writes them directly untravell'd.

Gal. Why, what if they be?

La. What if they be!

Meg. Good madam, let her go on.—What if they be? Why, if they be, I will justify, they cannot maintain discourse with a judicious lady, nor make a leg,[3] nor say "Excuse me."

Gal. Ha, ha, ha!

Meg. Do you laugh, madam?

Dion. Your desires upon you, ladies!

Meg. Then you must sit beside us.

Dion. I shall sit near you then, lady.

Meg. Near me, perhaps; but there 's a lady endures no stranger; and to me you appear a very strange fellow.

La. Methinks he 's not so strange; he would quickly be acquainted.

Thra. Peace, the King!

Enter King, Pharamond, Arethusa, and Train.

King. To give a stronger testimony of love
Than sickly promises (which commonly
In princes find both birth and burial
In one breath) we have drawn you, worthy sir,
To make your fair endearments to our daughter,

1 cheat.

2 The rocky promontories forming the Straits of Gibraltar were so called from the legend that they were torn asunder by Hercules.

3 bow.

And worthy services known to our subjects,
Now lov'd and wondered at; next, our intent
To plant you deeply our immediate heir
Both to our blood and kingdoms. For this lady,
(The best part of your life, as you confirm me,
And I believe,) though her few years and sex
Yet teach her nothing but her fears and blushes,
Desires without desire, discourse and knowledge
Only of what herself is to herself,
Make her feel moderate health; and when she sleeps,
In making no ill day, knows no ill dreams.
Think not, dear sir, these undivided parts,
That must mould up a virgin, are put on
To show her so, as borrowed ornaments
To speak her perfect love to you, or add
An artificial shadow to her nature,—
No, sir; I boldly dare proclaim her yet
No woman. But woo her still, and think her modesty
A sweeter mistress than the offer'd language
Of any dame, were she a queen, whose eye
Speaks common loves and comforts to her servants.[4]
Last, noble son (for so I now must call you),
What I have done thus public, is not only
To add a comfort in particular
To you or me, but all; and to confirm
The nobles and the gentry of these kingdoms
By oath to your succession, which shall be
Within this month at most.

Thra. This will be hardly done.

Cle. It must be ill done, if it be done.

Dion. When 't is at best, 't will be but half done, whilst
So brave a gentleman is wrong'd and flung off.

Thra. I fear.

Cle. Who does not?

Dion. I fear not for myself, and yet I fear too.
Well, we shall see, we shall see. No more.

Pha. Kissing your white hand, mistress, I take leave
To thank your royal father; and thus far
To be my own free trumpet. Understand,
Great King, and these your subjects, mine that must be,
(For so deserving you have spoke me, sir,
And so deserving I dare speak myself,)
To what a person, of what eminence,
Ripe expectation, of what faculties,
Manners and virtues, you would wed your kingdoms;
You in me have your wishes. Oh, this country!
By more than all the gods, I hold it happy;
Happy in their dear memories that have been
Kings great and good; happy in yours that is;
And from you (as a chronicle to keep
Your noble name from eating age) do I
Opine myself most happy. Gentlemen,
Believe me in a word, a prince's word,
There shall be nothing to make up a kingdom
Mighty and flourishing, defensed, fear'd,
Equal to be commanded and obeyed,
But through the travails of my life I'll find it,
And tie it to this country. By all the gods,
My reign shall be so easy to the subject,
That every man shall be his prince himself,
And his own law—yet I his prince and law.
And dearest lady, to your dearest self
(Dear in the choice of him whose name and lustre
Must make you more and mightier) let me say,
You are the blessed'st living; for, sweet princess,
You shall enjoy a man of men to be
Your servant; you shall make him yours, for whom
Great queens must die.

Thra. Miraculous!

Cle. This speech calls him Spaniard, being nothing but a large inventory of his own commendations.

Dion. I wonder what 's his price; for certainly

[4] lovers.

He 'll sell himself, he has so prais'd his shape.

Enter Philaster.

But here comes one more worthy those large speeches
Than the large speaker of them.
Let me be swallowed quick, if I can find,
In all the anatomy of yon man's virtues,
One sinew sound enough to promise for him
He shall be constable. By this sun,
He 'll ne'er make king unless it be of trifles,
In my poor judgment.

Phi. (*Kneeling.*) Right noble sir, as low as my obedience,
And with a heart as loyal as my knee,
I beg your favor.

King. Rise; you have it, sir.

Dion. Mark but the King, how pale he looks! He fears!
Oh, this same whoreson [5] conscience, how it jades us!

King. Speak your intents, sir.

Phi. Shall I speak 'em freely?
Be still my royal sovereign.

King. As a subject,
We give you freedom.

Dion. Now it heats.

Phi. Then thus I turn
My language to you, prince, you, foreign man!
Ne'er stare nor put on wonder, for you must
Endure me, and you shall. This earth you tread upon
(A dowry, as you hope, with this fair princess),
By my dead father (oh, I had a father,
Whose memory I bow to!) was not left
To your inheritance, and I up and living—
Having myself about me and my sword,
The souls of all my name and memories,
These arms and some few friends beside the gods—
To part so calmly with it, and sit still
And say, "I might have been." I tell thee, Pharamond,
When thou art king, look I be dead and rotten,
And my name ashes: for, hear me, Pharamond,
This very ground thou goest on, this fat earth
My father's friends made fertile with their faiths,
Before that day of shame shall gape and swallow
Thee and thy nation, like a hungry grave,
Into her hidden bowels. Prince, it shall;
By the just gods, it shall!

Pha. He 's mad; beyond cure, mad.

Dion. Here is a fellow has some fire in 's veins:
The outlandish prince looks like a tooth-drawer.

Phi. Sir Prince of popinjays, I 'll make it well
Appear to you I am not mad.

King. You displease us:
You are too bold.

Phi. No, sir, I am too tame,
Too much a turtle,[6] a thing born without passion,
A faint shadow, that every drunken cloud
Sails over, and makes nothing.

King. I do not fancy this.
Call our physicians; sure, he 's somewhat tainted.[7]

Thra. I do not think 't will prove so.

Dion. H'as given him a general purge already,
For all the right he has; and now he means
To let him blood. Be constant, gentlemen:
By heaven, I 'll run his hazard,
Although I run my name out of the kingdom!

Cle. Peace, we are all one soul.

Pha. What you have seen in me to stir offence
I cannot find, unless it be this lady,
Offer'd into mine arms with the succession;
Which I must keep, (though it hath pleas'd your fury
To mutiny within you,) without disputing
Your genealogies, or taking knowledge
Whose branch you are. The King will leave it me,
And I dare make it mine. You have your answer.

Phi. If thou wert sole inheritor to him
That made the world his,[8] and couldst see no sun
Shine upon any thing but thine; were Pharamond
As truly valiant as I feel him cold,
And ring'd amongst the choicest of his friends

5 plaguey.

6 turtledove.

7 unbalanced.

8 Alexander the Great.

(Such as would blush to talk such serious follies,
Or back such bellied [9] commendations),
And from this presence, spite of all these bugs,[10]
You should hear further from me.

King. Sir, you wrong the prince; I gave you not this freedom
To brave our best friends. You deserve our frown.
Go to; be better temper'd.

Phi. It must be, sir, when I am nobler us'd.

Gal. Ladies,
This would have been a pattern of succession,[11]
Had he ne'er met this mischief. By my life,
He is the worthiest the true name of man
This day within my knowledge.

Meg. I cannot tell what you may call your knowledge;
But the other is the man set in mine eye.
Oh, 't is a prince of wax! [12]

Gal. A dog it is.

King. Philaster, tell me
The injuries you aim at in your riddles.

Phi. If you had my eyes, sir, and sufferance,
My griefs upon you, and my broken fortunes,
My wants great, and now nought but hopes and fears,
My wrongs would make ill riddles to be laught at.
Dare you be still my king, and right me not?

King. Give me your wrongs in private.

Phi. Take them,
And ease me of a load would bow strong Atlas.

(*They whisper.*)

Cle. He dares not stand the shock.

Dion. I cannot blame him; there 's danger in 't. Every man in this age has not a soul of crystal, for all men to read their actions through: men's hearts and faces are so far asunder, that they hold no intelligence. Do but view yon stranger well, and you shall see a fever through all his bravery,[13] and feel him shake like a true tenant.[14] If he give not back his crown again upon the report of an elder-gun, I have no augury.

King. Go to;
Be more yourself, as you respect our favor;
You 'll stir us else. Sir, I must have you know,
That y' are and shall be, at our pleasure, what
Fashion we will put upon you. Smooth your brow,
Or by the gods——

Phi. I am dead, sir; y' are my fate. It was not I
Said, I was wrong'd: I carry all about me
My weak stars lead me to, all my weak fortunes.
Who dares in all this presence speak, (that is
But man of flesh, and may be mortal,) tell me
I do not most entirely love this prince,
And honor his full virtues!

King. Sure, he 's possess'd.

Phi. Yes, with my father's spirit. It 's here, O King,
A dangerous spirit! Now he tells me, King,
I was a king's heir, bids me be a king,
And whispers to me, these are all my subjects.
'T is strange he will not let me sleep, but dives
Into my fancy, and there gives me shapes
That kneel and do me service, cry me king.
But I 'll suppress him; he 's a factious spirit,
And will undo me.—(*To Phar.*) Noble sir, your hand;
I am your servant.

King. Away! I do not like this:
I 'll make you tamer, or I 'll dispossess you
Both of your life and spirit. For this time
I pardon your wild speech, without so much
As your imprisonment.

Exeunt King, Pharamond, Arethusa, and Train.

Dion. I thank you, sir; you dare not for the people.

Gal. Ladies, what think you now of this brave fellow?

Meg. A pretty talking fellow, hot at hand. But eye yon stranger: is he not a fine complete gentleman? Oh, these strangers, I do affect [15] them strangely! They do the rarest home-things, and

[9] swollen.
[10] bugbears.
[11] to succeeding kings.
[12] a model prince.
[13] ostentation.
[14] Probably corrupt. Q_1 *truant*.
[15] love.

please the fullest! As I live, I could love all the nation over and over for his sake.

Gal. Gods comfort your poor head-piece, lady! 'T is a weak one, and had need of a night-cap.

Exeunt Ladies.

Dion. See, how his fancy labors! Has he not
Spoke home and bravely? What a dangerous train
Did he give fire to! How he shook the King,
Made his soul melt within him, and his blood
Run into whey! It stood upon his brow
Like a cold winter dew.

Phi. Gentlemen,
You have no suit to me? I am no minion.
You stand, methinks, like men that would be courtiers,
If I could well be flatter'd at a price
Not to undo your children.[16] You 're all honest:
Go, get you home again, and make your country
A virtuous court, to which your great ones may,
In their diseased age, retire and live recluse.

Cle. How do you, worthy sir?

Phi. Well, very well;
And so well that, if the King please, I find
I may live many years.

Dion. The King must please,
Whilst we know what you are and who you are,
Your wrongs and virtues. Shrink not, worthy sir,
But add your father to you; in whose name
We'll waken all the gods, and conjure up
The rods of vengeance, the abused people,
Who, like to raging torrents, shall swell high,
And so begirt the dens of these male-dragons,
That, through the strongest safety, they shall beg
For mercy at your sword's point.

Phi. Friends, no more;
Our ears may be corrupted; 't is an age
We dare not trust our wills to. Do you love me?

Thra. Do we love heaven and honor?

Phi. My Lord Dion, you had
A virtuous gentlewoman call'd you father;
Is she yet alive?

Dion. Most honor'd sir, she is;
And for the penance but of an idle dream,
Has undertook a tedious pilgrimage.

Enter a Lady.

Phi. Is it to me, or any of these gentlemen, you come?

Lady. To you, brave lord; the princess would entreat
Your present company.

Phi. The princess send for me! You are mistaken.

Lady. If you be called Philaster, 't is to you.

Phi. Kiss her fair hand, and say I will attend her.

Exit Lady.

Dion. Do you know what you do?

Phi. Yes; go to see a woman.

Cle. But do you weigh the danger you are in?

Phi. Danger in a sweet face!
By Jupiter, I must not fear a woman!

Thra. But are you sure it was the princess sent?
It may be some foul train to catch your life.

Phi. I do not think it, gentlemen; she 's noble.
Her eye may shoot me dead, or those true red
And white friends in her cheeks may steal my soul out;
There 's all the danger in 't. But, be what may,
Her single[17] name hath arm'd me.

Exit.

Dion. Go on,
And be as truly happy as thou 'rt fearless!—
Come, gentlemen, let 's make our friends acquainted,
Lest the King prove false.

Exeunt.

SCENE 2. *Arethusa's apartment in the palace.*

Enter Arethusa and a Lady.

Are. Comes he not?

Lady. Madam?

Are. Will Philaster come?

16 Mason conj. Qq. F. *you.* If you could flatter me without ruining your families by antagonizing the king. (Neilson.)

17 mere.

Lady. Dear madam, you were wont to credit me
At first.
Are. But didst thou tell me so?
I am forgetful, and my woman's strength
Is so o'ercharg'd with dangers like to grow
About my marriage, that these under-things
Dare not abide in such a troubled sea.
How lookt he when he told thee he would come?
Lady. Why, well.
Are. And not a little fearful?
Lady. Fear, madam! Sure, he knows not what it is.
Are. You all are of his faction; the whole court
Is bold in praise of him; whilst I
May live neglected, and do noble things,
As fools in strife throw gold into the sea,
Drown'd in the doing. But I know he fears.
Lady. Fear, madam! Methought, his looks hid more
Of love than fear.
Are. Of love! To whom? To you?
Did you deliver those plain words I sent,
With such a winning gesture and quick look
That you have caught him?
Lady. Madam, I mean to you.
Are. Of love to me! Alas, thy ignorance
Lets thee not see the crosses of our births!
Nature, that loves not to be questioned
Why she did this or that, but has her ends,
And knows she does well, never gave the world
Two things so opposite, so contrary
As he and I am: if a bowl of blood
Drawn from this arm of mine would poison thee,
A draught of his would cure thee. Of love to me!
Lady. Madam, I think I hear him.
Are. Bring him in.
Exit Lady.
You gods, that would not have your dooms withstood,
Whose holy wisdoms at this time it is
To make the passion of a feeble maid
The way unto your justice, I obey.

Re-enter Lady with Philaster.

Lady. Here is my Lord Philaster.
Are. Oh, 't is well.
Withdraw yourself. *Exit Lady.*
Phi. Madam, your messenger
Made me believe you wish'd to speak with me.
Are. 'T is true, Philaster; but the words are such
I have to say, and do so ill beseem
The mouth of woman, that I wish them said,
And yet am loth to speak them. Have you known
That I have aught detracted from your worth?
Have I in person wrong'd you, or have set
My baser instruments to throw disgrace
Upon your virtues?
Phi. Never, madam, you.
Are. Why, then, should you, in such a public place,
Injure a princess, and a scandal lay
Upon my fortunes, fam'd to be so great,
Calling a great part of my dowry in question?
Phi. Madam, this truth which I shall speak will be
Foolish: but, for your fair and virtuous self,
I could afford myself to have no right
To any thing you wish'd.
Are. Philaster, know,
I must enjoy these kingdoms.
Phi. Madam, both?
Are. Both, or I die: by heaven, I die, Philaster,
If I not calmly may enjoy them both.
Phi. I would do much to save that noble life;
Yet would be loth to have posterity
Find in our stories, that Philaster gave
His right unto a scepter and a crown
To save a lady's longing.
Are. Nay, then, hear:
I must and will have them, and more——
Phi. What more?
Are. Or lose that little life the gods prepared
To trouble this poor piece of earth withal.
Phi. Madam, what more?
Are. Turn, then, away thy face.
Phi. No.
Are. Do.
Phi. I can endure it. Turn away my face!
I never yet saw enemy that lookt
So dreadfully, but that I thought myself

As great a basilisk[18] as he; or spake
So horrible, but that I thought my tongue
Bore thunder underneath, as much as his;
Nor beast that I could turn from. Shall I then
Begin to fear sweet sounds? A lady's voice,
Whom I do love? Say you would have my life;
Why, I will give it you; for 't is of me
A thing so loath'd, and unto you that ask
Of so poor use, that I shall make no price:
If you entreat, I will unmov'dly hear.
Are. Yet, for my sake, a little bend thy looks.
Phi. I do.
Are. Then know, I must have them and thee.
Phi. And me?
Are. Thy love; without which, all the land
Discovered yet will serve me for no use
But to be buried in.
Phi. Is 't possible?
Are. With it, it were too little to bestow
On thee. Now, though thy breath do strike me dead,
(Which, know, it may,) I have unript my breast.
Phi. Madam, you are too full of noble thoughts,
To lay a train for this contemned life,
Which you may have for asking. To suspect
Were base, where I deserve no ill. Love you!
By all my hopes, I do, above my life!
But how this passion should proceed from you
So violently, would amaze a man
That would be jealous.[19]
Are. Another soul into my body shot
Could not have fill'd me with more strength and spirit
Than this thy breath. But spend not hasty time
In seeking how I came thus: 't is the gods,
The gods, that make me so; and, sure, our love
Will be the nobler and the better blest,
In that the secret justice of the gods
Is mingled with it. Let us leave, and kiss;
Lest some unwelcome guest should fall betwixt us,
And we should part without it.
Phi. 'T will be ill
I should abide here long.
Are. 'T is true; and worse
You should come often. How shall we devise
To hold intelligence, that our true loves,
On any new occasion, may agree
What path is best to tread?
Phi. I have a boy,
Sent by the gods, I hope, to this intent,
Not yet seen in the court. Hunting the buck,
I found him sitting by a fountain's side,
Of which he borrow'd some to quench his thirst,
And paid the nymph again as much in tears.
A garland lay him by, made by himself
Of many several flowers bred in the vale,
Stuck in that mystic order that the rareness
Delighted me: but ever when he turn'd
His tender eyes upon 'em, he would weep,
As if he meant to make 'em grow again.
Seeing such pretty helpless innocence
Dwell in his face, I ask'd him all his story.
He told me that his parents gentle died,
Leaving him to the mercy of the fields,
Which gave him roots; and of the crystal springs,
Which did not stop their courses; and the sun,
Which still, he thank'd him, yielded him his light.
Then took he up his garland, and did show
What every flower, as country-people hold,
Did signify, and how all, ordered thus,
Exprest his grief; and, to my thoughts, did read
The prettiest lecture of his country-art
That could be wisht: so that methought I could
Have studied it. I gladly entertain'd
Him, who was glad to follow; and have got
The trustiest, loving'st, and the gentlest boy
That ever master kept. Him will I send
To wait on you, and bear our hidden love.
Are. 'T is well; no more.

Re-enter Lady.

Lady. Madam, the prince is come to do his service.

18 a fabulous serpent that killed with a glance.

19 suspicious.

Are. What will you do, Philaster, with yourself?
Phi. Why, that which all the gods have pointed out for me.
Are. Dear, hide thyself.—
Bring in the prince.
Exit Lady.
Phi. Hide me from Pharamond!
When thunder speaks, which is the voice of God,
Though I do reverence, yet I hide me not;
And shall a stranger-prince have leave to brag
Unto a foreign nation, that he made
Philaster hide himself?
Are. He cannot know it.
Phi. Though it should sleep for ever to the world,
It is a simple sin to hide myself,
Which will for ever on my conscience lie.
Are. Then, good Philaster, give him scope and way
In what he says; for he is apt to speak
What you are loth to hear. For my sake, do.
Phi. I will.

Re-enter Lady with Pharamond.

Pha. My princely mistress, as true lovers ought,
Exit Lady.
I come to kiss these fair hands, and to show,
In outward ceremonies, the dear love
Writ in my heart.
Phi. If I shall have an answer no directlier,
I am gone.
Pha. To what would he have answer?
Are. To his claim unto the kingdom.
Pha. Sirrah, I forbare you before the King—
Phi. Good sir, do so still; I would not talk with you.
Pha. But now the time is fitter. Do but offer
To make mention of right to any kingdom,
Though it be scarce habitable——
Phi. Good sir, let me go.
Pha. And by the gods—
Phi. Peace, Pharamond! if thou——
Are. Leave us, Philaster.
Phi. I have done.
(*Going.*)
Pha. You are gone! by Heaven, I'll fetch you back.
Phi. You shall not need.
(*Returning.*)
Pha. What now?
Phi. Know, Pharamond,
I loathe to brawl with such a blast as thou,
Who art nought but a valiant voice; but if
Thou shalt provoke me further, men shall say,
Thou wert, and not lament it.
Pha. Do you slight
My greatness so, and in the chamber of
The princess?
Phi. It is a place to which I must confess
I owe a reverence; but were 't the church,
Aye, at the altar, there 's no place so safe,
Where thou dar'st injure me, but I dare kill thee.
And for your greatness, know, sir, I can grasp
You and your greatness thus, thus into nothing.
Give not a word, not a word back! Farewell. *Exit.*
Pha. 'T is an odd fellow, madam; we must stop
His mouth with some office when we are married.
Are. You were best make him your controller.
Pha. I think he would discharge it well. But, madam,
I hope our hearts are knit; but yet so slow
The ceremonies of state are, that 't will be long
Before our hands be so. If then you please,
Being agreed in heart, let us not wait
For dreaming form, but take a little stolen
Delights, and so prevent[20] our joys to come.
Are. If you dare speak such thoughts,
I must withdraw in honor.
Exit.
Pha. The constitution of my body will never hold out till the wedding; I must seek elsewhere.
Exit.

ACT II.

SCENE 1. *An apartment in the palace.*

Enter Philaster and Bellario.

Phi. And thou shalt find her honorable, boy;

20 anticipate.

Full of regard unto thy tender youth,
For thine own modesty; and, for my sake,
Apter to give than thou wilt be to ask,
Aye, or deserve.

Bel. Sir, you did take me up
When I was nothing; and only yet am something
By being yours. You trusted me unknown;
And that which you were apt to conster[21]
A simple innocence in me, perhaps
Might have been craft, the cunning of a boy
Hard'ned in lies and theft: yet ventur'd you
To part my miseries and me: for which,
I never can expect to serve a lady
That bears more honor in her breast than you.

Phi. But, boy, it will prefer[22] thee. Thou art young,
And bear'st a childish overflowing love
To them that clap thy cheeks and speak thee fair yet;
But when thy judgment comes to rule those passions,
Thou wilt remember best those careful friends
That plac'd thee in the noblest way of life.
She is a princess I prefer thee to.

Bel. In that small time that I have seen the world,
I never knew a man hasty to part
With a servant he thought trusty. I remember,
My father would prefer the boys he kept
To greater men than he; but did it not
Till they were grown too saucy for himself.

Phi. Why, gentle boy, I find no fault at all
In thy behavior.

Bel. Sir, if I have made
A fault in ignorance, instruct my youth:
I shall be willing, if not apt, to learn;
Age and experience will adorn my mind
With larger knowledge; and if I have done
A wilful fault, think me not past all hope
For once. What master holds so strict a hand
Over his boy, that he will part with him
Without one warning? Let me be corrected
To break my stubbornness, if it be so,
Rather than turn me off; and I shall mend.

Phi. Thy love doth plead so prettily to stay,
That, trust me, I could weep to part with thee.
Alas, I do not turn thee off! Thou knowest
It is my business that doth call thee hence;
And when thou art with her, thou dwell'st with me,
Think so, and 't is so; and when time is full,
That thou hast well discharg'd this heavy trust,
Laid on so weak a one, I will again
With joy receive thee; as I live, I will!
Nay, weep not, gentle boy. 'T is more than time
Thou didst attend the princess.

Bel. I am gone.
But since I am to part with you, my lord,
And none knows whether I shall live to do
More service for you, take this little prayer:
Heaven bless your loves, your fights, all your designs!
May sick men, if they have your wish, be well;
And Heaven hate those you curse, though I be one! *Exit.*

Phi. The love of boys unto their lords is strange;
I have read wonders of it: yet this boy
For my sake (if a man may judge by looks
And speech) would out-do story. I may see
A day to pay him for his loyalty.
Exit.

SCENE 2. *A gallery in the palace.*

Enter Pharamond.

Pha. Why should these ladies stay so long? They must come this way. I know the queen employs 'em not; for the reverend mother[23] sent me word, they would all be for the garden. If they should all prove honest now, I were in a fair taking; I was never so long without sport in my life, and, in my conscience, 't is not my fault. Oh, for our country ladies!

21 construe. 22 advance. 23 in charge of the maids of honor.

Enter Galatea.

Here's one bolted; I'll hound at her.—
Madam!

Gal. Your grace!

Pha. Shall I not be a trouble?

Gal. Not to me, sir.

Pha. Nay, nay, you are too quick. By this sweet hand——

Gal. You'll be forsworn, sir; 't is but an old glove.
If you will talk at distance, I am for you:
But, good prince, be not bawdy, nor do not brag;
These two I bar;
And then, I think, I shall have sense enough
To answer all the weighty apophthegms
Your royal blood shall manage.

Pha. Dear lady, can you love?

Gal. Dear prince! how dear? I ne'er cost you a coach yet, nor put you to the dear repentance of a banquet. Here's no scarlet, sir, to blush the sin out it was given for. This wire [24] mine own hair covers; and this face has been so far from being dear to any, that it ne'er cost penny painting; and, for the rest of my poor wardrobe, such as you see, it leaves no hand [25] behind it, to make the jealous mercer's wife curse our good doings.

Pha. You mistake me, lady.

Gal. Lord, I do so; would you or I could help it!

Pha. You're very dangerous bitter, like a potion.

Gal. No, sir, I do not mean to purge you, though
I mean to purge a little time on you.

Pha. Do ladies of this country use to give
No more respect to men of my full being?

Gal. Full being! I understand you not, unless your grace means growing to fatness; and then your only remedy (upon my knowledge, prince) is, in a morning, a cup of neat white wine brewed with carduus,[26] then fast till supper; about eight you may eat; use exercise, and keep a sparrow-hawk; you can shoot in a tiller: [27] but, of all, your grace must fly phlebotomy,[28] fresh pork, conger,[29] and clarified whey; they are all dullers of the vital spirits.

Pha. Lady, you talk of nothing all this while.

Gal. 'T is very true, sir; I talk of you.

Pha. (*Aside.*) This is a crafty wench; I like her wit well; 't will be rare to stir up a leaden appetite. She's a Danaë, and must be courted in a shower of gold.—Madam, look here; all these, and more than——

Gal. What have you there, my lord? Gold! now, as I live, 't is fair gold! You would have silver for it, to play with the pages. You could not have taken me in a worse time; but, if you have present use, my lord, I'll send my man with silver and keep your gold for you.

Pha. Lady, lady!

Gal. She's coming, sir, behind, will take white money.—
(*Aside.*) Yet for all this I'll match ye.
Exit behind the hangings.

Pha. If there be but two such more in this kingdom, and near the court, we may even hang up our harps. Ten such camphire [30] constitutions as this would call the golden age again in question, and teach the old way for every ill-fac'd husband to get his own children; and what a mischief that would breed, let all consider!

Enter Megra.

Here's another: if she be of the same last, the devil shall pluck her on.—Many fair mornings, lady!

Meg. As many mornings bring as many days,
Fair, sweet and hopeful to your grace!

Pha. (*Aside.*) She gives good words yet; sure this wench is free.[31]—
If your more serious business do not call you,
Let me hold quarter with you; we will talk
An hour out quickly.

Meg. What would your grace talk of?

Pha. Of some such pretty subject as yourself:
I'll go no further than your eye, or lip;
There's theme enough for one man for an age.

Meg. Sir, they stand right, and my lips are yet even,
Smooth, young enough, ripe enough, and red enough,
Or my glass wrongs me.

Pha. Oh, they are two twinn'd cherries dy'd in blushes
Which those fair suns above with their bright beams
Reflect upon and ripen. Sweetest beauty,
Bow down those branches, that the longing taste

24 *i. e.* of a headdress.
25 note of indebtedness.
26 a thistle used for medicinal purposes.
27 cross-bow.
28 blood-letting.
29 conger-eel.
30 *i. e.* cold.
31 responsive.

Of the faint looker-on may meet those blessings,
And taste and live.
(*They kiss.*)

Meg. (*Aside.*) Oh, delicate sweet prince!
She that hath snow enough about her heart
To take the wanton spring of ten such lines off,
May be a nun without probation.—Sir,
You have in such neat poetry gathered a kiss,
That if I had but five lines of that number,
Such pretty begging blanks,[32] I should commend
Your forehead or your cheeks, and kiss you too.

Pha. Do it in prose; you cannot miss it, madam.

Meg. I shall, I shall.

Pha. By my life, but you shall not;
I'll prompt you first. (*Kisses her.*) Can you do it now?

Meg. Methinks 't is easy, now you ha' done 't before me;
But yet I should stick at it.
(*Kisses him.*)

Pha. Stick till to-morrow;
I'll ne'er part you, sweetest. But we lose time:
Can you love me?

Meg. Love you, my lord! How would you have me love you?

Pha. I'll teach you in a short sentence, 'cause I will not load your memory; this is all: love me, and lie with me.

Meg. Was it "lie with you" that you said? 'T is impossible.

Pha. Not to a willing mind, that will endeavor. If I do not teach you to do it as easily in one night as you'll go to bed, I'll lose my royal blood for 't.

Meg. Why, prince, you have a lady of your own
That yet wants teaching.

Pha. I'll sooner teach a mare the old measures than teach her anything belonging to the function. She 's afraid to lie with herself if she have but any masculine imaginations about her. I know, when we are married, I must ravish her.

Meg. By mine honor, that 's a foul fault, indeed;
But time and your good help will wear it out, sir.

Pha. And for any other I see, excepting your dear self, dearest lady, I had rather be Sir Tim the schoolmaster, and leap a dairy-maid, madam.

Meg. Has your grace seen the court-star, Galatea?

Pha. Out upon her! She 's as cold of her favor as an apoplex; she sail'd by but now.

Meg. And how do you hold her wit, sir?

Pha. I hold her wit? The strength of all the guard cannot hold it, if they were tied to it; she would blow 'em out of the kingdom. They talk of Jupiter; he 's but a squib-cracker to her: look well about you, and you may find a tongue-bolt. But speak, sweet lady, shall I be freely welcome?

Meg. Whither?

Pha. To your bed. If you mistrust my faith, you do me the unnoblest wrong.

Meg. I dare not, prince, I dare not.

Pha. Make your own conditions, my purse shall seal 'em, and what you dare imagine you can want, I'll furnish you withal. Give two hours to your thoughts every morning about it. Come I know you are bashful;
Speak in my ear, will you be mine? Keep this,
And with it, me: soon I will visit you.

Meg. My lord, my chamber 's most unsafe; but when 't is night,
I'll find some means to slip into your lodging;
Till when——

Pha. Till when, this and my heart go with thee! *Exeunt several ways.*

Re-enter Galatea from behind the hangings.

Gal. Oh, thou pernicious petticoat prince! are these your virtues? Well, if I do not lay a train to blow your sport up, I am no woman: and, Lady Towsabel, I'll fit you for 't.

Exit.

SCENE 3. *Arethusa's apartment in the palace.*

Enter Arethusa and a Lady.

Are. Where 's the boy?

Lady. Within, madam.

Are. Gave you him gold to buy him clothes?

Lady. I did.

Are. And has he done 't?

Lady. Yes, madam.

[32] blank verses.

Are. 'T is a pretty sad-talking boy, is it not?
Asked you his name?
Lady. No, madam.

Enter Galatea.

Are. Oh, you are welcome. What good news?
Gal. As good as any one can tell your grace,
That says she has done that you would have wish'd.
Are. Hast thou discovered?
Gal. I have strain'd a point of modesty for you.
Are. I prithee, how?
Gal. In list'ning after bawdry. I see, let a lady live never so modestly, she shall be sure to find a lawful time to hearken after bawdry. Your prince, brave Pharamond, was so hot on 't!
Are. With whom?
Gal. Why, with the lady I suspected. I can tell the time and place.
Are. Oh, when, and where?
Gal. To-night, his lodging.
Are. Run thyself into the presence; mingle there again
With other ladies; leave the rest to me.
Exit Galatea.
If destiny (to whom we dare not say,
"Why didst thou this?") have not decreed it so,
In lasting leaves (whose smallest characters
Were never alter'd yet), this match shall break.—
Where 's the boy?
Lady. Here, madam.

Enter Bellario.

Are. Sir, you are sad to change your service; is 't not so?
Bel. Madam, I have not chang'd; I wait on you,
To do him service.
Are. Thou disclaim'st in me.[33]
Tell me thy name.
Bel. Bellario.
Are. Thou canst sing and play?
Bel. If grief will give me leave, madam, I can.
Are. Alas, what kind of grief can thy years know?
Hadst thou a curst [34] master when thou went'st to school?
Thou art not capable of other grief;
Thy brows and cheeks are smooth as waters be
When no breath troubles them. Believe me, boy,
Care seeks out wrinkled brows and hollow eyes,
And builds himself caves, to abide in them.
Come, sir, tell me truly, doth your lord love me?
Bel. Love, madam! I know not what it is.
Are. Canst thou know grief, and never yet knew'st love?
Thou art deceiv'd, boy. Does he speak of me
As if he wish'd me well?
Bel. If it be love
To forget all respect of his own friends
With thinking of your face; if it be love
To sit cross-arm'd and sigh away the day,
Mingled with starts, crying your name as loud
And hastily as men i' the streets do fire;
If it be love to weep himself away
When he but hears of any lady dead
Or kill'd, because it might have been your chance;
If, when he goes to rest (which will not be),
'Twixt every prayer he says, to name you once,
As others drop a bead, be to be in love,
Then, madam, I dare swear he loves you.
Are. Oh, you 're a cunning boy, and taught to lie
For your lord's credit! But thou know'st a lie
That bears this sound is welcomer to me
Than any truth that says he loves me not.
Lead the way, boy.—(*To Lady.*) Do you attend me too.—
'T is thy lord's business hastes me thus. Away!
Exeunt.

SCENE 4. *Before Pharamond's lodging in the court of the palace.*

Enter Dion, Cleremont, Thrasiline, Megra, and Galatea.

Dion. Come, ladies, shall we talk a round? As men
Do walk a mile, women should talk an hour
After supper: 't is their exercise.

33 my right to your services.

34 cruel.

Gal. 'T is late.
Meg. 'T is all
My eyes will do to lead me to my bed.
Gal. I fear, they are so heavy, you 'll scarce find
The way to your own lodging with 'em to-night.

Enter Pharamond.

Thra. The prince!
Pha. Not a-bed, ladies? You 're good sitters-up.
What think you of a pleasant dream, to last
Till morning?
Meg. I should choose, my lord, a pleasing wake before it.

Enter Arethusa and Bellario.

Are. 'T is well, my lord; you 're courting of these ladies.—
Is 't not late, gentlemen?
Cle. Yes, madam.
Are. Wait you there.
Exit.
Meg. (*Aside.*) She 's jealous, as I live.—Look you, my lord,
The princess has a Hylas, an Adonis.
Pha. His form is angel-like.
Meg. Why, this is he that must, when you are wed,
Sit by your pillow, like young Apollo, with
His hand and voice binding your thoughts in sleep;
The princess does provide him for you and for herself.
Pha. I find no music in these boys.
Meg. Nor I:
They can do little, and that small they do,
They have not wit to hide.
Dion. Serves he the princess?
Thra. Yes.
Dion. 'T is a sweet boy: how brave[35] she keeps him!
Pha. Ladies all, good rest; I mean to kill a buck
To-morrow morning ere you 've done your dreams.
Meg. All happiness attend your grace!
Exit Pharamond.
Gentlemen, good rest.—
Come, shall we go to bed?
Gal. Yes.—All, good night.
Dion. May your dreams be true to you!—
Exeunt Galatea and Megra.
What shall we do, gallants? 't is late. The King
Is up still: see, he comes, a guard along
With him.

Enter King, Arethusa, and Guard.

King. Look your intelligence be true.
Are. Upon my life, it is; and I do hope
Your highness will not tie me to a man
That in the heat of wooing throws me off,
And takes another.
Dion. What should this mean?
King. If it be true,
That lady had been better have embrac'd
Cureless diseases. Get you to your rest:
You shall be righted.
Exeunt Arethusa and Bellario.
—Gentlemen, draw near;
We shall employ you. Is young Pharamond
Come to his lodging?
Dion. I saw him enter there.
King. Haste, some of you, and cunningly discover
If Megra be in her lodging.
Exit Dion.
Cle. Sir,
She parted hence but now, with other ladies.
King. If she be there, we shall not need to make
A vain discovery of our suspicion.
(*Aside.*) You gods, I see that who unrighteously
Holds wealth or state from others shall be curst
In that which meaner men are blest withal:
Ages to come shall know no male of him
Left to inherit, and his name shall be
Blotted from earth; if he have any child,
It shall be crossly match'd; the gods themselves
Shall sow wild strife betwixt her lord and her.
Yet, if it be your wills, forgive the sin
I have committed; let it not fall
Upon this understanding child of mine!
She has not broke your laws. But how can I
Look to be heard of gods that must be just,
Praying upon the ground I hold by wrong?

Re-enter Dion.

35 richly attired.

Dion. Sir, I have asked, and her women swear she is within; but they, I think, are bawds. I told 'em, I must speak with her; they laught, and said, their lady lay speechless. I said, my business was important; they said, their lady was about it. I grew hot, and cried, my business was a matter that concern'd life and death; they answered, so was sleeping, at which their lady was. I urg'd again, she had scarce time to be so since last I saw her: they smil'd again, and seem'd to instruct me that sleeping was nothing but lying down and winking.[36] Answers more direct I could not get: in short, sir, I think she is not there.

King. 'T is then no time to dally.—You o' th' guard,
Wait at the back door of the prince's lodging,
And see that none pass thence, upon your lives.
Exeunt Guards.
Knock, gentlemen; knock loud; louder yet.
(*They knock at the door of Pharamond's lodging.*)
What, has their pleasure taken off their hearing?—
I 'll break your meditations.—Knock again.—
Not yet? I do not think he sleeps, having this
Larum by him.—Once more.—Pharamond! prince!
(*Pharamond appears above.*)

Pha. What saucy groom knocks at this dead of night?
Where be our waiters?[37] By my vexed soul,
He meets his death that meets me, for his boldness.

King. Prince, prince, you wrong your thoughts; we are your friends:
Come down.

Pha. The King!

King. The same, sir. Come down, sir:
We have cause of present counsel with you.

Pha. If your grace please
To use me, I 'll attend you to your chamber.

Enter Pharamond below.

King. No, 't is too late, prince; I 'll make bold with yours.

Pha. I have some private reasons to myself
Makes me unmannerly, and say you cannot.—
(*They press to come in.*)
Nay, press not forward, gentlemen; he must
Come through my life that comes here.

King. Sir, be resolv'd I must and will come.—Enter.

Pha. I will not be dishonor'd.
He that enters, enters upon his death.
Sir, 't is a sign you make no stranger of me,
To bring these renegadoes to my chamber
At these unseasoned hours.

King. Why do you
Chafe yourself so? You are not wrong'd nor shall be;
Only I 'll search your lodging, for some cause
To ourself known.—Enter, I say.

Pha. I say, no.

Enter Megra above.

Meg. Let 'em enter, prince, let 'em enter;
I am up and ready:[38] I know their business;
'T is the poor breaking of a lady's honor
They hunt so hotly after; let 'em enjoy it.—
You have your business, gentlemen; I lay here.
Oh, my lord the King, this is not noble in you
To make public the weakness of a woman!

King. Come down.

Meg. I dare, my lord. Your hootings and your clamors,
Your private whispers and your broad fleerings,[39]
Can no more vex my soul than this base carriage.[40]
But I have vengeance yet in store for some
Shall, in the most contempt you can have of me,
Be joy and nourishment.

King. Will you come down?

Meg. Yes, to laugh at your worst; but I shall wring you,
If my skill fail me not.
Exit above.

King. Sir, I must dearly chide you for this looseness;
You have wrong'd a worthy lady; but, no more.—
Conduct him to my lodging and to bed.
Exeunt Pharamond and Attendants.

36 closing the eyes. 37 those that wait on us. 38 dressed. 39 gibes. 40 conduct

Cle. Get him another wench, and you bring him to bed indeed.

Dion. 'T is strange a man cannot ride a stage
Or two, to breathe himself, without a warrant.
If his gear hold, that lodgings be search'd thus,
Pray God we may lie with our own wives in safety,
That they be not by some trick of state mistaken!

Enter Attendants with Megra below.

King. Now, lady of honor, where 's your honor now?
No man can fit your palate but the prince.
Thou most ill-shrouded rottenness, thou piece
Made by a painter and a 'pothecary,
Thou troubled sea of lust, thou wilderness
Inhabited by wild thoughts, thou swoln cloud
Of infection, thou ripe mine of all diseases,
Thou all-sin, all-hell, and last, all-devils, tell me,
Had you none to pull on with your courtesies
But he that must be mine, and wrong my daughter?
By all the gods, all these, and all the pages,
And all the court, shall hoot thee through the court,
Fling rotten oranges, make ribald rhymes,
And sear thy name with candles upon walls!
Do you laugh, Lady Venus?

Meg. Faith, sir, you must pardon me;
I cannot choose but laugh to see you merry.
If you do this, O King! nay, if you dare do it,
By all those gods you swore by, and as many
More of my own, I will have fellows, and such
Fellows in it, as shall make noble mirth!
The princess, your dear daughter, shall stand by me
On walls, and sung in ballads, any thing.
Urge me no more; I know her and her haunts,
Her lays, leaps, and outlays, and will discover all;
Nay, will dishonor her. I know the boy
She keeps; a handsome boy, about eighteen;
Know what she does with him, where, and when.
Come, sir, you put me to a woman's madness,
The glory of a fury; and if I do not
Do 't to the height——

King. What boy is this she raves at?

Meg. Alas! good-minded prince, you know not these things!
I am loth to reveal 'em. Keep this fault,
As you would keep your health from the hot air
Of the corrupted people, or, by Heaven,
I will not fall alone. What I have known
Shall be as public as a print; all tongues
Shall speak it as they do the language they
Are born in, as free and commonly; I'll set it,
Like a prodigious[41] star, for all to gaze at,
And so high and glowing, that other kingdoms far and foreign
Shall read it there, nay, travel with it, till they find
No tongue to make it more, nor no more people;
And then behold the fall of your fair princess!

King. Has she a boy?

Cle. So please your grace, I have seen a boy wait
On her, a fair boy.

King. Go, get you to your quarter:
For this time I will study to forget you.

Meg. Do you study to forget me, and I'll study
To forget you.

Exeunt King, Megra, and Guard.

Cle. Why, here 's a male spirit fit for Hercules. If ever there be Nine Worthies of women, this wench shall ride astride and be their captain.

Dion. Sure, she has a garrison of devils in her tongue, she uttered such balls of wild-fire. She has so nettled the King, that all the doctors in the country will scarce cure him. That boy was a strange-found-out antidote to cure her infection; that boy, that princess' boy; that brave, chaste, virtuous lady's boy; and a fair

41 portentous.

boy, a well-spoken boy! All these considered, can make nothing else—but there I leave you, gentlemen.

Thra. Nay, we'll go wander with you.

Exeunt.

ACT III.

SCENE 1. *The court of the palace.*

Enter Dion, Cleremont, and Thrasiline.

Cle. Nay, doubtless, 't is true.

Dion. Aye; and 't is the gods
That rais'd this punishment, to scourge the King
With his own issue. Is it not a shame
For us that should write noble in the land,
For us that should be freemen, to behold
A man that is the bravery of his age,
Philaster, prest down from his royal right
By this regardless king? and only look
And see the sceptre ready to be cast
Into the hands of that lascivious lady
That lives in lust with a smooth boy, now to be married
To yon strange prince, who, but that people please
To let him be a prince, is born a slave
In that which should be his most noble part,
His mind?

Thra. That man that would not stir with you
To aid Philaster, let the gods forget
That such a creature walks upon the earth!

Cle. Philaster is too backward in 't himself.
The gentry do await it, and the people,
Against their nature, are all bent for him,
And like a field of standing corn, that 's moved
With a stiff gale, their heads bow all one way.

Dion. The only cause that draws Philaster back
From this attempt is the fair princess' love,
Which he admires, and we can now confute.

Thra. Perhaps he'll not believe it.

Dion. Why, gentlemen, 't is without question so.

Cle. Aye, 't is past speech she lives dishonestly.
But how shall we, if he be curious,[42] work
Upon his faith?

Thra. We all are satisfied within ourselves.

Dion. Since it is true, and tends to his own good,
I'll make this new report to be my knowledge;
I'll say I know it; nay, I'll swear I saw it.

Cle. It will be best.

Thra. 'T will move him.

Enter Philaster.

Dion. Here he comes.
Good morrow to your honor: we have spent
Some time in seeking you.

Phi. My worthy friends,
You that can keep your memories to know
Your friend in miseries, and cannot frown
On men disgrac'd for virtue, a good day
Attend you all! What service may I do
Worthy your acceptation?

Dion. My good lord,
We come to urge that virtue, which we know
Lives in your breast, forth. Rise, and make a head;[43]
The nobles and the people are all dull'd
With this usurping king; and not a man,
That ever heard the word, or knew such a thing
As virtue, but will second your attempts.

Phi. How honorable is this love in you
To me that have deserv'd none! Know, my friends,
(You, that were born to shame your poor Philaster
With too much courtesy,) I could afford
To melt myself in thanks: but my designs
Are not yet ripe. Suffice it, that ere long
I shall employ your loves; but yet the time
Is short of what I would.

Dion. The time is fuller, sir, than you expect;
That which hereafter will not, perhaps, be reach'd
By violence, may now be caught. As for the King,

42 scrupulous.

43 raise an army.

You know the people have long hated him;
But now the princess, whom they lov'd——
Phi. Why, what of her?
Dion. Is loath'd as much as he.
Phi. By what strange means?
Dion. She 's known a whore.
Phi. Thou liest!
Dion. My lord——
Phi. Thou liest,
(*Offers to draw and is held.*)
And thou shalt feel it! I had thought thy mind
Had been of honor. Thus to rob a lady
Of her good name is an infectious sin
Not to be pardon'd. Be it false as hell,
'T will never be redeem'd, if it be sown
Amongst the people, fruitful to increase
All evil they shall hear. Let me alone
That I may cut off falsehood whilst it springs!
Set hills on hills betwixt me and the man
That utters this, and I will scale them all,
And from the utmost top fall on his neck,
Like thunder from a cloud.
Dion. This is most strange:
Sure, he does love her.
Phi. I do love fair truth.
She is my mistress, and who injures her
Draws vengeance from me. Sirs, let go my arms.
Thra. Nay, good my lord, be patient.
Cle. Sir, remember this is your honor'd friend,
That comes to do his service, and will show you
Why he utter'd this.
Phi. I ask your pardon, sir;
My zeal to truth made me unmannerly:
Should I have heard dishonor spoke of you,
Behind your back, untruly, I had been
As much distemper'd and enrag'd as now.
Dion. But this, my lord, is truth.
Phi. Oh, say not so!
Good sir, forbear to say so: 't is then truth,
That womankind is false: urge it no more;
It is impossible. Why should you think
The princess light?
Dion. Why, she was taken at it.
Phi. 'T is false! by Heaven, 't is false! It cannot be!
Can it? Speak, gentlemen; for God's love, speak!
Is 't possible? Can women all be damn'd?
Dion. Why, no, my lord.
Phi. Why, then, it cannot be.
Dion. And she was taken with her boy.
Phi. What boy?
Dion. A page, a boy that serves her.
Phi. Oh, good gods!
A little boy?
Dion. Aye; know you him, my lord?
Phi. (*Aside.*) Hell and sin know him!—Sir, you are deceiv'd;
I 'll reason it a little coldly with you.
If she were lustful, would she take a boy,
That knows not yet desire? She would have one
Should meet her thoughts and know the sin he acts,
Which is the great delight of wickedness.
You are abus'd,[44] and so is she, and I.
Dion. How you, my lord?
Phi. Why, all the world 's abus'd
In an unjust report.
Dion. Oh, noble sir, your virtues
Cannot look into the subtle thoughts of woman!
In short, my lord, I took them; I myself.
Phi. Now, all the devils, thou didst! Fly from my rage!
Would thou hadst ta'en devils engend'ring plagues,
When thou didst take them! Hide thee from mine eyes!
Would thou hadst taken thunder on thy breast,
When thou didst take them; or been strucken dumb
For ever; that this foul deed might have slept
In silence!
Thra. Have you known him so ill-temper'd?
Cle. Never before.
Phi. The winds that are let loose
From the four several corners of the earth,
And spread themselves all over sea and land,
Kiss not a chaste one. What friend bears a sword
To run me through?
Dion. Why, my lord, are you
So mov'd at this?
Phi. When any fall from virtue,
I am distract; I have an interest in 't.
Dion. But, good my lord, recall yourself, and think

44 deceived.

What 's best to be done.
Phi. I thank you; I will do it.
Please you to leave me; I 'll consider of it.
To-morrow I will find your lodging forth,
And give you answer.
Dion. All the gods direct you
The readiest way!
Thra. He was extreme impatient.
Cle. It was his virtue and his noble mind.
Exeunt Dion, Cleremont, and Thrasiline.
Phi. I had forgot to ask him where he took them;
I 'll follow him. Oh that I had a sea
Within my breast, to quench the fire I feel!
More circumstances will but fan this fire:
It more afflicts me now, to know by whom
This deed is done, than simply that 't is done;
And he that tells me this is honorable,
As far from lies as she is far from truth.
Oh, that, like beasts, we could not grieve ourselves
With that we see not! Bulls and rams will fight
To keep their females standing in their sight;
But take 'em from them, and you take at once
Their spleens away; and they will fall again
Unto their pastures, growing fresh and fat,
And taste the waters of the springs as sweet
As 't was before, finding no start in sleep;
But miserable man——

Enter Bellario.

See, see, you gods!
He walks still; and the face you let him wear
When he was innocent is still the same,
Not blasted! Is this justice? Do you mean
To intrap mortality, that you allow
Treason so smooth a brow? I cannot now
Think he is guilty.
Bel. Health to you, my lord!
The princess doth commend her love, her life,
And this, unto you.
(*Gives a letter.*)
Phi. Oh, Bellario.
Now I perceive she loves me: she does show it
In loving thee, my boy; she has made thee brave.
Bel. My lord, she has attir'd me past my wish,
Past my desert; more fit for her attendant,
Though far unfit for me who do attend.
Phi. Thou art grown courtly, boy.—Oh, let all women,
That love black deeds, learn to dissemble here,
Here, by this paper! She does write to me
As if her heart were mines of adamant
To all the world besides; but, unto me,
A maiden-snow that melted with my looks.—
Tell me, my boy, how doth the princess use thee?
For I shall guess her love to me by that.
Bel. Scarce like her servant, but as if I were,
Something allied to her, or had preserv'd
Her life three times by my fidelity;
As mothers fond do use their only sons,
As I 'd use one that 's left unto my trust,
For whom my life should pay if he met harm,
So she does use me.
Phi. Why, this is wondrous well:
But what kind language does she feed thee with?
Bel. Why, she does tell me she will trust my youth
With all her loving secrets, and does call me
Her pretty servant; bids me weep no more
For leaving you; she 'll see my services
Regarded: and such words of that soft strain
That I am nearer weeping when she ends
Than ere she spake.
Phi. This is much better still.
Bel. Are you not ill, my lord?
Phi. Ill? No, Bellario.
Bel. Methinks your words
Fall not from off your tongue so evenly,
Nor is there in your looks that quietness
That I was wont to see.
Phi. Thou art deceiv'd, boy:
And she strokes thy head?
Bel. Yes.
Phi. And she does clap thy cheeks?
Bel. She does, my lord.
Phi. And she does kiss thee, boy? ha!

Bel. How, my lord?
Phi. She kisses thee?
Bel. Never, my lord, by heaven.
Phi. That 's strange, I know she does.
Bel. No, by my life!
Phi. Why then she does not love me. Come, she does.
I bade her do it; I charg'd her, by all charms
Of love between us, by the hope of peace
We should enjoy, to yield thee all delights
Naked as to her bed; I took her oath
Thou shouldst enjoy her. Tell me, gentle boy,
Is she not parallelless? Is not her breath
Sweet as Arabian winds when fruits are ripe?
Are not her breasts two liquid ivory balls?
Is she not all a lasting mine of joy?
Bel. Aye, now I see why my disturbed thoughts
Were so perplex'd. When first I went to her,
My heart held augury. You are abus'd;
Some villain has abus'd you; I do see
Whereto you tend. Fall rocks upon his head
That put this to you! 'T is some subtle train
To bring that noble frame of yours to nought.
Phi. Thou think'st I will be angry with thee. Come,
Thou shalt know all my drift. I hate her more
Than I love happiness, and plac'd thee there
To pry with narrow eyes into her deeds.
Hast thou discovered? Is she fallen to lust,
As I would wish her? Speak some comfort to me.
Bel. My lord, you did mistake the boy you sent.
Had she the lust of sparrows or of goats,
Had she a sin that way, hid from the world,
Beyond the name of lust, I would not aid
Her base desires; but what I came to know
As servant to her, I would not reveal,
To make my life last ages.
Phi. Oh, my heart!
This is a salve worse than the main disease.—
Tell me thy thoughts; for I will know the least
That dwells within thee, or will rip thy heart
To know it. I will see thy thoughts as plain
As I do now thy face.
Bel. Why, so you do.
She is (for aught I know) by all the gods,
As chaste as ice! But were she foul as hell,
And I did know it thus, the breath of kings,
The points of swords, tortures, nor bulls of brass,
Should draw it from me.
Phi. Then it is no time
To dally with thee; I will take thy life.
For I do hate thee. I could curse thee now.
Bel. If you do hate, you could not curse me worse;
The gods have not a punishment in store
Greater for me than is your hate.
Phi. Fie, fie,
So young and so dissembling! Tell me when
And where thou didst enjoy her, or let plagues
Fall on me, if I destroy thee not!
(*Draws his sword.*)
Bel. By heaven, I never did; and when I lie
To save my life, may I live long and loath'd!
Hew me asunder, and, whilst I can think,
I 'll love those pieces you have cut away
Better than those that grow, and kiss those limbs
Because you made 'em so.
Phi. Fear'st thou not death?
Can boys contemn that?
Bel. Oh, what boy is he
Can be content to live to be a man,
That sees the best of men thus passionate,
Thus without reason?
Phi. Oh, but thou dost not know
What 't is to die.
Bel. Yes, I do know, my lord:
'T is less than to be born; a lasting sleep;
A quiet resting from all jealousy,
A thing we all pursue. I know, besides,
It is but giving over of a game
That must be lost.

Phi. But there are pains, false boy,
For perjur'd souls. Think but on those, and then
Thy heart will melt, and thou wilt utter all.

Bel. May they fall all upon me whilst I live,
If I be perjur'd, or have ever thought
Of that you charged me with! If I be false,
Send me to suffer in those punishments
You speak of; kill me!

Phi. Oh, what should I do?
Why, who can but believe him? He does swear
So earnestly, that if it were not true,
The gods would not endure him. Rise, Bellario:
Thy protestations are so deep, and thou
Dost look so truly when thou utter'st them,
That, though I know 'em false as were my hopes,
I cannot urge thee further. But thou wert
To blame to injure me, for I must love
Thy honest looks, and take no revenge upon
Thy tender youth. A love from me to thee
Is firm, whate'er thou dost; it troubles me
That I have call'd the blood out of thy cheeks,
That did so well become thee. But, good boy,
Let me not see thee more: something is done
That will distract me, that will make me mad,
If I behold thee. If thou tender'st me,
Let me not see thee.

Bel. I will fly as far
As there is morning, ere I give distaste
To that most honor'd mind. But through these tears,
Shed at my hopeless parting, I can see
A world of treason practis'd upon you,
And her, and me. Farewell for evermore!
If you shall hear that sorrow struck me dead,
And after find me loyal, let there be
A tear shed from you in my memory,
And I shall rest in peace.

Exit.

Phi. Blessing be with thee,
Whatever thou deserv'st! Oh, where shall I
Go bathe this body? Nature too unkind.
That made no medicine for a troubled mind!

Exit.

Scene 2. *Arethusa's apartment in the palace.*

Enter Arethusa.

Are. I marvel my boy comes not back again:
But that I know my love will question him
Over and over,—how I slept, wak'd, talk'd,
How I rememb'red him when his dear name
Was last spoke, and how when I sigh'd, wept, sung,
And ten thousand such,—I should be angry at his stay.

Enter King.

King. What, at your meditations! Who attends you?

Are. None but my single self. I need no guard;
I do no wrong, nor fear none.

King. Tell me, have you not a boy?

Are. Yes, sir.

King. What kind of boy?

Are. A page, a waiting-boy.

King. A handsome boy?

Are. I think he be not ugly:
Well qualified and dutiful I know him;
I took him not for beauty.

King. He speaks and sings and plays?

Are. Yes, sir.

King. About eighteen?

Are. I never ask'd his age.

King. Is he full of service?

Are. By your pardon, why do you ask?

King. Put him away.

Are. Sir!

King. Put him away, I say.
He 's done you that good service shames me to speak of.

Are. Good sir, let me understand you.

King. If you fear me,
Show it in duty; put away that boy.

Are. Let me have reason for it, sir, and then
Your will is my command.

King. Do not you blush to ask it? Cast him off,
Or I shall do the same to you. You 're one
Shame with me, and so near unto myself,

That, by my life, I dare not tell myself
What you, myself, have done.
Are. What have I done, my lord?
King. 'T is a new language, that all love to learn:
The common people speak it well already;
They need no grammar. Understand me well;
There be foul whispers stirring. Cast him off,
And suddenly. Do it! Farewell.
Exit.
Are. Where may a maiden live securely free,
Keeping her honor fair? Not with the living;
They feed upon opinions, errors, dreams,
And make 'em truths; they draw a nourishment
Out of defamings, grow upon disgraces,
And, when they see a virtue fortified
Strongly above the batt'ry of their tongues,
Oh, how they cast[45] to sink it! and, defeated,
(Soul-sick with poison) strike the monuments
Where noble names lie sleeping, till they sweat,
And the cold marble melt.

Enter Philaster.

Phi. Peace to your fairest thoughts, dearest mistress!
Are. Oh, my dearest servant, I have a war within me!
Phi. He must be more than man that makes these crystals
Run into rivers. Sweetest fair, the cause?
And, as I am your slave, tied to your goodness,
Your creature, made again from what I was
And newly-spirited, I'll right your honor.
Are. Oh, my best love, that boy!
Phi. What boy?
Are. The pretty boy you gave me——
Phi. What of him?
Are. Must be no more mine.
Phi. Why?
Are. They are jealous of him.
Phi. Jealous! Who?
Are. The King.
Phi. (*Aside.*) Oh, my misfortune!
Then 't is no idle jealousy.—Let him go.
Are. Oh, cruel!
Are you hard-hearted too? Who shall now tell you
How much I lov'd you? Who shall swear it to you,
And weep the tears I send? Who shall now bring you
Letters, rings, bracelets? Lose his health in service?
Wake tedious nights in stories of your praise?
Who shall now sing your crying elegies,
And strike a sad soul into senseless pictures,
And make them mourn? Who shall take up his lute,
And touch it till he crown a silent sleep
Upon my eye-lids, making me dream, and cry,
"Oh, my dear, dear Philaster!"
Phi. (*Aside.*) Oh, my heart!
Would he had broken thee, that made me know
This lady was not loyal!—Mistress,
Forget the boy; I'll get thee a far better.
Are. Oh, never, never such a boy again
As my Bellario.
Phi. 'T is but your fond affection.
Are. With thee, my boy, farewell for ever
All secrecy in servants! Farewell, faith,
And all desire to do well for itself!
Let all that shall succeed thee for thy wrongs
Sell and betray chaste love!
Phi. And all this passion for a boy?
Are. He was your boy, and you put him to me,
And the loss of such must have a mourning for.
Phi. Oh, thou forgetful woman!
Are. How, my lord?
Phi. False Arethusa!
Hast thou a medicine to restore my wits,
When I have lost 'em? If not, leave to talk,
And do thus.
Are. Do what, sir? Would you sleep?
Phi. For ever, Arethusa. Oh, you gods
Give me a worthy patience! Have I stood,
Naked, alone, the shock of many fortunes?
Have I seen mischiefs numberless and mighty
Grow like a sea upon me? Have I taken

[45] plan.

Danger as stern as death into my bosom,
And laught upon it, made it but a mirth,
And flung it by? Do I live now like him,
Under this tyrant King, that languishing
Hears his sad bell and sees his mourners? Do I
Bear all this bravely, and must sink at length
Under a woman's falsehood? Oh, that boy,
That cursed boy! None but a villain boy
To ease your lust?

Are. Nay, then, I am betrayed:
I feel the plot cast for my overthrow.
Oh, I am wretched!

Phi. Now you may take that little right I have
To this poor kingdom. Give it to your joy,
For I have no joy in it. Some far place,
Where never womankind durst set her foot
For[46] bursting with her poisons, must I seek,
And live to curse you;
There dig a cave, and preach to birds and beasts
What woman is, and help to save them from you;
How heaven is in your eyes, but in your hearts
More hell than hell has; how your tongues, like scorpions,
Both heal and poison;[47] how your thoughts are woven
With thousand changes in one subtle web,
And worn so by you; how that foolish man,
That reads the story of a woman's face
And dies believing it, is lost for ever;
How all the good you have is but a shadow,
I' the morning with you, and at night behind you,
Past and forgotten; how your vows are frosts,
Fast for a night, and with the next sun gone;
How you are, being taken all together,
A mere confusion, and so dead a chaos,
That love cannot distinguish. These sad texts,
Till my last hour, I am bound to utter of you.
So, farewell all my woe, all my delight!

Exit.

Are. Be merciful, ye gods, and strike me dead!
What way have I deserv'd this? Make my breast
Transparent as pure crystal, that the world,
Jealous of me, may see the foulest thought
My heart holds. Where shall a woman turn her eyes,
To find out constancy?

Enter Bellario.

Save me, how black
And guilty, methinks, that boy looks now!
Oh, thou dissembler, that, before thou spak'st,
Wert in thy cradle false, sent to make lies
And betray innocents! Thy lord and thou
May glory in the ashes of a maid
Fool'd by her passion; but the conquest is
Nothing so great as wicked. Fly away!
Let my command force thee to that which shame
Would do without it. If thou understood'st
The loathed office thou hast undergone,
Why, thou wouldst hide thee under heaps of hills,
Lest men should dig and find thee.

Bel. Oh, what god,
Angry with men, hath sent this strange disease
Into the noblest minds! Madam, this grief
You add unto me is no more than drops
To seas, for which they are not seen to swell.
My lord hath struck his anger through my heart,
And let out all the hope of future joys.
You need not bid me fly; I came to part,
To take my latest leave. Farewell for ever!
I durst not run away in honesty
From such a lady, like a boy that stole
Or made some grievous fault. The power of gods

46 for fear of.

47 It was believed that scorpions if applied to the wound they made, cured it.

Assist you in your sufferings! Hasty time
Reveal the truth to your abused lord
And mine, that he may know your worth; whilst I
Go seek out some forgotten place to die!
Exit.

Are. Peace guide thee! Thou hast overthrown me once;
Yet, if I had another Troy to lose,
Thou, or another villain with thy looks,
Might talk me out of it, and send me naked,
My hair dishevell'd, through the fiery streets.

Enter a Lady.

Lady. Madam, the King would hunt, and calls for you
With earnestness.

Are. I am in tune to hunt!
Diana, if thou canst rage with a maid
As with a man, let me discover thee
Bathing, and turn me to a fearful hind,
That I may die pursued by cruel hounds,
And have my story written in my wounds![48]

Exeunt.

ACT IV.

Scene 1. *Before the palace.*

Enter King, Pharamond, Arethusa, Galatea, Megra, Dion, Cleremont, Thrasiline, and Attendants.

King. What, are the hounds before and all the woodmen?
Our horses ready and our bows bent?

Dion. All, sir.

King. (*To Pharamond.*) You are cloudy, sir. Come, we have forgotten
Your venial trepass; let not that sit heavy
Upon your spirit; here 's none dare utter it.

Dion. He looks like an old surfeited stallion, dull as a dormouse. See how he sinks! The wench has shot him between wind and water, and, I hope, sprung a leak.

Thra. He needs no teaching, he strikes sure enough. His greatest fault is, he hunts too much in the purlieus; would he would leave off poaching!

Dion. And for his horn, h'as left it at the lodge where he lay late. Oh, he 's a precious limehound![49] Turn him loose upon the pursuit of a lady, and if he lose her, hang him up i' the slip.[50] When my fox-bitch Beauty grows proud, I 'll borrow him.

King. Is your boy turn'd away?

Are. You did command, sir, and I obey'd you.

King. 'T is well done. Hark ye further.
(*They talk apart.*)

Cle. Is't possible this fellow should repent? Methinks, that were not noble in him; and yet he looks like a mortified member, as if he had a sick man's salve[51] in 's mouth. If a worse man had done this fault now, some physical[52] justice or other would presently (without the help of an almanac[53]) have opened the obstructions of his liver, and let him blood with a dog-whip.

Dion. See, see how modestly yon lady looks, as if she came from churching with her neighbors! Why, what a devil can a man see in her face but that she 's honest!

Thra. Faith, no great matter to speak of; a foolish twinkling with the eye, that spoils her coat;[54] but he must be a cunning herald that finds it.

Dion. See how they muster one another! Oh, there 's a rank regiment where the devil carries the colors and his dam drum-major! Now the world and the flesh come behind with the carriage.[55]

Cle. Sure this lady has a good turn done her against her will; before she was common talk, now none dare say cantharides[56] can stir her. Her face looks like a warrant, willing and commanding all tongues, as they will answer it, to be tied up and bolted when this lady means to let herself loose. As I live, she has got her a goodly protection and a gracious; and may use her body discreetly for her health's sake, once a week, excepting Lent and dog-days. Oh, if they were to be got for money, what a great sum would come out of the city for these licenses!

King. To horse, to horse! we lose the morning, gentlemen. *Exeunt.*

48 These five lines refer to the story of Actæon.
49 a hunting dog led on a line, or leash.
50 leash.
51 An allusion to a religious work, Thomas Bacon's *The Sicke Man's Salve*, 1561.
52 physic-administering.
53 Almanacs gave the proper seasons for blood-letting.
54 The allusion, suggested by *twinkling*, is to the introduction of stars into a coat of arms, denoting a younger and therefore inferior branch.
55 baggage.
56 a provocative drug.

SCENE 2. *A forest.*

Enter two Woodmen.

1 Wood. What, have you lodged[57] the deer?
2 Wood. Yes, they are ready for the bow.
1 Wood. Who shoots?
2 Wood. The princess.
1 Wood. No, she'll hunt.
2 Wood. She'll take a stand, I say.
1 Wood. Who else?
2 Wood. Why, the young stranger-prince.
1 Wood. He shall shoot in a stone-bow[58] for me. I never lov'd his beyond-sea-ship since he forsook the say,[59] for paying ten shillings. He was there at the fall of a deer, and would needs (out of his mightiness) give ten groats for the dowcets; marry, his steward would have the velvet-head[60] into the bargain, to turf[61] his hat withal. I think he should love venery; he is an old Sir Tristram;[62] for, if you be remembr'd, he forsook the stag once to strike a rascal[63] miching[64] in a meadow, and her he kill'd in the eye. Who shoots else?
2 Wood. The Lady Galatea.
1 Wood. That's a good wench, an she would not chide us for tumbling of her women in the brakes. She's liberal, and by the gods, they say she's honest, and whether that be a fault, I have nothing to do. There's all?
2 Wood. No, one more; Megra.
1 Wood. That's a firker,[65] i' faith, boy. There's a wench will ride her haunches as hard after a kennel of hounds as a hunting saddle, and when she comes home, get 'em clapt, and all is well again. I have known her lose herself three times in one afternoon (if the woods have been answerable),[66] and it has been work enough for one man to find her, and he has sweat for it. She rides well and she pays well. Hark! let's go.

Exeunt.

Enter Philaster.

Phi. Oh, that I had been nourish'd in these woods
With milk of goats and acorns, and not known
The right of crowns nor the dissembling trains
Of women's looks; but digg'd myself a cave
Where I, my fire, my cattle, and my bed,
Might have been shut together in one shed;
And then had taken me some mountain-girl,
Beaten with winds, chaste as the hard'ned rocks
Whereon she dwelt, that might have strewed my bed
With leaves and reeds, and with the skins of beasts,
Our neighbors, and have borne at her big breasts
My large coarse issue! This had been a life
Free from vexation.

Enter Bellario.

Bel. Oh, wicked men!
An innocent may walk safe among beasts;
Nothing assaults me here. See, my griev'd lord
Sits as his soul were searching out a way
To leave his body!—Pardon me, that must
Break thy last commandment; for I must speak.
You that are griev'd can pity; hear, my lord!

Phi. Is there a creature yet so miserable,
That I can pity?

Bel. Oh, my noble lord,
View my strange fortune, and bestow on me,
According to your bounty (if my service
Can merit nothing), so much as may serve
To keep that little piece I hold of life
From cold and hunger!

Phi. Is it thou? Be gone!
Go, sell those misbeseeming clothes thou wear'st,
And feed thyself with them.

Bel. Alas, my lord, I can get nothing for them!
The silly country-people think 't is treason
To touch such gay things.

Phi. Now, by the gods, this is
Unkindly done, to vex me with thy sight.
Thou 'rt fallen again to thy dissembling trade;
How shouldst thou think to cozen me again?

57 brought to covert.
58 with a cross-bow that shoots stones.
59 Gave up his right to the assay or slitting of the deer to test the quality of the flesh, in order to escape paying a fee to the keeper.
60 the hart's horns, covered with velvet pile when new.
61 cover.
62 Tristram, in the romances, was a famous hunter.
63 a lean doe.
64 lurking.
65 a fast one.
66 suitable.

Remains there yet a plague untried for me?
Even so thou wept'st, and lookt'st, and spok'st when first
I took thee up.
Curse on the time! If thy commanding tears
Can work on any other, use thy art;
I'll not betray it. Which way wilt thou take,
That I may shun thee, for thine eyes are poison
To mine, and I am loth to grow in rage?
This way, or that way?

Bel. Any will serve; but I will choose to have
That path in chase that leads unto my grave.

Exeunt severally.

Enter on one side Dion, and on the other the two Woodmen.

Dion. This is the strangest sudden chance!—You, woodmen!

1 Wood. My lord Dion?

Dion. Saw you a lady come this way on a sable horse studded with stars of white?

2 Wood. Was she not young and tall?

Dion. Yes. Rode she to the wood or to the plain?

2 Wood. Faith, my lord, we saw none.

Exeunt Woodmen.

Dion. Pox of your questions then!

Enter Cleremont.

What, is she found?

Cle. Nor will be, I think.

Dion. Let him seek his daughter himself. She cannot stray about a little necessary natural business, but the whole court must be in arms. When she has done, we shall have peace.

Cle. There's already a thousand fatherless tales amongst us. Some say, her horse ran away with her; some, a wolf pursued her; others, 't was a plot to kill her, and that arm'd men were seen in the wood: but questionless she rode away willingly.

Enter King and Thrasiline.

King. Where is she?

Cle. Sir, I cannot tell.

King. How's that?
Answer me so again!

Cle. Sir, shall I lie?

King. Yes, lie and damn, rather than tell me that.
I say again, where is she? Mutter not!—
Sir, speak you; where is she?

Dion. Sir, I do not know.

King. Speak that again so boldly, and, by Heaven,
It is thy last!—You, fellows, answer me;
Where is she? Mark me, all; I am your King:
I wish to see my daughter; show her me;
I do command you all, as you are subjects,
To show her me! What! am I not your King?
If aye, then am I not to be obeyed?

Dion. Yes, if you command things possible and honest.

King. Things possible and honest! Hear me, thou,—
Thou traitor, that dar'st confine thy King to things
Possible and honest! Show her me,
Or, let me perish, if I cover not
All Sicily with blood!

Dion. Faith, I cannot,
Unless you tell me where she is.

King. You have betray'd me; you have let me lose
The jewel of my life. Go bring her me,
And set her here before me. 'T is the King
Will have it so, whose breath can still the winds,
Uncloud the sun, charm down the swelling sea,
And stop the floods of heaven. Speak, can it not?

Dion. No.

King. No! cannot the breath of kings do this?

Dion. No; nor smell sweet itself, if once the lungs
Be but corrupted.

King. Is it so? Take heed!

Dion. Sir, take you heed how you dare the powers
That must be just.

King. Alas! what are we kings!
Why do you gods place us above the rest,
To be serv'd, flatter'd, and ador'd, till we
Believe we hold within our hands your thunder?
And when we come to try the power we have,
There's not a leaf shakes at our threat'nings.
I have sinn'd, 't is true, and here stand to be punish'd;

Yet would not thus be punish'd. Let me choose
My way, and lay it on!

Dion. (*Aside.*) He articles with the gods. Would somebody would draw bonds for the performance of covenants betwixt them!

Enter Pharamond, Galatea, and Megra.

King. What, is she found?
Pha. No; we have ta'en her horse;
He gallop'd empty by. There is some treason.
You, Galatea, rode with her into the wood;
Why left you her?
Gal. She did command me.
King. Command! you should not.
Gal. 'T would ill become my fortunes and my birth
To disobey the daughter of my king.
King. You 're all cunning to obey us for our hurt;
But I will have her.
Pha. If I have her not,
By this hand, there shall be no more Sicily.

Dion. (*Aside.*) What, will he carry it to Spain in 's pocket?

Pha. I will not leave one man alive, but the king,
A cook, and a tailor.

Dion. (*Aside.*) Yes; you may do well to spare your lady-bedfellow; and her you may keep for a spawner.

King. I see the injuries I have done must be reveng'd.

Dion. Sir, this is not the way to find her out.

King. Run all, disperse yourselves. The man that finds her,
Or (if she be kill'd) the traitor, I 'll make him great.

Dion. I know some would give five thousand pounds to find her.

Pha. Come, let us seek.
King. Each man a several way; here I myself.

Dion. Come, gentlemen, we here.
Cle. Lady, you must go search too.
Meg. I had rather be search'd myself.
Exeunt severally.

SCENE 3. *Another part of the forest.*

Enter Arethusa.

Are. Where am I now? Feet, find me out a way,
Without the counsel of my troubled head.
I 'll follow you boldly about these woods,
O'er mountains, thorough brambles, pits, and floods.
Heaven, I hope, will ease me: I am sick.
(*Sits down.*)

Enter Bellario.

Bel. Yonder 's my lady. God knows I want nothing,
Because I do not wish to live; yet I
Will try her charity.—Oh hear, you have plenty!
From that flowing store drop some on dry ground.—See,
The lively red is gone to guard her heart!
I fear she faints.—Madam, look up!—She breathes not.—
Open once more those rosy twins, and send
Unto my lord your latest farewell!—Oh, she stirs.—
How is it, Madam? Speak comfort.
Are. 'T is not gently done,
To put me in a miserable life,
And hold me there. I prithee, let me go;
I shall do best without thee; I am well.

Enter Philaster.

Phi. I am to blame to be so much in rage.
I 'll tell her coolly when and where I heard
This killing truth. I will be temperate
In speaking, and as just in hearing.——
Oh, monstrous! Tempt me not, you gods! good gods,
Tempt not a frail man! What 's he, that has a heart,
But he must ease it here!
Bel. My lord, help, help! The princess!
Are. I am well: forbear.
Phi. (*Aside.*) Let me love lightning, let me be embrac'd
And kist by scorpions, or adore the eyes
Of basilisks, rather than trust the tongues
Of hell-bred women! Some good god look down,
And shrink these veins up! Stick me here a stone,
Lasting to ages in the memory
Of this damn'd act!—Hear me, you wicked ones!
You have put hills of fire into this breast,
Not to be quench'd with tears; for which may guilt
Sit on your bosoms! At your meals and beds

Despair await you! What, before my face?
Poison of asps between your lips! Diseases
Be your best issues! Nature make a curse,
And throw it on you!

Are. Dear Philaster, leave
To be enrag'd, and hear me.

Phi. I have done;
Forgive my passion. Not the calmed sea,
When Æolus locks up his windy brood,
Is less disturb'd than I. I'll make you know 't.
Dear Arethusa, do but take this sword,
(*Offers his drawn sword.*)
And search how temperate a heart I have;
Then you and this your boy may live and reign
In lust without control.—Wilt thou, Bellario?
I prithee kill me; thou art poor, and may'st
Nourish ambitious thoughts; when I am dead,
Thy way were freer. Am I raging now?
If I were mad, I should desire to live.
Sirs,[67] feel my pulse, whether you have known
A man in a more equal tune to die.

Bel. Alas, my lord, your pulse keeps madman's time!
So does your tongue.

Phi. You will not kill me, then?

Are. Kill you!

Bel. Not for the world.

Phi. I blame not thee,
Bellario; thou hast done but that which gods
Would have transform'd themselves to do. Be gone,
Leave me without reply; this is the last
Of all our meetings.—

Exit Bellario.

Kill me with this sword;
Be wise, or worse will follow: we are two
Earth cannot bear at once. Resolve to do,
Or suffer.

Are. If my fortune be so good to let me fall
Upon thy hand, I shall have peace in death.
Yet tell me this, will there be no slanders,
No jealousy in the other world; no ill there?

Phi. No.

Are. Show me, then, the way.

Phi. Then guide my feeble hand,
You that have power to do it, for I must
Perform a piece of justice!—If your youth
Have any way offended Heaven, let prayers
Short and effectual reconcile you to it.

Are. I am prepared.

Enter a Country Fellow.

C. Fell. I'll see the King, if he be in the forest; I have hunted him these two hours. If I should come home and not see him, my sisters would laugh at me. I can see nothing but people better hors'd than myself, that outride me; I can hear nothing but shouting. These kings had need of good brains; this whooping is able to put a mean man out of his wits. There's a courtier with his sword drawn; by this hand, upon a woman, I think!

Phi. Are you at peace?

Are. With heaven and earth.

Phi. May they divide thy soul and body!
(*Wounds her.*)

C. Fell. Hold, dastard! strike a woman! Thou 'rt a craven. I warrant thee, thou wouldst be loth to play half a dozen venies[68] at wasters[69] with a good fellow for a broken head.

Phi. Leave us, good friend.

Are. What ill-bred man art thou, to intrude thyself
Upon our private sports, our recreation?

C. Fell. God 'uds[70] me, I understand you not; but
I know the rogue has hurt you.

Phi. Pursue thy own affairs: it will be ill
To multiply blood upon my head; which thou
Wilt force me to.

C. Fell. I know not your rhetoric; but I can lay it on, if you touch the woman.

Phi. Slave, take what thou deservest!
(*They fight.*)

Are. Heavens guard my lord!

C. Fell. Oh, do you breathe?

Phi. I hear the tread of people. I am hurt.

67 Formerly used to women as well as to men. 68 bouts. 69 cudgels. 70 God judge.

The gods take part against me: could this boor
Have held me thus else? I must shift for life,
Though I do loathe it. I would find a course
To lose it rather by my will than force.
Exit.

C. Fell. I cannot follow the rogue. I pray thee, wench, come and kiss me now.

Enter Pharamond, Dion, Cleremont, Thrasiline, and Woodmen.

Pha. What art thou?

C. Fell. Almost kill'd I am for a foolish woman; a knave has hurt her.

Pha. The princess, gentlemen!—Where 's the wound, madam! Is it dangerous?

Are. He has not hurt me.

C. Fell. By God, she lies; h'as hurt her in the breast;
Look else.

Pha. O sacred spring of innocent blood!

Dion. 'T is above wonder! Who should dare this?

Are. I felt it not.

Pha. Speak, villain, who has hurt the princess?

C. Fell. Is it the princess?

Dion. Aye.

C. Fell. Then I have seen something yet.

Pha. But who has hurt her?

C. Fell. I told you, a rogue; I ne'er saw him before, I.

Pha. Madam, who did it?

Are. Some dishonest wretch;
Alas, I know him not, and do forgive him!

C. Fell. He 's hurt too; he cannot go far; I made my father's old fox [71] fly about his ears.

Pha. How will you have me kill him?

Are. Not at all; 't is some distracted fellow.

Pha. By this hand, I 'll leave ne'er a piece of him bigger than a nut, and bring him all to you in my hat.

Are. Nay, good sir,
If you do take him, bring him quick [72] to me,
And I will study for a punishment
Great as his fault.

Phc. I will.

Are. But swear.

Pha. By all my love, I will.——
Woodmen, conduct the princess to the King,
And bear that wounded fellow to dressing.——
Come, gentlemen, we 'll follow the chase close.

Exeunt Arethusa, Pharamond, Dion, Cleremont, Thrasiline, and 1 Woodman.

C. Fell. I pray you, friend, let me see the King.

2 Wood. That you shall, and receive thanks.

C. Fell. If I get clear with this, I'll go see no more gay sights.
Exeunt.

SCENE 4. *Another part of the forest.*

Enter Bellario.

Bel. A heaviness near death sits on my brow,
And I must sleep. Bear me, thou gentle bank,
For ever, if thou wilt. You sweet ones all,
(*Lies down.*)
Let me unworthy press you; I could wish
I rather were a corse strew'd o'er with you
Than quick above you. Dulness [73] shuts mine eyes,
And I am giddy: oh, that I could take
So sound a sleep that I might never wake!
(*Sleeps.*)

Enter Philaster.

Phi. I have done ill; my conscience calls me false
To strike at her that would not strike at me.
When I did fight, methought I heard her pray
The gods to guard me. She may be abus'd,
And I a loathed villain; if she be,
She will conceal who hurt her. He has wounds
And cannot follow; neither knows he me.
Who 's this? Bellario sleeping! If thou be'st
Guilty, there is no justice that thy sleep
Should be so sound, and mine, whom thou hast wrong'd,
So broken. (*Cry within.*) Hark! I am pursued. You gods,
I 'll take this offer'd means of my escape.

71 broad sword. 72 alive. 73 drowsiness.

They have no mark to know me but my blood,
If she be true; if false, let mischief light
On all the world at once! Sword, print my wounds
Upon this sleeping boy! I ha' none, I think,
Are mortal, nor would I lay greater on thee.
(*Wounds Bellario.*)

Bel. Oh, death, I hope, is come! Blest be that hand!
It meant me well. Again, for pity's sake!

Phi. I have caught myself;
(*Falls.*)
The loss of blood hath stay'd my flight. Here, here,
Is he that struck thee: take thy full revenge;
Use me, as I did mean thee, worse than death;
I'll teach thee to revenge. This luckless hand
Wounded the princess; tell my followers[74]
Thou didst receive these hurts in staying me,
And I will second thee; get a reward.

Bel. Fly, fly, my lord, and save yourself!

Phi. How's this?
Wouldst thou I should be safe?

Bel. Else were it vain
For me to live. These little wounds I have
Ha' not bled much. Reach me that noble hand;
I'll help to cover you.

Phi. Art thou then true to me?

Bel. Or let me perish loath'd! Come, my good lord,
Creep in amongst those bushes; who does know
But that the gods may save your much-lov'd breath?

Phi. Then I shall die for grief, if not for this,
That I have wounded thee. What wilt thou do?

Bel. Shift for myself well. Peace! I hear 'em come.
(*Philaster creeps into a bush.*)

Voices within. Follow, follow, follow! that way they went.

Bel. With my own wounds I'll bloody my own sword.
I need not counterfeit to fall; Heaven knows
That I can stand no longer.
(*Falls.*)

Enter Pharamond, Dion, Cleremont, and Thrasiline.

Pha. To this place we have trackt him by his blood.

Cle. Yonder, my lord, creeps one away.

Dion. Stay, sir! what are you?

Bel. A wretched creature, wounded in these woods
By beasts. Relieve me, if your names be men,
Or I shall perish.

Dion. This is he, my lord,
Upon my soul, that hurt her. 'T is the boy,
That wicked boy, that serv'd her.

Pha. Oh, thou damn'd
In thy creation! What cause couldst thou shape
To hurt the princess?

Bel. Then I am betrayed.

Dion. Betrayed! No, apprehended.

Bel. I confess,
(Urge it no more) that, big with evil thoughts,
I set upon her, and did make my aim,
Her death. For charity let fall at once
The punishment you mean, and do not load
This weary flesh with tortures.

Pha. I will know
Who hir'd thee to this deed.

Bel. Mine own revenge.

Pha. Revenge! for what?

Bel. It pleas'd her to receive
Me as her page and, when my fortunes ebb'd,
That men strid o'er them careless, she did shower
Her welcome graces on me, and did swell
My fortunes till they overflow'd their banks,
Threat'ning the men that crost 'em; when, as swift
As storms arise at sea, she turn'd her eyes
To burning suns upon me, and did dry
The streams she had bestow'd, leaving me worse
And more contemn'd than other little brooks,
Because I had been great. In short, I knew
I could not live, and therefore did desire
To die reveng'd.

Pha. If tortures can be found

74 pursuers.

Long as thy natural life, resolve to feel
The utmost rigor.

(*Philaster creeps out of the bush.*)

Cle. Help to lead him hence.

Phi. Turn back, you ravishers of innocence!
Know ye the price of that you bear away
So rudely?

Pha. Who's that?

Dion. 'T is the Lord Philaster.

Phi. 'T is not the treasure of all kings in one,
The wealth of Tagus, nor the rocks of pearl
That pave the court of Neptune, can weigh down
That virtue. It was I that hurt the princess.
Place me, some god, upon a pyramis [75]
Higher than hills of earth, and lend a voice
Loud as your thunder to me, that from hence
I may discourse to all the under-world
The worth that dwells in him!

Pha. How 's this?

Bel. My lord, some man
Weary of life, that would be glad to die.

Phi. Leave these untimely courtesies, Bellario.

Bel. Alas, he 's mad! Come, will you lead me on?

Phi. By all the oaths that men ought most to keep,
And gods to punish most when men do break,
He touch'd her not.—Take heed, Bellario,
How thou dost drown the virtues thou hast shown
With perjury.—By all that 's good, 't was I!
You know she stood betwixt me and my right.

Pha. Thy own tongue be thy judge!

Cle. It was Philaster.

Dion. Is 't not a brave boy?
Well, sirs, I fear me we were all deceived.

Phi. Have I no friend here?

Dion. Yes.

Phi. Then show it: some
Good body lend a hand to draw us nearer.
Would you have tears shed for you when you die?
Then lay me gently on his neck, that there
I may weep floods and breathe forth my spirit.
'T is not the wealth of Plutus, nor the gold

(*Embraces Bellario.*)

Lockt in the heart of earth, can buy away
This arm-full from me; this had been a ransom
To have redeem'd the great Augustus Cæsar,
Had he been taken. You hard-hearted men,
More stony than these mountains, can you see
Such clear pure blood drop, and not cut your flesh
To stop his life, to bind whose bitter wounds,
Queens ought to tear their hair, and with their tears
Bathe 'em?—Forgive me, thou that art the wealth
Of poor Philaster!

Enter King, Arethusa, and Guard.

King. Is the villain ta'en?

Pha. Sir, here be two confess the deed; but sure
It was Philaster.

Phi. Question it no more;
It was.

King. The fellow that did fight with him,
Will tell us that.

Are. Ay me! I know he will.

King. Did not you know him?

Are. Sir, if it was he,
He was disguis'd.

Phi. I was so.[76]—Oh, my stars,
That I should live still!

King. Thou ambitious fool,
Thou that hast laid a train for thy own life!—
Now I do mean to do; I 'll leave to talk.[77]
Bear them to prison.

Are. Sir, they did plot together to take hence
This harmless life; should it pass unreveng'd,
I should to earth go weeping. Grant me, then,
By all the love a father bears his child,
Their custodies, and that I may appoint
Their tortures and their deaths.

Dion. Death! Soft; our law will not reach that for this fault.

King. 'T is granted; take 'em to you with a guard.—

75 pyramid. 76 *i.e.* out of my senses. 77 I 'll cease talking

Come, princely Pharamond, this business past,
We may with security go on
To your intended match.

Exeunt all except Dion, Cleremont, and Thrasiline.

Cle. I pray that his action lose not Philaster the hearts of the people.

Dion. Fear it not; their over-wise heads will think it but a trick.

Exeunt.

ACT V.

Scene 1. *Before the palace.*

Enter Dion, Cleremont, and Thrasiline.

Thra. Has the King sent for him to death?

Dion. Yes; but the King must know 't is not in his power to war with Heaven.

Cle. We linger time; the King sent for Philaster and the headsman an hour ago.

Thra. Are all his wounds well?

Dion. All; they were but scratches; but the loss of blood made him faint.

Cle. We dally, gentlemen.

Thra. Away!

Dion. We 'll scuffle hard before he perish.

Exeunt.

Scene 2. *A prison.*

Enter Philaster, Arethusa, and Bellario.

Are. Nay, faith, Philaster, grieve not; we are well.

Bel. Nay, good my lord, forbear; we 're wondrous well.

Phi. O Arethusa, O Bellario,
Leave to be kind!
I shall be shut from Heaven, as now from earth,
If you continue so. I am a man
False to a pair of the most trusty ones
That ever earth bore; can it bear us all?
Forgive, and leave me. But the King hath sent
To call me to my death: oh, show it me,
And then forget me! And for thee, my boy,
I shall deliver words will mollify
The hearts of beasts to spare thy innocence.

Bel. Alas, my lord, my life is not a thing
Worthy your noble thoughts! 'T is not a life,
'T is but a piece of childhood thrown away.
Should I outlive you, I should then outlive
Virtue and honor; and when that day comes,
If ever I shall close these eyes but once,
May I live spotted for my perjury,
And waste my limbs to nothing!

Are. And I (the woful'st maid that ever was,
Forc'd with my hands to bring my lord to death)
Do by the honor of a virgin swear
To tell no hours beyond it!

Phi. Make me not hated so.

Are. Come from this prison all joyful to our deaths!

Phi. People will tear me, when they find you true
To such a wretch as I; I shall die loath'd.
Enjoy your kingdoms peaceably whilst I
For ever sleep forgotten with my faults.
Every just servant, every maid in love,
Will have a piece of me, if you be true.

Are. My dear lord, say not so.

Bel. A piece of you!
He was not born of woman that can cut
It and look on.

Phi. Take me in tears betwixt you, for my heart
Will break with shame and sorrow.

Are. Why, 't is well.

Bel. Lament no more.

Phi. Why, what would you have done
If you had wrong'd me basely, and had found
Your life no price compar'd to mine? For love, sirs,
Deal with me truly.

Bel. 'T was mistaken, sir.

Phi. Why, if it were?

Bel. Then, sir, we would have ask'd
You pardon.

Phi. And have hope to enjoy it?

Are. Enjoy it! aye.

Phi. Would you indeed? Be plain.

Bel. We would, my lord.

Phi. Forgive me, then.

Are. So, so.

Bel. 'T is as it should be now.

Phi. Lead to my death.

Exeunt.

Scene 3. *A state-room in the palace.*

Enter King, Dion, Cleremont, Thrasiline, and Attendants.

King. Gentlemen, who saw the prince?

Cle. So please you, sir, he 's gone to see the city

And the new platform, with some gentlemen
Attending on him.
King. Is the princess ready
To bring her prisoner out?
Thra. She waits your grace.
King. Tell her we stay.
Exit Thrasiline.
Dion. (*Aside.*) King, you may be deceiv'd yet.
The head you aim at cost more setting on
Than to be lost so lightly. If it must off,—
Like a wild overflow, that swoops before him
A golden stack, and with it shakes down bridges,
Cracks the strong hearts of pines, whose cable-roots
Held out a thousand storms, a thousand thunders,
And, so made mightier, takes whole villages
Upon his back, and in that heat of pride
Charges strong towns, towers, castles, palaces,
And lays them desolate; so shall thy head,
Thy noble head, bury the lives of thousands,
That must bleed with thee like a sacrifice,
In thy red ruins.

Enter Arethusa, Philaster, Bellario in a robe and garland, and Thrasiline.

King. How now? What masque is this?
Bel. Right royal sir, I should
Sing you an epithalamion of these lovers,
But having lost my best airs with my fortunes,
And wanting a celestial harp to strike
This blessed union on, thus in glad story
I give you all. These two fair cedar-branches,
The noblest of the mountain where they grew,
Straightest and tallest, under whose still shades
The worthier beasts have made their lairs, and slept
Free from the fervor of the Sirian star [78]
And the fell thunder-stroke, free from the clouds
When they were big with humor, and deliver'd
In thousand spouts their issues to the earth;
Oh, there was none but silent quiet there!
Till never-pleased Fortune shot up shrubs,
Base under-brambles, to divorce these branches;
And for a while they did so, and did reign
Over the mountain, and choke up his beauty
With brakes, rude thorns and thistles, till the sun
Scorcht them even to the roots and dried them there.
And now a gentle gale hath blown again,
That made these branches meet and twine together,
Never to be divided. The god that sings
His holy numbers over marriage-beds
Hath knit their noble hearts; and here they stand
Your children, mighty King; and I have done.
King. How, how?
Are. Sir, if you love it in plain truth,
(For now there is no masquing in 't,) this gentleman,
The prisoner that you gave me, is become
My keeper, and through all the bitter throes
Your jealousies and his ill fate have wrought him,
Thus nobly hath he struggled, and at length
Arrived here my dear husband.
King. Your dear husband!—
Call in the Captain of the Citadel—
There you shall keep your wedding. I 'll provide
A masque shall make your Hymen turn his saffron [79]
Into a sullen coat, and sing sad requiems
To your departing souls.
Blood shall put out your torches; and, instead
Of gaudy flowers about your wanton necks,
An axe shall hang, like a prodigious meteor,
Ready to crop your loves' sweets. Hear, you gods!
From this time do I shake all title off
Of father to this woman, this base woman;
And what there is of vengeance in a lion
Chaf'd among dogs or robb'd of his dear young,

78 Sirius, the dog-star, was supposed to bring hot weather, the dog-days.
79 Hymen wore a saffron robe in the masques.

The same, enforc'd more terrible, more mighty,
Expect from me!

Are. Sir, by that little life I have left to swear by,
There's nothing that can stir me from myself.
What I have done, I have done without repentance,
For death can be no bugbear unto me,
So long as Pharamond is not my headsman.

Dion. (*Aside.*) Sweet peace upon thy soul, thou worthy maid,
Whene'er thou diest! For this time I'll excuse thee,
Or be thy prologue.

Phi. Sir, let me speak next;
And let my dying words be better with you
Than my dull living actions. If you aim
At the dear life of this sweet innocent,
You are a tyrant and a savage monster,
That feeds upon the blood you gave a life to;
Your memory shall be as foul behind you,
As you are living; all your better deeds
Shall be in water writ, but this in marble;
No chronicle shall speak you, though your own,
But for the shame of men. No monument,
Though high and big as Pelion, shall be able
To cover this base murder: make it rich
With brass, with purest gold, and shining jasper,
Like the Pyramides; lay on epitaphs
Such as make great men gods; my little marble,
That only clothes my ashes, not my faults,
Shall far outshine it. And for after-issues,
Think not so madly of the heavenly wisdoms,
That they will give you more for your mad rage
To cut off, unless it be some snake, or something
Like yourself, that in his birth shall strangle you.
Remember my father, King! There was a fault;
But I forgive it. Let that sin persuade you
To love this lady; if you have a soul,
Think, save her, and be saved. For myself,
I have so long expected this glad hour,
So languisht under you, and daily withered,
That, Heaven knows, it is a joy to die;
I find a recreation in't.

Enter a Messenger.

Mess. Where is the King?

King. Here.

Mess. Get you to your strength,
And rescue the Prince Pharamond from danger;
He's taken prisoner by the citizens,
Fearing[80] the Lord Philaster.

Dion. (*Aside.*) Oh, brave followers!
Mutiny, my fine dear countrymen, mutiny!
Now, my brave valiant foremen, show your weapons
In honor of your mistresses!

Enter a Second Messenger.

2 Mess. Arm, arm, arm, arm!

King. A thousand devils take 'em!

Dion. (*Aside.*) A thousand blessings on 'em!

2 Mess. Arm, O King! The city is in mutiny,
Led by an old gray ruffian, who comes on
In rescue of the Lord Philaster.

King. Away to the citadel! I'll see them safe,
And then cope with these burghers. Let the guard
And all the gentlemen give strong attendance.

Exeunt all except Dion, Cleremont, and Thrasiline.

Cle. The city up! This was above our wishes.

Dion. Aye, and the marriage too. By my life,
This noble lady has deceiv'd us all.
A plague upon myself, a thousand plagues,
For having such unworthy thoughts of her dear honor!
Oh, I could beat myself! Or do you beat me,
And I'll beat you; for we had all one thought.

Cle. No, no, 't will but lose time.

Dion. You say true. Are your swords sharp?—Well, my dear countrymen What-ye-lacks,[81] if you continue, and

80 fearing for.

81 *i.e.* shopkeepers, who thus addressed passers-by.

fall not back upon the first broken skin, I'll have you chronicled and chronicled, and cut and chronicled, and all-to-be-prais'd and sung in sonnets, and bawled in new brave ballads, that all tongues shall troll you *in saecula saeculorum,* my kind can-carriers.

Thra. What, if a toy [82] take 'em i' th' heels now, and they run all away, and cry, "the devil take the hindmost"?

Dion. Then the same devil take the foremost too, and souse him for his breakfast! If they all prove cowards, my curses fly among them, and be speeding! May they have murrains reign to keep the gentlemen at home unbound in easy frieze! May the moths branch [83] their velvets, and their silks only be worn before sore eyes! [84] May their false lights undo 'em, and discover presses,[85] holes, stains, and oldness in their stuffs, and make them shop-rid! May they keep whores and horses, and break; and live mewed up with necks of beef and turnips! May they have many children, and none like the father! May they know no language but that gibberish they prattle to their parcels, unless it be the goatish Latin they write in their bonds—and may they write that false, and lose their debts!

Re-enter King.

King. Now the vengeance of all the gods confound them! How they swarm together! What a hum they raise!—Devils choke your wild throats!—If a man had need to use their valors, he must pay a brokage for it, and then bring 'em on, and they will fight like sheep. 'T is Philaster, none but Philaster, must allay this heat. They will not hear me speak, but fling dirt at me and call me tyrant. Oh, run, dear friend, and bring the Lord Philaster! Speak him fair; call him prince; do him all the courtesy you can; commend me to him. Oh, my wits, my wits!

Exit Cleremont.

Dion. (*Aside.*) Oh, my brave countrymen! as I live, I will not buy a pin out of your walls [86] for this. Nay, you shall cozen me, and I'll thank you, and send you brawn and bacon, and soil [87] you every long vacation a brace of foremen,[88] that at Michaelmas shall come up fat and kicking.

King. What they will do with this poor prince, the gods know, and I fear.

Dion. (*Aside.*) Why, sir, they'll flay him, and make church-buckets on 's skin, to quench rebellion; then clap a rivet in 's sconce, and hang him up for a sign.

Enter Cleremont with Philaster.

King. Oh, worthy sir, forgive me! Do not make
Your miseries and my faults meet together,
To bring a greater danger. Be yourself,
Still sound amongst diseases. I have wrong'd you;
And though I find it last, and beaten to it,
Let first your goodness know it. Calm the people,
And be what you were born to. Take your love,
And with her my repentance, all my wishes,
And all my prayers. By the gods, my heart speaks this;
And if the least fall from me not perform'd,
May I be struck with thunder!

Phi. Mighty sir,
I will not do your greatness so much wrong,
As not to make your word truth. Free the princess
And the poor boy, and let me stand the shock
Of this mad sea-breach, which I'll either turn,
Or perish with it.

King. Let your own word free them.

Phi. Then thus I take my leave, kissing your hand,
And hanging on your royal word. Be kingly,
And be not mov'd, sir. I shall bring you peace,
Or never bring myself back.

King. All the gods go with thee.

Exeunt.

SCENE 4. *A street.*

Enter an old Captain and Citizens with Pharamond.

Cap. Come, my brave myrmidons, let us fall on.

82 whim.
83 eat patterns on.
84 *i. e.* for patches.
85 creases.
86 outside your shops.
87 fatten.
88 geese.

Let your caps swarm, my boys, and your nimble tongues
Forget your mother-gibberish of "what do you lack?"
And set your mouths ope, children, till your palates
Fall frighted half a fathom past the cure
Of bay-salt [89] and gross pepper, and then cry
"Philaster, brave Philaster!" Let Philaster
Be deeper in request, my ding-dongs,[90]
My pairs of dear indentures,[91] kings of clubs,[91]
Than your cold water-camlets,[92] or your paintings
Spitted with copper.[93] Let not your hasty [94] silks,
Or your branch'd cloth of bodkin,[95] or your tissues,
Dearly belov'd of spiced cake and custards,
You Robin Hoods, Scarlets, and Johns,[96] tie your affections
In darkness to your shops. No, dainty duckers,[97]
Up with your three-pil'd spirits, your wrought valors; [98]
And let your uncut cholers [99] make the King feel
The measure of your mightiness. Philaster!
Cry, my rose-nobles,[1] cry!

All. Philaster! Philaster!

Cap. How do you like this, my lord prince?
These are mad boys, I tell you; these are things
That will not strike their top-sails to a foist,[2]
And let a man of war, an argosy,
Hull [3] and cry cockles.[4]

Pha. Why, you rude slave, do you know what you do?

Cap. My pretty prince of puppets, we do know;
And give your greatness warning that you talk
No more such bug's-words,[5] or that solder'd crown
Shall be scratch'd with a musket.[6] Dear prince Pippin,[7]
Down with your noble blood, or, as I live,
I'll have you coddled.[8]—Let him loose, my spirits:
Make us a round ring with your bills,[9] my Hectors,
And let us see what this trim man dares do.
Now, sir, have at you! here I lie;
And with this swashing blow (do you see, sweet prince?)
I could hulk [10] your grace, and hang you up cross-legg'd,
Like a hare at a poulter's, and do this with this wiper.[11]

Pha. You will not see me murder'd, wicked villains?

1 Cit. Yes, indeed, will we, sir; we have not seen one
For a great while.

Cap. He would have weapons, would he?
Give him a broadside, my brave boys, with your pikes;
Branch me his skin in flowers like a satin,
And between every flower a mortal cut.—
Your royalty shall ravel!—Jag [12] him, gentlemen;
I'll have him cut to the kell,[13] then down the seams.
O for a whip to make him galloon-laces! [14]
I'll have a coach-whip.

Pha. Oh, spare me, gentlemen!

Cap. Hold, hold;
The man begins to fear and know himself.
He shall for this time only be seel'd up,[15]
With a feather through his nose, that he may only
See heaven, and think whither he is going.
Nay, my beyond-sea sir, we will proclaim you:
You would be king!
Thou tender heir apparent to a church-ale,[16]
Thou slight prince of single sarcenet,[17]

89 coarse-grained salt, obtained by evaporation from sea-water.
90 brave fellows.
91 apprentices, who were bound by indentures and whose usual weapons were clubs.
92 rich fabrics with a watered surface.
93 colored cloth interwoven with copper.
94 *i. e.* that soon wear out.
95 embroidered cloth of gold and silk.
96 Scarlet and Little John were two of Robin Hood's men.
97 cringers(?), duck-hunters(?).
98 a pun on velour.
99 a pun on collars.
1 another pun; rose-nobles were gold coins.
2 a small vessel.
3 float idly.
4 be basely occupied.
5 swaggering words.
6 a male sparrow-hawk, with a pun on the weapon.
7 Pepin, King of the Franks, with a pun on the fruit.
8 stewed.
9 pikes with a broad, spiked blade.
10 disembowel.
11 instrument for cleaning a gun.
12 slash.
13 membrane of the paunch.
14 ribbons, tape.
15 have his eyelids sewed together like a hawk's.
16 *i. e.* a bastard, one born after the convivialities of a church feast.
17 thin silk.

Thou royal ring-tail,[18] fit to fly at nothing
But poor men's poultry, and have every boy
Beat thee from that too with his bread and butter!

Pha. Gods keep me from these hell-hounds!

1 Cit. Shall 's geld him, captain?

Cap. No, you shall spare his dowcets, my dear donsels;[19]
As you respect the ladies, let them flourish.
The curses of a longing woman kill
As speedy as a plague, boys.

1 Cit. I 'll have a leg, that 's certain.

2 Cit. I 'll have an arm.

3 Cit. I 'll have his nose, and at mine own charge build
A college and clap 't upon the gate.[20]

4 Cit. I 'll have his little gut to string a kit[21] with;
For certainly a royal gut will sound like silver.

Pha. Would they were in thy belly, and I past
My pain once!

5 Cit. Good captain, let me have his liver to feed ferrets.

Cap. Who will have parcels[22] else? Speak.

Pha. Good gods, consider me! I shall be tortur'd.

1 Cit. Captain, I 'll give you the trimming of your two-hand sword,
And let me have his skin to make false scabbards.

2 Cit. He had no horns, sir, had he?

Cap. No, sir, he 's a pollard.[23]
What wouldst thou do with horns?

2 Cit. Oh, if he had had,
I would have made rare hafts and whistles of 'em;
But his shin-bones, if they be sound, shall serve me.

Enter Philaster.

All. Long live Philaster, the brave Prince Philaster!

Phi. I thank you, gentlemen. But why are these
Rude weapons brought abroad, to teach your hands
Uncivil trades?

Cap. My royal Rosicleer,[24]
We are thy myrmidons, thy guard, thy roarers;[25]
And when thy noble body is in durance,
Thus do we clap our musty murrions[26] on,
And trace the streets in terror. Is it peace,
Thou Mars of men? Is the King sociable,
And bids thee live? Art thou above thy foemen,
And free as Phœbus? Speak. If not, this stand[27]
Of royal blood shall be abroach, a-tilt,
And run even to the lees of honor.

Phi. Hold, and be satisfied. I am myself,
Free as my thoughts are; by the gods, I am!

Cap. Art thou the dainty darling of the King?
Art thou the Hylas to our Hercules?
Do the lords bow, and the regarded scarlets[28]
Kiss their gumm'd golls,[29] and cry, "We are your servants"?
Is the court navigable and the presence[30] stuck
With flags of friendship? If not, we are thy castle,
And this man sleeps.

Phi. I am what I desire to be, your friend;
I am what I was born to be, your prince.

Pha. Sir, there is some humanity in you;
You have a noble soul. Forget my name,
And know my misery; set me safe aboard
From these wild cannibals, and as I live,
I 'll quit this land for ever. There is nothing,—
Perpetual prisonment, cold, hunger, sickness
Of all sorts, of all dangers, and all together,
The worst company of the worst men madness, age,
To be as many creatures as a woman,
And do as all they do, nay, to despair,—
But I would rather make it a new nature.
And live with all these, than endure one hour
Amongst these wild dogs.

Phi. I do pity you.—Friends, discharge your fears;

18 kite, an inferior bird of prey.
19 youths aspiring to knighthood.
20 in allusion to Brasenose College, Oxford.
21 a small fiddle.
22 *i. e.* bits of him.
23 hornless stag.
24 A hero in *The Mirrour of Knighthood*, a romance translated from the Spanish.
25 bullies.
26 steel caps.
27 cask, *i. e.* Pharamond.
28 courtiers clad in scarlet.
29 perfumed hands.
30 presence chamber.

Deliver me the prince. I 'll warrant you
I shall be old enough to find my safety.

3 Cit. Good sir, take heed he does not hurt you;
He is a fierce man, I can tell you, sir.

Cap. Prince, by your leave, I 'll have a surcingle,[31]
And make [32] you like a hawk.

(*Pharamond strives.*)

Phi. Away, away, there is no danger in him:
Alas, he had rather sleep to shake his fit off!
Look you, friends, how gently he leads! Upon my word,
He 's tame enough, he needs no further watching.
Good, my friends, go to your houses,
And by me have your pardons and my love;
And know there shall be nothing in my power
You may deserve, but you shall have your wishes.
To give you more thanks, were to flatter you.
Continue still your love; and for an earnest,
Drink this.

(*Gives money.*)

All. Long mayst thou live, brave prince, brave prince, brave prince!

Exeunt Philaster and Pharamond.

Cap. Go thy ways, thou art the king of courtesy!
Fall off again, my sweet youths. Come,
And every man trace to his house again,
And hang his pewter [33] up; then to the tavern,
And bring your wives in muffs. We will have music;
And the red grape shall make us dance and rise, boys.

Exeunt.

Scene 5. *An apartment in the palace.*

Enter King, Arethusa, Galatea, Megra, Dion, Cleremont, Thrasiline, Bellario, and Attendants.

King. Is it appeas'd?

Dion. Sir, all is quiet as this dead of night,
As peaceable as sleep. My lord Philaster
Brings on the prince himself.

King. Kind gentleman!
I will not break the least word I have given
In promise to him. I have heap'd a world
Of grief upon his head, which yet I hope
To wash away.

Enter Philaster and Pharamond.

Cle. My lord is come.

King. My son!
Blest be the time that I have leave to call
Such virtue mine! Now thou art in mine arms,
Methinks I have a salve unto my breast
For all the stings that dwell there. Streams of grief
That I have wrong'd thee, and as much of joy
That I repent it, issue from mine eyes;
Let them appease thee. Take thy right; take her;
She is thy right too; and forget to urge
My vexed soul with that I did before.

Phi. Sir, it is blotted from my memory,
Past and forgotten.—For you, prince of Spain,
Whom I have thus redeem'd, you have full leave
To make an honorable voyage home.
And if you would go furnish'd to your realm
With fair provision, I do see a lady,
Methinks, would gladly bear you company.
How like you this piece?

Meg. Sir, he likes it well,
For he hath tried it, and hath found it worth
His princely liking. We were ta'en abed;
I know your meaning. I am not the first
That nature taught to seek a fellow forth;
Can shame remain perpetually in me,
And not in others? Or have princes salves
To cure ill names, that meaner people want?

Phi. What mean you?

Meg. You must get another ship,
To bear the princess and her boy together.

Dion. How now!

Meg. Others took me, and I took her and him

31 band. 32 train. 33 *i. e.* sword.

At that all women may be ta'en sometime.
Ship us all four, my lord; we can endure
Weather and wind alike.
King. Clear thou thyself, or know not me for father.
Are. This earth, how false it is! What means is left for me
To clear myself? It lies in your belief.
My lords, believe me; and let all things else
Struggle together to dishonor me.
Bel. Oh, stop your ears, great King, that I may speak
As freedom would! Then I will call this lady [34]
As base as are her actions. Hear me, sir;
Believe your heated blood when it rebels
Against your reason, sooner than this lady.
Meg. By this good light, he bears it handsomely.
Phi. This lady! I will sooner trust the wind
With feathers, or the troubled sea with pearl,
Than her with any thing. Believe her not.
Why, think you, if I did believe her words,
I would outlive 'em? Honor cannot take
Revenge on you; then what were to be known
But death?
King. Forget her, sir, since all is knit
Between us. But I must request of you
One favor, and will sadly [35] be denied.
Phi. Command, whate'er it be.
King. Swear to be true
To what you promise.
Phi. By the powers above,
Let it not be the death of her or him,
And it is granted!
King. Bear away that boy
To torture; I will have her clear'd or buried.
Phi. Oh, let me call my word back, worthy sir!
Ask something else: bury my life and right
In one poor grave; but do not take away
My life and fame at once.
King. Away with him! It stands irrevocable.
Phi. Turn all your eyes on me. Here stands a man,
The falsest and the basest of this world.
Set swords against this breast, some honest man,
For I have liv'd till I am pitied!
My former deeds were hateful; but this last
Is pitiful, for I unwillingly
Have given the dear preserver of my life
Unto his torture. Is it in the power
Of flesh and blood to carry this, and live?
(*Offers to stab himself.*)
Are. Dear sir, be patient yet! Oh, stay that hand!
King. Sirs, strip that boy.
Dion. Come, sir; your tender flesh
Will try your constancy.
Bel. Oh, kill me, gentlemen!
Dion. No.—Help, sirs.
Bel. Will you torture me?
King. Haste there;
Why stay you?
Bel. Then I shall not break my vow,
You know, just gods, though I discover all.
King. How 's that? Will he confess?
Dion. Sir, so he says.
King. Speak then.
Bel. Great King, if you command
This lord to talk with me alone, my tongue
Urg'd by my heart, shall utter all the thoughts
My youth hath known; and stranger things than these
You hear not often.
King. Walk aside with him.
(*Dion and Bellario walk apart.*)
Dion. Why speak'st thou not?
Bel. Know you this face, my lord?
Dion. No.
Bel. Have you not seen it, nor the like?
Dion. Yes, I have seen the like, but readily
I know not where.
Bel. I have been often told
In court of one Euphrasia, a lady,
And daughter to you; betwixt whom and me
They that would flatter my bad face would swear
There was such strange resemblance, that we two
Could not be known asunder, drest alike.
Dion. By Heaven, and so there is!
Bel. For her fair sake,
Who now doth spend the spring-time of her life
In holy pilgrimage, move to the King,

34 *i. e.* Megra.

35 I shall be sorry to be denied.

That I may scape this torture.
Dion. But thou speak'st
As like Euphrasia as thou dost look.
How came it to thy knowledge that she lives
In pilgrimage?
Bel. I know it not, my lord;
But I have heard it, and do scarce believe it.
Dion. Oh, my shame! is it possible? Draw near,
That I may gaze upon thee. Art thou she,
Or else her murderer?[36] Where wert thou born?
Bel. In Syracusa.
Dion. What 's thy name?
Bel. Euphrasia.
Dion. Oh, 't is just,[37] 't is she!
Now I do know thee. Oh, that thou hadst died,
And I had never seen thee nor my shame!
How shall I own thee? Shall this tongue of mine
E'er call thee daughter more?
Bel. Would I had died indeed! I wish it too;
And so I must have done by vow, ere publish'd
What I have told, but that there was no means
To hide it longer. Yet I joy in this,
The princess is all clear.
King. What, have you done?
Dion. All is discovered.
Phi. Why then hold you me?
All is discovered! Pray you, let me go.
(*Offers to stab himself.*)
King. Stay him.
Are. What is discovered?
Dion. Why, my shame.
It is a woman; let her speak the rest.
Phi. How? That again!
Dion. It is a woman.
Phi. Blest be you powers that favor innocence!
King. Lay hold upon that lady.
(*Megra is seized.*)
Phi. It is a woman, sir!—Hark, gentlemen,
It is a woman!—Arethusa, take
My soul into thy breast, that would be gone
With joy. It is a woman! Thou art fair,
And virtuous still to ages, in despite
Of malice.
King. Speak you, where lies his shame?
Bel. I am his daughter.
Phi. The gods are just.
Dion. I dare accuse none; but, before you two,
The virtue of our age, I bend my knee
For mercy.
(*Kneels.*)
Phi. (*Raising him.*) Take it freely; for I know,
Though what thou didst were undiscreetly done,
'T was meant well.
Are. And for me,
I have a power to pardon sins, as oft
As any man has power to wrong me.
Cle. Noble and worthy!
Phi. But, Bellario,
(For I must call thee still so,) tell me why
Thou didst conceal thy sex. It was a fault,
A fault, Bellario, though thy other deeds
Of truth outweigh'd it: all these jealousies
Had flown to nothing if thou hadst discovered
What now we know.
Bel. My father oft would speak
Your worth and virtue; and, as I did grow
More and more apprehensive,[38] I did thirst
To see the man so prais'd. But yet all this
Was but a maiden-longing, to be lost
As soon as found; till, sitting in my window,
Printing my thoughts in lawn, I saw a god,
I thought, (but it was you,) enter our gates.
My blood flew out and back again, as fast
As I had puft it forth and suckt it in
Like breath. Then was I call'd away in haste
To entertain you. Never was a man,
Heav'd from a sheep-cote to a scepter, rais'd
So high in thoughts as I. You left a kiss
Upon these lips then, which I mean to keep
From you for ever. I did hear you talk,

36 In some barbarous countries, it was believed that the murderer inherited the form and qualities of his victim. (Mason.)

37 true.

38 able to understand.

Far above singing. After you were gone,
I grew acquainted with my heart, and search'd
What stirr'd it so: alas, I found it love!
Yet far from lust; for, could I but have liv'd
In presence of you, I had had my end.
For this I did delude my noble father
With a feign'd pilgrimage, and drest myself
In habit of a boy; and, for I knew
My birth no match for you, I was past hope
Of having you; and, understanding well
That when I made discovery of my sex
I could not stay with you, I made a vow,
By all the most religious things a maid
Could call together, never to be known,
Whilst there was hope to hide me from men's eyes,
For other than I seem'd, that I might ever
Abide with you. Then sat I by the fount,
Where first you took me up.

King. Search out a match
Within our kingdom, where and when thou wilt,
And I will pay thy dowry; and thyself
Wilt well deserve him.

Bel. Never, sir, will I
Marry; it is a thing within my vow:
But, if I may have leave to serve the princess,
To see the virtues of her lord and her,
I shall have hope to live.

Are. I, Philaster,
Cannot be jealous, though you had a lady
Drest like a page to serve you; nor will I
Suspect her living here.—Come, live with me;
Live free as I do. She that loves my lord,
Curst be the wife that hates her!

Phi. I grieve such virtue should be laid in earth
Without an heir.—Hear me, my royal father:
Wrong not the freedom of our souls so much,
To think to take revenge of that base woman;
Her malice cannot hurt us. Set her free
As she was born, saving from shame and sin.

King. Set her at liberty.—But leave the court;
This is no place for such.—You, Pharamond,
Shall have free passage, and a conduct home
Worthy so great a prince. When you come there,
Remember 't was your faults that lost you her,
And not my purpos'd will.

Pha. I do confess,
Renowned sir.

King. Last, join your hands in one. Enjoy, Philaster,
This kingdom, which is yours, and, after me,
Whatever I call mine. My blessing on you!
All happy hours be at your marriage-joys,
That you may grow yourselves over all lands,
And live to see your plenteous branches spring
Wherever there is sun! Let princes learn
By this to rule the passions of their blood;
For what Heaven wills can never be withstood.

Exeunt

BEN JONSON

THE ALCHEMIST

Benjamin or Ben Jonson, as he has always been called (1572–1637), the stepson of a bricklayer, gained the beginnings of his solid classical learning in Westminster School under the celebrated Camden, but went to no university. After working as a bricklayer, fighting in Flanders, and being imprisoned for killing a man in a duel, he produced his first extant play, *Every Man in His Humor*, in 1598. In 1598–1602 he was concerned in a vigorous literary quarrel, especially with Dekker and Marston, during which they were fertile in dramas satirical of each other. His tragedies, *Sejanus* and *Catiline*, were first acted in 1603 and 1611, and his greatest comedies, those of his middle period, *Volpone*, *Epicene*, *The Alchemist* and *Bartholomew Fair*, from 1606 to 1614. Though his later plays were less meritorious, and though his lack of popular success often left him poor, toward the end of his life he held a station of commanding literary influence.

Jonson is the most vivid literary personality of the whole Elizabethan epoch; indeed, he is the first English writer whom we know intimately as a man. We know him through the self-expression in his candid, pugnacious prologues and epilogues, and in certain prose works; and we know him through one of the most delightful of seventeenth-century books, the *Conversations* with him recorded by William Drummond, whom he fascinated but repelled. With Jonson's classical sympathies and literary good-taste, his gifts as a talker, his trenchant humor and biting tongue, his influence over younger men, his solidity, his downright good-sense, he reminds us to an extraordinary degree of his namesake Samuel, a century and a half later, to whose biography by Boswell the *Conversations* by Drummond are like a sort of unflattering first sketch. Jonson, however, was no less inferior to Johnson as a Christian soul than he was superior in both the importance and variety of his literary work, which shows most remarkable versatility. The most vigorous and penetrating of early literary critics, author of an English grammar, yet also of some of the most limpid of songs, of strict and learned classical tragedy, of mordant realistic comedy, of highly poetic masques, he was the most weighty and versatile man of letters, though of course not the greatest poet or dramatist, in the entire Elizabethan period. While the other dramatists differ among themselves in degree, he stands apart in kind.

The foundation of Jonson's literary ideals was an admiration for the classics, their conscientious finish, their temperance and firmness, their reality. In the prologue to his first known comedy he cut loose from the extravagances of romantic drama in favor of

> deeds, and language, such as men do use,
> And persons such as comedy would choose,
> When she would show an image of the times,
> And sport with human follies, not with crimes.

Jonson was the real founder and first worthy exponent of classicism in English literature. But he was fortunate in living in a romantic age, so that the bonds of the classic were never tight upon him. The conventionality which lay heavy as frost and deep almost as life on so much of the literature of the eighteenth century and earlier is not to be seen in his work. In a word, he was free, and wrote as he did because it pleased him.

The Alchemist (first performed in 1610, and printed in 1612) has usually been recognized as his masterpiece. It was played till the theaters closed in 1642, and was one of the first comedies revived after the Restoration; Pepys the diarist thought it incomparable; indeed at this time Jonson was if anything preferred to Shakespeare, and Restoration comedy shows much of his influence. The play remained popular in the eighteenth century, when Garrick played both Face and Abel Drugger. Coleridge deemed the plots of Sophocles' *Œdipus*, *The Alchemist*, and Fielding's *Tom Jones* the three most perfect ever devised, and Swinburne called the play a faultless work of art. It is too hard and cold in its realism to be beloved or widely popular; Jonson wrote from and appeals to the head and not the heart; the play has been appreciated best in satirical times and by those who respond most to supreme technical skill.

The Alchemist is thoroughly typical of Jonson's plays. In his preface he censures the unrestrained extravagance of most of the dramatists, who he admits however will win more general favor than they who "use election and a mean" (selection and moderation). The play is a satirical picture of contemporary life, written with something of real moral purpose; his pen "did never aim to grieve, but better men"; a salutary result is said to have been actually effected by his exposure of the folly of those who trust charlatans. It contains little or nothing fantastic or improbable (save for the heightening essential to poetry). It follows classical precedent in its observance of the three unities; in *The Alchemist* the plot is single (though far from simple), and the action occurs in a single place and within one day. Though the plot, as usual with Jonson, is in general original, it shows much influence of Plautus, especially of the *Mostellaria*, or *Haunted House*. Both poets, like R. L. Stevenson, felt the fascinating possibilities, even the romance, of an empty house. In the *Mostellaria*, Philolaches in his father's absence introduces a disorderly crew into his house and holds high revel. A scene of lively quarreling at the opening of each play tells us the situation, but with such skill in *The Alchemist* that we hardly realize we are being informed; the peace-making Doll is soon as irate as the other two. Lovewit's return at the end of act four, and the complications which follow, reflect a similar situation toward the middle of the *Mostellaria*. These form the chief of Jonson's literary debts. The characters and most of the intrigue and situations, all that gives the play its vitality, are his own. Of a surety there is no anemic classicism in Sir Epicure Mammon, Face, and Tribulation Wholesome, in the scenes of bustling quackery, or in the deliciously human ending, where Lovewit, who cannot belie his name, smiles to himself so much over Face's cleverness that he must needs forgive him. Jonson did not understand his literary theory so narrowly as his successors in regard to moral teaching, poetic justice, and the like; he has even been censured by critics of our own day for letting off his rogues scot-free. But such critics miss the point of the play, and of Jonson's whole moral attitude. He would "sport with human follies, not with crimes." The real villains of the piece are the hypocritical and superstitious, who allow themselves to be duped through their avarice and self-seeking, and get the kind of punishment which they always get in life. But there was no more need of condemning the criminals, Subtle and Doll, than of organizing a crusade against the damned in the bottomless pit. Jonson could not have made their rascality alluring if he had wished, though he does leave us in a good humor with the rascals. They are the instruments with which he scourges his real villains.

It is in his refusal to dole out trivial poetic justice that Jonson shows himself most laudably free from the narrower classicism. The play shows a classical spirit vitally animating a native English body. The personages are types, as is announced by their names, of the significant sort to be used so largely in later comedies and novels of manners; but they are not the traditional types, as in other plays under classical influence, such as Lyly's *Mother Bombie*. The play is a comedy of manners, exhibiting the society of the day, or a part of it, in firmly but broadly sketched persons. In Jonson's satirical and moral realism, and his vividly typical personages, we feel almost equally the traits of the ancient comedy and the medieval morality. So vigorous yet so general is the characterization that we recognize much of it as permanently true of human nature, though the forms of embodiment may vary. The satire is mainly on gullibility and Puritan hypocrisy. The most imposing creation is Sir Epicure Mammon, in whom avarice and lust, without being made attractive, have become impressive through the force of his imagination. The two Puritans are distinguished from each other, Ananias narrow and more or less sincere, Tribulation intelligent but more of a hypocrite, the opportunist type which is to be found in all religions. It is of much interest to see this unflattering old English picture of the Puritans exiled in Amsterdam, who were to sail from Holland for New England a few years later, and be canonized among their descendants as the Pilgrim Fathers. There is also similar satire in *Bartholomew Fair*. It must be remembered, of course, that Jonson and other literary men, apostles of pagan culture and the drama, naturally were prejudiced against foes of the drama and apostles of a sometimes bigoted piety and asceticism. A figure of more temporary significance is that of "the angry boy," who would learn the etiquette of quarreling, much as Touchstone would have taught it (*As You Like It*, V. iv). The personage most suggestive of modern counterparts is Subtle, whose arts and methods are those of the quacks and confidence-men of all times, whether they capitalize a false science or a feigning religion; he has their dust-in-the-eyes methods, their skill in using decoys like Face, their pretense of personal sanctity and austerity.

A word should be said as to the pseudo-science which he exploits. Alchemy had long been studied in the Middle Ages, but the teaching of Paracelsus (1493–1541) had deprived it of much of its supposed basis, and it had always been in disrepute among the sensible. Chaucer had attacked it in the *Canon's Yeoman's Tale*, Lyly in *Gallathea*, Reginald Scot in his *Discovery of Witchcraft* (1584), and Jonson himself in *Eastward Ho:* he told Drummond that he had once fooled a woman by disguising himself as an astrologer. There is reason to believe that alchemy and other occult studies with which it was closely allied, astrology, magic, and forms of spiritualism, were particularly a pest about the time of this play. As is well known, the chief desire of the alchemists was to discover a recipe or stone or elixir by which other substances could be transformed into gold. Such a possibility was not discountenanced by medieval scientific conceptions, according to which gold was not an element wholly unrelated to others, but all metals were combined out of simpler elements; a view in fact not so inconsistent with the chemical theory of to-day as with that of some years ago. Gold might come into existence out of something else, just as animal life, to one unaware of the ubiquity of minute germs and eggs, seems to do out of putrefaction or stagnant water (cf. II. i.). A large amount of gold might grow from a small; therefore a goldmine was sometimes sealed up with the expectation that in time the gold would increase. The methods of the alchemists were largely based on the prevalent mystical conception of the universe, and on false analogies. Sex, likes and dislikes, goodness and badness, and other human traits, were attributed to physical matter. Besides this there was much traditional hocus-pocus. By no means all the votaries of alchemy were mere cranks or rogues; even those who extorted money by duping the foolish and dealing in other dubious and occult arts often did so in order to carry on experiments which the next day, they believed, might lay the world at their feet. Finally, though the subject and its terminology are too intricate and baffling to be fully explained here or in the notes, the reader may be assured that Jonson was not airily fluttering things he did not understand, but had read the masters of the subject and understood it thoroughly.

THE ALCHEMIST

By BEN JONSON

NAMES OF THE CHARACTERS

Subtle, *the* Alchemist.
Face, *the House-keeper.*
Dol Common, *their colleague.*
Dapper, *a Lawyer's clerk.*
Drugger, *a Tobacco-man.*
Lovewit, *Master of the House.*
Sir Epicure Mammon, *a Knight.*
Pertinax Surly, *a Gamester.*
Tribulation Wholesome, *a Pastor of Amsterdam.*
Ananias, *a Deacon there.*
Kastrill, *the angry boy.*
Dame Pliant, *his sister, a Widow.*
Neighbors.
Officers, Mutes.

Scene.—London

TO THE READER

If thou beest more, thou art an understander, and then I trust thee. If thou art one that tak'st up, and but a pretender, beware at what hands thou receiv'st thy commodity; for thou wert never more fair in the way to be coz'ned than in this age in poetry, especially in plays: wherein now the concupiscence of jigs and dances so reigneth, as to run away from nature and be afraid of her is the only point of art that tickles the spectators. But how out of purpose and place do I name art, when the professors are grown so obstinate contemners of it, and presumers on their own naturals,[1] as they are deriders of all diligence that way, and, by simple mocking at the terms when they understand not the things, think to get off wittily with their ignorance! Nay, they are esteem'd the more learned and sufficient for this by the multitude, through their excellent vice [2] of judgment. For they commend writers as they do fencers or wrastlers; who, if they come in robustiously and put for it with a great deal of violence, are receiv'd for the braver fellows; when many times their own rudeness is the cause of their disgrace, and a little touch of their adversary gives all that boisterous force the foil.[3] I deny not but that these men who always seek to do more than enough may some time happen on some thing that is good and great; but very seldom: and when it comes, it doth not recompense the rest of their ill. It sticks out, perhaps, and is more eminent, because all is sordid and vile about it; as lights are more discern'd in a thick darkness than a faint shadow. I speak not this out of a hope to do good on any man against his will; for I know, if it were put to the question of theirs and mine, the worse would find more suffrages, because the most favor common errors. But I give thee this warning, that there is a great difference between those that (to gain the opinion of copie [4]) utter all they can, however unfitly, and those that use election and a mean.[5] For it is only the disease of the unskillful to think rude things greater than polish'd, or scatter'd more numerous than compos'd.

1 natural endowments. 2 surpassing error. 3 check. 4 copiousness; Lat. *copia.* 5 moderation.

ARGUMENT

T he sickness[6] hot, a master quit, for fear,
H is house in town, and left one servant there.
E ase him corrupted, and gave means to know
A Cheater and his punk;[7] who now brought low,
L eaving their narrow practice, were become
C oz'ners[8] at large; and only wanting some
H ouse to set up, with him they here contract,
E ach for a share, and all begin to act.
M uch company they draw, and much abuse,
I n casting figures,[9] telling fortunes, news,
S elling of flies,[10] flat bawdry, with the stone,[11]
T ill it, and they, and all, in fume[12] are gone.

PROLOGUE

Fortune, that favors fools, these two short hours
  We wish away, both for your sakes and ours,
Judging spectators; and desire in place,
  To th' author justice, to ourselves but grace.
Our scene is London, 'cause we would make known,
  No country's mirth is better than our own.
No clime breeds better matter for your whore,
  Bawd, squire,[13] impostor, many persons more,
Whose manners, now call'd humors, feed the stage;
  And which have still been subject for the rage
Or spleen of comic writers. Though this pen
  Did never aim to grieve, but better men;
Howe'er the age he lives in doth endure
  The vices that she breeds, above their cure.
But when the wholesome remedies are sweet,
  And, in their working gain and profit meet,
He hopes to find no spirit so much diseas'
  But will with such fair correctives b
pleas'd.
For here he doth not fear who can appl
  If there be any that will sit so nigh
Unto the stream, to look what it doth rur
  They shall find things, they 'd think, o
wish, were done;
They are so natural follies, but so showr
  As even the doers may see, and yet no
own.

ACT I.

SCENE 1. *A room in Lovewit's house.*[1

Enter Face, in a captain's uniform, an Subtle with a vial, quarreling, and fol lowed by Dol Common.

Face. Believe 't, I will.
Sub. Thy worst. I fart at thee
Dol. Ha' you your wits? Why, gentle men! for love——
Face. Sirrah, I'll strip you——
Sub. What to do? Lick figs[1
Out at my——
Face. Rogue, rogue!—out of all you sleights.[16]
Dol. Nay, look ye, sovereign, general, ar you madmen?
Sub. O, let the wild sheep loose. I' gum your silks
With good strong water, an[17] you come
Dol. Will you hav
The neighbors hear you? Will you be tray all?
Hark! I hear somebody.
Face. Sirrah——
Sub. I shall ma
All that the tailor has made, if you approach.
Face. You most notorious whelp, you insolent slave,
Dare you do this?
Sub. Yes, faith; yes, faith.
Face. Why, whc
Am I, my mongrel, who am I?
Sub. I'll tell you
Since you know not yourself.
Face. Speak lower, rogue.
Sub. Yes. You were once (time's not long past) the good,
Honest, plain, livery-three-pound-thrum,[18] that kept

6 the plague.
7 mistress.
8 swindlers.
9 horoscopes.
10 dealing in familiar spirits.
11 philosophers' stone.
12 smoke.
13 pimp.
14 Jonson manages his action so cleverly that practically all the scenes can be conceived of as taking place in a single room; consequently changes of scene are rarely indicated in the stage directions.
15 The phrase has an insulting connotation.
16 drop your tricks.
17 if.
18 underpaid servant in livery.

Your master's worship's house here in the Friars,[19]
For the vacations [20]——
Face. Will you be so loud?
Sub. Since, by my means, translated [21] suburb-captain.
Face. By your means, doctor dog!
Sub. Within man's memory,
All this I speak of.
Face. Why, I pray you, have I
Been countenanc'd by you, or you by me?
Do but collect, sir, where I met you first.
Sub. I do not hear well.
Face. Not of this, I think it.
But I shall put you in mind, sir;—at Pie-corner,
Taking your meal of steam in, from cooks' stalls,
Where, like the father of hunger, you did walk
Piteously costive, with your pinch'd-horn-nose,
And your complexion of the Roman wash,[22]
Stuck full of black and melancholic worms,
Like powder-corns [23] shot at the artillery-yard.
Sub. I wish you could advance your voice a little.
Face. When you went pinn'd up in the several rags
You had rak'd and pick'd from dung-hills, before day;
Your feet in mouldy slippers, for your kibes; [24]
A felt of rug,[25] and a thin threaden cloak,
That scarce would cover your no-buttocks——
Sub. So, sir!
Face. When all your alchemy, and your algebra,
Your minerals, vegetals, and animals,
Your conjuring, coz'ning, and your dozen of trades,
Could not relieve your corpse with so much linen
Would make you tinder, but to see a fire; [26]
I ga' you count'nance, credit for your coals,
Your stills, your glasses, your materials;
Built you a furnace, drew you customers,
Advanc'd all your black arts; lent you, beside,
A house to practise in——
Sub. Your master's house!
Face. Where you have studied the more thriving skill
Of bawdry, since.
Sub. Yes, in your master's house.
You and the rats here kept possession.
Make it not strange.[27] I know you were one could keep
The buttery-hatch still lock'd, and save the chippings,
Sell the dole beer to aqua-vitae men,[28]
The which, together with your Christmas vails [29]
At post-and-pair,[30] your letting out of counters,[31]
Made you a pretty stock, some twenty marks,
And gave you credit to converse with cobwebs,
Here, since your mistress' death hath broke up house.
Face. You might talk softlier, rascal.
Sub. No, you scarab,[32]
I'll thunder you in pieces. I will teach you
How to beware to tempt a Fury again
That carries tempest in his hand and voice.
Face. The place has made you valiant.
Sub. No, your clothes.
Thou vermin, have I ta'en thee out of dung,
So poor, so wretched, when no living thing
Would keep thee company, but a spider or worse?
Rais'd thee from brooms, and dust, and wat'ring-pots,
Sublim'd thee, and exalted thee, and fix'd thee
In the third region, call'd our state of grace?
Wrought thee to spirit, to quintessence, with pains
Would twice have won me the philosopher's work?
Put thee in words and fashion? made thee fit
For more than ordinary fellowships?

19 Blackfriars; a quarter of London.
20 between the sessions of court.
21 changed to.
22 a cosmetic of some sort
23 grains of powder.
24 chilblains.
25 a rough hat.
26 tinder enough to make a fire that could be even seen.
27 don't feign ignorance.
28 It was usual to distribute at the pantry door (*buttery hatch*) of great houses, a daily or weekly *dole* of broken bread (*chippings*) and beer to the poor (Gifford); the latter, says Subtle, Face has sold to liquor dealers.
29 tips.
30 a game of cards.
31 renting of markers or chips.
32 beetle.

Giv'n thee thy oaths, thy quarreling dimensions? [33]
Thy rules to cheat at horse-race, cock-pit, cards,
Dice, or whatever gallant tincture [34] else?
Made thee a second in mine own great art?
And have I this for thanks! Do you rebel?
Do you fly out i' the projection? [35]
Would you be gone now?

Dol. Gentlemen, what mean you?
Will you mar all?

Sub. Slave, thou hadst had no name——

Dol. Will you undo yourselves with civil war?

Sub. Never been known, past *equi clibanum,*
The heat of horse-dung, under ground, in cellars,
Or an ale-house darker than deaf John's; been lost
To all mankind, but laundresses and tapsters,
Had not I been.

Dol. Do you know who hears you, sovereign?

Face. Sirrah——

Dol. Nay, general, I thought you were civil.

Face. I shall turn desperate, if you grow thus loud.

Sub. And hang thyself, I care not.

Face. Hang thee, collier,
And all thy pots and pans, in picture I will,
Since thou hast mov'd me——

Dol. (*Aside.*) O, this 'll o'erthrow all.

Face. Write thee up bawd in Paul's; [36] have all thy tricks
Of coz'ning with a hollow coal,[37] dust, scrapings.
Searching for things lost, with a sieve and shears,
Erecting figures in your rows of houses,
And taking in of shadows with a glass,
Told in red letters; and a face cut for thee,
Worse than Gamaliel Ratsey's.[38]

Dol. Are you sound?
Ha' you your senses, masters?

Face. I will have
A book, but barely reckoning thy impostures,
Shall prove a true philosopher's stone to printers.

Sub. Away, you trencher-rascal!

Face. Out, you dog-leech!
The vomit of all prisons——

Dol. Will you be
Your own destructions, gentlemen?

Face. Still spew'd out
For lying too heavy o' the basket.[39]

Sub. Cheater!

Face. Bawd!

Sub. Cow-herd!

Face. Conjurer!

Sub. Cutpurse!

Face. Witch!

Dol. O me!
We are ruin'd, lost! Ha' you no more regard
To your reputations? Where 's your judgment? 'Slight,
Have yet some care of me, o' your republic——

Face. Away, this brach! [40] I'll bring thee, rogue, within
The statute of sorcery, tricesimo tertio
Of Harry the Eighth: aye, and perhaps thy neck
Within a noose, for laund'ring gold and barbing it.[41]

Dol. You 'll bring your head within a cocks-comb,[42] will you?
(*She catcheth out Face his sword, and breaks Subtle's glass.*)
And you, sir, with your menstrue! [43]—
Gather it up.
'Sdeath, you abominable pair of stinkards,
Leave off your barking, and grow one again,
Or, by the light that shines, I'll cut your throats.
I'll not be made a prey unto the marshal
For ne'er a snarling dog-bolt [44] o' you both.
Ha' you together cozen'd all this while,
And all the world, and shall it now be said,
You 've made most courteous shift to cozen yourselves?
(*To Face.*) You will accuse him! You will bring him in
Within the statute! Who shall take your word?

33 rules.
34 inclination.
35 when the process is approaching completion.
36 Advertisements were posted in St. Paul's.
37 Chaucer exposes this practice in the *Canon's Yeoman's Tale.* Various tricks of astrologers are named in the following lines.
38 A highwayman, hanged in 1605, who wore a hideous mask.
39 eating more than his share of broken meats sent in to prisoners.
40 bitch.
41 "sweating" and clipping coins.
42 fool's cap.
43 a solvent.
44 blockhead.

A whoreson, upstart, apocryphal captain,
Whom not a Puritan in Blackfriars will trust
So much as for a feather:[45] and you, too,
(*To Subtle.*) Will give the cause, forsooth! You will insult,
And claim a primacy in the divisions!
You must be chief! As if you, only, had
The powder to project[46] with, and the work
Were not begun out of equality!
The venture tripartite! All things in common!
Without priority! 'Sdeath! you perpetual curs,
Fall to your couples again, and cozen kindly,
And heartily, and lovingly, as you should,
And lose not the beginning of a term,[47]
Or, by this hand, I shall grow factious too,
And take my part, and quit you.

Face. 'T is his fault;
He ever murmurs, and objects his pains,
And says, the weight of all lies upon him.

Sub. Why, so it does.

Dol. How does it? Do not we
Sustain our parts?

Sub. Yes, but they are not equal.

Dol. Why, if your part exceed to-day, I hope
Ours may to-morrow match it.

Sub. Aye, they *may.*

Dol. May, murmuring mastiff! Aye, and do. Death on me!
Help me to throttle him.
(*Seizes Subtle by the throat.*)

Sub. Dorothy! Mistress Dorothy!
'Ods precious, I 'll do anything. What do you mean?

Dol. Because o' your fermentation[48] and cibation?[49]

Sub. Not I, by heaven——

Dol. Your Sol and Luna——
(*To Face.*) Help me.

Sub. Would I were hang'd then! I 'll conform myself.

Dol. Will you, sir? Do so then, and quickly: swear.

Sub. What should I swear?

Dol. To leave your faction,[50] sir,
And labor kindly in the common work.

Sub. Let me not breathe if I meant aught beside.
I only us'd those speeches as a spur
To him.

Dol. I hope we need no spurs, sir. Do we?

Face. 'Slid, prove to-day who shall shark best.

Sub. Agreed.

Dol. Yes, and work close and friendly.

Sub. 'Slight, the knot
Shall grow the stronger for this breach, with me.
(*They shake hands.*)

Dol. Why, so, my good baboons! Shall we go make
A sort[51] of sober, scurvy, precise neighbors,
That scarce have smil'd twice sin' the king came in,[52]
A feast of laughter at our follies? Rascals,
Would run themselves from breath, to see me ride,[53]
Or you t' have but a hole to thrust your heads in,[54]
For which you should pay ear-rent?[55] No, agree.
And may Don Provost ride a feasting long,
In his old velvet jerkin and stain'd scarfs,
My noble sovereign, and worthy general,
Ere we contribute a new crewel[56] garter
To his most worsted worship.

Sub. Royal Dol!
Spoken like Claridiana,[57] and thyself.

Face. For which at supper, thou shalt sit in triumph,
And not be styl'd Dol Common, but Dol Proper,
Dol Singular: the longest cut at night,
Shall draw thee for his Dol Particular.
(*Bell rings without.*)

Sub. Who 's that? One rings. To the window, Dol: (*Exit Dol.*)—Pray heav'n,
The master do not trouble us this quarter.

Face. O, fear not him. While there dies one a week
O' the plague, he 's safe from thinking toward London.
Beside, he 's busy at his hop-yards now;
I had a letter from him. If he do,

45 Blackfriars was full of Puritans, many of whom were in the business of selling feathers.
46 change one metal to another.
47 term of court.
48 chemical change of a substance by something which worked on it like yeast.
49 supplying with fresh material to make up for evaporation.
50 factiousness.
51 crew.
52 In 1603.
53 be carted for a bawd.
54 the pillory.
55 have your ears cut off.
56 yarn; note puns on *crewel* and *worsted.*
57 The heroine of the "Mirror of Knighthood," a romance.

He 'll send such word, for airing o' the house,
As you shall have sufficient time to quit it:
Though we break up a fortnight, 't is no matter.

Re-enter Dol.

Sub. Who is it, Dol?
Dol. A fine young quodling.[58]
Face. O,
My lawyer's clerk, I lighted on last night,
In Holborn, at the Dagger. He would have
(I told you of him) a familiar,
To rifle[59] with at horses, and win cups.
Dol. O, let him in.
Sub. Stay. Who shall do 't?
Face. Get you
Your robes on; I will meet him, as going out.
Dol. And what shall I do?
Face. Not be seen; away!
Exit Dol.
Seem you very reserv'd.
Sub. Enough.
Exit.
Face. (*Aloud and retiring.*) God be wi' you, sir,
I pray you let him know that I was here:
His name is Dapper. I would gladly have stay'd, but——

SCENE 2.

Enter Face.

Dap. (*Within.*) Captain, I am here.
Face. Who 's that?—He 's come, I think, doctor.

Enter Dapper.

Good faith, sir, I was going away.
Dap. In truth,
I am very sorry, captain.
Face. But I thought
Sure I should meet you.
Dap. Aye, I am very glad.
I had a scurvy writ or two to make,
And I had lent my watch last night to one
That dines to-day at the sheriff's, and so was robb'd
Of my pass-time.

Re-enter Subtle in his velvet cap and gown.

Is this the cunning-man?
Face. This is his worship.
Dap. Is he a doctor?
Face. Yes.
Dap. And ha' you broke[60] with him, captain?
Face. Aye.
Dap. And how?
Face. Faith, he does make the matter, sir, so dainty,
I know not what to say.
Dap. Not so, good captain.
Face. Would I were fairly rid on 't, believe me.
Dap. Nay, now you grieve me, sir. Why should you wish so?
I dare assure you, I 'll not be ungrateful.
Face. I cannot think you will, sir. But the law
Is such a thing——and then he says, Reade's[61] matter
Falling so lately——
Dap. Reade! he was an ass,
And dealt, sir, with a fool.
Face. It was a clerk, sir.
Dap. A clerk!
Face. Nay, hear me, sir. You know the law
Better, I think——
Dap. I should, sir, and the danger:
You know, I show'd the statute to you.
Face. You did so.
Dap. And will I tell then! By this hand of flesh,
Would it might never write good court-hand more,
If I discover.[62] What do you think of me,
That I am a chiaus?
Face. What 's that?
Dap. The Turk was here.
As one would say, do you think I am a Turk?
Face. I 'll tell the doctor so.
Dap. Do, good sweet captain.
Face. Come, noble doctor, pray thee let 's prevail;
This is the gentleman, and he is no chiaus.
Sub. Captain, I have return'd you all my answer.
I would do much, sir, for your love——But this
I neither may, nor can.
Face. Tut, do not say so.
You deal now with a noble fellow, doctor,
One that will thank you richly; and he 's no chiaus:
Let that, sir, move you.

58 codling, green apple; hence, greenhorn.
59 raffle, gamble.
60 broached the matter.
61 A man named Reade had been indicted in 1608 for dealing with evil spirits.
62 disclose.

Sub. Pray you, forbear——
Face. He has
Four angels here.
Sub. You do me wrong, good sir.
Face. Doctor, wherein? To tempt you with these spirits?
Sub. To tempt my art and love, sir, to my peril.
'Fore heav'n, I scarce can think you are my friend,
That so would draw me to apparent danger.
Face. I draw you! A horse draw you, and a halter,
You, and your flies [63] together——
Dap. Nay, good captain.
Face. That know no difference of men.
Sub. Good words, sir.
Face. Good deeds, sir, doctor dogs'-meat.
'Slight, I bring you
No cheating Clim o' the Cloughs or Claribels,[64]
That look as big as five-and-fifty, and flush; [65]
And spit out secrets like hot custard——
Dap. Captain!
Face. Nor any melancholic underscribe,
Shall tell the vicar; but a special gentle,
That is the heir to forty marks a year,
Consorts with the small poets of the time,
Is the sole hope of his old grandmother;
That knows the law, and writes you six fair hands,
Is a fine clerk, and has his ciph'ring perfect.
Will take his oath o' the Greek Xenophon,
If need be, in his pocket; and can court
His mistress out of Ovid.
Dap. Nay, dear captain——
Face. Did you not tell me so?
Dap. Yes; but I 'd ha' you
Use master doctor with some more respect.
Face. Hang him, proud stag, with his broad velvet head! [66]—
But for your sake, I 'd choke ere I would change
An article of breath with such a puckfist! [67]
Come, let 's be gone.
(*Going.*)
Sub. Pray you le' me speak with you.
Dap. His worship calls you, captain.
Face. I am sorry
I e'er embark'd myself in such a business.
Dap. Nay, good sir; he did call you.
Face. Will he take then?
Sub. First, hear me——
Face. Not a syllable, 'less you take.
Sub. Pray ye, sir——
Face. Upon no terms but an *assumpsit.*[68]
Sub. Your humor must be law.
(*He takes the money.*)
Face. Why now, sir, talk.
Now I dare hear you with mine honor. Speak.
So may this gentleman too.
Sub. Why, sir——
(*Offering to whisper Face.*)
Face. No whisp'ring.
Sub. 'Fore heav'n, you do not apprehend the loss
You do yourself in this.
Face. Wherein? for what?
Sub. Marry, to be so importunate for one
That, when he has it, will undo you all:
He 'll win up all the money i' the town.
Face. How?
Sub. Yes, and blow up gamester after gamester,
As they do crackers in a puppet-play.
If I do give him a familiar,
Give you him all you play for; never set [69] him:
For he will have it.
Face. You 're mistaken, doctor.
Why, he does ask one but for cups and horses,
A rifling fly; none o' your great familiars.
Dap. Yes, captain, I would have it for all games.
Sub. I told you so.
Face. (*Taking Dap. aside.*) 'Slight, that is a new business!
I understood you, a tame bird, to fly
Twice in a term, or so, on Friday nights,
When you had left the office; for a nag
Of forty or fifty shillings.
Dap. Aye, 't is true, sir;
But I do think, now, I shall leave the law,
And therefore——
Face. Why, this changes quite the case.
Do you think that I dare move him?
Dap. If you please, sir;
All 's one to him, I see.
Face. What! for that money?
I cannot with my conscience; nor should you
Make the request, methinks.
Dap. No, sir, I mean

63 familiar spirits.
64 heroes of ballad and romance.
65 that show a tell-tale face when holding *five-and-fifty* and *flush*, the highest counts at primero. (Schelling.)
66 cap.
67 close-fisted person.
68 contract.
69 bet with.

To add consideration.
Face. Why, then, sir,
I'll try. (*Goes to Subtle.*) Say that it were for all games, doctor?
Sub. I say then, not a mouth shall eat for him
At any ordinary,[70] but o' the score;[71]
That is a gaming mouth, conceive me.
Face. Indeed!
Sub. He'll draw you all the treasure of the realm,
If it be set him.
Face. Speak you this from art?
Sub. Aye, sir, and reason too, the ground of art.
He is o' the only best complexion,
The queen of Fairy loves.
Face. What! Is he?
Sub. Peace.
He'll overhear you. Sir, should she but see him——
Face. What?
Sub. Do not you tell him.
Face. Will he win at cards too?
Sub. The spirits of dead Holland, living Isaac,[72]
You'd swear, were in him; such a vigorous luck
As cannot be resisted. 'Slight, he'll put
Six o' your gallants to a cloak,[73] indeed.
Face. A strange success, that some man shall be born to!
Sub. He hears you, man——
Dap. Sir, I'll not be ingrateful.
Face. Faith, I have a confidence in his good nature:
You hear, he says he will not be ingrateful.
Sub. Why, as you please; my venture follows yours.
Face. Troth, do it, doctor; think him trusty, and make him.
He may make us both happy in an hour;
Win some five thousand pound, and send us two on 't.
Dap. Believe it, and I will, sir.
Face. And you shall, sir.
You have heard all?
(*Face takes him aside.*)
Dap. No, what was 't? Nothing, I, sir.
Face. Nothing?
Dap. A little, sir.
Face. Well, a rare star
Reign'd at your birth.
Dap. At mine, sir! No.
Face. The doctor
Swears that you are——
Sub. Nay, captain, you'll tell all now.
Face. Allied to the queen of Fairy.
Dap. Who! That I am?
Believe it, no such matter——
Face. Yes, and that
You were born with a caul o' your head.[74]
Dap. Who says so?
Face. Come
You know it well enough, though you dissemble it.
Dap. I' fac,[75] I do not; you are mistaken.
Face. How!
Swear by your fac, and in a thing so known
Unto the doctor? How shall we, sir, trust you
I' the other matter? Can we ever think,
When you have won five or six thousand pound,
You'll send us shares in 't, by this rate?
Dap. By Jove, sir,
I'll win ten thousand pound, and send you half.
I' fac 's no oath.
Sub. No, no, he did but jest.
Face. Go to. Go thank the doctor. He's your friend,
To take it so.
Dap. I thank his worship.
Face. So!
Another angel.
Dap. Must I?
Face. Must you! 'Slight,
What else is thanks? Will you be trivial?—Doctor,
(*Dapper gives him the money.*)
When must he come for his familiar?
Dap. Shall I not ha' it with me?
Sub. O, good sir!
There must a world of ceremonies pass;
You must be bath'd and fumigated first:
Besides, the queen of Fairy does not rise
Till it be noon.
Face. Not if she danc'd to-night.
Sub. And she must bless it.
Face. Did you never see
Her royal grace yet?
Dap. Whom?
Face. Your aunt of Fairy?
Sub. Not since she kist him in the cradle, captain;
I can resolve you that.
Face. Well, see her grace,
Whate'er it cost you, for a thing that I know.
It will be somewhat hard to compass; but

70 eating house.
71 The gamblers (who frequented ordinaries) will be so impoverished through his winnings that they will have to eat on credit. (Neilson.)
72 Perhaps two gamblers of the time.
73 strip to the cloak.
74 a sign of good luck.
75 faith.

However, see her. You are made, believe it,
If you can see her. Her grace is a lone woman,
And very rich; and if she take a fancy,
She will do strange things. See her, at any hand.
'Slid, she may hap to leave you all she has!
It is the doctor's fear.

Dap. How will 't be done, then?

Face. Let me alone, take you no thought. Do you
But say to me, "Captain, I'll see her grace."

Dap. Captain, I'll see her grace.

Face. Enough.

(*One knocks without.*)

Sub. Who 's there?
Anon.—(*Aside to Face.*) Conduct him forth by the back way.
Sir, against one o'clock prepare yourself;
Till when you must be fasting; only take
Three drops of vinegar in at your nose,
Two at your mouth, and one at either ear;
Then bathe your fingers' ends and wash your eyes,
To sharpen your five senses, and cry *hum*
Thrice, and then *buz* as often; and then come.

Exit.

Face. Can you remember this?

Dap. I warrant you.

Face. Well then, away. It is but your bestowing
Some twenty nobles 'mong her grace's servants,
And put on a clean shirt. You do not know
What grace her grace may do you in clean linen.

Exeunt Face and Dapper.

SCENE 3.

Sub. (*Within.*) Come in! Good wives, I pray you forbear me now;
Troth, I can do you no good till afternoon.—

Enter Subtle, followed by Drugger.

Sub. What is your name, say you? Abel Drugger?

Drug. Yes, sir.

Sub. A seller of tobacco?

Drug. Yes, sir.

Sub. Umph!
Free of the grocers?[76]

Drug. Aye, an 't please you.

Sub. Well—
Your business, Abel?

Drug. This, an 't please your worship;
I am a young beginner, and am building
Of a new shop, an 't like your worship, just
At corner of a street:—Here is the plot[77] on 't——
And I would know by art, sir, of your worship,
Which way I should make my door, by necromancy,
And where my shelves; and which should be for boxes,
And which for pots. I would be glad to thrive, sir:
And I was wish'd[78] to your worship by a gentleman,
One Captain Face, that says you know men's planets,
And their good angels, and their bad.

Sub. I do,
If I do see 'em——

Enter Face.

Face. What! my honest Abel?
Thou art well met here.

Drug. Troth, sir, I was speaking,
Just as your worship came here, of your worship.
I pray you speak for me to master doctor.

Face. He shall do anything. Doctor, do you hear?
This is my friend, Abel, an honest fellow;
He lets me have good tobacco, and he does not
Sophisticate it with sack-lees or oil,
Nor washes it in muscadel and grains,
Nor buries it in gravel, under ground,
Wrapp'd up in greasy leather, or piss'd clouts:
But keeps it in fine lily pots, that, open'd,
Smell like conserve of roses, or French beans.
He has his maple block,[79] his silver tongs,
Winchester pipes, and fire of juniper:[80]
A neat, spruce, honest fellow, and no goldsmith.[81]

Sub. He 's a fortunate fellow, that I am sure on.

76 belonging to the Grocers' Guild.
77 plan.
78 recommended.
79 to shred tobacco on.
80 to light pipes with.
81 usurer; goldsmiths used to lend money.

Face. Already, sir, ha' you found it? Lo thee, Abel!
Sub. And in right way toward riches——
Face. Sir!
Sub. This summer.
He will be of the clothing [82] of his company,
And next spring call'd to the scarlet,[83] spend what he can.
Face. What, and so little beard?
Sub. Sir, you must think,
He may have a receipt to make hair come:
But he 'll be wise, preserve his youth, and fine for 't;
His fortune looks for him another way.
Face. 'Slid, doctor, how canst thou know this so soon?
I am amus'd [84] at that.
Sub. By a rule, captain,
In metoposcopy,[85] which I do work by;
A certain star i' the forehead, which you see not.
Your chestnut or your olive-color'd face
Does never fail: and your long ear doth promise.
I knew 't, by certain spots, too, in his teeth,
And on the nail of his mercurial finger.
Face. Which finger 's that?
Sub. His little finger. Look.
You were born upon a Wednesday?
Drug. Yes, indeed, sir.
Sub. The thumb, in chiromancy, we give Venus;
The forefinger to Jove; the midst to Saturn;
The ring to Sol; the least to Mercury,
Who was the lord, sir, of his horoscope,
His house of life being Libra; which forshow'd
He should be a merchant, and should trade with balance.
Face. Why, this is strange! Is it not, honest Nab?
Sub. There is a ship now coming from Ormus,
That shall yield him such a commodity
Of drugs——This is the west, and this the south?
(*Pointing to the plan.*)
Drug. Yes, sir.
Sub. And those are your two sides?
Drug. Aye, sir.
Sub. Make me your door then, south; your broad side, west:
And on the east side of your shop, aloft,
Write Mathlai, Tarmiel, and Baraborat;
Upon the north part, Rael, Velel, Thiel.
They are the names of those Mercurial spirits
That do fright flies from boxes.
Drug. Yes, sir.
Sub. And
Beneath your threshold, bury me a loadstone
To draw in gallants that wear spurs: the rest,
They 'll seem to follow.
Face. That 's a secret, Nab!
Sub. And, on your stall, a puppet, with a vice [86]
And a court-fucus,[87] to call city-dames:
You shall deal much with minerals.
Drug. Sir, I have.
At home, already——
Sub. Aye, I know, you 've arsenic,
Vitriol, sal-tartar, argaile, alkali,
Cinoper. I know all.—This fellow, captain,
Will come, in time, to be a great distiller,
And give a say [88]—I will not say directly,
But very fair—at the philosopher's stone.
Face. Why, how now, Abel! is this true?
Drug. (*Aside to Face.*) Good captain,
What must I give?
Face. Nay, I 'll not counsel thee.
Thou hear'st what wealth (he says, spend what thou canst)
Thou 'rt like to come to.
Drug. I would gi' him a crown.
Face. A crown! and toward such a fortune? Heart,
Thou shalt rather gi' him thy shop. No gold about thee?
Drug. Yes, I have a portague,[89] I ha' kept this half-year.
Face. Out on thee, Nab! 'Slight, there was such an offer—
Shalt keep 't no longer, I 'll gi' it him for thee. Doctor,
Nab prays your worship to drink this, and swears
He will appear more grateful, as your skill
Does raise him in the world.
Drug. I would entreat
Another favor of his worship.
Face. What is 't, Nab?
Drug. But to look over, sir, my almanac,
And cross out my ill-days,[90] that I may neither
Bargain, nor trust upon them.

82 be a full member.
83 be made sheriff.
84 amazed.
85 reading character by the face.
86 a mechanism to move the puppet.
87 cosmetic.
88 make an attempt.
89 a gold coin.
90 unlucky days

Face. That he shall, Nab:
Leave it, it shall be done, 'gainst afternoon.
Sub. And a direction for his shelves.
Face. Now, Nab,
Art thou well pleas'd, Nab?
Drug. 'Thank, sir, both your worships.
Face. Away.
Exit Drugger.
Why, now, you smoky persecutor of nature!
Now do you see, that something's to be done
Beside your beech-coal, and your cor'sive [91] waters,
Your crosslets,[92] crucibles, and cucurbites? [93]
You must have stuff brought home to you, to work on:
And yet you think, I am at no expense
In searching out these veins, then following 'em,
Then trying 'em out. 'Fore God, my intelligence
Costs me more money than my share oft comes to,
In these rare works.
Sub. You 're pleasant, sir.—How now!

SCENE 4.

Face, Subtle. Enter Dol.

Sub. What says my dainty Dolkin?
Dol. Yonder fish-wife
Will not away. And there's your giantess,
The bawd of Lambeth.
Sub. Heart, I cannot speak with 'em.
Dol. Not afore night, I have told 'em in a voice,
Thorough the trunk,[94] like one of your familiars.
But I have spied Sir Epicure Mammon——
Sub. Where?
Dol. Coming along, at far end of the lane,
Slow of his feet, but earnest of his tongue
To one that's with him.
Sub. Face, go you and shift.
Dol, you must presently make ready too.
Exit Face.
Dol. Why, what's the matter?
Sub. O, I did look for him
With the sun's rising: marvel he could sleep!
This is the day I am to perfect for him
The magisterium, our great work, the stone;
And yield it, made, into his hands; of which
He has, this month, talk'd as he were possess'd.
And now he's dealing pieces on 't away.
Methinks I see him ent'ring ordinaries,
Dispensing for the pox, and plaguy houses,
Reaching his dose, walking Moorfields for lepers,
And off'ring citizens' wives pomander-bracelets,[95]
As his preservative, made of the elixir;
Searching the 'spital, to make old bawds young;
And the highways, for beggars to make rich.
I see no end of his labors. He will make
Nature asham'd of her long sleep; when art,
Who's but a step-dame, shall do more than she,
In her best love to mankind, ever could.
If his dream last, he'll turn the age to gold.
Exeunt.

ACT II.

SCENE 1.

Enter Sir Epicure Mammon and Surly.

Mam. Come on, sir. Now you set your foot on shore
In *Novo Orbe;* here's the rich Peru:
And there within, sir, are the golden mines,
Great Solomon's Ophir! He was sailing to 't
Three years, but we have reach'd it in ten months.
This is the day wherein, to all my friends,
I will pronounce the happy word, BE RICH;
THIS DAY YOU SHALL BE SPECTATISSIMI.
You shall no more deal with the hollow die,
Or the frail card; no more be at charge of keeping
The livery-punk for the young heir, that must
Seal, at all hours, in his shirt: no more,
If he deny, ha' him beaten to 't, as he is
That brings him the commodity; no more

91 corrosive.
92 crucibles.
93 vessels for distilling.
94 speaking tube.
95 bracelets with perfume balls attached to guard against the plague.

Shall thirst of satin, or the covetous hunger
Of velvet entrails[96] for a rude-spun cloak,
To be display'd at Madam Augusta's, make
The sons of Sword and Hazard fall before
The golden calf, and on their knees, whole nights,
Commit idolatry with wine and trumpets:
Or go a-feasting after drum and ensign.
No more of this. You shall start up young viceroys,
And have your punks and punkettees, my Surly.
And unto thee I speak it first, BE RICH.
Where is my Subtle there? Within, ho!
Face. (*Within.*) Sir,
He 'll come to you by and by.
Mam. That is his fire-drake,
His Lungs, his Zephyrus, he that puffs his coals,
Till he firk[97] nature up, in her own center.
You are not faithful,[98] sir. This night I 'll change
All that is metal in my house to gold:
And, early in the morning, will I send
To all the plumbers and the pewterers,
And buy their tin and lead up; and to Lothbury
For all the copper.
Sur. What, and turn that, too?
Mam. Yes, and I 'll purchase Devonshire and Cornwall,
And make them perfect Indies! You admire now?
Sur. No, faith.
Mam. But when you see th' effects of the Great Med'cine,
Of which one part projected on a hundred
Of Mercury, or Venus,[99] or the Moon,[1]
Shall turn it to as many of the Sun;[2]
Nay, to a thousand, so *ad infinitum:*
You will believe me.
Sur. Yes, when I see 't, I will.
But if my eyes do cozen me so, and I
Giving 'em no occasion, sure I 'll have
A whore, shall piss 'em out next day.
Mam. Ha! why?
Do you think I fable with you? I assure you,
He that has once the flower of the sun,
The perfect ruby, which we call elixir,
Not only can do that, but by its virtue,
Can confer honor, love, respect, long life;
Give safety, valor, yea, and victory,
To whom he will. In eight and twenty days,
I 'll make an old man of fourscore, a child.
Sur. No doubt; he 's that already.
Mam. Nay, I mean,
Restore his years, renew him, like an eagle,
To the fifth age; make him get sons and daughters,
Young giants; as our philosophers have done,
The ancient patriarchs, afore the flood,
But taking, once a week, on a knife's point,
The quantity of a grain of mustard of it;
Become stout Marses, and beget young Cupids.
Sur. The decay'd vestals of Pickt-hatch[3] would thank you,
That keep the fire alive there.
Mam. 'T is the secret
Of nature naturiz'd 'gainst all infections,
Cures all diseases coming of all causes;
A month's grief in a day, a year's in twelve;
And, of what age soever, in a month.
Past all the doses of your drugging doctors.
I 'll undertake, withal, to fright the plague
Out o' the kingdom in three months.
Sur. And I 'll
Be bound, the players shall sing your praises then,
Without their poets.[4]
Mam. Sir, I 'll do 't. Meantime,
I 'll give away so much unto my man,
Shall serve th' whole city with preservative
Weekly; each house his[5] dose, and at the rate——
Sur. As he that built the Water-work does with water?
Mam. You are incredulous.
Sur. Faith, I have a humor,
I would not willingly be gull'd.[6] Your stone
Cannot transmute me.
Mam. Pertinax Surly,

96 lining.
97 rouse.
98 credulous.
99 copper.
1 silver.
2 gold.
3 a quarter in London of evil repute.
4 Because the banishment of the plague would mean that the theaters would never be obliged to close on account of its prevalence.
5 its.
6 tricked.

Will you believe antiquity? Records?
I 'll show you a book where Moses, and his sister,
And Solomon have written of the art;
Aye, and a treatise penn'd by Adam——
Sur. How!
Mam. Of the philosopher's stone, and in High Dutch.
Sur. Did Adam write, sir, in High Dutch?
Mam. He did;
Which proves it was the primitive tongue.
Sur. What paper?
Mam. On cedar board.
Sur. O that, indeed, they say,
Will last 'gainst worms.
Mam. 'T is like your Irish wood
'Gainst cobwebs. I have a piece of Jason's fleece too,
Which was no other than a book of alchemy,
Writ in large sheepskin, a good fat ram-vellum.
Such was Pythagoras' thigh, Pandora's tub,
And all that fable of Medea's charms,
The manner of our work; the bulls, our furnace,
Still breathing fire; our argent-vive,[7] the dragon:
The dragon's teeth, mercury sublimate,
That keeps the whiteness, hardness, and the biting;
And they are gather'd into Jason's helm,
Th' alembic, and then sow'd in Mars his field,
And thence sublim'd so often, till they're fix'd.
Both this, th' Hesperian garden, Cadmus' story,
Jove's shower,[8] the boon of Midas, Argus' eyes,
Boccace his Demogorgon, thousands more,
All abstract riddles of our stone.—How now!

SCENE 2.

Mammon, Surly. Enter Face, as a Servant.

Mam. Do we succeed? Is our day come? And holds it?
Face. The evening will set red upon you, sir;
You have color for it, crimson: the red ferment
Has done his office; three hours hence prepare you
To see projection.
Mam. Pertinax, my Surly.
Again I say to thee, aloud, BE RICH.
This day thou shalt have ingots; and to-morrow
Give lords th' affront.—Is it, my Zephyrus, right?
Blushes the bolt's-head?[9]
Face. Like a wench with child, sir,
That were but now discover'd to her master.
Mam. Excellent witty Lungs!—My only care is
Where to get stuff enough now, to project on;
This town will not half serve me.
Face. No, sir? Buy
The covering off o' churches.
Mam. That 's true.
Face. Yes.
Let 'em stand bare, as do their auditory;
Or cap 'em new with shingles.
Mam. No, good thatch:
Thatch will lie light upo' the rafters, Lungs.
Lungs, I will manumit thee from the furnace;
I will restore thee thy complexion, Puff,
Lost in the embers; and repair this brain,
Hurt wi' the fume o' the metals.
Face. I have blown, sir,
Hard, for your worship; thrown by many a coal,
When 't was not beech;[10] weigh'd those I put in, just
To keep your heat still even. These blear'd eyes
Have wak'd to read your several colors, sir,
Of the pale citron, the green lion, the crow,
The peacock's tail, the plumed swan.
Mam. And lastly,
Thou hast descried the flower, the *sanguis agni?*[11]
Face. Yes, sir.
Mam. Where 's master?
Face. At 's prayers, sir, he;
Good man, he 's doing his devotions
For the success.
Mam. Lungs, I will set a period
To all thy labors; thou shalt be the master
Of my seraglio.
Face. Good, sir.

[7] quicksilver.
[8] *i. e.* on Danaë.
[9] a flask with a long neck.
[10] Beech was the sovereign wood in making the alchemist's fire.
[11] red, the color of the last stage of the alchemical process.

Mam. But do you hear?
I 'll geld you, Lungs.
Face. Yes, sir.
Mam. For I do mean
To have a list of wives and concubines
Equal with Solomon, who had the stone
Alike with me; and I will make me a back
With the elixir, that shall be as tough
As Hercules, to encounter fifty a night.—
Thou 'rt sure thou saw 'st it blood?
Face. Both blood and spirit, sir.
Mam. I will have all my beds blown up, not stuft;
Down is too hard: and then, mine oval room
Fill'd with such pictures as Tiberius took
From Elephantis, and dull Aretine
But coldly imitated. Then, my glasses
Cut in more subtle angles, to disperse
And multiply the figures, as I walk
Naked between my succubae.[12] My mists
I'll have of perfume, vapor'd 'bout the room,
To lose our selves in; and my baths, like pits
To fall into; from whence we will come forth,
And roll us dry in gossamer and roses.—
Is it arrived ruby?——Where I spy
A wealthy citizen, or a rich lawyer,
Have a sublim'd[13] pure wife, unto that fellow
I'll send a thousand pound to be my cuckold.
Face. And I shall carry it?
Mam. No. I 'll ha' no bawds
But fathers and mothers: they will do it best,
Best of all others. And my flatterers
Shall be the pure and gravest of divines,
That I can get for money. My mere fools,
Eloquent burgesses, and then my poets
The same that writ so subtly of the fart,
Whom I will entertain still for that subject.
The few that would give out themselves to be
Court and town-stallions, and, eachwhere, belie
Ladies who are known most innocent, for them,—
Those will I beg, to make me eunuchs of:
And they shall fan me with ten estrich tails
A-piece, made in a plume to gather wind.
We will be brave, Puff, now we ha' the med'cine.
My meat shall all come in, in Indian shells,
Dishes of agate set in gold, and studded
With emeralds, sapphires, hyacinths, and rubies.
The tongues of carps, dormice, and camels' heels,
Boil'd i' the spirit of sol, and dissolv'd pearl
(Apicius'[14] diet, 'gainst the epilepsy):
And I will eat these broths with spoons of amber,
Headed with diamond and carbuncle.
My foot-boy shall eat pheasants, calver'd[15] salmons,
Knots,[16] godwits,[16] lampreys:[17] I myself will have
The beards of barbel[17] serv'd, instead of salads;
Oil'd mushrooms; and the swelling unctuous paps
Of a fat pregnant sow, newly cut off,
Drest with an exquisite and poignant sauce;
For which, I'll say unto my cook, *There 's gold;*
Go forth, and be a knight.[18]
Face. Sir, I'll go look
A little, how it heightens.
Exit.
Mam. Do.—My shirts
I 'll have of taffeta-sarsnet,[19] soft and light
As cobwebs; and for all my other raiment,
It shall be such as might provoke the Persian,
Were he to teach the world riot anew.
My gloves of fishes and birds' skins, perfum'd
With gums of paradise, and Eastern air——
Sur. And do you think to have the stone with this?
Mam. No, I do think t' have all this with the stone.
Sur. Why, I have heard he must be *homo frugi,*[20]

12 strumpets.
13 surpassing.
14 a famous epicure of Tiberius' time.
15 dressed in some particular fashion.
16 birds delicate to eat.
17 fish.
18 An allusion to James I's readiness to confer knighthood on all who could pay for the honor.
19 a fine, soft silk.
20 Piety was supposed to be an essential characteristic of a successful alchemist.

A pious, holy, and religious man,
One free from mortal sin, a very virgin.
Mam. That makes it, sir; he is so. But I buy it;
My venture brings it me. He, honest wretch,
A notable, superstitious, good soul,
Has worn his knees bare, and his slippers bald,
With prayer and fasting for it: and, sir, let him
Do it alone, for me, still. Here he comes.
Not a profane word afore him; 't is poison.—

SCENE 3.

Mammon, Surly. Enter Subtle.

Mam. Good morrow, father.
Sub. Gentle son, good morrow,
And to your friend there. What is he is with you?
Mam. An heretic, that I did bring along,
In hope, sir, to convert him.
Sub. Son, I doubt
You 're covetous, that thus you meet your time
I' the just point, prevent your day at morning.
This argues something worthy of a fear
Of importune and carnal appetite.
Take heed you do not cause the blessing leave you,
With your ungovern'd haste. I should be sorry
To see my labors, now e'en at perfection,
Got by long watching and large patience,
Not prosper where my love and zeal hath plac'd 'em.
Which (heaven I call to witness, with your self,
To whom I have pour'd my thoughts) in all my ends,
Have look'd no way, but unto public good,
To pious uses, and dear charity,
Now grown a prodigy with men. Wherein
If you, my son, should now prevaricate,
And to your own particular lusts employ
So great and catholic a bliss, be sure
A curse will follow, yea, and overtake
Your subtle and most secret ways.
Mam. I know, sir;
You shall not need to fear me; I but come
To ha' you confute this gentleman.
Sur. Who is,
Indeed, sir, somewhat costive of belief
Toward your stone; would not be gull'd.
Sub. Well, son,
All that I can convince him in, is this,
The work is done, bright Sol is in his robe.
We have a med'cine of the triple soul,
The glorified spirit. Thanks be to heaven,
And make us worthy of it!—*Ulen Spiegel!* [21]
Face. (*Within.*) Anon, sir.
Sub. Look well to the register.
And let your heat still lessen by degrees,
To the aludels.[22]
Face. (*Within.*) Yes, sir.
Sub. Did you look
O' the bolt's head yet?
Face. (*Within.*) Which? On D, sir?
Sub. Aye;
What 's the complexion?
Face. (*Within.*) Whitish.
Sub. Infuse vinegar,
To draw his volatile substance and his tincture:
And let the water in glass E be filt'red,
And put into the gripe's egg.[22] Lute [23] him well;
And leave him clos'd *in balneo.*[24]
Face. (*Within.*) I will, sir.
Sur. What a brave language here is! next to canting.[25]
Sub. I have another work you never saw, son,
That three days since past the philosopher's wheel,
In the lent [26] heat of Athanor; [27] and 's become
Sulphur o' Nature.
Mam. But 't is for me?
Sub. What need you?
You have enough, in that is, perfect.
Mam. O, but——
Sub. Why, this is covetise!
Mam. No, I assure you,
I shall employ it all in pious uses,
Founding of colleges and grammar schools,
Marrying young virgins, building hospitals,
And, now and then, a church.

Re-enter Face.

21 the rascally hero of a German jest-book.
22 vessels used in the alchemical process.
23 smear with clay for protection from the fire.
24 in the bath of warm water.
25 thieves' slang.
26 slow.
27 a furnace.

Sub. How now!
Face. Sir, please you,
Shall I not change the filter?
Sub. Marry, yes;
And bring me the complexion of glass B.
Exit Face.
Mam. Ha' you another?
Sub. Yes, son; were I assur'd
Your piety were firm, we would not want
The means to glorify it: but I hope the best.
I mean to tinct C in sand-heat to-morrow,
And give him imbibition.[28]
Mam. Of white oil?
Sub. No, sir, of red. F is come over the helm too,
I thank my maker, in S. Mary's bath,
And shows *lac virginis.* Blessed be heaven!
I sent you of his fæces there calcin'd:
Out of that calx, I ha' won the salt of mercury.
Mam. By pouring on your rectified water?
Sub. Yes, and reverberating[29] in Athanor.

Re-enter Face.

How now! what color says it?
Face. The ground black, sir.
Mam. That 's your crow's head?
Sur. Your cock's comb's, is it not?
Sub. No, 't is not perfect. Would it were the crow!
That work wants something.
Sur. (*Aside.*) O, I look'd for this,
The hay 's[30] a pitching.
Sub. Are you sure you loos'd 'em.
In their own menstrue?
Face. Yes, sir, and then married 'em,
And put 'em in a bolt's-head nipp'd to digestion,
According as you bade me, when I set
The liquor of Mars to circulation
In the same heat.
Sub. The process then was right.
Face. Yes, by the token, sir, the retort brake,
And what was sav'd was put into the pelican,[31]
And sign'd with Hermes' seal.[32]
Sub. I think 't was so.
We should have a new amalgama.
Sur. (*Aside.*) O, this ferret
Is rank as any polecat.
Sub. But I care not;
Let him e'en die; we have enough beside,
In embrion. H has his white shirt on?
Face. Yes, sir,
He 's ripe for inceration,[33] he stands warm,
In his ash-fire. I would not you should let
Any die now, if I might counsel, sir,
For luck's sake to the rest: it is not good.
Mam. He says right.
Sur. (*Aside.*) Aye, are you bolted? [34]
Face. Nay, I know 't, sir,
I 've seen th' ill fortune. What is some three ounces
Of fresh materials?
Mam. Is 't no more?
Face. No more, sir,
Of gold, t' amalgam with some six of mercury.
Mam. Away, here 's money. What will serve?
Face. Ask him, sir.
Mam. How much?
Sub. Give him nine pound: you may gi' him ten.
Sur. (*Aside.*) Yes, twenty, and be cozen'd, do.
Mam. There 't is.
(*Gives Face the money.*)
Sub. This needs not; but that you will have it so,
To see conclusions of all: for two
Of our inferior works are at fixation,
A third is in ascension. Go your ways.
Ha' you set the oil of Luna in kemia? [22]
Face. Yes, sir.
Sub. And the philosopher's vinegar?
Face. Aye. *Exit.*
Sur. We shall have a salad!
Mam. When do you make projection?
Sub. Son, be not hasty. I exalt our med'cine,
By hanging him *in balneo vaporoso,*
And giving him solution; then congeal him;
And then dissolve him; then again congeal him;
For look, how oft I iterate the work,
So many times I add unto his virtue.
As, if at first one ounce convert a hundred,
After his second loose, he 'll turn a thousand;

28 saturation.
29 heating by reflection.
30 a rabbit net; i.e. the snare is being laid.
31 alembic.
32 hermetically sealed.
33 softening.
34 driven out, like a rabbit.

His third solution, ten; his fourth, a hundred;
After his fifth, a thousand thousand ounces
Of any imperfect metal, into pure
Silver or gold, in all examinations,
As good as any of the natural mine.
Get you your stuff here against afternoon,
Your brass, your pewter, and your andirons.

Mam. Not those of iron?

Sub. Yes, you may bring them too;
We'll change all metals.

Sur. I believe you in that.

Mam. Then I may send my spits?

Sub. Yes, and your racks.

Sur. And dripping-pans, and pot-hangers, and hooks?
Shall he not?

Sub. If he please.

Sur. —To be an ass.

Sub. How, sir!

Mam. This gent'man you must bear withal.
I told you he had no faith.

Sur. And little hope, sir;
But much less charity, should I gull myself.

Sub. Why, what have you observ'd, sir, in our art,
Seems so impossible?

Sur. But your whole work, no more.
That you should hatch gold in a furnace, sir,
As they do eggs in Egypt!

Sub. Sir, do you
Believe that eggs are hatch'd so?

Sur. If I should?

Sub. Why, I think that the greater miracle.
No egg but differs from a chicken more
Than metals in themselves.

Sur. That cannot be.
The egg's ordain'd by nature to that end,
And is a chicken *in potentia.*

Sub. The same we say of lead and other metals,
Which would be gold if they had time.

Mam. And that
Our art doth further.

Sub. Aye, for 't were absurd
To think that nature in the earth bred gold
Perfect i' the instant: something went before.
There must be remote matter.

Sur. Aye, what is that?

Sub. Marry, we say——

Mam. Aye, now it heats: stand, father,
Pound him to dust.

Sub. It is, of the one part,
A humid exhalation, which we call
Materia liquida, or the unctuous water;
On th' other part, a certain crass and viscous
Portion of earth; both which, concorporate,
Do make the elementary matter of gold;
Which is not yet *propria materia,*
But common to all metals and all stones;
For, where it is forsaken of that moisture,
And hath more dryness, it becomes a stone:
Where it retains more of the humid fatness,
It turns to sulphur, or to quicksilver,
Who are the parents of all other metals.
Nor can this remote matter suddenly
Progress so from extreme unto extreme,
As to grow gold, and leap o'er all the means.
Nature doth first beget th' imperfect, then
Proceeds she to the perfect. Of that airy
And oily water, mercury is engend'red;
Sulphur o' the fat and earthy part; the one,
Which is the last, supplying the place of male,
The other of the female, in all metals.
Some do believe hermaphrodeity,
That both do act and suffer. But these two
Make the rest ductile, malleable, extensive.
And even in gold they are; for we do find
Seeds of them by our fire, and gold in them;
And can produce the species of each metal
More perfect thence, than nature doth in earth.
Beside, who doth not see in daily practice
Art can beget bees, hornets, beetles, wasps,
Out of the carcases and dung of creatures;
Yea, scorpions of an herb, being rightly plac'd?
And these are living creatures, far more perfect
And excellent than metals.

Mam. Well said, father!

Nay, if he take you in hand, sir, with an argument,
He 'll bray you in a mortar.
Sur. Pray you, sir, stay.
Rather than I'll be bray'd, sir, I'll believe
That Alchemy is a pretty kind of game,
Somewhat like tricks o' the cards, to cheat a man
With charming.
Sub. Sir?
Sur. What else are all your terms,
Whereon no one o' your writers 'grees with other?
Of your elixir, your *lac virginis*,
Your stone, your med'cine, and your chrysosperm,
Your sal, your sulphur, and your mercury,
Your oil of height, your tree of life, your blood,
Your marchesite, your tutie, your magnesia,
Your toad, your crow, your dragon, and your panther;
Your sun, your moon, your firmament, your adrop,
Your lato, azoch, zernich, chibrit, heautarit,
And then your red man, and your white woman,
With all your broths, your menstrues, and materials
Of piss and egg-shells, women's terms, man's blood,
Hair o' the head, burnt clouts, chalk, merds, and clay,
Powder of bones, scalings of iron, glass,
And worlds of other strange ingredients,
Would burst a man to name?
Sub. And all these, nam'd,
Intending but one thing; which art our writers
Us'd to obscure their art.
Mam. Sir, so I told him—
Because the simple idiot should not learn it.
And make it vulgar.
Sub. Was not all the knowledge
Of the Egyptians writ in mystic symbols?
Speak not the scriptures oft in parables?
Are not the choicest fables of the poets,
That were the fountains and first springs of wisdom,
Wrapt in perplexed allegories?
Mam. I urg'd that,
And clear'd to him, that Sisyphus was damn'd
To roll the ceaseless stone, only because
He would have made ours common. (*Dol is seen at the door.*)—Who is this?
Sub. God's precious!—What do you mean? Go in, good lady,
Let me entreat you. (*Dol retires.*)—Where 's this varlet?

Re-enter Face.

Face. Sir.
Sub. You very knave! do you use me thus?
Face. Wherein, sir?
Sub. Go in and see, you traitor. Go!
Exit Face.
Mam. Who is it, sir?
Sub. Nothing, sir; nothing.
Mam. What 's the matter, good sir?
I have not seen you thus distemp'red: who is 't?
Sub. All arts have still had, sir, their adversaries;
But ours the most ignorant.—

Face returns.

What now?
Face. 'T was not my fault, sir; she would speak with you.
Sub. Would she, sir! Follow me.
Exit.
Mam. (*Stopping him.*) Stay, Lungs.
Face. I dare not, sir.
Mam. How! pray thee, stay.
Face. She 's mad, sir, and sent hither—
Mam. Stay, man; what is she?
Face. A lord's sister, sir.
He 'll be mad too.—
Mam. I warrant thee.—Why sent hither?
Face. Sir, to be cur'd.
Sub. (*Within.*) Why, rascal!
Face. Lo you!—Here, sir!
Exit.
Mam. 'Fore God, a Bradamante,[35] a brave piece.
Sur. Heart, this is a bawdy-house! I'll be burnt else.
Mam. O, by this light, no: do not wrong him. He 's
Too scrupulous that way: it is his vice.
No, he 's a rare physician, do him right,
An excellent Paracelsian, and has done
Strange cures with mineral physic. He deals all
With spirits, he; he will not hear a word
Of Galen; or his tedious recipes.—

Face again.

35 a female warrior in Ariosto's *Orlando Furioso*.

How now, Lungs!
Face. Softly, sir; speak softly. I meant
To ha' told your worship all. This must not hear.
Mam. No, he will not be gull'd; let him alone.
Face. You 're very right, sir; she is a most rare scholar,
And is gone mad with studying Broughton's [36] works.
If you but name a word touching the Hebrew,
She falls into her fit, and will discourse
So learnedly of genealogies,
As you would run mad too, to hear her, sir.
Mam. How might one do t' have conference with her, Lungs?
Face. O, divers have run mad upon the conference.
I do not know, sir: I am sent in haste
To fetch a vial.
Sur. Be not gull'd, Sir Mammon.
Mam. Wherein? Pray ye, be patient.
Sur. Yes, as you are,
And trust confederate knaves and bawds and whores.
Mam. You are too foul, believe it.—Come here, *Ulen,*
One word.
Face. I dare not, in good faith. (*Going.*)
Mam. Stay, knave.
Face. He 's extreme angry that you saw her, sir.
Mam. Drink that. (*Gives him money.*) What is she when she 's out of her fit?
Face. O, the most affablest creature, sir! so merry!
So pleasant! She 'll mount you up, like quicksilver,
Over the helm; and circulate like oil,
A very vegetal: discourse of state,
Of mathematics, bawdry, anything——
Mam. Is she no way accessible? no means,
No trick to give a man a taste of her——wit——
Or so?
Sub. (*Within.*) *Ulen!*
Face. I 'll come to you again, sir. *Exit.*
Mam. Surly, I did not think one o' your breeding
Would traduce personages of worth.
Sur. Sir Epicure,
Your friend to use; yet still loth to be gull'd:
I do not like your philosophical bawds.
Their stone is lechery enough to pay for,
Without this bait.
Mam. Heart, you abuse yourself.
I know the lady, and her friends, and means,
The original of this disaster. Her brother
Has told me all.
Sur. And yet you ne'er saw her
Till now!
Mam. O yes, but I forgot. I have, believe it,
One o' the treacherous'st memories, I do think,
Of all mankind.
Sur. What call you her brother?
Mam. My lord——
He wi' not have his name known, now I think on 't.
Sur. A very treacherous memory!
Mam. O' my faith——
Sur. Tut, if you ha' it not about you, pass it
Till we meet next.
Mam. Nay, by this hand, 't is true.
He 's one I honor, and my noble friend;
And I respect his house.
Sur. Heart! can it be
That a grave sir, a rich, that has no need,
A wise sir, too, at other times, should thus,
With his own oaths, and arguments, make hard means
To gull himself? An this be your elixir,
Your *lapis mineralis,* and your lunary,[37]
Give me your honest trick yet at primero,[38]
Or gleek,[38] and take your *lutum sapientis,*
Your *menstruum simplex!* I 'll have gold before you,
And with less danger of the quicksilver,
Or the hot sulphur.

Re-enter Face.

Face. (*To Surly.*) Here 's one from Captain Face, sir,
Desires you meet him i' the Temple-church,
Some half-hour hence, and upon earnest business.
Sir (*Whispers Mammon*), if you please to quit us now, and come

36 Hugh Broughton (1549–1612), a rabbinical scholar.

37 The herb moonwort.

38 games at cards.

Again within two hours, you shall have
My master busy examining o' the works;
And I will steal you in unto the party,
That you may see her converse.—Sir, shall I say
You 'll meet the captain's worship?

Sur. Sir, I will.—
(*Walks aside.*)
But, by attorney, and to a second purpose.
Now, I am sure it is a bawdy-house;
I'll swear it, were the marshal here to thank me:
The naming this commander doth confirm it.
Don Face! why, he 's the most authentic dealer
I' these commodities, the superintendent
To all the quainter traffickers in town!
He is the visitor, and does appoint
Who lies with whom, and at what hour; what price;
Which gown, and in what smock; what fall,[39] what tire.[40]
Him will I prove, by a third person, to find
The subtleties of this dark labyrinth:
Which if I do discover, dear Sir Mammon,
You'll give your poor friend leave, though no philosopher,
To laugh; for you that are, 't is thought, shall weep.

Face. Sir, he does pray you 'll not forget.

Sur. I will not, sir.
Sir Epicure, I shall leave you.
Exit.

Mam. I follow you straight.

Face. But do so, good sir, to avoid suspicion.
This gent'man has a parlous head.

Mam. But wilt thou, *Ulen,*
Be constant to thy promise?

Face. As my life, sir.

Mam. And wilt thou insinuate what I am, and praise me,
And say I am a noble fellow?

Face. O, what else, sir?
And that you 'll make her royal with the stone,
An empress; and yourself King of Bantam.

Mam. Wilt thou do this?

Face. Will I, sir!

Mam. Lungs, my Lungs!
I love thee.

Face. Send your stuff, sir, that my master
May busy himself about projection.

Mam. Thou 'st witch'd me, rogue: take, go.
(*Gives him money.*)

Face. Your jack,[41] and all, sir.

Mam. Thou art a villain—I will send my jack,
And the weights too. Slave, I could bite thine ear.
Away, thou dost not care for me.

Face. Not I, sir!

Mam. Come, I was born to make thee, my good weasel,
Set thee on a bench, and ha' thee twirl a chain
With the best lord's vermin of 'em all.

Face. Away, sir.

Mam. A count, nay, a count palatine——

Face. Good sir, go.

Mam. Shall not advance thee better: no, nor faster.
Exit.

SCENE 4.

Face. Re-enter Subtle and Dol.

Sub. Has he bit? has he bit?

Face. And swallow'd, too, my Subtle.
I ha' given him line, and now he plays, i' faith.

Sub. And shall we twitch him?

Face. Thorough both the gills.
A wench is a rare bait, with which a man
No sooner 's taken, but he straight firks mad.

Sub. Dol, my Lord What's-hum's sister, you must now
Bear yourself *statelich.*

Dol. O, let me alone,
I'll not forget my race, I warrant you.
I'll keep my distance, laugh and talk aloud;
Have all the tricks of a proud scurvy lady,
And be as rude 's her woman.

Face. Well said, sanguine![42]

Sub. But will he send his andirons?

Face. His jack too,
And 's iron shoeing-horn; I ha' spoke to him. Well,
I must not lose my wary gamester yonder.

Sub. O, Monsieur Caution, that will not be gull'd?

Face. Aye,
If I can strike a fine hook into him, now!—

39 a collar, or a veil.
40 a head-dress.
41 a machine for turning a spit.
42 with light hair and ruddy complexion.

The Temple-church, there I have cast mine angle.
Well, pray for me. I'll about it.
(*One knocks.*)
Sub. What, more gudgeons![43]
Dol, scout, scout! (*Dol goes to the window.*) Stay, Face, you must go to the door;
'Pray God it be my anabaptist—Who is 't, Dol?
Dol. I know him not: he looks like a gold-end-man.[44]
Sub. Gods so! 't is he, he said he would send—what call you him?
The sanctified elder, that should deal
For Mammon's jack and andirons. Let him in.
Stay, help me off, first, with my gown.
(*Exit Face with the gown.*) Away,
Madam, to your withdrawing chamber. Now,
Exit Dol.
In a new tune, new gesture, but old language.—
This fellow is sent from one negotiates with me
About the stone too, for the holy brethren
Of Amsterdam, the exil'd saints, that hope
To raise their discipline[45] by it. I must use him
In some strange fashion now, to make him admire me.

Scene 5.

Subtle. Enter Ananias.

Where is my drudge?
Enter Face.
Face. Sir!
Sub. Take away the recipient,
And rectify your menstrue from the phlegma.
Then pour it on the Sol, in the cucurbite,
And let 'em macerate together.
Face. Yes, sir.
And save the ground?
Sub. No: *terra damnata*
Must not have entrance in the work.—Who are you?
Ana. A faithful brother, if it please you.
Sub. What's that?
A Lullianist? a Ripley?[46] *Filius artis?*
Can you sublime and dulcify? Calcine?
Know you the sapor pontic? Sapor stiptic?
Or what is homogene, or heterogene?
Ana. I understand no heathen language, truly.
Sub. Heathen! You Knipperdoling?[47] Is Ars sacra,
Or chrysopoeia, or spagyrica,
Or the pamphysic, or panarchic knowledge,
A heathen language?
Ana. Heathen Greek, I take it.
Sub. How! Heathen Greek?
Ana. All 's heathen but the Hebrew.
Sub. Sirrah my varlet, stand you forth and speak to him
Like a philosopher: answer i' the language.
Name the vexations, and the martyrizations
Of metals in the work.
Face. Sir, putrefaction,
Solution, ablution, sublimation,
Cohobation, calcination, ceration, and
Fixation.
Sub. This is heathen Greek, to you, now!—
And when comes vivification?
Face. After mortification.
Sub. What's cohobation?
Face. 'T is the pouring on
Your *aqua regis,* and then drawing him off,
To the trine circle of the seven spheres.
Sub. What's the proper passion of metals?
Face. Malleation.
Sub. What's your *ultimum supplicium auri?*
Face. Antimonium.
Sub. This's heathen Greek to you!—And what's your mercury?
Face. A very fugitive, he will be gone, sir.
Sub. How know you him?
Face. By his viscosity,
His oleosity, and his suscitability.
Sub. How do you sublime him?
Face. With the calce of egg-shells,
White marble, talc.
Sub. Your magisterium now,
What's that?
Face. Shifting, sir, your elements,
Dry into cold, cold into moist, moist into hot,

43 fools.
44 a buyer of broken pieces of gold.
45 Puritan form of church government. (Neilson.)
46 Lully and Ripley were writers on alchemy.
47 A German Anabaptist.

Hot into dry.
Sub. This is heathen Greek to you still!
Your *lapis philosophicus?*
Face. 'T is a stone,
And not a stone; a spirit, a soul, and a body:
Which if you do dissolve, it is dissolv'd;
If you coagulate, it is coagulated;
If you make it to fly, it flieth.
Sub. Enough.
Exit Face.
This 's heathen Greek to you! What are you, sir?
Ana. Please you, a servant of the exil'd brethren,
That deal with widows' and with orphans' goods,
And make a just account unto the saints:
A deacon.
Sub. O, you are sent from Master Wholesome,
Your teacher?
Ana. From Tribulation Wholesome,
Our very zealous pastor.
Sub. Good! I have
Some orphans' goods to come here.
Ana. Of what kind, sir?
Sub. Pewter and brass, andirons and kitchenware.
Metals, that we must use our med'cine on:
Wherein the brethren may have a penn'orth
For ready money.
Ana. Were the orphans' parents
Sincere professors?
Sub. Why do you ask?
Ana. Because
We then are to deal justly, and give, in truth,
Their utmost value.
Sub. 'Slid, you 'd cozen else,
An if their parents were not of the faithful!—
I will not trust you, now I think on it,
Till I ha' talk'd with your pastor. Ha' you brought money
To buy more coals?
Ana. No, surely.
Sub. No? How so?
Ana. The brethren bid me say unto you, sir,
Surely, they will not venture any more
Till they may see projection.
Sub. How!
Ana. You 've had
For the instruments, as bricks, and loam, and glasses,
Already thirty pound; and for materials,
They say, some ninety more: and they have heard since,
That one, at Heidelberg, made it of an egg,
And a small paper of pin-dust.
Sub. What 's your name?
Ana. My name is Ananias.
Sub. Out! the varlet
That cozen'd the apostles! Hence, away!
Flee, mischief! had your holy consistory
No name to send me, of another sound
Than wicked Ananias? Send your elders
Hither, to make atonement for you, quickly,
And gi' me satisfaction; or out goes
The fire; and down th' alembics, and the furnace,
Piger Henricus, or what not. Thou wretch!
Both *sericon* and *bufo* shall be lost,
Tell 'em. All hope of rooting out the bishops,
Or th' anti-Christian hierarchy shall perish,
If they stay threescore minutes: the aqueity,
Terreity, and sulphureity
Shall run together again, and all be annull'd,
Thou wicked Ananias! (*Exit Ananias.*) This will fetch 'em,
And make 'em haste towards their gulling more.
A man must deal like a rough nurse, and fright
Those that are froward, to an appetite.

Scene 6.

Subtle. Enter Face in his uniform, followed by Drugger.

Face. He 's busy with his spirits, but we 'll upon him.
Sub. How now! What mates, what Bayards [48] ha' we here?
Face. I told you he would be furious.—Sir, here 's Nab
Has brought you another piece of gold to look on;
—We must appease him. Give it me,—and prays you,

[48] "Bayard, the type of chivalry and soldierly bearing, in allusion to Face's uniform and Drugger's smart bearing." (Schelling.)

You would devise—what is it, Nab?
Drug. A sign, sir.
Face. Aye, a good lucky one, a thriving sign, doctor.
Sub. I was devising now.
Face. (*Aside to Subtle.*) 'Slight, do not say so,
He will repent he ga' you any more.—
What say you to his constellation, doctor,
The Balance?
Sub. No, that way is stale and common.
A townsman born in Taurus, gives the bull,
Or the bull's head: in Aries, the ram.—
A poor device! No, I will have his name
Form'd in some mystic character; whose *radii*,
Striking the senses of the passers-by,
Shall, by a virtual influence, breed affections,
That may result upon the party owns it:
As thus——
Face. Nab!
Sub. He first shall have *a bell*, that 's *Abel;*
And by it standing one whose name is *Dee*,[49]
In a *rug* gown, there 's *D*, and *Rug*, that 's *drug;*
And right anenst him a dog snarling *er;*
There 's Drugger, Abel Drugger. That 's his sign.
And here 's now mystery and hieroglyphic!
Face. Abel, thou art made.
Drug. Sir, I do thank his worship.
Face. Six o' thy legs[50] more will not do it, Nab.
He has brought you a pipe of tobacco, doctor.
Drug. Yes, sir;
I have another thing I would impart——
Face. Out with it, Nab.
Drug. Sir, there is lodg'd, hard by me,
A rich young widow——
Face. Good! a bona roba?[51]
Drug. But nineteen at the most.
Face. Very good, Abel.
Drug. Marry, she 's not in fashion yet; she wears
A hood, but 't stands a-cop.[52]
Face. No matter, Abel.
Drug. And I do now and then give her a fucus——
Face. What! dost thou deal, Nab?
Sub. I did tell you, captain.
Drug. And physic too, sometime, sir; for which she trusts me
With all her mind. She 's come up here of purpose
To learn the fashion.
Face. Good (his match too!)—On, Nab.
Drug. And she does strangely long to know her fortune.
Face. God's lid, Nab, send her to the doctor, hither.
Drug. Yes, I have spoke to her of his worship already;
But she 's afraid it will be blown abroad,
And hurt her marriage.
Face. Hurt it! 't is the way
To heal it, if 't were hurt; to make it more
Follow'd and sought. Nab, thou shalt tell her this.
She 'll be more known, more talk'd of; and your widows
Are ne'er of any price till they be famous;
Their honor is their multitude of suitors.
Send her, it may be thy good fortune. What!
Thou dost not know?
Drug. No, sir, she 'll never marry
Under a knight: her brother has made a vow.
Face. What! and dost thou despair, my little Nab,
Knowing what the doctor has set down for thee,
And seeing so many o' the city dubb'd?
One glass o' thy water, with a madam I know,
Will have it done, Nab. What 's her brother? a knight?
Drug. No, sir, a gentleman newly warm in 's land, sir,
Scarce cold in his one and twenty, that does govern
His sister here; and is a man himself
Of some three thousand a year, and is come up
To learn to quarrel, and to live by his wits,
And will go down again, and die i' the country.
Face. How! to quarrel?
Drug. Yes, sir, to carry quarrels,
As gallants do; to manage 'em by line.
Face. 'Slid, Nab, the doctor is the only man

49 Dr. John Dee (1527–1608), an astrologer of great repute.
50 bows.
51 handsome wench.
52 on the top of the head.

In Christendom for him. He has made a table,
With mathematical demonstrations,
Touching the art of quarrels: he will give him
An instrument to quarrel by. Go, bring 'em both,
Him and his sister. And, for thee, with her
The doctor happ'ly may persuade. Go to:
'Shalt give his worship a new damask suit
Upon the premises.
Sub. O, good captain!
Face. He shall;
He is the honestest fellow, doctor. Stay not,
No offers; bring the damask, and the parties.
Drug. I'll try my power, sir.
Face. And thy will too, Nab.
Sub. 'T is good tobacco, this! What is 't an ounce?
Face. He'll send you a pound, doctor.
Sub. O no.
Face. He will do 't.
It is the goodest soul!—Abel, about it.
Thou shalt know more anon. Away, be gone.
Exit Abel.
A miserable rogue, and lives with cheese,
And has the worms. That was the cause, indeed,
Why he came now: he dealt with me in private,
To get a med'cine for 'em.
Sub. And shall, sir. This works.
Face. A wife, a wife for one on 's, my dear Subtle!
We'll e'en draw lots, and he that fails, shall have
The more in goods, the other has in tail.
Sub. Rather the less; for she may be so light
She may want grains.
Face. Aye; or be such a burden,
A man would scarce endure her for the whole.
Sub. Faith, best let's see her first, and then determine.
Face. Content: but Dol must ha' no breath on 't.
Sub. Mum.
Away you, to your Surly yonder, catch him.
Face. Pray God I ha' not stay'd too long.
Sub. I fear it.
Exeunt.

ACT III.

SCENE 1. *The lane before Lovewit's house.*

Enter Tribulation Wholesome and Ananias.

Tri. These chastisements are common to the saints,
And such rebukes we of the separation
Must bear with willing shoulders, as the trials
Sent forth to tempt our frailties.
Ana. In pure zeal
I do not like the man; he is a heathen,
And speaks the language of Canaan, truly.
Tri. I think him a profane person indeed.
Ana. He bears
The visible mark of the beast in his forehead.
And for his stone, it is a work of darkness,
And with philosophy blinds the eyes of man.
Tri. Good brother, we must bend unto all means
That may give furtherance to the holy cause.
Ana. Which his cannot: the sanctified cause
Should have a sanctified course.
Tri. Not always necessary:
The children of perdition are oft times
Made instruments even of the greatest works.
Beside, we should give somewhat to man's nature,
The place he lives in, still about the fire,
And fume of metals, that intoxicate
The brain of man, and make him prone to passion.
Where have you greater atheists than your cooks?
Or more profane or choleric, than your glassmen?
More anti-Christian than your bell-founders?
What makes the devil so devilish, I would ask you,
Satan, our common enemy, but his being
Perpetually about the fire, and boiling
Brimstone and arsenic? We must give, I say,
Unto the motives, and the stirrers up
Of humors in the blood. It may be so,
When as the work is done, the stone is made,
This heat of his may turn into a zeal,

And stand up for the beauteous discipline
Against the menstrous[53] cloth and rag of Rome.
We must await his calling, and the coming
Of the good spirit. You did fault, t' upbraid him
With the brethren's blessing of Heidelberg, weighing
What need we have to hasten on the work,
For the restoring of the silenc'd saints,[54]
Which ne'er will be but by the philosopher's stone.
And so a learned elder, one of Scotland,
Assur'd me; *aurum potabile* being
The only med'cine for the civil magistrate,
T' incline him to a feeling of the cause;
And must be daily us'd in the disease.

Ana. I have not edified more, truly, by man;
Not since the beautiful light first shone on me:
And I am sad my zeal hath so offended.

Tri. Let us call on him then.

Ana. The motion 's good,
And of the spirit; I will knock first.
(*Knocks.*) Peace be within!

The door is opened, and they enter.

SCENE 2. *A room in Lovewit's house.*

Enter Subtle, followed by Tribulation and Ananias.

Sub. O, are you come? 'T was time. Your threescore minutes
Were at last thread, you see; and down had gone
Furnus acediae, turris circulatorius:
Lembic, bolt's-head, retort, and pelican
Had all been cinders. Wicked Ananias!
Art thou return'd? Nay, then it goes down yet.

Tri. Sir, be appeased; he is come to humble
Himself in spirit, and to ask your patience,
If too much zeal hath carried him aside
From the due path.

Sub. Why, this doth qualify!

Tri. The brethren had no purpose, verily,
To give you the least grievance; but are ready
To lend their willing hands to any project
The spirit and you direct.

Sub. This qualifies more!

Tri. And for the orphans' goods, let them be valu'd,
Or what is needful else to the holy work,
It shall be numb'red; here, by me, the saints
Throw down their purse before you.

Sub. This qualifies most!
Why, thus it should be, now you understand.
Have I discours'd so unto you of our stone,
And of the good that it shall bring your cause?
Show'd you (beside the main of hiring forces
Abroad, drawing the Hollanders, your friends,
From th' Indies, to serve you, with all their fleet)
That even the med'cinal use shall make you a faction
And party in the realm? As, put the case,
That some great man in state, he have the gout,
Why, you but send three drops of your elixir,
You help him straight: there you have made a friend.
Another has the palsy or the dropsy,
He takes of your incombustible stuff,
He 's young again: there you have made a friend.
A lady that is past the feat of body,
Though not of mind, and hath her face decay'd
Beyond all cure of paintings, you restore
With the oil of talc: there you have made a friend;
And all her friends. A lord that is a leper,
A knight that has the bone-ache, or a squire
That hath both these, you make 'em smooth and sound
With a bare fricace[55] of your med'cine; still
You increase your friends.

Tri. Aye, 't is very pregnant.

Sub. And then the turning of this lawyer's pewter
To plate at Christmas——

Ana. Christ-tide,[56] I pray you.

53 polluted.
54 Non-conformist ministers not allowed to preach. (Neilson.)
55 rubbing.
56 because the Puritans objected to the use of the word *mass* in *Christmas*

Sub. Yet, Ananias!
Ana. I have done.
Sub. Or changing
His parcel[57] gilt to massy gold. You cannot
But raise you friends. Withal, to be of power
To pay an army in the field, to buy
The King of France out of his realms, or Spain
Out of his Indies. What can you not do
Against lords spiritual or temporal,
That shall oppone[58] you?
Tri. Verily, 't is true.
We may be temporal lords ourselves, I take it.
Sub. You may be anything, and leave off to make
Long-winded exercises; or suck up
Your *ha!* and *hum!* in a tune. I not deny,
But such as are not graced in a state,
May, for their ends, be adverse in religion,
And get a tune to call the flock together:
For, to say sooth, a tune does much with women
And other phlegmatic people; it is your bell.
Ana. Bells are profane; a tune may be religious.
Sub. No warning with you? Then farewell my patience.
'Slight, it shall down; I will not be thus tortur'd.
Tri. I pray you, sir.
Sub. All shall perish. I have spoke it.
Tri. Let me find grace, sir, in your eyes; the man,
He stands corrected; neither did his zeal,
But as your self, allow a tune somewhere,
Which now, being tow'rd the stone, we shall not need.
Sub. No, nor your holy vizard, to win widows
To give you legacies; or make zealous wives
To rob their husbands for the common cause:
Nor take the start of bonds broke but one day,
And say they were forfeited by providence.
Nor shall you need o'er night to eat huge meals,
To celebrate your next day's fast the better;
The whilst the brethren and the sisters humbled,
Abate the stiffness of the flesh. Nor cast
Before your hungry hearers scrupulous bones;
As whether a Christian may hawk or hunt,
Or whether matrons of the holy assembly
May lay their hair out, or wear doublets,
Or have that idol, starch, about their linen.
Ana. It is indeed an idol.
Tri. Mind him not, sir.
I do command thee, spirit (of zeal, but trouble),
To peace within him! Pray you, sir, go on.
Sub. Nor shall you need to libel 'gainst the prelates,
And shorten so your ears[59] against the hearing
Of the next wire-drawn grace. Nor of necessity
Rail against plays, to please the alderman
Whose daily custard you devour; nor lie
With zealous rage till you are hoarse. Not one
Of these so singular arts. Nor call yourselves
By names of Tribulation, Persecution,
Restraint, Long-patience, and such like, affected
By the whole family or wood[60] of you,
Only for glory, and to catch the ear
Of the disciple.
Tri. Truly, sir, they are
Ways that the godly brethren have invented,
For propagation of the glorious cause,
As very notable means, and whereby also
Themselves grow soon, and profitably, famous.
Sub. O, but the stone, all's idle to't! Nothing!
The art of angels, nature's miracle,
The divine secret that doth fly in clouds
From east to west: and whose tradition
Is not from men, but spirits.
Ana. I hate traditions;
I do not trust them——
Tri. Peace!

57 partly. 58 oppose. 59 in the pillory. 60 crowd.

Ana. They are popish all.
I will not peace: I will not——

Tri. Ananias!

Ana. Please the profane, to grieve the godly; I may not.

Sub. Well, Ananias, thou shalt overcome.

Tri. It is an ignorant zeal that haunts him, sir:
But truly else a very faithful brother,
A botcher,[61] and a man by revelation
That hath a competent knowledge of the truth.

Sub. Has he a competent sum there i' the bag
To buy the goods within? I am made guardian,
And must, for charity and conscience' sake,
Now see the most be made for my poor orphan;
Though I desire the brethren, too, good gainers:
There they are within. When you have view'd and bought 'em,
And ta'en the inventory of what they are,
They are ready for projection; there 's no more
To do: cast on the med'cine, so much silver
As there is tin there, so much gold as brass,
I 'll gi' it you in by weight.

Tri. But how long time,
Sir, must the saints expect yet?

Sub. Let me see,
How 's the moon now? Eight, nine, ten days hence,
He will be silver potate; then three days
Before he citronise.[62] Some fifteen days,
The magisterium will be perfected.

Ana. About the second day of the third week,
In the ninth month?

Sub. Yes, my good Ananias.

Tri. What will the orphans' goods arise to, think you?

Sub. Some hundred marks, as much as fill'd three cars,
Unladed now: you 'll make six millions of 'em——
But I must ha' more coals laid in.

Tri. How?

Sub. Another load,
And then we ha' finish'd. We must now increase
Our fire to *ignis ardens;* we are past.
Fimus equinus, balnei, cineris,
And all those lenter [63] heats. If the holy purse
Should with this draught fall low, and that the saints
Do need a present sum, I have a trick
To melt the pewter you shall buy now instantly,
And with a tincture make you as good Dutch dollars
As any are in Holland.

Tri. Can you so?

Sub. Aye, and shall bide the third examination.

Ana. It will be joyful tidings to the brethren.

Sub. But you must carry it secret.

Tri. Aye; but stay,
This act of coining, is it lawful?

Ana. Lawful!
We know no magistrate: or, if we did,
This 's foreign coin.

Sub. It is no coining, sir.
It is but casting.

Tri. Ha! you distinguish well:
Casting of money may be lawful.

Ana. 'T is, sir.

Tri. Truly, I take it so.

Sub. There is no scruple,
Sir, to be made of it; believe Ananias;
This case of conscience he is studied in.

Tri. I 'll make a question of it to the brethren.

Ana. The brethren shall approve it lawful, doubt not.
Where shall 't be done?

Sub. For that we 'll talk anon.
(*Knock without.*)
There 's some to speak with me. Go in, I pray you,
And view the parcels. That 's the inventory.
I 'll come to you straight. (*Exeunt Tri. and Ana.*) Who is it?—Face! appear.

Scene 3.

Subtle. Enter Face in his uniform.

Sub. How now! good prize?

Face. Good pox! Yond' costive cheater
Never came on.

Sub. How then?

Face. I ha' walk'd the round
Till now, and no such thing.

Sub. And ha' you quit him?

61 a mender of clothes or shoes. 62 turn yellow. 63 gentler.

Face. Quit him! An hell would quit him too, he were happy.
'Slight! would you have me stalk like a mill-jade,
All day, for one that will not yield us grains?
I know him of old.

Sub. O, but to ha' gull'd him,
Had been a mastery.

Face. Let him go, black boy![64]
And turn thee, that some fresh news may possess thee.
A noble count, a don of Spain (my dear
Delicious compeer, and my party-bawd),
Who is come hither private for his conscience
And brought munition with him, six great slops,[65]
Bigger than three Dutch hoys,[66] beside round trunks,
Furnish'd with pistolets,[67] and pieces of eight,
Will straight be here, my rogue, to have thy bath,
(That is the color,[68]) and to make his batt'ry
Upon our Dol, our castle, our cinqueport,
Our Dover pier, our what thou wilt. Where is she?
She must prepare perfumes, delicate linen,
The bath in chief, a banquet, and her wit,
For she must milk his epididimis.
Where is the doxy?

Sub. I'll send her to thee:
And but despatch my brace of little John Leydens[69]
And come again myself.

Face. Are they within then?

Sub. Numb'ring the sun.

Face. How much?

Sub. A hundred marks, boy. *Exit.*

Face. Why, this is a lucky day. Ten pounds of Mammon!
Three o' my clerk! A portague o' my grocer!
This o' the brethren! Beside reversions
And states to come, i' the widow, and my count!
My share to-day will not be bought for forty——

Enter Dol.

Dol. What?

Face. Pounds, dainty Dorothy! Art thou so near?

Dol. Yes; say, lord general, how fares our camp?

Face. As with the few that had entrench'd themselves
Safe, by their discipline, against a world, Dol,
And laugh'd within those trenches, and grew fat
With thinking on the booties, Dol, brought in
Daily by their small parties. This dear hour,
A doughty don is taken with my Dol;
And thou mayst make his ransom what thou wilt,
My Dousabel; he shall be brought here, fetter'd
With thy fair looks, before he sees thee; and thrown
In a down-bed, as dark as any dungeon;
Where thou shalt keep him waking with thy drum;
Thy drum, my Dol, thy drum; till he be tame
As the poor blackbirds were i' the great frost,
Or bees are with a basin; and so hive him
I' the swan-skin coverlid and cambric sheets,
Till he work honey and wax, my little God's-gift.[70]

Dol. What is he, general?

Face. An adalantado,[71]
A grandee, girl. Was not my Dapper here yet?

Dol. No.

Face. Nor my Drugger?

Dol. Neither.

Face. A pox on 'em.
They are so long a-furnishing! such stinkards
Would not be seen upon these festival days.—

Re-enter Subtle.

How now! ha' you done?

Sub. Done. They are gone: the sum
Is here in bank, my Face. I would we knew
Another chapman now who would buy 'em outright.

Face. 'Slid, Nab shall do 't against he ha' the widow,
To furnish household.

64 knave.
65 large breeches.
66 small sloops.
67 Spanish coins.
68 pretext.
69 Leyden was an Anabaptist leader.
70 the literal meaning of *Dorothy*.
71 governor of a province.

Sub. Excellent, well thought on:
Pray God he come.
Face. I pray he keep away
Till our new business be o'erpast.
Sub. But, Face,
How camst thou by this secret don?
Face. A spirit
Brought me th' intelligence in a paper here,
As I was conjuring yonder in my circle
For Surly; I ha' my flies abroad. Your bath
Is famous, Subtle, by my means. Sweet Dol,
You must go tune your virginal, no losing
O' the least time. And—do you hear?—good action!
Firk like a flounder; kiss like a scallop, close;
And tickle him with thy mother-tongue. His great
Verdugoship has not a jot of language;
So much the easier to be cozen'd, my Dolly.
He will come here in a hir'd coach, obscure,
And our own coachman, whom I have sent as guide,
No creature else. (*One knocks.*) Who 's that?
Exit Dol.
Sub. It is not he?
Face. O no, not yet this hour.

Re-enter Dol.

Sub. Who is 't?
Dol. Dapper,
Your clerk.
Face. God's will then, Queen of Fairy,
On with your tire; (*Exit Dol.*) and, doctor, with your robes.
Let 's despatch him for God's sake.
Sub. 'T will be long.
Face. I warrant you, take but the cues I give you,
It shall be brief enough. (*Goes to the window.*) 'Slight, here are more!
Abel, and I think the angry boy, the heir,
That fain would quarrel.
Sub. And the widow?
Face. No,
Not that I see. Away!
Exit Sub.

Scene 4.

Face. Enter Dapper.

Face. O, sir, you are welcome.
The doctor is within a moving for you;
I have had the most ado to win him to it!—
He swears you 'll be the darling o' the dice:
He never heard her highness dote till now.
Your aunt has giv'n you the most gracious words
That can be thought on.
Dap. Shall I see her grace?
Face. See her, and kiss her too.—

Enter Abel, followed by Kastril.

What, honest Nab!
Hast brought the damask?
Drug. No, sir; here 's tobacco.
Face. 'T is well done, Nab; thou 'lt bring the damask too?
Drug. Yes. Here 's the gentleman, captain, Master Kastril,
I have brought to see the doctor.
Face. Where 's the widow?
Drug. Sir, as he likes, his sister, he says, shall come.
Face. O, is it so? Good time. Is your name Kastril, sir?
Kas. Aye, and the best o' the Kastrils, I 'd be sorry else,
By fifteen hundred a year. Where is this doctor?
My mad tobacco-boy here tells me of one
That can do things. Has he any skill?
Face. Wherein, sir?
Kas. To carry a business, manage a quarrel fairly,
Upon fit terms.
Face. It seems, sir, you 're but young
About the town, that can make that a question.
Kas. Sir, not so young but I have heard some speech
Of the angry boys,[72] and seen 'em take tobacco;
And in his shop; and I can take it too.
And I would fain be one of 'em, and go down
And practise i' the country.
Face. Sir, for the duello,
The doctor, I assure you, shall inform you,
To the least shadow of a hair; and show you

[72] "roaring boys," bravadoes.

An instrument he has of his own making,
Wherewith, no sooner shall you make report
Of any quarrel, but he will take the height on 't
Most instantly, and tell in what degree
Of safety it lies in, or mortality.
And how it may be borne, whether in a right line,
Or a half circle; or may else be cast
Into an angle blunt, if not acute:
And this he will demonstrate. And then, rules
To give and take the lie by.
Kas. How! to take it?
Face. Yes, in oblique he 'll show you, or in circle;[73]
But ne'er in diameter.[74] The whole town
Study his theorems, and dispute them ordinarily
At the eating academies.
Kas. But does he teach
Living by the wits too?
Face. Anything whatever.
You cannot think that subtlety but he reads it.
He made me a captain. I was a stark pimp,
Just o' your standing, 'fore I met with him;
It 's not two months since. I 'll tell you his method:
First, he will enter you at some ordinary.
Kas. No, I 'll not come there: you shall pardon me.
Face. For why, sir?
Kas. There 's gaming there, and tricks.
Face. Why, would you be
A gallant, and not game?
Kas. Aye, 't will spend a man.
Face. Spend you! It will repair you when you are spent.
How do they live by their wits there, that have vented
Six times your fortunes?
Kas. What, three thousand a year!
Face. Aye, forty thousand.
Kas. Are there such?
Face. Aye, sir,
And gallants yet. Here 's a young gentleman
Is born to nothing.—(*Points to Dapper.*) forty marks a year
Which I count nothing:—he 's to be initiated,
And have a fly o' the doctor. He will win you
By unresistible luck, within this fortnight,
Enough to buy a barony. They will set him
Upmost, at the groom porter's,[75] all the Christmas:
And for the whole year through at every place
Where there is play, present him with the chair,
The best attendance, the best drink, sometimes
Two glasses of Canary, and pay nothing;
The purest linen and the sharpest knife,
The partridge next his trencher: and somewhere
The dainty bed, in private, with the dainty.
You shall ha' your ordinaries bid for him,
As playhouses for a poet; and the master
Pray him aloud to name what dish he affects,
Which must be butter'd shrimps: and those that drink
To no mouth else, will drink to his, as being
The goodly president mouth of all the board.
Kas. Do you not gull one?
Face. 'Ods my life! Do you think it?
You shall have a cast[76] commander, (can but get
In credit with a glover, or a spurrier,
For some two pair of either's ware aforehand,)
Will, by most swift posts, dealing [but] with him,
Arrive at competent means to keep himself,
His punk, and naked boy, in excellent fashion,
And be admir'd for 't.
Kas. Will the doctor teach this?
Face. He will do more, sir: when your land is gone,
(As men of spirit hate to keep earth long),
In a vacation,[77] when small money is stirring,
And ordinaries suspended till the term,
He 'll show a perspective,[78] where on one side

73 the lie circumstantial
74 the lie direct.
75 an official having charge of the gaming at court.
76 discharged.
77 between terms of the law-courts.
78 conjuror's glass.

You shall behold the faces and the persons
Of all sufficient young heirs in town,
Whose bonds are current for commodity; [79]
On th' other side, the merchants' forms, and others,
That without help of any second broker,
Who would expect a share, will trust such parcels:
In the third square, the very street and sign
Where the commodity dwells, and does but wait
To be deliver'd, be it pepper, soap,
Hops, or tobacco, oatmeal, woad,[80] or cheeses.
All which you may so handle, to enjoy
To your own use, and never stand oblig'd.
Kas. I' faith! is he such a fellow?
Face. Why, Nab here knows him.
And then for making matches for rich widows,
Young gentlewomen, heirs, the fortunat'st man!
He 's sent to, far and near, all over England,
To have his counsel, and to know their fortunes.
Kas. God 's will, my suster shall see him.
Face. I'll tell you, sir,
What he did tell me of Nab. It 's a strange thing—
(By the way, you must eat no cheese, Nab, it breeds melancholy,
And that same melancholy breeds worms) but pass it:—
He told me, honest Nab here was ne'er at tavern
But once in 's life.
Drug. Truth, and no more I was not.
Face. And then he was so sick——
Drug. Could he tell you that too?
Face. How should I know it?
Drug. In troth, we had been a shooting,
And had a piece of fat ram-mutton to supper,
That lay so heavy o' my stomach——
Face. And he has no head
To bear any wine; for what with the noise o' the fiddlers,
And care of his shop, for he dares keep no servants——
Drug. My head did so ache——
Face. As he was fain to be brought home.
The doctor told me: and then a good old woman——
Drug. Yes, faith, she dwells in Seacoal-lane,—did cure me
With sodden ale, and pellitory o' the wall; [81]
Cost me but twopence. I had another sickness
Was worse than that.
Face. Aye, that was with the grief
Thou took'st for being cess'd [82] at eighteen-pence,
For the waterwork.
Drug. In truth, and it was like
T' have cost me almost my life.
Face. Thy hair went off?
Drug. Yes, sir; 't was done for spite.
Face. Nay, so says the doctor.
Kas. Pray thee, tobacco-boy, go fetch my suster;
I'll see this learned boy before I go;
And so shall she.
Face. Sir, he is busy now:
But if you have a sister to fetch hither,
Perhaps your own pains may command her sooner;
And he by that time will be free.
Kas. I go.
Exit.
Face. Drugger, she 's thine: the damask! —(*Exit Abel.*) Subtle and I
Must wrastle for her. (*Aside.*) Come on, Master Dapper,
You see how I turn clients here away,
To give your cause dispatch; ha' you perform'd
The ceremonies were enjoin'd you?
Dap. Yes, o' the vinegar,
And the clean shirt.
Face. 'T is well: that shirt may do you
More worship than you think. Your aunt's afire,
But that she will not show it, t' have a sight of you.
Ha' you provided for her grace's servants?
Dap. Yes, here are six score Edward shillings.
Face. Good!
Dap. And an old Harry's sovereign.
Face. Very good!
Dap. And three James shillings, and an Elizabeth groat,
Just twenty nobles.
Face. O, you are too just.

[79] The reference is to the "commodity" fraud, in which a borrower was obliged to take part of a loan in merchandise, which the lender frequently bought back by agents for much less than it represented in the loan. (Neilson.)

[80] used for blue dye.

[81] wall pellitory, a plant growing in old walls.

[82] assessed.

I would you had had the other noble in Maries.
Dap. I have some Philip and Maries.
Face. Aye, those same
Are best of all: where are they? Hark, the doctor.

SCENE 5.

Face, Dapper. Enter Subtle, disguised like a priest of Fairy with a strip of cloth.

Sub. (*In a feigned voice.*) Is yet her grace's cousin come?
Face. He is come.
Sub. And is he fasting?
Face. Yes.
Sub. And hath cried "hum"?
Face. Thrice, you must answer.
Dap. Thrice.
Sub. And as oft "buz"?
Face. If you have, say.
Dap. I have.
Sub. Then, to her coz,
Hoping that he hath vinegar'd his senses,
As he was bid, the Fairy queen dispenses,
By me, this robe, the petticoat of Fortune;
Which that he straight put on, she doth importune.
And though to Fortune near be her petticoat,
Yet nearer is her smock, the queen doth note:
And therefore, even of that a piece she hath sent,
Which, being a child, to wrap him in was rent;
And prays him for a scarf he now will wear it,
With as much love as then her grace did tear it,
About his eyes (*They blind him with the rag.*) to show he is fortunate.
And, trusting unto her to make his state,
He'll throw away all worldly pelf about him;
Which that he will perform, she doth not doubt him.
Face. She need not doubt him, sir. Alas, he has nothing
But what he will part withal as willingly,
Upon her grace's word—throw away your purse—
As she would ask it:—handkerchiefs and all—
She cannot bid that thing but he'll obey.—
If you have a ring about you, cast it off,
Or a silver seal at your wrist; her grace will send
(*He throws away, as they bid him.*)
Her fairies here to search you, therefore deal
Directly[83] with her highness: if they find
That you conceal a mite, you are undone.
Dap. Truly, there's all.
Face. All what?
Dap. My money; truly.
Face. Keep nothing that is transitory about you.
(*Aside to Subtle.*) Bid Dol play music.—Look, the elves are come
(*Dol enters with a cittern.*)
To pinch you, if you tell not the truth. Advise you.
(*They pinch him.*)
Dap. O! I have a paper with a spurryal[84] in 't.
Face. *Ti, ti.*
They knew 't, they say.
Sub. *Ti, ti, ti, ti.* He has more yet.
Face. *Ti, ti-ti-ti.* I' the other pocket?
Sub. *Titi, titi, titi, titi, titi.*
They must pinch him or he will never confess, they say.
(*They pinch him again.*)
Dap. O, O!
Face. Nay, pray you, hold: he is her grace's nephew.
Ti, ti, ti? What care you? Good faith, you shall care.—
Deal plainly, sir, and shame the fairies. Show
You are innocent,
Dap. By this good light, I ha' nothing.
Sub. *Ti, ti, ti, ti, to, ta.* He does equivocate she says:
Ti, ti do ti, ti ti do, ti da; and swears by the light when he is blinded.
Dap. By this good dark, I ha' nothing but a half-crown
Of gold about my wrist, that my love gave me;
And a leaden heart I wore sin' she forsook me.
Face. I thought 't was something. And would you incur
Your aunt's displeasure for these trifles? Come,

83 honestly.

84 a gold coin worth 15s.

I had rather you had thrown away twenty half-crowns.
(*Takes it off.*)
You may wear your leaden heart still.—How now!
Sub. What news, Dol?
Dol. Yonder's your knight, Sir Mammon.
Face. God's lid, we never thought of him till now!
Where is he?
Dol. Here hard by. He's at the door.
Sub. And you are not ready now! Dol, get his suit.
Exit Dol.
He must not be sent back.
Face. O, by no means.
What shall we do with this same puffin [85] here,
Now he's o' the spit?
Sub. Why, lay him back awhile,
With some device.

Re-enter Dol with Face's clothes.

—*Ti, ti, ti, ti, ti, ti.* Would her grace speak with me?
I come.—Help, Dol!
(*Knocking without.*)
Face. (*Speaks through the keyhole.*)—Who's there? Sir Epicure,
My master's i' the way. Please you to walk
Three or four turns, but till his back be turn'd,
And I am for you.—Quickly, Dol!
Sub. Her grace
Commends her kindly to you, Master Dapper.
Dap. I long to see her grace.
Sub. She now is set
At dinner in her bed, and she has sent you
From her own private trencher, a dead mouse,
And a piece of gingerbread, to be merry withal,
And stay your stomach, lest you faint with fasting:
Yet if you could hold out till she saw you, she says,
It would be better for you.
Face. Sir, he shall
Hold out, an't were this two hours, for her highness;
I can assure you that. We will not lose
All we ha' done.——
Sub. He must not see, nor speak
To anybody, till then.
Face. For that we'll put, sir,
A stay in's mouth.
Sub. Of what?
Face. Of gingerbread.
Make you it fit. He that hath pleas'd her grace
Thus far, shall not now crinkle [86] for a little.——
Gape, sir, and let him fit you.
(*They thrust a gag of gingerbread into his mouth.*)
Sub. ——Where shall we now
Bestow him?
Dol. I' the privy.——
Sub. Come along, sir,
I must now show you Fortune's privy lodgings.
Face. Are they perfum'd, and his bath ready?
Sub. All:
Only the fumigation's somewhat strong.
Face. (*Speaking through the keyhole.*) Sir Epicure, I am yours, sir, by and by.[87]
Exeunt with Dapper.

ACT IV.

Scene 1.

Enter Face and Mammon.

Face. O, sir, you're come i' the only finest time.——
Mam. Where's master?
Face. Now preparing for projection, sir.
Your stuff will be all chang'd shortly.
Mam. Into gold?
Face. To gold and silver, sir.
Mam. Silver I care not for.
Face. Yes, sir, a little to give beggars.
Mam. Where's the lady?
Face. At hand here. I ha' told her such brave things o' you,
Touching your bounty and your noble spirit——
Mam. Hast thou?
Face. As she is almost in her fit to see you.
But, good sir, no divinity i' your conference,
For fear of putting her in rage.——
Mam. I warrant thee.
Face. Six men will not hold her down. And then,

85 fool. 86 waver. 87 immediately.

If the old man should hear or see you——
Mam. Fear not.
Face. The very house, sir, would run mad. You know it,
How scrupulous he is, and violent,
'Gainst the least act of sin. Physic or mathematics,
Poetry, state,[88] or bawdry, as I told you,
She will endure, and never startle; but
No word of controversy.
Mam. I am school'd, good *Ulen.*
Face. And you must praise her house, remember that,
And her nobility.
Mam. Let me alone:
No herald, no, nor antiquary, Lungs,
Shall do it better. Go.
Face. (*Aside.*) Why, this is yet
A kind of modern happiness,[89] to have
Dol Common for a great lady.
Exit.
Mam. Now, Epicure,
Heighten thyself, talk to her all in gold:
Rain her as many showers as Jove did drops
Unto his Danaë; show the god a miser,
Compar'd with Mammon. What! the stone will do 't.
She shall feel gold, taste gold, hear gold, sleep gold;
Nay, we will *concumbere* gold: I will be puissant,
And mighty in my talk to her.—

Re-enter Face with Dol richly dressed.

Here she comes.
Face. To him, Dol, suckle him. This is the noble knight
I told your ladyship——
Mam. Madam, with your pardon,
I kiss your vesture.
Dol. Sir, I were uncivil
If I would suffer that; my lip to you, sir.
Mam. I hope my lord your brother be in health, lady.
Dol. My lord my brother is, though I no lady, sir.
Face. (*Aside.*) Well said, my Guinea bird.
Mam. Right noble madam——
Face. (*Aside.*) O, we shall have most fierce idolatry.
Mam. 'T is your prerogative.
Dol. Rather your courtesy.
Mam. Were there nought else t' enlarge your virtues to me,
These answers speak your breeding and your blood.
Dol. Blood we boast none, sir; a poor baron's daughter.
Mam. Poor! and gat you? Profane not. Had your father
Slept all the happy remnant of his life
After that act, lain but there still, and panted,
He 'd done enough to make himself, his issue,
And his posterity noble.
Dol. Sir, although
We may be said to want the gilt and trappings,
The dress of honor, yet we strive to keep
The seeds and the materials.
Mam. I do see
The old ingredient, virtue, was not lost,
Nor the drug money us'd to make your compound.
There is a strange nobility i' your eye,
This lip, that chin! Methinks you do resemble
One o' the Austriac princes.
Face. (*Aside.*) Very like!
Her father was an Irish costermonger.
Mam. The house of Valois just had such a nose,
And such a forehead yet the Medici
Of Florence boast.
Dol. Troth, and I have been lik'ned
To all these princes.
Face. (*Aside.*) I 'll be sworn, I heard it.
Mam. I know not how! it is not any one,
But e'en the very choice of all their features.
Face. (*Aside.*) I 'll in, and laugh.
Exit.
Mam. A certain touch, or air,
That sparkles a divinity beyond
An earthly beauty!
Dol. O, you play the courtier.
Mam. Good lady, gi' me leave——
Dol. In faith, I may not,
To mock me, sir.
Mam. To burn i' this sweet flame;
The phœnix never knew a nobler death.
Dol. Nay, now you court the courtier, and destroy
What you would build. This art, sir, i' your words,
Calls your whole faith in question.
Mam. By my soul——
Dol. Nay, oaths are made o' the same air, sir.
Mam. Nature
Never bestow'd upon mortality

88 politics.

89 up-to-date fitness.

A more unblam'd, a more harmonious feature;
She play'd the step-dame in all faces else:
Sweet madam, le' me be particular——
Dol. Particular, sir! I pray you, know your distance.
Mam. In no ill sense, sweet lady: but to ask
How your fair graces pass the hours? I see
You 're lodg'd here, i' the house of a rare man,
An excellent artist: but what 's that to you?
Dol. Yes, sir; I study here the mathematics and distillation.
Mam. O, I cry your pardon.
He 's a divine instructor! can extract
The souls of all things by his art; call all
The virtues, and the miracles of the sun,
Into a temperate furnace; teach dull nature
What her own forces are. A man, the emp'ror
Has courted above Kelly;[90] sent his medals
And chains, t' invite him.
Dol. Aye, and for his physic, sir——
Mam. Above the art of Æsculapius,
That drew the envy of the Thunderer!
I know all this, and more.
Dol. Troth, I am taken, sir,
Whole with these studies that contemplate nature.
Mam. It is a noble humor; but this form
Was not intended to so dark a use.
Had you been crooked, foul, of some coarse mould,
A cloister had done well; but such a feature,
That might stand up the glory of a kingdom,
To live recluse is a mere solecism,
Though in a nunnery. It must not be.
I muse, my lord your brother will permit it:
You should spend half my land first, were I he.
Does not this diamond better on my finger
Than i' the quarry?
Dol. Yes.
Mam. Why, you are like it.
You were created, lady, for the light.
Here, you shall wear it; take it, the first pledge
Of what I speak, to bind you to believe me.
Dol. In chains of adamant?
Mam. Yes, the strongest bands.
And take a secret too.—Here, by your side,
Doth stand this hour the happiest man in Europe.
Dol. You are contented, sir?
Mam. Nay, in true being,
The envy of princes and the fear of states.
Dol. Say you so, Sir Epicure?
Mam. Yes, and thou shalt prove it,
Daughter of honor. I have cast mine eye
Upon thy form, and I will rear this beauty
Above all styles.
Dol. You mean no treason, sir?
Mam. No, I will take away that jealousy.
I am the lord of the philosopher's stone,
And thou the lady.
Dol. How, sir! ha' you that?
Mam. I am the master of the mastery.
This day the good old wretch here o' the house
Has made it for us: now he 's at projection.
Think therefore thy first wish now, let me hear it;
And it shall rain into thy lap, no shower,
But floods of gold, whole cataracts, a deluge,
To get a nation on thee.
Dol. You are pleas'd, sir,
To work on the ambition of our sex.
Mam. I am pleas'd the glory of her sex should know,
This nook here of the Friars is no climate
For her to live obscurely in, to learn
Physic and surgery, for the constable's wife
Of some odd hundred in Essex; but come forth,
And taste the air of palaces; eat, drink
The toils of empirics, and their boasted practice;
Tincture of pearl, and coral, gold, and amber;
Be seen at feasts and triumphs; have it ask'd,
What miracle she is; set all the eyes
Of court a-fire, like a burning glass,
And work 'em into cinders, when the jewels

90 An astrologer, and associate of John Dee; the emperor is Rudolph II of Germany.

Of twenty states adorn thee, and the light
Strikes out the stars that, when thy name is mention'd,
Queens may look pale; and, we but showing our love,
Nero's Poppæa may be lost in story!
Thus will we have it.

Dol. I could well consent, sir.
But in a monarchy, how will this be?
The prince will soon take notice, and both seize
You and your stone, it being a wealth unfit
For any private subject.

Mam. If he knew it.

Dol. Yourself do boast it, sir.

Mam. To thee, my life.

Dol. O, but beware, sir! You may come to end
The remnant of your days in a loath'd prison,
By speaking of it.

Mam. 'T is no idle fear.
We 'll therefore go with all, my girl, and live
In a free state, where we will eat our mullets,
Sous'd in high-country wines, sup pheasants' eggs,
And have our cockles boil'd in silver shells;
Our shrimps to swim again, as when they liv'd,
In a rare butter made of dolphins' milk,
Whose cream does look like opals; and with these
Delicate meats set ourselves high for pleasure,
And take us down again, and then renew
Our youth and strength with drinking the elixir,
And so enjoy a perpetuity
Of life and lust! And thou shalt ha' thy wardrobe
Richer than Nature's, still to change thyself,
And vary oft'ner, for thy pride, than she,
Or Art, her wise and almost-equal servant.

Re-enter Face.

Face. Sir, you are too loud. I hear you every word
Into the laboratory. Some fitter place;
The garden, or great chamber above. How like you her?

Mam. Excellent! Lungs, There 's for thee.
(*Gives him money.*)

Face. But do you hear?
Good sir, beware, no mention of the rabbins.

Mam. We think not on 'em.

Exeunt Mam. and Dol.

Face. O, it is well, sir.—Subtle!

SCENE 2.

Face. Enter Subtle.

Dost thou not laugh?

Sub. Yes; are they gone?

Face. All 's clear.

Sub. The widow is come.

Face. And your quarreling disciple?

Sub. Aye.

Face. I must to my captainship again then.

Sub. Stay, bring 'em in first.

Face. So I meant. What is she?
A bonnibel?

Sub. I know not.

Face. We 'll draw lots:
You 'll stand to that?

Sub. What else?

Face. O, for a suit,
To fall now like a curtain, flap!

Sub. To th' door, man.

Face. You 'll ha' the first kiss, 'cause I am not ready.

Exit.

Sub. Yes, and perhaps hit you through both the nostrils.

Face. (*Within.*) Who would you speak with?

Kas. (*Within.*) Where 's the captain?

Face. (*Within.*) Gone, sir,
About some business.

Kas. (*Within.*) Gone!

Face. (*Within.*) He 'll return straight.
But, master doctor, his lieutenant, is here.

Enter Kastril, followed by Dame Pliant.

Sub. Come near, my worshipful boy, *my terrae fili,*
That is, my boy of land; make thy approaches:
Welcome; I know thy lusts and thy desires,
And I will serve and satisfy 'em. Begin,
Charge me from thence, or thence, or in this line;

Here is my centre: ground thy quarrel.
Kas. You lie.
Sub. How, child of wrath and anger! the loud lie?
For what, my sudden boy?
Kas. Nay, that look you to,
I am aforehand.
Sub. O, this is no true grammar,
And as ill logic! You must render causes, child,
Your first and second intentions, know your canons
And your divisions, moods, degrees, and differences,
Your predicaments, substance, and accident,
Series extern and intern, with their causes,
Efficient, material, formal, final,
And ha' your elements perfect?
Kas. What is this?
The angry tongue he talks in?
Sub. That false precept,
Of being aforehand, has deceiv'd a number,
And made 'em enter quarrels oftentimes
Before they were aware; and afterward,
Against their wills.
Kas. How must I do then, sir?
Sub. I cry this lady mercy; she should first
Have been saluted. (*Kisses her.*) I do call you lady,
Because you are to be one ere 't be long,
My soft and buxom widow.
Kas. Is she, i' faith?
Sub. Yes, or my art is an egregious liar.
Kas. How know you?
Sub. By inspection on her forehead,
And subtlety of her lip, which must be tasted
Often to make a judgment. (*Kisses her again.*) 'Slight, she melts
Like a myrobolane.[91] Here is yet a line,
In *rivo frontis,* tells me he is no knight.
Dame P. What is he then, sir?
Sub. Let me see your hand.
O, your *linea fortunae* makes it plain;
And *stella* here *in monte Veneris.*
But, most of all, *junctura annularis.*
He is a soldier, or a man of art, lady,
But shall have some great honor shortly.
Dame P. Brother,
He 's a rare man, believe me!

Re-enter Face, in his uniform.

Kas. Hold your peace.
Here comes t' other rare man.—'Save you, captain.
Face. Good Master Kastril! Is this your sister?
Kas. Aye, sir.
Please you to kuss her, and be proud to know her.
Face. I shall be proud to know you, lady. (*Kisses her.*)
Dame P. Brother,
He calls me lady, too.
Kas. Aye, peace: I heard it. (*Takes her aside.*)
Face. The count is come.
Sub. Where is he?
Face. At the door.
Sub. Why, you must entertain him.
Face. What will you do
With these the while?
Sub. Why, have 'em up, and show 'em
Some fustian[92] book, or the dark glass.
Face. 'Fore God,
She is a delicate dabchick! I must have her.
Exit.
Sub. (*Aside.*) Must you! Aye, if your fortune will, you must.—
Come, sir, the captain will come to us presently:
I 'll ha' you to my chamber of demonstrations,
Where I 'll show you both the grammar and logic,
And rhetoric of quarreling; my whole method
Drawn out in tables; and my instrument,
That hath the several scales upon 't shall make you
Able to quarrel at a straw's-breadth by moonlight.
And, lady, I 'll have you look in a glass,
Some half an hour, but to clear your eyesight,
Against you see your fortune; which is greater
Than I may judge upon the sudden, trust me.
Exeunt.

Scene 3.

Enter Face.

Face. Where are you, doctor?
Sub. (*Within.*) I 'll come to you presently.
Face. I will ha' this same widow, now I ha' seen her,

[91] a dried plum, a sweetmeat.
[92] full of incomprehensible jargon.

On any composition.[93]

Enter Subtle.

Sub. What do you say?
Face. Ha' you dispos'd of them?
Sub. I ha' sent 'em up.
Face. Subtle, in troth, I needs must have this widow.
Sub. Is that the matter?
Face. Nay, but hear me.
Sub. Go to.
If you rebel once, Dol shall know it all:
Therefore be quiet, and obey your chance.
Face. Nay, thou art so violent now. Do but conceive,
Thou art old, and canst not serve——
Sub. Who cannot? I?
'Slight, I will serve her with thee, for a——
Face. Nay,
But understand: I'll gi' you composition.
Sub. I will not treat with thee. What! sell my fortune?
'T is better than my birthright. Do not murmur:
Win her, and carry her. If you grumble, Dol
Knows it directly.
Face. Well, sir, I am silent.
Will you go help to fetch in Don in state?

Exit.

Sub. I follow you, sir. We must keep Face in awe,
Or he will overlook us like a tyrant.

Re-enter Face, introducing Surly like a Spaniard.

Brain of a tailor! who comes here? Don John!
Sur. *Senores, beso las manos a vuestras mercedes.*[94]
Sub. Would you had stoop'd a little, and kist our *anos.*
Face. Peace, Subtle!
Sub. Stab me; I shall never hold, man.
He looks in that deep ruff like a head in a platter,
Serv'd in by a short cloak upon two trestles.
Face. Or what do you say to a collar of brawn,[95] cut down
Beneath the souse,[96] and wriggled [97] with a knife?
Sub. 'Slud, he does look too fat to be a Spaniard.
Face. Perhaps some Fleming or some Hollander got him
In d'Alva's [98] time; Count Egmont's [99] bastard.
Sub. Don,
Your scurvy, yellow, Madrid face is welcome.
Sur. *Gratia.*
Sub. He speaks out of a fortification.
Pray God he ha' no squibs in those deep sets.[1]
Sur. *Por dios, senores, muy linda casa!* [2]
Sub. What says he?
Face. Praises the house, I think;
I know no more but 's action.
Sub. Yes, the *casa,*
My precious Diego, will prove fair enough
To cozen you in. Do you mark? You shall
Be cozened, Diego.
Face. Cozened, do you see,
My worthy Donzel,[3] cozened.
Sur. *Entiendo.*[4]
Sub. Do you intend it? So do we, dear Don.
Have you brought pistolets or portagues,
My solemn Don? (*To Face.*) Dost thou feel any?
Face. (*Feels his pockets.*) Full.
Sub. You shall be emptied, Don, pumped and drawn
Dry, as they say.
Face. Milked, in troth, sweet Don.
Sub. See all the monsters; the great lion of all, Don.
Sur. *Con licencia, se puede ver a esta senora?* [5]
Sub. What talks he now?
Face. Of the senora.
Sub. O, Don,
This is the lioness, which you shall see
Also, my Don.
Face. 'Slid, Subtle, how shall we do?
Sub. For what?
Face. Why, Dol 's employ'd, you know.
Sub. That 's true.
'Fore heav'n I know not: he must stay, that 's all.
Face. Stay! that he must not by no means.
Sub. No! why?
Face. Unless you 'll mar all. 'Slight, he 'll suspect it;

93 on any terms.
94 "Sirs, I kiss your hands."
95 a rolled-up piece of boar's flesh.
96 under the ears.
97 slashed (so that it looks like a ruff).
98 The Duke of Alva, governor of the Netherlands, 1567–73.
99 A Flemish leader, executed by Alva.
1 folds.
2 "Gad, sirs, a very pretty house."
3 squire.
4 "I understand"
5 "If you please, may I see the lady?"

And then he will not pay, not half so well.
This is a travell'd punk-master, and does know
All the delays; a notable hot rascal,
And looks already rampant.
Sub. 'Sdeath, and Mammon
Must not be troubled.
Face. Mammon! in no case.
Sub. What shall we do then?
Face. Think: you must be sudden.
Sur. *Entiendo que la senora es tan hermosa, que codicio tan a verla como la bien aventuranza de mi vida.*[6]
Face. *Mi vida!* 'Slid, Subtle, he puts me in mind o' the widow.
What dost thou say to draw her to 't, ha!
And tell her 't is her fortune? All our venture
Now lies upon 't. It is but one man more,
Which on 's chance to have her: and beside,
There is no maidenhead to be fear'd or lost.
What dost thou think on 't, Subtle?
Sub. Who, I? why——
Face. The credit of our house too is engag'd.
Sub. You made me an offer for my share ere-while.
What wilt thou gi' me, i' faith?
Face. O, by that light
I'll not buy now. You know your doom [7] to me.
E'en take your lot, obey your chance, sir; win her,
And wear her out, for me.
Sub. 'Slight, I'll not work her then.
Face. It is the common cause; therefore bethink you.
Dol else must know it, as you said.
Sub. I care not.
Sur. *Senores, porque se tarda tanto?* [8]
Sub. Faith, I am not fit, I am old.
Face. That 's now no reason, sir.
Sur. *Puede ser de hazer burla de mi amor?* [9]
Face. You hear the Don too? By this air I call,
And loose the hinges. Dol!
Sub. A plague of hell——
Face. Will you then do?
Sub. You 're a terrible rogue!
I 'll think of this. Will you, sir, call the widow?
Face. Yes, and I 'll take her too with all her faults,
Now I do think on 't better.
Sub. With all my heart, sir;
Am I discharg'd o' the lot?
Face. As you please.
Sub. Hands.
(*They shake hands.*)
Face. Remember now, that upon any change
You never claim her.
Sub. Much good joy and health to you, sir,
Marry a whore! Fate, let me wed a witch first.
Sur. *Por estas honradas barbas* [10]——
Sub. He swears by his beard.
Dispatch, and call the brother too.
Exit Face.
Sur. *Tengo duda, senores, que no me hagan alguna traycion.*[11]
Sub. How, issue on? Yes, *praesto, senor.* Please you
Enthratha the *chambratha*, worthy don:
Where if you please the fates, in your *bathada,*
You shall be soak'd, and strok'd, and tubb'd, and rubb'd,
And scrubb'd, and fubb'd,[12] dear Don, before you go.
You shall in faith, my scurvy baboon Don,
Be curried, claw'd, and flaw'd,[13] and taw'd,[14] indeed.
I will the heartlier go about it now,
And make the widow a punk so much the sooner,
To be reveng'd on this impetuous Face:
The quickly doing of it is the grace.
Exeunt Subtle and Surly.

Scene 4.

Enter Face, Kastril, and Dame Pliant.

Face. Come, lady: I knew the doctor would not leave
Till he had found the very nick of her fortune.
Kas. To be a countess, say you?
Face. A Spanish countess, sir.

6 "I understand that the lady is so handsome that I am as eager to see her as the good fortune of my life."
7 pledge.
8 "Sirs, why so long delay?"
9 "Can it be that you make sport of my love?"
10 "By this honored beard——"
11 "I fear, sirs, that you are playing me some trick."
12 gulled.
13 cracked.
14 soaked, like a hide in tanning.

Dame P. Why, is that better than an English countess?
Face. Better! 'Slight, make you that a question, lady?
Kas. Nay, she is a fool, captain, you must pardon her.
Face. Ask from your courtier to your inns-of-court-man,
To your mere milliner; they will tell you all,
Your Spanish jennet is the best horse; your Spanish
Stoop [15] is the best garb; [16] your Spanish beard
Is the best cut; your Spanish ruffs are the best
Wear; your Spanish pavin [17] the best dance;
Your Spanish titillation in a glove
The best perfume: and for your Spanish pike,
And Spanish blade, let your poor captain speak.—
Here comes the doctor.

Enter Subtle with a paper.

Sub. My most honor'd lady,
For so I am now to style you, having found
By this my scheme,[18] you are to undergo
An honorable fortune very shortly,
What will you say now, if some——
Face. I ha' told her all, sir,
And her right worshipful brother here, that she shall be
A countess; do not delay 'em, sir; a Spanish countess.
Sub. Still, my scarce-worshipful captain, you can keep
No secret! Well, since he has told you, madam,
Do you forgive him, and I do.
Kas. She shall do that, sir;
I'll look to it; 't is my charge.
Sub. Well then: nought rests
But that she fit her love now to her fortune.
Dame P. Truly I shall never brook a Spaniard.
Sub. No?
Dame P. Never sin' eighty-eight [19] could I abide 'em,
And that was some three years afore I was born, in truth.

Sub. Come, you must love him, or be miserable;
Choose which you will.
Face. By this good rush, persuade her,
She will cry [20] strawberries else within this twelve month.
Sub. Nay, shads and mackerel, which is worse.
Face. Indeed, sir!
Kas. God's lid, you shall love him, or I'll kick you.
Dame P. Why,
I'll do as you will ha' me, brother.
Kas. Do,
Or by this hand I'll maul you.
Face. Nay, good sir,
Be not so fierce.
Sub. No, my enraged child;
She will be rul'd. What, when she comes to taste
The pleasures of a countess! to be courted——
Face. And kiss'd and ruffled!
Sub. Aye, behind the hangings.
Face. And then come forth in pomp!
Sub. And know her state!
Face. Of keeping all th' idolators o' the chamber
Barer to her, than at their prayers!
Sub. Is serv'd
Upon the knee!
Face. And has her pages, ushers,
Footmen, and coaches——
Sub. Her six mares——
Face. Nay, eight!
Sub. To hurry her through London, to th' Exchange,[21]
Bet'lem,[22] the China-houses [23]——
Face. Yes, and have
The citizens gape at her, and praise her tires,
And my lord's goose-turd [24] bands, that rides with her!
Kas. Most brave! By this hand, you are not my suster
If you refuse.
Dame P. I will not refuse, brother.

Enter Surly.

Sur. *Que es esto, senores, que non se venga?*
Esta tardanza me mata! [25]
Face. It is the count come:
The doctor knew he would be here, by his art.

15 stooping posture.
16 fashion.
17 a stately dance.
18 horoscope.
19 1588, the year of the Armada.
20 hawk about town.
21 The Royal Exchange had arcades of small shops.
22 It was a fashionable amusement to visit Bedlam, the lunatic asylum.
23 where oriental wares were sold.
24 green.
25 "Why does n't she come, sirs? This delay is killing me."

Sub. *En gallanta, madama, Don! gallantissima!*
Sur. *Por todos los dioses, la mas acabada*
Hermosura, que he visto en ma vida! [26]
Face. Is 't not a gallant language that they speak?
Kas. An admirable language! Is 't not French?
Face. No, Spanish, sir.
Kas. It goes like law French,
And that, they say, is the court-liest language.
Face. List, sir.
Sur. *El sol ha perdito su lumbre, con el*
Resplandor que trae esta dana! Valga me dios! [27]
Face. H' admires your sister.
Kas. Must not she make curt'sy.
Sub. 'Ods will, she must go to him, man, and kiss him!
It is the Spanish fashion, for the women
To make first court.
Face. 'T is true he tells you, sir:
His art knows all.
Sur. *Porque no se acude?* [28]
Kas. He speaks to her, I think.
Face. That he does, sir.
Sur. *Por el amor de dios, que es esto que se tarda?* [29]
Kas. Nay, see: she will not understand him! Gull, noddy!
Dame P. What say you, brother?
Kas. Ass, my suster,
Go kuss him, as the cunning man would ha' you;
I 'll thrust a pin i' your buttocks else.
Face. O no, sir.
Sur. *Senora mia, mi persona muy indigna esta*
Allegar a tanta hermosura. [30]
Face. Does he not use her bravely?
Kas. Bravely, i' faith!
Face. Nay, he will use her better.
Kas. Do you think so?
Sur. *Senora, si sera servida, entremos.* [31]
Exit with Dame Pliant.
Kas. Where does he carry her?
Face. Into the garden, sir;
Take you no thought: I must interpret for her.
Sub. Give Dol the word.
(*Aside to Face, who goes out.*)
—Come, my fierce child, advance,
We 'll to our quarreling lesson again.
Kas. Agreed.
I love a Spanish boy with all my heart.
Sub. Nay, and by this means, sir, you shall be brother
To a great count.
Kas. Aye, I knew that at first.
This match will advance the house of the Kastrils.
Sub. 'Pray God your sister prove but pliant!
Kas. Why,
Her name is so, by her other husband.
Sub. How!
Kas. The Widow Pliant. Knew you not that?
Sub. No, faith, sir;
Yet, by the erection of her figure,[32] I guess'd it.
Come, let 's go practise.
Kas. Yes, but do you think, doctor,
I e'er shall quarrel well?
Sub. I warrant you.
Exeunt.

Scene 5.

Enter Dol followed by Mammon.

Dol. (*In her fit of talking.*) *For after Alexander's death——*
Mam. Good lady——
Dol. *That Perdiccas and Antigonus were slain,*
The two that stood, Seleuc' and Ptolomy——
Mam. Madam—
Dol. *Made up the two legs, and the fourth beast,*
That was Gog-north and Egypt-south: which after
Was called Gog-iron-leg and South-iron-leg——
Mam. Lady——
Dol. *And then Gog-horned. So was Egypt, too:*
Then Egypt-clay-leg, and Gog-clay-leg——
Mam. Sweet madam——
Dol. *And last Gog-dust, and Egypt-dust, which fall*
In the last link of the fourth chain. And these
Be stars in story, which none see, or look at——
Mam. What shall I do?
Dol. For, as he says, *except*

26 "By all the gods, the most perfect beauty I have seen in my life."
27 "The sun has lost his light with the splendor this lady brings, so help me God."
28 "Why don't you draw near?"
29 "For the love of God, why this delay?"
30 "Madam, my person is unworthy to approach such beauty."
31 "Madam, at your service, let us go in."
32 by her horoscope

We call the rabbins, and the heathen Greeks——
Mam. Dear lady——
Dol. *To come from Salem, and from Athens,*
And teach the people of Great Britain——

Enter Face hastily, in his servant's dress.

Face. What 's the matter, sir?
Dol. *To speak the tongue of Eber and Javan——*
Mam. Oh,
She 's in her fit.
Dol. *We shall know nothing——*
Face. Death, sir,
We are undone!
Dol. *Where then a learned linguist*
Shall see the ancient us'd communion
Of vowels and consonants——
Face. My master will hear!
Dol. *A wisdom, which Pythagoras held most high——*
Mam. Sweet honorable lady!
Dol. *To comprise*
All sounds of voices, in few marks of letters.
Face. Nay, you must never hope to lay her now.
(*They all speak together.*)
Dol. *And so we may arrive by Talmud skill,*[33]
And profane Greek, to raise the building up
Of Helen's house against the Ismaelite,
King of Thogarma, and his habergions
Brimstony, blue, and fiery; and the force
Of king Abadäon, and the beast of Cittim:
Which rabbi David Kimchi, Onkelos,
And Aben Ezra do interpret Rome.
Face. How did you put her into 't?
Mam. Alas, I talk'd
Of a fifth monarchy I would erect
With the philosopher's stone, by chance, and she
Falls on the other four straight.
Face. Out of Broughton![34]
I told you so. 'Slid, stop her mouth.
Mam. Is 't best?
Face. She 'll never leave else. If the old man hear her,
We are but fæces, ashes.
Sub. (*Within.*) What 's to do there?
Face. O, we are lost! Now she hears him, she is quiet.

Enter Subtle; upon Subtle's entry they disperse.

Mam. Where shall I hide me!
Sub. How! What sight is here?
Close deeds of darkness, and that shun the light!
Bring him again. Who is he? What, my son!
O, I have liv'd too long.
Mam. Nay, good, dear father,
There was no unchaste purpose.
Sub. Not? and flee me
When I come in?
Mam. That was my error.
Sub. Error?
Guilt, guilt, my son; give it the right name. No marvel
If I found check in our great work within,
When such affairs as these were managing!
Mam. Why, have you so?
Sub. It has stood still this half hour:
And all the rest of our less works gone back.
Where is the instrument of wickedness,
My lewd false drudge?
Mam. Nay, good sir, blame not him;
Believe me, 't was against his will or knowledge:
I saw her by chance.
Sub. Will you commit more sin,
T' excuse a varlet?
Mam. By my hope, 't is true, sir.
Sub. Nay, then I wonder less, if you, for whom
The blessing was prepar'd, would so tempt heaven,
And lose your fortunes.
Mam. Why, sir?
Sub. This will retard
The work a month at least.
Mam. Why, if it do,
What remedy? But think it not, good father:
Our purposes were honest.
Sub. As they were,
So the reward will prove. (*A great crack and noise within.*)—How now! ay me!
God and all saints be good to us.——

Re-enter Face.

33 In the early editions this speech is printed in parallel columns with the dialogue immediately following, to indicate simultaneous utterance. (Neilson.)

34 cf. p. 254, n. 36, Dol's jargon is taken from a book of Broughton's, *The Concent of Scripture*.

What's that?

Face. O, sir, we are defeated! All the works
Are flown *in fumo,* every glass is burst;
Furnace and all rent down, as if a bolt
Of thunder had been driven through the house.
Retorts, receivers, pelicans, bolt heads,
All struck in shivers!
(*Subtle falls down as in a swoon.*)
Help, good sir! alas,
Coldness and death invades him. Nay, Sir Mammon,
Do the fair offices of a man! You stand,
As you were readier to depart than he.
(*One knocks.*)
Who's there? My lord her brother is come.

Mam. Ha, Lungs!

Face. His coach is at the door. Avoid his sight,
For he's as furious as his sister's mad.

Mam. Alas!

Face. My brain is quite undone with the fume, sir,
I ne'er must hope to be mine own man again.

Mam. Is all lost, Lungs? Will nothing be preserv'd
Of all our cost?

Face. Faith, very little, sir;
A peck of coals or so, which is cold comfort, sir.

Mam. O, my voluptuous mind! I am justly punish'd.

Face. And so am I, sir.

Mam. Cast from all my hopes——

Face. Nay, certainties, sir.

Mam. By mine own base affections.

Sub. (*Seeming to come to himself.*) O, the curst fruits of vice and lust!

Mam. Good father,
It was my sin. Forgive it.

Sub. Hangs my roof
Over us still, and will not fall, O justice,
Upon us, for this wicked man!

Face. Nay, look, sir,
You grieve him now with staying in his sight.
Good sir, the nobleman will come too, and take you,
And that may breed a tragedy.

Mam. I'll go.

Face. Aye, and repent at home, sir. It may be,
For some good penance you may ha' it yet;
A hundred pound to the box at Bet'lem——

Mam. Yes.

Face. For the restoring such as—ha' their wits.

Mam. I'll do 't.

Face. I'll send one to you to receive it.

Mam. Do.
Is no projection left?

Face. All flown, or stinks, sir.

Mam. Will nought be sav'd that's good for med'cine, think'st thou?

Face. I cannot tell, sir. There will be perhaps
Something about the scraping of the shards,
Will cure the itch,—though not your itch of mind, sir. (*Aside.*)
It shall be sav'd for you, and sent home. Good sir,
This way, for fear the lord shall meet you.

Exit Mammon.

Sub. (*Raising his head.*) Face!

Face. Aye.

Sub. Is he gone?

Face. Yes, and as heavily
As all the gold he hop'd for were in 's blood.
Let us be light though.

Sub. (*Leaping up.*) Aye, as balls, and bound
And hit our heads against the roof for joy:
There's so much of our care now cast away.

Face. Now to our don.

Sub. Yes, your young widow by this time
Is made a countess, Face; she's been in travail
Of a young heir for you.

Face. Good, sir.

Sub. Off with your case,[35]
And greet her kindly, as a bridegroom should,
After these common hazards.

Face. Very well, sir.
Will you go fetch Don Diego off the while?

Sub. And fetch him over too, if you'll be pleas'd, sir.
Would Dol were in her place, to pick his pockets now!

Face. Why, you can do 't as well, if you would set to 't.
I pray you prove your virtue.[36]

Sub. For your sake, sir

Exeunt

35 change your clothes.

36 ability.

SCENE 6.

Enter Surly and Dame Pliant.

Sur. Lady, you see into what hands you are fall'n;
'Mongst what a nest of villains! and how near
Your honor was t' have catch'd a certain clap,
Through your credulity, had I but been
So punctually forward, as place, time,
And other circumstance would ha' made a man;
For you're a handsome woman: would you were wise too!
I am a gentleman come here disguis'd,
Only to find the knaveries of this citadel;
And where I might have wrong'd your honor, and have not,
I claim some interest in your love. You are,
They say, a widow, rich; and I'm a bachelor,
Worth nought: your fortunes may make me a man,
As mine ha' preserv'd you a woman. Think upon it,
And whether I have deserv'd you or no.
Dame P. I will, sir.
Sur. And for these household-rogues, let me alone
To treat with them.

Enter Subtle.

Sub. How doth my noble Diego,
And my dear madam countess? Hath the count
Been courteous, lady? liberal and open?
Donzel, methinks you look melancholic,
I do not like the dulness of your eye;
It hath a heavy cast, 't is upsee Dutch,[37]
And says you are a lumpish whore-master.
Be lighter, I will make your pockets so.
(*He falls to picking of them.*)
Sur. (*Throws open his cloak.*) Will you, Don bawd and pick-purse? (*Strikes him down.*) How now! Reel you?
Stand up, sir, you shall find, since I am so heavy,
I'll gi' you equal weight.
Sub. Help! murder!
Sur. No, sir,
There's no such thing intended. A good cart[38]
And a clean whip shall ease you of that fear.
I am the Spanish Don that should be cozened,
Do you see? Cozened? Where's your Captain Face,
That parcel-broker,[39] and whole-bawd, all rascal?

Enter Face in his uniform.

Face. How, Surly!
Sur. O, make your approach, good captain.
I've found from whence your copper rings and spoons
Come now, wherewith you cheat abroad in taverns.
'T was here you learn'd t' anoint your boot with brimstone,
Then rub men's gold on 't for a kind of touch,
And say, 't was naught, when you had chang'd the color,
That you might ha 't for nothing. And this doctor,
Your sooty, smoky-bearded compeer, he
Will close you so much gold, in a bolt's-head,
And, on a turn, convey i' the stead another
With sublim'd mercury, that shall burst i' the heat,
And fly out all *in fumo!* Then weeps Mammon;
Then swoons his worship. Or (*Face slips out.*) he is the Faustus,
That casteth figures and can conjure, cures
Plagues, piles, and pox, by the ephemerides.[40]
And holds intelligence with all the bawds
And midwives of three shires: while you send in——
Captain!—what! is he gone?—damsels with child,
Wives that are barren, or the waiting-maid
With the green sickness. (*Seizes Subtle as he is retiring.*)—Nay, sir, you must tarry,
Though he be scap'd; and answer by the ears, sir.

37 as if you were drunk as a Dutchman. 38 Bawds were carted through the streets. 39 part pawnbroker. 40 astrologer's almanac.

SCENE 7.

Re-enter Face with Kastril to Surly and Subtle.

Face. Why, now 's the time, if ever you will quarrel
Well, as they say, and be a true-born child:
The doctor and your sister both are abus'd.[41]
Kas. Where is he? Which is he? He is a slave.
Whate'er he is, and the son of a whore.—Are you
The man, sir, I would know?
Sur. I should be loth, sir.
To confess so much.
Kas. Then you lie i' your throat.
Sur. How!
Face. (*To Kastril.*) A very arrant rogue, sir, and a cheater,
Employ'd here by another conjurer
That does not love the doctor, and would cross him
If he knew how.
Sur. Sir, you are abus'd.
Kas. You lie:
And 't is no matter.
Face. Well said, sir! He is
The impudent'st rascal——
Sur. You are indeed. Will you hear me, sir?
Face. By no means: bid him be gone.
Kas. Begone, sir, quickly.
Sur. This is strange!—Lady, do you inform your brother.
Face. There is not such a foist[42] in all the town.
The doctor had him presently; and finds yet
The Spanish count will come here.—(*Aside.*) Bear up, Subtle.
Sub. Yes, sir, he must appear within this hour.
Face. And yet this rogue would come in a disguise,
By the temptation of another spirit,
To trouble our art, though he could not hurt it!
Kas. Aye,
I know—Away, (*To his sister.*) you talk like a foolish mauther.[43]
Sur. Sir, all is truth she says.
Face. Do not believe him, sir.
He is the lying'st swabber! Come your ways, sir.
Sur. You are valiant out of company!
Kas. Yes, how then, sir?

Enter Drugger with a piece of damask.

Face. Nay, here 's an honest fellow too that knows him,
And all his tricks. (Make good what I say, Abel.
This cheater would ha' cozen'd thee o' the widow.)
He owes this honest Drugger here seven pound,
He has had on him in twopenny'orths of tobacco.
Drug. Yes, sir. And he has damn'd himself three terms to pay me.
Face. And what does he owe for lotium?[44]
Drug. Thirty shillings, sir;
And for six syringes.
Sur. Hydra of villainy!
Face. Nay, sir, you must quarrel him out o' the house.
Kas. I will:
—Sir, if you get not out o' doors, you lie;
And you are a pimp.
Sur. Why, this is madness, sir,
Not valor in you; I must laugh at this.
Kas. It is my humor; you are a pimp and a trig.[45]
And an Amadis de Gaul, or a Don Quixote.
Drug. Or a knight o' the curious coxcomb, do you see?

Enter Ananias.

Ana. Peace to the household!
Kas. I'll keep peace for no man.
Ana. Casting of dollars is concluded lawful.
Kas. Is he the constable?
Sub. Peace, Ananias.
Face. No, sir.
Kas. Then you are an otter, and a shad, a whit,
A very tim.
Sur. You 'll hear me, sir?
Kas. I will not.
Ana. What is the motive?
Sub. Zeal in the young gentleman,
Against his Spanish slops.
Ana. They are profane,
Lewd, superstitious, and idolatrous breeches.
Sur. New rascals!
Kas. Will you be gone, sir?

41 deceived. 42 rogue. 43 country girl. 44 a lotion. 45 coxcomb.

Ana. Avoid, Satan!
Thou art not of the light! That ruff of pride
About thy neck, betrays thee; and is the same
With that which the unclean birds, in seventy-seven,
Were seen to prank it with on divers coasts:
Thou look'st like antichrist, in that lewd hat.
Sur. I must give way.
Kas. Be gone, sir.
Sur. But I'll take
A course with you.——
Ana. Depart, proud Spanish fiend!
Sur. Captain and doctor.
Ana. Child of perdition!
Kas. Hence, sir!—
Exit Surly.
Did I not quarrel bravely?
Face. Yes, indeed, sir.
Kas. Nay, an I give my mind to 't, I shall do 't.
Face. O, you must follow, sir, and threaten him tame:
He 'll turn again else.
Kas. I 'll re-turn him then.
Exit.
Face. Drugger, this rogue prevented [46] us, for thee:
We had determin'd that thou should'st ha' come
In a Spanish suit, and ha' carried her so; and he,
A brokerly slave, goes, puts it on himself.
Hast brought the damask?
Drug. Yes, sir.
Face. Thou must borrow
A Spanish suit. Hast thou no credit with the players?
Drug. Yes, sir; did you never see me play the fool?
Face. I know not, Nab;—thou shalt, if I can help it.—(*Aside.*)
Hieronimo's [47] old cloak, ruff, and hat will serve;
I 'll tell thee more when thou bring'st 'em.
Exit Drugger. Subtle hath whisper'd with Ana. this while.
Ana. Sir, I know.
The Spaniard hates the brethren, and hath spies
Upon their actions: and that this was one
I make no scruple.—But the holy synod
Have been in prayer and meditation for it;
And 't is reveal'd no less to them than me,
That casting of money is most lawful.
Sub. True.
But here I cannot do it: if the house
Should chance to be suspected, all would out,
And we be lock'd up in the Tower for ever,
To make gold there for th' state, never come out;
And then are you defeated.
Ana. I will tell
This to the elders and the weaker brethren,
That the whole company of the separation
May join in humble prayer again.
Sub. And fasting.
Ana. Yea, for some fitter place. The peace of mind
Rest with these walls!
Exit
Sub. Thanks, courteous Ananias.
Face. What did he come for?
Sub. About casting dollars,
Presently out of hand. And so I told him,
A Spanish minister came here to spy,
Against the faithful——
Face. I conceive. Come, Subtle,
Thou art so down upon the least disaster!
How wouldst thou ha' done, if I had not helpt thee out?
Sub. I thank thee, Face, for the angry boy, i' faith.
Face. Who would ha' look'd [48] it should ha' been that rascal
Surly? He had dy'd his beard and all Well, sir.
Here 's damask come to make you a suit.
Sub. Where 's Drugger?
Face. He is gone to borrow me a Spanish habit;
I 'll be the count now.
Sub. But where 's the widow?
Face. Within, with my lord's sister; Madam Dol
Is entertaining her.
Sub. By your favor, Face,
Now she is honest, I will stand again.
Face. You will not offer it?
Sub. Why?
Face. Stand to your word,
Or—here comes Dol. She knows——
Sub. You 're tyrannous still.

46 anticipated. 47 The hero of Kyd's *Spanish Tragedy*. 48 expected.

Enter Dol hastily.

Face. —Strict for my right.—How now, Dol! Hast told her
The Spanish count will come?
Dol. Yes; but another is come,
You little look'd for!
Face. Who's that?
Dol. Your master;
The master of the house.
Sub. How, Dol!
Face. She lies!
This is some trick. Come, leave your quiblins,[49] Dorothy.
Dol. Look out and see.
(*Face goes to the window.*)
Sub. Art thou in earnest?
Dol. 'Slight,
Forty o' the neighbors are about him, talking.
Face. 'T is he, by this good day.
Dol. 'T will prove ill day
For some on us.
Face. We are undone, and taken.
Dol. Lost, I'm afraid.
Sub. You said he would not come,
While there died one a week within the liberties.[50]
Face. No: 't was within the walls.
Sub. Was't so? Cry you mercy.
I thought the liberties. What shall we do now, Face?
Face. Be silent: not a word, if he call or knock.
I'll into mine old shape again and meet him,
Of Jeremy, the butler. I' the meantime,
Do you two pack up all the goods and purchase[51]
That we can carry i' the two trunks. I'll keep him
Off for to-day, if I cannot longer: and then
At night, I'll ship you both away to Ratcliff,
Where we will meet to-morrow, and there we'll share.
Let Mammon's brass and pewter keep the cellar;
We'll have another time for that. But, Dol,
Prithee go heat a little water quickly;
Subtle must shave me. All my captain's beard
Must off, to make me appear smooth Jeremy.
You'll do it?
Sub. Yes, I'll shave you as well as I can.
Face. And not cut my throat, but trim me?
Sub. You shall see, sir.
Exeunt.

ACT V.

SCENE 1. *Before Lovewit's door.*

Enter Lovewit, with several of the Neighbors.

Love. Has there been such resort, say you?
1 Nei. Daily, Sir.
2 Nei. And nightly, too.
3 Nei. Aye, some as brave as lords.
4 Nei. Ladies and gentlewomen.
5 Nei. Citizens' wives.
1 Nei. And knights.
6 Nei. In coaches.
2 Nei. Yes, and oyster-women.
1 Nei. Beside other gallants.
3 Nei. Sailors' wives.
4 Nei. Tobacco men.
5 Nei. Another Pimlico.[52]
Love. What should my knave advance,
To draw this company? He hung out no banners
Of a strange calf with five legs to be seen,
Or a huge lobster with six claws?
6 Nei. No, sir.
3 Nei. We had gone in then, sir.
Love. He has no gift
Of teaching i' the nose[53] that e'er I knew of.
You saw no bills set up that promis'd cure
Of agues or the tooth-ache?
2 Nei. No such thing, sir!
Love. Nor heard a drum struck for baboons or puppets?
5 Nei. Neither, sir.
Love. What device should he bring forth now?
I love a teeming wit as I love my nourishment:
'Pray God he ha' not kept such open house,
That he hath sold my hangings, and my bedding!
I left him nothing else. If he have eat 'em,

49 quibbling.
50 as long as there was one dead a week from the plague in the parts of the city outside the walls.
51 booty.
52 a summer resort, famous for cakes and ale.
53 preaching through the nose like a Puritan; or "perhaps ventriloquism." (Schelling.)

A plague o' the moth, say I! Sure he has got
Some bawdy pictures to call all this ging; [54]
The Friar and the Nun; or the new motion [55]
Of the knight's courser covering the parson's mare;
The boy of six year old, with the great thing:
Or 't may be, he has the fleas that run at tilt
Upon a table, or some dog to dance.
When saw you him?
1 Nei. Who, sir, Jeremy?
2 Nei. Jeremy butler?
We saw him not this month.
Love. How!
4 Nei. Not these five weeks, sir.
6 Nei. These six weeks, at the least.
Love. You amaze me, neighbors!
5 Nei. Sure, if your worship know not where he is,
He 's slipt away.
6 Nei. Pray God he be not made away.
(*He knocks.*)
Love. Ha! it 's no time to question, then.
6 Nei. About
Some three weeks since I heard a doleful cry,
As I sat up a-mending my wife's stockings.
Love. This 's strange that none will answer! Did'st thou hear
A cry, sayst thou?
6 Nei. Yes, sir, like unto a man
That had been strangled an hour, and could not speak.
2 Nei. I heard it, too, just this day three weeks, at two o'clock
Next morning.
Love. These be miracles, or you make 'em so!
A man an hour strangled, and could not speak,
And both you heard him cry?
3 Nei. Yes, downward, sir.
Love. Thou art a wise fellow. Give me thy hand, I pray thee.
What trade art thou on?
3 Nei. A smith, an 't please your worship.
Love. A smith! Then lend me thy help to get this door open.
3 Nei. That I will presently, sir, but fetch my tools—
Exit.
1 Nei. Sir, best to knock again afore you break it.

SCENE 2.

Lovewit, Neighbors.

Love. (*Knocks again.*) I will.

Enter Face in his butler's livery.

Face. What mean you, sir?
1, 2, 4 Nei. O, here 's Jeremy!
Face. Good sir, come from the door.
Love. Why, what 's the matter?
Face. Yet farther, you are too near yet.
Love. I' the name of wonder,
What means the fellow!
Face. The house, sir, has been visited.
Love. What, with the plague? Stand thou then farther.
Face. No, sir,
I had it not.
Love. Who had it then? I left
None else but thee i' the house.
Face. Yes, sir, my fellow,
The cat that kept the buttery, had it on her
A week before I spied it; but I got her
Convey'd away i' the night: and so I shut
The house for a month——
Love. How!
Face. Purposing then, sir,
To have burnt rose-vinegar, treacle, and tar,
And ha' made it sweet, that you should ne'er ha' known it;
Because I knew the news would but afflict you, sir.
Love. Breathe less, and farther off! Why this is stranger:
The neighbors tell me all here that the doors
Have still been open——
Face. How, sir!
Love. Gallants, men and women,
And of all sorts, tag-rag, been seen to flock here
In threaves,[56] these ten weeks, as to a second Hogsden,
In days of Pimlico and Eye-bright.[57]
Face. Sir,
Their wisdoms will not say so.
Love. To-day they speak
Of coaches and gallants; one in a French hood

[54] gang. [55] puppet show. [56] droves. [57] possibly the name of a tavern

Went in, they tell me; and another was seen
In a velvet gown at the window: divers more
Pass in and out.
Face. They did pass through the doors then,
Or walls, I assure their eye-sights, and their spectacles;
For here, sir, are the keys, and here have been,
In this my pocket, now above twenty days!
And for before, I kept the fort alone there.
But that 't is yet not deep i' the afternoon,
I should believe my neighbors had seen double
Through the black pot, and made these apparitions!
For, on my faith to your worship, for these three weeks
And upwards, the door has not been open'd.
Love. Strange!
1 Nei. Good faith, I think I saw a coach.
2 Nei. And I too,
I 'd ha' been sworn.
Love. Do you but think it now?
And but one coach?
4 Nei. We cannot tell, sir: Jeremy
Is a very honest fellow.
Face. Did you see me at all?
1 Nei. No; that we are sure on.
2 Nei. I 'll be sworn o' that.
Love. Fine rogues to have your testimonies built on!

Re-enter third Neighbor, with his tools.

3 Nei. Is Jeremy come!
1 Nei. O yes; you may leave your tools;
We were deceiv'd, he says.
2 Nei. He 's had the keys;
And the door has been shut these three weeks.
3 Nei. Like enough.
Love. Peace, and get hence, you changelings.

Enter Surly and Mammon.

Face. (*Aside.*) Surly come.
And Mammon made acquainted! They 'll tell all.
How shall I beat them off? What shall I do?
Nothing 's more wretched than a guilty conscience.

SCENE 3.

Surly, Mammon, Lovewit, Face, Neighbors.

Sur. No, sir, he was a great physician. This,
It was no bawdy-house, but a mere chancel!
You knew the lord and his sister.
Mam. Nay, good Surly.——
Sur. The happy word, BE RICH——
Mam. Play not the tyrant.—
Sur. Should be to-day pronounc'd to all your friends.
And where be your andirons now? And your brass pots,
That should ha' been golden flagons, and great wedges?
Mam. Let me but breathe. What, they ha' shut their doors,
Methinks!
(*He and Surly knock.*)
Sur. Aye, now 't is holiday with them.
Mam. Rogues,
Cozeners, impostors, bawds!
Face. What mean you, sir?
Mam. To enter if we can.
Face. Another man's house!
Here is the owner, sir; turn you to him,
And speak your business.
Mam. Are you, sir, the owner?
Love. Yes, sir.
Mam. And are those knaves within, your cheaters!
Love. What knaves, what cheaters?
Mam. Subtle and his Lungs.
Face. The gentleman is distracted, sir! No lungs
Nor lights [58] ha' been seen here these three weeks, sir,
Within these doors upon my word.
Sur. Your word,
Groom arrogant!
Face. Yes, sir, I am the housekeeper,
And know the keys ha' not been out o' my hands.
Sur. This 's a new Face.
Face. You do mistake the house, sir:
What sign was 't at? [59]
Sur. You rascal! This is one
Of the confederacy. Come, let 's get officers,
And force the door.

58 lungs, punningly. 59 Even private houses were sometimes distinguished by signs, like taverns or shops.

Love. Pray you stay, gentlemen.
Sur. No, sir, we'll come with warrant.
Mam. Aye, and then
We shall ha' your doors open.
Exeunt Mam. and Sur.
Love. What means this?
Face. I cannot tell, sir.
1 Nei. These are two o' the gallants
That we do think we saw.
Face. Two o' the fools!
You talk as idly as they. Good faith, sir,
I think the moon has craz'd 'em all.—
(*Aside.*) O me,

Enter Kastril.

The angry boy come too! He'll make a noise,
And ne'er away till he have betray'd us all.
Kas. (*Knocking.*) What, rogues, bawds, slaves, you'll open the door anon!
Punk, cockatrice, my suster! By this light
I'll fetch the marshal to you. You are a whore
To keep your castle——
Face. Who would you speak with, sir?
Kas. The bawdy doctor, and the cozening captain,
And puss my suster.
Love. This is something, sure.
Face. Upon my trust, the doors were never open, sir.
Kas. I have heard all their tricks told me twice over,
By the fat knight and the lean gentleman.
Love. Here comes another.

Enter Ananias and Tribulation.

Face. Ananias too!
And his pastor!
Tri. The doors are shut against us.
(*They beat too, at the door.*)
Ana. Come forth, you seed of sulphur, sons of fire!
Your stench it is broke forth; abomination
Is in the house.
Kas. Aye, my suster's there.
Ana. The place,
It is become a cage of unclean birds.
Kas. Yes, I will fetch the scavenger, and the constable.
Tri. You shall do well.
Ana. We'll join to weed them out.
Kas. You will not come then, punk device,[60] my suster!

Ana. Call her not sister; she's a harlot verily.
Kas. I'll raise the street.
Love. Good gentleman, a word.
Ana. Satan, avoid, and hinder not our zeal!
Exeunt Ana., Trib., and Kas.
Love. The world's turn'd Bet'lem.
Face. These are all broke loose,
Out of St. Katherine's, where they use to keep
The better sort of mad-folks.
1 Nei. All these persons
We saw go in and out here.
2 Nei. Yes, indeed, sir.
3 Nei. These were the parties.
Face. Peace, you drunkards! Sir,
I wonder at it. Please you to give me leave
To touch the door; I'll try an the lock be chang'd.
Love. It mazes me!
Face. (*Goes to the door.*) Good faith, sir, I believe
There's no such thing: 't is all *deceptio visus*.[61]—
(*Aside.*) Would I could get him away.
Dap. (*Within.*) Master captain! Master doctor!
Love. Who's that?
Face. (*Aside.*) Our clerk within, that I forgot!—I know not, sir.
Dap. (*Within.*) For God's sake, when will her grace be at leisure?
Face. Ha!
Illusions, some spirit o' the air!—
(*Aside.*) His gag is melted,
And now he sets out the throat.
Dap. (*Within.*) I am almost stifled——
Face. (*Aside.*) Would you were altogether!
Love. 'T is i' the house.
Ha! list!
Face. Believe it, sir, i' the air.
Love. Peace, you.
Dap. (*Within.*) Mine aunt's grace does not use me well.
Sub. (*Within.*) You fool,
Peace, you'll mar all.
Face. (*Speaks through the keyhole, while Lovewit advances to the door unobserved.*) Or you will else, you rogue.
Love. O, is it so? Then you converse with spirits!—
Come, sir. No more o' your tricks, good Jeremy.
The truth, the shortest way.

60 complete.

61 optical illusion.

Face. Dismiss this rabble, sir.—(*Aside.*) What shall I do? I am catch'd.

Love. Good neighbors,
I thank you all. You may depart. (*Exeunt Neighbors.*)—Come, sir,
You know that I am an indulgent master;
And therefore conceal nothing. What 's your medicine,
To draw so many several sorts of wild fowl?

Face. Sir, you were wont to affect mirth and wit—
But here 's no place to talk on 't i' the street.
Give me but leave to make the best of my fortune,
And only pardon me th' abuse of your house:
It 's all I beg. I 'll help you to a widow,
In recompense, that you shall gi' me thanks for,
Will make you seven years younger, and a rich one.
'T is but your putting on a Spanish cloak:
I have her within. You need not fear the house;
It was not visited.

Love. But by me, who came
Sooner than you expected.

Face. It is true, sir.
Pray you forgive me.

Love. Well: let 's see your widow.
Exeunt.

SCENE 4. *A room in the house.*

Enter Subtle leading in Dapper, with his eyes bound as before.

Sub. How! ha' you eaten your gag?

Dap. Yes, faith, it crumbled
Away i' my mouth.

Sub. You ha' spoil'd all then.

Dap. No!
I hope my aunt of Fairy will forgive me.

Sub. Your aunt 's a gracious lady; but in troth
You were to blame.

Dap. The fume did overcome me,
And I did do't to stay my stomach. Pray you,
So satisfy her grace.

Enter Face in his uniform.

Here comes the captain.

Face. How now! Is his mouth down?

Sub. Aye, he has spoken!

Face. A pox, I heard him, and you too. He 's undone then.—
(*Aside to Subtle.*) I have been fain to say, the house is haunted
With spirits, to keep churl back.

Sub. And hast thou done it?

Face. Sure, for this night.

Sub. Why, then triumph and sing
Of Face so famous, the precious king
Of present wits.

Face. Did you not hear the coil [62]
About the door?

Sub. Yes, and I dwindled with it.

Face. Show him his aunt, and let him be dispatch'd:
I 'll send her to you.

Exit Face.

Sub. Well, sir, your aunt her grace
Will give you an audience presently, on my suit,
And the captain's word that you did not eat your gag
In any contempt of her highness.

(*Unbinds his eyes.*)

Dap. Not I, in troth, sir.

Enter Dol like the Queen of Fairy.

Sub. Here she is come. Down o' your knees and wriggle:
She has a stately presence. (*Dapper kneels and shuffles towards her.*) Good! Yet nearer,
And bid, God save you!

Dap. Madam!

Sub. And your aunt.

Dap. And my most gracious aunt, God save your grace.

Dol. Nephew, we thought to have been angry with you;
But that sweet face of yours hath turn'd the tide,
And made it flow with joy, that ebb'd of love.
Arise, and touch our velvet gown.

Sub. The skirts,
And kiss 'em. So!

Dol. Let me now stroke that head.
Much, nephew, shalt thou win, much shalt thou spend;
Much shalt thou give away, much shalt thou lend.

Sub. (*Aside.*) Aye, much! indeed.—Why do you not thank her grace?

Dap. I cannot speak for joy.

62 hubbub.

Sub. See, the kind wretch!
Your grace's kinsman right.
Dol. Give me the bird.——
Here is your fly in a purse, about your neck, cousin;
Wear it, and feed it about this day sev'n-night,
On your right wrist——
Sub. Open a vein with a pin
And let it suck but once a week; till then,
You must not look on 't.
Dol. No: and, kinsman,
Bear yourself worthy of the blood you came on.
Sub. Her grace would ha' you eat no more Woolsack [63] pies
Nor Dagger [63] frumety.[64]
Dol. Nor break his fast
In Heaven [63] and Hell.[63]
Sub. She 's with you everywhere!
Nor play with costermongers, at mum-chance,[65] traytrip,[65]
God-make-you-rich [65] (when as your aunt has done it); but keep
The gallant'st company, and the best games——
Dap. Yes, sir.
Sub. Gleek [65] and primero; [65] and what you get, be true to us.
Dap. By this hand, I will.
Sub. You may bring 's a thousand pound
Before to-morrow night, if but three thousand
Be stirring, an you will.
Dap. I swear I will then.
Sub. Your fly will learn you all games.
Face. (*Within.*) Ha' you done there?
Sub. Your grace will command him no more duties?
Dol. No:
But come and see me often. I may chance
To leave him three or four hundred chests of treasure,
And some twelve thousand acres of fairy land,
If he game well and comely with good gamesters.
Sub. There 's a kind aunt: kiss her departing part.—
But you must sell your forty mark a year now.
Dap. Aye, sir, I mean.
Sub. Or, give 't away; pox on 't!
Dap. I 'll gi' 't mine aunt. I 'll go and fetch the writings.
Exit.
Sub. 'T is well; away.

Re-enter Face.

Face. Where 's Subtle?
Sub. Here: what news?
Face. Drugger is at the door; go take his suit,
And bid him fetch a parson presently.
Say he shall marry the widow. Thou shalt spend
A hundred pound by the service!
Exit Subtle.
Now, Queen Dol,
Have you pack'd up all?
Dol. Yes.
Face. And how do you like
The Lady Pliant?
Dol. A good dull innocent.

Re-enter Subtle.

Sub. Here 's your Hieronimo's cloak and hat.
Face. Give me 'em.
Sub. And the ruff too?
Face. Yes; I 'll come to you presently.
Exit.
Sub. Now he is gone about his project, Dol,
I told you of, for the widow.
Dol. 'T is direct
Against our articles.
Sub. Well, we will fit him, wench.
Hast thou gull'd her of her jewels or her bracelets?
Dol. No; but I will do 't.
Sub. Soon at night, my Dolly,
When we are shipt, and all our goods aboard,
Eastward for Ratcliff, we will turn our course
To Brainford, westward, if thou sayst the word,
And take our leaves of this o'erweening rascal,
This peremptory Face.
Dol. Content; I 'm weary of him.
Sub. Thou 'st cause, when the slave will run a-wiving, Dol,
Against the instrument that was drawn between us.
Dol. I 'll pluck his bird as bare as I can.
Sub. Yes, tell her
She must by any means address some present
To th' cunning man, make him amends for wronging
His art with her suspicion; send a ring,
Or chain of pearl; she will be tortur'd else

63 names of taverns. 64 wheat boiled in milk. 65 games of chance.

Extremely in her sleep, say, and ha' strange things
Come to her. Wilt thou?
Dol. Yes.
Sub. My fine flitter-mouse,[66]
My bird o' the night! We'll tickle it at the Pigeons,[67]
When we have all, and may unlock the trunks,
And say, this's mine, and thine; and thine, and mine. (*They kiss.*)

Re-enter Face.

Face. What now! a-billing?
Sub. Yes, a little exalted
In the good passage of our stock-affairs.
Face. Drugger has brought his parson; take him in, Subtle,
And send Nab back again to wash his face.
Sub. I will: and shave himself? *Exit.*
Face. If you can get him.
Dol. You are hot upon it, Face, whate'er it is!
Face. A trick that Dol shall spend ten pound a month by.

Re-enter Subtle.

Is he gone?
Sub. The chaplain waits you i' the hall, sir.
Face. I'll go bestow him. *Exit.*
Dol. He'll now marry her instantly.
Sub. He cannot yet, he is not ready. Dear Dol,
Cozen her of all thou canst. To deceive him
Is no deceit, but justice, that would break
Such an inextricable tie as ours was.
Dol. Let me alone to fit him.

Re-enter Face.

Face. Come, my venturers,
You ha' pack'd up all? Where be the trunks? Bring forth.
Sub. Here.
Face. Let us see 'em. Where's the money?
Sub. Here,
In this.
Face. Mammon's ten pound; eight score before:
The brethren's money this. Drugger's and Dapper's.
What paper's that?
Dol. The jewel of the waiting maid's,
That stole it from her lady, to know certain——
Face. If she should have precedence of her mistress?
Dol. Yes.
Face. What box is that?
Sub. The fish-wives' rings, I think,
And th' ale-wives' single money.[68] Is't not, Dol?
Dol. Yes; and the whistle that the sailor's wife
Brought you to know an her husband were with Ward.[69]
Face. We'll wet it to-morrow; and our silver beakers
And tavern cups. Where be the French petticoats
And girdles and hangers?
Sub. Here, i' the trunk,
And the bolts of lawn.
Face. Is Drugger's damask there,
And the tobacco?
Sub. Yes.
Face. Give me the keys.
Dol. Why you the keys?
Sub. No matter, Dol; because
We shall not open 'em before he comes.
Face. 'T is true, you shall not open them, indeed;
Nor have 'em forth, do you see? Not forth, Dol.
Dol. No!
Face. No, my smock-rampant. The right is, my master
Knows all, has pardon'd me, and he will keep 'em.
Doctor, 't is true—you look—for all your figures:
I sent for him, indeed.[70] Wherefore, good partners,
Both he and she, be satisfied: for here
Determines[71] the indenture tripartite
'Twixt Subtle, Dol, and Face. All I can do
Is to help you over the wall, o' the back-side,
Or lend you a sheet to save your velvet gown, Dol.
Here will be officers presently, bethink you
Of some course suddenly to scape the dock;
For thither you'll come else. (*Some knock.*) Hark you, thunder.
Sub. You are a precious fiend!
Offi. (*Without.*) Open the door.

66 bat. 67 an inn at Brentford. 68 small change. 69 a notorious pirate. 70 Face's crowning lie. 71 comes to an end.

Face. Dol, I am sorry for thee i' faith; but hear'st thou?
It shall go hard but I will place thee somewhere:
Thou shalt ha' my letter to Mistress Amo——
Dol. Hang you!
Face. Or Madam Cæsarean.
Dol. Pox upon you, rogue!
Would I had but time to beat thee!
Face. Subtle,
Let 's know where you 'll set up next; I will send you
A customer now and then, for old acquaintance.
What new course have you?
Sub. Rogue, I 'll hang myself,
That I may walk a greater devil than thou,
And haunt thee i' the flock-bed [72] and the buttery.
Exeunt.

SCENE 5.

Enter Lovewit in the Spanish dress, with the Parson. Loud knocking at the door.

Love. What do you mean, my masters?
Mam. (*Without.*) Open your door,
Cheaters, bawds, conjurers.
Offi. (*Without.*) Or we 'll break it open.
Love. What warrant have you?
Offi. (*Without.*) Warrant enough, sir, doubt not,
If you 'll not open it.
Love. Is there an officer there?
Offi. (*Without.*) Yes, two or three for failing.[73]
Love. Have but patience,
And I will open it straight.

Enter Face, as butler.

Face. Sir, ha' you done?
Is it a marriage? Perfect?
Love. Yes, my brain.
Face. Off with your ruff and cloak then; be yourself, sir.
Sur. (*Without.*) Down with the door.
Kas. (*Without.*) 'Slight, ding [74] it open.
Love. (*Opening the door.*) Hold,
Hold, gentlemen, what means this violence?

Mammon, Surly, Kastril, Ananias, Tribulation and Officers rush in.

Mam. Where is this collier?
Sur. And my Captain Face?
Mam. These day-owls.
Sur. They are birding in men's purses.
Mam. Madam Suppository.
Kas. Doxy, my suster.
Ana. Locusts
Of the foul pit.
Tri. Profane as Bel and the Dragon.
Ana. Worse than the grasshoppers, or the lice of Egypt.
Love. Good gentlemen, hear me. Are you officers,
And cannot stay this violence?
1 Offi. Keep the peace.
Love. Gentlemen, what is the matter? Whom do you seek?
Mam. The chemical cozener.
Sur. And the captain pander.
Kas. The nun my suster.
Mam. Madam Rabbi.
Ana. Scorpions,
And caterpillars.
Love. Fewer at once, I pray you.
1 Offi. One after another, gentlemen, I charge you,
By virtue of my staff.
Ana. They are the vessels
Of pride, lust, and the cart.
Love. Good zeal, lie still
A little while.
Tri. Peace, Deacon Ananias.
Love. The house is mine here, and the doors are open;
If there be any such persons as you seek for,
Use your authority, search on o' God's name,
I am but newly come to town, and finding
This tumult 'bout my door, to tell you true,
It somewhat maz'd me; till my man here, fearing
My more displeasure, told me he had done
Somewhat an insolent part, let out my house
(Belike presuming on my known aversion
From any air o' the town while there was sickness),
To a doctor and a captain: who, what they are
Or where they be, he knows not.
Mam. Are they gone?
Love. You may go in and search, sir. (*Mammon, Ana., and Trib. go in.*) Here, I find

72 mattress. 73 to prevent failure. 74 smash.

The empty walls worse than I left 'em, smok'd,
A few crack'd pots, and glasses, and a furnace;
The ceiling fill'd with poesies of the candle,
And "Madam with a dildo" [75] writ o' the walls.
Only one gentlewoman I met here
That is within, that said she was a widow——

Kas. Aye, that 's my suster; I 'll go thump her. Where is she?
(*Goes in.*)

Love. And should ha' married a Spanish count, but he,
When he came to 't, neglected her so grossly,
That I, a widower, am gone through with her.

Sur. How! have I lost her then?

Love. Were you the don, sir?
Good faith, now she does blame you extremely, and says
You swore, and told her you had ta'en the pains
To dye your beard, and umber o'er your face,
Borrowed a suit, and ruff, all for her love:
And then did nothing. What an oversight
And want of putting forward, sir, was this!
Well fare an old harquebusier [76] yet,
Could prime his powder, and give fire, and hit,
All in a twinkling!
(*Mammon comes forth.*)

Mam. The whole nest are fled!

Love. What sort of birds were they?

Mam. A kind of choughs,
Or thievish daws, sir, that have pick'd my purse,
Of eight score and ten pounds within these five weeks,
Beside my first materials; and my goods,
That lie i' the cellar, which I am glad they ha' left,
I may have home yet.

Love. Think you so, sir?

Mam. Aye.

Love. By order of law, sir, but not otherwise.

Mam. Not mine own stuff!

Love. Sir, I can take no knowledge
That they are yours, but by public means.
If you can bring certificate that you were gull'd of 'em,
Or any formal writ out of a court,
That you did cozen yourself, I will not hold them.

Mam. I'll rather lose 'em.

Love. That you shall not, sir,
By me, in troth; upon these terms, they 're yours.
What, should they ha' been, sir, turn'd into gold, all?

Mam. No.
I cannot tell.—It may be they should.—What then?

Love. What a great loss in hope have you sustain'd!

Mam. Not I; the commonwealth has.

Face. Aye, he would ha' built
The city new; and made a ditch about it
Of silver, should have run with cream from Hogsden;
That every Sunday in Moorfields the younkers,
And tits [77] and tom-boys should have fed on, gratis.

Mam. I will go mount a turnip-cart, and preach
The end o' the world within these two months. Surly,
What! in a dream?

Sur. Must I needs cheat myself
With that same foolish vice of honesty!
Come, let us go and hearken out the rogues:
That Face I 'll mark for mine, if e'er I meet him.

Face. If I can hear of him, sir, I'll bring you word
Unto your lodging; for in troth, they were strangers
To me; I thought 'em honest as myself, sir.
(*They come forth.*)

Re-enter Ananias and Tribulation.

Tri. 'T is well, the saints shall not lose all yet. Go
And get some carts——

Love. For what, my zealous friends?

Ana. To bear away the portion of the righteous
Out of this den of thieves.

Love. What is that portion?

Ana. The goods sometimes the orphans', that the brethren
Bought with their silver pence.

75 perhaps a ballad refrain. 76 musketeer. 77 strumpets.

Love. What, those i' the cellar,
The knight Sir Mammon claims?
Ana. I do defy
The wicked Mammon, so do all the brethren,
Thou profane man! I ask thee with what conscience
Thou canst advance that idol against us,
That have the seal?[78] Were not the shillings numb'red
That made the pounds; were not the pounds told out
Upon the second day of the fourth week,
In the eighth month, upon the table dormant,
The year of the last patience of the saints,
Six hundred and ten?
Love. Mine earnest vehement botcher,
And deacon also, I cannot dispute with you:
But if you get you not away the sooner,
I shall confute you with a cudgel.
Ana. Sir!
Tri. Be patient, Ananias.
Ana. I am strong,
And will stand up, well girt, against an host
That threatens Gad in exile.
Love. I shall send you
To Amsterdam, to your cellar.
Ana. I will pray there,
Against thy house. May dogs defile thy walls,
And wasps and hornets breed beneath thy roof,
This seat of falsehood, and this cave of coz'nage!

Exeunt Ana. and Tri.

Enter Drugger.

Love. Another too?
Drug. Not I, sir, I am no brother.
Love. (*Beats him.*) Away, you Harry Nicholas![79] do you talk?

Exit Drug.

Face. No, this was Abel Drugger. Good sir, go, (*To the Parson.*)
And satisfy him; tell him all is done:
He stay'd too long a washing of his face.
The doctor, he shall hear of him at Westchester;
And of the captain, tell him, at Yarmouth, or
Some good port-town else, lying for a wind.

Exit Parson.

If you can get off the angry child now, sir——

Enter Kastril, dragging in his sister.

Kas. Come on, you ewe, you have match'd most sweetly, ha' you not?
Did not I say, I would never ha' you tupt
But by a dubb'd boy,[80] to make you a lady-tom?
'Slight, you are a mammet![81] O, I could touse you now.
Death, mun[82] you marry with a pox!
Love. You lie, boy;
As sound as you; and I'm aforehand with you.
Kas. Anon!
Love. Come, will you quarrel? I will feeze[83] you, sirrah;
Why do you not buckle to your tools?
Kas. God's light,
This is a fine old boy as e'er I saw!
Love. What, do you change your copy now? Proceed;
Here stands my dove: stoop[84] at her if you dare.
Kas. 'Slight, I must love him! I cannot choose, i' faith,
An I should be hang'd for 't! Suster, I protest,
I honor thee for this match.
Love. O, do you so, sir?
Kas. Yes, an thou canst take tobacco and drink, old boy,
I 'll give her five hundred pound more to her marriage,
Than her own state.
Love. Fill a pipe full, Jeremy.
Face. Yes; but go in and take it, sir.
Love. We will.
I will be rul'd by thee in anything, Jeremy.
Kas. 'Slight, thou art not hide-bound, thou art a jovy[85] boy!
Come, let us in, I pray thee, and take our whiffs.
Love. Whiff in with your sister, brother boy.

Exeunt Kas. and Dame Pliant.

That master
That hath receiv'd such happiness by a servant,
In such a widow, and with so much wealth,
Were very ungrateful, if he would not be
A little indulgent to that servant's wit,

78 sealed as God's people.
79 a German religious fanatic, who founded a sect called "The Family of Love."
80 knight.
81 puppet.
82 must.
83 settle your business.
84 swoop, like a hawk on its prey.
85 jovial.

And help his fortune, though with some small strain
Of his own candor.[86] (*Advancing.*) Therefore, gentlemen,
And kind spectators, if I have outstript
An old man's gravity, or strict canon, think
What a young wife and a good brain may do;
Stretch age's truth sometimes, and crack it too.
Speak for thyself, knave.

Face. So I will, sir. (*Advancing to the front of the stage.*) Gentlemen,
My part a little fell in this last scene,
Yet 't was decorum.[87] And though I am clean
Got off from Subtle, Surly, Mammon, Dol,
Hot Ananias, Dapper, Drugger, all
With whom I traded; yet I put myself
On you, that are my country:[88] and this pelf
Which I have got, if you do quit me, rests,
To feast you often, and invite new guests.

Exeunt.

86 honor. 87 dramatic propriety. 88 jury.

JOHN WEBSTER

THE DUCHESS OF MALFI

Of the life of John Webster (c. 1580–1630), probably the son of a London tailor, almost nothing is known. He began writing for the stage as early as 1602, at first as a collaborator, more especially with Dekker, who strongly influenced his dramatic beginnings. Plays known to be by him alone number only four, all dating between 1607 and 1619. For reasons unknown to us, compared with his contemporaries he apparently lacked productiveness and therefore prominence, but was thought highly of by good judges.

Webster's reputation depends mainly on *The White Devil, or Vittoria Corombona* (1607–12) and *The Duchess of Malfi* (c. 1613), both romantic tragedies, the kind of play which most people are apt to think of, perhaps, as most typical of the Elizabethan drama, because the most intense of its plays are of this class. In the last hundred years and more these have been the chief models for writers of poetic drama (as in Shelley's *Cenci*). Both of Webster's plays mentioned belong to a subdivision of the type, the tragedy of blood. The most celebrated and influential early example is Thomas Kyd's *Spanish Tragedy* (1585–7) and the greatest is Shakespeare's *Hamlet* (1601–1603), though its original elements are so refined and ennobled as to gain a new character. The tragedy of blood abounds in crime, violence, madness, and bloodshed; ghosts glide through its scenes, much is made of physical horror, revenge is a frequent motive of its personages. Its obvious appeal was somewhat crude and popular; but the great strength of the Elizabethan drama was that while its roots ran deep into popular belief, taste and life, it was formed by the great geniuses of the age. A particular development of the tragedy of blood is seen in these two plays of Webster and some others. Here the horror is both intensified and refined; mere bloodshed is not enough, other and more elaborate physical horrors are added, and especially mental and moral horrors, inhuman wickedness, long-drawn and ingenious agonies, the subtleties of the sinner's inmost thought. The intensity is heightened by a more realistic setting; the ghosts are sometimes absent, as in *The Duchess of Malfi*, and we find ourselves in an almost contemporary age, often in Italy — which was regarded by the English, who had heard lurid tales of its corruption and had misunderstood Machiavelli, as the home of dire and subtle evil.

In *The Duchess of Malfi* there is no lack of murder and sudden death. All the chief characters die violently, four men, three women, two children. As often in Elizabethan tragedy, the play is closed by a group of lofty personages, unimportant for the play, with solemn and regretful comments on the general ruin. Strange and elaborate are the vehicles of dread and torment — the dancing and singing of lunatics, the feigned corpses of her husband and children which wring the Duchess' soul, the cold dead hand grasped in the dark, the coffin and bell, the dolorous echo, the poisoned book which slays by a kiss. The struggling and screaming of Cariola at her death not only serve as a foil to the Duchess' composure, but bring a new shock. The moral horror is not in the mere wickedness, common enough in all tragedy. Bosola is not a highly impressive villain, but an indifferent counterpart to Iago, with his pretense of frank honesty and success at dissimulation; with also, it is true, some individual traits, melancholy, railing and a meditative and scholarly turn. He has a conscience and a heart at bottom; he serves as a contrast to the more depraved brothers, and rebels against them; the gods are just, and of their own creature make an instrument to destroy them. Their motives are revenge and covetousness; both brothers resent the supposed dishonor brought by the Duchess on their royal blood, and Ferdinand hoped

> Had she continued widow, to have gained
> An infinite mass of treasure by her death (IV. ii; cf. I. i).

But their wickedness is so out of proportion to any advantage which it might produce that we feel it is the very air in which they live. We see it in the cold calculation with which they have planned all the accompaniments of their sister's murder. Ferdinand is the weaker and less abnormal of the two. Violent and impulsive as he is, when he sees his sister lying dead his shell of callousness is finally broken by resurgent family feeling and remembrances of their youth, and remorse invades his reason. As to the Cardinal, he is more discerning, abler, firmer than his brother, and it is he who claims responsibility for the strangling of the Duchess and her children. His frigid calm can be disturbed only by the fear of political disgrace, and by the brief moment when he permits himself to peer into the gulf of eternity which lies before him. One of the most abhorrent passages in Elizabethan tragedy is at the beginning of the final scene, where the Cardinal shudders over one of his theological books describing the fire of hell. He is a devil who half-believes and trembles. He recalls the political cardinal of two or three centuries earlier who is reported to have said that if he had a soul he had lost it for the Ghibellines.

Like Shakespeare, Webster is not borne down by the distressing, the negative, the destructive; he is strong enough to battle his way above them. We do not almost forget them, as in *Hamlet* — he has taken good care that we should not. But we concern ourselves more with the normal and benign personages who are finally engulfed in the murky, tempestuous ending. As usual with Webster, the most interesting person is a woman; indeed, for Julia too, as for Vittoria Corombona, he shows sympathy — for a bad woman who has heroic traits, a type always popular on the stage. The Duchess we fancy in the full ripeness of womanhood (though possibly meant to be younger), between youth and middle age, woman rather than sovereign, but both. Nothing could be more perfect than the scene where she reveals to Antonio her resolve to marry him; here is all the charm we feel when circumstances make it proper and necessary for a woman to do the wooing; the Duchess is mature enough to do it without embarrassment, but with the beaming eyes and roguish humor she always shows in talking with Antonio, as in the wonderfully human and dramatic scene (III. ii) where Ferdinand surprises them together. Yet she is almost more mother than wife, the sort of woman, the hope of the human race, who takes a husband to be the father of her children. Almost her last words are a domestic order (for a syrup for her boy's cold), which the situation raises to the highest poetry, but which turns to painful irony when we see the children strangled instantly after her. Antonio, though less fascinating and lifelike, is more elaborately studied than she, doubtless in order to reconcile an aristocratic age to seeing a sovereign marry beneath her; a soldier, diplomat, statesman, penetrating and with a remarkable knowledge of human nature, yet modest, honest, charitable, praised even by Bosola, and with a touch of modern-seeming cultivation in his love of ruins and history. He lacks interest a little through being passive and acted on throughout, for his status, in the drama as in his life, is that of a prince consort. Another curious modern trait is in both, a certain emancipation and liberalism as to religion, partly a reflection of the usual English prejudice against popery. The Duchess rebukes her woman as "a superstitious fool" because she objects to feigning a pilgrimage, and it is doubtless not only the unconsciously ironical Cardinal who would say that Antonio did "account religion but a school-name" (V. ii, and cf. III. iii). Both seem satisfied, as in the original source of the play, with a marriage certainly informal and barely legal. Julia too in her noble dying words "goes she knows not whither." A certain skepticism seems to have excited Webster's sympathy.

In truly Elizabethan manner, the construction and style of the play are ample and broad, not compact and minutely careful, like the work of such a man as Jonson. The verse is lax and irregular, sometimes unpardonably so, approaching mere rhythmical prose, as in some of the latest of the dramatists. Slurred and tumbling syllables often give a dramatic, easy, natural effect; but Webster's lines are sometimes difficult to read in any way which leaves the metrical norm still recognizable. In structure and incident he is at times a trifle careless. Antonio draws up an unnatural and dangerous memorandum for his son's horoscope, and drops it indifferently just when he should have been most careful; and at the end of the play this child who had been condemned by the stars to an early death is the only one of his family who survives! The play takes a sudden emotional turn toward the middle. The cloud in the sunny sky which beams over the first part is no bigger than a man's hand. The storm rolls up with speed, and nothing breaks the gloom of the last part. Webster daringly allows the interest to drop after the death of the Duchess, but towards the middle of the last act it revives, with new uncertainties and with the ingenious and appalling disasters which crush the sinners.

The source of the play is the story of the Duchess of Amalfi, perhaps partly historical, which forms the twenty-third novel in the second volume of Painter's *Palace of Pleasure* (1567), and which came through the French of Belle-Forest from the *Novelle* of Bandello. Painter's interest, like that of all contemporary novelists, is in sensational events, in rhetorical talk, and in drawing forced moral lessons; he censures the Duchess for her uncontrolled desire for marriage, and Antonio for his ambitious folly in marrying above him. The characterization is extremely simple and obvious; Bosola is inconspicuous, and Julia not present at all, nor most of the matter of Webster's fifth act.

A near kinship between Webster and Shakespeare has long been felt by both readers and spectators (the play was acted long and successfully, even as lately as 1851, with overwhelming effect, it is said). There are signs of Shakespeare's influence on it, as of the death of Desdemona in that of the Duchess: if a strangled person revived, as they both do, well enough to be able to speak, there is no reason why she should not recover. But it is doubtful whether Webster should be called a pupil of Shakespeare; if so he was not ready to admit it, for in the preface to *The White Devil*, after analyzing the merits of Chapman, Jonson, Beaumont and Fletcher, he dismisses Shakespeare, Dekker, and Heywood in one breath. He approaches Shakespeare on only one of his many dramatic sides, in his deeply human tragedy. Webster's two best plays put us more nearly in the frame of mind produced by *Hamlet*, *Lear*, and *Othello* than those of any other Elizabethan dramatist. The two men are alike in giving us more than we have any right to demand in a play. Without enlarging on abstract subjects, without mere talk, they give us glimpses into deep musings over human nature, life, and destiny. Both had wide intellectual interests. Both, in their greatest plays, though not pessimists, are somber. Their people are more than carefully drawn and individual pictures; they have the contrasting sides and the suggestions of strange possibilities, of the hidden and unknown, which we feel in the rare individual in real life. They give us the utterly unexpected, which we instantly accept. Webster knows what strangely commonplace, what terse and significant things, people will say at supreme moments, as in the staccato dialogue between Ferdinand and Bosola after the Duchess' murder (IV. ii). He makes us feel the moment of tense silence which divides the chatter of affectionate intimacy from the queenly acceptance of doom:

> I 'll assure you,
> You shall get no more children till my brothers
> Consent to be your gossips.— Have you lost your tongue?
> 'T is welcome:
> For know, whether I am doomed to live or die,
> I can do both like a prince.

We are aware, in both poets, of mental power and acuteness combined with warmth of heart and a living soul. In Swinburne's words, there is no poet nobler than Webster. Such likeness was not due to study, it was innate.

THE DUCHESS OF MALFI

By JOHN WEBSTER

NAMES OF THE CHARACTERS

FERDINAND, *Duke of Calabria.*
CARDINAL, *his brother.*
ANTONIO BOLOGNA, *Steward of the Household to the Duchess.*
DELIO, *his friend.*
DANIEL DE BOSOLA, *Gentleman of the Horse to the Duchess.*
CASTRUCCIO, *an old lord.*
MARQUIS OF PESCARA.
COUNT MALATESTE.
RODERIGO, SILVIO, GRISOLAN, } *Lords.*
Doctor.
Several Madmen.

DUCHESS OF MALFI.
CARIOLA, *her woman.*
JULIA, *wife to Castruccio, and mistress to the Cardinal.*
Old Lady.
Ladies, three young children, two pilgrims, executioners, court officers, and attendants.

Scene.—Amalfi, Rome, Loretto, Milan.

ACT I.

SCENE 1. *Amalfi. The presence-chamber in the Duchess's palace.*

Enter Antonio and Delio.

Del. You are welcome to your country, dear Antonio;
You have been long in France, and you return
A very formal Frenchman in your habit.
How do you like the French court?
Ant. I admire it.
In seeking to reduce both state and people
To a fix'd order, their judicious king
Begins at home; quits first his royal palace
Of flatt'ring sycophants, of dissolute
And infamous persons,—which he sweetly terms
His master's master-piece, the work of heaven;
Considering duly that a prince's court
Is like a common fountain, whence should flow
Pure silver drops in general, but if 't chance
Some curs'd example poison 't near the head,
Death and diseases through the whole land spread.
And what is 't makes this blessed government
But a most provident council, who dare freely

Inform him the corruption of the times?
Though some o' th' court hold it presumption
To instruct princes what they ought to do,
It is a noble duty to inform them
What they ought to foresee.[1]—Here comes Bosola,
The only court-gall; yet I observe his railing
Is not for simple love of piety:
Indeed, he rails at those things which he wants;
Would be as lecherous, covetous, or proud,
Bloody, or envious, as any man,
If he had means to be so.—Here 's the cardinal.

Enter Cardinal and Bosola.

Bos. I do haunt you still.
Card. So.
Bos. I have done you better service than to be slighted thus. Miserable age, where only the reward of doing well is the doing of it!
Card. You enforce your merit too much.
Bos. I fell into the galleys in your service; where, for two years together, I wore two towels instead of a shirt, with a knot on the shoulder, after the fashion of a Roman mantle. Slighted thus! I will thrive some way. Blackbirds fatten best in hard weather; why not I in these dog days?
Card. Would you could become honest!
Bos. With all your divinity do but direct me the way to it. I have known many travel far for it, and yet return as arrant knaves as they went forth, because they carried themselves always along with them. (*Exit Cardinal.*) Are you gone? Some fellows, they say, are possessed with the devil, but this great fellow were able to possess the greatest devil, and make him worse.
Ant. He hath denied thee some suit?
Bos. He and his brother are like plum-trees that grow crooked over standing[2] pools; they are rich and o'erladen with fruit, but none but crows, pies,[3] and caterpillars feed on them. Could I be one of their flatt'ring panders, I would hang on their ears like a horse-leech till I were full, and then drop off. I pray, leave me. Who would rely upon these miserable dependencies, in expectation to be advanc'd to morrow? What creature ever fed worse than hoping Tantalus? Nor ever died any man more fearfully than he that hop'd for a pardon. There are rewards for hawks and dogs when they have done us service; but for a soldier that hazards his limbs in a battle, nothing but a kind of geometry is his last supportation.
Delio. Geometry?
Bos. Aye, to hang in a fair pair of slings, take his latter swing in the world upon an honorable pair of crutches, from hospital to hospital. Fare ye well, sir: and yet do not you scorn us; for places in the court are but like beds in the hospital, where this man's head lies at that man's foot, and so lower and lower.
Exit.
Del. I knew this fellow seven years in the galleys
For a notorious murder; and 't was thought
The cardinal suborn'd it: he was releas'd
By the French general, Gaston de Foix,
When he recover'd Naples.
Ant. 'T is great pity
He should be thus neglected: I have heard
He 's very valiant. This foul melancholy
Will poison all his goodness; for, I 'll tell you,
If too immoderate sleep be truly said
To be an inward rust unto the soul,
It then doth follow want of action
Breeds all black malcontents; and their close rearing,
Like moths in cloth, do hurt for want of wearing.

SCENE 2. *The same.*

Antonio, Delio. Enter Silvio, Castruccio, Julia, Roderigo, and Grisolan.

Delio. The presence 'gins to fill: you promis'd me
To make me the partaker of the natures
Of some of your great courtiers.
Ant. The lord cardinal's
And other strangers' that are now in court?
I shall.—Here comes the great Calabrian duke.

Enter Ferdinand and Attendants.

Ferd. Who took the ring oft'nest?[4]

1 provide against.
2 stagnant.
3 magpies.
4 A sport in which a horseman tried to carry off on the point of his spear an iron ring hanging from the cross-piece of a post.

Sil. Antonio Bologna, my lord.

Ferd. Our sister duchess' great master of her household? Give him the jewel.—When shall we leave this sportive action, and fall to action indeed?

Cast. Methinks, my lord, you should not desire to go to war in person.

Ferd. Now for some gravity.—Why, my lord?

Cast. It is fitting a soldier arise to be a prince, but not necessary a prince descend to be a captain.

Ferd. No?

Cast. No, my lord; he were far better do it by a deputy.

Ferd. Why should he not as well sleep or eat by a deputy? This might take idle, offensive, and base office from him, whereas the other deprives him of honor.

Cast. Believe my experience, that realm is never long in quiet where the ruler is a soldier.

Ferd. Thou told'st me thy wife could not endure fighting.

Cast. True, my lord.

Ferd. And of a jest she broke of [5] a captain she met full of wounds: I have forgot it.

Cast. She told him, my lord, he was a pitiful fellow, to lie,[6] like the children of Ishmael, all in tents.[7]

Ferd. Why, there 's a wit were able to undo all the chirurgeons [8] o' the city; for although gallants should quarrel, and had drawn their weapons, and were ready to go to it, yet her persuasions would make them put up.

Cast. That she would, my lord.—How do you like my Spanish gennet? [9]

Rod. He is all fire.

Ferd. I am of Pliny's opinion, I think he was begot by the wind; he runs as if he were ballas'd [10] with quicksilver.

Sil. True, my lord, he reels from the tilt often.

Rod. Gris. Ha, ha, ha!

Ferd. Why do you laugh? Methinks you that are courtiers should be my touchwood, take fire when I give fire; that is, laugh when I laugh, were the subject never so witty.

Cast. True, my lord: I myself have heard a very good jest, and have scorn'd to seem to have so silly a wit as to understand it.

Ferd. But I can laugh at your fool, my lord.

Cast. He cannot speak, you know, but he makes faces; my lady cannot abide him.

Ferd. No?

Cast. Nor endure to be in merry company; for she says too full laughing, and too much company, fills her too full of the wrinkle.

Ferd. I would, then, have a mathematical instrument made for her face, that she might not laugh out of compass.—I shall shortly visit you at Milan, Lord Silvio.

Sil. Your grace shall arrive most welcome.

Ferd. You are a good horseman, Antonio: you have excellent riders in France; what do you think of good horsemanship?

Ant. Nobly, my lord: as out of the Grecian horse issued many famous princes, so out of brave horsemanship arise the first sparks of growing resolution, that raise the mind to noble action.

Ferd. You have bespoke it worthily.

Sil. Your brother, the lord cardinal, and sister duchess.

Enter Cardinal, Duchess, and Cariola.

Card. Are the galleys come about?

Gris. They are, my lord.

Ferd. Here 's the Lord Silvio is come to take his leave.

Delio. Now, sir, your promise: what 's that cardinal?
I mean his temper. They say he 's a brave fellow,
Will play his five thousand crowns at tennis, dance,
Court ladies, and one that hath fought single combats.

Ant. Some such flashes superficially hang on him for form; but observe his inward character: he is a melancholy churchman. The spring in his face is nothing but the engend'ring of toads; where he is jealous of any man, he lays worse plots for them than ever was impos'd on Hercules, for he strews in his way flatterers, panders, intelligencers, atheists, and a thousand such political [11] monsters. He should have been Pope; but instead of coming to it by the primitive decency of the church, he did bestow bribes so largely and so impudently as if he would have carried it away without heaven's knowledge. Some good he hath done——

Delio. You have given too much of him. What 's his brother?

Ant. The duke there? A most perverse and turbulent nature.

5 at the expense of.
6 lodge.
7 rolls of lint used for bandages.
8 surgeons.
9 a small horse.
10 ballasted.
11 intriguing.

What appears in him mirth is merely outside;
If he laught heartily, it is to laugh
All honesty out of fashion.

Delio. Twins?

Ant. In quality.
He speaks with others' tongues, and hears men's suits
With others' ears; will seem to sleep o' th' bench
Only to entrap offenders in their answers;
Dooms men to death by information;
Rewards by hearsay.

Delio. Then the law to him
Is like a foul, black cobweb to a spider,—
He makes it his dwelling and a prison
To entangle those shall feed him.

Ant. Most true:
He never pays debts unless they be shrewd turns,
And those he will confess that he doth owe.
Last, for his brother there, the cardinal,
They that do flatter him most say oracles
Hang at his lips; and verily I believe them,
For the devil speaks in them.
But for their sister, the right noble duchess,
You never fix'd your eye on three fair medals
Cast in one figure, of so different temper.
For her discourse, it is so full of rapture,
You only will begin then to be sorry
When she doth end her speech, and wish, in wonder,
She held it less vain-glory to talk much,
Than your penance to hear her. Whilst she speaks,
She throws upon a man so sweet a look
That it were able to raise one to a galliard[12]
That lay in a dead palsy, and to dote
On that sweet countenance; but in that look
There speaketh so divine a continence
As cuts off all lascivious and vain hope.
Her days are practis'd in such noble virtue,
That sure her nights, nay, more, her very sleeps,
Are more in heaven than other ladies' shrifts.
Let all sweet ladies break their flatt'ring glasses,
And dress themselves in her.

Delio. Fie, Antonio,
You play the wire-drawer with her commendations.

Ant. I'll case the picture up; only thus much:
All her particular worth grows to this sum,—
She stains[13] the time past, lights the time to come.

Cari. You must attend my lady in the gallery,
Some half an hour hence.

Ant. I shall.

Exeunt Antonio and Delio.

Ferd. Sister, I have a suit to you.

Duch. To me, sir?

Ferd. A gentleman here, Daniel de Bosola,
One that was in the galleys——

Duch. Yes, I know him.

Ferd. A worthy fellow he's: pray, let me entreat for
The provisorship of your horse.

Duch. Your knowledge of him
Commends him and prefers him.

Ferd. Call him hither.

Exeunt Attendants.

We [are] now upon parting.[14] Good Lord Silvio,
Do us commend to all our noble friends
At the leaguer.[15]

Sil. Sir, I shall.

Duch. You are for Milan?

Sil. I am.

Duch. Bring the caroches.[16]—We'll bring you down
To the haven.

Exeunt all but Cardinal and Ferdinand.

Card. Be sure you entertain that Bosola
For your intelligence.[17] I would not be seen in 't;
And therefore many times I have slighted him
When he did court our furtherance, as this morning.

Ferd. Antonio, the great master of her household,
Had been far fitter.

Card. You are deceiv'd in him.
His nature is too honest for such business.—
He comes: I'll leave you.

Exit.

Re-enter Bosola.

Bos. I was lur'd to you.

Ferd. My brother, here, the cardinal could never
Abide you.

12 a lively dance.
13 throws into the shade.
14 about to part.
15 camp.
16 coaches.
17 to give you a spy's information.

Bos. Never since he was in my debt.
Ferd. May be some oblique character in your face
Made him suspect you.
Bos. Doth he study physiognomy?
There 's no more credit to be given to th' face
Than to a sick man's urine, which some call
The physician's whore, because she cozens[18] him.
He did suspect me wrongfully.
Ferd. For that
You must give great men leave to take their times.
Distrust doth cause us seldom be deceiv'd.
You see the oft shaking of the cedar-tree
Fastens it more at root.
Bos. Yet take heed;
For to suspect a friend unworthily
Instructs him the next way to suspect you,
And prompts him to deceive you.
Ferd. There 's gold.
Bos. So:
What follows?—(*Aside.*) Never rain'd such showers as these
Without thunderbolts i' th' tail of them.
—Whose throat must I cut?
Ferd. Your inclination to shed blood rides post[19]
Before my occasion to use you. I give you that
To live i' th' court here, and observe the duchess;
To note all the particulars of her behavior,
What suitors do solicit her for marriage,
And whom she best affects.[20] She 's a young widow:
I would not have her marry again.
Bos. No, sir?
Ferd. Do not you ask the reason; but be satisfied.
I say I would not.
Bos. It seems you would create me
One of your familiars.
Ferd. Familiar! What 's that?
Bos. Why, a very quaint invisible devil in flesh,—
An intelligencer.[21]
Ferd. Such a kind of thriving thing
I would wish thee; and ere long thou mayst arrive
At a higher place by 't.
Bos. Take your devils,
Which hell calls angels![22] These curs'd gifts would make
You a corrupter, me an impudent traitor;
And should I take these, they 'd take me [to] hell.
Ferd. Sir, I 'll take nothing from you that I have given.
There is a place that I procur'd for you
This morning, the provisorship o' th' horse;
Have you heard on 't?
Bos. No.
Ferd. 'T is yours: is 't not worth thanks?
Bos. I would have you curse yourself now, that your bounty
(Which makes men truly noble) e'er should make me
A villain. Oh, that to avoid ingratitude
For the good deed you have done me, I must do
All the ill man can invent! Thus the devil
Candies all sins o'er: and what heaven terms vile,
That names he complimental.
Ferd. Be yourself;
Keep your old garb of melancholy; 't will express
You envy those that stand above your reach,
Yet strive not to come near 'em. This will gain
Access to private lodgings, where yourself
May, like a politic dormouse——
Bos. As I have seen some
Feed in a lord's dish, half asleep, not seeming
To listen to any talk; and yet these rogues
Have cut his throat in a dream. What 's my place?
The provisorship o' th' horse? Say, then, my corruption
Grew out of horse-dung: I am your creature.
Ferd. Away! *Exit.*
Bos. Let good men, for good deeds, covet good fame,
Since place and riches oft are bribes of shame.
Sometimes the devil doth preach. *Exit.*

SCENE 3. *Amalfi. Gallery in the Duchess's palace.*

Enter Ferdinand, Duchess, Cardinal, and Cariola.

18 cheats. 19 runs ahead of. 20 likes. 21 spy. 22 gold coins worth ten shillings.

Card. We are to part from you; and your own discretion
Must now be your director.
Ferd. You are a widow:
You know already what man is; and therefore
Let not youth, high promotion, eloquence——
Card. No,
Nor anything without the addition, honor,
Sway your high blood.
Ferd. Marry! They are most luxurious [23]
Will wed twice.
Card. O, fie!
Ferd. Their livers are more spotted
Than Laban's sheep.[24]
Duch. Diamonds are of most value,
They say, that have past through most jewelers' hands.
Ferd. Whores by that rule are precious.
Duch. Will you hear me?
I 'll never marry.
Card. So most widows say;
But commonly that motion [25] lasts no longer
Than the turning of an hour-glass: the funeral sermon
And it end both together.
Ferd. Now hear me:
You live in a rank pasture, here, i' th' court;
There is a kind of honey-dew that 's deadly;
'T will poison your fame; look to 't. Be not cunning;
For they whose faces do belie their hearts
Are witches ere they arrive at twenty years,
Aye, and give the devil suck.
Duch. This is terrible good counsel.
Ferd. Hypocrisy is woven of a fine small thread,
Subtler than Vulcan's engine: [26] yet, believe 't,
Your darkest actions, nay, your privat'st thoughts,
Will come to light.
Card. You may flatter yourself,
And take your own choice; privately be married
Under the eaves of night——
Ferd. Think 't the best voyage
That e'er you made; like the irregular crab,
Which, though 't goes backward, thinks that it goes right
Because it goes its own way: but observe,
Such weddings may more properly be said
To be executed than celebrated.
Card. The marriage night
Is the entrance into some prison.
Ferd. And those joys,
Those lustful pleasures, are like heavy sleeps
Which do fore-run man's mischief.
Card. Fare you well.
Wisdom begins at the end: remember it.
Exit.
Duch. I think this speech between you both was studied,
It came so roundly off.
Ferd. You are my sister;
This was my father's poniard, do you see?
I 'd be loth to see 't look rusty, 'cause 't was his.
I would have you give o'er these chargeable [27] revels:
A visor and a mask are whispering-rooms
That were ne'er built for goodness,—fare ye well—
And women like that part which, like the lamprey,
Hath ne'er a bone in 't.
Duch. Fie, sir!
Ferd. Nay,
I mean the tongue; variety of courtship.
What cannot a neat knave with a smooth tale
Make a woman believe? Farewell, lusty widow.
Exit.
Duch. Shall this move me? If all my royal kindred
Lay in my way unto this marriage,
I 'd make them my low footsteps. And even now,
Even in this hate, as men in some great battles,
By apprehending danger, have achiev'd
Almost impossible actions (I have heard soldiers say so),
So I through frights and threat'nings will assay
This dangerous venture. Let old wives report
I wink'd [28] and chose a husband.—Cariola,
To thy known secrecy I have given up

23 lustful.
24 *Genesis* xxx. 31–42.
25 resolve.
26 the net in which he caught Venus and Mars.
27 costly.
28 shut my eyes.

More than my life,—my fame.
Cari. Both shall be safe;
For I'll conceal this secret from the world
As warily as those that trade in poison
Keep poison from their children.
Duch. Thy protestation
Is ingenious and hearty; I believe it.
Is Antonio come?
Cari. He attends you.
Duch. Good dear soul,
Leave me; but place thyself behind the arras,
Where thou may'st overhear us. Wish me good speed;
For I am going into a wilderness,
Where I shall find nor path nor friendly clue
To be my guide.
Cariola goes behind the arras.

Enter Antonio.

I sent for you: sit down;
Take pen and ink, and write: are you ready?
Ant. Yes.
Duch. What did I say?
Ant. That I should write somewhat.
Duch. O, I remember.
After these triumphs and this large expense
It's fit, like thrifty husbands,[29] we inquire
What's laid up for to-morrow.
Ant. So please your beauteous excellence.
Duch. Beauteous!
Indeed, I thank you. I look young for your sake;
You have ta'en my cares upon you.
Ant. I'll fetch your grace
The particulars of your revenue and expense.
Duch. O, you are
An upright treasurer, but you mistook;
For when I said I meant to make inquiry
What's laid up for to-morrow, I did mean
What's laid up yonder for me.
Ant. Where?
Duch. In heaven.
I am making my will (as 't is fit princes should,
In perfect memory), and, I pray, sir, tell me,
Were not one better make it smiling, thus,
Than in deep groans and terrible ghastly looks,
As if the gifts we parted with procur'd[30]
That violent distraction?
Ant. O, much better.
Duch. If I had a husband now, this care were quit:
But I intend to make you overseer.
What good deed shall we first remember? Say.
Ant. Begin with that first good deed began i' th' world
After man's creation, the sacrament of marriage.
I'd have you first provide for a good husband;
Give him all.
Duch. All!
Ant. Yes, your excellent self.
Duch. In a winding sheet?
Ant. In a couple.[31]
Duch. Saint Winifred, that were a strange will!
Ant. 'T were stranger if there were no will in you
To marry again.
Duch. What do you think of marriage?
Ant. I take 't, as those that deny purgatory,
It locally contains or heaven or hell;
There 's no third place in 't.
Duch. How do you affect it?
Ant. My banishment, feeding my melancholy,
Would often reason thus:—
Duch. Pray, let's hear it.
Ant. Say a man never marry, nor have children,
What takes that from him? Only the bare name
Of being a father, or the weak delight
To see the little wanton ride a-cock-horse
Upon a painted stick, or hear him chatter
Like a taught starling.
Duch. Fie, fie, what's all this?
One of your eyes is blood-shot; use my ring to 't.
They say 't is very sovereign. 'T was my wedding-ring,
And I did vow never to part with it
But to my second husband.
Ant. You have parted with it now.
Duch. Yes, to help your eye-sight.
Ant. You have made me stark blind.
Duch. How?
Ant. There is a saucy and ambitious devil
Is dancing in this circle.
Duch. Remove him.
Ant. How?

29 housekeepers. 30 produced. 31 in marriage.

Duch. There needs small conjuration, when your finger
May do it: thus. Is it fit?
(*She puts the ring upon his finger: he kneels.*)
Ant. What said you?
Duch. Sir,
This goodly roof of yours is too low built;
I cannot stand upright in 't nor discourse,
Without I raise it higher. Raise yourself;
Or, if you please, my hand to help you: so.
(*Raises him.*)
Ant. Ambition, madam, is a great man's madness,
That is not kept in chains and close-pent rooms,
But in fair lightsome lodgings, and is girt
With the wild noise of prattling visitants,
Which makes it lunatic beyond all cure.
Conceive not I am so stupid but I aim [32]
Whereto your favors tend: but he 's a fool
That, being a-cold, would thrust his hands i' th' fire
To warm them.
Duch. So, now the ground 's broke,
You may discover what a wealthy mine
I make you lord of.
Ant. O my unworthiness!
Duch. You were ill to sell yourself: [33]
This dark'ning of your worth is not like that
Which tradesmen use i' th' city; their false lights [34]
Are to rid bad wares off: and I must tell you,
If you will know where breathes a complete man
(I speak it without flattery), turn your eyes,
And progress through yourself.
Ant. Were there nor heaven nor hell,
I should be honest: I have long serv'd virtue,
And ne'er ta'en wages of her.
Duch. Now she pays it.
The misery of us that are born great!
We are forc'd to woo, because none dare woo us;
And as a tyrant doubles with his words
And fearfully equivocates, so we
Are forc'd to express our violent passions
In riddles and in dreams, and leave the path
Of simple virtue, which was never made
To seem the thing it is not. Go, go brag
You have left me heartless; mine is in your bosom:
I hope 't will multiply love there. You do tremble:
Make not your heart so dead a piece of flesh,
To fear more than to love me. Sir, be confident.
What is 't distracts you? This is flesh and blood, sir;
'T is not the figure cut in alabaster
Kneels at my husband's tomb. Awake, awake, man!
I do here put off all vain ceremony,
And only do appear to you a young widow
That claims you for her husband, and, like a widow,
I use but half a blush in 't.
Ant. Truth speak for me;
I will remain the constant sanctuary
Of your good name.
Duch. I thank you, gentle love:
And 'cause you shall not come to me in debt,
Being now my steward, here upon your lips
I sign your *Quietus est.*[35] This you should have begg'd now.
I have seen children oft eat sweetmeats thus,
As fearful to devour them too soon.
Ant. But for your brothers?
Duch. Do not think of them:
All discord without this circumference
Is only to be pitied, and not fear'd:
Yet, should they know it, time will easily
Scatter the tempest.
Ant. These words should be mine,
And all the parts you have spoken, if some part of it
Would not have savor'd flattery.
Duch. Kneel.
(*Cariola comes from behind the arras.*)
Ant. Ha!
Duch. Be not amaz'd: this woman 's of my counsel.
I have heard lawyers say, a contract in a chamber
Per verba presenti [36] is absolute marriage.
Bless, heaven, this sacred gordian,[37] which let violence
Never untwine.

32 guess.
33 you would be a poor salesman of yourself.
34 the darkening of their shops.
35 The phrase used to indicate settlement of an account.
36 in the hearing of a third person.
37 knot.

Ant. And may our sweet affections, like the spheres,
Be still in motion!
Duch. Quick'ning, and make
The like soft music!
Ant. That we may imitate the loving palms,
Best emblem of a peaceful marriage,
That ne'er bore fruit, divided!
Duch. What can the church force more?
Ant. That fortune may not know an accident,
Either of joy or sorrow, to divide
Our fixed wishes!
Duch. How can the church build faster?[38]
We now are man and wife, and 't is the church
That must but echo this.—Maid, stand apart:
I now am blind.
Ant. What 's your conceit in this?
Duch. I would have you lead your fortune by the hand
Unto your marriage-bed:
(You speak in me this, for we now are one.)
We 'll only lie and talk together, and plot
T' appease my humorous[39] kindred; and if you please,
Like the old tale in *Alexander and Lodowick*,[40]
Lay a naked sword between us, keep us chaste.
O, let me shroud my blushes in your bosom,
Since 't is the treasury of all my secrets!
Exeunt Duchess and Antonio.
Cari. Whether the spirit of greatness or of woman
Reign most in her, I know not; but it shows
A fearful madness. I owe her much of pity.
Exit.

ACT II.

SCENE 1. *Amalfi. An apartment in the palace of the Duchess.*

Enter Bosola and Castruccio.

Bos. You say you would fain be taken for an eminent courtier?
Cast. 'T is the very main[41] of my ambition.
Bos. Let me see: you have a reasonable good face for 't already, and your night-cap expresses your ears sufficient largely. I would have you learn to twirl the strings of your band with a good grace, and in a set speech, at th' end of every sentence, to hum three or four times, or blow your nose till it smart again, to recover your memory. When you come to be a president in criminal causes, if you smile upon a prisoner, hang him; but if you frown upon him and threaten him, let him be sure to scape the gallows.
Cast. I would be a very merry president.
Bos. Do not sup o' nights; 't will beget you an admirable wit.
Cast. Rather it would make me have a good stomach to quarrel; for they say, your roaring boys[42] eat meat seldom, and that makes them so valiant. But how shall I know whether the people take me for an eminent fellow?
Bos. I will teach a trick to know it: give out you lie a-dying, and if you hear the common people curse you, be sure you are taken for one of the prime night-caps.

Enter an Old Lady.

You come from painting now.
Old Lady. From what?
Bos. Why, from your scurvy face-physic. To behold thee not painted inclines somewhat near a miracle. These in thy face here were deep ruts and foul sloughs the last progress.[43] There was a lady in France that, having had the small-pox, flayed the skin off her face to make it more level; and whereas before she looked like a nutmeg grater, after she resembled an abortive hedge-hog.
Old Lady. Do you call this painting?
Bos. No, no, but you call [it] careening[44] of an old morphew'd[45] lady, to make her disembogue[46] again: there 's rough-cast phrase to your plastic.[47]
Old Lady. It seems you are well acquainted with my closet.
Bos. One would suspect it for a shop of witchcraft, to find in it the fat of serpents, spawn of snakes, Jews' spittle, and their young children's ordure; and all these for the face. I would sooner eat a dead pigeon taken from the soles of the feet of one sick of the plague,[48] than kiss one of you fasting. Here are two

38 more drmly.
39 captious.
40 A sixteenth century ballad; a play so entitled, dealing with the same story, is mentioned in Henslowe's *Diary* as acted in 1597.
41 chief part.
42 bullies.
43 royal journey.
44 turning over.
45 scabbed.
46 discharge.
47 there's apppropriately rough language for your face modelling.
48 a prescription actually used at the time.

of you, whose sin of your youth is the very patrimony of the physician; makes him renew his foot-cloth with the spring, and change his high-pric'd courtesan with the fall of the leaf. I do wonder you do not loathe yourselves. Observe my meditation now.

What thing is in this outward form of man
To be belov'd? We account it ominous,
If nature do produce a colt, or lamb,
A fawn, or goat, in any limb resembling
A man, and fly from 't as a prodigy.
Man stands amaz'd to see his deformity
In any other creature but himself.
But in our own flesh though we bear diseases
Which have their true names only ta'en from beasts,—
As the most ulcerous wolf[49] and swinish measle,[50]—
Though we are eaten up of lice and worms,
And though continually we bear about us
A rotten and dead body, we delight
To hide it in rich tissue: all our fear,
Nay, all our terror, is, lest our physician
Should put us in the ground to be made sweet.—

Your wife's gone to Rome: you two couple, and get you to the wells at Lucca to recover your aches. I have other work on foot.

Exeunt Castruccio and Old Lady.

I observe our duchess
Is sick a-days, she pukes, her stomach seethes,
The fins of her eye-lids look most teeming blue,[51]
She wanes i' th' cheek, and waxes fat i' th' flank,
And, contrary to our Italian fashion,
Wears a loose-bodied gown: there's somewhat in 't.
I have a trick may discover it,
A pretty one; I have bought some apricocks,
The first our spring yields.

Enter Antonio and Delio, talking together apart.

Delio. And so long since married?
You amaze me.

Ant. Let me seal your lips for ever:
For, did I think that anything but th' air
Could carry these words from you, I should wish
You had no breath at all.—Now, sir, in your contemplation?
You are studying to become a great wise fellow.

Bos. O, sir, the opinion of wisdom is a foul tetter[52] that runs all over a man's body: if simplicity direct us to have no evil, it directs us to a happy being; for the subtlest folly proceeds from the subtlest wisdom. Let me be simply honest.

Ant. I do understand your inside.

Bos. Do you so?

Ant. Because you would not seem to appear to th' world
Puff'd up with your preferment, you continue
This out-of-fashion melancholy: leave it, leave it.

Bos. Give me leave to be honest in any phrase, in any compliment whatsoever. Shall I confess myself to you? I look no higher than I can reach: they are the gods that must ride on winged horses. A lawyer's mule of a slow pace will both suit my disposition and business; for, mark me, when a man's mind rides faster than his horse can gallop, they quickly both tire.

Ant. You would look up to heaven, but I think
The devil, that rules i' th' air, stands in your light.

Bos. O, sir, you are lord of the ascendant,[53] chief man with the duchess: a duke was your cousin-german remov'd. Say you were lineally descended from King Pepin, or he himself, what of this? Search the heads of the greatest rivers in the world, you shall find them but bubbles of water. Some would think the souls of princes were brought forth by some more weighty cause than those of meaner persons: they are deceiv'd, there's the same hand to them; the like passions sway them; the same reason that makes a vicar go to law for a tithe-pig, and undo his neighbors, makes them spoil a whole province, and batter down goodly cities with the cannon.

Enter Duchess and Ladies.

Duch. Your arm, Antonio: do I not grow fat?
I am exceeding short-winded.—Bosola,
I would have you, sir, provide for me a litter;

49 lupus. ulcer.
50 an eruptive disease of swine was called measles.
51 her eyelids look heavy and black as if she were pregnant.
52 scurf.
53 an astrological term for a position of importance

Such a one as the Duchess of Florence rode in.

Bos. The duchess us'd one when she was great with child.

Duch. I think she did.—Come hither, mend my ruff:

Here, when? thou art such a tedious lady; and

Thy breath smells of lemon-pills: would thou hadst done!

Shall I swoon under thy fingers? I am

So troubled with the mother![54]

Bos. (*Aside.*) I fear, too much.

Duch. I have heard you say that the French courtiers

Wear their hats on 'fore the king.

Ant. I have seen it.

Duch. In the presence?

Ant. Yes.

Duch. Why should not we bring up that fashion?

'T is ceremony more than duty that consists

In the removing of a piece of felt.

Be you the example to the rest o' th' court;

Put on your hat first.

Ant. You must pardon me:

I have seen, in colder countries than in France,

Nobles stand bare to th' prince; and the distinction

Methought show'd reverently.

Bos. I have a present for your grace.

Duch. For me, sir?

Bos. Apricocks, madam.

Duch. O, sir, where are they?

I have heard of none to-year.[55]

Bos. (*Aside.*) Good; her color rises.

Duch. Indeed, I thank you: they are wondrous fair ones.

What an unskilful fellow is our gardener!

We shall have none this month.

Bos. Will not your grace pare them?

Duch. No: they taste of musk, methinks; indeed they do.

Bos. I know not: yet I wish your grace had par'd 'em.

Duch. Why?

Bos. I forgot to tell you, the knave gardener,

Only to raise his profit by them the sooner,

Did ripen them in horse-dung.

Duch. O, you jest.—

You shall judge: pray, taste one.

Ant. Indeed, madam,

I do not love the fruit.

Duch. Sir, you are loth

To rob us of our dainties. 'T is a delicate fruit;

They say they are restorative.

Bos. 'T is a pretty art,

This grafting.

Duch. 'T is so; a bett'ring of nature.

Bos. To make a pippin grow upon a crab,

A damson on a black-thorn.—(*Aside.*) How greedily she eats them!

A whirlwind strike off these bawd farthingales!

For, but for that and the loose-bodied gown,

I should have discover'd apparently[56]

The young springal[57] cutting a caper in her belly.

Duch. I thank you, Bosola: they were right good ones,

If they do not make me sick.

Ant. How now, madam!

Duch. This green fruit and my stomach are not friends:

How they swell me!

Bos. (*Aside.*) Nay, you are too much swell'd already.

Duch. O, I am in an extreme cold sweat!

Bos. I am very sorry. *Exit.*

Duch. Lights to my chamber!—O good Antonio,

I fear I am undone!

Delio. Lights there, lights!

Exeunt Duchess and Ladies.

Ant. O my most trusty Delio, we are lost!

I fear she 's fall'n in labor; and there 's left

No time for her remove.

Delio. Have you prepar'd

Those ladies to attend her; and procur'd

That politic safe conveyance for the midwife

Your duchess plotted?

Ant. I have.

Delio. Make use, then, of this forc'd occasion.

Give out that Bosola hath poison'd her

With these apricocks; that will give some color

For her keeping close.

Ant. Fie, fie, the physicians

Will then flock to her.

Delio. For that you may pretend

She 'll use some prepar'd antidote of her own,

Lest the physicians should re-poison her.

Ant. I am lost in amazement: I know not what to think on 't. *Exeunt.*

54 hysteria. 55 this year. 56 clearly. 57 youngster.

SCENE 2. *A hall in the palace.*

Enter Bosola and Old Lady.

Bos. So, so, there 's no question but her techiness [58] and most vulturous eating of the apricocks are apparent signs of breeding.—Now?

Old Lady. I am in haste, sir.

Bos. There was a young waiting-woman had a monstrous desire to see the glass-house [59]—

Old Lady. Nay, pray, let me go.

Bos. And it was only to know what strange instrument it was should swell up a glass to the fashion of a woman's belly.

Old Lady. I will hear no more of the glass-house. You are still [60] abusing women!

Bos. Who? I? No; only, by the way now and then, mention your frailties. The orange-tree bears ripe and green fruit and blossoms all together; and some of you give entertainment for pure love, but more for more precious reward. The lusty spring smells well; but drooping autumn tastes well. If we have the same golden showers that rained in the time of Jupiter the thunderer, you have the same Danäes still, to hold up their laps to receive them. Didst thou never study the mathematics?

Old Lady. What 's that, sir?

Bos. Why, to know the trick how to make a many lines meet in one center. Go, go, give your foster-daughters good counsel: tell them, that the devil takes delight to hang at a woman's girdle, like a false rusty watch, that she cannot discern how the time passes.

Exit Old Lady.

Enter Antonio, Roderigo, and Grisolan.

Ant. Shut up the court-gates.
Rod. Why, sir? What 's the danger?
Ant. Shut up the posterns presently,[61] and call
All the officers o' th' court.
Gris. I shall instantly.

Exit.

Ant. Who keeps the key o' th' park-gate?
Rod. Forobosco.
Ant. Let him bring 't presently.

Re-enter Grisolan and Servants.

1 Serv. O, gentlemen o' th' court, the foulest treason!
Bos. (*Aside.*) If that these apricocks should be poison'd now,
Without my knowledge?

1 Serv. There was taken even now a Switzer in the duchess' bed-chamber—
2 Serv. A Switzer!
1 Serv. With a pistol in his great codpiece.
Bos. Ha, ha, ha!
1 Serv. The codpiece was the case for 't.
2 Serv. There was a cunning traitor. Who would have search'd his codpiece?
1 Serv. True; if he had kept out of the ladies' chambers. And all the molds of his buttons were leaden bullets.
2 Serv. O wicked cannibal! A fire-lock in 's codpiece!
1 Serv. 'T was a French plot, upon my life.
2 Serv. To see what the devil can do!
Ant. Are all the officers here?
Servants. We are.
Ant. Gentlemen,
We have lost much plate you know; and but this evening
Jewels, to the value of four thousand ducats,
Are missing in the duchess' cabinet.
Are the gates shut?
Serv. Yes.
Ant. 'T is the duchess' pleasure
Each officer be lock'd into his chamber
Till the sun-rising; and to send the keys
Of all their chests and of their outward doors
Into her bed-chamber. She is very sick.
Rod. At her pleasure.
Ant. She entreats you take 't not ill: the innocent
Shall be the more approv'd by it.
Bos. Gentlemen o' th' wood-yard, where 's your Switzer now?
1 Serv. By this hand, 't was credibly reported by one o' th' black guard.[62]

Exeunt all except Antonio and Delio.

Delio. How fares it with the duchess?
Ant. She 's expos'd
Unto the worst of torture, pain, and fear.
Delio. Speak to her all happy comfort.
Ant. How I do play the fool with mine own danger!
You are this night, dear friend, to post to Rome:
My life lies in your service.
Delio. Do not doubt me.
Ant. O, 't is far from me: and yet fear presents me
Somewhat that looks like danger.
Delio. Believe it,
'T is but the shadow of your fear, no more.

58 irritability.
59 glass factory; there was such a factory near the Blackfriars Theater, where this play was performed.
60 always.
61 at once.
62 scullions.

How superstitiously we mind our evils!
The throwing down salt, or crossing of a hare,
Bleeding at nose, the stumbling of a horse,
Or singing of a cricket, are of power
To daunt whole man in us. Sir, fare you well:
I wish you all the joys of a bless'd father;
And, for my faith, lay this unto your breast,—
Old friends, like old swords, still are trusted best.

Exit.

Enter Cariola.

Cari. Sir, you are the happy father of a son:
Your wife commends him to you.
Ant. Blessed comfort!—
For heaven' sake, tend her well: I'll presently
Go set a figure for 's nativity.[63]

Exeunt.

SCENE 3. *The inner court of the palace.*

Enter Bosola, with a dark lantern.

Bos. Sure I did hear a woman shriek: list, ha!
And the sound came, if I receiv'd it right,
From the duchess' lodgings. There 's some stratagem
In the confining all our courtiers
To their several wards: I must have part of it;
My intelligence will freeze else. List, again!
It may be 't was the melancholy bird,
Best friend of silence and of solitariness,
The owl, that scream'd so.—Ha! Antonio!

Enter Antonio with a candle, his sword drawn.

Ant. I heard some noise.—Who 's there? What art thou? Speak.
Bos. Antonio, put not your face nor body
To such a forc'd expression of fear;
I am Bosola, your friend.
Ant. Bosola!—
(*Aside.*) This mole does undermine me.— Heard you not
A noise even now?
Bos. From whence?
Ant. From the duchess' lodging.
Bos. Not I: did you?
Ant. I did, or else I dream'd.
Bos. Let 's walk towards it.
Ant. No: it may be 't was
But the rising of the wind.
Bos. Very likely.
Methinks 't is very cold, and yet you sweat:
You look wildly.
Ant. I have been setting a figure[64]
For the duchess' jewels.
Bos. Ah, and how falls your question?
Do you find it radical?[65]
Ant. What 's that to you?
'T is rather to be question'd what design,
When all men were commanded to their lodgings,
Makes you a night-walker.
Bos. In sooth, I'll tell you:
Now all the court 's asleep, I thought the devil
Had least to do here; I came to say my prayers;
And if it do offend you I do so,
You are a fine courtier.
Ant. (*Aside.*) This fellow will undo me.—
You gave the duchess apricocks to-day:
Pray heaven they were not poison'd!
Bos. Poison'd! a Spanish fig[66]
For the imputation!
Ant. Traitors are ever confident
Till they are discover'd. There were jewels stol'n too:
In my conceit, none are to be suspected
More than yourself.
Bos. You are a false steward.
Ant. Saucy slave, I'll pull thee up by the roots.
Bos. May be the ruin will crush you to pieces.
Ant. You are an impudent snake indeed, sir:
Are you scarce warm, and do you show your sting?
You libel[67] well, sir?
Bos. No, sir: copy it out,
And I will set my hand to 't.
Ant. (*Aside.*) My nose bleeds.
One that were superstitious would count
This ominous, when it merely comes by chance.
Two letters, that are wrought here for my name,[68]
Are drown'd in blood!
Mere accident.—For you, sir, I'll take order

63 cast his horoscope.
64 making an astrological calculation to discover the jewels.
65 going to the root of the matter.
66 an obscene gesture of contempt.
67 write.
68 *i.e.* on a handkerchief.

I' th' morn you shall be safe.—(*Aside.*)
'T is that must color
Her lying-in.—Sir, this door you pass not:
I do not hold it fit that you come near
The duchess' lodgings, till you have quit yourself.—
(*Aside.*) The great are like the base, nay, they are the same,
When they seek shameful ways to avoid shame. *Exit.*

Bos. Antonio hereabout did drop a paper:—
Some of your help, false friend.[69]—O, here it is.
What 's here? a child's nativity calculated!

(*Reads.*)

The duchess was deliver'd of a son, 'tween the hours twelve and one in the night, Anno Dom. 1504,—that 's this year—*decimo nono Decembris,*—that 's this night—*taken according to the meridian of Malfi,* —that 's our duchess: happy discovery!—*The lord of the first house being combust*[70] *in the ascendant signifies short life; and Mars being in a human sign,*[71] *joined to the tail of the Dragon, in the eighth house, doth threaten a violent death. Cætera non scrutantur.*[72]

Why, now 't is most apparent; this precise fellow
Is the duchess' bawd:—I have it to my wish!
This is a parcel of intelligency
Our courtiers were cas'd up[73] for: it needs must follow
That I must be committed on pretense
Of poisoning her; which I 'll endure, and laugh at.
If one could find the father now! but that
Time will discover. Old Castruccio
I' th' morning posts to Rome: by him I 'll send
A letter that shall make her brothers' galls
O'erflow their livers. This was a thrifty[74] way!
Though Lust do mask in ne'er so strange disguise,
She 's oft found witty, but is never wise. *Exit.*

SCENE 4. *Rome. A room in the Cardinal's palace.*

Enter Cardinal and Julia.

Card. Sit: thou art my best of wishes. Prithee, tell me
What trick didst thou invent to come to Rome
Without thy husband?

Julia. Why, my lord, I told him
I came to visit an old anchorite
Here for devotion.

Card. Thou art a witty false one,—
I mean, to him.

Julia. You have prevail'd with me
Beyond my strongest thoughts; I would not now
Find you inconstant.

Card. Do not put thyself
To such a voluntary torture, which proceeds
Out of your own guilt.

Julia. How, my lord!

Card. You fear
My constancy, because you have approv'd[75]
Those giddy and wild turnings in yourself.

Julia. Did you e'er find them?

Card. Sooth, generally for women,
A man might strive to make glass malleable,
Ere he should make them fixed.

Julia. So, my lord?

Card. We had need go borrow that fantastic glass
Invented by Galileo the Florentine
To view another spacious world i' th' moon,
And look to find a constant woman there.

Julia. This is very well, my lord.

Card. Why do you weep?
Are tears your justification? The selfsame tears
Will fall into your husband's bosom, lady,
With a loud protestation that you love him
Above the world. Come, I 'll love you wisely,
That 's jealously; since I am very certain
You cannot make me cuckold.

Julia. I 'll go home
To my husband.

Card. You may thank me, lady,
I have taken you off your melancholy perch,
Bore you upon my fist, and show'd you game,
And let you fly at it.[76] I pray thee, kiss me.

69 *i.e.* the lantern.
70 within eight degrees and thirty minutes of the sun.
71 one of the signs of the Zodiac with human form, e. g. Virgo.
72 *The rest not considered.*
73 shut up.
74 ingenious.
75 experienced.
76 The figure in the three lines is taken from falconry.

When thou wast with thy husband, thou wast watch'd
Like a tame elephant:—still you are to thank me:—
Thou hadst only kisses from him and high feeding;
But what delight was that? 'T was just like one
That hath a little fing'ring on the lute,
Yet cannot tune it:—still you are to thank me.

Julia. You told me of a piteous wound i' th' heart,
And a sick liver, when you woo'd me first,
And spake like one in physic.[77]

Card. Who 's that?—

Enter Servant.

Rest firm for my affection to thee,
Lightning moves slow to 't.

Serv. Madam, a gentleman
That 's come post from Malfi, desires to see you.

Card. Let him enter: I 'll withdraw. *Exit.*

Serv. He says
Your husband, old Castruccio, is come to Rome,
Most pitifully tir'd with riding post. *Exit.*

Enter Delio.

Julia. (*Aside.*) Signior Delio! 't is one of my old suitors.

Delio. I was bold to come and see you.

Julia. Sir, you are welcome.

Delio. Do you lie[78] here?

Julia. Sure, your own experience
Will satisfy you no: our Roman prelates
Do not keep lodging for ladies.

Delio. Very well.
I have brought you no commendations from your husband,
For I know none by him.

Julia. I hear he 's come to Rome.

Delio. I never knew man and beast, of a horse and a knight,
So weary of each other. If he had had a good back,
He would have undertook to have borne his horse,
His breech was so pitifully sore.

Julia. Your laughter
Is my pity.

Delio. Lady, I know not whether
You want money, but I have brought you some.

Julia. From my husband?

Delio. No, from mine own allowance.

Julia. I must hear the condition, ere I be bound to take it.

Delio. Look on 't, 't is gold; hath it not a fine color?

Julia. I have a bird more beautiful.

Delio. Try the sound on 't.

Julia. A lute-string far exceeds it.
It hath no smell, like cassia or civet;
Nor is it physical,[79] though some fond[80] doctors
Persuade us seethe 't in cullises.[81] I 'll tell you,
This is a creature bred by—

Re-enter Servant.

Serv. Your husband 's come,
Hath deliver'd a letter to the Duke of Calabria
That, to my thinking, hath put him out of his wits. *Exit.*

Julia. Sir, you hear:
Pray, let me know your business and your suit
As briefly as can be.

Delio. With good speed: I would wish you,
At such time as you are non-resident
With your husband, my mistress.

Julia. Sir, I 'll go ask my husband if I shall,
And straight return your answer. *Exit.*

Delio. Very fine!
Is this her wit, or honesty, that speaks thus?
I heard one say the duke was highly mov'd
With a letter sent from Malfi. I do fear
Antonio is betray'd. How fearfully
Shows his ambition now! Unfortunate fortune!
They pass through whirl-pools, and deep woes do shun,
Who the event weigh ere the action 's done. *Exit.*

SCENE 5. *Another room in the Cardinal's palace.*

Enter Cardinal and Ferdinand with a letter.

Ferd. I have this night digg'd up a mandrake.[82]

77 undergoing treatment.
78 lodge.
79 medicinal.
80 foolish.
81 broths.
82 Popular superstition found in the forked root of the mandrake resemblance to the human form, and alleged that the root shrieked on being torn out of the ground; the hearer of such shrieks went mad.

Card. Say you?
Ferd. And I am grown mad with 't.
Card. What 's the prodigy?
Ferd. Read there,—a sister damn'd: she 's loose i' th' hilts;[83]
Grown a notorious strumpet.
Card. Speak lower.
Ferd. Lower!
Rogues do not whisper 't now, but seek to publish 't
(As servants do the bounty of their lords)
Aloud; and with a covetous searching eye,
To mark who note them. O, confusion seize her!
She hath had most cunning bawds to serve her turn,
And more secure conveyances for lust
Than towns of garrison for service.
Card. Is 't possible?
Can this be certain?
Ferd. Rhubarb, O, for rhubarb
To purge this choler! Here 's the cursed day
To prompt my memory; and here 't shall stick
Till of her bleeding heart I make a sponge
To wipe it out.
Card. Why do you make yourself
So wild a tempest?
Ferd. Would I could be one,
That I might toss her palace 'bout her ears,
Root up her goodly forests, blast her meads,
And lay her general territory as waste
As she hath done her honors.
Card. Shall our blood,
The royal blood of Arragon and Castile,
Be thus attainted?
Ferd. Apply desperate physic:
We must not now use balsamum, but fire,
The smarting cupping-glass, for that 's the mean
To purge infected blood, such blood as hers.
I 'll give it to my handkercher; and now
There is a kind of pity in mine eye,—'t is here
I 'll bequeath this to her bastard.
Card. What to do?
Ferd. Why, to make soft lint for his mother's wounds,
When I have hew'd her to pieces.
Card. Curs'd creature!
Unequal nature, to place women's hearts
So far upon the left side![84]
Ferd. Foolish men,
That e'er will trust their honor in a bark
Made of so slight weak bulrush as is woman,
Apt every minute to sink it!
Card. Thus ignorance, when it hath purchas'd honor,
It cannot wield it.
Ferd. Methinks I see her laughing,—
Excellent hyena! Talk to me somewhat,[85] quickly,
Or my imagination will carry me
To see her in the shameful act of sin.
Card. With whom?
Ferd. Happily[86] with some strong-thigh'd bargeman,
Or one o' th' wood-yard that can quoit the sledge[87]
Or toss the bar, or else some lovely squire
That carries coals up to her privy lodgings.
Card. You fly beyond your reason.
Ferd. Go to, mistress!
'T is not your whore's milk that shall quench my wild-fire,
But your whore's blood.
Card. How idly shows this rage, which carries you,
As men convey'd by witches through the air,
On violent whirlwinds! This intemperate noise
Fitly resembles deaf men's shrill discourse,
Who talk aloud, thinking all other men
To have their imperfection
Ferd. Have not you
My palsy?
Card. Yes, [but] I can be angry
Without this rupture. There is not in nature
A thing that makes man so deform'd, so beastly,
As doth intemperate anger. Chide yourself.
You have divers men who never yet express'd
Their strong desire of rest but by unrest,
By vexing of themselves. Come, put yourself
In tune.
Ferd. So I will only study to seem
The thing I am not. I could kill her now,
In you, or in myself; for I do think
It is some sin in us heaven doth revenge
By her.

83 unchaste. 84 supposed to be a sign of folly. (N.) 85 on some subject. 86 haply. 87 throw the hammer.

Card. Are you stark mad?

Ferd. I would have their bodies
Burnt in a coal-pit with the ventage stopp'd,
That their curs'd smoke might not ascend to heaven;
Or dip the sheets they lie in in pitch or sulphur,
Wrap them in 't, and then light them like a match;
Or else to boil their bastard to a cullis,
And give 't his lecherous father to renew
The sin of his back.

Card. I'll leave you.

Ferd. Nay, I have done.
I am confident, had I been damn'd in hell,
And should have heard of this, it would have put me
Into a cold sweat. In, in; I'll go sleep.
Till I know who leaps my sister, I'll not stir:
That known, I'll find scorpions to string my whips,
And fix her in a general eclipse.
Exeunt.

ACT III.

SCENE 1. *Amalfi. A room in the Duchess's palace.*

Enter Antonio and Delio.

Ant. Our noble friend, my most beloved Delio!
O, you have been a stranger long at court:
Came you along with the Lord Ferdinand?

Delio. I did, sir: and how fares your noble duchess?

Ant. Right fortunately well: she's an excellent
Feeder of pedigrees; since you last saw her,
She hath had two children more, a son and daughter.

Delio. Methinks 't was yesterday. Let me but wink,
And not behold your face, which to mine eye
Is somewhat leaner, verily I should dream
It were within this half hour,

Ant. You have not been in law, friend Delio,
Nor in prison, nor a suitor at the court,
Nor begg'd the reversion of some great man's place,
Nor troubled with an old wife, which doth make
Your time so insensibly hasten.

Delio. Pray, sir, tell me,
Hath not this news arriv'd yet to the ear
Of the lord cardinal?

Ant. I fear it hath:
The Lord Ferdinand, that's newly come to court,
Doth bear himself right dangerously.

Delio. Pray, why?

Ant. He is so quiet that he seems to sleep
The tempest out, as dormice do in winter.
Those houses that are haunted are most still
Till the devil be up.

Delio. What say the common people?

Ant. The common rabble do directly say
She is a strumpet.

Delio. And your graver heads
Which would be politic, what censure they?

Ant. They do observe I grow to infinite purchase [88]
The left hand way; and all suppose the duchess
Would amend it, if she could; for, say they,
Great princes, though they grudge their officers
Should have such large and unconfined means
To get wealth under them, will not complain,
Lest thereby they should make them odious
Unto the people. For other obligation
Of love or marriage between her and me
They never dream of.

Delio. The Lord Ferdinand
Is going to bed.

Enter Duchess, Ferdinand, and Attendants.

Ferd. I'll instantly to bed,
For I am weary.—I am to bespeak
A husband for you.

Duch. For me, sir! Pray, who is 't?

Ferd. The great Count Malateste.

Duch. Fie upon him!
A count! He's a mere stick of sugar-candy;
You may look quite through him. When I choose
A husband, I will marry for your honor.

Ferd. You shall do well in 't.—How is 't, worthy Antonio?

88 wealth.

Duch. But, sir, I am to have private conference with you
About a scandalous report is spread
Touching mine honor.
Ferd. Let me be ever deaf to 't:
One of Pasquil's paper-bullets,[89] court-calumny,
A pestilent air, which princes' palaces
Are seldom purg'd of. Yet, say that it were true,
I pour it in your bosom, my fix'd love
Would strongly excuse, extenuate, nay, deny
Faults, were they apparent in you. Go, be safe
In your own innocency.
Duch. (*Aside.*) O bless'd comfort!
This deadly air is purg'd.
Exeunt Duchess, Antonio, Delio, and Attendants.
Ferd. Her guilt treads on
Hot-burning coulters.[90]

Enter Bosola.

Now, Bosola,
How thrives our intelligence?
Bos. Sir, uncertainly:
'T is rumor'd she hath had three bastards, but
By whom we may go read i' th' stars.
Ferd. Why, some
Hold opinion all things are written there.
Bos. Yes, if we could find spectacles to read them.
I do suspect there hath been some sorcery
Us'd on the duchess.
Ferd. Sorcery! to what purpose?
Bos. To make her dote on some desertless fellow
She shames to acknowledge.
Ferd. Can your faith give way
To think there's power in potions or in charms,
To make us love whether we will or no?
Bos. Most certainly.
Ferd. Away! these are mere gulleries,[91] horrid things,
Invented by some cheating mountebanks
To abuse us. Do you think that herbs or charms
Can force the will? Some trials have been made
In this foolish practice, but the ingredients
Were lenitive poisons, such as are of force
To make the patient mad; and straight the witch
Swears by equivocation they are in love.
The witch-craft lies in her rank blood. This night
I will force confession from her. You told me
You had got, within these two days, a false key
Into her bed-chamber.
Bos. I have.
Ferd. As I would wish.
Bos. What do you intend to do?
Ferd. Can you guess?
Bos. No.
Ferd. Do not ask, then:
He that can compass me, and know my drifts,
May say he hath put a girdle 'bout the world,
And sounded all her quick-sands.
Bos. I do not
Think so.
Ferd. What do you think, then, pray?
Bos. That you
Are your own chronicle[92] too much, and grossly
Flatter yourself.
Ferd. Give me thy hand; I thank thee:
I never gave pension but to flatterers,
Till I entertained thee. Farewell.
That friend a great man's ruin strongly checks,
Who rails into his belief all his defects.
Exeunt.

SCENE 2. *The bed-chamber of the Duchess in the same.*

Enter Duchess, Antonio, and Cariola.

Duch. Bring me the casket hither, and the glass.—
You get no lodging here to-night, my lord.
Ant. Indeed, I must persuade one.
Duch. Very good:
I hope in time 't will grow into a custom,
That noblemen shall come with cap and knee
To purchase a night's lodging of their wives.
Ant. I must lie here.
Duch. Must! You are a lord of mis-rule.[93]
Ant. Indeed, my rule is only in the night.

89 "Lampoons posted on a mutilated statue in Rome and commonly called *pasquils* from a satirical cobbler named Pasquin, who began the practice." (Thorndike.)
90 ploughshares.
91 deceptions.
92 chronicle your own deeds.
93 master of revels.

Duch. To what use will you put me?
Ant. We 'll sleep together.
Duch. Alas, what pleasure can two lovers find in sleep?
Cari. My lord, I lie with her often, and I know
She 'll much disquiet you.
Ant. See, you are complain'd of.
Cari. For she 's the sprawling'st bedfellow.
Ant. I shall like her the better for that.
Cari. Sir, shall I ask you a question?
Ant. I pray thee, Cariola.
Cari. Wherefore still when you lie with my lady
Do you rise so early?
Ant. Laboring men
Count the clock oft'nest, Cariola,
Are glad when their task 's ended.
Duch. I 'll stop your mouth.
(*Kisses him.*)
Ant. Nay, that 's but one; Venus had two soft doves
To draw her chariot; I must have another.—
(*She kisses him again.*)
When wilt thou marry, Cariola?
Cari. Never, my lord.
Ant. O, fie upon this single life! forgo it.
We read how Daphne, for her peevish flight,
Became a fruitless bay-tree; Syrinx turn'd
To the pale empty reed; Anaxarete
Was frozen into marble: whereas those
Which married, or prov'd kind unto their friends,
Were by a gracious influence trans-shap'd
Into the olive, pomegranate, mulberry,
Became flowers, precious stones, or eminent stars.
Cari. This is a vain poetry: but I pray you, tell me,
If there were propos'd me, wisdom, riches, and beauty,
In three several young men, which should I choose?
Ant. 'T is a hard question. This was Paris' case,
And he was blind in 't, and there was a great cause;
For how was 't possible he could judge right,
Having three amorous goddesses in view,
And they stark naked? 'T was a motion [94]
Were able to benight the apprehension
Of the severest counselor of Europe.
Now I look on both your faces so well form'd,
It puts me in mind of a question I would ask.
Cari. What is 't?
Ant. I do wonder why hard-favor'd ladies,
For the most part, keep worse-favor'd waiting-women
To attend them, and cannot endure fair ones.
Duch. O, that 's soon answered,
Did you ever in your life know an ill painter
Desire to have his dwelling next door to the shop
Of an excellent picture-maker? 'T would disgrace
His face-making, and undo him. I prithee,
When were we so merry? My hair tangles.
Ant. Pray thee, Cariola, let 's steal forth the room,
And let her talk to herself: I have divers times
Serv'd her the like, when she hath chaf'd extremely.
I love to see her angry. Softly, Cariola.
Exeunt Antonio and Cariola.
Duch. Doth not the color of my hair 'gin to change?
When I wax gray, I shall have all the court
Powder their hair with arras,[95] to be like me.
You have cause to love me; I ent'red you into my heart

Enter Ferdinand unseen.

Before you would vouchsafe to call for the keys.
We shall one day have my brothers take you napping.
Methinks his presence, being now in court,
Should make you keep your own bed; but you 'll say
Love mixt with fear is sweetest. I 'll assure you,
You shall get no more children till my brothers
Consent to be your gossips.[96] Have you lost your tongue?
(*Perceiving Ferdinand.*)
'T is welcome:
For know, whether I am doom'd to live or die,
I can do both like a prince.

94 proposal. 95 orris-root. 96 god-parents.

Ferd. Die, then, quickly.
(*Giving her a poniard.*)
Virtue, where art thou hid? What hideous thing
Is it that doth eclipse thee?
Duch. Pray, sir, hear me.
Ferd. Or is it true thou art but a bare name,
And no essential thing?
Duch. Sir—
Ferd. Do not speak.
Duch. No, sir:
I will plant my soul in mine ears, to hear you.
Ferd. O most imperfect light of human reason,
That mak'st [us] so unhappy to foresee
What we can least prevent! Pursue thy wishes,
And glory in them: there 's in shame no comfort
But to be past all bounds and sense of shame.
Duch. I pray, sir, hear me: I am married.
Ferd. So!
Duch. Happily, not to your liking: but for that,
Alas, your shears do come untimely now
To clip the bird's wings that 's already flown!
Will you see my husband?
Ferd. Yes, if I could change
Eyes with a basilisk.[97]
Duch. Sure, you came hither
By his confederacy.
Ferd. The howling of a wolf
Is music to thee, screech-owl: prithee, peace.—
Whate'er thou art that hast enjoy'd my sister,
For I am sure thou hear'st me, for thine own sake
Let me not know thee. I came hither prepar'd
To work thy discovery; yet am now persuaded
It would beget such violent effects
As would damn us both. I would not for ten millions
I had beheld thee: therefore use all means
I never may have knowledge of thy name;
Enjoy thy lust still, and a wretched life,
On that condition.—And for thee, vile woman,
If thou do wish thy lecher may grow old
In thy embracements, I would have thee build
Such a room for him as our anchorites
To holier use inhabit. Let not the sun
Shine on him till he 's dead; let dogs and monkeys
Only converse with him, and such dumb things
To whom nature denies use to sound his name;
Do not keep a paraquito, lest she learn it;
If thou do love him, cut out thine own tongue,
Lest it bewray him.
Duch. Why might not I marry?
I have not gone about in this to create
Any new world or custom.
Ferd. Thou art undone;
And thou hast ta'en that massy sheet of lead
That hid thy husband's bones, and folded it
About my heart.
Duch. Mine bleeds for 't.
Ferd. Thine! thy heart!
What should I name 't, unless a hollow bullet
Fill'd with unquenchable wild-fire?
Duch. You are in this
Too strict; and were you not my princely brother,
I would say, too wilful: my reputation
Is safe.
Ferd. Dost thou know what reputation is?
I 'll tell thee,—to small purpose, since th' instruction
Comes now too late.
Upon a time Reputation, Love, and Death,
Would travel o'er the world; and it was concluded
That they should part, and take three several ways.
Death told them, they should find him in great battles,
Or cities plagu'd with plagues; Love gives them counsel
To inquire for him 'mongst unambitious shepherds,
Where dowries were not talk'd of, and sometimes
'Mongst quiet kindred that had nothing left
By their dead parents: "Stay," quoth Reputation,
"Do not forsake me; for it is my nature,
If once I part from any man I meet,

[97] *i.e.* so that I could kill him with a glance (like the fabled basilisk).

I am never found again." And so for you:
You have shook hands with Reputation,
And made him invisible. So, fare you well:
I will never see you more.

Duch. Why should only I,
Of all the other princes of the world,
Be cas'd up, like a holy relic? I have youth
And a little beauty.

Ferd. So you have some virgins
That are witches. I will never see thee more.

Exit.

Re-enter Antonio with a pistol, and Cariola.

Duch. You saw this apparition?

Ant. Yes: we are
Betray'd. How came he hither? I should turn
This to thee, for that.

Cari. Pray, sir, do; and when
That you have cleft my heart, you shall read there
Mine innocence.

Duch. That gallery gave him entrance.

Ant. I would this terrible thing would come again,
That, standing on my guard, I might relate
My warrantable love.—

(*She shows the poniard.*)

Ha! what means this?

Duch. He left this with me,

Ant. And it seems did wish
You would use it on yourself.

Duch. His action seem'd
To intend so much.

Ant. This hath a handle to 't,
As well as a point: turn it towards him, and
So fasten the keen edge in his rank gall.

(*Knocking within.*)

How now! who knocks? More earthquakes?

Duch. I stand
As if a mine beneath my feet were ready
To be blown up.

Cari. 'T is Bosola.

Duch. Away!
O misery! methinks unjust actions
Should wear these masks and curtains, and not we.
You must instantly part hence: I have fashion'd it already.

Exit Antonio.

Enter Bosola.

Bos. The duke your brother is ta'en up in a whirlwind;
Hath took horse, and 's rid post to Rome.

Duch. So late?

Bos. He told me, as he mounted into th' saddle,
You were undone.

Duch. Indeed, I am very near it.

Bos. What 's the matter?

Duch. Antonio, the master of our household,
Hath dealt so falsely with me in 's accounts.
My brother stood engag'd with me for money
Ta'en up of certain Neapolitan Jews,
And Antonio lets the bonds be forfeit.

Bos. Strange!—(*Aside.*) This is cunning.

Duch. And hereupon
My brother's bills at Naples are protested
Against.—Call up our officers.

Bos. I shall.

Exit.

Re-enter Antonio.

Duch. The place that you must fly to is Ancona:
Hire a house there; I 'll send after you
My treasure and my jewels. Our weak safety
Runs upon enginous wheels:[98] short syllables
Must stand for periods. I must now accuse you
Of such a feigned crime as Tasso calls
Magnanima menzogna, a noble lie,
'Cause it must shield our honors.—Hark! they are coming.

Re-enter Bosola and Officers.

Ant. Will your grace hear me?

Duch. I have got well by you; you have yielded me
A million of loss: I am like to inherit
The people's curses for your stewardship.
You had the trick in audit-time to be sick,
Till I had sign'd your quietus;[99] and that cur'd you
Without help of a doctor.—Gentlemen,
I would have this man be an example to you all;
So shall you hold my favor; I pray, let him;[1]
For h' as done that, alas, you would not think of,
And, because I intend to be rid of him,

98 wheels swift as an engine's

99 Cf. n. 35, p. 302.

1 let him go.

I mean not to publish.—Use your fortune elsewhere.

Ant. I am strongly arm'd to brook my overthrow,
As commonly men bear with a hard year.
I will not blame the cause on 't; but do think
The necessity of my malevolent star
Procures this, not her humor. O, the inconstant
And rotten ground of service! You may see,
'T is even like him, that in a winter night,
Takes a long slumber o'er a dying fire,
A-loth to part from 't; yet parts thence as cold
As when he first sat down.

Duch. We do confiscate,
Towards the satisfying of your accounts,
All that you have.

Ant. I am all yours; and 't is very fit
All mine should be so.

Duch. So, sir, you have your pass.

Ant. You may see, gentlemen, what 't is to serve
A prince with body and soul.

Exit.

Bos. Here 's an example for extortion: what moisture is drawn out of the sea, when foul weather comes, pours down, and runs into the sea again.

Duch. I would know what are your opinions
Of this Antonio.

2 Off. He could not abide to see a pig's head gaping: I thought your grace would find him a Jew.

3 Off. I would you had been his officer, for your own sake.

4 Off. You would have had more money.

1 Off. He stopp'd his ears with black wool, and to those came to him for money said he was thick of hearing.

2 Off. Some said he was an hermaphrodite, for he could not abide a woman.

4 Off. How scurvy proud he would look when the treasury was full! Well, let him go.

1 Off. Yes, and the chippings of the buttery fly after him, to scour[2] his gold chain.[3]

Duch. Leave us.—

Exeunt Officers.

What do you think of these?

Bos. That these are rogues that in 's prosperity,
But to have waited on his fortune, could have wish'd
His dirty stirrup riveted through their noses,
And follow'd after 's mule, like a bear in a ring;
Would have prostituted their daughters to his lust;
Made their first-born intelligencers; thought none happy
But such as were born under his blest planet,
And wore his livery: and do these lice drop off now?
Well, never look to have the like again:
He hath left a sort[4] of flatt'ring rogues behind him;
Their doom must follow. Princes pay flatterers
In their own money: flatterers dissemble their vices,
And they dissemble their lies; that 's justice.
Alas, poor gentleman!

Duch. Poor! he hath amply fill'd his coffers.

Bos. Sure, he was too honest. Pluto,[5] the god of riches,
When he 's sent by Jupiter to any man,
He goes limping, to signify that wealth
That comes on God's name comes slowly; but when he 's sent
On the devil's errand, he rides post and comes in by scuttles.[6]
Let me show you what a most unvalu'd jewel
You have in a wanton humor thrown away,
To bless the man shall find him. He was an excellent
Courtier and most faithful; a soldier that thought it
As beastly to know his own value too little
As devilish to acknowledge it too much.
Both his virtue and form deserv'd a far better fortune:
His discourse rather delighted to judge itself than show itself:
His breast was fill'd with all perfection,
And yet it seem'd a private whisp'ring-room,
It made so little noise of 't.

Duch. But he was basely descended.

Bos. Will you make yourself a mercenary herald,

[2] polish. [3] the badge of a steward. [4] crew. [5] Properly *Plutus*. [6] quick steps.

Rather to examine men's pedigrees than virtues?
You shall want[7] him:
For know an honest statesman to a prince
Is like a cedar planted by a spring;
The spring bathes the tree's root, the grateful tree
Rewards it with his shadow: you have not done so.
I would sooner swim to the Bermoothes on
Two politicians' rotten bladders, tied
Together with an intelligencer's heart-string,
Than depend on so changeable a prince's favor.
Fare thee well, Antonio! Since the malice of the world
Would needs down with thee, it cannot be said yet
That any ill happen'd unto thee, considering thy fall
Was accompanied with virtue.

Duch. O, you render me excellent music!

Bos. Say you?

Duch. This good one that you speak of is my husband.

Bos. Do I not dream? Can this ambitious age
Have so much goodness in 't as to prefer
A man merely for worth, without these shadows
Of wealth and painted honors? Possible?

Duch. I have had three children by him.

Bos. Fortunate lady!
For you have made your private nuptial bed
The humble and fair seminary of peace,
No question but: many an unbenefic'd scholar
Shall pray for you for this deed, and rejoice
That some preferment in the world can yet
Arise from merit. The virgins of your land
That have no dowries shall hope your example
Will raise them to rich husbands. Should you want
Soldiers, 't would make the very Turks and Moors
Turn Christians, and serve you for this act.
Last, the neglected poets of your time,
In honor of this trophy of a man,
Rais'd by that curious engine, your white hand,
Shall thank you in your grave for 't, and make that
More reverend than all the cabinets
Of living princes. For Antonio,
His fame shall likewise flow from many a pen,
When heralds shall want coats to sell to men.

Duch. As I taste comfort in this friendly speech,
So would I find concealment.

Bos. O, the secret of my prince,
Which I will wear on th' inside of my heart!

Duch. You shall take charge of all my coin and jewels,
And follow him; for he retires himself
To Ancona.

Bos. So.

Duch. Whither, within few days,
I mean to follow thee.

Bos. Let me think:
I would wish your grace to feign a pilgrimage
To our Lady of Loretto,[8] scarce seven leagues
From fair Ancona; so may you depart
Your country with more honor, and your flight
Will seem a princely progress, retaining
Your usual train about you.

Duch. Sir, your direction
Shall lead me by the hand.

Cari. In my opinion,
She were better progress to the baths at Lucca,
Or go visit the Spa
In Germany; for, if you will believe me,
I do not like this jesting with religion,
This feigned pilgrimage.

Duch. Thou art a superstitious fool:
Prepare us instantly for our departure.
Past sorrows, let us moderately lament them,
For those to come, seek wisely to prevent them.

Exeunt Duchess and Cariola.

Bos. A politician is the devil's quilted anvil;
He fashions all sins on him, and the blows
Are never heard: he may work in a lady's chamber,
As here for proof. What rests[9] but I reveal

[7] miss. [8] Loretto boasted the possession of the house in which the Virgin Mary was born, miraculously taken there from Palestine; the shrine was famous. [9] remains.

All to my lord? O, this base quality [10]
Of intelligencer! Why, every quality i' th' world
Prefers but gain or commendation:
Now, for this act I am certain to be rais'd,
And men that paint weeds to the life are prais'd.
Exit.

SCENE 3. *Rome. A room in the Cardinal's palace.*

Enter Cardinal, Ferdinand, Malateste, Pescara, Delio, and Silvio.

Card. Must we turn soldier, then?
Mal. The emperor,
Hearing your worth that way, ere you attain'd
This reverend garment, joins you in commission
With the right fortunate soldier the Marquis of Pescara,
And the famous Lannoy.
Card. He that had the honor
Of taking the French king [11] prisoner?
Mal. The same.
Here 's a plot drawn for a new fortification
At Naples.
Ferd. This great Count Malateste, I perceive,
Hath got employment?
Delio. No employment, my lord;
A marginal note in the muster-book that he is
A voluntary lord.
Ferd. He 's no soldier?
Delio. He has worn gun-powder in 's hollow tooth for the tooth-ache.
Sil. He comes to the leaguer [12] with a full intent
To eat fresh beef and garlic, means to stay
Till the scent be gone, and straight return to court.
Delio. He hath read all the late service [13]
As the City Chronicle relates it;
And keeps two pewterers going, only to express
Battles in model.
Sil. Then he 'll fight by the book.[14]
Delio. By the almanac, I think,
To choose good days and shun the critical;
That 's his mistress' scarf.
Sil. Yes, he protests
He would do much for that taffeta.
Delio. I think he would run away from a battle,
To save it from taking [15] prisoner.
Sil. He is horribly afraid
Gun-powder will spoil the perfume on 't.
Delio. I saw a Dutchman break his pate once
For calling him pot-gun; he made his head
Have a bore in 't like a musket.
Sil. I would he had made a touch-hole to 't.
He is indeed a guarded sumpter-cloth,[16]
Only for the remove of the court.

Enter Bosola.

Pes. Bosola arriv'd! What should be the business?
Some falling-out among the cardinals?
These factions amongst great men, they are like
Foxes, when their heads are divided,[17]
They carry fire in their tails, and all the country
About them goes to wrack for 't.
Sil. What 's that Bosola?
Delio. I knew him in Padua,—a fantastical scholar, like such who study to know how many knots was in Hercules' club, of what color Achilles' beard was, or whether Hector were not troubled with the tooth-ache. He hath studied himself half blear-ey'd to know the true symmetry of Cæsar's nose by a shoeing-horn; and this he did to gain the name of a speculative man.
Pes. Mark Prince Ferdinand:
A very salamander lives in 's eye,
To mock the eager violence of fire.
Sil. That cardinal hath made more bad faces with his oppression than ever Michael Angelo made good ones. He lifts up 's nose, like a foul porpoise before a storm.
Pes. The Lord Ferdinand laughs.
Delio. Like a deadly cannon
That lightens ere it smokes.
Pes. These are your true pangs of death,
The pangs of life, that struggle with great statesmen.
Delio. In such a deformed silence witches whisper their charms.
Card. Doth she make religion her riding-hood

10 profession.
11 Francis I, at Pavia, in 1525.
12 camp.
13 an account of the late campaign.
14 *i.e.* he is a theoretical soldier.
15 being taken.
16 an elaborate saddle-cloth, used only when the court is making a journey.
17 Cf. *Judges*, xv. 4.

To keep her from the sun and tempest?
Ferd. That, that damns her. Methinks her fault and beauty,
Blended together, show like leprosy,
The whiter the fouler. I make it a question
Whether her beggarly brats were ever christ'ned.
Card. I will instantly solicit the state of Ancona
To have them banish'd.
Ferd. You are for Loretto:
I shall not be at your ceremony, fare you well—
Write to the Duke of Malfi, my young nephew,
She had by her first husband, and acquaint him
With 's mother's honesty.
Bos. I will.
Ferd. Antonio!
A slave that only smell'd of ink and counters,
And ne'er in 's life look'd like a gentleman,
But in the audit-time.—Go, go presently,
Draw me out an hundred and fifty of our horse,
And meet me at the foot-bridge.
Exeunt.

SCENE 4. *Loretto.*

Enter Two Pilgrims to the Shrine of our Lady of Loretto.

1 Pil. I have not seen a goodlier shrine than this;
Yet I have visited many.
2 Pil. The Cardinal of Arragon
Is this day to resign his cardinal's hat;
His sister duchess likewise is arriv'd
To pay her vow of pilgrimage. I expect
A noble ceremony.
1 Pil. No question.—They come.

Here the ceremony of the Cardinal's instalment in the habit of a soldier perform'd in delivering up his cross, hat, robes and ring at the shrine, and investing him with sword, helmet, shield, and spurs. Then Antonio, the Duchess and their children, having presented themselves at the shrine, are, by a form of banishment in dumb-show expressed towards them by the Cardinal and the state of Ancona, banished: during all which ceremony, this ditty is sung, to very solemn music, by divers church-men; and then exeunt all except the Two Pilgrims.

Arms and honors deck thy story,[18]
To thy fame's eternal glory!
Adverse fortune ever fly thee;
No disastrous fate come nigh thee!
I alone will sing thy praises,
Whom to honor virtue raises,
And thy study, that divine is,
Bent to martial discipline is;
Lay aside all those robes lie by thee;
Crown thy arts with arms, they 'll beautify thee.

O worthy of worthiest name, adorn'd in this manner,
Lead bravely thy forces on under war's warlike banner!
O, mayst thou prove fortunate in all martial courses!
Guide thou still by skill in arts and forces!
Victory attend thee nigh, whilst fame sings loud thy powers;
Triumphant conquest crown thy head, and blessings pour down showers!

1 Pil. Here 's a strange turn of state! who would have thought
So great a lady would have match'd herself
Unto so mean a person? Yet the cardinal
Bears himself much too cruel.
2 Pil. They are banish'd.
1 Pil. But I would ask what power hath this state
Of Ancona to determine[19] of a free prince?
2 Pil. They are a free state, sir, and her brother show'd
How that the Pope, fore-hearing of her looseness,
Hath seiz'd into th' protection of the church
The dukedom which she held as dowager.
1 Pil. But by what justice?
2 Pil. Sure, I think by none,
Only her brother's instigation.
1 Pil. What was it with such violence he took
Off from her finger?
2 Pil. 'T was her wedding-ring;
Which he vow'd shortly he would sacrifice
To his revenge.

18 The first quarto has in the margin: "The author disclaims this ditty to be his."
19 dispose.

1 Pil. Alas, Antonio!
If that a man be thrust into a well,
No matter who sets hand to 't, his own weight
Will bring him sooner to th' bottom. Come, let 's hence.
Fortune makes this conclusion general,
All things do help th' unhappy man to fall.

Exeunt.

SCENE 5. *Near Loretto.*

Enter Duchess, Antonio, Children, Cariola, and Servants.

Duch. Banish'd Ancona!
Ant. Yes, you see what power
Lightens in great men's breath.
Duch. Is all our train
Shrunk to this poor remainder?
Ant. These poor men,
Which have got little in your service, vow
To take your fortune: but your wiser buntings,
Now they are fledg'd, are gone.
Duch. They have done wisely.
This puts me in mind of death: physicians thus,
With their hands full of money, use to give o'er
Their patients.
Ant. Right the fashion of the world:
From decay'd fortunes every flatterer shrinks;
Men cease to build where the foundation sinks.
Duch. I had a very strange dream tonight.
Ant. What was 't?
Duch. Methought I wore my coronet of state,
And on a sudden all the diamonds
Were chang'd to pearls.
Ant. My interpretation
Is, you 'll weep shortly; for to me the pearls
Do signify your tears.
Duch. The birds, that live i' th' field
On the wild benefit of nature, live
Happier than we: for they may choose their mates,
And carol their sweet pleasures to the spring.

Enter Bosola with a letter.

Bos. You are happily o'erta'en.
Duch. From my brother?
Bos. Yes, from the Lord Ferdinand your brother
All love and safety.
Duch. Thou dost blanch mischief,
Would'st make it white. See, see, like to calm weather
At sea before a tempest, false hearts speak fair
To those they intend most mischief.

(*Reads.*)

"Send Antonio to me; I want his head in a business."
A politic equivocation!
He doth not want your counsel, but your head;
That is, he cannot sleep till you be dead.
And here 's another pitfall that 's strew'd o'er
With roses; mark it, 't is a cunning one:

(*Reads.*)

"I stand engaged for your husband for several debts at Naples: let not that trouble him; I had rather have his heart than his money."—
And I believe so too.
Bos. What do you believe?
Duch. That he so much distrusts my husband's love,
He will by no means believe his heart is with him
Until he see it: the devil is not cunning enough
To circumvent us in riddles.
Bos. Will you reject that noble and free league
Of amity and love which I present you?
Duch. Their league is like that of some politic kings,
Only to make themselves of strength and power
To be our after-ruin: tell them so.
Bos. And what from you?
Ant. Thus tell him: I will not come.
Bos. And what of this?
Ant. My brothers have dispers'd
Bloodhounds abroad; which till I hear are muzzl'd,
No truce, though hatch'd with ne'er such politic skill,
Is safe, that hangs upon our enemies' will.
I 'll not come at them.
Bos. This proclaims your breeding.
Every small thing draws a base mind to fear
As the adamant draws iron. Fare you well, sir;
You shall shortly hear from 's.

Exit.

Duch. I suspect some ambush;
Therefore by all my love I do conjure you
To take your eldest son, and fly towards Milan,
Let us not venture all this poor remainder
In one unlucky bottom.
Ant. You counsel safely.
Best of my life, farewell. Since we must part,
Heaven hath a hand in 't; but no otherwise
Than as some curious artist takes in sunder
A clock or watch, when it is out of frame,
To bring 't in better order.
Duch. I know not which is best,
To see you dead, or part with you. Farewell, boy:
Thou art happy that thou hast not understanding
To know thy misery; for all our wit
And reading brings us to a truer sense
Of sorrow.—In the eternal church, sir,
I do hope we shall not part thus.
Ant. O, be of comfort!
Make patience a noble fortitude,
And think not how unkindly we are us'd:
Man, like to cassia, is prov'd best, being bruis'd.
Duch. Must I, like to a slave-born Russian,
Account it praise to suffer tyranny?
And yet, O heaven, thy heavy hand is in 't!
I have seen my little boy oft scourge his top,[20]
And compar'd myself to 't: naught made me e'er
Go right but heaven's scourge-stick.
Ant. Do not weep:
Heaven fashion'd us of nothing; and we strive
To bring ourselves to nothing.—Farewell, Cariola,
And thy sweet armful.—If I do never see thee more,
Be a good mother to your little ones,
And save them from the tiger: fare you well.
Duch. Let me look upon you once more, for that speech
Came from a dying father. Your kiss is colder
Than that I have seen an holy anchorite
Give to a dead man's skull.
Ant. My heart is turn'd to a heavy lump of lead,
With which I sound my danger: fare you well.

Exeunt Antonio and his son.

Duch. My laurel is all withered.
Cari. Look, madam, what a troop of armed men
Make toward us!

Re-enter Bosola, masked, with a Guard.

Duch. O, they are very welcome:
When Fortune's wheel is over-charg'd with princes,
The weight makes it move swift: I would have my ruin
Be sudden.—I am your adventure, am I not?
Bos. You are: you must see your husband no more.
Duch. What devil art thou that counterfeit'st heaven's thunder?
Bos. Is that terrible? I would have you tell me whether
Is that note worse that frights the silly birds
Out of the corn, or that which doth allure them
To the nets? You have heark'ned to the last too much.
Duch. O misery! like to a rusty o'ercharg'd cannon,
Shall I never fly in pieces? Come, to what prison?
Bos. To none.
Duch. Whither, then?
Bos. To your palace.
Duch. I have heard
That Charon's boat serves to convey all o'er
The dismal lake, but brings none back again.
Bos. Your brothers mean you safety and pity.
Duch. Pity!
With such a pity men preserve alive
Pheasants and quails, when they are not fat enough
To be eaten.
Bos. These are your children?
Duch. Yes.
Bos. Can they prattle?
Duch. No:
But I intend, since they were born accurs'd,
Curses shall be their first language.
Bos. Fie, madam!
Forget this base, low fellow——

[20] Tops were spun with whips.

Duch. Were I a man,
I 'd beat that counterfeit face [21] into thy other.
Bos. One of no birth.
Duch. Say that he was born mean,
Man is most happy when 's own actions
Be arguments and examples of his virtue.
Bos. A barren, beggarly virtue.
Duch. I prithee, who is greatest? Can you tell?
Sad tales befit my woe: I 'll tell you one.
A salmon, as she swam unto the sea,
Met with a dog-fish, who encounters her
With this rough language: "Why art thou so bold
To mix thyself with our high state of floods,
Being no eminent courtier, but one
That for the calmest and fresh time o' th' year
Dost live in shallow rivers, rank'st thyself
With silly smelts and shrimps? And darest thou
Pass by our dog-ship without reverence?"
"O," quoth the salmon, "sister, be at peace:
Thank Jupiter we both have pass'd the net!
Our value never can be truly known,
Till in the fisher's basket we be shown:
I' th' market then my price may be the higher,
Even when I am nearest to the cook and fire."
So to great men the moral may be stretched;
Men oft are valu'd high, when they 're most wretched.—
But come, whither you please. I am arm'd 'gainst misery;
Bent to all sways of the oppressor's will.
There 's no deep valley but near some great hill.

Exeunt.

ACT IV.

SCENE 1. *Amalfi. A room in the Duchess's palace.*

Enter Ferdinand and Bosola.

Ferd. How doth our sister duchess bear herself
In her imprisonment?
Bos. Nobly: I 'll describe her.
She 's sad as one long us'd to 't, and she seems
Rather to welcome the end of misery
Than shun it; a behavior so noble
As gives a majesty to adversity:
You may discern the shape of loveliness
More perfect in her tears than in her smiles:
She will muse four hours together; and her silence,
Methinks, expresseth more than if she spake.
Ferd. Her melancholy seems to be fortified
With a strange disdain.
Bos. 'T is so; and this restraint,
Like English mastiffs that grow fierce with tying,
Makes her too passionately apprehend
Those pleasures she is kept from.
Ferd. Curse upon her!
I will no longer study in the book
Of another's heart. Inform her what I told you.

Exit.

Enter Duchess and Attendants.

Bos. All comfort to your grace!
Duch. I will have none.
Pray thee, why dost thou wrap thy poison'd pills
In gold and sugar?
Bos. Your elder brother, the Lord Ferdinand,
Is come to visit you, and sends you word,
'Cause once he rashly made a solemn vow
Never to see you more, he comes i' th' night;
And prays you gently neither torch nor taper
Shine in your chamber. He will kiss your hand,
And reconcile himself; but for his vow
He dares not see you.
Duch. At his pleasure.—
Take hence the lights.—He 's come.

Exeunt Attendants with lights.
Enter Ferdinand.

Ferd. Where are you?
Duch. Here, sir.
Ferd. This darkness suits you well.
Duch. I would ask you pardon.
Ferd. You have it;
For I account it the honorabl'st revenge,
Where I may kill, to pardon.—Where are your cubs?
Duch. Whom?

21 mask.

Ferd. Call them your children;
For though our national law distinguish bastards
From true legitimate issue, compassionate nature
Makes them all equal.
Duch. Do you visit me for this?
You violate a sacrament o' th' church
Shall make you howl in hell for 't.
Ferd. It had been well
Could you have liv'd thus always; for, indeed,
You were too much i' th' light:—but no more;
I come to seal my peace with you. Here 's a hand
(*Gives her a dead man's hand.*)
To which you have vow'd much love; the ring upon 't
You gave.
Duch. I affectionately kiss it.
Ferd. Pray, do, and bury the print of it in your heart.
I will leave this ring with you for a love-token;
And the hand as sure as the ring; and do not doubt
But you shall have the heart too. When you need a friend,
Send it to him that ow'd [22] it; you shall see
Whether he can aid you.
Duch. You are very cold:
I fear you are not well after your travel.—
Ha! lights!——O, horrible!
Ferd. Let her have lights enough.
Exit.
Duch. What witchcraft doth he practise, that he hath left
A dead man's hand here?
(*Here is discover'd, behind a traverse,[23] the artificial figures of Antonio and his children, appearing as if they were dead.*)
Bos. Look you, here 's the piece from which 't was ta'en.
He doth present you this sad spectacle,
That, now you know directly they are dead,
Hereafter you may wisely cease to grieve
For that which cannot be recovered.
Duch. There is not between heaven and earth one wish
I stay for after this. It wastes me more
Than were 't my picture,[24] fashion'd out of wax,
Stuck with a magical needle, and then buried
In some foul dung hill; and yon 's an excellent property
For a tyrant, which I would account mercy.
Bos. What 's that?
Duch. If they would bind me to that lifeless trunk,
And let me freeze to death.
Bos. Come, you must live.
Duch. That 's the greatest torture souls feel in hell,
In hell, that they must live, and cannot die.
Portia,[25] I 'll new kindle thy coals again,
And revive the rare and almost dead example
Of a loving wife.
Bos. O, fie! despair? Remember
You are a Christian.
Duch. The church enjoins fasting:
I 'll starve myself to death.
Bos. Leave this vain sorrow.
Things being at the worst begin to mend: the bee,
When he hath shot his sting into your hand,
May then play with your eye-lid.
Duch. Good comfortable fellow,
Persuade a wretch that 's broke upon the wheel
To have all his bones new set; entreat him live
To be executed again. Who must despatch me?
I account this world a tedious theater,
For I do play a part in 't 'gainst my will.
Bos. Come, be of comfort; I will save your life.
Duch. Indeed, I have not leisure to tend so small a business.
Bos. Now, by my life, I pity you.
Duch. Thou art a fool, then,
To waste thy pity on a thing so wretched
As cannot pity itself. I am full of daggers.
Puff, let me blow these vipers from me.

Enter Servant.

What are you?
Serv. One that wishes you long life.
Duch. I would thou wert hang'd for the horrible curse
Thou hast given me: I shall shortly grow one
Of the miracles of pity. I 'll go pray;—
Exit Serv.
No, I 'll go curse.

22 owned.
23 curtain.
24 image; as the image melted, the life of the person upon whom the spell was laid ebbed away.
25 The wife of Brutus, who committed suicide by swallowing burning coals.

Bos. O, fie!
Duch. I could curse the stars—
Bos. O, fearful!
Duch. And those three smiling seasons of the year
Into a Russian winter; nay, the world
To its first chaos.
Bos. Look you, the stars shine still.
Duch. O, but you must
Remember, my curse hath a great way to go.—
Plagues, that make lanes through largest families,
Consume them!—
Bos. Fie, lady!
Duch. Let them, like tyrants,
Never be remembered but for the ill they have done;
Let all the zealous prayers of mortified
Churchmen forget them!—
Bos. O, uncharitable!
Duch. Let heaven a little while cease crowning martyrs,
To punish them!—
Go, howl them this, and say, I long to bleed:
It is some mercy when men kill with speed.
Exit.

Re-enter Ferdinand.

Ferd. Excellent, as I would wish; she 's plagu'd in art.[26]
These presentations are but fram'd in wax
By the curious master in that quality,[27]
Vincentio Lauriola, and she takes them
For true substantial bodies.
Bos. Why do you do this?
Ferd. To bring her to despair.
Bos. Faith, end here,
And go no farther in your cruelty:
Send her a penitential garment to put on
Next to her delicate skin, and furnish her
With beads and prayer-books.
Ferd. Damn her! that body of hers,
While that my blood ran pure in 't, was more worth
Than that which thou wouldst comfort, call'd a soul.
I will send her masques of common courtesans,
Have her meat serv'd up by bawds and ruffians,
And, 'cause she 'll needs be mad, I am resolv'd
To remove forth the common hospital
All the mad-folk, and place them near her lodging;
There let them practise together, sing and dance,
And act their gambols to the full o' th' moon:
If she can sleep the better for it, let her.
Your work is almost ended.
Bos. Must I see her again?
Ferd. Yes.
Bos. Never.
Ferd. You must.
Bos. Never in mine own shape;
That 's forfeited by my intelligence
And this last cruel lie: when you send me next,
The business shall be comfort.
Ferd. Very likely,
Thy pity is nothing of kin to thee. Antonio
Lurks about Milan: thou shalt shortly thither,
To feed a fire as great as my revenge,
Which ne'er will slack till it hath spent his[28] fuel:
Intemperate agues make physicians cruel.
Exeunt.

SCENE 2. *Another room in the Duchess's palace.*

Enter Duchess and Cariola.

Duch. What hideous noise was that?
Cari. 'T is the wild consort[29]
Of madmen, lady, which your tyrant brother
Hath plac'd about your lodging. This tyranny,
I think, was never practis'd till this hour.
Duch. Indeed, I thank him. Nothing but noise and folly
Can keep me in my right wits; whereas reason
And silence make me stark mad. Sit down;
Discourse to me some dismal tragedy.
Cari. O, 't will increase your melancholy!
Duch. Thou art deceiv'd:
To hear of greater grief would lessen mine.
This is a prison?
Cari. Yes, but you shall live
To shake this durance off.
Duch. Thou art a fool:
The robin-red-breast and the nightingale
Never live long in cages.

26 by artifice. 27 profession. 28 its. 29 company.

Cari. Pray, dry your eyes.
What think you of, madam?
Duch. Of nothing;
When I muse thus, I sleep.
Cari. Like a madman, with your eyes open?
Duch. Dost thou think we shall know one another
In th' other world?
Cari. Yes, out of question.
Duch. O, that it were possible we might
But hold some two days' conference with the dead!
From them I should learn somewhat, I am sure,
I never shall know here. I 'll tell thee a miracle:
I am not mad yet, to my cause of sorrow:
Th' heaven o'er my head seems made of molten brass,
The earth of flaming sulphur, yet I am not mad.
I am acquainted with sad misery
As the tann'd galley-slave is with his oar;
Necessity makes me suffer constantly,
And custom makes it easy. Who do I look like now?
Cari. Like to your picture in the gallery,
A deal of life in show, but none in practice;
Or rather like some reverend monument
Whose ruins are even pitied.
Duch. Very proper;
And Fortune seems only to have her eyesight
To behold my tragedy.—How now!
What noise is that?

Enter Servant.

Serv. I am come to tell you
Your brother hath intended you some sport.
A great physician, when the Pope was sick
Of a deep melancholy, presented him
With several sorts [30] of madmen, which wild object,
Being full of change and sport, forc'd him to laugh,
And so th' imposthume [31] broke: the selfsame cure
The duke intends on you.
Duch. Let them come in.
Serv. There 's a mad lawyer; and a secular priest;
A doctor that hath forfeited his wits
By jealousy; an astrologian
That in his works said such a day o' th' month
Should be the day of doom, and, failing of 't,
Ran mad; an English tailor craz'd i' th' brain
With the study of new fashions; a gentleman-usher
Quite beside himself with care to keep in mind
The number of his lady's salutations,
Or "How do you," she employ'd him in each morning;
A farmer, too, an excellent knave in grain,[32]
Mad 'cause he was hind'red transportation: [33]
And let one broker that 's mad loose to these,
You 'd think the devil were among them.
Duch. Sit, Cariola.—Let them loose when you please,
For I am chain'd to endure all your tyranny.

Enter Madmen.

Here by a Madman this song is sung to a dismal kind of music.

O, let us howl some heavy note,
  Some deadly dogged howl,
Sounding as from the threat'ning throat
  Of beasts and fatal fowl!
As ravens, screech-owls, bulls, and bears,
  We 'll bell, and bawl our parts,
Till irksome noise have cloy'd your ears
  And corrosiv'd your hearts.
At last, when as our choir wants breath,
  Our bodies being blest,
We 'll sing, like swans, to welcome death,
  And die in love and rest.

1 Madman. Dooms-day not come yet! I 'll draw it nearer by a perspective,[34] or make a glass that shall set all the world on fire upon an instant. I cannot sleep; my pillow is stuft with a litter of porcupines.

2 Madman. Hell is a mere glass-house, where the devils are continually blowing up women's souls on hollow irons, and the fire never goes out.

3 Madman. I will lie with every woman in my parish the tenth night. I will tithe them over like hay-cocks.

4 Madman. Shall my 'pothecary out-go me, because I am a cuckold? I have

30 bands.
31 abscess.
32 a pun on *grain*= dye.
33 from exporting his grain.
34 telescope.

found out his roguery: he makes alum of his wife's urine, and sells it to Puritans that have sore throats with over-straining.

1 Madman. I have skill in heraldry.

2 Madman. Hast?

1 Madman. You do give for your crest a wood-cock's head with the brains pickt out on 't; you are a very ancient gentleman.

3 Madman. Greek is turn'd Turk: we are only to be sav'd by the Helvetian translation.[35]

1 Madman. Come on, sir, I will lay the law to you.

2 Madman. O, rather lay a corrosive: the law will eat to the bone.

3 Madman. He that drinks but to satisfy nature is damn'd.

4 Madman. If I had my glass here, I would show a sight should make all the women here call me mad doctor.

1 Madman. What 's he? A rope-maker?

2 Madman. No, no, no; a snuffling knave that while he shows the tombs, will have his hand in a wench's placket.[36]

3 Madman. Woe to the caroche[37] that brought home my wife from the masque at three o'clock in the morning! It had a large feather-bed in it.

4 Madman. I have pared the devil's nails forty times, roasted them in raven's eggs, and cur'd agues with them.

3 Madman. Get me three hundred milch-bats, to make possets[38] to procure sleep.

4 Madman. All the college[39] may throw their caps at me: I have made a soap-boiler costive; it was my masterpiece.

(*Here the dance, consisting of Eight Madmen, with music answerable thereunto; after which, Bosola, like an old man, enters.*)

Duch. Is he mad too?

Serv. Pray, question him. I 'll leave you.

Exeunt Servant and Madmen.

Bos. I am come to make thy tomb.

Duch. Ha! my tomb!
Thou speak'st as if I lay upon my death-bed,
Gasping for breath. Dost thou perceive me sick?

Bos. Yes, and the more dangerously, since thy sickness is insensible.

Duch. Thou art not mad, sure: dost know me?

Bos. Yes.

Duch. Who am I?

Bos. Thou art a box of worm-seed, at best but a salvatory[40] of green mummy.[41] What 's this flesh? A little crudded[42] milk, fantastical puff-paste. Our bodies are weaker than those paper-prisons boys use to keep flies in; more contemptible, since ours is to preserve earth-worms. Didst thou ever see a lark in a cage? Such is the soul in the body: this world is like her little turf of grass, and the heaven o'er our heads, like her looking-glass, only gives us a miserable knowledge of the small compass of our prison.

Duch. Am I not thy duchess?

Bos. Thou art some great woman, sure, for riot begins to sit on thy forehead (clad in gray hairs) twenty years sooner than on a merry milk-maid's. Thou sleep'st worst than if a mouse should be forc'd to take up her lodging in a cat's ear: a little infant that breeds its teeth, should it lie with thee, would cry out, as if thou wert the more unquiet bedfellow.

Duch. I am Duchess of Malfi still.

Bos. That makes thy sleeps so broken:
Glories, like glow-worms, afar off shine bright,
But, look'd to near, have neither heat nor light.

Duch. Thou art very plain.

Bos. My trade is to flatter the dead, not the living; I am a tomb-maker.

Duch. And thou com'st to make my tomb?

Bos. Yes.

Duch. Let me be a little merry:—of what stuff wilt thou make it?

Bos. Nay, resolve me first, of what fashion?

Duch. Why, do we grow fantastical on our deathbed?
Do we affect fashion in the grave?

Bos. Most ambitiously. Princes' images on their tombs do not lie, as they were wont, seeming to pray up to heaven; but with their hands under their cheeks, as if they died of the tooth-ache. They are not carved with their eyes fix'd upon the stars, but as their minds were wholly bent upon the world, the self-same way they seem to turn their faces.

Duch. Let me know fully therefore the effect
Of this thy dismal preparation,
This talk fit for a charnel.

Bos. Now I shall:—

35 the Geneva Bible.
36 petticoat.
37 coach.
38 hot milk curdled with liquor.
39 College of Physicians.
40 repository.
41 mummia, a pitchy substance supposedly derived from mummies, used as a medicine.
42 curdled.

Enter Executioners, with a coffin, cords, and a bell.

Here is a present from your princely brothers;
And may it arrive welcome, for it brings
Last benefit, last sorrow.

Duch. Let me see it:
I have so much obedience in my blood,
I wish it in their veins to do them good.

Bos. This is your last presence-chamber.

Cari. O my sweet lady!

Duch. Peace; it affrights not me.

Bos. I am the common bellman
That usually is sent to condemn'd persons
The night before they suffer.

Duch. Even now thou said'st
Thou wast a tomb-maker.

Bos. 'T was to bring you
By degrees to mortification. Listen.

Hark, now everything is still,
The screech-owl and the whistler shrill
Call upon our dame aloud,
And bid her quickly don her shroud!
Much you had of land and rent;
Your length in clay 's now competent:
A long war disturb'd your mind;
Here your perfect peace is sign'd.
Of what is 't fools make such vain keeping?
Sin their conception, their birth weeping,
Their life a general mist of error,
Their death a hideous storm of terror.
Strew your hair with powders sweet,
Don clean linen, bathe your feet,
And (the foul fiend more to check)
A crucifix let bless your neck.
'T is now full tide 'tween night and day;
End your groan, and come away.

Cari. Hence, villains, tyrants, murderers! Alas!
What will you do with my lady?—Call for help!

Duch. To whom? To our next neighbors? They are mad-folks.

Bos. Remove that noise.[43]

Duch. Farewell, Cariola.
In my last will I have not much to give:
A many hungry guests have fed upon me;
Thine will be a poor reversion.

Cari. I will die with her.

Duch. I pray thee, look thou giv'st my little boy
Some syrup for his cold, and let the girl
Say her prayers ere she sleep.

(*Cariola is forced out by the Executioners.*)

Now what you please:
What death?

Bos. Strangling; here are your executioners.

Duch. I forgive them:
The apoplexy, catarrh, or cough o' th' lungs,
Would do as much as they do.

Bos. Doth not death fright you?

Duch. Who would be afraid on 't,
Knowing to meet such excellent company
In th' other world?

Bos. Yet, methinks,
The manner of your death should much afflict you:
This cord should terrify you.

Duch. Not a whit:
What would it pleasure me to have my throat cut
With diamonds? or to be smothered
With cassia? or to be shot to death with pearls?
I know death hath ten thousand several doors
For men to take their exits; and 't is found
They go on such strange geometrical hinges,
You may open them both ways: any way, for heaven-sake,
So I were out of your whispering! Tell my brothers
That I perceive death, now I am well awake,
Best gift is they can give or I can take.
I would fain put off my last woman's-fault,
I 'd not be tedious to you.

1 Execut. We are ready.

Duch. Dispose my breath how please you; but my body
Bestow upon my women, will you?

1 Execut. Yes.

Duch. Pull, and pull strongly, for your able strength
Must pull down heaven upon me:—
Yet stay; heaven-gates are not so highly arch'd
As princes' palaces; they that enter there
Must go upon their knees (*Kneels*).—Come, violent death
Serve for mandragora to make me sleep!—
Go tell my brothers, when I am laid out,
They then may feed in quiet.

(*They strangle her.*)

[43] i.e. Cariola.

Bos. Where 's the waiting-woman?
Fetch her: some other strangle the children.

Enter Cariola.

Look you, there sleeps your mistress.
Cari. O, you are damn'd
Perpetually for this! My turn is next;
Is 't not so ordered?
Bos. Yes, and I am glad
You are so well prepar'd for 't.
Cari. You are deceiv'd, sir,
I am not prepar'd for 't, I will not die;
I will first come to my answer,[44] and know
How I have offended.
Bos. Come, despatch her.—
You kept her counsel; now you shall keep ours.
Cari. I will not die, I must not; I am contracted
To a young gentleman.
1 Execut. Here 's your wedding-ring.
Cari. Let me but speak with the duke: I 'll discover
Treason to his person.
Bos. Delays:—throttle her.
1 Execut. She bites and scratches.
Cari. If you kill me now,
I am damn'd; I have not been at confession
This two years.
Bos. (*To Executioners.*) When!
Cari. I am quick with child.
Bos. Why, then,
Your credit 's saved.
(*They strangle Cariola.*)
Bear her into th' next room;
Let this[45] lie still.
Exeunt Executioners with body of Cariola.

Enter Ferdinand.

Ferd. Is she dead?
Bos. She is what
You 'd have her. But here begin your pity:
(*Shows the Children strangled.*)
Alas, how have these offended?
Ferd. The death
Of young wolves is never to be pitied.
Bos. Fix your eye here.
Ferd. Constantly.
Bos. Do you not weep?
Other sins only speak; murder shrieks out.
The element of water moistens the earth,
But blood flies upwards and bedews the heavens.
Ferd. Cover her face; mine eyes dazzle: she died young.
Bos. I think not so; her infelicity
Seem'd to have years too many.
Ferd. She and I were twins;
And should I die this instant, I had liv'd
Her time to a minute.
Bos. It seems she was born first:
You have bloodily approv'd the ancient truth,
That kindred commonly do worse agree
Than remote strangers.
Ferd. Let me see her face
Again. Why didst thou not pity her? What
An excellent honest man mightst thou have been,
If thou hadst borne her to some sanctuary!
Or, bold in a good cause,—oppos'd thyself,
With thy advanced sword above thy head,
Between her innocence and my revenge!
I bade thee, when I was distracted of my wits,
Go kill my dearest friend, and thou hast done 't.
For let me but examine well the cause:
What was the meanness of her match to me?
Only I must confess I had a hope,
Had she continu'd widow, to have gain'd
An infinite mass of treasure by her death:
And that was the main cause,—her marriage,
That drew a stream of gall quite through my heart.
For thee, as we observe in tragedies
That a good actor many times is curs'd
For playing a villain's part, I hate thee for 't,
And, for my sake, say thou hast done much ill well.
Bos. Let me quicken your memory, for I perceive
You are falling into ingratitude: I challenge
The reward due to my service.
Ferd. I 'll tell thee
What I 'll give thee.
Bos. Do.
Ferd. I 'll give thee a pardon
For this murder.
Bos. Ha!
Ferd. Yes, and 't is

44 trial.

45 the Duchess's body.

The largest bounty I can study to do thee.
By what authority didst thou execute
This bloody sentence?

Bos. By yours.

Ferd. Mine! Was I her judge?
Did any ceremonial form of law
Doom her to not-being? Did a complete jury
Deliver her conviction up i' th' court?
Where shalt thou find this judgment register'd,
Unless in hell? See, like a bloody fool,
Thou 'st forfeited thy life, and thou shalt die for 't.

Bos. The office of justice is perverted quite
When one thief hangs another. Who shall dare
To reveal this?

Ferd. O, I 'll tell thee;
The wolf shall find her grave, and scrape it up,
Not to devour the corpse, but to discover
The horrid murder.

Bos. You, not I, shall quake for 't.

Ferd. Leave me.

Bos. I will first receive my pension.

Ferd. You are a villain.

Bos. When your ingratitude
Is judge, I am so.

Ferd. O horror,
That not the fear of him which binds the devils
Can prescribe man obedience!—
Never look upon me more.

Bos. Why, fare thee well.
Your brother and yourself are worthy men!
You have a pair of hearts are hollow graves,
Rotten, and rotting others; and your vengeance,
Like two chain'd-bullets, still goes arm in arm:
You may be brothers; for treason, like the plague,
Doth take much in a blood.[46] I stand like one
That long hath ta'en a sweet and golden dream:
I am angry with myself now, that I wake.

Ferd. Get thee into some unknown part o' the world,
That I may never see thee.

Bos. Let me know
Wherefore I should be thus neglected. Sir,
I serv'd your tyranny, and rather strove
To satisfy yourself than all the world:
And though I loath'd the evil, yet I lov'd
You that did counsel it; and rather sought
To appear a true servant than an honest man.

Ferd. I 'll go hunt the badger by owl-light:
'T is a deed of darkness.

Exit.

Bos. He 's much distracted. Off, my painted honor!
While with vain hopes our faculties we tire,
We seem to sweat in ice and freeze in fire.
What would I do, were this to do again?
I would not change my peace of conscience
For all the wealth of Europe.—She stirs;[47] here 's life:—
Return, fair soul, from darkness, and lead mine
Out of this sensible hell!—she 's warm, she breathes:—
Upon thy pale lips I will melt my heart,
To store them with fresh color.—Who 's there?
Some cordial drink!—Alas! I dare not call:
So pity would destroy pity.—Her eye opes,
And heaven in it seems to ope, that late was shut,
To take me up to mercy.

Duch. Antonio!

Bos. Yes, madam, he is living;
The dead bodies you saw were but feign'd statues.
He 's reconcil'd to your brothers; the Pope hath wrought
The atonement.

Duch. Mercy!
(*Dies.*)

Bos. O, she 's gone again! there the cords of life broke.
O sacred innocence, that sweetly sleeps
On turtles' feathers, whilst a guilty conscience
Is a black register wherein is writ
All our good deeds and bad, a perspective
That shows us hell! That we cannot be suffer'd
To do good when we have a mind to it!
This is manly sorrow;
These tears, I am very certain, never grew
In my mother's milk. My estate is sunk
Below the degree of fear: where were

[46] runs in a family.

[47] This revival of the Duchess is reminiscent of Desdemona's

These penitent fountains while she was living?
O, they were frozen up! Here is a sight
As direful to my soul as is the sword
Unto a wretch hath slain his father.
Come, I'll bear thee hence,
And execute thy last will: that's deliver
Thy body to the reverend dispose
Of some good women: that the cruel tyrant
Shall not deny me. Then I'll post to Milan,
Where somewhat I will speedily enact
Worth my dejection.
Exit with the body.

ACT V.

Scene 1. *Milan. A public place.*

Enter Antonio and Delio.

Ant. What think you of my hope of reconcilement
To the Arragonian brethren?
Delio. I misdoubt it;
For though they have sent their letters of safe-conduct
For your repair to Milan, they appear
But nets to entrap you. The Marquis of Pescara,
Under whom you hold certain land in cheat,[48]
Much 'gainst his noble nature hath been mov'd
To seize those lands; and some of his dependants
Are at this instant making it their suit
To be invested in your revenues.
I cannot think they mean well to your life
That do deprive you of your means of life,
Your living.
Ant. You are still an heretic
To any safety I can shape myself.
Delio. Here comes the marquis: I will make myself
Petitioner for some part of your land,
To know whither it is flying.
Ant. I pray, do.
Withdraws.

Enter Pescara.

Delio. Sir, I have a suit to you.
Pes. To me?
Delio. An easy one:
There is the Citadel of Saint Bennet,
With some demesnes, of late in the possession
Of Antonio Bologna,—please you bestow them on me.
Pes. You are my friend; but this is such a suit,
Nor fit for me to give, nor you to take.
Delio. No, sir?
Pes. I will give you ample reason for't
Soon in private:—here's the cardinal's mistress.

Enter Julia.

Julia. My lord, I am grown your poor petitioner,
And should be an ill beggar, had I not
A great man's letter here, the cardinal's,
To court you in my favor.
Pes. He entreats for you
The Citadel of Saint Bennet, that belong'd
To the banish'd Bologna.
Julia. Yes.
Pes. I could not have thought of a friend I could rather
Pleasure with it: 't is yours.
Julia. Sir, I thank you;
And he shall know how doubly I am engag'd
Both in your gift, and speediness of giving,
Which makes your grant the greater.
Exit.
Ant. How they fortify
Themselves with my ruin!
Delio. Sir, I am
Little bound to you.
Pes. Why?
Delio. Because you deni'd this suit to me, and gave 't
To such a creature.
Pes. Do you know what it was?
It was Antonio's land; not forfeited
By course of law, but ravish'd from his throat
By the cardinal's entreaty. It were not fit
I should bestow so main a piece of wrong
Upon my friend; 't is a gratification
Only due to a strumpet, for it is injustice.
Shall I sprinkle the pure blood of innocents
To make those followers I call my friends
Look ruddier upon me? I am glad
This land, ta'en from the owner by such wrong,

[48] in escheat; reverting to an overlord in the absence of heirs to the possessor.

Returns again unto so foul an use
As salary for his lust. Learn, good Delio,
To ask noble things of me, and you shall find
I 'll be a noble giver.

Delio. You instruct me well.

Ant. Why, here 's a man now would fright impudence
From sauciest beggars.

Pes. Prince Ferdinand 's come to Milan,
Sick, as they give out, of an apoplexy;
But some say 't is a frenzy: I am going
To visit him.

Exit.

Ant. 'T is a noble old fellow.

Delio. What course do you mean to take, Antonio?

Ant. This night I mean to venture all my fortune,
Which is no more than a poor ling'ring life,
To the cardinal's worst of malice. I have got
Private access to his chamber; and intend
To visit him about the mid of night,
As once his brother did our noble duchess.
It may be that the sudden apprehension
Of danger,—for I 'll go in mine own shape,—
When he shall see it fraught with love and duty,
May draw the poison out of him, and work
A friendly reconcilement. If it fail,
Yet it shall rid me of this infamous calling;
For better fall once than be ever falling.

Delio. I 'll second you in all danger; and, howe'er,
My life keeps rank with yours.

Ant. You are still my lov'd and best friend.

Exeunt.

SCENE 2. *A gallery in the Cardinal's palace.*

Enter Pescara and Doctor.

Pes. Now, doctor, may I visit your patient?

Doc. If 't please your lordship; but he 's instantly
To take the air here in the gallery
By my direction.

Pes. Pray thee, what 's his disease?

Doc. A very pestilent disease, my lord,
They call lycanthropia.

Pes. What 's that?
I need a dictionary to 't.

Doc. I 'll tell you.
In those that are possess'd with 't there o'erflows
Such melancholy humor they imagine
Themselves to be transformed into wolves;
Steal forth to church-yards in the dead of night,
And dig dead bodies up: as two nights since
One met the duke 'bout midnight in a lane
Behind Saint Mark's church, with the leg of a man
Upon his shoulder; and he howl'd fearfully;
Said he was a wolf, only the difference
Was, a wolf's skin was hairy on the outside,
His on the inside; bade them take their swords,
Rip up his flesh, and try. Straight I was sent for,
And, having minister'd to him, found his grace
Very well recovered.

Pes. I am glad on 't.

Doc. Yet not without some fear
Of a relapse. If he grow to his fit again,
I 'll go a nearer way to work with him
Than ever Paracelsus [49] dream'd of; if
They 'll give me leave, I 'll buffet his madness out of him.
Stand aside; he comes.

Enter Ferdinand, Cardinal, Malateste, and Bosola.

Ferd. Leave me.

Mal. Why doth your lordship love this solitariness?

Ferd. Eagles commonly fly alone: they are crows, daws, and starlings that flock together. Look, what 's that follows me?

Mal. Nothing, my lord.

Ferd. Yes.

Mal. 'T is your shadow.

Ferd. Stay it; let it not haunt me.

Mal. Impossible, if you move, and the sun shine.

Ferd. I will throttle it.

(*Throws himself down on his shadow.*)

Mal. O, my lord, you are angry with nothing.

Ferd. You are a fool: how is 't possible I should catch my shadow, unless I fall

[49] a famous physician and alchemist of the sixteenth century.

upon 't? When I go to hell, I mean to carry a bribe; for, look you, good gifts evermore make way for the worst persons.

Pes. Rise, good my lord.

Ferd. I am studying the art of patience.

Pes. 'T is a noble virtue.

Ferd. To drive six snails before me from this town to Moscow; neither use goad nor whip to them, but let them take their own time;—the patient'st man i' th' world match me for an experiment:—an I 'll crawl after like a sheep-biter.[50]

Card. Force him up.

(*They raise him.*)

Ferd. Use me well, you were best. What I have done, I have done: I 'll confess nothing.

Doc. Now let me come to him.—Are you mad, my lord?
Are you out of your princely wits?

Ferd. What 's he?

Pes. Your doctor.

Ferd. Let me have his beard saw'd off, and his eye-brows fil'd more civil.

Doc. I must do mad tricks with him, for that 's the only way on 't.—I have brought your grace a salamander's skin to keep you from sunburning.

Ferd. I have cruel sore eyes.

Doc. The white of a cockatrix's[51] egg is present[52] remedy.

Ferd. Let it be a new-laid one, you were best. Hide me from him: physicians are like kings,—They brook no contradiction.

Doc. Now he begins to fear me: now let me alone with him.

Card. How now! put off your gown!

Doc. Let me have some forty urinals filled with rose-water: he and I 'll go pelt one another with them.—Now he begins to fear me.—Can you fetch a frisk,[53] sir?—Let him go, let him go, upon my peril: I find by his eye he stands in awe of me; I 'll make him as tame as a dormouse.

Ferd. Can you fetch your frisks, sir!—I will stamp him into a cullis,[54] flay off his skin to cover one of the anatomies[55] this rogue hath set i' th' cold yonder in Barber-Chirurgeon's-hall.[56]—Hence, hence! you are all of you like beasts for sacrifice. (*Throws the Doctor down and beats him.*) There 's nothing left of you but tongue and belly, flattery and lechery.

Exit.

Pes. Doctor, he did not fear you thoroughly.

Doc. True; I was somewhat too forward.

Bos. Mercy upon me, what a fatal judgment
Hath fall'n upon this Ferdinand!

Pes. Knows your grace
What accident hath brought unto the prince
This strange distraction?

Card. (*Aside.*) I must feign somewhat.—Thus they say it grew.
You have heard it rumor'd, for these many years
None of our family dies but there is seen
The shape of an old woman, which is given
By tradition to us to have been murder'd
By her nephews for her riches. Such a figure
One night, as the prince sat up late at 's book,
Appear'd to him; when crying out for help,
The gentleman of 's chamber found his grace
All on a cold sweat, alter'd much in face
And language: since which apparition,
He hath grown worse and worse, and I much fear
He cannot live.

Bos. Sir, I would speak with you.

Pes. We 'll leave your grace,
Wishing to the sick prince, our noble lord,
All health of mind and body.

Card. You are most welcome.

Exeunt Pescara, Malateste, and Doctor.

Are you come? so.—(*Aside.*) This fellow must not know
By any means I had intelligence
In our duchess' death; for, though I counsel'd it,
The full of all th' engagement seem'd to grow
From Ferdinand.—Now, sir, how fares our sister?
I do not think but sorrow makes her look
Like to an oft-dy'd garment: she shall now
Take comfort from me. Why do you look so wildly?
O, the fortune of your master here, the prince,
Dejects you; but be you of happy comfort:
If you 'll do one thing for me I 'll entreat,
Though he had a cold tomb-stone o'er his bones,
I 'd make you what you would be.

50 a sheep-worrying dog.
51 a fabled serpent, whose glance, like the basilisk's, was deadly.
52 immediate.
53 cut a caper.
54 broth.
55 skeletons.
56 Guild-hall of the Barber-Surgeons (a London local allusion).

Bos. Any thing;
Give it me in a breath, and let me fly to 't.
They that think long small expedition win,
For musing much o' th' end cannot begin.

Enter Julia.

Julia. Sir, will you come in to supper?
Card. I am busy; leave me.
Julia. (*Aside.*) What an excellent shape hath that fellow!

Exit.

Card. 'T is thus. Antonio lurks here in Milan:
Inquire him out, and kill him. While he lives,
Our sister cannot marry; and I have thought
Of an excellent match for her. Do this, and style me
Thy advancement.
Bos. But by what means shall I find him out?
Card. There is a gentleman call'd Delio
Here in the camp, that hath been long approv'd
His loyal friend. Set eye upon that fellow;
Follow him to mass; may be Antonio,
Although he do account religion
But a school-name, for fashion of the world
May accompany him; or else go inquire out
Delio's confessor, and see if you can bribe
Him to reveal it. There are a thousand ways
A man might find to trace him; as to know
What fellows haunt the Jews for taking up
Great sums of money, for sure he 's in want;
Or else to go to th' picture-makers, and learn
Who bought her picture lately: some of these
Happily may take.
Bos. Well, I 'll not freeze i' th' business:
I would see that wretched thing, Antonio,
Above all sights i' th' world.
Card. Do, and be happy.

Exit.

Bos. This fellow doth breed basilisks in 's eyes,
He 's nothing else but murderer; yet he seems
Not to have notice of the duchess' death.
'T is his cunning: I must follow his example;
There cannot be a surer way to trace
Than that of an old fox.

Re-enter Julia, with a pistol.

Julia. So, sir, you are well met.
Bos. How now!
Julia. Nay, the doors are fast enough:
Now, sir, I will make you confess your treachery.
Bos. Treachery!
Julia. Yes, confess to me
Which of my women 't was you hir'd to put
Love-powder into my drink?
Bos. Love powder!
Julia. Yes, when I was at Malfi.
Why should I fall in love with such a face else?
I have already suffer'd for thee so much pain,
The only remedy to do me good
Is to kill my longing.
Bos. Sure, your pistol holds
Nothing but perfumes or kissing-comfits.[57] Excellent lady!
You have a pretty way on 't to discover
Your longing. Come, come, I 'll disarm you,
And arm you thus: yet this is wondrous strange.
Julia. Compare thy form and my eyes together,
You 'll find my love no such great miracle.
Now you 'll say
I am wanton: this nice modesty in ladies
Is but a troublesome familiar
That haunts them.
Bos. Know you me, I am a blunt soldier.
Julia. The better:
Sure, there wants fire where there are no lively sparks
Of roughness.
Bos. And I want [58] compliment.
Julia. Why, ignorance
In courtship cannot make you do amiss,
If you have a heart to do well.
Bos. You are very fair.
Julia. Nay, if you lay beauty to my charge,
I must plead unguilty.
Bos. Your bright eyes
Carry a quiver of darts in them, sharper
Than sun-beams.

57 perfumed candies for the breath.

58 lack.

Julia. You will mar me with commendation,
Put yourself to the charge of courting me,
Whereas now I woo you.
Bos. (*Aside.*) I have it, I will work upon this creature.—
Let us grow most amorously familiar:
If the great cardinal now should see me thus,
Would he not count me a villain?
Julia. No; he might count me a wanton,
Not lay a scruple of offense on you;
For if I see and steal a diamond,
The fault is not i' th' stone, but in me the thief
That purloins it. I am sudden with you.
We that are great women of pleasure use to cut off
These uncertain wishes and unquiet longings,
And in an instant join the sweet delight
And the pretty excuse together. Had you been i' th' street,
Under my chamber-window, even there
I should have courted you.
Bos. O, you are an excellent lady!
Julia. Bid me do somewhat for you presently
To express I love you.
Bos. I will; and if you love me,
Fail not to effect it.
The cardinal is grown wondrous melancholy;
Demand the cause, let him not put you off
With feign'd excuse; discover the main ground on 't.
Julia. Why would you know this?
Bos. I have depended on him,
And I hear that he is fall'n in some disgrace
With the emperor: if he be, like the mice
That forsake falling houses, I would shift
To other dependance.
Julia. You shall not need
Follow the wars: I'll be your maintenance.
Bos. And I your loyal servant: but I cannot
Leave my calling.
Julia. Not leave an ungrateful
General for the love of a sweet lady!
You are like some cannot sleep in feather-beds,
But must have blocks for their pillows.
Bos. Will you do this?
Julia. Cunningly.
Bos. To-morrow I'll expect th' intelligence.
Julia. To-morrow! Get you into my cabinet;
You shall have it with you. Do not delay me,
No more than I do you: I am like one
That is condemn'd; I have my pardon promis'd,
But I would see it seal'd. Go, get you in:
You shall see me wind my tongue about his heart
Like a skein of silk.

Exit Bosola.

Re-enter Cardinal.

Card. Where are you?

Enter Servants.

Servants. Here.
Card. Let none, upon your lives, have conference
With the Prince Ferdinand, unless I know it.—
(*Aside.*) In this distraction he may reveal
The murder.

Exeunt Servants.

Yond 's my lingering consumption:
I am weary of her, and by any means
Would be quit of.
Julia. How now, my lord! what ails you?
Card. Nothing.
Julia. O, you are much alter'd:
Come, I must be your secretary, and remove
This lead from off your bosom: what 's the matter?
Card. I may not tell you.
Julia. Are you so far in love with sorrow
You cannot part with part of it? Or think you
I cannot love your grace when you are sad
As well as merry? Or do you suspect
I, that have been a secret to your heart
These many winters, cannot be the same
Unto your tongue?
Card. Satisfy thy longing,—
The only way to make thee keep my counsel
Is, not to tell thee.
Julia. Tell your echo this,
Or flatterers, that like echoes still report
What they hear, though most imperfect, and not me;
For if that you be true unto yourself,
I'll know.

Card. Will you rack [59] me?
Julia. No, judgment shall
Draw it from you: it is an equal fault,
To tell one's secrets unto all or none.
Card. The first argues folly.
Julia. But the last tyranny.
Card. Very well: why, imagine I have committed
Some secret deed which I desire the world
May never hear of.
Julia. Therefore may not I know it?
You have conceal'd for me as great a sin
As adultery. Sir, never was occasion
For perfect trial of my constancy
Till now; sir, I beseech you——
Card. You'll repent it.
Julia. Never.
Card. It hurries thee to ruin: I'll not tell thee.
Be well advis'd, and think what danger 't is
To receive a prince's secrets. They that do,
Had need have their breasts hoop'd with adamant
To contain them. I pray thee, yet be satisfi'd;
Examine thine own frailty; 't is more easy
To tie knots than unloose them. 'T is a secret
That, like a ling'ring poison, may chance lie
Spread in thy veins, and kill thee seven year hence.
Julia. Now you dally with me.
Card. No more; thou shalt know it.
By my appointment, the great Duchess of Malfi
And two of her young children, four nights since,
Were strangled.
Julia. O heaven! sir, what have you done!
Card. How now? How settles this? Think you your bosom
Will be a grave dark and obscure enough
For such a secret?
Julia. You have undone yourself, sir.
Card. Why?
Julia. It lies not in me to conceal it.
Card. No?
Come, I will swear you to 't upon this book.
Julia. Most religiously.
Card. Kiss it.
(*She kisses the book.*)
Now you shall never utter it; thy curiosity
Hath undone thee; thou 'rt poison'd with that book.
Because I knew thou couldst not keep my counsel,
I have bound thee to 't by death.

Re-enter Bosola.

Bos. For pity sake, hold!
Card. Ha, Bosola!
Julia. I forgive you
This equal piece of justice you have done;
For I betray'd your counsel to that fellow.
He over-heard it; that was the cause I said
It lay not in me to conceal it.
Bos. O foolish woman,
Couldst not thou have poison'd him?
Julia. 'T is weakness
Too much to think what should have been done. I go,
I know not whither.
(*Dies.*)
Card. Wherefore com'st thou hither?
Bos. That I might find a great man like yourself,
Not out of his wits, as the Lord Ferdinand,
To remember my service.
Card. I'll have thee hew'd in pieces.
Bos. Make not yourself such a promise of that life
Which is not yours to dispose of.
Card. Who plac'd thee here?
Bos. Her lust, as she intended.
Card. Very well:
Now you know me for your fellow-murderer.
Bos. And wherefore should you lay fair marble colors
Upon your rotten purposes to me?
Unless you imitate some that do plot great treasons,
And when they have done, go hide themselves i' th' graves
Of those were actors in 't?
Card. No more; there is
A fortune attends thee.
Bos. Shall I go sue to Fortune any longer?
'T is the fool's pilgrimage.
Card. I have honors in store for thee.
Bos. There are a many ways that conduct to seeming
Honor, and some of them very dirty ones.

[59] torture me on the rack to reveal it.

Card. Throw to the devil
Thy melancholy. The fire burns well;
What need we keep a stirring of 't, and make
A greater smother?[60] Thou wilt kill Antonio?
Bos. Yes.
Card. Take up that body.
Bos. I think I shall
Shortly grow the common bier for church-yards.
Card. I will allow thee some dozen of attendants
To aid thee in the murder.
Bos. O, by no means. Physicians that apply horse-leeches to any rank swelling use to cut off their tails, that the blood may run through them the faster: let me have no train when I go to shed blood, less it make me have a greater when I ride to the gallows.
Card. Come to me after midnight, to help to remove
That body to her own lodging. I 'll give out
She died o' th' plague; 't will breed the less inquiry
After her death.
Bos. Where 's Castruccio her husband?
Card. He 's rode to Naples, to take possession
Of Antonio's citadel.
Bos. Believe me, you have done a very happy turn.
Card. Fail not to come. There is the master key
Of our lodgings; and by that you may conceive
What trust I plant in you.
Bos. You shall find me ready.
Exit Cardinal.
O poor Antonio, though nothing be so needful
To thy estate as pity, yet I find
Nothing so dangerous! I must look to my footing:
In such slippery ice-pavements men had need
To be frost-nail'd well, they may break their necks else;
The precedent 's here afore me. How this man
Bears up in blood! seems fearless! Why, 't is well:
Security some men call the suburbs of hell,
Only a dead wall between. Well, good Antonio,
I 'll seek thee out; and all my care shall be
To put thee into safety from the reach
Of these most cruel biters that have got
Some of thy blood already. It may be,
I 'll join with thee in a most just revenge.
The weakest arm is strong enough that strikes
With the sword of justice. Still methinks the duchess
Haunts me: there, there!—'T is nothing but my melancholy.
O Penitence, let me truly taste thy cup,
That throws men down only to raise them up!
Exit.

SCENE 3. *Milan. A fortification.*

Enter Antonio and Delio. Echo from the Duchess's Grave.

Delio. Yond 's the cardinal's window. This fortification
Grew from the ruins of an ancient abbey;
And to yond side o' th' river lies a wall,
Piece of a cloister, which in my opiuion
Gives the best echo that you ever heard,
So hollow and so dismal, and withal
So plain in the distinction of our words,
That many have suppos'd it is a spirit
That answers.
Ant. I do love these ancient ruins.
We never tread upon them but we set
Our foot upon some reverend history;
And, questionless, here in this open court,
Which now lies naked to the injuries
Of stormy weather, some men lie interr'd
Lov'd the church so well, and gave so largely to 't,
They thought it should have canopied their bones
Till dooms-day. But all things have their end;
Churches and cities, which have diseases like to men,
Must have like death that we have.
Echo. *Like death that we have.*
Delio. Now the echo hath caught you.
Ant. It groan'd methought, and gave
A very deadly accent.
Echo. *Deadly accent.*
Delio. I told you 't was a pretty one. You may make it
A huntsman, or a falconer, a musician,
Or a thing of sorrow.
Echo. *A thing of sorrow.*

60 smoke.

Ant. Aye, sure, that suits it best.
Echo. *That suits it best.*
Ant. 'T is very like my wife's voice.
Echo. *Aye, wife's voice.*
Delio. Come, let us walk further from 't.
I would not have you go to the cardinal's to-night:
Do not.
Echo. *Do not.*
Delio. Wisdom doth not more moderate wasting sorrow
Than time. Take time for 't; be mindful of thy safety.
Echo. *Be mindful of thy safety.*
Ant. Necessity compels me.
Make scrutiny throughout the passages
Of your own life, you 'll find it impossible
To fly your fate.
Echo. *O, fly your fate!*
Delio. Hark! the dead stones seem to have pity on you,
And give you good counsel.
Ant. Echo, I will not talk with thee,
For thou art a dead thing.
Echo. *Thou art a dead thing.*
Ant. My duchess is asleep now,
And her little ones, I hope sweetly. O heaven,
Shall I never see her more?
Echo. *Never see her more.*
Ant. I mark'd not one repetition of the echo
But that; and on the sudden a clear light
Presented me a face folded in sorrow.
Delio. Your fancy merely.
Ant. Come, I 'll be out of this ague.
For to live thus is not indeed to live:
It is a mockery and abuse of life.
I will not henceforth save myself by halves;
Lose all, or nothing.
Delio. Your own virtue save you!
I 'll fetch your eldest son, and second you.
It may be that the sight of his own blood
Spread in so sweet a figure may beget
The more compassion. However, fare you well.
Though in our miseries Fortune have a part,
Yet in our noble suff'rings she hath none.
Contempt of pain, that we may call our own.

Exeunt.

SCENE 4. *A room in the Cardinal's palace.*

Enter Cardinal, Pescara, Malateste, Roderigo, and Grisolan.

Card. You shall not watch to-night by the sick prince;
His grace is very well recover'd.
Mal. Good my lord, suffer us.
Card. O, by no means;
The noise, and change of object in his eye,
Doth more distract him. I pray, all to bed;
And though you hear him in his violent fit,
Do not rise, I entreat you.
Pes. So, sir; we shall not.
Card. Nay, I must have you promise
Upon your honors, for I was enjoin'd to 't
By himself; and he seem'd to urge it sensibly.
Pes. Let our honors bind this trifle.
Card. Nor any of your followers.
Mal. Neither.
Card. It may be, to make trial of your promise,
When he 's asleep, myself will rise and feign
Some of his mad tricks, and cry out for help,
And feign myself in danger.
Mal. If your throat were cutting,
I 'd not come at you, now I have protested against it.
Card. Why, I thank you.
Gris. 'T was a foul storm to-night.
Rod. The Lord Ferdinand's chamber shook like an osier.
Mal. 'T was nothing but pure kindness in the devil
To rock his own child.
Exeunt all except the Cardinal.
Card. The reason why I would not suffer these
About my brother, is, because at midnight
I may with better privacy convey
Julia's body to her own lodging. O, my conscience!
I would pray now; but the devil takes away my heart
For having any confidence in prayer.
About this hour I appointed Bosola
To fetch the body. When he hath serv'd my turn,
He dies.

Exit.

Enter Bosola.

Bos. Ha! 't was the cardinal's voice; I heard him name Bosola and my death.
Listen; I hear one's footing.

Enter Ferdinand.

Ferd. Strangling 's a very death.

Bos. (*Aside.*) Nay, then, I see I must stand upon my guard.

Ferd. What say to that? Whisper softly: do you agree to 't? So; it must be done i' th' dark; the cardinal would not for a thousand pounds the doctor should see it. *Exit.*

Bos. My death is plotted; here 's the consequence of murder.
We value not desert nor Christian breath,
When we know black deeds must be cur'd with death.

Enter Antonio and Servant.

Serv. Here stay, sir, and be confident, I pray;
I 'll fetch you a dark lantern. *Exit.*

Ant. Could I take him at his prayers,
There were hope of pardon.

Bos. Fall right, my sword!—
(*Stabs him.*)
I 'll not give thee so much leisure as to pray.

Ant. O, I am gone! Thou hast ended a long suit
In a minute.

Bos. What art thou?

Ant. A most wretched thing,
That only have thy benefit in death,
To appear myself.

Re-enter Servant with a lantern.

Serv. Where are you, sir?

Ant. Very near my home.—Bosola!

Serv. O, misfortune!

Bos. Smother thy pity, thou art dead else. —Antonio!
The man I would have sav'd 'bove mine own life!
We are merely the stars' tennis-balls, struck and bandied
Which way please them.—O good Antonio,
I 'll whisper one thing in thy dying ear
Shall make thy heart break quickly! Thy fair duchess
And two sweet children——

Ant. Their very names
Kindle a little life in me.

Bos. Are murder'd.

Ant. Some men have wish'd to die
At the hearing of sad tidings; I am glad
That I shall do 't in sadness.[61] I would not now
Wish my wounds balm'd nor heal'd, for I have no use
To put my life to. In all our quest of greatness,
Like wanton boys whose pastime is their care,
We follow after bubbles blown in th' air.
Pleasure of life, what is 't? Only the good hours
Of an ague; merely a preparative to rest,
To endure vexation. I do not ask
The process of my death; only commend me
To Delio.

Bos. Break, heart!

Ant. And let my son fly the courts of princes.
(*Dies.*)

Bos. Thou seem'st to have lov'd Antonio.

Serv. I brought him hither,
To have reconcil'd him to the cardinal.

Bos. I do not ask thee that.
Take him up, if thou tender thine own life,
And bear him where the lady Julia
Was wont to lodge.—O, my fate moves swift!
I have this cardinal in the forge already;
Now I 'll bring him to th' hammer. O direful misprision![62]
I will not imitate things glorious,
No more than base; I 'll be mine own example.—
On, on, and look thou represent, for silence,
The thing thou bear'st.[63] *Exeunt.*

SCENE 5. *Another room in the palace, with a gallery.*

Enter Cardinal, with a book.

Card. I am puzzl'd in a question about hell;
He says, in hell there 's one material fire,
And yet it shall not burn all men alike.
Lay him by. How tedious is a guilty conscience!
When I look into the fish-ponds in my garden,
Methinks I see a thing arm'd with a rake,
That seems to strike at me.

Enter Bosola, and Servant bearing Antonio's body.

Now, art thou come?
Thou look'st ghastly;
There sits in thy face some great determination
Mix'd with some fear.

61 reality. 62 mistake. 63 *i.e.* the dead body.

Bos. Thus it lightens into action:
I am come to kill thee.
Card. Ha!—Help! our guard!
Bos. Thou art deceiv'd; they are out of thy howling.
Card. Hold; and I will faithfully divide
Revenues with thee.
Bos. Thy prayers and proffers
Are both unseasonable.
Card. Raise the watch!
We are betray'd!
Bos. I have confin'd your flight:
I'll suffer your retreat to Julia's chamber,
But no further.
Card. Help! we are betray'd!

Enter, above, Pescara, Malateste, Roderigo, and Grisolan.

Mal. Listen.
Card. My dukedom for rescue!
Rod. Fie upon his counterfeiting!
Mal. Why, 't is not the cardinal.
Rod. Yes, yes, 't is he:
But I'll see him hang'd ere I'll go down to him.
Card. Here 's a plot upon me; I am assaulted! I am lost,
Unless some rescue!
Gris. He doth this pretty well;
But it will not serve to laugh me out of mine honor.
Card. The sword 's at my throat!
Rod. You would not bawl so loud then.
Mal. Come, come, let 's go to bed: he told us this much aforehand.
Pes. He wish'd you should not come at him; but, believe 't,
The accent of the voice sounds not in jest.
I'll down to him, howsoever, and with engines
Force ope the doors.
Exit above.
Rod. Let 's follow him aloof,
And note how the cardinal will laugh at him. *Exeunt above.*
Bos. There 's for you first,
'Cause you shall not unbarricade the door
To let in rescue.
(*Kills the Servant.*)
Card. What cause hast thou to pursue my life?
Bos. Look there.
Card. Antonio!
Bos. Slain by my hand unwittingly.
Pray, and be sudden. When thou kill'd'st thy sister,
Thou took'st from Justice her most equal balance,
And left her naught but her sword.
Card. O, mercy!
Bos. Now it seems thy greatness was only outward;
For thou fall'st faster of thyself than calamity
Can drive thee. I'll not waste longer time; there!
(*Stabs him.*)
Card. Thou hast hurt me.
Bos. Again!
Card. Shall I die like a leveret,
Without any resistance?—Help, help, help!
I am slain!

Enter Ferdinand.

Ferd. Th' alarum! Give me a fresh horse;
Rally the vaunt-guard, or the day is lost,
Yield, yield! I give you the honor of arms
Shake my sword over you; will you yield?
Card. Help me; I am your brother!
Ferd. The devil!
My brother fight upon the adverse party!
(*He wounds the Cardinal, and, in the scuffle, gives Bosola his death-wound.*)
There flies your ransom.
Card. O justice!
I suffer now for what hath former been:
Sorrow is held the eldest child of sin.
Ferd. Now you 're brave fellows. Cæsar's fortune was harder than Pompey's; Cæsar died in the arms of prosperity, Pompey at the feet of disgrace. You both died in the field. The pain 's nothing; pain many times is taken away with the apprehension of greater, as the toothache with the sight of a barber that comes to pull it out. There 's philosophy for you.
Bos. Now my revenge is perfect.—Sink, thou main cause
(*Kills Ferdinand.*)
Of my undoing!—The last part of my life
Hath done me best service.
Ferd. Give me some wet hay; I am broken-winded.
I do account this world but a dog-kennel:
I will vault credit[64] and affect high pleasures
Beyond death.

64 overleap belief.

Bos. He seems to come to himself,
Now he 's so near the bottom.
Ferd. My sister, O my sister! there 's the cause on 't.
Whether we fall by ambition, blood, or lust,
Like diamonds, we are cut with our own dust.
(*Dies.*)
Card. Thou hast thy payment too.
Bos. Yes, I hold my weary soul in my teeth;
'T is ready to part from me. I do glory
That thou, which stood'st like a huge pyramid
Begun upon a large and ample base,
Shalt end in a little point, a kind of nothing.

Enter, below, Pescara, Malateste, Roderigo, and Grisolan.

Pes. How now, my lord!
Mal. O sad disaster!
Rod. How comes this?
Bos. Revenge for the Duchess of Malfi murdered
By th' Arragonian brethren; for Antonio
Slain by this hand; for lustful Julia
Poison'd by this man; and lastly for myself,
That was an actor in the main of all
Much 'gainst mine own good nature, yet i' th' end
Neglected.
Pes. How now, my lord!
Card. Look to my brother:
He gave us these large wounds, as we were struggling
Here i' th' rushes.[65] And now, I pray, let me
Be laid by and never thought of.
(*Dies.*)
Pes. How fatally, it seems, he did withstand
His own rescue!
Mal. Thou wretched thing of blood,
How came Antonio by his death?
Bos. In a mist; I know not how;
Such a mistake as I have often seen
In a play. O, I am gone!
We are only like dead walls or vaulted graves,
That, ruin'd, yields no echo. Fare you well!
It may be pain, but no harm, to me to die
In so good a quarrel. O, this gloomy world!
In what a shadow, or deep pit of darkness,
Doth womanish and fearful mankind live!
Let worthy minds ne'er stagger in distrust
To suffer death or shame for what is just:
Mine is another voyage.
(*Dies.*)
Pes. The noble Delio, as I came to th' palace,
Told me of Antonio's being here, and show'd me
A pretty gentleman, his son and heir.

Enter Delio, and Antonio's Son.

Mal. O, sir, you come too late!
Delio. I heard so, and
Was arm'd for 't, ere I came. Let us make noble use
Of this great ruin; and join all our force
To establish this young hopeful gentleman
In 's mother's right. These wretched eminent things
Leave no more fame behind 'em, than should one
Fall in a frost, and leave his print in snow;
As soon as the sun shines, it ever melts,
Both form and matter. I have ever thought
Nature doth nothing so great for great men
As when she 's pleas'd to make them lords of truth:
Integrity of life is fame's best friend,
Which nobly, beyond death, shall crown the end.

Exeunt.

65 used as floor-coverings.

JOHN FLETCHER

THE WILD-GOOSE CHASE

The pursuit of the reluctant male by the predatory female suggested itself as a fit theme for comedy long before it was dignified in *Man and Superman* as an exhibition of the Life Force. As Shaw reminds us in his preface, several of Shakespeare's heroines take the offensive in vigorous campaigns to obtain the men of their choice. The wonder that we feel in such instances is not at the spectacle of the heroine flying in the face of tradition, for this she does with disarming grace, but that she should be at such pains to secure a husband so obviously her inferior in brains, as is Bassanio to Portia, in capacity for love, as Proteus to Julia, in everything but birth, as Bertram to Helena. A somewhat similar attitude is conceivable toward Oriana, the heroine of Fletcher's *Wild-Goose Chase.* We might cavil, "The Wild-Goose was n't worth chasing"; Fletcher's reply would be, "That 's not the question — was n't the chase amusing?" With all its freedom of speech and insinuation which may go beyond contemporary taste, no sensible critic will judge severely Fletcher's light-hearted representation of the triple man-hunt. To apply the test of morality to this play is to break a butterfly on a wheel. It is a perfect specimen of light comedy as practised by the wittiest and cleverest writer of it in the Elizabethan period. Comedy of manners in the strictest sense *The Wild-Goose Chase* is not. Fletcher makes no effort to hold the mirror up to nature and show "the very age and body of the time his form and pressure." There is here little observation of English life, and no particular attempt to portray manners exactly. In others of his comedies, in *Monsieur Thomas* and *Wit without Money,* for example, Fletcher approaches reality more closely. Nor is the play high comedy, as the term is sometimes applied to the Shakespearean romantic comedy like *Much Ado,* for that involves an idealization and a depth of characterization wanting here. It is only necessary to reflect upon the different impressions which Oriana and Viola or Rosalind make on us to perceive the difference; the situations are not dissimilar, but the glamour, the bloom of romance, the ideal reality, so to speak, of the Shakespearean work are altogether lacking. Although the influence of the Jonsonian humor comedy is evident in a figure like Belleur, comedy of humors presupposes a satirist's point of view, which Fletcher has not. Comedy of intrigue it might be called, though the name is too inclusive to be of much help in attempting a definition. The sole purpose of this play is to entertain, and light comedy is perhaps as good a name as can be found to describe it.

As in *Philaster,* the main interest of the play is in plot rather than in the characters. The plot is much slighter, but there is the same ingenuity of complication, the same use of surprise and suspense, the same development of episode at the expense of character, as for instance when Oriana reveals herself at the end of act IV. That part of the action, indeed, in which Oriana feigns madness in order to move Mirabel's heart to pity, the soft prelude to love, is strongly reminiscent of the method of tragicomedy. Neither the other characters nor the audience are let into Oriana's secret: she confesses that none set her on, "nor any knew or even dreamed" what she meant. Her adherents and sympathizers are as thoroughly deceived as Mirabel, and Fletcher plays on their emotions, and ours, to beguile us into a false sympathy which he exploits to its utmost before laughing it away. In this respect, the situation differs from the rest of the series of tricks composing the plot, for in all the others we are forewarned and are thus in a position to get the full comic flavor of the play of cross-purposes. The general criticism might be made of the plot that the scheming is rather too obvious. It is credible that Mirabel should have been deceived once, even twice, but that he should for a third time be hoodwinked passes belief. The devices employed by each side, moreover, are so much of one kind that the artificiality of structure is as apparent as in the case of *Mother Bombie.* The Wild-Goose is finally caught by the same sort of disguise that he had once before unmasked, and that he had himself unsuccessfully tried when he tricked out his English courtesan as a fine lady to advance Pinac in Lillia Bianca's esteem. It is, however, unreasonable to demand that work so obviously intended merely for diversion should stand close inspection, and the action moves forward so clearly through its plots and counterplots, the pace is so brisk and the interest so unflagging, that we are willing for the "two hours' traffic of the stage" to accept the story at its face value.

Dryden in a well-known passage in the *Essay of Dramatic Poesy* says of Beaumont and

Fletcher: "They understood and imitated the conversation of gentlemen much better [than Shakespeare]; whose wild debaucheries and quickness of wit in repartees, no poet before them could paint as they have done. . . . I am apt to believe the English language in them arrived to its highest perfection." *The Wild-Goose Chase* might well serve as a text for Dryden's comment. It was perfectly adapted to the audience before which it was produced in 1621, the gay, witty, cynical group of the Jacobean court. In its accurate reflection of the tone of the court it resembles the comedy of manners more closely than in its presentation of the manners themselves. It is not a play which a Puritan could see without abhorrence, nor which a modern Puritan can read with pleasure. Truly, these fine ladies and gentlemen of Fletcher's have little of the reticence in speech which we associate with breeding. The men are rakes by habit, and the women rakes at heart; Rosalura and Lillia Bianca are "honest" in the Elizabethan sense, and all too honest, we should say to-day, in the freedom with which they express their desires. "Why should we be ashamed to speak what we think?" queries Lillia. But the sprightly gaiety of dialogue and the smooth rapidity of the verse can delight us as they delighted Fletcher's auditors and as they delighted Dryden. The action moves fast from one amusing situation to the next, and the verse keeps pace with it. There are few speeches of any considerable length (only seven of more than fifteen lines); the dialogue consists mainly of thrust and parry, two or three lines to a speech. No pause, no time for reflection, simply a *mitrailleuse* gunfire of wit, with no quarter asked or given. For work of this sort Fletcher's light, easy-running verse is admirably suited. What in other writers is a device occasionally introduced for variety, the use of lines of eleven (or more) syllables, is with him a habit, a conscious artifice intended to banish rhetorical formality and to replace it with a flexibility giving the effect of colloquial prose. The proportion of lines running over the ten-syllable norm is so extraordinarily large that it is no exaggeration to call the verse hendecasyllabic. The familiar ease of such a style is enhanced by a limpid clearness of expression, a simplicity of vocabulary and absence of poetic adornment, meriting Dryden's praise of the language. No blank-verse dialogue resembles more the matchless prose of Congreve and Sheridan.

The mention of Congreve recalls the importance of Fletcher's work as pointing the way for Restoration comedy. *The Wild-Goose Chase* was one of the first plays revived on the reopening of the theaters in 1660 and its gay *abandon* pleased the audience of those days immensely. (Pepys, who saw it January 11, 1667, calls it a very famous play, but was disappointed in it.) We need not underrate the influence of Molière on Restoration comedy in order to appreciate what it owes to Fletcher. The atmosphere — frivolous, cynical, sophisticated, frankly immoral — is closer to that of Fletcher than it is to Molière's. The characters of this play are precisely those of the later period — fine ladies and gentlemen, sure of themselves, witty, and free of speech. The action, where the whole business of life is centered in amorous intrigue, foreshadows that of half a hundred Restoration plays. Mirabel in name and nonchalance prefigures his more famous namesake of *The Way of the World*, and his capitulation is as wittily contrived and his promised reformation as little convincing as those of the typical Restoration hero. The slightness of plot, the emphasis on dialogue, the repartee, the brilliance of style, received from the Restoration dramatists the sincerest flattery of imitation. Farquhar, indeed, remade this play as *The Inconstant*, not improving upon the original in the process. Through the Restoration writers and Sheridan, Fletcher's influence is yet alive in society comedy.

THE WILD-GOOSE CHASE

BY JOHN FLETCHER

NAMES OF THE CHARACTERS

DE GARD, *a noble staid Gentleman, that, being newly lighted from his travels, assists his sister Oriana in her chase of Mirabel the Wild-Goose.*
LA CASTRE, *the indulgent father to Mirabel.*
MIRABEL *the Wild-Goose, a traveled Monsieur, and great defier of all ladies in the way of marriage, otherwise their much loose servant, at last caught by the despised Oriana.*
PINAC, *his fellow-traveler, of a lively spirit, and servant to the no less sprightly Lillia Bianca.*
BELLEUR, *Companion to both, of a stout blunt humor, in love with Rosalura.*
NANTOLET, *father to Rosalura and Lillia Bianca.*
LUGIER, *the rough and confident tutor to the ladies, and chief engine to entrap the Wild-Goose.*
A Young Man disguised as a Factor.
Gentlemen, Foot-Boy, Singing-Boy, Two Men disguised as Merchants, Priest, Servants.

ORIANA, *the fair betrothed of Mirabel, and witty follower of the chase.*
ROSALURA, } *the airy daughters*
LILLIA BIANCA, } *of Nantolet.*
PETELLA, *their servant.*
MARIANA, *an English Courtesan.*
Four Women.

SCENE.—Paris.

ACT I.

SCENE 1. *A hall in the house of La Castre.*

Enter Monsieur De Gard and a Foot-boy.

De Gard. Sirrah, you know I have rid hard; stir my horse well,
And let him want no litter.
F. Boy. I am sure I have run hard;
Would somebody would walk me, and see me litter'd,
For I think my fellow-horse cannot in reason
Desire more rest, nor take up his chamber before me:
But we are the beasts now, and the beasts are our masters.
De Gard. When you have done, step to the ten-crown ordinary——
F. Boy. With all my heart, sir; for I have a twenty-crown stomach.
De Gard. And there bespeak a dinner.
F. Boy. (*Going.*) Yes, sir, presently.[1]
De Gard. For whom, I beseech you, sir?
F. Boy. For myself, I take it, sir.
De Gard. In truth, you shall not take it; 't is not meant for you.
There 's for your provender. (*Gives money.*) Bespeak a dinner
For Monsieur Mirabel and his companions;
They 'll be in town within this hour. When you have done, sirrah,
Make ready all things at my lodging for me,
And wait me there.
F. Boy. The ten-crown ordinary?
De Gard. Yes, sir, if you have not forgot it.
F. Boy. I 'll forget my feet first:
'T is the best part of a footman's faith.
Exit.
De Gard. These youths,
For all they have been in Italy to learn thrift,
And seem to wonder at men's lavish ways,
Yet they cannot rub off old friends, their French itches;
They must meet sometimes to disport their bodies
With good wine and good women, and good store too.
Let 'em be what they will, they are arm'd at all points,
And then hang saving, let the sea grow high!
This ordinary can fit 'em of all sizes.
They must salute their country with old customs.

[1] at once.

Enter La Castre and Oriana.

Ori. Brother!
De Gard. My dearest sister!
Ori. Welcome, welcome!
Indeed, ye are welcome home, most welcome!
De Gard. Thank ye.
You are grown a handsome woman, Oriana;
Blush at your faults. I am wondrous glad to see ye.—
Monsieur La Castre, let not my affection
To my fair sister make me be held unmannerly.
I am glad to see ye well, to see ye lusty,
Good health about ye, and in fair company;
Believe me, I am proud——
La Cast. Fair sir, I thank ye.
Monsieur De Gard, you are welcome from your journey;
Good men have still good welcome; give me your hand, sir.
Once more, you are welcome home. You look still younger.
De Gard. Time has no leisure to look after us;
We wander every where; age cannot find us.
La Cast. And how does all?
De Gard. All well, sir, and all lusty.
La Cast. I hope my son be so. I doubt not, sir,
But you have often seen him in your journeys,
And bring me some fair news.
De Gard. Your son is well, sir,
And grown a proper gentleman; he is well and lusty.
Within this eight hours I took leave of him,
And over-hied him, having some slight business
That forc'd me out o' th' way. I can assure you,
He will be here to-night.
La Cast. Ye make me glad, sir,
For, o' my faith, I almost long to see him.
Methinks, he has been away——
De Gard. 'T is but your tenderness.
What are three years? A love-sick wench will allow it.
His friends that went out with him are come back too,
Belleur and young Pinac. He bid me say little,
Because he means to be his own glad messenger.
La Cast. I thank ye for this news, sir. He shall be welcome,
And his friends too; indeed, I thank you heartily.
And how (for I dare say you will not flatter him)
Has Italy wrought on him? Has he mew'd [2] yet
His wild fantastic toys? They say that climate
Is a great purger of those humorous fluxes.
How is he improved, I pray ye?
De Gard. No doubt, sir, well;
H'as borne himself a full and noble gentleman:
To speak him farther is beyond my charter.
La Cast. I am glad to hear so much good. Come, I see
You long to enjoy your sister; yet I must entreat ye,
Before I go, to sup with me to-night,
And must not be deni'd.
De Gard. I am your servant.
La Cast. Where you shall meet fair, merry, and noble company:
My neighbor Nantolet and his two fair daughters.
De Gard. Your supper's season'd well, sir; I shall wait upon ye.
La Cast. Till then I'll leave ye; and y' are once more welcome.
Exit.
De Gard. I thank ye, noble sir! Now, Oriana,
How have ye done since I went? Have ye had your health well?
And your mind free?
Ori. You see, I am not bated; [3]
Merry, and eat my meat.
De Gard. A good preservative.
And how have you been us'd? You know, Oriana,
Upon my going out, at your request,
I left your portion in La Castre's hands,
The main means you must stick to. For that reason,
And 't is no little one, I ask ye, sister,
With what humanity he entertains ye,
And how ye find his courtesy?
Ori. Most ready.

[2] moulted, got rid of.

[3] reduced.

I can assure you, sir, I am us'd most nobly.
De Gard. I am glad to hear it; but, I prithee, tell me,
And tell me true, what end had you, Oriana,
In trusting your money here? He is no kinsman,
Nor any tie upon him of a guardian;
Nor dare I think ye doubt my prodigality.
Ori. No, certain, sir; none of all this provok'd[4] me;
Another private reason.
De Gard. 'T is not private,
Nor carried so; 't is common, my fair sister:
Your love to Mirabel; your blushes tell it.
'T is too much known, and spoken of too largely;
And with no little shame I wonder at it.
Ori. Is it a shame to love?
De Gard. To love undiscreetly:
A virgin should be tender of her honor,
Close, and secure.
Ori. I am as close as can be,
And stand upon as strong and honest guards too;
Unless this warlike age need a portcullis:
Yet I confess, I love him.
De Gard. Hear the people.
Ori. Now, I say, hang the people! He that dares
Believe what they say dares be mad, and give
His mother, nay, his own wife, up to rumor.
All grounds of truth they build on is a tavern,
And their best censure 's sack, sack in abundance;
For, as they drink, they think: they ne'er speak modestly,
Unless the wine be poor, or they want money.
Believe them! Believe *Amadis de Gaul, The Knight o' the Sun,* or *Palmerin of England;*[5]
For these, to them, are modest and true stories.
Pray, understand me; if their tongues be truth,
And if *in vino veritas* be an oracle,
What woman is, or has been ever, honest?
Give 'em but ten round cups, they 'll swear Lucretia
Died not for want of power to resist Tarquin,
But want of pleasure, that he stay'd no longer;
And Portia,[6] that was famous for her piety
To her lov'd lord, they 'll face ye out, died o' th' pox.
De Gard. Well, there is something, sister.
Ori. If there be, brother,
'T is none of their things; 't is not yet so monstrous:
My thing is marriage; and, at his return,
I hope to put their squint eyes right again.
De Gard. Marriage? 'T is true his father is a rich man,
Rich both in land and money; he his heir,
A young and handsome man, I must confess, too;
But of such qualities, and such wild flings,
Such admirable[7] imperfections, sister,
(For all his travel and bought experience,)
I should be loth to own him for my brother.
Methinks, a rich mind in a state indifferent
Would prove the better fortune.
Ori. If he be wild,
The reclaiming him to good and honest, brother,
Will make much for my honor; which, if I prosper,
Shall be the study of my love, and life too.
De Gard. Ye say well; would he thought as well, and loved too!
He marry! He 'll be hanged first. He knows no more
What the conditions and the ties of love are,
The honest purposes and grounds of marriage,
Nor will know, nor be ever brought t' endeavor,
Than I do how to build a church. He was ever
A loose and strong defier of all order;
His loves are wanderers, they knock at each door,
And taste each dish, but are no residents.
Or say, he may be brought to think of marriage,
(As 't will be no small labor), thy hopes are strangers.

[4] induced. [5] extravagant romantic tales. [6] Brutus's wife. [7] remarkable.

I know there is a labor'd match now follow'd,
Now at this time, for which he was sent for home too.
Be not abus'd:[8] Nantolet has two fair daughters,
And he must take his choice.

Ori. Let him take freely.
For all this I despair not; my mind tells me
That I, and only I, must make him perfect;
And in that hope I rest.

De Gard. Since y' are so confident,
Prosper your hope! I'll be no adversary;
Keep yourself fair and right, he shall not wrong ye.

Ori. When I forget my virtue, no man know me!

Exeunt.

SCENE 2. *A street before the same house.*

Enter Mirabel, Pinac, Belleur, and Servants.

Mir. Welcome to Paris, once more, gentlemen!
We have had a merry and a lusty ordinary,[9]
And wine, and good meat, and a bouncing reckoning;
And let it go for once; 't is a good physic.
Only the wenches are not for my diet;
They are too lean and thin, their embraces brawn-fallen.[10]
Give me the plump Venetian, fat and lusty,
That meets me soft and supple; smiles upon me,
As if a cup of full wine leap'd to kiss me,
These slight things I affect not.

Pin. They are ill-built;
Pin-buttocked,[11] like your dainty Barbaries,[12]
And weak i' the pasterns; they'll endure no hardness.

Mir. There's nothing good or handsome bred amongst us;
Till we are travel'd, and live abroad, we are coxcombs.
Ye talk of France—a slight unseason'd country,
Abundance of gross food, which makes us blockheads.
We are fair set out indeed, and so are fore-horses:—
Men say, we are great courtiers,—men abuse us;
We are wise, and valiant too,—*non credo, signor;*
Our women the best linguists,—they are parrots;
O' this side the Alps they are nothing but mere drolleries.[13]
Ha! *Roma la Santa,* Italy for my money!
Their policies, their customs, their frugalities,
Their courtesies so open, yet so reserv'd too,
As, when you think y' are known best, ye are a stranger.
Their very pick-teeth[14] speak more man than we do.
And season of more salt.

Pin. 'T is a brave country;
Not pester'd with your stubborn precise puppies,
That turn all useful and allow'd contentments
To scabs and scruples—hang 'em, capon-worshipers.

Bel. I like that freedom well, and like their women too,
And would fain do as others do; but I am so bashful,
So naturally an ass! Look ye, I can look upon 'em,
And very willingly I go to see 'em,
(There's no man willinger), and I can kiss 'em,
And make a shift——

Mir. But, if they chance to flout ye,
Or say, "Ye are too bold! Fie, sir, remember!
I pray, sit farther off——"

Bel. 'T is true—I am humbled,
I am gone; I confess ingenuously, I am silenced;
The spirit of amber[15] cannot force me answer.

Pin. Then would I sing and dance——

Bel. You have wherewithal, sir.

Pin. And charge her up again.

Bel. I can be hang'd first:
Yet, where I fasten well, I am a tyrant.

Mir. Why, thou dar'st fight?

Bel. Yes, certainly, I dare fight,
And fight with any man at any weapon.

8 deceived.
9 fare.
10 weak.
11 with narrow buttocks.
12 Barbary horses.
13 dolls.
14 tooth-picks.
15 a provocative.

Would th' other were no more! But, a pox on 't!
When I am sometimes in my height of hope,
And reasonable valiant that way, my heart harden'd,
Some scornful jest or other chops between me
And my desire. What would ye have me to do, then, gentlemen?

Mir. Belleur, you must be bolder. Travel three years,
And bring home such a baby to betray ye
As bashfulness! A great fellow, and a soldier!

Bel. You have the gift of impudence; be thankful.
Every man has not the like talent. I will study,
And, if it may be reveal'd to me——

Mir. Learn of me,
And of Pinac. No doubt, you 'll find employment;
Ladies will look for courtship.

Pin. 'T is but fleshing,[16]
But standing one good brunt or two. Hast thou any mind to marriage?
We 'll provide thee some soft-natur'd wench, that 's dumb too.

Mir. Or an old woman that cannot refuse thee in charity.

Bel. A dumb woman, or an old woman, that were eager,
And car'd not for discourse, I were excellent at.

Mir. You must now put on boldness, there 's no avoiding it,
And stand all hazards, fly at all games bravely;
They 'll say, you went out like an ox, and return'd like an ass, else.

Bel. I shall make danger,[17] sure.

Mir. I am sent for home now;
I know it is to marry; but my father shall pardon me:
Although it be a weighty ceremony,
And may concern me hereafter in my gravity,
I will not lose the freedom of a traveler.
A new strong lusty bark cannot ride at one anchor.
Shall I make divers suits to show to the same eyes?
'T is dull and homespun;—study several pleasures,
And want employments for 'em? I 'll be hang'd first.
Tie me to one smock? Make my travels fruitless?
I 'll none of that; for every fresh behavior,
By your leave, father, I must have a fresh mistress,
And a fresh favor [18] too.

Bel. I like that passingly;
As many as you will, so they be willing,
Willing, and gentle, gentle.

Pin. There 's no reason
A gentleman, and a traveler, should be clapt up,
(For 't is a kind of bilboes [19] to be married),
Before he manifest to the world his good parts;
Tug ever, like a rascal, at one oar?
Give me the Italian liberty!

Mir. That I study,
And that I will enjoy. Come, go in, gentlemen;
There mark how I behave myself, and follow.

Exeunt.

SCENE 3. *Room in the house of La Castre.*

Enter La Castre, Nantolet, Lugier, Rosalura, and Lillia Bianca.

La Cast. You and your beauteous daughters are most welcome.
Beshrew my blood, they are fair ones!—Welcome, beauties,
Welcome, sweet birds.

Nant. They are bound much to your courtesies.

La Cast. I hope we shall be nearer acquainted.

Nant. That 's my hope too:
For, certain, sir, I much desire your alliance.
You see 'em; they are no gypsies. For their breeding,
It has not been so coarse but they are able
To rank themselves with women of fair fashion;
Indeed, they have been trained well.

Lug. Thank me.

Nant. Fit for the heirs of that state I shall leave 'em:

16 satisfying desire. 17 make trial. 18 face. 19 shackles sliding on an iron bar.

To say more, is to sell 'em. They say your son,
Now he has travel'd, must be wondrous curious
And choice in what he takes; these are no coarse ones.
Sir, here 's a merry wench—let him look to himself—
All heart, i' faith—may chance to startle him;
For all his care, and travel'd caution,
May creep into his eye. If he love gravity,
Affect a solemn face, there 's one will fit him.

La Cast. So young and so demure?

Nant. She is my daughter,
Else I would tell you, sir, she is a mistress
Both of those manners and that modesty
You would wonder at. She is no often-speaker,
But, when she does, she speaks well; nor no reveler,
Yet she can dance, and has studied the court elements,
And sings, as some say, handsomely; if a woman,
With the decency of her sex, may be a scholar,
I can assure ye, sir, she understands too.

La Cast. These are fit garments, sir.

Lug. Thank them that cut 'em.
Yes, they are handsome women; they have handsome parts too,
Pretty becoming parts.

La Cast. 'T is like they have, sir.

Lug. Yes, yes, and handsome education they have had too,
Had it abundantly; they need not blush at it.
I taught it, I 'll avouch it.

La Cast. Ye say well, sir.

Lug. I know what I say, sir, and I say but right, sir.
I am no trumpet of their commendations
Before their father; else I should say farther.

La Cast. Pray ye, what 's this gentleman?

Nant. One that lives with me, sir;
A man well bred and learn'd, but blunt and bitter;
Yet it offends no wise man; I take pleasure in 't.
Many fair gifts he has, in some of which,
That lie most easy to their understandings,
H'as handsomely bred up my girls, I thank him.

Lug. I have put it to 'em, that 's my part, I have urg'd it.
It seems, they are of years now to take hold on 't.

Nant. He 's wondrous blunt.

La Cast. By my faith, I was afraid of him.
Does he not fall out with the gentlewomen sometimes?

Nant. No, no; he 's that way moderate and discreet, sir.

Ros. If he did, we should be too hard for him.

Lug. Well said, sulphur!
Too hard for thy husband's head, if he wear not armor.

Enter Mirabel, Pinac, Belleur, De Gard, and Oriana.

Nant. Many of these bickerings, sir.

La Cast. I am glad they are no oracles.
Sure as I live, he beats them, he 's so puissant.

Ori. Well, if ye do forget——

Mir. Prithee, hold thy peace.
I know thou art a pretty wench; I know thou lov'st me;
Preserve it till we have a fit time to discourse on 't,
And a fit place. I 'll ease thy heart, I warrant thee.
Thou seest I have much to do now.

Ori. I am answer'd, sir:
With me ye shall have nothing on these conditions.

De Gard. Your father and your friends.

La Cast. You are welcome home, sir;
Bless ye, ye are very welcome! Pray, know this gentleman,
And these fair ladies.

Nant. Monsieur Mirabel,
I am much affected with your fair return, sir;
You bring a general joy.

Mir. I bring you service,
And these bright beauties, sir.

Nant. Welcome home, gentlemen,
Welcome with all my heart!

Bel. and Pin. We thank ye, sir.

La Cast. Your friends will have their share too.

Bel. Sir, we hope
They 'll look upon us, though we show like strangers.

Nant. Monsieur De Gard, I must salute you also,

And this fair gentlewoman; you are welcome from your travel too.
All welcome, all.
De Gard. We render ye our loves, sir.
The best wealth we bring home.—By your favors, beauties.—
(*Aside to Ori.*) One of these two: you know my meaning.
Ori. Well, sir;
They are fair and handsome, I must needs confess it,
And, let it prove the worst, I shall live after it.
Whilst I have meat and drink, love cannot starve me;
For, if I die o' th' first fit, I am unhappy,
And worthy to be buried with my heels upward.
Mir. To marry, sir?
La Cast. You know I am an old man,
And every hour declining to my grave,
One foot already in; more sons I have not,
Nor more I dare not seek whilst you are worthy.
In you lies all my hope, and all my name,
The making good or wretched of my memory,
The safety of my state.
Mir. And you have provided,
Out of this tenderness, these handsome gentlewomen,
Daughters to this rich man, to take my choice of?
La Cast. I have, dear son.
Mir. 'T is true, ye are old and feebled;
Would ye were young again, and in full vigor!
I love a bounteous father's life, a long one;
I am none of those that, when they shoot to ripeness,
Do what they can to break the boughs they grew on.
I wish ye many years and many riches,
And pleasures to enjoy 'em; but, for marriage,
I neither yet believe in 't, nor affect[20] it;
Nor think it fit.
La Cast. You will render me your reasons?
Mir. Yes, sir, both short and pithy, and these they are:—
You would have me marry a maid?
La Cast. A maid! what else?
Mir. Yes, there be things called widows, dead men's wills,
I never lov'd to prove those; nor never long'd yet
To be buried alive in another man's cold monument.
And there be maids appearing, and maids being;
The appearing are fantastic things, mere shadows;
And, if you mark 'em well, they want their heads, too;
Only the world, to cozen[21] misty eyes,
Has clapt 'em on new faces: the maids being
A man may venture on, if he be so mad to marry,
If he have neither fear before his eyes, nor fortune;
And let him take heed how he gather these too;
For, look ye, father, they are just like melons,
Musk-melons are the emblems of these maids;
Now they are ripe, now cut 'em, they taste pleasantly,
And are a dainty fruit, digested easily;
Neglect this present time, and come to-morrow,
They are so ripe they are rotten gone, their sweetness
Run into humor, and their taste to surfeit.
La Cast. Why, these are now ripe, son.
Mir. I'll try them presently,
And, if I like their taste——
La Cast. 'Pray ye, please yourself, sir.
Mir. That liberty is my due, and I'll maintain it.—
Lady, what think you of a handsome man now?
Ros. A wholesome too, sir?
Mir. That 's as you make your bargain.
A handsome, wholesome man, then, and a kind man,
To cheer your heart up, to rejoice you, lady?
Ros. Yes, sir, I love rejoicing.
Mir. To lie close to you?
Close as a cockle? Keep the cold nights from ye?
Ros. That will be look'd for too; our bodies ask it.
Mir. And get two boys at every birth?
Ros. That 's nothing?
I have known a cobbler do it, a poor thin cobbler,

20 like.

21 cheat.

A cobbler out of moldy cheese perform it,
Cabbage, and coarse black bread. Methinks, a gentleman
Should take foul scorn to have an awl outname [22] him.
Two at a birth! Why, every house-dove has it.
That man that feeds well, promises as well too,
I should expect indeed something of worth from.
You talk of two!

Mir. (*Aside.*) She would have me get two dozen,
Like buttons, at a birth.

Ros. You love to brag, sir.
If you proclaim these offers at your marriage,
(You are a pretty-timber'd man, take heed,)
They may be taken hold of, and expected,
Yes, if not hoped for at a higher rate too.

Mir. I will take heed, and thank ye for your counsel.
Father, what think you?

La Cast. 'T is a merry gentlewoman;
Will make, no doubt, a good wife.

Mir. Not for me.
I marry her, and, happily,[23] get nothing;
In what a state am I then, father? I shall suffer,
For any thing I hear to the contrary, *more majorum;*
I were as sure to be a cuckold, father,
A gentleman of antler——

La Cast. Away, away, fool!

Mir. As I am sure to fail her expectation.
I had rather get the pox than get her babies.

La Cast. Ye are much to blame. If this do not affect [24] ye,
Pray, try the other; she 's of a more demure way.

Bel. (*Aside.*) That I had but the audacity to talk thus!
I love that plain-spoken gentlewoman admirably;
And, certain, I could go as near to please her,
If down-right doing—she has a per'lous countenance—
If I could meet one that would believe me,
And take my honest meaning without circumstance——

Mir. You shall have your will, sir; I will try the other;
But 't will be to small use.—I hope, fair lady,
(For, methinks, in your eyes I see more mercy,)
You will enjoin your lover a less penance;
And though I'll promise much, as men are liberal,
And vow an ample sacrifice of service,
Yet your discretion, and your tenderness,
And thriftiness in love, good huswife's carefulness
To keep the stock entire——

Lil. Good sir, speak louder,
That these may witness, too, you talk of nothing.
I should be loth alone to bear the burden
Of so much indiscretion.

Mir. Hark ye, hark ye!
'Ods-bobs, you are angry, lady.

Lil. Angry! no, sir;
I never own'd an anger to lose poorly.

Mir. But you can love, for all this; and delight too,
For all your set austerity to hear
Of a good husband, lady?

Lil. You say true, sir;
For, by my troth, I have heard of none these ten years,
They are so rare; and there are so many, sir,
So many longing women on their knees too,
That pray the dropping-down of these good husbands—
The dropping-down from heaven; for they are not bred here—
That you may guess at all my hope, but hearing——

Mir. Why may not I be one?

Lil. You were near 'em once, sir.
When ye came o'er the Alps; those are near heaven.
But since ye miss'd that happiness, there 's no hope of ye,

Mir. Can ye love a man?

Lil. Yes, if the man be lovely,
That is, be honest, modest. I would have him valiant,
His anger slow, but certain for his honor;
Travel'd he should be, but through himself exactly,
For 't is fairer to know manners well than countries.
He must be no vain talker, nor no lover

22 exceed. 23 haply. 24 please.

To hear himself talk; they are brags of a wanderer,
Of one finds no retreat for fair behavior.
Would ye learn more?
Mir. Yes.
Lil. Learn to hold your peace, then:
Fond [25] girls are got with tongues, women with tempers.
Mir. Women, with I know what; but let that vanish.
Go thy way, good-wife Bias! [26] Sure, thy husband
Must have a strong philosopher's stone, he will ne'er please thee else.—
Here 's a starch'd piece of austerity!—Do you hear, father?
Do you hear this moral lecture?
La Cast. Yes, and like it.
Mir. Why, there 's your judgment now; there 's an old bolt shot!
This thing must have the strangest observation,[27]
(Do you mark me, father?) when she is married once,
The strangest custom too of admiration
On all she does and speaks, 't will be past sufferance.
I must not lie with her in common language,
Nor cry, "Have at thee, Kate!"—I shall be hiss'd then;
Nor eat my meat without the sauce of sentences,[28]
Your powder'd [29] beef and problems, a rare diet!
My first son, Monsieur Aristotle, I know it,
Great master of the metaphysics, or so;
The second, Solon, and the best law-setter;
And I must look [30] Egyptian god-fathers,
Which will be no small trouble; my eldest daughter,
Sappho, or such a fiddling kind of poetess,
And brought up, *invita Minerva*,[31] at her needle!
My dogs must look their names too, and all Spartan,
Lelaps, Melampus; no more Fox and Bawdy-face.
I married to a sullen set of sentences!
To one that weighs her words and her behaviors
In the gold-weights [32] of discretion! I'll be hang'd first.
La Cast. Prithee, reclaim thyself.
Mir. Pray ye, give me time, then.
If they can set me any thing to play at,
That seems fit for a gamester, have at the fairest,
Till I see more, and try more!
La Cast. Take your time, then;
I 'll bar ye no fair liberty.—Come, gentlemen;
And ladies, come; to all, once more, a welcome!
And, now let 's in to supper.
Exeunt La Castre, Nantolet, Lugier, Rosalura, and Lillia Bianca.
Mir. How dost like 'em?
Pin. They are fair enough, but of so strange behaviors—
Mir. Too strange for me. I must have those have mettle,
And mettle to my mind. Come, let 's be merry.
Bel. Bless me from this woman! I would stand the cannon,
Before ten words of hers.
Exeunt Mirabel, Pinac, and Belleur.
De Gard. Do you find him now?
Do you think he will be ever firm?
Ori. I fear not.
Exeunt.

ACT II.

SCENE 1. *A garden belonging to the house of La Castre.*

Enter Mirabel, Pinac, and Belleur.

Mir. Ne'er tell me of this happiness; 't is nothing;
The state [33] they bring with being sought-to, scurvy:
I had rather make mine own play, and I will do.
My happiness is in mine own content,
And the despising of such glorious [34] trifles,
As I have done a thousand more. For my humor,
Give me a good free fellow, that sticks to me,
A jovial fair companion; there 's a beauty!
For women, I can have too many of them;
Good women too, as the age reckons 'em,
More than I have employment for.

25 foolish.
26 One of the "Seven Sages" of ancient Greece.
27 devoted attention.
28 maxims.
29 salted.
30 look for.
31 against her will.
32 most exact balances.
33 estate.
34 vain-glorious.

Pin. You are happy.
Mir. My only fear is, that I must be forced,
Against my nature, to conceal myself:
Health and an able body are two jewels.
Pin. If either of these two women were offered to me now,
I would think otherwise, and do accordingly;
Yes, and recant my heresies; I would, sir;
And be more tender of opinion,
And put a little of my travel'd liberty
Out of the way, and look upon 'em seriously.
Methinks, this grave-carried wench —
Bel. Methinks, the other,
The home-spoken gentlewoman, that desires to be fruitful,
That treats of the full manage of the matter,
(For there lies all my aim), that wench, methinks,
If I were but well set on, for she is affable,
If I were but hounded [35] right, and one to teach me —
She speaks to th' matter, and comes home to th' point —
Now do I know I have such a body to please her
As all the kingdom cannot fit her with, I am sure on 't,
If I could but talk myself into her favor.
Mir. That 's easily done.
Bel. That 's easily said; would 't were done!
You should see then how I would lay about me.
If I were virtuous, it would never grieve me,
Or any thing that might justify my modesty;
But when my nature is prone to do a charity,
And my calf's tongue will not help me—
Mir. Will ye go to 'em?
They cannot but take it courteously.
Pin. I'll do my part,
Though I am sure 't will be the hardest I e'er play'd yet,
A way I never tried too, which will stagger me;
And, if it do not shame me, I am happy.
Mir. Win 'em, and wear 'em; I give up my interest.
Pin. What say you, Monsieur Belleur?
Bel. Would I could say,
Or sing, or any thing that were but handsome!
I would be with her presently!
Pin. Yours is no venture;
A merry ready wench.
Bel. A vengeance squibber; [36]
She 'll fleer me out of faith too.
Mir. I 'll be near thee;
Pluck up thy heart; I 'll second thee at all brunts.
Be angry, if she abuse thee, and beat her a little;
Some women are won that way,
Bel. Pray, be quiet,
And let me think: I am resolv'd to go on;
But how I shall get off again—
Mir. I am persuaded
Thou wilt so please her, she will go near to ravish thee.
Bel. I would 't were come to that once! Let me pray a little.
Mir. Now, for thine honor, Pinac, board me this modesty;
Warm but this frozen snow-ball, 't will be a conquest
(Although I know thou art a fortunate wencher,
And hast done rarely in thy days) above all thy ventures.
Bel. You will be ever near?
Mir. At all necessities;
And take thee off, and set thee on again, boy,
And cherish thee, and stroke thee.
Bel. Help me out too;
For I know I shall stick i' th' mire. If you see us close once,
Be gone, and leave me to my fortune, suddenly,
For I am then determin'd to do wonders.
Farewell, and fling an old shoe. How my heart throbs!
Would I were drunk! Farewell, Pinac; Heaven send us
A joyful and a merry meeting, man!
Pin. Farewell,
And cheer thy heart up; and remember, Belleur,
They are but women.
Bel. I had rather they were lions.
Mir. About it; I 'll be with you instantly.—

Exeunt Belleur and Pinac.
Enter Oriana.

Shall I ne'er be at rest? No peace of conscience?

35 set on.

36 sarcastic jester.

No quiet for these creatures? Am I ordain'd
To be devour'd quick[37] by these she-cannibals?
Here 's another they call handsome; I care not for her,
I ne'er look after her. When I am half-tippled,
It may be I should turn her, and peruse her;
Or, in my want of women, I might call for her;
But to be haunted when I have no fancy,
No maw to th' matter—Now, why do you follow me?

Ori. I hope, sir, 't is no blemish to my virtue;
Nor need you, out of scruple, ask that question,
If you remember ye, before your travel,
The contract you tied to me. 'T is my love, sir,
That makes me seek ye, to confirm your memory;
And, that being fair and good, I cannot suffer.
I come to give ye thanks, too.

Mir. For what, prithee?

Ori. For that fair piece of honesty you show'd sir,
That constant nobleness.

Mir. How? for I am short-headed.[38]

Ori. I 'll tell you then; for refusing that free offer
Of Monsieur Nantolet's, those handsome beauties,
Those two prime ladies, that might well have press'd ye
If not to have broken, yet to have bow'd your promise.
I know it was for my sake, for your faith-sake,
You slipt 'em off; your honesty compell'd ye;
And let me tell ye, sir, it show'd most handsomely.

Mir. And let me tell thee, there was no such matter;
Nothing intended that way, of that nature.
I have more to do with my honesty than to fool it,
Or venture it in such leak barks as women.
I put 'em off because I lov'd 'em not,
Because they are too queasy[39] for my temper,
And not for thy sake, nor the contract-sake,
Nor vows, nor oaths; I have made a thousand of 'em;
They are things indifferent, whether kept or broken;
Mere venial slips, that grow not near the conscience;
Nothing concerns those tender parts; they are trifles;
For, as I think, there was never man yet hop'd for
Either constancy or secrecy from a woman,
Unless it were an ass ordain'd for sufferance;
Nor to contract with such can be a tie-all.
So let them know again; for 't is a justice
And a main point of civil policy,
Whate'er we say or swear, they being reprobates,
Out of the state of faith, we are clear of all sides,[40]
And 't is a curious blindness to believe us.

Ori. You do not mean this, sure?

Mir. Yes, sure, and certain;
And hold it positively, as a principle,
As ye are strange things, and made of strange fires and fluxes,
So we are allow'd as strange ways to obtain ye,
But not to hold; we are all created errant.

Ori. You told me other tales.

Mir. I not deny it;
I have tales of all sorts for all sorts of women,
And protestations likewise of all sizes,
As they have vanities to make us coxcombs.
If I obtain a good turn, so it is,
I am thankful for it; if I be made an ass,
The 'mends are in mine own hands, or the surgeon's,
And there 's an end on 't.

Ori. Do not you love me, then?

Mir. As I love others; heartily I love thee;
When I am high and lusty, I love thee cruelly.
After I have made a plenteous meal, and satisfied
My senses with all delicates, come to me,
And thou shalt see how I love thee.

Ori. Will not you marry me?

Mir. No, certain, no, for any thing I know yet.
I must not lose my liberty, dear lady,

37 alive.
38 short of memory.
39 critical.
40 An oath made to an unbeliever need not be kept.

And, like a wanton slave, cry for more shackles.
What should I marry for? Do I want any thing?
Am I an inch the farther from my pleasure?
Why should I be at charge to keep a wife of mine own,
When other honest married men will ease me,
And thank me too, and be beholding to me?
Thou think'st I am mad for a maidenhead; thou art cozen'd:
Or, if I were addicted to that diet,
Can you tell me where I should have one? Thou art eighteen now,
And, if thou hast thy maidenhead yet extant,
Sure, 't is as big as cods-head; and those grave dishes
I never love to deal withal. Dost thou see this book here?
Look over all these ranks; all these are women,
Maids, and pretenders to maidenheads; these are my conquests;
All these I swore to marry, as I swore to thee,
With the same reservation, and most righteously:
Which I need not have done neither; for, alas, they made no scruple,
And I enjoy'd 'em at my will, and left 'em.
Some of 'em are married since, and were as pure maids again,
Nay, o' my conscience, better than they were bred for;
The rest, fine sober women.

Ori. Are ye not ashamed, sir?

Mir. No, by my troth, sir;[41] there 's no shame belongs to it;
I hold it as commendable to be wealthy in pleasure,
As others do in rotten sheep and pasture.

Enter De Gard.

Ori. Are all my hopes come to this? Is there no faith,
No troth, nor modesty, in men? (*Weeps.*)

De Gard. How now, sister?
Why weeping thus? Did I not prophesy?
Come, tell me why—

Ori. I am not well; pray ye pardon me. *Exit.*

De Gard. Now, Monsieur Mirabel, what ails my sister?
You have been playing the wag with her.

Mir. As I take it,
She is crying for a cod-piece. Is she gone?
Lord, what an age is this! I was calling for ye;
For, as I live, I thought she would have ravish'd me.

De Gard. Ye are merry, sir.

Mir. Thou know'st this book, De Gard, this inventory?

De Gard. The debt-book of your mistresses; I remember it.

Mir. Why, this was it that anger'd her; she was stark mad
She found not her name here; and cried downright
Because I would not pity her immediately,
And put her in my list.

De Gard. Sure, she had more modesty.

Mir. Their modesty is anger to be overdone;
They 'll quarrel sooner for precedence here,
And take it in more dudgeon to be slighted,
Than they will in public meetings; 't is their natures:
And, alas, I have so many to despatch yet,
And to provide myself for my affairs too,
That, in good faith—

De Gard. Be not too glorious[42] foolish;
Sum not your travels up with vanities;
It ill becomes your expectation.[43]
Temper your speech, sir: whether your loose story
Be true or false (for you are so free, I fear[44] it),
Name not my sister in 't; I must not hear it.
Upon your danger, name her not! I hold her
A gentlewoman of those happy parts and carriage,
A good man's tongue may be right proud to speak her.

Mir. Your sister, sir! D' ye blench at that? D' ye cavil?
Do you hold her such a piece she may not be play'd withal?

41 formerly addressed to women also.
42 boastfully.
43 our expectation of you.
44 suspect.

I have had an hundred handsomer and nobler
Have su'd to me, too, for such a courtesy;
Your sister comes i' the rear. Since ye are so angry,
And hold your sister such a strong recusant,[45]
I tell ye, I may do it; and, it may be, will too;
It may be, have too; there 's my free confession;
Work upon that now!

De Gard. If I thought ye had, I would work,
And work such stubborn work should make your heart ache:
But I believe ye, as I ever knew ye,
A glorious talker, and a legend-maker
Of idle tales and trifles; a depraver
Of your own truth: their honors fly about ye!
And so, I take my leave; but with this caution,
Your sword be surer than your tongue; you 'll smart else.

Mir. I laugh at thee, so little I respect thee;
And I'll talk louder, and despise thy sister;
Set up a chamber-maid that shall outshine her,
And carry her in my coach too, and that will kill her.
Go, get thy rents up, go!

De Gard. Ye are a fine gentleman! *Exit.*

Mir. Now, have at my two youths! I 'll see how they do,
How they behave themselves; and then I 'll study
What wench shall love me next, and when I 'll lose her.

Exit.

SCENE 2. *A hall in Nantolet's house.*

Enter Pinac and Servant.

Pin. Art thou her servant, sayest thou?

Serv. Her poor creature;
But servant to her horse, sir.

Pin. Canst thou show me
The way to her chamber, or where I may conveniently
See her, or come to talk to her?

Serv. That I can, sir;
But the question is, whether I will or no.

Pin. Why, I 'll content thee.

Serv. Why, I 'll content thee, then; now ye come to me.

Pin. There 's for your diligence. (*Gives money.*)

Serv. There 's her chamber, sir,
And this way she comes out; stand ye but here, sir,
You have her at your prospect or your pleasure.

Pin. Is she not very angry?

Serv. You 'll find that quickly.
May be she 'll call ye saucy, scurvy fellow,
Or some such familiar name; may be she knows ye
And will fling a piss-pot at ye, or a pantofle,[46]
According as ye are in acquaintance. If she like ye,
May be she 'll look upon ye; may be no;
And two months hence call for ye.

Pin. This is fine.
She is monstrous proud, then?

Serv. She is a little haughty;
Of a small body, she has a mind well mounted.
Can ye speak Greek?

Pin. No, certain.

Serv. Get ye gone, then!—
And talk of stars, and firmaments, and fire-drakes?
Do you remember who was Adam's schoolmaster,
And who taught Eve to spin? She knows all these,
And will run ye over the beginning o' th' world
As familiar as a fiddler.
Can ye sit seven hours together, and say nothing?
Which she will do, and, when she speaks, speak oracles,
Speak things that no man understands, nor herself neither.

Pin. Thou mak'st me wonder.

Serv. Can ye smile?

Pin. Yes, willingly;
For naturally I bear a mirth about me.

Serv. She 'll ne'er endure ye, then; she is never merry;
If she see one laugh, she 'll swound past *aqua vitae.*
Never come near her, sir; if ye chance to venture,

45 rebel.

46 slipper.

And talk not like a doctor, you are damn'd too.
I have told ye enough for your crown, and so, good speed ye!
Exit.

Pin. I have a pretty task, if she be thus curious,[47]
As, sure, it seems she is! If I fall off now,
I shall be laugh'd at fearfully; if I go forward,
I can but be abus'd, and that I look for;
And yet I may hit right, but 't is unlikely.
Stay: in what mood and figure shall I attempt her?
A careless way? No, no, that will not waken her:
Besides, her gravity will give me line still,
And let me lose myself: yet this way often
Has hit, and handsomely. A wanton method?
Aye, if she give it leave to sink into her consideration:
But there 's the doubt: if it but stir her blood once,
And creep into the crannies of her fancy,
Set her a-gog;—but, if she chance to slight it,
And by the power of her modesty fling it back,
I shall appear the arrant'st rascal to her,
The most licentious knave, for I shall talk lewdly.
To bear myself austerely? Rate[48] my words?
And fling a general gravity about me.
As if I meant to give laws? But this I cannot do.
This is a way above my understanding;
Or, if I could, 't is odds she 'll think I mock her;
For serious and sad things are ever still suspicious.
Well, I 'll say something:
But learning I have none, and less good manners,
Especially for ladies. Well, I 'll set my best face.

Enter Lillia Bianca and Petella.

I hear some coming. This is the first woman
I ever fear'd yet, the first face that shakes me.
(*Retires.*)

Lil. Give me my hat, Petella; take this veil off,
This sullen cloud; it darkens my delights.
Come, wench, be free, and let the music warble:—
Play me some lusty measure.
(*Music within, to which presently Lillia dances.*)

Pin. (*Aside.*) This is she, sure,
The very same I saw, the very woman,
The gravity I wonder'd at. Stay, stay;
Let me be sure. Ne'er trust me, but she danceth!
Summer is in her face now, and she skippeth!
I 'll go a little nearer.

Lil. Quicker time, fellows!

Enter Mirabel, and remains at the side of the stage.

I cannot find my legs yet—Now, Petella!

Pin. (*Aside.*) I am amaz'd; I am founder'd in my fancy!

Mir. (*Aside.*) Ha! say you so? Is this your gravity?
This the austerity you put upon you?
I 'll see more o' this sport.

Lil. A song now!
Call in for a merry and a light song;
And sing it with a liberal spirit.

Enter a Man.

Man. Yes, madam.

Lil. And be not amaz'd, sirrah, but take us for your own company.—
(*A song by the Man, and exit.*)
Let 's walk ourselves; come, wench. Would we had a man or two!

Pin. (*Aside.*) Sure, she has spied me, and will abuse me dreadfully.
She has put on this for the purpose: yet I will try her.—
(*Advances.*)
Madam, I would be loth my rude intrusion,
Which I must crave a pardon for—

Lil. Oh, ye are welcome,
Ye are very welcome, sir! We want such a one.
Strike up again!—I dare presume ye dance well:
Quick, quick, sir, quick! the time steals on.

Pin. I would talk with you.

Lil. Talk as ye dance.
(*They dance.*)

47 captious.

48 weigh.

Mir. (*Aside.*) She 'll beat him off his legs first.
This is the finest masque!
Lil. Now, how do ye, sir?
Pin. You have given me a shrewd heat.
Lil. I 'll give ye a hundred.
Come, sing now, sing: for I know ye sing well;
I see ye have a singing face.
Pin. (*Aside.*) A fine modesty!
If I could, she 'd never give me breath.—
Madam, would
I might sit and recover!
Lil. Sit here, and sing now;
Let 's do things quickly, sir, and handsomely.—
Sit close, wench, close.—Begin, begin.
Pin. I am lesson'd.
(*A song.*)
Lil. 'T is very pretty, i' faith. Give me some wine now.
Pin. I would fain speak to you.
Lil. You shall drink first, believe me.
Here 's to ye a lusty health.
(*They drink.*)
Pin. I thank ye, lady.—
(*Aside.*) Would I were off again! I smell my misery;
I was never put to this rack: I shall be drunk too.
Mir. (*Aside.*) If thou be'st not a right one, I have lost mine aim much:
I thank Heaven that I have scap'd thee. To her, Pinac!
For thou art as sure to have her, and to groan for her.—
I 'll see how my other youth does; this speeds trimly.
A fine grave gentlewoman, and worth much honor!
Exit.
Lil. Now, how do ye like me, sir?
Pin. I like ye rarely.
Lil. Ye see, sir, though sometimes we are grave and silent,
And put on sadder dispositions,
Yet we are compounded of free parts, and sometimes too
Our lighter, airy, and our fiery mettles
Break out, and show themselves: and what think you of that, sir?
Pin. Good lady, sit (for I am very weary),
And then I 'll tell ye.
Lil. Fie! a young man idle!
Up, and walk; be still in action;
The motions of the body are fair beauties;
Besides, 't is cold. 'Ods me, sir, let 's walk faster!
What think ye now of the Lady Felicia?
And Bellafronte, the duke's fair daughter? ha!
Are they not handsome things? There is Duarta,
And brown Olivia.—
Pin. I know none of 'em.
Lil. But brown must not be cast away, sir.
If young Lelia
Had kept herself till this day from a husband,
Why, what a beauty, sir! You know Ismena,
The fair gem of Saint-Germains?
Pin. By my troth, I do not.
Lil. And, then, I know, you must hear of Brisac,
How unlike a gentleman—
Pin. As I live, I have heard nothing.
Lil. Strike me another galliard![49]
Pin. By this light, I cannot!
In troth, I have sprain'd my leg, madam.
Lil. Now sit ye down, sir,
And tell me why ye came hither? Why ye chose me out?
What is your business? Your errand? Despatch, despatch.
Maybe, you are some gentleman's man, and I mistook ye,
That have brought me a letter, or a haunch of venison,
Sent me from some friend of mine.
Pin. Do I look like a carrier?
You might allow me, what I am, a gentleman.
Lil. Cry ye mercy, sir! I saw ye yesterday;
You are new-come out of travel; I mistook ye.
And how do all our impudent friends in Italy?
Pin. Madam, I came with duty, and fair courtesy,
Service, and honor to ye.
Lil. Ye came to jeer me.
Ye see I am merry, sir; I have chang'd my copy;
None of the sages now: and, pray ye, proclaim it.
Fling on me what aspersion you shall please, sir,
Of wantonness or wildness; I look for it;
And tell the world I am an hypocrite,
Mask in a forc'd and borrow'd shape; I expect it;

49 a lively dance.

But not to have you believ'd: for, mark ye, sir,
I have won a nobler estimation,
A stronger tie, by my discretion,
Upon opinion (howe'er you think I forc'd it)
Than either tongue or art of yours can slubber;[50]
And, when I please, I will be what I please, sir,
So I exceed not mean;[51] and none shall brand it,
Either with scorn or shame, but shall be slighted.

Pin. Lady, I come to love ye.

Lil. Love yourself, sir;
And, when I want observers,[52] I'll send for ye.
Heigh-ho! my fit's almost off; for we do all by fits, sir.
If ye be weary, sit till I come again to ye.
Exit with Petella.

Pin. This is a wench of a dainty spirit; but
Hang me, if I know yet either what to think
Or make of her. She had her will of me,
And baited me abundantly, I thank her;
And, I confess, I never was so blurted,[53]
Nor never so abus'd. I must bear mine own sins.
Ye talk of travels; here's a curious country!
Yet I will find her out, or forswear my faculty.
Exit.

SCENE 3. *A garden belonging to the house of Nantolet, with a summer-house in the back-ground.*

Enter Rosalura, Oriana, and a Maid.

Ros. Ne'er vex yourself, nor grieve; ye are a fool, then.

Ori. I am sure I am made so: yet, before I suffer
Thus like a girl, and give him leave to triumph—

Ros. You say right; for, as long as he perceives ye
Sink under his proud scornings, he'll laugh at ye.
For me, secure yourself; and, for my sister,
I partly know her mind too: howsoever,
To obey my father, we have made a tender
Of our poor beauties to the travel'd monsieur;
Yet two words to a bargain. He slights us
As skittish things, and we shun him as curious.
May be, my free behavior turns his stomach,
And makes him seem to doubt a loose opinion.[54]
I must be so sometimes, though all the world saw it.

Ori. Why should not ye? Are our minds only measur'd?
As long as here ye stand secure—

Ros. Ye say true;
As long as mine own conscience makes no question,
What care I for report? That woman's miserable,
That's good or bad for their tongues' sake. Come, let's retire,
And get my veil, wench. (*Exit Maid.*) By my troth, your sorrow,
And the consideration of men's humorous maddings,
Have put me into a serious contemplation.

Enter Mirabel and Belleur, on one side.

Ori. Come, faith, let's sit and think.

Ros. That's all my business.

Mir. Why stand'st thou peeping here? Thou great slug, forward!

Bel. She is there; peace!

Mir. Why stand'st thou here, then,
Sneaking and peeking as thou wouldst steal linen?
Hast thou not place and time?

Bel. I had a rare speech
Studied, and almost ready; and your violence
Has beat it out of my brains.

Mir. Hang your rare speeches!
Go me on like a man.

Bel. Let me set my beard up.
How has Pinac performed?

Mir. He has won already;
He stands not thrumming of[55] caps thus.

Bel. Lord, what should I ail!
What a cold I have over my stomach! Would I had some hum![56]

50 soil.
51 moderation.
52 admirers at a distance.
53 flouted.
54 reputation.
55 fiddling with.
56 unusually strong ale.

Certain I have a great mind to be at her,
A mighty mind.
Mir. On, fool!
Bel. Good words, I beseech ye;
For I will not be abus'd by both.
Mir. Adieu, then
(I will not trouble you; I see you are valiant);
And work your own way.
Bel. Hist, hist! I will be rul'd;
I will, i' faith; I will go presently.
Will ye forsake me now, and leave me i' th' suds?
You know I am false-hearted this way, I beseech ye,
Good sweet Mirabel—I 'll cut your throat, if ye leave me,
Indeed I will—sweet-heart—
Mir. I will be ready,
Still at thine elbow. Take a man's heart to thee,
And speak thy mind; the plainer still the better.
She is a woman of that free behavior,
Indeed, that common courtesy, she cannot deny thee.
Go bravely on.
Bel. Madam—keep close about me,
Still at my back—Madam, sweet madam—
Ros. Ha!
What noise is that? What saucy sound to trouble me?
Mir. What said she?
Bel. I am saucy.
Mir. 'T is the better.
Bel. She comes; must I be saucy still?
Mir. More saucy.
Ros. Still troubled with these vanities? Heaven bless us!
What are we born to?—Would you speak with any of my people?
Go in, sir; I am busy.
Bel. This is not she, sure:
Is this two children at a birth? I 'll be hang'd, then:
Mine was a merry gentlewoman, talk'd daintily,
Talk'd of those matters that befitted women;
This is a parcel prayer-book.[57] I 'm serv'd sweetly!
And now I am to look to; I was prepar'd for th' other way.
Ros. Do you know that man?
Ori. Sure, I have seen him, lady.
Ros. Methinks 't is a pity such a lusty fellow
Should wander up and down, and want employment.
Bel. She takes me for a rogue!—You may do well, madam,
To stay this wanderer, and set him a-work, forsooth;
He can do something that may please your ladyship.
I have heard of women that desire good breedings,
Two at a birth, or so.
Ros. The fellow 's impudent.
Ori. Sure, he is craz'd.
Ros. I have heard of men too that have had good manners.
Sure, this is want of grace: indeed, 't is great pity
The young man has been bred so ill; but this lewd age
Is full of such examples.
Bel. I am founder'd,
And some shall rue the setting of me on.
Mir. Ha! so bookish, lady? Is it possible?
Turn'd holy at the heart too? I 'll be hang'd then:
Why, this is such a feat, such an activity,
Such fast and loose![58] A veil too for your knavery?

Enter Maid with veil.

O Dio, Dio!
Ros. What do you take me for, sir?
Mir. An hypocrite, a wanton, a dissembler,
Howe'er ye seem; and thus ye are to be handled!—
Mark me, Belleur;—and this you love, I know it.
Ros. Stand off, bold sir!
Mir. You wear good clothes to this end,
Jewels; love feasts and masques.
Ros. Ye are monstrous saucy.
Mir. All this to draw on fools: and thus, thus, lady,
(*Attempts to remove the veil.*)
You are to be lull'd.
Bel. Let her alone, I 'll swinge ye else,
I will, i' faith! for, though I cannot skill o' this matter
Myself, I will not see another do it before me,
And do it worse.
Ros. Away! ye are a vain thing.

57 partly a prayer-book.

58 Fast and loose was an old cheating game; hence shiftiness.

You have travel'd far, sir, to return again
A windy and poor bladder. You talk of women,
That are not worth the favor of a common one,
The grace of her grew in an hospital!
Against a thousand such blown [59] fooleries
I am able to maintain good women's honors,
Their freedoms, and their fames, and I will do it.—

Mir. She has almost struck me dumb too.

Ros. And declaim
Against your base malicious tongues, your noises,
For they are nothing else. You teach behaviors!
Or touch us for our freedoms! Teach yourselves manners,
Truth and sobriety, and live so clearly
That our lives may shine in ye; and then task [60] us.
It seems ye are hot; the suburbs [61] will supply ye:
Good women scorn such gamesters. So, I'll leave ye.
I am sorry to see this: faith, sir, live fairly.

Exit with Oriana.

Mir. This woman, if she hold on, may be virtuous;
'T is almost possible: we'll have a new day.

Bel. Ye brought me on, ye forc'd me to this foolery,
I am sham'd, I am scorn'd, I am flurted; [62] yes, I am so;
Though I cannot talk to a woman like your worship,
And use my phrases and my learned figures,
Yet I can fight with any man.

Mir. Fie!

Bel. I can, sir;
And I will fight.

Mir. With whom?

Bel. With you; with any man;
For all men now will laugh at me.

Mir. Prithee, be moderate.

Bel. And I'll beat all men. Come.

Mir. I love thee dearly.

Bel. I will beat all that love; love has undone me.
Never tell me; I will not be a history.

Mir. Thou art not.

Bel. 'Sfoot, I will not! Give me room,
And let me see the proudest of ye jeer me;
And I'll begin with you first.

Mir. Prithee, Belleur—
If I do not satisfy thee—

Bel. Well, look ye do.
But, now I think on't better, 't is impossible;
I must beat somebody. I am maul'd myself.
And I ought in justice—

Mir. No, no, no; ye are cozen'd:
But walk, and let me talk to thee.

Bel. Talk wisely,
And see that no man laugh, upon no occasion;
For I shall think then 't is at me.

Mir. I warrant thee.

Bel. Nor no more talk of this.

Mir. Dost think I am maddish?

Bel. I must needs fight yet, for I find it concerns me;
A pox on't, I must fight.

Mir. I' faith, thou shalt not.

Exeunt.

ACT III.

Scene 1. *A public walk.*

Enter De Gard and Lugier.

De Gard. I know ye are a scholar, and can do wonders.

Lug. There's no great scholarship belongs to this, sir;
What I am, I am. I pity your poor sister,
And heartily I hate these travelers,
These gim-cracks, made of mops [63] and motions.
There's nothing in their houses here but hummings;
A bee has more brains. I grieve and vex too
The insolent licentious carriage
Of this out-facing fellow Mirabel;
And I am mad to see him prick his plumes up.

De Gard. His wrongs [64] you partly know.

Lug. Do not you stir, sir;
Since he has begun with wit, let wit revenge it:

59 empty.
60 take to task.
61 Many of the London suburbs were notorious for their houses of ill-fame.
62 flouted.
63 grimaces.
64 insults.

Keep your sword close; we 'll cut his throat a new way.
I am asham'd the gentlewoman should suffer
Such base lewd wrongs.
De Gard. I will be rul'd; he shall live,
And left to your revenge.
Lug. Aye, aye, I 'll fit him.
He makes a common scorn of handsome women;
Modesty and good manners are his May-games;
He takes up maidenheads with a new commission,—
The church-warrant 's out of date. Follow my counsel,
For I am zealous in the cause.
De Gard. I will, sir,
And will be still directed; for the truth is,
My sword will make my sister seem more monstrous.
Besides, there is no honor won on reprobates.
Lug. You are i' th' right. The slight he has show'd my pupils
Sets me a-fire too. Go; I 'll prepare your sister,
And as I told ye.
De Gard. Yes; all shall be fit, sir.
Lug. And seriously, and handsomely.
De Gard. I warrant ye.
Lug. A little counsel more.
(*Whispers.*)
De Gard. 'T is well.
Lug. Most stately!
See that observ'd; and then—
De Gard. I have ye every way.
Lug. Away, then, and be ready.
De Gard. With all speed, sir.
Exit.

Enter Lillia Bianca, Rosalura, and Oriana.

Lug. We 'll learn to travel too, may be, beyond him.—
Good day, fair beauties!
Lil. You have beautified us,
We thank ye, sir; ye have set us off most gallantly
With your grave precepts.
Ros. We expected husbands
Out of your documents [65] and taught behaviors,
Excellent husbands; thought men would run stark mad on us,
Men of all ages and all states; we expected
An inundation of desires and offers,
A torrent of trim suitors; all we did,
Or said, or purpos'd, to be spells about us,
Spells to provoke.
Lil. Ye have provok'd us finely!
We follow'd your directions, we did rarely,
We were stately, coy, demure, careless, light, giddy,
And play'd at all points: this, you swore, would carry.
Ros. We made love, and contemn'd love; now seem'd holy,
With such a reverent put-on reservation [66]
Which could not miss, according to your principles;
Now gave more hope again; now close,[67] now public,
Still up and down we beat it like a billow;
And ever those behaviors you read to us,
Subtle and new: but all this will not help us.
Lil. They help to hinder us of all acquaintance,
They have frighted off all friends. What am I better,
For all my learning, if I love a dunce,
A handsome dunce? To what use serves my reading?
You should have taught me what belongs to horses,
Dogs, dice, hawks, banquets, masques, free and fair meetings,
To have studied gowns and dressings.
Lug. Ye are not mad, sure!
Ros. We shall be, if we follow your encouragements.
I 'll take mine own way now.
Lil. And I my fortune;
We may live maids else till the moon drop mill-stones.
I see, your modest women are taken for monsters;
A dowry of good breeding is worth nothing.
Lug. Since ye take it so to th' heart, pray ye, give me leave yet,
And ye shall see how I 'll convert this heretic.
Mark how this Mirabel—
Lil. Name him no more;
For, though I long for a husband, I hate him,
And would be married sooner to a monkey,

65 lessons. 66 reserve. 67 secret.

Or to a Jack of Straw, than such a juggler.

Ros. I am of that mind too. He is too nimble,
And plays at fast and loose too learnedly,
For a plain-meaning woman; that 's the truth on 't.
Here 's one too, that we love well, would be angry;
(*Pointing to Oriana.*)
And reason why.—No, no, we will not trouble ye,
Nor him at this time: may he make you happy!
We 'll turn ourselves loose now to our fair fortunes;
And the downright way—

Lil. The winning way we 'll follow;
We 'll bait that men may bite fair, and not be frighted.
Yet we 'll not be carried so cheap neither; we 'll have some sport,
Some mad-morris or other for our money, tutor.

Lug. 'T is like enough: prosper your own devices!
Ye are old enough to choose. But, for this gentlewoman,
So please her give me leave—

Ori. I shall be glad, sir,
To find a friend whose pity may direct me.

Lug. I 'll do my best, and faithfully deal for ye;
But then ye must be rul'd.

Ori. In all, I vow to ye.

Ros. Do, do: he has a lucky hand sometimes, I assure ye,
And hunts the recovery of a lost lover deadly.

Lug. You must away straight.

Ori. Yes.

Lug. And I 'll instruct ye:
Here ye can know no more.

Ori. By your leave, sweet ladies;
And all our fortunes arrive at our own wishes!

Lil. Amen, amen!

Lug. I must borrow your man.

Lil. Pray, take him;
He is within. To do her good, take any thing.
Take us and all.

Lug. No doubt, ye may find takers;
And so, we 'll leave ye to your own disposes.
Exeunt Lugier and Oriana.

Lil. Now, which way, wench?

Ros. We 'll go a brave way, fear not;
A safe and sure way too; and yet a by-way.
I must confess I have a great mind to be married.

Lil. So have I too a grudging [68] of good-will that way,
And would as fain be despatch'd. But this Monsieur Quicksilver—

Ros. No, no; we 'll bar him, bye and main.[69] Let him trample;
There is no safety in his surquedry.[70]
An army-royal of women are too few for him;
He keeps a journal of his gentleness,
And will go near to print his fair despatches,
And call it his "Triumph over time and women."
Let him pass out of memory! What think you
Of his two companions?

Lil. Pinac, methinks, is reasonable;
A little modesty he has brought home with him,
And might be taught, in time, some handsome duty.

Ros. They say he is a wencher too.

Lil. I like him better;
A free light touch or two becomes a gentleman,
And sets him seemly off: so he exceed not,
But keep his compass [71] clear, he may be lookt at.
I would not marry a man that must be taught,
And conjur'd up with kisses; the best game
Is play'd still by the best gamesters.

Ros. Fie upon thee!
What talk hast thou!

Lil. Are not we alone, and merry?
Why should we be ashamed to speak what we think? Thy gentleman,
The tall fat fellow, he that came to see thee—

Ros. Is 't not a goodly man?

Lil. A wondrous goodly!
H' as weight enough, I warrant thee. Mercy upon me,
What a serpent wilt thou seem under such a St. George!

Ros. Thou art a fool! Give me a man brings mettle,
Brings substance with him, needs no broths to lare [72] him.

68 inclination.
69 completely; a gambling phrase.
70 presumption.
71 bounds.
72 Possibly, as other editors suggest, a misprint for *lard* =fatten.

These little fellows shew like fleas in boxes,
Hop up and down, and keep a stir to vex us.
Give me the puissant pike; take you the small shot.
Lil. Of a great thing, I have not seen a duller;
Therefore, methinks, sweet sister—
Ros. Peace, he 's modest;
A bashfulness; which is a point of grace, wench:
But, when these fellows come to moulding, sister,
To heat, and handling—as I live, I like him;

Enter Mirabel.

And, methinks, I could form him.
Lil. Peace; the fire-drake.
Mir. Bless ye, sweet beauties, sweet incomparable ladies,
Sweet wits, sweet humors! Bless you, learned lady!
And you, most holy nun, bless your devotions!
Lil. And bless your brains, sir, your most pregnant brains, sir!
They are in travail; may they be delivered
Of a most hopeful wild-goose!
Ros. Bless your manhood!
They say ye are a gentleman of action,
A fair accomplish'd man, and a rare engineer.
You have a trick to blow up maidenheads,
A subtle trick, they say abroad.
Mir. I have, lady.
Ros. And often glory in their ruins.
Mir. Yes, forsooth;
I have a speedy trick, please you to try it;
My engine will despatch ye instantly.
Ros. I would I were a woman, sir, fit for ye!
As there be such, no doubt, may engine you too;
May, with a counter-mine, blow up your valor:
But in good faith, sir, we are both too honest;
And, the plague is, we cannot be persuaded;
For, look you, if we thought it were a glory
To be the last of all your lovely ladies—
Mir. Come, come, leave prating: this has spoil'd your market!
This pride and puft-up heart will make ye fast, ladies,
Fast when ye are hungry too.
Ros. The more our pain, sir.
Lil. The more our health, I hope too.
Mir. Your behaviors
Have made men stand amaz'd; those men that lov'd ye,
Men of fair states and parts. Your strange conversions
Into I know not what, nor how, nor wherefore;
Your scorns of those that came to visit ye;
Your studied whim-whams and your fine set faces—
What have these got ye? Proud and harsh opinions.
A travel'd monsieur was the strangest creature,
The wildest monster to be wond'red at;
His person made a public scoff, his knowledge
(As if he had been bred 'mongst bears or ban-dogs [73])
Shunn'd and avoided; his conversation snuff'd [74] at;—
What harvest brings all this?
Ros. I pray you, proceed, sir.
Mir. Now ye shall see in what esteem a traveler,
An understanding gentleman, and a monsieur,
Is to be held; and, to your griefs, confess it,
Both to your griefs and galls.
Lil. In what, I pray ye, sir?
We would be glad to understand your excellence.
Mir. Go on, sweet ladies; it becomes ye rarely!
For me, I have blest me from ye; scoff on seriously,
And note the man ye mock'd. You, Lady Learning,
Note the poor traveler that came to visit you,
That flat unfurnish'd fellow; note him throughly;
You may chance to see him anon.
Lil. 'T is very likely.
Mir. And see him courted by a travel'd lady,
Held dear and honor'd by a virtuous virgin;
May be, a beauty not far short of yours neither;
It may be, clearer.

73 fierce dogs.

74 sniffed.

Lil. Not unlikely.
Mir. Younger:
As killing eyes as yours, a wit as poignant;
May be, a state, too, that may top your fortune.
Inquire how she thinks of him, how she holds him;
His good parts, in what precious price already;
Being a stranger to him, how she courts him;
A stranger to his nation too, how she dotes on him.
Inquire of this; be sick to know; curse, lady,
And keep your chamber; cry, and curse; a sweet one,
A thousand in yearly land, well bred, well friended,
Travel'd, and highly followed for her fashions.
Lil. Bless his good fortune, sir!
Mir. This scurvy fellow,
I think they call his name Pinac, this serving-man
That brought ye venison, as I take it, madam,
Note but this scab: 't is strange that this coarse creature,
That has no more set-off[75] but his jugglings,
His travel'd tricks—
Lil. Good sir, I grieve not at him,
Nor envy not his fortune: yet I wonder.
He 's handsome; yet I see no such perfection.
Mir. Would I had his fortune! For 't is a woman
Of that sweet-temper'd nature, and that judgment,
Besides her state, that care, clear understanding,
And such a wife to bless him—
Ros. Pray you, whence is she?
Mir. Of England, and a most accomplish'd lady;
So modest that men's eyes are frighted at her,
And such a noble carriage—

Enter a Boy.

How now, sirrah?
Boy. Sir, the great English lady—
Mir. What of her, sir?
Boy. Has newly left her coach, and coming this way,
Where you may see her plain: Monsieur Pinac
The only man that leads her.

Enter Pinac, Mariana, and Attendants.

Mir. He is much honored;
Would I had such a favor! Now vex, ladies,
Envy, and vex, and rail!
Ros. You are short of us,[76] sir.
Mir. Bless your fair fortune, sir!
Pin. I nobly thank ye.
Mir. Is she married, friend?
Pin. No, no.
Mir. A goodly lady;
A sweet and delicate aspect!—Mark, mark, and wonder!—
Hast thou any hope of her?
Pin. A little.
Mir. Follow close, then;
Lose not that hope.
Pin. To you, sir.
(*Mariana courtesies to Mirabel.*)
Mir. Gentle lady!
Ros. She is fair, indeed.
Lil. I have seen a fairer; yet
She is well.
Ros. Her clothes sit handsome too.
Lil. She dresses prettily.
Ros. And, by my faith, she is rich; she looks still sweeter.
A well-bred woman, I warrant her.
Lil. Do you hear, sir?
May I crave this gentlewoman's name?
Pin. Mariana, lady.
Lil. I will not say I owe ye a quarrel, monsieur,
For making me your stale:[77] a noble gentleman
Would have had more courtesy, at least more faith,
Than to turn off his mistress at first trial.
You know not what respect I might have show'd ye;
I find ye have worth.
Pin. I cannot stay to answer ye;
Ye see my charge. I am beholding to ye
For all your merry tricks ye put upon me,
Your bobs,[78] and base accounts. I came to love ye,
To woo ye, and to serve ye; I am much indebted to ye
For dancing me off my legs, and then for walking me;
For telling me strange tales I never heard of,

75 attractiveness. 76 fail to do us justice. 77 decoy. 78 sneers.

More to abuse me; for mistaking me,
When you both knew I was a gentleman,
And one deserv'd as rich a match as you are.

Lil. Be not so bitter, sir.

Pin. You see this lady:
She is young enough and fair enough to please me;
A woman of a loving mind, a quiet,
And one that weighs the worth of him that loves her:
I am content with this, and bless my fortune.
Your curious wits, and beauties——

Lil. Faith, see me once more.

Pin. I dare not trouble ye.

Lil. May I speak to your lady?

Pin. I pray ye, content yourself. I know ye are bitter,
And, in your bitterness, ye may abuse her;
Which if she comes to know (for she understands ye not),
It may breed such a quarrel to your kindred,
And such an indiscretion fling on you too
(For she is nobly friended)——

Lil. (*Aside.*) I could eat her.

Pin. Rest as ye are, a modest noble gentlewoman,
And afford your honest neighbors some of your prayers.

Exeunt Pinac, Mariana, and Attendants.

Mir. What think you now?

Lil. Faith, she 's a pretty whiting;[79]
She has got a pretty catch too.

Mir. You are angry,
Monstrous angry now, grievously angry;
And the pretty heart does swell now.

Lil. No, in troth, sir.

Mir. And it will cry anon, "A pox upon it!"
And it will curse itself, and eat no meat, lady;
And it will sigh.

Lil. Indeed, you are mistaken;
It will be very merry.

Ros. Why, sir, do you think
There are no more men living, nor no handsomer,
Than he or you? By this light, there be ten thousand,
Ten thousand thousand! Comfort yourself, dear monsieur;
Faces, and bodies, wits, and all abiliments[80]—
There are so many we regard 'em not.

Enter Belleur and two Gentlemen.

Mir. That such a noble lady—I could burst now!—
So far above such trifles——

Bel. You did laugh at me;
And I know why ye laughed.

1 Gent. I pray ye, be satisfied:
If we did laugh, we had some private reason,
And not at you.

2 Gent. Alas, we know you not, sir!

Bel. I 'll make you know me. Set your faces soberly;
Stand this way, and look sad; I 'll be no May-game;
Sadder, demurer yet.

Ros. What is the matter?
What ails this gentleman?

Bel. Go off now backward, that I may behold ye;
And not a simper, on your lives!

Exeunt Gentlemen, walking backwards.

Lil. He 's mad, sure.

Bel. Do you observe me too?

Mir. I may look on ye.

Bel. Why do you grin? I know your mind.

Mir. You do not.
You are strangely humorous. Is there no mirth nor pleasure
But you must be the object?

Bel. Mark, and observe me. Wherever I am nam'd,
The very word shall raise a general sadness,
For the disgrace this scurvy woman did me,
This proud pert thing. Take heed ye laugh not at me,
Provoke me not; take heed.

Ros. I would fain please ye;
Do any thing to keep ye quiet.

Bel. Hear me.
Till I receive a satisfaction
Equal to the disgrace and scorn ye gave me,
Ye are a wretched woman; till thou woo'st me,
And I scorn thee as much, as seriously
Jeer and abuse thee; ask what gill[81] thou art,
Or any baser name; I will proclaim thee,
I will so sing thy virtue, so be-paint thee——

Ros. Nay, good sir, be more modest.

Bel. Do you laugh again?—
Because ye are a woman, ye are lawless,

79 a term of endearment.
80 faculties.
81 common woman.

And out of compass of an honest anger.
Ros. Good sir, have a better belief of me.
Lil. Away, dear sister!
Exit with Rosalura.
Mir. Is not this better now, this seeming madness,
Than falling out with your friends?
Bel. Have I not frighted her?
Mir. Into her right wits, I warrant thee. Follow this humor,
And thou shalt see how prosperously 't will guide thee.
Bel. I am glad I have found a way to woo yet; I was afraid once
I never should have made a civil suitor.
Well, I'll about it still.
Exit.
Mir. Do, do, and prosper.
What sport do I make with these fools! What pleasure
Feeds me, and fats my sides at their poor innocence!

Enter Lugier, disguised.

Wooing and wiving—hang it! Give me mirth,
Witty and dainty mirth! I shall grow in love, sure,
With mine own happy head. Who's this?—To me, sir?—
(*Aside.*) What youth is this?
Lug. Yes, sir, I would speak with you,
If your name be Monsieur Mirabel.
Mir. You have hit it:
Your business, I beseech you?
Lug. This it is, sir:
There is a gentlewoman hath long time affected ye,
And lov'd ye dearly.
Mir. Turn over, and end that story;
'T is long enough: I have no faith in women, sir.
Lug. It seems so, sir. I do not come to woo for her,
Or sing her praises, though she well deserve 'em;
I come to tell ye, ye have been cruel to her,
Unkind and cruel, falser of faith, and careless,
Taking more pleasure in abusing her,
Wresting her honor to your wild disposes,
Than noble in requiting her affection:
Which, as you are a man, I must desire ye
(A gentleman of rank) not to persist in,
No more to load her fair name with your injuries.
Mir. Why, I beseech you, sir?
Lug. Good sir, I'll tell ye.
And I'll be short; I'll tell ye because I love ye,
Because I would have you shun the shame may follow.
There is a nobleman, new come to town, sir,
A noble and a great man, that affects her,
(A countryman of mine, a brave Savoyan,
Nephew to th' duke) and so much honors her,
That 't will be dangerous to pursue your old way,
To touch at any thing concerns her honor,
Believe, most dangerous. Her name is Oriana,
And this great man will marry her. Take heed, sir;
For howsoe'er her brother, a staid gentleman,
Lets things pass upon better hopes, this lord, sir,
Is of that fiery and that poignant metal,
(Especially provok'd on by affection)
That 't will be hard—but you are wise.
Mir. A lord, sir?
Lug. Yes, and a noble lord.
Mir. Send her good fortune!
This will not stir her lord. A baroness!
Say ye so? Say ye so? By 'r lady, a brave title!
Top and top-gallant now! Save her great ladyship!
I was a poor servant of hers, I must confess, sir,
And in those days I thought I might be jovy,[82]
And make a little bold to call in to her;
But, *basta;*[83] now I know my rules and distance;
Yet, if she want an usher, such an implement,
One that is throughly pac'd, a clean-made gentleman,
Can hold a hanging[84] up with approbation,
Plant his hat formally, and wait with patience,
I do beseech you, sir——
Lug. Sir, leave your scoffing,
And, as ye are a gentleman, deal fairly.
I have given ye a friend's counsel; so, I'll leave ye.

82 iovial. 83 Ital. "enough." 84 portière.

Mir. But, hark ye, hark ye, sir; is 't possible
I may believe what you say?
Lug. You may choose, sir.
Mir. No baits, no fish-hooks, sir? No gins? no nooses?
No pitfalls to catch puppies?
Lug. I tell ye certain:
You may believe; if not, stand to the danger!
Exit.
Mir. A lord of Savoy, says he? The duke's nephew?
A man so mighty? By lady, a fair marriage!
By my faith, a handsome fortune! I must leave prating:
For, to confess the truth, I have abus'd her,
For which I should be sorry, but that will seem scurvy.
I must confess she was, ever since I knew her,
As modest as she was fair; I am sure she lov'd me;
Her means good, and her breeding excellent;
And for my sake she has refus'd fair matches.
I may play the fool finely.—Stay: who are these?

Re-enter De Gard, disguised, Oriana, and Attendants.

(*Aside.*) 'T is she, I am sure; and that the lord, it should seem.
He carries a fair port, is a handsome man too.
I do begin to feel I am a coxcomb.[85]
Ori. Good my lord, choose a nobler; for I know
I am so far below your rank and honor,
That what ye can say this way I must credit
But spoken to beget yourself sport. Alas, sir,
I am so far off from deserving you,
My beauty so unfit for your affection,
That I am grown the scorn of common railers,
Of such injurious things that, when they cannot
Reach at my person, lie with my reputation!
I am poor, besides.
De Gard. Ye are all wealth and goodness;
And none but such as are the scum of men,
The ulcers of an honest state, spite-weavers,
That live on poison only, like swoln spiders,
Dare once profane such excellence, such sweetness.
Mir. This man speaks loud indeed.
De Gard. Name but the men, lady;
Let me but know these poor and base depravers,
Lay but to my revenge their persons open,
And you shall see how suddenly, how fully,
For your most beauteous sake, how direfully,
I'll handle their despites. Is this thing one?
Be what he will——
Mir. Sir?
De Gard. Dare your malicious tongue, sir——
Mir. I know you not, nor what you mean.
Ori. Good my lord——
De Gard. If he, or any he——
Ori. I beseech your honor—
This gentleman 's a stranger to my knowledge;
And, no doubt, sir, a worthy man.
De Gard. Your mercy!—
But, had he been a tainter of your honor,
A blaster of those beauties reign within ye—
But we shall find a fitter time. Dear lady,
As soon as I have freed ye from your guardian,
And done some honor'd offices unto ye,
I'll take ye with those faults the world flings on ye,
And dearer than the whole world I'll esteem ye!
Exit with Oriana and Attendants.
Mir. This is a thund'ring lord: I am glad I scap'd him.
How lovingly the wench disclaim'd my villainy!
I am vex'd now heartily that he shall have her;
Not that I care to marry, or to lose her,
But that this bilbo-lord[86] shall reap that maidenhead
That was my due; that he shall rig and top her:
I'd give a thousand crowns now, he might miss her.

Enter a Servant.

[85] fool.

[86] swaggerer.

Serv. Nay, if I bear your blows, and keep your counsel,
You have good luck, sir: I'll teach ye to strike lighter.
Mir. Come hither, honest fellow: canst thou tell me
Where this great lord lies, this Savoy lord? Thou mett'st him;
He now went by thee, certain.
Serv. Yes, he did, sir;
I know him, and I know you are fool'd.
Mir. Come hither:
Here 's all this, give me truth.
(*Gives money.*)
Serv. Not for your money,
(And yet that may do much) but I have been beaten,
And by the worshipful contrivers beaten, and I'll tell ye:
This is no lord, no Savoy lord.
Mir. Go forward.
Serv. This is a trick, and put upon you grossly
By one Lugier. The lord is Monsieur De Gard, sir,
An honest gentleman, and a neighbor here;
Their ends you understand better than I, sure.
Mir. Now I know him; know him now plain.
Serv. I have discharg'd my colors,[87] so God b'y ye, sir!
Exit.
Mir. What a purblind puppy was I. Now I remember him;
All the whole cast on 's face, though it were umber'd,[88]
And mask'd with patches. What a dunderwhelp,[89]
To let him domineer thus! How he strutted,
And what a load of lord he clapt upon him!
Would I had him here again! I would so bounce him,
I would so thank his lordship for his lewd [90] plot!
Do they think to carry it away, with a great band made of bird-pots,[91]
And a pair of pin-buttock'd breeches?—Ha! 't is he again;
He comes, he comes, he comes! have at him!

Re-enter De Gard, Oriana, and Attendants.

My Savoy lord, why dost thou frown on me?
And will that favor never sweeter be?
Wilt thou, I say, for ever play the fool?
De Gard, be wise, and, Savoy, go to school!
My lord De Gard, I thank you for your antic;
My lady bright, that will be sometimes frantic;
You worthy train, that wait upon this pair,
Send you more wit, and them a bouncing bair? [92]
And so I take my humble leave of your honors!
Exit.
De Gard. We are discover'd; there 's no remedy.
Lillia Bianca's man, upon my life,
In stubbornness, because Lugier corrected him—
A shameless slave! Plague on him for a rascal!
Ori. I was in a perfect hope. The bane on 't is now,
He will make mirth on mirth, to persecute us.
De Gard. We must be patient; I am vex'd to the proof too.
I'll try once more; then, if I fail, here 's one speaks.
(*Puts his hand on his sword.*)
Ori. Let me be lost and scorn'd first!
De Gard. Well, we 'll consider.
Away, and let me shift; I shall be hooted else.
Exeunt.

ACT IV.

SCENE 1. *A street before the lodging of Pinac.*

Enter Lugier, Lillia Bianca, and Servant carrying a willow garland.

Lug. Faint not, but do as I direct ye: trust me;
Believe me too; for what I have told ye, lady,
As true as you are Lillia, is authentic;
I know it, I have found it: 't is a poor courage
Flies off for one repulse. These travelers

87 Exact meaning not known; apparently equivalent to "I have fulfilled my obligations."
88 stained brown.
89 blockhead.
90 vile.
91 apparently some extravagance of dress. (Neilson.)
92 bairn, child.

Shall find, before we have done, a homespun wit,
A plain French understanding, may cope with 'em.
They have had the better yet, thank your sweet squire here!
And let 'em brag. You would be reveng'd?

Lil. Yes, surely.

Lug. And married too?

Lil. I think so.

Lug. Then be counsel'd;
You know how to proceed. I have other irons
Heating as well as yours, and I will strike
Three blows with one stone home. Be rul'd, and happy;
And so, I leave ye. Now is the time.

Lil. I am ready,
If he do come to do[93] me.

Exit Lugier.

Serv. Will ye stand here,
And let the people think ye are God knows what, mistress?
Let boys and prentices presume upon ye?

Lil. Prithee, hold thy peace.

Serv. Stand at his door that hates ye?

Lil. Prithee, leave prating.

Serv. Pray ye, go to the tavern: I'll give ye a pint of wine there.
If any of the mad-cap gentlemen should come by,
That take up women upon special warrant,
You were in a wise case now.

Enter Mirabel, Pinac, Mariana, Priest, and Attendants.

Lil. Give me the garland;
And wait you here.

(*Takes the garland from Servant, who retires.*)

Mir. She is here to seek thee, sirrah.
I told thee what would follow; she is mad for thee.
Show, and advance.—So early stirring, lady?
It shows a busy mind, a fancy troubled.
A willow garland too? Is't possible?
'T is pity so much beauty should lie musty;
But 't is not to be help'd now.

Lil. The more 's my misery.—
Good fortune to ye, lady! you deserve it;
To me, too-late repentance! I have sought it.
I do not envy, though I grieve a little,
You are mistress of that happiness, those joys,
That might have been, had I been wise—but fortune—

Pin. She understands ye not; pray ye, do not trouble her:
And do not cross me like a hare thus; 't is as ominous.[94]

Lil. I come not to upbraid your levity
(Though ye made show of love, and though I lik'd ye),
To claim an interest (we are yet both strangers;
But what we might have been, had you persever'd, sir!)
To be an eye-sore to your loving lady:
This garland shows I give[95] myself forsaken
(Yet, she must pardon me, 't is most unwillingly);
And all the power and interest I had in ye
(As, I persuade myself, somewhat ye lov'd me)
Thus patiently I render up, I offer
To her that must enjoy ye, and so bless ye;
Only, I heartily desire this courtesy,
And would not be denied, to wait upon ye
This day, to see ye tied, then no more trouble ye.

Pin. It needs not, lady.

Lil. Good sir, grant me so much.

Pin. 'T is private, and we make no invitation.

Lil. My presence, sir, shall not proclaim it public.

Pin. May be, 't is not in town.

Lil. I have a coach, sir,
And a most ready will to do you service.

Mir. (*Aside to Pinac.*) Strike now or never; make it sure: I tell thee,
She will hang herself, if she have thee not.

Pin. Pray ye, sir,
Entertain my noble mistress: only a word or two
With this importunate woman, and I'll relieve ye.—
Now ye see what your flings are, and your fancies,
Your states, and your wild stubbornness; now ye find
What 't is to gird[96] and kick at men's fair services,

93 Sympson suggests *dor*=mock.

94 It was considered bad luck to have a hare cross in front of one.

95 grant.

96 jeer.

To raise your pride to such a pitch and glory
That goodness shows like gnats, scorn'd under ye.
'T is ugly, naught; a self-will in a woman,
Chain'd to an overweening thought, is pestilent,
Murders fair fortune first, then fair opinion.
There stands a pattern, a true patient pattern,
Humble and sweet.

Lil. I can but grieve my ignorance.
Repentance, some say too, is the best sacrifice;
For, sure, sir, if my chance had been so happy
(As I confess I was mine own destroyer)
As to have arriv'd at you, I will not prophesy,
But certain, as I think, I should have pleas'd ye;
Have made ye as much wonder at my courtesy,
My love, and duty, as I have dishearten'd ye.
Some hours we have of youth, and some of folly;
And being free-born maids, we take a liberty,
And, to maintain that, sometimes we strain highly.

Pin. Now you talk reason.

Lil. But, being yok'd and govern'd,
Married, and those light vanities purg'd from us,
How fair we grow, how gentle, and how tender!
We twine about those loves that shoot up with us!
A sullen woman fear, that talks not to ye;
She has a sad and darken'd soul, loves dully.
A merry and a free wench, give her liberty,
Believe her, in the lightest form she appears to ye,
Believe her excellent, though she despise ye;
Let but these fits and flashes pass, she will show to ye
As jewels rubb'd from dust, or gold new burnish'd:
Such had I been, had you believ'd.

Pin. Is 't possible?

Lil. And to your happiness, I dare assure ye,
If true love be accounted so: your pleasure,
Your will, and your command, had tied my motions:
But that hope 's gone. I know you are young and giddy,
And, till you have a wife can govern with ye,
You sail upon this world's sea light and empty,
Your bark in danger daily. 'T is not the name neither
Of wife can steer you, but the noble nature,
The diligence, the care, the love, the patience:
She makes the pilot, and preserves the husband,
That knows and reckons every rib he is built on.
But this I tell ye to my shame.

Pin. I admire ye;
And now am sorry that I aim beyond ye.

Mir. (*Aside.*) So, so, so: fair and softly! She is thine own, boy;
She comes now without lure.

Pin. But that it must needs
Be reckon'd to me as a wantonness,
Or worse, a madness, to forsake a blessing,
A blessing of that hope——

Lil. I dare not urge ye;
And yet, dear sir——

Pin. 'T is most certain, I had rather,
If 't were in mine own choice—for you are my country-woman,
A neighbor here, born by me; she a stranger,
And who knows how her friends——

Lil. Do as you please, sir;
If ye be fast, not all the world—I love ye.
It is most true, and clear I would persuade ye;
And I shall love you still.

Pin. Go, get before me—
So much you have won upon me—do it presently.
Here 's a priest ready—I 'll have you.

Lil. Not now, sir;
No, you shall pardon me. Advance your lady;
I dare not hinder your most high preferment:
'T is honor enough for me I have unmask'd you.

Pin. How 's that?

Lil. I have caught ye, sir. Alas, I am no stateswoman,

Nor no great traveler, yet I have found ye;
I have found your lady too, your beauteous lady;
I have found her birth and breeding too, her discipline,
Who brought her over, and who kept your lady,
And, when he laid her by, what virtuous nunnery
Receiv'd her in: I have found all these. Are ye blank now?
Methinks, such travel'd wisdoms should not fool thus,—
Such excellent indiscretions!

Mir. How could she know this?

Lil. 'T is true she's English-born; but most part French now,
And so I hope you'll find her to your comfort.
Alas, I am ignorant of what she cost ye!
The price of these hired clothes I do not know, gentlemen!
Those jewels are the broker's, how ye stand bound for 'em!

Pin. Will you make this good?

Lil. Yes, yes; and to her face, sir,
That she is an English whore, a kind of fling-dust,
One of your London light-o'-loves, a right one;
Came over in thin pumps and half a petticoat,
One faith, and one smock, with a broken haberdasher—
I know all this without a conjurer.
Her name is Jumping Joan, an ancient sin-weaver;
She was first a lady's chambermaid, there slipp'd,
And broke her leg above the knee; departed,
And set up shop herself; stood the fierce conflicts
Of many a furious term; there lost her colors,
And last shipp'd over hither.

Mir. We are betray'd!

Lil. Do you come to fright me with this mystery?
To stir me with a stink none can endure, sir?
I pray ye, proceed; the wedding will become ye:
Who gives the lady? You? An excellent father!
A careful man, and one that knows a beauty!
Send ye fair shipping, sir! and so, I'll leave ye.
Be wise and manly; then I may chance to love ye!

Exit with Servant.

Mir. As I live, I am asham'd this wench has reach'd me,
Monstrous asham'd; but there's no remedy.
This skew'd-ey'd carrion——

Pin. This I suspected ever.—
Come, come, uncase;[97] we have no more use of ye;
Your clothes must back again.

Mari. Sir, you shall pardon me;
'T is not our English use to be degraded.
If you will visit me, and take your venture,
You shall have pleasure for your properties.
And so, sweetheart——

Exit.

Mir. Let her go, and the devil go with her!
We have never better luck with these preludiums.
Come, be not daunted; think she is but a woman,
And, let her have the devil's wit, we'll reach her!

Exeunt.

Scene 2. *A public walk.*

Enter Rosalura and Lugier.

Ros. You have now redeem'd my good opinion, tutor,
And ye stand fair again.

Lug. I can but labor,
And sweat in your affairs. I am sure Belleur
Will be here instantly, and use his anger,
His wonted harshness.

Ros. I hope he will not beat me.

Lug. No, sure, he has more manners. Be you ready.

Ros. Yes, yes, I am; and am resolv'd to fit him,
With patience to outdo all he can offer.
But how does Oriana?

Lug. Worse and worse still;
There is a sad house for her;[98] she is now,
Poor lady, utterly distracted.

Ros. Pity,
Infinite pity! 't is a handsome lady:

97 take those clothes off.

98 her household is sad about her.

That Mirabel's a beast, worse than a monster,
If this affliction work not.

Enter Lillia Bianca.

Lil. Are you ready?
Belleur is coming on here, hard behind me:
I have no leisure to relate my fortune;
Only I wish you may come off as handsomely.
Upon the sign, you know what.

Ros. Well, well; leave me.

Exeunt Lillia Bianca and Lugier.

Enter Belleur.

Bel. How now?

Ros. Ye are welcome, sir.

Bel. 'T is well ye have manners.
That court'sy again, and hold your countenance staidly.
That look's too light; take heed: so; sit ye down now;
And, to confirm me that your gall is gone,
Your bitterness dispers'd (for so I'll have it),
Look on me steadfastly, and, whatsoe'er I say to ye,
Move not, nor alter in your face; ye are gone then;
For, if you do express the least distaste,
Or show an angry wrinkle, (mark me, woman!
We are now alone,) I will so conjure thee,
The third part of my execution
Cannot be spoke.

Ros. I am at your dispose, sir.

Bel. Now rise, and woo me a little; let me hear that faculty:
But touch me not; nor do not lie, I charge ye.
Begin now.

Ros. If so mean and poor a beauty
May ever hope the grace——

Bel. Ye cog,[99] ye flatter;
Like a lewd thing, ye lie: "May hope that grace!"
Why, what grace canst thou hope for? Answer not;
For, if thou dost, and liest again, I'll swinge thee.
Do not I know thee for a pestilent woman?
A proud at both ends? Be not angry,
Nor stir not, o' your life.

Ros. I am counsel'd, sir.

Bel. Art thou not now (confess, for I'll have the truth out)
As much unworthy of a man of merit,
Or any of ye all, nay, of mere man,
Though he were crooked, cold, all wants upon him,
Nay, of any dishonest thing that bears that figure,
As devils are of mercy?

Ros. We are unworthy.

Bel. Stick to that truth, and it may chance to save thee.
And is it not our bounty that we take ye?
That we are troubled, vex'd, or tortur'd with ye,
Our mere and special bounty?

Ros. Yes.

Bel. Our pity,
That for your wickedness we swinge ye soundly;
Your stubbornness and stout hearts, we belabor ye?
Answer to that!

Ros. I do confess your pity.

Bel. And dost not thou deserve in thine own person,
Thou impudent, thou pert—Do not change countenance.

Ros. I dare not, sir.

Bel. For, if ye do——

Ros. I am settled.

Bel. Thou wagtail, peacock, puppy, look on me:
I am a gentleman.

Ros. It seems no less, sir,

Bel. And dar'st thou in thy surquedry——

Ros. I beseech ye!—
It was my weakness, sir, I did not view ye,
I took not notice of your noble parts,
Nor call'd your person nor your fashion proper.[1]

Bel. This is some amends yet.

Ros. I shall mend, sir, daily,
And study to deserve.

Bel. Come a little nearer:
Canst thou repent thy villainy?

Ros. Most seriously.

Bel. And be asham'd?

Ros. I am asham'd.

Bel. Cry.

Ros. It will be hard to do, sir.

Bel. Cry now instantly;
Cry monstrously, that all the town may hear thee;
Cry seriously, as if thou hadst lost thy monkey;
And, as I like thy tears——

Ros. Now!

99 cheat.

1 handsome; original reading *proper fashion.*

Enter Lillia Bianca, and four Women, laughing.

Bel. How! how! Do ye jeer me?
Have ye broke your bounds again, dame?
Ros. Yes, and laugh at ye,
And laugh most heartily.
Bel. What are these? whirlwinds?
Is hell broke loose, and all the Furies flutter'd?
Am I greased [2] once again?
Ros. Yes, indeed are ye;
And once again ye shall be, if ye quarrel:
Do you come to vent your fury on a virgin?
Is this your manhood, sir?
1 Wom. Let him do his best;
Let's see the utmost of his indignation;
I long to see him angry.—Come, proceed, sir.—
Hang him, he dares not stir; a man of timber!
2 Wom. Come hither to fright maids with thy bull-faces!
To threaten gentlewomen! Thou a man! A Maypole,
A great dry pudding.[3]
3 Wom. Come, come, do your worst, sir;
Be angry, if thou dar'st.
Bel. The Lord deliver me!
4 Wom. Do but look scurvily upon this lady,
Or give us one foul word!—We are all mistaken;
This is some mighty dairy-maid in man's clothes.
Lil. I am of that mind too.
Bel. (*Aside.*) What will they do to me?
Lil. And hired to come and abuse us.—A man has manners;
A gentleman, civility and breeding:—
Some tinker's trull, with a beard glu'd on.
1 Wom. Let's search him,
And, as we find him——
Bel. Let me but depart from ye,
Sweet Christian women!
Lil. Hear the thing speak, neighbors.
Bel. 'T is but a small request: if e'er I trouble ye,
If e'er I talk again of beating women,
Or beating any thing that can but turn to me;
Of ever thinking of a handsome lady
But virtuously and well; of ever speaking
But to her honor,—this I'll promise ye,
I will take rhubarb, and purge choler mainly,[4]
Abundantly I'll purge.
Lil. I'll send ye broths, sir.
Bel. I will be laugh'd at, and endure it patiently;
I will do any thing.
Ros. I'll be your bail, then.
When ye come next to woo, pray come not boisterously,
And furnish'd like a bear-ward.[5]
Bel. No, in truth, forsooth.
Ros. I scented ye long since.
Bel. I was to blame, sure:
I will appear a gentleman.
Ros. 'T is the best for ye,
For a true noble gentleman's a brave thing.
Upon that hope, we quit ye. You fear seriously?
Bel. Yes, truly do I; I confess I fear ye,
And honor ye, and any thing.
Ros. Farewell, then.
Wom. And, when ye come to woo next, bring more mercy.
Exeunt all except Belleur.
Enter two Gentlemen.

Bel. A dairy-maid! A tinker's trull! Heaven bless me!
Sure, if I had provok'd 'em, they had quarter'd me.
I am a most ridiculous ass, now I perceive it;
A coward, and a knave too.
1 Gent. 'T is the mad gentleman;
Let's set our faces right.
Bel. No, no; laugh at me,
And laugh aloud.
2 Gent. We are better manner'd, sir.
Bel. I do deserve it; call me patch [6] and puppy,
And beat me, if you please.
1 Gent. No, indeed; we know ye.
Bel. 'Death, do as I would have ye!
2 Gent. Ye are an ass, then,
A coxcomb, and a calf!
Bel. I am a great calf.
Kick me a little now. Why, when! (*They kick him.*) Sufficient.
Now laugh aloud, and scorn me. So good b' ye!
And ever, when ye meet me, laugh.
Gentlemen. We will, sir.
Exeunt.

[2] fooled. [3] sausage. [4] vigorously. [5] bear-keeper. [6] fool.

SCENE 3. *A room in La Castre's house.*

Enter Nantolet, La Castre, De Gard, Lugier, and Mirabel.

Mir. Your patience, gentlemen; why do ye bait me?
Nant. Is 't not a shame you are so stubborn-hearted,
So stony and so dull, to such a lady,
Of her perfections and her misery?
Lug. Does she not love ye? Does not her distraction
For your sake only, her most pitied lunacy
Of all but you, show ye? Does it not compel ye?
Mir. Soft and fair, gentlemen; pray ye, proceed temperately.
Lug. If ye have any feeling, any sense in ye,
The least touch of a noble heart——
La Cast. Let him alone:
It is his glory that he can kill beauty.—
Ye bear my stamp, but not my tenderness;
Your wild unsavory courses let [7] that in ye!
For shame, be sorry, though ye cannot cure her;
Show something of a man, of a fair nature.
Mir. Ye make me mad!
De Gard. Let me pronounce this to ye:
You take a strange felicity in slighting
And wronging women, which my poor sister feels now;
Heaven's hand be gentle on her! Mark me, sir;
That very hour she dies (there 's small hope otherwise),
That minute, you and I must grapple for it;
Either your life or mine.
Mir. Be not so hot, sir;
I am not to be wrought on by these policies,
In truth, I am not; nor do I fear the tricks,
Or the high-sounding threats, of a Savoyan.
I glory not in cruelty, (ye wrong me,)
Nor grow up water'd with the tears of women.
This let me tell ye, howsoe'er I show to ye,
Wild, as you please to call it, or self-will'd,
When I see cause, I can both do and suffer,
Freely and feelingly, as a true gentleman.

Enter Rosalura and Lillia Bianca.

Ros. Oh, pity, pity! thousand, thousand pities!
Lil. Alas, poor soul, she will die! She is grown senseless;
She will not know nor speak now.
Ros. Die for love!
And love of such a youth! I would die for a dog first:
He that kills me, I'll give him leave to eat me;
I'll know men better, ere I sigh for any of 'em.
Lil. You have done a worthy act, sir, a most famous;
Ye have kill'd a maid the wrong way; ye are a conqueror.
Ros. A conqueror? A cobbler! Hang him, sowter! [8]—
Go hide thyself, for shame! Go lose thy memory!
Live not 'mongst men; thou art a beast, a monster,
A blatant beast!
Lil. If ye have yet any honesty,
Or ever heard of any, take my counsel:
Off with your garters, and seek out a bough,—
A handsome bough, for I would have ye hang like a gentleman;
And write some doleful matter to the world,
A warning to hard-hearted men.
Mir. Out, kitlings! [9]
What caterwauling 's here! What gibbing! [10]
Do you think my heart is soft'ned with a black santis? [11]
Show me some reason.

Enter Oriana on a bed.

Ros. Here then, here is a reason.
Nant. Now, if ye be a man, let this sight shake ye!
La Cast. Alas, poor gentlewoman!—Do ye know me, lady?
Lug. How she looks up, and stares!
Ori. I know ye very well;
You are my godfather: and that 's the monsieur.
De Gard. And who am I?
Ori. You are Amadis de Gaul, sir.—

7 prevent.
8 cobbler.
9 kitten.
10 Cat-like behavior (N. E. D.); possibly misprint for *gibing*.
11 *I. e.* black-sanctus, a burlesque hymn accompanied by discordant noises. (Neilson.)

Oh, oh, my heart!—Were you never in love, sweet lady?
And do you never dream of flowers and gardens?
I dream of walking fires: take heed; it comes now.
Who 's that? Pray, stand away. I have seen that face, sure.—
How light my head is!

Ros. Take some rest.

Ori. I cannot;
For I must be up to-morrow to go to church,
And I must dress me, put my new gown on,
And be as fine to meet my love! Heigh-ho!
Will you not tell me where my love lies buried?

Mir. He is not dead.—(*Aside.*) Beshrew my heart, she stirs me!

Ori. He is dead to me.

Mir. (*Aside.*) Is 't possible my nature
Should be so damnable to let her suffer?—
Give me your hand.

Ori. How soft you feel, how gentle!
I 'll tell you your fortune, friend.

Mir. How she stares on me!

Ori. You have a flattering face, but 't is a fine one;
I warrant you may have a hundred sweethearts.
Will ye pray for me? I shall die to-morrow;
And will ye ring the bells?

Mir. I am most unworthy,
I do confess, unhappy. Do you know me?

Ori. I would I did!

Mir. Oh, fair tears, how ye take me!

Ori. Do you weep too? You have not lost your lover?
You mock me: I 'll go home and pray.

Mir. Pray ye, pardon me;
Or, if it please ye to consider justly,
Scorn me, for I deserve it; scorn and shame me,
Sweet Oriana!

Lil. Let her alone; she trembles:
Her fits will grow more strong, if ye provoke her.

La Cast. Certain she knows ye not, yet loves to see ye.
How she smiles now!

Enter Belleur.

Bel. Where are ye? Oh, why do not ye laugh? Come, laugh at me:
Why a devil art thou sad, and such a subject,
Such a ridiculous subject, as I am,
Before thy face?

Mir. Prithee, put off this lightness;
This is no time for mirth, nor place; I have us'd too much on 't.
I have undone myself and a sweet lady
By being too indulgent to my foolery,
Which truly I repent. Look here.

Bel. What ails she?

Mir. Alas, she 's mad!

Bel. Mad!

Mir. Yes, too sure; for me too.

Bel. Dost thou wonder at that? By this good light, they are all so;
They are coz'ning-mad, they are brawling-mad, they are proud-mad;
They are all, all mad. I came from a world of mad women,
Mad as March hares. Get 'em in chains, then deal with 'em.
There 's one that 's mad; she seems well, but she is dog-mad.
Is she dead, dost think?

Mir. Dead! Heaven forbid!

Bel. Heaven further it!
For, till they be key-cold dead, there 's no trusting of 'em:
Whate'er they seem, or howsoe'er they carry it,
Till they be chap-fallen, and their tongues at peace,
Nail'd in their coffins sure, I 'll ne'er believe 'em.
Shall I talk with her?

Mir. No, dear friend, be quiet,
And be at peace a while.

Bel. I 'll walk aside,
And come again anon. But take heed to her:
You say she is a woman?

Mir. Yes.

Bel. Take great heed;
For, if she do not cozen thee, then hang me:
Let her be mad, or what she will, she 'll cheat thee!

Exit.

Mir. Away, wild fool!—How vile this shows in him now!—
Now take my faith (before ye all I speak it),
And with it my repentant love.

La Cast. This seems well.

Mir. Were but this lady clear again, whose sorrows
My very heart melts for, were she but perfect,

(For thus to marry her would be two miseries),
Before the richest and the noblest beauty,
France or the world could show me, I would take her.
As she is now, my tears and prayers shall wed her.

De Gard. This makes some small amends.
Ros. She beckons to ye;
To us, too, to go off.
Nant. Let's draw aside all.

Exeunt all except Oriana and Mirabel.

Ori. Oh, my best friend! I would fain—
Mir. (*Aside.*) What! she speaks well,
And with another voice.
Ori. But I am fearful,
And shame a little stops my tongue—
Mir. Speak boldly.
Ori. Tell ye, I am well. I am perfect well (pray ye, mock not);
And that I did this to provoke your nature;
Out of my infinite and restless love,
To win your pity. Pardon me!
Mir. Go forward:
Who set ye on?
Ori. None, as I live, no creature;
Not any knew or ever dream'd what I meant.
Will ye be mine?
Mir. 'T is true, I pity ye;
But, when I marry ye, ye must be wiser.
Nothing but tricks? devices?
Ori. Will ye shame me?
Mir. Yes, marry, will I.—Come near, come near! a miracle!
The woman's well; she was only mad for marriage.
Stark mad to be ston'd to death: give her good counsel.
Will this world never mend?—Are ye caught, damsel?

Enter Belleur, Nantolet, La Castre, De Gard, Lugier, Rosalura, and Lillia Bianca.

Bel. How goes it now?
Mir. Thou art a kind of prophet;
The woman's well again, and would have gull'd me;
Well, excellent well, and not a taint upon her.
Bel. Did not I tell ye? Let 'em be what can be,
Saints, devils, any thing, they will abuse us:
Thou wert an ass to believe her so long, a coxcomb:
Give 'em a minute, they'll abuse whole millions.
Mir. And am not I a rare physician, gentlemen,
That can cure desperate mad minds?
De Gard. Be not insolent.
Mir. Well, go thy ways: from this hour I disclaim thee,
Unless thou hast a trick above this; then I'll love thee.
Ye owe me for your cure.—Pray, have a care of her,
For fear she fall into relapse.—Come, Belleur;
We'll set up bills to cure diseased virgins.
Bel. Shall we be merry?
Mir. Yes.
Bel. But I'll no more projects:
If we could make 'em mad, it were some mastery.

Exeunt Mirabel and Belleur.

Lil. I am glad she is well again.
Ros. So am I, certain.—
Be not ashamed.
Ori. I shall never see a man more.
De Gard. Come, ye are a fool: had ye but told me this trick,
He should not have gloried thus.
Lug. He shall not long, neither.
La Cast. Be rul'd, and be at peace. Ye have my consent,
And what power I can work with.
Nant. Come, leave blushing;
We are your friends: an honest way compell'd ye:
Heaven will not see so true a love unrecompens'd.
Come in, and slight him too.
Lug. The next shall hit him.

Exeunt.

ACT V.

Scene 1. *A street.*

Enter De Gard and Lugier.

De Gard. 'T will be discover'd.
Lug. That's the worst can happen:
If there be any way to reach, and work upon him,
Upon his nature suddenly, and catch him—That he loves,
Though he dissemble it, and would show contrary,
And will at length relent, I'll lay my fortune;
Nay, more, my life.
De Gard. Is she won?

Lug. Yes, and ready,
And my designments set.
De Gard. They are now for travel;
All for that game again; they have forgot wooing.
Lug. Let 'em; we'll travel with 'em.
De Gard. Where's his father?
Lug. Within; he knows my mind too, and allows [12] it,
Pities your sister's fortune most sincerely,
And has appointed, for our more assistance,
Some of his secret friends.
De Gard. Speed the plough!
Lug. Well said!
And be you serious too.
De Gard. I shall be diligent.
Lug. Let's break the ice for one, the rest will drink too
(Believe me, sir) of the same cup. My young gentlewoman
Wait but who sets the game a-foot. Though they seem stubborn,
Reserv'd, and proud now, yet I know their hearts,
Their pulses how they beat, and for what cause, sir,
And how they long to venture their abilities
In a true quarrel. Husbands they must and will have,
Or nunneries and thin collations
To cool their bloods. Let's all about our business,
And, if this fail, let nature work.
De Gard. Ye have arm'd me.
Exeunt.

SCENE 2. *A public walk.*

Enter Mirabel, Nantolet, and La Castre.

La Cast. Will ye be wilful, then?
Mir. Pray, sir, your pardon;
For I must travel. Lie lazy here,
Bound to a wife! Chain'd to her subtleties,
Her humors, and her wills, which are mere fetters:
To have her to-day pleas'd, to-morrow peevish,
The third day mad, the fourth rebellious!
You see before they are married, what moriscoes,[13]
What masques and mummeries they put upon us:
To be tied here, and suffer their lavoltas! [14]
Nant. 'T is your own seeking.
Mir. Yes, to get my freedom,
Were they as I could wish 'em—
La Cast. Fools and meacocks,[15]
To endure what you think fit to put upon 'em.
Come, change your mind.
Mir. Not before I have chang'd air, father.
When I know women worthy of my company,
I will return again, and wait upon 'em;
Till then, dear sir, I'll amble all the world over,
And run all hazards, misery, and poverty,

Enter Pinac and Belleur.

So I escape the dangerous bay of matrimony.
Pin. Are ye resolv'd?
Mir. Yes, certain; I will out again.
Pin. We are for ye, sir; we are your servants once more;
Once more we'll seek our fortune in strange countries;
Ours is too scornful for us.
Bel. Is there ne'er a land
That you have read or heard of (for I care not how far it be,
Nor under what pestiferous star it lies),
A happy kingdom, where there are no women,
Nor have been ever, nor no mention
Of any such lewd things with lewder qualities,
(For thither would I travel) where 't is felony
To confess he had a mother; a mistress, treason?
La Cast. Are you for travel too?
Bel. For any thing,
For living in the moon, and stopping hedges,[16]
Ere I stay here to be abus'd and baffl'd.[17]
Nant. Why did ye not break your minds to me? They are my daughters;
And, sure, I think I should have that command over 'em,
To see 'em well bestow'd. I know ye are gentlemen,
Men of fair parts and states; I know your parents:

12 approves.
13 Morris-dances, in which the performers were fantastically dressed.
14 high-bounding dances.
15 cowards.
16 An allusion to the popular idea of the man in the moon, with his bundle of sticks, which Belleur supposes to be intended for mending hedges with. (Weber.)
17 disgraced; the term was used of the punishment given a knight for perjury, the displaying of a painting of him upside down.

And, had ye told me of your fair affections—
Make but one trial more, and let me second ye.
Bel. No; I'll make hob-nails first, and mend old kettles.
Can ye lend me an armor of high proof, to appear in,
And two or three field-pieces to defend me?
The king's guard are mere pigmies.
Nant. They will not eat ye.
Bel. Yes, and you too, and twenty fatter monsieurs,
If their high stomachs hold. They came with chopping-knives,
To cut me into rands[18] and sirloins, and so powder[19] me.—
Come, shall we go?
Nant. You cannot be so discourteous,
If ye intend to go, as not to visit 'em,
And take your leaves.
Mir. That we dare do, and civilly,
And thank 'em too.
Pin. Yes, sir, we know that honesty.
Bel. I'll come i' the rear, forty foot off, I'll assure ye,
With a good gun in my hand. I'll no more Amazons,
I mean, no more of their frights. I'll make my three legs,[20]
Kiss my hand twice, and, if I smell no danger,
If the interview be clear, may be I'll speak to her;
I'll wear a privy coat[21] too, and behind me,
To make those parts secure, a bandog.
La Cast. You are a merry gentleman.
Bel. A wary gentleman, I do assure ye.
I have been warn'd; and must be arm'd.
La Cast. Well, son,
These are your hasty thoughts; when I see you are bent to it,
Then I'll believe, and join with ye: so, we'll leave ye.—
(*Aside.*)
There's a trick will make ye stay.
Nant. (*Aside.*) I hope so.
Exeunt La Castre and Nantolet.
Mir. We have won immortal fame now, if we leave 'em.
Pin. You have; but we have lost.
Mir. Pinac, thou art cozen'd.
I know they love ye; and to gain ye handsomely,
Not to be thought to yield, they would give millions.
Their father's willingness, that must needs show ye.
Pin. If I thought so—
Mir. Ye shall be hang'd, ye recreant!
Would ye turn renegado now?
Bel. No; let's away, boys,
Out of the air and tumult of their villainies.
Though I were married to that grasshopper,
And had her fast by th' legs, I should think she would cozen me.

Enter a Young Man, disguised as a Factor.

Y. Man. Monsieur Mirabel, I take it?
Mir. Y' are i' th' right, sir.
Y. Man. I am come to seek ye, sir. I have been at your father's,
And, understanding you were here—
Mir. Ye are welcome.
May I crave your name?
Y. Man. Fosse, sir, and your servant.
That you may know me better, I am factor
To your old merchant, Leverdure.
Mir. How does he?
Y. Man. Well, sir, I hope; he is now at Orleans,
About some business.
Mir. You are once more welcome.
Your master's a right honest man, and one
I am much beholding to, and must very shortly
Trouble his love again.
Y. Man. You may be bold, sir.
Mir. Your business, if you please now?
Y. Man. This it is, sir.
I know ye well remember in your travel
A Genoa merchant—
Mir. I remember many.
Y. Man. But this man, sir, particularly; your own benefit
Must needs imprint him in ye; one Alberto,
A gentleman you sav'd from being murder'd
A little from Bologna:
I was then myself in Italy, and supplied ye;
Though haply you have forgot me now.
Mir. No, I remember ye,
And that Alberto too; a noble gentleman:
More to remember were to thank myself, sir.
What of that gentleman?
Y. Man. He is dead.

18 pieces. 19 salt. 20 bows. 21 secret coat of mail.

Mir. I am sorry.
Y. Man. But on his death-bed, leaving to his sister
All that he had, beside some certain jewels,
Which, with a ceremony, he bequeath'd to you
In grateful memory, he commanded strictly
His sister, as she lov'd him and his peace,
To see those jewels safe and true deliver'd,
And, with them, his last love. She, as tender
To observe his will, not trusting friend nor servant
With such a weight, is come herself to Paris
And at my master's house.
Mir. You tell me a wonder.
Y. Man. I tell ye a truth, sir. She is young and handsome,
And well attended; of much state and riches;
So loving and obedient to her brother,
That, on my conscience, if he had given her also,
She would most willingly have made her tender.
Mir. May not I see her?
Y. Man. She desires it heartily.
Mir. And presently?
Y. Man. She is now about some business,
Passing accounts of some few debts here owing,
And buying jewels of a merchant.
Mir. Is she wealthy?
Y. Man. I would ye had her, sir, at all adventure!
Her brother had a main state.[22]
Mir. And fair too?
Y. Man. The prime of all those parts of Italy,
For beauty and for courtesy.
Mir. I must needs see her.
Y. Man. 'T is all her business, sir. Ye may now see her;
But to-morrow will be fitter for your visitation,
For she is not yet prepared.
Mir. Only her sight, sir;
And, when you shall think fit, for further visit.
Y. Man. Sir, ye may see her, and I 'll wait your coming.
Mir. And I 'll be with ye instantly; I know the house;—
Meantime, my love and thanks, sir.
Y. Man. Your poor servant.
Exit.
Pin. Thou hast the strangest luck! What was that Alberto?
Mir. An honest noble merchant 't was my chance
To rescue from some rogues had almost slain him;
And he in kindness to remember this!
Bel. Now we shall have you
For all your protestations and your forwardness,
Find out strange fortunes in this lady's eyes,
And new enticements to put off your journey;
And who shall have honor then?
Mir. No, no, never fear it:
I must needs see her to receive my legacy.
Bel. If it be tied up in her smock, Heaven help thee!
May not we see too?
Mir. Yes, afore we go:
I must be known myself, ere I be able
To make thee welcome. Wouldst thou see more women?
I thought you had been out of love with all.
Bel. I may be
(I find that), with the least encouragement;
Yet I desire to see whether all countries
Are naturally possess'd with the same spirits,
For, if they be, I 'll take a monastery,
And never travel: for I had rather be a friar,
And live mew'd [23] up, than be a fool, and flouted.
Mir. Well, well, I 'll meet ye anon, then tell you more, boys;
However, stand prepared, prest [24] for our journey;
For certain we shall go, I think, when I have seen her,
And view'd her well.
Pin. Go, go, and we 'll wait for ye;
Your fortune directs ours.
Bel. You shall find us i' th' tavern,
Lamenting in sack and sugar for our losses.
If she be right Italian, and want servants,[25]
You may prefer the properest man. How I could
Worry a woman now!
Pin. Come, come, leave prating:

22 great estate. 23 confined, like a hawk in a mews. 24 ready. 25 lovers.

Ye may have enough to do, without this boasting.
Exeunt.

SCENE 3. *A room in Nantolet's house.*

Enter Lugier, De Gard, Rosalura, and Lillia Bianca.

Lug. This is the last adventure.
De Gard. And the happiest,
As we hope, too.
Ros. We should be glad to find it.
Lil. Who shall conduct us thither?
Lug. Your man is ready,
For I must not be seen; no, nor this gentleman;
That may beget suspicion; all the rest
Are people of no doubt. I would have ye, ladies,
Keep your old liberties, and as we instruct ye.
Come, look not pale; you shall not lose your wishes,
Nor beg 'em neither; but be yourselves and happy.
Ros. I tell you true, I cannot hold off longer,
Nor give no more hard language.
De Gard. You shall not need.
Ros. I love the gentleman, and must now show it:
Shall I beat a proper man out of heart?
Lug. There 's none advises ye.
Lil. Faith, I repent me too.
Lug. Repent and spoil all;
Tell what ye know, ye had best!
Lil. I 'll tell what I think;
For, if he ask me now if I can love him,
I 'll tell him, yes, I can. The man 's a kind man,
And out of his true honesty affects me.
Although he play'd the fool, which I requited,
Must I still hold him at the staff's end?
Lug. You are two strange women.
Ros. We may be, if we fool still.
Lug. Dare ye believe me?
Follow but this advice I have set you in now,
And if ye lose—Would ye yield now so basely?
Give up without your honors sav'd?
De Gard. Fie, ladies!
Preserve your freedom still.
Lil. Well, well, for this time.
Lug. And carry that full state—
Ros. That 's as the wind stands;
If it begin to chop about, and scant [26] us,
Hang me, but I know what I'll do! Come, direct us;
I make no doubt we shall do handsomely.
De Gard. Some part o' th' way we 'll wait upon ye, ladies;
The rest your man supplies.
Lug. Do well, I 'll honor ye.
Exeunt.

SCENE 4. *A room in a neighboring house, with a gallery.*

Oriana disguised as an Italian lady, and two persons disguised as Merchants discovered above. Enter, below, the Young Man disguised as a Factor, and Mirabel.

Y. Man. Look ye, sir, there she is; you see how busy.
Methinks you are infinitely bound to her for her journey.
Mir. How gloriously she shows! She is a tall woman.
Y. Man. Of a fair size, sir. My master not being at home,
I have been so out of my wits to get her company!
I mean, sir, of her own fair sex and fashion—
Mir. Afar off, she is most fair too.
Y. Man. Near, most excellent.—
At length, I have entreated two fair ladies
(And happily you know 'em), the young daughters
Of Monsieur Nantolet.
Mir. I know 'em well, sir.
What are those? Jewels?
Y. Man. All.
Mir. They make a rich show.
Y. Man. There is a matter of ten thousand pounds, too,
Was owing here. You see those merchants with her;
They have brought it in now.
Mir. How handsomely her shape shows!
Y. Man. Those are still neat; your Italians are most curious.[27]
Now she looks this way.
Mir. She has a goodly presence;
How full of courtesy!—Well, sir, I 'll leave ye;
And, if I may be bold to bring a friend or two,
Good noble gentlemen—
Y. Man. No doubt, ye may, sir;
For you have most command.

26 fail.

27 fastidious.

Mir. I have seen a wonder!
Exit.
Ori. Is he gone?
Y. Man. Yes.
Ori. How?
Y. Man. Taken to the utmost:
A wonder dwells about him.
Ori. He did not guess at me?
Y. Man. No, be secure; ye show another woman.
He is gone to fetch his friends.
Ori. Where are the gentlewomen?
Y. Man. Here, here: now they are come,
Sit still, and let them see ye.

Enter, below, Rosalura, Lillia Bianca, and Servant.

Ros. Pray ye, where's my friend, sir?
Y. Man. She is within, ladies; but here's another gentlewoman,
A stranger to this town: so please you visit her,
'T will be well taken.
Lil. Where is she?
Y. Man. There, above, ladies.
Serv. Bless me, what thing is this? Two pinnacles
Upon her pate! Is't not a glode [28] to catch woodcocks?
Ros. Peace, ye rude knave!
Serv. What a bouncing bum she has too!
There's sail enough for a carrack.[29]
Ros. What is this lady?
For, as I live, she is a goodly woman.
Y. Man. Guess, guess.
Lil. I have not seen a nobler presence.
Serv. 'T is a lusty wench: now could I spend my forty-pence,
With all my heart, to have but one fling at her,
To give her but a swashing blow.
Lil. Ye rascal!
Serv. Aye, that's all a man has for's good will. 'T will be long enough
Before ye cry, "Come, Anthony, and kiss me."
Lil. I'll have ye whipt.
Ros. Has my friend seen this lady?
Y. Man. Yes, yes, and is well known to her.
Ros. I much admire her presence.
Lil. So do I too;
For, I protest, she is the handsomest,
The rarest, and the newest to mine eye,
That ever I saw yet.
Ros. I long to know her;
My friend shall do that kindness.
Ori. So she shall, ladies:
Come, pray ye, come up.
Ros. Oh me!
Lil. Hang me, if I knew her!—
Were I a man myself, I should now love ye;
Nay, I should dote.
Ros. I dare not trust mine eyes;
For, as I live, ye are the strangest alter'd!
I must come up to know the truth.
Serv. So must I, lady:
For I'm a kind of unbeliever too.
Lil. Get ye gone, sirrah;
And what ye have seen be secret in; you are paid else!
No more of your long tongue.
Y. Man. Will ye go in, ladies,
And talk with her? These venturers will come straight.
Away with this fellow.
Lil. There, sirrah; go, disport ye.
Serv. I would the trunk-hos'd [30] woman would go with me.
Exeunt.

Scene 5. *The street, before the same house.*

Enter Mirabel, Pinac, and Belleur.

Pin. Is she so glorious handsome?
Mir. You would wonder;
Our women look like gipsies, like gills [31] to her;
Their clothes and fashions beggarly and bankrupt,
Base, old, and scurvy.
Bel. How looks her face?
Mir. Most heavenly;
And the becoming motion of her body
So sets her off!
Bel. Why then, we shall stay.
Mir. Pardon me,
That's more than I know. If she be that woman
She appears to be—
Bel. As 't is impossible.
Mir. I shall then tell ye more.
Pin. Did ye speak to her?
Mir. No, no, I only saw her; she was busy.
Now I go for that end; and mark her, gentlemen,
If she appear not to ye one of the sweetest,
The handsomest, the fairest in behavior!
We shall meet the two wenches there too; they come to visit her,

[28] glade, an opening in a wood utilized for snaring birds. (N. E. D.)
[29] galleon.
[30] Trunk hose were large, loose breeches: evidently Oriana was attired in the manner of an Oriental woman.
[31] common wenches.

To wonder, as we do.
Pin. Then we shall meet 'em.
Bel. I had rather meet two bears.
Mir. There you may take your leaves, despatch that business,
And, as ye find their humors—
Pin. Is your love there too?
Mir. No, certain; she has no great heart to set out again.
This is the house; I 'll usher ye.
Bel. I 'll bless me,
And take a good heart, if I can.
Mir. Come, nobly. *Exeunt.*

SCENE 6. *A room in the same house.*

Enter the Young Man disguised as a Factor, Rosalura, Lillia Bianca, and Oriana disguised as before.

Y. Man. They are come in. Sit you two off, as strangers.—
There, lady.—Where 's the boy?

Enter Boy.

Be ready, sirrah,
And clear your pipes.[32]—The music now; they enter.

(*Music.*)

Enter Mirabel, Pinac, and Belleur.

Pin. What a state she keeps! How far off they sit from her!
How rich she is! Aye, marry, this shows bravely!
Bel. She is a lusty wench, and may allure a good man;
But, if she have a tongue, I 'll not give twopence for her.
There sits my Fury; how I shake to see her!
Y. Man. Madam, this is the gentleman.
Mir. How sweet she kisses!
She has a spring dwells on her lips, a paradise!
This is the legacy?
(*Song by the Boy, while he presents a casket to Mirabel.*)

From the honor'd dead I bring
Thus his love and last off'ring.
Take it nobly, 't is your due,
From a friendship ever true;
From a faith, &c.

Ori. Most noble sir,
This from my now-dead brother, as his love,
And grateful memory of your great benefit;
From me my thanks, my wishes, and my service.
Till I am more acquainted, I am silent;
Only I dare say this,—you are truly noble.
Mir. What should I think?
Pin. Think ye have a handsome fortune:
Would I had such another!
Ros. Ye are all well met, gentlemen;
We hear ye are for travel.
Pin. You hear true, lady;
And come to take our leaves.
Lil. We 'll along with ye:
We see you are grown so witty by your journey,
We cannot choose but step out too. This lady
We mean to wait upon as far as Italy.
Bel. I 'll travel into Wales, amongst the mountains,
In hope they cannot find me.
Ros. If you go further,
So good and free society we hold ye,
We 'll jog along too.
Pin. Are you so valiant, lady?
Lil. And we 'll be merry, sir, and laugh.
Pin. It may be
We 'll go by sea.
Lil. Why, 't is the only voyage!
I love a sea-voyage, and a blust'ring tempest;
And let all split!
Pin. This is a dainty damosel!—
I think 't will tame ye. Can ye ride post?
Lil. Oh, excellently! I am never weary that way:
A hundred mile a day is nothing with me.
Bel. I 'll travel under ground. Do you hear, sweet lady?
I find it will be dangerous for a woman.
Ros. No danger, sir, I warrant; I love to be under.
Bel. I see she will abuse me all the world over.—
But say we pass through Germany, and drink hard?
Ros. We 'll learn to drink, and swagger too.
Bel. She 'll beat me!—
Lady, I 'll live at home.
Ros. And I 'll live with thee;
And we 'll keep house together.
Bel. I 'll keep hounds first:
And those I hate right heartily.
Pin. I go for Turkey;
And so, it may be, up into Persia.
Lil. We cannot know too much; I 'll travel with ye.

[32] throat.

Pin. And you 'll abuse me?
Lil. Like enough.
Pin. 'T is dainty!
Bel. I will live in a bawdy-house.
Ros. I dare come to ye.
Bel. Say I am dispos'd to hang myself?
Ros. There I 'll leave ye.
Bel. I am glad I know how to avoid ye.
Mir. May I speak yet?
Y. Man. She beckons to ye.
Mir. Lady, I could wish I knew to recompense,
Even with the service of my life, those pains,
And those high favors you have thrown upon me:
Till I be more desertful in your eye,
And till my duty shall make known I honor ye,
Noblest of women, do me but this favor,
To accept this back again as a poor testimony.
(*Offering the casket.*)
Ori. I must have you too with 'em; else the will,
That says they must rest with ye, is infring'd, sir;
Which, pardon me, I dare not do.
Mir. Take me then,
And take me with the truest love.
Ori. 'T is certain
My brother lov'd ye dearly, and I ought
As dearly to preserve that love: but, sir,
Though I were willing, these are but your ceremonies.
Mir. As I have life, I speak my soul!
Ori. I like ye:
But how you can like me, without I have testimony,
A stranger to ye—
Mir. I 'll marry ye immediately;
A fair state I dare promise ye.
Bel. Yet she 'll cozen thee.
Ori. Would some fair gentleman durst promise for ye!
Mir. By all that 's good—

Enter La Castre, Nantolet, Lugier, and De Gard.

La Cast., Nant., &c. And we 'll make up the rest, lady.
Ori. Then Oriana takes ye! Nay, she has caught ye;
If ye start now, let all the world cry shame on ye!
I have out-travell'd ye.
Bel. Did not I say she would cheat thee?
Mir. I thank ye: I am pleas'd ye have deceiv'd me,
And willingly I swallow it, and joy in 't;
And yet, perhaps, I knew ye. Whose plot was this?
Lug. He is not asham'd that cast[33] it; he that executed,
Follow'd your father's will.
Mir. What a world 's this!
Nothing but craft and cozenage!
Ori. Who begun, sir?
Mir. Well; I do take thee upon mere compassion;
And I do think I shall love thee. As a testimony,
I 'll burn my book, and turn a new leaf over.
But these fine clothes you shall wear still.
Ori. I obey you, sir, in all.
Nant. And how, how, daughters? What say you to these gentlemen?—
What say ye, gentlemen, to the girls?
Pin. By my troth—if she can love me—
Lil. How long?
Pin. Nay, if once ye love—
Lil. Then take me,
And take your chance.
Pin. Most willingly: ye are mine, lady;
And, if I use ye not that ye may love me—
Lil. A match, i' faith.
Pin. Why, now ye travel with me.
Ros. How that thing stands!
Bel. It will, if ye urge it:
Bless your five wits!
Ros. Nay, prithee, stay; I 'll have thee.
Bel. You must ask me leave first.
Ros. Wilt thou use me kindly,
And beat me but once a week?
Bel. If you deserve no more.
Ros. And wilt thou get me with child?
Bel. Dost thou ask me seriously?
Ros. Yes, indeed, do I.
Bel. Yes, I will get thee with child. Come, presently,
An 't be but in revenge, I 'll do thee that courtesy.
Well, if thou wilt fear God and me, have at thee!
Ros. I 'll love ye, and I 'll honor ye
Bel. I am pleas'd, then.
Mir. This *Wild-Goose Chase* is done; we have won o' both sides.
Brother, your love: and now to church of all hands;
Let 's lose no time.
Pin. Our travelling lay by.
Bel. No more for Italy; for the Low Countries, I. *Exeunt.*

33 contrived.

MIDDLETON AND ROWLEY

THE CHANGELING

Thomas Middleton (1580–1627), after studying at Oxford but not as once fancied at Gray's Inn, was by 1612 writing for Henslowe, and about 1600 began the series of realistic comedies of London life which established his reputation. He also wrote a considerable number of masques and Lord Mayor's pageants, and held the post of City Chronologer from 1620 till his death. The most striking incident of his career was connected with his play *The Game at Chess*, satirizing the proposed marriage of Prince Charles with a Spanish princess, which roused the anger of the Spanish ambassador and led to a warrant for the arrest of the players and author.

William Rowley (1585?–c. 1625), an actor and playwright of whose life we know nothing, did most of his work in collaboration, with Fletcher, Dekker, Heywood, and others. The year 1614, when the Prince's Company, for whom Rowley was writing, and the Lady Elizabeth's men, who had been acting Middleton's plays, were united, is the date assigned for the beginning of the collaboration which, next to that of Beaumont and Fletcher, was most fruitful of good work.

Whatever the circumstances that brought Middleton and Rowley together, the partnership was a fortunate one, for it produced two plays of the first water, *A Fair Quarrel* (1616) and *The Changeling* (1623). By 1614 Middleton had written most of the comedies which stamp him as a chief realist of his time. *A Mad World My Masters, A Chaste Maid in Cheapside, A Trick to Catch the Old One, No Wit No Help like a Woman's*, racy, bustling plays of intrigue, the plot centering in the pursuit of a rich widow by a young scapegrace, or the fooling of a miserly father or greedy usurer, introducing just the sort of figures that would come under the observation of a young lawyer with a keen eye for the *comédie humaine*, prodigal sons beset by creditors, country gentlemen swindled by sharpers, widows with more money than prudence, old men overreaching themselves in craft, knaves and swaggerers of every sort, constables and police magistrates, once an Amazon in doublet and hose, courtesans masquerading as fine ladies — all the seething underworld of London set forth with the veracity of first-hand acquaintance — plays of this kind are Middleton's contribution to the comedy of manners. Not a pleasant world, my masters, and depicted without a touch of romance, without moral ideality, without a breath of the fresh air that blows through *The Shoemakers' Holiday*. The plotting is deft, the action is brisk, the characters are firmly drawn, the dialogue, shifting easily from verse to prose and back, is clear and fluent. Rowley, on the other hand, both in style and structure offers a striking contrast. His plotting is slovenly; the conception may be good, for the man had dramatic instinct, but the execution is frequently marred by a huddling of incident and violent straining for theatrical effect. The verse exhibits the same faults; it is often rugged to uncouthness, shambling in meter, exaggerated in its effort for distinction of phrase. Rowley's humor is characteristic: genuine, but tending to buffoonery, rough and ready, and all too commonly depending on mere horseplay and on violent attempts at verbal cleverness, for Rowley was an inveterate bad punster. Yet with all his faults Rowley displays an honesty and human sympathy, a capacity for imagination of the higher, idealizing sort, not felt in Middleton's more artistic product.

An ill-assorted pair this, we should be tempted to say, with no promise of the sympathy of taste and poetic gift which made the union of Beaumont and Fletcher so happy. Yet something in each man seemed to call forth the best in the other, and in their first united work there comes an indescribable lift, a nobility of conception and a power to interpret life and express it in terms of poetry, utterly unheralded by the previous work of either man. *A Fair Quarrel*, with its problem of the attitude of a finely grained youth toward a mother who has admitted her own dishonor (though untruthfully, in order to prevent the boy from fighting a duel), and toward her accuser, strikes the reader as surprisingly modern in idea, and in execution the plot is not unworthy of the theme. But it is in the romantic tragedy, *The Changeling*, of the same class as Beaumont and Fletcher's *The Maid's Tragedy* and Webster's *The Duchess of Malfi*, that Middleton and Rowley reach their highest achievement and produce one of the greatest plays of the period.

The Changeling is an illustration of the dual-plot construction common at the time in Elizabethan plays, in *A Woman Killed with Kindness*, for instance. A superbly conceived main-plot is disfigured by a trashy comic sub-plot, of which the best thing to be said is that it soon fades from memory. The mad-house scenes are by all critics assigned to Rowley. Worthless in themselves, revolting to modern taste, exhibiting Rowley's coarse and clumsy humor at its worst, they are united to the main plot in the flimsiest fashion; the only connection between the two actions is that Antonio and Franciscus are for a time suspected of Piracquo's murder, and that the final scene is almost ruined by the intrusion of these buffoons. The story of De Flores and Beatrice-Joanna is taken from *God's Revenge against Murder* (1621) by John Reynolds, a collection of gory murder stories, while the Diaphanta episode is borrowed from an old French fabliau. In its cheap sensationalism and offensive tone this latter shows the evil influence of the Fletcherian romantic work in the decadence of the drama. There are notable differences between Reynolds's narrative and the play, among them being a very decided change in the relations of De Flores and Beatrice, of which more hereafter, and a skilful compression of the ending. In the story, Alsemero kills his wife and her paramour and slays Tomaso Piracquo by treachery. On being arrested and tried for the latter crime he reveals the facts of Alonzo Piracquo's death, whereupon he is beheaded, and the bodies of De Flores and Beatrice exhumed and burned. The new ending not only ennobles Alsemero, but raises the sordid end of the paramours to the dignity of a tragic catastrophe by making the chief mover in the villainy the instrument of just retribution.

It is the characters that make the play great, and it is Rowley who introduces them. The first scene is undoubtedly his. The setting aside by a lady of a suitor favored by her father is used several times by Rowley; the bad punning is in his fashion; and Beatrice's action in throwing her glove at De Flores is of a piece with the violent behavior of other Rowley heroines. The verse, moreover, betrays metrical differences from Middleton's: it has fewer feminine endings, more run-on lines, is less smooth and colloquial in effect. But coming to the more important question of the conception of the characters as they appear in this scene, it is unwise to give to Rowley the entire credit for a masterly exposition. In a fundamental matter like characterization there must have been discussion and agreement between the collaborators as to the lines along which the people should be developed. De Flores and Beatrice are done with extreme care. The relations between them are so improbable that the exposition must be unusually thorough. Now almost the entire first scene is given to portraying the actual physical repulsion inspired in Beatrice by De Flores. The mere sight of the man fills her with loathing, expressed in her reception of his message, enforced in the following conversation with Alsemero, and driven sharply home by the glove incident. This antipathy, so dramatic in its conflict of wills, so provocative of curiosity as to what it will lead to, is a stroke of genius on the part of the dramatists. There is no hint of it in the source, for there De Flores is "a gallant young gentleman," to whose advances Beatrice makes no resistance. In the handling of De Flores there is a noteworthy restrained power. He appears, is repulsed, retires, and is kept at the back of the stage until the end of the scene. Exposition is managed by the very lack of action, the situation made clear by Beatrice's scorn and studied neglect. With act II Middleton takes up the pen, and is mainly responsible for the conduct of the story till the final scene. The verse becomes more fluent and yet more pointed, and an even excellence of dialogue is maintained of which Rowley seemed incapable. Between the first scene of the act, wherein the hatred of Beatrice for De Flores is emphasized, and the second, in which she accepts him as her tool for murder, the contrast is striking. The second scene in particular is masterly in its latent power, as Beatrice, confident that she is mistress of the situation, thinks she is playing upon De Flores by her seeming reluctance to divulge the service she requires, while he accepts the task open-eyed, in full assurance of its possibilities. Effective too is the laconic brevity of his reply to her promise of reward —"Aye, aye; we'll talk of that hereafter"; Beatrice disregards it, but its full significance appears in the finest scene of the play, III. iv. Here is Beatrice, rejoicing that Piracquo is out of her way, and thinking only of ridding herself at once and forever of De Flores; and here is De Flores, gloating over the fact that she is completely in his power. How subtly he weaves the web of complicity about her, how slowly she awakens to the fearful consciousness that he is her master! How simple the dialogue is, but how it cuts! Not even when she at last understands his demand can she comprehend that there is no escape:

> Why, 't is impossible thou canst be so wicked,
> Or shelter such a cunning cruelty
> To make his death the murderer of my honor!"

The cold logic whereby he convinces her that she has become "the deed's creature," and one with him in crime and reward is unanswerable indeed. When Lamb was making his excerpts for his *Specimens of the English Dramatic Poets* he, oddly enough, omitted *The Changeling*, and it was left for Leigh Hunt to say of De Flores' conduct in this scene that for "effect at once tragical, probable, and poetical it surpasses anything . . . in the drama of domestic life." It is interesting that a somewhat similar situation appears in our day in Sir A. W. Pinero's *Iris*.

There is, almost inevitably, a distinct letting down with the Diaphanta episode of the fourth and fifth acts. The chemical test of virtue and the method by which Diaphanta is disposed of, strike us as excessively curious. The whole episode, indeed, is so far below the level of the preceding scenes that it can be justified only on the ground that it exhibits the swift degradation of Beatrice's character under the influence of De Flores. In V. i, we see how absolutely she accepts him as her equal. The introduction of Alonzo's ghost is a cheap device, but it calls forth a superb speech from De Flores:

> Ha! what art thou that tak'st away the light
> Betwixt that star and me? I dread thee not;
> 'T was but a mist of conscience; all 's clear again.

In the last scene "rough Rowley's Esau hand," as Swinburne liked to say, is discernible in the more labored movement of the verse, the overcharged language, and the physical violence. We do not object to the deaths of Beatrice and De Flores — only in a scene of terror could such a story end. But it is undeniable that the solution of the action is inferior to the complication.

The play stands comparison with the work of Webster and of Beaumont and Fletcher, with all but the very greatest of its time. Not even Webster, indeed, gave us such a masterly piece of character-drawing as De Flores; Bosola is faltering in comparison. Nor, though the Duchess of Malfi and Vittoria Corombona are magnificent in fortitude of virtue and of crime respectively, is Webster's analysis of his women so profound, his understanding of them so thorough, as Middleton's of Beatrice. Had the last two acts been written with the restraint and poetic beauty of the first three, it would not be with Webster's tragedy that we should be forced to compare *The Changeling*, but with *Lear* and *Macbeth* and *Hamlet*.

THE CHANGELING

By THOMAS MIDDLETON and WILLIAM ROWLEY

NAMES OF THE CHARACTERS

Vermandero, *governor of the castle of Alicant, father to Beatrice.*
Tomaso De Piracquo, *a noble lord.*
Alonzo De Piracquo, *his brother, suitor to Beatrice.*
Alsemero, *a nobleman, afterwards married to Beatrice.*
Jasperino, *his friend.*
Alibius, *a jealous doctor.*
Lollio, *his man.*
Pedro, *friend to Antonio.*
Antonio, *the changeling.*
Franciscus, *a counterfeit madman.*
De Flores, *servant to Vermandero.*
Madmen.
Servants.
Beatrice-Joanna, *daughter to Vermandero.*
Diaphanta, *her waiting-woman.*
Isabella, *wife of Alibius.*

Scene.—Alicant.

ACT I.

Scene 1. *A street.*

Enter Alsemero.

Als. 'T was in the temple where I first beheld her,
And now again the same: what omen yet
Follows of that? None but imaginary.
Why should my hopes or fate be timorous?
The place is holy, so is my intent:
I love her beauties to the holy purpose;
And that, methinks, admits comparison
With man's first creation, the place blessed,
And is his right home back, if he achieve it.
The church hath first begun our interview,
And that 's the place must join us into one;
So there 's beginning and perfection too.

Enter Jasperino.

Jas. O sir, are you here? Come, the wind 's fair with you;
You 're like to have a swift and pleasant passage.
Als. Sure, you 're deceived, friend, 't is contrary,
In my best judgment.
Jas. What, for Malta?

If you could buy a gale amongst the witches,
They could not serve you such a lucky penny-worth
As comes a' God's name.

Als. Even now I observ'd
The temple's vane to turn full in my face;
I know it is against me.

Jas. Against you?
Then you know not where you are.

Als. Not well, indeed.

Jas. Are you not well, sir?

Als. Yes, Jasperino,
Unless there be some hidden malady
Within me, that I understand not.

Jas. And that
I began to doubt,[1] sir. I never knew
Your inclinations to travels at a pause
With any cause to hinder it, till now.
Ashore you were wont to call your servants up,
And help to trap your horses for the speed;
At sea I 've seen you weigh the anchor with 'em,
Hoist sails for fear to lose the foremost breath,
Be in continual prayers for fair winds;
And have you chang'd your orisons?

Als. No, friend;
I keep the same church, same devotion.

Jas. Lover I 'm sure you 're none; the stoic was
Found in you long ago; your mother nor
Best friends, who have set snares of beauty, aye,
And choice ones too, could never trap you that way.
What might be the cause?

Als. Lord, how violent
Thou art! I was but meditating of
Somewhat I heard within the temple.

Jas. Is this
Violence? 'T is but idleness compar'd
With your haste yesterday.

Als. I 'm all this while
A-going, man.

Enter Servants.

Jas. Backwards, I think, sir. Look,
Your servants.

1 Ser. The seamen call; shall we board your trunks?

Als. No, not to-day.

Jas. 'T is the critical day, it seems, and the sign in Aquarius.

2 Serv. We must not to sea to-day; this smoke will bring forth fire.

Als. Keep all on shore; I do not know the end,
Which needs I must do, of an affair in hand
Ere I can go to sea.

1 Serv. Well, your pleasure.

2 Serv. Let him e'en take his leisure too; we are safer on land.

Exeunt Servants.

Enter Beatrice, Diaphanta, and Servants. Alsemero accosts Beatrice and then kisses her.

Jas. (*Aside.*) How now? The laws of the Medes are chang'd sure; salute a woman! He kisses too; wonderful! Where learnt he this? and does it perfectly too. In my conscience, he ne'er rehearst it before. Nay, go on; this will be stranger and better news at Valencia than if he had ransom'd half Greece from the Turk.

Beat. You are a scholar, sir?

Als. A weak one, lady.

Beat. Which of the sciences is this love you speak of?

Als. From your tongue I take it to be music.

Beat. You 're skilful in it, can sing at first sight.

Als. And I have show'd you all my skill at once;
I want more words to express me further,
And must be forc'd to repetition;
I love you dearly.

Beat. Be better advis'd, sir;
Our eyes are sentinels unto our judgments,
And should give certain judgment what they see;
But they are rash sometimes, and tell us wonders
Of common things, which when our judgments find,
They can then check the eyes, and call them blind.

Als. But I am further, lady; yesterday
Was mine eyes' employment, and hither now
They brought my judgment, where are both agreed.
Both houses then consenting, 't is agreed;
Only there wants the confirmation
By the hand royal; that 's your part, lady.

Beat. Oh, there 's one above me, sir.—(*Aside.*) For five days past

[1] suspect.

To be recall'd! Sure mine eyes were mistaken;
This was the man was meant me. That he should come
So near his time, and miss it!

Jas. We might have come by the carriers from Valencia, I see, and sav'd all our sea-provision; we are at farthest sure. Methinks I should do something too;
I meant to be a venturer in this voyage.
Yonder 's another vessel, I 'll board her;
If she be lawful prize, down goes her topsail.

(*Accosts Diaphanta.*)

Enter De Flores.

De F. Lady, your father—

Beat. Is in health, I hope.

De F. Your eye shall instantly instruct you, lady;
He 's coming hitherward.

Beat. What needed then
Your duteous preface? I had rather
He had come unexpected; you must stall[2]
A good presence with unnecessary blabbing;
And how welcome for your part you are,
I 'm sure you know.

De F. (*Aside.*) Will 't never mend, this scorn,
One side nor other? Must I be enjoin'd
To follow still whilst she flies from me? Well,
Fates, do your worst, I 'll please myself with sight
Of her at all opportunities,
If but to spite her anger. I know she had
Rather see me dead than living; and yet
She knows no cause for 't but a peevish will.

Als. You seem'd displeased, lady, on the sudden.

Beat. Your pardon, sir, 't is my infirmity;
Nor can I other reason render you
Than his or hers, of some particular thing
They must abandon as a deadly poison,
Which to a thousand other tastes were wholesome;
Such to mine eyes is that same fellow there,
The same that report speaks of the basilisk.[3]

Als. This is a frequent frailty in our nature;
There 's scarce a man amongst a thousand found
But hath his imperfection: one distastes
The scent of roses, which to infinites
Most pleasing is and odoriferous;
One oil, the enemy of poison;
Another wine, the cheerer of the heart
And lively refresher of the countenance.
Indeed this fault, if so it be, is general;
There 's scarce a thing but is both lov'd and loath'd:
Myself, I must confess, have the same frailty.

Beat. And what may be your poison, sir? I 'm bold with you.

Als. What might be your desire, perhaps; a cherry.

Beat. I am no enemy to any creature
My memory has, but yon gentleman.

Als. He does ill to tempt your sight, if he knew it.

Beat. He cannot be ignorant of that, sir,
I have not spar'd to tell him so; and I want
To help myself, since he 's a gentleman
In good respect with my father, and follows him.

Als. He 's out of his place then now.

(*They talk apart.*)

Jas. I am a mad wag, wench.

Dia. So methinks; but for your comfort, I can tell you, we have a doctor in the city that undertakes the cure of such.

Jas. Tush, I know what physic is best for the state of mine own body.

Dia. 'T is scarce a well-govern'd state, I believe.

Jas. I could show thee such a thing with an ingredient that we two would compound together, and if it did not tame the maddest blood i' th' town for two hours after, I 'll ne'er profess[4] physic again.

Dia. A little poppy, sir, were good to cause you sleep.

Jas. Poppy? I 'll give thee a pop i' th' lips for that first, and begin there. Poppy is one simple[5] indeed, and cuckoo (what-you-call 't) another. I 'll discover no more now; another time I 'll show thee all.

Exit.

Enter Vermandero and Servants.

Beat. My father, sir.

Ver. O Joanna, I came to meet thee.
Your devotion 's ended?

Beat. For this time, sir.—
(*Aside.*) I shall change my saint, I fear me; I find
A giddy turning in me.—Sir, this while
I am beholding to this gentleman,

2 forestall. 3 a fabled snake whose mere glance was fatal. 4 claim skill in. 5 medicinal herb.

Who left his own way to keep me company,
And in discourse I find him much desirous
To see your castle. He hath deserv'd it, sir,
If ye please to grant it.

Ver. With all my heart, sir.
Yet there 's an article between; I must know
Your country; we use not to give survey
Of our chief strengths to strangers; our citadels
Are plac'd conspicuous to outward view,
On promonts'[6] tops, but within our secrets.

Als. A Valencian, sir.

Ver. A Valencian?
That 's native, sir. Of what name, I beseech you?

Als. Alsemero, sir.

Ver. Alsemero? Not the son
Of John de Alsemero?

Als. The same, sir.

Ver. My best love bids you welcome.

Beat. He was wont
To call me so, and then he speaks a most
Unfeign'd truth.

Ver. O sir, I knew your father;
We two were in acquaintance long ago,
Before our chins were worth iulan[7] down,
And so continued till the stamp of time
Had coin'd us into silver. Well, he 's gone;
A good soldier went with him.

Als. You went together in that, sir.

Ver. No, by Saint Jacques, I came behind him;
Yet I 've done somewhat too: an unhappy day
Swallowed him at last at Gibraltar,
In fight with those rebellious Hollanders.
Was it not so?

Als. Whose death I had reveng'd,
Or followed him in fate, had not the late league
Prevented me.

Ver. Aye, aye, 't was time to breathe.—
O Joanna, I should ha' told thee news;
I saw Piracquo lately.

Beat. (*Aside.*) That 's ill news.

Ver. He 's hot preparing for this day of triumph:
Thou must be a bride within this seven-night.

Als. (*Aside.*) Ha!

Beat. Nay, good sir, be not so violent; with speed
I cannot render satisfaction
Unto the dear companion of my soul,
Virginity, whom I thus long have liv'd with,
And part with it so rude and suddenly.
Can such friends divide, never to meet again,
Without a solemn farewell?

Ver. Tush, tush! there 's a toy.[8]

Als. (*Aside.*) I must now part, and never meet again
With any joy on earth.—Sir, your pardon;
My affairs call on me.

Ver. How, sir? By no means:
Not chang'd so soon, I hope? You must see my castle,
And her best entertainment, e'er we part;
I shall think myself unkindly us'd else.
Come, come, let 's on; I had good hope your stay
Had been a while with us in Alicant;
I might have bid you to my daughter's wedding.

Als. (*Aside.*) He means to feast me, and poisons me beforehand.—
I should be dearly glad to be there, sir,
Did my occasions suit as I could wish.

Beat. I shall be sorry if you be not there
When it is done, sir; but not so suddenly.

Ver. I tell you, sir, the gentleman 's complete,
A courtier and a gallant, enricht
With many fair and noble ornaments;
I would not change him for a son-in-law
For any he in Spain, the proudest he,
And we have great ones, that you know.

Als. He 's much
Bound to you, sir.

Ver. He shall be bound to me
As fast as this tie can hold him; I 'll want
My will else.

Beat. (*Aside.*) I shall want mine, if you do it.

Ver. But come, by the way I 'll tell you more of him.

Als. (*Aside.*) How shall I dare to venture in his castle,
When he discharges murderers[9] at the gate?
But I must on, for back I cannot go.

Beat. (*Aside.*) Not this serpent gone yet?

(*Drops a glove.*)

6 promontories'. 7 Of the first growth of the beard. (N.E.D.) 8 whim. 9 small cannon.

Ver. Look, girl, thy glove 's fallen.
Stay, stay; De Flores, help a little.
Exeunt Vermandero, Alsemero, and Servants.

De F. Here, lady.
(*Offers her the glove.*)

Beat. Mischief on your officious forwardness;
Who bade you stoop? They touch my hand no more:
There! For t' other's sake I part with this:
(*Takes off and throws down the other glove.*)
Take 'em, and draw thine own skin off with 'em!
Exit with Diaphanta and Servants.

De F. Here 's a favor come with a mischief now! I know
She had rather wear my pelt tann'd in a pair
Of dancing pumps, than I should thrust my fingers
Into her sockets here. I know she hates me,
Yet cannot choose but love her. No matter,
If but to vex her, I will haunt her still;
Though I get nothing else, I 'll have my will.
Exit.

SCENE 2. *A room in the house of Alibius.*

Enter Alibius and Lollio.

Alib. Lollio, I must trust thee with a secret,
But thou must keep it.

Lol. I was ever close to a secret, sir.

Alib. The diligence that I have found in thee,
The care and industry already past,
Assures me of thy good continuance.
Lollio, I have a wife.

Lol. Fie, sir, 't is too late to keep her secret; she 's known to be married all the town and country over.

Alib. Thou goest too fast, my Lollio. That knowledge
I allow no man can be barr'd it;
But there is a knowledge which is nearer,
Deeper, and sweeter, Lollio.

Lol. Well, sir, let us handle that between you and I.

Alib. 'T is that I go about, man. Lollio,
My wife is young.

Lol. So much the worse to be kept secret, sir.

Alib. Why, now thou meet'st the substance of the point;
I am old, Lollio.

Lol. No, sir, 't is I am old Lollio.

Alib. Yet why may not this concord and sympathize?
Old trees and young plants often grow together,
Well enough agreeing.

Lol. Aye, sir, but the old trees raise themselves higher and broader than the young plants.

Alib. Shrewd application! There 's the fear, man;
I would wear my ring on my own finger;
Whilst it is borrowed, it is none of mine,
But his that useth it.

Lol. You must keep it on still then; if it but lie by, one or other will be thrusting into 't.

Alib. Thou conceiv'st me, Lollio; here thy watchful eye
Must have employment; I cannot always be
At home.

Lol. I dare swear you cannot.

Alib. I must look out.

Lol. I know 't, you must look out; 't is every man's case.

Alib. Here, I do say, must thy employment be;
To watch her treadings, and in my absence
Supply my place.

Lol. I 'll do my best, sir; yet surely I cannot see who you should have cause to be jealous of.

Alib. Thy reason for that, Lollio? It is
A comfortable question.

Lol. We have but two sorts of people in the house, and both under the whip, that 's fools [10] and madmen; the one has not wit enough to be knaves, and the other not knavery enough to be fools.

Alib. Aye, those are all my patients, Lollio;
I do profess the cure of either sort;
My trade, my living 't is; I thrive by it;
But here 's the care that mixes with my thrift:
The daily visitants, that come to see
My brain-sick patients, I would not have
To see my wife. Gallants I do observe
Of quick enticing eyes, rich in habits,
Of stature and proportion very comely:
These are most shrewd temptations, Lollio.

Lol. They may be easily answered, sir; if

10 idiots.

they come to see the fools and madmen, you and I may serve the turn, and let my mistress alone; she 's of neither sort.

Alib. 'T is a good ward;[11] indeed, come they to see
Our madmen or our fools, let 'em see no more
Than what they come for; by that consequent
They must not see her; I 'm sure she 's no fool.

Lol. And I 'm sure she 's no madman.

Alib. Hold that buckler fast; Lollio, my trust
Is on thee, and I account it firm and strong.
What hour is 't, Lollio?

Lol. Towards belly-hour, sir.

Alib. Dinner-time? Thou mean'st twelve o'clock?

Lol. Yes, sir, for every part has his hour: we wake at six and look about us, that 's eye hour; at seven we should pray, that 's knee-hour: at eight walk, that 's leg-hour; at nine gather flowers and pluck a rose, that 's nose-hour; at ten we drink, that 's mouth-hour; at eleven lay about us for victuals, that 's hand-hour; at twelve go to dinner, that 's belly-hour.

Alib. Profoundly, Lollio! It will be long
Ere all thy scholars learn this lesson, and
I did look to have a new one ent'red;—stay,
I think my expectation is come home.

Enter Pedro, and Antonio disguised as an idiot.

Ped. Save you, sir; my business speaks itself:
This sight takes off the labor of my tongue.

Alib. Aye, aye, sir, it is plain enough, you mean
Him for my patient.

Ped. And if your pains prove but commodious, to give but some little strength to his sick and weak part of nature in him, these are (*Gives him money.*) but patterns to show you of the whole pieces that will follow to you, beside the charge of diet, washing, and other necessaries, fully defrayed.

Alib. Believe it, sir, there shall no care be wanting.

Lol. Sir, an officer in this place may deserve something. The trouble will pass through my hands.

Ped. 'T is fit something should come to your hands then, sir.
(*Gives him money.*)

Lol. Yes, sir, 't is I must keep him sweet, and read to him: what is his name?

Ped. His name is Antonio; marry, we use but half to him, only Tony.

Lol. Tony, Tony, 't is enough, and a very good name for a fool.—What 's your name, Tony?

Ant. He, he, he! well, I thank you, cousin; he, he, he!

Lol. Good boy! hold up your head.—He can laugh; I perceive by that he is no beast.

Ped. Well, sir,
If you can raise him but to any height,
Any degree of wit; might he attain,
As I might say, to creep on but all four
Towards the chair of wit, or walk on crutches,
'T would add an honor to your worthy pains,
And a great family might pray for you,
To which he should be heir, had he discretion
To claim and guide his own. Assure you, sir,
He is a gentleman.

Lol. Nay, there 's nobody doubted that; at first sight I knew him for a gentleman, he looks no other yet.

Ped. Let him have good attendance and sweet lodging.

Lol. As good as my mistress lies in, sir; and as you allow us time and means, we can raise him to the higher degree of discretion.

Ped. Nay, there shall no cost want, sir.

Lol. He will hardly be stretcht up to the wit of a magnifico.

Ped. O no, that 's not to be expected; far shorter will be enough.

Lol. I 'll warrant you I 'll make him fit to bear office in five weeks; I 'll undertake to wind him up to the wit of constable.

Ped. If it be lower than that, it might serve turn.

Lol. No, fie; to level him with a headborough,[12] beadle, or watchman, were but little better than he is. Constable I 'll able[13] him; if he do come to be a justice afterwards, let him thank the keeper: or I 'll go further with you; say I do bring him up to my own pitch, say I make him as wise as myself.

Ped. Why, there I would have it.

Lol. Well, go to; either I 'll be as arrant a

11 guard (in fencing). 12 constable. 13 fit him for.

fool as he, or he shall be as wise as I, and then I think 't will serve his turn.

Ped. Nay, I do like thy wit passing well.

Lol. Yes, you may; yet if I had not been a fool, I had had more wit than I have too. Remember what state you found me in.

Ped. I will, and so leave you. Your best cares, I beseech you.

Exit Pedro.

Alib. Take you none with you, leave 'em all with us.

Ant. O, my cousin 's gone! cousin, cousin, O!

Lol. Peace, peace, Tony; you must not cry, child, you must be whipt if you do; your cousin is here still; I am your cousin, Tony.

Ant. He, he! then I 'll not cry, if thou be'st my cousin; he, he, he!

Lol. I were best try his wit a little, that I may know what form [14] to place him in.

Alib. Aye, do, Lollio, do.

Lol. I must ask him easy questions at first.—Tony, how many true [15] fingers has a tailor on his right hand?

Ant. As many as on his left, cousin.

Lol. Good: and how many on both?

Ant. Two less than a deuce, cousin.

Lol. Very well answered. I come to you again, cousin Tony; how many fools goes to a wise man?

Ant. Forty in a day sometimes, cousin.

Lol. Forty in a day? How prove you that?

Ant. All that fall out amongst themselves, and go to a lawyer to be made friends.

Lol. A parlous fool! he must sit in the fourth form at least. I perceive that.—I come again, Tony; how many knaves make an honest man?

Ant. I know not that, cousin.

Lol. No, the question is too hard for you. I 'll tell you, cousin; there 's three knaves may make an honest man,—a sergeant, a jailor, and a beadle; the sergeant catches him, the jailor holds him, and the beadle lashes him; and if he be not honest then, the hangman must cure him.

Ant. Ha, ha, ha! that 's fine sport, cousin.

Alib. This was too deep a question for the fool, Lollio.

Lol. Yes, this might have serv'd yourself, though I say 't.—Once more and you shall go play, Tony.

Ant. Aye, play at push-pin,[16] cousin; ha, he!

Lol. So thou shalt: say how many fools are here——

Ant. Two, cousin; thou and I.

Lol. Nay, you 're too forward there, Tony. Mark my question; how many fools and knaves are here; a fool before a knave, a fool behind a knave, between every two fools a knave; how many fools, how many knaves?

Ant. I never learnt so far, cousin.

Alib. Thou puttest too hard questions to him, Lollio.

Lol. I 'll make him understand it easily.—Cousin, stand there.

Ant. Aye, cousin.

Lol. Master, stand you next the fool.

Alib. Well, Lollio.

Lol. Here 's my place. Mark now, Tony, there 's a fool before a knave.

Ant. That 's I, cousin.

Lol. Here 's a fool behind a knave, that 's I; and between us two fools there is a knave, that 's my master, 't is but we three, that 's all.

Ant. We three, we three, cousin.

1 Mad. (*Within.*) Put 's head i' th' pillory, the bread 's too little.

2 Mad. (*Within.*) Fly, fly, and he catches the swallow.

3 Mad. (*Within.*) Give her more onion, or the devil put the rope about her crag.[17]

Lol. You may hear what time of day it is, the chimes of Bedlam goes.

Alib. Peace, peace, or the wire [18] comes!

3 Mad. (*Within.*) Cat whore, cat whore! her permasant, her permasant! [19]

Alib. Peace, I say!—Their hour 's come, they must be fed, Lollio.

Lol. There 's no hope of recovery of that Welsh madman; was undone by a mouse that spoil'd him a permasant; lost his wits for 't.

Alib. Go to your charge, Lollio; I 'll to mine.

Lol. Go you to your madmen's ward, let me alone with your fools.

Alib. And remember my last charge, Lollio.

Exit.

Lol. Of which your patients do you think I am? Come, Tony, you must amongst your school-fellows now; there 's pretty scholars amongst 'em, I can tell you; there 's some of 'em at *stultus, stulta, stultum.*

Ant. I would see the madmen, cousin, if they would not bite me.

14 class.
15 honest.
16 a child's game.
17 neck.
18 whip made of wire.
19 Parmesan cheese.

Lol. No, they shall not bite thee, Tony.
Ant. They bite when they are at dinner, do they not, coz?
Lol. They bite at dinner, indeed, Tony. Well, I hope to get credit by thee; I like thee the best of all the scholars that ever I brought up, and thou shalt prove a wise man, or I 'll prove a fool myself.
Exeunt.

ACT II.

SCENE 1. *An apartment in the Castle.*

Enter Beatrice and Jasperino severally.

Beat. O sir, I'm ready now for that fair service
Which makes the name of friend sit glorious on you!
Good angels and this conduct be your guide!
(*Giving a paper.*)
Fitness of time and place is there set down, sir.
Jas. The joy I shall return rewards my service.
Exit.
Beat. How wise is Alsemero in his friend!
It is a sign he makes his choice with judgment;
Then I appear in nothing more approv'd
Than making choice of him; for 't is a principle,
He that can choose
That bosom well who of his thoughts partakes,
Proves most discreet in every choice he makes.
Methinks I love now with the eyes of judgment,
And see the way to merit, clearly see it.
A true deserver like a diamond sparkles;
In darkness you may see him, that 's in absence,
Which is the greatest darkness falls on love;
Yet is he best discern'd then
With intellectual eyesight. What 's Piracquo,
My father spends his breath for? And his blessing
Is only mine as I regard his name,
Else it goes from me, and turns head against me,
Transform'd into a curse. Some speedy way
Must be rememb'red. He 's so forward too,
So urgent that way, scarce allows me breath
To speak to my new comforts.

Enter De Flores.

De F. (*Aside.*) Yonder 's she;
Whatever ails me, now a-late especially,
I can as well be hang'd as refrain seeing her;
Some twenty times a day, nay, not so little,
Do I force errands, frame ways and excuses,
To come into her sight; and I 've small reason for 't,
And less encouragement, for she baits me still
Every time worse than other; does profess herself
The cruellest enemy to my face in town;
At no hand can abide the sight of me,
As if danger or ill-luck hung in my looks.
I must confess my face is bad enough,
But I know far worse has better fortune,
And not endur'd alone, but doted on;
And yet such pick-hair'd [20] faces, chins like witches',
Here and there five hairs whispering in a corner,
As if they grew in fear one of another,
Wrinkles like troughs, where swine-deformity swills
The tears of perjury, that lie there like wash
Fallen from the slimy and dishonest eye,—
Yet such a one plucks sweets without restraint,
And has the grace of beauty to his sweet.
Though my hard fate has thrust me out to servitude,
I tumbled into th' world a gentleman.
She turns her blessed eye upon me now,
And I 'll endure all storms before I part with 't.
Beat. (*Aside.*) Again?
This ominous ill-fac'd fellow more disturbs me
Than all my other passions.
De F. (*Aside.*) Now 't begins again;
I 'll stand this storm of hail, though the stones pelt me.
Beat. Thy business? What 's thy business?
De F. (*Aside.*) Soft and fair!
I cannot part so soon now.

[20] thin-bearded.

Beat. (*Aside.*) The villain 's fixt.—
Thou standing toad-pool——
De F. (*Aside.*) The shower falls amain now.
Beat. Who sent thee? What 's thy errand? Leave my sight!
De F. My lord your father charg'd me to deliver
A message to you.
Beat. What, another since?
Do 't, and be hang'd then; let me be rid of thee.
De F. True service merits mercy.
Beat. What 's thy message?
De F. Let beauty settle but in patience,
You shall hear all.
Beat. A dallying, trifling torment!
De F. Signor Alonzo de Piracquo, lady,
Sole brother to Tomaso de Piracquo——
Beat. Slave, when wilt make an end?
De F. Too soon I shall.
Beat. What all this while of him?
De F. The said Alonzo,
With the foresaid Tomaso——
Beat. Yet again?
De F. Is new alighted.
Beat. Vengeance strike the news!
Thou thing most loath'd, what cause was there in this
To bring thee to my sight?
De F. My lord your father
Charg'd me to seek you out.
Beat. Is there no other
To send his errand by?
De F. It seems 't is my luck
To be i' th' way still.
Beat. Get thee from me!
De F. So:—
(*Aside.*) Why, am not I an ass to devise ways
Thus to be rail'd at? I must see her still!
I shall have a mad qualm within this hour again,
I know 't; and, like a common Garden-bull,[21]
I do but take breath to be lugg'd [22] again.
What this may bode I know not; I 'll despair the less,
Because there 's daily precedents of bad faces
Belov'd beyond all reason. These foul chops
May come into favor one day 'mongst their fellows.
Wrangling has prov'd the mistress of good pastime;
As children cry themselves asleep, I ha' seen
Women have chid themselves a-bed to men.
Exit.
Beat. I never see this fellow but I think
Of some harm towards me; danger 's in my mind still;
I scarce leave trembling of an hour after.
The next good mood I find my father in,
I 'll get him quite discarded. O, I was
Lost in this small disturbance, and forgot
Affliction's fiercer torrent that now comes
To bear down all my comforts!

Enter Vermandero, Alonzo, and Tomaso.

Ver. You 're both welcome,
But an especial one belongs to you, sir,
To whose most noble name our love presents
Th' addition of a son, our son Alonzo.
Alon. The treasury of honor cannot bring forth
A title I should more rejoice in, sir.
Ver. You have improv'd it well.—Daughter, prepare;
The day will steal upon thee suddenly.
Beat. (*Aside.*) Howe'er, I will be sure to keep the night,
If it should come so near me.
(*Beatrice and Vermandero talk apart.*)
Tom. Alonzo?
Alon. Brother?
Tom. In troth I see small welcome in her eye.
Alon. Fie, you are too severe a censurer
Of love in all points, there 's no bringing on you.
If lovers should mark everything a fault,
Affection would be like an ill-set book,
Whose faults might prove as big as half the volume.
Beat. That 's all I do entreat.
Ver. It is but reasonable;
I 'll see what my son says to 't.—Son Alonzo,
Here is a motion made but to reprieve
A maidenhead three days longer; the request
Is not far out of reason, for indeed
The former time is pinching.
Alon. Though my joys
Be set back so much time as I could wish
They had been forward, yet since she desires it,
The time is set as pleasing as before,
I find no gladness wanting.

21 The sport of bull-baiting was carried on in Paris Garden on the Bankside. 22 dragged by the ear.

Ver. May I ever
Meet it in that point still! You 're nobly welcome, sirs.
Exit with Beatrice.
Tom. So; did you mark the dulness of her parting now?
Alon. What dulness? Thou art so exceptious still!
Tom. Why, let it go then; I am but a fool
To mark your harms so heedfully.
Alon. Where 's the oversight?
Tom. Come, your faith 's cozened in her, strongly cozened.
Unsettle your affection with all speed
Wisdom can bring it to; your peace is ruin'd else.
Think what a torment 't is to marry one
Whose heart is leapt into another's bosom:
If ever pleasure she receive from thee,
It comes not in thy name, or of thy gift;
She lies but with another in thine arms,
He the half-father unto all thy children
In the conception; if he get 'em not,
She helps to get 'em for him; and how dangerous
And shameful her restraint may go in time to,
It is not to be thought on without sufferings.
Alon. You speak as if she lov'd some other, then.
Tom. Do you apprehend so slowly?
Alon. Nay, an that
Be your fear only, I am safe enough.
Preserve your friendship and your counsel, brother,
For times of more distress; I should depart
An enemy, a dangerous, deadly one,
To any but thyself, that should but think
She knew the meaning of inconstancy,
Much less the use and practice: yet we 're friends.
Pray, let no more be urg'd; I can endure
Much, till I meet an injury to her,
Then I am not myself. Farewell, sweet brother;
How much we 're bound to Heaven to depart lovingly. *Exit.*
Tom. Why, here is love's tame madness; thus a man
Quickly steals into his vexation.
Exit.

SCENE 2. *Another apartment in the Castle.*

Enter Diaphanta and Alsemero.

Dia. The place is my charge; you have kept your hour,
And the reward of a just meeting bless you!
I hear my lady coming. Complete gentleman,
I dare not be too busy with my praises,
They 're dangerous things to deal with.
Exit.
Als. This goes well;
These women are the ladies' cabinets,
Things of most precious trust are lockt into 'em.

Enter Beatrice.

Beat. I have within mine eye all my desires.
Requests that holy prayers ascend Heaven for,
And brings 'em down to furnish our defects,
Come not more sweet to our necessities
Than thou unto my wishes.
Als. We 're so like
In our expressions, lady, that unless I borrow
The same words, I shall never find their equals.
Beat. How happy were this meeting, this embrace,
If it were free from envy! This poor kiss
It has an enemy, a hateful one,
That wishes poison to 't. How well were I now,
If there were none such name known as Piracquo,
Nor no such tie as the command of parents!
I should be but too much bless'd.
Als. One good service
Would strike off both your fears, and I 'll go near 't too,
Since you are so distrest. Remove the cause,
The command ceases; so there 's two fears blown out
With one and the same blast.
Beat. Pray, let me find you,[23] sir:
What might that service be, so strangely happy?
Als. The honorablest piece about man, valor:
I 'll send a challenge to Piracquo instantly.
Beat. How? Call you that extinguishing of fear,

23 get your meaning.

When 't is the only way to keep it flaming?
Are not you ventured in the action,
That 's all my joys and comforts? Pray, no more, sir.
Say you prevail'd, you 're danger's and not mine then;
The law would claim you from me, or obscurity
Be made the grave to bury you alive.
I 'm glad these thoughts come forth; O, keep not one
Of this condition, sir! Here was a course
Found to bring sorrow on her way to death;
The tears would ne'er ha' dried, till dust had chok'd 'em.
Blood-guiltiness becomes a fouler visage;—
(*Aside.*) And now I think on one; I was to blame,
I ha' marr'd so good a market with my scorn;
'T had been done questionless: the ugliest creature
Creation fram'd for some use: yet to see
I could not mark so much where it should be!

Als. Lady——

Beat. (*Aside.*) Why, men of art make much of poison,
Keep one to expel another. Where was my art?

Als. Lady, you hear not me.

Beat. I do especially, sir.
The present times are not so sure of our side
As those hereafter may be; we must use 'em then
As thrifty folks their wealth, sparingly now,
Till the time opens.

Als. You teach wisdom, lady.

Beat. Within there! Diaphanta!

Re-enter Diaphanta.

Dia. Do you call, madam?

Beat. Perfect your service, and conduct this gentleman
The private way you brought him.

Dia. I shall, madam.

Als. My love 's as firm as love e'er built upon.

Exit with Diaphanta.

Enter De Flores.

De F. (*Aside.*) I've watcht this meeting, and do wonder much
What shall become of t' other; I 'm sure both
Cannot be serv'd unless she transgress; haply
Then I 'll put in for one; for if a woman
Fly from one point, from him she makes a husband,
She spreads and mounts then like arithmetic;
One, ten, a hundred, a thousand, ten thousand,
Proves in time sutler to an army royal.
Now do I look to be most richly rail'd at,
Yet I must see her.

Beat. (*Aside.*) Why, put case I loath'd him
As much as youth and beauty hates a sepulchre,
Must I needs show it? Cannot I keep that secret,
And serve my turn upon him? See, he 's here.—
De Flores.

De F. (*Aside.*) Ha, I shall run mad with joy!
She call'd me fairly by my name De Flores,
And neither rogue nor rascal.

Beat. What ha' you done
To your face a' late? You 've met with some good physician;
You 've prun'd[24] yourself, methinks: you were not wont
To look so amorously.

De F. Not I;—
(*Aside.*) 'T is the same physnomy, to a hair and pimple,
Which she called scurvy scarce an hour ago:
How is this?

Beat. Come hither; nearer, man.

De F. (*Aside.*) I 'm up to the chin in Heaven!

Beat. Turn, let me see;
Faugh, 't is but the heat of the liver, I perceive 't;
I thought it had been worse.

De F. (*Aside.*) Her fingers toucht me!
She smells all amber.[25]

Beat. I 'll make a water for you shall cleanse this
Within a fortnight.

De F. With your own hands, lady?

Beat. Yes, mine own, sir; in a work of cure
I 'll trust no other.

De F. (*Aside.*) 'T is half an act of pleasure

24 preened, trimmed.

25 ambergris.

To hear her talk thus to me.
Beat. When we 're us'd
To a hard face, it is not so unpleasing:
It mends still in opinion, hourly mends;
I see it by experience.
De F. (*Aside.*) I was blest
To light upon this minute; I 'll make use on 't.
Beat. Hardness becomes the visage of a man well;
It argues service, resolution, manhood,
If cause were of employment.
De F. 'T would be soon seen
If e'er your ladyship had cause to use it;
I would but wish the honor of a service
So happy as that mounts to.
Beat. We shall try you.—
O my De Flores!
De F. (*Aside.*) How 's that? She calls me hers
Already! *My* De Flores!—You were about
To sigh out somewhat, madam?
Beat. No, was I?
I forgot,—O!——
De F. There 't is again, the very fellow on 't.
Beat. You are too quick, sir.
De F. There 's no excuse for 't now; I heard it twice, madam;
That sigh would fain have utterance: take pity on 't,
And lend it a free word. 'Las, how it labors
For liberty! I hear the murmur yet
Beat at your bosom.
Beat. Would creation——
De F. Aye, well said, that is it.
Beat. Had form'd me man!
De F. Nay, that 's not it.
Beat. O, 't is the soul of freedom!
I should not then be forc'd to marry one
I hate beyond all depths; I should have power
Then to oppose my loathings, nay, remove 'em
For ever from my sight.
De F. (*Aside.*) O blest occasion!——
Without change to your sex you have your wishes;
Claim so much man in me.
Beat. In thee, De Flores?
There is small cause for that.
De F. Put it not from me,
It is a service that I kneel for to you.
(*Kneels.*)
Beat. You are too violent to mean faithfully.
There 's horror in my service, blood, and danger;
Can those be things to sue for?
De F. If you knew
How sweet it were to me to be employed
In any act of yours, you would say then
I fail'd, and us'd not reverence enough
When I receive[d] the charge on 't.
Beat. (*Aside.*) This is much,
Methinks; belike his wants are greedy; and
To such gold tastes like angel's food. Rise.
De F. I 'll have the work first.
Beat. (*Aside.*) Possible his need
Is strong upon him.—There 's to encourage thee;
(*Gives money.*)
As thou art forward, and thy service dangerous,
Thy reward shall be precious.
De F. That I 've thought on;
I have assur'd myself of that beforehand,
And know it will be precious; the thought ravishes!
Beat. Then take him to thy fury!
De F. I thirst for him.
Beat. Alonzo de Piracquo.
De F. (*Rising.*) His end 's upon him;
He shall be seen no more.
Beat. How lovely now
Dost thou appear to me! Never was man
Dearlier rewarded.
De F. I do think of that.
Beat. Be wondrous careful in the execution.
De F. Why, are not both our lives upon the cast?
Beat. Then I throw all my fears upon thy service.
De F. They ne'er shall rise to hurt you.
Beat. When the deed 's done,
I 'll furnish thee with all things for thy flight;
Thou may'st live bravely in another country.
De F. Aye, aye;
We 'll talk of that hereafter.
Beat. (*Aside.*) I shall rid myself
Of two inveterate loathings at one time,
Piracquo, and his dog-face.
Exit.
De F. O my blood!
Methinks I feel her in mine arms already;
Her wanton fingers combing out this beard,

And, being pleased, praising this bad face.
Hunger and pleasure, they'll commend sometimes
Slovenly dishes, and feed heartily on 'em.
Nay, which is stranger, refuse daintier for 'em:
Some women are odd feeders.—I am too loud.
Here comes the man goes supperless to bed,
Yet shall not rise to-morrow to his dinner.

Enter Alonzo.

Alon. De Flores.
De F. My kind, honorable lord?
Alon. I'm glad I ha' met with thee.
De F. Sir?
Alon. Thou canst show me
The full strength of the castle?
De F. That I can, sir.
Alon. I much desire it.
De F. And if the ways and straits
Of some of the passages be not too tedious for you,
I'll assure you, worth your time and sight, my lord.
Alon. Pooh, that shall be no hindrance.
De F. I'm your servant, then.
'T is now near dinner-time; 'gainst your lordship's rising
I'll have the keys about me.
Alon. Thanks, kind De Flores.
De F. (*Aside.*) He's safely thrust upon me beyond hopes.

Exeunt.

ACT III.

SCENE 1. *A narrow passage in the Castle.*

Enter Alonzo and De Flores. In the act-time[26] *De Flores hides a naked rapier.*

De Flores. Yes, here are all the keys; I was afraid, my lord,
I'd wanted for the postern, this is it.
I've all, I've all, my lord: this for the sconce.[27]
Alon. 'T is a most spacious and impregnable fort.
De F. You'll tell me more, my lord. This descent
Is somewhat narrow, we shall never pass
Well with our weapons, they'll but trouble us.
Alon. Thou sayest true.
De F. Pray, let me help your lordship.
Alon. 'T is done: thanks, kind De Flores.
De F. Here are hooks, my lord,
To hang such things on purpose.
(*Hanging up his own sword and that of Alonzo.*)
Alon. Lead, I'll follow thee.

Exeunt.

SCENE 2. *A vault.*

Enter Alonzo and De Flores.

De F. All this is nothing; you shall see anon
A place you little dream on.
Alon. I am glad
I have this leisure; all your master's house
Imagine I ha' taken a gondola.
De F. All but myself, sir,—(*Aside.*) which makes up my safety.
My lord, I'll place you at a casement here
Will show you the full strength of all the castle.
Look, spend your eye awhile upon that object.
Alon. Here's rich variety, De Flores.
De F. Yes, sir.
Alon. Goodly munition.
De F. Aye, there's ordnance, sir,
No bastard metal, will ring you a peal like bells
At great men's funerals. Keep your eye straight, my lord;
Take special notice of that sconce before you,
There you may dwell awhile.
(*Takes the rapier which he had hid behind the door.*)
Alon. I am upon 't.
De F. And so am I.
(*Stabs him.*)
Alon. De Flores! O De Flores!
Whose malice hast thou put on?
De F. Do you question
A work of secrecy? I must silence you.
(*Stabs him.*)
Alon. O, O, O!
De F. I must silence you.
(*Stabs him.*)
So here's an undertaking well accomplish'd.
This vault serves to good use now: ha, what's that
Threw sparkles in my eye? O, 't is a diamond

[26] between the acts.

[27] small fort.

He wears upon his finger; 't was well found;
This will approve the work.[28] What, so fast on?
Not part in death? I'll take a speedy course then.
Finger and all shall off. (*Cuts off the finger.*) So, now, I'll clear
The passages from all suspect or fear.
Exit with body.

SCENE 3. *An apartment in the house of Alibius.*

Enter Isabella and Lollio.

Isa. Why, sirrah, whence have you commission
To fetter the doors against me?
If you keep me in a cage, pray, whistle to me,
Let me be doing something.

Lol. You shall be doing, if it please you; I'll whistle to you, if you'll pipe after.

Isa. Is it your master's pleasure, or your own,
To keep me in this pinfold?[29]

Lol. 'T is for my master's pleasure, lest being taken in another man's corn, you might be pounded[30] in another place.

Isa. 'T is very well, and he'll prove very wise.

Lol. He says you have company enough in the house, if you please to be sociable, of all sorts of people.

Isa. Of all sorts? Why, here's none but fools and madmen.

Lol. Very well: and where will you find any other, if you should go abroad? There's my master and I to boot too.

Isa. Of either sort one, a madman and a fool.

Lol. I would ev'n participate of both then if I were as you; I know you're half mad already, be half foolish too.

Isa. You're a brave saucy rascal! Come on, sir,
Afford me then the pleasure of your bedlam.
You were commending once to-day to me
Your last-come lunatic; what a proper[31]
Body there was without brains to guide it,
And what a pitiful delight appear'd
In that defect, as if your wisdom had found
A mirth in madness; pray, sir, let me partake,
If there be such a pleasure.

Lol. If I do not show you the handsomest, discreetest madman, one that I may call the understanding madman, then say I am a fool.

Isa. Well, a match, I will say so.

Lol. When you have had a taste of the madman, you shall, if you please, see Fool's College, o' th' other side. I seldom lock there; 't is but shooting a bolt or two, and you are amongst 'em. (*Exit. Enter presently.*)—Come on, sir; let me see how handsomely you'll behave yourself now.

Enter Franciscus.

Fran. How sweetly she looks! O, but there's a wrinkle in her brow as deep as philosophy. Anacreon, drink to my mistress' health, I'll pledge it. Stay, stay, there's a spider in the cup! No, 't is but a grape-stone; swallow it, fear nothing, poet; so, so, lift higher.

Isa. Alack, alack, it is too full of pity
To be laught at! How fell he mad?
Canst thou tell?

Lol. For love, mistress. He was a pretty poet, too, and that set him forwards first; the muses then forsook him; he ran mad for a chambermaid, yet she was but a dwarf neither.

Fran. Hail, bright Titania!
Why stand'st thou idle on these flow'ry banks?
Oberon is dancing with his Dryades;
I'll gather daisies, primrose, violets,
And bind them in a verse of poesy.

Lol. (*Holding up a whip.*) Not too near! You see your danger.

Fran. O, hold thy hand, great Diomede!
Thou feed'st thy horses well, they shall obey thee:
Get up, Bucephalus kneels.
(*Kneels.*)

Lol. You see how I awe my flock; a shepherd has not his dog at more obedience.

Isa. His conscience is unquiet; sure that was
The cause of this: a proper gentleman!

Fran. Come hither, Æsculapius; hide the poison.

Lol. Well, 't is hid.
(*Hides the whip.*)

Fran. Didst thou ne'er hear of one Tiresias,
A famous poet?

Lol. Yes, that kept tame wild geese.

Fran. That's he; I am the man.

28 prove that the work has been done. (Bullen.)
29 a pound for confining stray cattle.
30 confined in a pound.
31 handsome.

Lol. No?

Fran. Yes; but make no words on 't. I was a man
Seven years ago.

Lol. A stripling, I think, you might.

Fran. Now I 'm a woman, all feminine.

Lol. I would I might see that!

Fran. Juno struck me blind.

Lol. I 'll ne'er believe that; for a woman, they say, has an eye more than a man.

Fran. I say she struck me blind.

Lol. And Luna made you mad: you have two trades to beg with.

Fran. Luna is now big-bellied, and there 's room
For both of us to ride with Hecate;
I 'll drag thee up into her silver sphere,
And there we 'll kick the dog—and beat the bush[32]—
That barks against the witches of the night;
The swift lycanthropi[33] that walks the round,
We 'll tear their wolvish skins, and save the sheep.
(*Attempts to seize Lollio.*)

Lol. Is 't come to this? Nay, then, my poison comes forth again. (*Showing the whip.*) Mad slave, indeed, abuse your keeper!

Isa. I prithee, hence with him, now he grows dangerous.

Fran. (*Sings.*)
Sweet love, pity me,
Give me leave to lie with thee.

Lol. No, I 'll see you wiser first. To your own kennel!

Fran. No noise, she sleeps; draw all the curtains round,
Let no soft sound molest the pretty soul
But love, and love creeps in at a mouse-hole.

Lol. I would you would get into your hole! (*Exit Franciscus.*)—Now, mistress, I will bring you another sort; you shall be fool'd another while. (*Exit, and brings in Antonio.*)—Tony, come hither, Tony: look who 's yonder, Tony.

Ant. Cousin, is it not my aunt?[34]

Lol. Yes, 't is one of 'em, Tony.

Ant. He, he! how do you, uncle?

Lol. Fear him not, mistress, 't is a gentle nigget;[35] you may play with him, as safely with him as with his bauble.

Isa. How long hast thou been a fool?

Ant. Ever since I came hither, cousin.

Isa. Cousin? I 'm none of thy cousins, fool.

Lol. O, mistress, fools have always so much wit as to claim their kindred.

Madman. (*Within.*) Bounce, bounce! he falls, he falls!

Isa. Hark you, your scholars in the upper room
Are out of order.

Lol. Must I come amongst you there?—Keep you the fool, mistress; I 'll go up and play left-handed Orlando amongst the madmen.

Exit.

Isa. Well, sir.

Ant. 'T is opportuneful now, sweet lady! nay,
Cast no amazing eye upon this change.

Isa. Ha!

Ant. This shape of folly shrouds your dearest love,
The truest servant to your powerful beauties,
Whose magic had this force thus to transform me.

Isa. You 're a fine fool indeed!

Ant. O, 't is not strange!
Love has an intellect that runs through all
The scrutinous[36] sciences; and, like a cunning poet,
Catches a quantity of every knowledge,
Yet brings all home into one mystery,
Into one secret that he proceeds in.

Isa. You 're a parlous fool.

Ant. No danger in me; I bring nought but love
And his soft-wounding shafts to strike you with.
Try but one arrow; if it hurt you, I
Will stand you twenty back in recompense.
(*Kisses her.*)

Isa. A forward fool too!

Ant. This was love's teaching:
A thousand ways he fashion'd out my way,
And this I found the safest and the nearest,
To tread the galaxia to my star.

Isa. Profound withal! certain you dream'd of this,
Love never taught it waking.

Ant. Take no acquaintance
Of these outward follies, there 's within
A gentleman that loves you.

Isa. When I see him,
I 'll speak with him; so, in the meantime, keep

---

32 the dog and the thorn bush belonging to the man in the moon.
33 afflicted with *lycanthropia*, or wolf-madness. Cf. *Duchess of Malfi*, V. ii.
34 bawd.
35 idiot.
36 exact.

Your habit, it becomes you well enough.
As you 're a gentleman, I 'll not discover you;
That 's all the favor that you must expect.
When you are weary, you may leave the school,
For all this while you have but play'd the fool.

Re-enter Lollio.

Ant. And must again.—He, he! I thank you, cousin;
I 'll be your valentine to-morrow morning.

Lol. How do you like the fool, mistress?

Isa. Passing well, sir.

Lol. Is he not witty, pretty well, for a fool?

Isa. If he holds on as he begins, he 's like
To come to something.

Lol. Aye, thank a good tutor. You may put him to 't; he begins to answer pretty hard questions.—Tony, how many is five times six?

Ant. Five times six is six times five.

Lol. What arithmetician could have answer'd better? How many is one hundred and seven?

Ant. One hundred and seven is seven hundred and one, cousin.

Lol. This is no wit to speak on!—Will you be rid of the fool now?

Isa. By no means; let him stay a little.

Madman. (*Within.*) Catch there, catch the last couple in hell! [37]

Lol. Again! must I come amongst you? Would my master were come home! I am not able to govern both these wards together. *Exit.*

Ant. Why should a minute of love's hour be lost?

Isa. Fie, out again! I had rather you kept
Your other posture; you become not your tongue
When you speak from [38] your clothes.

Ant. How can he freeze
Lives near so sweet a warmth? Shall I alone
Walk through the orchard of th' Hesperides,
And, cowardly, not dare to pull an apple?

Enter Lollio above.

This with the red cheeks I must venture for.

(*Attempts to kiss her.*)

Isa. Take heed, there 's giants keep 'em.

Lol. (*Aside.*) How now, fool, are you good at that? Have you read Lipsius? [39] He 's past *Ars Amandi;* I believe I must put harder questions to him, I perceive that.

Isa. You 're bold without fear too.

Ant. What should I fear,
Having all joys about me? Do you smile,
And love shall play the wanton on your lip,
Meet and retire, retire and meet again;
Look you but cheerfully, and in your eyes
I shall behold mine own deformity,
And dress myself up fairer. I know this shape
Becomes me not, but in those bright mirrors
I shall array me handsomely.

(*Cries of madmen are heard within, some as birds, others as beasts.*)

Lol. Cuckoo, cuckoo! *Exit, above.*

Ant. What are these?

Isa. Of fear enough to part us;
Yet are they but our schools of lunatics,
That act their fantasies in any shapes,
Suiting their present thoughts: if sad, they cry;
If mirth be their conceit, they laugh again:
Sometimes they imitate the beasts and birds,
Singing or howling, braying, barking; all
As their wild fancies prompt 'em.

Enter Lollio.

Ant. These are no fears.

Isa. But here 's a large one, my man.

Ant. Ha, he! that 's fine sport, indeed, cousin.

Lol. I would my master were come home! 'T is too much for one shepherd to govern two of these flocks; nor can I believe that one churchman can instruct two benefices at once; there will be some incurable mad of the one side, and very fools on the other.—Come, Tony.

Ant. Prithee, cousin, let me stay here still.

37 An allusion to the game of barley-break, the ground for which was divided into three compartments, of which the middle one was termed "hell." (Ellis.)

38 foreign to.

39 A Flemish scholar of the sixteenth century; introduced only for the pun on *lip.*

Lol. No, you must to your book now; you have play'd sufficiently.
Isa. Your fool has grown wondrous witty.
Lol. Well, I'll say nothing: but I do not think but he will put you down one of these days.
Exit with Antonio.
Isa. Here the restrained current might make breach,
Spite of the watchful bankers. Would a woman stray,
She need not gad abroad to seek her sin,
It would be brought home one way or another:
The needle's point will to the fixed north;
Such drawing arctics women's beauties are.

Re-enter Lollio.

Lol. How dost thou, sweet rogue?
Isa. How now?
Lol. Come, there are degrees; one fool may be better than another.
Isa. What's the matter?
Lol. Nay, if thou giv'st thy mind to fool's flesh, have at thee!
Isa. You bold slave, you!
Lol. I could follow now as t' other fool did:
"What should I fear,
Having all joys about me? Do you but smile,
And love shall play the wanton on your lip,
Meet and retire, retire and meet again;
Look you but cheerfully, and in your eyes
I shall behold my own deformity,
And dress myself up fairer. I know this shape
Becomes me not—"
And so as it follows: but is not this the most foolish way? Come, sweet rogue; kiss me, my little Lacedæmonian; let me feel how thy pulses beat. Thou hast a thing about thee would do a man pleasure, I'll lay my hand on 't.
Isa. Sirrah, no more! I see you have discovered
This love's knight errant, who hath made adventure
For purchase[40] of my love: be silent, mute,
Mute as a statue, or his injunction
For me enjoying, shall be to cut thy throat;
I'll do it, though for no other purpose; and
Be sure he'll not refuse it.
Lol. My share, that's all;
I'll have my fool's part with you.
Isa. No more! Your master.

Enter Alibius.

Alib. Sweet, how dost thou?
Isa. Your bounden servant, sir.
Alib. Fie, fie, sweetheart, no more of that.
Isa. You were best lock me up.
Alib. In my arms and bosom, my sweet Isabella,
I'll lock thee up most nearly.—Lollio,
We have employment, we have task in hand.
At noble Vermandero's, our castle's captain,
There is a nuptial to be solemniz'd—
Beatrice-Joanna, his fair daughter, bride,—
For which the gentleman hath bespoke our pains,
A mixture of our madmen and our fools,
To finish, as it were, and make the fag[41]
Of all the revels, the third night from the first;
Only an unexpected passage over,
To make a frightful pleasure, that is all,
But not the all I aim at. Could we so act it,
To teach it in a wild distracted measure,
Though out of form and figure, breaking time's head,
It were no matter, 't would be heal'd again
In one age or other, if not in this:
This, this, Lollio, there's a good reward begun,
And will beget a bounty, be it known.
Lol. This is easy, sir, I'll warrant you: you have about you fools and madmen that can dance very well; and 't is no wonder, your best dancers are not the wisest men; the reason is, with often jumping they jolt their brains down into their feet, that their wits lie more in their heels than in their heads.
Alib. Honest Lollio, thou giv'st me a good reason,
And a comfort in it.
Isa. You've a fine trade on 't.
Madmen and fools are a staple commodity.
Alib. O wife, we must eat, wear clothes, and live.
Just at the lawyer's haven we arrive,
By madmen and by fools we both do thrive. *Exeunt.*

40 winning.

41 end.

SCENE 4. *An apartment in the Castle.*

Enter Vermandero, Beatrice, Alsemero, and Jasperino.

Ver. Valencia speaks so nobly of you, sir,
I wish I had a daughter now for you.
Als. The fellow of this creature were a partner
For a king's love.
Ver. I had her fellow once, sir,
But Heaven has married her to joys eternal;
'T were sin to wish her in this vale again.
Come, sir, your friend and you shall see the pleasures
Which my health chiefly joys in.
Als. I hear
The beauty of this seat largely commended.
Ver. It falls much short of that.
Exit with Alsemero and Jasperino.
Beat. So, here 's one step
Into my father's favor; time will fix him;
I've got him now the liberty of the house.
So wisdom, by degrees, works out her freedom;
And if that eye be dark'ned that offends me,—
I wait but that eclipse,—this gentleman
Shall soon shine glorious in my father's liking,
Through the refulgent virtue of my love.

Enter De Flores.

De F. (*Aside.*) My thoughts are at a banquet; for the deed,
I feel no weight in 't; 't is but light and cheap
For the sweet recompense that I set down for 't.
Beat. De Flores?
De F. Lady?
Beat. Thy looks promise cheerfully.
De F. All things are answerable, time, circumstance,
Your wishes, and my service.
Beat. Is it done, then?
De F. Piracquo is no more.
Beat. My joys start at mine eyes; our sweet'st delights
Are evermore born weeping.
De F. I've a token for you.
Beat. For me?
De F. But it was sent somewhat unwillingly;
I could not get the ring without the finger.
(*Produces the finger and ring.*)
Beat. Bless me, what hast thou done?
De F. Why, is that more
Than killing the whole man? I cut his heart-strings;
A greedy hand thrust in a dish at court,
In a mistake hath had as much as this.
Beat. 'T is the first token my father made me send him.
De F. And I have made him send it back again
For his last token. I was loth to leave it,
And I 'm sure dead men have no use of jewels;
He was as loth to part with 't, for it stuck
As if the flesh and it were both one substance.
Beat. At the stag's fall, the keeper has his fees;
'T is soon appli'd, all dead men's fees are yours, sir.
I pray, bury the finger, but the stone
You may make use on shortly; the true value,
Take 't of my truth, is near three hundred ducats.
De F. 'T will hardly buy a capcase [42] for one's conscience though,
To keep it from the worm, as fine as 't is.
Well, being my fees, I 'll take it;
Great men have taught me that, or else my merit
Would scorn the way on 't.
Beat. It might justly, sir.
Why, thou mistak'st, De Flores; 't is not given
In state [43] of recompense.
De F. No, I hope so, lady;
You should soon witness my contempt to 't then.
Beat. Prithee,—thou look'st as if thou wert offended.
De F. That were strange, lady; 't is not possible
My service should draw such a cause from you.
Offended! Could you think so? That were much
For one of my performance, and so warm
Yet in my service.
Beat. 'T were misery in me to give you cause, sir.
De F. I know so much, it were so; misery
In her most sharp condition.
Beat. 'T is resolv'd then;
Look you, sir, here 's three thousand golden florins;

[42] casket.

[43] instead of.

I have not meanly thought upon thy merit.

De F. What! salary? Now you move me.

Beat. How, De Flores?

De F. Do you place me in the rank of verminous fellows,
To destroy things for wages? Offer gold
For the life-blood of man? Is anything
Valued too precious for my recompense?

Beat. I understand thee not.

De F. I could ha' hir'd
A journeyman in murder at this rate,
And mine own conscience might have [slept at ease],[44]
And have had the work brought home.

Beat. (*Aside.*) I'm in a labyrinth;
What will content him? I'd fain be rid of him.—
I'll double the sum, sir.

De F. You take a course
To double my vexation, that's the good you do.

Beat. (*Aside.*) Bless me, I'm now in worse plight than I was;
I know not what will please him.—For my fear's sake,
I prithee, make away with all speed possible;
And if thou be'st so modest not to name
The sum that will content thee, paper blushes not,
Send thy demand in writing, it shall follow thee;
But, prithee, take thy flight.

De F. You must fly too, then.

Beat. I?

De F. I'll not stir a foot else.

Beat. What's your meaning?

De F. Why, are not you as guilty? In, I'm sure,
As deep as I; and we should stick together.
Come, your fears counsel you but ill; my absence
Would draw suspect upon you instantly;
There were no rescue for you.

Beat. (*Aside.*) He speaks home!

De F. Nor is it fit we two, engag'd so jointly,
Should part and live asunder.

Beat. How now, sir?
This shows not well.

De F. What makes your lip so strange?
This must not be 'twixt us.

Beat. The man talks wildly!

De F. Come, kiss me with a zeal now.

Beat. (*Aside.*) Heaven, I doubt him!

De F. I will not stand so long to beg 'em shortly.

Beat. Take heed, De Flores, of forgetfulness,
'T will soon betray us.

De F. Take you heed first;
Faith, you're grown much forgetful, you're to blame in 't.

Beat. (*Aside.*) He's bold, and I am blam'd for 't.

De F. I have eas'd you
Of your trouble, think on it; I am in pain,
And must be eas'd of[45] you; 't is a charity:
Justice invites your blood to understand me.

Beat. I dare not.

De F. Quickly!

Beat. O, I never shall!
Speak it yet further off, that I may lose
What has been spoken, and no sound remain on 't;
I would not hear so much offence again
For such another deed.

De F. Soft, lady, soft!
The last is not yet paid for. O, this act
Has put me into spirit; I was as greedy on 't
As the parcht earth of moisture, when the clouds weep.
Did you not mark, I wrought myself into 't,
Nay, su'd and kneel'd for 't? Why was all that pains took?
You see I've thrown contempt upon your gold;
Not that I want it not, for I do piteously,
In order I'll come unto 't, and make use on 't,
But 't was not held so precious to begin with,
For I place wealth after the heels of pleasure;
And were not I resolv'd in my belief
That thy virginity were perfect in thee,
I should but take my recompense with grudging,
As if I had but half my hopes I agreed for.

Beat. Why, 't is impossible thou canst be so wicked,
Or shelter such a cunning cruelty,
To make his death the murderer of my honor!
Thy language is so bold and vicious,
I cannot see which way I can forgive it
With any modesty.

[44] Added in an edition of 1816.

[45] by.

De F. Pish! you forget yourself;
A woman dipt in blood, and talk of modesty!

Beat. O misery of sin! would I'd been bound
Perpetually unto my living hate
In that Piracquo, than to hear these words!
Think but upon the distance that creation
Set 'twixt thy blood and mine, and keep thee there.

De F. Look but into your conscience, read me there;
'T is a true book, you'll find me there your equal.
Pish! fly not to your birth, but settle you
In what the act has made you; you're no more now.
You must forget your parentage to me;
You're the deed's creature; by that name
You lost your first condition, and I challenge you,
As peace and innocency has turn'd you out,
And made you one with me.

Beat. With thee, foul villain!

De F. Yes, my fair murd'ress. Do you urge me,
Though thou writ'st maid, thou whore in thy affection?
'T was chang'd from thy first love, and that's a kind
Of whoredom in thy heart; and he's chang'd now
To bring thy second on, thy Alsemero,
Whom, by all sweets that ever darkness tasted,
If I enjoy thee not, thou ne'er enjoy'st!
I'll blast the hopes and joys of marriage,
I'll confess all; my life I rate at nothing.

Beat. De Flores!

De F. I shall rest from all love's plagues then;
I live in pain now; that shooting eye
Will burn my heart to cinders.

Beat. O sir, hear me!

De F. She that in life and love refuses me,
In death and shame my partner she shall be.

Beat. (*Kneeling.*) Stay, hear me once for all; I make thee master
Of all the wealth I have in gold and jewels;
Let me go poor unto my bed with honor,
And I am rich in all things!

De F. Let this silence thee:
The wealth of all Valencia shall not buy
My pleasure from me;
Can you weep Fate from its determin'd purpose?
So soon may you weep me.

Beat. Vengeance begins;
Murder, I see, is followed by more sins.
Was my creation in the womb so curst,
It must engender with a viper first?

De F. (*Raising her.*) Come, rise and shroud your blushes in my bosom;
Silence is one of pleasure's best receipts:
Thy peace is wrought for ever in this yielding.
'Las! how the turtle pants! Thou'lt love anon
What thou so fear'st and faint'st to venture on.

Exeunt.

ACT IV.

Dumb Show.

Enter Gentlemen, Vermandero meeting them with action of wonderment at the flight of Piracquo. Enter Alsemero with Jasperino and gallants: Vermandero points to him, the gentlemen seeming to applaud the choice. Alsemero, Jasperino, and Gentlemen; Beatrice the bride following in great state. accompanied with Diaphanta, Isabella, and other gentlewomen; De Flores after all, smiling at the accident: Alonzo's ghost appears to De Flores in the midst of his smile, startles him, showing him the hand whose finger he had cut off. They pass over in great solemnity.

SCENE 1. *Alsemero's apartment in the Castle.*

Enter Beatrice.

Beat. This fellow has undone me endlessly;
Never was bride so fearfully distrest.
The more I think upon th' ensuing night,
And whom I am to cope with in embraces,
One who's ennobled both in blood and mind,
So clear in understanding,—that's my plague now—
Before whose judgment will my fault appear
Like malefactors' crimes before tribunals,
There is no hiding on 't, the more I dive
Into my own distress. How a wise man
Stands for a great calamity! There's no venturing
Into his bed, what course soe'er I light upon,

Without my shame, which may grow up
to danger.
He cannot but in justice strangle me
As I lie by him; as a cheater use me;
'T is a precious craft to play with a false
die
Before a cunning gamester. Here 's his
closet;
The key left in 't, and he abroad i' th'
park!
Sure 't was forgot; I 'll be so bold as look
in 't.

(*Opens closet.*)

Bless me! a right physician's closet 't is,
Set round with vials; every one her
mark too.
Sure he does practise physic for his own
use,
Which may be safely call'd your great
man's wisdom.
What manuscript lies here? "The Book
of Experiment,
Call'd Secrets in Nature." So 't is: 't is
so.

(*Reads.*)

"How to know whether a woman be with
child or no."
I hope I am not yet; if he should try
though!
Let me see (*reads*) "folio forty-five,"
here 't is,
The leaf tuckt down upon 't, the place
suspicious.

(*Reads.*)

"If you would know whether a woman be with child or not, give her two spoonfuls of the white water in glass C—"
Where 's that glass C? O yonder, I see 't
now— (*reads*) "and if she be with child, she sleeps full twelve hours after; if not, not:"
None of that water comes into my belly;
I 'll know you from a hundred; I could
break you now,
Or turn you into milk, and so beguile
The master of the mystery; but I 'll look
to you.
Ha! that which is next is ten times worse:

(*Reads.*)

"How to know whether a woman be a maid or not:"
If that should be appli'd, what would be-
come of me?
Belike he has a strong faith of my purity,
That never yet made proof; but this he
calls

(*Reads.*)

"A merry slight,[46] but true experiment; the author Antonius Mizaldus. Give the party you suspect the quantity of a spoonful of the water in the glass M, which, upon her that is a maid, makes three several effects; 't will make her incontinently [47] gape, then fall into a sudden sneezing, last into a violent laughing; else, dull, heavy, and lumpish."
Where had I been?
I fear it, yet 't is seven hours to bed-time.

Enter Diaphanta.

Dia. Cuds, madam, are you here?
Beat. Seeing that wench now,
A trick comes in my mind; 't is a nice
piece
Gold cannot purchase. (*Aside.*)—I come
hither, wench,
To look my lord.
Dia. Would I had such a cause
To look him too!—Why, he 's i' th' park,
madam.
Beat. There let him be.
Dia. Aye, madam, let him compass
Whole parks and forests, as great rangers
do,
At roosting-time a little lodge can hold
'em.
Earth-conquering Alexander, that
thought the world
Too narrow for him, in th' end had but
his pit-hole.
Beat. I fear thou art not modest, Dia-
phanta.
Dia. Your thoughts are so unwilling to be
known, madam.
'T is ever the bride's fashion, toward bed-
time,
To set light by her joys, as if she ow'd
'em not.
Beat. Her joys? Her fears thou wouldst
say.
Dia. Fear of what?
Beat. Art thou a maid, and talk'st so to a
maid?
You leave a blushing business behind;
Beshrew your heart for 't!
Dia. Do you mean good sooth, madam?
Beat. Well, if I 'd thought upon the fear
at first,
Man should have been unknown.
Dia. Is 't possible?
Beat. I 'd give a thousand ducats to that
woman
Would try what my fear were, and tell
me true
To-morrow, when she gets from 't; as she
likes,

46 trick.

47 immediately.

I might perhaps be drawn to 't.

Dia. Are you in earnest?

Beat. Do you get the woman, then challenge me,
And see if I'll fly from 't; but I must tell you
This by the way, she must be a true maid;
Else there 's no trial, my fears are not her's else.

Dia. Nay, she that I would put into your hands, madam,
Shall be a maid.

Beat. You know I should be sham'd else,
Because she lies for me.

Dia. 'T is a strange humor!
But are you serious still? Would you resign
Your first night's pleasure, and give money too?

Beat. As willingly as live.—(*Aside.*) Alas, the gold
Is but a by-bet to wedge in the honor!

Dia. I do not know how the world goes abroad
For faith or honesty; there 's both requir'd in this.
Madam, what say you to me, and stray no further?
I've a good mind, in troth, to earn your money.

Beat. You are too quick, I fear, to be a maid.

Dia. How? Not a maid? Nay, then you urge me, madam;
Your honorable self is not a truer,
With all your fears upon you—

Beat. (*Aside.*) Bad enough then.

Dia. Then I with all my lightsome joys about me.

Beat. I'm glad to hear 't. Then you dare put your honesty [48]
Upon an easy trial.

Dia. Easy? Anything.

Beat. I'll come to you straight.
(*Goes to the closet.*)

Dia. She will not search me, will she,
Like the forewoman of a female jury?

Beat. Glass M: aye, this is it. (*Brings vial.*) Look, Diaphanta,
You take no worse than I do.
(*Drinks.*)

Dia. And in so doing,
I will not question what it is, but take it.
(*Drinks.*)

Beat. (*Aside.*) Now if th' experiment be true, 't will praise itself,
And give me noble ease: begins already;
(*Diaphanta gapes.*)
There 's the first symptom; and what haste it makes
To fall into the second, there by this time!
(*Diaphanta sneezes.*)
Most admirable secret! on the contrary,
It stirs not me a whit, which most concerns it.

Dia. Ha, ha, ha!

Beat. (*Aside.*) Just in all things, and in order
As if 't were circumscrib'd; one accident [49]
Gives way unto another.

Dia. Ha, ha, ha!

Beat. How now, wench?

Dia. Ha, ha, ha! I'm so—so light
At heart—ha, ha, ha!—so pleasurable!
But one swig more, sweet madam.

Beat. Aye, to-morrow,
We shall have time to sit by 't.

Dia. Now I'm sad [50] again.

Beat. (*Aside.*) It lays itself so gently too!—Come, wench.
Most honest Diaphanta I dare call thee now.

Dia. Pray, tell me, madam, what trick call you this?

Beat. I'll tell thee all hereafter; we must study
The carriage of this business.

Dia. I shall carry 't well,
Because I love the burthen.

Beat. About midnight
You must not fail to steal forth gently,
That I may use the place.

Dia. O, fear not, madam,
I shall be cool by that time. The bride's place,
And with a thousand ducats! I'm for a justice now,
I bring a portion [51] with me; I scorn small fools.

Exeunt.

SCENE 2. *Another apartment in the Castle.*

Enter Vermandero and Servant.

Ver. I tell thee, knave, mine honor is in question,
A thing till now free from suspicion,
Nor ever was there cause. Who of my gentlemen
Are absent? Tell me, and truly, how many and who?

Ser. Antonio, sir, and Franciscus.

Ver. When did they leave the castle?

[48] chastity. [49] symptom. [50] serious. [51] *i. e.* marriage portion.

Ser. Some ten days since, sir; the one intending to
Briamata, th' other for Valencia.
Ver. The time accuses 'em; a charge of murder
Is brought within my castle-gate, Piracquo's murder;
I dare not answer[52] faithfully their absence.
A strict command of apprehension[53]
Shall pursue 'em suddenly, and either wipe
The stain off clear, or openly discover[54] it.
Provide me winged warrants for the purpose.
Exit Servant.
See, I am set on again.

Enter Tomaso.

Tom. I claim a brother of you.
Ver. You 're too hot;
Seek him not here.
Tom. Yes, 'mongst your dearest bloods,
If my peace find no fairer satisfaction.
This is the place must yield account for him,
For here I left him; and the hasty tie
Of this snatcht marriage gives strong testimony
Of his most certain ruin.
Ver. Certain falsehood!
This is the place indeed; his breach of faith
Has too much marr'd both my abused love,
The honorable love I reserv'd for him,
And mockt my daughter's joy; the prepar'd morning
Blusht at his infidelity; he left
Contempt and scorn to throw upon those friends
Whose belief hurt 'em. O, 't was most ignoble
To take his flight so unexpectedly,
And throw such public wrongs on those that lov'd him!
Tom. Then this is all your answer?
Ver. 'T is too fair
For one of his alliance; and I warn you
That this place no more see you.
Exit.

Enter De Flores.

Tom. The best is,
There is more ground to meet a man's revenge on.—
Honest De Flores?
De F. That 's my name indeed.
Saw you the bride? Good sweet sir, which way took she?
Tom. I 've blest mine eyes from seeing such a false one.
De F. (*Aside.*) I 'd fain get off, this man 's not for my company;
I smell his brother's blood when I come near him.
Tom. Come hither, kind and true one; I remember
My brother lov'd thee well.
De F. O, purely, dear sir!—
(*Aside.*) Methinks I 'm now again a-killing on him,
He brings it so fresh to me.
Tom. Thou canst guess, sirrah—
An honest friend has an instinct of jealousy—
At some foul guilty person.
De F. Alas! sir,
I am so charitable, I think none
Worse than myself! You did not see the bride then?
Tom. I prithee, name her not: is she not wicked?
De F. No, no; a pretty, easy, round-packt sinner,
As your most ladies are, else you might think
I flattered her; but, sir, at no hand wicked,
Till they 're so old their chins and noses[55] meet,
And they salute witches. I 'm call'd, I think, sir.—
(*Aside.*) His company ev'n overlays my conscience.
Exit.
Tom. That De Flores has a wondrous honest heart!
He 'll bring it out in time, I 'm assur'd on 't.
O, here 's the glorious master of the day's joy!
'T will not be long till he and I do reckon.—

Enter Alsemero.

Sir.
Als. You 're most welcome.
Tom. You may call that word back;
I do not think I am, nor wish to be.
Als. 'T is strange you found the way to this house, then.
Tom. Would I 'd ne'er known the cause! I 'm none of those, sir,

52 account for.
53 arrest.
54 reveal.
55 Dyce's correction for the quarto reading *sins and vices*.

That come to give you joy, and swill your wine;
'T is a more precious liquor that must lay
The fiery thirst I bring.

Als. Your words and you
Appear to me great strangers.

Tom. Time and our swords
May make us more acquainted. This the business:
I should have had a brother in your place;
How treachery and malice have dispos'd of him,
I 'm bound to inquire of him which holds his right,
Which never could come fairly.

Als. You must look
To answer for that word, sir.

Tom. Fear you not,
I 'll have it ready drawn at our next meeting.
Keep your day solemn; farewell, I disturb it not;
I 'll bear the smart with patience for a time.

Exit.

Als. 'T is somewhat ominous this; a quarrel ent'red
Upon this day; my innocence relieves me,

Enter Jasperino.

I should be wondrous sad else.—Jasperino,
I 've news to tell thee, strange news.

Jas. I ha' some too
I think as strange as yours. Would I might keep
Mine, so my faith and friendship might be kept in 't!
Faith, sir, dispense a little with my zeal,
And let it cool in this.

Als. This puts me on,
And blames thee for thy slowness.

Jas. All may prove nothing,
Only a friendly fear that leapt from me, sir.

Als. No question, 't may prove nothing; let 's partake it though.

Jas. 'T was Diaphanta's chance—for to that wench
I pretend [56] honest love, and she deserves it—
To leave me in a back part of the house,
A place we chose for private conference.
She was no sooner gone, but instantly
I heard your bride's voice in the next room to me;
And lending more attention, found De Flores
Louder than she.

Als. De Flores! Thou art out now.

Jas. You 'll tell me more anon.

Als. Still I 'll prevent [57] thee,
The very sight of him is poison to her.

Jas. That made me stagger too; but Diaphanta
At her return confirm'd it.

Als. Diaphanta!

Jas. Then fell we both to listen, and words past
Like those that challenge interest in a woman.

Als. Peace: quench thy zeal, 't is dangerous to thy bosom.

Jas. Then truth is full of peril.

Als. Such truths are.
O, were she the sole glory of the earth,
Had eyes that could shoot fire into king's breasts,
And toucht,[58] she sleeps not here! Yet I have time,
Though night be near, to be resolv'd hereof;
And, prithee, do not weigh me by my passions.

Jas. I never weigh'd friend so.

Als. Done charitably!
That key will lead thee to a pretty secret,
(*Giving key.*)
By a Chaldean taught me, and I have
My study upon some. Bring from my closet
A glass inscrib'd there with the letter M,
And question not my purpose.

Jas. It shall be done, sir.

Exit.

Als. How can this hang together? Not an hour since
Her woman came pleading her lady's fears,
Deliver'd her for the most timorous virgin
That ever shrunk at man's name, and so modest,
She charg'd her weep out her request to me,
That she might come obscurely to my bosom.

Enter Beatrice.

Beat. (*Aside.*) All things go well; my woman's preparing yonder
For her sweet voyage, which grieves me to lose;
Necessity compels it; I lose all, else.

56 profess. 57 anticipate. 58 polluted.

Als. (*Aside.*) Pish! modesty's shrine is set in yonder forehead:
I cannot be too sure though.—My Joanna!

Beat. Sir, I was bold to weep a message to you;
Pardon my modest fears.

Als. The dove 's not meeker;
(*Aside.*) She 's abus'd, questionless.

Re-enter Jasperino with vial.

O, are you come, sir?

Beat. (*Aside.*) The glass, upon my life!
I see the letter.

Jas. Sir, this is M. (*Giving vial.*)

Als. 'T is it.

Beat. (*Aside.*) I am suspected.

Als. How fitly our bride comes to partake with us!

Beat. What is 't, my lord?

Als. No hurt.

Beat. Sir, pardon me,
I seldom taste of any composition.

Als. But this, upon my warrant, you shall venture on.

Beat. I fear 't will make me ill.

Als. Heaven forbid that.

Beat. (*Aside.*) I 'm put now to my cunning: th' effects I know,
If I can now but feign 'em handsomely.
(*Drinks.*)

Als. It has that secret virtue, it ne'er mist, sir,
Upon a virgin.

Jas. Treble-qualitied?
(*Beatrice gapes and sneezes.*)

Als. By all that 's virtuous it takes there! proceeds!

Jas. This is the strangest trick to know a maid by.

Beat. Ha, ha, ha!
You have given me joy of heart to drink, my lord.

Als. No, thou hast given me such joy of heart,
That never can be blasted.

Beat. What 's the matter, sir?

Als. (*Aside.*) See now 't is settled in a melancholy;
Keeps both the time and method.—My Joanna,
Chaste as the breath of Heaven, or morning's womb,
That brings the day forth! thus my love encloses thee.

Exeunt.

Scene 3. *A room in the house of Alibius.*

Enter Isabella and Lollio.

Isa. O Heaven! is this the waning moon?
Does love turn fool, run mad, and all at once?
Sirrah, here 's a madman, akin to the fool too,
A lunatic lover.

Lol. No, no, not he I brought the letter from?

Isa. Compare his inside with his out, and tell me.

Lol. The out 's mad, I 'm sure of that; I had a taste on 't. (*Reads letter.*) "To the bright Andromeda, chief chambermaid to the Knight of the Sun, at the sign of Scorpio, in the middle region, sent by the bellows-mender of Æolus. Pay the post." This is stark madness!

Isa. Now mark the inside. (*Takes the letter and reads.*) "Sweet lady, having now cast off this counterfeit cover of a madman, I appear to your best judgment a true and faithful lover of your beauty."

Lol. He is mad still.

Isa. (*Reads.*) "If any fault you find, chide those perfections in you which have made me imperfect; 't is the same sun that causeth to grow and enforceth to wither—"

Lol. O rogue!

Isa. (*Reads.*) "Shapes and transhapes, destroys and builds again. I come in winter to you, dismantled of my proper ornaments; by the sweet splendor of your cheerful smiles, I spring and live a lover."

Lol. Mad rascal still!

Isa. (*Reads.*) "Tread him not under foot, that shall appear an honor to your bounties. I remain—mad till I speak with you, from whom I expect my cure, yours all, or one beside himself, Franciscus."

Lol. You are like to have a fine time on 't. My master and I may give over our professions; I do not think but you can cure fools and madmen faster than we, with little pains too.

Isa. Very likely.

Lol. One thing I must tell you, mistress: you perceive that I am privy to your skill; if I find you minister once, and set up the trade, I put in for my thirds; I shall be mad or fool else.

Isa. The first place is thine, believe it, Lollio,
If I do fall.

Lol. I fall upon you.
Isa. So.
Lol. Well, I stand to my venture.
Isa. But thy counsel now; how shall I deal with 'em?
Lol. Why, do you mean to deal with 'em?
Isa. Nay, the fair understanding,[59] how to use 'em.
Lol. Abuse[60] 'em! That 's the way to mad the fool, and make a fool of the madman, and then you use 'em kindly.
Ia. 'T is easy, I 'll practise; do thou observe it.
The key of thy wardrobe.
Lol. There (*Gives key.*); fit yourself for 'em, and I 'll fit 'em both for you.
Isa. Take thou no further notice than the outside.
Exit.
Lol. Not an inch; I 'll put you to the inside.

Enter Alibius.

Alib. Lollio, art there? Will all be perfect, think'st thou?
To-morrow night, as if to close up the Solemnity, Vermandero expects us.
Lol. I mistrust the madmen most; the fools will do well enough; I have taken pains with them.
Alib. Tush! they cannot miss; the more absurdity.
The more commends it, so no rough behaviors
Affright the ladies; they 're nice[61] things, thou know'st.
Lol. You need not fear, sir; so long as we are there with our commanding pizzles,[62] they 'll be as tame as the ladies themselves.
Alib. I 'll see them once more rehearse before they go.
Lol. I was about it, sir: look you to the madmen's morris, and let me alone with the other. There is one or two that I mistrust their fooling; I 'll instruct them, and then they shall rehearse the whole measure.
Alib. Do so; I 'll see the music prepar'd: but, Lollio,
By the way, how does my wife brook her restraint?
Does she not grudge at it?
Lol. So, so; she takes some pleasure in the house, she would abroad else. You must allow her a little more length, she 's kept too short.
Alib. She shall along to Vermandero's with us,
That will serve her for a month's liberty.
Lol. What 's that on your face, sir?
Alib. Where, Lollio? I see nothing.
Lol. Cry you mercy,[63] sir, 't is your nose; it show'd like the trunk of a young elephant.
Alib. Away, rascal! I 'll prepare the music, Lollio.
Exit.
Lol. Do, sir, and I 'll dance the whilst.—Tony, where art thou, Tony?

Enter Antonio.

Ant. Here, cousin; where art thou?
Lol. Come, Tony, the footmanship I taught you.
Ant. I had rather ride, cousin.
Lol. Aye, a whip take you! but I 'll keep you out; vault in: look you, Tony; fa, la, la, la, la.
(*Dances.*)
Ant. Fa, la, la, la, la.
(*Sings and dances.*)
Lol. There, an honor.[64]
Ant. Is this an honor, coz?
Lol. Yes, an it please your worship.
Ant. Does honor bend in the hams, coz?
Lol. Marry does it, as low as worship, squireship, nay, yeomanry itself sometimes, from whence it first stiffened: there rise, a caper.
Ant. Caper after an honor, coz?
Lol. Very proper, for honor is but a caper, rises as fast and high, has a knee or two, and falls to th' ground again. You can remember your figure, Tony?
Ant. Yes, cousin; when I see thy figure, I can remember mine.
Exit Lollio.

Re-enter Isabella dressed as a madwoman.

Isa. Hey, how he treads the air! Shough, shough, t' other way! he burns his wings else. Here 's wax enough below, Icarus, more than will be cancelled these eighteen moons. He 's down, he 's down! what a terrible fall he had! Stand up, thou son of Cretan Daedalus,
And let us tread the lower labyrinth;
I 'll bring thee to the clue.
Ant. Prithee, coz, let me alone.
Isa. Art thou not drown'd?
About thy head I saw a heap of clouds
Wrapt like a Turkish turban; on thy back
A crookt chameleon-color'd rainbow hung
Like a tiara down unto thy hams.

59 take the words in their modest sense.
60 deceive.
61 delicate.
62 whips.
63 beg pardon.
64 bow.

Let me suck out those billows in thy belly;
Hark, how they roar and rumble in the straits![65]
Bless thee from the pirates!

Ant. Pox upon you, let me alone!

Isa. Why shouldst thou mount so high as Mercury,
Unless thou hadst reversion of his place?
Stay in the moon with me, Endymion,
And we will rule these wild rebellious waves,
That would have drown'd my love.

Ant. I'll kick thee, if
Again thou touch me, thou wild unshapen antic;
I am no fool, you bedlam!

Isa. But you are, as sure as I am, mad.
Have I put on this habit of a frantic,
With love as full of fury, to beguile
The nimble eye of watchful jealousy,
And am I thus rewarded?

Ant. Ha! dearest beauty!

Isa. No, I have no beauty now,
Nor ever had but what was in my garments.
You a quick-sighted lover! Come not near me:
Keep your caparisons, you're aptly clad;
I came a feigner, to return stark mad.
Exit.

Ant. Stay, or I shall change condition,
And become as you are.

Re-enter Lollio.

Lol. Why, Tony, whither now? Why fool—

Ant. Whose fool, usher of idiots? You coxcomb!
I have fool'd too much.

Lol. You were best be mad another while then.

Ant. So I am, stark mad; I have cause enough;
And I could throw the full effects on thee,
And beat thee like a fury.

Lol. Do not, do not; I shall not forbear the gentleman under the fool, if you do. Alas! I saw through your fox-skin before now! Come, I can give you comfort; my mistress loves you; and there is as arrant a madman i' th' house as you are a fool, your rival, whom she loves not. If after the masque we can rid her of him, you earn her love, she says, and the fool shall ride her.

Ant. May I believe thee?

Lol. Yes, or you may choose whether you will or no.

Ant. She's eas'd of him; I've a good quarrel on't.

Lol. Well, keep your old station yet, and be quiet.

Ant. Tell her I will deserve her love.
Exit.

Lol. And you are like to have your desert.

Enter Franciscus.

Fran. (*sings.*) "Down, down, down, a-down a-down,"—and then with a horse-trick
To kick Latona's forehead, and break her bow-string.

Lol. This is t' other counterfeit; I'll put him out of his humor. (*Aside. Takes out a letter and reads.*) "Sweet lady, having now cast this counterfeit cover of a madman, I appear to your best judgment a true and faithful lover of your beauty." This is pretty well for a madman.

Fran. Ha! what's that?

Lol. (*reads*) "Chide those perfections in you which have made me imperfect."

Fran. I am discover'd to the fool.

Lol. I hope to discover the fool in you ere I have done with you. (*Reads.*) "Yours all, or one beside himself, Franciscus." This madman will mend sure.

Fran. What do you read, sirrah?

Lol. Your destiny, sir; you'll be hang'd for this trick, and another that I know.

Fran. Art thou of counsel with thy mistress?

Lol. Next her apron-strings.

Fran. Give me thy hand.

Lol. Stay, let me put yours in my pocket first. (*Putting letter into his pocket.*) Your hand is true,[66] is it not? It will not pick?[67] I partly fear it, because I think it does lie.

Fran. Not in a syllable.

Lol. So if you love my mistress so well as you have handled the matter here, you are like to be cur'd of your madness.

Fran. And none but she can cure it.

Lol. Well, I'll give you over then, and she shall cast your water next.

Fran. Take for thy pains past.
(*Gives him money.*)

Lol. I shall deserve more, sir, I hope. My mistress loves you, but must have some proof of your love to her.

Fran. There I meet my wishes.

65 Q. *streets.* 66 honest. 67 steal.

Lol. That will not serve, you must meet her enemy and yours.

Fran. He 's dead already.

Lol. Will you tell me that, and I parted but now with him?

Fran. Show me the man.

Lol. Aye, that 's a right course now; see him before you kill him, in any case; and yet it needs not go so far neither. 'T is but a fool that haunts the house and my mistress in the shape of an idiot; bang but his fool's coat well-favoredly, and 't is well.

Fran. Soundly, soundly!

Lol. Only reserve him till the masque be past; and if you find him not now in the dance yourself, I 'll show you. In, in! my master!

Fran. He handles him like a feather. Hey!

Exit.

Enter Alibius.

Alib. Well said: in a readiness, Lollio?

Lol. Yes, sir.

Alib. Away then, and guide them in, Lollio:
Entreat your mistress to see this sight.
Hark, is there not one incurable fool
That might be begg'd?[68] I 've friends.

Lol. I have him for you,
One that shall deserve it too.

Alib. Good boy, Lollio!

(*The madmen and fools dance.*)

'T is perfect: well, fit but once these strains,
We shall have coin and credit for our pains.

Exeunt.

ACT V.

SCENE 1. *A gallery in the Castle.*

Enter Beatrice: a clock strikes one.

Beat. One struck, and yet she lies by 't!
O my fears!
This strumpet serves her own ends, 't is apparent now,
Devours the pleasure with a greedy appetite,
And never minds my honor or my peace,
Makes havoc of my right. But she pays dearly for 't;
No trusting of her life with such a secret
That cannot rule her blood to keep her promise;
Beside, I 've some suspicion of her faith to me,
Because I was suspected of my lord,
And it must come from her. (*Strikes two.*) Hark! by my horrors,
Another clock strikes two!

Enter De Flores.

De F. Pist! where are you?

Beat. De Flores?

De F. Aye. Is she not come from him yet?

Beat. As I 'm a living soul, not!

De F. Sure the devil
Hath sow'd his itch within her. Who would trust
A waiting-woman?

Beat. I must trust somebody.

De F. Pish! they 're termagants;
Especially when they fall upon their masters
And have their ladies' first fruits; they 're mad whelps
You cannot stave 'em off from game royal: then
You are so rash and hardy, ask no counsel;
And I could have helpt you to a 'pothecary's daughter
Would have fall'n off before eleven, and thankt you too.

Beat. O me, not yet; this whore forgets herself.

De F. The rascal fares so well: look, you 're undone;
The day-star, by this hand! see Phosphorus plain yonder.

Beat. Advise me now to fall upon some ruin;
There is no counsel safe else.

De F. Peace! I ha 't now,
For we must force a rising, there 's no remedy.

Beat. How? take heed of that.

De F. Tush! be you quiet, or else give over all.

Beat. Prithee, I ha' done then.

De F. This is my reach:[69] I 'll set
Some part a-fire of Diaphanta's chamber.

Beat. How? Fire, sir? That may endanger the whole house.

De F. You talk of danger when your fame 's on fire?

Beat. That 's true; do what thou wilt now.

De F. Pish! I aim
At a most rich success strikes all dead sure.

68 for the sake of the income from his estate.

69 device.

The chimney being a-fire, and some light parcels
Of the least danger in her chamber only,
If Diaphanta should be met by chance then
Far from her lodging, which is now suspicious,
It would be thought her fears and affrights then
Drove her to seek for succor; if not seen
Or met at all, as that 's the likeliest,
For her own shame she 'll hasten towards her lodging;
I will be ready with a piece[70] high-charg'd,
As 't were to cleanse the chimney, there 't is proper now
But she shall be the mark.

Beat. I 'm forc'd to love thee now,
'Cause thou provid'st so carefully for my honor.

De F. 'Slid, it concerns the safety of us both,
Our pleasure and continuance.

Beat. One word now,
Prithee; how for the servants?

De F. I 'll despatch them,
Some one way, some another in the hurry,
For buckets, hooks, ladders; fear not you,
The deed shall find its time; and I 've thought since
Upon a safe conveyance for the body too:
How this fire purifies wit! Watch you your minute.

Beat. Fear keeps my soul upon 't, I cannot stray from 't.

Enter Alonzo's Ghost.

De F. Ha! what art thou that tak'st away the light
Betwixt that star and me? I dread thee not.—
'T was but a mist of conscience; all 's clear again.

Exit.

Beat. Who 's that, De Flores? Bless me, it slides by!

Exit Ghost.

Some ill thing haunts the house; 't has left behind it
A shivering sweat upon me; I 'm afraid now.
This night hath been so tedious! O this strumpet!
Had she a thousand lives, he should not leave her
Till he had destroy'd the last. List! O my terrors!

(*Clock strikes three.*)

Three struck by St. Sebastian's!

Within. Fire, fire, fire!

Beat. Already? How rare is that man's speed!
How heartily he serves me! his face loathes one;
But look upon his care, who would not love him?
The east is not more beauteous than his service.

Within. Fire, fire, fire!

Re-enter De Flores: Servants pass over: bell rings.

De F. Away, despatch! hooks, buckets, ladders! that 's well said.[71]
The fire-bell rings; the chimney works, my charge;
The piece is ready.

Exit.

Beat. Here 's a man worth loving!

Enter Diaphanta.

O you 're a jewel!

Dia. Pardon frailty, madam;
In troth, I was so well, I ev'n forgot myself.

Beat. You 've made trim work!

Dia. What?

Beat. Hie quickly to your chamber;
Your reward follows you.

Dia. I never made
So sweet a bargain.

Exit.

Enter Alsemero.

Als. O my dear Joanna,
Alas! art thou risen too? I was coming,
My absolute treasure!

Beat. When I mist you,
I could not choose but follow.

Als. Thou 'rt all sweetness:
The fire is not so dangerous.

Beat. Think you so, sir?

Als. I prithee, tremble not; believe me, 't is not.

Enter Vermandero and Jasperino.

Ver. O bless my house and me!

Als. My lord your father.

Re-enter De Flores with a gun.

Ver. Knave, whither goes that piece?

De F. To scour the chimney.

Exit.

Ver. O, well said, well said!
That fellow 's good on all occasions.

70 gun.

71 well done.

Beat. A wondrous necessary man, my lord.
Ver. He hath a ready wit; he 's worth 'em all, sir;
Dog at a house of fire; I ha' seen him singed ere now.—
(*The piece goes off.*)
Ha, there he goes!
Beat. 'T is done!
Als. Come, sweet, to bed now;
Alas! thou wilt get cold.
Beat. Alas! the fear keeps that out!
My heart will find no quiet till I hear
How Diaphanta, my poor woman, fares;
It is her chamber, sir, her lodging chamber.
Ver. How should the fire come there?
Beat. As good a soul as ever lady countenanc'd,
But in her chamber negligent and heavy:
She scapt a mine twice.
Ver. Twice?
Beat. Strangely twice, sir.
Ver. Those sleepy sluts are dangerous in a house,
An they be ne'er so good.

Re-enter De Flores, with the body of Diaphanta.

De F. O poor virginity,
Thou hast paid dearly for 't!
Ver. Bless us, what 's that?
De F. A thing you all knew once, Diaphanta 's burnt.
Beat. My woman! O my woman!
De F. Now the flames
Are greedy of her; burnt, burnt, burnt to death, sir!
Beat. O my presaging soul!
Als. Not a tear more!
I charge you by the last embrace I gave you
In bed, before this rais'd us.
Beat. Now you tie me;
Were it my sister, now she gets no more.

Enter Servant.

Ver. How now?
Ser. All danger 's past; you may now take
Your rests, my lords; the fire is throughly quencht.
Ah, poor gentlewoman, how soon was she stifled!
Beat. De Flores, what is left of her inter,
And we as mourners all will follow her.
I will entreat that honor to my servant
Ev'n of my lord himself.
Als. Command it, sweetness.
Beat. Which of you spied the fire first?
De F. 'T was I, madam.
Beat. And took such pains in 't too? A double goodness!
'T were well he were rewarded.
Ver. He shall be.—
De Flores, call upon me.
Als. And upon me, sir.
Exeunt all except De Flores.
De F. Rewarded? Precious! here 's a trick beyond me.
I see in all bouts, both of sport and wit,
Always a woman strives for the last hit.
Exit.

SCENE 2. *Another apartment in the Castle.*

Enter Tomaso.

Tom. I cannot taste the benefits of life
With the same relish I was wont to do.
Man I grow weary of, and hold his fellowship
A treacherous bloody friendship; and because
I 'm ignorant in whom my wrath should settle,
I must think all men villains, and the next
I meet, whoe'er he be, the murderer
Of my most worthy brother. Ha! what 's he?
(*De Flores passes over the stage.*)
O, the fellow that some call honest De Flores;
But methinks honesty was hard bestead
To come there for a lodging; as if a queen
Should make her palace of a pest-house.
I find a contrariety in nature
Betwixt that face and me; the least occasion
Would give me game upon him; yet he 's so foul
One would scarce touch him with a sword he lov'd
And made account of; so most deadly venomous,
He would go near to poison any weapon
That should draw blood on him; one must resolve
Never to use that sword again in fight
In way of honest manhood that strikes him;
Some river must devour it; 't were not fit
That any man should find it. What, again?

Re-enter De Flores.

He walks a' purpose by, sure, to choke me up,
T' infect my blood.

De F. My worthy noble lord!
Tom. Dost offer to come near and breathe upon me?
(*Strikes him.*)
De F. A blow!
(*Draws.*)
Tom. Yea, are you so prepar'd?
I'll rather like a soldier die by th' sword,
Than like a politician by thy poison.
(*Draws.*)
De F. Hold, my lord, as you are honorable!
Tom. All slaves that kill by poison are still cowards.
De F. (*Aside.*) I cannot strike; I see his brother's wounds
Fresh bleeding in his eye, as in a crystal.—
I will not question this, I know you're noble;
I take my injury with thanks given, sir,
Like a wise lawyer, and as a favor
Will wear it for the worthy hand that gave it.—
(*Aside.*) Why this from him that yesterday appear'd
So strangely loving to me?
O, but instinct is of a subtler strain!
Guilt must not walk so near his lodge again;
He came near me now.
Exit.
Tom. All league with mankind I renounce for ever,
Till I find this murderer; not so much
As common courtesy but I'll lock up;
For in the state of ignorance I live in,
A brother may salute his brother's murderer,
And wish good speed to th' villain in a greeting.

Enter Vermandero, Alibius, and Isabella.

Ver. Noble Piracquo!
Tom. Pray, keep on your way, sir;
I've nothing to say to you.
Ver. Comforts bless you, sir;
Tom. I've forsworn compliment, in troth I have, sir;
As you are merely man, I have not left
A good wish for you, nor for any here.
Ver. Unless you be so far in love with grief,
You will not part from't upon any terms,
We bring that news will make a welcome for us.
Tom. What news can that be?
Ver. Throw no scornful smile
Upon the zeal I bring you, 't is worth more, sir.
Two of the chiefest men I kept about me
I hide not from the law of your just vengeance.
Tom. Ha!
Ver. To give your peace more ample satisfaction,
Thank these discoverers.
Tom. If you bring that calm,
Name but the manner I shall ask forgiveness in
For that contemptuous smile [I threw] upon you;
I'll perfect it with reverence that belongs
Unto a sacred altar.
(*Kneels.*)
Ver. (*Raising him.*) Good sir, rise;
Why, now you overdo as much a' this hand
As you fell short a' t' other.—Speak, Alibius.
Alib. 'T was my wife's fortune, as she is most lucky
At a discovery, to find out lately,
Within our hospital of fools and madmen,
Two counterfeits slipt into these disguises,
Their names Franciscus and Antonio.
Ver. Both mine, sir, and I ask no favor for 'em.
Alib. Now that which draws suspicion to their habits,
The time of their disguisings agrees justly
With the day of the murder.
Tom. O blest revelation!
Ver. Nay, more, nay, more, sir—I'll not spare mine own
In way of justice—they both feign'd a journey
To Briamata, and so wrought out their leaves;[72]
My love was so abus'd in 't.
Tom. Time's too precious
To run in waste now; you have brought a peace
The riches of five kingdoms could not purchase.
Be my most happy conduct; I thirst for 'em:
Like subtle lightning will I wind about 'em,
And melt their marrow in 'em.
Exeunt.

72 obtained permission to leave.

SCENE 3. *Alsemero's apartment in the Castle.*

Enter Alsemero and Jasperino.

Jas. Your confidence, I 'm sure, is now of proof;
The prospect from the garden has show'd
Enough for deep suspicion.

Als. The black mask
That so continually was worn upon 't
Condemns the face for ugly ere 't be seen,
Her despite to him, and so seeming bottomless.

Jas. Touch it home then; 't is not a shallow probe
Can search this ulcer soundly; I fear you 'll find it
Full of corruption. 'T is fit I leave you,
She meets you opportunely from that walk;
She took the back door at his parting with her.
Exit.

Als. Did my fate wait for this unhappy stroke
At my first sight of woman? She is here.

Enter Beatrice.

Beat. Alsemero!

Als. How do you?

Beat. How do I?
Alas, sir! how do you? You look not well.

Als. You read me well enough; I am not well.

Beat. Not well, sir? Is 't in my power to better you?

Als. Yes.

Beat. Nay, then you 're cur'd again.

Als. Pray, resolve[73] me one question, lady.

Beat. If I can.

Als. None can so sure: are you honest?

Beat. Ha, ha, ha! that 's a broad question, my lord.

Als. But that 's not a modest answer, my lady.
Do you laugh? My doubts are strong upon me.

Beat. 'T is innocence that smiles, and no rough brow
Can take away the dimple in her cheek.
Say I should strain a tear to fill the vault,
Which would you give the better faith to?

Als. 'T were but hypocrisy of a sadder color,
But the same stuff; neither your smiles nor tears
Shall move or flatter me from my belief:
You are a whore!

Beat. What a horrid sound it hath!
It blasts a beauty to deformity;
Upon what face soever that breath falls,
It strikes it ugly. O, you have ruin'd
What you can ne'er repair again?

Als. I 'll all
Demolish, and seek out truth within you,
If there be any left; let your sweet tongue
Prevent your heart's rifling; there I 'll ransack
And tear out my suspicion.

Beat. You may, sir;
It is an easy passage; yet, if you please,
Show me the ground whereon you lost your love;
My spotless virtue may but tread on that
Before I perish.

Als. Unanswerable;
A ground you cannot stand on; you fall down
Beneath all grace and goodness when you set
Your ticklish heel on 't. There was a visor
Over that cunning face, and that became you;
Now Impudence in triumph rides upon 't.
How comes this tender reconcilement else
'Twixt you and your despite, your rancorous loathing,
De Flores? he that your eye was sore at sight of,
He 's now become your arm's supporter, your
Lip's saint!

Beat. Is there the cause?

Als. Worse, your lust's devil,
Your adultery!

Beat. Would any but yourself say that,
'T would turn him to a villain!

Als. It was witnest
By the counsel of your bosom, Diaphanta.

Beat. Is your witness dead then?

Als. 'T is to be fear'd
It was the wages of her knowledge; poor soul,
She liv'd not long after the discovery.

Beat. Then hear a story of not much less horror
Than this your false suspicion is beguil'd with;

73 answer.

To your bed's scandal I stand up innocence,
Which even the guilt of one black other deed
Will stand for proof of; your love has made me
A cruel murd'ress.

Als. Ha!

Beat. A bloody one;
I have kist poison for it, strokt a serpent:
That thing of hate, worthy in my esteem
Of no better employment, and him most worthy
To be so employ'd, I caus'd to murder
That innocent Piracquo, having no
Better means than that worst to assure
Yourself to me.

Als. O, the place itself e'er since
Has crying been for vengeance! The temple,
Where blood and beauty first unlawfully
Fir'd their devotion and quencht the right one;
'T was in my fears at first, 't will have it now:
O, thou art all deform'd!

Beat. Forget not, sir,
It for your sake was done. Shall greater dangers
Make the less welcome?

Als. O, thou should'st have gone
A thousand leagues about to have avoided
This dangerous bridge of blood! Here we are lost.

Beat. Remember, I am true unto your bed.

Als. The bed itself 's a charnel, the sheets shrouds
For murdered carcasses. It must ask pause
What I must do in this; meantime you shall
Be my prisoner only: enter my closet;

Exit Beatrice.

I 'll be your keeper yet. O, in what part
Of this sad story shall I first begin? Ha!
This same fellow has put me in.[74]—De Flores!

Enter De Flores.

De F. Noble Alsemero!

Als. I can tell you
News, sir; my wife has her commended to you.

De F. That 's news indeed, my lord; I think she would
Commend me to the gallows if she could,
She ever lov'd me so well; I thank her.

Als. What 's this blood upon your band, De Flores?

De F. Blood! no, sure 't was washt since.

Als. Since when, man?

De F. Since 't other day I got a knock
In a sword-and-dagger school; I think 't is out.

Als. Yes, 't is almost out, but 't is perceiv'd though.
I had forgot my message; this it is,
What price goes murder?

De F. How, sir?

Als. I ask you, sir;
My wife 's behindhand with you, she tells me,
For a brave bloody blow you gave for her sake
Upon Piracquo.

De F. Upon? 'T was quite through him sure:
Has she confest it?

Als. As sure as death to both of you;
And much more than that.

De F. It could not be much more;
'T was but one thing, and that—she is a whore.

Als. It could not choose but follow. O cunning devils!
How should blind men know you from fair-fac'd saints?

Beat. (*Within.*) He lies! the villain does belie me!

De F. Let me go to her, sir.

Als. Nay, you shall to her.—
Peace, crying crocodile, your sounds are heard;
Take your prey to you;—get you into her, sir:

Exit De Flores.

I 'll be your pander now; rehearse again
Your scene of lust, that you may be perfect
When you shall come to act it to the black audience,
Where howls and gnashings shall be music to you.
Clip[75] your adulteress freely, 't is the pilot
Will guide you to the *mare mortuum*,
Where you shall sink to fathoms bottomless.

Enter Vermandero, Tomaso, Alibius, Isabella, Franciscus, and Antonio.

Ver. O Alsemero! I 've a wonder for you.

74 given me my cue.

75 hug.

Als. No, sir, 't is I, I have a wonder for you.
Ver. I have suspicion near as proof itself
For Piracquo's murder.
Als. Sir, I have proof
Beyond suspicion of Piracquo's murder.
Ver. Beseech you, hear me; these who have been disguis'd
E'er since the deed was done.
Als. I have two other
That were more close disguis'd than your two could be
E'er since the deed was done.
Ver. You'll hear me—these mine own servants——
Als. Hear me—those nearer than your servants
That shall acquit them, and prove them guiltless.
Fran. That may be done with easy truth, sir.
Tom. How is my cause bandied through your delays!
'T is urgent in my blood and calls for haste.
Give me a brother or alive or dead;
Alive, a wife with him; if dead, for both
A recompense for murder and adultery.
Beat. (*Within.*) O, O, O!
Als. Hark! 't is coming to you.
De F. (*Within.*) Nay, I'll along for company.
Beat. (*Within.*) O, O!
Ver. What horrid sounds are these?
Als. Come forth, you twins
Of mischief!

Re-enter De Flores, bringing in Beatrice wounded.

De F. Here we are; if you have any more
To say to us, speak quickly, I shall not
Give you the hearing else; I am so stout yet,
And so, I think, that broken rib of mankind.
Ver. A host of enemies ent'red my citadel
Could not amaze like this: Joanna! Beatrice-Joanna!
Beat. O, come not near me, sir, I shall defile you!
I that was of your blood was taken from you,
For your better health; look no more upon 't,
But cast it to the ground regardlessly,
Let the common sewer take it from distinction.
Beneath the stars, upon yon meteor
(*Pointing to De Flores.*)
Ever hung my fate 'mongst things corruptible;
I ne'er could pluck it from him; my loathing
Was prophet to the rest, but ne'er believ'd.
Mine honor fell with him, and now my life.—
Alsemero, I'm a stranger to your bed;
Your bed was coz'ned on the nuptial night,—
For which your false bride died.
Als. Diaphanta?
De F. Yes, and the while I coupled with your mate
At barley-break; now we are left in hell.[76]
Ver. We are all there, it circumscribes us here.
De F. I lov'd this woman in spite of her heart:
Her love I earn'd out of Piracquo's murder.
Tom. Ha! my brother's murderer?
De F. Yes, and her honor's prize
Was my reward; I thank life for nothing
But that pleasure; it was so sweet to me,
That I have drunk up all, left none behind
For any man to pledge me.
Ver. Horrid villain!
Keep life in him for future tortures.
De F. No!
I can prevent you; here 's my pen-knife still;
It is but one thread more (*Stabbing himself*), and now 't is cut.—
Make haste, Joanna, by that token to thee,
Canst not forget, so lately put in mind;
I would not go to leave thee far behind.
(*Dies.*)
Beat. Forgive me, Alsemero, all forgive!
'T is time to die when 't is a shame to live.
(*Dies.*)
Ver. O, my name 's ent'red now in that record
Where till this fatal hour 't was never read.
Als. Let it be blotted out; let your heart lose it,
And it can never look you in the face,
Nor tell a tale behind the back of life
To your dishonor. Justice hath so right
The guilty hit, that innocence is quit
By proclamation, and may joy again.—

76 Cf. n. 37, p. 400.

Sir, you are sensible of what truth hath done;
'T is the best comfort that your grief can find.

Tom. Sir, I am satisfied; my injuries
Lie dead before me; I can exact no more,
Unless my soul were loose, and could o'ertake
Those black fugitives that are fled from hence,
To take a second vengeance; but there are wraths
Deeper than mine, 't is to be fear'd, about 'em.

Als. What an opacous body had that moon
That last chang'd on us! Here is beauty chang'd
To ugly whoredom; here servant-obedience
To a master-sin, imperious murder;
I, a suppos'd husband, chang'd embraces
With wantonness,—but that was paid before.—
Your change is come too, from an ignorant wrath
To knowing friendship.—Are there any more on 's?

Ant. Yes, sir, I was chang'd too from a little ass as I was to a great fool as I am; and had like to ha' been chang'd to the gallows, but that you know my innocence[77] always excuses me.

Fran. I was chang'd from a little wit to be stark mad,
Almost for the same purpose.

Isa. Your change is still behind,
But deserve best your transformation:
You are a jealous coxcomb, keep schools of folly,
And teach your scholars how to break your own head.

Alib. I see all apparent, wife, and will change now
Into a better husband, and ne'er keep
Scholars that shall be wiser than myself.

Als. Sir, you have yet a son's duty living,
Please you, accept it; let that your sorrow,
As it goes from your eye, go from your heart,
Man and his sorrow at the grave must part.

EPILOGUE

Als. All we can do to comfort one another,
To stay a brother's sorrow for a brother,
To dry a child from the kind father's eyes,
Is to no purpose, it rather multiplies:
Your only smiles have power to cause re-live
The dead again, or in their rooms to give
Brother a new brother, father a child;
If these appear, all griefs are reconcil'd.

Exeunt omnes.

77 simple-mindedness.

III. THE RESTORATION

JOHN DRYDEN

ALMANZOR AND ALMAHIDE, OR THE CONQUEST OF GRANADA

John Dryden (1631–1700) was the leading literary man of the last quarter of the seventeenth century. He came of a Puritan family, and graduated at Cambridge. After the Restoration he transferred his loyalty from Oliver Cromwell's weak son Richard to Charles II, and at the accession of James II he became a Roman Catholic. In such changes there was probably not so much time-serving as a desire to support a strong autocratic governmental system. It is certain that he was interested in politics, and liked to be on the winning side. In his literary work he was remarkable for his versatility; besides nearly thirty tragedies and comedies, he excelled in prose criticism, translation, and satirical, lyric, and narrative poetry. For many years he exercised a controlling influence on literature, and is generally recognized as the first great leader in the era of classicism.

Since poetry expresses both the ideals and the realities of the age which produces it, we should expect a strong contrast between the drama of the Elizabethan period and that of so different an age as the forty years or so of the Restoration period. The earlier form in large measure survived, since a dramatic form is too complex to be often renewed, but the spirit is greatly altered. In 1642 the Puritan parliament, always opposed to the stage, took advantage of the beginnings of the Civil War to close the theaters, and for eighteen years such performances as were given were rude and clandestine. Many other innocent amusements were proscribed, and the sober and ascetic spirit of Puritanism was at least theoretically supreme in the land. The era of the Puritan Revolution saw England's great experiment in a moral idealism compulsory for all. It produced a far-reaching effect, for to it more than to any other cause are due the differences which every one feels between English (and partly American) life and that of the whole of continental Europe. But on the whole it failed, and the violence of the reaction when Charles II's return released the tense spring is nowhere more apparent than in the drama. That of the Restoration lacked the fine, steady, normal, masculine spirit of the greater Elizabethan dramatists — their universality and depth of insight; it became contracted lengthwise and crosswise, became superficial and narrower. It was aristocratic rather than democratic, met the taste of a smaller part of the community; it exhibited the irresponsible life they led, and when it expressed moral ideality, this was sometimes an insincere, weak, and unnatural ideality. With all these limitations as to spirit and matter, technically and as to literary style the drama was never more brilliant. It does not fail in what it sets out to do, and from the point of view of moral and social history is unusually significant. All this is vividly shown in the comedy, but the serious plays, if understood, are quite as characteristic.

Dryden's *Conquest of Granada*, his greatest popular success (first performed in 1670, printed 1672), is the best example of a type of serious drama differing from tragedy in having a happy ending — the "heroic play." Though a relation can be seen to some of the Elizabethan dramas, and though he expressed obligation to D'Avenant's *Siege of Rhodes*, Dryden is regarded as the originator of the type. There is a certain amount of resemblance to the French classical drama of Corneille and Racine; and as in them the three "classical" unities (see page 46 above) were observed. But these plays were largely an attempt to bring into the drama the supposed manner and spirit of Greek and Italian epic, and especially of the prose romances of seventeenth-century France, such as those of la Calprenède, Gomberville, and Mlle. de Scudéry. Three romances by the last-named underlie respectively the three parts of the plot in *The Conquest of Granada;* which is also founded on a Spanish history of Granada. For this, like other "heroic plays," has a historical background, which was felt to impart a weighty dignity. The locality is always remote, classical, among the Aztecs or Peruvians, or as with this play among the orientals. This too, was felt to give a romantic dignity, and made less noticeable certain departures from nature and probability. There is little attempt at "local color"; the Moors invoke the saints, observe knightly usages, and even sing of "Phyllis."

The plot is apt to be loose and episodic, with no prolonged suspense (opportunities for it are rejected), not working up to a crisis, not intimately growing out of the personalities, but accidental and successive, and made up of commonplace elements. Dryden was far from being a born dramatist. In all these plays the general formula for plot is the conflict between love and honor. In this play the plot is of three parts, well interwoven, dealing with the loves of Almanzor, Almahide, and Boabdelin, with those of Abdalla, Lyndaraxa, and Abdelmelech, and with those of Ozmyn and Benzayda. The Second Part is equally intricate, ending in the capture of Granada by the Spaniards, the death of Boabdelin, the prospective union of his widow Almahide with Almanzor, and the wholly unprepared-for recognition of the latter as the long-lost son of the Duke of Arcos. The commonplaceness of the plot is somewhat concealed by the incessant changeful action, and the amorous framework by the constant drums and tramplings of conquests, the alarums and excursions of domestic malice and foreign levies. As a critic has well said, the play combines French artificial gallantry with the English love of sound and fury. The noisy motion was doubtless one reason for its popularity on the stage. There being no one point of deep interest, the focus of attention is constantly shifted. The outline of the play is narrative, epic, rather than dramatic.

This point bears equally on the most characteristic feature of the heroic play, its treatment of personality. Here too its nature and origin is rather epic than dramatic. As in the epic, the characters are of the highest rank. Dryden stated that his originals for Almanzor were Homer's Achilles and Tasso's Rinaldo. Almanzor, however, did not perfectly please contemporary critics. To us it seems more odd to censure him as "no perfect pattern of heroic virtue," a "contemner of kings," who changes sides, than to carp at him for performing impossibilities — he falls short of, and exceeds, the conventional notion of his kind. Dryden makes the defence that heroic plays are not subject to the laws of probability, and that, being a foreigner, Almanzor was bound to neither of the Moorish factions. The hero's very first words, as he goes to aid one of them, are

> I cannot stay to ask which cause is best:
> But this is so to me because oppress;

and later he declares,

> True, I would wish my friend the juster side;
> But, in the unjust, my kindness more is tried.

Thus from the first he declares his indifference to ordinary rules of conduct. With his frantic self-assertion and megalomania, "a confidence of himself, almost approaching to an arrogance," Dryden moderately says, Almanzor and his fellow-heroes are the completest example in English of the Superman-type, of "the will to power." Almanzor's biggest talk does no more than justice to his deeds, he faces kings, armies and ghosts (Part II.) with like equanimity.

> What, in another, vanity would seem,
> Appears but noble confidence in him.

But heroic arrogance is not exhibited merely for its own sake. Almanzor's chief virtues Dryden meant to be "a frank and open nobleness of nature, an easiness to forgive his conquered enemies, and to protect them in distress; and, above all, an inviolable faith in his affection." He towers above the world of men that his subjection to woman and love may be more flattering and delightful. Love is the giant's only weakness; what a tribute to love! Love is at first sight, but as constant as it is sudden. An etiquette controls it, even if repented of. Almahide, though loving Almanzor, feels as much bound by her betrothal to the weak Boabdelin as by her marriage-vow, and must be faithful not only to his person but to his memory; at the end of Part II she dedicates a year's widowhood to *les convenances*. What a tribute to the virtue of constancy and loyalty, when even the almighty Almanzor is kept waiting! But if love and honor hopelessly conflict, usually honor goes to the wall. Boabdelin prefers his love to his crown.

Hardly less important than the characters, in the mind of Dryden and his auditors, were the "sentiments," the views and ideals discoursed upon. Some of these plays devote much space to arguments and controversies among the characters, as here in the second act. The ideals are mainly of love and honor; "betwixt their love and virtue they are tost;" honor being partly glory and partly a rigid sense of propriety. In each case the ideal is a thoroughly individualistic one; the love is passion, and the honor is largely selfish virtue. Though occasionally a personage is so Quixotic as to contemplate killing himself to spare another the guilt of killing him, of patriotism there is scarcely a hint. "Honor is what myself and friends I owe," Almanzor announces. "*L'état c'est moi*" is the principle of all of them. With an empire of eight hundred years nearing its fall the Moors think only of private revenge, private ambition, and private passion. Here as elsewhere Dryden sacrificed nature and breadth to intensity. Yet insight is not wholly wanting; a passage in Part II has often been quoted:

> A blush remains in a forgiven face:
> It wears the silent tokens of disgrace.
> Forgiveness to the injur'd does belong;
> But they ne'er pardon who have done the wrong.

Such passages, and even rhodomontade and commonplace, gain impressiveness by Dryden's matchless style. Not always great as an imaginative poet, or as a dramatist, he was a master of dramatic rhetoric, unsubtle, bold. His verse sweeps one along like a wave on its rhythmic rise and fall, with endless nerve and verve and never a sign of faltering; it reads aloud superbly. The form of verse is, as regularly in the heroic plays, the ten-syllable couplet, the "heroic couplet," treated with some variety, such as occasional short lines. His lyric gift enabled him also to introduce charming songs, which contrast with the masculine march of the other verse, and also sometimes with its high moral tone.

An artificial idealism, in a word, is what this play embodies. There is plenty of idealism in Shakespeare, but it comes from a heightening of human nature as it is; his people are merely more fully and intensely what they are than they would be in life. Dryden's are not imitated from life, but from the vague ideals of the unideal, artificial aristocrats for whom he wrote. The reality of these people appears in the comedy of the age. Sexual morality and personal honor were at a low ebb; in these plays they are lauded in an unreal and exaggerated manner. Because such people cared little for ideals, these serious plays are artificial. They are the somewhat perfunctory homage which Restoration vice paid to virtue. Their artificiality links them closely to another highly artificial dramatic type, which grew up about the same time and from much the same origin — the opera. Both were felt to be independent of nature and probability, both were remote and aristocratic, both were simple and conventional in their elements, both dealt largely with the heroic and with love. The sonorous lyric verse which is the accompaniment of Dryden's plays in a sense takes the place of the music which is that of the opera. The spirit of *The Conquest of Granada* therefore still survives on the boards of the opera-house.

ALMANZOR AND ALMAHIDE, OR THE CONQUEST OF GRANADA

PART I

Major rerum mihi nascitur ordo;
Majus opus moveo.
VIRGIL, *Æneid,* vii, 44, 45.

PROLOGUE TO PART I

Spoken by Mrs. Ellen Gwyn, in a Broad-brimmed Hat, and Waist-belt.

This jest[1] was first of t' other house's making,
And five times tried, has never failed of taking;
For 't were a shame a poet should be killed
Under the shelter of so broad a shield.
This is that hat, whose very sight did win ye
To laugh and clap as though the devil were in ye.
As then, for Nokes, so now I hope you 'll be
So dull, to laugh once more for love of me.
"I 'll write a play," says one, "for I have got
A broad-brimmed hat, and waist-belt, towards a plot."
Says t'other, "I have one more large than that."
Thus they out-write each other with a hat!
The brims still grew with every play they writ;
And grew so large, they covered all the wit.
Hat was the play; 't was language, wit, and tale:
Like them that find meat, drink, and cloth in ale.
What dulness do these mongrel wits confess,
When all their hope is acting of a dress!
Thus, two the best comedians of the age
Must be worn out, with being blocks o' the stage;
Like a young girl, who better things has known,
Beneath their poet's impotence they groan.
See now what charity it was to save!
They thought you liked, what only you forgave;
And brought you more dull sense, dull sense much worse
Than brisk gay nonsense, and the heavier curse.
They bring old iron, and glass upon the stage,
To barter with the Indians of our age.

[1] Nokes, an actor at a rival theater, is said to have caricatured French styles in the above-mentioned costume.

Still they write on, and like great authors show;
But 't is as rollers in wet gardens grow
Heavy with dirt, and gathering as they go.
May none, who have so little understood,
[2] To like such trash, presume to praise what 's good!
And may those drudges of the stage, whose fate
Is damn'd dull farce more dully to translate,
Fall under that excise the state thinks fit
To set on all French wares, whose worst is wit.
French farce, worn out at home, is sent abroad;
And, patched up here, is made our English mode.
Henceforth, let poets, ere allowed to write,
Be searched, like duellists before they fight,
For wheel-broad hats, dull humor, all that chaff,
Which makes you mourn, and makes the vulgar laugh:
For these, in plays, are as unlawful arms
As, in a combat, coats of mail, and charms.

NAMES OF THE CHARACTERS

PERSONS REPRESENTED[3]

MEN

MAHOMET BOABDELIN, *the last king of Granada.*
PRINCE ABDALLA, *his brother.*
ABDELMELECH, *chief of the Abencerrages.*[4]
ZULEMA, *chief of the Zegrys.*[4]
ABENAMAR, *an old Abencerrago.*
SELIN, *an old Zegry.*
OZMYN, *a brave young Abencerrago, son to Abenamar.*
HAMET, *brother to Zulema, a Zegry.*
GOMEL, *a Zegry.*
ALMANZOR.
FERDINAND, *King of Spain.*
DUKE OF ARCOS, *his General.*
DON ALONZO D'AGUILAR, *a Spanish Captain.*

WOMEN

ALMAHIDE, *queen of Granada.*
LYNDARAXA, *sister of Zulema, a Zegry lady.*
BENZAYDA, *daughter to Selin.*
ESPERANZA, *slave to the queen.*
HALYMA, *slave to Lyndaraxa.*
ISABELLA, *Queen of Spain.*
Messengers, Guards, Attendants, Men, and Women.

The Scene in Granada, and the Christian Camp besieging it.

ACT I.

(*Boabdelin, Abenamar, Abdelmelech, Guards.*)

Boab. Thus, in the triumphs of soft peace, I reign;
And, from my walls, defy the powers of Spain;
With pomp and sports my love I celebrate,
While they keep distance, and attend my state.—

(*To Aben.*)

Parent to her, whose eyes my soul enthral,
Whom I, in hope, already father call,
Abenamar, thy youth these sports has known,
Of which thy age is now spectator grown;
Judge-like thou sit'st, to praise, or to arraign
The flying skirmish of the darted cane:[5]
But, when fierce bulls run loose upon the place,
And our bold Moors their loves with danger grace,
Then heat new-bends thy slackened nerves again,
And a short youth runs warm through every vein.

Aben. I must confess the encounters of this day
Warmed me indeed, but quite another way:
Not with the fire of youth; but generous rage,
To see the glories of my youthful age
So far out-done.

Abdelm. Castile could never boast, in all its pride,
A pomp so splendid, when the lists, set wide,
Gave room to the fierce bulls, which wildly ran
In Sierra Ronda, ere the war began;
Who, with high nostrils snuffing up the wind,

[2] as to like. [4] Tribes or parties among the Moors, whose enmities hastened the fall of Granada.
[3] Some of these personages appear only in Part II.

Now stood the champions of the savage kind.
Just opposite, within the circled place,
Ten of our bold Abencerrages' race
(Each brandishing his bull-spear in his hand)
Did their proud jennets gracefully command.
On their steeled heads their demi-lances wore
Small pennons, which their ladies' colors bore.
Before this troop did warlike Ozmyn go;
Each lady, as he rode, saluting low;
At the chief stands, with reverence more profound,
His well-taught courser, kneeling, touched the ground;
Thence raised, he sidelong bore his rider on,
Still facing, till he out of sight was gone.

Boab. You praise him like a friend; and I confess,
His brave deportment merited no less.

Abdelm. Nine bulls were launched by his victorious arm,
Whose wary jennet, shunning still the harm,
Seemed to attend the shock, and then leaped wide:
Meanwhile, his dext'rous rider, when he spied
The beast just stooping, 'twixt the neck and head
His lance, with never-erring fury, sped.

Aben. My son did well, and so did Hamet too;
Yet did no more than we were wont to do;
But what the stranger did was more than man.

Abdelm. He finished all those triumphs we began.
One bull, with curled black head, beyond the rest,
And dew-laps hanging from his brawny chest,
With nodding front a while did daring stand,
And with his jetty hoof spurned back the sand;
Then, leaping forth, he bellowed out aloud:
The amazed assistants back each other crowd,
While monarch-like he ranged the listed field;
Some tossed, some gored, some trampling down he killed.
The ignobler Moors from far his rage provoke
With woods of darts, which from his sides he shook.
Meantime your valiant son, who had before
Gained fame, rode round to every mirador;[6]
Beneath each lady's stand a stop he made,
And, bowing, took the applauses which they paid,
Just in that point of time, the brave unknown
Approached the lists.

Boab. I marked him, when alone
(Observed by all, himself observing none)
He entered first, and with a graceful pride
His fiery Arab dext'rously did guide,
Who while his rider every stand surveyed,
Sprung loose, and flew into an escapade;[7]
Not moving forward, yet, with every bound,
Pressing, and seeming still to quit his ground:
What after passed
Was far from the ventanna[8] where I sate,
But you were near, and can the truth relate.

(*To Abdelm.*)

Abdelm. Thus while he stood, the bull, who saw this foe,
His easier conquests proudly did forego;
And, making at him with a furious bound,
From his bent forehead aimed a double wound.
A rising murmur ran through all the field,
And every lady's blood with fear was chilled:
Some shrieked, while others, with more helpful care,
Cried out aloud, "Beware, brave youth, beware!"
At this he turned, and, as the bull drew near,
Shunned and received him on his pointed spear:

5 javelin. 7 Uncontrolled prancing, bounding or running (French technical term in horsemanship).
6 gallery or balcony for spectators. 8 window.

The lance broke short, the beast then bellowed loud
And his strong neck to a new onset bowed.
The undaunted youth
Then drew; and from his saddle bending low,
Just where the neck did to the shoulders grow,
With his full force discharged a deadly blow.
Not heads of poppies (when they reap the grain)
Fall with more ease before the laboring swain,
Than fell this head:
It fell so quick, it did even death prevent,[9]
And made imperfect bellowings as it went.
Then all the trumpets victory did sound,
And yet their clangors in our shouts were drown'd.

(*A confused noise within.*)

Boab. The alarm-bell rings from our Alhambra walls,
And from the streets sound drums and atabals.[10]

(*Within, a bell, drums, and trumpets.*)

(*To them a Messenger.*)

How now? from whence proceed these new alarms?

Mess. The two fierce factions are again in arms;
And, changing into blood the day's delight,
The Zegrys with the Abencerrages fight;
On each side their allies and friends appear;
The Maças here, the Alabezes there:
The Gazuls with the Bencerrages join,
And, with the Zegrys, all great Gomel's line.

Boab. Draw up behind the Vivarambla place;
Double my guards,—these factions I will face;
And try if all the fury they can bring,
Be proof against the presence of their king.

(*Exit Boab.*)

(*The Factions appear: At the head of the Abencerrages, Ozmyn; at the head of the Zegrys, Zulema, Hamet, Gomel, and Selin: Abenamar and Abdelmelech joined with the Abencerrages.*)

Zul. The faint Abencerrages quit their ground;
Press 'em; put home your thrusts to every wound.

Abdelm. Zegry, on manly force our line relies;
Thine poorly takes the advantage of surprise:
Unarmed and much out-numbered we retreat;
You gain no fame, when basely you defeat.
If thou art brave, seek nobler victory;
Save Moorish blood; and, while our bands stand by,
Let two to two an equal combat try.

Ham. 'T is not for fear the combat we refuse,
But we our gained advantage will not lose.

Zul. In combating, but two of you will fall;
And we resolve we will despatch you all.

Ozm. We'll double yet the exchange before we die,
And each of ours two lives of yours shall buy.

(*Almanzor enters betwixt them, as they stand ready to engage.*)

Alm. I cannot stay to ask which cause is best;
But this is so to me, because oppress'd.

(*Goes to the Abencerrages.*)

(*To them Boabdelin and his Guards, going betwixt them.*)

Boab. On your allegiance, I command you stay;
Who passes here, through me must make his way;
My life's the Isthmus; through this narrow line
You first must cut, before those seas can join.
What fury, Zegrys, has possessed your minds?
What rage the brave Abencerrages blinds?
If of your courage you new proofs would show,
Without much travel you may find a foe.
Those foes are neither so remote nor few,
That you should need each other to pursue.
Lean times and foreign wars should minds unite;
When poor, men mutter, but they seldom fight.
O holy Allah! that I live to see
Thy Granadines assist their enemy!

9 anticipate, get ahead of.

10 kettle-drums or tabors.

You fight the Christians' battles; every life
You lavish thus, in this intestine strife,
Does from our weak foundations take one prop
Which helped to hold our sinking country up.

Ozm. 'T is fit our private enmity should cease;
Though injured first, yet I will first seek peace.

Zul. No, murderer, no; I never will be won
To peace with him, whose hand has slain my son.

Ozm. Our prophet's curse
On me, and all the Abencerrages light,
If, unprovoked, I with your son did fight.

Abdelm. A band of Zegrys ran within the place,
Matched with a troop of thirty of our race.
Your son and Ozmyn the first squadrons led,
Which, ten by ten, like Parthians, charged and fled;
The ground was strowed with canes where we did meet,
Which crackled underneath our coursers' feet:
When Tarifa (I saw him ride apart)
Changed his blunt cane for a steel-pointed dart,
And, meeting Ozmyn next,—
Who wanted time for treason to provide,—
He basely threw it at him, undefied.

Ozm. (*Showing his arm.*) Witness this blood—which when by treason sought,
That followed, sir, which to myself I ought.[11]

Zul. His hate to thee was grounded on a grudge,
Which all our generous Zegrys just did judge:
Thy villain-blood thou openly didst place
Above the purple of our kingly race.

Boab. From equal stems their blood both houses draw,
They from Morocco, you from Cordova.

Ham. Their mongrel race is mixed with Christian breed;
Hence 't is that they those dogs in prisons feed.

Abdelm. Our holy prophet wills, that charity
Should even to birds and beasts extended be:
None knows what fate is for himself designed;
The thought of human chance should make us kind.

Gom. We waste that time we to revenge should give:
Fall on: let no Abencerrago live.

(*Advancing before the rest of his party. Almanzor, advancing on the other side, and describing a line with his sword.*)

Almanz. Upon thy life pass not this middle space;
Sure death stands guarding the forbidden place.

Gom. To dare that death, I will approach yet nigher;
Thus,—wert thou compassed in with circling fire.

(*They fight.*)

Boab. Disarm 'em both; if they resist you, kill.

(*Almanzor, in the midst of the Guards, kills Gomel, and then is disarmed.*)

Almanz. Now you have but the leavings of my will.

Boab. Kill him! this insolent unknown shall fall,
And be the victim to atone[12] you all.

Ozm. If he must die, not one of us will live:
That life he gave for us, for him we give.

Boab. It was a traitor's voice that spoke those words;
So are you all, who do not sheathe your swords.

Zul. Outrage unpunished, when a prince is by,
Forfeits to scorn the rights of majesty:
No subject his protection can expect,
Who what he owes himself does first neglect.

Aben. This stranger, sir, is he,
Who lately in the Vivarambla place
Did, with so loud applause, your triumphs grace.

Boab. The word which I have given, I'll not revoke;
If he be brave, he's ready for the stroke.

Almanz. No man has more contempt than I of breath,
But whence hast thou the right to give me death?
Obeyed as sovereign by thy subjects be,
But know, that I alone am king of me.
I am as free as nature first made man,
Ere the base laws of servitude began,

11 owed.

12 reconcile.

When wild in woods the noble savage ran.

Boab. Since, then, no power above your own you know,
Mankind should use you like a common foe;
You should be hunted like a beast of prey:
By your own law I take your life away.

Almanz. My laws are made but only for my sake;
No king against himself a law can make.
If thou pretend'st to be a prince like me,
Blame not an act, which should thy pattern be.
I saw the oppressed, and thought it did belong
To a king's office to redress the wrong:
I brought that succor, which thou ought'st to bring,
And so, in nature, am thy subjects' king.

Boab. I do not want your counsel to direct,
Or aid to help me punish or protect.

Almanz. Thou want'st 'em both, or better thou wouldst know,
Than to let factions in thy kingdom grow.
Divided interests, while thou think'st to sway,
Draw, like two brooks, thy middle stream away:
For though they band and jar, yet both combine
To make their greatness by the fall of thine.
Thus, like a buckler, thou art held in sight,
While they behind thee with each other fight.

Boab. Away, and execute him instantly!
(*To his Guards.*)

Almanz. Stand off; I have not leisure yet to die.
(*To them Abdalla, hastily.*)

Abdal. Hold, sir! for heaven sake hold!
Defer this noble stranger's punishment,
Or your rash orders you will soon repent.

Boab. Brother, you know not yet his insolence.

Abdal. Upon yourself you punish his offence:
If we treat gallant strangers in this sort,
Mankind will shun the inhospitable court;
And who, henceforth, to our defence will come,
If death must be the brave Almanzor's doom?
From Africa I drew him to your aid,
And for his succor have his life betrayed.

Boab. Is this the Almanzor whom at Fez you knew,
When first their swords the Xeriff brothers drew?

Abdal. This, sir, is he, who for the elder fought,
And to the juster cause the conquest brought;
Till the proud Santo, seated in the throne,
Disdained the service, he had done, to own:
Then to the vanquished part his fate he led:
The vanquished triumphed, and the victor fled.
Vast is his courage, boundless is his mind,
Rough as a storm, and humorous [13] as wind:
Honor 's the only idol of his eyes;
The charms of beauty like a pest he flies;
And, raised by valor from a birth unknown,
Acknowledges no power above his own.
(*Boabdelin coming to Almanzor.*)

Boab. Impute your danger to our ignorance;
The bravest men are subject most to chance:
Granada much does to your kindness owe;
But towns, expecting sieges, cannot show
More honor, than to invite you to a foe.

Almanz. I do not doubt but I have been to blame:
But, to pursue the end for which I came,
Unite your subjects first; then let us go,
And pour their common rage upon the foe.

Boab. (*To the Factions.*) Lay down your arms, and let me beg you cease
Your enmities.

Zul. We will not hear of peace,
Till we by force have first revenged our slain.

Abdelm. The action we have done we will maintain.

Selin. Then let the king depart, and we will try
Our cause by arms.

Zul. For us and victory!

Boab. A king entreats you.

Almanz. What subjects will precarious [14] kings regard?
A beggar speaks too softly to be heard:

13 capricious, self-willed.

14 suppliant.

Lay down your arms! 't is I command you now.
Do it—or, by our prophet's soul I vow,
My hands shall right your king on him I seize.
Now let me see whose look but disobeys!

Omnes. Long live king Mahomet Boabdelin!

Almanz. No more; but hushed as midnight silence go:
He will not have your acclamations now
Hence, you unthinking crowd!—

(*The common people go off on both parties.*)

Empire, thou poor and despicable thing,
When such as these unmake or make a king!

Abdal. How much of virtue lies in one great soul,

(*Embracing him.*)

Whose single force can multitudes control!

(*A trumpet within.*)

(*Enter a Messenger.*)

Mess. The Duke of Arcos, sir,
Does with a trumpet from the foe appear.

Boab. Attend him; he shall have his audience here.

(*Enter the Duke of Arcos.*)

D. Arcos. The monarchs of Castile and Aragon
Have sent me to you, to demand this town,
To which their just and rightful claim is known.

Boab. Tell Ferdinand, my right to it appears
By long possession of eight hundred years:
When first my ancestors from Afric sailed,
In Rodrique's death your Gothic title failed.

D. Arcos. The successors of Rodrique still remain,
And ever since have held some part of Spain:
Even in the midst of your victorious powers,
The Asturias, and all Portugal, were ours.
You have no right, except you force allow;
And if yours then was just, so ours is now.

Boab. 'T is true from force the noblest title springs;
I therefore hold from that, which first made kings.

D. Arcos. Since then by force you prove your title true,
Ours must be just, because we claim from you.
When with your father you did jointly reign,
Invading with your Moors the south of Spain,
I, who that day the Christians did command,
Then took, and brought you bound to Ferdinand.

Boab. I'll hear no more; defer what you would say:
In private we'll discourse some other day.

D. Arcos. Sir, you shall hear, however you are loth,
That, like a perjured prince, you broke your oath:
To gain your freedom you a contract signed,
By which your crown you to my king resigned,
From thenceforth as his vassal holding it,
And paying tribute such as he thought fit;
Contracting, when your father came to die,
To lay aside all marks of royalty,
And at Purchena privately to live,
Which, in exchange, king Ferdinand did give.

Boab. The force used on me made that contract void.

D. Arcos. Why have you then its benefits enjoyed?
By it you had not only freedom then,
But, since, had aid of money and of men;
And, when Granada for your uncle held,
You were by us restored, and he expelled.
Since that, in peace we let you reap your grain,
Recalled our troops, that used to beat your plain;
And more——

Almanz. Yes, yes, you did with wondrous care,
Against his rebels prosecute the war,
While he secure in your protection slept;
For him you took, but for yourselves you kept.
Thus, as some fawning usurer does feed,
With present sums, the unwary unthrift's need,
You sold your kindness at a boundless rate,

And then o'erpaid the debt from his estate;
Which, mouldering piecemeal, in your hands did fall
Till now at last you came to swoop it all.
D. Arcos. The wrong you do my king I cannot bear;
Whose kindness you would odiously compare.
The estate was his; which yet, since you deny,
He 's now content, in his own wrong, to buy.
Almanz. And he shall buy it dear what his he calls—
We will not give one stone from out these walls.
Boab. Take this for answer, then,—
Whate'er your arms have conquered of my land,
I will, for peace, resign to Ferdinand.
To harder terms my mind I cannot bring;
But, as I still have lived, will die a king.
D. Arcos. Since thus you have resolved, henceforth prepare
For all the last extremities of war:
My king his hope from heaven's assistance draws.
Almanz. The Moors have heaven, and me, t' assist their cause.

(*Exit Arcos.*)

(*Enter Esperanza.*)

Esper. Fair Almahide,
(Who did with weeping eyes these discords see,
And fears the omen may unlucky be,)
Prepares a zambra [15] to be danced this night,
In hope soft pleasures may your minds unite.
Boab. My mistress gently chides the fault I made:
But tedious business has my love delayed,—
Business, which dares the joys of kings invade.
Almanz. First let us sally out, and meet the foe.
Abdal. Led on by you, we on to triumph go.
Boab. Then with the day let war and tumult cease;
The night be sacred to our love and peace:
'T is just some joys on weary kings should wait;
'T is all we gain by being slaves of state.

(*Exeunt omnes.*)

15 Festivity of dancing and music.

ACT II.

(*Abdalla, Abdelmelech, Ozmyn, Zulema, Hamet, as returning from the sally.*)

Abdal. This happy day does to Granada bring
A lasting peace, and triumphs to the king:
The two fierce factions will no longer jar,
Since they have now been brothers in the war.
Those who, apart, in emulation fought,
The common danger to one body brought;
And, to his cost, the proud Castilian finds
Our Moorish courage in united minds.
Abdelm. Since to each other's aid our lives we owe,
Lose we the name of faction, and of foe;
Which I to Zulema can bear no more,
Since Lyndaraxa's beauty I adore.
Zul. I am obliged to Lyndaraxa's charms,
Which gain the conquest I should lose by arms;
And wish my sister may continue fair,
That I may keep a good,
Of whose possession I should else despair.
Ozm. While we indulge our common happiness,
He is forgot, by whom we all possess;
The brave Almanzor, to whose arms we owe
All that we did, and all that we shall do;
Who, like a tempest, that outrides the wind,
Made a just battle ere the bodies joined.
Abdelm. His victories we scarce could keep in view,
Or polish 'em so fast as he rough-drew.
Abdal. Fate, after him, below with pain did move,
And victory could scarce keep pace above:
Death did at length so many slain forget,
And lost the tale, and took 'em by the great.[16]

(*To them Almanzor with the Duke of Arcos, prisoner.*)

Hamet. See, here he comes,
And leads in triumph him who did command
The vanquished army of king Ferdinand.
Almanz. (*To the Duke of Arcos.*) Thus far your master's arms a fortune find
Below the swelled ambition of his mind;
And Allah shuts a misbeliever's reign

16 Lost count and took wholesale.

From out the best and goodliest part of Spain.
Let Ferdinand Calabrian conquests make,
And from the French contested Milan take;
Let him new worlds discover to the old,
And break up shining mountains, big with gold;
Yet he shall find this small domestic foe,
Still sharp and pointed, to his bosom grow.

D. Arcos. Of small advantages too much you boast;
You beat the out-guards of my master's host:
This little loss, in our vast body, shows
So small, that half have never heard the news.
Fame 's out of breath, ere she can fly so far,
To tell 'em all that you have e'er made war.

Almanz. It pleases me your army is so great;
For now I know there 's more to conquer yet.
By heaven, I 'll see what troops you have behind:
I 'll face this storm, that thickens in the wind;
And, with bent forehead, full against it go,
Till I have found the last and utmost foe.

D. Arcos. Believe, you shall not long attend in vain:
To-morrow's dawn shall cover all your plain;
Bright arms shall flash upon you from afar,
A wood of lances, and a moving war.
But I, unhappy, in my bands must yet
Be only pleased to hear of your defeat,
And with a slave's inglorious ease remain,
Till conquering Ferdinand has broke my chain.

Almanz. Vain man, thy hopes of Ferdinand are weak!
I hold thy chain too fast for him to break.
But since thou threaten'st us, I 'll set thee free,
That I again may fight, and conquer thee.

D. Arcos. Old as I am, I take thee at thy word,
And will to-morrow thank thee with my sword.

Almanz. I 'll go, and instantly acquaint the king,
And sudden orders for thy freedom bring;
Thou canst not be so pleased at liberty
As I shall be to find thou dar'st be free.

(*Exeunt Almanzor, Arcos, and the rest, excepting only Abdalla and Zulema.*)

Abdal. Of all those Christians who infest[17] this town,
This Duke of Arcos is of most renown.

Zul. Oft have I heard, that in your father's reign,
His bold adventurers beat the neighboring plain;
Then under Ponce Leon's name he fought,
And from our triumphs many prizes brought;
Till in disgrace from Spain at length he went,
And since continued long in banishment.

Abdal. But see, your beauteous sister does appear.

(*To them Lyndaraxa.*)

Zul. By my desire she came to find me here.

(*Zulema and Lyndaraxa whisper; then Zulema goes out, and Lyndaraxa is going after.*)

Abdal. Why, fairest Lyndaraxa, do you fly

(*Staying her.*)

A prince, who at your feet is proud to die?

Lyndar. Sir, I should blush to own so rude a thing,

(*Staying.*)

As 't is to shun the brother of my king.

Abdal. In my hard fortune I some ease should find,
Did your disdain extend to all mankind.
But give me leave to grieve, and to complain,
That you give others what I beg in vain.

Lyndar. Take my esteem, if you on that can live;
For, frankly, sir, 't is all I have to give:
If from my heart you ask or hope for more,
I grieve the place is taken up before.

Abdal. My rival merits you.—
To Abdelmelech I will justice do;
For he wants worth, who dares not praise a foe.

Lyndar. That for his virtue, sir, you make defence,
Shows in your own a noble confidence.
But him defending, and excusing me,

17 Trouble by attacks.

I know not what can your advantage be.
Abdal. I fain would ask, ere I proceed in this,
If, as by choice, you are by promise his?
Lyndar. The engagement only in my love does lie,
But that 's a knot which you can ne'er untie.
Abdal. When cities are besieged, and treat to yield,
If there appear relievers from the field,
The flag of parley may be taken down,
Till the success of those without be known.
Lyndar. Though Abdelmelech has not yet possess'd,
Yet I have sealed the treaty for my breast.
Abdal. Your treaty has not tied you to a day;
Some chance might break it, would you but delay.
If I can judge the secrets of your heart,
Ambition in it has the greatest part;
And wisdom, then, will show some difference
Betwixt a private person and a prince.
Lyndar. Princes are subjects still,—
Subject and subject can small diff'rence bring:
The diff'rence is 'twixt subjects and a king.
And since, sir, you are none, your hopes remove;
For less than empire I 'll not change my love.
Abdal. Had I a crown, all I should prize in it,
Should be the power to lay it at your feet.
Lyndar. Had you that crown which you but wish, not hope,
Then I, perhaps, might stoop and take it up.
But till your wishes and your hopes agree,
You shall be still a private man with me.
Abdal. If I am king, and if my brother die,——
Lyndar. Two if's scarce make one possibility.
Abdal. The rule of happiness by reason scan;
You may be happy with a private man.
Lyndar. That happiness I may enjoy, 't is true;
But then that private man must not be you.
Where'er I love, I'm happy in my choice;
If I make you so, you shall pay my price.
Abdal. Why would you be so great?
Lyndar. Because I 've seen,
This day, what 't is to hope to be a queen.
Heaven, how you all watched each motion of her eye!
None could be seen while Almahide was by,
Because she is to be Her Majesty!—
Why would I be a queen? Because my face
Would wear the title with a better grace.
If I became it not, yet it would be
Part of your duty, then, to flatter me.
These are not half the charms of being great;
I would be somewhat—that I know not yet:
Yes! I avow the ambition of my soul,
To be that one, to live without control!
And that 's another happiness to me,
To be so happy as but one can be.
Abdal. Madam,—because I would all doubts remove,—
Would you, were I a king, accept my love?
Lyndar. I would accept it; and, to show 't is true,
From any other man as soon as you.
Abdal. Your sharp replies make me not love you less;
But make me seek new paths to happiness.
What I design, by time will best be seen:
You may be mine, and yet may be a queen.
When you are so, your word your love assures.
Lyndar. Perhaps not love you,—but I will be yours.—
(*He offers to take her hand, and kiss it.*)
Stay, sir, that grace I cannot yet allow,
Before you set the crown upon my brow.—
That favor which you seek,
Or Abdelmelech, or a king, must have;
When you are so, then you may be my slave.
(*Exit; but looks smiling back on him.*)
Abdal. Howe'er imperious in her words she were,
Her parting looks had nothing of severe;
A glancing smile allured me to command,
And her soft fingers gently pressed my hand:
I felt the pleasure glide through every part;

Her hand went through me to my very heart.
For such another pleasure, did he live,
I could my father of a crown deprive.
What did I say?—
Father?—That impious thought has shocked my mind:
How bold our passions are, and yet how blind!—
She 's gone; and now,
Methinks there is less glory in a crown:
My boiling passions settle, and go down.
Like amber chafed, when she is near, she acts;
When farther off, inclines, but not attracts.

(*To him Zulema.*)

Assist me, Zulema, if thou wouldst be
That friend thou seem'st, assist me against me.
Betwixt my love and virtue I am tossed;
This must be forfeited, or that be lost.
I could do much to merit thy applause;
Help me to fortify the better cause.
My honor is not wholly put to flight,
But would, if seconded, renew the fight.

Zul. I met my sister, but I do not see
What difficulty in your choice can be:
She told me all; and 't is so plain a case,
You need not ask what counsel to embrace.

Abdal. I stand reproved, that I did doubt at all;
My waiting virtue stayed but for thy call:
'T is plain that she, who for a kingdom now
Would sacrifice her love, and break her vow,
Not out of love, but interest, acts alone,
And would, even in my arms, lie thinking of a throne.

Zul. Add to the rest this one reflection more:
When she is married, and you still adore,
Think then—and think what comfort it will bring—
She had been mine,
Had I but only dared to be a king!

Abdal. I hope you only would my honor try;
I 'm loth to think you virtue's enemy.

Zul. If, when a crown and mistress are in place,
Virtue intrudes, with her lean holy face,
Virtue 's then mine, and not I virtue's foe.
Why does she come where she has nought to do?
Let her with anchorites, not with lovers, lie;
Statesmen and they keep better company.

Abdal. Reason was given to curb our headstrong will.

Zul. Reason but shows a weak physician's skill;
Gives nothing, while the raging fit does last,
But stays to cure it, when the worst is past.
Reason 's a staff for age, when nature 's gone;
But youth is strong enough to walk alone.

Abdal. In curs'd ambition I no rest should find,
But must for ever lose my peace of mind.

Zul. Methinks that peace of mind were bravely lost.
A crown, whate'er we give, is worth the cost.

Abdal. Justice distributes to each man his right;
But what she gives not, should I take by might?

Zul. If justice will take all, and nothing give,
Justice, methinks, is not distributive.

Abdal. Had fate so pleased, I had been eldest born,
And then, without a crime, the crown had worn.

Zul. Would you so please, fate yet a way would find;
Man makes his fate according to his mind.
The weak low spirit fortune makes her slave;
But she 's a drudge when hectored by the brave:
If fate weaves common thread, he 'll change the doom,
And with new purple spread a nobler loom.

Abdal. No more!—I will usurp the royal seat;
Thou, who hast made me wicked, make me great.

Zul. Your way is plain: the death of Tarifa
Does on the king our Zegrys' hatred draw;
Though with our enemies in show we close,
'T is but while we to purpose can be foes.
Selin, who heads us, would revenge his son;
But favor hinders justice to be done.

Proud Ozmyn with the king his power maintains,
And in him each Abencerrago reigns.

Abdal. What face of any title can I bring?

Zul. The right an eldest son has to be king.
Your father was at first a private man,
And got your brother ere his reign began:
When, by his valor, he the crown had won,
Then you were born, a monarch's eldest son.

Abdal. To sharp-eyed reason this would seem untrue;
But reason I through love's false optics view.

Zul. Love's mighty power has led me captive too;
I am in it unfortunate as you.

Abdal. Our loves and fortunes shall together go;
Thou shalt be happy, when I first am so.

Zul. The Zegrys at old Selin's house are met,
Where, in close council, for revenge they sit:
There we our common interest will unite;
You their revenge shall own, and they your right.
One thing I had forgot which may import:
I met Almanzor coming back from court,
But with a discomposed and speedy pace,
A fiery color kindling all his face:
The king his prisoner's freedom has denied,
And that refusal has provoked his pride.

Abdal. Would he were ours!—
I'll try to gild the injustice of the cause,
And court his valor with a vast applause.

Zul. The bold are but the instruments o' the wise;
They undertake the dangers we advise:
And, while our fabric with their pains we raise,
We take the profit, and pay them with praise.

(*Exeunt.*)

ACT III.

Scene 1.

(*Almanzor and Abdalla.*)

Almanz. That he should dare to do me this disgrace!—
Is fool or coward writ upon my face?
Refuse my prisoner!—I such means will use,
He shall not have a prisoner to refuse.

Abdal. He said you were not by your promise tied;
That he absolved your word, when he denied.

Almanz. He break my promise and absolve my vow!
'T is more than Mahomet himself can do!
The word which I have given shall stand like fate;
Not like the king's, that weathercock of state.
He stands so high, with so unfixed a mind,
Two factions turn him with each blast of wind:
But now, he shall not veer! My word is passed;
I'll take his heart by the roots, and hold it fast.

Abdal. You have your vengeance in your hand this hour;
Make me the humble creature of your power:
The Granadins will gladly me obey
Tired with so base and impotent a sway;
And, when I show my title, you shall see
I have a better right to reign than he.

Almanz. It is sufficient that you make the claim;
You wrong our friendship when your right you name.
When for myself I fight, I weigh the cause,
But friendship will admit of no such laws:
That weighs by the lump; and, when the cause is light,
Puts kindness in to set the balance right.
True, I would wish my friend the juster side;
But, in the unjust, my kindness more is tried:
And all the opposition I can bring,
Is that I fear to make you such a king.

Abdal. The majesty of kings we should not blame,
When royal minds adorn the royal name;
The vulgar, greatness too much idolize,
But haughty subjects it too much despise.

Almanz. I only speak of him,
Whom pomp and greatness sit so loose about,
That he wants majesty to fill 'em out.

Abdal. Haste, then, and lose no time!—
The business must be enterprised this night:

We must surprise the court in its delight.
Almanz. For you to will, for me 't is to obey:
But I would give a crown in open day;
And, when the Spaniards their assault begin,
At once beat those without, and these within.
(*Exit Almanzor.*)
(*Enter Abdelmelech.*)

Abdelm. Abdalla, hold!—There 's somewhat I intend
To speak, not as your rival, but your friend.
Abdal. If as a friend, I am obliged to hear;
And what a rival says I cannot fear.
Abdelm. Think, brave Abdalla, what it is you do:
Your quiet, honor, and our friendship too,
All for a fickle beauty you forego.
Think, and turn back, before it be too late.
Behold in me the example of your fate:
I am your sea-mark;[18] and, though wracked and lost,
My ruins stand to warn you from the coast.
Abdal. Your counsels, noble Abdelmelech, move
My reason to accept 'em, not my love.
Ah, why did heaven leave man so weak defence,
To trust frail reason with the rule of sense![19]
'T is overpoised and kicked up in the air,
While sense weighs down the scale, and keeps it there;
Or, like a captive king, 't is borne away,
And forced to countenance its own rebel's sway.
Abdelm. No, no; our reason was not vainly lent;
Nor is a slave, but by its own consent:
If reason on his subject's triumph wait,
An easy king deserves no better fate.
Abdal. You speak too late; my empire 's lost too far:
I cannot fight.
Abdelm. Then make a flying war;
Dislodge betimes before you are beset.
Abdal. Her tears, her smiles, her every look 's a net.
Her voice is like a Siren's of the land;
And bloody hearts lie panting in her hand.
Abdelm. This do you know, and tempt the danger still?
Abdal. Love, like a lethargy, has seized my will.
I 'm not myself, since from her sight I went;
I lean my trunk that way, and there stand bent.
As one who, in some frightful dream, would shun
His pressing foe, labors in vain to run;
And his own slowness in his sleep bemoans,
With thick short sighs, weak cries, and tender groans,
So I—
Abdelm. Some friend, in charity, should shake,
And rouse, and call you loudly till you wake.
Too well I know her blandishments to gain,
Usurper-like, till settled in her reign;
Then proudly she insults, and gives you cares
And jealousies, short hopes and long despairs.
To this hard yoke you must hereafter bow,
Howe'er she shines all golden to you now.
Abdal. Like him, who on the ice
Slides swiftly on, and sees the water near,
Yet cannot stop himself in his career,
So am I carried. This enchanted place,
Like Circe's isle, is peopled with a race
Of dogs and swine; yet, though their fate I know,
I look with pleasure, and am turning too.
(*Lyndaraxa passes over the stage.*)
Abdelm. Fly, fly, before the allurements of her face,
Ere she return with some resistless grace,
And with new magic covers all the place.
Abdal. I cannot, will not,—nay, I would not fly:
I 'll love, be blind, be cozened till I die;
And you, who bid me wiser counsel take,
I 'll hate, and, if I can, I 'll kill you for her sake.
Abdelm. Even I, that counselled you, that choice approve:
I 'll hate you blindly, and her blindly love.
Prudence, that stemmed the stream, is out of breath;
And to go down it is the easier death.

18 beacon

19 sensuous desire.

(*Lyndaraxa re-enters, and smiles on Abdalla.*)

(*Exit Abdalla.*)

Abdelm. That smile on Prince Abdalla seems to say,
You are not in your killing mood to-day:
Men brand, indeed, your sex with cruelty,
But you 're too good to see poor lovers die.
This godlike pity in you I extol;
And more, because, like heaven's, 't is general.

Lyndar. My smile implies not that I grant his suit:
'T was but a bare return of his salute.

Abdelm. It said, you were engaged, and I in place;[20]
But, to please both, you would divide the grace.

Lyndar. You 've cause to be contented with your part,
When he has but the look, and you the heart.

Abdelm. In giving but that look, you give what 's mine:
I 'll not one corner of a glance resign.
All 's mine; and I am covetous of my store:
I have not love enough; I 'll tax you more.

Lyndar. I gave not love; 't was but civility:
He is a prince; that 's due to his degree.

Abdelm. That prince you smiled on is my rival still,
And should, if me you loved, be treated ill.

Lyndar. I know not how to show so rude a spite.

Abdelm. That is, you know not how to love aright;
Or, if you did, you would more difference see
Betwixt our souls, than 'twixt our quality.
Mark, if his birth makes any difference,
If to his words it adds one grain of sense.
That duty which his birth can make his due
I 'll pay, but it shall not be paid by you:
For, if a prince courts her whom I adore,
He is my rival, and a prince no more.

Lyndar. And when did I my power so far resign,
That you should regulate each look of mine?

Abdelm. Then, when you gave your love, you gave that power.

Lyndar. 'T was during pleasure, 't is revoked this hour.
Now call me false, and rail on womankind,—
'T is all the remedy you 're like to find.

Abdelm. Yes, there 's one more;
I 'll hate you, and this visit is my last.

Lyndar. Do 't if you can; you know I hold you fast:
Yet, for your quiet, would you could resign
Your love, as easily as I do mine.

Abdelm. Furies and hell, how unconcerned she speaks!
With what indifference all her vows she breaks!
Curse on me, but she smiles!

Lyndar. That smile 's a part of love, and all 's your due:
I take it from the prince, and give it you.

Abdelm. Just heaven, must my poor heart your May-game prove,
To bandy, and make children's play in love?

(*Half crying.*)

Ah! how have I this cruelty deserved?
I, who so truly and so long have served!
And left so easily! oh, cruel maid!
So easily! 'T was too unkindly said.
That heart which could so easily remove
Was never fixed, nor rooted deep in love.

Lyndar. You lodged it so uneasy in your breast,
I thought you had been weary of the guest.
First, I was treated like a stranger there;
But, when a household friend I did appear,
You thought, it seems, I could not live elsewhere.
Then, by degrees, your feigned respect withdrew;
You marked my actions, and my guardian grew.
But I am not concerned your acts to blame:
My heart to yours but upon liking came;
And, like a bird whom prying boys molest,
Stays not to breed where she had built her nest.

Abdelm. I have done ill,
And dare not ask you to be less displeased;
Be but more angry, and my pain is eased.

Lyndar. If I should be so kind a fool, to take
This little satisfaction which you make,
I know you would presume some other time

[20] in the way (a meaning not noticed by the *Oxf. Dict.*)

Upon my goodness, and repeat your crime.
Abdelm. Oh never, never, upon no pretence;
My life 's too short to expiate this offence.
Lyndar. No, now I think on 't, 't is in vain to try;
'T is in your nature, and past remedy.
You 'll still disquiet my too loving heart:
Now we are friends, 't is best for both to part.
Abdelm. (*taking her hand.*) By this—will you not give me leave to swear?
Lyndar. You would be perjured if you should, I fear:
And, when I talk with Prince Abdalla next,
I with your fond[21] suspicions shall be vexed.
Abdelm. I cannot say I 'll conquer jealousy,
But, if you 'll freely pardon me, I 'll try.
Lyndar. And, till you that submissive servant prove,
I never can conclude you truly love.
(*To them the King, Almahide, Abenamar, Esperanza, Guards, Attendants.*)
Boab. Approach, my Almahide, my charming fair,
Blessing of peace, and recompense of war.
This night is yours; and may your life still be
The same in joy, though not solemnity.

SONG

I

Beneath a myrtle shade,
Which love for none but happy lovers made,
I slept; and straight my love before me brought
Phyllis, the object of my waking thought.
Undressed she came my flames to meet,
While love strowed flowers beneath her feet;
Flowers which, so pressed by her, became more sweet.

II

From the bright vision's head
A careless veil of lawn was loosely spread:
From her white temples fell her shaded hair,
Like cloudy sunshine, not too brown nor fair;
Her hands, her lips, did love inspire;
Her every grace my heart did fire;
But most her eyes, which languished with desire.

III

"Ah, charming fair," said I,
"How long can you my bliss and yours deny?
By nature and by love this lonely shade
Was for revenge of suffering lovers made.
Silence and shades with love agree;
Both shelter you and favor me:
You cannot blush, because I cannot see."

IV

"No, let me die," she said,
"Rather than lose the spotless name of maid!"
Faintly, methought, she spoke; for all the while
She bid me not believe her, with a smile.
"Then die," said I: she still denied;
"And is it thus, thus, thus," she cried,
"You use a harmless maid?"—and so she died!

V

I waked, and straight I knew,
I loved so well, it made my dream prove true:
Fancy, the kinder mistress of the two,
Fancy had done what Phyllis would not do!
Ah, cruel nymph, cease your disdain;
While I can dream, you scorn in vain,—
Asleep or waking, you must ease my pain.

(*The Zambra Dance.*)
(*After the dance, a tumultuous noise of drums and trumpets.*)
(*To them Ozmyn; his sword drawn.*)
Ozm. Arm, quickly, arm; yet all, I fear, too late;
The enemy 's already at the gate.
Boab. The Christians are dislodged; what foe is near?
Ozm. The Zegrys are in arms, and almost here:
The streets with torches shine, with shoutings ring,
And Prince Abdalla is proclaimed the king.
What man could do, I have already done,
But bold Almanzor fiercely leads 'em on.
Aben. The Alhambra yet is safe in my command;
(*To the King.*)
Retreat you thither, while their shock we stand.

21 foolish.

Boab. I cannot meanly for my life provide;
I 'll either perish in 't, or stem this tide.
To guard the palace, Ozmyn, be your care:
If they o'ercome, no sword will hurt the fair.

Ozm. I 'll either die, or I 'll make good the place.

Abdelm. And I with these will bold Almanzor face.

(*Exeunt all but the Ladies. An alarm within.*)

Almah. What dismal planet did my triumphs light!
Discord the day, and death does rule the night:
The noise my soul does through my senses wound.

Lyndar. Methinks it is a noble, sprightly sound,
The trumpet's clangor, and the clash of arms!
This noise may chill your blood, but mine it warms.

(*Shouting and clashing of swords within.*)

We have already passed the Rubicon;
The dice are mine; now, fortune, for a throne!

(*A shout within, and clashing of swords afar off.*)

The sound goes farther off, and faintly dies;
Curse of this going back, these ebbing cries!
Ye winds, waft hither sounds more strong and quick;
Beat faster, drums, and mingle deaths more thick.
I 'll to the turrets of the palace go,
And add new fire to those that fight below:
Thence, Hero-like,[22] with torches by my side
(Far be the omen, though) my love I 'll guide.
No; like his better fortune I 'll appear,
With open arms, loose veil, and flowing hair,
Just flying forward from my rolling sphere:
My smiles shall make Abdalla more than man;
Let him look up, and perish if he can.

(*Exit.*)

(*An alarm nearer: then enter Almanzor and Selin at the head of the Zegrys; Ozmyn, prisoner.*)

Almanz. We have not fought enough; they fly too soon;
And I am grieved the noble sport is done.
This only man, of all whom chance did bring

(*Pointing to Ozmyn.*)

To meet my arms, was worth the conquering.
His brave resistance did my fortune grace;
So slow, so threatening forward, he gave place.
His chains be easy, and his usage fair.

Selin. I beg you would commit him to my care.

Almanz. Next, the brave Spaniard free without delay;
And with a convoy send him safe away.

(*Exit a Guard.*)

(*To them Hamet and others.*)

Hamet. The king by me salutes you; and, to show
That to your valor he his crown does owe,
Would from your mouth I should the word receive,
And that to these you would your orders give.

Almanz. He much o'errates the little I have done.

(*Almanzor goes to the door, and there seems to give out orders by sending people several ways.*)

Selin (*to Ozmyn*). Now, to revenge the murder of my son,
To-morrow for thy certain death prepare;
This night I only leave thee to despair.

Ozmyn. Thy idle menaces I do not fear:
My business was to die or conquer here.
Sister, for you I grieve I could no more:
My present state betrays my want of power;
But, when true courage is of force bereft,
Patience, the noblest fortitude, is left.

(*Exit cum Selin.*)

Almah. Ah, Esperanza, what for me remains
But death, or, worse than death, inglorious chains!

Esper. Madam, you must not to despair give place;
Heaven never meant misfortune to that face.
Suppose there were no justice in your cause,
Beauty 's a bribe that gives her judges laws.

22 Hero set a light to guide her lover Leander in swimming the Hellespont.

That you are brought to this deplored estate,
Is but the ingenious flattery of your fate;
Fate fears her succor like an alms to give;
And would you, God-like, from yourself should live.

Almah. Mark but how terrible his eyes appear!
And yet there 's something roughly noble there,
Which, in unfashioned nature, looks divine,
And, like a gem, does in the quarry shine.

(*Almanzor returns; she falls at his feet, being veiled.*)

Almah. Turn, mighty conqueror, turn your face this way,
Do not refuse to hear the wretched pray!

Almanz. What business can this woman have with me?

Almah. That of the afflicted to the Deity.
So may your arms success in battles find;
So may the mistress of your vows be kind,
If you have any; or, if you have none,
So may your liberty be still your own!

Almanz. Yes, I will turn my face, but not my mind:
You bane and soft destruction of mankind,
What would you have with me?

Almah. I beg the grace

(*Unveiling.*)

You would lay by those terrors of your face.
Till calmness to your eyes you first restore,
I am afraid, and I can beg no more.

Almanz. (*looking fixedly on her*). Well; my fierce visage shall not murder you.
Speak quickly, woman; I have much to do.

Almah. Where should I find the heart to speak one word?
Your voice, sir, is as killing as your sword.
As you have left the lightning of your eye,
So would you please to lay your thunder by.

Almanz. I 'm pleased and pained, since first her eyes I saw,
As I were stung with some tarantula.
Arms, and the dusty field, I less admire,
And soften strangely in some new desire;
Honor burns in me not so fiercely bright,
But pale as fires when mastered by the light:
Even while I speak and look, I change yet more,
And now am nothing that I was before.
I 'm numbed, and fixed, and scarce my eyeballs move;
I fear it is the lethargy of love!
'T is he; I feel him now in every part:
Like a new lord he vaunts about my heart;
Surveys, in state, each corner of my breast,
While poor fierce I, that was, am dispossessed.
I 'm bound; but I will rouse my rage again;
And, though no hope of liberty remain,
I 'll fright my keeper when I shake my chain.
You are——

(*Angrily.*)

Almah. I know I am your captive, sir.

Almanz. You are—You shall—And I can scarce forbear——

Almah. Alas!

Almanz. 'T is all in vain; it will not do:

(*Aside.*)

I cannot now a seeming anger show:
My tongue against my heart no aid affords;
For love still rises up, and chokes my words.

Almah. In half this time a tempest would be still.

Almanz. 'T is you have raised that tempest in my will.
I wonnot [23] love you; give me back my heart;
But give it, as you had it, fierce and brave.
It was not made to be a woman's slave:
But, lion-like, has been in deserts bred,
And, used to range, will ne'er be tamely led.
Restore its freedom to my fettered will,
And then I shall have power to use you ill.

Almah. My sad condition may your pity move;
But look not on me with the eyes of love.—
I must be brief, though I have much to say.

Almanz. No, speak; for I can hear you now all day.

(*Softly.*)

Her suing soothes me with a secret pride:

23 wol (will) not. won't. a line seems to be lost just before this

A suppliant beauty cannot be denied:
(*Aside.*)
Even while I frown, her charms and furrows seize;
And I'm corrupted with the power to please.

Almah. Though in your worth no cause of fear I see,
I fear the insolence of victory;
As you are noble, sir, protect me then
From the rude outrage of insulting men.

Almanz. Who dares touch her I love? I'm all o'er love:
Nay, I am Love; Love shot, and shot so fast,
He shot himself into my breast at last.

Almah. You see before you her who should be queen,
Since she is promised to Boabdelin.

Almanz. Are you beloved by him? O wretched fate,
First, that I love at all; then, love too late!
Yet, I must love!

Almah. Alas, it is in vain;
Fate for each other did not us ordain.
The chances of this day too clearly show
That heaven took care that it should not be so.

Almanz. Would heaven had quite forgot me this one day!
But fate's yet hot——
I'll make it take a bent another way.
(*He walks swiftly and discomposedly, studying.*)
I bring a claim which does his right remove;
You're his by promise, but you're mine by love.
'T is all but ceremony which is past;
The knot's to tie which is to make you fast.
Fate gave not to Boabdelin that power;
He wooed you but as my ambassador.

Almah. Our souls are tied by holy vows above.

Almanz. He signed but his; but I will seal my love.
I love you better, with more zeal than he.

Almah. This day
I gave my faith to him, he his to me.

Almanz. Good heaven, thy book of fate before me lay,
But to tear out the journal of this day:
Or, if the order of the world below
Will not the gap of one whole day allow,
Give me that minute when she made her vow!
"That minute, ev'n the happy from their bliss might give;
"And those, who live in grief, a shorter time would live.[24]
So small a link, if broke, the eternal chain
Would, like divided waters, join again.—
It wonnot be; the fugitive is gone,
Pressed by the crowd of following minutes on:
That precious moment's out of nature fled,
And in the heap of common rubbish laid,
Of things that once have been, and are decayed.

Almah. Your passion, like a fright, suspends my pain;
It meets, o'erpowers, and bears mine back again:
But as, when tides against the current flow,
The native stream runs its own course below,
So, though your griefs possess the upper part,
My own have deeper channels in my heart.

Almanz. Forgive that fury which my soul does move;
'T is the essay of an untaught first love:
Yet rude, unfashioned truth it does express;
'T is love just peeping in a hasty dress.
Retire, fair creature, to your needful rest;
There's something noble laboring in my breast:
This raging fire which through the mass does move
Shall purge my dross, and shall refine my love.
(*Exeunt Almahide and Esperanza.*)
She goes, and I like my own ghost appear;
It is not living when she is not here.
(*To him Abdalla as King, attended.*)

Abdal. My first acknowledgments to heaven are due;
My next, Almanzor, let me pay to you.

Almanz. A poor surprise, and on a naked foe,
Whatever you confess, is all you owe;
And I no merit own, or understand
That fortune did you justice by my hand:
Yet, if you will that little service pay
With a great favor, I can show the way.

Abdal. I have a favor to demand of you;
That is, to take the thing for which you sue.

24 The quotation marks seem to be for emphasis, or ability for quotation, not to indicate a borrower (Noyes).

Almanz. Then, briefly, thus: when I the Albayzin won,
I found the beauteous Almahide alone,
Whose sad condition did my pity move;
And that compassion did produce my love.
Abdal. This needs no suit; in justice, I declare,
She is your captive by the right of war.
Almanz. She is no captive then; I set her free;
And, rather than I will her jailer be,
I'll nobly lose her in her liberty.
Abdal. Your generosity I much approve;
But your excess of that shows want of love.
Almanz. No, 't is the excess of love which mounts so high
That, seen far off, it lessens to the eye.
Had I not loved her, and had set her free,
That, sir, had been my generosity;
But 't is exalted passion, when I show
I dare be wretched, not to make her so:
And, while another passion fills her breast,
I'll be all wretched rather than half blest.
Abdal. May your heroic act so prosperous be,
That Almahide may sigh you set her free.

(*Enter Zulema.*)

Zul. Of five tall towers which fortify this town,
All but the Alhambra your dominion own:
Now, therefore, boldly I confess a flame,
Which is excused in Almahida's name.
If you the merit of this night regard,
In her possession I have my reward.
Almanz. She your reward! why, she's a gift so great,
That I myself have not deserved her yet;
And therefore, though I won her with my sword,
I have, with awe, my sacrilege restored.
Zul. What you deserve
I'll not dispute because I do not know;
This only I will say, she shall not go.
Almanz. Thou, single, art not worth my answering:
But take what friends, what armies thou canst bring;
What worlds; and, when you are united all,
Then I will thunder in your ears: "She shall!"
Zul. I'll not one tittle of my right resign.
Sir, your implicit promise made her mine;
When I in general terms my love did show,
You swore our fortunes should together go.
Abdal. The merits of the cause I'll not decide,
But, like my love, I would my gift divide.
Your equal titles, then, no longer plead;
But one of you, for love of me, recede.
Almanz. I have receded to the utmost line,
When, by my free consent, she is not mine:
Then let him equally recede with me,
And both of us will join to set her free.
Zul. If you will free your part of her, you may;
But, sir, I love not your romantic way.
Dream on, enjoy her soul, and set that free;
I'm pleased her person should be left for me.
Almanz. Thou shalt not wish her thine; thou shalt not dare
To be so impudent as to despair.
Zul. The Zegrys, sir, are all concerned to see
How much their merit you neglect in me.
Hamet. Your slighting Zulema this very hour
Will take ten thousand subjects from your power.
Almanz. What are ten thousand subjects such as they?
If I am scorned—I'll take myself away.
Abdal. Since both cannot possess what both pursue,
I grieve, my friend, the chance should fall on you;
But when you hear what reasons I can urge——
Almanz. None, none that your ingratitude can purge.
Reason's a trick, when it no grant affords;
It stamps the face of majesty on words.
Abdal. Your boldness to your services I give:
Now take it, as your full reward—to live.
Almanz. To live!
If from thy hands alone my death can be,
I am immortal, and a god, to thee.
If I would kill thee now, thy fate's so low,
That I must stoop ere I can give the blow;

But mine is fixed so far above thy crown,
That all thy men,
Piled on thy back, can never pull it down.
But at my ease thy destiny I send,
By ceasing from this hour to be thy friend.
Like heaven, I need but only to stand still,
And, not concurring to thy life, I kill.
Thou canst no title to my duty bring;
I'm not thy subject, and my soul's thy king.
Farewell. When I am gone,
There's not a star of thine dare stay with thee:
I'll whistle thy tame fortune after me;
And whirl fate with me wheresoe'er I fly,
As winds drive storms before 'em in the sky.

(*Exit.*)

Zul. Let not this insolent unpunished go;
Give your commands; your justice is too slow.

(*Zulema, Hamet, and others are going after him.*)

Abdal. Stay, and what part he pleases let him take:
I know my throne's too strong for him to shake.
But my fair mistress I too long forget;
The crown I promised is not offered yet.
Without her presence all my joys are vain,
Empire a curse, and life itself a pain.

(*Exeunt.*)

ACT IV

Scene 1.

(*Boabdelin, Abenamar, Guards.*)

Boab. Advise, or aid, but do not pity me:
No monarch born can fall to that degree.
Pity descends from kings to all below;
But can, no more than fountains, upward flow.
Witness, just heaven, my greatest grief has been,
I could not make your Almahide a queen.

Aben. I have too long the effects of fortune known,
Either to trust her smiles, or fear her frown.
Since in their first attempt you were not slain,
Your safety bodes you yet a second reign.
The people like a headlong torrent go,
And every dam they break, or overflow;
But, unopposed, they either lose their force,
Or wind in volumes to their former course.

Boab. In walls we meanly must our hopes enclose,
To wait our friends, and weary out our foes:
While Almahide
To lawless rebels is exposed a prey,
And forced the lustful victor to obey.

Aben. One of my blood, in rules of virtue bred!
Think better of her, and believe she's dead.

(*To them Almanzor.*)

Boab. We are betrayed, the enemy is here;
We have no farther room to hope or fear.

Almanz. It is indeed Almanzor whom you see,
But he no longer is your enemy.
You were ungrateful, but your foes were more;
What your injustice lost you, theirs restore.
Make profit of my vengeance while you may;
My two-edged sword can cut the other way.—
I am your fortune, but am swift like her,
And turn my hairy front if you defer:
That hour when you deliberate, is too late;
I point you the white moment of your fate.

Aben. Believe him sent as prince Abdalla's spy;
He would betray us to the enemy.

Almanz. Were I, like thee, in cheats of state grown old
(Those public markets, where for foreign gold
The poorer prince is to the richer sold),
Then thou mightst think me fit for that low part;
But I am yet to learn the statesman's art.
My kindness and my hate unmasked I wear;
For friends to trust, and enemies to fear.
My heart's so plain
That men on every passing thought may look,
Like fishes gliding in a crystal brook;
When troubled most, it does the bottom show;
'T is weedless all above, and rockless all below.

Aben. Ere he be trusted, let him first be tried;

He may be false, who once has changed his side.
Almanz. In that you more accuse yourselves than me;
None who are injured can unconstant be.
You were unconstant, you, who did the wrong;
To do me justice does to me belong.
Great souls by kindness only can be tied;
Injured again, again I 'll leave your side.
Honor is what myself, and friends, I owe;
And none can lose it who forsake a foe.
Since, then, your foes now happen to be mine,
Though not in friendship, we 'll in interest join:
So while my loved revenge is full and high,
I 'll give you back your kingdom by the by.
Boab. (*Embracing him.*) That I so long delayed what you desire,
Was not to doubt your worth, but to admire.
Almanz. This counsellor an old man's caution shows,
Who fears that little he has left to lose:
Age sets to [24] fortune; while youth boldly throws.
But let us first your drooping soldiers cheer;
Then seek out danger, ere it dare appear:
This hour I fix your crown upon your brow;
Next hour fate gives it, but I give it now.
(*Exeunt.*)

SCENE 2.

(*Lyndaraxa alone.*)

Lyndar. O, could I read the dark decrees of fate,
That I might once know whom to love, or hate!
For I myself scarce my own thoughts can guess,
So much I find 'em varied by success.
As in some weather-glass, my love I hold;
Which falls or rises with the heat or cold.
I will be constant yet, if Fortune can;
I love the king,—let her but name the man.
(*To her Halyma.*)
Hal. Madam, a gentleman, to me unknown,
Desires that he may speak with you alone.
Lyndar. Some message from the king. Let him appear.
(*To her Abdelmelech; who entering throws off his disguise. She starts.*)
Abdelm. I see you are amazed that I am here:
But let at once your fear and wonder end.
In the usurper's guard I found a friend,
Who led me to you safe in this disguise.
Lyndar. Your danger brings this trouble in my eyes.
But what affair this venturous visit drew?
Abdelm. The greatest in the world,—the seeing you.
Lyndar. The courage of your love I so admire
That, to preserve you, you shall straight retire.
(*She leads him to the door.*)
Go, dear! each minute does new dangers bring;
You will be taken; I expect the king.
Abdelm. The king!—the poor usurper of an hour:
His empire's but a dream of kingly power.—
I warn you, as a lover and a friend,
To leave him ere his short dominion end:
The soldier I suborned will wait at night,
And shall alone be conscious of your flight.
Lyndar. I thank you that you so much care bestow;
But, if his reign be short, I need not go.
For why should I expose my life and yours
For what, you say, a little time assures?
Abdelm. My danger in the attempt is very small;
And, if he loves you, yours is none at all.
But, though his ruin be as sure as fate,
Your proof of love to me would come too late.
This trial I in kindness would allow;
'T is easy; if you love me, show it now.
Lyndar. It is because I love you, I refuse;
For all the world my conduct would accuse,
If I should go with him I love away:
And, therefore, in strict virtue I will stay.
Abdelm. You would in vain dissemble love to me;
Through that thin veil your artifice I see.
You would expect the event, and then declare;
But do not, do not drive me to despair:

24 "Gambles (methodically) against" (?) (Noyes.)

For, if you now refuse with me to fly,
Rather than love you after this, I 'll die;
And therefore weigh it well before you speak;
My king is safe, his force within not weak.

Lyndar. The counsel you have given me may be wise;
But, since the affair is great, I will advise.

Abdelm. Then that delay I for denial take.
(*Is going.*)

Lyndar. Stay; you too swift an exposition make.
If I should go, since Zulema will stay,
I should my brother to the king betray.

Abdelm. There is no fear; but, if there were, I see
You value still your brother more than me.
Farewell! some ease I in your falsehood find;
It lets a beam in that will clear my mind:
My former weakness I with shame confess,
And, when I see you next, shall love you less.
(*Is going again.*)

Lyndar. Your faithless dealing you may blush to tell;
(*Weeping.*)
This is a maid's reward, who loves too well.—
(*He looks back.*)
Remember that I drew my latest breath
In charging your unkindness with my death.

Abdelm. (*coming back*). Have I not answered all you can invent,
Even the least shadow of an argument?

Lyndar. You want not cunning what you please to prove,
But my poor heart knows only how to love;
And, finding this, you tyrannize the more:
'T is plain, some other mistress you adore;
And now, with studied tricks of subtilty,
You come prepared to lay the fault on me.
(*Wringing her hands.*)
But, O, that I should love so false a man!

Abdelm. Hear me, and then disprove it, if you can.

Lyndar. I 'll hear no more; your breach of faith is plain:
You would with wit your want of love maintain.
But, by my own experience, I can tell,
They who love truly cannot argue well.—
Go, faithless man!
Leave me alone to mourn my misery;
I cannot cease to love you, but I 'll die.
(*Leans her head on his arm.*)

Abdelm. What man but I so long unmoved could hear
(*Weeping.*)
Such tender passion, and refuse a tear!
But do not talk of dying any more,
Unless you mean that I should die before.

Lyndar. I fear your feigned repentance comes too late;
I die, to see you still thus obstinate:
But yet, in death my truth of love to show,
Lead me; if I have strength enough, I 'll go.

Abdelm. By heaven, you shall not go! I will not be
O'ercome in love or generosity.
All I desire, to end the unlucky strife,
Is but a vow that you will be my wife.

Lyndar. To tie me to you by a vow is hard;
It shows my love you as no tie regard.
Name anything but that, and I 'll agree.

Abdelm. Swear, then, you never will my rival's be.

Lyndar. Nay, pr'ythee, this is harder than before.
Name anything, good dear, but that thing more.

Abdelm. Now I too late perceive I am undone;
Living and seeing, to my death I run.
I know you false, yet in your snares I fall;
You grant me nothing, and I grant you all.

Lyndar. I would grant all; but I must curb my will,
Because I love to keep you jealous still.
In your suspicion I your passion find;
But I will take a time to cure your mind.

Halyma. O, madam, the new king is drawing near!

Lyndar. Haste quickly hence, lest he should find you here!

Abdelm. How much more wretched than I came, I go!
I more my weakness and your falsehood know;
And now must leave you with my greatest foe!
(*Exit Abdelm.*)

Lyndar. Go!—How I love thee, heaven can only tell:
And yet I love thee, for a subject, well.—

Yet, whatsoever charms a crown can bring,
A subject 's greater than a little king.
I will attend till time this throne secure;
And, when I climb, my footing shall be sure.—
(*Music without.*)
Music! and, I believe, addressed to me.

SONG

I

Wherever I am, and whatever I do,
My Phyllis is still in my mind;
When angry, I mean not to Phyllis to go,
My feet, of themselves, the way find;
Unknown to myself I am just at her door,
And, when I would rail, I can bring out no more,
Than, "Phyllis too fair and unkind!"

II

When Phyllis I see, my heart bounds in my breast,
And the love I would stifle is shown;
But asleep, or awake, I am never at rest,
When from my eyes Phyllis is gone.
Sometimes a sad dream does delude my sad mind;
But, alas! when I wake, and no Phyllis I find,
How I sigh to myself all alone!

III

Should a king be my rival in her I adore,
He should offer his treasure in vain.
O, let me alone to be happy and poor,
And give me my Phyllis again!
Let Phyllis be mine, and but ever be kind,
I could to a desert with her be confined,
And envy no monarch his reign.

IV

Alas! I discover too much of my love,
And she too well knows her own power!
She makes me each day a new martyrdom prove,
And makes me grow jealous each hour:
But let her each minute torment my poor mind,
I had rather love Phyllis, both false and unkind,
Than ever be freed from her power.

(*Abdalla enters, with Guards.*)

Abdal. Now, madam, at your feet a king you see;
Or, rather, if you please, a sceptred slave:
'T is just you should possess the power you gave.
Had love not made me yours, I yet had been
But the first subject to Boabdelin.
Thus heaven declares the crown I bring your due;
And had forgot my title, but for you.

Lyndar. Heaven to your merits will, I hope, be kind;
But, sir, it has not yet declared its mind.
'T is true, it holds the crown above your head;
But does not fix it till your brother 's dead.

Abdal. All but the Alhambra is within my power;
And that my forces go to take this hour.

Lyndar. When, with its keys, your brother's head you bring,
I shall believe you are indeed a king.

Abdal. But since the events of all things doubtful are,
And, of events, most doubtful those of war;
I beg to know before, if fortune frown,
Must I then lost your favor with my crown?

Lyndar. You 'll soon return a conqueror again;
And, therefore, sir, your question is in vain.

Abdal. I think to certain victory I move;
But you may more assure it by your love,
That grant will make my arms invincible.

Lyndar. My prayers and wishes your success foretell.—
Go then, and fight, and think you fight for me;
I wait but to reward your victory.

Abdal. But if I lose it, must I lose you too?

Lyndar. You are too curious, if you more would know.
I know not what my future thoughts will be:
Poor women's thoughts are all *extempore.*
Wise men, indeed,
Beforehand a long chain of thoughts produce;
But ours are only for our present use.

Abdal. Those thoughts, you will not know, too well declare
You mean to wait the final doom of war.

Lyndar. I find you come to quarrel with me now;

Would you know more of me than I allow?
Whence are you grown that great divinity
That with such ease into my thoughts can pry?
Indulgence does not with some tempers suit;
I see I must become more absolute.

Abdal. I must submit,
On what hard terms soe'er my peace be bought.

Lyndar. Submit!—you speak as you were not in fault.
'T is evident the injury is mine;
For why should you my secret thoughts divine?

Abdal. Yet if we might be judged by reason's laws!—

Lyndar. Then you would have your reason judge my cause!—
Either confess your fault, or hold your tongue;
For I am sure I 'm never in the wrong.

Abdal. Then I acknowledge it.

Lyndar. Then I forgive.

Abdal. Under how hard a law poor lovers live!
Who, like the vanquished, must their right release,
And with the loss of reason buy their peace.—
(*Aside.*)
Madam, to show that you my power command,
I put my life and safety in your hand.
Dispose of the Albayzin as you please,
To your fair hands I here resign the keys.

Lyndar. I take your gift, because your love it shows,
And faithful Selin for Alcalde [25] choose.

Abdal. Selin, from her alone your orders take.
This one request, yet, madam, let me make,
That from those turrets you the assault will see;
And crown, once more, my arms with victory.
(*Leads her out.*)

(*Selin remains with Gazui and Reduan, his servants.*)

Selin. Gazul, go tell my daughter that I wait.
You, Reduan, bring the prisoner to his fate.
(*Exeunt Gaz. and Red.*)
Ere of my charge I will possession take,
A bloody sacrifice I mean to make:
The manes [26] of my son shall smile this day,
While I, in blood, my vows of vengeance pay.

(*Enter at one door Benzayda, with Gazul; at the other, Ozmyn bound, with Reduan.*)

Selin. I sent, Benzayda, to glad your eyes:
These rites we owe your brother's obsequies.—
You two (*to Gaz. and Red.*) the accurst Abencerrago bind:
You need no more to instruct you in my mind.

(*They bind him to one corner of the stage.*)

Benz. In what sad object am I called to share?
Tell me, what is it, sir, you here prepare?

Selin. 'T is what your dying brother did bequeath:
A scene of vengeance, and a pomp of death!

Benz. The horrid spectacle my soul does fright;
I want the heart to see the dismal sight.

Selin. You are my principal invited guest,
Whose eyes I would not only feed, but feast:
You are to smile at his last groaning breath,
And laugh to see his eyeballs roll in death;
To judge the lingering soul's convulsive strife,
When thick short breath catches at parting life.

Benz. And of what marble do you think me made?

Selin. What! can you be of just revenge afraid?

Benz. He killed my brother in his own defence.
Pity his youth, and spare his innocence.

Selin. Art thou so soon to pardon murder won?
Can he be innocent, who killed my son?
Abenamar shall mourn as well as I;
His Ozmyn, for my Tarifa, shall die.
But since thou plead'st so boldly, I will see
That justice thou wouldst hinder done by thee.
(*Gives her his sword.*)
Here—take the sword, and do a sister's part:
Pierce his, fond girl, or I will pierce thy heart.

25 magistrate (three syllables).

26 ghost.

Ozm. To his commands I join my own request;
All wounds from you are welcome to my breast:
Think only, when your hand this act has done,
It has but finished what your eyes begun.
I thought with silence to have scorned my doom;
But now your noble pity has o'ercome;
Which I acknowledge with my latest breath,—
The first whoe'er began a love in death.

Benz. (*to Selin*). Alas, what aid can my weak hand afford?
You see I tremble when I touch a sword:
The brightness dazzles me, and turns my sight;
Or, if I look, 't is but to aim less right.

Ozm. I 'll guide the hand which must my death convey;
My leaping heart shall meet it half the way.

Selin (*to Benz.*). Waste not the precious time in idle breath.

Benz. Let me resign this instrument of death.

(*Giving the sword to her father, and then pulling it back.*)

Ah, no! I was too hasty to resign:
'T is in your hand more mortal than in mine.

(*To them Hamet.*)

Hamet. The king is from the Alhambra beaten back,
And now preparing for a new attack;
To favor which, he wills that instantly
You reinforce him with a new supply.

Selin (*to Benz.*). Think not, although my duty calls me hence,
That with the breach of yours I will dispense.
Ere my return see my commands you do:
Let me find Ozmyn dead, and killed by you.—
Gazul and Reduan, attend her still;
And, if she dares to fail, perform my will.

(*Exeunt Selin and Hamet.*)

(*Benzayda looks languishing on him, with her sword down; Gazul and Reduan standing with drawn swords by her.*)

Ozm. Defer not, fair Benzayda, my death:
Looking for you,
I should but live to sigh away my breath.
My eyes have done the work they had to do:
I take your image with me, which they drew;
And, when they close, I shall die full of you.

Benz. When parents their commands unjustly lay,
Children are privileged to disobey;
Yet from that breach of duty I am clear,
Since I submit the penalty to bear.
To die, or kill you, is the alternative;
Rather than take your life, I will not live.

Ozm. This shows the excess of generosity;
But, madam, you have no pretence to die.
I should defame the Abencerrages' race,
To let a lady suffer in my place.
But neither could that life you would bestow,
Save mine; nor do you so much pity owe
To me, a stranger, and your house's foe.

Benz. From whencesoe'er their hate our houses drew,
I blush to tell you, I have none for you.
'T is a confession which I should not make,
Had I more time to give, or you to take:
But, since death 's near, and runs with so much force,
We must meet first, and intercept his course.

Ozm. O, how unkind a comfort do you give!
Now I fear death again, and wish to live.
Life were worth taking, could I have it now;
But 't is more good than heaven can e'er allow
To one man's portion, to have life and you.

Benz. Sure, at our births,
Death with our meeting planets danced above,
Or we were wounded by a mourning love!

(*Shouts within.*)

Red. The noise returns, and doubles from behind;
It seems as if two adverse armies joined.—
Time presses us.

Gaz. If longer you delay,
We must, though loth, your father's will obey.

Ozm. Haste, madam, to fulfil his hard commands,
And rescue me from their ignoble hands.
Let me kiss yours, when you my wound begin,
Then easy death will slide with pleasure in.

Benz. Ah, gentle soldiers, some short time allow!

(*To Gaz. and Red.*)

My father has repented him ere now;
Or will repent him, when he finds me dead.
My clue of life is twined with Ozmyn's thread.

Red. 'T is fatal to refuse her, or obey.
But where is our excuse? what can we say?

Benz. Say anything—
Say that to kill the guiltless you were loth;
Or if you did, say I would kill you both.

Gaz. To disobey our orders is to die.—
I 'll do 't: who dare oppose it?

Red. That dare I.

(*Reduan stands before Ozmyn, and fights with Gazul. Benzayda unbinds Ozmyn, and gives him her sword.*)

Benz. Stay not to see the issue of the fight;
(*Red. kills Gaz.*)
But haste to save yourself by speedy flight.

Ozm. (*kneeling to kiss her hand*) Did all mankind against my life conspire,
Without this blessing I would not retire.
But, madam, can I go and leave you here?
Your father's anger now for you I fear:
Consider, you have done too much to stay.

Benz. Think not of me, but fly yourself away.

Red. Haste quickly hence; the enemies are nigh!
From every part I see our soldiers fly.
The foes not only our assailants beat,
But fiercely sally out on their retreat,
And, like a sea broke loose, come on amain.

(*To them Abenamar, and a party with their swords drawn, driving in some of the enemies.*)

Aben. Traitors, you hope to save yourselves in vain!
Your forfeit lives shall for your treason pay;
And Ozmyn's blood shall be revenged this day.

Ozm. (*kneeling to his father*). No, sir, your Ozmyn lives; and lives to own
A father's piety to free his son.

Aben. (*embracing him*). My Ozmyn!—O, thou blessing of my age!
And art thou safe from their deluded rage!—
Whom must I praise for thy deliverance?
Was it thy valor, or the work of chance?

Ozm. Nor chance, nor valor, could deliver me;
But 't was a noble pity set me free.
My liberty, and life,
And what your happiness you 're pleased to call,
We to this charming beauty owe it all.

Aben. (*to her*). Instruct me, visible divinity!
Instruct me by what name to worship thee!
For to thy virtue I would altars raise,
Since thou art much above all human praise.
But see——

(*Enter Almanzor, his sword bloody, leading in Almahide, attended by Esperanza.*)

My other blessing, Almahide, is here!
I 'll to the king, and tell him she is near:
You, Ozmyn, on your fair deliverer wait,
And with your private joys the public celebrate.
(*Exeunt.*)

Almanz. The work is done; now, madam, you are free;
At least, if I can give you liberty:
But you have chains which you yourself have chose;
And, O, that I could free you too from those!
But you are free from force, and have full power
To go, and kill my hopes and me, this hour.
I see, then, you will go; but yet my toil
May be rewarded with a looking-while.

Almah. Almanzor can from every subject raise
New matter for our wonder and his praise.
You bound and freed me; but the difference is,
That showed your valor; but your virtue this.

Almanz. Madam, you praise a funeral victory,
At whose sad pomp the conqueror must die.

Almah. Conquest attends Almanzor everywhere;
I am too small a foe for him to fear:
But heroes still must be opposed by some,
Or they would want occasion to o'ercome.

Almanz. Madam, I cannot on bare praises live;
Those who abound in praises seldom give.

Almah. While I to all the world your worth make known,

May heaven reward the pity you have shown!
Almanz. My love is languishing, and starved to death;
And would you give me charity—in breath?
Prayers are the alms of churchmen to the poor:
They send to heaven's, but drive us from their door.
Almah. Cease, cease a suit
So vain to you, and troublesome to me,
If you will have me think that I am free.
If I am yet a slave, my bonds I 'll bear;
But what I cannot grant, I will not hear.
Almanz. You wonnot hear! You must both hear and grant;
For, madam, there 's an impudence in want.
Almah. Your way is somewhat strange to ask relief;
You ask with threatening, like a begging thief.
Once more, Almanzor, tell me, am I free?
Almanz. Madam, you are, from all the world,—but me!
But as a pirate, when he frees the prize
He took from friends, sees the rich merchandise,
And, after he has freed it, justly buys;
So, when I have restored your liberty—
But then, alas, I am too poor to buy!
Almah. Nay, now you use me just as pirates do:
You free me; but expect a ransom too.
Almanz. You 've all the freedom that a prince can have;
But greatness cannot be without a slave.
A monarch never can in private move,
But still is haunted with officious love.
So small an inconvenience you may bear;
'T is all the fine Fate sets upon the fair.
Almah. Yet princes may retire whene'er they please,
And breathe free air from out [27] their palaces:
They go sometimes unknown, to shun their state;
And then 't is manners not to know or wait.
Almanz. If not a subject, then a ghost I 'll be;
And from a ghost, you know, no place is free.
Asleep, awake, I 'll haunt you everywhere;
From my white shroud groan love into your ear:
When in your lover's arms you sleep at night,
I 'll glide in cold betwixt, and seize my right:
And is 't not better, in your nuptial bed,
To have a living lover than a dead?
Almah. I can no longer bear to be accused,
As if, what I could grant you, I refused.
My father's choice I never will dispute;
And he has chosen ere you moved your suit.
You know my case; if equal you can be,
Plead for yourself, and answer it for me.
Almanz. Then, madam, in that hope you bid me live;
I ask no more than you may justly give:
But in strict justice there may favor be,
And may I hope that you have that for me?
Almah. Why do you thus my secret thoughts pursue,
Which, known, hurt me, and cannot profit you?
Your knowledge but new troubles does prepare,
Like theirs who curious in their fortunes are.
To say, I could with more content be yours,
Tempts you to hope; but not that hope assures.
For since the king has right,
And favored by my father in his suit,
It is a blossom which can bear no fruit.
Yet, if you dare attempt so hard a task,
May you succeed; you have my leave to ask.
Almanz. I can with courage now my hopes pursue,
Since I no longer have to combat you.
That did the greatest difficulty bring;
The rest are small, a father and a king!
Almah. Great souls discern not when the leap 's too wide,
Because they only view the farther side.
Whatever you desire, you think is near;
But, with more reason, the event I fear.
Almanz. No; there is a necessity in fate,
Why still the brave bold man is fortunate:
He keeps his object ever full in sight,
And that assurance holds him firm and right.
True, 't is a narrow path that leads to bliss,
But right before there is no precipice:

27 outside of.

Fear makes men look aside, and then their footing miss.

Almah. I do your merit all the right I can;
Admiring virtue in a private man;
I only wish the king may grateful be,
And that my father with my eyes may see.
Might I not make it as my last request,—
Since humble carriage suits a suppliant best,—
That you would somewhat of your fierceness hide—
That inborn fire—I do not call it pride?

Almanz. Born, as I am, still to command, not sue,
Yet you shall see that I can beg for you;
And if your father will require a crown,
Let him but name the kingdom, 't is his own.
I am, but while I please, a private man;
I have that soul which empires first began.
From the dull crowd, which every king does lead,
I will pick out whom I will choose to head:
The best and bravest souls I can select,
And on their conquered necks my throne erect.

(*Exeunt.*)

ACT V.

Scene 1.

(*Abdalla alone, under the walls of the Albayzin.*)

Abdal. While she is mine, I have not yet lost all,
But in her arms shall have a gentle fall:
Blest in my love, although in war o'ercome,
I fly, like Antony from Actium,
To meet a better Cleopatra here.—
You of the watch! you of the watch! appear.

Sold. (*Above.*) Who calls below? What 's your demand?

Abdal. 'T is I:
Open the gate with speed; the foe is nigh.

Sold. What orders for admittance do you bring?

Abdal. Slave, my own orders: look, and know the king.

Sold. I know you; but my charge is so severe
That none, without exception, enter here.

Abdal. Traitor, and rebel! thou shalt shortly see
Thy orders are not to extend to me.

Lyndar. (*Above.*) What saucy slave so rudely does exclaim,
And brands my subject with a rebel's name?

Abdal. Dear Lyndaraxa, haste; the foes pursue.

Lyndar. My lord, the Prince Abdalla, is it you?
I scarcely can believe the words I hear;
Could you so coarsely treat my officer?

Abdal. He forced me; but the danger nearer draws:
When I am entered, you shall know the cause.

Lyndar. Entered! Why, have you any business here?

Abdal. I am pursued, the enemy is near.

Lyndar. Are you pursued, and do you thus delay
To save yourself? Make haste, my lord, away.

Abdal. Give me not cause to think you mock my grief:
What place have I, but this, for my relief?

Lyndar. This favor does your handmaid much oblige,
But we are not provided for a siege:
My subjects few; and their provision thin;
The foe is strong without, we weak within.
This to my noble lord may seem unkind,
But he will weigh it in his princely mind;
And pardon her, who does assurance want
So much, she blushes when she cannot grant.

Abdal. Yes, you may blush; and you have cause to weep.
Is this the faith you promised me to keep?
Ah yet, if to a lover you will bring
No succor, give your succor to a king.

Lyndar. A king is he, whom nothing can withstand;
Who men and money can with ease command.
A king is he, whom fortune still does bless;
He is a king, who does a crown possess.
If you would have me think that you are he,
Produce to view your marks of sovereignty;

But if yourself alone for proof you bring,
You 're but a single person, not a king.

Abdal. Ingrateful maid, did I for this rebel?
I say no more; but I have loved too well.

Lyndar. Who but yourself did that rebellion move?
Did I e'er promise to receive your love?
Is it my fault you are not fortunate?
I love a king, but a poor rebel hate.

Abdal. Who follow fortune, still are in the right;
But let me be protected here this night.

Lyndar. The place to-morrow will be circled round;
And then no way will for your flight be found.

Abdal. I hear my enemies just coming on;
(*Trampling within.*)
Protect me but one hour, till they are gone.

Lyndar. They 'll know you have been here; it cannot be;
That very hour you stay, will ruin me:
For if the foe behold our interview,
I shall be thought a rebel too, like you.
Haste hence; and that your flight may prosperous prove,
I 'll recommend you to the powers above.
(*Exit Lynd. from above.*)

Abdal. She 's gone! Ah, faithless and ingrateful maid!
I hear some tread; and fear I am betrayed.
I 'll to the Spanish king; and try if he,
To countenance his own right, will succor me:
There is more faith in Christian dogs, than thee.
(*Exit.*)

SCENE 2.

(*Ozmyn, Benzayda, Abenamar.*)

Benz. I wish
(To merit all these thanks) I could have said,
My pity only did his virtue aid;
'T was pity, but 't was of a love-sick maid.
His manly suffering my esteem did move;
That bred compassion, and compassion love.

Ozm. O blessing sold me at too cheap a rate!
(*To his father.*)
My danger was the benefit of fate.
But that you may my fair deliverer know,
She was not only born our house's foe,
But to my death by powerful reasons led;
At least, in justice, she might wish me dead.

Aben. But why thus long do you her name conceal?

Ozm. To gain belief for what I now reveal:
Even thus prepared, you scarce can think it true,
The saver of my life from Selin drew
Her birth; and was his sister whom I slew.

Aben. No more; it cannot, was not, must not be:
Upon my blessing, say not it was she.
The daughter of the only man I hate!
Two contradictions twisted in a fate!

Ozm. The mutual hate, which you and Selin bore,
Does but exalt her generous pity more.
Could she a brother's death forgive to me,
And cannot you forget her family?
Can you so ill requite the life I owe,
To reckon her, who gave it, still your foe?
It lends too great a lustre to her line,
To let her virtue ours so much outshine.

Aben. Thou giv'st her line the advantage which they have,
By meanly taking of the life they gave.
Grant that it did in her a pity show;
But would my son be pitied by a foe?
She has the glory of thy act defaced:
Thou killedst her brother; but she triumphs last:
Poorly for us our enmity would cease;
When we are beaten, we receive a peace.

Benz. If that be all in which you disagree,
I must confess 't was Ozmyn conquered me.
Had I beheld him basely beg his life,
I should not now submit to be his wife;
But when I saw his courage death control,
I paid a secret homage to his soul;
And thought my cruel father much to blame,
Since Ozmyn's virtue his revenge did shame.

Aben. What constancy canst thou e'er hope to find
In that unstable, and soon conquered mind?

What piety canst thou expect from her,
Who could forgive a brother's murderer?
Or, what obedience hop'st thou to be paid,
From one who first her father disobeyed?

Ozm. Nature, that bids us parents to obey,
Bids parents their commands by reason weigh;
And you her virtue by your praise did own,
Before you knew by whom the act was done.

Aben. Your reasons speak too much of insolence;
Her birth 's a crime past pardon or defence.
Know, that as Selin was not won by thee,
Neither will I by Selin's daughter be.
Leave her, or cease henceforth to be my son:
This is my will; and this I will have done.

(*Exit Aben.*)

Ozm. It is a murdering will,
That whirls along with an impetuous sway,
And, like chain-shot, sweeps all things in its way.
He does my honor want of duty call;
To that, and love, he has no right at all.

Benz. No, Ozmyn, no; it is a much less ill
To leave me, than dispute a father's will:
If I had any title to your love,
Your father's greater right does mine remove:
Your vows and faith I give you back again,
Since neither can be kept without a sin.

Ozm. Nothing but death my vows can give me back:
They are not yours to give, nor mine to take.

Benz. Nay, think not, though I could your vows resign,
My love or virtue could dispense with mine.
I would extinguish your unlucky fire,
To make you happy in some new desire:
I can preserve enough for me and you,
And love, and be unfortunate, for two.

Ozm. In all that 's good and great
You vanquish me so fast, that in the end
I shall have nothing left me to defend.
From every post you force me to remove;
But let me keep my last retrenchment, love.

Benz. Love then, my Ozmyn; I will be content

(*Giving her hand.*)

To make you wretched by your own consent:
Live poor, despised, and banished for my sake,
And all the burden of my sorrows take;
For, as for me, in whatsoe'er estate,
While I have you, I must be fortunate.

Ozm. Thus then, secured of what we hold most dear,
(Each other's love) we 'll go—I know not where.
For where, alas, should we our flight begin?
The foe 's without; our parents are within.

Benz. I 'll fly to you, and you shall fly to me;
Our flight but to each other's arms shall be.
To providence and chance permit the rest;
Let us but love enough, and we are blest.

(*Exeunt.*)

Scene 3.

(*Enter Boabdelin, Abenamar, Abdelmelech, Guard: Zulema and Hamet, prisoners.*)

Abdelm. They 're Lyndaraxa's brothers; for her sake,
Their lives and pardon my request I make.

Boab. Then, Zulema and Hamet, live; but know,
Your lives to Abdelmelech's suit you owe.

Zul. The grace received so much my hope exceeds
That words come weak and short to answer deeds.
You 've made a venture, sir, and time must show
If this great mercy you did well bestow.

Boab. You, Abdelmelech, haste before 't is night,
And close pursue my brother in his flight.

(*Exeunt Abdelmelech, Zulema, Hamet. Enter Almanzor, Almahide, and Esperanza.*)

But see, with Almahide
The brave Almanzor comes, whose conquering sword
The crown, it once took from me, has restored.
How can I recompense so great desert!

Almanz. I bring you, sir, performed in every part,
My promise made; your foes are fled or slain;

Without a rival, absolute you reign.
Yet though, in justice, this enough may be,
It is too little to be done by me:
I beg to go,
Where my own courage and your fortune calls,
To chase these misbelievers from our walls.
I cannot breathe within this narrow space;
My heart 's too big, and swells beyond the place.

Boab. You can perform, brave warrior, what you please;
Fate listens to your voice, and then decrees.
Now I no longer fear the Spanish powers;
Already we are free, and conquerors.

Almanz. Accept, great king, to-morrow, from my hand,
The captive head of conquered Ferdinand.
You shall not only what you lost regain,
But o'er the Biscayn mountains to the main,
Extend your sway, where never Moor did reign.

Aben. What, in another, vanity would seem,
Appears but noble confidence in him;
No haughty boasting, but a manly pride;
A soul too fiery, and too great to guide:
He moves eccentric, like a wandering star,
Whose motion 's just, though 't is not regular.

Boab. It is for you, brave man, and only you,
Greatly to speak, and yet more greatly do.
But, if your benefits too far extend,
I must be left ungrateful in the end:
Yet somewhat I would pay,
Before my debts above all reckoning grow,
To keep me from the shame of what I owe.
But you
Are conscious to yourself of such desert,
That of your gift I fear to offer part.

Almanz. When I shall have declared my high request,
So much presumption there will be confessed,
That you will find your gifts I do not shun,
But rather much o'er-rate the service done.

Boab. Give wing to your desires, and let 'em fly,
Secure they cannot mount a pitch too high.
So bless me, Allah, both in peace and war,
As I accord whate'er your wishes are.

Almanz. Emboldened by the promise of a prince,
(*Putting one knee on the ground.*)
I ask this lady now with confidence.

Boab. You ask the only thing I cannot grant.
(*The King and Abenamar look amazedly on each other.*)
But, as a stranger, you are ignorant
Of what by public fame my subjects know;
She is my mistress.

Aben. —And my daughter too.

Almanz. Believe, old man, that I her father knew:
What else should make Almanzor kneel to you?
Nor doubt, sir, but your right to her was known:
For had you had no claim but love alone,
I could produce a better of my own.

Almah. (*Softly to him.*) Almanzor, you forget my last request:
Your words have too much haughtiness expressed.
Is this the humble way you were to move?

Almanz. (*To her.*) I was too far transported by my love.
Forgive me; for I had not learned to sue
To anything before, but heaven and you,—
Sir, at your feet, I make it my request—
(*To the King.*)
(*First line kneeling: second, rising, and boldly.*)
Though, without boasting, I deserve her best;
For you her love with gaudy titles sought,
But I her heart with blood and dangers bought.

Boab. The blood which you have shed in her defence
Shall have in time a fitting recompence:
Or, if you think your services delayed,
Name but your price, and you shall soon be paid.

Almanz. My price! Why, king, you do not think you deal

With one who sets his services to sale?
Reserve your gifts for those who gifts regard;
And know, I think myself above reward.

Boab. Then sure you are some godhead; and our care
Must be to come with incense and with prayer.

Almanz. As little as you think yourself obliged,
You would be glad to do 't, when next besieged.
But I am pleased there should be nothing due;
For what I did was for myself, not you.

Boab. You with contempt on meaner gifts look down;
And, aiming at my queen, disdain my crown.
That crown, restored, deserves no recompense,
Since you would rob the fairest jewel thence.
Dare not henceforth ungrateful me to call;
Whate'er I owed you, this has cancelled all.

Almanz. I 'll call thee thankless, king, and perjured both:
Thou swor'st by Allah, and hast broke thy oath.
But thou dost well; thou tak'st the cheapest way;
Not to own services thou canst not pay.

Boab. My patience more than pays thy service past;
But know this insolence shall be thy last.
Hence from my sight! and take it as a grace,
Thou liv'st, and art but banished from the place.

Almanz. Where'er I go, there can no exile be;
But from Almanzor's sight I banish thee:
I will not now, if thou wouldst beg me, stay;
But I will take my Almahide away.
Stay thou with all thy subjects here; but know,
We leave thy city empty when we go.
(*Takes Almahide's hand.*)

Boab. Fall on; take; kill the traitor.

(*The Guards fall on him; he makes at the King through the midst of them, and falls upon him; they disarm him, and rescue the King.*)

Almanz. —Base and poor,
Blush that thou art Almanzor's conqueror.
(*Almahide wrings her hands, then turns and veils her face.*)
Farewell, my Almahide!
Life of itself will go, now thou art gone,
Like flies in winter, when they lose the sun.

(*Abenamar whispers the King a little, then speaks aloud.*)

Aben. Revenge, and taken so secure a way,
Are blessings which heaven sends not every day.

Boab. I will at leisure now revenge my wrong;
And, traitor, thou shalt feel my vengeance long:
Thou shalt not die just at thy own desire,
But see my nuptials, and with rage expire.

Almanz. Thou darest not marry her while I 'm in sight:
With a bent brow thy priest and thee I 'll fright;
And in that scene
Which all thy hopes and wishes should content,
The thought of me shall make thee impotent.
(*He is led off by Guards.*)

Boab. (*To Almah.*) As some fair tulip, by a storm oppressed,
Shrinks up, and folds its silken arms to rest;
And, bending to the blast, all pale and dead,
Hears from within the wind sing round its head;
So, shrouded up, your beauty disappears:
Unveil, my love, and lay aside your fears.
The storm that caused your fright is passed and done.

(*Almahide unveiling, and looking round for Almanzor.*)

Almah. So flowers peep out too soon, and miss the sun.
(*Turning from him.*)

Boab. What mystery in this strange behavior lies?

Almah. Let me for ever hide these guilty eyes
Which lighted my Almanzor to his tomb;
Or, let 'em blaze, to show me there a room.

Boab. Heaven lent their lustre for a nobler end:

A thousand torches must their light attend,
To lead you to a temple and a crown.
Why does my fairest Almahida frown?
Am I less pleasing than I was before,
Or is the insolent Almanzor more?
Almah. I justly own that I some pity have,
Not for the insolent, but for the brave.
Aben. Though to your king your duty you neglect,
Know, Almahide, I look for more respect:
And, if a parent's charge your mind can move,
Receive the blessing of a monarch's love.
Almah. Did he my freedom to his life prefer,
And shall I wed Almanzor's murderer?
No, sir; I cannot to your will submit;
Your way 's too rugged for my tender feet.
Aben. You must be driven where you refuse to go;
And taught, by force, your happiness to know.
Almah. (*Smiling scornfully.*) To force me, sir, is much unworthy you,
And, when you would, impossible to do.
If force could bend me, you might think, with shame,
That I debased the blood from whence I came.
My soul is soft, which you may gently lay
In your loose palm; but, when 't is pressed to stay,
Like water, it deludes your grasp and slips away.
Boab. I find I must revoke what I decreed:
Almanzor's death my nuptials must precede.
Love is a magic which the lover ties;
But charms still end when the magician dies.
Go; let me hear my hated rival 's dead;
(*To his Guards.*)
And, to convince my eyes, bring back his head.
Almah. Go on: I wish no other way to prove
That I am worthy of Almanzor's love.
We will in death, at least, united be:
I 'll show you I can die as well as he.
Boab. What should I do! when equally I dread
Almanzor living and Almanzor dead!—
Yet, by your promise, you are mine alone.
Almah. How dare you claim my faith, and break your own?
Aben. This for your virtue is a weak defence:
No second vows can with your first dispense.
Yet, since the king did to Almanzor swear,
And in his death ingrateful may appear,
He ought, in justice, first to spare his life,
And then to claim your promise as his wife.
Almah. Whate'er my secret inclinations be,
To this, since honor ties me, I agree:
Yet I declare, and to the world will own,
That, far from seeking, I would shun the throne,
And with Almanzor lead a humble life:
There is a private greatness in his wife.
Boab. That little love I have, I hardly buy;
You give my rival all, while you deny:
Yet, Almahide, to let you see your power,
Your loved Almanzor shall be free this hour.
You are obeyed; but 't is so great a grace,
That I could wish me in my rival's place.
(*Exeunt King and Abenamar.*)
Almah. How blest was I before this fatal day,
When all I knew of love, was to obey!
'T was life becalmed, without a gentle breath;
Though not so cold, yet motionless as death.
A heavy, quiet state; but love, all strife,
All rapid, is the hurricane of life.
Had love not shown me, I had never seen
An excellence beyond Boabdelin.
I had not, aiming higher, lost my rest;
But with a vulgar good been dully blest:
But, in Almanzor, having seen what 's rare,
Now I have learnt too sharply to compare;
And, like a favorite quickly in disgrace,
Just know the value ere I lose the place.
(*To her Almanzor, bound and guarded.*)
Almanz. I see the end for which I 'm hither sent,
(*Looking down.*)
To double, by your sight, my punishment.
There is a shame in bonds I cannot bear;
Far more than death, to meet your eyes I fear.

Almah. (*Unbinding him.*) That shame of long continuance shall not be:
The king, at my entreaty, sets you free.
Almanz. The king! my wonder's greater than before;
How did he dare my freedom to restore?
He like some captive lion uses me;
He runs away before he sets me free,
And takes a sanctuary in his court:
I'll rather lose my life than thank him for't.
Almah. If any subject for your thanks there be,
The king expects 'em not; you owe 'em me.
Our freedoms through each other's hands have passed;
You give me my revenge in winning last.
Almanz. Then fate commodiously for me has done;
To lose mine there where I would have it won.
Almah. Almanzor, you too soon will understand,
That what I win is on another's hand.
The king (who doomed you to a cruel fate)
Gave to my prayers both his revenge and hate;
But at no other price would rate your life,
Than my consent and oath to be his wife.
Almanz. Would you, to save my life, my love betray?
Here; take me; bind me; carry me away;
Kill me! I'll kill you if you disobey.
(*To the Guards.*)
Almah. That absolute command your love does give,
I take, and charge you by that power to live.
Almanz. When death, the last of comforts, you refuse,
Your power, like heaven upon the damned, you use;
You force me in my being to remain,
To make me last, and keep me fresh for pain.
When all my joys are gone,
What cause can I for living longer give,
But a dull, lazy habitude to live?
Almah. Rash men, like you, and impotent of will,
Give Chance no time to turn, but urge her still;
She would repent; you push the quarrel on,
And once because she went, she must be gone.
Almanz. She shall not turn; what is it she can do,
To recompense me for the loss of you?
Almah. Heaven will reward your worth some better way:
At least, for me, you have but lost one day.
Nor is't a real loss which you deplore;
You sought a heart that was engaged before.
'T was a swift love which took you in his way;
Flew only through your heart, but made no stay:
'T was but a dream, where truth had not a place;
A scene of fancy, moved so swift a pace,
And shifted, that you can but think it was;
Let, then, the short vexatious vision pass.
Almanz. My joys, indeed, are dreams; but not my pain:
'T was a swift ruin, but the marks remain.
When some fierce fire lays goodly buildings waste,
Would you conclude
There had been none, because the burning's past?
Almah. It was your fault that fire seized all your breast;
You should have blown up some to save the rest:
But 't is, at worst, but so consumed by fire,
As cities are, that by their falls rise higher.
Build love a nobler temple in my place;
You'll find the fire has but enlarged your space.
Almanz. Love has undone me; I am grown so poor,
I sadly view the ground I had before,
But want a stock, and ne'er can build it more.
Almah. Then say what charity I can allow;
I would contribute if I knew but how.
Take friendship; or, if that too small appear,
Take love which sisters may to brothers bear.
Almanz. A sister's love! that is so palled a thing,
What pleasure can it to a lover bring?
'T is like thin food to men in fevers spent;
Just keeps alive, but gives no nourishment.

What hopes, what fears, what transports can it move?
'T is but the ghost of a departed love.

Almah. You, like some greedy cormorant, devour
All my whole life can give you, in an hour.
What more I can do for you is to die,
And that must follow, if you this deny.
Since I gave up my love, that you might live,
You, in refusing life, my sentence give.

Almanz. Far from my breast be such an impious thought!
Your death would lose the quiet mine had sought.
I'll live for you, in spite of misery;
But you shall grant that I had rather die.
I'll be so wretched, filled with such despair,
That you shall see to live was more to dare.

Almah. Adieu, then, O my soul's far better part!
Your image sticks so close,
That the blood follows from my rending heart.
A last farewell!
For, since a last must come, the rest are vain,
Like gasps in death, which but prolong our pain.
But, since the king is now a part of me,
Cease from henceforth to be his enemy.
Go now, for pity go! for, if you stay,
I fear I shall have something still to say.
Thus—I for ever shut you from my sight.

(*Veils.*)

Almanz. Like one thrust out in a cold winter's night,
Yet shivering underneath your gate I stay;
One look—I cannot go before 't is day.—
(*She beckons him to be gone.*)
Not one—Farewell: Whate'er my sufferings be
Within, I'll speak farewell as loud as she:
I will not be outdone in constancy.—
(*She turns her back.*)
Then like a dying conqueror I go;
At least I have looked last upon my foe.
I go—but if too heavily I move,
I walk encumbered with a weight of love.
Fain I would leave the thought of you behind,
But still, the more I cast you from my mind,
You dash, like water, back, when thrown against the wind.

(*Exit.*)

(*As he goes off, the King meets him with Abenamar; they stare at each other without saluting.*)

Boab. With him go all my fears. A guard there wait,
And see him safe without the city gate.
(*To them Abdelmelech.*)
Now, Abdelmelech, is my brother dead?

Abdelm. The usurper to the Christian camp is fled;
Whom as Granada's lawful king they own,
And vow, by force, to seat him in the throne.
Meantime the rebels in the Albayzin rest;
Which is in Lyndaraxa's name possessed.

Boab. Haste and reduce it instantly by force.

Abdelm. First give me leave to prove a milder course.
She will, perhaps, on summons yield the place.

Boab. We cannot to your suit refuse her grace.

(*One enters hastily, and whispers Abenamar.*)

Aben. How fortune persecutes this hoary head!
My Ozmyn is with Selin's daughter fled.
But he's no more my son:
My hate shall like a Zegry him pursue,
Till I take back what blood from me he drew.

Boab. Let war and vengeance be to-morrow's care;
But let us to the temple now repair.
A thousand torches make the mosque more bright:
This must be mine and Almahida's night.
Hence, ye importunate affairs of state,
You should not tyrannize on love, but wait.
Had life no love, none would for business live;
Yet still from love the largest part we give;
And must be forced, in empire's weary toil,
To live long wretched, to be pleased a while.

(*Exeunt.*)

EPILOGUE

Success, which can no more than beauty last,
Makes our sad poet mourn your favors past:
For, since without desert he got a name,
He fears to lose it now with greater shame.
Fame, like a little mistress of the town,
Is gained with ease, but then she 's lost as soon:
For, as those tawdry misses, soon or late,
Jilt such as keep 'em at the highest rate;
(And oft the lacquey, or the brawny clown,
Gets what is hid in the loose-bodied gown),—
So, Fame is false to all that keep her long;
And turns up to the fop that 's brisk and young.
Some wiser poet now would leave Fame first;
But elder wits are, like old lovers, cursed:
Who, when the vigor of their youth is spent,
Still grow more fond, as they grow impotent.
This, some years hence, our poet's case may prove:
But yet, he hopes, he 's young enough to love.
When forty comes, if e'er he live to see
That wretched, fumbling age of poetry,
'T will be high time to bid his Muse adieu:
Well he may please himself, but never you.
Till then, he 'll do as well as he began,
And hopes you will not find him less a man.
Think him not duller for this year's delay;[28]
He was prepared, the women were away;
And men, without their parts, can hardly play.
If they, through sickness, seldom did appear,
Pity the virgins of each theatre:
For at both houses 't was a sickly year!
And pity us, your servants, to whose cost,
In one such sickness, nine whole months are lost.
Their stay, he fears, has ruined what he writ:
Long waiting both disables love and wit.
They thought they gave him leisure to do well;
But, when they forced him to attend, he fell!
Yet, though he much has failed, he begs, to-day,
You will excuse his unperforming play:
Weakness sometimes great passion does express;
He had pleased better, had he loved you less.

28 "This apparently alludes to the lapse of a year since the production of Dryden's last play." (Noyes.) Nell Gwyn, who played Almahide, had borne a son to Charles II in May, 1670.

THOMAS OTWAY

VENICE PRESERVED, OR, A PLOT DISCOVERED

Thomas Otway (1652–1685) led a checquered and stormy life. Rejected by an actress whom he long loved, he fought in the Low Countries in 1678–9. After failing as an actor, he had taken to writing plays with remarkable fertility, at first in the manner of Dryden and the seventeenth-century French dramatists. His comedies are not highly thought of; but two of his tragedies, *The Orphan* (1680), and the present one (first acted in 1682), rise to the highest excellence.

Venice Preserved is of a style less peculiar to the Restoration period than *The Conquest of Granada,* is a more normal and to us more interesting play, and nearer the regular line of dramatic development. It is at once more Elizabethan and more modern. The student can hardly overlook certain Shakespearean reminiscences, or the influence of Fletcher, especially on the characterization and the verse. The chief sign that it dates from the Restoration period is that the dramatist observes the three unities, of action, time, and place. Accordingly, the action is single, admitting no side-issue or "sub-plot," and takes place within twenty-four hours, and within the limits of one city. These rules were partly drawn from Aristotle's *Poetics* and from the practice of the ancients, but were first laid down as a strict law (as stated earlier) by Castelvetro in 1570. Founded on an error as to the nature of dramatic illusion, they hampered the drama for centuries, and exacted heavy sacrifices from freedom and naturalness. In this play, however, as occasionally elsewhere, there is no conspicuous loss in their observance, and they may even be thought to have heightened the intensity.

With this classical body, a body at least which a classicist could hardly censure, the spirit of the play is thoroughly romantic. We have not only such imposing circumstances as the tolling bell, the rising ghosts, the madness of Belvidera, the violent action and bloodshed on the stage; the emotional pitch of the play is soft, pathetic, and almost sentimental. Except in the figure of Pierre, there is nothing sturdy about it. It strives to melt us. The sentimental tragedy for which Otway is known has its analogues in the Elizabethan drama (as in that of Fletcher and Ford); it also looks forward to the sentimentalism of the eighteenth century, as in the comedies of Steele and Cumberland. We miss the strong, truer emotions of the greater Elizabethans. In this soft emotionality we may perhaps see something characteristic of the age. This play, like *The Conquest of Granada,* sets at nought the feeling of patriotism, and reminds us that it was written in an age when England was full of discord, and when the very sovereign had sold himself and was ready to sell his country to a foreign prince.

The sentimentalism is not in what is said, its vehicle in the later comedy, but is perhaps only half conscious, springing from Otway's own gentle soul, and appearing in the sort of characters with whom he felt sympathy. The characterization is at once a source of strength and weakness in the play. Jaffeir, structurally the hero, excites pity abundantly, but little respect and no admiration. A private wrong, inflicted by an individual senator, makes him join a band of irresponsible traitors, largely foreigners at that (we are nowhere told that he was a foreigner). His own trustful carelessness for his wife puts him in a position where he betrays their secret to her. And he makes haste to justify the worst suspicions of the hateful Renault. Another private wrong, threatened by an individual conspirator, and his first realization of the horrors which would follow the success of the plot, lead him to betray them to the Council of Ten, with the childish expectation that their lives will be spared. He is a lifelike but unattractive figure of a weak emotional character at the mercy of circumstance, of his own feelings, and even of every last speaker, capable of instantaneous but not of sustained courage and resolution. He excites, not terror like a tragic hero, but only pity, like a sentimental one. We tolerate him for the sake of his friend and his wife. Pierre is admirably contrasted with Jaffeir, a fine example of cheerful devil-may-care generosity and loyalty. "Revenge!" cries Jaffeir, when he has joined the conspirators.

Pierre. And liberty!

Jaff. Revenge! revenge! [*Exeunt.*

Few heroines surpass Belvidera, unintellectual, but courageous, tender, with an infinite capacity for strong love, and a woman's conservatism and dread of sedition, privy conspiracy, and rebellion. Otway's women are always better done than his men; with good reason Collins in his *Ode to Pity* pays a tribute to "gentlest Otway," who "sung the female heart." It is notable, however, that the emotional interest has no aid from the uncertainties of a romantic love-affair; the love is either married or bought love.

Well done as they are, Otway's strength is less in his characters than in the situations and the action. In this play the construction is admirable. Clear as crystal, simple and single, with no assistance from a sub-action to maintain the interest, and with no cheap devices, the play holds the reader, still more the spectator, without slackening. A most notable means is the skillful use of suspense. In the fourth act the conspiracy is betrayed and the plotters all seized; no visible hope remains for either it or them. As in the fourth act of Jonson's *Alchemist*, we wonder what can remain for a fifth. But presently the only two senators whom we know are won over to mercy, the one by his daughter, the other by his self-sacrificing mistress. In the following scene of poignant pathos between the married lovers, broken in upon by the gloomy tolling bell, we begin to fear all is in vain, but are not sure of it till the end. Even the silly and distasteful scenes between the senator Antonio (a repulsive portrait of the Earl of Shaftsbury) and his "Nacky," poorly done as they are, and indeed disproportionate and needless, have prepared for this moment of hope. Nothing could surpass the death-scene of Jaffeir and Pierre, completely surprising yet completely satisfying.

For all the intensity of interest in the play, the power of holding us, and the compassion we feel for the characters, there is a certain aloofness in the emotion it excites. This is because we cannot perfectly give our sympathy to either side. On the one hand, our human feelings are all for the conspirators. Yet, unlovely as are the two officials whom we see, Priuli with his cowardice and hardness, Antonio with his impotent senility, our indignation goes out against the attempt by a gang of foreigners to wreck a great historic state. The very title of the play bespeaks our support for this side. At the moment when he is about to join the conspirators,

> Hell! hell! why sleepest thou?

cries the desperate Jaffeir, and then with great dramatic effectiveness enters the unconscious Pierre muttering,

> Sure I have stayed too long!

The plotters have not been injured enough to win even our temporary approval. There results a state of mind somewhat like that excited by *Macbeth*, in which we feel deeply for persons who we know should and will be punished. With all our painful interest, we look down with a certain intellectual serenity. A tragedy of this sort has a fine and unusual character of its own.

The play is founded on the Abbé St. Réal's *Conjuration des espagnols contre la Venise en 1618*, probably through an English translation (1675). The groundwork therefore is historical, but Otway has made great changes, raising Jaffeir and Pierre to importance and introducing the character of Belvidera. It has been one of the most popular of post-Elizabethan tragedies, having been translated and acted in various European languages, and having held the English stage until well into the nineteenth century (revived in 1904), with the help of such actors as Betterton, Garrick, J. P. Kemble, and Macready, and of such actresses as Mrs. Barry, Mrs. Siddons, and Miss O'Neill.

VENICE PRESERVED, OR, A PLOT DISCOVERED

A TRAGEDY

BY THOMAS OTWAY

PROLOGUE

In these distracted times,[1] when each man dreads
The bloody stratagems of busy heads;
When we have feared three years we know not what,
Till witnesses begin to die o' th' rot,
What made our poet meddle with a plot?
Was 't that he fancied, for the very sake
And name of plot, his trifling play might take?
For there 's not in 't one inch-board evidence,[2]
But 't is, he says, to reason plain and sense,[3]
And that he thinks a plausible defence.
Were truth by sense and reason to be tried,
Sure, all our swearers might be laid aside:
No, of such tools our author has no need,

1 Otway, a strong Tory, ridicules the Whig excitement over the supposed Popish plot of 1678. The later part of the prologue makes various allusions to contemporary incidents and personages.
2 imaginary evidence (such as would be got by pretending to see through a board an inch thick).
3 perception.

To make his plot, or [make] his play succeed;
He, of black bills, has no prodigious tales,
Or Spanish pilgrims cast ashore in Wales;
Here 's not one murthered magistrate at least,
Kept rank like ven'son for a city feast,
Grown four days stiff, the better to prepare
And fit his pliant limbs to ride in chair:
Yet here 's an army raised, though under ground,
But no man seen, nor one commission found;
Here is a traitor too, that 's very old,
Turbulent, subtle, mischievous, and bold,
Bloody, revengeful, and to crown his part,
Loves fumbling with a wench, with all his heart;
Till after having many changes passed,
In spite of age (thanks Heaven) is hanged at last:
Next is a senator that keeps a whore,[4]
In Venice none a higher office bore;
To lewdness every night the lecher ran,
Show me, all London, such another man,
Match him at Mother Creswold's if you can.
O Poland, Poland! had it been thy lot,
T' have heard in time of this Venetian plot,
Thou surely chosen hadst one king from thence,
And honored them, as thou hast England since.

PERSONÆ DRAMATIS

Duke of Venice.
Priuli, *Father to Belvidera, a Senator.*
Antonio, *a Fine Speaker in the Senate.*
Jaffeir,
Pierre,
Renault, Bedamar, Spinosa, Theodore, Eliot, Revillido, Durand, Mezzana, Bra[in]veil, Ternon, [Retrosi] Brabe, — *Conspirators.*

Belvidera.
Aquilina.
Two Women, Attendants on Belvidera.
Two Women, Servants to Aquilina.
The Council of Ten.[5]
Officer.
Guards.
Friar.
Executioner and Rabble.

ACT I.

Scene 1.

(*Enter Priuli and Jaffeir.*)

Priu. No more! I'll hear no more; begone and leave.
Jaff. Not hear me! by my sufferings but you shall!
My lord, my lord! I'm not that abject wretch
You think me: patience! where 's the distance throws
Me back so far, but I may boldly speak
In right, though proud oppression will not hear me!
Priu. Have you not wronged me?
Jaff. Could my nature e'er
Have brooked injustice or the doing wrongs,
I need not now thus low have bent myself
To gain a hearing from a cruel father!
Wronged you?
Priu. Yes! wronged me, in the nicest point:
The honor of my house; you have done me wrong;
You may remember (for I now will speak,
And urge its baseness): when you first came home
From travel, with such hopes as made you looked on
By all men's eyes, a youth of expectation;

4 Antonio is a ferocious portrait of the dissolute elderly Earl of Shaftsbury, who schemed to secure the crown of Poland.

5 From the 14th century a part of the Venetian machinery of government; originally executive, afterwards also judicial, and in the 17th century the chief power in the state. In IV, ii, the poet seems to err in making the Doge a member of it.

Pleased with your growing virtue, I received you:
Courted, and sought to raise you to your merits:
My house, my table, nay my fortune too,
My very self, was yours; you might have used me
To your best service; like an open friend,
I treated, trusted you, and thought you mine;
When, in requital of my best endeavors,
You treacherously practised[6] to undo me,
Seduced the weakness of my age's darling,
My only child, and stole her from my bosom:
Oh Belvidera!

Jaff. 'T is to me you owe her,
Childless you had been else, and in the grave
Your name extinct, nor no more Priuli heard of.
You may remember, scarce five years are past,
Since in your brigandine you sailed to see
The Adriatic wedded by our Duke,[7]
And I was with you: your unskilful pilot
Dashed us upon a rock; when to your boat
You made for safety; entered first yourself;
The affrighted Belvidera following next,
As she stood trembling on the vessel side,
Was by a wave washed off into the deep,
When instantly I plunged into the sea,
And buffeting the billows to her rescue,
Redeemed her life with half the loss of mine;
Like a rich conquest in one hand I bore her,
And with the other dashed the saucy waves,
That thronged and pressed to rob me of my prize:
I brought her, gave her to your despairing arms:
Indeed you thanked me; but a nobler gratitude
Rose in her soul: for from that hour she loved me,
Till for her life she paid me with herself.

Priu. You stole her from me; like a thief you stole her,
At dead of night; that cursed hour you chose
To rifle me of all my heart held dear.
May all your joys in her prove false like mine;
A sterile fortune, and a barren bed,
Attend you both; continual discord make
Your days and nights bitter and grievous: still
May the hard hand of a vexatious need
Oppress, and grind you; till at last you find
The curse of disobedience all your portion.

Jaff. Half of your curse you have bestowed in vain;
Heaven has already crowned our faithful loves
With a young boy, sweet as his mother's beauty.
May he live to prove more gentle than his grandsire,
And happier than his father!

Priu. Rather live
To bait thee for his bread, and din your ears
With hungry cries; whilst his unhappy mother
Sits down and weeps in bitterness of want.

Jaff. You talk as if it would please you.

Priu. 'T would, by Heaven.
Once she was dear indeed; the drops that fell
From my sad heart, when she forgot her duty,
The fountain of my life was not so precious:
But she is gone, and if I am a man
I will forget her.

Jaff. Would I were in my grave!

Priu. And she too with thee;
For, living here, you're but my curst remembrancers
I once was happy.

Jaff. You use me thus, because you know my soul
Is fond of Belvidera: you perceive
My life feeds on her, therefore thus you treat me;
Oh! could my soul ever have known satiety,
Were I that thief, the doer of such wrongs
As you upbraid me with, what hinders me,
But I might send her back to you with contumely,
And court my fortune where she would be kinder!

Priu. You dare not do 't——

6 plotted. 7 The Doge annually "wedded" the Adriatic by dropping a ring into it, in token of dominion.

Jaff. Indeed, my lord, I dare not.
My heart that awes me is too much my master:
Three years are past since first our vows were plighted,
During which time, the world must bear me witness,
I have treated Belvidera like your daughter,
The daughter of a senator of Venice;
Distinction, place, attendance and observance,
Due to her birth, she always has commanded;
Out of my little fortune I have done this;
Because (though hopeless e'er to win your nature)
The world might see, I loved her for herself,
Not as the heiress of the great Priuli——

Priu. No more!

Jaff. Yes! all, and then adieu for ever.
There 's not a wretch that lives on common charity
But 's happier than me: for I have known
The luscious sweets of plenty; every night
Have slept with soft content about my head,
And never waked but to a joyful morning;
Yet now must fall like a full ear of corn,
Whose blossom scaped, yet 's withered in the ripening.

Priu. Home and be humble, study to retrench;
Discharge the lazy vermin of thy hall,
Those pageants of thy folly,
Reduce the glittering trappings of thy wife
To humble weeds, fit for thy little state;
Then to some suburb cottage both retire;
Drudge, to feed loathsome life: get brats, and starve—
Home, home, I say.——

(*Exit Priuli.*)

Jaff. Yes, if my heart would let me—
This proud, this swelling heart: home I would go,
But that my doors are hateful to my eyes,
Filled and dammed up with gaping creditors,
Watchful as fowlers when their game will spring;
I have now not fifty ducats in the world,
Yet still I am in love, and pleased with ruin.
O Belvidera! oh, she [i]s my wife—
And we will bear our wayward fate together,
But ne'er know comfort more.

(*Enter Pierre.*)

Pierr. My friend, good morrow!
How fares the honest partner of my heart?
What, melancholy! not a word to spare me?

Jaff. I 'm thinking, Pierre, how that damned starving quality,
Called honesty, got footing in the world.

Pierr. Why, powerful villainy first set it up,
For its own ease and safety: honest men
Are the soft easy cushions on which knaves
Repose and fatten. Were all mankind villains,
They 'd starve each other; lawyers would want practice,
Cut-throats rewards; each man would kill his brother
Himself, none would be paid or hanged for murder.
Honesty was a cheat invented first
To bind the hands of bold deserving rogues,
That fools and cowards might sit safe in power,
And lord it uncontrolled above their betters.

Jaff. Then honesty is but a notion.

Pierr. Nothing else,
Like wit, much talked of, not to be defined:
He that pretends to most, too, has least share in 't;
'T is a ragged virtue: honesty! no more on 't.

Jaff. Sure thou art honest?

Pierr. So indeed men think me;
But they 're mistaken, Jaffeir: I am a rogue
As well as they;
A fine gay bold-faced villain, as thou seest me;
'T is true, I pay my debts when they 're contracted;
I steal from no man; would not cut a throat
To gain admission to a great man's purse,
Or a whore's bed; I 'd not betray my friend,
To get his place or fortune: I scorn to flatter

A blown-up fool above me, or crush the wretch beneath me,
Yet, Jaffeir, for all this, I am a villain!
Jaff. A villain——
Pierr. Yes, a most notorious villain:
To see the suff'rings of my fellow-creatures,
And own myself a man: to see our senators
Cheat the deluded people with a show
Of liberty, which yet they ne'er must taste of;
They say, by them our hands are free from fetters,
Yet whom they please they lay in basest bonds;
Bring whom they please to infamy and sorrow;
Drive us like wracks down the rough tide of power,
Whilst no hold's left to save us from destruction;
All that bear this are villains; and I one,
Not to rouse up at the great call of nature,
And check the growth of these domestic spoilers,
That makes us slaves and tells us 't is our charter.
Jaff. O Aquilina! friend, to lose such beauty,
The dearest purchase of thy noble labors;
She was thy right by conquest, as by love.
Pierr. O Jaffeir! I'd so fixed my heart upon her,
That wheresoe'er I framed a scheme of life
For time to come, she was my only joy
With which I wished to sweeten future cares;
I fancied pleasures, none but one that loves
And dotes as I did can imagine like 'em:
When in the extremity of all these hopes,
In the most charming hour of expectation,
Then when our eager wishes soar the highest,
Ready to stoop and grasp the lovely game,
A haggard owl, a worthless kite of prey,
With his foul wings sailed in and spoiled my quarry.
Jaff. I know the wretch, and scorn him as thou hat'st him.
Pierr. Curse on the common good that's so protected.
Where every slave that heaps up wealth enough
To do much wrong, becomes a lord of right!
I, who believed no ill could e'er come near me,
Found in the embraces of my Aquilina
A wretched, old but itching senator;
A wealthy fool, that had bought out my title,
A rogue, that uses beauty like a lambskin,
Barely to keep him warm: that filthy cuckoo too
Was in my absence crept into my nest,
And spoiling all my brood of noble pleasure.
Jaff. Didst thou not chase him thence?
Pierr. I did; and drove
The rank old bearded Hirco[8] stinking home:
The matter was complained of in the Senate,
I summoned to appear, and censured basely,
For violating something they call *privilege*—
This was the recompense of [all] my service:
Would I'd been rather beaten by a coward!
A soldier's mistress, Jaffeir, 's his religion;
When that's profaned, all other ties are broken;
That even dissolves all former bonds of service,
And from that hour I think myself as free
To be the foe as e'er the friend of Venice.—
Nay, dear Revenge, whene'er thou call'st I'm ready.
Jaff. I think no safety can be here for virtue,
And grieve, my friend, as much as thou to live
In such a wretched state as this of Venice;
Where all agree to spoil the public good,
And villains fatten with the brave man's labors.
Pierr. We have neither safety, unity, nor peace,
For the foundation's lost of common good;
Justice is lame as well as blind amongst us;

8 goat (Spanish, apparently; Lat. *hircus*).

The laws (corrupted to their ends that make 'em)
Serve but for instruments of some new tyranny,
That every day starts up to enslave us deeper:
Now could this glorious cause but find out friends
To do it right! O Jaffeir! then might'st thou
Not wear these seals of woe upon thy face,
The proud Priuli should be taught humanity,
And learn to value such a son as thou art.
I dare not speak! But my heart bleeds this moment!

Jaff. Curst be the cause, though I thy friend be part on 't:
Let me partake the troubles of thy bosom,
For I am used to misery, and perhaps
May find a way to sweeten 't to thy spirit.

Pierr. Too soon it will reach thy knowledge——

Jaff. Then from thee
Let it proceed. There 's virtue in thy friendship
Would make the saddest tale of sorrow pleasing,
Strengthen my constancy, and welcome ruin.

Pierr. Then thou art ruined!

Jaff. That I long since knew,
I and ill-fortune have been long acquaintance.

Pierr. I passed this very moment by thy doors,
And found them guarded by a troop of villains;
The sons of public rapine were destroying:
They told me, by the sentence of the law
They had commission to seize all thy fortune,
Nay more, Priuli's cruel hand hath signed it.
Here stood a ruffian with a horrid face
Lording it o'er a pile of massy plate,
Tumbled into a heap for public sale:
There was another making villainous jests
At thy undoing; he had ta'en possession
Of all thy ancient most domestic ornaments,
Rich hangings, intermixed and wrought with gold;
The very bed, which on thy wedding-night
Received thee to the arms of Belvidera,
The scene of all thy joys, was violated
By the coarse hands of filthy dungeon villains,
And thrown amongst the common lumber.

Jaff. Now, thanks, Heaven——

Pierr. Thank Heaven! for what?

Jaff. That I am not worth a ducat.

Pierr. Curse thy dull stars, and the worse fate of Venice,
Where brothers, friends, and fathers, all are false;
Where there 's no trust, no truth; where innocence
Stoops under vile oppression, and vice lords it.
Hadst thou but seen, as I did, how at last
Thy beauteous Belvidera, like a wretch
That 's doomed to banishment, came weeping forth,
Shining through tears, like April suns in showers
That labor to o'ercome the cloud that loads 'em,
Whilst two young virgins, on whose arms she leaned,
Kindly looked up, and at her grief grew sad,
As if they catched the sorrows that fell from her!
Even the lewd rabble that were gathered round
To see the sight, stood mute when they beheld her;
Governed their roaring throats and grumbled pity:
I could have hugged the greasy rogues; they pleased me.

Jaff. I thank thee for this story, from my soul,
Since now I know the worst that can befall me:
Ah, Pierre! I have a heart, that could have borne
The roughest wrong my fortune could have done me;
But when I think what Belvidera feels,
The bitterness her tender spirit tastes of,
I own myself a coward: bear my weakness,
If throwing thus my arms about thy neck,
I play the boy, and blubber in thy bosom.
Oh! I shall drown thee with my sorrows!

Pierr. Burn!
First burn, and level Venice to thy ruin.
What! starve like beggars' brats in frosty weather,
Under a hedge, and whine ourselves to death!

Thou, or thy cause, shall never want assistance,
Whilst I have blood or fortune fit to serve thee;
Command my heart: thou art every way its master.

Jaff. No; there 's a secret pride in bravely dying.

Pierr. Rats die in holes and corners, dogs run mad;
Man knows a braver remedy for sorrow:
Revenge! the attribute of gods, they stamped it
With their great image on our natures; die!
Consider well the cause that calls upon thee,
And if thou 'rt base enough, die then. Remember
Thy Belvidera suffers; Belvidera!
Die!—damn first!—what! be decently interred
In a churchyard, and mingle thy brave dust
With stinking rogues that rot in dirty winding-sheets,
Surfeit-slain fools, the common dung o' th' soil.

Jaff. Oh!

Pierr. Well said, out with it, swear a little——

Jaff. Swear!
By sea and air! by earth, by heaven and hell,
I will revenge my Belvidera's tears!
Hark thee, my friend—Priuli—is—a senator!

Pierr. A dog!

Jaff. Agreed.

Pierr. Shoot him.

Jaff. With all my heart.
No more: where shall we meet at night?

Pierr. I'll tell thee;
On the Rialto [9] every night at twelve
I take my evening's walk of meditation,
There we two will meet, and talk of precious
Mischief——

Jaff. Farewell.

Pierr. At twelve.

Jaff. At any hour, my plagues
Will keep me waking.

(*Exit Pierre.*)

Tell me why, good Heaven.
Thou mad'st me what I am, with all the spirit,
Aspiring thoughts and elegant desires
That fill the happiest man? Ah! rather why
Didst thou not form me sordid as my fate,
Base-minded, dull, and fit to carry burdens?
Why have I sense [10] to know the curse that 's on me?
Is this just dealing, Nature? Belvidera!

(*Enter Belvidera.*)

Poor Belvidera!

Belv. Lead me, lead me, my virgins,
To that kind voice. My lord, my love, my refuge!
Happy my eyes, when they behold thy face:
My heavy heart will leave its doleful beating
At sight of thee, and bound with sprightful joys.
O smile, as when our loves were in their spring,
And cheer my fainting soul.

Jaff. As when our loves
Were in their spring? has then my fortune changed?
Art thou not Belvidera, still the same,
Kind, good, and tender, as my arms first found thee?
If thou art altered, where shall I have harbor?
Where ease my loaded heart? Oh! where complain?

Belv. Does this appear like change, or love decaying?
When thus I throw myself into thy bosom,
With all the resolution of a strong truth:
Beats not my heart, as 't would al[a]rum thine
To a new charge of bliss? I joy more in thee,
Than did thy mother when she hugged thee first,
And blessed the gods for all her travail past.

Jaff. Can there in women be such glorious faith?
Sure all ill stories of thy sex are false;
O woman! lovely woman! Nature made thee
To temper man: we had been brutes without you;
Angels are painted fair, to look like you;
There 's in you all that we believe of heaven,
Amazing brightness, purity and truth,
Eternal joy, and everlasting love.

9 The celebrated bridge over the Grand Canal.

10 perception.

Belv. If love be treasure, we 'll be wondrous rich;
I have so much, my heart will surely break with 't;
Vows cannot express it; when I would declare
How great 's my joy, I am dumb with the big thought;
I swell, and sigh, and labor with my longing.
O lead me to some desert wide and wild,
Barren as our misfortunes, where my soul
May have its vent: where I may tell aloud
To the high heavens, and every listening planet,
With what a boundless stock my bosom 's fraught;
Where I may throw my eager arms about thee,
Give loose to love with kisses, kindling joy,
And let off all the fire that 's in my heart.

Jaff. O Belvidera! double I am a beggar,
Undone by fortune, and in debt to thee;
Want! worldly want! that hungry meagre fiend
Is at my heels, and chases me in view.
Canst thou bear cold and hunger? Can these limbs,
Framed for the tender offices of love,
Endure the bitter gripes of smarting poverty?
When banished by our miseries abroad
(As suddenly we shall be), to seek out
(In some far climate where our names are strangers)
For charitable succor; wilt thou then,
When in a bed of straw we shrink together,
And the bleak winds shall whistle round our heads,
Wilt thou then talk thus to me? Wilt thou then
Hush my cares thus, and shelter me with love?

Belv. O, I will love thee, even in madness love thee.
Though my distracted senses should forsake me,
I 'd find some intervals, when my poor heart
Should suage itself and be let loose to thine.
Though the bare earth be all our resting-place,
Its roots our food, some clift our habitation,
I 'll make this arm a pillow for thy head;
And as thou sighing liest, and swelled with sorrow,
Creep to thy bosom, pour the balm of love
Into thy soul, and kiss thee to thy rest;
Then praise our God, and watch thee till the morning.

Jaff. Hear this, you Heavens, and wonder how you made her!
Reign, reign, ye monarchs that divide the world,
Busy rebellion ne'er will let you know
Tranquility and happiness like mine;
Like gaudy ships, the obsequious billows fall
And rise again, to lift you in your pride;
They wait but for a storm and then devour you:
I, in my private bark, already wrecked,
Like a poor merchant driven on unknown land,
That had by chance packed up his choicest treasure
In one dear casket, and saved only that,
Since I must wander further on the shore,
Thus hug my little, but my precious store;
Resolved to scorn, and trust my fate no more.

(*Exeunt.*)

ACT II

Scene 1.

(*Enter Pierre and Aquilina.*)

Aquil. By all thy wrongs, thou 'rt dearer to my arms
Than all the wealth of Venice: prithee stay,
And let us love to-night.

Pierr. No: there 's fool,
There 's fool about thee: when a woman sells
Her flesh to fools, her beauty 's lost to me;
They leave a taint, a sully where they 've past,
There 's such a baneful quality about 'em,
Even spoils complexions with their own nauseousness.
They infect all they touch; I cannot think
Of tasting anything a fool has palled.

Aquil. I loathe and scorn that fool thou mean'st, as much
Or more than thou canst; but the beast has gold
That makes him necessary; power too,

To qualify my character, and poise me
Equal with peevish[11] virtue, that beholds
My liberty with envy; in their hearts
Are loose as I am; but an ugly power
Sits in their faces, and frights pleasures from 'em.

Pierr. Much good may 't do you, madam, with your senator.

Aquil. My senator! why, canst thou think that wretch
E'er filled thy Aquilina's arms with pleasure?
Think'st thou, because I sometimes give him leave
To foil himself at what he is unfit for;
Because I force myself to endure and suffer him,
Think'st thou I love him? No, by all the joys
Thou ever gav'st me, his presence is my penance;
The worst thing an old man can be 's a lover,
A mere *memento mori* to poor woman.
I never lay by his decrepit side,
But all that night I pondered on my grave.

Pierr. Would he were well sent thither!

Aquil. That 's my wish too:
For then, my Pierre, I might have cause with pleasure
To play the hypocrite. Oh! how I could weep
Over the dying dotard, and kiss him too,
In hopes to smother him quite; then, when the time
Was come to pay my sorrows at his funeral,
For he has already made me heir to treasures,
Would make me out-act a real widow's whining:
How could I frame my face to fit my mourning!
With wringing hands attend him to his grave,
Fall swooning on his hearse:[12] take mad possession
Even of the dismal vault where he lay buried;
There like the Ephesian matron[13] dwell, till thou,
My lovely soldier, com'st to my deliverance;
Then throwing up my veil, with open arms
And laughing eyes, run to new dawning joy.

Pierr. No more! I have friends to meet me here to-night,
And must be private. As you prize my friendship,
Keep up your coxcomb:[14] let him not pry nor listen
Nor fisk[15] about the house as I have seen him,
Like a tame mumping[16] squirrel with a bell on;
Curs will be abroad to bite him if you do.

Aquil. What friends to meet? may I not be of your council?

Pierr. How! a woman ask questions out of bed?
Go to your senator, ask him what passes
Amongst his brethren, he 'll hide nothing from you
But pump not me for politics. No more!
Give order that whoever in my name
Comes here, receive admittance: so good-night.

Aquil. Must we ne'er meet again! Embrace no more!
Is love so soon and utterly forgotten!

Pierr. As you henceforward treat your fool, I 'll think on 't.

Aquil. Curst be all fools, and doubly curst myself,
The worst of fools—I die if he forsakes me;
And now to keep him, heaven or hell instruct me.

(*Exeunt.*)

SCENE 2. *The Rialto.*

(*Enter Jaffeir.*)

Jaff. I am here, and thus, the shades of night around me,
I look as if all hell were in my heart,
And I in hell. Nay, surely 't is so with me;—
For every step I tread, methinks some fiend
Knocks at my breast, and bids it not be quiet:
I 've heard, how desperate wretches, like myself,
Have wandered out at this dead time of night

11 ill-humored.
12 Framework supporting lights, etc., on which a coffin rested before burial.
13 The allusion is to the widespread cynical story of the Widow of Ephesus, who intrigued with the soldier set to watch her dead husband, and even mutilated the corpse.
14 restrain your fool.
15 scamper, whisk.
16 munching, nibbling (?); grimacing (?).

To meet the foe of mankind in his walk:
Sure I 'm so curst, that, tho' of Heaven forsaken,
No minister of darkness cares to tempt me.
Hell! hell! why sleepest thou?

(*Enter Pierre.*)

Pierr. Sure I have stayed too long:
The clock has struck, and I may lose my proselyte.
Speak, who goes there?

Jaff. A dog, that comes to howl
At yonder moon: what 's he that asks the question?

Pierr. A friend of dogs, for they are honest creatures
And ne'er betray their masters; never fawn
On any that they love not. Well met, friend:
Jaffeir!

Jaff. The same. O Pierre! thou art come in season,
I was just going to pray.

Pierr. Ah, that 's mechanic,
Priests make a trade on 't, and yet starve by it too:
No praying, it spoils business, and time 's precious;
Where 's Belvidera?

Jaff. For a day or two
I 've lodged her privately till I see farther
What fortune will do with me. Prithee, friend,
If thou wouldst have me fit to hear good counsel,
Speak not of Belvidera——

Pierr. Speak not of her?

Jaff. Oh no!

Pierr. Nor name her? May be I wish her well.

Jaff. Who well?

Pierr. Thy wife, thy lovely Belvidera;
I hope a man may wish his friend's wife well,
And no harm done!

Jaff. Y' are merry, Pierre!

Pierr. I am so:
Thou shalt smile too, and Belvidera smile;
We 'll all rejoice; here 's something to buy pins,
Marriage is chargeable.

Jaff. I but half wished
To see the Devil, and he 's here already.
Well!
What must this buy, rebellion, murder, treason?
Tell me which way I must be damned for this.

Pierr. When last we parted, we had no qualms like these,
But entertained each other's thoughts like men
Whose souls were well acquainted. Is the world
Reformed since our last meeting? What new miracles
Have happened? Has Priuli's heart relented?
Can he be honest?

Jaff. Kind Heaven! let heavy curses
Gall his old age; cramps, aches, rack his bones;
And bitterest disquiet wring his heart;
Oh, let him live till life become his burden!
Let him groan under 't long, linger an age
In the worst agonies and pangs of death,
And find its ease but late!

Pierr. Nay, couldst thou not
As well, my friend, have stretched the curse to all
The Senate round, as to one single villain?

Jaff. But curses stick not: could I kill with cursing,
By Heaven, I know not thirty heads in Venice
Should not be blasted; senators should rot
Like dogs on dunghills; but their wives and daughters
Die of their own diseases. Oh, for a curse
To kill with!

Pierr. Daggers, daggers, are much better!

Jaff. Ha!

Pierr. Daggers.

Jaff. But where are they?

Pierr. Oh, a thousand
May be disposed in honest hands in Venice.

Jaff. Thou talk'st in clouds.

Pierr. But yet a heart half wronged
As thine has been, would find the meaning, Jaffeir.

Jaff. A thousand daggers, all in honest hands;
And have not I a friend will stick one here?

Pierr. Yes, if I thought thou wert not to be cherished
To a nobler purpose, I 'd be that friend.
But thou hast better friends, friends, whom thy wrongs

Have made thy friends; friends worthy to be called so;
I'll trust thee with a secret: there are spirits
This hour at work. But as thou art a man,
Whom I have picked and chosen from the world,
Swear, that thou wilt be true to what I utter,
And when I have told thee, that which only gods
And men like gods are privy to, then swear,
No chance or change shall wrest it from thy bosom.

Jaff. When thou wouldst bind me, is there need of oaths?
(Greensickness[17] girls lose maidenheads with such counters)
For thou 'rt so near my heart, that thou mayst see
Its bottom, sound its strength, and firmness to thee:
Is coward, fool, or villain, in my face?
If I seem none of these, I dare believe
Thou wouldst not use me in a little cause,
For I am fit for honor's toughest task;
Nor ever yet found fooling was my province;
And for a villainous inglorious enterprise,
I know thy heart so well, I dare lay mine
Before thee, set it to what point thou wilt.

Pierr. Nay, it 's a cause thou wilt be fond of, Jaffeir.
For it is founded on the noblest basis,
Our liberties, our natural inheritance;
There 's no religion, no hypocrisy in 't;
We 'll do the business, and ne'er fast and pray for 't:
Openly act a deed, the world shall gaze
With wonder at, and envy when it is done.

Jaff. For liberty!

Pierr. For liberty, my friend!
Thou shalt be freed from base Priuli's tyranny.
And thy sequestered fortunes healed again.
I shall be freed from opprobrious wrongs,
That press me now, and bend my spirit downward:
All Venice free, and every growing merit
Succeed to its just right; fools shall be pulled
From wisdom's seat; those baleful unclean birds,
Those lazy owls, who (perched near Fortune's top)
Sit only watchful with their heavy wings
To cuff down new-fledged virtues, that would rise
To nobler heights, and make the grove harmonious.

Jaff. What can I do?

Pierr. Canst thou not kill a senator?

Jaff. Were there one wise or honest, I could kill him
For herding with that nest of fools and knaves.
By all my wrongs, thou talk'st as if revenge
Were to be had, and the brave story warms me.

Pierr. Swear, then!

Jaff. I do, by all those glittering stars
And yond great ruling planet of the night!
By all good powers above, and ill below!
By love and friendship, dearer than my life!
No power or death shall make me false to thee.

Pierr. Here we embrace, and I 'll unlock my heart.
A council 's held hard by, where the destruction
Of this great empire 's hatching: there I 'll lead thee!
But be a man, for thou art to mix with men
Fit to disturb the peace of all the world,
And rule it when it 's wildest——

Jaff. I give thee thanks
For this kind warning: yes, I will be a man,
And charge thee, Pierre, whene'er thou seest my fears
Betray me less, to rip this heart of mine
Out of my breast, and show it for a coward's.
Come, let 's begone, for from this hour I chase
All little thoughts, all tender humane follies
Out of my bosom: vengeance shall have room:
Revenge!

Pierr. And liberty!

Jaff. Revenge! revenge!

(*Exeunt.*)

SCENE 3. *The Scene changes to Aquilina's house, the Greek Courtesan.*

(*Enter Renault.*)

[17] anæmic.

Renault. Why was my choice ambition, the first ground
A wretch can build on? It's indeed at distance
A good prospect, tempting to the view,
The height delights us, and the mountain top
Looks beautiful, because it's nigh to heaven,
But we ne'er think how sandy 's the foundation,
What storm will batter, and what tempest shake us!
Who 's there?

(*Enter Spinosa.*)

Spin. Renault, good morrow! for by this time
I think the scale of night has turned the balance,
And weighs up morning: has the clock struck twelve?
Ren. Yes, clocks will go as they are set. But man,
Irregular man 's ne'er constant, never certain:
I 've spent at least three precious hours of darkness
In waiting dull attendance; 't is the curse
Of diligent virtue to be mixed like mine,
With giddy tempers, souls but half resolved.
Spin. Hell seize that soul amongst us it can frighten!
Ren. What 's then the cause that I am here alone?
Why are we not together?

(*Enter Eliot.*)

O sir, welcome!
You are an Englishman: when treason 's hatching
One might have thought you 'd not have been behindhand.
In what whore's lap have you been lolling?
Give but an Englishman his whore and ease,
Beef and a sea-coal fire, he 's yours for ever.
Eliot. Frenchman, you are saucy.
Ren. How!

(*Enter Bedamar the Ambassador, Theodore, Brainveil, Durand, Brabe, Rev[i]llido, Mezzana, Ternon, Retrosi, Conspirators.*)

Beda. At difference, fie!
Is this a time for quarrels? Thieves and rogues
Fall out and brawl: should men of your high calling,
Men separated by the choice of Providence
From the gross heap of mankind, and set here
In this great assembly as in one great jewel,
To adorn the bravest purpose it e'er smiled on,—
Should you like boys wrangle for trifles?
Ren. Boys!
Beda. Renault, thy hand!
Ren. I thought I'd given my heart
Long since to every man that mingles here;
But grieve to find it trusted with such tempers,
That can't forgive my froward age its weakness.
Beda. Eliot, thou once hadst virtue; I have seen
Thy stubborn temper bend with godlike goodness,
Not half thus courted: 't is thy nation's glory,
To hug the foe that offers brave alliance.
Once more embrace, my friends—we 'll all embrace—
United thus, we are the mighty engine
Must twist this rooted empire from its basis!
Totters it not already?
Eliot. Would it were tumbling!
Beda. Nay, it shall down: this night we seal its ruin.

(*Enter Pierre.*)

O Pierre! thou art welcome!
Come to my breast, for by its hopes thou look'st
Lovelily dreadful, and the fate of Venice
Seems on thy sword already. O my Mars!
The poets that first feigned a god of war
Sure prophesied of thee.
Pierr. Friends! was not Brutus,
(I mean that Brutus who in open senate
Stabbed the first Cæsar that usurped the world)
A gallant man?
Ren. Yes, and Catiline too;
Though story wrong his fame; for he conspired
To prop the reeling glory of his country:
His cause was good.
Beda. And ours as much above it,
As, Renault, thou art superior to Cethegus,

Or Pierre to Cassius.

Pierr. Then to what we aim at,
When do we start? or must we talk for ever?

Beda. No, Pierre, the deed's near birth: fate seems to have set
The business up, and given it to our care;
I hope there's not a heart nor hand amongst us
But is firm and ready.

All. All! We'll die with Bedamar.

Beda. O men,
Matchless, as will your glory be hereafter!
The game is for a matchless prize, if won;
If lost, disgraceful ruin.

Ren. What can lose it?
The public stock's a beggar; one Venetian
Trusts not another. Look into their stores
Of general safety; empty magazines,
A tattered fleet, a murmuring unpaid army,
Bankrupt nobility, a harassed commonalty,
A factious, giddy, and divided Senate,
Is all the strength of Venice. Let's destroy it;
Let's fill their magazines with arms to awe them,
Man out their fleet, and make their trade maintain it;
Let loose the murmuring army on their masters,
To pay themselves with plunder; lop their nobles
To the base roots, whence most of 'em first sprung;
Enslave the rout, whom smarting will make humble;
Turn out their droning Senate, and possess
That seat of empire which our souls were framed for.

Pierr. Ten thousand men are armed at your nod,
Commanded all by leaders fit to guide
A battle for the freedom of the world;
This wretched state has starved them in its service,
And by your bounty quickened, they're resolved
To serve your glory, and revenge their own!
Th' have all their different quarters in this city,
Watch for the alarm, and grumble 't is so tardy.

Beda. I doubt not, friend, but thy unwearied diligence
Has still kept waking, and it shall have ease.
After this night it is resolved we meet
No more, till Venice own us for her lords.

Pierr. How love[li]ly the Adriatic whore,
Dressed in her flames, will shine! devouring flames!
Such as shall burn her to the watery bottom
And hiss in her foundation.

Beda. Now if any
Amongst us that owns this glorious cause
Have friends or interest he'd wish to save,
Let it be told; the general doom is sealed;
But I'd forego the hopes of a world's empire,
Rather than wound the bowels of my friend.

Pierr. I must confess, you there have touched my weakness,
I have a friend; hear it, such a friend!
My heart was ne'er shut to him: nay, I'll tell you,
He knows the very business of this hour;
But he rejoices in the cause, and loves it;
We've changed a vow to live and die together,
And he's at hand to ratify it here.

Ren. How! all betrayed?

Pierr. No—I've dealt nobly with you;
I've brought my all into the public stock;
I had but one friend, and him I'll share amongst you!
Receive and cherish him: or if, when seen
And searched, you find him worthless, as my tongue
Has lodged this secret in his faithful breast,
To ease your fears I wear a dagger here
Shall rip it out again, and give you rest.
Come forth, thou only good I e'er could boast of.

(*Enter Jaffeir with a dagger.*)

Beda. His presence bears the show of manly virtue.

Jaff. I know you'll wonder all, that thus uncalled,
I dare approach this place of fatal counsels;
But I'm amongst you, and by Heaven it glads me,
To see so many virtues thus united,
To restore justice and dethrone oppression.
Command this sword, if you would have it quiet,

Into this breast; but if you think it worthy
To cut the throats of reverend rogues in robes,
Send me into the curst assembled Senate;
It shrinks not, though I meet a father there.
Would you behold this city flaming? Here 's
A hand shall bear a lighted torch at noon
To the arsenal, and set its gates on fire.
Ren. You talk this well, sir.
Jaff. Nay—by Heaven I 'll do this.
Come, come, I read distrust in all your faces;
You fear me a villain, and indeed it 's odd
To hear a stranger talk thus at first meeting,
Of matters, that have been so well debated;
But I come ripe with wrongs as you with counsels,
I hate this Senate, am a foe to Venice;
A friend to none, but men resolved like me,
To push on mischief; oh, did you but know me,
I need not talk thus!
Beda. Pierre! I must embrace him,
My heart beats to this man as if it knew him.
Ren. I never loved these huggers.
Jaff. Still I see
The cause delights me not. Your friends survey me,
As I were dangerous—but I come armed
Against all doubts, and to your trust will give
A pledge, worth more than all the world can pay for.
My Belvidera! Ho! My Belvidera!
Reda. What wonder next?
Jaff. Let me entreat you,
As I have henceforth hopes to call ye friends,
That all but the ambassador, [and] this
Grave guide of councils, with my friend that owns me,
Withdraw a while to spare a woman's blushes.
(*Exeunt all but Bedamar, Renault, Jaffeir, Pierre.*)
Beda. Pierre, whither will this ceremony lead us?
Jaff. My Belvidera! Belvidera!

(*Enter Belvidera.*)

Belv. Who?
Who calls so loud at this late peaceful hour?
That voice was wont to come in gentler whispers,
And fill my ears with the soft breath of love:
Thou hourly image of my thoughts, where art thou?
Jaff. Indeed, 't is late.
Belv. Oh! I have slept and dreamt,
And dreamt again. Where hast thou been, thou loiterer?
Though my eyes closed, my arms have still been opened;
Stretched every way betwixt my broken slumbers,
To search if thou wert come to crown my rest;
There 's no repose without thee. Oh, the day
Too soon will break, and wake us to our sorrow;
Come, come to bed, and bid thy cares good-night.
Jaff. O Belvidera! we must change the scene
In which the past delights of life were tasted:
The poor sleep little, we must learn to watch
Our labors late, and early every morning,
Midst winter frosts, thin clad and fed with sparing,
Rise to our toils, and drudge away the day.
Belv. Alas! where am I? whither is 't you lead me?
Methinks I read distraction in your face,
Something less gentle than the fate you tell me:
You shake and tremble too! your blood runs cold!
Heavens guard my love, and bless his heart with patience!
Jaff. That I have patience, let our fate bear witness,
Who has ordained it so, that thou and I,
(Thou the divinest good man e'er possessed,
And I the wretched'st of the race of man)
This very hour, without one tear, must part.
Belv. Part! must we part? O! am I then forsaken?
Will my love cast me off? have my misfortunes

Offended him so highly, that he'll leave me?
Why drag you from me; whither are you going?
My dear! my life! my love!

Jaff. Oh friends!

Belv. Speak to me.

Jaff. Take her from my heart;
She'll gain such hold else, I shall ne'er get loose.
I charge thee take her, but with tenderest care
Relieve her troubles and assuage her sorrows.

Ren. Rise, madam! and command amongst your servants!

Jaff. To you, sirs, and your honors, I bequeath her,
And with her this, when I prove unworthy—

(*Gives a dagger.*)

You know the rest—then strike it to her heart;
And tell her, he, who three whole happy years
Lay in her arms, and each kind night repeated
The passionate vows of still-increasing love,
Sent that reward for all her truth and sufferings.

Belv. Nay, take my life, since he has sold it cheaply;
Or send me to some distant clime your slave,
But let it be far off, lest my complainings
Should reach his guilty ears, and shake his peace.

Jaff. No, Belvidera, I've contrived thy honor.
Trust to my faith, and be but fortune kind
To me, as I'll preserve that faith unbroken,
When next we meet, I'll lift thee to a height,
Shall gather all the gazing world about thee,
To wonder what strange virtue placed thee there.
But if we ne'er meet more——

Belv. O thou unkind one,
Never meet more? have I deserved this from you?
Look on me, tell me, tell me, speak, thou dear deceiver,
Why am I separated from thy love?
If I am false, accuse me; but if true,
Don't, prithee, don't in poverty forsake me,
But pity the sad heart, that's torn with parting.
Yet hear me! yet recall me——

(*Exeunt Renault, Bedamar, and Belvidera.*)

Jaff. O my eyes!
Look not that way, but turn yourselves awhile
Into my heart, and be weaned all together.
My friend, where art thou?

Pierr. Here, my honor's brother.

Jaff. Is Belvidera gone?

Pierr. Renault has led her
Back to her own apartment; but, by Heaven!
Thou must not see her more till our work's over.

Jaff. No?

Pierr. Not for your life.

Jaff. O Pierre, wert thou but she,
How I could pull thee down into my heart,
Gaze on thee till my eye-strings cracked with love,
Till all my sinews with its fire extended
Fixed me upon the rack of ardent longing;
Then swelling, sighing, raging to be blest,
Come like a panting turtle to thy breast,
On thy soft bosom, hovering, bill and play,
Confess the cause why last I fled away;
Own 't was a fault, but swear to give it o'er
And never follow false ambition more.

(*Exeunt ambo.*)

ACT III

Scene 1.

(*Enter Aquilina and her Maid.*)

Aquil. Tell him I am gone to bed: tell him I am not at home; tell him I've better company with me, or any thing; tell him, in short, I will not see him, the eternal, troublesome, vexatious fool: he's worse company than an ignorant physician—I'll not be disturbed at these unseasonable hours.

Maid. But madam! He's here already, just entered the doors.

Aquil. Turn him out again, you unnecessary, useless, giddy-brained ass! If he will not be gone, set the house a-fire and burn us both; I had rather meet a toad in my dish than that old hideous animal in my chamber to-night.

(*Enter Antonio.*)

Anto. Nacky, Nacky, Nacky—how dost do, Nacky? Hurry durry. I am come, little Nacky; past eleven o'clock, a late hour; time in all conscience to go to bed, Nacky—Nacky, did I say? Ay Nacky; Aquilina, lina, lina, quilina, quilina, quilina, Aquilina, Naquilina, Naquilina, Acky, Acky, Nacky, Nacky, Queen Nacky—come let 's to bed—you fubbs, you pugg you—you little puss—purree tuzzey—I am a senator.

Aquil. You are a fool, I am sure.

Anto. May be so too, sweetheart. Never the worse senator for all that. Come Nacky, Nacky, let 's have a game at rump, Nacky.

Aquil. You would do well, signior, to be troublesome here no longer, but leave me to myself; be sober and go home, sir.

Anto. Home, Madonna!

Aquil. Ay, home, sir. Who am I?

Anto. Madonna, as I take it, you are my—you are—thou art my little Nicky Nacky—that 's all!

Aquil. I find you are resolved to be troublesome, and so to make short of the matter in few words, I hate you, detest you, loathe you, I am weary of you, sick of you—hang you, you are an old, silly, impertinent, impotent, solicitous coxcomb, crazy in your head, and lazy in your body, love to be meddling with everything, and if you had not money, you are good for nothing.

Anto. "Good for nothing!" Hurry durry, I 'll try that presently. Sixty-one years old, and good for nothing: that 's brave! (*To the Maid.*) Come, come, come, Mistress Fiddle-faddle, turn you out for a season; go turn out, I say, it is our will and pleasure to be private some moments—out, out when you are bid to—(*Puts her out and locks the door.*) "Good for nothing," you say.

Aquil. Why, what are you good for?

Anto. In the first place, madam, I am old, and consequently very wise, very wise, Madonna, d' ye mark that? in the second place, take notice, if you please, that I am a senator, and when I think fit can make speeches, Madonna. Hurry durry, I can make a speech in the Senate-house now and then—would make your hair stand on end, Madonna.

Aquil. What care I for your speeches in the Senate-house? If you would be silent here, I should thank you.

Anto. Why, I can make speeches to thee too, my lovely Madonna; for example—my cruel fair one, (*takes out a purse of gold and at every pause shakes it*), since it is my fate, that you should with your servant angry prove; tho' late at night—I hope 't is not too late with this to gain reception for my love—there 's for thee, my little Nicky Nacky—take it, here take it—I say take it, or I 'll throw it at your head—how now, rebel!

Aquil. Truly, my illustrious Senator, I must confess your honor is at present most profoundly eloquent indeed.

Anto. Very well; come, now let 's sit down and think upon 't a little—come sit I say—sit down by me a little, my Nicky Nacky, ha!—(*Sits down.*) Hurry durry "good for nothing!"

Aquil. No, sir, if you please, I can know my distance and stand.

Anto. Stand: how? Nacky up and I down! Nay, then, let me exclaim with the poet.

Show me a case more pitiful who can,
A standing woman, and a falling man.

Hurry durry—not sit down—see this, ye gods—You won't sit down?

Aquil. No, sir.

Anto. Then look you now, suppose me a bull, a Basan-bull, the bull of bulls, or any bull. Thus up I get and with my brows thus bent—I broo, I say I broo, I broo, I broo. You won't sit down, will you?—I broo——

(*Bellows like a bull, and drives her about.*)

Aquil. Well, sir, I must endure this. (*She sits down.*) Now your honor has been a bull, pray what beast will your worship please to be next?

Anto. Now I 'll be a senator again, and thy lover, little Nicky Nacky! (*He sits by her.*) Ah toad, toad, toad, toad! spit in my face, a little, Nacky—spit in my face prithee, spit in my face, never so little: spit but a little bit—spit, spit, spit, spit, when you are bid, I say; do prithee spit—now, now, now, spit: what, you won't spit, will you? Then I 'll be a dog.

Aquil. A dog, my lord?

Anto. Ay, a dog—and I 'll give thee this t'other purse to let me be a dog—and to use me like a dog a little. Hurry durry—I will—here 't is.

(*Gives the purse.*)

Aquil. Well, with all my heart. But let me beseech your dogship to play your tricks over as fast as you can, that you may come to stinking the sooner, and be turned out of doors as you deserve.

Anto. Ay, ay—no matter for that—that—(*He gets under the table.*)—shan't move me——Now, bow wow, wow, bow wow . . .

(*Barks like a dog.*)

Aquil. Hold, hold, hold, sir, I beseech you: what is't you do? If curs bite, they must be kicked, sir. Do you see, kicked thus?

Anto. Ay, with all my heart: do kick, kick on, now I am under the table, kick again—kick harder—harder yet, bow wow wow, wow, bow—'od, I'll have a snap at thy shins—bow wow wow, wow, bow—'od, she kicks bravely.——

Aquil. Nay, then I'll go another way to work with you; and I think here's an instrument fit for the purpose. (*Fetches a whip and bell.*) What, bite your mistress, sirrah! out, out of doors, you dog, to kennel and be hanged—bite your mistress by the legs, you rogue——

(*She whips him.*)

Anto. Nay, prithee, Nacky, now thou art too loving: hurry durry, 'od I'll be a dog no longer.

Aquil. Nay, none of your fawning and grinning: but be gone, or here's the discipline: what, bite your mistress by the legs, you mongrel? out of doors—hout, hout, to kennel, sirrah! go.

Anto. This is very barbarous usage, Nacky, very barbarous: look you, I will not go—I will not stir from the door, that I resolve—hurry durry, what, shut me out?

(*She whips him out.*)

Aquil. Ay, and if you come here any more to-night I'll have my footman lug you, you cur: what, bite your poor mistress Nacky, sirrah!

(*Enter Maid.*)

Maid. Heavens, madam! What's the matter?

(*He howls at the door like a dog.*)

Aquil. Call my footmen hither presently.

(*Enter two Footmen.*)

Maid. They are here already, madam, the house is all alarmed with a strange noise, that nobody knows what to make of.

Aquil. Go all of you and turn that troublesome beast in the next room out of my house—if I ever see him within these walls again, without my leave for his admittance, you sneaking rogues, I'll have you poisoned all, poisoned like rats; every corner of the house shall stink of one of you; go, and learn hereafter to know my pleasure. So now for my Pierre:
Thus when godlike lover was displeased,
We sacrifice our fool and he's appeased.

(*Exeunt.*)

Scene 2.

(*Enter Belvidera.*)

Belv. I'm sacrificed! I am sold! betrayed to shame!
Inevitable ruin has inclosed me!
No sooner was I to my bed repaired
To weigh, and (weeping) ponder my condition,
But the old hoary wretch, to whose false care
My peace and honor was entrusted, came
(Like Tarquin) ghastly with infernal lust.
O thou, Roman Lucrece! Thou couldst find friends
To vindicate thy wrong;
I never had but one, and he's proved false;
He that should guard my virtue has betrayed it;
Left me! undone me! O that I could hate him!
Where shall I go? O whither, whither wander?

(*Enter Jaffeir.*)

Jaff. Can Belvidera want a resting place,
When these poor arms are open to receive her?
Oh, 't is in vain to struggle with desires
Strong as my love to thee; for every moment
I am from thy sight, the heart within my bosom
Moans like a tender infant in its cradle
Whose nurse has left it; come, and with the songs
Of gentle love persuade it to its peace.

Belv. I fear the stubborn wanderer will not own me,
'T is grown a rebel to be ruled no longer,
Scorns the indulgent bosom that first lulled it,
And like a disobedient child disdains
The soft authority of Belvidera.

Jaff. There was a time——

Belv. Yes, yes, there was a time
When Belvidera's tears, her cries, and sorrows.

Were not despised; when if she chanced to sigh,
Or look but sad—there was indeed a time
When Jaffeir would have ta'en her in his arms,
Eased her declining head upon his breast,
And never left her till he found the cause.
But let her now weep seas,
Cry, till she rend the earth; sigh till she burst
Her heart asunder; still he bears it all;
Deaf as the wind, and as the rocks unshaken.

Jaff. Have I been deaf? am I that rock unmoved,
Against whose root tears beat and sighs are sent?
In vain have I beheld thy sorrows calmly!
Witness against me, Heavens, have I done this?
Then bear me in a whirlwind back again,
And let that angry dear one ne'er forgive me!
O thou too rashly censurest of my love!
Couldst thou but think how I have spent this night,
Dark and alone, no pillow to my head,
Rest in my eyes, nor quiet in my heart,
Thou wouldst not, Belvidera, sure thou wouldst not
Talk to me thus, but like a pitying angel,
Spreading thy wings, come settle on my breast,
And hatch warm comfort there, ere sorrows freeze it.

Belv. Why, then, poor mourner, in what baleful corner
Hast thou been talking with that witch the Night?
On what cold stone hast thou been stretched along,
Gathering the grumbling winds about thy head,
To mix with theirs the accents of thy woes!
Oh, now I find the cause my love forsakes me!
I am no longer fit to bear a share
In his concernments: my weak female virtue
Must not be trusted; 't is too frail and tender.

Jaff. O Portia! Portia! what a soul was thine!

Belv. That Portia was a woman, and when Brutus,
Big with the fate of Rome (Heaven guard thy safety!),
Concealed from her the labors of his mind,
She let him see her blood was great as his,
Flowed from a spring as noble, and a heart
Fit to partake his troubles, as his love.
Fetch, fetch that dagger back, the dreadful dower
Thou gavest last night in parting with me; strike it
Here to my heart; and as the blood flows from it,
Judge if it run not pure as Cato's daughter's.

Jaff. Thou art too good, and I indeed unworthy,
Unworthy so much virtue: teach me how
I may deserve such matchless love as thine,
And see with what attention I'll obey thee.

Belv. Do not despise me: that 's the all I ask.

Jaff. Despise thee! Hear me——

Belv. Oh, thy charming tongue
Is but too well acquainted with my weakness,
Knows, let it name but love, my melting heart
Dissolves within my breast; till with closed eyes
I reel into thy arms, and all 's forgotten.

Jaff. What shall I do?

Belv. Tell me! be just, and tell me
Why dwells that busy cloud upon thy face?
Why am I made a stranger? why that sigh,
And I not know the cause? Why, when the world
Is wrapt in rest, why chooses then my love
To wander up and down in horrid darkness,
Loathing his bed, and these desiring arms?
Why are these eyes bloodshot with tedious watching?
Why starts he now? and looks as if he wished
His fate were finished? Tell me, ease my fears;
Lest, when we next time meet, I want the power
To search into the sickness of thy mind,
But talk as wildly then as thou look'st now.

Jaff. O Belvidera!

Belv. Why was I last night delivered to a villain?
Jaff. Ha, a villain!
Belv. Yes! to a villain! Why at such an hour
Meets that assembly all made up of wretches
That look as hell had drawn 'em into league?
Why, I in this hand, and in that a dagger,
Was I delivered with such dreadful ceremonies?
"To you, sirs, and to your honor I bequeath her,
And with her this: whene'er I prove unworthy—
You know the rest,—then strike it to her heart?"
Oh! why 's that *rest* concealed from me? Must I
Be made the hostage of a hellish trust?
For such I know I am; that 's all my value!
But by the love and loyalty I owe thee,
I 'll free thee from the bondage of these slaves;
Straight to the Senate, tell 'em all I know,
All that I think, all that my fears inform me!
Jaff. Is this the Roman virtue! this the blood
That boasts its purity with Cato's daughter!
Would she have e'er betrayed her Brutus?
Belv. No:
For Brutus trusted her: wert thou so kind,
What would not Belvidera suffer for thee?
Jaff. I shall undo myself, and tell thee all.
Belv. Look not upon me, as I am a woman,
But as a bone,[18] thy wife, thy friend, who long
Has had admission to thy heart, and there
Studied the virtues of thy gallant nature;
Thy constancy, thy courage and thy truth,
Have been my daily lesson: I have learnt them,
Am bold as thou, can suffer or despise
The worst of fates for thee, and with thee share them.
Jaff. Oh you divinest powers! look down and hear
My prayers! instruct me to reward this virtue!
Yet think a little ere thou tempt me further:
Think I have a tale to tell, will shake thy nature,
Melt all this boasted constancy thou talk'st of
Into vile tears and despicable sorrows:
Then if thou shouldst betray me!
Belv. Shall I swear?
Jaff. No: do not swear: I would not violate
Thy tender nature with so rude a bond:
But as thou hopest to see me live my days,
And love thee long, lock this within thy breast;
I 've bound myself by all the strictest sacraments
Divine and human——
Belv. Speak!
Jaff. To kill thy father——
Belv. My father!
Jaff. Nay, the throats of the whole Senate
Shall bleed, my Belvidera: he amongst us
That spares his father, brother, or his friend,
Is damned. How rich and beauteous will the face
Of ruin look, when these wide streets run blood;
I and the glorious partners of my fortune
Shouting, and striding o'er the prostrate dead,
Still to new waste; whilst thou, far off in safety
Smiling, shalt see the wonders of our daring;
And when night comes, with praise and love receive me!
Belv. Oh!
Jaff. Have a care, and shrink not even in thought!
For if thou dost——
Belv. I know it, thou wilt kill me.
Do, strike thy sword into this bosom: lay me
Dead on the earth, and then thou wilt be safe:
Murder my father! though his cruel nature
Has persecuted me to my undoing,
Driven me to basest wants, can I behold him,
With smiles of vengeance, butchered in his age?
The sacred fountain of my life destroyed?

18 *i. e.* "bone of thy bone, flesh of thy flesh."

And canst thou shed the blood that gave me being?
Nay, be a traitor too, and sell thy country?
Can thy great heart descend so vilely low,
Mix with hired slaves, bravos, and common stabbers,
Nose-slitters, alley-lurking villains? join
With such a crew and take a ruffian's wages
To cut the throats of wretches as they sleep?

Jaff. Thou wrong'st me, Belvidera! I 've engaged
With men of souls, fit to reform the ills
Of all mankind: there 's not a heart amongst them,
But 's stout as death, yet honest as the nature
Of man first made, ere fraud and vice were fashions.

Belv. What 's he, to whose curst hands last night thou gav'st me?
Was that well done! Oh! I could tell a story
Would rouse thy lion-heart out of its den,
And make it rage with terrifying fury.

Jaff. Speak on, I charge thee!

Belv. O my love! if e'er
Thy Belvidera's peace deserved thy care,
Remove me from this place: last night, last night——

Jaff. Distract me not, but give me all the truth.

Belv. No sooner wert thou gone, and I alone,
Left in the power of that old son of mischief;
No sooner was I lain on my sad bed,
But that vile wretch approached me, loose, unbuttoned,
Ready for violation: then my heart
Throbbed with its fears: oh, how I wept and sighed
And shrunk and trembled; wished in vain for him
That should protect me. Thou, alas! wert gone!

Jaff. Patience, sweet Heaven, till I make vengeance sure!

Belv. He drew the hideous dagger forth thou gav'st him,
And with upbraiding smiles, he said, "Behold it;
This is the pledge of a false husband's love:"
And in my arms then pressed, and would have clasped me;
But with my cries I scared his coward heart,
Till he withdrew, and muttered vows to hell.
These are thy friends! with these thy life, thy honor,
Thy love, all 's staked, and all will go to ruin.

Jaff. No more: I charge thee keep this secret close;
Clear up thy sorrows, look as if thy wrongs
Were all forgot, and treat him like a friend,
As no complaint were made. No more; retire,
Retire, my life, and doubt not of my honor;
I 'll heal its failings, and deserve thy love.

Belv. Oh, should I part with thee, I fear thou wilt
In anger leave me, and return no more.

Jaff. Return no more! I would not live without thee
Another night, to purchase the creation.

Belv. When shall we meet again?

Jaff. Anon at twelve!
I 'll steal myself to thy expecting arms,
Come like a travelled dove and bring thee peace.

Belv. Indeed!

Jaff. By all our loves!

Belv. 'T is hard to part:
But sure no falsehood e[v]er looked so fairly.
Farewell—remember twelve.

(*Exit Belvidera.*)

Jaff. Let Heaven forget me
When I remember not thy truth, thy love.
How curst is my condition! tossed and justled
From every corner; fortune's common fool,
The jest of rogues, an instrumental ass
For villains to lay loads of shame upon,
And drive about just for their ease and scorn.

(*Enter Pierre.*)

Pierr. Jaffeir!

Jaff. Who calls?

Pierr. A friend, that could have wished

To have found thee otherwise employed: what, hunt
A wife on the dull foil![19] sure a staunch husband
Of all hounds is the dullest! Wilt thou never,
Never be weaned from caudles and confections?
What feminine tale hast thou been listening to,
Of unaired shirts; catarrhs and toothache got
By thin-soled shoes? Damnation! that a fellow
Chosen to be sharer in the destruction
Of a whole people, should sneak thus in corners
To ease his fulsome lusts, and fool his mind!

Jaff. May not a man then trifle out an hour
With a kind woman and not wrong his calling?

Pierr. Not in a cause like ours.

Jaff. Then, friend, our cause
Is in a damned condition: for I'll tell thee,
That canker-worm called lechery has touched it;
'T is tainted vilely: wouldst thou think it, Renault
(That mortified, old, withered, winter rogue)
Loves simple fornication like a priest;
I found him out for watering at my wife:
He visited her last night like a kind guardian:
Faith, she has some temptations, that's the truth on 't.

Pierr. He durst not wrong his trust!

Jaff. 'T was something late, though,
To take the freedom of a lady's chamber.

Pierr. Was she in bed?

Jaff. Yes, faith, in virgin sheets
White as her bosom, Pierre, dished neatly up,
Might tempt a weaker appetite to taste.
Oh, how the old fox stunk, I warrant thee,
When the rank fit was on him!

Pierr. Patience guide me!
He used no violence?

Jaff. No, no! out on 't, violence!
Played with her neck, brushed her with his grey-beard,
Struggled and towzed, tickled her till she squeaked a little,
May be, or so—but not a jot of violence——

Pierr. Damn him!

Jaff. Ay, so say I: but hush, no more on 't;
All hitherto is well, and I believe
Myself no monster[20] yet: though no man knows
What fate he's born to: sure 't is near the hour
We all should meet for our concluding orders:
Will the ambassador be here in person?

Pierr. No; he has sent commission to that villain,
Renault, to give the executing charge.
I'd have thee be a man, if possible,
And keep thy temper; for a brave revenge
Ne'er comes too late.

Jaff. Fear not, I'm cool as patience:
Had he completed my dishonor, rather
Than hazard the success our hopes are ripe for,
I'd bear it all with mortifying virtue.

Pierr. He's yonder coming this way through the hall;
His thoughts seem full.

Jaff. Prithee retire, and leave me
With him alone: I'll put him to some trial,
See how his rotten part will bear the touching.

Pierr. Be careful, then.

(*Exit Pierre.*)

Jaff. Nay, never doubt, but trust me.
What, be a devil! take a damning oath
For shedding native blood! can there be a sin
In merciful repentance? O this villain!

(*Enter Renault.*)

Ren. Perverse! and peevish! what a slave is man!
To let his itching flesh thus get the better of him!
Despatch the tool her husband—that were well.
Who's there!

Jaff. A man.

Ren. My friend, my near ally!
The hostage of your faith, my beauteous charge,
Is very well.

Jaff. Sir, are you sure of that?
Stands she in perfect health? beats her pulse even?
Neither too hot nor cold?

19 The track of a hunted animal.

20 *I.e.* A cuckold (supposed to wear horns).

Ren. What means that question?
Jaff. Oh, women have fantastic constitutions,
Inconstant as their wishes, always wavering,
And ne'er fixed; was it not boldly done
Even at first sight to trust the thing I loved
(A tempting treasure too!) with youth so fierce
And vigorous as thine? but thou art honest.
Ren. Who dares accuse me?
Jaff. Curst be him that doubts
Thy virtue: I have tried it, and declare,
Were I to choose a guardian of my honor,
I'd put it into thy keeping; for I know thee.
Ren. Know me!
Jaff. Ay, know thee: there's no falsehood in thee.
Thou look'st just as thou art: let us embrace.
Now wouldst thou cut my throat or I cut thine?
Ren. You dare not do't.
Jaff. You lie, sir.
Ren. How!
Jaff. No more.
'T is a base world, and must reform, that's all.

(*Enter Spinosa, Theodore, Eliot, Revillido, Durand, Brainveil, and the rest of the Conspirators.*)

Ren. Spinosa, Theodore!
Spin. The same.
Ren. You are welcome!
Spin. You are trembling, sir.
Ren. 'T is a cold night indeed, I am aged,
Full of decay and natural infirmities;
We shall be warm, my friend, I hope, to-morrow.

(*Pierre re-enters.*)

Pierr. (*aside*). 'T was not well done, thou shouldst have stroked him
And not have galled him.
Jaff. (*aside*). Damn him, let him chew on't.
Heaven! where am I? beset with cursed fiends,
That wait to damn me: what a devil's man,
When he forgets his nature—hush, my heart.
Ren. My friends, 't is late: are we assembled all?
Where's Theodore?
Theo. At hand.
Ren. Spinosa.
Spin. Here.
Ren. Bra[in]veil.
Brain. I'm ready.
Ren. Durand and Brabe.
Dur. Command us,
We are both prepared!
Ren. Mezzana, Revillido,
Ternon, Retrosi; oh, you are men, I find,
Fit to behold your fate, and meet her summons.
To-morrow's rising sun must see you all
Decked in your honors! Are the soldiers ready?
Omn. All, all.
Ren. You, Durand, with your thousand must possess
St. Mark's; you, captain, know your charge already:
'T is to secure the Ducal Palace: you,
Brabe, with a hundred more must gain the Secque.[21]
With the like number Brainveil to the Procuralle.[22]
Be all this done with the least tumult possible,
Till in each place you post sufficient guards:
Then sheathe your swords in every breast you meet.
Jaff. (*aside*). O reverend cruelty! damned bloody villain!
Ren. During this execution, Durand, you
Must in the midst keep your battalia fast,
And, Theodore, be sure to plant the cannon
That may command the streets; whilst Revillido,
Mezzana, Ternon, and Retrosi, guard you.
This done, we'll give the general alarm,
Apply petards, and force the arsenal gates;
Then fire the city round in several places,
Or with our cannon, if it dare resist,
Batter it to ruin. But above all I charge you
Shed blood enough, spare neither sex nor age,

21 A French spelling (derived from the French source) for *Zecca*; the mint, just off the Piazza of St. Mark.

22 This is a misprint for *Procuratie*, two palaces on the Piazza of St. Mark, the Venetian "civic center," once the residences of the nine procurators, financial officers.

Name nor condition; if there live a senator
After to-morrow, though the dullest rogue
That e'er said nothing, we have lost our ends;
If possible, let 's kill the very name
Of senator, and bury it in blood.

Jaff. (*aside*). Merciless, horrid slave!— Ay, blood enough!
Shed blood enough, old Renault: how thou charm'st me!

Ren. But one thing more, and then farewell till fate
Join us again, or separate us ever:
First, let 's embrace. Heaven knows who next shall thus
Wing ye together: but let 's all remember
We wear no common cause upon our swords;
Let each man think that on his single virtue
Depends the good and fame of all the rest,
Eternal honor or perpetual infamy.
Let 's remember through what dreadful hazards
Propitious fortune hitherto has led us,
How often on the brink of some discovery
Have we stood tottering, and yet still kept our ground
So well, the busiest searchers ne'er could follow
Those subtle tracks which puzzled all suspicion:
You droop, sir.

Jaff. No; with a most profound attention
I 've heard it all, and wonder at thy virtue.

Ren. Though there be yet few hours 'twixt them and ruin,
Are not the Senate lulled in full security,
Quiet and satisfied, as fools are always!
Never did so profound repose forerun
Calamity so great: nay, our good fortune
Has blinded the most piercing of mankind;
Strengthened the fearful'st, charmed the most suspectful,
Confounded the most subtle; for we live,
We live, my friends, and quickly shall our life
Prove fatal to these tyrants: let 's consider
That we destroy oppression, avarice,
A people nursed up equally with vices
And loathsome lusts, which nature most abhors,
And such as without shame she cannot suffer.

Jaff. (*aside*). O Belvidera, take me to thy arms
And show me where 's my peace, for I have lost it.

(*Exit Jaffeir.*)

Ren. Without the least remorse then let 's resolve
With fire and sword to exterminate these tyrants,
And when we shall behold those curst tribunals,
Stained by the tears and sufferings of the innocent,
Burning with flames rather from Heaven than ours,
The raging, furious and unpitying soldier
Pulling his reeking dagger from the bosoms
Of gasping wretches; death in every quarter,
With all that sad disorder can produce,
To make a spectacle of horror: then,
Then let 's call to mind, my dearest friends,
That there is nothing pure upon the earth,
That the most valued things have most allays,
And that in change of all those vile enormities,
Under whose weight this wretched country labors,
The means are only in our hands to crown them.

Pierr. And may those powers above that are propitious
To gallant minds record this cause, and bless it.

Ren. Thus happy, thus secure of all we wish for,
Should there, my friends, be found amongst us one
False to this glorious enterprise, what fate,
What vengeance were enough for such a villain?

Eliot. Death here without repentance, hell hereafter.

Ren. Let that be my lot, if as here I stand
Listed by fate amongst her darling sons,

Though I had one only brother, dear by all
The strictest ties of nature; though one hour
Had given us birth, one fortune fed our wants,
One only love, and that but of each other,
Still filled our minds: could I have such a friend
Joined in this cause, and had but ground to fear
Meant foul play; may this right hand drop from me,
If I 'd not hazard all my future peace,
And stab him to the heart before you. Who
Would not do less? Wouldst not thou, Pierre, the same?

Pierr. You 've singled me, sir, out for this hard question,
As if 't were started only for my sake!
Am I the thing you fear? Here, here 's my bosom,
Search it with all your swords! Am I a traitor?

Ren. No: but I fear your late commended friend
Is little less. Come, sirs, 't is now no time
To trifle with our safety. Where 's this Jaffeir?

Spin. He left the room just now in strange disorder.

Ren. Nay, there is danger in him: I observed him,
During the time I took for explanation,
He was transported from most deep attention,
To a confusion which he could not smother.
His looks grew full of sadness and surprise,
All which betrayed a wavering spirit in him,
That labored with reluctancy and sorrow.
What 's requisite for safety must be done
With speedy execution: he remains
Yet in our power: I for my own part wear
A dagger.

Pierr. Well.

Ren. And I could wish it——

Pierr. Where?

Ren. Buried in his heart.

Pierr. Away! we 're yet all friends;
No more of this, 't will breed ill blood amongst us.

Spin. Let us all draw our swords, and search the house,
Pull him from the dark hole where he sits brooding
O'er his cold fears, and each man kill his share of him.

Pierr. Who talks of killing? Who 's he 'll shed the blood
That 's dear to me! Is 't you? or you? or you, sir?
What, not one speak? how you stand gaping all
On your grave oracle, your wooden god there;
Yet not a word: (*to Renault*) then, sir, I 'll tell you a secret,
Suspicion 's but at best a coward's virtue!

Ren. A coward——

(*Handles his sword.*)

Pierr. Put, put up the sword, old man,
Thy hand shakes at it; come, let 's heal this breach,
I am too hot; we yet may live [as] friends.

Spin. Till we are safe, our friendship cannot be so.

Pierr. Again: who 's that?

Spin. 'Twas I.

Theo. And I.

Revill. And I.

Eliot. And all.

Ren. Who are on my side?

Spin. Every honest sword;
Let 's die like men and not be sold like slaves.

Pierr. One such word more, by Heaven, I 'll to the Senate
And hang ye all, like dogs in clusters.
Why peep your coward swords half out their shells?
Why do you not all brandish them like mine?
You fear to die, and yet dare talk of killing?

Ren. Go to the Senate and betray us, hasten,
Secure thy wretched life, we fear to die
Less than thou dar'st be honest.

Pierr. That 's rank falsehood.
Fear'st not thou death? fie, there 's a knavish itch
In that salt blood, an utter foe to smarting.
Had Jaffeir's wife proved kind, he had still been true.
Foh—how that stinks!
Thou die! thou kill my friend, or thou, or thou.

Or thou, with that lean, withered, wretched face!
Away! disperse all to your several charges,
And meet to-morrow where your honor calls you;
I'll bring that man, whose blood you so much thirst for,
And you shall see him venture for you fairly—
Hence, hence, I say.
(*Exit Renault angrily.*)

Spin. I fear we've been to blame:
And done too much.

Theo. 'T was too far urged against the man you loved.

Revill. Here, take our swords and crush 'em with your feet.

Spin. Forgive us, gallant friend.

Pierr. Nay, now you've found
The way to melt and cast me as you will:
I'll fetch this friend and give him to your mercy:
Nay, he shall die if you will take him from me;
For your repose I'll quit my heart's jewel,
But would not have him torn away by villains
And spiteful villainy.

Spin. No; may you both
For ever live and fill the world with fame!

Pierr. Now you are too kind. Whence rose all this discord?
Oh, what a dangerous precipice have we scaped!
How near a fall was all we had long been building!
What an eternal blot had stained our glories,
If one, the bravest and the best of men,
Had fallen a sacrifice to rash suspicion,
Butchered by those whose cause he came to cherish!
Oh, could you know him all as I have known him,
How good he is, how just, how true, how brave,
You would not leave this place till you had seen him;
Humbled yourselves before him, kissed his feet,
And gained remission for the worst of follies;
Come but to-morrow, all your doubts shall end,
And to your loves me better recommend,
That I've preserved your fame, and saved my friend.
(*Exeunt omnes.*)

ACT IV.

Scene 1.

[*A Public Place.*]

(*Enter Jaffeir and Belvidera.*)

Jaff. Where dost thou lead me? Every step I move,
Methinks I tread upon some mangled limb
Of a racked friend. O my dear charming ruin!
Where are we wandering?

Belv. To eternal honor;
To do a deed shall chronicle thy name,
Among the glorious legends of those few
That have saved sinking nations: thy renown
Shall be the future song of all the virgins,
Who by thy piety have been preserved
From horrid violation: every street
Shall be adorned with statues to thy honor,
And at thy feet this great inscription written,
Remember him that propped the fall of Venice.

Jaff. Rather, remember him who after all
The sacred bonds of oaths and holier friendship,
In fond compassion to a woman's tears
Forgot his manhood, virtue, truth and honor,
To sacrifice the bosom that relieved him.
Why wilt thou damn me?

Belv. O inconstant man!
How will you promise? how will you deceive?
Do, return back, replace me in my bondage,
Tell all thy friends how dangerously thou lov'st me,
And let thy dagger do its bloody office;
O that kind dagger, Jaffeir, how 't will look
Stuck through my heart, drenched in my blood to the hilts!
Whilst these poor dying eyes shall with their tears
No more torment thee, then thou wilt be free:

Or if thou think'st it nobler, let me live
Till I'm a victim to the hateful lust
Of that infernal devil, that old fiend
That's damned himself and would undo mankind:
Last night, my love!

Jaff. Name, name it not again,
It shows a beastly image to my fancy,
Will wake me into madness. Oh, the villain!
That durst approach such purity as thine
On terms so vile: destruction, swift destruction
Fall on my coward-head, and make my name
The common scorn of fools if I forgive him;
If I forgive him, if I not revenge
With utmost rage and most unstaying fury,
Thy sufferings, thou dear darling of my life, love!

Belv. Delay no longer, then, but to the Senate;
And tell the dismal'st story e'er was uttered,
Tell them what bloodshed, rapines, desolations,
Have been prepared, how near's the fatal hour!
Save thy poor country, save the reverend blood
Of all its nobles, which to-morrow's dawn
Must else see shed: save the poor tender lives
Of all those little infants which the swords
Of murtherers are whetting for this moment:
Think thou already hear'st their dying screams,
Think that thou seest their sad distracted mothers
Kneeling before thy feet, and begging pity
With torn dishevell'd hair and streaming eyes,
Their naked mangled breasts besmeared with blood,
And even the milk with which their fondled babes,
Softly they hushed, dropping in anguish from 'em.
Think thou seest this, and then consult thy heart.

Jaff. Oh!

Belv. Think too, if thou lose this present minute,
What miseries the next day bring[s] upon thee.
Imagine all the horrors of that night,
Murder and rapine, waste and desolation,
Confusedly ranging. Think what then may prove
My lot! the ravisher may then come safe,
And midst the terror of the public ruin
Do a damned deed; perhaps to lay a train
May catch thy life; then where will be revenge,
The dear revenge that's due to such a wrong?

Jaff. By all Heaven's powers, prophetic truth dwells in thee,
For every word thou speak'st strikes through my heart
Like a new light, and shows it how 't has wandered;
Just what th' hast made me, take me, Belvidera,
And lead me to the place where I'm to say
This bitter lesson, where I must betray
My truth, my virtue, constancy and friends:
Must I betray my friends? Ah, take me quickly,
Secure me well before that thought's renewed;
If I relapse once more, all's lost for ever.

Belv. Hast thou a friend more dear than Belvidera?

Jaff. No, thou'rt my soul itself; wealth, friendship, honor,
All present joys, and earnest of all future,
Are summed in thee: methinks when in thy arms
Thus leaning on thy breast, one minute's more
Than a long thousand years of vulgar hours.
Why was such happiness not given me pure?
Why dashed with cruel wrongs, and bitter wantings?
Come, lead me forward now like a tame lamb
To sacrifice, thus in his fatal garlands,
Decked fine and pleased, the wanton skips and plays,

Trots by the enticing flattering priestess' side,
And much transported with his little pride,
Forgets his dear companions of the plain
Till, by her bound, he 's on the altar lain,
Yet then too hardly bleats, such pleasure 's in the pain.

(*Enter Officer and six Guards.*)

Offic. Stand; who goes there?
Belv. Friends.
Jaff. Friends, Belvidera! hide me from my friends:
By Heaven, I 'd rather see the face of hell,
Than meet the man I love.
Offic. But what friends are you?
Belv. Friends to the Senate and the state of Venice.
Offic. My orders are to seize on all I find
At this late hour, and bring 'em to the Council,
Who now are sitting.
Jaff. Sir, you shall be obeyed.
Hold, brutes, stand off, none of your paws upon me.
Now the lot 's cast, and fate, do what thou wilt!
(*Exeunt guarded.*)

SCENE 2. *The Senate-house.*

(*Where appear sitting, the Duke of Venice, Priuli, Antonio, and eight other Senators.*)

Duke. Antony, Priuli, senators of Venice,
Speak; why are we assembled here this night?
What have you to inform us of, concerns
The state of Venice, honor, or its safety?
Priu. Could words express the story I have to tell you,
Fathers, these tears were useless, these sad tears
That fall from my old eyes; but there is cause
We all should weep; tear off these purple robes,
And wrap ourselves in sackcloth, sitting down
On the sad earth, and cry aloud to Heaven.
Heaven knows if yet there be an hour to come
Ere Venice be no more.
All Senators. How!
Priu. Nay, we stand
Upon the very brink of gaping ruin.
Within this city 's formed a dark conspiracy,
To massacre us all, our wives and children,
Kindred and friends, our palaces and temples
To lay in ashes: nay, the hour, too, fixed;
The swords, for aught I know, drawn e'en this moment,
And the wild waste begun: from unknown hands
I had this warning: but if we are men,
Let 's not be tamely butchered, but do something
That may inform the world in after ages,
Our virtue was not ruined though we were.
(*A noise without.*)
Room, room, make room for some prisoners——
Second Senator. Let 's raise the city.

(*Enter Officer and Guard.*)

Priu. Speak there, what disturbance?
Offic. Two prisoners have the guard seized in the streets,
Who say they come to inform this reverend Senate
About the present danger.
(*Enter Jaffeir and Belvidera guarded.*)
All. Give 'em entrance——
Well, who are you?
Jaff. A villain.
Anto. Short and pithy.
The man speaks well.
Jaff. Would every man that hears me
Would deal so honestly, and own his title.
Duke. 'T is rumored that a plot has been contrived
Against this state; that you have a share in 't too.
If you 're a villain, to redeem your honor,
Unfold the truth and be restored with mercy.
Jaff. Think not that I to save my life come hither,
I know its value better; but in pity
To all those wretches whose unhappy dooms

Are fixed and sealed. You see me here before you,
The sworn and covenanted foe of Venice;
But use me as my dealings may deserve
And I may prove a friend.

Duke. The slave capitulates;
Give him the tortures.

Jaff. That you dare not do,
Your fears won't let you, nor the longing itch
To hear a story which you dread the truth of,
Truth which the fear of smart shall ne'er get from me.
Cowards are scared with threat'nings; boys are whipp'd
Into confessions: but a steady mind
Acts of itself, ne'er asks the body counsel.
"Give him the tortures!" Name but such a thing
Again, by Heaven I'll shut these lips for ever,
Not all your racks, your engines, or your wheels
Shall force a groan away—that you may guess at.

Anto. A bloody-minded fellow, I'll warrant;
A damned bloody-minded fellow.

Duke. Name your conditions.

Jaff. For myself full pardon,
Besides the lives of two and twenty friends
(*Delivers a list.*)
Whose names are here enrolled: nay, let their crimes
Be ne'er so monstrous, I must have the oaths
And sacred promise of this reverend council,
That in a full assembly of the Senate
The thing I ask be ratified. Swear this,
And I'll unfold the secrets of your danger.

All. We'll swear.

Duke. Propose the oath.

Jaff. By all the hopes
Ye have of peace and happiness hereafter,
Swear.

All. We all swear,

Jaff. To grant me what I've asked,
Ye swear?

All. We swear.

Jaff. And as ye keep the oath,
May you and your posterity be blest
Or curst for ever.

All. Else be curst for ever.

Jaff. (*Delivers another paper.*) Then here's the list, and with't the full disclose
Of all that threatens you.
Now, fate, thou hast caught me.

Anto. Why, what a dreadful catalogue of cut-throats is here! I'll warrant you, not one of these fellows but has a face like a lion. I dare not so much as read their names over.

Duke. Give orders that all diligent search be made
To seize these men, their characters are public;
The paper intimates their rendezvous
To be at the house of a famed Grecian courtesan
Called Aquilina; see that place secured.

Anto.
What, my Nicky Nacky, hurry durry,
Nicky Nacky in the plot—I'll make a speech.
Most noble Senators,
What headlong apprehension drives you on,
Right noble, wise and truly solid senators,
To violate the laws and rights of nations?
The lady is a lady of renown.
'T is true, she holds a house of fair reception,
And though I say't myself, as many more
Can say as well as I.

Second Senator. My lord, long speeches
Are frivolous here when dangers are so near us;
We all know your interest in that lady,
The world talks loud on't.

Anto. Verily, I have done,
I say no more.

Duke. But since he has declared
Himself concerned, pray, captain, take great caution
To treat the fair one as becomes her character,
And let her bed-chamber be searched with decency.
You, Jaffeir, must with patience bear till morning
To be our prisoner.

Jaff. Would the chains of death
Had bound me fast ere I had known this minute.
I've done a deed will make my story hereafter
Quoted in competition with all ill ones:

The history of my wickedness shall run
Down through the low traditions of the vulgar,
And boys be [taught] to tell the tale of Jaffeir.

Duke. Captain, withdraw your prisoner.

Jaff. Sir, if possible,
Lead me where my own thoughts themselves may lose me,
Where I may doze out what I've left of life,
Forget myself and this day's guilt and falsehood.
Cruel remembrance, how shall I appease thee!

(*Exit guarded.*)

(*Noise without.*)

More traitors; room, room, make room there.

Duke. How's this? guards?
Where are our guards? Shut up the gates, the treason's
Already at our doors.

(*Enter Officer.*)

Offic. My lords, more traitors:
Seized in the very act of consultation;
Furnished with arms and instruments of mischief.
Bring in the prisoners.

(*Enter Pierre, Renault, Theodore, Eliot, Revillido, and other conspirators, in fetters, guarded.*)

Pierr. You, my lords and fathers
(As you are pleased to call yourselves) of Venice,
If you sit here to guide the course of justice,
Why these disgraceful chains upon the limbs
That have so often labored in your service?
Are these the wreaths of triumph ye bestow
On those that bring you conquests home and honors?

Duke. Go on: you shall be heard, sir.

Anto. And be hanged too, I hope.

Pierr. Are these the trophies I've deserved for fighting
Your battles with confederated powers?
When winds and seas conspired to overthrow you,
And brought the fleets of Spain to your own harbors?
When you, great Duke, shrunk trembling in your palace,
And saw your wife, the Adriatic, ploughed
Like a lewd whore by bolder prows than yours,
Stepped not I forth, and taught your loose Venetians,
The task of honor and the way to greatness,
Rais'd you from your capitulating fears
To stipulate the terms of sued-for peace?
And this my recompense? If I am a traitor
Produce my charge; or show the wretch that's base enough
And brave enough to tell me I am a traitor.

Duke. Know you one Jaffeir?

(*All the Conspirators murmur.*)

Pierr. Yes, and know his virtue,
His justice, truth; his general worth and sufferings
From a hard father taught me first to love him.

(*Enter Jaffeir.*)

Duke. See him brought forth.

Pierr. My friend too bound! nay then
Our fate has conquered us, and we must fall.
Why droops the man whose welfare's so much mine
They're but one thing? These reverend tyrants, Jaffeir,
Call us all traitors: art thou one, my brother?

Jaff. To thee I am the falsest, veriest slave
That e'er betrayed a generous, trusting friend,
And gave up honor to be sure of ruin.
All our fair hopes which morning was to have crowned
Has this curst tongue o'erthrown.

Pierr. So, then, all's over;
Venice has lost her freedom; I my life;
No more; farewell.

Duke. Say, will you make confession
Of your vile deeds and trust the Senate's mercy?

Pierr. Curst be your Senate; curst your constitution;
The curse of growing factions and division
Still vex your councils, shake your public safety,
And makes the robes of government you wear,

Hateful to you, as these base chains to me!
Duke. Pardon or death?
Pierr. Death, honorable death!
Ren. Death' s the best thing we ask or you can give.
All Conspir. No shameful bonds, but honorable death.
Duke. Break up the council: captain, guard your prisoners.
Jaffeir, you are free, but these must wait for judgment.
(*Exeunt all the Senators.*)
Pierr. Come, where 's my dungeon? lead me to my straw:
It will not be the first time I 've lodged hard
To do your Senate service.
Jaff. Hold one moment.
Pierr. Who 's he disputes the judgment of the Senate?
Presumptuous rebel—on——
(*Strikes Jaffeir.*)
Jaff. By Heaven, you stir not.
I must be heard, I must have leave to speak;
Thou hast disgraced me, Pierre, by a vile blow:
Had not a dagger done thee nobler justice?
But use me as thou wilt, thou canst not wrong me,
For I am fallen beneath the basest injuries;
Yet look upon me with an eye of mercy,
With pity and with charity behold me;
Shut not thy heart against a friend's repentance,
But as there dwells a god-like nature in thee
Listen with mildness to my supplications.
Pierr. What whining monk art thou? what holy cheat,
That wouldst encroach upon my credulous ears
And canst thus vilely? Hence. I know thee not.
Dissemble and be nasty: leave me, hypocrite.
Jaff. Not know me, Pierre?
Pierr. No, I know thee not! what art thou?
Jaff. Jaffeir, thy friend, thy once loved, valued friend!
Though now deservedly scorned, and used most hardly.
Pierr. Thou Jaffeir! Thou my once loved valued friend?
By Heaven, thou liest; the man so-called, my friend,
Was generous, honest, faithful, just and valiant,
Noble in mind, and in his person lovely,
Dear to my eyes and tender to my heart:
But thou a wretched, base, false, worthless coward,
Poor even in soul, and loathsome in thy aspect,
All eyes must shun thee, and all hearts detest thee.
Prithee avoid, nor longer cling thus round me,
Like something baneful, that my nature's chilled at.
Jaff. I have not wronged thee, by these tears I have not.
But still am honest, true, and hope too, valiant;
My mind still full of thee, therefore still noble;
Let not thy eyes then shun me, nor thy heart
Detest me utterly: oh, look upon me,
Look back and see my sad, sincere submission!
How my heart swells, as even 't would burst my bosom;
Fond of its goal, and laboring to be at thee!
What shall I do? what say to make thee hear me?
Pierr. Hast thou not wronged me? dar'st thou call thyself
Jaffeir, that once loved, valued friend of mine,
And swear thou hast not wronged me? Whence these chains?
Whence the vile death which I may meet this moment?
Whence this dishonor, but from thee, thou false one?
Jaff. All 's true, yet grant one thing, and I 've done asking.
Pierr. What 's that?
Jaff. To take thy life on such conditions
The Council have proposed: thou and thy friends
May yet live long, and to be better treated.
Pierr. Life! ask my life! confess! record myself
A villain for the privilege to breath[e],
And carry up and down this cursed city
A discontented and repining spirit,
Burthensome to itself a few years longer,
To lose it, may be, at last in a lewd quarrel

For some new friend, treacherous and false as thou art!
No, this vile world and I have long been jangling,
And cannot part on better terms than now,
When only men like thee are fit to live in 't.

Jaff. By all that 's just——

Pierr. Swear by some other powers,
For thou hast broke that sacred oath too lately.

Jaff. Then by that hell I merit, I 'll not leave thee,
Till to thyself at least thou'rt reconciled,
However thy resentments deal with me.

Pierr. Not leave me!

Jaff. No, thou shalt not force me from thee.
Use me reproachfully, and like a slave,
Tread on me, buffet me, heap wrongs on wrongs
On my poor head; I 'll bear it all with patience,
Shall weary out thy most unfriendly cruelty,
Lie at thy feet and kiss 'em, though they spurn me,
Till, wounded by my sufferings, thou relent,
And raise me to thy arms with dear forgiveness.

Pierr. Art thou not——

Jaff. What?

Pierr. A traitor?

Jaff. Yes.

Pierr. A villain?

Jaff. Granted.

Pierr. A coward, a most scandalous coward,
Spiritless, void of honor, one who has sold
Thy everlasting fame for shameless life?

Jaff. All, all, and more, much more: my faults are numberless.

Pierr. And wouldst thou have me live on terms like thine?
Base as thou art false——

Jaff. No, 't is to me that 's granted.
The safety of thy life was all I aimed at,
In recompense for faith and trust so broken.

Pierr. I scorn it more because preserved by thee.
And as when first my foolish heart took pity
On thy misfortunes, sought thee in thy miseries,
Relieved thy wants, and raised thee from thy state
Of wretchedness in which thy fate had plunged thee,
To rank thee in my list of noble friends;
All I received in surety for thy truth,
Were unregarded oaths; and this, this dagger,
Given with a worthless pledge, thou since hast stoln,
So I restore it back to thee again,
Swearing by all those powers which thou hast violated,
Never from this curst hour to hold communion,
Friendship or interest with thee, though our years
Were to exceed those limited the world.
Take it—farewell—for now I owe thee nothing.

Jaff. Say thou wilt live, then.

Pierr. For my life, dispose it
Just as thou wilt, because 't is what I 'm tired with.

Jaff. O Pierre!

Pierr. No more.

Jaff. My eyes won't lose the sight of thee,
But languish after thine, and ache with gazing.

Pierr. Leave me—nay, then, thus, thus, I throw thee from me,
And curses, great as is thy falsehood, catch thee.

Jaff. Amen.—He 's gone, my father, friend, preserver,
And here 's the portion he has left me.
(*Holds the dagger up.*)
This dagger, well remembered, with this dagger
I gave a solemn vow of dire importance,
Parted with this and Belvidera together;
Have a care, memory, drive that thought no farther;
No, I 'll esteem it as a friend's last legacy,
Treasure it up within this wretched bosom,
Where it may grow acquainted with my heart,
That when they meet, they start not from each other.
So; now for thinking: a blow, called traitor, villain,
Coward, dishonorable coward, faugh!
O for a long sound sleep, and so forget it!
Down, busy devil—

(*Enter Belvidera.*)

Belv. Whither shall I fly?
Where hide me and my miseries together?
Where 's now the Roman constancy I boasted?
Sunk into trembling fears and desperation!
Not daring to look up to that dear face
Which used to smile even on my faults, but down
Bending these miserable eyes to earth,
Must move in penance, and implore much mercy.

Jaff. "Mercy," kind Heaven has surely endless stores
Hoarded for thee of blessings yet untasted;
Let wretches loaded hard with guilt as I am,
Bow [with] the weight and groan beneath the burthen,
Creep with a remnant of that strength th' have left,
Before the footstool of that Heaven th' have injured.
O Belvidera! I 'm the wretched'st creature
E'er crawled on earth; now if thou hast virtue, help me.
Take me into thy arms, and speak the words of peace
To my divided soul, that wars within me,
And raises every sense to my confusion;
By Heaven, I 'm tottering on the very brink
Of peace; and thou art all the hold I 've left.

Belv. Alas! I know thy sorrows are most mighty;
I know thou'st cause to mourn; to mourn, my Jaffeir,
With endless cries, and never-ceasing wailings,
Th' hast lost——

Jaff. Oh, I have lost what can't be counted;
My friend too, Belvidera, that dear friend,
Who, next to thee, was all my health rejoiced in,
Has used me like a slave; shamefully used me;
'T would break thy pitying heart to hear the story.
What shall I do? resentment, indignation,
Love, pity, fear and memory, how I 've wronged him,
Distract my quiet with the very thought on 't,
And tear my heart to pieces in my bosom.

Belv. What has he done?

Jaff. Thou'dst hate me, should I tell thee.

Belv. Why?

Jaff. Oh, he has used me! yet, by Heaven, I bear it:
He has used me, Belvidera, but first swear
That when I 've told thee, thou'lt not loathe me utterly,
Though vilest blots and stains appear upon me;
But still at least with charitable goodness,
Be near me in the pangs of my affliction,
Not scorn me, Belvidera, as he has done.

Belv. Have I then e'er been false that now I am doubted?
Speak, what 's the cause I am grown into distrust,
Why thought unfit to hear my love's complaining?

Jaff. Oh!

Belv. Tell me.

Jaff. Bear my failings, for they are many.
O my dear angel! in that friend I 've lost
All my soul's peace; for every thought of him
Strikes my sense hard, and deads it in my brains;
Wouldst thou believe it?

Belv. Speak.

Jaff. Before we parted,
Ere yet his guards had led him to his prison,
Full of severest sorrows for his sufferings,
With eyes o'erflowing and a bleeding heart,
Humbling myself almost beneath my nature,
As at his feet I kneeled, and sued for mercy,
Forgetting all our friendship, all the dearness,
In which w' have lived so many years together,
With a reproachful hand, he dashed a blow,
He struck me, Belvidera, by Heaven, he struck me,
Buffeted, called me traitor, villain, coward.

Am I a coward? am I a villain? tell me:
Thou'rt the best judge, and mad'st me, if I am so.
Damnation; coward!

Belv. Oh! forgive him, Jaffeir.
And if his sufferings wound thy heart already,
What will they do to-morrow?

Jaff. Hah!

Belv. To-morrow,
When thou shalt see him stretched in all the agonies
Of a tormenting and a shameful death,
His bleeding bowels, and his broken limbs,
Insulted o'er by a vile butchering villain;
What will thy heart do then? Oh, sure 't will stream
Like my eyes now.

Jaff. What means thy dreadful story?
Death, and to-morrow! broken limbs and bowels!
Insulted o'er by a vile butchering villain!
By all my fears I shall start out to madness,
With barely guessing, if the truth 's hid longer.

Belv. The faithless senators, 't is they 've decreed it:
They say according to our friends' request,
They shall have death, and not ignoble bondage:
Declare their promised mercy all as forfeited,
False to their oaths, and deaf to intercession;
Warrants are passed for public death to-morrow.

Jaff. Death! doomed to die! condemned unheard! unpleaded!

Belv. Nay, cruell'st racks and torments are preparing,
To force confessions from their dying pangs.
Oh, do not look so terribly upon me,
How your lips shake, and all your face disordered!
What means my love?

Jaff. Leave me, I charge thee, leave me—strong temptations
Wake in my heart.

Belv. For what?

Jaff. No more, but leave me.

Belv. Why?

Jaff. Oh! by Heaven, I love thee with that fondness
I would not have thee stay a moment longer,
Near these curst hands; are they not cold upon thee?

(*Pulls the dagger half out of his bosom and puts it back again.*)

Belv. No, everlasting comfort 's in thy arms.
To lean thus on thy breast is softer ease
Than downy pillows decked with leaves of roses.

Jaff. Alas! thou think'st not of the thorns 't is filled with:
Fly ere they [g]all thee: there 's a lurking serpent,
Ready to leap and sting thee to thy heart;
Art thou not terrified?

Belv. No.

Jaff. Call to mind,
What thou hast done, and whither thou hast brought me.

Belv. Hah!

Jaff. Where 's my friend? my friend, thou smiling mischief?
Nay, shrink not, now 't is too late, thou shouldst have fled
When thy guilt first had cause, for dire revenge
Is up and raging for my friend. He groans,
Hark how he groans, his screams are in my ears
Already; see, th' have fixed him on the wheel,
And now they tear him—Murther! perjured Senate!
Murther—Oh! hark thee, traitress, thou hast done this:
Thanks to thy tears and false persuading love.

(*Fumbling for his dagger.*)

How her eyes speak! O thou bewitching creature!
Madness cannot hurt thee: come, thou little trembler,
Creep even into my heart, and there lie safe:
'T is thy own citadel—ha!—yet stand off,
Heaven must have justice, and my broken vows
Will sink me else beneath its reaching mercy;
I 'll wink and then 't is done——

Belv. What means the lord
Of me, my life and love? what 's in thy bosom,

Thou grasp'st at so? Nay, why am I thus treated?
(*Draws the dagger, offers to stab her.*)
What wilt thou do? Ah! do not kill me, Jaffeir,
Pity these panting breasts, and trembling limbs,
That used to clasp thee when thy looks were milder,
That yet hang heavy on my unpurged soul,
And plunge it not into eternal darkness.

Jaff. No, Belvidera, when we parted last,
I gave this dagger with thee as in trust
To be thy portion, if I e'er proved false.
On such condition was my truth believed:
But now 't is forfeited and must be paid for.
(*Offers to stab her again.*)

Belv. (*Kneeling.*) Oh, mercy!

Jaff. Nay, no struggling.

Belv. Now, then, kill me.
(*Leaps upon his neck and kisses him.*)
While thus I cling about thy cruel neck,
Kiss thy revengeful lips and die in joys
Greater than any I can guess hereafter.

Jaff. I am, I am a coward; witness it, Heaven,
Witness it, earth, and every being witness;
'T is but one blow; yet, by immortal love,
I cannot longer bear a thought to harm thee;
(*He throws away the dagger and embraces her.*)
The seal of Providence is sure upon thee,
And thou wert born for yet unheard-of wonders:
Oh, thou wert either born to save or damn me!
By all the power that 's given thee o'er my soul,
By thy resistless tears and conquering smiles,
By the victorious love that still waits on thee,
Fly to thy cruel father: save my friend,
Or all our future quiet 's lost for ever:
Fall at his feet, cling round his reverend knees;
Speak to him with thy eyes, and with thy tears
Melt his hard heart, and wake dead nature in him;
Crush him in th' arms, and torture him with thy softness:
Nor, till thy prayers are granted, set him free,
But conquer him, as thou hast vanquished me.
(*Exeunt ambo.*)

ACT V.

SCENE 1

(*Enter Priuli, solus.*)

Priu. Why, cruel Heaven, have my unhappy days
Been lengthened to this sad one? Oh, dishonor
And deathless infamy is fall'n upon me!
Was it my fault? Am I a traitor? No.
But then, my only child, my daughter, wedded;
There my best blood runs foul, and a disease
Incurable has seized upon my memory,
To make it rot and stink to after ages.
Curst be the fatal minute when I got her;
Or would that I'd been anything but man,
And raised an issue which would ne'er have wronged me.
The miserablest creatures (man excepted)
Are not the less esteemed, though their posterity
Degenerate from the virtues of their fathers;
The vilest beasts are happy in their offsprings,
While only man gets traitors, whores and villains.
Curst be the names, and some swift blow from fate
Lay his head deep, where mine may be forgotten.

(*Enter Belvidera in a long mourning veil.*)

Belv. He 's there, my father, my inhuman father,
That, for three years, has left an only child
Exposed to all the outrages of fate,
And cruel ruin—oh!——

Priu. What child of sorrow
Art thou that com'st thus wrapt in weeds of sadness,
And mov'st as if thy steps were towards a grave?

Belv. A wretch, who from the very top of happiness
Am fallen into the lowest depths of misery,

And want your pitying hand to raise me up again.
Priu. Indeed thou talk'st as thou hadst tasted sorrows;
Would I could help thee!
Belv. 'T is greatly in your power.
The world, too, speaks you charitable, and I,
Who ne'er asked alms before, in that dear hope
Am come a-begging to you, sir.
Priu. For what?
Belv. O well regard me, is this voice a strange one?
Consider, too, when beggars once pretend
A case like mine, no little will content 'em.
Priu. What wouldst thou beg for?
Belv. Pity and forgiveness.
(*Throws up her veil.*)
By the kind tender names of child and father,
Hear my complaints and take me to your love.
Priu. My daughter?
Belv. Yes, your daughter, by a mother
Virtuous and noble, faithful to your honor,
Obedient to your will, kind to your wishes,
Dear to your arms: by all the joys she gave you,
When in her blooming years she was your treasure,
Look kindly on me; in my face behold
The lineaments of hers you 've kissed so often,
Pleading the cause of your poor cast-off child.
Priu. Thou art my daughter.
Belv. Yes—and y' have oft told me,
With smiles of love and chaste paternal kisses,
I 'd much resemblance of my mother.
Priu. Oh!
Hadst thou inherited her matchless virtues,
I 'd been too bless'd.
Belv. Nay, do not call to memory
My disobedience, but let pity enter
Into your heart, and quite deface the impression;
For could you think how mine 's perplexed, what sadness,
Fears and despairs distract the peace within me,
Oh, you would take me in your dear, dear arms.
Hover with strong compassion o'er your young one,
To shelter me with a protecting wing,
From the black gathered storm, that 's just, just breaking.
Priu. Don't talk thus.
Belv. Yes, I must, and you must hear too.
I have a husband.
Priu. Damn him!
Belv. Oh, do not curse him!
He would not speak so hard a word towards you
On any terms, howe'er he deal with me.
Priu. Ha! what means my child?
Belv. Oh, there 's but this short moment
'Twixt me and fate, yet send me not with curses
Down to my grave, afford me one kind blessing
Before we part: just take me in your arms,
And recommend me with a prayer to Heaven,
That I may die in peace, and when I 'm dead——
Priu. How my soul 's catched!
Belv. Lay me, I beg you, lay me
By the dear ashes of my tender mother.
She would have pitied me, had fate yet spared her.
Priu. By Heaven, my aching heart forebodes much mischief;
Tell me thy story, for I 'm still thy father.
Belv. No, I 'm contented.
Priu. Speak.
Belv. No matter.
Priu. Tell me.
By yon blest Heaven, my heart runs o'er with fondness.
Belv. Oh!
Priu. Utter it.
Belv. O my husband, my dear husband
Carries a dagger in his once kind bosom,
To pierce the heart of your poor Belvidera.
Priu. Kill thee?
Belv. Yes, kill me. When he passed his faith
And covenant, against your state and Senate,
He gave me up as hostage for his truth,
With me a dagger and a dire commission,
Whene'er he failed, to plunge it through this bosom.
I learnt the danger, chose the hour of love

T' attempt his heart, and bring it back to honor.
Great love prevailed and blessed me with success:
He came, confessed, betrayed his dearest friends
For promised mercy; now they 're doomed to suffer,
Galled with remembrance of what then was sworn,
If they are lost, he vows t' appease the gods
With this poor life, and make my blood th' atonement.

Priu. Heavens!

Belv. Think you saw what passed at our last parting;
Think you beheld him like a raging lion,
Pacing the earth and tearing up his steps,
Fate in his eyes, and roaring with the pain
Of burning fury; think you saw his one hand
Fixed on my throat, while the extended other
Grasped a keen threatening dagger: oh, 't was thus
We last embraced, when, trembling with revenge,
He dragged me to the ground, and at my bosom
Presented horrid death, cried out: "My friends,
Where are my friends?" swore, wept, raged, threatened, loved,
For he yet loved, and that dear love preserved me,
To this last trial of a father's pity.
I fear not death, but cannot bear a thought
That that dear hand should do the unfriendly office;
If I was ever then your care, now hear me;
Fly to the Senate, save the promised lives
Of his dear friends, ere mine be made the sacrifice.

Priu. O my heart's comfort!

Belv. Will you not, my father?
Weep not, but answer me.

Priu. By Heaven, I will.
Not one of 'em but what shall be immortal.
Canst thou forgive me all my follies past,
I 'll henceforth be indeed a father; never,
Never more thus expose, but cherish thee,
Dear as the vital warmth that feeds my life,
Dear as these eyes that weep in fondness o'er thee.
Peace to thy heart. Farewell.

Belv. Go, and remember
'T is Belvidera's life her father pleads for.

(*Exeunt severally.*)

(*Enter Antonio.*)

Anto. Hum, hum, ha, Seignior Priuli, my lord Priuli, my lord, my lord, my lord: [h]ow we lords love to call one another by our titles! My lord, my lord, my lord—pox on him, I am a lord as well as he; and so let him fiddle—I 'll warrant him he 's gone to the Senate-house, and I 'll be there too, soon enough for somebody. 'Od, here 's a tickling speech about the plot, I 'll prove there 's a plot with a vengeance—would I had it without book; let me see——
"Most reverend Senators,
That there is a plot, surely by this time no man that hath eyes or understanding in his head will presume to doubt, 't is as plain as the light in the cowcumber"—no —hold there—cowcumber does not come in yet—" 't is as plain as the light in the sun, or as the man in the moon, even at noon-day; it is indeed a pumpkin-plot, which, just as it was mellow, we have gathered, and now we have gathered it, prepared and dressed it, shall we throw it like a pickled cowcumber out at the window? no: that it is not only a bloody, horrid, execrable, damnable and audacious plot, but it is, as I may so say, a saucy plot: and we all know, most reverend fathers, that what is sauce for a goose is sauce for a gander: therefore, I say, as those bloodthirsty ganders of the conspiracy would have destroyed us geese of the Senate, let us make haste to destroy them, so I humbly move for hanging"—ha! hurry durry—I think this will do; though I was something out, at first, about the sun and the cowcumber.

(*Enter Aquilina.*)

Aquil. Good-morrow, senator.

Anto. Nacky, my dear Nacky, morrow, Nacky, 'od, I am very brisk, very merry, very pert, very jovial—ha-a-a-a-a—kiss me, Nacky; how dost thou do, my little Tory, rory strumpet, kiss me, I say, hussy, kiss me.

Aquil. Kiss me, Nacky, hang you, sir, coxcomb, hang you, sir.

Anto. Hayty, tayty, is it so indeed, with all my heart, faith—*hey then up go we,* faith—*hey then up go we,* dum dum derum dump.

(*Sings.*)

Aquil. Seignior.

Anto. Madonna.

Aquil. Do you intend to die in your bed?——

Anto. About threescore years hence, much may be done, my dear.

Aquil. You 'll be hanged, seignior.

Anto. Hanged, sweetheart, prithee be quiet, hanged quotha, that 's a merry conceit, with all my heart, why thou jok'st, Nacky, thou art given to joking, I 'll swear; well, I protest, Nacky, nay, I must protest, and will protest that I love joking dearly, man. And I love thee for joking, and I 'll kiss thee for joking, and towse thee for joking, and 'od, I have a devilish mind to take thee aside about that business for joking too, 'od, I have, and *Hey then up go we,* dum dum derum dump.

(*Sings.*)

Aquil. (*Draws a dagger.*) See you this, sir?

Anto. O laud, a dagger! O laud! it is naturally my aversion, I cannot endure the sight on 't, hide it for Heaven's sake, I cannot look that way till it be gone—hide it, hide it, oh, oh, hide it!

Aquil. Yes, in your heart I 'll hide it.

Anto. My heart; what, hide a dagger in my heart's blood?

Aquil. Yes, in thy heart, thy throat, thou pampered devil;
Thou hast helped to spoil my peace, and I 'll have vengeance
On thy curst life, for all the bloody Senate,
The perjured faithless Senate: where 's my lord,
My happiness, my love, my god, my hero,
Doomed by thy accursed tongue, amongst the rest,
T' a shameful wrack? By all the rage that 's in me
I 'll be whole years in murthering thee.

Anto. Why, Nacky, wherefore so passionate? what have I done? what 's the matter, my dear Nacky? am not I thy love, thy happiness, thy lord, thy hero, thy senator, and everything in the world, Nacky?

Aquil. Thou! think'st thou, thou art fit to meet my joys;
To bear the eager clasps of my embraces?
Give me my Pierre, or——

Anto. Why, he 's to be hanged, little Nacky, trussed up for treason, and so forth, child.

Aquil. Thou liest: stop down thy throat that hellish sentence,
Or 't is thy last: swear that my love shall live,
Or thou art dead.

Anto. Ah-h-h-h.

Aquil. Swear to recall his doom,
Swear at my feet, and tremble at my fury.

Anto. I do. Now if she would but kick a little bit, one kick now. Ah-h-h-h.

Aquil. Swear, or——

Anto. I do, by these dear fragrant foots and little toes sweet as, e-e-e-e my Nacky, Nacky, Nacky.

Aquil. How!

Anto. Nothing but untie thy shoe-string a little, faith and troth, that 's all, as I hope to live, Nacky, that 's all.

Aquil. Nay, then——

Anto. Hold, hold, thy love, thy lord, thy hero shall be preserved and safe.

Aquil. Or may this poniard
Rust in thy heart.

Anto. With all my soul.

Aquil. Farewell——

(*Exit Aquilina.*)

Anto. Adieu. Why, what a bloody-minded, inveterate, termagant strumpet have I been plagued with! Oh-h-h yet more! nay then I die, I die—I am dead already.

(*Stretches himself out.*)

Scene 2.

[*A Street near Priuli's House.*]

(*Enter Jaffeir.*)

Jaff. Final destruction seize on all the world:
Bend down, ye Heavens, and shutting round this earth,
Crush the vile globe into its first confusion;
Scorch it with elemental flames, to one curst cinder,
And all us little creepers in 't, called men,
Burn, burn to nothing: but let Venice burn

Hotter than all the rest: here kindle hell
Ne'er to extinguish, and let souls hereafter
Groan here, in all those pains which mine feels now!

(*Enter Belvidera.*)

Belv. (*Meeting him.*) My life——
Jaff. (*Turning from her.*) My plague——
Belv. Nay then I see my ruin,
If I must die!
Jaff. No, Death 's this day too busy,
Thy father's ill-timed mercy came too late.
I thank thee for thy labors though and him too,
But all my poor betrayed unhappy friends
Have summons to prepare for fate's black hour;
And yet I live.
Belv. Then be the next my doom.
I see thou'st passed my sentence in thy heart,
And I 'll no longer weep or plead against it,
But with the humblest, most obedient patience
Meet thy dear hands, and kiss 'em when they wound me;
Indeed I am willing, but I beg thee do it
With some remorse, and where thou giv'st the blow,
View me with eyes of a relenting love,
And show me pity, for 't will sweeten justice.
Jaff. Show pity to thee?
Belv. Yes, and when thy hands,
Charged with my fate, come trembling to the deed,
As thou hast done a thousand thousand dear times,
To this poor breast, when kinder rage has brought thee,
When our stinged hearts have leaped to meet each other,
And melting kisses sealed our lips together,
When joys have left me gasping in thy arms,
So let my death come now, and I 'll not shrink from 't.
Jaff. Nay, Belvidera, do not fear my cruelty,
Nor let the thoughts of death perplex thy fancy,
But answer me to what I shall demand
With a firm temper and unshaken spirit.
Belv. I will when I 've done weeping——
Jaff. Fie, no more on 't—
How long is 't since the miserable day
We wedded first——
Belv. Oh-h-h!
Jaff. Nay, keep in thy tears
Lest they unman me too.
Belv. Heaven knows I cannot;
The words you utter sound so very sadly
These streams will follow——
Jaff. Come, I 'll kiss 'em dry, then.
Belv. But was 't a miserable day?
Jaff. A curs'd one.
Belv. I thought it otherwise, and you 've oft sworn
In the transporting hours of warmest love
When sure you spoke the truth, you 've sworn you blessed it.
Jaff. 'T was a rash oath.
Belv. Then why am I not curs'd too?
Jaff. No, Belvidera; by th' eternal truth,
I dote with too much fondness.
Belv. Still so kind?
Still then do you love me?
Jaff. Nature, in her workings,
Inclines not with more ardor to creation,
Than I do now towards thee: man ne'er was blessed,
Since the first pair first met, as I have been.
Belv. Then sure you will not curse me.
Jaff. No, I 'll bless thee.
I came on purpose, Belvidera, to bless thee.
'T is now, I think, three years we 've lived together.
Belv. And may no fatal minute ever part us,
Till, reverend grown, for age and love, we go
Down to one grave, as our last bed together,
There sleep in peace till an eternal morning.
Jaff. (*Sighing.*) When will that be?
Belv. I hope long ages hence.
Jaff. Have I not hitherto (I beg thee tell me
Thy very fears) used thee with tenderest love?
Did e'er my soul rise up in wrath against thee?
Did I e'er frown when Belvidera smiled,
Or, by the least unfriendly word, betray
A bating passion? have I ever wronged thee?
Belv. No.
Jaff. Has my heart, or have my eyes e'er wandered

To any other woman?
Belv. Never, never—
I were the worst of false ones should I accuse thee;
I own I've been too happy, blessed above
My sex's charter.
Jaff. Did I not say I came to bless thee?
Belv. Yes.
Jaff. Then hear me, bounteous Heaven!
Pour down your blessings on this beauteous head,
Where everlasting sweets are always springing.
With a continual giving hand, let peace,
Honor, and safety always hover round her:
Feed her with plenty, let her eyes ne'er see
A sight of sorrow, nor her heart know mourning:
Crown all her days with joy, her nights with rest,
Harmless as her own thoughts, and prop her virtue,
To bear the loss of one that too much loved,
And comfort her with patience in our parting.
Belv. How, parting! parting!
Jaff. Yes, for ever parting.
I have sworn, Belvidera, by yon Heaven,
That best can tell how much I lose to leave thee,
We part this hour for ever.
Belv. Oh, call back
Your cruel blessings, stay with me and curse me!
Jaff. No, 't is resolved.
Belv. Then hear me too, just Heaven!
Pour down your curses on this wretched head
With never-ceasing vengeance: let despair,
Danger or infamy, nay, all surround me;
Starve me with wantings; let my eyes ne'er see
A sight of comfort, nor my heart know peace,
But dash my days with sorrow, nights with horrors
Wild as my own thoughts now, and let loose fury
To make me mad enough for what I lose,
If I must lose him. If I must! I will not.
O turn and hear me!
Jaff. Now hold, heart, or never!
Belv. By all the tender days we've lived together,
By all our charming nights, and joys that crowned 'em:
Pity my sad condition, speak, but speak.
Jaff. Oh-h-h!
Belv. By these arms that now cling round thy neck:
By this dear kiss and by ten thousand more,
By these poor streaming eyes——
Jaff. Murther! unhold me:
By the immortal destiny that doomed me
(*Draws his dagger.*)
To this curs'd minute, I'll not live one longer.
Resolve to let me go or see me fall——
Belv. Hold, sir, be patient.
(*Passing bell tolls.*)
Jaff. Hark, the dismal bell
Tolls out for death; I must attend its call too,
For my poor friend, my dying Pierre expects me:
He sent a message to require I'd see him
Before he died, and take his last forgiveness.
Farewell for ever.
Belv. Leave thy dagger with me.
Bequeath me something.—Not one kiss at parting?
(*Going out looks back at her.*)
O my poor heart, when wilt thou break?
Jaff. Yet stay,
We have a child, as yet a tender infant.
Be a kind mother to him when I am gone:
Breed him in virtue and the paths of honor,
But let him never know his father's story:
I charge thee guard him from the wrongs my fate
May do his future fortune or his name.
Now—nearer yet—
(*Approaching each other.*)
O that my arms were riveted
Thus round thee ever! But my friends, my oath!
(*Kisses her.*)
This and no more.
Belv. Another, sure another,
For that poor little one you've ta'en care of,
I'll give 't him truly.
Jaff. So, now farewell.
Belv. For ever?
Jaff. Heaven knows for ever; all good angels guard thee.
[*Exit.*]

Belv. All ill ones sure had charge of me this moment.
Curst be my days, and doubly curst my nights,
Which I must now mourn out in widowed tears;
Blasted be every herb and fruit and tree;
Curst be the rain that falls upon the earth.
And may the general curse reach man and beast;
Oh, give me daggers, fire or water!
How I could bleed, how burn, how drown, the waves
Huzzing and booming round my sinking head,
Till I descended to the peaceful bottom!
Oh, there's all quiet, here all rage and fury:
The air's too thin, and pierces my weak brain:
I long for thick substantial sleep: hell, hell,
Burst from the centre, rage and roar aloud,
If thou art half so hot, so mad as I am.

(*Enter Priuli and Servants.*)

Who's there?
Priu. Run, seize and bring her safely home.
(*They seize her.*)
Guard her as you would life: alas, poor creature!
Belv. What? to my husband then conduct me quickly.
Are all things ready? shall we die most gloriously?
Say not a word of this to my old father.
Murmuring streams, soft shades, and springing flowers,
Lutes, laurels, seas of milk, and ships of amber.
(*Exeunt.*)

SCENE 3.

(*Opening discovers a scaffold and a wheel prepared for the executing of Pierre, then enter Officers, Pierre and Guards, a Friar, Executioner, and a great Rabble.*)

Officer. Room, room there—stand all by, make room for the prisoner.
Pierr. My friend not come yet?
Father. Why are you so obstinate?
Pierr. Why you so troublesome, that a poor wretch
Cannot die in peace?
But you, like ravens, will be croaking round him—
Fath. Yet Heaven——
Pierr. I tell thee Heaven and I are friends.
I ne'er broke peace with 't yet, by cruel murthers,
Rapine or perjury, or vile deceiving,
But lived in moral justice towards all men,
Nor am a foe to the most strong believers,
Howe'er my own short-sighted faith confine me.
Fath. But an all-seeing Judge——
Pierr. You say my conscience
Must be mine accuser: I have searched that conscience,
And find no records there of crimes that scare me.
Fath. 'T is strange you should want faith.
Pierr. You want to lead
My reason blindfold, like a hampered lion,
Checked of its nobler vigor; then, when baited
Down to obedient tameness, make it couch,
And show strange tricks, which you call signs of faith.
So silly souls are gulled and you get money.
Away, no more! Captain, I would hereafter
This fellow write no lies of my conversion,
Because he has crept upon my troubled hours.

(*Enter Jaffeir.*)

Jaff. Hold: eyes, be dry! Heart, strengthen me to bear
This hideous sight, and humble me, to take
The last forgiveness of a dying friend,
Betrayed by my vile falsehood, to his ruin.
O Pierre!
Pierr. Yet nearer.
Jaff. Crawling on my knees,
And prostrate on the earth, let me approach thee.
How shall I look up to thy injured face,
That always used to smile with friendship on me?
It darts an air of so much manly virtue,
That I, methinks, look little in thy sight,

And stripes are fitter for me than embraces.
Pierr. Dear to my arms, though thou hast undone my fame,
I cannot forget to love thee: prithee, Jaffeir,
Forgive that filthy blow my passion dealt thee;
I am now preparing for the land of peace,
And fain would have the charitable wishes
Of all good men, like thee, to bless my journey.
Jaff. Good! I am the vilest creature; worse than e'er
Suffered the shameful fate thou art going to taste of.
Why was I sent for to be used thus kindly?
Call, call me villain, as I am, describe
The foul complexion of my hateful deeds,
Lead me to the rack, and stretch me in thy stead,
I 've crimes enough to give it its full load,
And do it credit. Thou wilt but spoil the use on 't,
And honest men hereafter bear its figure
About 'em, as a charm from treacherous friendship.
Offic. The time grows short, your friends are dead already.
Jaff. Dead!
Pierr. Yes, dead, Jaffeir; they 've all died like men too,
Worthy their character.
Jaff. And what must I do?
Pierr. O Jaffeir!
Jaff. Speak aloud thy burthened soul
And tell thy troubles to thy tortured friend.
Pierr. Friend!
Couldst thou yet be a friend, a generous friend,
I might hope comfort from thy noble sorrows.
Heaven knows I want a friend.
Jaff. And I a kind one,
That would not thus scorn my repenting virtue,
Or think when he is to die, my thoughts are idle.
Pierr. No! live, I charge thee, Jaffeir.
Jaff. Yes, I will live,
But it shall be to see thy fall revenged
At such a rate, as Venice long shall groan for.
Pierr. Wilt thou?
Jaff. I will, by Heav'n.
Pierr. Then still thou 'rt noble.
And I forgive thee, oh—yet—shall I trust thee?
Jaff. No: I 've been false already.
Pierr. Dost thou love me?
Jaff. Rip up my heart, and satisfy thy doubtings.
Pierr. (*he weeps*). Curse on this weakness.
Jaff. Tears! Amazement! Tears!
I never saw thee melted thus before,
And know there 's something laboring in thy bosom
That must have vent: though I 'm a villain, tell me.
Pierr. (*pointing to the wheel.*) Seest thou that engine?
Jaff. Why?
Pierr. Is 't fit a soldier, who has lived with honor,
Fought nations' quarrels, and been crowned with conquest,
Be exposed a common carcase on a wheel?
Jaff. Ha!
Pierr. Speak! is't fitting?
Jaff. Fitting?
Pierr. Yes, is 't fitting?
Jaff. What 's to be done?
Pierr. I 'd have thee undertake
Something that 's noble, to preserve my memory
From the disgrace that 's ready to attaint it.
Offic. The day grows late, sir.
Pierr. I 'll make haste! O Jaffeir,
Though thou 'st betrayed me, do me some way justice.
Jaff. No more of that: thy wishes shall be satisfied.
I have a wife, and she shall bleed, my child too
Yield up his little throat, and all t' appease thee——
Pierr. No—this—no more!
(*He whispers Jaffeir.*)
Jaff. Ha! is 't then so?
Pierr. Most certainly.
(*Going away, Pierre holds him.*)
Jaff. I 'll do 't.
Pierr. Remember.
Offic. Sir.
Pierr. Come, now I 'm ready.
Captain, you should be a gentleman of honor.
(*He and Jaffeir ascend the scaffold.*)

Keep off the rabble, that I may have room
To entertain my fate and die with decency.
Come!
(*Takes off his gown. Executioner prepares to bind him.*)

Fath. Son!

Pierr. Hence, tempter.

Offic. Stand off, priest.

Pierr. I thank you, sir. You'll think on 't.
(*To Jaffeir.*)

Jaff. 'T won't grow stale before to-morrow.

Pierr. Now, Jaffeir! now I am going.
Now;—
(*Executioner having bound him.*)

Jaff. Have at thee,
Thou honest heart, then—here—
(*Stabs him.*)
And this is well too.
(*Then stabs himself.*)

Fath. Damnable deed!

Pierr. Now thou hast indeed been faithful.
This was done nobly—we have deceived the Senate.

Jaff. Bravely.

Pierr. Ha! ha! ha!—oh! oh!——
(*Dies.*)

Jaff. Now, ye curs'd rulers,
Thus of the blood y' have shed I make libation,
And sprinkle 't mingling: may it rest upon you,
And all your race: be henceforth peace a stranger
Within your walls; let plagues and famine waste
Your generations—O poor Belvidera!
Sir, I have a wife, bear this in safety to her,—
A token that with my dying breath I blessed her,
And the dear little infant left behind me.
I am sick—I'm quiet——
(*Jaffeir dies.*)

Offic. Bear this news to the Senate,
And guard their bodies till there's farther order:
Heaven grant I die so well!
(*Scene shuts upon them.*)

SCENE 4. [*A Room in Priuli's House.*]

(*Soft music. Enter Belvidera distracted, led by two of her Women, Priuli and Servants.*)

Priu. Strengthen her heart with patience, pitying Heaven.

Belv. Come, come, come, come, come, nay, come to bed!
Prithee, my love. The winds! hark how they whistle!
And the rain beats: oh, how the weather shrinks me!
You are angry now, who cares? pish, no indeed.
Choose then; I say you shall not go, you shall not;
Whip your ill nature; get you gone then! oh,
(*Jaffeir's Ghost rises.*)
Are you return'd? See, father, here he's come again!
Am I to blame to love him? O thou dear one!
(*Ghost sinks.*)
Why do you fly me? Are you angry still, then?
Jaffeir! where art thou? Father, why do you do thus?
Stand off, don't hide him from me. He's here somewhere.
Stand off, I say! what, gone? remember it, tyrant!
I may revenge myself for this trick one day.
I'll do 't—I'll do 't! Renault's a nasty fellow.
Hang him, hang him, hang him.

(*Enter Officer and others.*)

Priu. News, what news?
(*Officer whispers Priuli.*)

Offic. Most sad, sir.
Jaffeir, upon the scaffold, to prevent
A shameful death, stabbed Pierre, and next himself:
Both fell together.
(*The Ghosts of Jaffeir and Pierre rise together both bloody.*)

Priu. Daughter.

Belv. Ha, look there!
My husband bloody, and his friend too! Murther!
Who has done this? Speak to me, thou sad vision,
(*Ghosts sink.*)
On these poor trembling knees I beg it. Vanished!
Here they went down; oh, I'll dig, dig the den up.
You shan't delude me thus. Ho, Jaffeir, Jaffeir,
Peep up and give me but a look. I have him!

I've got him, father: oh, now how I'll smuggle[23] him!
My love! my dear! my blessing! help me, help me!
They have hold on me, and drag me to the bottom.
Nay—now they pull so hard—farewell——

(*She dies.*)

Maid. She's dead,
Breathless and dead.

Priu. Then guard me from the sight on't;
Lead me into some place that's fit for mourning;
Where the free air, light, and the cheerful sun
May never enter: hang it round with black:
Set up one taper that may last a day
As long as I've to live: and there all leave me,
Sparing no tears when you this tale relate,
But bid all cruel fathers dread my fate.

(*Curtain falls. Exeunt omnes.*)

EPILOGUE.

The text is done, and now for application,
And when that's ended, pass your approbation.
Though the conspiracy's prevented here,
Methinks I see another hatching there;
And there's a certain faction fain would sway,
If they had strength enough, and damn this play,
But this the author bade me boldly say:
If any take his plainness in ill part,
He's glad on't from the bottom of his heart;
Poets in honor of the truth should write,
With the same spirit brave men for it fight;
And though against him causeless hatreds rise,
And daily where he goes of late, he spies
The scowls of sullen and revengeful eyes;
'T is what he knows with much contempt to bear,
And serves a cause too good to let him fear:
He fears no poison from an incensed drab,
No ruffian's five-foot sword, nor rascal's stab;
Nor any other snares of mischief laid,
Not a Rose-alley[24] cudgel-ambuscade,
From any private cause where malice reigns,
Or general pique all blockheads have to brains:
Nothing shall daunt his pen when truth does call,
No, not the picture-mangler * at Guildhall.
The rebel tribe, of which that vermin's one,
Have now set forward and their course begun;
And while that Prince's figure they deface,
As they before had massacred his name,
Durst their base fears but look him in the face,
They'd use his person as they've used his fame;
A face, in which such lineaments they read
Of that great martyr's,[25] whose rich blood they shed,
That their rebellious hate they still retain,
And in his son would murther him again.
With indignation then, let each brave heart
Rouse and unite to take his injured part;
Till royal love and goodness call him home,
And songs of triumph meet him as he come;
Till Heaven his honor and our peace restore,
And villains never wrong his virtue more.

23 fondle.
24 Dryden, who was friendly with Otway, in 1679 was beaten by hired ruffians in Rose St.
* *The Rascal that cut the Duke of York's Picture.* [Note in the original.]
25 Charles I., father of James, Duke of York.

WILLIAM CONGREVE

THE WAY OF THE WORLD

William Congreve (1669–1729), brought up and highly educated in Ireland, passed his early manhood in fashionable life in London, where he held small government offices and was made much of by the great; later he lived more retired. His four comedies and one tragedy were produced early in his life — the first, *The Old Bachelor*, when he was but twenty or so, and the last, *The Way of the World*, when he was thirty. In spite of his success as a dramatist, that of his last play did not come up to his desires, and, his health failing, he withdrew from the stage. He also wrote a novel, criticism, and poems.

The Way of the World represents a large, distinguished, and notorious body of drama, Restoration comedy. The chief foreign influence under which it arose is that of Molière, though by no means all its traits can be fathered on him. The type is well-marked as to its characterization, its plotting, its style, and its morals. The characterization is broad and slight, typical rather than individual. As Congreve says in the epilogue to *The Way of the World*, in disclaiming satire of real persons,

> as when painters form a matchless face,
> They from each fair one catch some different grace;
>
> . . . .
>
> So poets oft do in one piece expose
> Whole *belles-assemblées* of coquettes and beaux.

Occasionally distinctive traits (superficial ones) are given the various persons, such as Lady Wishfort's trick of asseverating "As I am a person," and occasional "low" language spoken by the servants, like Mincing "crips" (II. i) and "I vow, mem, I thought once they would have fit" (III. i). Usually, however, the very servants talk like their betters and are almost as witty — perhaps less so in this than in other Restoration comedies; in striking contrast with the ignorant in Shakespeare's plays, who divert us by their dialect and blunders. The contrast strikingly illustrates the prevalence in the romantic drama of humor and the characteristic and individual, and in the "classical" eighteenth-century drama of wit and the typical. Sir Wilful Witwoud, the person who most conspicuously stands out among the others, with his downrightness and coarseness, would have melted into his social background if he had joined it as early as his half-brother did. Petulant, unlike Mirabell and Fainall, who are to the manner born, is impertinent and ill-bred, and Witwoud is a snob, but this is merely because they are still climbing. We may know that one of the female characters, Millamant, differs from the others in the important point of being virtuous; in most of Congreve's plays there is one such part, which he always wrote for Mrs. Bracegirdle, many years his friend, a charming actress who stood out equally among actresses for her discretion. But Millamant breathes the same atmosphere as the others, and for the purposes of the play really differs only in being a little more fascinating. In *The Way of the World* it may almost be said that all the persons, men and women, servants and all, under the same circumstances speak alike and act alike. The play represents the life and especially the standards of one of the most unified, limited, conventional societies ever known. Under the fascinating surface glitter, the people are all alike hard and cold, and much as we delight to hear them talk, Charles Lamb truly says we care not a farthing for any one of them (unless, like George Meredith, we cherish a pious opinion that Millamant might grow into a human being).

The Way of the World is one of the most brilliant examples in English of the "comedy of manners," which gives an external picture of social life, with all its activity, intrigues, and foibles. In the Elizabethan drama the picture is a much broader one, taking in various social strata, the whole life of the community with its activity and enjoyment. In some of Fletcher's and Shirley's comedies, however, we find the same tendency to limit the picture to "society" in the small sense; and this is the rule in the comedy of the Restoration period. In other words it is what is now called high comedy. The matters at issue are love and marriage (often rather, love or marriage), and it is no accident that in *The Way of the World* the *dramatis personæ* are mostly women. The play may very properly be called a *picture* of life, for the main interest in it is in seeing how things are, not in seeing what happens. True, it is unjust to censure the play, as has been done, for lacking plot. After the earlier part the action is constant, with abundance of suspense and surprise, and our interest would be fairly maintained for the time being even if there were nothing else. But the first two acts consist mostly of talk and of very leisurely exposition. When the complicated plot begins to unfold, it is not lifelike, we do not feel that by itself it brings us nearer the life of the time. It is fantastic and borders on farce, turning on the all but successful scheme to marry a dressed-up footman to a fine lady, in order to blackmail her into giving up her niece's fortune; it is also hardly likely that Fainall and Mrs. Marwood could squander her fortune between them under the nose of the gossips without arousing scandal. Congreve's claim in the prologue is barely true,—

Some plot we think he has, and some new thought;
Some humor too, no farce.

All that saves the plot from being farce is that there are no farcical situations. But any plot would have been brilliantly carried off. Long after we have forgotten the story, the impression of the whole play is almost as sharp as ever, the impression of a gay unscrupulous social life, and of unparalleled mental agility and cleverness.

If Congreve is not the most brilliant English writer of dialogue certainly none is more brilliant. His dialogue is a series of flashes so close together that they impress one as a continuous radiance. Nothing can surpass the combination of sheer inventive cleverness with good breeding, restraint and literary polish of style. Among the best passages are that with Lady Wishfort at her toilet (III. i), and above all Mrs. Marwood's picture of the consequences of divulging the family scandal (V. i). Nobody ever talked as well as Congreve's people; we have here a conversational idealism more genuine than the moral idealism of *The Conquest of Granada*. Vituperation has become a fine art. The cleverness of the talk actually gives us somewhat the same heightened sense of the value of life and the dignity of human nature that we gain from the beauty and heroism in a play of a different sort.

And all this in spite of the frivolous, heartless, and vicious set of people who do the talking. But the picture may easily be misunderstood. The dramatist's purpose is to show the surface and the surface only of a fashionable society. "Good Mirabell," says Mrs. Millamant, "don't let us be familiar or fond, nor kiss before folks; but let us be very strange and well-bred: let us be as strange as if we had been married a great while; and as well-bred as if we were not married at all"; to which he replies, "Your demands are pretty reasonable." To conceal deeper feeling, and to turn everything into mirth, are two of the ten commandments of such a society. We must forgive, too, even Millamant's malice for the sake of her high spirits; and after all Mrs. Marwood is fair game. Aside from the occasional free-and-easy language, which is that of its age, the air of cynicism is inevitable; even Congreve could not have written five acts of incessant splendor without an occasional joke at the expense of virtue, or the pose that marriage is bondage, or the like. Wit being his commodity, we have to pay for it. But we are paying merely imitation money; we are sacrificing no real convictions. In other words, the cynical wit is no more to be taken seriously than the cynical wit of a good talker in a club. Whether there is anything worthy under the attractive outside we are not supposed to ask, either in the play or in the society it represents. We are to eat such meat as is set before us, asking no questions for conscience' sake.

But if the moral issue will not stay down, if we must allow the much-debated question as to the moral effect of Restoration comedy in general, what then? Few persons have been able to accept Charles Lamb's theory that the life represented in it is a purely imaginary life with which morality has nothing to do. In such plays as those of Wycherley we are asked to follow with sympathetic interest deep-laid plans to debauch ignorant and innocent women. If a play has sufficient reality to interest us aside from the interest of its wit, it cannot escape the moral question which is so important a part of reality. The greater part of Restoration comedy from this point of view is brutal and repulsive; it surrounds us, in the words of Macaulay, "with foreheads of bronze, hearts like the nether millstone, and tongues set on fire of hell." But even Voltaire esteemed Congreve as more decent than his predecessors. There is nothing brutal or repulsive in the ethics of *The Way of the World*, unless it be so to scheme light-heartedly to outwit a stingy and tyrannical old coquette, and to associate with people who have been no better than they should be. We are not asked to give our sympathy or liking to anything or anybody whatever; nor even to watch with interest anything which involves moral turpitude. The play does not make vice attractive, though it grants that vicious people may be. It does not sentimentalize over illicit passion; there is no passion in it. No one can carp at the morality of the ending. *The Way of the World* is therefore in the fortunate position of being one of the most characteristic specimens of the type on its best side, with but little of the qualities that have made the type notorious.

THE WAY OF THE WORLD

Audire est operæ pretium, procedere recte
Qui mœchos non vultis, [ut omni parte laborent].
—HORAT. Lib. i. Sat. 2. [37–38].

[Hæc] metuat, doti deprensa.—*Ibid.*, Lib. i. Sat. 2. [131].

PROLOGUE.

Spoken by Mr. Betterton.

Of those few fools who with ill stars are curst,
Sure scribbling fools, called poets, fare the worst:
For they 're a sort of fools which Fortune makes,
And after she has made 'em fools, forsakes.
With Nature's oafs[1] 't is quite a different case,
For Fortune favors all her idiot-race.
In her own nest the cuckoo-eggs[2] we find,
O'er which she broods to hatch the changeling-kind.
No portion for her own she has to spare,
So much she dotes on her adopted care.
Poets are bubbles, by the town drawn in,
Suffered at first some trifling stakes to win;
But what unequal hazards do they run!
Each time they write they venture all they 've won:
The squire that 's buttered still[3] is sure to be undone.
This author heretofore has found your favor;
But pleads no merit from his past behavior.
To build on that might prove a vain presumption,
Should grants, to poets made, admit resumption:
And in Parnassus he must lose his seat,
If that be found a forfeited estate.
He owns with toil he wrought the following scenes;
But, if they 're naught,[4] ne'er spare him for his pains:
Damn him the more; have no commiseration
For dullness on mature deliberation,
He swears he 'll not resent one hissed-off scene,
Nor, like those peevish wits, his play maintain,
Who, to assert their sense, your taste arraign.
Some plot we think he has, and some new thought;
Some humor too, no farce; but that 's a fault.
Satire, he thinks, you ought not to expect;
For so reformed a town who dares correct?
To please, this time, has been his sole pretence,
He 'll not instruct, lest it should give offence.
Should he by chance a knave or fool expose,
That hurts none here, sure here are none of those:
In short, our play shall (with your leave to show it)
Give you one instance of a passive poet,
Who to your judgments yields all resignation;
So save or damn, after your own discretion.

DRAMATIS PERSONÆ

FAINALL, *in love with* MRS. MARWOOD.
MIRABELL, *in love with* MRS. MILLAMANT.
WITWOUD, PETULANT. } *Followers of* MRS. MILLAMANT.
SIR WILFULL WITWOUD, *Half-brother to* WITWOUD, *and Nephew to* LADY WISHFORT.
WAITWELL, *Servant to* MIRABELL.
Coachmen, Dancers, Footmen, and Attendants.
LADY WISHFORT, *Enemy to* MIRABELL, *for having falsely pretended love to her.*
MRS.[5] MILLAMANT, *a fine Lady, Niece to* LADY WISHFORT, *and loves* MIRABELL.
MRS. MARWOOD, *Friend to* MR. FAINALL, *and likes* MIRABELL.
MRS. FAINALL, *Daughter to* LADY WISHFORT, *and Wife to* FAINALL, *formerly Friend to* MIRABELL.
FOIBLE, *Woman to* LADY WISHFORT.
MINCING, *Woman to* MRS. MILLAMANT.
[BETTY, *Waiting-maid at a Chocolate-house.*]
[PEG, *Maid to* LADY WISHFORT.]

SCENE.—London.

1 simpleton.
2 *I. e.*, the eggs laid by Nature in Fortune's nest, as cuckoos are supposed to lay their own eggs in other birds' nests.
3 Constantly flattered.
4 No good.
5 Mistress, formerly used with the name of an unmarried as well as a married woman.

ACT I.

Scene 1. *A Chocolate-house.*

(*Mirabell and Fainall, rising from cards, Betty waiting.*)

Mir. You are a fortunate man, Mr. Fainall!

Fain. Have we done?

Mir. What you please: I'll play on to entertain you.

Fain. No, I'll give you your revenge another time, when you are not so indifferent; you are thinking of something else now, and play too negligently; the coldness of a losing gamester lessens the pleasure of the winner. I'd no more play with a man that slighted his ill fortune than I'd make love to a woman who undervalued the loss of her reputation.

Mir. You have a taste extremely delicate, and are for refining on your pleasures.

Fain. Prithee, why so reserved? Something has put you out of humor.

Mir. Not at all: I happen to be grave today, and you are gay; that's all.

Fain. Confess, Millamant and you quarrelled last night after I left you; my fair cousin has some humors that would tempt the patience of a Stoic. What, some coxcomb came in, and was well received by her, while you were by?

Mir. Witwoud and Petulant; and what was worse, her aunt, your wife's mother, my evil genius; or to sum up all in her own name, my old Lady Wishfort came in.

Fain. O, there it is then! She has a lasting passion for you, and with reason.—What, then my wife was there?

Mir. Yes, and Mrs. Marwood, and three or four more, whom I never saw before. Seeing me, they all put on their grave faces, whispered one another; then complained aloud of the vapors,[6] and after fell into a profound silence.

Fain. They had a mind to be rid of you.

Mir. For which reason I resolved not to stir. At last the good old lady broke through her painful taciturnity with an invective against long visits. I would not have understood her, but Millamant joining in the argument, I rose, and, with a constrained smile, told her I thought nothing was so easy as to know when a visit began to be troublesome. She reddened, and I withdrew, without expecting her reply.

Fain. You were to blame to resent what she spoke only in compliance with her aunt.

Mir. She is more mistress of herself than to be under the necessity of such a resignation.

Fain. What! though half her fortune depends upon her marrying with my lady's approbation?

Mir. I was then in such a humor, that I should have been better pleased if she had been less discreet.

Fain. Now I remember, I wonder not they were weary of you; last night was one of their cabal[7] nights; they have 'em three times a-week, and meet by turns at one another's apartments, where they come together like a coroner's inquest, to sit upon the murdered reputations of the week. You and I are excluded; and it was once proposed that all the male sex should be excepted; but somebody moved that, to avoid scandal, there might be one man of the community; upon which motion Witwoud and Petulant were enrolled members.

Mir. And who may have been the foundress of this sect? My Lady Wishfort, I warrant, who publishes her detestation of mankind; and full of the vigor of fifty-five, declares for a friend and ratafia[8]; and let posterity shift for itself, she'll breed no more.

Fain. The discovery of your sham addresses to her, to conceal your love to her niece, has provoked this separation; had you dissembled better, things might have continued in the state of nature.

Mir. I did as much as man could, with any reasonable conscience; I proceeded to the very last act of flattery with her, and was guilty of a song in her commendation. Nay, I got a friend to put her into a lampoon, and compliment her with the imputation of an affair with a young fellow, which I carried so far, that I told her the malicious town took notice that she was grown fat of a sudden; and when she lay in of a dropsy, persuaded her she was reported to be in labor. The devil's in't, if an old woman is to be flattered further, unless

6 A fit of peevishness or "the blues."

7 A small private clique.

8 "A cordial or liqueur flavoured with certain fruits or their kernels" (*Oxf. Dict.*); pronounced "ratafēa."

a man should endeavor downright personally to debauch her; and that my virtue forbade me. But for the discovery of that amour I am indebted to your friend, or your wife's friend, Mrs. Marwood.

Fain. What should provoke her to be your enemy, without she has made you advances which you have slighted? Women do not easily forgive omissions of that nature.

Mir. She was always civil to me till of late.—I confess I am not one of those coxcombs who are apt to interpret a woman's good manners to her prejudice, and think that she who does not refuse 'em everything, can refuse 'em nothing.

Fain. You are a gallant man, Mirabell; and though you may have cruelty enough not to satisfy a lady's longing, you have too much generosity not to be tender of her honor. Yet you speak with an indifference which seems to be affected, and confesses you are conscious of a negligence.

Mir. You pursue the argument with a distrust that seems to be unaffected, and confesses you are conscious of a concern for which the lady is more indebted to you than is your wife.

Fain. Fy, fy, friend! if you grow censorious I must leave you.—I'll look upon the gamesters in the next room.

Mir. Who are they?

Fain. Petulant and Witwoud.—(*To Betty.*) Bring me some chocolate.

(*Exit.*)

Mir. Betty, what says your clock?

Bet. Turned of the last canonical hour,[9] sir.

(*Exit.*)

Mir. How pertinently the jade answers me! Ha! almost one o'clock!—(*Looking on his watch.*)—Oh, y' are come!

(*Enter a Servant.*)

Well, is the grand affair over? You have been something tedious.

Serv. Sir, there 's such coupling at Pancras that they stand behind one another, as 't were in a country dance. Ours was the last couple to lead up; and no hopes appearing of dispatch, besides the parson growing hoarse, we were afraid his lungs would have failed before it came to our turn; so we drove round to Duke's-place; and there they were rivetted in a trice.

Mir. So, so, you are sure they are married?

Serv. Married and bedded, sir; I am witness.

Mir. Have you the certificate?

Serv. Here it is, sir.

Mir. Has the tailor brought Waitwell's clothes home, and the new liveries?

Serv. Yes, sir.

Mir. That 's well. Do you go home again, d 'ye hear, and adjourn the consummation till farther orders. Bid Waitwell shake his ears, and Dame Partlet[10] rustle up her feathers, and meet me at one o'clock by Rosamond's Pond, that I may see her before she returns to her lady; and as you tender your ears be secret.

(*Exit Servant.*)

(*Re-enter Fainall and Betty.*)

Fain. Joy of your success, Mirabell; you look pleased.

Mir. Aye; I have been engaged in a matter of some sort of mirth, which is not yet ripe for discovery. I am glad this is not a cabal night. I wonder, Fainall, that you who are married and of consequence should be discreet, will suffer your wife to be of such a party.

Fain. Faith, I am not jealous. Besides, most who are engaged are women and relations; and for the men, they are of a kind too contemptible to give scandal.

Mir. I am of another opinion. The greater the coxcomb, always the more the scandal: for a woman who is not a fool can have but one reason for associating with a man who is one.

Fain. Are you jealous as often as you see Witwoud entertained by Millamant?

Mir. Of her understanding I am, if not of her person.

Fain. You do her wrong; for, to give her her due, she has wit.

Mir. She has beauty enough to make any man think so; and complaisance enough not to contradict him who shall tell her so.

Fain. For a passionate lover, methinks you are a man somewhat too discerning in the failings of your mistress.

Mir. And for a discerning man, somewhat too passionate a lover; for I like her with all her faults; nay, like her for her faults. Her follies are so natural, or

9 The latest hour (formerly noon) at which a marriage might be performed in a parish church.
10 A traditional humorous name for a hen (or woman).

so artful, that they become her; and those affectations which in another woman would be odious, serve but to make her more agreeable. I 'll tell thee, Fainall, she once used me with that insolence, that in revenge I took her to pieces; sifted her, and separated her failings; I studied 'em, and got 'em by rote. The catalogue was so large, that I was not without hopes one day or other to hate her heartily: to which end I so used myself to think of 'em, that at length, contrary to my design and expectation, they gave me every hour less and less disturbance; till in a few days it became habitual to me to remember 'em without being displeased. They are now grown as familiar to me as my own frailties; and in all probability, in a little time longer, I shall like 'em as well.

Fain. Marry her, marry her! Be half as well acquainted with her charms, as you are with her defects, and my life on 't, you are your own man again.

Mir. Say you so?

Fain. Ay, ay, I have experience: I have a wife, and so forth.

(*Enter Messenger.*)

Mes. Is one squire Witwoud here?

Bet. Yes, what 's your business?

Mes. I have a letter for him, from his brother Sir Wilfull, which I am charged to deliver into his own hands.

Bet. He 's in the next room, friend—that way.

(*Exit Messenger.*)

Mir. What, is the chief of that noble family in town, Sir Wilfull Witwoud?

Fain. He is expected to-day. Do you know him?

Mir. I have seen him. He promises to be an extraordinary person; I think you have the honor to be related to him.

Fain. Yes; he is half-brother to this Witwoud by a former wife, who was sister to my Lady Wishfort, my wife's mother. If you marry Millamant, you must call cousins too.

Mir. I had rather be his relation than his acquaintance.

Fain. He comes to town in order to equip himself for travel.

Mir. For travel! Why, the man that I mean is above forty.

Fain. No matter for that; 't is for the honor of England, that all Europe should know we have blockheads of all ages.

Mir. I wonder there is not an act of parliament to save the credit of the nation, and prohibit the exportation of fools.

Fain. By no means; 't is better as 't is. 'T is better to trade with a little loss, than to be quite eaten up with being overstocked.

Mir. Pray, are the follies of this knight-errant, and those of the squire his brother, anything related?

Fain. Not at all; Witwoud grows by the knight, like a medlar grafted on a crab.[11] One will melt in your mouth, and t' other set your teeth on edge; one is all pulp, and the other all core.

Mir. So one will be rotten before he be ripe, and the other will be rotten without ever being ripe at all.

Fain. Sir Wilfull is an odd mixture of bashfulness and obstinacy.—But when he 's drunk he 's as loving as the monster in *The Tempest*,[12] and much after the same manner. To give t' other his due, he has something of good nature, and does not always want wit.

Mir. Not always: but as often as his memory fails him, and his commonplace [13] of comparisons. He is a fool with a good memory, and some few scraps of other folks' wit. He is one whose conversation can never be approved, yet it is now and then to be endured. He has indeed one good quality, he is not exceptious [14]; for he so passionately affects the reputation of understanding raillery, that he will construe an affront into a jest; and call downright rudeness and ill language, satire and fire.

Fain. If you have a mind to finish his picture, you have an opportunity to do it at full length. Behold the original.

(*Enter Witwoud.*)

Wit. Afford me your compassion, my dears! Pity me, Fainall! Mirabel, pity me!

Mir. I do from my soul.

Fain. Why, what 's the matter?

Wit. No letters for me, Betty?

Bet. Did not the messenger bring you one but now, sir?

Wit. Ay, but no other?

Bet. No, sir.

11 Crab-apple; a medlar is a small fruit like an apple, eaten when decayed to softness.

12 Caliban, who made beastly love to Miranda.

13 A commonplace book, or note book of bits for conversation.

14 captious, censorious.

Wit. That 's hard, that 's very hard.—A messenger! a mule, a beast of burden! he has brought me a letter from the fool my brother, as heavy as a panegyric in a funeral sermon, or a copy of commendatory verses from one poet to another: and what 's worse, 't is as sure a forerunner of the author, as an epistle dedicatory.

Mir. A fool, and your brother, Witwoud!

Wit. Ay, ay, my half-brother. My half-brother he is; no nearer, upon honor.

Mir. Then 't is possible he may be but half a fool.

Wit. Good, good, Mirabell, *le drôle!* [15] Good, good; hang him, don't let 's talk of him.—Fainall, how does your lady? Gad, I say anything in the world to get this fellow out of my head. I beg pardon that I should ask a man of pleasure, and the town, a question at once so foreign and domestic. But I talk like an old maid at a marriage; I don't know what I say: but she 's the best woman in the world.

Fain. 'T is well you don't know what you say, or else your commendation would go near to make me either vain or jealous.

Wit. No man in town lives well with a wife but Fainall.—Your judgment, Mirabell.

Mir. You had better step and ask his wife, if you would be credibly informed.

Wit. Mirabell?

Mir. Ay.

Wit. My dear, I ask ten thousand pardons;—gad, I have forgot what I was going to say to you!

Mir. I thank you heartily, heartily.

Wit. No, but prithee excuse me:—my memory is such a memory.

Mir. Have a care of such apologies, Witwoud; for I never knew a fool but he affected to complain, either of the spleen [16] or his memory.

Fain. What have you done with Petulant?

Wit. He 's reckoning his money—my money it was.—I have no luck today.

Fain. You may allow him to win of you at play: for you are sure to be too hard for him at repartee; since you monopolize the wit that is between you, the fortune must be his of course.

Mir. I don't find that Petulant confesses the superiority of wit to be your talent, Witwoud.

Wit. Come, come, you are malicious now, and would breed debates.—Petulant 's my friend; and a very honest fellow, and a very pretty [17] fellow, has a smattering—faith and troth, a pretty deal of an odd sort of a small wit: nay, I 'll do him justice. I 'm his friend, I won't wrong him, neither.—And if he had but any judgment in the world, he would not be altogether contemptible. Come, come, don't detract from the merits of my friend.

Fain. You don't take your friend to be over-nicely bred?

Wit. No, no, hang him, the rogue has no manners at all, that I must own:—no more breeding than a bum-baily, [18] that I grant you:—'t is pity; the fellow has fire and life.

Mir. What, courage?

Wit. Hum, faith, I don't know as to that, I can't say as to that. Yes, faith, in a controversy, he 'll contradict anybody.

Mir. Though 't were a man whom he feared, or a woman whom he loved.

Wit. Well, well, he does not always think before he speaks;—we have all our failings: you are too hard upon him, you are, faith. Let me excuse him—I can defend most of his faults, except one or two: one he has, that 's the truth on 't; if he were my brother, I could not acquit him:—that, indeed, I could wish were otherwise.

Mir. Ay, marry, what 's that, Witwoud?

Wit. O pardon me!—Expose the infirmities of my friend!—No, my dear, excuse me there.

Fain. What, I warrant he 's unsincere, or 't is some such trifle.

Wit. No, no; what if he be? 't is no matter for that, his wit will excuse that: a wit should no more be sincere, than a woman constant; one argues a decay of parts, as t' other of beauty.

Mir. Maybe you think him too positive?

Wit. No, no, his being positive is an incentive to argument, and keeps up conversation.

Fain. Too illiterate?

Wit. That! that 's his happiness:—his want of learning gives him the more opportunities to show his natural parts.

Mir. He wants words?

Wit. Ay: but I like him for that now;

15 The funny fellow. 16 melancholy. 17 "fine."
18 A contemptuous word for a bailiff who makes arrests.

for his want of words gives me the pleasure very often to explain his meaning.

Fain. He 's impudent?

Wit. No, that 's not it.

Mir. Vain?

Wit. No.

Mir. What! He speaks unseasonable truths sometimes, because he has not wit enough to invent an evasion?

Wit. Truths! ha! ha! ha! No, no; since you will have it,—I mean, he never speaks truth at all,—that 's all. He will lie like a chambermaid, or a woman of quality's porter. Now that is a fault.

(*Enter Coachman.*)

Coach. Is Master Petulant here, mistress?

Bet. Yes.

Coach. Three gentlewomen in a coach would speak with him.

Fain. O brave Petulant! three!

Bet. I 'll tell him.

Coach. You must bring two dishes of chocolate and a glass of cinnamon-water.

(*Exeunt Betty and Coachman.*)

Wit. That should be for two fasting strumpets, and a bawd troubled with wind. Now you may know what the three are.

Mir. You are very free with your friend's acquaintance.

Wit. Ay, ay, friendship without freedom is as dull as love without enjoyment, or wine without toasting. But to tell you a secret, these are trulls that he allows coach-hire, and something more, by the week, to call on him once a day at public places.

Mir. How!

Wit. You shall see he won't go to 'em, because there 's no more company here to take notice of him.—Why, this is nothing to what he used to do:—before he found out this way, I have known him to call for himself.

Fain. Call for himself! What dost thou mean?

Wit. Mean! Why, he would slip you[19] out of this chocolate-house, just when you had been talking to him—as soon as your back was turned—whip he was gone!—then trip to his lodging, clap on a hood and scarf, and a mask, slap into a hackney-coach, and drive hither to the door again in a trice, where he would send in for himself; that I mean, call for himself, wait for himself; nay, and what 's more, not finding himself, sometimes leave a letter for himself.

Mir. I confess this is something extraordinary.—I believe he waits for himself now, he is so long a-coming: Oh! I ask his pardon.

(*Enter Petulant and Betty.*)

Bet. Sir, the coach stays.

Pet. Well, well;—I come.—'Sbud, a man had as good be a professed midwife as a professed whoremaster, at this rate! to be knocked up and raised at all hours, and in all places! Pox on 'em, I won't come!—D' ye hear, tell 'em I won't come:—let 'em snivel and cry their hearts out.

Fain. You are very cruel, Petulant.

Pet. All 's one, let it pass: I have a humor to be cruel.

Mir. I hope they are not persons of condition that you use at this rate.

Pet. Condition! condition 's a dried fig, if I am not in humor!—By this hand, if they were your—a—a—your what d 'ye-call-'ems themselves, they must wait or rub off, if I want appetite.

Mir. What d 'ye-call-'ems! What are they, Witwoud?

Wit. Empresses, my dear:—by your what-d' ye-call-'ems he means sultana queens.

Pet. Ay, Roxalanas.[20]

Mir. Cry you mercy!

Fain. Witwoud says they are—

Pet. What does he say th' are?

Wit. I? Fine ladies, I say.

Pet. Pass on, Witwoud.—Hark'ee, by this light, his relations:—two co-heiresses his cousins, and an old aunt, that loves caterwauling better than a conventicle.

Wit. Ha! ha! ha! I had a mind to see how the rogue would come off.—Ha! ha! ha! Gad, I can't be angry with him, if he said they were my mother and my sisters.

Mir. No!

Wit. No; the rogue's wit and readiness of invention charm me. Dear Petulant!

Bet. They are gone, sir, in great anger.

Pet. Enough, let 'em trundle. Anger helps complexion, saves paint.

Fain. This continence is all dissembled; this is in order to have something to brag of the next time he makes court to Millamant, and swear he has abandoned the whole sex for her sake.

Mir. Have you not left off your impu-

19 A kind of "dative of interest," common in earlier English.
20 The Sultana in D'Avenant's *Siege of Rhodes*.

dent pretensions there yet? I shall cut your throat some time or other, Petulant, about that business.

Pet. Ay, ay, let that pass—there are other throats to be cut.

Mir. Meaning mine, sir?

Pet. Not I—I mean nobody—I know nothing:—but there are uncles and nephews in the world—and they may be rivals—what, then! All 's one for that.

Mir. How! hark'ee, Petulant, come hither:—explain, or I shall call your interpreter.

Pet. Explain! I know nothing. Why, you have an uncle, have you not, lately come to town, and lodges by my Lady Wishfort's?

Mir. True.

Pet. Why, that 's enough—you and he are not friends; and if he should marry and have a child, you may be disinherited, ha?

Mir. Where hast thou stumbled upon all this truth?

Pet. All 's one for that; why, then, say I know something.

Mir. Come, thou art an honest fellow, Petulant, and shalt make love to my mistress, thou sha't, faith. What hast thou heard of my uncle?

Pet. I? Nothing, I. If throats are to be cut, let swords clash! snug 's the word, I shrug and am silent.

Mir. Oh, raillery, raillery! Come, I know thou art in the women's secrets.—What, you 're a cabalist; I know you stayed at Millamant's last night, after I went. Was there any mention made of my uncle or me? Tell me. If thou hadst but good nature equal to thy wit, Petulant, Tony Witwoud, who is now thy competitor in fame, would show as dim by thee as a dead whiting's eye by a pearl of orient; he would no more be seen by thee, than Mercury is by the sun. Come, I 'm sure thou wo't tell me.

Pet. If I do, will you grant me common sense then for the future?

Mir. Faith, I 'll do what I can for thee, and I 'll pray that Heaven may grant it thee in the meantime.

Pet. Well, hark'ee.

Fain. Petulant and you both will find Mirabel as warm a rival as a lover.

Wit. Pshaw! pshaw! that she laughs at Petulant is plain. And for my part, but that it is almost a fashion to admire her, I should—hark'ee—to tell you a secret, but let it go no further—between friends, I shall never break my heart for her.

Fain. How!

Wit. She 's handsome; but she 's a sort of an uncertain woman.

Fain. I thought you had died for her.

Wit. Umh—no—

Fain. She has wit.

Wit. 'T is what she will hardly allow anybody else:—now, demme, I should hate that, if she were as handsome as Cleopatra. Mirabell is not so sure of her as he thinks for.

Fain. Why do you think so?

Wit. We stayed pretty late there last night, and heard something of an uncle to Mirabell, who is lately come to town—and is between him and the best part of his estate. Mirabell and he are at some distance, as my Lady Wishfort has been told; and you know she hates Mirabell worse than a quaker hates a parrot, or than a fishmonger hates a hard frost. Whether this uncle has seen Mrs. Millamant or not, I cannot say, but there were items of such a treaty being in embryo; and if it should come to life, poor Mirabell would be in some sort unfortunately fobbed,[21] i' faith.

Fain. 'T is impossible Millamant should hearken to it.

Wit. Faith, my dear, I can't tell; she 's a woman, and a kind of a humorist.[22]

Mir. And this is the sum of what you could collect last night?

Pet. The quintessence. Maybe Witwoud knows more, he stayed longer:—besides, they never mind him; they say anything before him.

Mir. I thought you had been the greatest favorite.

Pet. Ay, *tête-à-tête,* but not in public, because I make remarks.

Mir. Do you?

Pet. Ay, ay; pox, I 'm malicious, man! Now he 's soft you know; they are not in awe of him—the fellow 's well-bred; he 's what you call a—what-d' ye-call-'em, a fine gentleman; but he 's silly withal.

Mir. I thank you. I know as much as my curiosity requires.—Fainall, are you for the Mall?[23]

Fain. Ay, I 'll take a turn before dinner.

Wit. Ay, we 'll all walk in the Park; the ladies talked of being there.

Mir. I thought you were obliged to watch

21 tricked.

22 Capricious person.

23 A promenade in St. James' Park, fashionable in the 17th and 18th centuries.

for your brother Sir Wilfull's arrival.

Wit. No, no; he comes to his aunt's, my lady Wishfort. Pox on him! I shall be troubled with him, too; what shall I do with the fool?

Pet. Beg him for his estate, that I may beg you afterwards: and so have but one trouble with you both.

Wit. O, rare Petulant! Thou art as quick as a fire in a frosty morning: thou shalt to the Mall with us, and we'll be very severe.

Pet. Enough, I'm in a humor to be severe.

Mir. Are you? Pray, then, walk by yourselves: let us not be accessary to your putting the ladies out of countenance with your senseless ribaldry, which you roar out aloud as often as they pass by you; and when you have made a handsome woman blush, then you think you have been severe.

Pet. What, what! Then let 'em either show their innocence by not understanding what they hear, or else show their discretion by not hearing what they would not be thought to understand.

Mir. But hast not thou then sense enough to know that thou ought'st to be most ashamed thyself, when thou hast put another out of countenance?

Pet. Not I, by this hand!—I always take blushing either for a sign of guilt, or ill breeding.

Mir. I confess you ought to think so. You are in the right, that you may plead the error of your judgment in defence of your practice.

Where modesty's ill manners, 't is but fit
That impudence and malice pass for wit.

(*Exeunt.*)

ACT II.

Scene 1. *St. James' Park.*

(*Mrs. Fainall and Mrs. Marwood.*)

Mrs. Fain. Ay, ay, dear Marwood, if we will be happy, we must find the means in ourselves, and among ourselves. Men are ever in extremes; either doting or averse. While they are lovers, if they have fire and sense, their jealousies are insupportable; and when they cease to love (we ought to think at least) they loathe; they look upon us with horror and distaste; they meet us like the ghosts of what we were, and as such, fly from us.

Mrs. Mar. True, 't is an unhappy circumstance of life, that love should ever die before us; and that the man so often should outlive the lover. But say what you will, 't is better to be left than never to have been loved. To pass our youth in dull indifference, to refuse the sweets of life because they once must leave us, is as preposterous as to wish to have been born old, because we one day must be old. For my part, my youth may wear and waste, but it shall never rust in my possession.

Mrs. Fain. Then it seems you dissemble an aversion to mankind, only in compliance with my mother's humor?

Mrs. Mar. Certainly. To be free; I have no taste of those insipid dry discourses, with which our sex of force must entertain themselves, apart from men. We may affect endearments to each other, profess eternal friendships, and seem to dote like lovers; but 't is not in our natures long to persevere. Love will resume his empire in our breasts; and every heart, or soon or late, receive and re-admit him as its lawful tyrant.

Mrs. Fain. Bless me, how have I been deceived! Why, you profess a libertine.

Mrs. Mar. You see my friendship by my freedom. Come, be as sincere, acknowledge that your sentiments agree with mine.

Mrs. Fain. Never!

Mrs. Mar. You hate hankind?

Mrs. Fain. Heartily, inveterately.

Mrs. Mar. Your husband?

Mrs. Fain. Most transcendently; ay, though I say it, meritoriously.

Mrs. Mar. Give me your hand upon it.

Mrs. Fain. There.

Mrs. Mar. I join with you; what I have said has been to try you.

Mrs. Fain. Is it possible? Dost thou hate those vipers, men?

Mrs. Mar. I have done hating 'em, and am now come to despise 'em; the next thing I have to do, is eternally to forget 'em.

Mrs. Fain. There spoke the spirit of an Amazon, a Penthesilea!

Mrs. Mar. And yet I am thinking sometimes to carry my aversion further.

Mrs. Fain. How?

Mrs. Mar. Faith, by marrying; if I could but find one that loved me very well, and would be thoroughly sensible of ill usage, I think I should do myself the violence of undergoing the ceremony.

Mrs. Fain. You would not make him a cuckold?

Mrs. Mar. No; but I'd make him believe I did, and that's as bad.

Mrs. Fain. Why, had not you as good do it?

Mrs. Mar. Oh! if he should ever discover it, he would then know the worst, and be out of his pain; but I would have him ever to continue upon the rack of fear and jealousy.

Mrs. Fain. Ingenious mischief! would thou wert married to Mirabell.

Mrs. Mar. Would I were!

Mrs. Fain. You change color.

Mrs. Mar. Because I hate him.

Mrs. Fain. So do I; but I can hear him named. But what reason have you to hate him in particular?

Mrs. Mar. I never loved him; he is, and always was, insufferably proud.

Mrs. Fain. By the reason you give for your aversion, one would think it dissembled;[24] for you have laid a fault to his charge, of which his enemies must acquit him.

Mrs. Mar. Oh, then it seems you are one of his favorable enemies! Methinks you look a little pale, and now you flush again.

Mrs. Fain. Do I? I think I am a little sick o' the sudden.

Mrs. Mar. What ails you?

Mrs. Fain. My husband. Don't you see him? He turned short upon me unawares, and has almost overcome me.

(*Enter Fainall and Mirabell.*)

Mrs. Mar. Ha! ha! ha! He comes opportunely for you.

Mrs. Fain. For you, for he has brought Mirabell with him.

Fain. My dear!

Mrs. Fain. My soul!

Fain. You don't look well to-day, child.

Mrs. Fain. D' ye think so?

Mir. He is the only man that does, madam.

Mrs. Fain. The only man that would tell me so at least; and the only man from whom I could hear it without mortification.

Fain. O, my dear, I am satisfied of your tenderness; I know you cannot resent anything from me; especially what is an effect of my concern.

Mrs. Fain. Mr. Mirabell, my mother interrupted you in a pleasant relation[25] last night; I would fain hear it out.

Mir. The persons concerned in that affair have yet a toelrable reputation.—I am afraid Mr. Fainall will be censorious.

Mrs. Fain. He has a humor more prevailing than his curiosity, and will willingly dispense with the hearing of one scandalous story, to avoid giving an occasion to make another by being seen to walk with his wife. This way, Mr. Mirabell, and I dare promise you will oblige us both.

(*Exeunt Mrs. Fainall and Mirabell.*)

Fain. Excellent creature! Well, sure if I should live to be rid of my wife, I should be a miserable man.

Mrs. Mar. Ay!

Fain. For having only that one hope, the accomplishment of it, of consequence, must put an end to all my hopes; and what a wretch is he who must survive his hopes! Nothing remains when that day comes, but to sit down and weep like Alexander, when he wanted other worlds to conquer.

Mrs. Mar. Will you not follow 'em?

Fain. Faith, I think not.

Mrs. Mar. Pray let us; I have a reason.

Fain. You are not jealous?

Mrs. Mar. Of whom?

Fain. Of Mirabell.

Mrs. Mar. If I am, is it inconsistent with my love to you that I am tender of your honor?

Fain. You would intimate, then, as if there were a fellow-feeling between my wife and him?

Mrs. Mar. I think she does not hate him to that degree she would be thought.

Fain. But he, I fear, is too insensible.

Mrs. Mar. It may be you are deceived.

Fain. It may be so. I do not now begin to apprehend it.

Mrs. Mar. What?

Fain. That I have been deceived, madam, and you are false.

Mrs. Mar. That I am false! What mean you?

Fain. To let you know I see through all your little arts.—Come, you both love him; and both have equally dissembled your aversion. Your mutual jealousies of one another have made you clash till

24 feigned.

25 Amusing story.

you have both struck fire. I have seen the warm confession reddening on your cheeks, and sparkling from your eyes.

Mrs. Mar. You do me wrong.

Fain. I do not. 'T was for my ease to oversee and wilfully neglect the gross advances made him by my wife; that by permitting her to be engaged, I might continue unsuspected in my pleasures; and take you oftener to my arms in full security. But could you think, because the nodding husband would not wake, that e'er the watchful lover slept?

Mrs. Mar. And wherewithal can you reproach me?

Fain. With infidelity, with loving another, with love of Mirabell.

Mrs. Mar. 'T is false! I challenge you to show an instance that can confirm your groundless accusation. I hate him.

Fain. And wherefore do you hate him? He is insensible, and your resentment follows his neglect. An instance! the injuries you have done him are a proof: your interposing in his love. What cause had you to make discoveries of his pretended passion? To undeceive the credulous aunt, and be the officious obstacle of his match with Millamant?

Mrs. Mar. My obligations to my lady urged me; I had professed a friendship to her; and could not see her easy nature so abused by that dissembler.

Fain. What, was it conscience, then? Professed a friendship! O, the pious friendships of the female sex!

Mrs. Mar. More tender, more sincere, and more enduring than all the vain and empty vows of men, whether professing love to us or mutual faith to one another.

Fain. Ha! ha! ha! You are my wife's friend, too.

Mrs. Mar. Shame and ingratitude! Do you reproach me? You, you upbraid me? Have I been false to her, through strict fidelity to you, and sacrificed my friendship to keep my love inviolate? And have you the baseness to charge me with the guilt, unmindful of the merit? To you it should be meritorious, that I have been vicious: and do you reflect that guilt upon me, which should lie buried in your bosom?

Fain. You misinterpret my reproof. I meant but to remind you of the slight account you once could make of strictest ties, when set in competition with your love to me.

Mrs. Mar. 'T is false, you urged it with deliberate malice! 't was spoken in scorn, and I never will forgive it.

Fain. Your guilt, not your resentment, begets your rage. If yet you loved, you could forgive a jealousy: but you are stung to find you are discovered.

Mrs. Mar. It shall be all discovered. You too shall be discovered; be sure you shall. I can but be exposed.—If I do it myself I shall prevent your baseness.

Fain. Why, what will you do?

Mrs. Mar. Disclose it to your wife; own what has passed between us.

Fain. Frenzy!

Mrs. Mar. By all my wrongs I 'll do 't!—I 'll publish to the world the injuries you have done me, both in my fame and fortune! With both I trusted you, you bankrupt in honor, as indigent of wealth.

Fain. Your fame I have preserved: your fortune has been bestowed as the prodigality of your love would have it, in pleasures which we both have shared. Yet, had not you been false, I had ere this repaid it—'t is true—had you permitted Mirabell with Millamant to have stolen their marriage, my lady had been incensed beyond all means of reconcilement: Millamant had forfeited the moiety of her fortune; which then would have descended to my wife; and wherefore did I marry, but to make lawful prize of a rich widow's wealth, and squander it on love and you?

Mrs. Mar. Deceit and frivolous pretence!

Fain. Death, am I not married? What 's pretence? Am I not imprisoned, fettered? Have I not a wife? nay a wife that was a widow, a young widow, a handsome widow; and would be again a widow, but that I have a heart of proof, and something of a constitution to bustle through the ways of wedlock and this world! Will you yet be reconciled to truth and me?

Mrs. Mar. Impossible. Truth and you are inconsistent: I hate you, and shall for ever.

Fain. For loving you?

Mrs. Mar. I loathe the name of love after such usage; and next to the guilt with which you would asperse me, I scorn you most. Farewell!

Fain. Nay, we must not part thus.

Mrs. Mar. Let me go.

Fain. Come, I 'm sorry.

Mrs. Mar. I care not—let me go—break my hands, do—I 'd leave 'em to get loose.

Fain. I would not hurt you for the world. Have I no other hold to keep you here?

Mrs. Mar. Well, I have deserved it all.

Fain. You know I love you.

Mrs. Mar. Poor dissembling!—Oh, that—well, it is not yet—

Fain. What? What is it not? What is it not yet? It is not yet too late—

Mrs. Mar. No, it is not yet too late;—I have that comfort.

Fain. It is, to love another.

Mrs. Mar. But not to loathe, detest, abhor mankind, myself, and the whole treacherous world.

Fain. Nay, this is extravagance.—Come, I ask your pardon—no tears—I was to blame, I could not love you and be easy in my doubts. Pray forbear—I believe you; I'm convinced I've done you wrong; and anyway, every way will make amends. I'll hate my wife yet more, damn her! I'll part with her, rob her of all she's worth, and we'll retire somewhere, anywhere, to another world. I'll marry thee—be pacified.—'Sdeath, they come, hide your face, your tears;—you have a mask, wear it a moment. This way, this way—be persuaded.

(*Exeunt.*)

(*Enter Mirabell and Mrs. Fainall.*)

Mrs. Fain. They are here yet.

Mir. They are turning into the other walk.

Mrs. Fain. While I only hated my husband, I could bear to see him; but since I have despised him, he's too offensive.

Mir. O, you should hate with prudence.

Mrs. Fain. Yes, for I have loved with indiscretion.

Mir. You should have just so much disgust for your husband, as may be sufficient to make you relish your lover.

Mrs. Fain. You have been the cause that I have loved without bounds, and would you set limits to that aversion of which you have been the occasion? Why did you make me marry this man?

Mir. Why do we daily commit disagreeable and dangerous actions? To save that idol, reputation. If the familiarities of our loves had produced that consequence of which you were apprehensive, where could you have fixed a father's name with credit, but on a husband? I knew Fainall to be a man lavish of his morals, an interested and professing friend, a false and a designing lover; yet one whose wit and outward fair behavior have gained a reputation with the town enough to make that woman stand excused who has suffered herself to be won by his addresses. A better man ought not to have been sacrificed to the occasion; a worse had not answered to the purpose. When you are weary of him, you know your remedy.

Mrs. Fain. I ought to stand in some degree of credit with you, Mirabell.

Mir. In justice to you, I have made you privy to my whole design, and put it in your power to ruin or advance my fortune.

Mrs. Fain. Whom have you instructed to represent your pretended uncle?

Mir. Waitwell, my servant.

Mrs. Fain. He is an humble servant to Foible my mother's woman, and may win her to your interest.

Mir. Care is taken for that—she is won and worn by this time. They were married this morning.

Mrs. Fain. Who?

Mir. Waitwell and Foible. I would not tempt my servant to betray me by trusting him too far. If your mother, in hopes to ruin me, should consent to marry my pretended uncle, he might, like Mosca in *The Fox*, stand upon terms;[26] so I made him sure beforehand.

Mrs. Fain. So if my poor mother is caught in a contract, you will discover the imposture betimes, and release her by producing a certificate of her gallant's former marriage?

Mir. Yes, upon condition she consent to my marriage with her niece, and surrender the moiety of her fortune in her possession.

Mrs. Fain. She talked last night of endeavoring at a match between Millamant and your uncle.

Mir. That was by Foible's direction, and my instruction, that she might seem to carry it more privately.

Mrs. Fain. Well, I have an opinion of your success; for I believe my lady will do anything to get a husband; and when she has this, which you have provided for her, I suppose she will submit to anything to get rid of him.

Mir. Yes, I think the good lady would marry anything that resembled a man, though 't were no more than what a butler could pinch out of a napkin.

[26] **Hold to the arrangement, refuse to give her up. Mosca, in Jonson's *Volpone, or The Fox*, played off his dupes against each other.**

Mrs. Fain. Female frailty! We must all come to it, if we live to be old, and feel the craving of a false appetite when the true is decayed.

Mir. An old woman's appetite is depraved like that of a girl—'t is the green sickness of a second childhood; and, like the faint offer of a latter spring, serves but to usher in the fall, and withers in an affected bloom.

Mrs. Fain. Here 's your mistress.

(*Enter Mrs. Millamant, Witwoud, and Mincing.*)

Mir. Here she comes, i' faith, full sail, with her fan spread and her streamers out, and a shoal of fools for tenders; ha, no, I cry her mercy!

Mrs. Fain. I see but one poor empty sculler; and he tows her woman after him.

Mir. You seem to be unattended, madam—you used to have the *beau monde* throng after you; and a flock of gay fine perukes hovering round you.

Wit. Like moths about a candle.—I had like to have lost my comparison for want of breath.

Mrs. Mil. O, I have denied myself airs to-day, I have walked as fast through the crowd—

Wit. As a favorite in disgrace; and with as few followers.

Mrs. Mil. Dear Mr. Witwoud, truce with your similitudes; for I 'm as sick of 'em—

Wit. As a physician of a good air.—I cannot help it, madam, though 't is against myself.

Mrs. Mil. Yet again! Mincing, stand between me and his wit.

Wit. Do, Mrs. Mincing, like a screen before a great fire.—I confess I do blaze to-day; I am too bright.

Mrs. Fain. But, dear Millamant, why were you so long?

Mrs. Mil. Long! Lord, have I not made violent haste? I have asked every living thing I met for you; I have inquired after you, as after a new fashion.

Wit. Madam, truce with your similitudes.—No, you met her husband, and did not ask him for her.

Mrs. Mil. By your leave, Witwoud, that were like inquiring after an old fashion, to ask a husband for his wife.

Wit. Hum, a hit! a hit! a palpable hit! I confess it.

Mrs. Fain. You were dressed before I came abroad.

Mrs. Mil. Ay, that 's true.—O, but then I had—Mincing, what had I? Why was I so long?

Min. O mem, your la'ship stayed to peruse a pecquet of letters.

Mrs. Mil. O, ay, letters—I had letters—I am persecuted with letters—I hate letters.—Nobody knows how to write letters, and yet one has 'em, one does not know why. They serve one to pin up one's hair.

Wit. Is that the way? Pray, madam, do you pin up your hair with all your letters? I find I must keep copies.

Mrs. Mil. Only with those in verse, Mr. Witwoud; I never pin up my hair with prose. I fancy one's hair would not curl if it were pinned up with prose.—I think I tried once, Mincing.

Min. O mem, I shall never forget it.

Mrs. Mil. Ay, poor Mincing tift and tift [27] all the morning.

Min. Till I had the cremp in my fingers, I 'll vow, mem: and all to no purpose. But when your la'ship pins it up with poetry, it sits so pleasant the next day as anything, and is so pure and so crips.[28]

Wit. Indeed, so crips?

Min. You 're such a critic, Mr. Witwoud.

Mrs. Mil. Mirabell, did not you take exceptions last night? O, ay, and went away.—Now I think on 't I 'm angry—no, now I think on 't I 'm pleased—for I believe I gave you some pain.

Mir. Does that please you?

Mrs. Mil. Infinitely; I love to give pain.

Mir. You would affect a cruelty which is not in your nature; your true vanity is in the power of pleasing.

Mrs. Mil. Oh, I ask your pardon for that—one's cruelty is one's power; and when one parts with one's cruelty, one parts with one's power; and when one has parted with that, I fancy one 's old and ugly.

Mir. Ay, ay, suffer your cruelty to ruin the object of your power, to destroy your lover—and then how vain, how lost a thing you 'll be! Nay, 't is true: you are no longer handsome when you 've lost your lover; your beauty dies upon the instant; for beauty is the lover's gift; 't is he bestows your charms—your glass is all a cheat. The ugly and the old, whom the looking-glass mortifies, yet

27 Dressed, arranged (my hair).

28 A dialectical form for "crisp."

after commendation can be flattered by it, and discover beauties in it; for that reflects our praises, rather than your face.

Mrs. Mil. Oh, the vanity of these men!—Fainall, d' ye hear him? If they did not commend us, we were not handsome! Now you must know they could not commend one, if one was not handsome. Beauty the lover's gift!—Lord, what is a lover, that it can give? Why, one makes lovers as fast as one pleases, and they live as long as one pleases, and they die as soon as one pleases; and then, if one pleases, one makes more.

Wit. Very pretty. Why, you make no more of making of lovers, madam, than of making so many card-matches.

Mrs. Mil. One no more owes one's beauty to a lover, than one's wit to an echo. They can but reflect what we look and say; vain empty things if we are silent or unseen, and want a being.

Mir. Yet to those two vain empty things you owe two the greatest pleasures of your life.

Mrs. Mil. How so?

Mir. To your lover you owe the pleasure of hearing yourselves praised; and to an echo the pleasure of hearing yourselves talk.

Wit. But I know a lady that loves talking so incessantly, she won't give an echo fair play; she has that everlasting rotation of tongue, that an echo must wait till she dies, before it can catch her last words.

Mrs. Mil. Oh, fiction!—Fainall, let us leave these men.

Mir. Draw off Witwoud.
(*Aside to Mrs. Fainall.*)

Mrs. Fain. Immediately.—I have a word or two for Mr. Witwoud.

Mir. I would beg a little private audience too.—(*Exeunt Witwoud and Mrs. Fainall.*) You had the tyranny to deny me last night; though you knew I came to impart a secret to you that concerned my love.

Mrs. Mil. You saw I was engaged.

Mir. Unkind! You had the leisure to entertain a herd of fools; things who visit you from their excessive idleness; bestowing on your easiness that time which is the encumbrance of their lives. How can you find delight in such society? It is impossible they should admire you, they are not capable: or if they were, it should be to you as a mortification; for sure to please a fool is some degree of folly.

Mrs. Mil. I please myself:—besides, sometimes to converse with fools is for my health.

Mir. Your health! Is there a worse disease than the conversation of fools?

Mrs. Mil. Yes, the vapors; fools are physic for it, next to assafœtida.

Mir. You are not in a course of fools?

Mrs. Mil. Mirabell, if you persist in this offensive freedom, you 'll displease me.—I think I must resolve, after all, not to have you; we shan't agree.

Mir. Not in our physic, it may be.

Mrs. Mil. And yet our distemper, in all likelihood, will be the same; for we shall be sick of one another. I shan't endure to be reprimanded nor instructed: 't is so dull to act always by advice, and so tedious to be told of one's faults—I can't bear it. Well, I won't have you, Mirabell,—I 'm resolved—I think—you may go.—Ha! ha! ha! What would you give, that you could help loving me?

Mir. I would give something that you did not know I could not help it.

Mrs. Mil. Come, don't look grave, then. Well, what do you say to me?

Mir. I say that a man may as soon make a friend by his wit, or a fortune by his honesty, as win a woman with plain dealing and sincerity.

Mrs. Mil. Sententious Mirabell!—Prithee, don't look with that violent and inflexible wise face, like Solomon at the dividing of the child in an old tapestry hanging.

Mir. You are merry, madam, but I would persuade you for a moment to be serious.

Mrs. Mil. What, with that face? No, if you keep your countenance, 't is impossible I should hold mine. Well, after all, there is something very moving in a love-sick face. Ha! ha! ha!—Well, I won't laugh, don't be peevish—Heigho! now I 'll be melancholy, as melancholy as a watch-light. Well, Mirabell, if ever you will win me woo me now.—Nay, if you are so tedious, fare you well;—I see they are walking away.

Mir. Can you not find in the variety of your disposition one moment—

Mrs. Mil. To hear you tell me that Foible 's married, and your plot like to speed—no.

Mir. But how you came to know it—

Mrs. Mil. Unless by the help of the devil, you can't imagine; unless she should tell me herself. Which of the two it may have been I will leave you to consider; and when you have done thinking of that, think of me.

(*Exit.*)

Mir. I have something more.—Gone!—Think of you? To think of a whirlwind, though 't were in a whirlwind, were a case of more steady contemplation; a very tranquillity of mind and mansion. A fellow that lives in a windmill has not a more whimsical dwelling than the heart of a man that is lodged in a woman. There is no point of the compass to which they cannot turn, and by which they are not turned; and by one as well as another; for motion, not method, is their occupation. To know this, and yet continue to be in love, is to be made wise from the dictates of reason, and yet persevere to play the fool by the force of instinct.—Oh, here come my pair of turtles!—What, billing so sweetly! Is not Valentine's Day over with you yet?

(*Enter Waitwell and Foible.*)

Sirrah, Waitwell, why sure you think you were married for your own recreation, and not for my conveniency.

Wait. Your pardon, sir. With submission, we have indeed been solacing in lawful delights; but still with an eye to business, sir. I have instructed her as well as I could. If she can take your directions as readily as my instructions, sir, your affairs are in a prosperous way.

Mir. Give you joy, Mrs. Foible.

Foib. Oh, 'las, sir, I'm so ashamed!—I'm afraid my lady has been in a thousand inquietudes for me. But I protest, sir, I made as much haste as I could.

Wait. That she did indeed, sir. It was my fault that she did not make more.

Mir. That I believe.

Foib. But I told my lady as you instructed me, sir, that I had a prospect of seeing Sir Rowland your uncle; and that I would put her ladyship's picture in my pocket to show him; which I'll be sure to say has made him so enamored of her beauty, that he burns with impatience to lie at her ladyship's feet, and worship the original.

Mir. Excellent Foible! Matrimony has made you eloquent in love.

Wait. I think she has profited, sir, I think so.

Foib. You have seen Madam Millamant, sir?

Mir. Yes.

Foib. I told her, sir, because I did not know that you might find an opportunity; she had so much company last night.

Mir. Your diligence will merit more—in the meantime—

(*Gives money.*)

Foib. O dear sir, your humble servant!

Wait. Spouse.

Mir. Stand off, sir, not a penny!—Go on and prosper, Foible:—the lease shall be made good, and the farm stocked, if we succeed.

Foib. I don't question your generosity, sir: and you need not doubt of success. If you have no more commands, sir, I'll be gone; I'm sure my lady is at her toilet, and can't dress till I come.—O dear, I'm sure that (*Looking out*) was Mrs. Marwood that went by in a mask! If she has seen me with you I'm sure she'll tell my lady. I'll make haste home and prevent her. Your servant, sir.—B'w'y,[29] Waitwell.

(*Exit.*)

Wait. Sir Rowland, if you please.—The jade's so pert upon her preferment she forgets herself.

Mir. Come, sir, will you endeavor to forget yourself, and transform into Sir Rowland?

Wait. Why, sir, it will be impossible I should remember myself.—Married, knighted, and attended all in one day! 't is enough to make any man forget himself. The difficulty will be how to recover my acquaintance and familiarity with my former self, and fall from my transformation to a reformation into Waitwell. Nay, I shan't be quite the same Waitwell neither; for now, I remember me, I'm married, and can't be my own man again.

Ay, there's the grief; that's the sad
change of life,
To lose my title, and yet keep my wife.

(*Exeunt.*)

ACT III

Scene 1. *A Room in Lady Wishfort's House.*

(*Lady Wishfort at her toilet, Peg waiting.*)

Lady Wish. Merciful! no news of Foible yet?

29 [God-]be-with-you, good-bye.

Peg. No, madam.

Lady Wish. I have no more patience.—If I have not fretted myself till I am pale again, there 's no veracity in me! Fetch me the red—the red, do you hear, sweetheart?—An arrant ash-color, as I am a person! Look you how this wench stirs! —Why dost thou not fetch me a little red? Didst thou not hear me, Mopus? [30]

Peg. The red ratafia, does your ladyship mean, or the cherry-brandy?

Lady Wish. Ratafia, fool? No, fool. Not the ratafia, fool—grant me patience!—I mean the Spanish paper, idiot—complexion, darling. Paint, paint, paint, dost thou understand that, changeling, dangling thy hands like bobbins before thee? Why dost thou not stir, puppet? Thou wooden thing upon wires!

Peg. Lord, madam, your ladyship is so impatient!—I cannot come at the paint, madam; Mrs. Foible has locked it up, and carried the key with her.

Lady Wish. A pox take you both!—Fetch me the cherry-brandy then. (*Exit Peg.*) I 'm as pale and as faint, I look like Mrs. Qualmsick, the curate's wife, that 's always breeding.—Wench, come, come, wench, what art thou doing? sipping, tasting?—Save thee, dost thou not know the bottle?

(*Re-enter Peg with a bottle and china cup.*)

Peg. Madam, I was looking for a cup.

Lady Wish. A cup, save thee! and what a cup hast thou brought!—Dost thou take me for a fairy, to drink out of an acorn? Why didst thou not bring thy thimble? Hast thou ne'er a brass thimble clinking in thy pocket with a bit of nutmeg?—I warrant thee. Come, fill, fill!—So—again—See who that is.—(*One knocks.*) —Set down the bottle first—here, here, under the table.—What, wouldst thou go with the bottle in thy hand, like a tapster? As I am a person, this wench has lived in an inn upon the road, before she came to me, like Maritornes the Asturian in Don Quixote!—No Foible yet?

Peg. No, madam; Mrs. Marwood.

Lady Wish. Oh, Marwood; let her come in.—Come in, good Marwood.

(*Enter Mrs. Marwood.*)

Mrs. Mar. I 'm surprised to find your ladyship in dishabille at this time of day.

Lady Wish. Foible 's a lost thing; has been abroad since morning, and never heard of since.

Mrs. Mar. I saw her but now, as I came masked through the park, in conference with Mirabell.

Lady Wish. With Mirabell!—You call my blood into my face, with mentioning that traitor. She durst not have the confidence! I sent her to negotiate an affair, in which, if I 'm detected, I 'm undone. If that wheedling villain has wrought upon Foible to detect me, I 'm ruined. O my dear friend, I 'm a wretch of wretches if I 'm detected.

Mrs. Mar. O madam, you cannot suspect Mrs. Foible's integrity!

Lady Wish. Oh, he carries poison in his tongue that would corrupt integrity itself! If she has given him an opportunity, she has as good as put her integrity into his hands. Ah, dear Marwood, what 's integrity to an opportunity?—Hark! I hear her!—Go, you thing, and send her in. (*Exit Peg.*) Dear friend, retire into my closet,[31] that I may examine her with more freedom.—You 'll pardon me, dear friend; I can make bold with you.—There are books over the chimney—Quarles and Prynne, and *The Short View of the Stage*,[32] with Bunyan's works, to entertain you.—

(*Exit Mrs. Marwood.*)

(*Enter Foible.*)

Lady Wish. O Foible, where hast thou been? What hast thou been doing?

Foib. Madam, I have seen the party.

Lady Wish. But what hast thou done?

Foib. Nay, 't is your ladyship has done, and are to do; I have only promised—But a man so enamored—so transported! —Well, here it is, all that is left, all that is not kissed away. Well, if worshipping of pictures be a sin—poor Sir Rowland, I say.

Lady Wish. The miniature has been counted like;—but hast thou not betrayed me, Foible? Hast thou not detected me to that faithless Mirabell?—What hadst thou to do with him in the Park? Answer me, has he got nothing out of thee?

Foib. (*Aside.*) So, the devil has been beforehand with me. What shall I say?—(*Aloud.*)—Alas, madam, could I help it, if I met that confident thing? Was I in fault? If you had heard how he used me, and all upon your ladyship's account,

30 Mope, stupid creature.

31 Small private room.

32 Quarles was a religious writer. Prynne's *Histriomastix* and Collier's *Short View* were harsh attacks on the stage.

I'm sure you would not suspect my fidelity. Nay, if that had been the worst, I could have borne; but he had a fling at your ladyship too; and then I could not hold; but i' faith I gave him his own.

Lady Wish. Me? What did the filthy fellow say?

Foib. O madam! 't is a shame to say what he said—with his taunts and his fleers, tossing up his nose. Humh! (says he) what, you are a-hatching some plot (says he), you are so early abroad, or catering (says he), ferreting for some disbanded officer, I warrant.—Half-pay is but thin subsistence (says he);—well, what pension does your lady propose? Let me see (says he), what, she must come down pretty deep now, she's superannuated (says he) and—

Lady Wish. Odds my life, I'll have him, I'll have him murdered! I'll have him poisoned! Where does he eat?—I'll marry a drawer to have him poisoned in his wine. I'll send for Robin from Locket's [33] immediately.

Foib. Poison him! poisoning's too good for him. Starve him, madam, starve him: marry Sir Rowland, and get him disinherited. Oh, you would bless yourself to hear what he said!

Lady Wish. A villain! Superannuated!

Foib. Humh (says he), I hear you are laying designs against me too (says he) and Mrs. Millamant is to marry my uncle (he does not suspect a word of your ladyship); but (says he) I'll fit you for that, I warrant you (says he), I'll hamper you for that (says he); you and your old frippery [34] too (says he); I'll handle you—

Lady Wish. Audacious villain! Handle me! would he durst!—Frippery! old frippery! Was there ever such a foul-mouthed fellow? I'll be married tomorrow, I'll be contracted to-night.

Foib. The sooner the better, madam.

Lady Wish. Will Sir Rowland be here, sayest thou? when, Foible?

Foib. Incontinently, madam. No new sheriff's wife expects the return of her husband after knighthood with that impatience in which Sir Rowland burns for the dear hour of kissing your ladyship's hands after dinner.

Lady Wish. Frippery! superannuated frippery! I'll frippery the villain; I'll reduce him to frippery and rags! a tatterdemalion! I hope to see him hung with tatters, like a Long-Lane penthouse [35] or a gibbet thief. A slander-mouthed railer! I warrant the spendthrift prodigal's in debt as much as the million lottery, or the whole court upon a birthday. I'll spoil his credit with his tailor. Yes, he shall have my niece with her fortune, he shall!

Foib. He! I hope to see him lodge in Ludgate [36] first, and angle into Blackfriars for brass farthings with an old mitten.

Lady Wish. Ay, dear Foible; thank thee for that, dear Foible. He has put me out of all patience. I shall never recompose my features to receive Sir Rowland with any economy of face. This wretch has fretted me that I am absolutely decayed. Look, Foible.

Foib. Your ladyship has frowned a little too rashly, indeed, madam. There are some cracks discernible in the white varnish.

Lady Wish. Let me see the glass.—Cracks, say'st thou?—why, I am arrantly flayed—I look like an old peeled wall. Thou must repair me, Foible, before Sir Rowland comes, or I shall never keep up to my picture.

Foible. I warrant you, madam, a little art once made your picture like you; and now a little of the same art must make you like your picture. Your picture must sit for you, madam.

Lady Wish. But art thou sure Sir Rowland will not fail to come? Or will 'a not fail when he does come? Will he be importunate, Foible, and push? For if he should not be importunate, I shall never break decorums:—I shall die with confusion, if I am forced to advance.—Oh, no, I can never advance!—I shall swoon if he should expect advances. No, I hope Sir Rowland is better bred than to put a lady to the necessity of breaking her forms. I won't be too coy, neither.—I won't give him despair—but a little disdain is not amiss; a little scorn is alluring.

Foib. A little scorn becomes your ladyship.

Lady Wish. Yes, but tenderness becomes me best—a sort of a dyingness—you see that picture has a sort of a—ha, Foible!

33 A waiter from Locket's Ordinary, a well-known tavern.

34 "A stand or horse for dresses" (*Oxf. Dict.*).

35 A street in Smithfield, full of second-hand clothes dealers' booths (Tupper).

36 There was a debtors' prison here, whose inmates begged from passers-by in the street.

a swimmingness in the eyes—yes, I'll look so—my niece affects it; but she wants features. Is Sir Rowland handsome? Let my toilet be removed—I'll dress above. I'll receive Sir Rowland here. Is he handsome? Don't answer me. I won't know; I'll be surprised, I'll be taken by surprise.

Foib. By storm, madam, Sir Rowland 's a brisk man.

Lady Wish. Is he! O, then he'll importune, if he's a brisk man. I shall save decorums if Sir Rowland importunes. I have a mortal terror at the apprehension of offending against decorums. Nothing but importunity can surmount decorums. O, I'm glad he's a brisk man. Let my things be removed, good Foible.

(*Exit.*)

(*Enter Mrs. Fainall.*)

Mrs. Fain. O Foible, I have been in a fright, lest I should come too late! That devil Marwood saw you in the Park with Mirabell, and I'm afraid will discover it to my lady.

Foib. Discover what, madam?

Mrs. Fain. Nay, nay, put not on that strange face, I am privy to the whole design, and know that Waitwell, to whom thou wert this morning married, is to personate Mirabell's uncle, and as such, winning my lady, to involve her in those difficulties from which Mirabell only must release her, by his making his conditions to have my cousin and her fortune left to her own disposal.

Foib. O dear madam, I beg your pardon. It was not my confidence in your ladyship that was deficient; but I thought the former good correspondence between your ladyship and Mr. Mirabell might have hindered his communicating this secret.

Mrs. Fain. Dear Foible, forget that.

Foib. O dear madam, Mr. Mirabell is such a sweet, winning gentleman—but your ladyship is the pattern of generosity.[37]—Sweet lady, to be so good! Mr. Mirabell cannot choose but be grateful. I find your ladyship has his heart still. Now, madam, I can safely tell your ladyship our success; Mrs. Marwood had told my lady; but I warrant I managed myself; I turned it all for the better. I told my lady that Mr. Mirabell railed at her; I laid horrid things to his charge, I'll vow; and my lady is so incensed that she'll be contracted to Sir Rowland to-night, she says; I warrant I worked her up, that he may have her for asking for, as they say of a Welsh maidenhead.

Mrs. Fain. O rare Foible!

Foib. Madam, I beg your ladyship to acquaint Mr. Mirabell of his success. I would be seen as little as possible to speak to him: besides, I believe Madam Marwood watches me.—She has a month's mind[38]; but I know Mr. Mirabell can't abide her.—(*Enter Footman.*) John!—remove my lady's toilet.—Madam, your servant: my lady is so impatient, I fear she'll come for me if I stay.

Mrs. Fain. I'll go with you up the back-stairs, lest I should meet her.

(*Exeunt.*)

(*Enter Mrs. Marwood.*)

Mrs. Mar. Indeed, Mrs. Engine, is it thus with you? Are you become a go-between of this importance? Yes, I shall watch you. Why this wench is the *passe-partout,* a very master-key to everybody's strong-box. My friend Fainall, have you carried it so swimmingly? I thought there was something in it; but it seems it's over with you. Your loathing is not from a want of appetite, then, but from a surfeit. Else you could never be so cool to fall from a principal to be an assistant; to procure for him! A pattern of generosity, that I confess. Well, Mr. Fainall, you have met with your match.—O man, man! woman, woman, the devil's an ass: if I were a painter, I would draw him like an idiot, a driveller with a bib and bells: man should have his head and horns, and woman the rest of him. Poor simple fiend!—"Madam Marwood has a month's mind, but he can't abide her."—'T were better for him you had not been his confessor in that affair, without you could have kept his counsel closer. I shall not prove another pattern of generosity, and stalk for him till takes his stand to aim at a fortune: he has not obliged me to that with those excesses of himself! and now I'll have none of him. Here comes the good lady, panting ripe; with a heart full of hope, and a head full of care, like any chemist upon the day of projection.

(*Enter Lady Wishfort.*)

Lady Wish. O dear Marwood, what shall

37 Of course Mrs. Fainall has just tipped her.

38 A liking, a hankering.

I say for this rude forgetfulness?—but my dear friend is all goodness.

Mrs. Mar. No apologies, dear madam, I have been very well entertained.

Lady Wish. As I 'm a person, I am in a very chaos to think I should so forget myself: but I have such an olio [39] of affairs, really I know not what to do.—(*Calls.*) Foible!—I expect my nephew, Sir Wilfull, every moment too.—Why, Foible!—He means to travel for improvement.

Mrs. Mar. Methinks Sir Wilfull should rather think of marrying than travelling at his years. I hear he is turned of forty.

Lady Wish. O, he 's in less danger of being spoiled by his travels—I am against my nephew's marrying too young. It will be time enough when he comes back, and has acquired discretion to choose for himself.

Mrs. Mar. Methinks Mrs. Millamant and he would make a very fit match. He may travel afterwards. 'T is a thing very usual with young gentlemen.

Lady Wish. I promise you I have thought on 't—and since 't is your judgment, I 'll think on 't again. I assure you I will; I value your judgment extremely. On my word, I 'll propose it.

(*Enter Foible.*)

Lady Wish. Come, come, Foible—I had forgot my nephew will be here before dinner—I must make haste.

Foib. Mr. Witwoud and Mr. Petulant are come to dine with your ladyship.

Lady Wish. O dear, I can't appear till I 'm dressed.—Dear Marwood, shall I be free with you again, and beg you to entertain 'em? I 'll make all imaginable haste. Dear friend, excuse me.

(*Exeunt Lady Wish. and Foible.*)

(*Enter Mrs. Millamant and Mincing.*)

Mrs. Mil. Sure, never anything was so unbred as that odious man!—Marwood, your servant.

Mrs. Mar. You have a color; what 's the matter?

Mrs. Mil. That horrid fellow, Petulant, has provoked me into a flame: I have broke my fan.—Mincing, lend me yours; is not all the powder out of my hair?

Mrs. Mar. No. What has he done?

Mrs. Mil. Nay, he has done nothing; he has only talked—nay, he has said nothing neither; but he has contradicted everything that has been said. For my part, I thought Witwoud and he would have quarrelled.

Min. I vow, mem, I thought once they would have fit.

Mrs. Mil. Well, 't is a lamentable thing, I 'll swear, that one has not the liberty of choosing one's acquaintance as one does one's clothes.

Mrs. Mar. If we had that liberty, we should be as weary of one set of acquaintance, though never so good, as we are of one suit, though never so fine. A fool and a doily stuff [40] would now and then find days of grace, and be worn for variety.

Mrs. Mil. I could consent to wear 'em, if they would wear alike; but fools never wear out—they are such *drap-du-Berri* [41] things! Without [42] one could give 'em to one's chambermaid after a day or two.

Mrs. Mar. 'T were better so indeed. Or what think you of the playhouse? A fine gay glossy fool should be given there, like a new masking habit, after the masquerade is over, and we have done with the disguise. For a fool's visit is always a disguise; and never admitted by a woman of wit, but to blind her affair with a lover of sense. If you would but appear barefaced now, and own Mirabell, you might as easily put off Petulant and Witwoud as your hood and scarf. And indeed, 't is time, for the town has found it; the secret is grown too big for the pretence. 'T is like Mrs. Primly's great belly; she may lace it down before, but it burnishes on her hips. Indeed, Millamant, you can no more conceal it than my Lady Strammel can her face; that goodly face, which in defiance of her Rhenish wine tea, will not be comprehended in a mask.

Mrs. Mil. I 'll take my death, Marwood, you are more censorious than a decayed beauty, or a discarded toast.—Mincing, tell the men they may come up.—My aunt is not dressing [here]; their folly is less provoking than your malice. The town has found it! (*Exit Mincing.*) What has it found? That Mirabell loves me is no more a secret than it is a secret that you discovered it to my aunt, or than the reason why you discovered it is a secret.

Mrs. Mar. You are nettled.

Mrs. Mil. You 're mistaken. Ridiculous!

Mrs. Mar. Indeed, my dear, you 'll tear

39 "Mix-up" (originally a stew of meat and vegetables).

40 A woolen material. "at once cheap and genteel" (*Oxf. Dict.*).

41 A kind of French woolen cloth, apparently very durable.

42 unless.

another fan, if you don't mitigate those violent airs.

Mrs. Mil. O, silly! ha! ha! ha! I could laugh immoderately. Poor Mirabell! His constancy to me has quite destroyed his complaisance for all the world beside. I swear, I never enjoined it him to be so coy.—If I had the vanity to think he would obey me, I would command him to show more gallantry—'t is hardly well-bred to be so particular on one hand, and so insensible on the other. But I despair to prevail, and so let him follow his own way. Ha! ha! ha! pardon me, dear creature, I must laugh, ha! ha! ha! though I grant you 't is a little barbarous, ha! ha! ha!

Mrs. Mar. What pity 't is so much fine raillery, and delivered with so significant gesture, should be so unhappily directed to miscarry!

Mrs. Mil. Ha? dear creature, I ask your pardon—I swear I did not mind you.

Mrs. Mar. Mr. Mirabell and you both may think it a thing impossible, when I shall tell him by telling you—

Mrs. Mil. O dear, what? for it is the same thing if I hear it—ha! ha! ha!

Mrs. Mar. That I detest him, hate him, madam.

Mrs. Mil. O madam, why, so do I—and yet the creature loves me, ha! ha! ha! How can one forebear laughing to think of it!—I am a sibyl if I am not amazed to think what he can see in me. I'll take my death, I think you are handsomer—and within a year or two as young—if you could but stay for me, I should overtake you—but that cannot be.—Well, that thought makes me melancholic.—Now, I'll be sad.

Mrs. Mar. Your merry note may be changed sooner than you think.

Mrs. Mil. D'ye say so? Then I'm resolved I'll have a song to keep up my spirits.

(*Enter Mincing.*)

Min. The gentlemen stay but to comb, madam, and will wait on you.

Mrs. Mil. Desire Mrs. —— that is in the next room to sing the song I would have learned yesterday.—You shall hear it, madam—not that there's any great matter in it—but 't is agreeable to my humor.

(*Set by Mr. John Eccles, and sung by Mrs. Hodgson.*)

SONG

Love 's but the frailty of the mind,
  When 't is not with ambition joined;
A sickly flame, which, if not fed, expires,
And feeding, wastes in self-consuming fires.

'T is not to wound a wanton boy
  Or amorous youth, that gives the joy;
But 't is the glory to have pierced a swain,
For whom inferior beauties sighed in vain.

Then I alone the conquest prize,
  When I insult a rival's eyes:
If there 's delight in love, 't is when I see
That heart, which others bleed for, bleed for me.

(*Enter Petulant and Witwoud.*)

Mrs. Mil. Is your animosity composed, gentlemen?

Wit. Raillery, raillery, madam; we have no animosity—we hit off a little wit now and then, but no animosity.—The falling-out of wits is like the falling-out of lovers: we agree in the main, like treble and bass.—Ha, Petulant?

Pet. Ay, in the main—but when I have a humor to contradict—

Wit. Ay, when he has a humor to contradict, then I contradict too. What, I know my cue. Then we contradict one another like two battledores; for contradictions beget one another like Jews.

Pet. If he says black 's black—if I have a humor to say 't is blue—let that pass—all 's one for that. If I have a humor to prove it, it must be granted.

Wit. Not positively must—but it may—it may.

Pet. Yes, it positively must, upon proof positive.

Wit. Ay, upon proof positive it must; but upon proof presumptive it only may.—That 's a logical distinction now, madam.

Mrs. Mar. I perceive your debates are of importance, and very learnedly handled.

Pet. Importance is one thing, and learning 's another; but a debate 's a debate, that I assert.

Wit. Petulant 's an enemy to learning; he relies altogether on his parts.

Pet. No, I 'm no enemy to learning; it hurts not me.

Mrs. Mar. That 's a sign indeed it 's no enemy to you.

Pet. No, no, it 's no enemy to anybody but them that have it.

Mrs. Mil. Well, an illiterate man 's my

aversion: I wonder at the impudence of any illiterate man to offer to make love.

Wit. That I confess I wonder at too.

Mrs. Mil. Ah! to marry an ignorant that can hardly read or write!

Pet. Why should a man be ever further from being married, though he can't read, than he is from being hanged? The ordinary's[43] paid for setting the psalm, and the parish priest for reading the ceremony. And for the rest which is to follow in both cases, a man may do it without book—so all's one for that.

Mrs. Mil. D' ye hear the creature?—Lord, here's company, I'll be gone.

(*Exeunt Mrs. Mil. and Mincing.*)

Wit. In the name of Bartlemew and his fair,[44] what have we here?

Mrs. Mar. 'T is your brother, I fancy. Don't you know him?

Wit. Not I.—Yes, I think it is he—I've almost forgot him; I have not seen him since the Revolution.[45]

(*Enter Sir Wilfull Witwoud in a country riding habit, and Servant to Lady Wishfort.*)

Serv. Sir, my lady's dressing. Here's company; if you please to walk in, in the mean time.

Sir Wil. Dressing! What, it's but morning here, I warrant, with you in London; we should count it towards afternoon in our parts, down in Shropshire.—Why then, belike, my aunt han't dined yet, ha, friend?

Serv. Your aunt, sir?

Sir Wil. My aunt, sir! Yes, my aunt, sir, and your lady, sir; your lady is my aunt, sir.—Why, what, dost thou not know me, friend? why then send somebody here that does. How long hast thou lived with thy lady, fellow, ha?

Serv. A week, sir; longer than anybody in the house, except my lady's woman.

Sir Wil. Why then belike thou dost not know thy lady, if thou seest her, ha, friend?

Serv. Why, truly, sir, I cannot safely swear to her face in a morning, before she is dressed. 'T is like I may give a shrewd guess at her by this time.

Sir Wil. Well, prithee try what thou canst do; if thou canst not guess, inquire her out, dost hear, fellow? and tell her, her nephew, Sir Wilfull Witwoud, is in the house.

Serv. I shall, sir.

Sir Wil. Hold ye, hear me, friend; a word with you in your ear; prithee who are these gallants?

Serv. Really, sir, I can't tell; here come so many here, 't is hard to know 'em all. (*Exit.*)

Sir Wil. Oons,[46] this fellow knows less than a starling; I don't think 'a knows his own name.

Mrs. Mar. Mr. Witwoud, your brother is not behindhand in forgetfulness—I fancy he has forgot you too.

Wit. I hope so—the devil take him that remembers first, I say.

Sir Wil. Save you, gentlemen and lady!

Mrs. Mar. For shame, Mr. Witwoud; why won't you speak to him?—And you, sir.

Wit. Petulant, speak.

Pet. And you, sir.

Sir Wil. No offence, I hope.

(*Salutes Mrs. Marwood.*)

Mrs. Mar. No, sure, sir.

Wit. This is a vile dog, I see that already. No offence! ha! ha! ha! To him; to him, Petulant, smoke[47] him.

Pet. It seems as if you had come a journey, sir; hem, hem.

(*Surveying him round.*)

Sir Wil. Very likely, sir, that it may seem so.

Pet. No offence, I hope, sir.

Wit. Smoke the boots, the boots; Petulant, the boots: ha! ha! ha!

Sir Wil. May be not, sir; thereafter, as 't is meant, sir.

Pet. Sir, I presume upon the information of your boots.

Sir Wil. Why, 't is like you may, sir: if you are not satisfied with the information of my boots, sir, if you will step to the stable, you may inquire further of my horse, sir.

Pet. Your horse, sir! your horse is an ass, sir!

Sir Wil. Do you speak by way of offence, sir?

Mrs. Mar. The gentleman's merry, that's all, sir.—(*Aside.*) S' life,[48] we shall have a quarrel betwixt an horse and an ass before they find one another out.—(*Aloud.*) You must not take anything

43 The chaplain of a prison, who apparently set the passage to be read (usually the beginning of the 51st psalm) by those who wished to secure "benefit of clergy."

44 A fair was held on St. Bartholomew's Day in Smithfield.

45 1688, when James II was dethroned.

46 Zounds, by God's wounds!

47 "Take him in," "get on to him."

48 By God's life!

amiss from your friends, sir. You are among your friends here, though it may be you don't know it.—If I am not mistaken, you are Sir Wilfull Witwoud.

Sir Wilfull. Right, lady; I am Sir Wilfull Witwoud, so I write myself; no offence to anybody, I hope; and nephew to the Lady Wishfort of this mansion.

Mrs. Mar. Don't you know this gentleman, sir?

Sir Wil. Hum! what, sure 't is not—yea by 'r Lady, but 't is—s' heart, I know not whether 't is or no—yea, but 't is, by the Wrekin![49] Brother Anthony! what, Tony, i' faith! what, dost thou not know me? By 'r Lady, nor I thee, thou art so becravated, and beperiwigged.—S' heart, why dost not speak? art thou o'erjoyed?

Wit. Odso, brother, is it you? your servant, brother.

Sir Wil. Your servant! why yours, sir. Your servant again—s 'heart, and your friend and servant to that—and a (*puff*) and a flap-dragon[50] for your service, sir! and a hare's foot and a hare's scut[51] for your service, sir! an you be so cold and so courtly.

Wit. No offence, I hope, brother.

Sir Wil. S' heart, sir, but there is, and much offence!—A pox, is this your inns o' court breeding, not to know your friends and your relations, your elders and your betters?

Wit. Why, brother Wilfull of Salop,[52] you may be as short as a Shrewsbury-cake, if you please. But I tell you 't is not modish to know relations in town: you think you 're in the country, where great lubberly brothers slabber and kiss one another when they meet, like a call of serjeants—'t is not the fashion here; 't is not indeed, dear brother.

Sir Wil. The fashion 's a fool; and you 're a fop, dear brother. S' heart, I 've suspected this—by 'r Lady, I conjectured you were a fop, since you began to change the style of your letters, and write on a scrap of paper gilt round the edges, no broader than a *subpœna.* I might expect this when you left off, "Honored brother"; and "hoping you are in good health," and so forth—to begin with a "Rat me, knight, I 'm so sick of a last night's debauch"—'ods heart, and then tell a familiar tale of a cock and a bull, and a whore and a bottle, and so conclude.—You could write news before you were out of your time, when you lived with honest Pumple Nose the attorney of Furnival's Inn[53]—you could entreat to be remembered then to your friends round the Wrekin. We could have gazettes, then, and Dawks's Letter, and the Weekly Bill,[54] till of late days.

Pet. S 'life, Witwoud, were you ever an attorney's clerk? of the family of the Furnivals? Ha! ha! ha!

Wit. Ay, ay, but that was for a while: not long, not long. Pshaw! I was not in my own power then; an orphan, and this fellow was my guardian; ay, ay, I was glad to consent to that man, to come to London: he had the disposal of me then. If I had not agreed to that, I might have been bound 'prentice to a felt-maker in Shrewsbury; this fellow would have bound me to a maker of felts.

Sir Wil. S' heart, and better than to be bound to a maker of fops; where, I suppose, you have served your time; and now you may set up for yourself.

Mrs. Mar. You intend to travel, sir, as I 'm informed.

Sir Wil. Belike I may, madam. I may chance to sail upon the salt seas, if my mind hold.

Pet. And the wind serve.

Sir Wil. Serve or not serve, I shan't ask license of you, sir; nor the weathercock your companion: I direct my discourse to the lady, sir.—'T is like my aunt may have told you, madam—yes, I have settled my concerns, I may say now, and am minded to see foreign parts. If an how that the peace holds, whereby that is, taxes abate.

Mrs. Mir. I thought you had designed for France at all adventures.[55]

Sir Wil. I can't tell that; 't is like I may, and 't is like I may not. I am somewhat dainty in making a resolution—because when I make it I keep it. I don't stand shill I, shall I, then; if I say 't, I 'll do 't; but I have thoughts to tarry a small matter in town, to learn somewhat of your lingo first, before I cross the seas. I 'd gladly have a spice of your French as they say, whereby to hold discourse in foreign countries.

Mrs. Mar. Here 's an academy in town for that use.

Sir Wil. There is? 'T is like there may.

49 A hill in Shropshire, Sir Wilfull's native county.

50 A raisin burning in brandy, swallowed as a sport; hence something valueless.

51 tail; a natural synonym for a trifle, with a sporting squire.

52 Shropshire, in which the chief town is Shrewsbury.

53 One of the Inns of Chancery.

54 Periodicals.

55 in any case.

Mrs. Mar. No doubt you will return very much improved.

Wil. Yes, refined, like a Dutch skipper from a whale-fishing.

(*Enter Lady Wishfort and Fainall.*)

Lady Wish. Nephew, you are welcome.

Sir Wil. Aunt, your servant.

Fain. Sir Wilfull, your most faithful servant.

Sir Wil. Cousin Fainall, give me your hand.

Lady Wish. Cousin Witwoud, your servant; Mr. Petulant, your servant—nephew, you are welcome again. Will you drink anything after your journey, nephew, before you eat? Dinner 's almost ready.

Sir Wil. I 'm very well, I thank you, aunt—however, I thank you for your courteous offer. S' heart, I was afraid you would have been in the fashion too, and have remembered to have forgot your relations. Here 's your cousin Tony, belike, I may n't call him brother for fear of offence.

Lady Wish. Oh, he 's a rallier, nephew—my cousin 's a wit: and your great wits always rally their best friends to choose. When you have been abroad, nephew, you 'll understand raillery better.

(*Fainall and Mrs. Marwood talk apart.*)

Sir Wil. Why then let him hold his tongue in the mean time; and rail when that day comes.

(*Enter Mincing.*)

Min. Mem, I come to acquaint your la' ship that dinner is impatient.

Sir Wil. Impatient! why then belike it won't stay till I pull off my boots.—Sweetheart, can you help me to a pair of slippers?—My man 's with his horses, I warrant.

Lady Wish. Fy, fy, nephew! you would not pull off your boots here?—Go down into the hall—dinner shall stay for you.—My nephew 's a little unbred, you 'll pardon him, madam.—Gentlemen, will you walk?—Marwood?

Mrs. Mar. I 'll follow you, madam—before Sir Wilfull is ready.

(*Exeunt all but Mrs. Marwood and Fainall.*)

Fain. Why then, Foible 's a bawd, an errant, rank, match-making bawd: and I, it seems, am a husband, a rank husband; and my wife a very errant, rank wife—all in the way of the world. 'S death, to be an anticipated cuckold, a cuckold in embryo! sure I was born with budding antlers, like a young satyr, or a citizen's child. S' death! to be out-witted—to be out-jilted—out-matrimony'd!—If I had kept my speed like a stag, 't were somewhat,—but to crawl after, with my horns, like a snail, and outstripped by my wife—'t is scurvy wedlock.

Mrs. Mar. Then shake it off; you have often wished for an opportunity to part—and now you have it. But first prevent their plot—the half of Millamant's fortune is too considerable to be parted with to a foe, to Mirabell.

Fain. Damn him! that had been mine—had you not made that fond discovery [56]—that had been forfeited, had they been married. My wife had added lustre to my horns by that increase of fortune; I could have worn 'em tipped with gold, though my forehead had been furnished like a deputy-lieutenant's hall.

Mrs. Mar. They may prove a cap of maintenance [57] to you still, if you can away with [58] your wife. And she 's no worse than when you had her—I dare swear she had given up her game before she was married.

Fain. Hum! that may be. She might throw up her cards, but I 'll be hanged if she did not put Pam [59] in her pocket.

Mrs. Mar. You married her to keep you; and if you can contrive to have her keep you better than you expected, why should you not keep her longer than you intended?

Fain. The means, the means?

Mrs Mar. Discover to my lady your wife's conduct; threaten to part with her!—my lady loves her, and will come to any composition to save her reputation. Take the opportunity of breaking it, just upon the discovery of this imposture. My lady will be enraged beyond bounds, and sacrifice niece, and fortune, and all, at that conjuncture. And let me alone to keep her warm; if she should flag in her part, I will not fail to prompt her.

Fain. Faith, this has an appearance.

Mrs. Mar. I 'm sorry I hinted to my lady to endeavor a match between Millamant and Sir Wilfull; that may be an obstacle.

Fain. Oh, for that matter, leave me to manage him: I 'll disable him for that; he

56 Foolish disclosure (of Millamant's and Mirabell's love).

57 A cap with horns pictured in armorial bearings (obviously there is a pun).

58 put up with.

59 The knave of clubs, the highest card in the game of loo.

will drink like a Dane; after dinner, I 'll set his hand in.

Mrs. Mar. Well, how do you stand affected towards your lady?

Fain. Why, faith, I 'm thinking of it.—Let me see—I am married already, so that 's over:—my wife has played the jade with me—well, that 's over too:—I never loved her, or if I had, why that would have been over too by this time:—jealous of her I cannot be for I am certain; so there 's an end of jealousy:—weary of her I am, and shall be—no, there 's no end of that—no, no, that were too much to hope. Thus far concerning my repose; now for my reputation. As to my own, I married not for it, so that 's out of the question;—and as to my part in my wife's—why, she had parted with hers before; so bringing none to me, she can take none from me; 't is against all rule of play, that I should lose to one who has not wherewithal to stake.

Mrs. Mar. Besides, you forget, marriage is honorable.

Fain. Hum, faith, and that 's well thought on; marriage is honorable as you say; and if so, wherefore should cuckoldom be a discredit, being derived from so honorable a root?

Mrs. Mar. Nay, I know not; if the root be honorable, why not the branches?

Fain. So, so, why this point 's clear—well, how do we proceed?

Mrs. Mar. I will contrive a letter which shall be delivered to my lady at the time when that rascal who is to act Sir Rowland is with her. It shall come as from an unknown hand—for the less I appear to know of the truth, the better I can play the incendiary. Besides, I would not have Foible provoked if I could help it—because you know she knows some passages—nay, I expect all will come out—but let the mine be sprung first, and then I care not if I am discovered.

Fain. If the worst come to the worst—I 'll turn my wife to grass—I have already a deed of settlement of the best part of her estate, which I wheedled out of her; and that you shall partake at least.

Mrs. Mar. I hope you are convinced that I hate Mirabell; now you 'll be no more jealous.

Fain. Jealous! no—by this kiss—let husbands be jealous; but let the lover still believe; or if he doubt, let it be only to endear his pleasure, and prepare the joy that follows, when he proves his mistress true. But let husbands' doubts convert to endless jealousy; or if they have belief, let it corrupt to superstition and blind credulity. I am single, and will herd no more with 'em. True, I wear the badge, but I 'll disown the order. And since I take my leave of 'em, I care not if I leave 'em a common motto to their common crest:—

All husbands must or pain or shame endure;
The wise too jealous are, fools too secure.[60]

(*Exeunt.*)

ACT IV

SCENE 1. *Scene continues.*

(*Enter Lady Wishfort and Foible.*)

Lady Wish. Is Sir Rowland coming, sayest thou, Foible? And are things in order?

Foib. Yes, madam, I have put wax lights in the sconces, and placed the footmen in a row in the hall, in their best liveries, with the coachman and postillion to fill up the equipage.[61]

Lady Wish. Have you pulvilled[62] the coachman and postillion, that they may not stink of the stable when Sir Rowland comes by?

Foib. Yes, madam.

Lady Wish. And are the dancers and the music ready, that he may be entertained in all points with correspondence to his passion?

Foib. All is ready, madam.

Lady Wish. And—well—and how do I look, Foible?

Foib. Most killing well, madam.

Lady Wish. Well, and how shall I receive him? in what figure shall I give his heart the first impression? there is a great deal in the first impression. Shall I sit?—no, I won't sit—I 'll walk—ay, I 'll walk from the door upon his entrance; and then turn full upon him—no, that will be too sudden. I 'll lie,—ay, I 'll lie down—I 'll receive him in my little dressing-room, there 's a couch—yes, yes, I 'll give the first impression on a couch.—I won't lie neither, but loll and lean upon one elbow: with one foot a little dangling

60 confident 61 retinue, "establishment." 62 perfumed with powder.

off, jogging in a thoughtful way—yes—and then as soon as he appears, start, ay, start and be surprised, and rise to meet him in a pretty disorder—yes,—O, nothing is more alluring than a levee from a couch, in some confusion:—it shows the foot to advantage, and furnishes with blushes, and recomposing airs beyond comparison. Hark! there's a coach.

Foib. 'T is he, madam.

Lady Wish. Oh, dear!—Has my nephew made his addresses to Millamant? I ordered him.

Foib. Sir Wilfull is set in to drinking, madam, in the parlor.

Lady Wish. Odds my life,[63] I'll send him to her. Call her down, Foible; bring her hither. I'll send him as I go—when they are together, then come to me, Foible, that I may not be too long alone with Sir Rowland.

(*Exit.*)

(*Enter Mrs. Millamant and Mrs. Fainall.*)

Foib. Madam, I stayed here, to tell your ladyship that Mr. Mirabell has waited this half hour for an opportunity to talk with you: though my lady's orders were to leave you and Sir Wilfull together. Shall I tell Mr. Mirabell that you are at leisure?

Mrs. Mil. No,—what would the dear man have? I am thoughtful, and would amuse myself—bid him come another time.

"There never yet was woman made
Nor shall, but to be cursed." [64]

(*Repeating and walking about.*)

That's hard!

Mrs. Fain. You are very fond of Sir John Suckling to-day, Millamant, and the poets.

Mrs. Mil. He? Ay, and filthy verses—so I am.

Foib. Sir Wilfull is coming, madam. Shall I send Mr. Mirabell away?

Mrs. Mil. Ay, if you please, Foible, send him away—or send him hither—just as you will, dear Foible.—I think I'll see him—shall I? Ay, let the wretch come.

(*Exit Foible.*)

"Thyrsis, a youth of the inspir'd train."

(*Repeating.*)

Dear Fainall, entertain Sir Wilfull—thou hast philosophy to undergo a fool, thou art married and hast patience—I would confer with my own thoughts.

Mrs. Fain. I am obliged to you, that you would make me your proxy in this affair; but I have business of my own.

(*Enter Sir Wilfull.*)

Mrs. Fain. O Sir Wilfull, you are come at the critical instant. There's your mistress up to the ears in love and contemplation; pursue your point now or never.

Sir Wil. Yes; my aunt would have it so—I would gladly have been encouraged with a bottle or two, because I'm somewhat wary at first before I am acquainted.—(*This while Millamant walks about repeating to herself.*)—But I hope, after a time, I shall break my mind—that is, upon further acquaintance—so for the present, cousin, I'll take my leave—if so be you'll be so kind to make my excuse, I'll return to my company—

Mrs. Fain. O, fy, Sir Wilfull! What, you must not be daunted.

Sir Wil. Daunted! no, that's not it, it is not so much for that—for if so be that I set on't, I'll do't. But only for the present, 't is sufficient till further acquaintance, that's all—your servant.

Mrs. Fain. Nay, I'll swear you shall never lose so favorable an opportunity, if I can help it. I'll leave you together, and lock the door.

(*Exit.*)

Sir Wil. Nay, nay, cousin—I have forgot my gloves—what d'ye do?—S'heart, a'has locked the door indeed, I think—nay, Cousin Fainall, open the door—pshaw, what a vixen trick is this?—Nay, now a' has seen me too.—Cousin, I made bold to pass through as it were—I think this door's enchanted!

Mrs. Mil. (*Repeating.*)
"I prithee spare me, gentle boy,
Press me no more for that slight toy."

Sir Wil. Anan?[65] Cousin, your servant.

Mrs. Mil. (*Repeating.*)
"That foolish trifle of a heart."
Sir Wilfull!

Sir Wil. Yes—your servant. No offence, I hope, cousin.

Mrs. Mil. (*Repeating.*)
"I swear it will not do its part,
Though thou dost thine, employ'st thy power and art."
Natural, easy Suckling.

---

63 A corrupted oath or asseveration; perhaps "God save my life!"

64 This and the later bits of verse are from Suckling and Waller (mid-17th century lyric poets).

65 "I beg your pardon, I don't understand you" (originally *anon*, meaning *immediately*).

Sir Wil. Anan? Suckling! no such suckling neither, cousin, nor stripling: I thank Heaven, I 'm no minor.

Mrs. Mil. Ah, rustic, ruder than Gothic!

Sir Wil. Well, well, I shall understand your lingo one of these days, cousin; in the meanwhile I must answer in plain English.

Mrs. Mil. Have you any business with me, Sir Wilfull?

Sir Wil. Not at present, cousin—yes, I make bold to see, to come and know if that how you were disposed to fetch a walk this evening, if so be that I might not be troublesome, I would have sought a walk with you.

Mrs. Mil. A walk! what then?

Sir Wil. Nay, nothing—only for the walk's sake, that 's all.

Mrs. Mil. I nauseate walking; 't is a country diversion; I loathe the country, and everything that relates to it.

Sir Wil. Indeed! ha! Look ye, look ye, you do? Nay, 't is like you may—here are choice of pastimes here in town, as plays and the like; that must be confessed indeed.

Mrs. Mil. Ah, *l'étourdi!*[66] I hate the town too.

Sir Wil. Dear heart, that 's much—ha! that you should hate 'em both! Ha! 't is like you may; there are some can't relish the town, and others can't away with the country—'t is like you may be one of those, cousin.

Mrs. Mil. Ha! ha! ha! yes, 't is like I may.—You have nothing further to say to me?

Sir Wil. Not at present, cousin.—'T is like when I have an opportunity to be more private—I may break my mind in some measure—I conjecture you partly guess—however, that 's as time shall try —but spare to speak and spare to speed,[67] as they say.

Mrs. Mil. If it is of no great importance, Sir Wilfull, you will oblige me to leave me; I have just now a little business—

Sir Wil. Enough, enough, cousin: yes, yes, all a case—when you 're disposed, when you 're disposed: now 's as well as another time; and another time as well as now. All 's one for that—yes, yes, if your concerns call you, there 's no haste; it will keep cold, as they say.—Cousin, your servant—I think this door 's locked.

Mrs. Mil. You may go this way, sir.

Sir Wil. Your servant; then with your leave I 'll return to my company.

(*Exit.*)

Mrs. Mil. Ay, ay; ha! ha! ha!
"Like Phœbus sung the no less amorous boy."

(*Enter Mirabell.*)

Mir. "Like Daphne she, as lovely and as coy." Do you lock yourself up from me, to make my search more curious? or is this pretty artifice contrived to signify that here the chase must end, and my pursuit be crowned? For you can fly no further.

Mrs. Mil. Vanity! no—I 'll fly, and be followed to the last moment. Though I am upon the very verge of matrimony, I expect you should solicit me as much as if I were wavering at the grate of a monastery, with one foot over the threshold. I 'll be solicited to the very last, nay, and afterwards.

Mir. What, after the last?

Mrs. Mil. Oh, I should think I was poor and had nothing to bestow, if I were reduced to an inglorious ease, and freed from the agreeable fatigues of solicitation.

Mir. But do not you know, that when favors are conferred upon instant[68] and tedious solicitation, that they diminish in their value, and that both the giver loses the grace, and the receiver lessens his pleasure?

Mrs. Mil. It may be in things of common application; but never sure in love. Oh, I hate a lover than can dare to think he draws a moment's air, independent on the bounty of his mistress. There is not so impudent a thing in nature, as the saucy look of an assured man, confident of success. The pedantic arrogance of a very husband has not so pragmatical an air. Ah! I 'll never marry, unless I am first made sure of my will and pleasure.

Mir. Would you have 'em both before marriage? or will you be contented with the first now, and stay for the other till after grace?

Mrs. Mil. Ah! don't be impertinent.—My dear liberty, shall I leave thee? my faithful solitude, my darling contemplation, must I bid you then adieu? Ay-h adieu —my morning thoughts, agreeable wakings, indolent slumbers, all ye *douceurs*, ye *sommeils du matin*, adieu!—I can't

66 The giddy creature! (The title of a play by Molière.)

67 prosper.

68 insistent.

do 't, 't is more than impossible—positively, Mirabell, I 'll lie abed in a morning as long as I please.

Mir. Then I 'll get up in a morning as early as I please.

Mrs. Mil. Ah! idle creature, get up when you will—and d' ye hear, I won't be called names after I 'm married; positively I won't be called names.

Mir. Names!

Mrs. Mil. Ay, as wife, spouse, my dear, joy, jewel, love, sweetheart, and the rest of that nauseous cant, in which men and their wives are so fulsomely familiar—I shall never bear that—good Mirabell, don't let us be familiar or fond, nor kiss before folks, like my Lady Fadler and Sir Francis: nor go to Hyde Park together the first Sunday in a new chariot, to provoke eyes and whispers, and then never to be seen there together again; as if we were proud of one another the first week, and ashamed of one another for ever after. Let us never visit together, nor go to a play together; but let us be very strange and well-bred: let us be as strange as if we had been married a great while; and as well-bred as if we were not married at all.

Mir. Have you any more conditions to offer? Hitherto your demands are pretty reasonable.

Mrs. Mil. Trifles!—As liberty to pay and receive visits to and from whom I please; to write and receive letters, without interrogatories or wry faces on your part; to wear what I please; and choose conversation with regard only to my own taste; to have no obligation upon me to converse with wits that I don't like, because they are your acquaintance: or to be intimate with fools, because they may be your relations. Come to dinner when I please; dine in my dressing-room when I 'm out of humor, without giving a reason. To have my closet inviolate; to be sole empress of my tea-table, which you must never presume to approach without first asking leave. And lastly, wherever I am, you shall always knock at the door before you come in. These articles subscribed, if I continue to endure you a little longer, I may by degrees dwindle into a wife.

Mir. Your bill of fare is something advanced in this latter account.—Well, have I liberty to offer conditions—that when you are dwindled into a wife, I may not be beyond measure enlarged into a husband?

Mrs. Mil. You have free leave; propose your utmost, speak and spare not.

Mir. I thank you.—*Imprimis* then, I covenant, that your acquaintance be general; that you admit no sworn confidant, or intimate of your own sex; no she-friend to screen her affairs under your countenance, and tempt you to make trial of a mutual secrecy. No decoy-duck to wheedle you a fop-scrambling to the play in a mask—then bring you home in a pretended fright, when you think you shall be found out—and rail at me for missing the play, and disappointing the frolic which you had to pick me up, and prove my constancy.

Mrs. Mil. Detestable *imprimis!* I go to the play in a mask!

Mir. *Item,* I article, that you continue to like your own face, as long as I shall: and while it passes current with me, that you endeavor not to new-coin it. To which end, together with all vizards [69] for the day, I prohibit all masks for the night, made of oiled-skins, and I know not what—hogs' bones, hares' gall, pig-water, and the marrow of a roasted cat. In short, I forbid all commerce with the gentlewoman in what-d'ye-call-it court. *Item,* I shut my doors against all bawds with baskets, and pennyworths of muslin, china, fans, atlases, [70] etc.—*Item,* when you shall be breeding—

Mrs. Mil. Ah! name it not.

Mir. Which may be presumed with a blessing on our endeavors—

Mrs. Mil. Odious endeavors!

Mir. I denounce against all strait lacing, squeezing for a shape, till you mould my boy's head like a sugar-loaf, and instead of a man-child, make me the father to a crooked billet. Lastly, to the dominion of the tea-table I submit—but with proviso, that you exceed not in your province; but restrain yourself to native and simple tea-table drinks, as tea, chocolate, and coffee: as likewise to genuine and authorized tea-table talk—such as mending of fashions, spoiling reputations, railing at absent friends, and so forth—but that on no account you encroach upon the men's prerogative, and presume to drink healths, or toast fellows; for prevention of which I banish all foreign forces, all auxiliaries to the tea-table, as orange-brandy, all aniseed, cinnamon,

69 A kind of mask.

70 An oriental silk or satin.

citron, and Barbadoes waters, together with ratafia, and the most noble spirit of clary [71]—but for cowslip wine, poppy water, and all dormitives, those I allow. —These provisos admitted, in other things I may prove a tractable and complying husband.

Mrs. Mil. O horrid provisos! filthy strong-waters! I toast fellows! odious men! I hate your odious provisos.

Mir. Then we are agreed! Shall I kiss your hand upon the contract? And here comes one to be a witness to the sealing of the deed.

(*Enter Mrs. Fainall.*)

Mrs. Mil. Fainall, what shall I do? shall I have him? I think I must have him.

Mrs. Fain. Ay, ay, take him, take him, what should you do?

Mrs. Mil. Well then—I'll take my death I'm in a horrid fright—Fainall, I shall never say it—well—I think—I'll endure you.

Mrs. Fain. Fy! fy! have him, have him, and tell him so in plain terms: for I am sure you have a mind to him.

Mrs. Mil. Are you? I think I have—and the horrid man looks as if he thought so too—well, you ridiculous thing you, I'll have you—I won't be kissed, nor I won't be thanked—here kiss my hand though.—So, hold your tongue now, and don't say a word.

Mrs. Fain. Mirabell, there's a necessity for your obedience; you have neither time to talk nor stay. My mother is coming; and in my conscience if she should see you, would fall into fits, and maybe not recover time enough to return to Sir Rowland, who, as Foible tells me, is in a fair way to succeed. Therefore spare your ecstasies for another occasion, and slip down the backstairs, where Foible waits to consult you.

Mrs. Mil. Ay, go, go. In the meantime I suppose you have said something to please me.

Mir. I am all obedience.

(*Exit.*)

Mrs. Fain. Yonder Sir Wilfull's drunk, and so noisy that my mother has been forced to leave Sir Rowland to appease him; but he answers her only with singing and drinking—what they may have done by this time I know not; but Petulant and he were upon quarrelling as I came by.

Mrs. Mil. Well, if Mirabell should not make a good husband, I am a lost thing, for I find I love him violently.

Mrs. Fain. So it seems, when you mind not what's said to you.—If you doubt him, you had best take up with Sir Wilfull.

Mrs. Mil. How can you name that superannuated lubber? foh!

(*Enter Witwoud from drinking.*)

Mrs. Fain. So, is the fray made up, that you have left 'em?

Wit. Left 'em? I could stay no longer—I have laughed like ten christenings—I am tipsy with laughing—if I had stayed any longer I should have burst—I must have been let out and pieced in the sides like an unsized camlet.[72]—Yes, yes, the fray is composed; my lady came in like a *noli prosequi,*[73] and stopped their proceedings.

Mrs. Mil. What was the dispute?

Wit. That's the jest; there was no dispute. They could neither of 'em speak for rage, and so fell a sputtering at one another like two roasting apples.

(*Enter Petulant, drunk.*)

Wit. Now, Petulant, all's over, all's well. Gad, my head begins to whim it about—why dost thou not speak? thou art both as drunk and as mute as a fish.

Pet. Look you, Mrs. Millamant—if you can love me, dear nymph—say it—and that's the conclusion—pass on, or pass off—that's all.

Wit. Thou hast uttered volumes, folios, in less than *decimo sexto,* my dear Lacedemonian. Sirrah, Petulant, thou art an epitomizer of words.

Pet. Witwoud—you are an annihilator of sense.

Wit. Thou art a retailer of phrases; and dost deal in remnants of remnants, like a maker of pincushions—thou art in truth (metaphorically speaking) a speaker of shorthand.

Pet. Thou art (without a figure) just one-half of an ass, and Baldwin yonder, thy half-brother, is the rest.—A Gemini of asses split would make just four of you.

Wit. Thou dost bite, my dear mustard seed; kiss me for that.

Pet. Stand off!—I'll kiss no more males —I have kissed your twin yonder in a humor of reconciliation, till he (*Hiccup*)

71 Sweetened and flavored wine.

72 A kind of woolen material; unsized, unstiffened.

73 A notice to stop a prosecution.

rises upon my stomach like a radish.

Mrs. Mil. Eh? filthy creature! what was the quarrel?

Pet. There was no quarrel—there might have been a quarrel.

Wit. If there had been words enow between 'em to have expressed provocation, they had gone together by the ears like a pair of castanets.

Pet. You were the quarrel.

Mrs. Mil. Me!

Pet. If I have a humor to quarrel, I can make less matters conclude premises.—If you are not handsome, what then, if I have a humor to prove it? If I shall have my reward, say so; if not, fight for your face the next time yourself—I'll go sleep.

Wit. Do, wrap thyself up like a woodlouse, and dream revenge—and hear me, if thou canst learn to write by to-morrow morning, pen me a challenge.—I'll carry it for thee.

Pet. Carry your mistress's monkey a spider!—Go flea dogs, and read romances!—I'll go to bed to my maid.

(*Exit.*)

Mrs. Fain. He's horribly drunk.—How came you all in this pickle?

Wit. A plot! a plot! to get rid of the night—your husband's advice; but he sneaked off.

(*Enter Lady Wishfort, and Sir Wilfull, drunk.*)

Lady Wish. Out upon 't, out upon 't! At years of discretion, and comport yourself at this rantipole [74] rate!

Sir Wil. No offence, aunt.

Lady Wish. Offence! as I'm a person, I'm ashamed of you—foh! how you stink of wine! D'ye think my niece will ever endure such a Borachio! [75] you're an absolute Borachio.

Sir Wil. Borachio?

Lady Wish. At a time when you should commence an amour, and put your best foot foremost—

Sir Wit. S'heart, an you grutch me your liquor, make a bill—give me more drink, and take my purse.—

(*Sings.*)

"Prithee fill me the glass,
Till it laugh in my face,
With ale that is potent and mellow;
He that whines for a lass,
Is an ignorant ass,
For a bumper has not its fellow."

But if you would have me marry my cousin—say the word, and I'll do 't—Wilfull will do 't, that 's the word—Wilfull will do 't, that 's my crest—my motto I have forgot.

Lady Wish. My nephew 's a little overtaken, cousin—but 't is with drinking your health.—O' my word you are obliged to him.

Sir Wil. *In vino veritas,* aunt.—If I drunk your health to-day, cousin—I am a Borachio. But if you have a mind to be married, say the word, and send for the piper; Wilfull will do 't. If not, dust it away, and let 's have t' other round.—Tony!—Odds heart, where 's Tony!—Tony 's an honest fellow; but he spits after a bumper, and that 's a fault.—

(*Sings.*)

"We'll drink, and we'll never ha' done, boys,
Put the glass then around with the sun, boys,
Let Apollo's example invite us;
For he 's drunk every night,
And that makes him so bright,
That he 's able next morning to light us."

The sun 's a good pimple,[76] an honest soaker; he has a cellar at your Antipodes. If I travel, aunt, I touch at your Antipodes.—Your Antipodes are a good, rascally sort of topsy-turvy fellows: if I had a bumper, I'd stand upon my head and drink a health to 'em.—A match or no match, cousin with the hard name?—Aunt, Wilfull will do 't. If she has her maidenhead, let her look to 't; if she has not, let her keep her own counsel in the meantime, and cry out at the nine months' end.

Mrs. Mil. Your pardon, madam, I can stay no longer—Sir Wilfull grows very powerful. Eh! how he smells! I shall be overcome, if I stay.—Come, cousin.

(*Exeunt Mrs. Millamant and Mrs. Fainall.*)

Lady Wish. Smells! He would poison a tallow-chandler and his family! Beastly creature, I know not what to do with him!—Travel, quotha! ay, travel, travel, get thee gone, get thee gone, get thee but far enough, to the Saracens, or the Tartars, or the Turks!—for thou art not fit to live in a Christian commonwealth, thou beastly pagan!

Sir Wil. Turks, no; no Turks, aunt: your Turks are infidels, and believe not in the grape. Your Mahometan, your Mussulman, is a dry stinkard—no offence, aunt.

74 disorderly.

75 Wine-bag used in Spain; hence a drunkard.

76 boon companion

My map says that your Turk is not so honest a man as your Christian. I cannot find by the map that your Mufti is orthodox—whereby it is a plain case, that orthodox is a hard word, aunt, and (*Hiccup*) Greek for claret.—

(*Sings.*)

"To drink is a Christian diversion,
Unknown to the Turk and the Persian:
Let Mahometan fools
Live by heathenish rules,
And be damned over tea-cups and coffee.
But let British lads sing,
Crown a health to the king,
And a fig for your sultan and sophy!"[77]

Ah, Tony!

(*Enter Foible, and whispers Lady Wishfort.*)

Lady Wish. Sir Rowland impatient? Good lack! what shall I do with this beastly tumbril?[78] Go lie down and sleep, you sot!—or, as I'm a person, I'll have you bastinadoed with broomsticks.—Call up the wenches.

(*Exit Foible.*)

Sir Wil. Ahey! wenches, where are the wenches?

Lady Wish. Dear Cousin Witwoud, get him away, and you will bind me to you inviolably. I have an affair of moment that invades me with some precipitation—you will oblige me to all futurity.

Wit. Come, knight.—Pox on him, I don't know what to say to him.—Will you go to a cock-match?

Sir Wil. With a wench, Tony! Is she a shakebag,[79] sirrah? Let me bite your cheek for that.

Wit. Horrible! he has a breath like a bagpipe!—Ay, ay; come, will you march, my Salopian?

Sir Wil. Lead on, little Tony—I'll follow thee, my Anthony, my Tantony, sirrah, thou sha't be my Tantony,[80] and I'll be thy pig.

"And a fig for your sultan and sophy."

(*Exeunt singing with Witwoud.*)

Lady Wish. This will never do. It will never make a match—at least before he has been abroad.

(*Enter Waitwell, disguised as Sir Rowland.*)

Lady Wish. Dear Sir Rowland, I am confounded with confusion at the retrospection of my own rudeness!—I have more pardons to ask than the pope distributes in the year of jubilee. But I hope, where there is likely to be so near an alliance, we may unbend the severity of decorums, and dispense with a little ceremony.

Wait. My impatience, madam, is the effect of my transport; and till I have the possession of your adorable person, I am tantalized on a rack; and do but hang, madam, on the tenter[81] of expectation.

Lady Wish. You have excess of gallantry, Sir Rowland, and press things to a conclusion with a most prevailing vehemence.—But a day or two for decency of marriage—

Wait. For decency of funeral, madam! The delay will break my heart—or, if that should fail, I shall be poisoned. My nephew will get an inkling of my designs, and poison me—and I would willingly starve him before I die—I would gladly go out of the world with that satisfaction.—That would be some comfort to me, if I could but live so long as to be revenged on that unnatural viper!

Lady Wish. Is he so unnatural, say you? Truly I would contribute much both to the saving of your life, and the accomplishment of your revenge.—Not that I respect myself, though he has been a perfidious wretch to me.

Wait. Perfidious to you!

Lady Wish. O Sir Rowland, the hours that he has died away at my feet, the tears that he has shed, the oaths that he has sworn, the palpitations that he has felt, the trances and the tremblings, the ardors and the ecstasies, the kneelings and the risings, the heart-heavings and the handgripings, the pangs and the pathetic regards of his protesting eyes!—Oh, no memory can register!

Wait. What, my rival! is the rebel my rival?—a' dies.

Lady Wish. No, don't kill him at once, Sir Rowland, starve him gradually, inch by inch.

Wait. I'll do't. In three weeks he shall be barefoot; in a month out at knees with begging an alms.—He shall starve upward and upward, till he has nothing living but his head, and then go out in a stink like a candle's end upon a save-all.[82]

Lady Wish. Well, Sir Rowland, you have

77 Shah.
78 Drunken fellow (originally a cart or boat for carrying a heavy load).
79 A fighting-cock.
80 St. Anthony, patron saint of pigs.
81 Frame for stretching cloth.
82 Candlestick which allows the candle to burn to the end.

the way—you are no novice in the labyrinth of love—you have the clue.—But as I am a person, Sir Rowland, you must not attribute my yielding to any sinister appetite, or indigestion of widowhood; nor impute my complacency to any lethargy of continence—I hope you do not think me prone to any iteration of nuptials—

Wait. Far be it from me—

Lady Wish. If you do, I protest I must recede—or think that I have made a prostitution of decorums; but in the vehemence of compassion, and to save the life of a person of so much importance—

Wait. I esteem it so.

Lady Wish. Or else you wrong my condescension.

Wait. I do not, I do not!

Lady Wish. Indeed you do.

Wait. I do not, fair shrine of virtue!

Lady Wish. If you think the least scruple of carnality was an ingredient,—

Wait. Dear madam, no. You are all camphor and frankincense, all chastity and odor.

Lady Wish. Or that—

(*Enter Foible.*)

Foib. Madam, the dancers are ready; and there 's one with a letter, who must deliver it into your own hands.

Lady Wish. Sir Rowland, will you give me leave? Think favorably, judge candidly, and conclude you have found a person who would suffer racks in honor's cause, dear Sir Rowland, and will wait on you incessantly.

(*Exit.*)

Wait. Fy, fy!—What a slavery have I undergone! Spouse, hast thou any cordial? I want spirits.

Foib. What a washy [83] rogue art thou, to pant thus for a quarter of an hour's lying and swearing to a fine lady!

Wait. Oh, she is the antidote to desire! Spouse, thou wilt fare the worst for 't—I shall have no appetite to iteration of nuptials this eight-and-forty hours.—By this hand I 'd rather be a chairman [84] in the dog-days—than act Sir Rowland till this time to-morrow!

(*Enter Lady Wishfort, with a letter.*)

Lady Wish. Call in the dancers.—Sir Rowland, we 'll sit, if you please, and see the entertainment. (*Dance.*) Now, with your permission, Sir Rowland, I will peruse my letter.—I would open it in your presence, because I would not make you uneasy. If it should make you uneasy, I would burn it.—Speak, if it does—but you may see the superscription is like a woman's hand.

Foib. By Heaven! Mrs. Marwood's, I know it.—My heart aches—get it from her.

(*To him.*)

Wait. A woman's hand! no, madam, that 's no woman's hand, I see that already. That 's somebody whose throat must be cut.

Lady Wish. Nay, Sir Rowland, since you give me a proof of your passion by your jealousy, I promise you I 'll make a return, by a frank communication.—You shall see it—we 'll open it together—look you here.—(*Reads.*)—"Madam, though unknown to you"—Look you there, 't is from nobody that I know—"I have that honor for your character, that I think myself obliged to let you know you are abused. He who pretends to be Sir Rowland, is a cheat and a rascal."—Oh, Heavens! what 's this?

Foib. (*Aside.*) Unfortunate! all 's ruined!

Wait. How, how, let me see, let me see!—(*Reading.*) "A rascal, and disguised and suborned for that imposture,"—O villainy! O villainy!—"by the contrivance of—"

Lady Wish. I shall faint, I shall die, I shall die; oh!

Foib. Say 't is your nephew's hand—quickly, his plot, swear, swear it!

(*To him.*)

Wait. Here 's a villain! Madam, don't you perceive it, don't you see it?

Lady Wish. Too well, too well! I have seen too much.

Wait. I told you at first I knew the hand.—A woman's hand! The rascal writes a sort of a large hand; your Roman hand—I saw there was a throat to be cut presently. If he were my son, as he is my nephew, I 'd pistol him!

Foib. O treachery!—But are you sure, Sir Rowland, it is his writing?

Wait. Sure! am I here? Do I live? Do I love this pearl of India? I have twenty letters in my pocket from him in the same character.

Lady Wish. How!

Foib. Oh, what luck it is, Sir Rowland,

83 feeble.

84 A carrier of a sedan-chair.

that you were present at this juncture!—This was the business that brought Mr. Mirabell disguised to Madam Millamant this afternoon. I thought something was contriving, when he stole by me and would have hid his face.

Lady Wish. How, how!—I heard the villain was in the house indeed; and now I remember, my niece went away abruptly, when Sir Wilfull was to have made his addresses.

Foib. Then, then, madam, Mr. Mirabell waited for her in her chamber! but I would not tell your ladyship to discompose you when you were to receive Sir Rowland.

Wait. Enough, his date is short.

Foib. No, good Sir Rowland, don't incur the law.

Wait. Law! I care not for law. I can but die, and 't is in a good cause.—My lady shall be satisfied of my truth and innocence, though it cost me my life.

Lady Wish. No, dear Sir Rowland, don't fight; if you should be killed I must never show my face; or hanged—O, consider my reputation, Sir Rowland!—No, you shan't fight—I 'll go in and examine my niece; I 'll make her confess. I conjure you, Sir Rowland, by all your love, not to fight.

Wait. I am charmed, madam, I obey. But some proof you must let me give you; I 'll go for a black box, which contains the writings of my whole estate, and deliver that into your hands.

Lady Wish. Ay, dear Sir Rowland, that will be some comfort, bring the black box.

Wait. And may I presume to bring a contract to be signed this night? may I hope so far?

Lady Wish. Bring what you will; but come alive, pray come alive. Oh, this is a happy discovery!

Wait. Dead or alive I 'll come—and married we will be in spite of treachery; ay, and get an heir that shall defeat the last remaining glimpse of hope in my abandoned nephew. Come, my buxom widow:

Ere long you shall substantial proofs receive,
That I 'm an arrant [85] knight—

Foib. (*Aside.*) Or arrant knave.

ACT V.

Scene 1. *Scene continues.*

(*Lady Wishfort and Foible.*)

Lady Wish. Out of my house, out of my house, thou viper! thou serpent, that I have fostered! thou bosom traitress, that I raised from nothing!—Begone! begone! begone!—go! go!—That I took from washing of old gauze and weaving of dead hair, with a bleak blue nose over a chafing-dish of starved embers, and dining behind a traverse rag, in a shop no bigger than a bird-cage!—Go, go! starve again, do, do!

Foib. Dear madam, I 'll beg pardon on my knees.

Lady Wish. Away! out! out!—Go, set up for yourself again!—Do, drive a trade, do, with your three-pennyworth of small ware, flaunting upon a packthread, under a brandy-seller's bulk, or against a dead wall by a ballad-monger! Go, hang out an old Frisoneer gorget, with a yard of yellow colbertine again! Do; an old gnawed mask, two rows of pins, and a child's fiddle; a glass necklace with the beads broken, and a quilted night-cap with one ear! Go, go, drive a trade!—These were your commodities, you treacherous trull! this was your merchandise you dealt in when I took you into my house, placed you next myself, and made you governante of my whole family! You have forgot this, have you, now you have feathered your nest?

Foib. No, no, dear madam. Do but hear me, have but a moment's patience, I 'll confess all. Mr. Mirabell seduced me; I am not the first that he has wheedled with his dissembling tongue; your ladyship's own wisdom has been deluded by him; then how should I, a poor ignorant, defend myself? O madam, if you knew but what he promised me, and how he assured me your ladyship should come to no damage!—Or else the wealth of the Indies should not have bribed me to conspire against so good, so sweet, so kind a lady as you have been to me.

Lady Wish. No damage! What, to betray me, to marry me to a cast servingman! to make me a receptacle, an hospital for a decayed pimp! No damage! O thou frontless impudence, more than a big-bellied actress!

Foib. Pray, do but hear me, madam; he

[85] *i.e.*, errant.

could not marry your ladyship, madam. —No, indeed, his marriage was to have been void in law, for he was married to me first, to secure your ladyship. He could not have bedded your ladyship; for if he had consummated with your ladyship, he must have run the risk of the law, and been put upon his clergy.[86]—Yes, indeed, I inquired of the law in that case before I would meddle or make.

Lady Wish. What, then, I have been your property, have I? I have been convenient to you, it seems!—While you were catering for Mirabell, I have been broker for you! What, have you made a passive bawd of me?—This exceeds all precedent; I am brought to fine uses, to become a botcher of second-hand marriages between Abigails and Andrews![87]—I'll couple you!—Yes, I'll baste you together, you and your Philander! I'll Duke's-place you, as I'm a person! Your turtle is in custody already: you shall coo in the same cage, if there be constable or warrant in the parish.

(*Exit.*)

Foib. Oh, that ever I was born! Oh, that I was ever married!—A bride!—ay, I shall be a Bridewell-bride.—Oh!

(*Enter Mrs. Fainall.*)

Mrs. Fain. Poor Foible, what's the matter?

Foib. O madam, my lady's gone for a constable. I shall be had to a justice, and put to Bridewell to beat hemp. Poor Waitwell's gone to prison already.

Mrs. Fain. Have a good heart, Foible; Mirabell's gone to give security for him. This is all Marwood's and my husband's doing.

Foib. Yes, yes; I know it, madam: she was in my lady's closet, and overheard all that you said to me before dinner. She sent the letter to my lady; and that missing effect, Mr. Fainall laid this plot to arrest Waitwell, when he pretended to go for the papers; and in the meantime Mrs. Marwood declared all to my lady.

Mrs. Fain. Was there no mention made of me in the letter? My mother does not suspect my being in the confederacy? I fancy Marwood has not told her, though she has told my husband.

Foib. Yes, madam; but my lady did not see that part; we stifled the letter before she read so far.—Has that mischievous devil told Mr. Fainall of your ladyship, then?

Mrs. Fain. Ay, all's out—my affair with Mirabell—everything discovered. This is the last day of our living together, that's my comfort.

Foib. Indeed, madam; and so 't is a comfort if you knew all;—he has been even with your ladyship, which I could have told you long enough since, but I love to keep peace and quietness by my good-will. I had rather bring friends together, than set 'em at distance: but Mrs. Marwood and he are nearer related than ever their parents thought for.

Mrs. Fain. Sayest thou so, Foible? Canst thou prove this?

Foib. I can take my oath of it, madam; so can Mrs. Mincing. We have had many a fair word from Madam Marwood, to conceal something that passed in our chamber one evening when you were at Hyde Park; and we were thought to have gone a-walking, but we went up unawares;—though we were sworn to secrecy, too. Madam Marwood took a book and swore us upon it, but it was but a book of verses and poems. So long as it was not a bible-oath, we may break it with a safe conscience.

Mrs. Fain. This discovery is the most opportune thing I could wish.—Now, Mincing!

(*Enter Mincing.*)

Min. My lady would speak with Mrs. Foible, mem. Mr. Mirabell is with her; he has set your spouse at liberty, Mrs. Foible, and would have you hide yourself in my lady's closet till my old lady's anger is abated. Oh, my old lady is in a perilous passion at something Mr. Fainall has said; he swears, and my old lady cries. There's a fearful hurricane, I vow. He says, mem, how that he'll have my lady's fortune made over to him, or he'll be divorced.

Mrs. Fain. Does your lady and Mirabell know that?

Min. Yes, mem; they have sent me to see if Sir Wilfull be sober, and to bring him to them. My lady is resolved to have him, I think, rather than lose such a vast sum as six thousand pound.—Oh, come, Mrs. Foible, I hear my old lady.

Mrs. Fain. Foible, you must tell Mincing that she must prepare to vouch when I call her.

86 *i. e.*, have been arraigned (had to claim benefit of clergy).

87 Maids and valets.

Foib. Yes, yes, madam.

Min. Oh, yes, mem, I'll vouch anything for your ladyship's service, be what it will.

(*Exeunt Mincing and Foible.*)

(*Enter Lady Wishfort, and Mrs. Marwood.*)

Lady Wish. Oh, my dear friend, how can I enumerate the benefits that I have received from your goodness! To you I owe the timely discovery of the false vows of Mirabell; to you the detection of the impostor Sir Rowland. And now you are become an intercessor with my son-in-law, to save the honor of my house, and compound for the frailties of my daughter. Well, friend, you are enough to reconcile me to the bad world, or else I would retire to deserts and solitudes, and feed harmless sheep by groves and purling streams. Dear Marwood, let us leave the world, and retire by ourselves and be shepherdesses.

Mrs. Mar. Let us first dispatch the affair in hand, madam. We shall have leisure to think of retirement afterwards. Here is one who is concerned in the treaty.

Lady Wish. Oh, daughter, daughter! is it possible thou shouldst be my child, bone of my bone, and flesh of my flesh, and, as I may say, another me, and yet transgress the most minute particle of severe virtue? Is it possible you should lean aside to iniquity, who have been cast in the direct mould of virtue? I have not only been a mould but a pattern for you, and a model for you, after you were brought into the world.

Mrs. Fain. I don't understand your ladyship.

Lady Wish. Not understand! Why, have you not been naught? [88] have you not been sophisticated? Not understand! here I am ruined to compound for your caprices and your cuckoldoms. I must pawn my plate and my jewels, and ruin my niece, and all little enough—

Mrs. Fain. I am wronged and abused, and so are you. 'T is a false accusation, as false as hell, as false as your friend there, ay, or your friend's friend, my false husband.

Mrs. Mar. My friend, Mrs. Fainall! your husband my friend! what do you mean?

Mrs. Fain. I know what I mean, madam, and so do you; and so shall the world at a time convenient.

Mrs. Mar. I am sorry to see you so passionate, madam. More temper [89] would look more like innocence. But I have done. I am sorry my zeal to serve your ladyship and family should admit of misconstruction, or make me liable to affronts. You will pardon me, madam, if I meddle no more with an affair in which I am not personally concerned.

Lady Wish. O dear friend, I am so ashamed that you should meet with such returns!—(*To Mrs. Fainall.*) You ought to ask pardon on your knees, ungrateful creature! she deserves more from you than all your life can accomplish.—(*To Mrs. Marwood.*) Oh, don't leave me destitute in this perplexity!—no, stick to me, my good genius.

Mrs. Fain. I tell you, madam, you're abused.—Stick to you; ay, like a leech, to suck your best blood—she'll drop off when she's full. Madam, you sha'not pawn a bodkin, nor part with a brass counter, in composition for me. I defy 'em all. Let 'em prove their aspersions; I know my own innocence, and dare stand a trial.

(*Exit.*)

Lady Wish. Why, if she should be innocent, if she should be wronged after all, ha?—I don't know what to think;—and I promise you her education has been unexceptionable—I may say it; for I chiefly made it my own care to initiate her very infancy in the rudiments of virtue, and to impress upon her tender years a young odium and aversion to the very sight of men: ay, friend, she would ha' shrieked if she had but seen a man, till she was in her teens. As I'm a person 't is true;—she was never suffered to play with a male child, though but in coats; nay, her very babies [90] were of the feminine gender. Oh, she never looked a man in the face but her own father, or the chaplain, and him we made a shift to put upon her for a woman, by the help of his long garments, and his sleek face, till she was going in her fifteen.

Mrs. Mar. 'T was much she should be deceived so long.

Lady Wish. I warrant you, or she would never have borne to have been catechized by him; and have heard his long lectures against singing and dancing, and such debaucheries; and going to filthy plays, and profane music-meetings, where the lewd trebles squeak nothing but bawdy,

88 Frail, no better than you should be.

89 composure.

90 dolls

and the basses roar blasphemy. Oh, she would have swooned at the sight or name of an obscene play-book!—and can I think, after all this, that my daughter can be naught? What, a whore? and thought it excommunication to set her foot within the door of a playhouse! O dear friend, I can't believe it, no, no! As she says, let him prove it, let him prove it.

Mrs. Mar. Prove it, madam! What, and have your name prostituted in a public court! Yours and your daughter's reputation worried at the bar by a pack of bawling lawyers! To be ushered in with an *O Yez*[91] of scandal; and have your case opened by an old fumbling lecher in a quoif[92] like a man-midwife; to bring your daughter's infamy to light; to be a theme for legal punsters and quibblers by the statute; and become a jest against a rule of court, where there is no precedent for a jest in any record—not even in doomsday-book;[93] to discompose the gravity of the bench, and provoke naughty interrogatories in more naughty law Latin; while the good judge, tickled with the proceeding, simpers under a grey beard, and fidges[94] off and on his cushion as if he had swallowed cantharides, or sat upon cow-itch!—

Lady Wish. Oh, 't is very hard!

Mrs. Mar. And then to have my young revellers of the Temple take notes, like 'prentices at a conventicle; and after talk it over again in commons, or before drawers in an eating-house.

Lady Wish. Worse and worse!

Mrs. Mar. Nay, this is nothing; if it would end here 't were well. But it must, after this, be consigned by the shorthand writers to the public press; and from thence be transferred to the hands, nay into the throats and lungs of hawkers, with voices more licentious than the loud flounder-man's or the woman that cries grey-pease; and this you must hear till you are stunned; nay, you must hear nothing else for some days.

Lady Wish. Oh, 't is insupportable! No, no, dear friend, make it up, make it up; ay, ay, I'll compound. I'll give up all, myself and my all, my niece and her all—anything, everything for composition.

Mrs. Mar. Nay, madam, I advise nothing, I only lay before you, as a friend, the inconveniences which perhaps you have overseen. Here comes Mr. Fainall; if he will be satisfied to huddle up all in silence, I shall be glad. You must think I would rather congratulate than condole with you.

(*Enter Fainall.*)

Lady Wish. Ay, ay, I do not doubt it, dear Marwood; no, no, I do not doubt it.

Fain. Well, madam; I have suffered myself to be overcome by the importunity of this lady your friend; and am content you shall enjoy your own proper estate during life, on condition you oblige yourself never to marry, under such penalty as I think convenient.

Lady Wish. Never to marry!

Fain. No more Sir Rowlands; the next imposture may not be so timely detected.

Mrs. Mar. That condition, I dare answer, my lady will consent to without difficulty; she has already but too much experienced the perfidiousness of men.—Besides, madam, when we retire to our pastoral solitude we shall bid adieu to all other thoughts.

Lady Wish. Ay, that 's true; but in case of necessity, as of health, or some such emergency—

Fain. Oh, if you are prescribed marriage, you shall be considered; I will only reserve to myself the power to choose for you. If your physic be wholesome, it matters not who is your apothecary. Next, my wife shall settle on me the remainder of her fortune, not made over already; and for her maintenance depend entirely on my discretion.

Lady Wish. This is most inhumanly savage; exceeding the barbarity of a Muscovite husband.

Fain. I learned it from his Czarish majesty's retinue, in a winter evening's conference over brandy and pepper, amongst other secrets of matrimony and policy, as they are at present practised in the northern hemisphere. But this must be agreed unto, and that positively. Lastly, I will be endowed, in right of my wife, with that six thousand pound, which is the moiety of Mrs. Millamant's fortune in your possession; and which she has forfeited (as will appear by the last will and testament of your deceased husband, Sir Jonathan Wishfort) by her disobedi-

91 *Oyez* (French, *hear ye*), used to proclaim silence at the opening of court.

92 A white cap formerly worn by lawyers.

93 A record of land dating from the reign of William the Conqueror; an unlikely place for a jest.

94 *Fidge*, to move restlessly, fidget.

ence in contracting herself against your consent or knowledge; and by refusing the offered match with Sir Wilfull Witwoud, which you, like a careful aunt, had provided for her.

Lady Wish. My nephew was *non compos,*[95] and could not make his addresses.

Fain. I come to make demands—I'll hear no objections.

Lady Wish. You will grant me time to consider?

Fain. Yes, while the instrument is drawing, to which you must set your hand till more sufficient deeds can be perfected: which I will take care shall be done with all possible speed. In the meanwhile I will go for the said instrument, and till my return you may balance this matter in your own discretion.

(*Exit.*)

Lady Wish. This insolence is beyond all precedent, all parallel: must I be subject to this merciless villain?

Mrs. Mar. 'T is severe indeed, madam, that you should smart for your daughter's wantonness.

Lady Wish. 'T was against my consent that she married this barbarian, but she would have him, though her year was not out.—Ah! her first husband, my son Languish, would not have carried it thus. Well, that was my choice, this is hers: she is matched now with a witness.—I shall be mad, dear friend, is there no comfort for me? must I live to be confiscated at this rebel-rate?—Here come two more of my Egyptian plagues too.

(*Enter Millamant and Sir Wilfull.*)

Sir Wil. Aunt, your servant.

Lady Wish. Out, caterpillar, call not me aunt! I know thee not!

Sir Wil. I confess I have been a little in disguise, as they say.—S'heart! and I'm sorry for 't. What would you have? I hope I committed no offence, aunt—and if I did I am willing to make satisfaction; and what can a man say fairer? If I have broke anything I'll pay for 't, an it cost a pound. And so let that content for what 's past, and make no more words. For what 's to come, to pleasure you I 'm willing to marry my cousin. So pray let 's all be friends; she and I are agreed upon the matter before a witness.

Lady Wish. How 's this, dear niece? Have I any comfort? Can this be true?

Mrs. Mil. I am content to be a sacrifice to your repose, madam; and to convince you that I had no hand in the plot, as you were misinformed, I have laid my commands on Mirabell to come in person, and be a witness that I give my hand to this flower of knighthood: and for the contract that passed between Mirabell and me, I have obliged him to make a resignation of it in your ladyship's presence;—he is without, and waits your leave for admittance.

Lady Wish. Well, I'll swear I am something revived at this testimony of your obedience: but I cannot admit that traitor.—I fear I cannot fortify myself to support his appearance. He is as terrible to me as a gorgon; if I see him I fear I shall turn to stone, and petrify incessantly.

Mrs. Mil. If you disoblige him, he may resent your refusal, and insist upon the contract still. Then 't is the last time he will be offensive to you.

Lady Wish. Are you sure it will be the last time?—If I were sure of that—shall I never see him again?

Mrs. Mil. Sir Wilfull, you and he are to travel together, are you not?

Sir. Wil. S'heart, the gentleman 's a civil gentleman, aunt, let him come in; why, we are sworn brothers and fellow-travellers.—We are to be Pylades and Orestes, he and I.—He is to be my interpreter in foreign parts. He has been over-seas once already; and with proviso that I marry my cousin, will cross 'em once again, only to bear me company.—S'heart, I'll call him in,—an I set on 't once, he shall come in; and see who 'll hinder him.

(*Exit.*)

Mrs. Mar. This is precious fooling, if it would pass; but I'll know the bottom of it.

Lady Wish. O dear Marwood, you are not going?

Mrs. Mar. Not far, madam; I'll return immediately.

(*Exit.*)

(*Re-enter Sir Wilfull and Mirabell.*)

Sir Wil. Look up, man, I'll stand by you; 'sbud,[96] an she do frown, she can't kill you; besides—harkee, she dare not frown desperately, because her face is none of her own. S'heart, an she should, her forehead would wrinkle like the coat

95 Not himself (not sober).

96 A corrupted oath.

of a cream-cheese; but mum for that, fellow-traveller.

Mir. If a deep sense of the many injuries I have offered to so good a lady, with a sincere remorse, and a hearty contrition, can but obtain the least glance of compassion, I am too happy.—Ah, madam, there was a time!—but let it be forgotten—I confess I have deservedly forfeited the high place I once held of sighing at your feet. Nay, kill me not, by turning from me in disdain.—I come not to plead for favor; nay, not for pardon; I am a suppliant only for your pity—I am going where I never shall behold you more—

Sir Wil. How, fellow-traveller! you shall go by yourself then.

Mir. Let me be pitied first, and afterwards forgotten.—I ask no more.

Sir Wil. By'r Lady, a very reasonable request, and will cost you nothing, aunt! Come, come, forgive and forget, aunt. Why, you must, an you are a Christian.

Mir. Consider, madam, in reality, you could not receive much prejudice; it was an innocent device; though I confess it had a face of guiltiness,—it was at most an artifice which love contrived; and errors which love produces have ever been accounted venial. At least think it is punishment enough, that I have lost what in my heart I hold most dear, that to your cruel indignation I have offered up this beauty, and with her my peace and quiet; nay, all my hopes of future comfort.

Sir Wil. An he does not move me, would I may never be o' the quorum![97]—an it were not as good a deed as to drink, to give her to him again, I would I might never take shipping!—Aunt, if you don't forgive quickly, I shall melt, I can tell you that. My contract went no farther than a little mouth glue, and that 's hardly dry;—one doleful sigh more from my fellow-traveller, and 't is dissolved.

Lady Wish. Well, nephew, upon your account—Ah, he has a false insinuating tongue!—Well, sir, I will stifle my just resentment at my nephew's request.—I will endeavor what I can to forget, but on proviso that you resign the contract with my niece immediately.

Mir. It is in writing, and with papers of concern; but I have sent my servant for it, and will deliver it to you, with all acknowledgments for your transcendent goodness.

Lady Wish. Oh, he has witchcraft in his eyes and tongue!—When I did not see him, I could have bribed a villain to his assassination; but his appearance rakes the embers which have so long lain smothered in my breast.

(*Apart.*)

(*Enter Fainall and Mrs. Marwood.*)

Fain. Your date of deliberation, madam, is expired. Here is the instrument; are you prepared to sign?

Lady Wish. If I were prepared, I am not impowered. My niece exerts a lawful claim, having matched herself by my direction to Sir Wilfull.

Fain. That sham is too gross to pass on me—though 't is imposed on you, madam.

Mrs. Mil. Sir, I have given my consent.

Mir. And, sir, I have resigned my pretensions.

Sir Wil. And, sir, I assert my right: and will maintain it in defiance of you, sir, and of your instrument. S'heart, an you talk of an instrument, sir, I have an old fox[98] by my thigh that shall hack your instrument of ram vellum to shreds, sir! It shall not be sufficient for a mittimus[99] or a tailor's measure. Therefore withdraw your instrument, sir, or by'r Lady, I shall draw mine.

Lady Wish. Hold, nephew, hold!

Mrs. Mil. Good Sir Wilfull, respite your valor.

Fain. Indeed! Are you provided of your guard, with your single beef-eater there? but I'm prepared for you, and insist upon my first proposal. You shall submit your own estate to my management, and absolutely make over my wife's to my sole use. As pursuant to the purport and tenor of this other covenant, I suppose, madam, your consent is not requisite in this case; nor, Mr. Mirabell, your resignation; nor, Sir Wilfull, your right. —You may draw your fox if you please, sir, and make a bear-garden flourish somewhere else: for here it will not avail. This, my Lady Wishfort, must be subscribed, or your darling daughter's turned adrift, like a leaky hulk, to sink or swim, as she and the current of this lewd town can agree.

Lady Wish. Is there no means, no rem-

97 Sit as one of the justices of the peace.

98 sword.

99 Order for some one's imprisonment, addressed to the keeper of a prison.

edy to stop my ruin? Ungrateful wretch! dost thou not owe thy being, thy subsistence, to my daughter's fortune?

Fain. I'll answer you when I have the rest of it in my possession.

Mir. But that you would not accept of a remedy from my hands—I own I have not deserved you should owe any obligation to me; or else perhaps I could advise—

Lady Wish. O, what? what? To save me and my child from ruin, from want, I'll forgive all that's past; nay, I'll consent to anything to come, to be delivered from this tyranny.

Mir. Ay, madam; but that is too late, my reward is intercepted. You have disposed of her who only could have made me a compensation for all my services; but be it as it may, I am resolved I'll serve you! you shall not be wronged in this savage manner.

Lady Wish. How! dear Mr. Mirabell, can you be so generous at last! But it is not possible. Harkee, I'll break my nephew's match; you shall have my niece yet, and all her fortune, if you can but save me from this imminent danger.

Mir. Will you? I take you at your word, I ask no more. I must have leave for two criminals to appear.

Lady Wish. Ay, ay, anybody, anybody!

Mir. Foible is one, and a penitent.

(*Enter Mrs. Fainall, Foible, and Mincing.*)

Mrs. Mar. Oh, my shame! (*Mirabell and Lady Wishfort go to Mrs. Fainall and Foible.*) These corrupt things are bought and brought hither to expose me. (*To Fainall.*)

Fain. If it must all come out, why let 'em know it; 't is but the way of the world. That shall not urge me to relinquish or abate one tittle of my terms; no, I will insist the more.

Foib. Yes, indeed, madam, I'll take my bible-oath of it.

Min. And so will I, mem.

Lady Wish. O Marwood, Marwood, art thou false? my friend deceive me! hast thou been a wicked accomplice with that profligate man?

Mrs. Mar. Have you so much ingratitude and injustice to give credit against your friend, to the aspersions of two such mercenary trulls?

Min. Mercenary, mem? I scorn your words. 'T is true we found you and Mr. Fainall in the blue garret; by the same token, you swore us to secrecy upon Messalinas's [1] poems. Mercenary! No, if we would have been mercenary, we should have held our tongues; you would have bribed us sufficiently.

Fain. Go, you are an insignificant thing! —Well, what are you the better for this; is this Mr. Mirabell's expedient? I'll be put off no longer.—You thing, that was a wife, shall smart for this! I will not leave thee wherewithal to hide thy shame; your body shall be as naked as your reputation.

Mrs. Fain. I despise you, and defy your malice!—you have aspersed me wrongfully—I have proved your falsehood—go, you and your treacherous—I will not name it, but starve together—perish!

Fain. Not while you are worth a groat, indeed, my dear.—Madam, I'll be fooled no longer.

Lady Wish. Ah, Mr. Mirabell, this is small comfort, the detection of this affair.

Mir. Oh, in good time—your leave for the other offender and penitent to appear, madam.

(*Enter Waitwell with a box of writings.*)

Lady Wish. O Sir Rowland!—Well, rascal!

Wait. What your ladyship pleases. I have brought the black box at last, madam.

Mir. Give it me.—Madam, you remember your promise.

Lady Wish. Ay, dear sir.

Mir. Where are the gentlemen?

Wait. At hand, sir, rubbing their eyes—just risen from sleep.

Fain. 'Sdeath, what's this to me? I'll not wait your private concerns.

(*Enter Petulant and Witwoud.*)

Pet. How now? What's the matter? Whose hand's out?

Wit. Heyday! what, are you all got together, like players at the end of the last act?

Mir. You may remember, gentlemen, I once requested your hands at witnesses to a certain parchment.

Wit. Ay, I do, my hand I remember—Petulant set his mark.

Mir. You wrong him, his name is fairly written, as shall appear.—You do not remember, gentlemen, anything of what that parchment contained?— (*Undoing the box.*)

[1] Of course Messalina, the wife of the Emperor Claudius, left no poems; but Congreve's joke is that she was a very vicious woman.

Wit. No.

Pet. Not I; I writ, I read nothing.

Mir. Very well, now you shall know.—Madam, your promise.

Lady Wish. Ay, ay, sir, upon my honor.

Mir. Mr. Fainall, it is now time that you should know that your lady, while she was at her own disposal, and before you had by your insinuations wheedled her out of a pretended settlement of the greatest part of her fortune—

Fain. Sir! pretended!

Mir. Yes, sir. I say that this lady while a widow, having it seems received some cautions respecting your inconstancy and tyranny of temper, which from her own partial opinion and fondness of you she could never have suspected—she did, I say, by the wholesome advice of friends, and of sages learned in the laws of this land, deliver this same as her act and deed to me in trust, and to the uses within mentioned. You may read if you please—(*Holding out the parchment*) though perhaps what is inscribed on the back may serve your occasions.

Fain. Very likely, sir. What's here?—Damnation! (*Reads.*) *A deed of conveyance of the whole estate real of Arabella Languish, widow, in trust to Edward Mirabell.*—Confusion!

Mir. Even so, sir; 't is the way of the world, sir, of the widows of the world. I suppose this deed may bear an elder date than what you have obtained from your lady.

Fain. Perfidious fiend! then thus I'll be revenged.

(*Offers to run at Mrs. Fainall.*)

Sir Wil. Hold, sir! Now you may make your bear-garden flourish somewhere else, sir.

Fain. Mirabell, you shall hear of this, sir, be sure you shall.—Let me pass, oaf![2]

(*Exit.*)

Mrs. Fain. Madam, you seem to stifle your resentment; you had better give it vent.

Mrs. Mar. Yes, it shall have vent—and to your confusion; or I'll perish in the attempt.

(*Exit.*)

Lady Wish. O daughter, daughter! 'T is plain thou hast inherited thy mother's prudence.

Mrs. Fain. Thank Mr. Mirabell, a cautious friend, to whose advice all is owing.

Lady Wish. Well, Mr. Mirabell, you have kept your promise—and I must perform mine.—First, I pardon, for your sake, Sir Rowland there, and Foible; the next thing is to break the matter to my nephew—and how to do that—

Mir. For that, madam, give yourself no trouble; let me have your consent. Sir Wilfull is my friend; he has had compassion upon lovers, and generously engaged a volunteer in this action, for our service; and now designs to prosecute his travels.

Sir Wil. S'heart, aunt, I have no mind to marry. My cousin 's a fine lady, and the gentleman loves her, and she loves him, and they deserve one another; my resolution is to see foreign parts—I have set on 't—and when I 'm set on 't I must do 't. And if these two gentlemen would travel too, I think they may be spared.

Pet. For my part, I say little—I think things are best off or on.[3]

Wit. I'gad, I understand nothing of the matter; I 'm in a maze yet, like a dog in a dancing-school.

Lady Wish. Well, sir, take her, and with her all the joy I can give you.

Mrs. Mil. Why does not the man take me? Would you have me give myself to you over again?

Mir. Ay, and over and over again; for (*Kisses her hand*) I would have you as often as possibly I can. Well, Heaven grant I love you not too well, that 's all my fear.

Sir Wil. S'heart, you'll have him time enough to toy after you 're married; or if you will toy now, let us have a dance in the meantime, that we who are not lovers may have some other employment besides looking on.

Mir. With all my heart, dear Sir Wilfull. What shall we do for music?

Foib. Oh, sir, some that were provided for Sir Rowland's entertainment are yet within call.

(*A dance.*)

Lady Wish. As I am a person, I can hold out no longer; I have wasted my spirits so to-day already, that I am ready to sink under the fatigue; and I cannot but have some fears upon me yet, that my son Fainall will pursue some desperate course.

Mir. Madam, disquiet not yourself on that account; to my knowledge his circumstances are such he must of force comply. For my part, I will contribute all that in me lies to a reunion; in the meantime,

2 dolt, booby.

3 Either one way or the other.

madam, let me—(*To Mrs. Fainall*) before these witnesses restore to you this deed of trust: it may be a means, well-managed, to make you live easily together.

From hence let those be warned, who mean to wed;
Lest mutual falsehood stain the bridal bed;
For each deceiver to his cost may find
That marriage-frauds too oft are paid in kind.

(*Exeunt omnes.*)

EPILOGUE.

Spoken by Mrs. Bracegirdle.

After our Epilogue this crowd dismisses,
I 'm thinking how this play 'll be pulled to pieces.
But pray consider, ere you doom its fall,
How hard a thing 't would be to please you all.
There are some critics so with spleen diseased,
They scarcely come inclining to be pleased:
And sure he must have more than mortal skill,
Who pleases any one against his will.
Then all bad poets we are sure are foes,
And how their number 's swelled, the town well knows:
In shoals I 've marked 'em judging in the pit;
Though they 're, on no pretence, for judgment fit,
But that they have been damned for want of wit.
Since when, they by their own offences taught,
Set up for spies on plays, and finding fault.
Others there are whose malice we 'd prevent;
Such who watch plays with scurrilous intent
To mark out who by characters are meant.
And though no perfect likeness they can trace,
Yet each pretends to know the copied face.
These with false glosses feed their own ill nature,
And turn to libel what was meant a satire.
May such malicious fops this fortune find,
To think themselves alone the fools designed:
If any are so arrogantly vain,
To think they singly can support a scene,
And furnish fool enough to entertain.
For well the learn'd and the judicious know
That satire scorns to stoop so meanly low,
As any one abstracted fop to show,
For, as when painters form a matchless face,
They from each fair one catch some different grace;
And shining features in one portrait blend,
To which no single beauty must pretend;
So poets oft do in one piece expose
Whole *belles-assemblees* of coquettes and beaux.

IV. THE EIGHTEENTH CENTURY

JOSEPH ADDISON

CATO

Joseph Addison (1672–1719), distinguished himself at Oxford for "elegant scholarship," knowledge of Latin poetry, and skill in composing it. He first rose to prominence through his poem, *The Campaign* (1704), which celebrated Marlborough's victory at Blenheim, and for which the Whigs gave him a government office. He was in Parliament from 1708 till his death, and became a Secretary of State. In a literary way he is best known, of course, for his essays, of a somewhat fresh type, the short familiar essay, contributed especially to *The Tatler* and *The Spectator* (1709–12).

The eighteenth century, though not highly distinguished in drama, was notably an era of comedy. Its best work followed the example less of the Elizabethan than of the Restoration comic writers, but raised their moral tone. The chief new feature in comedy was the taste for the superficially ethical and emotional, generally known as sentimentalism. In tragedy the age did not excel. Addison's *Cato* is the most celebrated tragedy, and as representative as any.

Cato, mostly written as early as 1703, was finished, performed in London twenty times and published in eight editions, in 1713. As a curious illustration of the lack of historical knowledge and imagination in that day, it is interesting to know that (in Macaulay's words) "Juba's waistcoat blazed with gold lace; Marcia's hoop was worthy of a Duchess on the birthday; and Cato wore a wig worth fifty guineas." The play was based on Plutarch's life of Cato, and perhaps on reminiscences of a poor tragedy which Addison had seen in Venice. Its great success with both spectators and readers was partly due to Addison's prestige and the loyalty of his friends, partly to its merits, partly to circumstances. Though he disclaimed partizan intentions, the play was timely. The end of Queen Anne's reign was approaching (she died in 1714), there was no direct heir, and the prospective coming of the Hanoverian dynasty involved danger to English liberty through insurrections in favor of the tyrannical Stuarts, such as actually followed in 1715. A play exciting sympathy for old Roman liberty was sure of attention. The Whigs, Dr. Johnson said, applauded all references to freedom, and the Tories applauded just as loudly lest they should be thought less zealous in its behalf. The Duke of Marlborough's attempt to gain the office of Captain General for life was felt to give point to Cato's denunciation of Cæsar the military dictator. Though some critics felt the play, as we do, to be undramatic, its success at the time passed into permanent appreciation; Voltaire praised it as the first regular English tragedy, because it followed French rules (an outward and visible sign of which is its observance of the French practice of beginning a new scene on an important exit or entrance); and its popularity in the past is shown by numerous bits which have become proverbial, such as

> The woman that deliberates is lost,

and

> Plato, thou reason'st well.

But taste has changed; the play in our time would be impossible to put on the stage, and is read chiefly because Addison wrote it.

Addison was looked up to in his own age as a man of high character, perfect taste, and highly developed sense of propriety, but lacked the spontaneity and warmth for the love of which some men will readily forgive lapses from propriety, taste, and even virtue. It would excite an unfair prejudice against him to compare him to a Pharisee or the Prodigal Son's elder brother, for his caution and moderation were due to his modesty and diffidence, and all testify to his personal charm; but he was more akin to them than to the Publican or the Prodigal himself. He had another side, which expressed itself in the grace, the gentle irony, the human nature, of his essays. But he was well fitted to determine and express the more ambitious literary orthodoxy of the age of Queen Anne, a classicism Latin and critical rather than Greek and original, uninterested in feeling, restrained, dignified. The more formal literary ideals of the age, and the personality of Addison, are not unfairly represented by *Cato*.

No criticism of it has oftener been made than that it is emotionally frigid, and the charge is true. None of the characters excites vivid interest, none except Cato excites much sympathy. Hardest of all for us is to give ourselves up to the love-episodes. A man whose first known love-affair was at the age of forty-four with an elderly widowed peeress was perhaps not likely to excel in portraying passion. When Sempronius, Juba, and Marcia, Portius, Marcus, and Lucia talk, and even when they rant, we have to take their word for it that they are in love. There is not one of those simple natural phrases which show a poet's insight, not one syllable which speaks the language of the heart. The language of emotion in poetry of course is not always necessarily that of emotion in real life; Romeo speaks not as a lover would, but as a romantic lover would if he could. But no lover would wish to speak as Addison's do. The polished style, faultily faultless some call it, indirect and highly literary, heightens the sense of coolness, but the feeling throughout is one of detachment.

The composition of the play is what we might expect of the early eighteenth century, and of Addison. More than at any other time men felt then that literary art might be produced by rule rather than by inspiration. Addison had no innate dramatic gift, and little dramatic experience. The creator of Sir Roger de Coverley might have done well in comedy, especially in a delicate and subtle kind such as was scarcely written in the eighteenth century. His literary convictions, rather than his genius, drew him to tragedy. Even in his day the play was censured as not well constructed. The love-stories have little to do with the main action, yet most of what suspense and surprise exists is in them. The strict observance of the unities of time and place leads to an artificiality. Yet throughout we can see conscientious and well-informed workmanship, according to classical taste. The characters may not be vividly human or individual, but still they are clearly and broadly distinguished from each other. Portius is cool and reflective, Marcus is emotional. Juba the Numidian has the fiery impulsiveness commonly associated with the south. The treachery of Sempronius and Syphax are well motivated. Addison follows the convention of giving his various characters confidantes, by conversation with whom their feelings are disclosed to the audience without excessive use of the artificial soliloquy. He also complied in this play with the preference of the modern classicists for dealing out strict poetic justice, so that all shall end as nearly as possible in complete satisfaction. This they esteemed more than the crash of ruin, involving guilty and innocent alike, with which Elizabethan tragedy ends, and from which the spectator almost feels that he himself has barely escaped, alive but shaken. In *Cato* the traitors meet their deserved harsh end, which we relish the more for Sempronius because of his carelessness and stupidity. The good Marcus by a heroic death escapes the pain he could not have avoided receiving and giving, had he lived to learn that his brother was his favored rival. Cato's willing death was his only way out of a situation impossible for him. Nothing better than this play could illustrate the fundamental optimism of the eighteenth century, the most optimistic because the most theoretical period in history.

One truth is clear, Whatever is, is right,

announced its greatest English poet; and people expected literary art to support their faith that this was a truth.

The most permanently valuable thing in the play, which enables us still to read it with esteem if not with admiration, is the stately pathos of the central situation — the grand old man of Rome at the end of the strait and narrow path whence he had never deviated, and finding an impassable wall; and his calm acceptance of the only way out; though Addison makes a concession to Christian morals at the end, where Cato regrets his suicide when it is too late, and there is a tragic irony in the summons to him as he is dying to lead the forces of Pompey against Cæsar. In portraying Cato Addison had not to make the effort which he could not conceal in the love-scenes. And here his calm style is not out of place. Cato is hardly a dramatic hero, for he has no struggle, and the emotions he excites are hardly those that warm; the average playgoer is unfortunately but little stirred by "inward greatness, unaffected wisdom, and sanctity of manners." But Addison's tribute is no less sincere and worthy than Dante's. In the *Purgatorio* the greatest of Christian poets, who has just witnessed the pains of suicides and pagans in hell, places this pagan suicide as the director of righteous souls upon the path of complete purification; this he did because he regarded Cato as the type of perfect freedom of the will, which Dante exalts throughout his poem. Addison's Cato, though the world and the future may be against him, is firm in his convictions. As a late Roman poet says,

Victrix causa deis placuit, sed victa Catoni.

CATO

A Tragedy

PROLOGUE.

By Mr. Pope.

To wake the soul by tender strokes of art,
To raise the genius and to mend the heart,
To make mankind in conscious virtue bold,
Live o'er each scene, and be what they behold;—
For this the tragic muse first trod the stage,
Commanding tears to stream through every age;
Tyrants no more their savage nature kept,
And foes to virtue wondered how they wept.
Our author shuns by vulgar springs to move
The hero's glory, or the virgin's love,
In pitying love, we but our weakness show,
And wild ambition well deserves its woe.
Here tears shall flow from a more generous cause,
Such tears as patriots shed for dying laws.
He bids your breasts with ancient ardor rise,
And calls forth Roman drops from British eyes.
Virtue confessed in human shape he draws,
What Plato thought, and godlike Cato was:
No common object to your sight displays,
But, what with pleasure heaven itself surveys,
A brave man struggling in the storms of fate,
And greatly falling with a falling state!
While Cato gives his little senate laws,
What bosom beats not in his country's cause?
Who sees him act, but envies every deed?
Who hears him groan, and does not wish to bleed?
Ev'n when proud Cæsar, 'midst triumphal cars,
The spoils of nations, and the pomp of wars,
Ignobly vain, and impotently great,
Showed Rome her Cato's figure drawn in state;
As her dead father's reverend image past,
The pomp was darkened, and the day o'ercast,
The triumph ceased—tears gushed from every eye,
The world's great victor passed unheeded by;
Her last good man dejected Rome adored,
And honored Cæsar's less than Cato's sword.
Britons, attend: be worth like this approved,
And show you have the virtue to be moved.
With honest scorn the first famed Cato viewed
Rome learning arts from Greece, whom she subdued.
Our scene precariously subsists too long
On French translation, and Italian song:
Dare to have sense yourselves; assert the stage,
Be justly warmed with your own native rage.
Such plays alone should please a British ear,
As Cato's self had not disdained to hear.

DRAMATIS PERSONÆ

MEN

CATO.
LUCIUS, *a Senator.*
SEMPRONIUS, *a Senator.*
JUBA, *Prince of Numidia.*
SYPHAX, *General of the Numidians.*
PORTIUS, } *Sons of* CATO.
MARCUS, }
DECIUS, *Ambassador from Cæsar.*
Mutineers, Guards, etc.

WOMEN

MARCIA, *Daughter to* CATO.
LUCIA, *Daughter to* LUCIUS

SCENE.—A Large Hall in the Governor's Palace of Utica.

ACT I.

Scene 1.

(*Portius, Marcus.*)

Por. The dawn is overcast, the morning lowers,
And heavily in clouds brings on the day,
The great, the important day, big with the fate
Of Cato and of Rome. Our father's death
Would fill up all the guilt of civil war,
And close the scene of blood. Already Cæsar
Has ravaged more than half the globe, and sees
Mankind grown thin by his destructive sword:
Should he go further, numbers would be wanting
To form new battles,[1] and support his crimes.
Ye gods, what havoc does ambition make
Among your works!

Mar. Thy steady temper, Portius,
Can look on guilt, rebellion, fraud, and Cæsar,
In the calm lights of mild philosophy;
I'm tortured ev'n to madness, when I think
On the proud victor: every time he's named
Pharsalia rises to my view!—I see
The insulting tyrant, prancing o'er the field
Strowed with Rome's citizens, and drenched in slaughter,
His horse's hoofs wet with patrician blood.
Oh, Portius! is there not some chosen curse,
Some hidden thunder in the stores of heaven,
Red with uncommon wrath, to blast the man
Who owes his greatness to his country's ruin?

Por. Believe me, Marcus, 't is an impious greatness,
And mixed with too much horror to be envied.
How does the luster of our father's actions,
Through the dark cloud of ills that cover him,
Break out, and burn with more triumphant brightness!
His sufferings shine, and spread a glory around him;
Greatly unfortunate, he fights the cause
Of honor, virtue, liberty, and Rome.
His sword ne'er fell but on the guilty head;
Oppression, tyranny, and power usurped,
Draw all the vengeance of his arm upon 'em.

Mar. Who knows not this? But what can Cato do
Against a world, a base, degenerate world,
That courts the yoke, and bows the neck to Cæsar?
Pent up in Utica he vainly forms
A poor epitome of Roman greatness,
And, covered with Numidian guards, directs
A feeble army, and an empty senate,
Remnants of mighty battles fought in vain.
By heavens, such virtues, joined with such success,
Distract my very soul: our father's fortune
Would almost tempt us to renounce his precepts.

Por. Remember what our father oft has told us:
The ways of heaven are dark and intricate,
Puzzled in mazes, and perplexed with errors;
Our understanding traces 'em in vain,
Lost and bewildered in the fruitless search;
Nor sees with how much art the windings run,
Nor where the regular confusion ends.

Mar. These are suggestions of a mind at ease:
Oh, Portius! didst thou taste but half the griefs
That wring my soul, thou couldst not talk thus coldly.
Passion unpitied, and successless love,
Plant daggers in my heart, and aggravate
My other griefs. Were but my Lucia kind!—

Por. Thou seest not that thy brother is thy rival;
But I must hide it, for I know thy temper.
(*Aside.*)
Now, Marcus, now, thy virtue's on the proof:

1 Battalions.

Put forth thy utmost strength, work every nerve,
And call up all thy father in thy soul:
To quell the tyrant Love, and guard thy heart
On this weak side, where most our nature fails,
Would be a conquest worthy Cato's son.

Mar. Portius, the counsel which I cannot take,
Instead of healing, but upbraids my weakness.
Bid me for honor plunge into a war
Of thickest foes, and rush on certain death,
Then shalt thou see that Marcus is not slow
To follow glory, and confess his father.
Love is not to be reasoned down, or lost
In high ambition, and a thirst of greatness;
'T is second life, it grows into the soul,
Warms every vein, and beats in every pulse,
I feel it here: my resolution melts—

Por. Behold young Juba, the Numidian prince!
With how much care he forms himself to glory,
And breaks the fierceness of his native temper
To copy out our father's bright example.
He loves our sister Marcia, greatly loves her,
His eyes, his looks, his actions all betray it:
But still the smothered fondness burns within him.
When most it swells, and labors for a vent,
The sense of honor and desire of fame
Drive the big passion back into his heart.
What! shall an African, shall Juba's heir,
Reproach great Cato's son, and show the world
A virtue wanting in a Roman soul?

Mar. Portius, no more! your words leave stings behind 'em.
Whene'er did Juba, or did Portius, show
A virtue that has cast me at a distance,
And thrown me out in the pursuits of honor?

Por. Marcus, I know thy generous temper well;
Fling but the appearance of dishonor on it,
It straight takes fire, and mounts into a blaze.

Mar. A brother's sufferings claim a brother's pity.

Por. Heaven knows I pity thee: behold my eyes
Even whilst I speak.—Do they not swim in tears?
Were but my heart as naked to thy view,
Marcus would see it bleed in his behalf.

Mar. Why then dost treat me with rebukes, instead
Of kind, condoling cares and friendly sorrow?

Por. O Marcus! did I know the way to ease
Thy troubled heart, and mitigate thy pains,
Marcus, believe me, I could die to do it.

Mar. Thou best of brothers, and thou best of friends!
Pardon a weak, distempered soul, that swells
With sudden gusts, and sinks as soon in calms,
The sport of passions—but Sempronius comes:
He must not find this softness hanging on me.

(*Exit.*)

Scene 2.

(*Sempronius, Portius.*)

Sem. Conspiracies no sooner should be formed
Than executed. What means Portius here?
I like not that cold youth. I must dissemble,
And speak a language foreign to my heart.

(*Aside.*)

Good-morrow, Portius! let us once embrace,
Once more embrace; whilst yet we both are free.
To-morrow should we thus express our friendship,
Each might receive a slave into his arms:
This sun, perhaps, this morning sun 's the last,
That e'er shall rise on Roman liberty.

Por My father has this morning called together
To this poor hall his little Roman senate,
(The leavings of Pharsalia) to consult
If yet he can oppose the mighty torrent
That bears down Rome, and all her gods, before it,

Or must at length give up the world to Cæsar.
Sem. Not all the pomp and majesty of Rome
Can raise her senate more than Cato's presence.
His virtues render our assembly awful,
They strike with something like religious fear,
And make ev'n Cæsar tremble at the head
Of armies flushed with conquest: O my Portius,
Could I but call that wondrous man my father,
Would but thy sister Marcia be propitious
To thy friend's vows, I might be blessed indeed!
Por. Alas! Sempronius, wouldst thou talk of love
To Marcia, whilst her father's life 's in danger?
Thou might'st as well court the pale trembling vestal,
When she beholds the holy flame expiring.
Sem. The more I see the wonders of thy race,
The more I 'm charmed. Thou must take heed, my Portius!
The world has all its eyes on Cato's son.
Thy father's merit sets thee up to view,
And shows thee in the fairest point of light,
To make thy virtues or thy faults conspicuous.
Por. Well dost thou seem to check my lingering here
On this important hour!—I 'll straight away,
And while the fathers of the senate meet
In close debate to weigh the events of war,
I 'll animate the soldiers' drooping courage,
With love of freedom, and contempt of life.
I 'll thunder in their ears their country's cause,
And try to rouse up all that 's Roman in 'em.
'T is not in mortals to command success,
But we 'll do more, Sempronius; we 'll deserve it.
(*Exit.*)
Sem., solus. Curse on the stripling! how he apes his sire!
Ambitiously sententious!—but I wonder
Old Syphax comes not; his Numidian genius
Is well disposed to mischief, were he prompt
And eager on it; but he must be spurred,
And every moment quickened to the course.
Cato has used me ill: he has refused
His daughter Marcia to my ardent vows.
Besides, his baffled arms and ruined cause
Are bars to my ambition. Cæsar's favor,
That showers down greatness on his friends, will raise me
To Rome's first honors. If I give up Cato,
I claim in my reward his captive daughter.
But Syphax comes!—

SCENE 3.

(*Syphax, Sempronius.*)

Syph. Sempronius, all is ready;
I 've sounded my Numidians, man by man,
And find 'em ripe for a revolt: they all
Complain aloud of Cato's discipline,
And wait but the command to change their master.
Sem. Believe me, Syphax, there 's no time to waste;
Even whilst we speak, our conqueror comes on,
And gathers ground upon us every moment.
Alas! thou know'st not Cæsar's active soul,
With what a dreadful course he rushes on
From war to war: in vain has nature formed
Mountains and oceans to oppose his passage;
He bounds o'er all, victorious in his march,
The Alps and Pyreneans sink before him;
Through winds and waves and storms he works his way,
Impatient for the battle: one day more
Will set the victor thundering at our gates.
But tell me, hast thou yet drawn o'er young Juba?
That still would recommend thee more to Cæsar,
And challenge better terms.
Syph. Alas, he 's lost,

He 's lost, Sempronius; all his thoughts are full
Of Cato's virtues:—but I 'll try once more
(For every instant I expect him here)
If yet I can subdue those stubborn principles
Of faith, of honor, and I know not what,
That have corrupted his Numidian temper,
And struck the infection into all his soul.

Sem. Be sure to press upon him every motive.
Juba's surrender, since his father's death,
Would give up Afric into Cæsar's hands,
And make him lord of half the burning zone.

Syph. But is it true, Sempronius, that your senate
Is called together? Gods! thou must be cautious!
Cato has piercing eyes, and will discern
Our frauds, unless they 're covered thick with art.

Sem. Let me alone, good Syphax, I 'll conceal
My thoughts in passion ('t is the surest way);
I 'll bellow out for Rome and for my country,
And mouth at Cæsar till I shake the senate.
Your cold hypocrisy 's a stale device,
A worn-out trick: wouldst thou be thought in earnest?
Clothe thy feigned zeal in rage, in fire, in fury!

Syph. In troth, thou 'rt able to instruct grey hairs,
And teach the wily African deceit!

Sem. Once more, be sure to try thy skill on Juba.
Meanwhile I 'll hasten to my Roman soldiers,
Inflame the mutiny, and underhand
Blow up their discontents, till they break out
Unlooked for, and discharge themselves on Cato.
Remember, Syphax, we must work in haste:
Oh think what anxious moments pass between
The birth of plots and their last fatal periods.
Oh! 't is a dreadful interval of time,
Filled up with horror all, and big with death!
Destruction hangs on every word we speak,
On every thought, till the concluding stroke
Determines all, and closes our design.
(*Exit.*)

Syph., solus. I 'll try if yet I can reduce to reason
This headstrong youth, and make him spurn at Cato.
The time is short, Cæsar comes rushing on us—
But hold! young Juba sees me, and approaches.

Scene 4.

(*Juba, Syphax.*)

Juba. Syphax, I joy to meet thee thus alone.
I have observed of late thy looks are fallen,
O'ercast with gloomy cares and discontent;
Then tell me, Syphax, I conjure thee, tell me,
What are the thoughts that knit thy brow in frowns,
And turn thine eye thus coldly on thy prince?

Syph. 'T is not my talent to conceal my thoughts,
Or carry smiles and sunshine in my face,
When discontent sits heavy at my heart.
I have not yet so much the Roman in me.

Juba. Why dost thou cast out such ungenerous terms
Against the lords and sovereigns of the world?
Dost thou not see mankind fall down before them,
And own the force of their superior virtue?
Is there a nation in the wilds of Afric,
Amidst our barren rocks and burning sands,
That does not tremble at the Roman name?

Syph. Gods! where 's the worth that sets this people up
Above your own Numidia's tawny sons!
Do they with tougher sinews bend the bow?
Or flies the javelin swifter to its mark,
Launched from the vigor of a Roman arm?
Who like our active African instructs

The fiery steed, and trains him to his hand?
Or guides in troops the embattled elephant,
Loaden with war? these, these are arts, my prince,
In which your Zama does not stoop to Rome.

Juba. These all are virtues of a meaner rank,
Perfections that are placed in bones and nerves.
A Roman soul is bent on higher views:
To civilize the rude, unpolished world,
And lay it under the restraint of laws;
To make man mild and sociable to man;
To cultivate the wild, licentious savage
With wisdom, discipline, and liberal arts—
The embellishments of life; virtues like these
Make human nature shine, reform the soul,
And break our fierce barbarians into men.

Syph. Patience, kind heavens!—excuse an old man's warmth.
What are these wondrous civilizing arts,
This Roman polish, and this smooth behavior,
That render man thus tractable and tame?
Are they not only to disguise our passions,
To set our looks at variance with our thoughts,
To check the starts and sallies of the soul,
And break off all its commerce with the tongue;
In short, to change us into other creatures
Than what our nature and the gods designed us?

Juba. To strike thee dumb, turn up thy eyes to Cato!
There may'st thou see to what a godlike height
The Roman virtues lift up mortal man.
While good, and just, and anxious for his friends,
He's still severely bent against himself;
Renouncing sleep, and rest, and food, and ease,
He strives with thirst and hunger, toil and heat;
And when his fortune sets before him all
The pomps and pleasures that his soul can wish,
His rigid virtue will accept of none.

Syph. Believe me, prince, there's not an African
That traverses our vast Numidian deserts
In quest of prey, and lives upon his bow,
But better practises these boasted virtues.
Coarse are his meals, the fortune of the chase,
Amidst the running stream he slakes his thirst,
Toils all the day, and at the approach of night
On the first friendly bank he throws him down,
Or rests his head upon a rock till morn:
Then rises fresh, pursues his wonted game,
And if the following day he chance to find
A new repast, or an untasted spring,
Blesses his stars, and thinks it luxury.

Juba. Thy prejudices, Syphax, won't discern
What virtues grow from ignorance and choice,
Nor how the hero differs from the brute.
But grant that others could with equal glory
Look down on pleasures, and the baits of sense;
Where shall we find the man that bears affliction,
Great and majestic in his griefs, like Cato?
Heavens, with what strength, what steadiness of mind,
He triumphs in the midst of all his sufferings!
How does he rise against a load of woes,
And thank the gods that throw the weight upon him!

Syph. 'T is pride, rank pride, and haughtiness of soul:
I think the Romans call it stoicism.
Had not your royal father thought so highly
Of Roman virtue, and of Cato's cause,
He had not fallen by a slave's hand, inglorious;
Nor would his slaughtered army now have lain
On Afric's sands, disfigured with their wounds,
To gorge the wolves and vultures of Numidia.

Juba. Why dost thou call my sorrows up afresh?
My father's name brings tears into my eyes.
Syph. Oh, that you'd profit by your father's ills!
Juba. What wouldst thou have me do?
Syph. Abandon Cato.
Juba. Syphax, I should be more than twice an orphan
By such a loss.
Syph. Ay, there's the tie that binds you!
You long to call him father. Marcia's charms
Work in your heart unseen, and plead for Cato.
No wonder you are deaf to all I say.
Juba. Syphax, your zeal becomes importunate;
I've hitherto permitted it to rave,
And talk at large; but learn to keep it in,
Lest it should take more freedom than I'll give it.
Syph. Sir, your great father never used me thus.
Alas! he's dead! but can you e'er forget
The tender sorrows, and the pangs of nature,
The fond embraces, and repeated blessings,
Which you drew from him in your last farewell?
Still must I cherish the dear, sad remembrance,
At once to torture and to please my sou[illegible]
The good old king at parting wrung [illegible] hand,
(His eyes brimful of tears) then s[illegible] cried,
Prithee, be careful of my son!—h[illegible] grief
Swelled up so high, he could not utter more.
Juba. Alas, thy story melts away my soul.
That best of fathers! how shall I discharge
The gratitude and duty which I owe him!
Syph. By laying up his counsels in your heart.
Juba. His counsels bade me yield to thy directions:
Then, Syphax, chide me in severest terms,
Vent all thy passion, and I'll stand its shock,
Calm and unruffled as a summer sea,
When not a breath of wind flies o'er its surface.
Syph. Alas, my prince, I'd guide you to your safety.
Juba. I do believe thou wouldst: but tell me how?
Syph. Fly from the fate that follows Cæsar's foes.
Juba. My father scorned to do it.
Syph. And therefore died.
Juba. Better to die ten thousand thousand deaths,
Than wound my honor.
Syph. Rather say, your love.
Juba. Syphax, I've promised to preserve my temper.
Why wilt thou urge me to confess a flame
I long have stifled, and would fain conceal?
Syph. Believe me, prince, though hard to conquer love,
'T is easy to divert and break its force:
Absence might cure it, or a second mistress
Light up another flame, and put out this.
The glowing dames of Zama's royal court
Have faces flushed with more exalted charms,
The sun, that rolls his chariot o'er their heads,
Works up more fire and color in their cheeks:
Were you with these, my prince, you'd soon forget
[illegible]he pale, unripened beauties of the north.
[illegible] is not a set of features, or com[illegible]
[illegible]f a skin, that I admire.
[illegible]s familiar to the lover,
[illegible] and palls upon the [illegible]
Th[illegible]ers above her s[illegible]
True, she[illegible] fair!),
But still th[illegible] her charms
With inward grea[illegible]dom,
And sanctity of manne[illegible]
Shines out in everything [illegible] speaks,
While winning mildness and a[illegible] smiles
Dwell in her looks, and with becomin[illegible] grace
Soften the rigor of her father's virtues.

Syph. How does your tongue grow wanton in her praise!
But on my knees I beg you would consider—

Juba. Hah! Syphax, is 't not she?—she moves this way:
And with her Lucia, Lucius's fair daughter.
My heart beats thick—I prithee, Syphax, leave me.

Syph. Ten thousand curses fasten on 'em both!
Now will this woman, with a single glance,
Undo what I 've been laboring all this while.

(*Exit.*)

Scene 5.

(*Juba, Marcia, Lucia.*)

Juba. Hail, charming maid! How does thy beauty smooth
The face of war, and make even horror smile!
At sight of thee my heart shakes off its sorrows;
I feel a dawn of joy break in upon me,
And for a while forget the approach of Cæsar.

Mar. I should be grieved, young prince, to think my presence
Unbent your thoughts, and slackened 'em to arms,
While, warm with slaughter, our victorious foe
Threatens aloud, and calls you to the field.

Juba. O Marcia, let me hope thy kind concerns
And gentle wishes follow me to battle!
The thought will give new vigor to my arm,
And strength and weight to my descending sword,
And drive it in a tempest on the foe.

Mar. My prayers and wishes always shall attend
The friends of Rome, the glorious cause of virtue,
And men approved of by the gods and Cato.

Juba. That Juba may deserve thy pious cares,
I 'll gaze forever on thy godlike father,
Transplanting, one by one, into my life,
His bright perfections, till I shine like him.

Mar. My father never, at a time like this,
Would lay out his great soul in words, and waste
Such precious moments.

Juba. Thy reproofs are just,
Thou virtuous maid; I 'll hasten to my troops,
And fire their languid souls with Cato's virtue;
If e'er I lead them to the field, when all
The war shall stand ranged in its just array,
And dreadful pomp; then will I think on thee!
O lovely maid, then will I think on thee!
And, in the shock of charging hosts, remember
What glorious deeds should grace the man who hopes
For Marcia's love.

(*Exit.*)

Scene 6.

(*Lucia, Marcia.*)

Luc. Marcia, you 're too severe:
How could you chide the young good-natured prince,
And drive him from you with so stern an air,
A prince that loves and dotes on you to death?

Mar. 'T is therefore, Lucia, that I chide him from me.
His air, his voice, his looks, and honest soul
Speak all so movingly in his behalf.
I dare not trust myself to hear him talk.

Luc. Why will you fight against so sweet a passion,
And steel your heart to such a world of charms?

Mar. How, Lucia, wouldst thou have me sink away
In pleasing dreams, and lose myself in love,
When every moment Cato's life 's at stake?
Cæsar comes armed with terror and revenge,
And aims his thunder at my father's head.
Should not the sad occasion swallow up
My other cares, and draw them all into it?

Luc. Why have not I this constancy of mind,
Who have so many griefs to try its force?

Sure, nature formed me of her softest mould,
Enfeebled all my soul with tender passions,
And sunk me ev'n below my own weak sex:
Pity and love, by turns, oppress my heart.

Mar. Lucia, disburthen all thy cares on me,
And let me share thy most retired distress;
Tell me who raises up this conflict in thee?

Luc. I need not blush to name them, when I tell thee
They're Marcia's brothers, and the sons of Cato.

Mar. They both behold thee with their sister's eyes,
And often have revealed their passion to me.
But tell me whose address thou favorest most;
I long to know, and yet I dread to hear it.

Luc. Which is it Marcia wishes for?

Mar. For neither—
And yet for both;—the youths have equal share
In Marcia's wishes, and divide their sister:
But tell me, which of them is Lucia's choice?

Luc. Marcia, they both are high in my esteem,
But in my love—why wilt thou make me name him?
Thou know'st it is a blind and foolish passion,
Pleased and disgusted with it knows not what—

Mar. O Lucia, I'm perplexed, oh tell me which
I must hereafter call my happy brother.

Luc. Suppose 't were Portius, could you blame my choice?
O Portius, thou hast stolen away my soul!
With what a graceful tenderness he loves!
And breathes the softest, the sincerest vows!
Complacency,[2] and truth, and manly sweetness
Dwell ever on his tongue, and smooth his thoughts.
Marcus is over-warm, his fond complaints
Have so much earnestness and passion in them,
I hear him with a secret kind of horror,
And tremble at his vehemence of temper.

Mar. Alas, poor youth! how canst thou throw him from thee?
Lucia, thou know'st not half the love he bears thee;
Whene'er he speaks of thee, his heart's in flames.
He sends out all his soul in every word,
And thinks, and talks, and looks like one transported.
Unhappy youth! how will thy coldness raise
Tempests and storms in his afflicted bosom!
I dread the consequence.

Luc. You seem to plead
Against your brother Portius.

Mar. Heaven forbid!
Had Portius been the unsuccessful lover,
The same compassion would have fallen on him.

Luc. Was ever virgin love distressed like mine!
Portius himself oft falls in tears before me,
As if he mourned his rival's ill success,
Then bids me hide the motions of my heart,
Nor show which way it turns. So much he fears
The sad effects that it would have on Marcus.

Mar. He knows too well how easily he's fired,
And would not plunge his brother in despair,
But waits for happier times, and kinder moments.

Luc. Alas! too late I find myself involved
In endless griefs, and labyrinths of woe,
Born to afflict my Marcia's family,
And sow dissension in the hearts of brothers.
Tormenting thought! it cuts into my soul.

Mar. Let us not, Lucia, aggravate our sorrows,
But to the gods permit the event of things.
Our lives, discolored with our present woes,
May still grow white, and smile with happier hours.
So the pure limpid stream, when foul with stains

2 Desire to please.

Of rushing torrents and descending rains,
Works itself clear, and as it runs, refines;
Till, by degrees, the floating mirror shines,
Reflects each flower that on the border grows,
And a new heaven in its fair bosom shows.

(*Exeunt.*)

ACT II.

Scene 1. *The Senate.*

Sem. Rome still survives in this assembled senate!
Let us remember we are Cato's friends,
And act like men who claim that glorious title.

Luc. Cato will soon be here, and open to us
The occasion of our meeting. Hark! he comes!
(*A sound of trumpets.*)
May all the guardian gods of Rome direct him!

(*Enter Cato.*)

Cato. Fathers, we once again are met in council.
Cæsar's approach has summoned us together,
And Rome attends her fate from our resolves:
How shall we treat this bold, aspiring man?
Success still follows him and backs his crimes;
Pharsalia gave him Rome; Egypt has since
Received his yoke, and the whole Nile is Cæsar's.
Why should I mention Juba's overthrow,
And Scipio's death? Numidia's burning sands
Still smoke with blood. 'T is time we should decree
What course to take. Our foe advances on us,
And envies us even Libya's sultry deserts.
Fathers, pronounce your thoughts, are they still fixed
To hold it out, and fight it to the last?
Or are your hearts subdued at length, and wrought
By time and ill success to a submission?
Sempronius, speak.

Sem. My voice is still for war.
Gods, can a Roman senate long debate
Which of the two to choose, slavery or death!
No, let us rise at once, gird on our swords,
And, at the head of our remaining troops,
Attack the foe, break through the thick array
Of his throng'd legions, and charge home upon him.
Perhaps some arm, more lucky than the rest,
May reach his heart, and free the world from bondage.
Rise, fathers, rise! 't is Rome demands your help!
Rise, and revenge her slaughtered citizens,
Or share their fate! the corps of half her senate
Manure the fields of Thessaly, while we
Sit here, deliberating in cold debates,
If we should sacrifice our lives to honor,
Or wear them out in servitude and chains.
Rouse up, for shame! our brothers of Pharsalia
Point at their wounds, and cry aloud—To battle!
Great Pompey's shade complains that we are slow,
And Scipio's ghost walks unrevenged amongst us!

Cato. Let not a torrent of impetuous zeal
Transport thee thus beyond the bounds of reason:
True fortitude is seen in great exploits,
That justice warrants, and that wisdom guides,
All else is towering frenzy and distraction.
Are not the lives of those who draw the sword
In Rome's defence intrusted to our care?
Should we thus lead them to a field of slaughter,
Might not the impartial world with reason say
We lavished at our deaths the blood of thousands,
To grace our fall, and make our ruin glorious?
Lucius, we next would know what 's your opinion.

Luc. My thoughts, I must confess, are turned on peace.
Already have our quarrels filled the world

With widows and with orphans: Scythia mourns
Our guilty wars, and earth's remotest regions
Lie half unpeopled by the feuds of Rome:
'T is time to sheathe the sword, and spare mankind.
It is not Cæsar, but the gods, my fathers,
The gods declare against us, and repel
Our vain attempts. To urge the foe to battle,
(Prompted by blind revenge and wild despair)
Were to refuse the awards of Providence,
And not to rest in heaven's determination.
Already have we shown our love to Rome,
Now let us show submission to the gods,
We took up arms, not to revenge ourselves,
But free the commonwealth; when this end fails,
Arms have no further use: our country's cause,
That drew our swords, now wrests 'em from our hands,
And bids us not delight in Roman blood,
Unprofitably shed; what men could do
Is done already: heaven and earth will witness,
If Rome must fall, that we are innocent.

Sem. This smooth discourse and mild behavior oft
Conceal a traitor—something whispers me
All is not right—Cato, beware of Lucius.
(*Aside to Cato.*)

Cato. Let us appear nor rash nor diffident:
Immoderate valor swells into a fault,
And fear, admitted into public councils,
Betrays like treason. Let us shun 'em both.
Fathers, I cannot see that our affairs
Are grown thus desperate. We have bulwarks round us;
Within our walls are troops inured to toil
In Afric's heats, and seasoned to the sun;
Numidia's spacious kingdom lies behind us,
Ready to rise at its young prince's call.
While there is hope, do not distrust the gods;
But wait at least till Cæsar's near approach
Force us to yield. 'T will never be too late
To sue for chains and own a conqueror.
Why should Rome fall a moment ere her time?
No, let us draw her term of freedom out
In its full length, and spin it to the last,
So shall we gain still one day's liberty;
And let me perish, but in Cato's judgment,
A day, an hour, of virtuous liberty
Is worth a whole eternity in bondage.

(*Enter Marcus.*)

Mar. Fathers, this moment, as I watched the gates,
Lodged on my post, a herald is arrived
From Cæsar's camp, and with him comes old Decius,
The Roman knight; he carries in his looks
Impatience, and demands to speak with Cato.

Cato. By your permission, fathers, bid him enter.
(*Exit Marcus.*)
Decius was once my friend, but other prospects
Have loosed those ties, and bound him fast to Cæsar.
His message may determine our resolves.

Scene 2.

(*Decius, Cato, &c.*)

Dec. Cæsar sends health to Cato.—

Cato. Could he send it
To Cato's slaughtered friends, it would be welcome.
Are not your orders to address the senate?

Dec. My business is with Cato: Cæsar sees
The straits to which you 're driven; and, as he knows
Cato's high worth, is anxious for your life.

Cato. My life is grafted on the fate of Rome:
Would he save Cato, bid him spare his country.
Tell your dictator this: and tell him, Cato
Disdains a life which he has power to offer.

Dec. Rome and her senators submit to Cæsar;
Her generals and her consuls are no more,

Who checked his conquests, and denied his triumphs.
Why will not Cato be this Cæsar's friend?

Cato. Those very reasons thou hast urged forbid it.

Dec. Cato, I 've orders to expostulate
And reason with you, as from friend to friend:
Think on the storm that gathers o'er your head,
And threatens every hour to burst upon it;
Still may you stand high in your country's honors,
Do but comply, and make your peace with Cæsar.
Rome will rejoice, and cast its eyes on Cato,
As on the second of mankind.

Cato. No more!
I must not think of life on such conditions.

Dec. Cæsar is well acquainted with your virtues,
And therefore sets this value on your life:
Let him but know the price of Cato's friendship,
And name your terms.

Cato. Bid him disband his legions;
Restore the commonwealth to liberty,
Submit his actions to the public censure,
And stand the judgment of a Roman senate:
Bid him do this, and Cato is his friend.

Dec. Cato, the world talks loudly of your wisdom—

Cato. Nay more, though Cato's voice was ne'er employed
To clear the guilty, and to varnish crimes,
Myself will mount the rostrum in his favor,
And strive to gain his pardon from the people.

Dec. A style like this becomes a conqueror.

Cato. Decius, a style like this becomes a Roman.

Dec. What is a Roman, that is Cæsar's foe?

Cato. Greater than Cæsar, he 's a friend to virtue.

Dec. Consider, Cato, you 're in Utica,
And at the head of your own little senate;
You don't now thunder in the Capitol,
With all the mouths of Rome to second you.

Cato. Let him consider that who drives us hither:
'T is Cæsar's sword has made Rome's senate little,
And thinned its ranks. Alas! thy dazzled eye
Beholds this man in a false glaring light,
Which conquest and success have thrown upon him;
Didst thou but view him right, thou 'dst see him black
With murder, treason, sacrilege, and crimes
That strike my soul with horror but to name 'em.
I know thou look'st on me, as on a wretch
Beset with ills, and covered with misfortunes;
But, by the gods I swear, millions of worlds
Should never buy me to be like that Cæsar.

Dec. Does Cato send this answer back to Cæsar,
For all his generous cares, and proffered friendship?

Cato. His cares for me are insolent and vain:
Presumptuous man! the gods take care of Cato.
Would Cæsar show the greatness of his soul,
Bid him employ his care for these my friends,
And make good use of his ill-gotten power,
By sheltering men much better than himself.

Dec. Your high unconquered heart makes you forget
You are a man. You rush on your destruction—
But I have done. When I relate hereafter
The tale of this unhappy embassy,
All Rome will be in tears.
(*Exit Decius.*)

SCENE 3.

(*Sempronius, Lucius, Cato, &c.*)

Sem. Cato, we thank thee.
The mighty genius of immortal Rome
Speaks in thy voice, thy soul breathes liberty:
Cæsar will shrink to hear the words thou utterest,

And shudder in the midst of all his conquests.
Luc. The senate owns its gratitude to Cato,
Who with so great a soul consults its safety,
And guards our lives, while he neglects his own.
Sem. Sempronius gives no thanks on this account.
Lucius seems fond of life; but what is life?
'T is not to stalk about, and draw fresh air
From time to time, or gaze upon the sun;
'T is to be free. When liberty is gone,
Life grows insipid, and has lost its relish.
Oh, could my dying hand but lodge a sword
In Cæsar's bosom, and revenge my country,
By heavens, I could enjoy the pangs of death,
And smile in agony.
Luc. Others perhaps
May serve their country with as warm a zeal,
Though 't is not kindled into so much rage.
Sem. This sober conduct is a mighty virtue
In lukewarm patriots.
Cato. Come! no more, Sempronius,
All here are friends to Rome, and to each other.
Let us not weaken still the weaker side
By our divisions.
Sem. Cato, my resentments
Are sacrificed to Rome—I stand reproved.
Cato. Fathers, 't is time you come to a resolve.
Luc. Cato, we all go into your opinion,
Cæsar's behavior has convinced the senate
We ought to hold it out till terms arrive.
Sem. We ought to hold it out till death; but, Cato,
My private voice is drowned amid the senate's.
Cato. Then let us rise, my friends, and strive to fill
This little interval, this pause of life,
(While yet our liberty and fates are doubtful)
With resolution, friendship, Roman bravery,
And all the virtues we can crowd into it;
That heaven may say, it ought to be prolonged.
Fathers, farewell—The young Numidian prince
Comes forward, and expects to know our counsels.

Scene 4.

(*Cato, Juba.*)

Cato. Juba, the Roman Senate has resolved,
Till time give better prospects, still to keep
The sword unsheathed, and turn its edge on Cæsar.
Juba. The resolution fits a Roman senate.
But, Cato, lend me for a while thy patience,
And condescend to hear a young man speak.
My father, when some days before his death
He ordered me to march for Utica,
(Alas! I thought not then his death so near)
Wept o'er me, pressed me in his aged arms,
And, as his griefs gave way, "My son," said he,
"Whatever fortune shall befall thy father,
Be Cato's friend; he'll train thee up to great
And virtuous deeds: do but observe him well,
Thou'lt shun misfortunes, or thou'lt learn to bear 'em."
Cato. Juba, thy father was a worthy prince,
And merited, alas! a better fate;
But heaven thought otherwise.
Juba. My father's fate,
In spite of all the fortitude that shines
Before my face, in Cato's great example,
Subdues my soul, and fills my eyes with tears.
Cato. It is an honest sorrow, and becomes thee.
Juba. My father drew respect from foreign climes:
The kings of Afric sought him for their friend;
Kings far remote, that rule, as fame reports,
Behind the hidden sources of the Nile,
In distant worlds, on t' other side the sun:

Oft have their black ambassadors appeared,
Loaden with gifts, and filled the courts of Zama.
Cato. I am no stranger to thy father's greatness.
Juba. I would not boast the greatness of my father,
But point out new alliances to Cato.
Had we not better leave this Utica,
To arm Numidia in our cause, and court
The assistance of my father's powerful friends?
Did they know Cato, our remotest kings
Would pour embattled multitudes about him;
Their swarthy hosts would darken all our plains,
Doubling the native horror of the war,
And making death more grim.
Cato. And canst thou think
Cato will fly before the sword of Cæsar?
Reduced, like Hannibal, to seek relief
From court to court, and wander up and down,
A vagabond in Afric!
Juba. Cato, perhaps
I 'm too officious, but my forward cares
Would fain preserve a life of so much value.
My heart is wounded, when I see such virtue
Afflicted by the weight of such misfortunes.
Cato. Thy nobleness of soul obliges me.
But know, young prince, that valor soars above
What the world calls misfortune and affliction.
These are not ills; else would they never fall
On heaven's first favorites, and the best of men:
The gods, in bounty, work up storms about us,
That give mankind occasion to exert
Their hidden strength, and throw out into practice
Virtues that shun the day, and lie concealed
In the smooth seasons and the calms of life.
Juba. I 'm charmed whene'er thou talk'st! I pant for virtue
And all my soul endeavors at perfection.
Cato. Dost thou love watchings, abstinence, and toil,
Laborious virtues all? learn them from Cato:
Success and fortune must thou learn from Cæsar.
Juba. The best good fortune that can fall on Juba,
The whole success at which my heart aspires,
Depends on Cato.
Cato. What does Juba say?
Thy words confound me.
Juba. I would fain retract them,
Give 'em me back again. They aimed at nothing.
Cato. Tell me thy wish, young prince; make not my ear
A stranger to thy thoughts.
Juba. Oh! they 're extravagant;
Still let me hide them.
Cato. What can Juba ask
That Cato will refuse?
Juba. I fear to name it.
Marcia—inherits all her father's virtues.
Cato. What wouldst thou say?
Juba. Cato, thou hast a daughter.
Cato. Adieu, young prince; I would not hear a word
Should lessen thee in my esteem: remember
The hand of fate is over us, and heaven
Exacts severity from all our thoughts:
It is not now a time to talk of aught
But chains or conquest, liberty or death.

Scene 5.

(*Syphax, Juba.*)

Syph. How 's this, my prince, what! covered with confusion?
You look as if yon stern philosopher
Had just now chid you.
Juba. Syphax, I 'm undone!
Syph. I know it well.
Juba. Cato thinks meanly of me.
Syph. And so will all mankind.
Juba. I 've opened to him
The weakness of my soul, my love for Marcia.
Syph. Cato 's a proper person to intrust
A love-tale with!
Juba. Oh! I could pierce my heart,
My foolish heart! was ever wretch like Juba?
Syph. Alas! my prince, how are you changed of late!
I 've known young Juba rise before the sun,
To beat the thicket where the tiger slept,
Or seek the lion in his dreadful haunts:
How did the color mount into your cheeks,

When first you roused him to the chase! I 've seen you,
Even in the Libyan dog-days, hunt him down,
Then charge him close, provoke him to the rage
Of fangs and claws, and stooping from your horse
Rivet the panting savage to the ground.

Juba. Prithee, no more!

Syph. How would the old king smile
To see you weigh the paws, when tipped with gold,
And throw the shaggy spoils about your shoulders!

Juba. Syphax, this old man's talk (though honey flowed
In every word) would now lose all its sweetness.
Cato 's displeased, and Marcia lost forever!

Syph. Young prince, I yet could give you good advice.
Marcia might still be yours.

Juba. What say'st thou, Syphax?
By heavens, thou turn'st me all into attention.

Syph. Marcia might still be yours.

Juba. As how, dear Syphax?

Syph. Juba commands Numidia's hardy troops,
Mounted on steeds, unused to the restraint
Of curbs or bits, and fleeter than the winds:
Give but the word, we 'll snatch this damsel up
And bear her off.

Juba. Can such dishonest thoughts
Rise up in man! wouldst thou seduce my youth
To do an act that would destroy my honor?

Syph. Gods! I could tear my beard to hear you talk!
Honor 's a fine imaginary notion,
That draws in raw and unexperienced men
To real mischiefs, while they hunt a shadow.

Juba. Wouldst thou degrade thy prince into a ruffian?

Syph. The boasted ancestors of these great men,
Whose virtues you admire were all such ruffians.
This dread of nations, this almighty Rome,
That comprehends in her wide empire's bounds
All under heaven, was founded on a rape.
Your Scipios, Cæsars, Pompeys, and your Catos,
(These gods on earth) are all the spurious brood
Of violated maids, of ravished Sabines.

Juba. Syphax, I fear that hoary head of thine
Abounds too much in our Numidian wiles.

Syph. Indeed, my prince, you want to know the world;
You have not read mankind; your youth admires
The throws and swellings of a Roman soul,
Cato's bold flights, the extravagance of virtue.

Juba. If knowledge of the world makes man perfidious,
May Juba ever live in ignorance!

Syph. Go, go, you 're young.

Juba. Gods! must I tamely bear
This arrogance unanswered! thou 'rt a traitor,
A false old traitor.

Syph. I have gone too far.
(*Aside.*)

Juba. Cato shall know the baseness of thy soul.

Syph. I must appease this storm, or perish in it.
(*Aside.*)
Young prince, behold these locks that are grown white
Beneath a helmet in your father's battles.

Juba. Those locks shall ne'er protect thy insolence.

Syph. Must one rash word, the infirmity of age,
Throw down the merit of my better years?
This the reward of a whole life of service?
Curse on the boy! how steadily he hears me!
(*Aside.*)

Juba. Is it because the throne of my forefathers
Still stands unfilled, and that Numidia's crown
Hangs doubtful yet, whose head it shall enclose,
Thou thus presumest to treat thy prince with scorn?

Syph. Why will you rive my heart with such expressions?
Does not old Syphax follow you to war?

What are his aims? why does he load with darts
His trembling hand, and crush beneath a casque
His wrinkled brows? what is it he aspires to?
Is it not this, to shed the slow remains,
His last poor ebb of blood, in your defense?

Juba. Syphax, no more! I would not hear you talk.

Syph. Not hear me talk! what, when my faith to Juba,
My royal master's son, is called in question?
My prince may strike me dead, and I 'll be dumb:
But whilst I live, I must not hold my tongue,
And languish out old age in his displeasure.

Juba. Thou know'st the way too well into my heart,
I do believe thee loyal to thy prince.

Syph. What greater instance can I give? I 've offered
To do an action which my soul abhors,
And gain you whom you love at any price.

Juba. Was this thy motive? I have been too hasty.

Syph. And 't is for this my prince has called me traitor.

Juba. Sure thou mistakest; I did not call thee so.

Syph. You did indeed, my prince, you called me traitor:
Nay, further, threatened you 'd complain to Cato.
Of what, my prince, would you complain to Cato?
That Syphax loves you, and would sacrifice
His life, nay, more, his honor in your service.

Juba. Syphax, I know thou lov'st me, but indeed
Thy zeal for Juba carried thee too far.
Honor 's a sacred tie, the law of kings,
The noble mind's distinguishing perfection,
That aids and strengthens virtue where it meets her,
And imitates her actions, where she is not:
It ought not to be sported with.

Syph. By heavens,
I 'm ravished when you talk thus, though you chide me!
Alas! I 've hitherto been used to think
A blind, officious zeal to serve my king
The ruling principle that ought to burn
And quench all others in a subject's heart.
Happy the people, who preserve their honor
By the same duties that oblige their prince!

Juba. Syphax, thou now begin'st to speak thyself.
Numidia 's grown a scorn among the nations
For breach of public vows. Our Punic faith
Is infamous, and branded to a proverb.
Syphax, we 'll join our cares, to purge away
Our country's crimes, and clear her reputation.

Syph. Believe me, prince, you make old Syphax weep
To hear you talk—but 't is with tears of joy.
If e'er your father's crown adorn your brows,
Numidia will be blest by Cato's lectures.

Juba. Syphax, thy hand! we 'll mutually forget
The warmth of youth, and frowardness of age:
Thy prince esteems thy worth, and loves thy person.
If e'er the scepter comes into my hand,
Syphax shall stand the second in my kingdom.

Syph. Why will you overwhelm my age with kindness?
My joy grows burdensome, I shan't support it.

Juba. Syphax, farewell, I 'll hence, and try to find
Some blest occasion that may set me right
In Cato's thoughts. I 'd rather have that man
Approve my deeds, than worlds for my admirers.

(*Exit.*)

Syph. solus. Young men soon give, and soon forget affronts;
Old age is slow in both—A false old traitor!
Those words, rash boy, may chance to cost thee dear.
My heart had still some foolish fondness for thee:
But hence! 't is gone: I give it to the winds:
Cæsar, I 'm wholly thine—

Scene 6.

(*Syphax, Sempronius.*)

Syph. All hail, Sempronius!
Well, Cato's senate is resolved to wait
The fury of a siege before it yields.
Sem. Syphax, we both were on the verge of fate:
Lucius declared for peace, and terms were offered
To Cato by a messenger from Cæsar.
Should they submit, ere our designs are ripe,
We both must perish in the common wreck,
Lost in a general, undistinguished ruin.
Syph. But how stands Cato?
Sem. Thou hast seen Mount Atlas:
While storms and tempests thunder on its brows,
And oceans break their billows at its feet,
It stands unmoved, and glories in its height.
Such is that haughty man; his towering soul,
'Midst all the shocks and injuries of fortune,
Rises superior, and looks down on Cæsar.
Syph. But what 's this messenger?
Sem. I 've practised with him,
And found a means to let the victor know
That Syphax and Sempronius are his friends.
But let me now examine in my turn:
Is Juba fixed?
Syph. Yes—but it is to Cato.
I 've tried the force of every reason on him,
Soothed and caressed, been angry, soothed again,
Laid safety, life, and interest in his sight,
But all are vain, he scorns them all for Cato.
Sem. Come, 't is no matter, we shall do without him.
He 'll make a pretty figure in a triumph,
And serve to trip before the victor's chariot.
Syphax, I now may hope thou hast forsook
Thy Juba's cause, and wishest Marcia mine.
Syph. May she be thine as fast as thou wouldst have her!
Sem. Syphax, I love that woman; though I curse
Her and myself, yet, spite of me, I love her.
Syph. Make Cato sure, and give up Utica,
Cæsar will ne'er refuse thee such a trifle.
But are thy troops prepared for a revolt?
Does the sedition catch from man to man,
And run among their ranks?
Sem. All, all is ready.
The factious leaders are our friends, that spread
Murmurs and discontents among the soldiers.
They count their toilsome marches, long fatigues,
Unusual fastings, and will bear no more
This medley of philosophy and war.
Within an hour they 'll storm the senate-house.
Syph. Meanwhile I 'll draw up my Numidian troops
Within the square, to exercise their arms,
And, as I see occasion, favor thee.
I laugh to think how your unshaken Cato
Will look aghast, while unforeseen destruction
Pours in upon him thus from every side.
So, where our wide Numidian wastes extend,
Sudden, the impetuous hurricanes descend,
Wheel through the air, in circling eddies play,
Tear up the sands, and sweep whole plains away.
The helpless traveller, with wild surprise,
Sees the dry desert all around him rise,
And smothered in the dusty whirlwind dies.

ACT III.

Scene 1.

(*Marcus, Portius.*)

Mar. Thanks to my stars, I have not ranged about
The wilds of life, ere I could find a friend;
Nature first pointed out my Portius to me,
And early taught me, by her secret force,
To love thy person, ere I knew thy merit;

Till, what was instinct, grew up into friendship.
Por. Marcus, the friendships of the world are oft
Confederacies in vice, or leagues of pleasure;
Ours has severest virtue for its basis,
And such a friendship ends not but with life.
Mar. Portius, thou know'st my soul in all its weakness;
Then prithee spare me on its tender side,
Indulge me but in love, my other passions
Shall rise and fall by virtue's nicest rules.
Por. When love 's well-timed, 't is not a fault to love.
The strong, the brave, the virtuous, and the wise
Sink in the soft captivity together.
I would not urge thee to dismiss thy passion,
(I know 't were vain) but to suppress its force,
Till better times may make it look more graceful.
Mar. Alas! thou talk'st like one who never felt
The impatient throbs and longings of a soul
That pants and reaches after distant good.
A lover does not live by vulgar time:
Believe me, Portius, in my Lucia's absence
Life hangs upon me, and becomes a burden;
And yet, when I behold the charming maid,
I 'm ten times more undone; while hope, and fear,
And grief, and rage, and love, rise up at once,
And with variety of pain distract me.
Por. What can thy Portius do to give thee help?
Mar. Portius, thou oft enjoy'st the fair one's presence:
Then undertake my cause, and plead it to her
With all the strength and heats of eloquence
Fraternal love and friendship can inspire.
Tell her thy brother languishes to death,
And fades away, and withers in his bloom;
That he forgets his sleep, and loathes his food,
That youth, and health, and war, are joyless to him.
Describe his anxious days and restless nights,
And all the torments that thou seest me suffer.
Por. Marcus, I beg thee give me not an office
That suits with me so ill. Thou know'st my temper.
Mar. Wilt thou behold me sinking in my woes?
And wilt thou not reach out a friendly arm,
To raise me from amidst this plunge of sorrows?
Por. Marcus, thou canst not ask what I 'd refuse.
But here, believe me, I 've a thousand reasons—
Mar. I know thou 'lt say my passion 's out of season;
That Cato's great example and misfortunes
Should both conspire to drive it from my thoughts.
But what 's all this to one who loves like me!
Oh, Portius, Portius, from my soul I wish
Thou didst but know thyself what 't is to love!
Then wouldst thou pity and assist thy brother.
Por. What should I do? If I disclose my passion,
Our friendship 's at an end: if I conceal it,
The world will call me false to a friend and brother.
(*Aside.*)
Mar. But see where Lucia, at her wonted hour,
Amid the cool of yon high marble arch,
Enjoys the noon-day breeze! observe her, Portius!
That face, that shape, those eyes, that heaven of beauty!
Observe her well, and blame me, if thou canst.
Por. She sees us, and advances—
Mar. I 'll withdraw,
And leave you for a while. Remember, Portius,
Thy brother's life depends upon thy tongue.

SCENE 2.

(*Lucia, Portius.*)

Luc. Did not I see your brother Marcus here?
Why did he fly the place, and shun my presence?
Por. Oh, Lucia, language is too faint to show
His rage of love; it preys upon his life;
He pines, he sickens, he despairs, he dies:
His passions and his virtues lie confused,
And mixed together in so wild a tumult,
That the whole man is quite disfigured in him.
Heavens! would one think 't were possible for love
To make such ravage in a noble soul!
Oh, Lucia, I'm distrest! my heart bleeds for him;
Even now, while thus I stand blest in thy presence,
A secret damp of grief comes o'er my thoughts,
And I'm unhappy, though thou smil'st upon me.
Luc. How wilt thou guard thy honor, in the shock
Of love and friendship! think betimes, my Portius,
Think how the nuptial tie, that might insure
Our mutual bliss, would raise to such a height
Thy brother's griefs, as might perhaps destroy him.
Por. Alas, poor youth! what dost thou think, my Lucia?
His generous, open, undesigning heart
Has begged his rival to solicit for him.
Then do not strike him dead with a denial,
But hold him up in life, and cheer his soul
With the faint glimmering of a doubtful hope:
Perhaps when we have passed these gloomy hours,
And weathered out the storm that beats upon us—
Luc. No, Portius, no! I see thy sister's tears,
Thy father's anguish, and thy brother's death,
In the pursuit of our ill-fated loves.
And, Portius, here I swear, to heaven I swear,
To heaven, and all the powers that judge mankind,
Never to mix my plighted hands with thine,
While such a cloud of mischiefs hangs about us,
But to forget our loves, and drive thee out
From all my thoughts, as far—as I am able.
Por. What hast thou said! I'm thunder-struck!—recall
Those hasty words, or I am lost for ever.
Luc. Has not the vow already passed my lips?
The gods have heard it, and 't is sealed in heaven.
May all the vengeance that was ever poured
On perjured heads o'erwhelm me, if I break it!
Por. Fixed in astonishment, I gaze upon thee;
Like one just blasted by a stroke from heaven,
Who pants for breath, and stiffens, yet alive,
In dreadful looks—a monument of wrath!
Luc. At length I've acted my severest part,
I feel the woman breaking in upon me.
And melt about my heart! my tears will flow.
But oh I'll think no more! the hand of fate
Has torn thee from me, and I must forget thee.
Por. Hard-hearted, cruel maid!
Luc. Oh stop those sounds,
Those killing sounds! why dost thou frown upon me?
My blood runs cold, my heart forgets to heave,
And life itself goes out at thy displeasure.
The gods forbid us to indulge our loves,
But oh! I cannot bear thy hate and live!
Por. Talk not of love, thou never knew'st its force,
I've been deluded, led into a dream
Of fancied bliss. Oh Lucia, cruel maid!
Thy dreadful vow, loaden with death, still sounds
In my stunned ears. What shall I say or do?
Quick, let us part! perdition's in thy presence,

And horror dwells about thee!—hah, she faints!
Wretch that I am! what has my rashness done!
Lucia, thou injured innocence! thou best
And loveliest of thy sex! awake, my Lucia,
Or Portius rushes on his sword to join thee.
—Her imprecations reach not to the tomb,
They shut not out society in death—
But, hah! she moves! life wanders up and down
Through all her face, and lights up every charm.

Luc. O Portius, was this well!— to frown on her
That lives upon thy smiles! to call in doubt
The faith of one expiring at thy feet,
That loves thee more than ever woman loved!
—What do I say? my half-recovered sense
Forgets the vow in which my soul is bound.
Destruction stands betwixt us! we must part.

Por. Name not the word, my frighted thoughts run back,
And startle into madness at the sound.

Luc. What wouldst thou have me do? consider well
The train of ills our love would draw behind it.
Think, Portius, think, thou seest thy dying brother
Stabbed at his heart, and all besmeared with blood,
Storming at heaven and thee! thy awful sire
Sternly demands the cause, th' accursed cause,
That robs him of his son! poor Marcia trembles,
Then tears her hair, and frantic in her griefs
Calls out on Lucia! What could Lucia answer?
Or how stand up in such a scene of sorrow?

Por. To my confusion and eternal grief,
I must approve the sentence that destroys me.
The mist that hung about my mind clears up;
And now, athwart the terrors that thy vow
Has planted round thee, thou appear'st more fair,
More amiable, and risest in thy charms.
Loveliest of women! heaven is in thy soul,
Beauty and virtue shine for ever round thee,
Brightening each other! thou art all divine!

Luc. Portius, no more! thy words shoot through my heart,
Melt my resolves, and turn me all to love.
Why are those tears of fondness in thy eyes?
Why heaves thy heart? Why swells thy soul with sorrow?
It softens me too much—farewell, my Portius,
Farewell, though death is in the word, forever.

Por. Stay, Lucia, stay! what dost thou say? Forever?

Luc. Have I not sworn? if, Portius, thy success
Must throw thy brother on his fate, farewell—
Oh, how shall I repeat the word?—forever!

Por. Thus o'er the dying lamp the unsteady flame
Hangs quivering on a point, leaps off by fits,
And falls again, as loth to quit its hold.
Thou must not go, my soul still hovers o'er thee,
And can't get loose.

Luc. If the firm Portius shake
To hear of parting, think what Lucia suffers!

Por. 'T is true; unruffled and serene I 've met
The common accidents of life, but here
Such an unlooked-for storm of ills falls on me,
It beats down all my strength. I cannot bear it.
We must not part.

Luc. What dost thou say? not part?
Hast thou forgot the vow that I have made?
Are there not heavens, and gods, and thunder o'er us?
—But see! thy brother Marcus bends this way!
I sicken at the sight. Once more, farewell,
Farewell, and know thou wrong'st me, if thou think'st
Ever was love, or ever grief, like mine.

Scene 3.

(*Marcus, Portius.*)

Mar. Portius, what hopes? how stands she? am I doomed
To life or death?

Por. What wouldst thou have me say?

Mar. What means this pensive posture? thou appear'st
Like one amazed and terrified.

Por. I've reason.

Mar. Thy downcast looks and thy disordered thoughts
Tell me my fate. I ask not the success
My cause has found.

Por. I'm grieved I undertook it.

Mar. What! does the barbarous maid insult my heart,
My aching heart! and triumph in my pains?
That I could cast her from my thoughts for ever!

Por. Away! you're too suspicious in your griefs;
Lucia, though sworn never to think of love,
Compassionates your pains, and pities you!

Mar. Compassionates my pains, and pities me!
What is compassion when 't is void of love?
Fool that I was to choose so cold a friend
To urge my cause! compassionate my pains!
Prithee what art, what rhetoric didst thou use
To gain this mighty boon? She pities me!
To one that asks the warm return of love,
Compassion's cruelty, 't is scorn, 't is death—

Por. Marcus, no more! have I deserved this treatment?

Mar. What have I said! O Portius, O forgive me!
A soul exasperated in ills falls out
With everything, its friend, its self—but, hah!
What means that shout, big with the sounds of war?
What new alarm?

Por. A second, louder yet,
Swells in the winds, and comes more full upon us.

Mar. Oh for some glorious cause to fall in battle!
Lucia, thou hast undone me! thy disdain
Has broke my heart: 't is death must give me ease.

Por. Quick, let us hence; who knows if Cato's life
Stands sure? O Marcus, I am warmed; my heart
Leaps at the trumpet's voice, and burns for glory.

Scene 4.

(*Sempronius with the leaders of the mutiny.*)

Sem. At length the winds are raised, the storm blows high,
Be it your care, my friends, to keep it up
In its full fury, and direct it right,
Till it has spent itself on Cato's head.
Meanwhile I'll herd among his friends, and seem
One of the number, that whate'er arrive,
My friends and fellow soldiers may be safe.

First Lead. We all are safe, Sempronius is our friend,
Sempronius is as brave a man as Cato.
But, hark! he enters. Bear up boldly to him;
Be sure you beat him down, and bind him fast.
This day will end our toils, and give us rest;
Fear nothing, for Sempronius is our friend.

Scene 5.

(*Cato, Sempronius, Lucius, Portius, Marcus.*)

Cato. Where are these bold, intrepid sons of war,
That greatly turn their backs upon the foe,
And to their general send a brave defiance?

Sem. Curse on their dastard souls, they stand astonished!
(*Aside.*)

Cato. Perfidious men! and will you thus dishonor
Your past exploits, and sully all your wars?
Do you confess 't was not a zeal for Rome

Nor love of liberty, nor thirst of honor,
Drew you thus far; but hopes to share the spoil
Of conquered towns and plundered provinces?
Fired with such motives you do well to join
With Cato's foes, and follow Cæsar's banners.
Why did I scape the envenomed aspic's rage,
And all the fiery monsters of the desert,
To see this day? why could not Cato fall
Without your guilt? Behold, ungrateful men,
Behold my bosom naked to your swords,
And let the man that 's injured strike the blow.
Which of you all suspects that he is wronged,
Or thinks he suffers greater ills than Cato?
Am I distinguished from you but by toils,
Superior toils, and heavier weight of cares?
Painful pre-eminence!

Sem. By heavens they droop!
Confusion to the villains! all is lost. (*Aside.*)

Cato. Have you forgotten Libya's burning waste,
Its barren rocks, parched earth, and hills of sand,
Its tainted air, and all its broods of poison?
Who was the first to explore th' untrodden path,
When life was hazarded in every step?
Or, fainting in the long, laborious march,
When on the banks of an unlooked-for stream
You sunk the river with repeated draughts,
Who was the last in all your host that thirsted?

Sem. If some penurious source by chance appeared,
Scanty of waters, when you scooped it dry,
And offered the full helmet up to Cato,
Did he not dash the untasted moisture from him?
Did he not lead you through the mid-day sun,
And clouds of dust? did not his temples glow
In the same sultry winds and scorching heats?

Cato. Hence, worthless men! hence! and complain to Cæsar
You could not undergo the toils of war,
Nor bear the hardships that your leader bore.

Luc. See, Cato, see th' unhappy men! they weep!
Fear, and remorse, and sorrow for their crime,
Appear in every look, and plead for mercy.

Cato. Learn to be honest men, give up your leaders,
And pardon shall descend on all the rest.

Sem. Cato, commit these wretches to my care.
First let 'em each be broken on the rack,
Then, with what life remains, impaled and left
To writhe at leisure round the bloody stake.
There let 'em hang, and taint the southern wind.
The partners of their crime will learn obedience,
When they look up and see their fellow-traitors
Stuck on a fork, and blackening in the sun.

Luc. Sempronius, why, why wilt thou urge the fate
Of wretched men?

Sem. How! wouldst thou clear rebellion?
Lucius (good man) pities the poor offenders,
That would imbrue their hands in Cato's blood.

Cato. Forbear, Sempronius!—see they suffer death,
But in their deaths remember they are men.
Strain not the laws to make their tortures grievous.
Lucius, the base, degenerate age requires
Severity and justice in its rigor;
This awes an impious, bold, offending world,
Commands obedience, and gives force to laws.
When by just vengeance guilty mortals perish,
The gods behold their punishment with pleasure,
And lay th' uplifted thunderbolt aside.

Sem. Cato, I execute thy will with pleasure.

Cato. Meanwhile we 'll sacrifice to liberty.

Remember, O my friends, the laws, the rights,
The generous plan of power delivered down,
From age to age by your renowned forefathers,
(So dearly bought, the price of so much blood)
Oh let it never perish in your hands!
But piously transmit it to your children.
Do thou, great Liberty, inspire our souls,
And make our lives in thy possession happy,
Or our deaths glorious in thy just defense.

SCENE 6.

(*Sempronius and the leaders of the mutiny.*)

1st Lead. Sempronius, you have acted like yourself,
One would have thought you had been half in earnest.

Sem. Villain, stand off! base, grovelling, worthless wretches,
Mongrels in faction, poor faint-hearted traitors!

2d Lead. Nay, now you carry it too far, Sempronius:
Throw off the mask, there are none here but friends.

Sem. Know, villains, when such paltry slaves presume
To mix in treason, if the plot succeeds,
They 're thrown neglected by: but if it fails,
They 're sure to die like dogs, as you shall do.
Here, take these factious monsters, drag 'em forth
To sudden death.

(*Enter Guards.*)

1st Lead. Nay, since it comes to this—

Sem. Despatch 'em quick, but first pluck out their tongues,
Lest with their dying breath they sow sedition.

SCENE 7.

(*Syphax, Sempronius.*)

Syph. Our first design, my friend, has proved abortive;
Still there remains an after-game to play:
My troops are mounted; their Numidian steeds
Snuff up the wind, and long to scour the desert:
Let but Sempronius head us in our flight,
We 'll force the gate where Marcus keeps his guard,
And hew down all that would oppose our passage.
A day will bring us into Cæsar's camp.

Sem. Confusion! I have failed of half my purpose:
Marcia, the charming Marcia 's left behind!

Syph. How! will Sempronius turn a woman's slave?

Sem. Think not thy friend can ever feel the soft
Unmanly warmth and tenderness of love.
Syphax, I long to clasp that haughty maid,
And bend her stubborn virtue to my passion:
When I have gone thus far, I 'd cast her off.

Syph. Well said! that 's spoken like thyself, Sempronius.
What hinders then, but that thou find her out,
And hurry her away by manly force?

Sem. But how to gain admission? for access
Is given to none but Juba and her brothers.

Syph. Thou shalt have Juba's dress and Juba's guards:
The doors will open, when Numidia's prince
Seems to appear before the slaves that watch them.

Sem. Heavens, what a thought is there! Marcia 's my own!
How will my bosom swell with anxious joy,
When I behold her struggling in my arms,
With glowing beauty and disordered charms,
While fear and anger, with alternate grace,
Pant in her breast, and vary in her face!
So Pluto, seized of[1] Proserpine, conveyed
To hell's tremendous gloom th' affrighted maid,
There grimly smiled, pleased with the beauteous prize,
Nor envied Jove his sunshine and his skies.

1 possessed of.

ACT IV.

Scene 1.

(*Lucia and Marcia.*)

Luc. Now tell me, Marcia, tell me from thy soul,
If thou believ'st 't is possible for woman
To suffer greater ills than Lucia suffers?
Mar. O Lucia, Lucia, might my big-swoln heart
Vent all its griefs, and give a loose to sorrow:
Marcia could answer thee in sighs, keep pace
With all thy woes, and count out tear for tear.
Luc. I know thou 'rt doomed, alike, to be beloved
By Juba and thy father's friend, Sempronius;
But which of these has power to charm like Portius?
Mar. Still must I beg thee not to name Sempronius?
Lucia, I like not that loud, boisterous man;
Juba to all the bravery of a hero
Adds softest love, and more than female sweetness;
Juba might make the proudest of our sex,
Any of woman-kind, but Marcia, happy.
Luc. And why not Marcia? come, you strive in vain
To hide your thoughts from one who knows too well
The inward glowings of a heart in love.
Mar. While Cato lives, his daughter has no right
To love or hate, but as his choice directs.
Luc. But should this father give you to Sempronius?
Mar. I dare not think he will: but if he should—
Why wilt thou add to all the griefs I suffer
Imaginary ills, and fancied tortures?
I hear the sound of feet! they march this way!
Let us retire, and try if we can drown
Each softer thought in sense of present danger.
When love once pleads admission to our hearts,
(In spite of all the virtue we can boast)
The woman that deliberates is lost.

Scene 2.

(*Sempronius, dressed like Juba, with Numidian guards.*)

Sem. The deer is lodged. I 've tracked her to her covert.
Be sure you mind the word, and when I give it,
Rush in at once, and seize upon your prey.
Let not her cries or tears have force to move you.
—How will the young Numidian rave, to see
His mistress lost! if aught could glad my soul,
Beyond th' enjoyment of so bright a prize,
'T would be to torture that young gay barbarian.
—But, hark, what noise! death to my hopes! 't is he,
'T is Juba's self! there is but one way left—
He must be murdered, and a passage cut
Through those his guards—Hah! dastards, do you tremble!
Or act like men, or by yon azure heaven—

(*Enter Juba.*)

Juba. What do I see? who 's this that dare usurp
The guards and habit of Numidia's prince?
Sem. One that was born to scourge thy arrogance,
Presumptuous youth!
Juba. What can this mean? Sempronius!
Sem. My sword shall answer thee. Have at thy heart.
Juba. Nay, then beware thy own, proud, barbarous man!
(*Sempronius falls. His guards surrender.*)
Sem. Curse on my stars! am I then doomed to fall
By a boy's hand, disfigured in a vile
Numidian dress, and for a worthless woman?
Gods, I'm distracted! this my close of life!
Oh for a peal of thunder that would make
Earth, sea, and air, and heaven, and Cato tremble!
(*Dies.*)
Juba. With what a spring his furious soul broke loose.

And left the limbs still quivering on the ground!
Hence let us carry off those slaves to Cato,
That we may there at length unravel all
This dark design, this mystery of fate.

SCENE 3.

(*Lucia and Marcia.*)

Luc. Sure 't was the clash of swords; my troubled heart
Is so cast down, and sunk amidst its sorrows,
It throbs with fear and aches at every sound.
O Marcia, should thy brothers for my sake!—
I die away with horror at the thought.

Mar. See, Lucia, see! here 's blood! here 's blood and murder!
Hah, a Numidian! heavens preserve the prince;
The face lies muffled up within the garment.
But hah! death to my sight, a diadem,
And purple robes! O Gods! 't is he, 't is he!
Juba, the loveliest youth that ever warmed
A virgin's heart, Juba lies dead before us!

Luc. Now, Marcia, now call up to thy assistance
Thy wonted strength and constancy of mind;
Thou canst not put it to a greater trial.

Mar. Lucia, look there, and wonder at my patience.
Have I not cause to rave, and beat my breast,
To rend my heart with grief, and run distracted?

Luc. What can I think or say to give thee comfort?

Mar. Talk not of comfort, 't is for lighter ills:
Behold a sight that strikes all comfort dead.

(*Enter Juba, listening.*)

I will indulge my sorrows, and give way
To all the pangs and fury of despair,
That man, that best of men, deserved it from me.

Juba. What do I hear! and was the false Sempronius
The best of men? Oh had I fallen like him,
And could have thus been mourned, I had been happy!

Luc. Here will I stand, companion in thy woes,
And help thee with my tears! when I behold
A loss like thine, I half forget my own.

Mar. 'T is not in fate to ease my tortured breast.
This empty world, to me a joyless desert,
Has nothing left to make poor Marcia happy.

Juba. I 'm on the rack! was he so near her heart?

Mar. Oh! he was all made up of love and charms,
Whatever maid could wish or man admire:
Delight of every eye! when he appeared,
A secret pleasure gladdened all that saw him;
But when he talked, the proudest Roman blushed
To hear his virtues, and old age grew wise.

Juba. I shall run mad—

Mar. O Juba! Juba! Juba!

Juba. What means that voice? did she not call on Juba?

Mar. Why do I think on what he was! he 's dead!
He 's dead, and never knew how much I loved him.
Lucia, who knows but his poor bleeding heart,
Amidst its agonies, remembered Marcia,
And the last words he uttered called me cruel!
Alas! he knew not, hapless youth, he knew not
Marcia's whole soul was full of love and Juba.

Juba. Where am I? do I live! or am indeed
What Marcia thinks! all is Elysium round me!

Mar. Ye dear remains of the most loved of men!
Nor modesty nor virtue here forbid
A last embrace, while thus—

Juba. —See, Marcia, see,

(*Throwing himself before her.*)

The happy Juba lives! he lives to catch
That dear embrace, and to return it too
With mutual warmth and eagerness of love.

Mar. With pleasure and amaze, I stand transported!
Sure 't is a dream! dead and alive at once!
If thou art Juba, who lies there?
Juba. A wretch,
Disguised like Juba, on a cursed design.
The tale is long, nor have I heard it out;
Thy father knows it all. I could not bear
To leave thee in the neighborhood of death,
But flew, in all the haste of love, to find thee;
I found thee weeping, and confess this once,
Am rapt with joy to see my Marcia's tears.
Mar. I've been surprised in an unguarded hour,
But must not now go back: the love, that lay
Half smothered in my breast, has broke through all
Its weak restraints, and burns in its full luster;
I cannot, if I would, conceal it from thee.
Juba. I'm lost in ecstasy! and dost thou love,
Thou charming maid?
Mar. And dost thou live to ask it?
Juba. This, this is life indeed! life worth preserving,
Such life as Juba never felt till now!
Mar. Believe me, prince, before I thought thee dead,
I did not know myself how much I loved thee.
Juba. O fortunate mistake!
Mar. Oh happy Marcia!
Juba. My joy! my best beloved! my only wish!
How shall I speak the transport of my soul?
Mar. Lucia, thy arm! oh let me rest upon it!—
The vital blood, that had forsook my heart,
Returns again in such tumultuous tides,
It quite o'ercomes me. Lead to my apartment.—
O prince! I blush to think what I have said,
But fate has wrested the confession from me;
Go on, and prosper in the paths of honor,
Thy virtue will excuse my passion for thee,
And make the gods propitious to our love.

(*Exeunt Marcia and Lucia.*)

Juba. I am so blest, I fear 't is all a dream.
Fortune, thou now hast made amends for all
Thy past unkindness. I absolve my stars.
What though Numidia add her conquered towns
And provinces to swell the victor's triumph!
Juba will never at his fate repine;
Let Cæsar have the world, if Marcia 's mine.

SCENE 4. *A March at a Distance.*

(*Cato and Lucius.*)

Luc. I stand astonished! what, the bold Sempronius!
That still broke foremost through the crowd of patriots,
As with a hurricane of zeal transported,
And virtuous even to madness—
Cato. Trust me, Lucius,
Our civil discords have produced such crimes,
Such monstrous crimes, I am surprised at nothing.
—O Lucius! I am sick of this bad world!
The day-light and the sun grow painful to me.

(*Enter Portius.*)

But see where Portius comes! What means this haste?
Why are thy looks thus changed?
Por. My heart is grieved.
I bring such news as will afflict my father.
Cato. Has Cæsar shed more Roman blood?
Por. Not so.
The traitor Syphax, as within the square
He exercised his troops, the signal given,
Flew off at once with his Numidian horse
To the south gate, where Marcus holds the watch.
I saw, and called to stop him, but in vain,
He tossed his arm aloft, and proudly told me,

He would not stay and perish like Sempronius.

Cato. Perfidious men! but haste, my son, and see
Thy brother Marcus acts a Roman's part.

(*Exit Por.*)

—Lucius, the torrent bears too hard upon me:
Justice gives way to force: the conquered world
Is Cæsar's: Cato has no business in it.

Luc. While pride, oppression, and injustice reign,
The world will still demand her Cato's presence.
In pity to mankind, submit to Cæsar,
And reconcile thy mighty soul to life.

Cato. Would Lucius have me live to swell the number
Of Cæsar's slaves, or by a base submission
Give up the cause of Rome, and own a tyrant?

Luc. The victor never will impose on Cato
Ungenerous terms. His enemies confess
The virtues of humanity are Cæsar's.

Cato. Curse on his virtues! they 've undone his country.
Such popular humanity is treason—
But see young Juba! the good youth appears
Full of the guilt of his perfidious subjects.

Luc. Alas! poor prince! his fate deserves compassion.

(*Enter Juba.*)

Juba. I blush and am confounded to appear
Before thy presence, Cato.

Cato. What 's thy crime?

Juba. I 'm a Numidian.

Cato. And a brave one too.
Thou hast a Roman soul.

Juba. Hast thou not heard
Of my false countrymen?

Cato. Alas! young prince,
Falsehood and fraud shoot up in every soil,
The product of all climes—Rome has its Cæsars.

Juba. 'T is generous thus to comfort the distressed.

Cato. 'T is just to give applause where 't is deserved;
Thy virtue, prince, has stood the test of fortune,
Like purest gold, that, tortured in the furnace,
Comes out more bright, and brings forth all its weight.

Juba. What shall I answer thee? my ravished heart
O'erflows with secret joy; I'd rather gain
Thy praise, O Cato, than Numidia's empire.

(*Re-enter Portius.*)

Por. Misfortune on misfortune! grief on grief!
My brother Marcus—

Cato. Hah! what has he done?
Has he forsook his post? has he given way?
Did he look tamely on, and let 'em pass?

Por. Scarce had I left my father, but I met him
Borne on the shields of his surviving soldiers,
Breathless and pale, and covered o'er with wounds.
Long, at the head of his few faithful friends,
He stood the shock of a whole host of foes.
Till, obstinately brave, and bent on death,
Oppressed with multitudes, he greatly fell.

Cato. I 'm satisfied.

Por. Nor did he fall before
His sword had pierc'd through the false heart of Syphax.
Yonder he lies. I saw the hoary traitor
Grin in the pangs of death, and bite the ground.

Cato. Thanks to the gods! my boy has done his duty.
—Portius, when I am dead, be sure thou place
His urn near mine.

Por. Long may they keep asunder.

Luc. O Cato! arm thy soul with all its patience;
See where the corpse of thy dead son approaches!
The citizens and senators, alarmed,
Have gathered round it, and attend it weeping.

(*Cato, meeting the corpse.*)

Welcome, my son! here lay him down, my friends,
Full in my sight, that I may view at leisure

The bloody corse, and count those glorious wounds.
How beautiful is death, when earned by virtue!
Who would not be that youth? what pity is it
That we can die but once to serve our country!
Why sits this sadness on your brows, my friends?
I should have blushed if Cato's house had stood
Secure, and flourished in a civil war.
—Portius, behold thy brother, and remember
Thy life is not thy own, when Rome demands it.

Juba. Was ever man like this! (*Aside.*)

Cato. Alas! my friends!
Why mourn you thus? let not a private loss
Afflict your hearts. 'T is Rome requires our tears,
The mistress of the world, the seat of empire,
The nurse of heroes, the delight of gods,
That humbled the proud tyrants of the earth,
And set the nations free, Rome is no more.
Oh liberty! Oh virtue! Oh my country!

Juba. Behold that upright man! Rome fills his eyes
With tears, that flowed not o'er his own dead son. (*Aside.*)

Cato. Whate'er the Roman virtue has subdued,
The sun's whole course, the day and year, are Cæsar's.
For him the self-devoted Decii died,
The Fabii fell, and the great Scipios conquered;
Even Pompey fought for Cæsar. Oh! my friends!
How is the toil of fate, the work of ages,
The Roman empire fallen! Oh curst ambition!
Fallen into Cæsar's hands! Our great forefathers
Had left him nought to conquer but his country.

Juba. While Cato lives, Cæsar will blush to see
Mankind enslaved, and be ashamed of empire.

Cato. Cæsar ashamed! has not he seen Pharsalia?

Luc. Cato, 't is time thou save thyself and us.

Cato. Lose not a thought on me; I 'm out of danger.
Heaven will not leave me in the victor's hand.
Cæsar shall never say, I conquered Cato.
But, oh! my friends, your safety fills my heart
With anxious thoughts: a thousand secret terrors
Rise in my soul: how shall I save my friends!
'T is now, O Cæsar, I begin to fear thee.

Luc. Cæsar has mercy, if we ask it of him.

Cato. Then ask it, I conjure you! let him know
Whate'er was done against him, Cato did it.
Add, if you please, that I request it of him,
The virtue of my friends may pass unpunished.
—Juba, my heart is troubled for thy sake.
Should I advise thee to regain Numidia,
Or seek the conqueror?—

Juba. If I forsake thee
Whilst I have life, may heaven abandon Juba!

Cato. Thy virtues, prince, if I foresee aright,
Will one day make thee great; at Rome, hereafter,
'T will be no crime to have been Cato's friend.
Portius, draw near! my son, thou oft hast seen
Thy sire engaged in a corrupted state,
Wrestling with vice and faction: now thou seest me
Spent, overpowered, despairing of success;
Let me advise thee to retreat betimes
To thy paternal seat, the Sabine field,
Where the great Censor toiled with his own hands,
And all our frugal ancestors were blessed
In humble virtues, and a rural life.
There live retired, pray for the peace of Rome:
Content thyself to be obscurely good.
When vice prevails, and impious men bear sway,
The post of honor is a private station.

Por. I hope my father does not recommend
A life to Portius that he scorns himself.

Cato. Farewell, my friends! if there be any of you
Who dare not trust the victor's clemency,
Know, there are ships prepared by my command,
(Their sails already opening to the winds)
That shall convey you to the wished-for port.
Is there aught else, my friends, I can do for you?
The conqueror draws near. Once more farewell!
If e'er we meet hereafter, we shall meet
In happier climes, and on a safer shore,
Where Cæsar never shall approach us more.
(*Pointing to his dead son.*)
There the brave youth, with love of virtue fired,
Who greatly in his country's cause expired,
Shall know he conquered. The firm patriot there,
(Who made the welfare of mankind his care)
Though still, by faction, vice, and fortune crost,
Shall find the generous labor was not lost.

ACT V.

Scene 1.

(*Cato solus, sitting in a thoughtful posture: in his hand Plato's Book on the Immortality of the Soul. A drawn sword on the table by him.*)

It must be so—Plato, thou reason'st well!—
Else whence this pleasing hope, this fond desire,
This longing after immortality?
Or whence this secret dread, and inward horror,
Of falling into naught? why shrinks the soul
Back on herself, and startles at destruction?
'T is the divinity that stirs within us;
'T is heaven itself, that points out an hereafter,
And intimates eternity to man.
Eternity! thou pleasing, dreadful thought!
Through what variety of untried being,
Through what new scenes and changes must we pass!
The wide, th' unbounded prospect, lies before me;
But shadows, clouds, and darkness, rest upon it.
Here will I hold. If there 's a power above us,
(And that there is all nature cries aloud
Through all her works) he must delight in virtue:
And that which he delights in, must be happy.
But when! or where!—This world was made for Cæsar.
I 'm weary of conjectures—This must end 'em.
(*Laying his hand on his sword.*)
Thus am I doubly armed: my death and life,
My bane and antidote, are both before me:
This in a moment brings me to an end;
But this informs me I shall never die.
The soul secured in her existence, smiles
At the drawn dagger, and defies its point.
The stars shall fade away, the sun himself
Grow dim with age, and nature sink in years;
But thou shalt flourish in immortal youth,
Unhurt amidst the war of elements,
The wrecks of matter, and the crush of worlds.
What means this heaviness that hangs upon me?
This lethargy that creeps through all my senses?
Nature, oppressed and harassed out with care,
Sinks down to rest. This once I 'll favor her,
That my awakened soul may take her flight,
Renewed in all her strength, and fresh with life,
An offering fit for heaven. Let guilt or fear
Disturb man's rest: Cato knows neither of 'em,
Indifferent in his choice to sleep or die.

SCENE 2.

(*Cato, Portius.*)

Cato. But, hah! how 's this, my son? why this intrusion?
Were not my orders that I would be private?
Why am I disobeyed?
Por. Alas! my father!
What means this sword, this instrument of death?
Let me convey it hence!
Cato. Rash youth, forbear!
Por. Oh let the prayers, th' entreaties of your friends,
Their tears, their common danger, wrest it from you.
Cato. Wouldst thou betray me? wouldst thou give me up
A slave, a captive, into Cæsar's hands?
Retire, and learn obedience to a father,
Or know, young man!—
Por. Look not thus sternly on me;
You know I 'd rather die than disobey you.
Cato. 'T is well! again I 'm master of myself.
Now, Cæsar, let thy troops beset our gates,
And bar each avenue, thy gathering fleets
O'erspread the sea, and stop up every port;
Cato shall open to himself a passage,
And mock thy hopes—
Por. Oh, sir! forgive your son,
Whose grief hangs heavy on him! Oh my father!
How am I sure it is not the last time
I e'er shall call you so! be not displeased,
Oh be not angry with me whilst I weep,
And, in the anguish of my heart beseech you
To quit the dreadful purpose of your soul!
Cato. Thou hast been ever good and dutiful.
(*Embracing him.*)
Weep not, my son. All will be well again.
The righteous gods, whom I have sought to please,
Will succor Cato, and preserve his children.
Por. Your words give comfort to my drooping heart.
Cato. Portius, thou may'st rely upon my conduct.
Thy father will not act what misbecomes him.
But go, my son, and see if aught be wanting
Among thy father's friends; see them embarked;
And tell me if the winds and seas befriend them.
My soul is quite weighed down with care, and asks
The soft refreshment of a moment's sleep.
(*Exit.*)
Por. My thoughts are more at ease, my heart revives.

SCENE 3.

(*Portius and Marcia.*)

Por. O Marcia, O my sister, still there 's hope!
Our father will not cast away a life
So needful to us all, and to his country.
He is retired to rest, and seems to cherish
Thoughts full of peace. He has despatched me hence
With orders, that bespeak a mind composed,
And studious for the safety of his friends.
Marcia, take care that none disturb his slumbers.
Mar. O ye immortal powers, that guard the just,
Watch round his couch, and soften his repose,
Banish his sorrows, and becalm his soul
With easy dreams; remember all his virtues!
And show mankind that goodness is your care.

SCENE 4.

(*Lucia and Marcia.*)

Luc. Where is your father, Marcia, where is Cato?
Mar. Lucia, speak low, he is retired to rest.
Lucia, I feel a gently-dawning hope
Rise in my soul. We shall be happy still.
Luc. Alas! I tremble when I think on Cato,
In [e]very view, in every thought I tremble!

Cato is stern, and awful as a god;
He knows not how to wink at human frailty,
Or pardon weakness that he never felt.

Mar. Though stern and awful to the foes of Rome,
He is all goodness, Lucia, always mild,
Compassionate, and gentle to his friends.
Fill'd with domestic tenderness, the best,
The kindest father! I have ever found him
Easy, and good, and bounteous to my wishes.

Luc. 'T is his consent alone can make us blest.
Marcia, we both are equally involved
In the same intricate, perplexed distress.
The cruel hand of fate, that has destroyed
Thy brother Marcus, whom we both lament—

Mar. And ever shall lament, unhappy youth!

Luc. Has set my soul at large, and now I stand
Loose of my vow. But who knows Cato's thoughts?
Who knows how yet he may dispose of Portius,
Or how he has determined of thyself?

Mar. Let him but live! commit the rest to heaven.

(*Enter Lucius.*)

Luc. Sweet are the slumbers of the virtuous man!
O Marcia, I have seen thy godlike father:
Some power invisible supports his soul,
And bears it up in all its wonted greatness.
A kind refreshing sleep is fallen upon him:
I saw him stretched at ease, his fancy lost
In pleasing dreams: as I drew near his couch,
He smiled, and cried, "Cæsar, thou canst not hurt me."

Mar. His mind still labors with some dreadful thought.

Luc. Lucia, why all this grief, these floods of sorrow?
Dry up thy tears, my child, we all are safe
While Cato lives—his presence will protect us.

(*Enter Juba.*)

Juba. Lucius, the horsemen are returned from viewing
The number, strength, and posture of our foes,
Who now encamp within a short hour's march.
On the high point of yon bright western tower
We ken them from afar, the setting sun
Plays on their shining arms and burnished helmets,
And covers all the field with gleams of fire.

Luc. Marcia, 't is time we should awake thy father.
Cæsar is still disposed to give us terms,
And waits at distance till he hears from Cato.

(*Enter Portius.*)

Portius, thy looks speak somewhat of importance,
What tidings dost thou bring? methinks I see
Unusual gladness sparkling in thy eyes.

Por. As I was hasting to the port, where now
My father's friends, impatient for a passage,
Accuse the lingering winds, a sail arrived
From Pompey's son, who through the realms of Spain
Calls out for vengeance on his father's death,
And rouses the whole nation up to arms.
Were Cato at their head, once more might Rome
Assert her rights and claim her liberty.
But, hark! what means that groan! Oh give me way,
And let me fly into my father's presence.
(*Exit Portius.*)

Luc. Cato, amidst his slumbers, thinks on Rome,
And in the wild disorder of his soul
Mourns o'er his country,—Hah! a second groan!—
Heaven guard us all—

Mar. Alas! 't is not the voice
Of one who sleeps! 't is agonizing pain,
'T is death is in that sound—

(*Re-enter Portius.*)

Por. Oh sight of woe!
O Marcia, what we feared is come to pass!
Cato is fallen upon his sword—

Luc. O Portius,

Hide all the horrors of thy mournful tale,
And let us guess the rest.

Por. I 've raised him up,
And placed him in his chair, where, pale and faint,
He gasps for breath, and, as his life flows from him,
Demands to see his friends. His servants weeping,
Obsequious to his orders, bear him hither.

(*The back scene opens and discovers Cato.*)

Mar. O heaven, assist me in this dreadful hour
To pay the last sad duties to my father.

Juba. These are thy triumphs, thy exploits, O Cæsar!

Luc. Now is Rome fallen indeed!

(*Cato brought forward in his chair.*)

Cato. Here set me down—
Portius, come near me—are my friends embarked?
Can anything be thought of for their service?
Whilst I yet live, let me not live in vain.
—O Lucius, art thou here?—thou art too good!—
Let this our friendship live between our children;
Make Portius happy in thy daughter Lucia.
Alas! poor man, he weeps!—Marcia, my daughter—
—Oh bend me forward!—Juba loves thee, Marcia.
A senator of Rome, while Rome survived,
Would not have match'd his daughter with a king,
But Cæsar's arms have thrown down all distinction;
Whoe'er is brave and virtuous, is a Roman.—
—I 'm sick to death—Oh when shall I get loose
From this vain world, th' abode of guilt and sorrow!
—And yet methinks a beam of light breaks in
On my departing soul. Alas! I fear
I 've been too hasty! O ye powers that search
The heart of man, and weigh his inmost thoughts,
If I have done amiss, impute it not!—
The best may err, but you are good, and—oh!

(*Dies.*)

Luc. There fled the greatest soul that ever warmed
A Roman breast. O Cato! O my friend!
Thy will shall be religiously observed.
But let us bear this awful corpse to Cæsar,
And lay it in his sight, that it may stand
A fence betwixt us and the victor's wrath;
Cato, though dead, shall still protect his friends.
From hence, let fierce contending nations know
What dire effects from civil discord flow.
'T is this that shakes our country with alarms,
And gives up Rome a prey to Roman arms,
Produces fraud, and cruelty, and strife,
And robs the guilty world of Cato's life.

SIR RICHARD STEELE

THE CONSCIOUS LOVERS

Sir Richard Steele (1672–1729), born in Dublin, son of a well-to-do Irish attorney, was educated and passed most of his life in England. Like the later Irish dramatist Sheridan, he rose to prominence in both politics and literature. Active and versatile, he passed some of his early years in the army, and later contributed to political journalism, entered Parliament and was knighted. A lifelong friend of Addison, from the age of fourteen, like him he won his chief fame by contributing essays to *The Tatler* and *The Spectator*, 1709–12.

The origin and influence of *The Conscious Lovers* and its type of play are what give the work its main interest. Of itself it is not a particularly good play, and makes us smile oftener when the author did not intend we should than when he did. But all the same it is a landmark of a profound change in social history and in the drama. In Steele's plays conscious morality, and sentimentalism, came into the drama of real life. In Elizabethan domestic tragedy, such as Heywood's *A Woman Killed with Kindness*, there had been conscious morality, but with Steele we get a new combination and a new literary effect.

Two chief influences led Steele to make the innovation. In 1698 Jeremy Collier, a Nonjuring clergyman, had attacked the contemporary drama in his book *A Short View of the Immorality and Profaneness of the English Stage*, a work, though not without fallacies, remarkable for learning, wit, sobriety, and sense. On Steele it created a profound impression. Further, in 1701, while still in the army, he had published *The Christian Hero*, as a check on his own expansive though conscientious nature, declaring Christian principles a better guide for a man than the principles of honor so-called which were the ideals of most persons of station; the chief result of which book among his mates was "that from being reckoned no undelightful companion he was soon reckoned a disagreeable fellow." Feeling a challenge to prove himself after all no prig, he undertook in 1701 "to enliven his character" by the production of a comedy — with the unexpected title *The Funeral*. This and several which followed, though not lacking cleverness and humor, are notable chiefly for their attempt to teach or at least not to offend morality and virtue. Thus he served both God and Mammon.

The Conscious Lovers was written later in Steele's life, after the *Spectator* period. He worked over it for some two years; it appeared in 1722, and ran for twenty-six nights, which then meant a considerable success. It evoked much discussion, especially as to act IV, where Bevil as a matter of principle avoids fighting a duel, the strongest and most genuine scene in the play. Steele states in his preface that he wrote the play for the sake of this point. Early in his life he had been forced into a duel, and came to feel keenly the iniquity of the conventional code of honor; in the play he imaginatively embodies and applies the principles which he had laid down in *The Christian Hero.* Other timely and practical matters which find a voice in the play are the question as to the relative dignity of the landed aristocracy and the merchant class, discussed by Sealand and the elder Bevil in act IV, and the duty of a father to look sharply into the character of the man to whom he is to intrust his daughter. At such points we feel a decidedly new and modern spirit, and are conscious, under the artificial exterior, of a humane and independent thinker. In other places we get a vivid light on the roughness of contemporary life, even among the sentimental; the coarse talk of Cimberton seems to anger the pride rather than to shock the modesty even of the proper Lucinda. Likewise we are surprised, though rather relieved, to hear this well-conducted young woman now and then exclaim "Deuce on 'em!" On the whole, however, the play represents rather things as they supposedly ought to be than as they are. Its moral idealism is more prominent than its realism. Some credit must doubtless be given to such plays as Steele's, as to novels like Godwin's *Caleb Williams* (1794), also written against duelling, for such changes in public feeling as have, for example, abolished the duel from the Anglo-Saxon world. The seriousness which was genially satirized by Fielding through the mouth of Parson Adams in *Joseph Andrews* was one reason for the play's long hold on people —"I never heard of any plays fit for a Christian to read, but *Cato* and the *Conscious Lovers;* and, I must own, in the latter there are some things almost solemn enough for a sermon." The appealing emotionality of sentimental drama fitted it to be an instrument of social reform.

The words sentiment and sentimentalism as used of this and later plays have really two applications. They refer to a soft emotionalism — pity, mild unpassionate love, gentle admiration, over-delicacy, and sensitiveness; and also to the fondness of the characters for sententious expression of laudable opinions. A "man of sentiment" is a man of feeling, and given to moralizing. The development of sentimentalism, unlike that of classicism and romanticism, was not well defined enough to be called a movement; but all of them were alike in this, that each was at bottom merely a *taste*, a liking for a certain kind of esthetic impression, a liking which has always existed, but at a particular time became especially general and self-expressive. Since these plays attempted to substitute something harmless for the reckless wit and unscrupulous intrigue of Restoration comedy, they were cut off from a source of strong sensation; and it may truly be said that sentimentalism is an endeavor not only to secure the ethical character which the earlier comedy had lacked, but also to retain the interest and piquancy which it had secured in another way. It remained for Goldsmith and Sheridan to show that comedy could abandon its licentiousness without substituting tears for laughter. Yet such was the genuine originality and vitality of sentimentalism that even these men, its enemies, could not escape its influence.

The sentimentalism of this play is not extreme or offensive, yet it is ever present. The delicacy of young Bevil toward his father is almost as fine-drawn as that of Mrs. Ann Radcliffe's romantic heroine, later in the century, who had too much delicacy to tell her parents of a proposal of marriage. Old Bevil is arrogant and domineering, "yet their fear of giving each other pain is attended with constant mutual uneasiness." The music-master is introduced merely to let Bevil show that "the distinguishing part of a gentleman" is "to make his superiority of fortune as easy to his inferiors as he can," and to win for him Indiana's "smile of approbation." When we first see him he is laying in moral fuel for the day's run by reading Addison's *Vision of Mirza*. Bevil appears to us a prig, and we dislike him; he pays the penalty of practically all faultless heroes in realistic fiction. The reason for this all but universal feeling is not a mean and envious streak in human nature, but a pardonable resentment at seeing what we know to be rare and difficult represented as so easy as complete virtue is to these unnatural heroes. Indiana has all the swooning, clinging sensibility of a long line of later heroines; in the epoch of sensibility women were not expected to control themselves. The moral delicacy of the play is expressed in its very title. Alluding to the couplet with which Indiana closes the second act,—

> As conscious honor all his actions steers,
> So conscious innocence dispels my fears,—

the word "conscious" in "*Conscious Lovers*" means "who know what they are about." "Conscious love" was a household substitute for the reckless passion which the drama has usually preferred.

The ideality, representing things as better or more convenient than in life, is not confined to the characters. As a further substitute for dash and wit, we have an elaborate plot in which probability is not allowed to stand in the way of somewhat crude humor, or the niceties of poetic justice — in which all things work together for good for those who love good, and in which the most childish disguises and intrigues are made to work. The facts of the world give way before the interests of both the characters and the dramatist. Sentimental comedy is thoroughly artificial and conventional in the elements of its plot. There is a curious contrast between the highly sophisticated and fragile characters and the traditional sort of story through which they move, with its disguises, long-lost children, new-found wills, and the like. For free comedy in this play we have to resort to Tom and Phillis, who are not bound by the code which trammels their betters, and who are an early instance of a device common in later novel and drama, a comic and every-day pair of lovers alongside a romantic pair. No critic has failed to relish Tom's description (III. i) of his Pyramus-like courtship of Phillis through the window-glass which she was cleaning. But unfortunately this is only told, not acted.

The traditional, artificial character of the plot is partly accounted for by its source, the *Andria* of Terence, to which the first two acts and the last are especially indebted; almost every character and every essential incident in Steele's work has its counterpart in the admirable Latin play. Glycerium, lost by her father in infancy and now kept mistress of Pamphilus, turns into the delicate-minded Indiana, innocently supported for a time by Bevil's bounty. Charinus, in love with the girl whom Pamphilus' father would have him marry, jealously quarrels with his unwilling rival; from this Steele develops the incident of the averted duel. The recognition of the long-lost daughter at the end he does his best to make as plausible as it seems in Terence; even the change of old Sealand's name is paralleled in Terence by a change of the daughter's. It is of the greatest interest to see how the stock characters of Latin comedy — the tyrannical old man, the wild son, the rascally slave — have been translated as it were into the native English vernacular, or refined into ideality.

The soundest estimate of this and like plays is that they are a hybrid, attempting to combine the entertainment afforded by comedy with the dignity and "uplift" of tragedy. The comic muse, grown too wild, was to be reformed by the influence of her sedate sister. The idealized personalties, the indifference to every-day probability, and the moral teaching of contemporary tragedy are fully adopted; its violent emotions are toned down to a degree which will not rend the frailer fabric of comedy, and become sentimentalism; so far as possible its poetic vesture is preserved. In *The Conscious Lovers* much of the talk is not meant to be that of daily life; it is formal, rhetorical, rhythmical, and, toward the end especially, much of it is actually blank verse (though printed as prose). This heavy and edifying side of the play is relieved by comic elements, partly realistic (as in the talk of Tom), partly fantastic (as in the figure of Cimberton and in the various disguises). But the lighter element is made to know its place; sentimentalism in the person of Lucinda rebukes comedy in the person of Phillis as "a pert merry hussy" (III. i). The novelty and a certain merit in the combination gave it success with the uncritical; and though it was fair game for the ridicule it was to receive from the great comic dramatists, Goldsmith and Sheridan, even the critical will give a certain sympathy to its well-meaning optimism. This is the fundamental trait it has in common with contemporary tragedy, and is also what gave the type its long life. The improving sentiments poured out, and the upright intentions of the characters, seem to gain validity and even divine approval from the complete satisfaction in which everything ends. The picture of life afforded by the play justifies the moral optimism of the concluding couplet:

> Whate'er the generous mind itself denies,
> The secret care of Providence supplies.

The Conscious Lovers was played in the principal theaters of London for generations, and sentimentalism more or less modified has lived on even to the present day, in dramas of lower grade; more important yet, it built itself a more stately mansion in the novel, beginning with Richardson. Sometimes combined with romance, it flourished in the nineteenth century, and is one of the main elements in the novels of Dickens.

THE CONSCIOUS LOVERS

"Illud genus narrationis, quod in personis positum est, debet habere sermonis festivitatem, animorum dissimilitudinem, gravitatem, lenitatem, spem, metum, suspicionem, desiderium, dissimulationem, misericordiam, rerum varietates, fortunæ commutationem, insperatum incommodum, subitam letitiam, jucundum exitum rerum." *— CICERO, Rhetor. ad Herenn. Lib. i.

DRAMATIS PERSONÆ

SIR JOHN BEVIL.
MR. SEALAND.
BEVIL, JUN., *in love with* INDIANA.
MYRTLE, *in love with* LUCINDA.
CIMBERTON, *a Coxcomb.*
HUMPHRY, *an old Servant to* SIR JOHN.
TOM, *Servant to* BEVIL, JUN.
DANIEL, *a Country Boy, Servant to* INDIANA.

MRS. SEALAND, *second Wife to* SEALAND.
ISABELLA, *Sister to* SEALAND.
INDIANA, SEALAND'S *Daughter, by his first Wife.*
LUCINDA, SEALAND'S *Daughter, by his second Wife.*
PHILLIS, *Maid to* LUCINDA.

SCENE.—*London.*

ACT THE FIRST.

SCENE 1. *Sir John Bevil's House.*

(*Enter Sir John Bevil and Humphry.*)

Sir J. Bev. Have you ordered that I should not be interrupted while I am dressing?

Humph. Yes, sir; I believed you had something of moment to say to me.

Sir J. Bev. Let me see, Humphry; I think it is now full forty years since I first took thee to be about myself.

Humph. I thank you, sir, it has been an easy forty years; and I have passed 'em without much sickness, care, or labor.

Sir J. Bev. Thou hast a brave constitution; you are a year or two older than I am, sirrah.

Humph. You have ever been of that mind, sir.

Sir J. Bev. You knave, you know it; I took thee for thy gravity and sobriety, in my wild years.

Humph. Ah, sir! our manners were

* The kind of story which is presented on the stage ought to be marked by gaiety of dialogue, diversity of character, seriousness, tenderness, hope, fear, suspicion, desire, dissimulation, pity, variety of events, changes of fortune, unexpected disaster, sudden joy, and a happy ending. (Not really by Cicero.)

formed from our different fortunes, not our different age. Wealth gave a loose to your youth, and poverty put a restraint upon mine.

Sir J. Bev. Well, Humphry, you know I have been a kind master to you; I have used you, for the ingenuous nature I observed in you from the beginning, more like an humble friend than a servant.

Humph. I humbly beg you'll be so tender of me as to explain your commands, sir, without any farther preparation.

Sir J. Bev. I'll tell thee, then: In the first place, this wedding of my son's in all probability—shut the door—will never be at all.

Humph. How, sir! not be at all? for what reason is it carried on in appearance?

Sir J. Bev. Honest Humphry, have patience; and I'll tell thee all in order. I have, myself, in some part of my life, lived (indeed) with freedom, but, I hope, without reproach. Now, I thought liberty would be as little injurious to my son; therefore, as soon as he grew towards man, I indulged him in living after his own manner. I knew not how, otherwise, to judge of his inclination; for what can be concluded from a behavior under restraint and fear? But what charms me above all expression is, that my son has never, in the least action, the most distant hint or word, valued himself upon that great estate of his mother's, which, according to our marriage settlement, he has had ever since he came to age.

Humph. No, sir; on the contrary, he seems afraid of appearing to enjoy it, before you or any belonging to you. He is as dependent and resigned to your will as if he had not a farthing but what must come from your immediate bounty. You have ever acted like a good and generous father, and he like an obedient and grateful son.

Sir J. Bev. Nay, his carriage is so easy to all with whom he converses, that he is never assuming, never prefers himself to others, nor ever is guilty of that rough sincerity which a man is not called to, and certainly disobliges most of his acquaintance; to be short, Humphry, his reputation was so fair in the world, that old Sealand, the great Indian merchant, has offered his only daughter, and sole heiress to that vast estate of his, as a wife for him. You may be sure I made no difficulties, the match was agreed on, and this very day named for the wedding.

Humph. What hinders the proceeding?

Sir J. Bev. Don't interrupt me. You know I was last Thursday at the masquerade; my son, you may remember, soon found us out. He knew his grandfather's habit, which I then wore; and though it was the mode, in the last age, yet the masquers, you know, followed us as if we had been the most monstrous figures in that whole assembly.

Humph. I remember, indeed, a young man of quality in the habit of a clown, that was particularly troublesome.

Sir J. Bev. Right; he was too much what he seemed to be. You remember how impertinently he followed and teased us, and would know who we were.

Humph. I know he has a mind to come into that particular.
(*Aside.*)

Sir J. Bev. Ay, he followed us till the gentleman who led the lady in the Indian mantle presented that gay creature to the rustic, and bid him (like Cymon in the fable) grow polite by falling in love, and let that worthy old gentleman alone, meaning me. The clown was not reformed, but rudely persisted, and offered to force off my mask; with that, the gentleman, throwing off his own, appeared to be my son, and in his concern for me, tore off that of the nobleman; at this they seized each other; the company called the guards, and in the surprise the lady swooned away; upon which my son quitted his adversary, and had now no care but of the lady. When raising her in his arms, "Art thou gone," cried he, "for ever?—forbid it, Heaven!" She revived at his known voice, and with the most familiar, though modest, gesture, hangs in safety over his shoulder weeping, but wept as in the arms of one before whom she could give herself a loose, were she not under observation; while she hides her face in his neck, he carefully conveys her from the company.

Humph. I have observed this accident has dwelt upon you very strongly.

Sir J. Bev. Her uncommon air, her noble modesty, the dignity of her person, and the occasion itself, drew the whole assembly together; and I soon heard it buzzed about she was the adopted daughter of a famous sea-officer who had served in France. Now this unexpected and public discovery of my son's so deep concern for her——

Humph. Was what, I suppose, alarmed Mr. Sealand, in behalf of his daughter, to break off the match?

Sir J. Bev. You are right. He came to me yesterday and said he thought himself disengaged from the bargain; being credibly informed my son was already married, or worse, to the lady at the masquerade. I palliated matters, and insisted on our agreement; but we parted with little less than a direct breach between us.

Humph. Well, sir; and what notice have you taken of all this to my young master?

Sir J. Bev. That 's what I wanted to debate with you. I have said nothing to him yet—but look you, Humphry, if there is so much in this amour of his, that he denies upon my summons to marry, I have cause enough to be offended; and then by my insisting upon his marrying to-day, I shall know how far he is engaged to this lady in masquerade, and from thence only shall be able to take my measures. In the meantime I would have you find out how far that rogue, his man, is let into his secret. He, I know, will play tricks as much to cross me, as to serve his master.

Humph. Why do you think so of him, sir? I believe he is no worse than I was for you, at your son's age.

Sir J. Bev. I see it in the rascal's looks. But I have dwelt on these things too long; I 'll go to my son immediately, and while I 'm gone, your part is to convince his rogue, Tom, that I am in earnest.—I 'll leave him to you.

(*Exit Sir John Bevil.*)

Humph. Well, though this father and son live as well together as possible, yet their fear of giving each other pain is attended with constant mutual uneasiness. I 'm sure I have enough to do to be honest, and yet keep well with them both. But they know I love 'em, and that makes the task less painful, however. Oh, here 's the prince of poor coxcombs, the representative of all the better fed than taught. Ho! ho! Tom, whither so gay and so airy this morning?

(*Enter Tom, singing.*)

Tom. Sir, we servants of single gentlemen are another kind of people than you domestic ordinary drudges that do business; we are raised above you. The pleasures of board wages, tavern dinners, and many a clear gain; vails,[1] alas! you never heard or dreamt of.

Humph. Thou hast follies and vices enough for a man of ten thousand a year, though 't is but as t'other day that I sent for you to town to put you into Mr. Sealand's family, that you might learn a little before I put you to my young master, who is too gentle for training such a rude thing as you were into proper obedience. You then pulled off your hat to every one you met in the street, like a bashful great awkward cub as you were. But your great oaken cudgel, when you were a booby, became you much better than that dangling stick at your button, now you are a fop. That 's fit for nothing, except it hangs there to be ready for your master's hand when you are impertinent.

Tom. Uncle Humphry, you know my master scorns to strike his servants. You talk as if the world was now just as it was when my old master and you were in your youth; when you went to dinner because it was so much o'clock, when the great blow was given in the hall at the pantry door, and all the family came out of their holes in such strange dresses and formal faces as you see in the pictures in our long gallery in the country.

Humph. Why, you wild rogue!

Tom. You could not fall to your dinner till a formal fellow in a black gown said something over the meat, as if the cook had not made it ready enough.

Humph. Sirrah, who do you prate after? Despising men of sacred characters! I hope you never heard my good young master talk so like a profligate.

Tom. Sir, I say you put upon me, when I first came to town, about being orderly, and the doctrine of wearing shams to make linen last clean a fortnight, keeping my clothes fresh, and wearing a frock within doors.

Humph. Sirrah, I gave you those lessons because I supposed at that time your master and you might have dined at home every day, and cost you nothing; then you might have made a good family servant. But the gang you have fre-

[1] tips.

quented since at chocolate houses and taverns, in a continual round of noise and extravagance——

Tom. I don't know what you heavy inmates call noise and extravagance; but we gentlemen, who are well fed, and cut a figure, sir, think it a fine life, and that we must be very pretty fellows who are kept only to be looked at.

Humph. Very well, sir, I hope the fashion of being lewd and extravagant, despising of decency and order, is almost at an end, since it is arrived at persons of your quality.

Tom. Master Humphry, ha! ha! you were an unhappy lad to be sent up to town in such queer days as you were. Why, now, sir, the lackeys are the men of pleasure of the age, the top gamesters; and many a laced coat about town have had their education in our party-colored regiment. We are false lovers; have a taste of music, poetry, billet-doux, dress, politics; ruin damsels; and when we are tired of this lewd town, and have a mind to take up,[2] whip into our masters' wigs and linen, and marry fortunes.

Humph. Hey-day!

Tom. Nay, sir, our order is carried up to the highest dignities and distinctions; step but into the Painted Chamber,[3] and by our titles you'd take us all for men of quality. Then, again, come down to the Court of Requests,[3] and you see us all laying our broken heads together for the good of the nation; and though we never carry a question *nemine contradicente,*[4] yet this I can say, with a safe conscience (and I wish every gentleman of our cloth could lay his hand upon his heart and say the same), that I never took so much as a single mug of beer for my vote in all my life.

Humph. Sirrah, there is no enduring your extravagance; I'll hear you prate no longer. I wanted to see you to enquire how things go with your master, as far as you understand them; I suppose he knows he is to be married to-day.

Tom. Ay, sir, he knows it, and is dressed as gay as the sun; but, between you and I, my dear, he has a very heavy heart under all that gaiety. As soon as he was dressed I retired, but overheard him sigh in the most heavy manner. He walked thoughtfully to and fro in the room, then went into his closet; when he came out he gave me this for his mistress, whose maid, you know——

Humph. Is passionately fond of your fine person.

Tom. The poor fool is so tender, and loves to hear me talk of the world, and the plays, operas, and ridottos[5] for the winter, the parks and Belsize[6] for our summer diversions; and "Lard!" says she, "you are so wild, but you have a world of humor."

Humph. Coxcomb! Well, but why don't you run with your master's letter to Mrs. Lucinda, as he ordered you?

Tom. Because Mrs. Lucinda is not so easily come at as you think for.

Humph. Not easily come at? Why, sirrah, are not her father and my old master agreed that she and Mr. Bevil are to be one flesh before to-morrow morning?

Tom. It's no matter for that; her mother, it seems, Mrs. Sealand, has not agreed to it; and you must know, Mr. Humphry, that in that family the grey mare is the better horse.

Humph. What dost thou mean?

Tom. In one word, Mrs. Sealand pretends to have a will of her own, and has provided a relation of hers, a stiff, starched philosopher, and a wise fool, for her daughter; for which reason, for these ten days past, she has suffered no message nor letter from my master to come near her.

Humph. And where had you this intelligence?

Tom. From a foolish fond soul that can keep nothing from me; one that will deliver this letter too, if she is rightly managed.

Humph. What! her pretty handmaid, Mrs. Phillis?

Tom. Even she, sir; this is the very hour, you know, she usually comes hither, under a pretence of a visit to your housekeeper, forsooth, but in reality to have a glance at——

Humph. Your sweet face, I warrant you.

Tom. Nothing else in nature; you must know, I love to fret and play with the little wanton.

Humph. Play with the little wanton! What will this world come to!

2 reform.
3 Apparently taverns or rooms in a tavern, named after rooms in the old Parliament House.
4 unanimously.
5 Parties with music and dancing, introduced into England in the year of this play (*Oxf. Dict.*).
6 A fashionable pleasure-resort in the northwest of London.

Tom. I met her this morning in a new manteau and petticoat, not a bit the worse for her lady's wearing; and she has always new thoughts and new airs with new clothes—then she never fails to steal some glance or gesture from every visitant at their house; and is, indeed, the whole town of coquets at second-hand. But here she comes; in one motion she speaks and describes herself better than all the words in the world can.

Humph. Then I hope, dear sir, when your own affair is over, you will be so good as to mind your master's with her.

Tom. Dear Humphry, you know my master is my friend, and those are people I never forget.

Humph. Sauciness itself! but I'll leave you to do your best for him.

(*Exit.*)

(*Enter Phillis.*)

Phil. Oh, Mr. Thomas, is Mrs. Sugarkey at home? Lard, one is almost ashamed to pass along the streets! The town is quite empty, and nobody of fashion left in it; and the ordinary people do so stare to see anything dressed like a woman of condition, as it were on the same floor with them, pass by. Alas! alas! it is a sad thing to walk. O fortune! fortune!

Tom. What! a sad thing to walk? Why, Madam Phillis, do you wish yourself lame?

Phil. No, Mr. Tom, but I wish I were generally carried in a coach or chair, and of a fortune neither to stand nor go, but to totter, or slide, to be short-sighted, or stare, to fleer in the face, to look distant, to observe, to overlook, yet all become me; and, if I was rich, I could twire [7] and loll as well as the best of them. Oh, Tom! Tom! is it not a pity that you should be so great a coxcomb, and I so great a coquet, and yet be such poor devils as we are?

Tom. Mrs. Phillis, I am your humble servant for that——

Phil. Yes, Mr. Thomas, I know how much you are my humble servant, and know what you said to Mrs. Judy, upon seeing her in one of her lady's cast manteaus: That any one would have thought her the lady, and that she had ordered the other to wear it till it sat easy; for now only it was becoming. To my lady it was only a covering, to Mrs. Judy it was a habit. This you said, after somebody or other. Oh, Tom! Tom! thou art as false and as base as the best gentleman of them all; but, you wretch, talk to me no more on the old odious subject—don't, I say.

Tom. I know not how to resist your commands, madam.

(*In a submissive tone, retiring.*)

Phil. Commands about parting are grown mighty easy to you of late.

Tom. Oh, I have her; I have nettled and put her into the right temper to be wrought upon and set a-prating. (*Aside.*)—Why, truly, to be plain with you, Mrs. Phillis, I can take little comfort of late in frequenting your house.

Phil. Pray, Mr. Thomas, what is it all of a sudden offends your nicety at our house?

Tom. I don't care to speak particulars, but I dislike the whole.

Phil. I thank you, sir, I am a part of that whole.

Tom. Mistake me not, good Phillis.

Phil. Good Phillis! Saucy enough. But however——

Tom. I say, it is that thou art a part, which gives me pain for the disposition of the whole. You must know, madam, to be serious, I am a man, at the bottom, of prodigious nice honor. You are too much exposed to company at your house. To be plain, I don't like so many, that would be your mistress's lovers, whispering to you.

Phil. Don't think to put that upon me. You say this, because I wrung you to the heart when I touched your guilty conscience about Judy.

Tom. Ah, Phillis! Phillis! if you but knew my heart!

Phil. I know too much on 't.

Tom. Nay, then, poor Crispo's [8] fate and mine are one. Therefore give me leave to say, or sing at least, as he does upon the same occasion—

"Se vedette," &c.

(*Sings.*)

Phil. What, do you think I'm to be fobbed [9] off with a song? I don't question but you have sung the same to Mrs. Judy too.

Tom. Don't disparage your charms, good Phillis, with jealousy of so worthless an object; besides, she is a poor hussy, and if you doubt the sincerity of my love,

7 "Make eyes," ogle.
8 See note on II. ii.
9 Put off, cajoled.

you will allow me true to my interest. You are a fortune, Phillis.

Phil. What would the fop be at now? In good time, indeed, you shall be setting up for a fortune!

Tom. Dear Mrs. Phillis, you have such a spirit that we shall never be dull in marriage when we come together. But I tell you, you are a fortune, and you have an estate in my hands.

(*He pulls out a purse, she eyes it.*)

Phil. What pretence have I to what is in your hands, Mr. Tom?

Tom. As thus: there are hours, you know, when a lady is neither pleased or displeased; neither sick or well; when she lolls or loiters; when she 's without desires—from having more of everything than she knows what to do with.

Phil. Well, what then?

Tom. When she has not life enough to keep her bright eyes quite open, to look at her own dear image in the glass.

Phil. Explain thyself, and don't be so fond of thy own prating.

Tom. There are also prosperous and good-natured moments: as when a knot or a patch is happily fixed; when the complexion particularly flourishes.

Phil. Well, what then? I have not patience!

Tom. Why, then—or on the like occasions—we servants who have skill to know how to time business, see when such a pretty folded thing as this (*Shows a letter.*) may be presented, laid, or dropped, as best suits the present humor. And, madam, because it is a long wearisome journey to run through all the several stages of a lady's temper, my master, who is the most reasonable man in the world, presents you this to bear your charges on the road.

(*Gives her the purse.*)

Phil. Now you think me a corrupt hussy.

Tom. O fie, I only think you 'll take the letter.

Phil. Nay, I know you do, but I know my own innocence; I take it for my mistress's sake.

Tom. I know it, my pretty one, I know it.

Phil. Yes, I say I do it, because I would not have my mistress deluded by one who gives no proof of his passion; but I 'll talk more of this as you see me on my way home. No, Tom, I assure thee, I take this trash of thy master's, not for the value of the thing, but as it convinces me he has a true respect for my mistress. I remember a verse to the purpose—

They may be false who languish and complain,
But they who part with money never feign.

(*Exeunt.*)

SCENE 2. *Bevil, Jun.'s Lodgings.*

(*Bevil, Jun., reading.*)

Bev. Jun. These moral writers practise virtue after death. This charming vision of Mirza![10] Such an author consulted in a morning sets the spirit for the vicissitudes of the day better than the glass does a man's person. But what a day have I to go through! to put on an easy look with an aching heart! If this lady my father urges me to marry should not refuse me, my dilemma is insupportable. But why should I fear it? Is not she in equal distress with me? Has not the letter I have sent her this morning confessed my inclination to another? Nay, have I not moral assurances of her engagements, too, to my friend Myrtle? It 's impossible but she must give in to it; for, sure, to be denied is a favor any man may pretend to. It must be so—Well, then, with the assurance of being rejected, I think I may confidently say to my father, I am ready to marry her. Then let me resolve upon, what I am not very good at, though it is an honest dissimulation.

(*Enter Tom.*)

Tom. Sir John Bevil, sir, is in the next room.

Bev. Jun. Dunce! Why did not you bring him in?

Tom. I told him, sir, you were in your closet.

Bev. Jun. I thought you had known, sir, it was my duty to see my father anywhere.

(*Going himself to the door.*)

Tom. The devil 's in my master! he has always more wit[11] than I have.

(*Aside.*)

(*Bevil, Jun., introducing Sir John.*)

Bev. Jun. Sir, you are the most gallant, the most complaisant of all parents. Sure, 't is not a compliment to say these

10 Here Steele compliments his friend Addison's moralizing vision in the Spectator (No. 159).
11 Cleverness, sense.

lodgings are yours. Why would you not walk in, sir?

Sir J. Bev. I was loth to interrupt you unseasonably on your wedding-day.

Bev. Jun. One to whom I am beholden for my birthday might have used less ceremony.

Sir J. Bev. Well, son, I have intelligence you have writ to your mistress this morning. It would please my curiosity to know the contents of a wedding-day letter; for courtship must then be over.

Bev. Jun. I assure you, sir, there was no insolence in it upon the prospect of such a vast fortune 's being added to our family; but much acknowledgment of the lady's greater desert.

Sir J. Bev. But, dear Jack, are you in earnest in all this? And will you really marry her?

Bev. Jun. Did I ever disobey any command of yours, sir? nay, any inclination that I saw you bent upon?

Sir J. Bev. Why, I can't say you have, son; but methinks in this whole business, you have not been so warm as I could have wished you. You have visited her, it 's true, but you have not been particular. Every one knows you can say and do as handsome things as any man; but you have done nothing but lived in the general—been complaisant only.

Bev. Jun. As I am ever prepared to marry if you bid me, so I am ready to let it alone if you will have me.

(*Humphry enters, unobserved.*)

Sir J. Bev. Look you there now! why, what am I to think of this so absolute and so indifferent a resignation?

Bev. Jun. Think? that I am still your son, sir. Sir, you have been married, and I have not. And you have, sir, found the inconvenience there is when a man weds with too much love in his head. I have been told, sir, that at the time you married, you made a mighty bustle on the occasion. There was challenging and fighting, scaling walls, locking up the lady, and the gallant under an arrest for fear of killing all his rivals. Now, sir, I suppose you having found the ill consequences of these strong passions and prejudices, in preference of one woman to another, in case of a man's becoming a widower——

Sir J. Bev. How is this?

Bev. Jun. I say, sir, experience has made you wiser in your care of me; for, sir, since you lost my dear mother, your time has been so heavy, so lonely, and so tasteless, that you are so good as to guard me against the like unhappiness, by marrying me prudentially by way of bargain and sale. For, as you well judge, a woman that is espoused for a fortune, is yet a better bargain, if she dies; for then a man still enjoys what he did marry, the money, and is disencumbered of what he did not marry, the woman.

Sir J. Bev. But pray, sir, do you think Lucinda, then, a woman of such little merit?

Bev. Jun. Pardon me, sir, I don't carry it so far neither; I am rather afraid I shall like her too well; she has, for one of her fortune, a great many needless and superfluous good qualities.

Sir J. Bev. I am afraid, son, there 's something I don't see yet, something that 's smothered under all this raillery.

Bev. Jun. Not in the least, sir. If the lady is dressed and ready, you see I am. I suppose the lawyers are ready too.

Humph. This may grow warm if I don't interpose. (*Aside.*)—Sir, Mr. Sealand is at the coffee-house, and has sent to speak with you.

Sir J. Bev. Oh! that 's well! Then I warrant the lawyers are ready. Son, you 'll be in the way, you say.

Bev. Jun. If you please, sir, I 'll take a chair,[12] and go to Mr. Sealand's, where the young lady and I will wait your leisure.

Sir J. Bev. By no means. The old fellow will be so vain if he sees——

Bev. Jun. Ay; but the young lady, sir, will think me so indifferent.

Humph. Ay, there you are right; press your readiness to go to the bride—he won't let you.

(*Aside to Bev. Jun.*)

Bev. Jun. Are you sure of that?

(*Aside to Humph.*)

Humph. How he likes being prevented!

(*Aside.*)

Sir J. Bev. No, no. You are an hour or two too early.

(*Looking on his watch.*)

Bev. Jun. You 'll allow me, sir, to think it too late to visit a beautiful, virtuous young woman, in the pride and bloom of

12 sedan-chair.

life, ready to give herself to my arms; and to place her happiness or misery, for the future, in being agreeable or displeasing to me, is a——Call a chair.

Sir J. Bev. No, no, no, dear Jack; this Sealand is a moody old fellow. There 's no dealing with some people but by managing with indifference. We must leave to him the conduct of this day. It is the last of his commanding his daughter.

Bev. Jun. Sir, he can't take it ill, that I am impatient to be hers.

Sir J. Bev. Pray let me govern in this matter; you can't tell how humorsome old fellows are. There 's no offering reason to some of 'em, especially when they are rich.—If my son should see him before I 've brought old Sealand into better temper, the match would be impracticable.

(*Aside.*)

Humph. Pray, sir, let me beg you to let Mr. Bevil go.—See whether he will or not. (*Aside to Sir John*)—(*Then to Bev.*)—Pray, sir, command yourself; since you see my master is positive, it is better you should not go.

Bev. Jun. My father commands me, as to the object of my affections; but I hope he will not, as to the warmth and height of them.

Sir J. Bev. So! I must even leave things as I found them; and in the meantime, at least, keep old Sealand out of his sight—Well, son, I 'll go myself and take orders in your affair. You 'll be in the way, I suppose, if I send to you. I 'll leave your old friend with you—Humphry, don't let him stir, d'ye hear?—Your servant, your servant.

(*Exit Sir John.*)

Humph. I have a sad time on 't, sir, between you and my master. I see you are unwilling, and I know his violent inclinations for the match.—I must betray neither, and yet deceive you both, for your common good. Heaven grant a good end of this matter.—But there is a lady, sir, that gives your father much trouble and sorrow.—You 'll pardon me.

Bev. Jun. Humphry, I know thou art a friend to both, and in that confidence I dare tell thee, that lady is a woman of honor and virtue. You may assure yourself I never will marry without my father's consent. But give me leave to say, too, this declaration does not come up to a promise that I will take whomsoever he pleases.

Humph. Come, sir, I wholly understand you. You would engage my services to free you from this woman whom my master intends you, to make way, in time, for the woman you have really a mind to.

Bev. Jun. Honest Humphry, you have always been a useful friend to my father and myself; I beg you continue your good offices, and don't let us come to the necessity of a dispute; for, if we should dispute, I must either part with more than life, or lose the best of fathers.

Humph. My dear master, were I but worthy to know this secret, that so near concerns you, my life, my all should be engaged to serve you. This, sir, I dare promise, that I am sure I will and can be secret: your trust, at worst, but leaves you where you were; and if I cannot serve you, I will at once be plain and tell you so.

Bev. Jun. That 's all I ask. Thou hast made it now my interest to trust thee. Be patient, then, and hear the story of my heart.

Humph. I am all attention, sir.

Bev. Jun. You may remember, Humphry, that in my last travels my father grew uneasy at my making so long a stay at Toulon.

Humph. I remember it; he was apprehensive some woman had laid hold of you.

Bev. Jun. His fears were just; for there I first saw this lady. She is of English birth: her father's name was Danvers—a younger brother of an ancient family, and originally an eminent merchant of Bristol, who, upon repeated misfortunes, was reduced to go privately to the Indies. In this retreat, Providence again grew favorable to his industry, and, in six years' time, restored him to his former fortunes. On this he sent directions over that his wife and little family should follow him to the Indies. His wife, impatient to obey such welcome orders, would not wait the leisure of a convoy, but took the first occasion of a single ship, and, with her husband's sister only, and this daughter, then scarce seven years old, undertook the fatal voyage—for here, poor creature, she lost her liberty and life. She and her family, with all they had, were, unfortunately, taken by a privateer from Toulon. Being thus made a prisoner, though as such not ill-treated, yet the fright, the shock, and cruel disappointment, seized with such violence upon her unhealthy frame, she sickened, pined, and died at sea.

Humph. Poor soul! O the helpless infant!

Bev. Her sister yet survived, and had the care of her. The captain, too, proved to have humanity, and became a father to her; for having himself married an English woman, and being childless, he brought home into Toulon this her little country-woman, presenting her, with all her dead mother's movables of value, to his wife, to be educated as his own adopted daughter.

Humph. Fortune here seemed again to smile on her.

Bev. Only to make her frowns more terrible; for, in his height of fortune, this captain, too, her benefactor, unfortunately was killed at sea; and dying intestate, his estate fell wholly to an advocate, his brother, who, coming soon to take possession, there found (among his other riches) this blooming virgin at his mercy.

Humph. He durst not, sure, abuse his power?

Bev. No wonder if his pampered blood was fired at the sight of her—in short, he loved; but when all arts and gentle means had failed to move, he offered, too, his menaces in vain, denouncing vengeance on her cruelty, demanding her to account for all her maintenance from her childhood; seized on her little fortune as his own inheritance, and was dragging her by violence to prison, when Providence at the instant interposed, and sent me, by miracle, to relieve her.

Humph. 'T was Providence, indeed. But pray, sir, after all this trouble, how came this lady at last to England?

Bev. The disappointed advocate, finding she had so unexpected a support, on cooler thoughts, descended to a composition, which I, without her knowledge, secretly discharged.

Humph. That generous concealment made the obligation double.

Bev. Having thus obtained her liberty, I prevailed, not without some difficulty, to see her safe to England; where, no sooner arrived, but my father, jealous of my being imprudently engaged, immediately proposed this other fatal match that hangs upon my quiet.

Humph. I find, sir, you are irrecoverably fixed upon this lady.

Bev. As my vital life dwells in my heart —and yet you see what I do to please my father: walk in this pageantry of dress, this splendid covering of sorrow— But, Humphry, you have your lesson.

Humph. Now, sir, I have but one material question——

Bev. Ask it freely.

Humph. Is it, then, your own passion for this secret lady, or hers for you, that gives you this aversion to the match your father has proposed you?

Bev. I shall appear, Humphry, more romantic in my answer than in all the rest of my story; for though I dote on her to death, and have no little reason to believe she has the same thoughts for me, yet in all my acquaintance and utmost privacies with her, I never once directly told her that I loved.

Humph. How was it possible to avoid it?

Bev. My tender obligations to my father have laid so inviolable a restraint upon my conduct that, till I have his consent to speak, I am determined, on that subject, to be dumb for ever.

Humph. Well, sir, to your praise be it spoken, you are certainly the most unfashionable lover in Great Britain.

(*Enter Tom.*)

Tom. Sir, Mr. Myrtle 's at the next door, and, if you are at leisure, will be glad to wait on you.

Bev. Whenever he pleases——hold, Tom! did you receive no answer to my letter?

Tom. Sir, I was desired to call again; for I was told her mother would not let her be out of her sight; but about an hour hence, Mrs. Lettice said, I should certainly have one.

Bev. Very well.

(*Exit Tom.*)

Humph. Sir, I will take another opportunity. In the meantime, I only think it proper to tell you that, from a secret I know, you may appear to your father as forward as you please, to marry Lucinda without the least hazard of its coming to a conclusion—Sir, your most obedient servant.

Bev. Honest Humphry, continue but my friend in this exigence, and you shall always find me yours. (*Exit Humph.*)— I long to hear how my letter has succeeded with Lucinda—but I think it cannot fail; for, at worst, were it possible she could take it ill, her resentment of my indifference may as probably occasion a delay as her taking it right. Poor Myrtle, what terrors must he be in all this while? Since he knows she is offered to me, and refused to him, there is no conversing or taking any measures with him for his own service. —But I ought to bear with my friend, and use him as one in adversity—

All his disquiets by my own I prove,
The greatest grief 's perplexity in love
(*Exit.*)

ACT II.

SCENE 1. *Bevil, Jun.'s Lodgings.*

(*Enter Bevil, Jun., and Tom.*)

Tom. Sir, Mr. Myrtle.

Bev. Jun. Very well—do you step again, and wait for an answer to my letter.

(*Exit Tom.*)

(*Enter Myrtle.*)

Bev. Jun. Well, Charles, why so much care in thy countenance? Is there anything in this world deserves it? You, who used to be so gay, so open, so vacant![13]

Myrt. I think we have of late changed complexions. You, who used to be much the graver man, are now all air in your behavior.—But the cause of my concern may, for aught I know, be the same object that gives you all this satisfaction. In a word, I am told that you are this very day—and your dress confirms me in it—to be married to Lucinda.

Bev. Jun. You are not misinformed.—Nay, put not on the terrors of a rival till you hear me out. I shall disoblige the best of fathers if I don't seem ready to marry Lucinda; and you know I have ever told you you might make use of my secret resolution never to marry her for your own service as you please; but I am now driven to the extremity of immediately refusing or complying unless you help me to escape the match.

Myrt. Escape? Sir, neither her merit or her fortune are below your acceptance—Escaping do you call it?

Bev. Jun. Dear sir, do you wish I should desire the match?

Myrt. No; but such is my humorous[14] and sickly state of mind since it has been able to relish nothing but Lucinda, that though I must owe my happiness to your aversion to this marriage, I can't bear to hear her spoken of with levity or unconcern.

Bev. Jun. Pardon me, sir, I shall transgress that way no more. She has understanding, beauty, shape, complexion, wit——

Myrt. Nay, dear Bevil, don't speak of her as if you loved her neither.

Bev. Jun. Why, then, to give you ease at once, though I allow Lucinda to have good sense, wit, beauty, and virtue, I know another in whom these qualities appear to me more amiable than in her.

Myrt. There you spoke like a reasonable and good-natured friend. When you acknowledge her merit, and own your prepossession for another, at once you gratify my fondness and cure my jealousy.

Bev. Jun. But all this while you take no notice, you have no apprehension, of another man that has twice the fortune of either of us.

Myrt. Cimberton! hang him, a formal, philosophical, pedantic coxcomb; for the sot, with all these crude notions of divers things, under the direction of great vanity and very little judgment, shows his strongest bias is avarice; which is so predominant in him that he will examine the limbs of his mistress with the caution of a jockey, and pays no more compliment to her personal charms than if she were a mere breeding animal.

Bev. Jun. Are you sure that is not affected? I have known some women sooner set on fire by that sort of negligence than by——

Myrt. No, no; hang him, the rogue has no art; it is pure, simple insolence and stupidity.

Bev. Jun. Yet, with all this, I don't take him for a fool.

Myrt. I own the man is not a natural;[15] he has a very quick sense,[16] though very slow understanding.. He says, indeed, many things that want only the circumstances of time and place to be very just and agreeable.

Bev. Jun. Well, you may be sure of me if you can disappoint him; but my intelligence says the mother has actually sent for the conveyancer to draw articles for his marriage with Lucinda, though

13 care-free.

14 capricious.

15 idiot.

16 perception

those for mine with her are, by her father's orders, ready for signing; but it seems she has not thought fit to consult either him or his daughter in the matter.

Myrt. Pshaw! a poor troublesome woman. Neither Lucinda nor her father will ever be brought to comply with it. Besides, I am sure Cimberton can make no settlement upon her without the concurrence of his great uncle, Sir Geoffry, in the west.

Bev. Jun. Well, sir, and I can tell you that 's the very point that is now laid before her counsel, to know whether a firm settlement can be made without his uncle's actual joining in it. Now, pray consider, sir, when my affair with Lucinda comes, as it soon must, to an open rupture, how are you sure that Cimberton's fortune may not then tempt her father, too, to hear his proposals?

Myrt. There you are right, indeed; that must be provided against. Do you know who are her counsel?

Bev. Jun. Yes, for your service I have found out that, too. They are Serjeant Bramble and Old Target—by the way, they are neither of them known in the family. Now, I was thinking why you might not put a couple of false counsel upon her to delay and confound matters a little; besides, it may probably let you into the bottom of her whole design against you.

Myrt. As how, pray?

Bev. Jun. Why, can't you slip on a black wig and a gown, and be Old Bramble yourself?

Myrt. Ha! I don't dislike it.—But what shall I do for a brother in the case?

Bev. Jun. What think you of my fellow, Tom? The rogue 's intelligent, and is a good mimic. All his part will be but to stutter heartily, for that 's old Target's case. Nay, it would be an immoral thing to mock him were it not that his impertinence is the occasion of its breaking out to that degree. The conduct of the scene will chiefly lie upon you.

Myrt. I like it of all things. If you 'll send Tom to my chambers, I will give him full instructions. This will certainly give me occasion to raise difficulties, to puzzle or confound her project for a while at least.

Bev. Jun. I 'll warrant you success.—So far we are right, then. And now, Charles, your apprehension of my marrying her is all you have to get over.

Myrt. Dear Bevil, though I know you are my friend, yet when I abstract myself from my own interest in the thing, I know no objection she can make to you, or you to her, and therefore hope——

Bev. Jun. Dear Myrtle, I am as much obliged to you for the cause of your suspicion, as I am offended at the effect; but, be assured, I am taking measures for your certain security, and that all things with regard to me will end in your entire satisfaction.

Myrt. Well, I 'll promise you to be as easy and as confident as I can, though I cannot but remember that I have more than life at stake on your fidelity.

(*Going.*)

Bev. Jun. Then depend upon it, you have no chance against you.

Myrt. Nay, no ceremony, you know I must be going.

(*Exit Myrt.*)

Bev. Jun. Well, this is another instance of the perplexities which arise, too, in faithful friendship. We must often in this life go on in our good offices, even under the displeasure of those to whom we do them, in compassion to their weaknesses and mistakes.—But all this while poor Indiana is tortured with the doubt of me. She has no support or comfort but in my fidelity, yet sees me daily pressed to marriage with another. How painful, in such a crisis, must be every hour she thinks on me! I 'll let her see at least my conduct to her is not changed. I 'll take this opportunity to visit her; for though the religious vow I have made to my father restrains me from ever marrying without his approbation, yet that confines me not from seeing a virtuous woman that is the pure delight of my eyes and the guiltless joy of my heart. But the best condition of human life is but a gentler misery—

To hope for perfect happiness is vain,
And love has ever its allays [17] of pain.

(*Exit.*)

SCENE 2. *Indiana's Lodgings.*

(*Enter Isabella and Indiana.*)

Isab. Yes, I say 't is artifice, dear child. I say to thee again and again 't is all skill and management.

17 allovs.

Ind. Will you persuade me there can be an ill design in supporting me in the condition of a woman of quality? attended, dressed, and lodged like one; in my appearance abroad and my furniture at home, every way in the most sumptuous manner, and he that does it has an artifice, a design in it?

Isab. Yes, yes.

Ind. And all this without so much as explaining to me that all about me comes from him!

Isab. Ay, ay, the more for that. That keeps the title to all you have the more in him.

Ind. The more in him! He scorns the thought——

Isab. Then he—he—he——

Ind. Well, be not so eager. If he is an ill man, let us look into his stratagems. Here is another of them. (*Showing a letter.*) Here 's two hundred and fifty pounds in bank notes, with these words: "To pay for the set of dressing-plate which will be brought home to-morrow." Why, dear aunt, now here 's another piece of skill for you, which I own I cannot comprehend; and it is with a bleeding heart I hear you say anything to the disadvantage of Mr. Bevil. When he is present I look upon him as one to whom I owe my life and the support of it; then, again, as the man who loves me with sincerity and honor. When his eyes are cast another way, and I dare survey him, my heart is painfully divided between shame and love. Oh! could I tell you——

Isab. Ah! you need not; I imagine all this for you.

Ind. This is my state of mind in his presence; and when he is absent, you are ever dinning my ears with notions of the arts of men; that his hidden bounty, his respectful conduct, his careful provision for me, after his preserving me from utmost misery, are certain signs he means nothing but to make I know not what of me.

Isab. Oh! You have a sweet opinion of him, truly.

Ind. I have, when I am with him, ten thousand things, besides my sex's natural decency and shame, to suppress my heart, that yearns to thank, to praise, to say it loves him. I say, thus it is with me while I see him; and in his absence I am entertained with nothing but your endeavors to tear his amiable image from my heart; and in its stead, to place a base dissembler, an artful invader of my happiness, my innocence, my honor.

Isab. Ah, poor soul! has not his plot taken? don't you die for him? has not the way he has taken been the most proper with you? Oh! oh! He has sense, and has judged the thing right.

Ind. Go on then, since nothing can answer you; say what you will of him. Heigh! ho!

Isab. Heigh! ho! indeed. It is better to say so, as you are now, than as many others are. There are, among the destroyers of women, the gentle, the generous, the mild, the affable, the humble, who all, soon after their success in their designs, turn to the contrary of those characters. I will own to you, Mr. Bevil carries his hypocrisy the best of any man living, but still he is a man, and therefore a hypocrite. They have usurped an exemption from shame for any baseness, any cruelty towards us. They embrace without love; they make vows without conscience of obligation; they are partners, nay, seducers to the crime, wherein they pretend to be less guilty.

Ind. That 's truly observed. (*Aside.*)—But what 's all this to Bevil?

Isab. This it is to Bevil and all mankind. Trust not those who will think the worse of you for your confidence in them; serpents who lie in wait for doves. Won't you be on your guard against those who would betray you? Won't you doubt those who would contemn you for believing 'em? Take it from me, fair and natural dealing is to invite injuries; 't is bleating to escape wolves who would devour you! Such is the world—and such (since the behavior of one man to myself) have I believed all the rest of the sex. (*Aside.*)

Ind. I will not doubt the truth of Bevil, I will not doubt it. He has not spoke it by an organ that is given to lying. His eyes are all that have ever told me that he was mine. I know his virtue, I know his filial piety, and ought to trust his management with a father to whom he has uncommon obligations. What have I to be concerned for? my lesson is very short. If he takes me for ever, my purpose of life is only to please him. If he leaves me (which Heaven avert) I know he 'll do it nobly, and I shall have nothing to do but to learn to die, after worse than death has happened to me.

Isab. Ay, do, persist in your credulity! flatter yourself that a man of his figure and fortune will make himself the jest of the town, and marry a handsome beggar for love.

Ind. The town! I must tell you, madam, the fools that laugh at Mr. Bevil will but make themselves more ridiculous; his actions are the result of thinking, and he has sense enough to make even virtue fashionable.

Isab. O' my conscience he has turned her head.—Come, come, if he were the honest fool you take him for, why has he kept you here these three weeks, without sending you to Bristol in search of your father, your family, and your relations?

Ind. I am convinced he still designs it, and that nothing keeps him here, but the necessity of not coming to a breach with his father in regard to the match he has proposed him. Beside, has he not writ to Bristol? and has not he advice that my father has not been heard of there almost these twenty years?

Isab. All sham, mere evasion; he is afraid, if he should carry you thither, your honest relations may take you out of his hands, and so blow up all his wicked hopes at once.

Ind. Wicked hopes! did I ever give him any such?

Isab. Has he ever given you any honest ones? Can you say, in your conscience, he has ever once offered to marry you?

Ind. No! but by his behavior I am convinced he will offer it, the moment 't is in his power, or consistent with his honor, to make such a promise good to me.

Isab. His honor!

Ind. I will rely upon it; therefore desire you will not make my life uneasy, by these ungrateful jealousies of one, to whom I am, and wish to be, obliged. For from his integrity alone, I have resolved to hope for happiness.

Isab. Nay, I have done my duty; if you won't see, at your peril be it!

Ind. Let it be—This is his hour of visiting me.

Isab. Oh! to be sure, keep up your form; don't see him in a bed-chamber—This is pure prudence, when she is liable, wherever he meets her, to be conveyed where'er he pleases. (*Apart.*)

Ind. All the rest of my life is but waiting till he comes. I live only when I'm with him. (*Exit.*)

Isab. Well, go thy ways, thou wilful innocent!—I once had almost as much love for a man, who poorly left me to marry an estate; and I am now, against my will, what they call an old maid—but I will not let the peevishness of that condition grow upon me, only keep up the suspicion of it, to prevent this creature's being any other than a virgin, except upon proper terms.

(*Exit.*)

(*Re-enter Indiana, speaking to a Servant.*)

Ind. Desire Mr. Bevil to walk in—Design! impossible! A base designing mind could never think of what he hourly puts in practice. And yet, since the late rumor of his marriage, he seems more reserved than formerly—he sends in too, before he sees me, to know if I am at leisure—such new respect may cover coldness in the heart; it certainly makes me thoughtful—I'll know the worst at once; I'll lay such fair occasions in his way, that it shall be impossible to avoid an explanation, for these doubts are insupportable!—But see, he comes, and clears them all.

(*Enter Bevil.*)

Bev. Madam, your most obedient—I am afraid I broke in upon your rest last night; 't was very late before we parted, but 't was your own fault. I never saw you in such agreeable humor.

Ind. I am extremely glad we were both pleased; for I thought I never saw you better company.

Bev. Me, madam! you rally; I said very little.

Ind. But I am afraid you heard me say a great deal; and, when a woman is in the talking vein, the most agreeable thing a man can do, you know, is to have patience to hear her.

Bev. Then it 's pity, madam, you should ever be silent, that we might be always agreeable to one another.

Ind. If I had your talent or power, to make my actions speak for me, I might indeed be silent, and yet pretend to something more than the agreeable.

Bev. If I might be vain of anything in my power, madam, 't is that my understanding, from all your sex, has marked you out as the most deserving object of my esteem.

Ind. Should I think I deserve this, 't were enough to make my vanity forfeit the very esteem you offer me.

Bev. How so, madam?

Ind. Because esteem is the result of reason, and to deserve it from good sense, the height of human glory. Nay, I had rather a man of honor should pay me that, than all the homage of a sincere and humble love.

Bev. You certainly distinguish right, madam; love often kindles from external merit only.

Ind. But esteem rises from a higher source, the merit of the soul.

Bev. True—and great souls only can deserve it.

(*Bowing respectfully.*)

Ind. Now I think they are greater still, that can so charitably part with it.

Bev. Now, madam, you make me vain, since the utmost pride and pleasure of my life is, that I esteem you as I ought.

Ind. (*Aside.*) As he ought! still more perplexing! he neither saves nor kills my hope.

Bev. But, madam, we grow grave, methinks. Let 's find some other subject—Pray how did you like the opera last night?

Ind. First give me leave to thank you for my tickets.

Bev. Oh! your servant, madam. But pray tell me, you now, who are never partial to the fashion, I fancy must be the properest judge of a mighty dispute among the ladies, that is, whether *Crispo* or *Griselda*[18] is the more agreeable entertainment.

Ind. With submission now, I cannot be a proper judge of this question.

Bev. How so, madam?

Ind. Because I find I have a partiality for one of them.

Bev. Pray which is that?

Ind. I do not know; there 's something in that rural cottage of Griselda, her forlorn condition, her poverty, her solitude, her resignation, her innocent slumbers, and that lulling *dolce sogno*[19] that 's sung over her; it had an effect upon me that—in short I never was so well deceived, at any of them.

Bev. Oh! Now then, I can account for the dispute. Griselda, it seems, is the distress of an injured innocent woman, Crispo, that only of a man in the same condition; therefore the men are mostly concerned for Crispo, and, by a natural indulgence, both sexes for Griselda.

Ind. So that judgment, you think, ought to be for one, though fancy and complaisance have got ground for the other. Well! I believe you will never give me leave to dispute with you on any subject; for I own, Crispo has its charms for me too. Though, in the main, all the pleasure the best opera gives us is but mere sensation. Methinks it 's pity the mind can't have a little more share in the entertainment. The music 's certainly fine, but, in my thoughts, there 's none of your composers come up to old Shakespeare and Otway.

Bev. How, madam! why, if a woman of your sense were to say this in the drawing-room——

(*Enter a Servant.*)

Serv. Sir, here 's Signor Carbonelli says he waits your commands in the next room.

Bev. Apropos! you were saying yesterday, madam, you had a mind to hear him. Will you give him leave to entertain you now?

Ind. By all means; desire the gentleman to walk in.

(*Exit Servant.*)

Bev. I fancy you will find something in this hand that is uncommon.

Ind. You are always finding ways, Mr. Bevil, to make life seem less tedious to me.

(*Enter Music Master.*)

When the gentleman pleases.

(*After a Sonata is played, Bevil waits on the Master to the door, etc.*)

Bev. You smile, madam, to see me so complaisant to one whom I pay for his visit. Now, I own, I think it is not enough barely to pay those whose talents are superior to our own (I mean such talents as would become our condition, if we had them). Methinks we ought to do something more than barely gratify them for what they do at our command, only because their fortune is below us.

Ind. You say I smile. I assure you it was a smile of approbation; for, indeed, I cannot but think it the distinguishing part of a gentleman to make his superiority of fortune as easy to his inferiors as he can.—Now once more to try him. (*Aside.*)—I was saying just now, I be-

18 Operas by G. B. Buononcini (d. about 1750). then popular in London. 19 A lullaby.

lieved you would never let me dispute with you, and I dare say it will always be so. However, I must have your opinion upon a subject which created a debate between my aunt and me, just before you came hither; she would needs have it that no man ever does any extraordinary kindness or service for a woman, but for his own sake.

Bev. Well, madam! Indeed I can't but be of her mind.

Ind. What, though he should maintain and support her, without demanding anything of her, on her part?

Bev. Why, madam, is making an expense in the service of a valuable woman (for such I must suppose her), though she should never do him any favor, nay, though she should never know who did her such service, such a mighty heroic business?

Ind. Certainly! I should think he must be a man of an uncommon mould.

Bev. Dear madam, why so? 't is but, at best, a better taste in expense. To bestow upon one, whom he may think one of the ornaments of the whole creation, to be conscious, that from his superfluity, an innocent, a virtuous spirit is supported above the temptations and sorrows of life! That he sees satisfaction, health, and gladness in her countenance, while he enjoys the happiness of seeing her (as that I will suppose too, or he must be too abstracted, too insensible), I say, if he is allowed to delight in that prospect; alas, what mighty matter is there in all this?

Ind. No mighty matter in so disinterested a friendship!

Bev. Disinterested! I can't think him so; your hero, madam, is no more than what every gentleman ought to be, and I believe very many are. He is only one who takes more delight in reflections than in sensations. He is more pleased with thinking than eating; that 's the utmost you can say of him. Why, madam, a greater expense than all this men lay out upon an unnecessary stable of horses.

Ind. Can you be sincere in what you say?

Bev. You may depend upon it, if you know any such man, he does not love dogs inordinately.

Ind. No, that he does not.

Bev. Nor cards, nor dice.

Ind. No.

Bev. Nor bottle companions.

Ind. No.

Bev. Nor loose women.

Ind. No, I 'm sure he does not.

Bev. Take my word, then, if your admired hero is not liable to any of these kind of demands, there 's no such preeminence in this as you imagine. Nay, this way of expense you speak of is what exalts and raises him that has a taste for it; and, at the same time, his delight is incapable of satiety, disgust, or penitence.

Ind. But still, I insist, his having no private interest in the action makes it prodigious, almost incredible.

Bev. Dear madam, I never knew you more mistaken. Why, who can be more a usurer than he who lays out his money in such valuable purchases? If pleasure be worth purchasing, how great a pleasure is it to him, who has a true taste of life, to ease an aching heart; to see the human countenance lighted up into smiles of joy, on the receipt of a bit of ore which is superfluous and otherwise useless in a man's own pocket? What could a man do better with his cash? This is the effect of an humane disposition, where there is only a general tie of nature and common necessity. What then must it be when we serve an object of merit, of admiration!

Ind. Well! the more you argue against it the more I shall admire the generosity.

Bev. Nay, nay—Then, madam, 't is time to fly, after a declaration that my opinion strengthens my adversary's argument. I had best hasten to my appointment with Mr. Myrtle, and begone while we are friends, and before things are brought to an extremity.

(*Exit, carelessly.*)

(*Enter Isabella.*)

Isab. Well, madam, what think you of him now, pray?

Ind. I protest, I begin to fear he is wholly disinterested in what he does for me. On my heart, he has no other view but the mere pleasure of doing it, and has neither good or bad designs upon me.

Isab. Ah! dear niece! don't be in fear of both! I 'll warrant you, you will know time enough that he is not indifferent.

Ind. You please me when you tell me so; for, if he has any wishes towards me, I know he will not pursue them but with honor.

Isab. I wish I were as confident of one as t' other. I saw the respectful downcast of his eye, when you catch'd him gazing at you during the music. He, I warrant, was surprised, as if he had been taken stealing your watch. Oh! the undissembled guilty look!

Ind. But did you observe any such thing, really? I thought he looked most charmingly graceful! How engaging is modesty in a man, when one knows there is a great mind within. So tender a confusion! and yet, in other respects, so much himself, so collected, so dauntless, so determined!

Isab. Ah! niece! there is a sort of bashfulness which is the best engine to carry on a shameless purpose. Some men's modesty serves their wickedness, as hypocrisy gains the respect due to piety. But I will own to you, there is one hopeful symptom, if there could be such a thing as a disinterested lover. But it 's all a perplexity—till—till—till——

Ind. Till what?

Isab. Till I know whether Mr. Myrtle and Mr. Bevil are really friends or foes. —And that I will be convinced of before I sleep; for you shall not be deceived.

Ind. I 'm sure I never shall, if your fears can guard me. In the meantime I 'll wrap myself up in the integrity of my own heart, nor dare to doubt of his.

As conscious honor all his actions steers,
So conscious innocence dispels my fears.

(*Exeunt.*)

ACT III.

Scene 1. *Sealand's House.*

(*Enter Tom, meeting Phillis.*)

Tom. Well, Phillis! What, with a face as if you had never seen me before!—What a work have I to do now? She has seen some new visitant at their house whose airs she has catcht, and is resolved to practise them upon me. Numberless are the changes she 'll dance through before she 'll answer this plain question: videlicet, have you delivered my master's letter to your lady? Nay, I know her too well to ask an account of it in an ordinary way; I 'll be in my airs as well as she. (*Aside.*)—Well, madam, as unhappy as you are at present pleased to make me, I would not, in the general, be any other than what I am. I would not be a bit wiser, a bit richer, a bit taller, a bit shorter than I am at this instant.

(*Looking steadfastly at her.*)

Phil. Did ever anybody doubt, Master Thomas, but that you were extremely satisfied with your sweet self?

Tom. I am, indeed. The thing I have least reason to be satisfied with is my fortune, and I am glad of my poverty. Perhaps if I were rich I should overlook the finest woman in the world, that wants nothing but riches to be thought so.

Phil. How prettily was that said! But I 'll have a great deal more before I 'll say one word.

(*Aside.*)

Tom. I should, perhaps, have been stupidly above her had I not been her equal; and by not being her equal, never had opportunity of being her slave. I am my master's servant for hire—I am my mistress's from choice, would she but approve my passion.

Phil. I think it 's the first time I ever heard you speak of it with any sense of the anguish, if you really do suffer any.

Tom. Ah, Phillis! can you doubt, after what you have seen?

Phil. I know not what I have seen, nor what I have heard; but since I 'm at leisure, you may tell me when you fell in love with me; how you fell in love with me; and what you have suffered or are ready to suffer for me.

Tom. Oh, the unmerciful jade! when I 'm in haste about my master's letter. But I must go through it. (*Aside.*)—Ah! too well I remember when, and how, and on what occasion I was first surprised. It was on the 1st of April, 1715, I came into Mr. Sealand's service; I was then a hobble-dehoy, and you a pretty little tight girl, a favorite handmaid of the housekeeper. At that time we neither of us knew what was in us. I remember I was ordered to get out of the window, one pair of stairs, to rub the sashes clean; the person employed on the inner side was your charming self, whom I had never seen before.

Phil. I think I remember the silly accident. What made ye, you oaf, ready to fall down into the street?

Tom. You know not, I warrant you—you could not guess what surprised me. You took no delight when you immediately grew wanton in your conquest, and put your lips close, and breathed upon the glass, and when my lips approached, a dirty cloth you rubbed against my face, and hid your beauteous form! When I again drew near, you spit, and rubbed, and smiled at my undoing.

Phil. What silly thoughts you men have!

Tom. We were Pyramus and Thisbe—but ten times harder was my fate. Pyramus could peep only through a wall; I saw her, saw my Thisbe in all her beauty, but as much kept from her as if a hundred walls between—for there was more: there was her will against me. Would she but yet relent! O Phillis! Phillis! shorten my torment, and declare you pity me.

Phil. I believe it 's very sufferable; the pain is not so exquisite but that you may bear it a little longer.

Tom. Oh! my charming Phillis, if all depended on my fair one's will, I could with glory suffer—but, dearest creature, consider our miserable state.

Phil. How! Miserable!

Tom. We are miserable to be in love, and under the command of others than those we love; with that generous passion in the heart, to be sent to and fro on errands, called, checked, and rated for the meanest trifles. Oh, Phillis! you don't know how many china cups and glasses my passion for you has made me break. You have broke my fortune as well as my heart.

Phil. Well, Mr. Thomas, I cannot but own to you that I believe your master writes and you speak the best of any men in the world. Never was woman so well pleased with a letter as my young lady was with his; and this is an answer to it.

(*Gives him a letter.*)

Tom. This was well done, my dearest; consider, we must strike out some pretty livelihood for ourselves by closing their affairs. It will be nothing for them to give us a little being of our own, some small tenement, out of their large possessions. Whatever they give us, it will be more than what they keep for themselves. One acre with Phillis would be worth a whole county without her.

Phil. O, could I but believe you!

Tom. If not the utterance, believe the touch of my lips.

(*Kisses her.*)

Phil. There 's no contradicting you. How closely you argue, Tom!

Tom. And will closer, in due time. But I must hasten with this letter, to hasten towards the possession of you. Then, Phillis, consider how I must be revenged, look to it, of all your skittishness, shy looks, and at best but coy compliances.

Phil. Oh, Tom, you grow wanton, and sensual, as my lady calls it; I must not endure it. Oh! foh! you are a man—an odious, filthy, male creature—you should behave, if you had a right sense or were a man of sense, like Mr. Cimberton, with distance and indifference; or, let me see, some other becoming hard word, with seeming in-in-in-advertency, and not rush on one as if you were seizing a prey.—But hush! the ladies are coming.—Good Tom, don't kiss me above once, and be gone. Lard, we have been fooling and toying, and not considered the main business of our masters and mistresses.

Tom. Why, their business is to be fooling and toying as soon as the parchments are ready.

Phil. Well remembered, parchments; my lady, to my knowledge, is preparing writings between her coxcomb cousin, Cimberton, and my mistress, though my master has an eye to the parchments already prepared between your master, Mr. Bevil, and my mistress; and, I believe, my mistress herself has signed and sealed, in her heart, to Mr. Myrtle.—Did I not bid you kiss me but once, and be gone? But I know you won't be satisfied.

Tom. No, you smooth creature, how should I?

(*Kissing her hand.*)

Phil. Well, since you are so humble, or so cool, as to ravish my hand only, I 'll take my leave of you like a great lady, and you a man of quality.

(*They salute formally.*)

Tom. Pox of all this state.

(*Offers to kiss her more closely.*)

Phil. No, prithee, Tom, mind your business. We must follow that interest which will take, but endeavor at that which will be most for us, and we like most. Oh, here 's my young mistress! (*Tom taps her neck behind, and kisses his fingers.*) Go, ye liquorish [20] fool.

(*Exit Tom.*)

(*Enter Lucinda.*)

Luc. Who was that you was hurrying away?

Phil. One that I had no mind to part with.

20 greedy.

Luc. Why did you turn him away then?

Phil. For your ladyship's service—to carry your ladyship's letter to his master. I could hardly get the rogue away.

Luc. Why, has he so little love for his master?

Phil. No; but he hath so much love for his mistress.

Luc. But I thought I heard him kiss you. Why did you suffer that?

Phil. Why, madam, we vulgar take it to be a sign of love—We servants, we poor people, that have nothing but our persons to bestow or treat for, are forced to deal and bargain by way of sample, and therefore as we have no parchments or wax necessary in our agreements, we squeeze with our hands and seal with our lips, to ratify vows and promises.

Luc. But can't you trust one another without such earnest down?

Phil. We don't think it safe, any more than you gentry, to come together without deeds executed.

Luc. Thou art a pert merry hussy.

Phil. I wish, madam, your lover and you were as happy as Tom and your servant are.

Luc. You grow impertinent.

Phil. I have done, madam; and I won't ask you what you intend to do with Mr. Myrtle, what your father will do with Mr. Bevil, nor what you all, especially my lady, mean by admitting Mr. Cimberton as particularly here as if he were married to you already; nay, you are married actually as far as people of quality are.

Luc. How is that?

Phil. You have different beds in the same house.

Luc. Pshaw! I have a very great value for Mr. Bevil, but have absolutely put an end to his pretensions in the letter I gave you for him. But my father, in his heart, still has a mind to him, were it not for this woman they talk of; and I am apt to imagine he is married to her, or never designs to marry at all.

Phil. Then Mr. Myrtle——

Luc. He had my parents' leave to apply to me, and by that he has won me and my affections; who is to have this body of mine without 'em, it seems, is nothing to me. My mother says 't is indecent for me to let my thoughts stray about the person of my husband; nay, she says a maid, rigidly virtuous, though she may have been where her lover was a thousand times, should not have made observations enough to know him from another man when she sees him in a third place.

Phil. That is more than the severity of a nun, for not to see when one may is hardly possible; not to see when one can't is very easy. At this rate, madam, there are a great many whom you have not seen who——

Luc. Mamma says the first time you see your husband should be at that instant he is made so. When your father, with the help of the minister, gives you to him, then you are to see him; then you are to observe and take notice of him; because then you are to obey him.

Phil. But does not my lady remember you are to love as well as obey?

Luc. To love is a passion, 't is a desire, and we must have no desires.—Oh, I cannot endure the reflection! With what insensibility on my part, with what more than patience have I been exposed and offered to some awkward booby or other in every county of Great Britain!

Phil. Indeed, madam, I wonder I never heard you speak of it before with this indignation.

Luc. Every corner of the land has presented me with a wealthy coxcomb. As fast as one treaty has gone off, another has come on, till my name and person have been the tittle-tattle of the whole town. What is this world come to?—no shame left—to be bartered for like the beasts of the field, and that in such an instance as coming together to an entire familiarity and union of soul and body. Oh! and this without being so much as well-wishers to each other, but for increase of fortune.

Phil. But, madam, all these vexations will end very soon in one for all. Mr. Cimberton is your mother's kinsman, and three hundred years an older gentleman than any lover you ever had; for which reason, with that of his prodigious large estate, she is resolved on him, and has sent to consult the lawyers accordingly; nay, has (whether you know it or no) been in treaty with Sir Geoffry, who, to join in the settlement, has accepted of a sum to do it, and is every moment expected in town for that purpose.

Luc. How do you get all this intelligence?

Phil. By an art I have, I thank my stars, beyond all the waiting-maids in Great

Britain—the art of listening, madam, for your ladyship's service.

Luc. I shall soon know as much as you do; leave me, leave me, Phillis, begone. Here, here! I'll turn you out. My mother says I must not converse with my servants, though I must converse with no one else. (*Exit Phil.*)—How unhappy are we who are born to great fortunes! No one looks at us with indifference, or acts towards us on the foot of plain dealing; yet, by all I have been heretofore offered to or treated for I have been used with the most agreeable of all abuses —flattery. But now, by this phlegmatic fool I'm used as nothing, or a mere thing. He, forsooth, is too wise, too learned to have any regard to desires, and I know not what the learned oaf calls sentiments of love and passion—Here he comes with my mother—It's much if he looks at me, or if he does, takes no more notice of me than of any other movable in the room.

(*Enter Mrs. Sealand, and Mr. Cimberton.*)

Mrs. Seal. How do I admire this noble, this learned taste of yours, and the worthy regard you have to our own ancient and honorable house in consulting a means to keep the blood as pure and as regularly descended as may be.

Cim. Why, really, madam, the young women of this age are treated with discourses of such a tendency, and their imaginations so bewildered in flesh and blood, that a man of reason can't talk to be understood. They have no ideas of happiness, but what are more gross than the gratification of hunger and thirst.

Luc. With how much reflection he is a coxcomb!

(*Aside.*)

Cim. And in truth, madam, I have considered it as a most brutal custom that persons of the first character in the world should go as ordinarily, and with as little shame, to bed as to dinner with one another. They proceed to the propagation of the species as openly as to the preservation of the individual.

Luc. She that willingly goes to bed to thee must have no shame, I'm sure.

(*Aside.*)

Mrs. Seal. Oh, cousin Cimberton! cousin Cimberton! how abstracted, how refined is your sense of things! But, indeed, it is too true there is nothing so ordinary as to say, in the best governed families, my master and lady are gone to bed; one does not know but it might have been said of one's self.

(*Hiding her face with her fan.*)

Cim. Lycurgus, madam, instituted otherwise; among the Lacedæmonians the whole female world was pregnant, but none but the mothers themselves knew by whom; their meetings were secret, and the amorous congress always by stealth; and no such professed doings between the sexes as are tolerated among us under the audacious word, marriage.

Mrs. Seal. Oh, had I lived in those days and been a matron of Sparta, one might with less indecency have had ten children, according to that modest institution, than one, under the confusion of our modern, barefaced manner.

Luc. And yet, poor woman, she has gone through the whole ceremony, and here I stand a melancholy proof of it.

(*Aside.*)

Mrs. Seal. We will talk then of business. That girl walking about the room there is to be your wife. She has, I confess, no ideas, no sentiments, that speak her born of a thinking mother.

Cimb. I have observed her; her lively look, free air, and disengaged countenance speak her very——

Luc. Very what?

Cimb. If you please, madam—to set her a little that way.

Mrs. Seal. Lucinda, say nothing to him, you are not a match for him; when you are married, you may speak to such a husband when you're spoken to. But I am disposing of you above yourself every way.

Cimb. Madam, you cannot but observe the inconveniences I expose myself to, in hopes that your ladyship will be the consort of my better part. As for the young woman, she is rather an impediment than a help to a man of letters and speculation. Madam, there is no reflection, no philosophy, can at all times subdue the sensitive life, but the animal shall sometimes carry away the man. Ha! ay, the vermilion of her lips.

Luc. Pray, don't talk of me thus.

Cimb. The pretty enough—pant of her bosom.

Luc. Sir! madam, don't you hear him?

Cimb. Her forward chest.

Luc. Intolerable!

Cimb. High health.

Luc. The grave, easy impudence of him!

Cimb. Proud heart.

Luc. Stupid coxcomb!

Cimb. I say, madam, her impatience, while we are looking at her, throws out all attractions—her arms—her neck—what a spring in her step!

Luc. Don't you run me over thus, you strange unaccountable!

Cimb. What an elasticity in her veins and arteries!

Luc. I have no veins, no arteries.

Mrs. Seal. Oh, child! hear him, he talks finely; he 's a scholar, he knows what you have.

Cimb. The speaking invitation of her shape, the gathering of herself up, and the indignation you see in the pretty little thing—Now, I am considering her, on this occasion, but as one that is to be pregnant.

Luc. The familiar, learned, unseasonable puppy!

(*Aside.*)

Cimb. And pregnant undoubtedly she will be yearly. I fear I shan't, for many years, have discretion enough to give her one fallow season.

Luc. Monster! there 's no bearing it. The hideous sot! there 's no enduring it, to be thus surveyed like a steed at sale.

Cimb. At sale! She 's very illiterate—But she 's very well limbed too; turn her in; I see what she is.

(*Exit Lucinda, in a rage.*)

Mrs. Seal. Go, you creature, I am ashamed of you.

Cimb. No harm done—you know, madam, the better sort of people, as I observed to you, treat by their lawyers of weddings (*Adjusting himself at the glass.*)—and the woman in the bargain, like the mansion house in the sale of the estate, is thrown in, and what that is, whether good or bad, is not at all considered.

Mrs. Seal. I grant it; and therefore make no demand for her youth and beauty, and every other accomplishment, as the common world think 'em, because she is not polite.

Cimb. Madam, I know your exalted understanding, abstracted, as it is, from vulgar prejudices, will not be offended, when I declare to you, I marry to have an heir to my estate, and not to beget a colony, or a plantation. This young woman's beauty and constitution will demand provision for a tenth child at least.

Mrs. Seal. With all that wit and learning, how considerate! What an economist! (*Aside.*)—Sir, I cannot make her any other than she is; or say she is much better than the other young women of this age, or fit for much besides being a mother; but I have given directions for the marriage settlements, and Sir Geoffry Cimberton's counsel is to meet ours here, at this hour, concerning his joining in the deed, which, when executed, makes you capable of settling what is due to Lucinda's fortune. Herself, as I told you, I say nothing of.

Cimb. No, no, no, indeed, madam, it is not usual; and I must depend upon my own reflection and philosophy not to overstock my family.

Mrs. Seal. I cannot help her, cousin Cimberton; but she is, for aught I see, as well as the daughter of anybody else.

Cimb. That is very true, madam.

(*Enter a Servant, who whispers Mrs. Sealand.*)

Mrs. Seal. The lawyers are come, and now we are to hear what they have resolved as to the point whether it 's necessary that Sir Geoffry should join in the settlement, as being what they call in the remainder. But, good cousin, you must have patience with 'em. These lawyers, I am told, are of a different kind; one is what they call a chamber counsel, the other a pleader. The conveyancer is slow, from an imperfection in his speech, and therefore shunned the bar, but extremely passionate and impatient of contradiction. The other is as warm as he; but has a tongue so voluble, and a head so conceited, he will suffer nobody to speak but himself.

Cimb. You mean old Serjeant Target and Counsellor Bramble? I have heard of 'em.

Mrs. Seal. The same. Show in the gentlemen.

(*Exit Servant.*)

(*Re-enter Servant, introducing Myrtle and Tom disguised as Bramble and Target.*)

Mrs. Seal. Gentlemen, this is the party concerned, Mr. Cimberton; and I hope you have considered of the matter.

Tar. Yes, madam, we have agreed that it must be by indent——dent——dent——dent——

Bram. Yes, madam, Mr. Serjeant and myself have agreed, as he is pleased to inform you, that it must be an indenture tripartite, and tripartite let it be, for Sir

Geoffry must needs be a party; old Cimberton, in the year 1619, says, in that ancient roll in Mr. Serjeant's hands, as recourse thereto being had, will more at large appear——

Tar. Yes, and by the deeds in your hands, it appears that——

Bram. Mr. Serjeant, I beg of you to make no inferences upon what is in our custody; but speak to the titles in your own deeds. I shall not show that deed till my client is in town.

Cimb. You know best your own methods.

Mrs. Seal. The single question is, whether the entail is such that my cousin, Sir Geoffry, is necessary in this affair?

Bram. Yes, as to the lordship of Tretriplet, but not as to the messuage of Grimgribber.

Tar. I say that Gr—gr— that Gr—gr—Grimgribber, Grimgribber is in us; that is to say the remainder thereof, as well as that of Tr—tr—Triplet.

Bram. You go upon the deed of Sir Ralph, made in the middle of the last century, precedent to that in which old Cimberton made over the remainder, and made it pass to the heirs general, by which your client comes in; and I question whether the remainder even of Tretriplet is in him—But we are willing to waive that, and give him a valuable consideration. But we shall not purchase what is in us for ever, as Grimgribber is, at the rate, as we guard against the contingent of Mr. Cimberton having no son—Then we know Sir Geoffry is the first of the collateral male line in this family—yet——

Tar. Sir, Gr——gr——ber is——

Bram. I apprehend you very well, and your argument might be of force, and we would be inclined to hear that in all its parts—But, sir, I see very plainly what you are going into. I tell you, it is as probable a contingent that Sir Geoffry may die before Mr. Cimberton, as that he may outlive him.

Tar. Sir, we are not ripe for that yet, but I must say——

Bram. Sir, I allow you the whole extent of that argument; but that will go no farther than as to the claimants under old Cimberton. I am of opinion that, according to the instruction of Sir Ralph, he could not dock the entail, and then create a new estate for the heirs general.

Tar. Sir, I have not patience to be told that, when Gr——gr——ber——

Bram. I will allow it you, Mr. Serjeant; but there must be the word heirs for ever, to make such an estate as you pretend.

Cimb. I must be impartial, though you are counsel for my side of the question. Were it not that you are so good as to allow him what he has not said, I should think it very hard you should answer him without hearing him—But, gentlemen, I believe you have both considered this matter, and are firm in your different opinions. 'T were better, therefore, you proceeded according to the particular sense of each of you, and gave your thoughts distinctly in writing. And do you see, sirs, pray let me have a copy of what you say in English.

Bram. Why, what is all we have been saying? In English! Oh! but I forgot myself, you 're a wit. But, however, to please you, sir, you shall have it, in as plain terms as the law will admit of.

Cimb. But I would have it, sir, without delay.

Bram. That, sir, the law will not admit of. The Courts are sitting at Westminster, and I am this moment obliged to be at every one of them, and 't would be wrong if I should not be in the hall to attend one of 'em at least; the rest would take it ill else. Therefore, I must leave what I have said to Mr. Serjeant's consideration, and I will digest his arguments on my part, and you shall hear from me again, sir.

(*Exit Bramble.*)

Tar. Agreed, agreed.

Cimb. Mr. Bramble is very quick; he parted a little abruptly.

Tar. He could not bear my argument; I pinched him to the quick about that Gr——gr——ber.

Mrs. Seal. I saw that, for he durst not so much as hear you. I shall send to you, Mr. Serjeant, as soon as Sir Geoffry comes to town, and then I hope all may be adjusted.

Tar. I shall be at my chambers, at my usual hours.

(*Exit.*)

Cimb. Madam, if you please, I 'll now attend you to the tea table, where I shall hear from your ladyship reason and good sense, after all this law and gibberish.

Mrs. Seal. 'T is a wonderful thing, sir, that men of professions do not study to talk the substance of what they have to say in the language of the rest of the world. Sure, they 'd find their account in it.

Cim. They might, perhaps, madam, with people of your good sense; but with the generality 't would never do. The vulgar would have no respect for truth and knowledge, if they were exposed to naked view.

Truth is too simple, of all art bereaved:
Since the world will—why let it be deceived.

(*Exeunt.*)

ACT IV.

SCENE 1. *Bevil, Jun.'s Lodgings.*

(*Bevil, Jun., with a letter in his hand, followed by Tom.*)

Tom. Upon my life, sir, I know nothing of the matter. I never opened my lips to Mr. Myrtle about anything of your honor's letter to Madam Lucinda.

Bev. What 's the fool in such a fright for? I don't suppose you did. What I would know is, whether Mr. Myrtle showed any suspicion, or asked you any questions, to lead you to say casually that you had carried any such letter for me this morning.

Tom. Why, sir, if he did ask me any questions, how could I help it?

Bev. I don't say you could, oaf! I am not questioning you, but him. What did he say to you?

Tom. Why, sir, when I came to his chambers, to be dressed for the lawyer's part your honor was pleased to put me upon, he asked me if I had been at Mr. Sealand's this morning? So I told him, sir, I often went thither—because, sir, if I had not said that he might have thought there was something more in my going now than at another time.

Bev. Very well!—The fellow's caution, I find, has given him this jealousy. (*Aside.*)—Did he ask you no other questions?

Tom. Yes, sir; now I remember, as we came away in the hackney coach from Mr. Sealand's, Tom, says he, as I came in to your master this morning, he bade you go for an answer to a letter he had sent. Pray did you bring him any? says he. Ah! says I, sir, your honor is pleased to joke with me; you have a mind to know whether I can keep a secret or no?

Bev. And so, by showing him you could, you told him you had one?

Tom. Sir——

(*Confused.*)

Bev. What mean actions does jealousy make a man stoop to! How poorly has he used art with a servant to make him betray his master!—Well! and when did he give you this letter for me?

Tom. Sir, he writ it before he pulled off his lawyer's gown, at his own chambers.

Bev. Very well; and what did he say when you brought him my answer to it?

Tom. He looked a little out of humor, sir, and said it was very well.

Bev. I knew he would be grave upon 't; wait without.

Tom. Hum! 'gad, I don't like this; I am afraid we are all in the wrong box here.

(*Exit Tom.*)

Bev. I put on a serenity while my fellow was present; but I have never been more thoroughly disturbed. This hot man! to write me a challenge, on supposed artificial dealing, when I professed myself his friend! I can live contented without glory; but I cannot suffer shame. What 's to be done? But first let me consider Lucinda's letter again.

(*Reads.*)

"SIR,

"I hope it is consistent with the laws a woman ought to impose upon herself, to acknowledge that your manner of declining a treaty of marriage in our family, and desiring the refusal may come from me, has something more engaging in it than the courtship of him who, I fear, will fall to my lot, except your friend exerts himself for our common safety and happiness. I have reasons for desiring Mr. Myrtle may not know of this letter till hereafter, and am your most obliged humble servant,

"LUCINDA SEALAND."

Well, but the postscript—

(*Reads.*)

"I won't, upon second thoughts, hide anything from you. But my reason for concealing this is, that Mr. Myrtle has a jealousy in his temper which gives me some terrors; but my esteem for him inclines me to hope that only an ill effect which sometimes accompanies a tender love, and what may be cured by a careful and unblamable conduct."

Thus has this lady made me her friend and confidant, and put herself, in a kind, under my protection. I cannot tell him immediately the purport of her letter, except I could cure him of the violent and untractable passion of jealousy, and so serve him, and her, by disobeying her, in the article of secrecy, more than I should by complying with her directions. —But then this duelling, which custom has imposed upon every man who would live with reputation and honor in the world—how must I preserve myself from imputations there? He 'll, forsooth, call it or think it fear, if I explain without fighting.—But his letter—I 'll read it again—

"SIR,

"You have used me basely in corresponding and carrying on a treaty where you told me you were indifferent. I have changed my sword since I saw you; which advertisement I thought proper to send you against the next meeting between you and the injured

"CHARLES MYRTLE."

(*Enter Tom.*)

Tom. Mr. Myrtle, sir. Would your honor please to see him?

Bev. Why, you stupid creature! Let Mr. Myrtle wait at my lodgings? Show him up. (*Exit Tom.*) Well! I am resolved upon my carriage to him. He is in love, and in every circumstance of life a little distrustful, which I must allow for—but here he is.

(*Enter Tom, introducing Myrtle.*)

Sir, I am extremely obliged to you for this honor.—(*To Tom.*) But, sir, you, with your very discerning face, leave the room. (*Exit Tom.*)—Well, Mr. Myrtle, your commands with me?

Myrt. The time, the place, our long acquaintance, and many other circumstances which affect me on this occasion, oblige me, without farther ceremony or conference, to desire you would not only, as you already have, acknowledge the receipt of my letter, but also comply with the request in it. I must have farther notice taken of my message than these half lines—"I have yours," "I shall be at home."

Bev. Sir, I own I have received a letter from you in a very unusual style; but as I design everything in this matter shall be your own action, your own seeking, I shall understand nothing but what you are pleased to confirm face to face, and I have already forgot the contents of your epistle.

Myrt. This cool manner is very agreeable to the abuse you have already made of my simplicity and frankness; and I see your moderation tends to your own advantage and not mine—to your own safety, not consideration of your friend.

Bev. My own safety, Mr. Myrtle?

Myrt. Your own safety, Mr. Bevil.

Bev. Look you, Mr. Myrtle, there 's no disguising that I understand what you would be at; but, sir, you know I have often dared to disapprove of the decisions a tyrant custom has introduced, to the breach of all laws, both divine and human.

Myrt. Mr. Bevil, Mr. Bevil, it would be a good first principle, in those who have so tender a conscience that way, to have as much abhorrence of doing injuries, as——

Bev. As what?

Myrt. As fear of answering for 'em.

Bev. As fear of answering for 'em! But that apprehension is just or blamable according to the object of that fear. I have often told you, in confidence of heart, I abhorred the daring to offend the Author of life, and rushing into His presence—I say, by the very same act, to commit the crime against Him, and immediately to urge on to His tribunal.

Myrt. Mr. Bevil, I must tell you, this coolness, this gravity, this show of conscience, shall never cheat me of my mistress. You have, indeed, the best excuse for life, the hopes of possessing Lucinda. But consider, sir, I have as much reason to be weary of it, if I am to lose her; and my first attempt to recover her shall be to let her see the dauntless man who is to be her guardian and protector.

Bev. Sir, show me but the least glimpse of argument, that I am authorised, by my own hand, to vindicate any lawless insult of this nature, and I will show thee—to chastise thee hardly deserves the name of courage—slight, inconsiderate man!—There is, Mr. Myrtle, no such terror in quick anger; and you shall, you know not why, be cool, as you have, you know not why, been warm.

Myrt. Is the woman one loves so little an occasion of anger? You perhaps, who know not what it is to love, who have your ready, your commodious, your foreign trinket, for your loose hours; and from your fortune, your specious outward carriage, and other lucky circumstances, as easy a way to the possession of a woman of honor; you know nothing of what it is to be alarmed, to be distracted with anxiety and terror of losing more than life. Your marriage, happy man, goes on like common business, and in the interim you have your rambling captive, your Indian princess, for your soft moments of dalliance, your convenient, your ready Indiana.

Bev. You have touched me beyond the patience of a man; and I 'm excusable, in the guard of innocence (or from the infirmity of human nature, which can bear no more), to accept your invitation, and observe your letter—Sir, I 'll attend you.

(*Enter Tom.*)

Tom. Did you call, sir? I thought you did; I heard you speak aloud.

Bev. Yes; go call a coach.

Tom. Sir—master—Mr. Myrtle—friends—gentlemen—what d'ye mean? I am but a servant, or——

Bev. Call a coach. (*Exit Tom.*)—(*A long pause, walking sullenly by each other.*)—(*Aside.*) Shall I (though provoked to the uttermost) recover myself at the entrance of a third person, and that my servant too, and not have respect enough to all I have ever been receiving from infancy, the obligation to the best of fathers, to an unhappy virgin too, whose life depends on mine? (*Shutting the door.*)—(*To Myrtle.*) I have, thank Heaven, had time to recollect myself, and shall not, for fear of what such a rash man as you think of me, keep longer unexplained the false appearances under which your infirmity of temper makes you suffer; when perhaps too much regard to a false point of honor makes me prolong that suffering.

Myrt. I am sure Mr. Bevil cannot doubt but I had rather have satisfaction from his innocence than his sword.

Bev. Why, then, would you ask it first that way?

Myrt. Consider, you kept your temper yourself no longer than till I spoke to the disadvantage of her you loved.

Bev. True; but let me tell you, I have saved you from the most exquisite distress, even though you had succeeded in the dispute. I know you so well, that I am sure to have found this letter about a man you had killed would have been worse than death to yourself—Read it.—(*Aside.*) When he is thoroughly mortified, and shame has got the better of jealousy, when he has seen himself throughly, he will deserve to be assisted towards obtaining Lucinda.

Myrt. With what a superiority has he turned the injury on me, as the aggressor! I begin to fear I have been too far transported—*A treaty in our family!* is not that saying too much? I shall relapse.—But I find (on the postscript) *something like jealousy.* With what face can I see my benefactor, my advocate, whom I have treated like a betrayer! (*Aside.*)—Oh, Bevil, with what words shall I——

Bev. There needs none; to convince is much more than to conquer.

Myrt. But can you——

Bev. You have o'erpaid the inquietude you gave me, in the change I see in you towards me. Alas! what machines are we! thy face is altered to that of another man; to that of my companion, my friend.

Myrt. That I could be such a precipitant wretch!

Bev. Pray, no more.

Myrt. Let me reflect how many friends have died, by the hands of friends, for want of temper; and you must give me leave to say again, and again, how much I am beholden to that superior spirit you have subdued me with. What had become of one of us, or perhaps both, had you been as weak as I was, and as incapable of reason?

Bev. I congratulate to us both the escape from ourselves, and hope the memory of it will make us dearer friends than ever.

Myrt. Dear Bevil, your friendly conduct has convinced me that there is nothing manly but what is conducted by reason, and agreeable to the practice of virtue and justice. And yet how many have been sacrificed to that idol, the unreasonable opinion of men! Nay, they are so ridiculous in it, that they often use their swords against each other with dissembled anger and real fear.

Betrayed by honor, and compelled by shame,
They hazard being, to preserve a name:
Nor dare inquire into the dread mistake,
Till plunged in sad eternity they wake.

(*Exeunt.*)

SCENE 2. *St. James's Park.*

(*Enter Sir John Bevil and Mr. Sealand.*)

Sir J. Bev. Give me leave, however, Mr. Sealand, as we are upon a treaty for uniting our families, to mention only the business of an ancient house. Genealogy and descent are to be of some consideration in an affair of this sort.

Mr. Seal. Genealogy and descent! Sir, there has been in our family a very large one. There was Galfrid the father of Edward, the father of Ptolomey, the father of Crassus, the father of Earl Richard, the father of Henry the Marquis, the father of Duke John——

Sir J. Bev. What, do you rave, Mr. Sealand? all these great names in your family?

Mr. Seal. These? yes, sir. I have heard my father name 'em all, and more.

Sir J. Bev. Ay, sir? and did he say they were all in your family?

Mr. Seal. Yes, sir, he kept 'em all. He was the greatest cocker [21] in England. He said Duke John won him many battles, and never lost one.

Sir J. Bev. Oh, sir, your servant! you are laughing at my laying any stress upon descent; but I must tell you, sir, I never knew anyone but he that wanted that advantage turn it into ridicule.

Mr. Seal. And I never knew any one who had many better advantages put that into his account.—But, Sir John, value yourself as you please upon your ancient house, I am to talk freely of everything you are pleased to put into your bill of rates on this occasion; yet, sir, I have made no objections to your son's family. 'T is his morals that I doubt.

Sir J. Bev. Sir, I can't help saying, that what might injure a citizen's credit may be no stain to a gentleman's honor.

Mr. Seal. Sir John, the honor of a gentleman is liable to be tainted by as small a matter as the credit of a trader. We are talking of a marriage, and in such a case, the father of a young woman will not think it an addition to the honor or credit of her lover that he is a keeper——

Sir J. Bev. Mr. Sealand, don't take upon you to spoil my son's marriage with any woman else.

Mr. Seal. Sir John, let him apply to any woman else, and have as many mistresses as he pleases.

Sir J. Bev. My son, sir, is a discreet and sober gentleman.

Mr. Seal. Sir, I never saw a man that wenched soberly and discreetly, that ever left it off; the decency observed in the practice hides, even from the sinner, the iniquity of it. They pursue it, not that their appetites hurry 'em away, but, I warrant you, because 't is their opinion they may do it.

Sir J. Bev. Were what you suspect a truth—do you design to keep your daughter a virgin till you find a man unblemished that way?

Mr. Seal. Sir, as much a cit [22] as you take me for, I know the town and the world; and give me leave to say, that we merchants are a species of gentry that have grown into the world this last century, and are as honorable, and almost as useful, as you landed folks, that have always thought yourselves so much above us; for your trading, forsooth, is extended no farther than a load of hay or a fat ox. You are pleasant people, indeed, because you are generally bred up to be lazy; therefore, I warrant you, industry is dishonorable.

Sir J. Bev. Be not offended, sir; let us go back to our point.

Mr. Seal. Oh! not at all offended; but I don't love to leave any part of the account unclosed. Look you, Sir John, comparisons are odious, and more particularly so on occasions of this kind, when we are projecting races that are to be made out of both sides of the comparisons.

Sir J. Bev. But, my son, sir, is, in the eye of the world, a gentleman of merit.

Mr. Seal. I own to you, I think him so.—But, Sir John, I am a man exercised and experienced in chances and disasters. I lost, in my earlier years, a very fine wife, and with her a poor little infant. This makes me, perhaps, over cautious to preserve the second bounty of providence to me, and be as careful as I can of this child. You 'll pardon me, my poor girl, sir, is as valuable to me as your boasted son to you.

Sir J. Bev. Why, that 's one very good reason, Mr. Sealand, why I wish my son had her.

Mr. Seal. There is nothing but this strange lady here, this *incognita*, that can be objected to him. Here and there a man falls in love with an artful crea-

21 Lover of cock-fights.

22 A bourgeois.

ture, and gives up all the motives of life to that one passion.

Sir J. Bev. A man of my son's understanding cannot be supposed to be one of them.

Mr. Seal. Very wise men have been so enslaved; and, when a man marries with one of them upon his hands, whether moved from the demand of the world or slighter reasons, such a husband soils with [23] his wife for a month perhaps—then good be w' ye,[24] madam, the show 's over—Ah! John Dryden points out such a husband to a hair, where he says,—

"And while abroad so prodigal the dolt is,
Poor spouse at home as ragged as a colt is."

Now, in plain terms, sir, I shall not care to have my poor girl turned a-grazing, and that must be the case when——

Sir J. Bev. But pray consider, sir, my son——

Mr. Seal. Look you, sir, I 'll make the matter short. This unknown lady, as I told you, is all the objection I have to him; but, one way or other, he is, or has been, certainly engaged to her. I am therefore resolved, this very afternoon, to visit her. Now from her behavior, or appearance, I shall soon be let into what I may fear or hope for.

Sir J. Bev. Sir, I am very confident there can be nothing inquired into relating to my son, that will not, upon being understood, turn to his advantage.

Mr. Seal. I hope that as sincerely as you believe it.—Sir John Bevil, when I am satisfied, in this great point, if your son's conduct answers the character you give him, I shall wish your alliance more than that of any gentleman in Great Britain; and so your servant.

(*Exit.*)

Sir J. Bev. He is gone in a way but barely civil; but his great wealth, and the merit of his only child, the heiress of it, are not to be lost for a little peevishness.

(*Enter Humphry.*)

Oh! Humphry, you are come in a seasonable minute. I want to talk to thee, and to tell thee that my head and heart are on the rack about my son.

Humph. Sir, you may trust his discretion; I am sure you may.

Sir J. Bev. Why, I do believe I may, and yet I 'm in a thousand fears when I lay this vast wealth before me; when I consider his prepossessions, either generous to a folly, in an honorable love, or abandoned, past redemption, in a vicious one; and, from the one or the other, his insensibility to the fairest prospect towards doubling our estate: a father, who knows how useful wealth is, and how necessary, even to those who despise it—I say a father, Humphry, a father cannot bear it.

Humph. Be not transported, sir; you will grow incapable of taking any resolution in your perplexity.

Sir J. Bev. Yet, as angry as I am with him, I would not have him surprised in anything. This mercantile rough man may go grossly into the examination of this matter, and talk to the gentlewoman so as to——

Humph. No, I hope, not in an abrupt manner.

Sir J. Bev. No, I hope not! Why, dost thou know anything of her, or of him, or of anything of it, or all of it?

Humph. My dear master, I know so much that I told him this very day you had reason to be secretly out of humor about her.

Sir J. Bev. Did you go so far? Well, what said he to that?

Humph. His words were, looking upon me steadfastly: "Humphry," says he, "that woman is a woman of honor."

Sir J. Bev. How! Do you think he is married to her, or designs to marry her?

Humph. I can say nothing to the latter; but he says he can marry no one without your consent while you are living.

Sir J. Bev. If he said so much, I know he scorns to break his word with me.

Humph. I am sure of that.

Sir J. Bev. You are sure of that—well! that 's some comfort. Then I have nothing to do but to see the bottom of this matter during this present ruffle—Oh, Humphry——

Humph. You are not ill, I hope, sir.

Sir J. Bev. Yes, a man is very ill that 's in a very ill-humor. To be a father is to be in care for one whom you oftener disoblige than please by that very care—Oh! that sons could know the duty to a father before they themselves are fathers

23 lives with.

24 good-by.

—But, perhaps, you'll say now that I am one of the happiest fathers in the world; but, I assure you, that of the very happiest is not a condition to be envied.

Humph. Sir, your pain arises, not from the thing itself, but your particular sense of it. You are overfond, nay, give me leave to say, you are unjustly apprehensive from your fondness. My master Bevil never disobliged you, and he will, I know he will, do everything you ought to expect.

Sir J. Bev. He won't take all this money with this girl—For ought I know, he will, forsooth, have so much moderation as to think he ought not to force his liking for any consideration.

Humph. He is to marry her, not you; he is to live with her, not you, sir.

Sir J. Bev. I know not what to think. But, I know, nothing can be more miserable than to be in this doubt—Follow me; I must come to some resolution.

(*Exeunt.*)

SCENE 3. *Bevil, Jun.'s Lodgings.*

(*Enter Tom and Phillis.*)

Tom. Well, madam, if you must speak with Mr. Myrtle, you shall; he is now with my master in the library.

Phil. But you must leave me alone with him, for he can't make me a present, nor I so handsomely take anything from him before you; it would not be decent.

Tom. It will be very decent, indeed, for me to retire, and leave my mistress with another man.

Phil. He is a gentleman, and will treat one properly.

Tom. I believe so; but, however, I won't be far off, and therefore will venture to trust you. I'll call him to you.

(*Exit Tom.*)

Phil. What a deal of pother and sputter here is between my mistress and Mr. Myrtle from mere punctilio! I could, any hour of the day, get her to her lover, and would do it—but she, forsooth, will allow no plot to get him; but, if he can come to her, I know she would be glad of it. I must, therefore, do her an acceptable violence, and surprise her into his arms. I am sure I go by the best rule imaginable. If she were my maid, I should think her the best servant in the world for doing so by me.

(*Enter Myrtle and Tom.*)

Oh sir! You and Mr. Bevil are fine gentlemen to let a lady remain under such difficulties as my poor mistress, and no attempt to set her at liberty, or release her from the danger of being instantly married to Cimberton.

Myrt. Tom has been telling——But what is to be done?

Phil. What is to be done—when a man can't come at his mistress! Why, can't you fire our house, or the next house to us, to make us run out, and you take us?

Myrt. How, Mrs. Phillis?

Phil. Ay; let me see that rogue deny to fire a house, make a riot, or any other little thing, when there were no other way to come at me.

Tom. I am obliged to you, madam.

Phil. Why, don't we hear every day of people's hanging themselves for love, and won't they venture the hazard of being hanged for love? Oh, were I a man——

Myrt. What manly thing would you have me undertake, according to your ladyship's notion of a man?

Phil. Only be at once what, one time or other, you may be, and wish to be, or must be.

Myrt. Dear girl, talk plainly to me, and consider I, in my condition, can't be in very good humor—you say, to be at once what I must be.

Phil. Ay, ay; I mean no more than to be an old man; I saw you do it very well at the masquerade. In a word, old Sir Geoffry Cimberton is every hour expected in town, to join in the deeds and settlements for marrying Mr. Cimberton. He is half blind, half lame, half deaf, half dumb; though, as to his passions and desires, he is as warm and ridiculous as when in the heat of youth.

Tom. Come to the business, and don't keep the gentleman in suspense for the pleasure of being courted, as you serve me.

Phil. I saw you at the masquerade act such a one to perfection. Go, and put on that very habit, and come to our house as Sir Geoffry. There is not one there but myself knows his person; I was born in the parish where he is Lord of the Manor. I have seen him often and often at church in the country. Do not hesitate, but come hither; they will think you bring a certain security against Mr. Myrtle, and you bring Mr. Myrtle.

Leave the rest to me; I leave this with you, and expect—They don't, I told you, know you; they think you out of town, which you had as good be for ever, if you lose this opportunity—I must be gone; I know I am wanted at home.

Myrt. My dear Phillis!

(*Catches and kisses her, and gives her money.*)

Phil. O fie! my kisses are not my own; you have committed violence; but I'll carry 'em to the right owner. (*Tom kisses her.*)—Come, see me downstairs (*To Tom*) and leave the lover to think of his last game for the prize.

(*Exeunt Tom and Phillis.*)

Myrt. I think I will instantly attempt this wild expedient. The extravagance of it will make me less suspected, and it will give me opportunity to assert my own right to Lucinda, without whom I cannot live. But I am so mortified at this conduct of mine towards poor Bevil. He must think meanly of me—I know not how to reassume myself, and be in spirit enough for such an adventure as this; yet I must attempt it, if it be only to be near Lucinda under her present perplexities; and sure——

The next delight to transport, with the fair,
Is to relieve her in her hours of care.

(*Exit.*)

ACT V.

Scene 1. *Sealand's House.*

(*Enter Phillis, with lights, before Myrtle, disguised like old Sir Geoffry; supported by Mrs. Sealand, Lucinda, and Cimberton.*)

Mrs. Seal. Now I have seen you thus far, Sir Geoffry, will you excuse me a moment while I give my necessary orders for your accommodation?

(*Exit Mrs. Seal.*)

Myrt. I have not seen you, cousin Cimberton, since you were ten years old; and as it is incumbent on you to keep up our name and family, I shall, upon very reasonable terms, join with you in a settlement to that purpose. Though I must tell you, cousin, this is the first merchant that has married into our house.

Luc. Deuce on 'em! am I a merchant because my father is?

(*Aside.*)

Myrt. But is he directly a trader at this time?

Cimb. There's no hiding the disgrace, sir; he trades to all parts of the world.

Myrt. We never had one of our family before who descended from persons that did anything.

Cimb. Sir, since it is a girl that they have, I am, for the honor of my family, willing to take it in again, and to sink her into our name, and no harm done.

Myrt. 'T is prudently and generously resolved—Is this the young thing?

Cimb. Yes, sir.

Phil. Good madam, don't be out of humor, but let them run to the utmost of their extravagance.—Hear them out.

(*To Luc.*)

Myrt. Can't I see her nearer? My eyes are but weak.

Phil. Beside, I am sure the uncle has something worth your notice. I'll take care to get off the young one, and leave you to observe what may be wrought out of the old one for your good.

(*To Luc. Exit.*)

Cimb. Madam, this old gentleman, your great uncle, desires to be introduced to you, and to see you nearer!—Approach, sir.

Myrt. By your leave, young lady. (*Puts on spectacles.*)—Cousin Cimberton! She has exactly that sort of neck and bosom for which my sister Gertrude was so much admired in the year sixty-one, before the French dresses first discovered anything in women below the chin.

Luc. (*Aside.*) What a very odd situation am I in! though I cannot but be diverted at the extravagance of their humors, equally unsuitable to their age—Chin, quotha—I don't believe my passionate lover there knows whether I have one or not. Ha! ha!

Myrt. Madam, I would not willingly offend, but I have a better glass.

(*Pulls out a large one.*)

(*Enter Phillis.*)

Phil. (*To Cimberton.*) Sir, my lady desires to show the apartment to you that she intends for Sir Geoffry.

Cimb. Well, sir! by that time you will have sufficiently gazed and sunned yourself in the beauties of my spouse there.—I will wait on you again.

(*Exit Cimb. and Phil.*)

Myrt. Were it not, madam, that I might be troublesome, there is something of importance, though we are alone, which I would say more safe from being heard.

Luc. There is something in this old fellow, methinks, that raises my curiosity.

(*Aside.*)

Myrt. To be free, madam, I as heartily contemn this kinsman of mine as you do, and am sorry to see so much beauty and merit devoted by your parents to so insensible a possessor.

Luc. Surprising!—I hope, then, sir, you will not contribute to the wrong you are so generous as to pity, whatever may be the interest of your family.

Myrt. This hand of mine shall never be employed to sign anything against your good and happiness.

Luc. I am sorry, sir, it is not in my power to make you proper acknowledgments; but there is a gentleman in the world whose gratitude will, I am sure, be worthy of the favor.

Myrt. All the thanks I desire, madam, are in your power to give.

Luc. Name them and command them.

Myrt. Only, madam, that the first time you are alone with your lover, you will, with open arms, receive him.

Luc. As willingly as his heart could wish it.

Myrt. Thus, then, he claims your promise. O Lucinda!

Luc. Oh! a cheat! a cheat! a cheat!

Myrt. Hush! 't is I, 't is I, your lover, Myrtle himself, madam.

Luc. O bless me! what a rashness and folly to surprise me so—But hush—my mother.

(*Enter Mrs. Sealand, Cimberton, and Phillis.*)

Mrs. Seal. How now! what 's the matter?

Luc. O madam! as soon as you left the room my uncle fell into a sudden fit, and —and—so I cried out for help to support him and conduct him to his chamber.

Mrs. Seal. That was kindly done! Alas! sir, how do you find yourself?

Myrt. Never was taken in so odd a way in my life—pray lead me! Oh! I was talking here—(pray carry me)—to my cousin Cimberton's young lady.

Mrs. Seal. (*Aside.*) My cousin Cimberton's young lady! How zealous he is, even in his extremity, for the match! A right Cimberton.

(*Cimberton and Lucinda lead him, as one in pain.*)

Cimb. Pox! Uncle, you will pull my ear off.

Luc. Pray, uncle! you will squeeze me to death.

Mrs. Seal. No matter, no matter—he knows not what he does.—Come, sir, shall I help you out?

Myrt. By no means! I 'll trouble nobody but my young cousins here.

(*They lead him off.*)

Phil. But pray, madam, does your ladyship intend that Mr. Cimberton shall really marry my young mistress at last? I don't think he likes her.

Mrs. Seal. That 's not material! Men of his speculation are above desires—but be it as it may. Now I have given old Sir Geoffry the trouble of coming up to sign and seal, with what countenance can I be off?

Phil. As well as with twenty others, madam. It is the glory and honor of a great fortune to live in continual treaties, and still to break off: it looks great, madam.

Mrs. Seal. True, Phillis—yet to return our blood again into the Cimbertons is an honor not to be rejected—But were not you saying that Sir John Bevil's creature, Humphry, has been with Mr. Sealand?

Phil. Yes, madam; I overheard them agree that Mr. Sealand should go himself and visit this unknown lady that Mr. Bevil is so great with; and if he found nothing there to fright him, that Mr. Bevil should still marry my young mistress.

Mrs. Seal. How! nay, then, he shall find she is my daughter as well as his. I 'll follow him this instant, and take the whole family along with me. The disputed power of disposing of my own daughter shall be at an end this very night. I 'll live no longer in anxiety for a little hussy that hurts my appearance wherever I carry her: and for whose sake I seem to be at all regarded, and that in the best of my days.

Phil. Indeed, madam, if she were married, your ladyship might very well be taken for Mr. Sealand's daughter.

Mrs. Seal. Nay, when the chit has not been with me, I have heard the men say as much. I 'll no longer cut off the greatest pleasure of a woman's life (the shining in assemblies) by her forward anticipation of the respect that 's due to her superior. She shall down to Cimberton-Hall—she shall—she shall.

Phil. I hope, madam, I shall stay with your ladyship.

Mrs. Seal. Thou shalt, Phillis, and I'll place thee then more about me—But order chairs immediately; I'll be gone this minute.

(*Exeunt.*)

SCENE 2. *Charing Cross.*

(*Enter Mr. Sealand and Humphry.*)

Mr. Seal. I am very glad, Mr. Humphry, that you agree with me that it is for our common good I should look thoroughly into this matter.

Humph. I am, indeed, of that opinion; for there is no artifice, nothing concealed, in our family, which ought in justice to be known. I need not desire you, sir, to treat the lady with care and respect.

Mr. Seal. Master Humphry, I shall not be rude, though I design to be a little abrupt, and come into the matter at once, to see how she will bear upon a surprise.

Humph. That's the door, sir; I wish you success.—(*While Humphry speaks, Sealand consults his table book.*)—I am less concerned what happens there, because I hear Mr. Myrtle is well lodged as old Sir Geoffry; so I am willing to let this gentleman employ himself here, to give them time at home; for I am sure 't is necessary for the quiet of our family Lucinda were disposed of out of it, since Mr. Bevil's inclination is so much otherwise engaged.

(*Exit.*)

Mr. Seal. I think this is the door. (*Knocks.*) I'll carry this matter with an air of authority, to inquire, though I make an errand, to begin discourse.

(*Knocks again, and enter a foot-boy.*)

So, young man! is your lady within?

Boy. Alack, sir! I am but a country boy —I dant know whether she is or noa; but an you'll stay a bit, I'll goa and ask the gentlewoman that's with her.

Mr. Seal. Why, sirrah, though you are a country boy, you can see, can't you? You know whether she is at home, when you see her, don't you?

Boy. Nay, nay, I'm not such a country lad neither, master, to think she's at home because I see her. I have been in town but a month, and I lost one place already for believing my own eyes.

Mr. Seal. Why, sirrah! have you learnt to lie already?

Boy. Ah, master! things that are lies in the country are not lies at London. I begin to know my business a little better than so—But an you please to walk in, I'll call a gentlewoman to you that can tell you for certain—she can make bold to ask my lady herself.

Mr. Seal. Oh! then, she is within, I find, though you dare not say so.

Boy. Nay, nay! that's neither here nor there: what's matter whether she is within or no, if she has not a mind to see anybody?

Mr. Seal. I can't tell, sirrah, whether you are arch or simple; but, however, get me a direct answer, and here's a shilling for you.

Boy. Will you please to walk in; I'll see what I can do for you.

Mr. Seal. I see you will be fit for your business in time, child; but I expect to meet with nothing but extraordinaries in such a house.

Boy. Such a house! Sir, you han't seen it yet. Pray walk in.

Mr. Seal. Sir, I'll wait upon you.

(*Exeunt.*)

SCENE 3. *Indiana's House.*

(*Enter Isabella.*)

Isab. What anxiety do I feel for this poor creature! What will be the end of her? Such a languishing unreserved passion for a man that at last must certainly leave or ruin her! and perhaps both! Then the aggravation of the distress is, that she does not believe he will—not but, I must own, if they are both what they would seem, they are made for one another, as much as Adam and Eve were, for there is no other of their kind but themselves.

(*Enter Boy.*)

So, Daniel! what news with you?

Boy. Madam, there's a gentleman below would speak with my lady.

Isab. Sirrah! don't you know Mr. Bevil yet?

Boy. Madam, 't is not the gentleman who comes every day, and asks for you, and won't go in till he knows whether you are with her or no.

Isab. Ha! that's a particular I did not know before. Well! be it who it will, let him come up to me.

(*Exit Boy; and re-enters with Mr. Sealand; Isabella looks amazed.*)

Mr. Seal. Madam, I can't blame your being a little surprised to see a perfect stranger make a visit, and——

Isab. I am indeed surprised!—I see he does not know me.

(*Aside.*)

Mr. Seal. You are very prettily lodged here, madam; in troth you seem to have everything in plenty—A thousand a year, I warrant you, upon this pretty nest of rooms, and the dainty one within them.

(*Aside, and looking about.*)

Isab. (*Apart.*) Twenty years, it seems, have less effect in the alteration of a man of thirty than of a girl of fourteen—he 's almost still the same; but alas! I find, by other men, as well as himself, I am not what I was. As soon as he spoke, I was convinced 't was he; how shall I contain my surprise and satisfaction! He must not know me yet.

Mr. Seal. Madam, I hope I don't give you any disturbance; but there is a young lady here with whom I have a particular business to discourse, and I hope she will admit me to that favor.

Isab. Why, sir, have you had any notice concerning her? I wonder who could give it you.

Mr. Seal. That, madam, is fit only to be communicated to herself.

Isab. Well, sir! you shall see her.—(*Aside.*) I find he knows nothing yet, nor shall from me. I am resolved I will observe this interlude, this sport of nature and of fortune.—You shall see her presently, sir; for now I am as a mother, and will trust her with you.

(*Exit.*)

Mr. Seal. As a mother! right; that 's the old phrase for one of those commode[25] ladies, who lend out beauty for hire to young gentlemen that have pressing occasions. But here comes the precious lady herself. In troth a very sightly woman——

(*Enter Indiana.*)

Ind. I am told, sir, you have some affair that requires your speaking with me.

Mr. Seal. Yes, madam, there came to my hands a bill drawn by Mr. Bevil, which is payable to-morrow; and he, in the intercourse of business, sent it to me, who have cash of his, and desired me to send a servant with it; but I have made bold to bring you the money myself.

Ind. Sir! was that necessary?

Mr. Seal. No, madam; but to be free with you, the fame of your beauty, and the regard which Mr. Bevil is a little too well known to have for you, excited my curiosity.

Ind. Too well known to have for me! Your sober appearance, sir, which my friend described, made me expect no rudeness, or absurdity, at least—Who 's there?[26]—Sir, if you pay the money to a servant, 't will be as well.

Mr. Seal. Pray, madam, be not offended; I came hither on an innocent, nay, a virtuous design; and, if you will have patience to hear me, it may be as useful to you, as you are in a friendship with Mr. Bevil, as to my only daughter, whom I was this day disposing of.

Ind. You make me hope, sir, I have mistaken you. I am composed again; be free, say on—(*Aside.*)—what I am afraid to hear.

Mr. Seal. I feared, indeed, an unwarranted passion here, but I did not think it was in abuse of so worthy an object, so accomplished a lady as your sense and mien bespeak; but the youth of our age care not what merit and virtue they bring to shame, so they gratify——

Ind. Sir, you are going into very great errors; but as you are pleased to say you see something in me that has changed at least the color of your suspicions, so has your appearance altered mine, and made me earnestly attentive to what has any way concerned you to inquire into my affairs and character.

Mr. Seal. How sensibly, with what an air she talks!

Ind. Good sir, be seated, and tell me tenderly; keep all your suspicions concerning me alive, that you may in a proper and prepared way acquaint me why the care of your daughter obliges a person of your seeming worth and fortune to be thus inquisitive about a wretched, helpless, friendless——(*Weeping.*) But I beg your pardon; though I am an orphan, your child is not; and your concern for her, it seems, has brought you hither.—I 'll be composed; pray go on, sir.

Mr. Seal. How could Mr. Bevil be such a monster, to injure such a woman?

Ind. No, sir, you wrong him; he has not injured me. My support is from his bounty.

Mr. Seal. Bounty! when gluttons give

25 accommodating.

26 A way of calling a servant.

high prices for delicates, they are prodigious bountiful.

Ind. Still, still you will persist in that error. But my own fears tell me all. You are the gentleman, I suppose, for whose happy daughter he is designed a husband by his good father, and he has, perhaps, consented to the overture. He was here this morning, dressed beyond his usual plainness—nay, most sumptuously—and he is to be, perhaps, this night a bridegroom.

Mr. Seal. I own he was intended such; but, madam, on your account, I have determined to defer my daughter's marriage till I am satisfied from your own mouth of what nature are the obligations you are under to him.

Ind. His actions, sir; his eyes have only made me think he designed to make me the partner of his heart. The goodness and gentleness of his demeanor made me misinterpret all. 'T was my own hope, my own passion, that deluded me; he never made one amorous advance to me. His large heart, and bestowing hand, have only helped the miserable; nor know I why, but from his mere delight in virtue, that I have been his care and the object on which to indulge and please himself with pouring favors.

Mr. Seal. Madam, I know not why it is, but I, as well as you, am methinks afraid of entering into the matter I came about; but 't is the same thing as if we had talked never so distinctly——he ne'er shall have a daughter of mine.

Ind. If you say this from what you think of me, you wrong yourself and him. Let not me, miserable though I may be, do injury to my benefactor. No, sir, my treatment ought rather to reconcile you to his virtues. If to bestow without a prospect of return; if to delight in supporting what might, perhaps, be thought an object of desire, with no other view than to be her guard against those who would not be so disinterested; if these actions, sir, can in a careful parent's eye commend him to a daughter, give yours, sir, give her to my honest, generous Bevil. What have I to do but sigh, and weep, and rave, run wild, a lunatic in chains, or, hid in darkness, mutter in distracted starts and broken accents my strange, strange story!

Mr. Seal. Take comfort, madam.

Ind. All my comfort must be to expostulate in madness, to relieve with frenzy my despair, and shrieking to demand of fate why—why was I born to such variety of sorrows.

Mr. Seal. If I have been the least occasion——

Ind. No, 't was Heaven's high will I should be such; to be plundered in my cradle! tossed on the seas! and even there an infant captive! to lose my mother, hear but of my father! to be adopted! lose my adopter! then plunged again into worse calamities!

Mr. Seal. An infant captive!

Ind. Yet then, to find the most charming of mankind, once more to set me free from what I thought the last distress, to load me with his services, his bounties, and his favors; to support my very life in a way that stole, at the same time, my very soul itself from me.

Mr. Seal. And has young Bevil been this worthy man?

Ind. Yet then, again, this very man to take another! without leaving me the right, the pretence of easing my fond heart with tears! For, oh! I can't reproach him, though the same hand that raised me to this height now throws me down the precipice.

Mr. Seal. Dear lady! Oh, yet one moment's patience: my heart grows full with your affliction.—But yet there 's something in your story that——

Ind. My portion here is bitterness and sorrow.

Mr. Seal. Do not think so. Pray answer me: does Bevil know your name and family?

Ind. Alas! too well! Oh, could I be any other thing than what I am——I 'll tear away all traces of my former self, my little ornaments, the remains of my first state, the hints of what I ought to have been——

(*In her disorder she throws away a bracelet, which Sealand takes up, and looks earnestly on it.*)

Mr. Seal. Ha! what 's this? My eyes are not deceived! It is, it is the same! the very bracelet which I bequeathed to my wife at our last mournful parting.

Ind. What said you, sir? Your wife? Whither does my fancy carry me? What means this unfelt motion at my heart? And yet, again my fortune but deludes me; for if I err not, sir, your name is Sealand; but my lost father's name was——

Mr. Seal. Danvers; was it not?

Ind. What new amazement? That is, indeed, my family.

Mr. Seal. Know, then, when my misfortunes drove me to the Indies, for reasons too tedious now to mention, I changed my name of Danvers into Sealand.

(*Enter Isabella.*)

Isab. If yet there wants an explanation of your wonder, examine well this face (yours, sir, I well remember), gaze on and read in me your sister, Isabella.

Mr. Seal. My sister!

Isab. But here 's a claim more tender yet ——your Indiana, sir, your long-lost daughter.

Mr. Seal. Oh, my child! my child!

Ind. All-gracious Heaven! is it possible! do I embrace my father?

Mr. Seal. And do I hold thee?—These passions are too strong for utterance. Rise, rise, my child, and give my tears their way.—Oh, my sister!

(*Embracing her.*)

Isab. Now, dearest niece, my groundless fears, my painful cares no more shall vex thee. If I have wronged thy noble lover with too much suspicion, my just concern for thee, I hope, will plead my pardon.

Mr. Seal. Oh! make him, then, the full amends, and be yourself the messenger of joy. Fly this instant! tell him all these wondrous turns of Providence in his favor! Tell him I have now a daughter to bestow which he no longer will decline; that this day he still shall be a bridegroom; nor shall a fortune, the merit which his father seeks, be wanting. Tell him the reward of all his virtues waits on his acceptance. (*Exit Isab.*) My dearest Indiana!

(*Turns and embraces her.*)

Ind. Have I, then, at last, a father's sanction on my love? His bounteous hand to give, and make my heart a present worthy of Bevil's generosity?

Mr. Seal. Oh, my child! how are our sorrows past o'erpaid by such a meeting! Though I have lost so many years of soft paternal dalliance with thee, yet, in one day to find thee thus, and thus bestow thee, in such perfect happiness, is ample, ample reparation!—And yet, again, the merit of thy lover——

Ind. Oh! had I spirits left to tell you of his actions! how strongly filial duty has suppressed his love; and how concealment still has doubled all his obligations; the pride, the joy of his alliance, sir, would warm your heart, as he has conquered mine.

Mr. Seal. How laudable is love when born of virtue! I burn to embrace him——

Ind. See, sir, my aunt already has succeeded, and brought him to your wishes.

(*Enter Isabella, with Sir John Bevil, Bevil, Jun., Mrs. Sealand, Cimberton, Myrtle, and Lucinda.*)

Sir J. Bev. (*Entering.*) Where, where 's this scene of wonder? Mr. Sealand, I congratulate, on this occasion, our mutual happiness——Your good sister, sir, has, with the story of your daughter's fortune, filled us with surprise and joy. Now all exceptions are removed; my son has now avowed his love, and turned all former jealousies and doubts to approbation; and, I am told, your goodness has consented to reward him.

Mr. Seal. If, sir, a fortune equal to his father's hopes can make this object worthy his acceptance.

Bev. Jun. I hear your mention, sir, of fortune, with pleasure only as it may prove the means to reconcile the best of fathers to my love. Let him be provident, but let me be happy.—My ever-destined, my acknowledged wife!

(*Embracing Indiana.*)

Ind. Wife! Oh, my ever loved! My lord! my master!

Sir J. Bev. I congratulate myself, as well as you, that I had a son who could, under such disadvantages, discover your great merit.

Mr. Seal. Oh, Sir John! how vain, how weak is human prudence! What care, what foresight, what imagination could contrive such blest events, to make our children happy, as Providence in one short hour has laid before us?

Cimb. (*To Mrs. Sealand.*) I am afraid, madam, Mr. Sealand is a little too busy for our affair. If you please, we 'll take another opportunity.

Mrs. Seal. Let us have patience, sir.

Cimb. But we make Sir Geoffry wait, madam.

Myrt. O, sir, I am not in haste.

(*During this Bev. Jun. presents Lucinda to Indiana.*)

Mr. Seal. But here! here 's our general benefactor! Excellent young man, that could be at once a lover to her beauty and a parent to her virtue.

Bev. Jun. If you think that an obligation,

sir, give me leave to overpay myself, in the only instance that can now add to my felicity, by begging you to bestow this lady on Mr. Myrtle.

Mr. Seal. She is his without reserve; I beg he may be sent for. Mr. Cimberton, notwithstanding you never had my consent, yet there is, since I last saw you, another objection to your marriage with my daughter.

Cimb. I hope, sir, your lady has concealed nothing from me?

Mr. Seal. Troth, sir, nothing but what was concealed from myself—another daughter, who has an undoubted title to half my estate.

Cimb. How, Mr. Sealand? Why, then, if half Mrs. Lucinda's fortune is gone, you can't say that any of my estate is settled upon her. I was in treaty for the whole; but if that is not to be come at, to be sure there can be no bargain. Sir, I have nothing to do but to take my leave of your good lady, my cousin, and beg pardon for the trouble I have given this old gentleman.

Myrt. That you have, Mr. Cimberton, with all my heart.

(*Discovers himself.*)

All. Mr. Myrtle!

Myrt. And I beg pardon of the whole company that I assumed the person of Sir Geoffry, only to be present at the danger of this lady's being disposed of, and in her utmost exigence to assert my right to her; which, if her parents will ratify, as they once favored my pretensions, no abatement of fortune shall lessen her value to me.

Luc. Generous man!

Mr. Seal. If, sir, you can overlook the injury of being in treaty with one who as meanly left her, as you have generously asserted your right in her, she is yours.

Luc. Mr. Myrtle, though you have ever had my heart, yet now I find I love you more, because I bring you less.

Myrt. We have much more than we want; and I am glad any event has contributed to the discovery of our real inclinations to each other.

Mrs. Seal. Well! however, I'm glad the girl's disposed of, anyway.

(*Aside.*)

Bev. Myrtle, no longer rivals now, but brothers!

Myrt. Dear Bevil, you are born to triumph over me! but now our competition ceases; I rejoice in the pre-eminence of your virtue, and your alliance adds charms to Lucinda.

Sir J. Bev. Now, ladies and gentlemen, you have set the world a fair example: your happiness is owing to your constancy and merit; and the several difficulties you have struggled with evidently show—

Whate'er the generous mind itself denies,
The secret care of Providence supplies.

(*Exeunt.*)

HENRY FIELDING

THE TRAGEDY OF TRAGEDIES; OR, THE LIFE AND DEATH OF TOM THUMB THE GREAT

Henry Fielding (1707–1754), of aristocratic birth and pleasure-loving disposition, began writing plays as the best-paying form of literature, most of them being comedies more or less after the pattern of Molière and Congreve. He best shows his comic ability in his burlesques and farces. *Tom Thumb* (the fourth of twenty-seven plays) was first acted, at the Haymarket Theater, in 1730, was enlarged to three acts in 1731, and published in both years; in an altered form it held the stage till well on in the nineteenth century. At the age of thirty Fielding abandoned the stage for the law, and a few years later began the series of great novels which mainly support his fame; a word of admiration can be spared also for his essays.

Fielding was a born parodist. Endlessly clever, versatile, vigorous, with a strong though not fine feeling for style, a great sense of the ridiculous, and exhaustless common-sense, he could have had no mercy on unreality, pomposity, pretentiousness, and sentimentality. His fling at sentimentality is in a novel, later and more celebrated than this play. In 1740 Samuel Richardson had published *Pamela, or Virtue Rewarded,* which seemed to Fielding petty and fine-drawn, and he responded in 1742 with *Joseph Andrews.* Thus from the first fully-developed novel of emotion was born the first fully-developed novel of incident. For the mood of mockery died away as Fielding became more interested, and a creative spirit replaced it.

In the present burlesque he maintains throughout the spirit of delicious derision. There was no new type of fiction ready for the birth. In a highly diverting Preface to *Tom Thumb*, all as fictitious as the fantastic name, H. Scriblerus Secundus, under which he wrote it, he states that "some publicly affirmed that no author could produce so fine a piece but Mr. P— [Pope]; others have with as much vehemence insisted that no one could write anything so bad but Mr. F— [Fielding]." After recording the ponderous praises it had received from universities and critics, and how "though it hath, among other languages, been translated into Dutch, and celebrated with great applause at Amsterdam (where burlesque never came) by the title of Mynheer Vander Thumb, the burgomasters received it with that reverend and silent attention which becometh an audience at a deep tragedy,"— he rejects with seeming indignation the notion that it was meant to be ludicrous, and, hinting that it may be by Shakespeare, confidently dates it in the reign of Queen Elizabeth. He continues by applauding, in received critical style, "the Fable, the Moral, the Characters, the Sentiments, and the Diction." Thus in the Preface, as well as in some of the notes, he has his joke at the expense of the portentous style and deficient insight of some scholars and critics of his day, who he avers have wagged their heavy heads over this eminent work. The similarities between it and other plays of the preceding seventy years he affects to be uncertain whether to attribute to coincidence or to their imitation of his author; but in the notes intimates that it has been pillaged right and left, till, like *Hamlet*, it seems to be made up of nothing but quotations.

The "heroic plays" are particularly though not wholly the object of his mirth, and among them *The Conquest of Granada* comes in for its full share. Like Almanzor, though probably not especially imitated from him, Tom Thumb has his moments of modesty or at least of courtesy, but not unlike the other he announces,

> I ask not kingdoms, I can conquer those.

Like Almanzor he is devoted to honor only less than to love, and comes from preterhuman victory to lay his heart at the feet of the fair. Like Almanzor (in part II) King Arthur not only faces but threatens a ghost; a scene which poor saturnine Dean Swift said was one of the two things in his life which had made him laugh. Several scenes are in the rhymed couplet, which Fielding sometimes varies by such grotesque Browning-like rhymes as "Are you drunk, ha?" "Huncamunca." The unities are observed with a strictness to set the heart of Castelvetro aglow. Like the classical tragedies of the day, the play has a moral, which when stated is, as usually, a platitude; "it teaches these two instructive lessons," says the Preface, "viz., that human happiness is exceeding transient; and that death is the certain end of all men: the former whereof is inculcated by the fatal end of Tom Thumb; the latter by that of all the other personages." As is natural in a burlesque, the height of the absurd is reached at the end, in the anticlimax where the hero is swallowed by a cow, and in the concluding extravagance, where the spectator's head fairly swims watching all the other characters fall dead. Thus he has his fling at the exaggerated and unnatural violences of some artificial tragedy. On the whole the several dozen plays by sixteen writers thus ridiculed are fair game. They are almost without exception tragedies of the Restoration and early eighteenth century, more especially those of Dryden, Banks, and Lee. Earlier tragedies he leaves almost entirely alone. While one or two of the plays at which he shoots his arrows, such as Dryden's *All for Love*, are still admired, most of them met only a temporary taste, and have ceased to please and even to be read. Passion, freedom of feeling, are essential to great tragedy, and an age when it was literary good breeding to repress and make light of feeling was ill adapted to it. Poets did not wait till the fire kindled and at last they spake with their tongue. They thought more of rule than of spontaneity, as was pointed out in the discussion of *Cato*. There never was a time when poets made such elaborate effort to write tragedy, or more often dismally failed. They were like the men of Babel, who said, "Go to, let us build us a tower, whose top may reach unto heaven, and let us make us a name"; and the Lord confounded their language, that they might not understand one another's speech.

"Which brings me to speak of his diction," as the Preface says. "Here I shall only beg one postulatum, viz., that the greatest perfection of the language of a tragedy is, that it is not to be understood; which granted (as I think it must be), it will necessarily follow that the only way to avoid this is by being too high or too low for the understanding. . . . What can be so proper for tragedy as a set of big sounding words, so contrived together as to convey no meaning?" He has no mercy on the artificial and the inflated, especially the frigid and long similes bedecking the tragedies of poets "who liken things not like at all." "Our author" "is very rarely within sight through the whole play, either rising higher than the eye of your imagination can soar, or sinking lower than it careth to stoop." Such a parody as

> Oh! Huncamunca, Huncamunca, oh!,

which chastises Thomson's notorious effort

> Oh! Sophonisba; Sophonisba, oh!,

illustrates how faint a line parts the ludicrous from the intolerably touching, for it differs in but one word from Shakespeare's

> O Desdemona, Desdemona, dead,!

With the incongruity which is the essence of humor, he varies this sort of thing by the prosaic and grotesque, which made particularly effective satire in an age when a poet had better be in jail than be "low." His laughter rings out at the too-literary device of attributing human traits to non-human things (smiling dolphins, a blushing sun), which John Ruskin a century later scolded at as the "pathetic fallacy"; and at the puffing up of a frog-commonplace into an ox-grandiloquence. Fielding relishes nothing in his play more than the dressing up in burlesque solemnity of some proverb like "Between two stools the breech falls to the ground" (II. x). With his common-sense liking for pithy reality, he says in the note, "It were to be wished that, instead of filling their pages with the fabulous theology of the pagans, our modern poets would think it worth their while to enrich their works with the proverbial sayings of their ancestors." There speaks not only eighteenth-century prosaic sense against pseudo-classicism, but also the later romantic spirit, with its fondness for the popular and traditional.

But, after all, Tom Thumb must not be taken too seriously, even as a burlesque. Fielding was no prophet, or reformer, with deep convictions on literature, but a playwright who needed money and wanted to "make a hit." He saw a chance in cleverly parodying what everybody would recognize, not only what deserved ridicule and might be discredited by it, but also what could bear ridicule. There are almost as many reminiscences of Shakespeare as of any later dramatist, though Fielding has too much reverence to point them out in the notes (he also spares *Venice Preserved*). There is no more humor in his parody of Thomson's Sophonisba-scream than of Juliet in "O Tom Thumb! Tom Thumb! wherefore art thou Tom Thumb?"; or than in his parody of Don John's "Leonato's Hero, your Hero, every man's Hero," in "Your Huncamunca, Tom Thumb's Huncamunca, every man's Huncamunca." The only difference is that Shakespeare can stand it and Thomson cannot. It must not be supposed that Fielding condemned everything in the plays he parodied, or even every parodied passage. It must be admitted too that his mockery is often undeserved; a clever writer can always take passable or even good things out of their context and make them look silly. Young's "with these eyes I saw him," ridiculed in III. ix, is the natural emphatic language of strong feeling. With a mind full of scraps of plays, Fielding parodied from memory anything that could be made to raise a laugh, and when he came to print set the originals in the footnotes (so far as he could remember them), and sometimes inaccurately. These notes make the play more suitable to read than to witness, for few things are less intelligible than a burlesque of something unknown. They explain to us a play which is rather a free-and-easy boiling over of humor than a harsh and serious satire. Much of Fielding's spirit reappeared a century later in Thackeray, and one can hardly fail to see the manner and style of *Tom Thumb* (combined with Thackeray's own novelist-style) in his delicious Christmas-burlesque, *The Rose and the Ring.*

The chief origin or models of the work (aside from the plays already discussed) were the Duke of Buckingham's *Rehearsal* (1671), a dramatic satire on Dryden's plays, and especially *A Commentary on the History of Tom Thumb* (1711), a burlesque ballad with a commentary much like Fielding's, supposedly by Dr. William Wagstaffe, and written to ridicule Addison's appreciation of the ballad of Chevy Chase in the *Spectator.* The play quotes the *History* (III. viii), and borrows some of its incidents. In such burlesques there is really much more of the vital energy of the age than in the works they parodied. Its greatest literary men, Swift, Pope, Addison, were critics, and the critical spirit of the earlier eighteenth century was more vigorous and more characteristic than the imaginative. Any collection of eighteenth-century dramas would be incomplete without a specimen of it.

THE TRAGEDY OF TRAGEDIES; OR, THE LIFE AND DEATH OF TOM THUMB THE GREAT

With the Annotations of H. Scriblerus Secundus.
First acted in 1730, and altered in 1731.

DRAMATIS PERSONÆ

MEN

KING ARTHUR, *a passionate sort of king, husband to* QUEEN DOLLALLOLLA, *of whom he stands a little in fear; father to* HUNCAMUNCA, *whom he is very fond of and in love with* GLUMDALCA.

TOM THUMB THE GREAT, *a little hero with a great soul, something violent in his temper, which is a little abated by his love for* HUNCAMUNCA.

GHOST OF GAFFER THUMB, *a whimsical sort of Ghost.*

LORD GRIZZLE, *extremely zealous for the liberty of the subject, very choleric in his temper, and in love with* HUNCAMUNCA.

MERLIN, *a conjurer, and in some sort father to* TOM THUMB.

NOODLE, DOODLE, } *courtiers in place, and consequently of that party that is uppermost.*

FOODLE, *a courtier that is out of place, and consequently of that party that is undermost.*

BAILIFF, FOLLOWER, } *of the party of the plaintiff.*

PARSON, *of the side of the church.*

WOMEN

QUEEN DOLLALLOLLA, *wife to* KING ARTHUR, *and mother to* HUNCAMUNCA, *a woman entirely faultless, saving that she is a little given to drink, a little too much a virago towards her husband, and in love with* TOM THUMB.

THE PRINCESS HUNCAMUNCA, *daughter to their Majesties* KING ARTHUR *and* QUEEN DOLLALLOLLA, *of a very sweet, gentle, and amorous disposition, equally in love with* LORD GRIZZLE *and* TOM THUMB, *and desirous to be married to them both.*

GLUMDALCA, *of the giants, a captive queen, beloved by the king, but in love with* TOM THUMB.

CLEORA, MUSTACHA, *maids of honor in love with* NOODLE *and* DOODLE.

Courtiers, Guards, Rebels, Drums, Trumpets, Thunder and Lightning.

Scene.—The Court of King Arthur, and a Plain Thereabouts.

ACT I.

SCENE 1. *The Palace.*

(*Doodle, Noodle.*)

Doodle. Sure such a[1] day as this was never seen!
The sun himself, on this auspicious day,
Shines like a beau in a new birth-day suit:
This down the seams embroidered, that the beams.
All nature wears one universal grin.

Nood. This day, O Mr. Doodle, is a day

1 Corneille recommends some very remarkable day wherein to fix the action of a tragedy. This the best of our tragical writers have understood to mean a day remarkable for the serenity of the sky, or what we generally call a fine summer's day: so that according to this their exposition, the same months are proper for tragedy which are proper for pastoral. Most of our celebrated English tragedies as *Cato, Marianne, Tamerlane,** &c., begin with their observations on the morning. Lee seems to have come the

* By Addison, Fenton, and Rowe.

Indeed!—A day,[2] we never saw before.
The mighty [3] Thomas Thumb victorious comes;
Millions of giants crowd his chariot wheels,
[4] Giants! to whom the giants in Guildhall *
Are infant dwarfs. They frown, and foam and roar,
While Thumb, regardless of their noise, rides on.
So some cock-sparrow in a farmer's yard,
Hops at the head of an huge flock of turkeys.

Dood. When Goody Thumb first brought this Thomas forth,
The Genius of our land triumphant reigned;
Then, then, O Arthur! did thy Genius reign.

Nood. They tell me it is [5] whispered in the books
Of all our sages, that this mighty hero,
By Merlin's art begot, hath not a bone
Within his skin, but is a lump of gristle.

Dood. Then 't is a gristle of no mortal
Some God, my Noodle, stept into the place
Of Gaffer Thumb, and more than [6] half begot
This mighty Tom.

Nood. [7]—Sure he was sent express
From Heaven to be the pillar of our state.
Though small his body be, so very small,
A chairman's ‖ leg is more than twice as large,
Yet is his soul like any mountain big;
And as a mountain once brought forth a mouse,
[8] So doth this mouse contain a mighty mountain.

nearest to this beautiful description of our author's:
The morning dawns with an unwonted crimson,
The flowers all odorous seem, the garden birds
Sing louder, and the laughing sun ascends
The gaudy earth with an unusual brightness:
All nature smiles. *Cæs. Borg.*
Massinissa, in the New *Sophonisba* [by Thomson], is also a favorite of the sun:
—The sun too seems
As conscious of my joy, with broader eye
To look abroad the world, and all things smile
Like Sophonisba.
Memnon, in the *Persian Princess* [by Theobald], makes the sun decline rising, that he may not peep on objects which would profane his brightness:
—The morning rises slow,
And all those ruddy streaks that used to paint
The day's approach are lost in clouds, as if
The horrors of the night had sent 'em back,
To warn the sun he should not leave the sea,
To peep, &c.

2 This line is highly conformable to the beautiful simplicity of the ancients. It hath been copied by almost every modern.
Not to be is not to be in woe.
[Dryden's] *State of Innocence.*
Love is not sin but where 'tis sinful love.
[Dryden's] *Don Sebastian.*
Nature is nature, Lælius. [Lee's] *Sophonisba.*
Men are but men, we did not make ourselves.
[Young's] *Revenge.*

3 Dr. B—y reads, The mighty Tall-mast Thumb. Mr. D—s, The mighty Thumbing Thumb. Mr. T—d † reads, Thundering. I think Thomas more agreeable to the great simplicity so apparent in our author.

4 That learned historian Mr. S—n.‡ in the third number of his criticism on our author, takes great pains to explode this passage. "It is," says he, "difficult to guess what giants are here meant, unless the giant Despair in the *Pilgrim's Progress,* or the giant Greatness in the *Royal Villain;* for I have heard of no other sort of giants in the reign of King Arthur." Petrus Burmannus makes three Tom Thumbs, one whereof he supposes to have been the same person whom the Greeks call Hercules; and that by these giants are to be understood the Centaurs slain by that hero. Another Tom Thumb he contends to have been no other than the Hermes Trismegistus of the ancients. The third Tom Thumb he places under the reign of king Arthur; to which third Tom Thumb, says he, the actions of the other two were attributed. Now, though I know that this opinion is supported by an assertion of Justus Lipsius, "Thomam illum Thumbum non alium quàm Herculem fuisse satis constat," yet shall I venture to oppose one line of Mr. Midwinter ¶ against them all:
In Arthur's court Tom Thumb did live.
"But then," says Dr. B—y, "if we place Tom Thumb in the court of king Arthur, it will be proper to place that court out of Britain, where no giants were ever heard of." Spenser, in his *Fairy Queen,* is of another opinion, where, describing Albion, he says,
——Far within a savage nation dwelt
Of hideous giants.
And in the same canto:
Then Elfar, with two brethren giants had,
The one of which had two heads —
The other three.
Risum teneatis, amici.**

5 "To whisper in books," says Mr. D—s, "is arrant nonsense." I am afraid this learned man does not sufficiently understand the extensive meaning of the word whisper. If he had rightly understood what is meant by the "senses whispering the soul," in the *Persian Princess,* or what "whispering like winds" is in [Dryden's] *Aurengzebe,* or like thunder in another author, he would have understood this. Emmeline in Dryden sees a voice, but she was born blind, which is an excuse Panthea cannot plead in [Banks'] *Cyrus,* who hears a sight:
——Your description will surpass
All fiction, painting, or dumb show of horror,
That ever ears yet heard, or eyes beheld.
When Mr. D—s understands these, he will understand whispering in books.

6 —Some ruffian stept into his father's place,
And more than half begot him.
Mary Queen of Scots.††

7 —For Ulamar seems sent express from Heaven,
To civilize this rugged Indian clime.
[Dennis'] *Liberty Asserted.*

8 "Omne majus continet in se minus, sed minus

* Two wooden figures 14½ feet high, of mythical British giants.
† Bentley, Dennis and Theobald are meant.
‡ One of the two Salmon brothers, writers on history and geography (Tupper).
¶ "The supposititious author of the ballad of Tom Thumb" (Tupper).
‖ A carrier of a sedan-chair.
** Don't laugh, my friends.
†† Banks' *The Island* [later *Albion*] *Queens; or, The Death of Mary Queen of Scotland.*

Dood. Mountain indeed! So terrible his name,
[9] The giant nurses frighten children with it,
And cry Tom Thumb is come, and if you are
Naughty, will surely take the child away.
Nood. But hark! [10] these trumpets speak the king's approach.
Dood. He comes most luckily for my petition.

(*Flourish.*)

SCENE 2.

(*King, Queen, Grizzle, Noodle, Doodle, Foodle.*)

King. [11] Let nothing but a face of joy appear;
The man who frowns this day shall lose his head,
That he may have no face to frown withal.
Smile, Dollallolla—Ha! what wrinkled sorrow
[12] Hangs, sits, lies, frowns upon thy knitted brow?
Whence flow those tears fast down thy blubbered cheeks,
Like a swoln gutter, gushing through the streets?
Queen. [13] Excess of joy, my lord, I've heard folks say,
Gives tears as certain as excess of grief.
King. If it be so, let all men cry for joy,
[14] Till my whole court be drowned with their tears;
Nay, till they overflow my utmost land,
And leave me nothing but the sea to rule.
Dood. My liege, I a petition have here got.
King. Petition me no petitions, sir, to-day:
Let other hours be set apart for business.
To-day it is our pleasure to be [15] drunk.
And this our queen shall be as drunk as we.
Queen. (Though I already [16] half seas over am)
If the capacious goblet overflow
With arrack punch—'fore George! I'll see it out:
Of rum and brandy I'll not taste a drop.
King. Though rack, in punch, eight shillings be a quart,
And rum and brandy be no more than six,
Rather than quarrel you shall have your will.

(*Trumpets.*)

non in se majus continere potest," says Scaliger * in Thumbo. I suppose he would have cavilled at these beautiful lines in the *Earl of Essex:*

——Thy most inveterate soul,
That looks through the foul prison of thy body.

And at those of Dryden:

The palace is without too well designed;
Conduct me in, for I will view thy mind.
Aurengzebe.

9 Mr. Banks hath copied this almost verbatim:

It was enough to say, here's Essex come,
And nurses stilled their children with the fright.
Earl of Essex.

10 The trumpet in a tragedy is generally as much as to say Enter king, which makes Mr. Banks, in one of his plays, call it the trumpet's formal sound.

11 Phraortes, in the *Captives* [by Gay], seems to have been acquainted with king Arthur:

Proclaim a festival for seven days' space.
Let the court shine in all its pomp and lustre,
Let all our streets resound with shouts of joy;
Let music's care-dispelling voice be heard;
The sumptuous banquet and the flowing goblet
Shall warm the cheek and fill the heart with gladness.
Astarbe shall sit mistress of the feast.

12 Repentance frowns on thy contracted brow.
Sophonisba.
Hung on his clouded brow, I marked despair. *Ibid.*
——A sullen gloom
Scowls on his brow. [Young's] *Busiris.*

13 Plato is of this opinion, and so is Mr. Banks:

Behold these tears sprung from fresh pain and joy.
[Banks'] *Earl of Essex.*

14 These floods are very frequent in the tragic authors:

Near to some murmuring brook I'll lay me down,
Whose waters, if they should too shallow flow,
My tears shall swell them up till I will drown.
Lee's *Sophonisba.*

Pouring forth tears at such a lavish rate,
That were the world on fire they might have drowned
The wrath of heaven, and quenched the mighty ruin.
[Lee's] *Mithridates.*

One author changes the waters of grief to those of joy:

——These tears, that sprung from tides of grief,
Are now augmented to a flood of joy.
[Banks'] *Cyrus the Great.*

Another:

Turns all the streams of heat, and makes them flow
In pity's channel. *Royal Villain.*†

One drowns himself:

——Pity like a torrent pours me down,
Now I am drowning all within a deluge.
[Banks' *Virtue Betray'd, or*] *Anne Bullen.*

Cyrus drowns the whole world:

Our swelling grief
Shall melt into a deluge, and the world
Shall drown in tears. *Cyrus the Great.*

15 An expression vastly beneath the dignity of tragedy, says Mr. D—s, yet we find the word he cavils at in the mouth of Mithridates less properly used, and applied to a more terrible idea:

I would be drunk with death. *Mithridates.*

The author of the new *Sophonisba* taketh hold of this monosyllable, and uses it pretty much to the same purpose:

The Carthaginian sword with Roman blood
Was drunk.

I would ask Mr. D—s which gives him the best idea, a drunken king, or a drunken sword?

Mr. Tate dresses up king Arthur's resolution in heroic [*Injured Love,* 1707]:

Merry, my lord, o' th' captain's humor right,
I am resolved to be dead drunk to-night.

Lee also uses this charming word:

Love 's the drunkenness of the mind. **Gloriana.**

16 Dryden hath borrowed this, and applied it improperly:

I'm half seas o'er in death.
Cleomenes.

* A noted French critic (1540–1609).

† *The Persian Princess;* or, *The Royal Villain,* by Theobald.

But, ha! the warrior comes—the great
Tom Thumb.
The little hero, giant-killing boy,
Preserver of my kingdom, is arrived.

Scene 3.

(Tom Thumb to them, with Officers, Prisoners, and Attendants.)

King. [17] Oh! welcome most, most welcome to my arms.
What gratitude can thank away the debt
Your valor lays upon me?
Queen. ———[18] Oh! ye gods! (*Aside.*)
Thumb. When I'm not thanked at all, I'm thanked enough.
[19] I've done my duty, and I've done no more.
Queen. Was ever such a godlike creature seen? (*Aside.*)
King. Thy modesty's a [20] candle to thy merit,
It shines itself, and shows thy merit too.
But say, my boy, where didst thou leave the giants?
Thumb. My liege, without the castle gates they stand,
The castle gates too low for their admittance.
King. What look they like?
Thumb. Like nothing but themselves.
Queen. [21] And sure thou art like nothing but thyself. (*Aside.*)
King. Enough! the vast idea fills my soul.
I see them—yes, I see them now before me:
The monstrous, ugly, barb'rous sons of whores.
But ha! what form majestic strikes our eyes?
[22] So perfect, that it seems to have been drawn
By all the gods in council: so fair she is,
That surely at her birth the council paused,
And then at length cried out, This is a woman!
Thumb. Then were the gods mistaken—she is not
A woman, but a giantess——whom we,
[23] With much ado, have made a shift to hawl
Within the town: [24] for she is by a foot
Shorter than all her subject giants were.
Glum. We yesterday were both a queen and wife,
One hundred thousand giants owned our sway.
Twenty whereof were married to ourself.
Queen. Oh! happy state of giantism where husbands
Like mushrooms grow, whilst hapless we are forced
To be content, nay, happy thought, with one.
Glum. But then to lose them all in one black day,
That the same sun which, rising, saw me wife
To twenty giants, setting should behold
Me widowed of them all.——[25] My worn-out heart,
That ship, leaks fast, and the great heavy lading,
My soul, will quickly sink.
Queen. Madam, believe
I view your sorrows with a woman's eye:

17 This figure is in great use among the tragedians:
'T is therefore, therefore 't is.
[Charles Johnson's] *Victim.*
I long, repent, repent, and long again.
[Young's] *Busiris.*

18 A tragical exclamation.

19 This line is copied verbatim in the *Captives.*

20 We find a candlestick for this candle in two celebrated authors:—
——Each star withdraws
His golden head, and burns within the socket.
[Lee's] *Nero.*
A soul grown old and sunk into the socket.
[Dryden's *Don*] *Sebastian.*

21 This simile occurs very frequently among the dramatic writers of both kinds.

22 Mr. Lee hath stolen this thought from our author:
This perfect face, drawn by the gods in council,
Which they were long a making.
Luc. Jun. Brut.
——At his birth the heavenly council paused,
And then at last cried out, This is a man! Dryden hath improved this hint to the utmost perfection:
So perfect, that the very gods who formed you wondered
At their own skill, and cried, A lucky hit
Has mended our design! Their envy hindered,
Or you had been immortal, and a pattern,
When Heaven would work for ostentation sake.
To copy out again. [Dryden's] *All for Love.*
Banks prefers the works of Michael Angelo to that of the gods:
A pattern for the gods to make a man by,
Or Michael Angelo to form a statue.

23 It is impossible, says Mr. W—,* sufficiently to admire this natural easy line.

24 This tragedy, which in most points resembles the ancients, differs from them in this—that it assigns the same honor to lowness of stature which they did to height. The gods and heroes in Homer and Virgil are continually described higher by the head than their followers, the contrary of which is observed by our author. In short, to exceed on either side is equally admirable; and a man of three foot is as wonderful a sight as a man of nine.

25 My blood leaks fast, and the great heavy lading,
My soul will quickly sink. *Mithridates.*
My soul is like a ship. [Tate's] *Injured Love.*

* It is not clear who is meant.

But learn to bear them with what strength you may,
To-morrow we will have our grenadiers
Drawn out before you, and you then shall choose
What husbands you think fit.

Glum. [26] Madam, I am
Your most obedient and most humble servant.

King. Think, mighty princess, think this court your own,
Nor think the landlord me, this house my inn;
Call for whate'er you will, you 'll nothing pay.
[27] I feel a sudden pain within my breast,
Nor know I whether it arise from love
Or only the wind-colic. Time must show.
Oh Thumb! what do we to thy valor owe!
Ask some reward, great as we can bestow.

Thumb. [28] I ask not kingdoms, I can conquer those;
I ask not money, money I 've enough;
For what I 've done, and what I mean to do,
For giants slain, and giants yet unborn,
Which I will slay——if this be called a debt,
Take my receipt in full: I ask but this,—
[29] To sun myself in Huncamunca's eyes.

King. Prodigious bold request.

Queen. ——[30] Be still, my soul.
(*Aside.*)

Thumb. [31] My heart is at the threshold of your mouth,
And waits its answer there.——Oh! do not frown.
I 've tried to reason's tune to tune my soul,
But love did overwind and crack the string.
Though Jove in thunder had cried out, YOU SHAN'T,
I should have loved her still——for oh, strange fate!
Then when I loved her least I loved her most!

King. It is resolved—the princess is your own.

Thumb. Oh! [32] happy, happy, happy, happy Thumb!

Queen. Consider, sir; reward your soldier's merit,
But give not Huncamunca to Tom Thumb.

King. Tom Thumb! Odzooks! my wide-extended realm
Knows not a name so glorious as Tom Thumb.
Let Macedonia Alexander boast,
Let Rome her Cæsars and her Scipios show,
Her Messieurs France, let Holland boast Mynheers,
Ireland her O's, her Macs let Scotland boast,
Let England boast no other than Tom Thumb.

Queen. Though greater yet his boasted merit was,
He shall not have my daughter, that is pos'.*

King. Ha! sayest thou, Dollallolla?

Queen. I say he shan't.

King. [33] Then by our royal self we swear you lie.

Queen. [34] Who, but a dog, who, but a dog
Would use me as thou dost? Me, who have lain
[35] These twenty years so loving by thy side!
But I will be revenged. I 'll hang myself.
Then tremble all who did this match persuade,

26 This well-bred line seems to be copied in the *Persian Princess*:—
To be your humblest and most faithful slave.

27 This doubt of the king puts me in mind of a passage in the *Captives*, where the noise of feet is mistaken for the rustling of leaves.
————Methinks I hear
The sound of feet:
No; 't was the wind that shook yon cypress boughs.

28 Mr. Dryden seems to have had this passage in his eye in the first page of *Love Triumphant*.

29 Don Carlos, in the *Revenge*, suns himself in the charms of his mistress:
While in the lustre of her charms I lay.

30 A tragical phrase much in use.

31 This speech hath been taken to pieces by several tragical authors, who seem to have rifled it, and shared its beauties among them.
My soul waits at the portal of thy breast,
To ravish from thy lips the welcome news.
Anne Bullen.
My soul stands listening at my ears.
Cyrus the Great.
Love to his tune my jarring heart would bring,
But reason overwinds, and cracks the string.
[Dryden and Lee's] *Duke of Guise.*
————I should have loved,
Though Jove, in muttering thunder had forbid it.
New Sophonisba.
And when it (*my heart*) wild resolves to love no more,
Then is the triumph of excessive love. *Ibid.*

32 Massinissa is one-fourth less happy than Tom Thumb.
Oh! happy, happy, happy! *New Sophonisba.*

33 No, by myself. *Anne Bullen.*

34 ————Who caused
This dreadful revolution in my fate.
Ulamar. Who, but a dog—who, but a dog?
Liberty Ass[erted].

35 ————A bride,
Who twenty years lay loving by your side.
Banks.

* An old colloquialism for *positive*.

[36] For, riding on a cat, from high I 'll fall,
And squirt down royal vengeance on you all.

Food. [37] Her majesty the queen is in a passion.

King. [38] Be she, or be she not, I 'll to the girl
And pave thy way, oh Thumb.—Now by ourself,
We were indeed a pretty king of clouts
To truckle to her will.——For when by force
Or art the wife her husband over-reaches,
Give him the petticoat, and her the breeches.

Thumb. [39] Whisper ye winds, that Huncamunca 's mine!
Echoes repeat, that Huncamunca 's mine!
The dreadful business of the war is o'er,
And beauty, heavenly beauty! crowns my toils!
I 've thrown the bloody garment now aside
And hymeneal sweets invite my bride.
So when some chimney-sweeper all the day
Hath through dark paths pursued the sooty way,
At night to wash his hands and face he flies,
And in his t'other shirt with his Brickdusta lies.

Scene 4.

Grizzle. (*Solus.*) [40] Where art thou, Grizzle? where are now thy glories?
Where are the drums that waken thee to honor?
Greatness is a laced coat from Monmouth-street,*
Which fortune lends us for a day to wear,
To-morrow puts it on another's back.
The spiteful sun but yesterday surveyed
His rival high as Saint Paul's cupola;
Now may he see me as Fleet-ditch laid low.

Scene 5.

(*Queen, Grizzle.*)

Queen. [41] Teach me to scold, prodigious-minded Grizzle.
Mountain of treason, ugly as the devil,
Teach this confounded hateful mouth of mine
To spout forth words malicious as thyself,
Words which might shame all Billingsgate † to speak.

Griz. Far be it from my pride to think my tongue
Your royal lips can in that art instruct,
Wherein you so excel. But may I ask,
Without offence, wherefore my queen would scold?

Queen. Wherefore? Oh! blood and thunder! ha' n't you heard
(What every corner of the court resounds)
That little Thumb will be a great man made?

Griz. I heard it. I confess—for who, alas!
[42] Can always stop his ears?—But would my teeth,
By grinding knives, had first been set on edge!

Queen. Would I had heard, at the still noon of night,
The hallalloo of fire in every street!
Odsbobs! I have a mind to hang myself,
To think I should a grandmother be made
By such a rascal!—Sure the king forgets
When in a pudding, by his mother put,
The bastard, by a tinker, on a stile
Was dropped.—O, good lord Grizzle! can I bear
To see him from a pudding mount the throne?
Or can, Oh can, my Huncamunca bear
To take a pudding's offspring to her arms?

Griz. Oh horror! horror! horror! cease, my queen.

36 For, borne upon a cloud, from high I 'll fall,
And rain down royal vengeance on you all.
Alb. Queens.

37 An information very like this we have in the *Tragedy of Love* [Banks' *Cyrus*], where, Cyrus having stormed in the most violent manner, Cyaxares observes very calmly,
Why, nephew Cyrus, you are moved.
38 'T is in your choice.
Love me, or love me not.
[Dryden's] *Conquest of Granada.*

39 There is not one beauty in this charming speech but hath been borrowed by almost every tragic writer.

40 Mr. Banks has (I wish I could not say too servilely) imitated this of Grizzle in his *Earl of Essex:*
Where art thou, Essex, &c.

41 The countess of Nottingham, in the *Earl of Essex*, is apparently acquainted with Dollallolla.

42 Grizzle was not probably possessed of that glue of which Mr. Banks speaks in his *Cyrus.*
I 'll glue my ears to every word.

* Noted for its second-hand clothing shops; now called Dudley Street.
† The principal fish-market of London; the bad language used at it has become proverbial.

[43] Thy voice, like twenty screech-owls, wracks my brain.
Queen. Then rouse thy spirit—we may yet prevent
This hated match.
Griz. ——We will; [44] nor fate itself,
Should it conspire with Thomas Thumb, should cause it.
I'll swim through seas; I'll ride upon the clouds;
I'll dig the earth; I'll blow out every fire;
I'll rave; I'll rant; I'll rise; I'll rush; I'll roar;
Fierce as the man whom [45] smiling dolphins bore
From the prosaic to poetic shore.
I'll tear the scoundrel into twenty pieces.
Queen. Oh, no! prevent the match, but hurt him not;
For, though I would not have him have my daughter,
Yet can we kill the man that killed the giants?
Griz. I tell you, madam, it was all a trick;
He made the giants first, and then he killed them;
As fox-hunters bring foxes to the wood,
And then with hounds they drive them out again.
Queen. How! have you seen no giants? Are there not
Now, in the yard, ten thousand proper giants?
Griz. [46] Indeed I cannot positively tell,
But firmly do believe there is not one.
Queen. Hence! from my sight! thou traitor, hie away;
By all my stars! thou enviest Tom Thumb.
Go, sirrah! go,[47] hie away! hie!—thou art
A setting-dog: be gone.
Griz. Madam, I go.
Tom Thumb shall feel the vengeance you have raised.
So, when two dogs are fighting in the streets,
With a third dog one of the two dogs meets,
With angry teeth he bites him to the bone,
And this dog smarts for what that dog had done.

SCENE 6.

Queen. (*Sola.*) And whither shall I go? —Alack a day!
I love Tom Thumb—but must not tell him so;
For what's a woman when her virtue's gone?
A coat without its lace; wig out of buckle;
A stocking with a hole in't——I can't live
Without my virtue, or without Tom Thumb.
[48] Then let me weigh them in two equal scales;
In this scale put my virtue, that Tom Thumb.
Alas! Tom Thumb is heavier than my virtue.
But hold!—perhaps I may be left a widow:
This match prevented, then Tom Thumb is mine:
In that dear hope I will forget my pain.
So, when some wench to Tothill Bridewell's sent,
With beating hemp and flogging she's content;
She hopes in time to ease her present pain,
At length is free, and walks the streets again.

43 Screech-owls, dark ravens, and amphibious monsters,
Are screaming in that voice.
Mary Queen of Scots.

44 The reader may see all the beauties of this speech in a late ode, called the Naval Lyric. [Not identified.]

45 This epithet to a dolphin doth not give one so clear an idea as were to be wished; a smiling fish seeming a little more difficult to be imagined than a flying fish. Mr. Dryden is of opinion that smiling is the property of reason, and that no irrational creature can smile:
Smiles not allowed to beasts from reason move.
State of Innocence.

46 These lines are written in the same key with those in the *Earl of Essex:*
Why, sayest thou so? I love thee well, indeed
I do, and thou shalt find by this 't is true.
Or with this in *Cyrus:*
The most heroic mind that ever was.
And with above half of the modern tragedies.

47 Aristotle, in that excellent work of his which is very justly styled his masterpiece, earnestly recommends using the terms of art, however coarse or even indecent they may be. Mr. Tate is of the same opinion.
Bru. Do not, like young hawks, fetch a course about:
Your game flies fair.
Fra. Do not fear it.
He answers you in your hawking phrase.
Injured Love.
I think these two great authorities are sufficient to justify Dollallolla in the use of the phrase, "Hie away, hie!" when in the same line she says she is speaking to a setting-dog.

48 We meet with such another pair of scales in Dryden's *King Arthur:*
Arthur and Oswald, and their different fates,
Are weighing now within the scales of heaven.
Also in *Sebastian:*
This hour my lot is weighing in the scales.

ACT II

Scene 1. *The Street.*

(*Bailiff, Follower.*)

Bail. Come on, my trusty [follower], come on;
This day discharge thy duty, and at night
A double mug of beer, and beer shall glad thee.
Stand here by me, this way must Noodle pass.

Fol. No more, no more, oh Bailiff! every word
Inspires my soul with virtue. Oh! I long
To meet the enemy in the street—and nab him:
To lay arresting hands upon his back,
And drag him trembling to the sponging-house.*

Bail. There when I have him, I will sponge upon him.
[49] Oh! glorious thought! by the sun, moon, and stars,
I will enjoy it, though it be in thought!
Yes, yes, my follower, I will enjoy it.

Fol. Enjoy it then some other time, for now
Our prey approaches.

Bail. Let us retire.

Scene 2.

(*Tom Thumb, Noodle, Bailiff, Follower.*)

Thumb. Trust me, my Noodle, I am wondrous sick;
For, though I love the gentle Huncamunca,
Yet at the thought of marriage I grow pale:
For, oh!—[50] but swear thou'll keep it ever secret,
I will unfold a tale will make thee stare.

Nood. I swear by lovely Huncamunca's charms.

Thumb. Then know [51] my grandmamma hath often said,
Tom Thumb, beware of marriage.

Nood. Sir, I blush
To think a warrior, great in arms as you,
Should be affrighted by his grandmamma.
Can an old woman's empty dreams deter
The blooming hero from the virgin's arms?
Think of the joy that will your soul alarm,
When in her fond embraces clasped you lie,
While on her panting breast, dissolved in bliss,
You pour out all Tom Thumb in every kiss.

Thumb. Oh! Noodle, thou hast fired my eager soul
Spite of my grandmother she shall be mine;
I'll hug, caress, I'll eat her up with love:
Whole days, and nights, and years shall be too short
For our enjoyment; every sun shall rise
[52] Blushing to see us in our bed together.

Nood. Oh! sir! this purpose of your soul pursue.

Bail. Oh! sir! I have an action against you.

Nood. At whose suit is it?

Bail. At your tailor's, sir.
Your tailor put this warrant in my hands,
And I arrest you, sir, at his commands.

Thumb. Ha! dogs! Arrest my friend before my face!
Think you Tom Thumb will suffer this disgrace?
But let vain cowards threaten by their word,
Tom Thumb shall show his anger by his sword.

(*Kills the Bailiff and his Follower.*)

Bail. Oh, I am slain!

Fol. I am murdered also

[49] Mr. † Rowe is generally imagined to have taken some hints from this scene in his character of Bajazet; but as he, of all the tragic writers, bears the least resemblance to our author in his diction, I am unwilling to imagine he would condescend to copy him in this particular.

[50] This method of surprising an audience, by raising their expectation to the highest pitch, and then baulking it, hath been practised with great success by most of our tragical authors.

[51] Almeyda, in *Sebastian*, is in the same distress:
Sometimes methinks I hear the groan of ghosts,
Thin hollow sounds and lamentable screams;
Then, like a dying echo from afar,
My mother's voice that cries, Wed not, Almeyda;
Forewarned, Almeyda, marriage is thy crime.

[52] "As very well he may, if he hath any modesty in him," says Mr. D—s. The author of *Busiris* is extremely zealous to prevent the sun's blushing at any indecent object; and therefore on all such occasions he addresses himself to the sun, and desires him to keep out of the way.
Rise never more, O sun! let night prevail,
Eternal darkness close the world's wide scene.
Busiris.
Sun, hide thy face, and put the world in mourning.
Ibid.

Mr. Banks makes the sun perform the office of Hymen, and therefore not likely to be disgusted at such a sight:
The sun sets forth like a gay brideman with you.
Mary Queen of Scots.

* A place of preliminary confinement for debtors.

† Nicholas Rowe (1674–1718), the first editor of Shakespeare, and author of *Jane Shore* and other excellent plays. Observe the compliment Fielding pays him.

And to the shades, the dismal shades below,
My bailiff's faithful follower I go.

Nood. [53] Go then to hell, like rascals as you are,
And give our service to the bailiffs there.

Thumb. Thus perish all the bailiffs [in the land],
Till debtors at noon-day shall walk the streets,
And no one fear a bailiff or his writ.

Scene 3. *The Princess Huncamunca's Apartment.*

(*Huncamunca, Cleora, Mustacha.*)

Hunc. [54] Give me some music—see that it be sad.

(*Cleora sings.*)

I

Cupid, ease a love-sick maid,
Bring thy quiver to her aid;
With equal ardor wound the swain,
Beauty should never sigh in vain.

II

Let him feel the pleasing smart,
Drive thy arrow through his heart:
When one you wound, you then destroy;
When both you kill, you kill with joy.

Hunc. [55] O Tom Thumb! Tom Thumb! wherefore art thou Tom Thumb?
Why hadst thou not been born of royal race?
Why had not mighty Bantam * been thy father?
Or else the king of Brentford, Old or New? †

Must. I am surprised that your highness can give yourself a moment's uneasiness about that little insignificant fellow,[56] Tom Thumb the Great—one properer for a plaything than a husband. Were he my husband his horns should be as long as his body. If you had fallen in love with a grenadier, I should not have wondered at it. If you had fallen in love with something; but to fall in love with nothing!

Hunc. Cease, my Mustacha, on thy duty [c]ease.
The zephyr, when in flowery vales it plays,
Is not so soft, so sweet as Thummy's breath.
The dove is not so gentle to its mate.

Must. The dove is every bit as proper for a husband.—Alas! Madam, there's not a beau about the court looks so little like a man. He is a perfect butterfly, a thing without substance, and almost without shadow too.

Hunc. This rudeness is unseasonable: desist;
Or I shall think this railing comes from love.
Tom Thumb's a creature of that charming form,
That no one can abuse, unless they love him.

Must. Madam, the king.

Scene 4.

(*King, Huncamunca.*)

King. Let all but Huncamunca leave the room.

(*Exeunt Cleora and Mustacha.*)

Daughter, I have observed of late some grief
Unusual in your countenance: your eyes
[57] That, like two open windows, used to show
The lovely beauty of the rooms within,
Have now two blinds before them. What is the cause?
Say, have you not enough of meat and drink?
We've given strict orders not to have you stinted.

Hunc. Alas! my lord, I value not myself

[53] Nourmahal sends the same message to heaven:
For I would have you when you upwards move,
Speak kindly of us to our friends above.
Aurengzebe.
We find another "to hell," in the *Persian Princess:*
Villain, get thee down
To hell, and tell them that the fray's begun.

[54] Anthony gives the same command in the same words. [Dryden's *All for Love*, I, i.]

[55] Oh! Marius, Marius, wherefore art thou Marius?
Otway's *Marius.*

[56] Nothing is more common than these seeming contradictions: such as,
Haughty weakness. *Victim.*
Great small world. [Ecclestone's] *Noah's Flood.*

[57] Lee hath improved this metaphor:
Dost thou not view joy peeping from my eyes,
The casements opened wide to gaze on thee,
So Rome's glad citizens to windows rise,
When they some young triumpher fain would see.
[Lee's] *Gloriana.*

* The King of Bantam in Java, with a pun on the name of a small kind of fowl, perhaps imported thence.
† The two kings of Brentford were fantastic characters in the Duke of Buckingham's play, *The Rehearsal.*

That once I eat two fowls and half a pig;
[58] Small is that praise! but oh! a maid may want
What she can neither eat nor drink.
King. What 's that?
Hunc. O [59] spare my blushes; but I mean a husband.
King. If that be all, I have provided one,
A husband great in arms, whose warlike sword
Streams with the yellow blood of slaughter'd giants,
Whose name in Terra Incognita is known,
Whose valor, wisdom, virtue make a noise
Great as the kettle-drums of twenty armies.
Hunc. Whom does my royal father mean?
King. Tom Thumb.
Hunc. Is it possible?
King. Ha! the window-blinds are gone;
[60] A country-dance of joy is in your face.
Your eyes spit fire, your cheeks grow red as beef.
Hunc. O, there 's a magic-music in that sound,
Enough to turn me into beef indeed!
Yes, I will own, since licensed by your word,
I 'll own Tom Thumb the cause of all my grief.
For him I 've sighed, I 've wept, I 've gnawed my sheets.
King. Oh! thou shalt gnaw thy tender sheets no more.
A husband thou shalt have to mumble now.
Hunc. Oh! happy sound! henceforth let no one tell
That Huncamunca shall lead apes in hell.*
Oh! I am overjoyed!
King. I see thou art.
[61] Joy lightens in thy eyes, and thunders from thy brows;
Transports, like lightning, dart along thy soul,
As small-shot through a hedge.
Hunc. Oh! say not small.
King. This happy news shall on our tongue ride post,
Ourself we bear the happy news to Thumb.
Yet think not, daughter, that your powerful charms
Must still detain the hero from his arms;
Various his duty, various his delight;
Now is his turn to kiss, and now to fight,
And now to kiss again. So, mighty [62] Jove,
When with excessive thundering tired above,
Comes down to earth, and takes a bit—and then
Flies to his trade of thundering back again.

Scene 5.

(*Grizzle, Huncamunca.*)

[63] *Griz.* Oh! Huncamunca, Huncamunca, oh!
Thy pouting breasts, like kettle-drums of brass,
Beat everlasting loud alarms of joy;
As bright as brass they are, and oh, as hard.
Oh! Huncamunca, Huncamunca, oh!

58 Almahide hath the same contempt for these appetites:
To eat and drink can no perfection be.
Conquest of Granada.
The Earl of Essex is of a different opinion, and seems to place the chief happiness of a general therein:
Were but commanders half so well rewarded,
Then they might eat.
Banks's *Earl of Essex.*
But, if we may believe one who knows more than either, the devil himself, we shall find eating to be an affair of more moment than is generally imagined:
Gods are immortal only by their food.
Lucifer, in the *State of Innocence* [by Dryden].

59 "This expression is enough of itself," says Mr. D—s, "utterly to destroy the character of Huncamunca!" Yet we find a woman of no abandoned character in Dryden adventuring farther, and thus excusing herself:
To speak our wishes first, forbid it pride,
Forbid it modesty; true, they forbid it,
But Nature does not. When we are athirst,
Or hungry, will imperious Nature stay,
Nor eat, nor drink, before 't is bid fall on?
Cleomenes.
Cassandra speaks before she is asked: Huncamunca afterwards. Cassandra speaks her wishes to her lover: Huncamunca only to her father.

60 Her eyes resistless magic bear;
Angels, I see, and gods are dancing there.
Lee's *Sophonisba.*

61 Mr. Dennis, in that excellent tragedy called *Liberty Asserted*, which is thought to have given so great a stroke to the late French king, hath frequent imitations of this beautiful speech of king Arthur:
Conquest lightening in his eyes, and thundering in his arm.
Joy lightened in her eyes.
Joys like lightning dart along my soul.

62 Jove, with excessive thundering tired above,
Comes down for ease, enjoys a nymph, and then
Mounts dreadful, and to thundering goes again.
Gloriana.

63 This beautiful line, which ought, says Mr. W—, to be written in gold, is imitated in the New *Sophonisba:*
Oh! Sophonisba; Sophonisba, oh!
Oh! Narva; Narva, oh!
The author of a song called *Duke upon Duke* hath improved it:
Alas! O Nick! O Nick, alas!
Where, by the help of a little false spelling, you have two meanings in the repeated words.

* It was a jocose tradition that unmarried women must lead apes in hell.

Hunc. Ha! dost thou know me, princess as I am,
[64] That thus of me you dare to make your game?
Griz. Oh! Huncamunca, well I know that you
A princess are, and a king's daughter, too;
But love no meanness scorns, no grandeur fears;
Love often lords into the cellar bears,
And bids the sturdy porter come up stairs.
For what's too high for love, or what's too low?
Oh! Huncamunca, Huncamunca, oh!
Hunc. But, granting all you say of love were true,
My love, alas! is to another due.
In vain to me a suitoring you come,
For I'm already promised to Tom Thumb.
Griz. And can my princess such a durgen * wed?
One fitter for your pocket than your bed!
Advised by me, the worthless baby shun,
Or you will ne'er be brought to bed of one.
Oh take me to thy arms, and never flinch,
Who am a man, by Jupiter! every inch.
[65] Then, while in joys together lost we lie,
I'll press thy soul while gods stand wishing by.
Hunc. If, sir, what you insinuate you prove,
All obstacles of promise you remove;
For all engagements to a man must fall,
Whene'er that man is proved no man at all.
Griz. Oh! let him seek some dwarf, some fairy miss,
Where no joint-stool must lift him to the kiss!
But, by the stars and glory! you appear
Much fitter for a Prussian grenadier; †
One globe alone on Atlas' shoulders rests,
Two globes are less than Huncamunca's breasts;
The milky way is not so white, that's flat,
And sure thy breasts are full as large as that.
Hunc. Oh, sir, so strong your eloquence I find,
It is impossible to be unkind.
Griz. Ah! speak that o'er again; and let the [66] sound
From one pole to another pole rebound;
The earth and sky each be a battledore,
And keep the sound, that shuttlecock, up an hour:
To Doctors-Commons ‡ for a licence I
Swift as an arrow from a bow will fly.
Hunc. Oh, no! lest some disaster we should meet,
'T were better to be married at the Fleet.¶
Griz. Forbid it, all ye powers, a princess should
By that vile place contaminate her blood;
My quick return shall to my charmer prove
I travel on the [67] post-horses of love.
Hunc. Those post-horses to me will seem too slow
Though they should fly swift as the gods, when they
Ride on behind that post-boy, Opportunity.

Scene 6.

(*Tom Thumb, Huncamunca.*)

Thumb. Where is my princess? where's my Huncamunca?
Where are those eyes, those card-matches ‖ of love,
That [68] light up all with love my waxen soul?
Where is that face which artful nature made

64 Edith, in the *Bloody Brother* [by Fletcher], speaks to her lover in the same familiar language:
Your grace is full of game.

65 Traverse the glittering chambers of the sky,
Borne on a cloud in view of fate I'll lie,
And press her soul while gods stand wishing by.
[Lee's *Sophonisba; or*] *Hannibal['s Overthrow]*.

66 Let the four winds from distant corners meet,
And on their wings first bear it into France;
Then back again to Edina's proud walls,
Till victim to the sound th' aspiring city falls.
Albion Queens.

67 I do not remember any metaphors so frequent in the tragic poets as those borrowed from riding post:
The gods and opportunity ride post.
Hannibal.
——Let's rush together,
For death rides post: *Duke of Guise.*
Destruction gallops to thy murder post.
Gloriana.

68 This image, too, very often occurs:
——Bright as when thy eye
First lighted up our loves. *Aurengzebe.*
'T is not a crown alone lights up my name.
Busiris.

* dwarf.
† The allusion is to the regiment of very tall men in the army of King Frederick William I, of Prussia, father of Frederick the Great.
‡ The body which issued marriage licenses, and dealt with divorces, wills, etc.
¶ A prison frequented by disreputable clergymen ready to perform secret marriages.
‖ "A piece of card dipped in melted sulphur" (*Oxf. Dict.*), used to start a fire.

[69] In the same moulds where Venus' self was cast?
Hunc. [70] Oh! what is music to the ear that 's deaf,
Or a goose-pie to him that has no taste?
What are these praises now to me, since I
Am promised to another?
Thumb. Ha! promised?
Hunc. Too sure; 't is written in the book of fate.
Thumb. [71] Then I will tear away the leaf
Wherein it 's writ; or, if fate won't allow
So large a gap within its journal-book,
I 'll blot it out at least.

Scene 7.

(*Glumdalca, Tom Thumb, Huncamunca.*)

Glum. [72] I need not ask if you are Huncamunca,
Your brandy-nose proclaims——
Hunc. I am a princess;
Nor need I ask who you are.
Glum. A giantess;
The queen of those who made and unmade queens.
Hunc. The man whose chief ambition is to be
My sweetheart hath destroyed these mighty giants.
Glum. Your sweetheart? Dost thou think the man who once
Hath worn my easy chains will e'er wear thine?
Hunc. Well may your chains be easy, since, if fame
Says true, they have been tried on twenty husbands.
[73] The glove or boot, so many times pulled on,
May well sit easy on the hand or foot.
Glum. I glory in the number, and when I
Sit poorly down, like thee, content with one,
Heaven change this face for one as bad as thine.
Hunc. Let me see nearer what this beauty is
That captivates the heart of men by scores.
(*Holds a candle to her face.*)
Oh! Heaven, thou art as ugly as the devil.
Glum. You 'd give the best of shoes within your shop
To be but half so handsome.
Hunc. Since you come
[74] To that, I 'll put my beauty to the test:
Tom Thumb, I 'm yours, if you with me will go.
Glum. Oh! stay, Tom Thumb, and you alone shall fill
That bed where twenty giants used to lie.
Thumb. In the balcony that o'erhangs the stage,
I 've seen a whore two 'prentices engage;
One half-a-crown does in his fingers hold,
The other shows a little piece of gold;

69 There is great dissension among the poets concerning the method of making man. One tells his mistress that the mould she was made in being lost, Heaven cannot form such another. Lucifer, in Dryden, gives a merry description of his own formation:
Whom heaven, neglecting, made and scarce designed,
But threw me in for number to the rest.
State of Innoc[ence].
In one place the same poet supposes man to be made of metal: I was formed
Of that coarse metal which, when she was made,
The gods threw by for rubbish.
All for Love.
In another of dough:
When the gods moulded up the paste of man,
Some of their clay was left upon their hands,
And so they made Egyptians. *Cleomenes.*
In another of clay:
——Rubbish of remaining clay. *Sebastian.*
One makes the soul of wax:
Her waxen soul begins to melt apace.
Anne Bullen.
Another of flint:
Sure our two souls have somewhere been acquainted
In former beings, or, struck out together,
One spark to Afric flew, and one to Portugal.
Sebastian.
To omit the great quantities of iron, brazen, and leaden souls which are so plenty in modern authors—I cannot omit the dress of a soul as we find it in Dryden:
Souls shirted but with air. *King Arthur.*
Nor can I pass by a particular sort of soul in a particular sort of description in the New *Sophonisba.*
Ye mysterious powers,
——Whether through your gloomy depths I wander,
Or on the mountains walk, give me the calm,
The steady smiling soul, where wisdom sheds
Eternal sunshine, and eternal joy.

70 This line Mr. Banks has plundered entire in his *Anne Bullen.*

71 Good Heaven! the book of fate before me lay,
But to tear out the journal of that day.
Or, if the order of the world below
Will not the gap of one whole day allow,
Give me that minute when she made her vow.
Conquest of Granada.

72 I know some of the commentators have imagined that Mr. Dryden, in the altercative scene between Cleopatra and Octavia, a scene which Mr. Addison inveighs against with great bitterness, is much beholden to our author. How just this their observation is I will not presume to determine.

73 "A cobbling poet indeed," says Mr. D.; and yet I believe we may find as monstrous images in the tragic authors: I 'll put down one:
Untie your folded thoughts, and let them dangle loose as a bride's hair. *Injured Love.*
Which line seems to have as much title to a milliner's shop as our author's to a shoemaker's.

74 Mr. L— [Lee] takes occasion in this place to commend the great care of our author to preserve the metre of blank verse, in which Shakespeare, Jonson, and Fletcher were so notoriously negligent; and the moderns, in imitation of our author, so laudably observant:
Then does
Your majesty believe that he can be
A traitor? *Earl of Essex.*
Every page of *Sophonisba* gives us instances of this excellence.

She the half-guinea wisely does purloin,
And leaves the larger and the baser coin.
Glum. Left, scorned, and loathed for such a chit as this;
[75] I feel the storm that's rising in my mind,
Tempests and whirlwinds rise, and roll, and roar.
I'm all within a hurricane, as if
[76] The world's four winds were pent within my carcase.
[77] Confusion, horror, murder, guts, and death!

Scene 8.

(*King, Glumdalca.*)

King. [78] Sure never was so sad a king as I!
[79] My life is worn as ragged as a coat
A beggar wears; a prince should put it off.
[80] To love a captive and a giantess!
Oh love! oh love! how great a king art thou!
My tongue's thy trumpet, and thou trumpetest,
Unknown to me, within me. [81] Oh, Glumdalca!
Heaven thee designed a giantess to make,
But an angelic soul was shuffled in.
[82] I am a multitude of walking griefs,
And only on her lips the balm is found
[83] To spread a plaster that might cure them all.

Glum. What do I hear?
King. What do I see?
Glum. Oh!
King. Ah!
[84] *Glum.* Ah! wretched queen!
King. Oh! wretched king!
[85] *Glum.* Ah!
King. Oh!

Scene 9.

(*Tom Thumb, Huncamunca, Parson.*)

Par. Happy's the wooing that's not long a doing;
For, if I guess right, Tom Thumb this night
Shall give a being to a new Tom Thumb.
Thumb. It shall be my endeavor so to do.
Hunc. Oh! fie upon you, sir, you make me blush.
Thumb. It is the virgin's sign, and suits you well:
[86] I know not where, nor how, nor what I am;
[87] I'm so transported, I have lost myself.

---

75 Love mounts and rolls about my stormy mind.
Aurengzebe.
Tempests and whirlwinds through my bosom move.
Cleom[enes].

76 With such a furious tempest on his brow,
As if the world's four winds were pent within
His blustering carcase. *Anne Bullen.*

77 Verba Tragica. [*i. e., stock words in tragedy.*]

78 This speech has been terribly mauled by the poet.

79 ——My life is worn to rags,
Not worth a prince's wearing.
Love Triumphant.

80 Must I beg the pity of my slave?
Must a king beg? But love's a greater king,
A tyrant, nay, a devil, that possesses me.
He tunes the organ to my voice and speaks,
Unknown to me, within me. *Sebastian.*

81 When thou wert formed heaven did a man begin;
But a brute soul by chance was shuffled in.
Aurengzebe.

82 I am a multitude
Of walking griefs.
New *Sophonisba.*

83 I will take thy scorpion blood,
And lay it to my grief till I have ease.
Anne Bullen.

84 Our author, who everywhere shows his great penetration into human nature, here outdoes himself: where a less judicious poet would have raised a long scene of whining love, he, who understood the passions better, and that so violent an affection as this must be too big for utterance, chooses rather to send his characters off in this sullen doleful manner, in which admirable conduct he is imitated by the author of the justly celebrated *Eurydice.* Dr. Young seems to point at this violence of passion:

——Passion chokes
Their words, and they're the statues of despair.

And Seneca tells us, "Curæ leves loquuntur, ingentes stupent." The story of the Egyptian king in Herodotus is too well known to need to be inserted; I refer the more curious reader to the excellent Montaigne, who hath written an essay on this subject.

85 To part is death.
'Tis death to part.
Ah!
Oh!
[Otway's] *Don Carlos.*

86 Nor know I whether
What am I, who, or where.
Busiris.
I was I know not what, and am I know not how.
Gloriana.

87 To understand sufficiently the beauty of this passage, it will be necessary that we comprehend every man to contain two selfs. I shall not attempt to prove this from philosophy, which the poets make so plainly evident.

One runs away from the other:
—Let me demand your majesty,
Why fly you from yourself?
Duke of Guise.

In a second one self is a guardian to the other:
Leave me the care of me.
Conquest of Granada.

Again:
Myself am to myself less near.
Ibid.

In the same, the first self is proud of the second:
I myself am proud of me.
State of Innocence.

In a third, distrustful of him:
Fain I would tell, but whisper it in my ear,
That none besides might hear, nay, not myself.
Earl of Essex.

In a fourth, honors him:
I honor Rome,
And honor too myself.
Sophonisba.

Hunc. Forbid it, all ye stars, for you 're so small,
That were you lost, you 'd find yourself no more.
So the unhappy sempstress once, they say,
Her needle in a pottle,* lost, of hay;
In vain she looked, and looked, and made her moan,
For ah, the needle was for ever gone.

Par. Long may they live, and love, and propagate,
Till the whole land be peopled with Tom Thumbs!
[88] So, when the Cheshire cheese a maggot breeds,
Another and another still succeeds:
By thousands and ten thousands they increase,
Till one continued maggot fills the rotten cheese.

Scene 10.

(*Noodle, and then Grizzle.*)

Nood. [89] Sure, Nature means to break her solid chain,
Or else unfix the world, and in a rage
To hurl it from its axletree and hinges;
All things are so confused, the king 's in love,
The queen is drunk, the princess married is.

Griz. Oh, Noodle! Hast thou Huncamunca seen?

Nood. I 've seen a thousand sights this day, where none
Are by the wonderful bitch herself outdone.
The king, the queen, and all the court, are sights.

Griz. [90] D—n your delay, you trifler! are you drunk, ha?
I will not hear one word but Huncamunca.

Nood. By this time she is married to Tom Thumb.

Griz. [91] My Huncamunca!

Nood. Your Huncamunca,
Tom Thumb's Huncamunca, every man's Huncamunca.

Griz. If this be true, all womankind are damned.

Nood. If it be not, may I be so myself.

Griz. See where she comes! I 'll not believe a word
Against that face, upon whose [92] ample brow
Sits innocence with majesty enthroned.

(*Grizzle, Huncamunca.*)

Griz. Where has my Huncamunca been? See here.
The licence in my hand!

Hunc. Alas! Tom Thumb.

Griz. Why dost thou mention him?

Hunc. Ah, me! Tom Thumb.

Griz. What means my lovely Huncamunca?

Hunc. Hum!

Griz. Oh! speak.

Hunc. Hum!

Griz. Ha! your every word is hum:
[93] You force me still to answer you, Tom Thumb.
Tom Thumb—I 'm on the rack—I 'm in a flame.
[94] Tom Thumb, Tom Thumb, Tom Thumb—you love the name;
So pleasing is that sound, that, were you dumb,
You still would find a voice to cry Tom Thumb.

Hunc. Oh! be not hasty to proclaim my doom!
My ample heart for more than one has room:
A maid like me Heaven formed at least for two.

In a fifth, at variance with him:
Leave me not thus at variance with myself.
Busiris.

Again, in a sixth:
I find myself divided from myself.
[Charles Johnson's] *Medea.*

She seemed the sad effigies of herself.
Banks.

Assist me, Zulema, if thou wouldst be
The friend thou seemst, assist me against me.
Albion Queens.

From all which it appears that there are two selfs; and therefore Tom Thumb's losing himself is no such solecism as it hath been represented by men rather ambitious of criticising than qualified to criticise.

88 Mr. F— [Fielding] imagines this parson to have been a Welsh one, from his simile.

89 Our author hath been plundered here, according to custom:
Great Nature, break thy chain that links together
The fabric of the world, and make a chaos
Like that within my soul. *Love Triumphant.*
——Startle Nature, unfix the globe,
And hurl it from its axletree and hinges.
Albion Queens.
The tottering earth seems sliding off its props.

90 D—n your delay, ye torturers, proceed;
I will not hear one word but Almahide.
Conquest of Granada.

91 Mr. Dryden hath imitated this in *All for Love.*

92 This Miltonic style abounds in the New *Sophonisba:*
——And on her ample brow
Sat majesty.

93 Your every answer still so ends in that,
You force me still to answer you Morat.
Aurengzebe.

94 Morat, Morat, Morat! you love the name. *Ibid.*

* For *bottle,* meaning *bundle.*

[95] I married him, and now I'll marry you.
Griz. Ha! dost thou own thy falsehood to my face?
Thinkest thou that I will share thy husband's place?
Since to that office one cannot suffice,
And since you scorn to dine one single dish on,
Go, get your husband put into commission.
Commissioners to discharge (ye gods! it fine is)
The duty of a husband to your highness.
Yet think not long I will my rival bear,
Or unrevenged the slighted willow wear;
The gloomy, brooding tempest, now confined
Within the hollow caverns of my mind,
In dreadful whirl shall roll along the coasts,
Shall thin the land of all the men it boasts,
[96] And cram up every chink of hell with ghosts.
[97] So have I seen, in some dark winter's day,
A sudden storm rush down the sky's highway,
Sweep through the streets with terrible ding-dong,
Gush through the spouts, and wash whole c[r]owds along.
The crowded shops the thronging vermin screen,
Together cram the dirty and the clean,
And not one shoe-boy in the street is seen.

Hunc. Oh, fatal rashness! should his fury slay
My hapless bridegroom on his wedding-day,
I, who this morn of two chose which to wed,
May go again this night alone to bed.
[98] So have I seen some wild unsettled fool,
Who had her choice of this and that joint-stool,
To give the preference to either loth,
And fondly coveting to sit on both,
While the two stools her sitting-part confound,
Between 'em both fall squat upon the ground.

ACT III.

Scene 1. *King Arthur's Palace.*

[99] *Ghost* (*solus*). Hail! ye black horrors of midnight's midnoon!
Ye fairies, goblins, bats, and screech-owls, hail!

95 "Here is a sentiment for the virtuous Huncamunca!" says Mr. D—s. And yet, with the leave of this great man, the virtuous Panthea, in *Cyrus*, hath an heart every whit as ample:

For two I must confess are gods to me,
Which is my Abradatus first, and thee.
Cyrus the Great.

Nor is the lady in *Love Triumphant* more reserved, though not so intelligible:

I am so divided,
That I grieve most for both, and love both most.

96 A ridiculous supposition to any one who considers the great and extensive largeness of hell, says a commentator; but not so to those who consider the great expansion of immaterial substance. Mr. Banks makes one soul to be so expanded, that heaven could not contain it:

The heavens are all too narrow for her soul.
Virtue Betrayed.

The *Persian Princess* hath a passage not unlike the author of this:

We will send such shoals of murdered slaves,
Shall glut hell's empty regions.

This threatens to fill hell, even though it was empty: Lord Grizzle, only to fill up the chinks, supposing the rest already full.

97 Mr. Addison is generally thought to have had this simile in his eye when he wrote that beautiful one at the end of the third act of his *Cato*

98 This beautiful simile is founded on a proverb which does honor to the English language:

Between two stools the breech falls to the ground.

I am not so well pleased with any written remains of the ancients as with those little aphorisms which verbal tradition hath delivered down to us under the title of proverbs. It were to be wished that, instead of filling their pages with the fabulous theology of the pagans, our modern poets would think it worth their while to enrich their works with the proverbial sayings of their ancestors. Mr. Dryden hath chronicled one in heroic:

Two ifs scarce make one possibility.
Conquest of Granada.

My Lord Bacon is of opinion that, whatever is known of arts and sciences might be proved to have lurked in the Proverbs of Solomon. I am of the same opinion in relation to those above mentioned; at least I am confident that a more perfect system of ethics, as well as economy, might be compiled out of them than is at present extant, either in the works of the ancient philosophers, or those more valuable, as more voluminous ones of the modern divines.

99 Of all the particulars in which the modern stage falls short of the ancient, there is none so much to be lamented as the great scarcity of ghosts. Whence this proceeds I will not presume to determine. Some are of opinion that the moderns are unequal to that sublime language which a ghost ought to speak. One says, ludicrously, that ghosts are out of fashion; another that they are properer for comedy; forgetting, I suppose, that Aristotle hath told us that a ghost is the soul of tragedy; for so I render the ψυχὴ ὁ μῦθος τῆς τραγωδίας which M. Dacier, amongst others, hath mistaken; I suppose misled by not understanding the Fabula of the Latins which signifies a ghost as well as fable.

"Te premet nox, fabulæque manes."
Horace.

Of all the ghosts that have ever appeared on the stage, a very learned and judicious foreign critic gives the preference to this of our author. These are his words, speaking of this tragedy:—"Nec quidquam in illâ admirabilius quàm phasma quoddam horrendum, quod omnibus aliis spectris, quibuscum scatet Angelorum tragœdia, longè (pace D—ysii V. Doctiss dixerim) prætulerim."

And, oh! ye mortal watchmen, whose hoarse throats
The immortal ghosts' dread croakings counterfeit,
All hail!—Ye dancing phantoms, who, by day,
Are some condemned to fast, some feast in fire,
Now play in churchyards, skipping o'er the graves,
To the [100] loud music of the silent bell,
All hail!

SCENE 2.

(*King and Ghost.*)

King. What noise is this? What villain dares,
At this dread hour, with feet and voice profane,
Disturb our royal walls?
Ghost. One who defies
Thy empty power to hurt him; [101] one who dares
Walk in thy bedchamber.
King. Presumptuous slave!
Thou diest.
Ghost. Threaten others with that word:
[102] I am a ghost, and am already dead.
King. Ye stars! 't is well. Were thy last hour to come,
This moment had been it; [103] yet by thy shroud
I 'll pull thee backward, squeeze thee to a bladder,
Till thou dost groan thy nothingness away.
Thou flyest! 'T is well.
(*Ghost retires.*)
[104] I thought what was the courage of a ghost!
Yet, dare not, on thy life—Why say I that,
Since life thou hast not?—Dare not walk again
Within these walls, on pain of the Red Sea.
For, if henceforth I ever find thee here,
As sure, sure as a gun, I 'll have thee laid——
Ghost. Were the Red Sea a sea of Holland's gin,
The liquor (when alive) whose very smell
I did detest, did loathe—yet, for the sake
Of Thomas Thumb, I would be laid therein.
King. Ha! said you?
Ghost. Yes, my liege, I said Tom Thumb,
Whose father's ghost I am—once not unknown
To mighty Arthur. But, I see, 't is true,
The dearest friend, when dead, we all forget.
King. 'T is he—it is the honest Gaffer Thumb.
Oh! let me press thee in my eager arms,
Thou best of ghosts! thou something more than ghost!
Ghost. Would I were something more, that we again
Might feel each other in the warm embrace.
But now I have th' advantage of my king,
[105] For I feel thee, whilst thou dost not feel me.
King. But say, [106] thou dearest air, Oh! say what dread,
Important business sends thee back to earth?
Ghost. Oh! then prepare to hear—which but to hear
Is full enough to send thy spirit hence.
Thy subjects up in arms, by Grizzle led,
Will, ere the rosy-fingered morn shall ope
The shutters of the sky, before the gate

100 We have already given instances of this figure.

101 Almanzor reasons in the same manner:

A ghost I 'll be;
And from a ghost, you know, no place is free.
Conquest of Granada.

102 "The man who writ this wretched pun," says Mr. D., "would have picked your pocket:" which he proceeds to show not only bad in itself, but doubly so on so solemn an occasion. And yet, in that excellent play of *Liberty Asserted*, we find something very much resembling a pun in the mouth of a mistress, who is parting with the lover she is fond of:

Ul. Oh, mortal woe! one kiss, and then farewell.
Irene. The gods have given to others to fare well.
O! miserably must Irene fare.

Agamemnon, in the *Victim*, is full as facetious on the most solemn occasion—that of sacrificing his daughter:

Yes, daughter, yes; you will assist the priest;
Yes, you must offer up your—vows for Greece.

103 I 'll pull thee backwards by thy shroud to light,
Or else I 'll squeeze thee, like a bladder, there,
And make thee groan thyself away to air.
Conquest of Granada
Snatch me, ye gods, this moment into nothing.
Cyrus the Great.

104 So, art thou gone? Thou canst no conquest boast.
I thought what was the courage of a ghost.
Conquest of Granada

King Arthur seems to be as brave a fellow as Almanzor, who says most heroically,

In spite of ghosts I 'll on.

105 The ghost of Lausaria, in *Cyrus*, is a plain copy of this, and is therefore worth reading:

Ah, Cyrus!
Thou mayest as well grasp water, or fleet air,
As think of touching my immortal shade.
Cyrus the Great

106 Thou better part of heavenly air.
Conquest of Granada

Of this thy royal palace, swarming spread.
[107] So have I seen the bees in clusters swarm,
So have I seen the stars in frosty nights,
So have I seen the sand in windy days,
So have I seen the ghost[s] on Pluto's shore,
So have I seen the flowers in spring arise,
So have I seen the leaves in autumn fall,
So have I seen the fruits in summer smile,
So have I seen the snow in winter frown.

King. D—n all thou hast seen! dost thou, beneath the shape
Of Gaffer Thumb, come hither to abuse me
With similes, to keep me on the rack?
Hence—or, by all the torments of thy hell,
[108] I 'll run thee through the body, though thou 'st none.

Ghost. Arthur, beware! I must this moment hence,
Not frighted by your voice, but by the cocks!
Arthur beware, beware, beware, beware!
Strive to avert thy yet impending fate;
For if thou 'rt killed to-day,
To-morrow all thy care will come too late.

SCENE 3.

(*King, solus.*)

King. Oh! stay, and leave me not uncertain thus!
And, whilst thou tellest me what 's like my fate,
Oh! teach me how I may avert it too!
Cursed be the man who first a simile made!
Cursed every bard who writes!—So have I seen
Those whose comparisons are just and true,
And those who liken things not like at all.
The devil is happy that the whole creation
Can furnish out no simile to his fortune.

107 "A string of similes," says one, "proper to be hung up in the cabinet of a prince."

108 This passage hath been understood several different ways by the commentators. For my part, I find it difficult to understand it at all. Mr. Dryden says—
I 've heard something how two bodies meet,
But how two souls join I know not.
So that, till the body of a spirit be better understood, it will be difficult to understand how it is possible to run him through it.

SCENE 4.

(*King, Queen.*)

Queen. What is the cause, my Arthur, that you steal
Thus silently from Dollallolla's breast?
Why dost thou leave me in the [109] dark alone,
When well thou knowest I am afraid of sprites?

King. Oh, Dollallolla! do not blame my love!
I hoped the fumes of last night's punch had laid
Thy lovely eyelids fast.—But, oh! I find
There is no power in drams to quiet wives;
Each morn, as the returning sun, they wake,
And shine upon their husbands.

Queen. Think, Oh think!
What a surprise it must be to the sun,
Rising, to find the vanished world away.
What less can be the wretched wife's surprise
When, stretching out her arms to fold thee fast,
She folds her useless bolster in her arms.
[110] Think, think, on that.—Oh! think, think well on that!
I do remember also to have read
[111] In Dryden's Ovid's Metamorphoses,
That Jove in form inanimate did lie
With beauteous Danaë: and, trust me, love,
[112] I feared the bolster might have been a Jove.

King. Come to my arms, most virtuous of thy sex;
Oh, Dollallolla! were all wives like thee,
So many husbands never had worn horns.
Should Huncamunca of thy worth partake,
Tom Thumb indeed were blest.—Oh, fatal name!
For didst thou know one quarter what I know,
Then wouldst thou know—Alas! what thou wouldst know!

109 Cydaria is of the same fearful temper with Dollallolla.
I never durst in darkness be alone.
[Dryden's] *Indian Emperor.*

110 Think well of this, think that, think every way.
Sophonisba.

111 These quotations are more usual in the comic than in the tragic writers.

112 "This distress," says Mr. D— [Dennis], "I must allow to be extremely beautiful, and tends to heighten the virtuous character of Dollallolla, who is so exceedingly delicate, that she is in the highest apprehension from the inanimate embrace of a bolster. An example worthy of imitation [for] all our writers of tragedy."

Queen. What can I gather hence? Why dost thou speak
Like men who carry rareeshows * about?
"Now you shall see, gentlemen, what you shall see."
O, tell me more, or thou hast told too much.

SCENE 5.

(*King, Queen, Noodle.*)

Nood. Long life attend your majesties serene,
Great Arthur, king, and Dollallolla, queen!
Lord Grizzle, with a bold rebellious crowd,
Advances to the palace, threatening loud,
Unless the princess be delivered straight,
And the victorious Thumb, without his pate,
They are resolved to batter down the gate.

SCENE 6.

(*King, Queen, Huncamunca, Noodle.*)

King. See where the princess comes! Where is Tom Thumb?
Hunc. Oh! sir, about an hour and half ago
He sallied out to encounter with the foe,
And swore, unless his fate had him misled,
From Grizzle's shoulders to cut off his head,
And serve 't up with your chocolate in bed.
King. 'T is well, I found one devil told us both.
Come, Dollallolla, Huncamunca, come;
Within we'll wait for the victorious Thumb:
In peace and safety we secure may stay,
While to his arm we trust the bloody fray;
Though men and giants should conspire with gods,
[113] He is alone equal to all these odds.

Queen. He is, indeed, [114] a helmet to us all;
While he supports we need not fear to fall;
His arm dispatches all things to our wish,
And serves up every foe's head in a dish.
Void is the mistress of the house of care,
While the good cook presents the bill of fare;
Whether the cod, that northern king of fish,
Or duck, or goose, or pig, adorn the dish,
No fears the number of her guests afford,
But at her hour she sees the dinner on the board.

SCENE 7. *A Plain.*

(*Grizzle, Foodle, Rebels.*)

Griz. Thus far our arms with victory are crowned;
For, though we have not fought, yet we have found
[115] No enemy to fight withal.
Food. Yet I,
Methinks, would willingly avoid this day,
[116] This first of April, to engage our foes.
Griz. This day, of all the days of th' year, I'd choose,
For on this day my grandmother was born.
Gods! I will make Tom Thumb an April-fool;

113 "Credat Judæus Appella,
Non ego,"
says Mr. D—. "For, passing over the absurdity of being equal to odds, can we possibly suppose a little insignificant fellow—I say again, a little insignificant fellow—able to vie with a strength which all the Samsons and Herculeses of antiquity would be unable to encounter?" I shall refer this incredulous critic to Mr. Dryden's defence of his Almanzor; and, lest that should not satisfy him, I shall quote a few lines from the speech of a much braver fellow than Almanzor, Mr. Johnson's Achilles:

Though human race rise in embattled hosts,
To force her from my arms—Oh! son of Atreus!
By that immortal power, whose deathless spirit
Informs this earth, I will oppose them all.
Victim.

114 "I have heard of being supported by a staff," says Mr. D., "but never of being supported by an helmet." I believe he never heard of sailing with wings, which he may read in no less a poet than Mr. Dryden:

Unless we borrow wings, and sail through air.
Love Triumphant.

What will he say to a kneeling valley?
————I'll stand
Like a safe valley, that low bends the knee
To some aspiring mountain. *Injured Love.*

I am ashamed of so ignorant a carper, who doth not know that an epithet in tragedy is very often no other than an expletive. Do not we read in the New *Sophonisba* of "grinding chains, blue plagues, white occasions, and blue serenity?" Nay, it is not the adjective only, but sometimes half a sentence is put by way of expletive, as, "Beauty pointed high with spirit," in the same play; and, "In the lap of blessing, to be most curst," in the *Revenge*.

115 A victory like that of Almanzor:
Almanzor is victorious without fight.
Conquest of Granada.

116 Well have we chose an happy day for fight;
For every man, in course of time, has found
Some days are lucky, some unfortunate.
King Arthur.

* A peep-show, carried around in a box.

[117] Will teach his wit an errand it ne'er knew,
And send it post to the Elysian shades.

Food. I'm glad to find our army is so stout,
Nor does it move my wonder less than joy.

Griz. [118] What friends we have, and how we came so strong,
I'll softly tell you as we march along.

SCENE 8. *Thunder and Lightning.*

(*Tom Thumb, Glumdalca, cum suis.**)

Thumb. Oh, Noodle! hast thou seen a day like this?
[119] The unborn thunder rumbles o'er our heads,
[120] As if the gods meant to unhinge the world;
And heaven and earth in wild confusion hurl;
Yet will I boldly tread the tottering ball.

Merl. Tom Thumb!

Thumb. What voice is this I hear?

Merl. Tom Thumb!

Thumb. Again it calls.

Merl. Tom Thumb!

Glum. It calls again.

Thumb. Appear, whoe'er thou art; I fear thee not.

Merl. Thou hast no cause to fear, I am thy friend,
Merlin by name, a conjurer by trade,
And to my art thou dost thy being owe.

Thumb. How!

Merl. Hear then the mystic getting of Tom Thumb.

[121] His father was a ploughman plain,
His mother milked the cow;
And yet the way to get a son
This couple knew not how.
Until such time the good old man
To learned Merlin goes,
And there to him, in great distress,
In secret manner shows;
How in his heart he wished to have
A child, in time to come,
To be his heir, though it may be
No bigger than his thumb:
Of which old Merlin was foretold
That he his wish should have;
And so a son of stature small
The charmer to him gave.

Thou'st heard the past, look up and see the future.

Thumb. [122] Lost in amazement's gulf, my senses sink;
See there, Glumdalca, see another [123] me!

Glum. O, sight of horror! see, you are devoured
By the expanded jaws of a red cow.

Merl. Let not these sights deter thy noble mind,
[124] For, lo! a sight more glorious courts thy eyes.
See from afar a theatre arise;
There ages, yet unborn, shall tribute pay
To the heroic actions of this day;
Then buskin tragedy at length shall choose
Thy name the best supporter of her muse.

Thumb. Enough: let every warlike music sound.
We fall contented, if we fall renown'd.

SCENE 9.

(*Lord Grizzle, Foodle, Rebels, on one side; Tom Thumb, Glumdalca, on the other.*)

Food. At length the enemy advances nigh,
[125] I hear them with my ear, and see them with my eye.

Griz. Draw all your swords: for liberty we fight,
[126] And liberty the mustard is of life.

---

117 We read of such another in Lee:
Teach his rude wit a flight she never made,
And send her post to the Elysian shade.
Gloriana.

118 These lines are copied verbatim in the *Indian Emperor.*

119 Unborn thunder rolling in a cloud.
Conquest of Granada.

120 Were heaven and earth in wild confusion hurled,
Should the rash gods unhinge the rolling world,
Undaunted would I tread the tottering ball,
Crushed, but unconquered, in the dreadful fall.
[Hopkins'] *Female Warrior.*

121 See the *History of Tom Thumb*, page 2.

122 Amazement swallows up my sense,
And in the impetuous whirl of circling fate
Drinks down my reason. *Persian Princess.*

123 I have outfaced myself.
What! am I two? Is there another me?
King Arthur.

124 The character of Merlin is wonderful throughout; but most so in this prophetic part. We find several of these prophecies in the tragic authors, who frequently take this opportunity to pay a compliment to their country, and sometimes to their prince. None but our author (who seems to have detested the least appearance of flattery) would have passed by such an opportunity of being a political prophet.

125 I saw the villain, Myron; with these eyes I saw him. *Busiris.*
In both which places it is intimated that it is sometimes possible to see with other eyes than your own.

126 "This mustard," says Mr. D., "is enough to turn one's stomach. I would be glad to know what idea the author had in his head when he wrote it." This will be, I believe, best explained by a line of Mr. Dennis:
And gave him liberty, the salt of life.
Liberty Asserted.
The understanding that can digest the one will not rise at the other.

* With their followers.

Thumb. Are you the man whom men famed Grizzle name?
Griz. [127] Are you the much more famed Tom Thumb?
Thumb. The same.
Griz. Come on; our worth upon ourselves we 'll prove;
For liberty I fight.
Thumb. And I for love.
(*A bloody engagement between the two armies here; drums beating, trumpets sounding, thunder and lightning. They fight off and on several times. Some fall. Griz. and Glum. remain.*)
Glum. Turn, coward, turn; nor from a woman fly.
Griz. Away—thou art too ignoble for my arm.
Glum. Have at thy heart.
Griz. Nay, then I thrust at thine.
Glum. You push too well; you 've run me through the guts.
And I am dead.
Griz. Then there 's an end of one.
Thumb. When thou art dead, then there 's an end of two,
[128] Villain.
Griz. Tom Thumb!
Thumb. Rebel!
Griz. Tom Thumb!
Thumb. Hell!
Griz. Huncamunca!
Thumb. Thou hast it there.
Griz. Too sure I feel it.
Thumb. To hell then, like a rebel as you are,
And give my service to the rebels there.
Griz. Triumph not, Thumb, nor think thou shalt enjoy
Thy Huncamunca undisturbed; I 'll send
[129] My ghost to fetch her to the other world;
[130] It shall but bait at heaven, and then return.
[131] But, ha! I feel death rumbling in my brains:
[132] Some kinder sprite knocks softly at my soul,
And gently whispers it to haste away.
I come, I come, most willingly I come.
[133] So when some city wife, for country air,
To Hampstead or to Highgate does repair,
Her to make haste her husband does implore,
And cries, "My dear, the coach is at the door:"
With equal wish, desirous to be gone,
She gets into the coach, and then she cries—"Drive on!"
Thumb. With those last words [134] he vomited his soul,
Which, [135] like whipt cream, the devil will swallow down.
Bear off the body, and cut off the head,
Which I will to the king in triumph lug.
Rebellion 's dead, and now I 'll go to breakfast.

Scene 10.

(*King, Queen, Huncamunca, Courtiers.*)

King. Open the prisons, set the wretched free,
And bid our treasurer disburse six pounds
To pay their debts.—Let no one weep to-day.
Come, Dollallolla; [136] curse that odious name!
It is so long, it asks an hour to speak it.
By heavens! I 'll change it into Doll, or Loll,
Or any other civil monosyllable,
That will not tire my tongue.—Come, sit thee down.

127 *Han.* Are you the chief whom men famed Scipio call?
Scip. Are you the much more famous Hannibal?
Hannibal.

128 Dr. Young seems to have copied this engagement in his *Busiris.*
Myr. Villain!
Mem. Myron!
Myr. Rebel!
Mem. Myron!
Myr. Hell!
Mem. Mandane!

129 This last speech of my Lord Grizzle hath been of great service to our poets:
I 'll hold it fast
As life, and when life's gone I'll hold this last;
And if thou takest it from me when I'm slain,
I'll send my ghost, and fetch it back again.
Conquest of Granada.

130 My soul should with such speed obey,
It should not bait at heaven to stop its way.
Lee seems to have had this last in his eye:
'T was not my purpose, sir, to tarry there;
I would but go to heaven to take the air.
Gloriana.

131 A rising vapor rumbling in my brains.
Cleomenes.

132 Some kind sprite knocks softly at my soul,
To tell me fate 's at hand.

133 Mr. Dryden seems to have had this simile in his eye, when he says,
My soul is packing up, and just on wing.
Conquest of Granada.

134 And in a purple vomit poured his soul.
Cleomenes.

135 The devil swallows vulgar souls
Like whipt cream. *Sebastian.*

136 How I could curse my name of Ptolemy!
It is so long, it asks an hour to write it.
By heaven! I 'll change it into Jove or Mars!
Or any other civil monosyllable,
That will not tire my hand. *Cleomenes.*

Here seated let us view the dancers' sports;
Bid 'em advance. This is the wedding-day
Of Princess Huncamunca and Tom Thumb;
Tom Thumb! who wins two victories [137] to-day,
And this way marches, bearing Grizzle's head.

A dance here.

Nood. Oh! monstrous, dreadful, terrible, Oh! Oh!
Deaf be my ears, for ever blind my eyes!
Dumb be my tongue! feet lame! all senses lost!
[138] Howl wolves, grunt bears, hiss snakes, shriek all ye ghosts!

King. What does the blockhead mean?

Nood. I mean, my liege,
[139] Only to grace my tale with decent horror.
Whilst from my garret, twice two stories high,
I looked abroad into the streets below,
I saw Tom Thumb attended by the mob;
Twice twenty shoe-boys, twice two dozen links,
Chairmen and porters, hackney-coachmen, whores;
Aloft he bore the grizly head of Grizzle;
When of a sudden through the streets there came
A cow, of larger than the usual size,
And in a moment—guess, Oh! guess the rest!—
And in a moment swallowed up Tom Thumb.

King. Shut up again the prisons, bid my treasurer
Not give three farthings out—hang all the culprits,
Guilty or not—no matter.—Ravish virgins:
Go bid the schoolmasters whip all their boys!
Let lawyers, parsons, and physicians loose,
To rob, impose on, and to kill the world.

Nood. Her majesty the queen is in a swoon.

Queen. Not so much in a swoon but I have still
Strength to reward the messenger of ill news.

(*Kills Noodle.*)

Nood. O! I am slain.

Cle. My lover's killed, I will revenge him so.

(*Kills the Queen.*)

Hunc. My mamma killed! vile murderess, beware.

(*Kills Cleora.*)

Dood. This for an old grudge to thy heart.

(*Kills Huncamunca.*)

Must. And this
I drive to thine, O Doodle! for a new one.

(*Kills Doodle.*)

King. Ha! murderess vile, take that.

(*Kills Must.*)

[140] And take thou this.

(*Kills himself, and falls.*)

So when the child, whom nurse from danger guards,
Sends Jack for mustard * with a pack of cards,
Kings, queens, and knaves, throw one another down,
Till the whole pack lies scattered and o'erthrown;
So all our pack upon the floor is cast,
And all I boast is—that I fall the last.

(*Dies.*)

137 Here is a visible conjunction of two days in one, by which our author may have either intended an emblem of a wedding, or to insinuate that men in the honey-moon are apt to imagine time shorter than it is. It brings into my mind a passage in the comedy called *The Coffee-House Politician:*
We will celebrate this day at my house to-morrow.

138 These beautiful phrases are all to be found in one single speech of *King Arthur, or The British Worthy.*

139 I was but teaching him to grace his tale
With decent horror. *Cleomenes.*

140 We may say with Dryden [*Conquest of Granada*]:
Death did at length so many slain forget,
And left the tale, and took them by the great.
I know of no tragedy which comes nearer to this charming and bloody catastrophe than *Cleomenes,* where the curtain covers five principal characters dead on the stage. These lines too—
I asked no questions then, of who killed who?
The bodies tell the story as they lie—
seem to have belonged more properly to this scene of our author; nor can I help imagining they were originally his. *The Rival Ladies* [by Dryden], too, seem beholden to this scene:
We're now a chain of lovers linked in death;
Julia goes first, Gonsalvo hangs on her,
And Angelina hangs upon Gonsalvo,
As I on Angelina.
No scene, I believe, ever received greater honors than this. It was applauded by several encores, a word very unusual in tragedy. And it was very difficult for the actors to escape without a second slaughter. This I take to be a lively assurance of that fierce spirit of liberty which remains among us, and which Mr. Dryden in his *Essay on Dramatic Poetry,* hath observed: "Whether custom," says he, "hath so insinuated itself into our countrymen, or nature hath so formed them to fierceness, I know not; but they will scarcely suffer combats and other objects of horror to be taken from them." And indeed I am for having them encouraged in this martial disposition: nor do I believe our victories over the French have been owing to anything more than to those bloody spectacles daily exhibited in our tragedies, of which the French stage is so entirely clear.

* Apparently a trick or game in which cards are stood up on end and then knocked over.

GEORGE LILLO

THE LONDON MERCHANT: OR, THE HISTORY OF GEORGE BARNWELL

George Lillo (1693–1739), a Netherlander in name and paternity, was outside the main current of literary fashion, being a tradesman and a Dissenter; and therefore, being independent-minded, was in a position to perceive fresh literary subjects, and even to dignify the humdrum pursuit of commerce (I. i, III. i), as Steele had done. He wrote several plays of merit. *Fatal Curiosity*, a rather fine blank-verse tragedy, is the best of all of them; but the most celebrated, original and influential is the play here given.

The modern moral subject of *The London Merchant* (1731) strongly recalls the similar subjects ("The Harlot's Progress," "The Rake's Progress") of several series of paintings by William Hogarth, a London contemporary. But the plot is taken from the old ballad *George Barnwell*, of the mid-seventeenth century or earlier. Lillo sets the time in the reign of Elizabeth, but in essentials follows the original plot closely, even to the names of Barnwell and Millwood; except that in the ballad the former flees the country and is hanged in Poland. There is no reason for believing deviations and additions due to anything but Lillo's invention. His fidelity to the ballad was not quite happy in its results, for it has made the play narrative rather than dramatic in structure, and has almost excluded surprise and suspense (save when Barnwell's theft is made good by Maria, III. iii); the play presents Barnwell's even and almost expected progress from folly to crime after crime, from ensnarement by the harlot's wiles to murder and the gallows. Any possible semblance of the inexorable march of destiny is really due to Barnwell's blind amorousness and flimsy character. Even the introduction of Trueman and Maria makes no important contribution to the plot, for they are hardly more than spectators. Maria contributes a little, it is true, both to suspense and to pathos and dramatic irony; the besotted George might have ended as his master's son-in-law; but even a reader can see that she would never have had a chance with the sensual George against the skilled siren Millwood.

The style and wording may strike some readers as over-literary, stiff and artificial; in fact much of the dialogue, as in Steele's *Conscious Lovers*, is actually in blank verse, though printed as prose. But wholly to condemn the style on such grounds would be uncritical. Dramatic dialogue is no mere transcript of ordinary talk, with all its hesitations, verbosities and inaptnesses, but gives something felt to be better; needless to illustrate from the poetic beauty of Shakespeare's dialogue, the wit of Congreve's, the simplicity stripped to essentials of Pinero's. Their characters would have talked thus if they could. Taste has so changed that few to-day would wish to talk like Lillo's people; but in his day many people did try to do so, and would feel his dialogue to be a fitting beautification of the ordinary. Lillo, conscious of his daring in bespeaking the town's interest for shopkeepers and apprentices, felt such beautification necessary. And indeed, if we can forget the taste of our own day, some of it has beauty.

Much the same is true of the sentiments and the characters. People of the eighteenth century, from Dr. Johnson down, approved sententious expression of moral truths, and also practised it; taste here too has changed, but the truths are none the less true for all that, and one can understand the strengthening of faith in the goodness of the universe which people found in such solemn epigrams when they were the fashion. Lillo and contemporary sentimentalists however did not shut their eyes to vice or the seamy side of human nature, like later, romantic, sentimentalists. The characterization is broad and simple; this agrees with the classic principles then accepted in tragedy, where the persons were not highly individualized but tended to be typical or ideal for their station in life, age and temperament. The dramatic contrasts are of the most obvious, — that of the faithful Trueman with Barnwell, the delicate Maria with Millwood; even the latter's rascally servants by recoiling from murder and by repenting throw into relief the remorseless craft and strength of their mistress. She of course is the outstanding character; there is power in her savage arraignment of unscrupulous man (I. iii, IV. xviii), which even bespeaks a little tolerance for her, and in her despairing end; and in writing the scenes (I. v, viii, II. ix) where she seduces Barnwell, rarer in literature than the seduction of a woman by a man, assuredly Lillo was not over-delicate. Compared with her, Barnwell is a shadow, though not unlifelike; at first as much a moralizer as any (which shows how little moralizing was worth), and yielding with his eyes open to every temptation. Yet understanding readers have found his last long speech impressive (V. x). Such eminent actors as Sir Henry Irving (1838–1905) and Mrs. Siddons (1755–

1831), in their youth but while playing leading parts in other important dramas, played Barnwell and Millwood.

The London Merchant is a "domestic tragedy," a type of play which disregards the principle of Aristotle and other Greeks, followed by moderns, that tragedy deals with characters of rank and of heroic magnitude. This principle undoubtedly secures a grandeur which can be got in no other way; but domestic tragedies may come home to our bosoms more intimately. As noticed earlier in this book, there were a few of them in English before Lillo, notably Heywood's *A Woman Killed with Kindness*, a few among anonymous Elizabethan plays, and some plays by Otway and Rowe. But Lillo's play is on a more prosaic level of style and in a humbler walk of society. In spite of the contemporary esteem it won, only one other such play reached eminence in that generation, — Edward Moore's *Gamester* (1753). Lillo's influence was greater in France, and especially in Germany. It is needless to say that, largely owing to the influence of Ibsen, tragedies dealing with the struggles and ruin of ordinary people are one of the features of the drama in our own day. However great or small his direct influence, Lillo has distinction as a forerunner.

THE LONDON MERCHANT: OR, THE HISTORY OF GEORGE BARNWELL

PROLOGUE

Spoke by Mr. Cibber, Jun.

The Tragic Muse, sublime, delights to show
Princes distrest and scenes of royal woe;
In awful pomp, majestic, to relate
The fall of nations or some hero's fate;
That scepter'd chiefs may by example know
The strange vicissitude of things below:
What dangers on security attend;
How pride and cruelty in ruin end;
Hence Providence supreme to know, and own
Humanity, adds glory to a throne.
 In every former age and foreign tongue
With native grandeur thus the Goddess sung.
Upon our stage indeed, with wish'd success,
You've sometimes seen her in a humbler dress—
Great only in distress. When she complains
In *Southern's, Rowe's,* or *Otway's* moving strains,
The brilliant drops that fall from each bright eye
The absent pomp with brighter gems supply.
Forgive us then, if we attempt to show,
In artless strains, a tale of private woe.
A *London* 'Prentice ruin'd is our theme,
Drawn from the fam'd old song that bears his name.
We hope your taste is not so high to scorn
A moral tale, esteem'd ere you were born;
Which, for a century of rolling years,
Has fill'd a thousand-thousand eyes with tears.
If thoughtless youth to warn, and shame the age
From vice destructive, well becomes the stage;
If this example innocence secure,
Prevent our guilt, or by reflection cure;
If *Millwood's* dreadful guilt and sad despair
Commend the virtue of the good and fair:
Though art be wanting, and our numbers fail,
Indulge th' attempt in justice to the tale!

DRAMATIS PERSONAE

MEN

THOROWGOOD	Mr. Bridgwater
BARNWELL, *uncle to* GEORGE	Mr. Roberts
GEORGE BARNWELL	Mr. Cibber, *Jun.*
TRUEMAN	Mr. W. Mills
BLUNT	Mr. R. Wetherilt
[JAILER	
JOHN]	

WOMEN

MARIA	Mrs. Cibber
MILLWOOD	Mrs. Butler
LUCY	Mrs. Charke

Officers with their Attendants, Keeper, and Footmen.

SCENE: London, and an adjacent Village.

ACT I.

Scene I. *A Room in Thorowgood's House.*

Enter Thorowgood and Trueman.

Trueman. Sir, the packet from Genoa is arrived. (*Gives letters.*)

Thorowgood. Heaven be praised, the storm that threatened our royal mistress, pure religion, liberty and laws, is for a time diverted; the haughty and revengeful Spaniard, disappointed of the loan on which he depended from Genoa, must now attend the slow return of wealth from his new world, to supply his empty coffers, ere he can execute his purposed invasion of our happy island; by which means time is gained to make such preparations on our part as may, Heaven concurring, prevent [1] his malice, or turn the meditated mischief on himself.

True. He must be insensible indeed, who is not affected when the safety of his country is concerned.—Sir, may I know by what means—if I am too bold—

Thor. Your curiosity is laudable; and I gratify it with the greater pleasure, because from thence you may learn how honest merchants, as such, may sometimes contribute to the safety of their country, as they do at all times to its happiness; that if hereafter you should be tempted to any action that has the appearance of vice or meanness in it, upon reflecting on the dignity of our profession, you may with honest scorn reject whatever is unworthy of it.

True. Should Barnwell, or I, who have the benefit of your example, by our ill conduct bring any imputation on that honorable name, we must be left without excuse.

Thor. You compliment, young man. (*Trueman bows respectfully.*) Nay, I'm not offended. As the name of merchant never degrades the gentleman, so by no means does it exclude him; only take heed not to purchase the character of complaisant at the expense of your sincerity.—But to answer your question. The bank of Genoa had agreed, at excessive interest and on good security, to advance the King of Spain a sum of money sufficient to equip his vast Armada; of which our peerless Elizabeth (more than in name the Mother of her People) being well informed, sent Walsingham, her wise and faithful secretary, to consult the merchants of this loyal city, who all agreed to direct their several agents to influence, if possible, the Genoese to break their contract with the Spanish court. 'T is done; the state and bank of Genoa, having maturely weighed and rightly judged of their true interest, prefer the friendship of the merchants of London to that of a monarch who proudly styles himself King of both Indies.

True. Happy success of prudent counsels! What an expense of blood and treasure is here saved! Excellent Queen! O how unlike to former princes, who made the danger of foreign enemies a pretense to oppress their subjects by taxes great and grievous to be borne.

Thor. Not so our gracious Queen, whose richest exchequer is her people's love, as their happiness her greatest glory.

True. On these terms to defend us, is to make our protection a benefit worthy her who confers it, and well worth our acceptance.—Sir, have you any commands for me at this time?

Thor. Only to look carefully over the files to see whether there are any tradesmen's bills unpaid; and if there are, to send and discharge 'em. We must not let artificers lose their time, so useful to the public and their families, in unnecessary attendance. (*Exit Trueman.*)

Scene II.

Thorowgood and Maria.

Thorowgood. Well, Maria, have you given orders for the entertainment? I would have it in some measure worthy the guests. Let there be plenty, and of the best; that the courtiers, though they should deny us citizens politeness,[2] may at least commend our hospitality.

Maria. Sir, I have endeavored not to wrong your well-known generosity by an ill-timed parsimony.

Thor. Nay, 'twas a needless caution; I have no cause to doubt your prudence.

Ma. Sir, I find myself unfit for conversation at present; I should but increase the number of the company without adding to their satisfaction.

Thor. Nay, my child, this melancholy must not be indulged.

Ma. Company will but increase it. I wish you would dispense with [3] my ab-

1 Anticipate. 2 Elegance. 3 Put up with.

sence; solitude best suits my present temper.

Thor. You are not insensible that it is chiefly on your account these noble lords do me the honor so frequently to grace my board; should you be absent, the disappointment may make them repent their condescension, and think their labor lost.

Ma. He that shall think his time or honor lost in visiting you can set no real value on your daughter's company, whose only merit is that she is yours. The man of quality, who chooses to converse with a gentleman and merchant of your worth and character may confer honor by so doing, but he loses none.

Thor. Come, come, Maria; I need not tell you that a young gentleman may prefer your conversation to mine, yet intend me no disrespect at all; for, though he may lose no honor in my company, 't is very natural for him to expect more pleasure in yours. I remember the time when the company of the greatest and wisest man in the kingdom would have been insipid and tiresome to me, if it had deprived me of an opportunity of enjoying your mother's.

Ma. Yours no doubt was as agreeable to her; for generous minds know no pleasure in society but where 't is mutual.

Thor. Thou know'st I have no heir, no child but thee; the fruits of many years' successful industry must all be thine. Now, it would give me pleasure great as my love, to see on whom you would bestow it. I am daily solicited by men of the greatest rank and merit for leave to address you; but I have hitherto declined it, in hopes that by observation I should learn which way your inclination tends; for, as I know love to be essential to happiness in the marriage state, I had rather my approbation should confirm your choice than direct it.

Ma. What can I say? How shall I answer, as I ought, this tenderness, so uncommon even in the best of parents? But you are without example; yet had you been less indulgent, I had been most wretched. That I look on the crowd of courtiers that visit here with equal esteem, but equal indifference, you have observed, and I must needs confess; yet had you asserted your authority, and insisted on a parent's right to be obeyed, I had submitted, and to my duty sacrificed my peace.

Thor. From your perfect obedience in every other instance, I feared as much; and therefore would leave you without a bias in an affair wherein your happiness is so immediately concerned.

Ma. Whether from a want of that just ambition that would become your daughter, or from some other cause, I know not; but I find high birth and titles don't recommend the man who owns them to my affections.

Thor. I would not that they should, unless his merit recommends him more. A noble birth and fortune, though they make not a bad man good, yet they are a real advantage to a worthy one, and place his virtues in the fairest light.

Ma. I cannot answer for my inclinations, but they shall ever be submitted to your wisdom and authority; and, as you will not compel me to marry where I cannot love, so love shall never make me act contrary to my duty. Sir, have I your permission to retire?

Thor. I'll see you to your chamber. (*Exeunt.*)

Scene III.

A Room in Millwood's House.

Millwood at her toilet. Lucy, waiting.

Millwood. How do I look today, Lucy?

Lucy. O, killingly, madam! A little more red, and you 'll be irresistible! But why this more than ordinary care of your dress and complexion? What new conquest are you aiming at?

Mill. A conquest would be new indeed!

Lucy. Not to you, who make 'em every day, but to me.—Well! 'tis what I 'm never to expect, unfortunate as I am. But your wit and beauty—

Mill. First made me a wretch, and still continue me so. Men, however generous or sincere to one another, are all selfish hypocrites in their affairs with us. We are no otherwise esteemed or regarded by them, but as we contribute to their satisfaction.

Lucy. You are certainly, madam, on the wrong side in this argument. Is not the expense all theirs? And I am sure it is our own fault, if we haven't our share of the pleasure.

Mill. We are but slaves to men.

Lucy. Nay, 'tis they that are slaves most certainly; for we lay them under contribution.

Mill. Slaves have no property; no, not even in themselves. All is the victor's.

Lucy. You are strangely arbitrary in your principles, madam.

Mill. I would have my conquests complete, like those of the Spaniards in the New World: who first plundered the natives of all the wealth they had, and then condemned the wretches to the mines for life to work for more.

Lucy. Well, I shall never approve of your scheme of government; I should think it much more politic, as well as just, to find my subjects an easier employment.

Mill. It 's a general maxim among the knowing part of mankind, that a woman without virtue, like a man without honor or honesty, is capable of any action, though never so vile; and yet what pains will they not take, what arts not use, to seduce us from our innocence, and make us contemptible and wicked, even in their own opinions! Then is it not just, the villains, to their cost, should find us so?—But guilt makes them suspicious, and keeps them on their guard; therefore we can take advantage only of the young and innocent part of the sex, who, having never injured women, apprehend no injury from them.

Lucy. Ay, they must be young indeed.

Mill. Such a one, I think, I have found.—As I 've passed through the City, I have often observed him receiving and paying considerable sums of money; from thence I conclude he is employed in affairs of consequence.

Lucy. Is he handsome?

Mill. Ay, ay, the stripling is well made.

Lucy. About—

Mill. Eighteen.

Lucy. Innocent, handsome, and about eighteen.—You 'll be vastly happy.—Why, if you manage well, you may keep him to yourself these two or three years.

Mill. If I manage well, I shall have done with him much sooner. Having long had a design on him; and, meeting him yesterday, I made a full stop, and gazing wishfully on his face, asked him his name; he blushed, and bowing very low, answered: 'George Barnwell.' I begged his pardon for the freedom I had taken, and told him that he was the person I had long wished to see, and to whom I had an affair of importance to communicate at a proper time and place. He named a tavern; I talked of honor and reputation, and invited him to my house: he swallowed the bait, promised to come, and this is the time I expect him. (*Knocking at the door.*) Somebody knocks—d' ye hear? I am at home to nobody today but him. (*Exit Lucy.*)

Scene IV.

Millwood.

Millwood. Less affairs must give way to those of more consequence; and I am strangely mistaken if this does not prove of great importance to me and him too, before I have done with him.—Now, after what manner shall I receive him? Let me consider—what manner of person am I to receive? He is young, innocent, and bashful; therefore I must take care not to shock him at first.—But then, if I have any skill in physiognomy, he is amorous, and, with a little assistance, will soon get the better of his modesty.—I'll trust to nature, who does wonders in these matters.—If to seem what one is not, in order to be the better liked for what one really is; if to speak one thing, and mean the direct contrary, be art in a woman,—I know nothing of nature.

Scene V.

Millwood. To her Barnwell, bowing very low. Lucy at a distance.

Millwood. Sir! the surprise and joy—

Barnwell. Madam—

Mill. (*Advancing.*) This is such a favor—

Barn. (*Still advances.*) Pardon me, madam—

Mill. So unhoped for—(*Barnwell salutes her, and retires in confusion.*) To see you here!—Excuse the confusion—

Barn. I fear I am too bold.

Mill. Alas, sir! All my apprehensions proceed from my fears of your thinking me so.—Please, sir, to sit.—I am as much at a loss how to receive this honor as I ought, as I am surprised at your goodness in conferring it.

Barn. I thought you had expected me—I promised to come.

Mill. That is the more surprising; few men are such religious observers of their word.

Barn. All who are honest are.

Mill. To one another.—But we silly women are seldom thought of consequence enough to gain a place in your remembrance.

(*Laying her hand on his, as if by accident.*)

Barn. (*Aside.*) Her disorder is so great, she don't perceive she has laid her hand on mine.—Heaven! how she trembles!—What can this mean?

Mill. The interest I have in all that relates to you (the reason of which you shall know hereafter) excites my curiosity; and, were I sure you would pardon my presumption, I should desire to know your real sentiments on a very particular affair.

Barn. Madam, you may command my poor thoughts on any subject; I have none that I would conceal.

Mill. You 'll think me bold.

Barn. No, indeed.

Mill. What then are your thoughts of love?

Barn. If you mean the love of women, I have not thought of it [at] all.—My youth and circumstances make such thoughts improper in me yet. But if you mean the general love we owe to mankind, I think no one has more of it in his temper than myself.—I don't know that person in the world whose happiness I don't wish, and wouldn't promote, were it in my power.—In an especial manner I love my uncle, and my master, but, above all, my friend.

Mill. You have a friend then whom you love?

Barn. As he does me, sincerely.

Mill. He is, no doubt, often blessed with your company and conversation?

Barn. We live in one house together, and both serve the same worthy merchant.

Mill. Happy, happy youth! Whoe'er thou art, I envy thee, and so must all who see and know this youth. What have I lost, by being formed a woman! I hate my sex, myself. Had I been a man, I might, perhaps, have been as happy in your friendship, as he who now enjoys it; but, as it is— Oh!

Barn. (*Aside.*) I never observed women before, or this is sure the most beautiful of her sex! You seem disordered, madam! May I know the cause?

Mill. Do not ask me,—I can never speak it, whatever is the cause.—I wish for things impossible.—I would be a servant, bound to the same master as you are, to live in one house with you.

Barn. (*Aside.*) How strange, and yet how kind, her words and actions are! And the effect they have on me is as strange. I feel desires I never knew before;—I must be gone, while I have power to go. Madam, I humbly take my leave.

Mill. You will not sure leave me so soon!

Barn. Indeed I must.

Mill. You cannot be so cruel!—I have prepared a poor supper, at which I promised myself your company.

Barn. I am sorry I must refuse the honor that you designed me—but my duty to my master calls me hence. I never yet neglected his service; he is so gentle, and so good a master, that, should I wrong him, though he might forgive me, I never should forgive myself.

Mill. Am I refused, by the first man, the second favor I ever stooped to ask?—Go then, thou proud hard-hearted youth! But know, you are the only man that could be found, who would let me sue twice for greater favors.

Barn. What shall I do!—How shall I go or stay!

Mill. Yet do not, do not, leave me! I wish my sex's pride would meet your scorn:—But when I look upon you,—when I behold those eyes,—Oh! spare my tongue, and let my blushes speak.—This flood of tears to that will force their way, and declare—what woman's modesty should hide.

Barn. Oh, heavens! she loves me, worthless as I am; her looks, her words, her flowing tears confess it;—and can I leave her then?—Oh, never, never!—Madam, dry up those tears! You shall command me always; I will stay here for ever, if you 'd have me.

Lucy. (*Aside.*) So! she has wheedled him out of his virtue of obedience already, and will strip him of all the rest, one after another, till she has left him as few as her ladyship, or myself.

Mill. Now you are kind, indeed; but I mean not to detain you always. I would have you shake off all slavish obedience to your master; but you may serve him still.

Lucy. (*Aside.*) Serve him still!—Aye, or he 'll have no opportunity of fingering his cash, and then he 'll not serve your end, I 'll be sworn.

Scene VI.

To them, Blunt.

Blunt. Madam, supper 's on the table.

Mill. Come, sir, you 'll excuse all defects.—My thoughts were too much employed on my guest to observe the entertainment. (*Exeunt Millwood and Barnwell.*)

Scene VII.

Lucy and Blunt.

Blunt. What! is all this preparation, this elegant supper, variety of wines, and music, for the entertainment of that young fellow?

Lucy. So it seems.

Blunt. What! is our mistress turned fool at last? She 's in love with him, I suppose.

Lucy. I suppose not; but she designs to make him in love with her, if she can.

Blunt. What will she get by that? He seems under age, and can't be supposed to have much money.

Lucy. But his master has; and that 's the same thing, as she 'll manage it.

Blunt. I don't like this fooling with a handsome young fellow; while she 's endeavoring to ensnare him, she may be caught herself.

Lucy. Nay, were she like me, that would certainly be the consequence; for, I confess, there is something in youth and innocence that moves me mightily.

Blunt. Yes, so does the smoothness and plumpness of a partridge move a mighty desire in the hawk to be the destruction of it.

Lucy. Why, birds are their prey, as men are ours; though, as you observed, we are sometimes caught ourselves; but that I dare say will never be the case with our mistress.

Blunt. I wish it may prove so; for you know we all depend upon her. Should she trifle away her time with a young fellow, that there 's nothing to be got by, we must all starve.

Lucy. There 's no danger of that, for I am sure she has no view in this affair but interest.

Blunt. Well, and what hopes are there of success in that?

Lucy. The most promising that can be. 'T is true, the youth has his scruples; but she 'll soon teach him to answer them, by stifling his conscience. O, the lad is in a hopeful way, depend upon 't. (*Exeunt.*)

Scene VIII.

Barnwell and Millwood at an entertainment.

Barnwell. What can I answer? All that I know is, that you are fair, and I am miserable.

Millwood. We are both so, and yet the fault is in ourselves.

Barn. To ease our present anguish, by plunging into guilt, is to buy a moment's pleasure with an age of pain.

Mill. I should have thought the joys of love as lasting as they are great. If ours prove otherwise, 't is your inconstancy must make them so.

Barn. The law of Heaven will not be reversed; and that requires us to govern our passions.

Mill. To give us sense of beauty and desires, and yet forbid us to taste and be happy, is cruelty to nature.—Have we passions only to torment us?

Barn. To hear you talk, though in the cause of vice—to gaze upon your beauty —press your hand—and see your snow-white bosom heave and fall—enflames my wishes. My pulse beats high—my senses all are in a hurry, and I am on the rack of wild desire. Yet, for a moment's guilty pleasure, shall I lose my innocence, my peace of mind, and hopes of solid happiness?

Mill. Chimeras all!—Come on with me and prove:
No joy 's like woman kind, nor Heaven like love.

Barn. I would not, yet must on.—
Reluctant thus, the merchant quits his ease,
And trusts to rocks, and sands, and stormy seas;
In hopes some unknown golden coast to find,
Commits himself, though doubtful, to the wind;
Longs much for joys to come, yet mourns those left behind.

The End of the First Act.

ACT II.

Scene I. *A Room in Thorowgood's House.*

Enter Barnwell.

Barnwell. How strange are all things round me! Like some thief, who treads forbidden ground, fearful I enter each apartment of this well-known house. To guilty love, as if that was too little, already have I added breach of trust.—A thief!—Can I know myself that wretched thing, and look my honest friend and injured master in the face? Though hypocrisy may a while conceal my guilt, at length it will be known, and public shame and ruin must ensue. In the mean time, what must be my life? Ever to speak a language foreign to my heart; hourly to add to the number of my crimes in order to conceal 'em.—Sure, such was the condition of the grand apostate, when first he lost his purity; like me, disconsolate he wandered, and, while yet in Heaven, bore all his future Hell about him.

(*Enter Trueman.*)

Scene II.

Barnwell and Trueman.

Trueman. Barnwell! O how I rejoice to see you safe! So will our master and his gentle daughter, who during your absence often inquired after you.

Barnwell. (*Aside.*) Would he were gone! His officious love will pry into the secrets of my soul.

True. Unless you knew the pain the whole family has felt on your account, you can't conceive how much you are beloved. But why thus cold and silent? When my heart is full of joy for your return, why do you turn away? why thus avoid me? What have I done? how am I altered since you saw me last? Or rather, what have you done? and why are you thus changed, for I am still the same.

Barn. (*Aside.*) What have I done, indeed?

True. Not speak nor look upon me!

Barn. (*Aside.*) By my face he will discover all I would conceal; methinks, already I begin to hate him.

True. I cannot bear this usage from a friend—one whom till now I ever found so loving, whom yet I love, though this unkindness strikes at the root of friendship, and might destroy it in any breast but mine.

Barn. (*Turning to him.*) I am not well. Sleep has been a stranger to these eyes since you beheld them last.

True. Heavy they look indeed, and swoln with tears;—now they o'erflow. Rightly did my sympathizing heart forbode last night, when thou wast absent, something fatal to our peace.

Barn. Your friendship engages you too far. My troubles, whate'er they are, are mine alone; you have no interest in them, nor ought your concern for me give you a moment's pain.

True. You speak as if you knew of friendship nothing but the name. Before I saw your grief I felt it. Since we parted last I have slept no more than you, but pensive in my chamber sat alone, and spent the tedious night in wishes for your safety and return; e'en now, though ignorant of the cause, your sorrow wounds me to the heart.

Barn. 'T will not be always thus. Friendship and all engagements cease, as circumstances and occasions vary; and, since you once may hate me, perhaps it might be better for us both that now you loved me less.

True. Sure, I but dream! Without a cause would Barnwell use me thus? Ungenerous and ungrateful youth, farewell! —I shall endeavor to follow your advice. (*Going.*) (*Aside.*) Yet stay, perhaps I am too rash, and angry when the cause demands compassion. Some unforeseen calamity may have befallen him, too great to bear.

Barn. (*Aside.*) What part am I reduced to act! 'T is vile and base to move his temper thus—the best of friends and men!

True. I am to blame; prithee forgive me, Barnwell!—Try to compose your ruffled mind; and let me know the cause that thus transports you from yourself: my friendly counsel may restore your peace.

Barn. All that is possible for man to do for man, your generous friendship may effect; but here even that 's in vain.

True. Something dreadful is laboring in your breast. O give it vent, and let me share your grief; 't will ease your pain, should it admit no cure, and make it lighter by the part I bear.

Barn. Vain supposition! My woes increase by being observed; should the cause be known, they would exceed all bounds.

True. So well I know thy honest heart, guilt cannot harbor there.

Barn. (*Aside.*) O torture insupportable!

True. Then why am I excluded? Have I a thought I would conceal from you?

Barn. If still you urge me on this hated subject, I 'll never enter more beneath this roof, nor see your face again.

True. 'T is strange—but I have done. Say but you hate me not!

Barn. Hate you! I am not that monster yet.

True. Shall our friendship still continue?

Barn. It 's a blessing I never was worthy of; yet now must stand on terms, and but upon conditions can confirm it.

True. What are they?

Barn. Never hereafter, though you should wonder at my conduct, desire to know more than I am willing to reveal.

True. 'T is hard; but upon any conditions I must be your friend.

Barn. Then, as much as one lost to himself can be another's, I am yours.

(*Embracing.*)

True. Be ever so, and may Heaven restore your peace!

Barn. Will yesterday return? We have heard the glorious sun, that till then incessant rolled, once stopped his rapid course, and once went back. The dead have risen, and parched rocks poured forth a liquid stream to quench a people's thirst; the sea divided, and formed walls of water, while a whole nation passed in safety through its sandy bosom; hungry lions have refused their prey, and men unhurt have walked amidst consuming flames. But never yet did time, once past, return.

True. Though the continued chain of time has never once been broke, nor ever will, but uninterrupted must keep on its course, till lost in eternity it ends there where it first begun: yet, as Heaven can repair whatever evils time can bring upon us, he who trusts Heaven ought never to despair. But business requires our attendance—business, the youth's best preservative from ill, as idleness his worst of snares. Will you go with me?

Barn. I'll take a little time to reflect on what has passed, and follow you.

(*Exit Trueman.*)

Scene III.

Barnwell.

Barnwell. I might have trusted Trueman to have applied to my uncle to have repaired the wrong I have done my master,—but what of Millwood? Must I expose her too? Ungenerous and base! Then Heaven requires it not.—But Heaven requires that I forsake her. What! never see her more! Does Heaven require that?—I hope I may see her, and Heaven not be offended. Presumptuous hope—dearly already have I proved my frailty; should I once more tempt Heaven, I may be left to fall never to rise again. Yet shall I leave her, forever leave her, and not let her know the cause? She who loves me with such a boundless passion—can cruelty be duty? I judge of what she then must feel by what I now endure. The love of life and fear of shame, opposed by inclination strong as death or shame, like wind and tide in raging conflict met, when neither can prevail, keep me in doubt. How then can I determine?

Scene IV.

Enter Thorowgood.

Thorowgood and Barnwell.

Thorowgood. Without a cause assigned, or notice given, to absent yourself last night was a fault, young man, and I came to chide you for it, but hope I am prevented.[4] That modest blush, the confusion so visible in your face, speak grief and shame. When we have offended Heaven, it requires no more; and shall man, who needs himself to be forgiven, be harder to appease? If my pardon or love be of moment to your peace, look up, secure of both.

Barnwell. (*Aside.*) This goodness has o'ercome me.—O sir! you know not the nature and extent of my offense; and I should abuse your mistaken bounty to receive 'em. Though I had rather die than speak my shame; though racks could not have forced the guilty secret from my breast, your kindness has.

Thor. Enough, enough, whate'er it be, this concern shows you 're convinced, and I am satisfied. (*Aside.*) How painful is the sense of guilt to an ingenuous mind—some youthful folly which it were prudent not to enquire into.—When we consider the frail condition of humanity, it may raise our pity, not our wonder, that youth should go astray: when reason, weak at the best when opposed to inclination, scarce formed, and wholly unassisted by experience, faintly contends, or willingly becomes the slave of sense. The state of youth is much to be deplored;

4 Anticipated.

and the more so, because they see it not: they being then to danger most exposed, when they are least prepared for their defense.

Barn. It will be known, and you recall your pardon and abhor me.

Thor. I never will; so Heaven confirm to me the pardon of my offenses! Yet be upon your guard in this gay, thoughtless season of your life; now, when the sense of pleasure 's quick, and passion high, the voluptuous appetites raging and fierce demand the strongest curb, take heed of a relapse: when vice becomes habitual, the very power of leaving it is lost.

Barn. Hear me, then, on my knees confess—

Thor. I will not hear a syllable more upon this subject; it were not mercy, but cruelty, to hear what must give you such torment to reveal.

Barn. This generosity amazes and distracts me.

Thor. This remorse makes thee dearer to me than if thou hadst never offended; whatever is your fault, of this I 'm certain: 't was harder for you to offend than me to pardon. (*Exit.*)

Scene V.

Barnwell.

Barnwell. Villain, villain, villain! basely to wrong so excellent a man! Should I again return to folly—detested thought—but what of Millwood then?—Why, I renounce her;—I give her up:—the struggle 's over and virtue has prevailed. Reason may convince, but gratitude compels. This unlooked-for generosity has saved me from destruction. (*Going.*)

Scene VI.

Barnwell. To him a Footman.

Footman. Sir, two ladies from your uncle in the country desire to see you.

Barn. (*Aside.*) Who should they be?—Tell them I 'll wait upon 'em.

(*Exit Footman.*)

Scene VII.

Barnwell.

Barnwell. Methinks I dread to see 'em. Guilt, what a coward hast thou made me! Now everything alarms me.

Scene VIII.

Another Room in Thorowgood's House.

Millwood and Lucy; and to them a Footman.

Footman. Ladies, he 'll wait upon you immediately.

Millwood. 'T is very well.—I thank you.

(*Exit Footman.*)

Scene IX.

Millwood and Lucy.

Enter Barnwell.

Barnwell. Confusion! Millwood!

Millwood. That angry look tells me that here I 'm an unwelcome guest. I feared as much—the unhappy are so everywhere.

Barn. Will nothing but my utter ruin content you?

Mill. Unkind and cruel! Lost myself, your happiness is now my only care.

Barn. How did you gain admission?

Mill. Saying we were desired by your uncle to visit and deliver a message to you, we were received by the family without suspicion, and with much respect directed here.

Barn. Why did you come at all?

Mill. I never shall trouble you more; I 'm come to take my leave for ever. Such is the malice of my fate. I go hopeless, despairing ever to return. This hour is all I have left me. One short hour is all I have to bestow on love and you, for whom I thought the longest life too short.

Barn. Then we are met to part for ever?

Mill. It must be so—yet think not that time or absence ever shall put a period to my grief or make me love you less; though I must leave you, yet condemn me not!

Barn. Condemn you? No, I approve your resolution, and rejoice to hear it. 'T is just; 't is necessary; I have well weighed, and found it so.

Lucy. (*Aside.*) I 'm afraid the young man has more sense than she thought he had.

Barn. Before you came, I had determined never to see you more.

Mill. (*Aside.*) Confusion!

Lucy. (*Aside.*) Ay! we are all out; this is a turn so unexpected, that I shall make nothing of my part; they must e'en play the scene betwixt themselves.

Mill. 'T was some relief to think, though absent, you would love me still. But to find, though fortune had been kind, that you, more cruel and inconstant, had resolved to cast me off—this, as I never could expect, I have not learnt to bear.

Barn. I am sorry to hear you blame in me a resolution that so well becomes us both.

Mill. I have reason for what I do, but you have none.

Barn. Can we want a reason for parting, who have so many to wish we never had met?

Mill. Look on me, Barnwell! Am I deformed or old, that satiety so soon succeeds enjoyment? Nay, look again, am I not she whom yesterday you thought the fairest and the kindest of her sex? whose hand, trembling with ecstasy, you pressed and moulded[5] thus, while on my eyes you gazed with such delight, as if desire increased by being fed?

Barn. No more; let me repent my former follies, if possible, without remembering what they were.

Mill. Why?

Barn. Such is my frailty that 't is dangerous.

Mill. Where is the danger, since we are to part?

Barn. The thought of that already is too painful.

Mill. If it be painful to part, then I may hope at least you do not hate me?

Barn. No—no—I never said I did.—O my heart!—

Mill. Perhaps you pity me?

Barn. I do—I do—indeed, I do.

Mill. You 'll think upon me?

Barn. Doubt it not, while I can think at all!

Mill. You may judge an embrace at parting too great a favor, though it would be the last? (*He draws back.*) A look shall then suffice—farewell for ever.

(*Exit with Lucy.*)

Scene X.

Barnwell.

Barnwell. If to resolve to suffer be to conquer, I have conquered. Painful victory!

Scene XI.

Reënter Millwood and Lucy.

Barnwell, Millwood and Lucy.

Millwood. One thing I had forgot: I never must return to my own house again. This I thought proper to let you know, lest your mind should change, and you should seek in vain to find me there. Forgive this second intrusion; I only came to give you this caution; and that perhaps was needless.

Barnwell. I hope it was; yet it is kind, and I must thank you for it.

Mill. (*To Lucy.*) My friend, your arm.—Now I am gone for ever. (*Going.*)

Barn. One thing more: sure, there 's no danger in my knowing where you go?—If you think otherwise—

Mill. (*Weeping.*) Alas!

Lucy. (*Aside.*) We are right, I find; that 's my cue. Ah; dear sir, she 's going she knows not whither; but go she must.

Barn. Humanity obliges me to wish you well: why will you thus expose yourself to needless troubles?

Lucy. Nay, there 's no help for it. She must quit the town immediately, and the kingdom as soon as possible; it was no small matter, you may be sure, that could make her resolve to leave you.

Mill. No more, my friend; since he for whose dear sake alone I suffer, and am content to suffer, is kind and pities me. Where'er I wander through wilds and deserts, benighted and forlorn, that thought shall give me comfort.

Barn. For my sake! O tell me how; which way am I so cursed as to bring such ruin on thee?

Mill. No matter, I am contented with my lot.

Barn. Leave me not in this uncertainty!

Mill. I have said too much.

Barn. How, how am I the cause of your undoing?

Mill. 'T will but increase your troubles.

Barn. My troubles can't be greater than they are.

Lucy. Well, well, sir; if she won't satisfy you, I will.

Barn. I am bound to you beyond expression.

Mill. Remember, sir, that I desired you not to hear it.

5 Fondled.

Barn. Begin, and ease my racking expectation!

Lucy. Why, you must know, my lady here was an only child; but her parents, dying while she was young, left her and her fortune (no inconsiderable one, I assure you) to the care of a gentleman who has a good estate of his own.

Mill. Ay, ay, the barbarous man is rich enough—but what are riches when compared to love?

Lucy. For a while he performed the office of a faithful guardian, settled her in a house, hired her servants—but you have seen in what manner she lived, so I need say no more of that.

Mill. How I shall live hereafter, Heaven knows!

Lucy. All things went on as one could wish, till, some time ago, his wife dying, he fell violently in love with his charge, and would fain have married her. Now, the man is neither old nor ugly, but a good personable sort of a man; but I don't know how it was she could never endure him. In short, her ill-usage so provoked him, that he brought in an account of his executorship, wherein he makes her debtor to him—

Mill. A trifle in itself, but more than enough to ruin me, whom, by this unjust account, he had stripped of all before.

Lucy. Now, she having neither money, nor friend, except me, who am as unfortunate as herself, he compelled her to pass his account, and give bond for the sum he demanded; but still provided handsomely for her, and continued his courtship, till, being informed by his spies (truly I suspect some in her own family) that you were entertained at her house, and stayed with her all night, he came this morning raving and storming like a madman; talks no more of marriage—so there 's no hopes of making up matters that way—but vows her ruin, unless she 'll allow him the same favor that he supposes she granted you.

Barn. Must she be ruined, or find her refuge in another's arms?

Mill. He gave me but an hour to resolve in. That 's happily spent with you—and now I go.—

Barn. To be exposed to all the rigors of the various seasons, the summer's parching heat, and winter's cold; unhoused to wander friendless through the unhospitable world, in misery and want, attended with fear and danger, and pursued by malice and revenge—would'st thou endure all this for me, and can I do nothing, nothing to prevent it?

Lucy. 'T is really a pity there can be no way found out!

Barn. O where are all my resolutions now? Like early vapors, or the morning dew, chased by the sun's warm beams, they 're vanished and lost, as though they had never been.

Lucy. Now I advised her, sir, to comply with the gentleman; that would not only put an end to her troubles, but make her fortune at once.

Barn. Tormenting fiend, away!—I had rather perish, nay, see her perish, than have her saved by him; I will myself prevent her ruin, though with my own.—A moment's patience; I 'll return immediately. (*Exit.*)

Scene XII.

Millwood and Lucy.

Lucy. 'T was well you came; or, by what I can perceive, you had lost him.

Millwood. That, I must confess, was a danger I did not foresee; I was only afraid he should have come without money. You know a house of entertainment like mine is not kept with nothing.

Lucy. That 's very true; but then you should be reasonable in your demands; 't is pity to discourage a young man.

Scene XIII.

Enter Barnwell with a bag of money.

Millwood and Lucy.

Barnwell. (*Aside.*) What am I about to do!—Now you, who boast your reason all-sufficient, suppose yourselves in my condition, and determine for me: whether it 's right to let her suffer for my faults, or, by this small addition to my guilt, prevent the ill effects of what is past.

Lucy. These young sinners think everything in the ways of wickedness so strange; but I could tell him that this is nothing but what 's very common; for one vice as naturally begets another, as a father a son. But he 'll find out that himself, if he lives long enough.

Barn. Here, take this, and with it purchase your deliverance; return to your house, and live in peace and safety.

Mill. So I may hope to see you there again.

Barn. Answer me not, but fly—lest, in the agonies of my remorse, I take again what is not mine to give, and abandon thee to want and misery!

Mill. Say but you 'll come!

Barn. You are my fate, my heaven, or my hell; only leave me now, dispose of me hereafter as you please.

(*Exeunt Millwood and Lucy.*)

Scene XIV.

Barnwell.

Barnwell. What have I done!—Were my resolutions founded on reason, and sincerely made—why then has Heaven suffered me to fall? I sought not the occasion; and, if my heart deceives me not, compassion and generosity were my motives.—Is virtue inconsistent with itself, or are vice and virtue only empty names? Or do they depend on accidents, beyond our power to produce or to prevent—wherein we have no part, and yet must be determined by the event? But why should I attempt to reason? All is confusion, horror, and remorse: I find I am lost, cast down from all my late erected hopes, and plunged again in guilt, yet scarce know how or why—

Such undistinguished horrors make my brain,
Like Hell, the seat of darkness and of pain.

The End of the Second Act.

ACT III.

Scene I. *A Room in Thorowgood's House.*

Thorowgood and Trueman sitting at a table with account books.

Thorowgood. Methinks I would not have you only learn the method of merchandise, and practise it hereafter, merely as a means of getting wealth. 'T will be well worth your pains to study it as a science. See how it is founded in reason, and the nature of things; how it has promoted humanity, as it has opened and yet keeps up an intercourse between nations, far remote from one another in situation, customs and religion; promoting arts, industry, peace and plenty; by mutual benefits diffusing mutual love from pole to pole.

Trueman. Something of this I have considered, and hope, by your assistance, to extend my thoughts much farther. I have observed those countries, where trade is promoted and encouraged, do not make discoveries to destroy, but to improve, mankind by love and friendship; to tame the fierce and polish the most savage; to teach them the advantages of honest traffic, by taking from them, with their own consent, their useless superfluities, and giving them, in return, what, from their ignorance in manual arts, their situation, or some other accident, they stand in need of.

Thor. 'T is justly observed: the populous East, luxuriant, abounds with glittering gems, bright pearls, aromatic spices, and health-restoring drugs. The late-found Western World glows with unnumbered veins of gold and silver ore. On every climate and on every country, Heaven has bestowed some good peculiar to itself. It is the industrious merchant's business to collect the various blessings of each soil and climate, and, with the product of the whole, to enrich his native country.—Well! I have examined your accounts: they are not only just, as I have always found them, but regularly kept, and fairly entered. I commend your diligence. Method in business is the surest guide. He who neglects it frequently stumbles, and always wanders perplexed, uncertain, and in danger.—Are Barnwell's accounts ready for my inspection? He does not use to be the last on these occasions.

True. Upon receiving your orders he retired, I thought, in some confusion. If you please, I 'll go and hasten him.—I hope he hasn't been guilty of any neglect.

Thor. I 'm now going to the Exchange; let him know, at my return, I expect to find him ready. (*Exeunt.*)

Scene II.

Enter Maria with a book; sits and reads.

Maria. How forcible is truth! The weakest mind, inspired with love of that, fixed and collected in itself, with indifference beholds—the united force of earth and hell opposing. Such souls are raised above the sense of pain, or so supported that they regard it not. The martyr cheaply purchases his heaven. Small are his sufferings, great is his reward; not so the wretch, who combats love with duty; when the mind, weakened and dissolved by the soft passion, feeble and hopeless opposes its own desires.—What is an hour, a day, a year of pain, to a whole life of tortures such as these?

Scene III.

Enter Trueman.

Trueman and Maria.

Trueman. O, Barnwell! O, my friend, how art thou fallen!

Maria. Ha! Barnwell! What of him? Speak, say, what of Barnwell?

True. 'T is not to be concealed. I 've news to tell of him that will afflict your generous father, yourself, and all who knew him.

Ma. Defend us, Heaven!

True. I cannot speak it.—See there.

(*Gives a letter. Maria reads.*)

Trueman,

I know my absence will surprise my honored master and yourself; and the more, when you shall understand that the reason of my withdrawing, is my having embezzled part of the cash with which I was entrusted. After this, 't is needless to inform you that I intend never to return again. Though this might have been known by examining my accounts, yet, to prevent that unnecessary trouble, and to cut off all fruitless expectations of my return, I have left this from the lost

George Barnwell.

True. Lost indeed! Yet, how he should be guilty of what he there charges himself withal, raises my wonder equal to my grief. Never had youth a higher sense of virtue: justly he thought, and as he thought he practised; never was life more regular than his; an understanding uncommon at his years—an open, generous manliness of temper—his manners easy, unaffected and engaging.

Ma. This and much more you might have said with truth. He was the delight of every eye, and joy of every heart that knew him.

True. Since such he was, and was my friend, can I support his loss?—See! the fairest and happiest maid this wealthy city boasts, kindly condescends to weep for thy unhappy fate, poor ruined Barnwell!

Ma. Trueman, do you think a soul so delicate as his, so sensible of shame, can e'er submit to live a slave to vice?

True. Never, never! So well I know him, I 'm sure this act of his, so contrary to his nature, must have been caused by some unavoidable necessity.

Ma. Is there no means yet to preserve him?

True. O, that there were! But few men recover reputation lost—a merchant never. Nor would he, I fear, though I should find him, ever be brought to look his injured master in the face.

Ma. I fear as much—and therefore would never have my father know it.

True. That 's impossible.

Ma. What 's the sum?

True. 'T is considerable. I 've marked it here, to show it, with the letter, to your father, at his return.

Ma. If I should supply the money, could you so dispose of that, and the account, as to conceal this unhappy mismanagement from my father?

True. Nothing more easy. But can you intend it? Will you save a helpless wretch from ruin? Oh! 't were an act worthy such exalted virtue as Maria's. Sure, Heaven, in mercy to my friend, inspired the generous thought!

Ma. Doubt not but I would purchase so great a happiness at a much dearer price. —But how shall he be found?

True. Trust to my diligence for that. In the mean time, I 'll conceal his absence from your father, or find such excuses for it that the real cause shall never be suspected.

Ma. In attempting to save from shame one whom we hope may yet return to virtue, to Heaven, and you, the judges of this action, I appeal, whether I have done anything misbecoming my sex and character.

True. Earth must approve the deed, and Heaven, I doubt not, will reward it.

Ma. If Heaven succeed [6] it, I am well rewarded. A virgin's fame is sullied by suspicion's slightest breath; and therefore as this must be a secret from my father and the world, for Barnwell's sake, for mine, let it be so to him! (*Exeunt.*)

6 Prosper.

SCENE IV.

Millwood's House. Enter Lucy and Blunt.

Lucy. Well! what do you think of Millwood's conduct now!

Blunt. I own it is surprising; I don't know which to admire most, her feigned or his real passion—though I have sometimes been afraid that her avarice would discover[7] her. But his youth and want of experience make it the easier to impose on him.

Lucy. No, it is his love. To do him justice, notwithstanding his youth, he don't want understanding; but you men are much easier imposed on, in these affairs, than your vanity will allow you to believe. Let me see the wisest of you all as much in love with me as Barnwell is with Millwood, and I 'll engage to make as great a fool of him.

Blunt. And all circumstances considered, to make as much money of him too.

Lucy. I can't answer for that. Her artifice in making him rob his master at first, and the various stratagems by which she has obliged him to continue in that course, astonish even me, who know her so well.

Blunt. But then you are to consider that the money was his master's.

Lucy. There was the difficulty of it. Had it been his own it had been nothing. Were the world his, she might have it for a smile.—But those golden days are done; he 's ruined, and Millwood's hopes of farther profits there are at an end.

Blunt. That 's no more than we all expected.

Lucy. Being called by his master to make up his accounts, he was forced to quit his house and service, and wisely flies to Millwood for relief and entertainment.

Blunt. I have not heard of this before! How did she receive him?

Lucy. As you would expect. She wondered what he meant; was astonished at his impudence; and, with an air of modesty peculiar to herself, swore so heartily that she never saw him before, that she put me out of countenance.

Blunt. That 's much indeed! But how did Barnwell behave?

Lucy. He grieved, and, at length, enraged at this barbarous treatment, was preparing to be gone; and, making toward the door, showed a bag of money, which he had stolen from his master—the last he 's ever like to have from thence.

Blunt. But then, Millwood?

Lucy. Aye, she, with her usual address, returned to her old arts of lying, swearing and dissembling. Hung on his neck, and wept, and swore 't was meant in jest; till the easy fool, melted into tears, threw the money into her lap, and swore he had rather die than think her false.

Blunt. Strange infatuation!

Lucy. But what followed was stranger still. As doubts and fears, followed by reconcilement, ever increase love, where the passion is sincere: so in him it caused so wild a transport of excessive fondness, such joy, such grief, such pleasure, and such anguish, that nature in him seemed sinking with the weight, and the charmed soul disposed to quit his breast for hers. Just then, when every passion with lawless anarchy prevailed, and reason was in the raging tempest lost, the cruel, artful Millwood prevailed upon the wretched youth to promise what I tremble but to think on.

Blunt. I am amazed![8] What can it be?

Lucy. You will be more so, to hear it is to attempt the life of his nearest relation, and best benefactor.

Blunt. His uncle, whom we have often heard him speak of as a gentleman of a large estate and fair character in the country where he lives?

Lucy. The same. She was no sooner possessed of the last dear purchase of his ruin, but her avarice, insatiate as the grave, demands this horrid sacrifice—Barnwell's near relation; and unsuspected virtue must give too easy means to seize the good man's treasure, whose blood must seal the dreadful secret, and prevent the terrors of her guilty fears.

Blunt. Is it possible she could persuade him to do an act like that? He is, by nature, honest, grateful, compassionate, and generous; and though his love and her artful persuasions have wrought him to practise what he most abhors; yet we all can witness for him with what reluctance he has still complied! So many tears he shed o'er each offense, as might, if possible, sanctify theft, and make a merit of a crime.

Lucy. 'T is true; at the naming the murder of his uncle he started into rage, and, breaking from her arms, where she still then had held him with well dissembled

[7] Betray.

[8] Confounded.

love and false endearments, called her 'cruel monster, devil,' and told her she was born for his destruction. She thought it not for her purpose to meet his rage with rage, but affected a most passionate fit of grief—railed at her fate, and cursed her wayward stars: that still her wants should force her to press him to act such deeds as she must needs abhor, as well as he; but told him, necessity had no law, and love no bounds; that therefore he never truly loved, but meant, in her necessity, to forsake her; then kneeled and swore, that since, by his refusal, he had given her cause to doubt his love, she never would see him more—unless, to prove it true, he robbed his uncle to supply her wants, and murdered him, to keep it from discovery.

Blunt. I am astonished! What said he?

Lucy. Speechless he stood; but in his face you might have read that various passions tore his very soul. Oft he, in anguish, threw his eyes towards Heaven, and then as often bent their beams on her; then wept and groaned, and beat his breast; at length, with horror not to be expressed, he cried: 'Thou cursed fair! have I not given dreadful proofs of love! What drew me from my youthful innocence, to stain my then unspotted soul, but love? What caused me to rob my gentle master but cursed love? What makes me now a fugitive from his service, loathed by myself, and scorned by all the world, but love? What fills my eyes with tears, my soul with torture, never felt on this side death before? Why, love, love, love! And why, above all, do I resolve' (for, tearing his hair, he cried 'I do resolve') 'to kill my uncle?'

Blunt. Was she not moved? It makes me weep to hear the sad relation.

Lucy. Yes, with joy, that she had gained her point. She gave him no time to cool, but urged him to attempt it instantly. He 's now gone; if he performs it, and escapes, there 's more money for her; if not, he 'll ne'er return, and then she 's fairly rid of him.

Blunt. 'T is time the world was rid of such a monster.

Lucy. If we don't do our endeavors to prevent this murder, we are as bad as she.

Blunt. I 'm afraid it is too late.

Lucy. Perhaps not.—Her barbarity to Barnwell makes me hate her. We 've run too great a length with her already. I did not think her or myself so wicked as I find, upon reflection, we are.

Blunt. 'T is true, we have all been too much so. But there is something so horrid in murder, that all other crimes seem nothing when compared to that. I would not be involved in the guilt of that for all the world.

Lucy. Nor I, Heaven knows; therefore let us clear ourselves by doing all that is in our power to prevent it. I have just thought of a way that, to me, seems probable. Will you join with me to detect [8] this cursed design?

Blunt. With all my heart.—How else shall I clear myself? He who knows of a murder intended to be committed and does not discover [9] it, in the eye of the law and reason is a murderer.

Lucy. Let us lose no time; I 'll acquaint you with the particulars as we go.

(*Exeunt.*)

Scene V.

A Walk at some distance from a Country Seat.

Enter Barnwell.

Barnwell. A dismal gloom obscures the face of day; either the sun has slipped behind a cloud, or journeys down the west of Heaven, with more than common speed, to avoid the sight of what I 'm doomed to act. Since I set forth on this accursed design, where'er I tread, methinks, the solid earth trembles beneath my feet.—Yonder limpid stream, whose hoary fall has made a natural cascade, as I passed by, in doleful accents seemed to murmur 'Murder.' The earth, the air, and water, seem concerned—but that 's not strange: the world is punished, and nature feels the shock, when Providence permits a good man's fall!—Just Heaven! Then what should I be! For him, that was my father's only brother, and since his death has been to me a father, who took me up an infant, and an orphan; reared me with tenderest care, and still indulged me with most paternal fondness—yet here I stand avowed his destined murderer.—I stiffen with horror at my own impiety.—'T is yet unperformed. What if I quit my bloody purpose, and fly the place! (*Going, then stops.*)—But whither, O whither, shall I fly? My master's once friendly doors are ever shut against me; and without money Mill-

9 Reveal.

wood will never see me more, and life is not to be endured without her. She 's got such firm possession of my heart, and governs there with such despotic sway—aye, there 's the cause of all my sin and sorrow! 'T is more than love: 't is the fever of the soul, and madness of desire. In vain does nature, reason, conscience, all oppose it; the impetuous passion bears down all before it, and drives me on to lust, to theft and murder. Oh conscience! feeble guide to virtue, who only shows us when we go astray, but wants the power to stop us in our course.—Ha, in yonder shady walk I see my uncle. He 's alone. Now for my disguise! (*Plucks out a vizor.*[10]) This is his hour of private meditation. Thus daily he prepares his soul for Heaven, whilst I—but what have I to do with Heaven? Ha! No struggles, conscience!

Hence, hence, remorse, and every thought that 's good:
The storm that lust began must end in blood.

(*Puts on the vizor, draws a pistol and exit.*)

SCENE VI.

A close Walk in a Wood.

Enter Uncle.

Uncle. If I was superstitious, I should fear some danger lurked unseen, or death were nigh.—A heavy melancholy clouds my spirits; my imagination is filled with gashly [11] forms of dreary graves and bodies changed by death; when the pale, lengthened visage attracts each weeping eye, and fills the musing soul, at once, with grief and horror, pity and aversion.—I will indulge the thought. The wise man prepares himself for death, by making it familiar to his mind. When strong reflections hold the mirror near, and the living in the dead behold their future selves, how does each inordinate passion and desire cease, or sicken at the view! The mind scarce moves; the blood, curdling and chilled, creeps slowly through the veins; fixed, still, and motionless, like the solemn object of our thoughts, we are almost at present what we must be hereafter, till curiosity awakes the soul, and sets it on inquiry.

10 Mask.

SCENE VII.

Uncle. George Barnwell at a distance.

Uncle. O Death, thou strange mysterious power,—seen every day, yet never understood but by the incommunicative dead—what art thou? The extensive mind of man, that with a thought circles the earth's vast globe, sinks to the centre, or ascends above the stars; that worlds exotic finds, or thinks it finds—thy thick clouds attempts to pass in vain, lost and bewildered in the horrid gloom; defeated, she returns more doubtful than before; of nothing certain but of labor lost.

(*During this speech, Barnwell sometimes presents the pistol and draws it back again; at last he drops it, at which his uncle starts, and draws his sword.*)

Barnwell. Oh, 't is impossible!

Uncle. A man so near me, armed and masked!

Barn. Nay, then there 's no retreat.

(*Plucks a poniard from his bosom, and stabs him.*)

Uncle. Oh! I am slain! All-gracious Heaven regard the prayer of thy dying servant! Bless, with thy choicest blessings, my dearest nephew; forgive my murderer, and take my fleeting soul to endless mercy!

(*Barnwell throws off his mask, runs to him, and, kneeling by him, raises and chafes him.*)

Barn. Expiring saint! Oh, murdered, martyred uncle! Lift up your dying eyes, and view your nephew in your murderer! O, do not look so tenderly upon me! Let indignation lighten from your eyes, and blast me e'er you die!—By Heaven, he weeps in pity of my woes. Tears,—tears, for blood! The murdered, in the agonies of death, weeps for his murderer.—Oh, speak our pious purpose—pronounce my pardon then—and take me with you!—He would, but cannot. O why with such fond affection do you press my murdering hand!—What! will you kiss me! (*Kisses him. Uncle groans and dies.*) He 's gone for ever—and oh! I follow. (*Swoons away upon his uncle's dead body.*) Do I still live to press the suffering bosom of the earth? Do I still breathe, and taint with my infectious breath the wholesome air! Let Heaven from its high throne, in justice

11 Ghastly.

or in mercy, now look down on that dear murdered saint, and me the murderer. And, if his vengeance spares, let pity strike and end my wretched being!—Murder the worst of crimes, and parricide the worst of murders, and this the worst of parricides! Cain, who stands on record from the birth of time, and must to its last final period, as accursed, slew a brother, favored above him. Detested Nero by another's hand dispatched a mother that he feared and hated. But I, with my own hand, have murdered a brother, mother, father, and a friend, most loving and beloved. This execrable act of mine 's without a parallel. O may it ever stand alone—the last of murders, as it is the worst!

The rich man thus, in torment and despair,
Preferred his vain, but charitable prayer.
The fool, his own soul lost, would fain be wise
For others' good; but Heaven his suit denies.
By laws and means well known we stand or fall,
And one eternal rule remains for all.

The End of the Third Act.

ACT IV.

Scene I. *A Room in Thorowgood's House. Maria.*

Maria. How falsely do they judge who censure or applaud as we 're afflicted or rewarded here! I know I am unhappy, yet cannot charge myself with any crime, more than the common frailties of our kind, that should provoke just Heaven to mark me out for sufferings so uncommon and severe. Falsely to accuse ourselves, Heaven must abhor; then it is just and right that innocence should suffer, for Heaven must be just in all its ways. Perhaps by that they are kept from moral evils much worse than penal, or more improved in virtue; or may not the lesser ills that they sustain be the means of greater good to others? Might all the joyless days and sleepless nights that I have passed but purchase peace for thee!

Thou dear, dear cause of all my grief and pain,
Small were the loss, and infinite the gain;
Though to the grave in secret love I pine,
So life, and fame, and happiness were thine.

Scene II.

Enter Trueman.

Trueman and Maria.

Maria. What news of Barnwell?

Trueman. None. I have sought him with the greatest diligence, but all in vain.

Ma. Doth my father yet suspect the cause of his absenting himself?

True. All appeared so just and fair to him, it is not possible he ever should; but his absence will no longer be concealed. Your father 's wise; and, though he seems to hearken to the friendly excuses I would make for Barnwell, yet, I am afraid, he regards 'em only as such, without suffering them to influence his judgment.

Ma. How does the unhappy youth defeat all our designs to serve him! Yet I can never repent what we have done. Should he return, 't will make his reconciliation with my father easier, and preserve him from future reproach from a malicious, unforgiving world.

Scene III.

To them, Thorowgood and Lucy.

Thorowgood. This woman here has given me a sad, and (bating some circumstances) too probable account of Barnwell's defection.

Lucy. I am sorry, sir, that my frank confession of my former unhappy course of life should cause you to suspect my truth on this occasion.

Thor. It is not that; your confession has in it all the appearance of truth. (*To them.*) Among many other particulars, she informs me that Barnwell has been influenced to break his trust, and wrong me, at several times, of considerable sums of money; now, as I know this to be false, I would fain doubt the whole of her relation, too dreadful to be willingly believed.

Maria. Sir, your pardon; I find myself on a sudden so indisposed, that I must retire.—(*Aside.*) Providence opposes all attempts to save him. Poor ruined Barnwell! Wretched, lost Maria! (*Exit.*)

Scene IV.

Thorowgood, Trueman and Lucy.

Thorowgood. How am I distressed on every side! Pity for that unhappy youth, fear for the life of a much valued friend —and then my child, the only joy and hope of my declining life! Her melancholy increases hourly, and gives me painful apprehensions of her loss.—O Trueman! this person informs me that your friend, at the instigation of an impious woman, is gone to rob and murder his venerable uncle.

Trueman. O execrable deed! I am blasted with the horror of the thought.

Lucy. This delay may ruin all.

Thor. What to do or think I know not. That he ever wronged me, I know is false; the rest may be so too—there 's all my hope.

True. Trust not to that; rather suppose all true than lose a moment's time. Even now the horrid deed may be a-doing —dreadful imagination! Or it may be done, and we are vainly debating on the means to prevent what is already past.

Thor. (*Aside.*) This earnestness convinces me that he knows more than he has yet discovered.—What ho! without there! who waits?

Scene V.

To them, a Servant.

Thorowgood. Order the groom to saddle the swiftest horse, and prepare himself to set out with speed!—An affair of life and death demands his diligence. (*Exit Servant.*)

Scene VI.

Thorowgood, Trueman and Lucy.

Thorowgood. For you, whose behavior on this occasion I have no time to commend as it deserves, I must engage your farther assistance. Return and observe this Millwood till I come. I have your directions, and will follow you as soon as possible. (*Exit Lucy.*)

Scene VII.

Thorowgood and Trueman.

Thorowgood. Trueman, you I am sure would not be idle on this occasion. (*Exit.*)

Scene VIII.

Trueman.

Trueman. He only who is a friend can judge of my distress. (*Exit.*)

Scene IX.

Millwood's House.

Millwood.

Millwood. I wish I knew the event[12] of his design; the attempt without success would ruin him.—Well! what have I to apprehend from that? I fear too much. The mischief being only intended, his friends, in pity of his youth, turn all their rage on me. I should have thought of that before.—Suppose the deed done: then, and then only, I shall be secure; or what if he returns without attempting it at all?

Scene X.

Millwood, and enter Barnwell, bloody.

Millwood. But he is here, and I have done him wrong; his bloody hands show he has done the deed, but show he wants the prudence to conceal it.

Barnwell. Where shall I hide me? whither shall I fly to avoid the swift, unerring hand of justice?

Mill. Dismiss those fears: though thousands had pursued you to the door, yet being entered here you are safe as innocence. I have such a cavern, by art so cunningly contrived, that the piercing eyes of jealousy and revenge may search in vain, nor find the entrance to the safe retreat. There will I hide you, if any danger 's near.

Barn. O hide me from myself, if it be possible; for while I bear my conscience in my bosom, though I were hid, where man's eye never saw, nor light e'er dawned, 't were all in vain. For that inmate,—that impartial judge, will try, convict and sentence me for murder; and execute me with never-ending torments. Behold these hands all crimsoned o'er with my dear uncle's blood! Here 's a sight to make a statue start with horror, or turn a living man into a statue.

Mill. Ridiculous! Then it seems you are afraid of your own shadow, or, what 's less than a shadow, your conscience.

Barn. Though to man unknown I did the accursed act, what can we hide from Heaven's omniscient eye?

Mill. No more of this stuff! What advantage have you made of his death? or what advantage may yet be made of it? Did you secure the keys of his treasure

12 Outcome.

—those no doubt were about him. What gold, what jewels, or what else of value have you brought me?

Barn. Think you I added sacrilege to murder? Oh! had you seen him as his life flowed from him in a crimson flood, and heard him praying for me by the double name of nephew and of murderer—alas, alas! he knew not then that his nephew was his murderer: how would you have wished, as I did, though you had a thousand years of life to come, to have given them all to have lengthened his one hour! But being dead, I fled the sight of what my hands had done, nor could I, to have gained the empire of the world, have violated by theft his sacred corpse.

Mill. Whining, preposterous, canting villain, to murder your uncle, rob him of life, nature's first, last, dear prerogative, after which there 's no injury, then fear to take what he no longer wanted; and bring to me your penury and guilt! Do you think I 'll hazard my reputation, nay my life, to entertain you?

Barn. Oh! Millwood! this from thee!—but I have done—if you hate me, if you wish me dead, then are you happy—for oh! 't is sure my grief will quickly end me.

Mill. In his madness he will discover [13] all, and involve me in his ruin. We are on a precipice from whence there 's no retreat for both—then, to preserve myself! (*Pauses.*) There is no other way,—'t is dreadful; but reflection comes too late when danger 's pressing, and there 's no room for choice.—It must be done. (*Stamps.*)

Scene XI.

To them, a Servant.

Millwood. Fetch me an officer, and seize this villain: he has confessed himself a murderer. Should I let him escape, I justly might be thought as bad as he. (*Exit Servant.*)

Scene XII.

Millwood and Barnwell.

Barnwell. O Millwood! sure thou dost not, cannot mean it. Stop the messenger, upon my knees I beg you, call him back! 'T is fit I die indeed, but not by you. I will this instant deliver myself into the hands of justice; indeed I will, for death is all I wish. But thy ingratitude so tears my wounded soul, 't is worse ten thousand times than death with torture.

Millwood. Call it what you will, I am willing [14] to live, and live secure; which nothing but your death can warrant.

Barn. If there be a pitch of wickedness that seats the author beyond the reach of vengeance, you must be secure. But what remains for me but a dismal dungeon, hard-galling fetters, an awful trial, and ignominious death—justly to fall unpitied and abhorred; after death to be suspended between Heaven and earth, a dreadful spectacle, the warning and horror of a gaping crowd. This I could bear, nay wish not to avoid, had it come from any hand but thine.

Scene XIII.

Millwood, Barnwell. Enter Blunt, Officer and Attendants.

Millwood. Heaven defend me! Conceal a murderer! Here, sir; take this youth into your custody. I accuse him of murder, and will appear to make good my charge. (*They seize him.*)

Barnwell. To whom, of what, or how shall I complain? I 'll not accuse her: the hand of Heaven is in it, and this the punishment of lust and parricide. Yet Heaven, that justly cuts me off, still suffers her to live, perhaps to punish others. Tremendous mercy! so fiends are cursed with immortality, to be the executioners of Heaven.—

Be warned, ye youths, who see my sad despair,
Avoid lewd women, false as they are fair;
By reason guided, honest joys pursue;
The fair, to honor and to virtue true,
Just to herself, will ne'er be false to you.
By my example learn to shun my fate;
(How wretched is the man who 's wise too late!)
Ere innocence, and fame, and life, be lost,
Here purchase wisdom, cheaply, at my cost!
(*Exit with Officers.*)

Scene XIV.

Millwood and Blunt.

Millwood. Where 's Lucy? Why is she absent at such a time?

13 Reveal.

14 Disposed.

Blunt. Would I had been so too, thou devil!

Mill. Insolent! This to me!

Blunt. The worst that we know of the devil is that he first seduces to sin and then betrays to punishment. (*Exit.*)

Scene XV.

Millwood.

Millwood. They disapprove of my conduct, and mean to take this opportunity to set up for themselves. My ruin is resolved. I see my danger, but scorn it and them. I was not born to fall by such weak instruments. (*Going.*)

Scene XVI.

Enter Thorowgood.

Thorowgood and Millwood.

Thorowgood. Where is this scandal of her own sex, and curse of ours?

Millwood. What means this insolence? Who do you seek?

Thor. Millwood.

Mill. Well, you have found her, then. I am Millwood.

Thor. Then you are the most impious wretch that e'er the sun beheld.

Mill. From your appearance I should have expected wisdom and moderation, but your manners belie your aspect.—What is your business here? I know you not.

Thor. Hereafter you may know me better; I am Barnwell's master.

Mill. Then you are master to a villain; which, I think, is not much to your credit.

Thor. Had he been as much above thy arts as my credit is superior to thy malice, I need not blush to own him.

Mill. My arts? I don't understand you, sir. If he has done amiss, what 's that to me? Was he my servant, or yours? You should have taught him better.

Thor. Why should I wonder to find such uncommon impudence in one arrived to such a height of wickedness? When innocence is banished, modesty soon follows. Know, sorceress, I 'm not ignorant of any of your arts, by which you first deceived the unwary youth. I know how, step by step, you 've led him on, reluctant and unwilling, from crime to crime, to this last horrid act, which you contrived, and, by your cursed wiles, even forced him to commit—and then betrayed him.

Mill. (*Aside.*) Ha! Lucy has got the advantage of me, and accused me first. Unless I can turn the accusation, and fix it upon her and Blunt, I am lost.

Thor. Had I known your cruel design sooner, it had been prevented. To see you punished as the law directs, is all that now remains.—Poor satisfaction—for he, innocent as he is, compared to you, must suffer too. But Heaven, who knows our frame, and graciously distinguishes between frailty and presumption, will make a difference, though man cannot, who sees not the heart, but only judges by the outward action.—

Mill. I find, sir, we are both unhappy in our servants. I was surprised at such ill treatment from a gentleman of your appearance, without cause, and therefore too hastily returned it; for which I ask your pardon. I now perceive you have been so far imposed on as to think me engaged in a former correspondence with your servant, and. some way or other, accessary to his undoing.

Thor. I charge you as the cause, the sole cause of all his guilt and all his suffering—of all he now endures, and must endure, till a violent and shameful death shall put a dreadful period to his life and miseries together.

Mill. 'T is very strange! But who 's secure from scandal and detraction?—So far from contributing to his ruin, I never spoke to him till since that fatal accident, which I lament as much as you. 'T is true, I have a servant, on whose account he has of late frequented my house; if she has abused my good opinion of her, am I to blame? Hasn't Barnwell done the same by you?

Thor. I hear you; pray, go on!

Mill. I have been informed he had a violent passion for her, and she for him; but I always thought it innocent; I know her poor, and given to expensive pleasures. Now who can tell but she may have influenced the amorous youth to commit this murder, to supply her extravagancies? It must be so; I now recollect a thousand circumstances that confirm it. I'll have her and a man-servant, that I suspect as an accomplice, secured immediately. I hope, sir, you will lay aside your ill-grounded suspicions of me, and join to punish the real contrivers of this bloody deed. (*Offers to go.*)

Thor. Madam, you pass not this way! I see your design, but shall protect them from your malice.

Mill. I hope you will not use your influence, and the credit of your name, to screen such guilty wretches. Consider, sir, the wickedness of persuading a thoughtless youth to such a crime!

Thor. I do—and of betraying him when it was done.

Mill. That which you call betraying him, may convince you of my innocence. She who loves him, though she contrived the murder, would never have delivered him into the hands of justice, as I, struck with the horror of his crimes, have done.

Thor. (*Aside.*) How should an unexperienced youth escape her snares? The powerful magic of her wit and form might betray the wisest to simple dotage, and fire the blood that age had froze long since. Even I, that with just prejudice came prepared, had, by her artful story, been deceived, but that my strong conviction of her guilt makes even a doubt impossible.—Those whom subtly you would accuse, you know are your accusers; and, what proves unanswerably their innocence and your guilt, they accused you before the deed was done, and did all that was in their power to have prevented it.

Mill. Sir, you are very hard to be convinced; but I have such a proof, which, when produced, will silence all objections. (*Exit.*)

Scene XVII.

Thorowgood. Enter Lucy, Trueman, Blunt, Officers, etc.

Lucy. Gentlemen, pray, place yourselves, some on one side of that door, and some on the other; watch her entrance, and act as your prudence shall direct you—this way! (*to Thorowgood*) and note her behavior. I have observed her: she 's driven to the last extremity, and is forming some desperate resolution.—I guess at her design.—

Scene XVIII.

To them Millwood with a pistol.—Trueman secures her.

Trueman. Here thy power of doing mischief ends, deceitful, cruel, bloody woman!

Millwood. Fool, hypocrite, villain—man! Thou can'st not call me that.

True. To call thee woman were to wrong the sex, thou devil!

Mill. That imaginary being is an emblem of thy cursed sex collected—a mirror, wherein each particular man may see his own likeness, and that of all mankind.

True. Think not by aggravating the fault of others to extenuate thy own, of which the abuse of such uncommon perfections of mind and body is not the least!

Mill. If such I had, well may I curse your barbarous sex, who robbed me of 'em, ere I knew their worth, then left me, too late, to count their value by their loss. Another and another spoiler came; and all my gain was poverty and reproach. My soul disdained, and yet disdains, dependence and contempt. Riches, no matter by what means obtained, I saw secured the worst of men from both; I found it therefore necessary to be rich; and, to that end, I summoned all my arts. You call 'em wicked; be it so! They were such as my conversation with your sex had furnished me withal.

Thorowgood. Sure, none but the worst of men conversed with thee.

Mill. Men of all degrees and all professions I have known, yet found no difference, but in their several capacities; all were alike wicked to the utmost of their power. In pride, contention, avarice, cruelty and revenge, the reverend priesthood were my unerring guides. From suburb-magistrates, who live by ruined reputations, as the unhospitable natives of Cornwall do by shipwrecks, I learned that to charge my innocent neighbors with my crimes was to merit their protection; for to screen the guilty is the less scandalous, when many are suspected, and detraction, like darkness and death, blackens all objects and levels all distinction. Such are your venal magistrates, who favor none but such as, by their office, they are sworn to punish. With them, not to be guilty is the worst of crimes; and large fees privately paid is every needful virtue.

Thor. Your practice has sufficiently discovered your contempt of laws, both human and divine; no wonder then that you should hate the officers of both.

Mill. I hate you all; I know you, and expect no mercy. Nay, I ask for none; I have done nothing that I am sorry for; I followed my inclinations, and that the best of you does every day. All actions are alike natural and indifferent to man and beast, who devour, or are devoured, as they meet with others weaker or stronger than themselves.

Thor. What pity it is, a mind so comprehensive, daring and inquisitive should be a stranger to religion's sweet but powerful charms.

Mill. I am not fool enough to be an atheist, though I have known enough of men's hypocrisy to make a thousand simple women so. Whatever religion is in itself—as practised by mankind, it has caused the evils you say it was designed to cure. War, plague, and famine, has not destroyed so many of the human race as this pretended piety has done, and with such barbarous cruelty—as if the only way to honor Heaven, were to turn the present world into Hell.

Thor. Truth is truth, though from an enemy and spoke in malice. You bloody, blind, and superstitious bigots, how will you answer this?

Mill. What are your laws, of which you make your boast, but the fool's wisdom, and the coward's valor; the instrument and screen of all your villainies, by which you punish in others what you act yourselves, or would have acted, had you been in their circumstances. The judge who condemns the poor man for being a thief had been a thief himself, had he been poor. Thus you go on deceiving, and being deceived, harassing, and plaguing, and destroying one another: but women are your universal prey.

Women, by whom you are, the source of joy,
With cruel arts you labor to destroy;
A thousand ways our ruin you pursue,
Yet blame in us those arts first taught by you.
O may, from hence, each violated maid,
By flattering, faithless, barbarous man betrayed,
When robbed of innocence, and virgin fame,
From your destruction raise a nobler name;
To right their sex's wrongs devote their mind,
And future Millwoods prove, to plague mankind!

The End of the Fourth Act.

ACT V.

SCENE I. *A Room in a Prison.*

Thorowgood, Blunt and Lucy.

Thorowgood. I have recommended to Barnwell a reverend divine, whose judgment and integrity I am well acquainted with. Nor has Millwood been neglected; but she, unhappy woman, still obstinate, refuses his assistance.

Lucy. This pious charity to the afflicted well becomes your character; yet pardon me, sir, if I wonder you were not at their trial.

Thor. I knew it was impossible to save him, and I and my family bear so great a part in his distress that to have been present would have aggravated our sorrows without relieving his.

Blunt. It was mournful indeed. Barnwell's youth and modest deportment, as he passed, drew tears from every eye: when placed at the bar, and arraigned before the reverend judges, with many tears and interrupting sobs he confessed and aggravated his offenses, without accusing, or once reflecting on Millwood, the shameless author of his ruin; who dauntless and unconcerned stood by his side, viewing with visible pride and contempt the vast assembly, who all with sympathizing sorrow wept for the wretched youth. Millwood, when called upon to answer, loudly insisted upon her innocence, and made an artful and a bold defense; but, finding all in vain, the impartial jury and the learned bench concurring to find her guilty, how did she curse herself, poor Barnwell, us, her judges, all mankind! But what could that avail? She was condemned, and is this day to suffer with him.

Thor. The time draws on. I am going to visit Barnwell, as you are Millwood.

Lucy. We have not wronged her, yet I dread this interview. She 's proud, impatient, wrathful, and unforgiving. To be the branded instruments of vengeance, to suffer in her shame, and sympathize with her in all she suffers, is the tribute we must pay for our former ill-spent lives, and long confederacy with her in wickedness.

Thor. Happy for you it ended when it did! What you have done against Millwood, I know, proceeded from a just abhorrence of her crimes, free from interest, malice, or revenge. Proselytes to virtue should be encouraged. Pursue your proposed reformation, and know me hereafter for your friend.

Lucy. This is a blessing as unhoped for as unmerited; but Heaven, that snatched us from impending ruin, sure, intends you as its instrument to secure us from apostasy.

Thor. With gratitude to impute your deliverance to Heaven is just. Many, less virtuously disposed than Barnwell was, have never fallen in the manner he has done;—may not such owe their safety rather to Providence than to themselves? With pity and compassion let us judge him! Great were his faults, but strong was the temptation. Let his ruin learn us diffidence, humanity and circumspection; for we, who wonder at his fate—perhaps, had we like him been tried, like him we had fallen too. (*Exeunt.*)

Scene II.

A Dungeon. A table and lamp.

Barnwell, reading. Enter Thorowgood.

Thorowgood. See there the bitter fruits of passion's detested reign and sensual appetite indulged—severe reflections, penitence and tears.

Barnwell. My honored, injured master, whose goodness has covered me a thousand times with shame, forgive this last unwilling disrespect! Indeed, I saw you not.

Thor. 'T is well; I hope you were better employed in viewing of yourself. Your journey 's long, your time for preparation almost spent. I sent a reverend divine to teach you to improve it, and should be glad to hear of his success.

Barn. The word of truth, which he recommended for my constant companion in this my sad retirement, has at length removed the doubts I labored under. From thence I 've learned the infinite extent of heavenly mercy; that my offenses, though great, are not unpardonable; and that 't is not my interest only, but my duty, to believe and to rejoice in that hope: so shall Heaven receive the glory, and future penitents the profit of my example.

Thor. Go on! How happy am I who live to see this!

Barn. 'T is wonderful that words should charm despair, speak peace and pardon to a murderer's conscience! But truth and mercy flow in every sentence attended with force and energy divine. How shall I describe my present state of mind? I hope in doubt, and trembling I rejoice. I feel my grief increase, even as my fears give way. Joy and gratitude now supply more tears than the horror and anguish of despair before.

Thor. These are the genuine signs of true repentance, the only preparatory certain way to everlasting peace.—O the joy it gives to see a soul formed and prepared for Heaven! For this the faithful minister devotes himself to meditation, abstinence and prayer, shunning the vain delights of sensual joys, and daily dies, that others may live for ever. For this he turns the sacred volumes o'er, and spends his life in painful search of truth. The love of riches and the lust of power he looks on with just contempt and detestation, who only counts for wealth the souls he wins, and whose highest ambition is to serve mankind. If the reward of all his pains be to preserve one soul from wandering, or turn one from the error of his ways, how does he then rejoice, and own his little labors overpaid!

Barn. What do I owe for all your generous kindness? But, though I cannot, Heaven can and will reward you.

Thor. To see thee thus is joy too great for words. Farewell! Heaven strengthen thee! Farewell!

Barn. O, sir, there 's something I could say, if my sad swelling heart would give me leave.

Thor. Give it vent a while, and try.

Barn. I had a friend—'t is true I am unworthy, yet methinks your generous example might persuade—could I not see him once before I go from whence there 's no return?

Thor. He 's coming, and as much thy friend as ever; but I 'll not anticipate his sorrow: too soon he 'll see the sad effect of this contagious ruin.—(*Aside.*) This torrent of domestic misery bears too hard upon me; I must retire to indulge a weakness I find impossible to overcome.—Much loved and much lamented youth, farewell! Heaven strengthen thee! Eternally farewell!

Barn. The best of masters and of men, farewell! While I live, let me not want your prayers!

Thor. Thou shalt not. Thy peace being made with Heaven, death 's already vanquished; bear a little longer the pains that attend this transitory life, and cease from pain for ever. (*Exit.*)

Scene III.

Barnwell.

Barnwell. I find a power within that bears my soul above the fears of death, and, spite of conscious shame and guilt, gives me a taste of pleasure more than mortal.

Scene IV.

To him Trueman and Keeper.

Keeper. Sir, there 's the prisoner. (*Exit.*)

Scene V.

Barnwell and Trueman.

Barnwell. Trueman—my friend, whom I so wished to see! Yet now he 's here I dare not look upon him. (*Weeps.*)

Trueman. Oh Barnwell! Barnwell!

Barn. Mercy, mercy, gracious Heaven! For death, but not for this, was I prepared.

True. What have I suffered since I saw you last! What pain has absence given me!—But oh! to see thee thus!

Barn. I know it is dreadful! I feel the anguish of thy generous soul—but I was born to murder all who love me. (*Both weep.*)

True. I came not to reproach you; I thought to bring you comfort. But I 'm deceived, for I have none to give. I came to share thy sorrow, but cannot bear my own.

Barn. My sense of guilt indeed you cannot know—'t is what the good and innocent, like you, can ne'er conceive. But other griefs at present I have none, but what I feel for you. In your sorrow I read you love me still. But yet methinks 'tis strange, when I consider what I am.

True. No more of that! I can remember nothing but thy virtues, thy honest, tender friendship, our former happy state, and present misery.—O, had you trusted me when first the fair seducer tempted you, all might have been prevented.

Barn. Alas, thou know'st not what a wretch I 've been! Breach of friendship was my first and least offense. So far was I lost to goodness, so devoted to the author of my ruin, that, had she insisted on my murdering thee, I think I should have done it.

True. Prithee, aggravate thy faults no more!

Barn. I think I should! Thus, good and generous as you are, I should have murdered you!

True. We have not yet embraced, and may be interrupted. Come to my arms!

Barn. Never, never will I taste such joys on earth; never will I so soothe my just remorse! Are those honest arms and faithful bosom fit to embrace and to support a murderer? These iron fetters only shall clasp, and flinty pavement bear me (*throwing himself on the ground*)—even these too good for such a bloody monster.

True. Shall fortune sever those whom friendship joined? Thy miseries cannot lay thee so low, but love will find thee. (*Lies down by him.*) Upon this rugged couch then let us lie; for well it suits our most deplorable condition. Here will we offer to stern calamity, this earth the altar, and ourselves the sacrifice! Our mutual groans shall echo to each other through the dreary vault. Our sighs shall number the moments as they pass, and mingling tears communicate such anguish as words were never made to express.

Barn. Then be it so! Since you propose an intercourse of woe, pour all your griefs into my breast, and in exchange take mine! (*Embracing.*) Where 's now the anguish that you promised? You 've taken mine, and make me no return. Sure, peace and comfort dwell within these arms, and sorrow can't approach me while I 'm here! This too is the work of Heaven, who, having before spoke peace and pardon to me, now sends thee to confirm it. O take, take some of the joy that overflows my breast!

True. I do, I do. Almighty Power, how have you made us capable to bear, at once, the extremes of pleasure and of pain?

Scene VI.

To them, Keeper.

Keeper. Sir!

Trueman. I come. (*Exit Keeper.*)

Scene VII.

Barnwell and Trueman.

Barnwell. Must you leave me? Death would soon have parted us for ever.

Trueman. O my Barnwell, there 's yet another task behind; again your heart must bleed for others' woes.

Barn. To meet and part with you, I thought was all I had to do on earth! What is there more for me to do or suffer?

True. I dread to tell thee; yet it must be known!—Maria—

Barn. Our master's fair and virtuous daughter?

True. The same.

Barn. No misfortune, I hope, has reached that lovely maid! Preserve her, Heaven, from every ill, to show mankind that goodness is your care!

True. Thy, thy misfortunes, my unhappy friend, have reached her. Whatever you and I have felt, and more, if more be possible, she feels for you.

Barn. (*Aside.*) I know he doth abhor a lie, and would not trifle with his dying friend. This is, indeed, the bitterness of death!

True. You must remember, for we all observed it, for some time past, a heavy melancholy weighed her down. Disconsolate she seemed, and pined and languished from a cause unknown;—till, hearing of your dreadful fate,—the long stifled flame blazed out. She wept, she wrung her hands, and tore her hair, and, in the transport of her grief, discovered her own lost state, whilst she lamented yours.

Barn. Will all the pain I feel restore thy ease, lovely unhappy maid? (*Weeping.*) Why didn't you let me die and never know it?

True. It was impossible; she makes no secret of her passion for you, and is determined to see you ere you die. She waits for me to introduce her. (*Exit.*)

Scene VIII.

Barnwell.

Barnwell. Vain, busy thoughts, be still! What avails it to think on what I might have been? I now am what I 've made myself.

Scene IX.

To him, Trueman and Maria.

Trueman. Madam, reluctant I lead you to this dismal scene. This is the seat of misery and guilt. Here awful justice reserves her public victims. This is the entrance to shameful death.

Maria. To this sad place, then, no improper guest, the abandoned, lost Maria brings despair—and see the subject and the cause of all this world of woe! Silent and motionless he stands, as if his soul had quitted her abode, and the lifeless form alone was left behind—yet that so perfect that beauty and death, ever at enmity, now seem united there.

Barnwell. I groan, but murmur not. Just Heaven, I am your own; do with me what you please.

Ma. Why are your streaming eyes still fixed below, as though thou 'dst give the greedy earth thy sorrows, and rob me of my due? Were happiness within your power, you should bestow it where you pleased; but in your misery I must and will partake!

Barn. Oh! say not so, but fly, abhor, and leave me to my fate! Consider what you are—how vast your fortune, and how bright your fame; have pity on your youth, your beauty, and unequalled virtue, for which so many noble peers have sighed in vain! Bless with your charms some honorable lord! Adorn with your beauty, and by your example improve, the English court, that justly claims such merit: so shall I quickly be to you as though I had never been.

Ma. When I forget you, I must be so indeed. Reason, choice, virtue, all forbid it. Let women like Millwood, if there be more such women, smile in prosperity, and in adversity forsake! Be it the pride of virtue to repair, or to partake, the ruin such have made.

True. Lovely, ill-fated maid! Was there ever such generous distress before? How must this pierce his grateful heart, and aggravate his woes?

Barn. Ere I knew guilt or shame—when fortune smiled, and when my youthful hopes were at the highest—if then to have raised my thoughts to you, had been presumption in me, never to have been pardoned: think how much beneath yourself you condescend, to regard me now!

Ma. Let her blush, who, professing love,

invades the freedom of your sex's choice, and meanly sues in hopes of a return! Your inevitable fate hath rendered hope impossible as vain. Then, why should I fear to avow a passion so just and so disinterested?

True. If any should take occasion, from Millwood's crimes, to libel the best and fairest part of the creation, here let them see their error! The most distant hopes of such a tender passion from so bright a maid might add to the happiness of the most happy, and make the greatest proud. Yet here 't is lavished in vain: though by the rich present, the generous donor is undone, he on whom it is bestowed receives no benefit.

Barn. So the aromatic spices of the East, which all the living covet and esteem, are, with unavailing kindness, wasted on the dead.

Ma. Yes, fruitless is my love, and unavailing all my sighs and tears. Can they save thee from approaching death—from such a death? O, terrible idea! What is her misery and distress, who sees the first last object of her love, for whom alone she 'd live—for whom she 'd die a thousand, thousand deaths, if it were possible—expiring in her arms? Yet she is happy, when compared to me. Were millions of worlds mine, I 'd gladly give them in exchange for her condition. The most consummate woe is light to mine. The last of curses to other miserable maids is all I ask; and that 's denied me.

True. Time and reflection cure all ills.

Ma. All but this; his dreadful catastrophe virtue herself abhors. To give a holiday to suburb slaves, and passing entertain the savage herd, who, elbowing each other for a sight, pursue and press upon him like his fate! A mind with piety and resolution armed may smile on death. But public ignominy, everlasting shame, —shame, the death of souls—to die a thousand times, and yet survive even death itself, in never dying infamy—is this to be endured? Can I, who live in him, and must, each hour of my devoted life, feel all these woes renewed, can I endure this?

True. Grief has impaired her spirits; she pants as in the agonies of death.

Barn. Preserve her, Heaven, and restore her peace; nor let her death be added to my crime! (*Bell tolls.*) I am summoned to my fate.

Scene X.

To them Keeper.

Keeper. The officers attend you, sir. Mrs. Millwood is already summoned.

Barnwell. Tell 'em, I 'm ready.—And now, my friend, farewell! (*Embracing.*) Support and comfort the best you can this mourning fair.—No more! Forget not to pray for me!—(*Turning to Maria.*) Would you, bright excellence, permit me the honor of a chaste embrace, the last happiness this world could give were mine. (*She inclines toward him; they embrace.*) Exalted goodness! O turn your eyes from earth, and me to Heaven, where virtue like yours is ever heard. Pray for the peace of my departing soul! Early my race of wickedness began, and soon has reached the summit. Ere nature has finished her work, and stamped me man—just at the time that others begin to stray—my course is finished. Though short my span of life, and few my days, yet, count my crimes for years, and I have lived whole ages. Justice and mercy are in Heaven the same: its utmost severity is mercy to the whole, thereby to cure man's folly and presumption, which else would render even infinite mercy vain and ineffectual. Thus justice, in compassion to mankind, cuts off a wretch like me, by one such example to secure thousands from future ruin.

If any youth, like you, in future times
Shall mourn my fate, though he abhor my crimes;
Or tender maid, like you, my tale shall hear,
And to my sorrows give a pitying tear;
To each such melting eye, and throbbing heart,
Would gracious Heaven this benefit impart,
Never to know my guilt, nor feel my pain,
Then must you own, you ought not to complain;
Since you nor weep, nor shall I die, in vain. (*Exeunt.*)

Scene XI.

The Place of Execution. The gallows and ladders at the farther end of the stage. A crowd of spectators. Blunt and Lucy.

Lucy. Heavens! what a throng!

Blunt. How terrible is death, when thus prepared!

Lucy. Support them, Heaven; thou only can support them; all other help is vain.

Officer. (*Within.*) Make way there; make way, and give the prisoners room!

Lucy. They are here; observe them well! How humble and composed young Barnwell seems! But Millwood looks wild, ruffled with passion, confounded and amazed.

(*Enter Barnwell, Millwood, Officers and Executioners.*)

Barnwell. See, Millwood, see: our journey 's at an end. Life, like a tale that 's told, is passed away; that short but dark and unknown passage, death, is all the space 'tween us and endless joys, or woes eternal.

Millwood. Is this the end of all my flattering hopes? Were youth and beauty given me for a curse, and wisdom only to insure my ruin? They were, they were! Heaven, thou hast done thy worst. Or, if thou hast in store some untried plague —somewhat that 's worse than shame, despair and death, unpitied death, confirmed despair and soul-confounding shame—something that men and angels can't describe, and only fiends, who bear it, can conceive: now pour it, now, on this devoted head, that I may feel the worst thou canst inflict, and bid defiance to thy utmost power!

Barn. Yet, ere we pass the dreadful gulf of death—yet, ere you 're plunged in everlasting woe: O bend your stubborn knees and harder heart, humbly to deprecate the wrath divine! Who knows but Heaven, in your dying moments, may bestow that grace and mercy which your life despised!

Mill. Why name you mercy to a wretch like me? Mercy 's beyond my hope—almost beyond my wish. I can't repent, nor ask to be forgiven.

Barn. O think what 't is to be for ever, ever miserable; nor with vain pride oppose a Power that 's able to destroy you!

Mill. That will destroy me; I feel it will. A deluge of wrath is pouring on my soul. Chains, darkness, wheels, racks, sharp stinging scorpions, molten lead, and seas of sulphur, are light to what I feel.

Barn. O! add not to your vast account despair, a sin more injurious to Heaven than all you 've yet committed.

Mill. O! I have sinned beyond the reach of mercy.

Barn. O say not so; 't is blasphemy to think it. As yon bright roof is higher than the earth, so, and much more, does Heaven's goodness pass our apprehension. O! what created being shall presume to circumscribe mercy, that knows no bounds?

Mill. This yields no hope. Though mercy may be boundless, yet 't is free; and I was doomed, before the world began, to endless pains, and thou to joys eternal.

Barn. O gracious Heaven! extend thy pity to her! Let thy rich mercy flow in plenteous streams, to chase her fears and heal her wounded soul!

Mill. It will not be. Your prayers are lost in air, or else returned, perhaps with double blessing, to your bosom; but me they help not.

Barn. Yet hear me, Millwood!

Mill. Away, I will not hear thee. I tell thee, youth, I am by Heaven devoted a dreadful instance of its power to punish. (*Barnwell seems to pray.*) If thou wilt pray, pray for thyself, not me! How doth his fervent soul mount with his words, and both ascend to Heaven—that Heaven whose gates are shut with adamantine bars against my prayers, had I the will to pray.—I cannot bear it! Sure, 't is the worst of torments to behold others enjoy that bliss that we must never taste!

Officer. The utmost limit of your time 's expired.

Mill. Encompassed with horror, whither must I go? I would not live—nor die. That I could cease to be, or ne'er had been!

Barn. Since peace and comfort are denied her here, may she find mercy where she least expects it, and this be all her hell! —From our example may all be taught to fly the first approach of vice; but, if o'ertaken

By strong temptation, weakness, or surprise,
Lament their guilt and by repentance rise!
Th' impenitent alone die unforgiven;
To sin 's like man, and to forgive like Heaven. (*Exeunt.*)

Scene XII.

Enter Trueman, to Blunt and Lucy.

Lucy. Heart-breaking sight! O wretched, wretched Millwood!

Trueman. You came from her, then; how is she disposed to meet her fate?

Blunt. Who can describe unalterable woe?

Lucy. She goes to death encompassed with horror, loathing life, and yet afraid to die; no tongue can tell her anguish and despair.

True. Heaven be better to her than her fears: may she prove a warning to others, a monument of mercy in herself!

Lucy. O sorrow insupportable! Break, break, my heart!

True. In vain

With bleeding hearts and weeping eyes we show
A humane generous sense of others' woe,
Unless we mark what drew their ruin on,
And, by avoiding that, prevent our own.

FINIS.

OLIVER GOLDSMITH

SHE STOOPS TO CONQUER, OR, THE MISTAKES OF A NIGHT

Oliver Goldsmith (1728–1774), born in central Ireland, was educated in Dublin, later studying medicine in various parts of Great Britain and the Continent. After attempts as schoolmaster and physician, he settled down to miscellaneous or hack writing; in this he was very successful, though nothing could have made him rich. Careless, mercurial, unpractical, generous, he like Steele and Sheridan was an example of some of the traits often associated with the Irishman and with the artistic temperament. Most of his literary work was made-to-order and mediocre; with now and then a masterpiece, like *The Deserted Village* among poems, *The Vicar of Wakefield* among novels, and *She Stoops to Conquer* among plays, which advance him close to the front rank of eighteenth-century writers.

Goldsmith's principal other play, *The Good Natur'd Man*, only moderately good and only moderately successful, in 1768 had earned him £400 or £500, while *The Vicar of Wakefield* seems to have fetched only some £63; though others of his non-dramatic works had made more than this, it is no wonder that in his needs he turned to the stage again, and in 1771 wrote *She Stoops to Conquer*, which was published and performed two years later. Since he badly needed money, it is the more to the credit of his literary conscience that he set himself against the prevailing fashion of sentimentalism, and even publicly ridiculed it; but he had the personal reason that Hugh Kelly's *False Delicacy*, a rather wishy-washy specimen of the type, had come out as a rival to his own earlier play. George Colman, the manager of the Covent Garden theater, doubting the success of *She Stoops to Conquer*, accepted it only through the persuasions and almost the compulsion of Dr. Johnson, a warm friend of Goldsmith's. Johnson and other friends went the first night to force applause, but when the nervous author entered the theater behind the scenes during the fifth act, and heard a hiss (at the supposed improbability of Mrs. Hardcastle in her own garden believing herself forty miles from home), Colman maliciously said to him, "Pshaw, Doctor, don't be fearful of squibs, when we have been sitting almost these two hours upon a barrel of gunpowder." So strong had been the tide of sentimentalism. But the tide was turned back. The hiss was understood next day to have come only from Cumberland, the high-priest of sentimental comedy; the play "succeeded prodigiously," according to even Horace Walpole, who disliked it; everybody watching Dr. Johnson, and laughing when he did. No wonder the author dedicated his play to its greatest supporter.

The ridicule of sentimentalism is most apparent in the prologue and in scene ii of act I. In the former, which was written by David Garrick the actor, the play is represented as a last effort to revive the dying muse of sound legitimate comedy, and to save the world from the deluge of maudlin sentimentality and platitude-sentiments poured out by her rival. The parody of the manner and speeches of the sentimental hero was highly diverting to sensible people. In the other passage, the fellows at The Three Pigeons love to hear the booby Tony Lumpkin sing, "bekeays he never gives us nothing that's *low*." "May this be my poison if my bear ever dances but to the very genteelest of tunes." Elsewhere also there is plenty of satire, as in that on the insincere talk of the conventional hero in the embarrassed Marlowe's stuttering attempts at genteel conversation with Miss Hardcastle (II. i), who speaks satirically of "a man of *sentiment*." Yet, so hard is it to escape the mental atmosphere in which one lives, there are some slight signs of the disease even in the physician who is to cure it, notably in Miss Neville's somewhat exaggerated sense of propriety. When she at last refuses to elope, "prudence once more comes to her relief, and she will obey its dictates," but she is restrained less by sense than by sensibility. It would have harmonized better with the high spirits of the play if she had been allowed to rattle off toward Scotland; but this would have prevented not only a grand *finale*, with all the chief personages on the stage, but also a sense of complete and dutiful propriety at the end, of all for the very best, of submitting oneself to all one's governors, teachers, spiritual pastors, and masters. "Pshaw, pshaw!" cries Mrs. Hardcastle, apparently conscious of it, "this is all but the whining end of a modern novel."

Instead of the edification afforded by the over-sweet new style of play, Goldsmith meant simply to amuse. He asked a friend to whom he had given a ticket how he had liked the play. To the reply that it had made him laugh he said, "That is all I ask." He would stick to good old-fashioned styles in comedy, as old Hardcastle in dress: "Is not the whole age in a combination to drive sense and discretion out of doors?" He aimed but little, after all, at either satire or the exhibition of truth for its own sake; rather to excite a state of mind as different as possible from that produced by a Kelly or a Cumberland. *She Stoops to Conquer* is in the main a comedy of intrigue. Even Horace Walpole, who thought it mean and "low," worse than the sort of comedy it satirized, allowed merit in the situations, and that it made one laugh; its admirer Johnson, while admitting that the plot, with its confusion of a gentleman's house with an inn, bordered upon farce, felt that the incidents were so prepared for as not to seem improbable. The preparation is fairly obvious, as where in the first scene Mrs. Hardcastle calls the audience's attention to the inn-like look of the house, and Miss Hardcastle informs her father that she is wont at night to wear a "housewive's dress, to please him"; and elsewhere information is given the audience in a sufficiently deliberate way. Like Sheridan, Goldsmith cared less to surprise the spectator than to gratify him by sharing secrets with him. It may make us a little readier in accepting two of the most surprising incidents, to know that Goldsmith as a boy spent a night in a squire's house in Ardagh thinking it an inn, and that Sheridan played on Mme. de Genlis a trick like Tony's on his mother. Chance constantly favors the deceptions, as in the play of cross-purposes between Marlow and old Hardcastle (IV. i), where the former thinks he is doing his landlord a favor by instructing his servants to drink heavily and thus increase the bill. Hastings is too much absorbed in his own amorous schemes to undeceive his friend (his fear of disconcerting him is hardly enough). The light is dim when the bashful Marlow sees Miss Hardcastle so little as not to recognize her the next time. We are willing to give the dramatist the benefit of every doubt; though our generosity is somewhat tried where Miss Neville returns to Tony her lover's letter. The gaiety and rapidity of the action keep such improbabilities from offending us. The farther any play departs from probability — the nearer it comes to farce —, the more crowded must be the action; which here is quick and abundant, with an unusual amount of surprise and reversal. Assuredly it well fulfilled its purpose, as Dr. Johnson said: "I know of no comedy for many years that has so much exhilarated an audience, that has answered so much the great end of comedy — making an audience merry."

The characterization, as fits a comedy of intrigue, is simple but firm. Few sketches of a heroine have more charm than Miss Hardcastle. If her talk to her father sometimes sounds a trifle prim, that was only to be expected in a patriarchal century, and her merry impudence and tact in talking with Marlow, her freedom from prudishness, her living vigor, recall the heroines of Shakespeare's comedies, the Rosalinds and the Beatrices. Hastings, who realizes that more flies are caught by honey than vinegar, is the soft-tongued sort that gets what he wants, yet keeps the good-will of those who would have withheld it; Mrs. Hardcastle has never a harsh word for him. He is the off-spring of an Irishman's heart. His one slip, if it is such, is assuring Mrs. Hardcastle that jewels do not befit a woman under forty, and so making it harder for Miss Neville to filch her own. Tony Lumpkin, the inspired hobbledehoy, is the most enlivening creation in the play (suggested by Humphry Gubbin in Steele's *The Tender Husband*). Though critics have protested that a fellow who could scarcely read should not have composed the admirable drinking-song in the first act, a light comedy may take full advantage of the license of art to make any type of person more perfect in the type than he would be in life; and is not a clever drinking-song directly in the line of this resourceful lover of the bottle? Marlow and his adventures bring us nearest to farce, but his timidity or boldness with different sorts of women are only heightened beyond those of Thackeray's Harry Foker.

She Stoops to Conquer prevailed over its adversary not only with a sling and with a stone, but also by temperate and sincere use of what had been overdone in the other. With all the merriment and extravagance, there is no lack of genuine sentiment, and old Hardcastle even manages to slip in *sotto voce* a moral (V. ii) more practical than the edifying commonplaces of the rival type of play. It follows the sentimental tradition as started by Steele in its entire freedom from vulgarity. Garrick's promise in the prologue is well fulfilled;

> No *poisonous drugs* are mixed in what he gives.

If it is too much to say, though it has been said, that this play gave a deadly blow to the sentimental drama, it certainly reinstated pure comedy, and no reader needs to be told that, along with Sheridan's best two plays, alone among eighteenth-century dramas, it still excites spontaneous delight on the stage.

SHE STOOPS TO CONQUER, OR, THE MISTAKES OF A NIGHT

TO SAMUEL JOHNSON, LL.D.

Dear Sir,—By inscribing this slight performance to you, I do not mean so much to compliment you as myself. It may do me some honor to inform the public, that I have lived many years in intimacy with you. It may serve the interests of mankind also to inform them, that the greatest wit may be found in a character, without impairing the most unaffected piety.

I have, particularly, reason to thank you for your partiality to this performance. The undertaking a comedy, not merely sentimental, was very dangerous; and Mr. Colman, who saw this piece in its various stages, always thought it so. However, I ventured to trust it to the public; and, though it was necessarily delayed till late in the season, I have every reason to be grateful.—I am, dear Sir, your most sincere friend and admirer,

Oliver Goldsmith.

PROLOGUE

By David Garrick, Esq.

(*Enter Mr. Woodward,*[1] *dressed in black, and holding a Handkerchief to his Eyes.*)

Excuse me, sirs, I pray—I can't yet speak—
I'm crying now—and have been all the week!
'T is not alone this mourning suit, good masters;
I 've that within—for which there are no plasters!
Pray would you know the reason why I'm crying?
The Comic muse, long sick, is now a-dying!
And if she goes, my tears will never stop;
For as a player, I can't squeeze out one drop:
I am undone, that 's all—shall lose my bread—
I'd rather, but that 's nothing—lose my head.
When the sweet maid is laid upon the bier,
Shuter[2] and *I* shall be chief mourners here.
To *her* a mawkish drab of spurious breed,
Who deals in *sentimentals* will succeed!
Poor *Ned* and *I* are dead to all intents,
We can as soon speak *Greek* as *sentiments!*
Both nervous grown, to keep our spirits up,
We now and then take down a hearty cup.
What shall we do?—If Comedy forsake us!
They 'll turn us out, and no one else will take us,
But why can't I be moral?—Let me try—
My heart thus pressing—fixed my face and eye—
With a sententious look, that nothing means
(Faces are blocks, in sentimental scenes),
Thus I begin—*All is not gold that glitters,*
Pleasure seems sweet, but proves a glass of bitters.
When ignorance enters, folly is at hand;
Learning is better far than house and land.
Let not your virtue trip, who trips may stumble,
And virtue is not virtue, if she tumble.
I give it up—morals won't do for me;
To make you laugh I must play tragedy.
One hope remains—hearing the maid was ill,
A *doctor* comes this night to show his skill.
To cheer her heart, and give your muscles motion,
He in *five draughts* prepared, presents a potion:
A kind of magic charm—for be assured,
If you will *swallow it,* the maid is cured.
But desperate the Doctor, and her case is,
If you reject the dose, and make wry faces!
This truth he boasts, will boast it while he lives,
No *poisonous drugs* are mixed in what he gives;
Should he succeed, you 'll give him his degree;
If not, within he will receive no fee!
The college *you,* must his pretentions back,
Pronounce him *regular,* or dub him *quack.*

1 An actor.

2 An actor who played old Hardcastle.

DRAMATIS PERSONÆ

MEN

Sir Charles Marlow.
Young Marlow (His Son).
Hardcastle.
Hastings.
Tony Lumpkin.
Diggory.

WOMEN

Mrs. Hardcastle.
Miss Hardcastle.
Miss Neville.
Maid.

Landlord, Servants, &c., &c.

ACT I.

Scene 1. *A Chamber in an Old-Fashioned House.*

(*Enter Mrs. Hardcastle and Mr. Hardcastle.*)

Mrs. Hard. I vow, Mr. Hardcastle, you 're very particular. Is there a creature in the whole country, but ourselves, that does not take a trip to town now and then, to rub off the rust a little? There 's the two Miss Hoggs, and our neighbor, Mrs. Grigsby, go to take a month's polishing every winter.

Hard. Ay, and bring back vanity and affectation to last them the whole year. I wonder why London cannot keep its own fools at home. In my time, the follies of the town crept slowly among us, but now they travel faster than a stage-coach. Its fopperies come down, not only as inside passengers, but in the very basket.[3]

Mrs. Hard. Ay, *your* times were fine times, indeed; you have been telling us of *them* for many a long year. Here we live in an old rumbling mansion, that looks for all the world like an inn, but that we never see company. Our best visitors are old Mrs. Oddfish, the curate's wife, and little Cripplegate, the lame dancing-master: and all our entertainment your old stories of Prince Eugene and the Duke of Marlborough. I hate such old-fashioned trumpery.

Hard. And I love it. I love everything that 's old: old friends, old times, old manners, old books, old wine; and, I believe, Dorothy (*taking her hand*), you 'll own I have been pretty fond of an old wife.

Mrs. Hard. Lord, Mr. Hardcastle, you 're for ever at your Dorothy's and your old wife's. You may be a Darby, but I 'll be no Joan, I promise you.[4] I 'm not so old as you 'd make me, by more than one good year. Add twenty to twenty, and make money of that.

Hard. Let me see; twenty added to twenty, makes just fifty and seven!

Mrs. Hard. It 's false, Mr. Hardcastle: I was but twenty when I was brought to bed of Tony, that I had by Mr. Lumpkin, my first husband; and he 's not come to years of discretion yet.

Hard. Nor ever will, I dare answer for him. Ay, you have taught *him* finely!

Mrs. Hard. No matter, Tony Lumpkin has a good fortune. My son is not to live by his learning. I don't think a boy wants much learning to spend fifteen hundred a year.

Hard. Learning, quotha! A mere composition of tricks and mischief!

Mrs. Hard. Humor, my dear: nothing but humor. Come, Mr. Hardcastle, you must allow the boy a little humor.

Hard. I 'd sooner allow him an horse-pond! If burning the footmen's shoes, frighting the maids, and worrying the kittens, be humor, he has it. It was but yesterday he fastened my wig to the back of my chair, and when I went to make a bow, I popped my bald head in Mrs. Frizzle's face!

Mrs. Hard. And am I to blame? The poor boy was always too sickly to do any good. A school would be his death. When he comes to be a little stronger, who knows what a year or two's Latin may do for him?

Hard. Latin for him! A cat and fiddle! No, no, the ale-house and the stable are the only schools he 'll ever go to!

Mrs. Hard. Well, we must not snub the poor boy now, for I believe we shan't have him long among us. Anybody that looks in his face may see he 's consumptive.

Hard. Ay, if growing too fat be one of the symptoms.

Mrs. Hard. He coughs sometimes.

Hard. Yes, when his liquor goes the wrong way.

Mrs. Hard. I 'm actually afraid of his lungs.

3 The back-part of a stage-coach, a poor place to travel in.

4 Darby and Joan, in tradition, are a devoted elderly couple.

Hard. And truly, so am I; for he sometimes whoops like a speaking-trumpet—(*Tony hallooing behind the scenes*)—O, there he goes—A very consumptive figure, truly!

(*Enter Tony, crossing the stage.*)

Mrs. Hard. Tony, where are you going, my charmer? Won't you give papa and I a little of your company, lovey?

Tony. I 'm in haste, mother, I cannot stay.

Mrs. Hard. You shan't venture out this raw evening, my dear: you look most shockingly.

Tony. I can't stay, I tell you. The Three Pigeons expects me down every moment. There 's some fun going forward.

Hard. Ay; the ale-house, the old place: I thought so.

Mrs. Hard. A low, paltry set of fellows.

Tony. Not so low, neither. There 's Dick Muggins the exciseman, Jack Slang the horse doctor, Little Aminadab that grinds the music box, and Tom Twist that spins the pewter platter.

Mrs. Hard. Pray, my dear, disappoint them for one night, at least.

Tony. As for disappointing *them,* I should not so much mind; but I can't abide to disappoint *myself!*

Mrs. Hard. (*Detaining him.*) You shan't go.

Tony. I will, I tell you.

Mrs. Hard. I say you shan't.

Tony. We 'll see which is strongest, you or I.

(*Exit hauling her out.*)

(*Hardcastle solus.*)

Hard. Ay, there goes a pair that only spoil each other. But is not the whole age in a combination to drive sense and discretion out of doors? There 's my pretty darling, Kate; the fashions of the times have almost infected her too. By living a year or two in town, she is as fond of gauze and French frippery as the best of them.

(*Enter Miss Hardcastle.*)

Hard. Blessings on my pretty innocence! Dressed out as usual, my Kate! Goodness! What a quantity of superfluous silk has thou got about thee, girl! I could never teach the fools of this age, that the indigent world could be clothed out of the trimmings of the vain.

Miss Hard. You know our agreement, sir. You allow me the morning to receive and pay visits, and to dress in my own manner; and in the evening, I put on my housewife's dress, to please you.

Hard. Well, remember, I insist on the terms of our agreement; and, by-the-bye, I believe I shall have occasion to try your obedience this very evening.

Miss Hard. I protest, sir, I don't comprehend your meaning.

Hard. Then, to be plain with you, Kate, I expect the young gentleman I have chosen to be your husband from town this very day. I have his father's letter, in which he informs me his son is set out, and that he intends to follow himself shortly after.

Miss Hard. Indeed! I wish I had known something of this before. Bless me, how shall I behave? It 's a thousand to one I shan't like him; our meeting will be so formal, and so like a thing of business, that I shall find no room for friendship or esteem.

Hard. Depend upon it, child, I 'll never control your choice; but Mr. Marlow, whom I have pitched upon, is the son of my old friend, Sir Charles Marlow, of whom you have heard me talk so often. The young gentleman has been bred a scholar, and is designed for an employment in the service of his country. I am told he 's a man of an excellent understanding.

Miss Hard. Is he?

Hard. Very generous.

Miss Hard. I believe I shall like him.

Hard. Young and brave.

Miss Hard. I 'm sure I shall like him.

Hard. And very handsome.

Miss Hard. My dear papa, say no more (*kissing his hand*), he 's mine, I 'll have him!

Hard. And, to crown all, Kate, he 's one of the most bashful and reserved young fellows in all the world.

Miss Hard. Eh! you have frozen me to death again. That word reserved has undone all the rest of his accomplishments. A reserved lover, it is said, always makes a suspicious husband.

Hard. On the contrary, modesty seldom resides in a breast that is not enriched with nobler virtues. It was the very feature in his character that first struck me.

Miss Hard. He must have more striking features to catch me, I promise you. However, if he be so young, so handsome, and so everything, as you mention, I believe he 'll do still. I think I 'll have him.

Hard. Ay, Kate, but there is still an obstacle. It is more than an even wager, he may not have *you.*

Miss Hard. My dear papa, why will you mortify one so?—Well, if he refuses, instead of breaking my heart at his indifference, I 'll only break my glass for its flattery. Set my cap to some newer fashion, and look out for some less difficult admirer.

Hard. Bravely resolved! In the meantime I 'll go prepare the servants for his reception; as we seldom see company, they want as much training as a company of recruits the first day's muster.

(*Exit.*)

(*Miss Hardcastle sola.*)

Miss Hard. Lud, this news of papa's puts me all in a flutter. Young, handsome; these he put last; but I put them foremost. Sensible, good-natured; I like all that. But then reserved, and sheepish, that 's much against him. Yet can't he be cured of his timidity, by being taught to be proud of his wife? Yes, and can't I—but I vow I 'm disposing of the husband before I have secured the lover!

(*Enter Miss Neville.*)

Miss Hard. I 'm glad you 're come, Neville, my dear. Tell me, Constance, how do I look this evening? Is there anything whimsical about me? Is it one of my well-looking days, child? Am I in face to-day?

Miss Neville. Perfectly, my dear. Yet, now I look again—bless me!—sure no accident has happened among the canary birds or the goldfishes? Has your brother or the cat been meddling? Or has the last novel been too moving?

Miss Hard. No; nothing of all this. I have been threatened—I can scarce get it out—I have been threatened with a lover!

Miss Neville. And his name——

Miss Hard. Is Marlow.

Miss Neville. Indeed!

Miss Hard. The son of Sir Charles Marlow.

Miss Neville. As I live, the most intimate friend of Mr. Hastings, *my* admirer. They are never asunder. I believe you must have seen him when we lived in town.

Miss Hard. Never.

Miss Neville. He 's a very singular character, I assure you. Among women of reputation and virtue, he is the modestest man alive; but his acquaintance give him a very different character among creatures of another stamp: you understand me.

Miss Hard. An odd character, indeed! I shall never be able to manage him. What shall I do? Pshaw, think no more of him, but trust to occurrences for success. But how goes on your own affair, my dear? Has my mother been courting you for my brother Tony, as usual?

Miss Neville. I have just come from one of our agreeable *tête-à-têtes.* She has been saying a hundred tender things, and setting off her pretty monster as the very pink of perfection.

Miss Hard. And her partiality is such, that she actually thinks him so. A fortune like yours is no small temptation. Besides, as she has the sole management of it, I 'm not surprised to see her unwilling to let it go out of the family.

Miss Neville. A fortune like mine, which chiefly consists in jewels, is no such mighty temptation. But, at any rate, if my dear Hastings be but constant, I make no doubt to be too hard for her at last. However, I let her suppose that I am in love with her son, and she never once dreams that my affections are fixed upon another.

Miss Hard. My good brother holds out stoutly. I could almost love him for hating you so.

Miss Neville. It is a good-natured creature at bottom, and I 'm sure would wish to see me married to anybody but himself. But my aunt's bell rings for our afternoon's walk round the improvements. *Allons.*[5] Courage is necessary, as our affairs are critical.

Miss Hard. Would it were bed-time and all were well.

(*Exeunt.*)

Scene 2. *An Ale-house Room.*

(*Several shabby fellows, with punch and tobacco. Tony at the head of the table, a little higher than the rest: a mallet in his hand.*)

Omnes. Hurrea, hurrea, hurrea, bravo!

First Fellow. Now, gentlemen, silence for a song. The 'Squire is going to knock himself down for a song.

Omnes. Ay, a song, a song.

Tony. Then I 'll sing you, gentlemen, a

5 *Let's go.*

song I made upon this ale-house, the Three Pigeons.

SONG

Let school-masters puzzle their brain
With grammar, and nonsense, and learning;
Good liquor, I stoutly maintain,
Gives *genus* [6] a better discerning.
Let them brag of their Heathenish Gods,
Their Lethes, their Styxes, and Stygians;
Their Quis, and their Quæs, and their Quods,
They 're all but a parcel of pigeons.
Toroddle, toroddle, toroll!

When Methodist preachers come down,
A-preaching that drinking is sinful,
I 'll wager the rascals a crown,
They always preach best with a skinful.
But when you come down with your pence,
For a slice of their scurvy religion,
I 'll leave it to all men of sense,
But you, my good friend, are the pigeon.[7]
Toroddle, toroddle, toroll!

Then come, put the jorum [8] about,
And let us be merry and clever,
Our hearts and our liquors are stout,
Here 's the Three Jolly Pigeons for ever.
Let some cry up woodcock or hare,
Your bustards, your ducks, and your widgeons;
But of all the birds in the air,
Here 's a health to the Three Jolly Pigeons.
Toroddle, toroddle, toroll!

Omnes. Bravo, bravo!

First Fellow. The 'Squire has got spunk in him.

Second Fellow. I loves to hear him sing, bekeays he never gives us nothing that 's *low.*

Third Fellow. O damn anything that 's *low,* I cannot bear it!

Fourth Fellow. The genteel thing is the genteel thing at any time. If so be that a gentleman bees in a concatenation accordingly.

Third Fellow. I like the maxum of it, Master Muggins. What, though I am obligated to dance a bear, a man may be a gentleman for all that. May this be my poison if my bear ever dances but to the very genteelest of tunes. *Water Parted,* or the minuet in *Ariadne.*

Second Fellow. What a pity it is the 'Squire is not come to his own. It would be well for all the publicans within ten miles round of him.

Tony. Ecod, and so it would, Master Slang. I 'd then show what it was to keep choice of company.

Second Fellow. O, he takes after his own father for that. To be sure, old 'Squire Lumpkin was the finest gentleman I ever set my eyes on. For winding the straight horn, or beating a thicket for a hare, or a wench, he never had his fellow. It was a saying in the place, that he kept the best horses, dogs, and girls in the whole county.

Tony. Ecod, and when I 'm of age I 'll be no bastard, I promise you. I have been thinking of Bet Bouncer and the miller's grey mare to begin with. But come, my boys, drink about and be merry, for you pay no reckoning. Well, Stingo, what 's the matter?

(*Enter Landlord.*)

Landlord. There be two gentlemen in a postchaise at the door. They have lost their way upo' the forest; and they are talking something about Mr. Hardcastle.

Tony. As sure as can be, one of them must be the gentleman that 's coming down to court my sister. Do they seem to be Londoners?

Landlord. I believe they may. They look woundily [9] like Frenchmen.

Tony. Then desire them to step this way, and I 'll set them right in a twinkling. (*Exit Landlord.*) Gentlemen, as they may n't be good enough company for you, step down for a moment, and I 'll be with you in the squeezing of a lemon.

(*Exeunt Mob.*)

(*Tony solus.*)

Tony. Father-in-law [10] has been calling me whelp and hound, this half year. Now, if I pleased, I could be so revenged upon the old grumbletonian. But then I 'm afraid—afraid of what? I shall soon be worth fifteen hundred a year, and let him frighten me out of *that* if he can!

(*Enter Landlord, conducting Marlow and Hastings.*)

Marlow. What a tedious uncomfortable day have we had of it! We were told it was but forty miles across the country, and we have come above threescore!

6 Presumably for *genius.*
7 gull, dupe.
8 bowl.
9 extremely (a provincial word).
10 Sometimes wrongly used in England for *stepfather.*

Hastings. And all, Marlow, from that unaccountable reserve of yours, that would not let us enquire more frequently on the way.

Harlow. I own, Hastings, I am unwilling to lay myself under an obligation to every one I meet; and often stand the chance of an unmannerly answer.

Hastings. At present, however, we are not likely to receive any answer.

Tony. No offence, gentlemen. But I'm told you have been enquiring for one Mr. Hardcastle, in [these] parts. Do you know what part of the country you are in?

Hastings. Not in the least, sir, but should thank you for information.

Tony. Nor the way you came?

Hastings. No, sir, but if you can inform us——

Tony. Why, gentlemen, if you know neither the road you are going, nor where you are, nor the road you came, the first thing I have to inform you is, that—you have lost your way.

Marlow. We wanted no ghost to tell us that.

Tony. Pray, gentlemen, may I be so bold as to ask the place from whence you came?

Marlow. That's not necessary towards directing us where we are to go.

Tony. No offence; but question for question is all fair, you know. Pray, gentlemen, is not this same Hardcastle a cross-grained, old-fashioned, whimsical fellow with an ugly face, a daughter, and a pretty son?

Hastings. We have not seen the gentleman, but he has the family you mention.

Tony. The daughter, a tall, trapesing, trolloping, talkative maypole——The son, a pretty, well-bred, agreeable youth, that everybody is fond of!

Marlow. Our information differs in this. The daughter is said to be well-bred and beautiful; the son, an awkward booby, reared up and spoiled at his mother's apron-string.

Tony. He-he-hem—then, gentlemen, all I have to tell you is, that you won't reach Mr. Hardcastle's house this night, I believe.

Hastings. Unfortunate!

Tony. It's a damned long, dark, boggy, dirty, dangerous way. Stingo, tell the gentlemen the way to Mr. Hardcastle's. (*Winking upon the Landlord.*) Mr. Hardcastle's of Quagmire Marsh, you understand me.

Landlord. Master Hardcastle's! Lack-a-daisy, my masters, you're come a deadly deal wrong! When you came to the bottom of the hill, you should have crossed down Squash Lane.

Marlow. Cross down Squash Lane!

Landlord. Then you were to keep straight forward, until you came to four roads.

Marlow. Come to where four roads meet!

Tony. Ay, but you must be sure to take only one of them.

Marlow. O, sir, you're facetious!

Tony. Then, keeping to the right, you are to go sideways till you come upon Crack-skull Common: there you must look sharp for the track of the wheel, and go forward, till you come to Farmer Murrain's barn. Coming to the farmer's barn, you are to turn to the right, and then to the left, and then to the right about again, till you find out the old mill——

Marlow. Zounds, man! we could as soon find out the longitude!

Hastings. What's to be done, Marlow?

Marlow. This house promises but a poor reception, though, perhaps, the landlord can accommodate us.

Landlord. Alack, master, we have but one spare bed in the whole house.

Tony. And to my knowledge, that's taken up by three lodgers already. (*After a pause, in which the rest seem disconcerted.*) I have hit it. Don't you think, Stingo, our landlady could accommodate the gentlemen by the fire-side, with——three chairs and a bolster?

Hastings. I hate sleeping by the fire-side.

Marlow. And I detest your three chairs and a bolster.

Tony. You do, do you?—then let me see—what—if you go on a mile further, to the Buck's Head; the old Buck's Head on the hill, one of the best inns in the whole county?

Hastings. O ho! so we have escaped an adventure for this night, however.

Landlord. (*Apart to Tony.*) Sure, you be n't sending them to your father's as an inn, be you?

Tony. Mum, you fool, you. Let *them* find that out. (*To them.*) You have only to keep on straight forward, till you come to a large old house by the roadside. You'll see a pair of large horns over the door. That's the sign. Drive up the yard, and call stoutly about you.

Hastings. Sir, we are obliged to you. The servants can't miss the way?

Tony. No, no: but I tell you though, the

landlord is rich, and going to leave off business; so he wants to be thought a gentleman, saving your presence, he! he! he! He'll be for giving you his company, and, ecod, if you mind him, he'll persuade you that his mother was an alderman, and his aunt a justice of peace!

Landlord. A troublesome old blade, to be sure; but 'a keeps as good wines and beds as any in the whole country.

Marlow. Well, if he supplies us with these, we shall want no further connection. We are to turn to the right, did you say?

Tony. No, no; straight forward. I'll just step myself, and show you a piece of the way. (*To the Landlord.*) Mum.

Landlord. Ah, bless your heart, for a sweet, pleasant,—damned mischievous son of a whore.

(*Exeunt.*)

ACT II

SCENE 1. *An Old-Fashioned House.*

(*Enter Hardcastle, followed by three or four awkward Servants.*)

Hardcastle. Well, I hope you're perfect in the table exercise I have been teaching you these three days. You all know your posts and your places, and can show that you have been used to good company, without ever stirring from home.

Omnes. Ay, ay.

Hard. When company comes, you are not to pop out and stare, and then run in again, like frighted rabbits in a warren.

Omnes. No, no.

Hard. You, Diggory, whom I have taken from the barn, are to make a show at the side-table; and you, Roger, whom I have advanced from the plough, are to place yourself behind *my* chair. But you're not to stand so, with your hands in your pockets. Take your hands from your pockets, Roger; and from your head, you blockhead, you. See how Diggory carries his hands. They're a little too stiff, indeed, but that's no great matter.

Diggory. Ay, mind how I hold them. I learned to hold my hands this way, when I was upon drill for the militia. And so being upon drill——

Hard. You must not be so talkative, Diggory. You must be all attention to the guests. You must hear us talk, and not think of talking; you must see us drink, and not think of drinking; you must see us eat, and not think of eating.

Diggory. By the laws, your worship, that's parfectly unpossible. Whenever Diggory sees yeating going forward, ecod, he's always wishing for a mouthful himself.

Hard. Blockhead! Is not a bellyful in the kitchen as good as a bellyful in the parlor? Stay your stomach with that reflection.

Diggory. Ecod, I thank your worship, I'll make a shift to stay my stomach with a slice of cold beef in the pantry.

Hard. Diggory, you are too talkative. Then, if I happen to say a good thing, or tell a good story at table, you must not all burst out a-laughing, as if you made part of the company.

Diggory. Then, ecod, your worship must not tell the story of Ould Grouse in the gun-room: I can't help laughing at that —he! he! he!—for the soul of me! We have laughed at that these twenty years —ha! ha! ha!

Hard. Ha! ha! ha! The story is a good one. Well, honest Diggory, you may laugh at that—but still remember to be attentive. Suppose one of the company should call for a glass of wine, how will you behave? A glass of wine, sir, if you please (*to Diggory*)—Eh, why don't you move?

Diggory. Ecod, your worship, I never have courage till I see the eatables and drinkables brought upo' the table, and then I'm as bauld as a lion.

Hard. What, will nobody move?

First Servant. I'm not to leave this pleace.

Second Servant. I'm sure it's no pleace of mine.

Third Servant. Not mine, for sartain.

Diggory. Wauns, and I'm sure it canna be mine.

Hard. You numskulls! and so while, like your betters, you are quarrelling for places, the guests must be starved. O, you dunces! I find I must begin all over again.—But don't I hear a coach drive into the yard? To your posts, you blockheads! I'll go in the meantime and give my old friend's son a hearty reception at the gate.

(*Exit Hardcastle.*)

Diggory. By the elevens,[11] my pleace is gone quite out of my head.

11 A meaningless exclamation.

Roger. I know that my pleace is to be everywhere!

First Servant. Where the devil is mine?

Second Servant. My pleace is to be nowhere at all; and so I 'ze go about my business!

(*Exeunt Servants, running about as if frighted, different ways.*)

(*Enter Servant with candles, showing in Marlow and Hastings.*)

Servant. Welcome, gentlemen, very welcome. This way.

Hastings. After the disappointments of the day, welcome once more, Charles, to the comforts of a clean room and a good fire. Upon my word, a very well-looking house; antique but creditable.

Marlow. The usual fate of a large mansion. Having first ruined the master by good housekeeping, it at last comes to levy contributions as an inn.

Hastings. As you say, we passengers are to be taxed to pay all these fineries. I have often seen a good sideboard, or a marble chimney-piece, though not actually put in the bill, inflame a reckoning confoundedly.

Marlow. Travellers, George, must pay in all places. The only difference, is, that in good inns, you pay dearly for luxuries; in bad inns, you are fleeced and starved.

Hastings. You have lived pretty much among them. In truth, I have been often surprised, that you who have seen so much of the world, with your natural good sense, and your many opportunities, could never yet acquire a requisite share of assurance.

Marlow. The Englishman's malady. But tell me, George, where could I have learned that assurance you talk of? My life has been chiefly spent in a college, or an inn, in seclusion from that lovely part of the creation that chiefly teach men confidence. I don't know that I was ever familiarly acquainted with a single modest woman—except my mother—But among females of another class, you know——

Hastings. Ay, among them you are impudent enough of all conscience!

Marlow. They are of *us,* you know.

Hastings. But in the company of women of reputation I never saw such an idiot, such a trembler; you look for all the world as if you wanted an opportunity of stealing out of the room.

Marlow. Why, man, that 's because I *do* want to steal out of the room. Faith, I have often formed a resolution to break the ice, and rattle away at any rate. But I don't know how, a single glance from a pair of fine eyes has totally overset my resolution. An impudent fellow may counterfeit modesty, but I 'll be hanged if a modest man can ever counterfeit impudence.

Hastings. If you could but say half the fine things to them that I have heard you lavish upon the barmaid of an inn, or even a college bedmaker——

Marlow. Why, George, I can't say fine things to them. They freeze, they petrify me. They may talk of a comet, or a burning mountain, or some such bagatelle. But to me, a modest woman, dressed out in all her finery, is the most tremendous object of the whole creation.

Hastings. Ha! ha! ha! At this rate, man, how can you ever expect to marry!

Marlow. Never, unless, as among kings and princes, my bride were to be courted by proxy. If, indeed, like an Eastern bridegroom, one were to be introduced to a wife he never saw before, it might be endured. But to go through all the terrors of a formal courtship, together with the episode of aunts, grandmothers and cousins, and at last to blurt out the broad staring question of, *madam, will you marry me?* No, no, that 's a strain much above me, I assure you!

Hastings. I pity you. But how do you intend behaving to the lady you are come down to visit at the request of your father?

Marlow. As I behave to all other ladies. Bow very low. Answer yes, or no, to all her demands—But for the rest, I don't think I shall venture to look in her face, till I see my father's again.

Hastings. I 'm surprised that one who is so warm a friend can be so cool a lover.

Marlow. To be explicit, my dear Hastings, my chief inducement down was to be instrumental in forwarding your happiness, not my own. Miss Neville loves you, the family don't know you, as my friend you are sure of a reception, and let honor do the rest.

Hastings. My dear Marlow! But I 'll suppress the emotion. Were I a wretch, meanly seeking to carry off a fortune, you should be the last man in the world I would apply to for assistance. But Miss Neville's person is all I ask, and that is mine, both from her deceased father's consent, and her own inclination.

Marlow. Happy man! You have talents and art to captivate any woman. I'm doomed to adore the sex, and yet to converse with the only part of it I despise. This stammer in my address, and this awkward [un]prepossessing visage of mine, can never permit me to soar above the reach of a milliner's apprentice, or one of the duchesses of Drury Lane.[12] Pshaw! this fellow here to interrupt us.

(*Enter Hardcastle.*)

Hard. Gentlemen, once more you are heartily welcome. Which is Mr. Marlow? Sir, you're heartily welcome. It's not my way, you see, to receive my friends with my back to the fire. I like to give them a hearty reception in the old style at my gate. I like to see their horses and trunks taken care of.

Marlow. (*Aside.*) He has got our names from the servants already. (*To him.*) We approve your caution and hospitality, sir. (*To Hastings.*) I have been thinking, George, of changing our travelling dresses in the morning. I am grown confoundedly ashamed of mine.

Hard. I beg, Mr. Marlow, you'll use no ceremony in this house.

Hastings. I fancy, George, you're right: the first blow is half the battle. I intend opening the campaign with the white and gold.

Hard. Mr. Marlow—Mr. Hastings—gentlemen—pray be under no constraint in this house. This is Liberty Hall, gentlemen. You may do just as you please here.

Marlow. Yet, George, if we open the campaign too fiercely at first, we may want ammunition before it is over. I think to reserve the embroidery to secure a retreat.

Hard. Your talking of a retreat, Mr. Marlow, puts me in mind of the Duke of Marlborough, when we went to besiege Denain.[13] He first summoned the garrison——

Marlow. Don't you think the *ventre d'or* waistcoat will do with the plain brown?

Hard. He first summoned the garrison, which might consist of about five thousand men——

Hastings. I think not: brown and yellow mix but very poorly.

Hard. I say, gentlemen, as I was telling you, he summoned the garrison, which might consist of about five thousand men——

Marlow. The girls like finery.

Hard. Which might consist of about five thousand men, well appointed with stores, ammunition, and other implements of war. "Now," says the Duke of Marlborough to George Brooks, that stood next to him—you must have heard of George Brooks; "I'll pawn my dukedom," says he, "but I take that garrison without spilling a drop of blood!" So——

Marlow. What, my good friend, if you gave us a glass of punch in the meantime, it would help us to carry on the siege with vigor.

Hard. Punch, sir!—(*Aside.*) This is the most unaccountable kind of modesty I ever met with!

Marlow. Yes, sir, punch! A glass of warm punch, after our journey, will be comfortable. This is Liberty Hall, you know.

Hard. Here's cup, sir.

Marlow. (*Aside.*) So this fellow, in his Liberty Hall, will only let us have just what he pleases.

Hard. (*Taking the cup.*) I hope you'll find it to your mind. I have prepared it with my own hands, and I believe you'll own the ingredients are tolerable. Will you be so good as to pledge me, sir? Here, Mr. Marlow, here is our better acquaintance!

(*Drinks.*)

Marlow. (*Aside.*) A very impudent fellow this! but he's a character, and I'll humor him a little. Sir, my service to you.

(*Drinks.*)

Hastings. (*Aside.*) I see this fellow wants to give us his company, and forgets that he's an innkeeper, before he has learned to be a gentleman.

Marlow. From the excellence of your cup, my old friend, I suppose you have a good deal of business in this part of the country. Warm work, now and then, at elections, I suppose?

Hard. No, sir, I have long given that work over. Since our betters have hit upon the expedient of electing each other, there's no business *for us that sell ale.*

Hastings. So, then you have no turn for politics, I find.

Hard. Not in the least. There was a time, indeed, I fretted myself about the mis-

12 courtesans.

13 Where the English and their allies were beaten by the French in 1712.

takes of government, like other people; but, finding myself every day grow more angry, and the government growing no better, I left it to mend itself. Since that, I no more trouble my head about *Heyder Ally,* or *Ally Cawn,* than about *Ally Croaker.*[14] Sir, my service to you.

Hastings. So that, with eating above stairs, and drinking below, with receiving your friends within, and amusing them without, you lead a good pleasant bustling life of it.

Hard. I do stir about a great deal, that 's certain. Half the differences of the parish are adjusted in this very parlor.

Marlow. (*After drinking.*) And you have an argument in your cup, old gentleman, better than any in Westminster Hall.

Hard. Ay, young gentleman, that, and a little philosophy.

Marlow. (*Aside.*) Well, this is the first time I ever heard of an innkeeper's philosophy.

Hastings. So then, like an experienced general, you attack them on every quarter. If you find their reason manageable, you attack it with your philosophy; if you find they have no reason, you attack them with this. Here 's your health, my philosopher.

(*Drinks.*)

Hard. Good, very good, thank you; ha! ha! Your generalship puts me in mind of Prince Eugene, when he fought the Turks at the battle of Belgrade.[15] You shall hear.

Marlow. Instead of the battle of Belgrade, I believe it 's almost time to talk about supper. What has your philosophy got in the house for supper?

Hard. For supper, sir!——(*Aside.*) Was ever such a request to a man in his own house!

Marlow. Yes, sir, supper, sir; I begin to feel an appetite. I shall make devilish work to-night in the larder, I promise you.

Hard. (*Aside.*) Such a brazen dog sure never my eyes beheld. (*To him.*) Why, really, sir, as for supper I can't well tell. My Dorothy, and the cook maid, settle these things between them. I leave these kind of things entirely to them.

Marlow. You do, do you?

Hard. Entirely. By-the-bye, I believe they are in actual consultation upon what 's for supper this moment in the kitchen.

Marlow. Then I beg they 'll admit *me* as one of their privy council. It 's a way I have got. When I travel, I always choose to regulate my own supper. Let the cook be called. No offence, I hope, sir.

Hard. O, no, sir, none in the least; yet, I don't know how: our Bridget, the cook maid, is not very communicative upon these occasions. Should we send for her, she might scold us all out of the house.

Hastings. Let 's see your list of the larder, then. I ask it as a favor. I always match my appetite to my bill of fare.

Marlow. (*To Hardcastle, who looks at them with surprise.*) Sir, he 's very right, and it 's my way, too.

Hard. Sir, you have a right to command here. Here, Roger, bring us the bill of fare for to-night's supper. I believe it 's drawn out. Your manner, Mr. Hastings, puts me in mind of my uncle, Colonel Wallop. It was a saying of his, that no man was sure of his supper till he had eaten it.

Hastings. (*Aside.*) All upon the high ropes! His uncle a colonel! We shall soon hear of his mother being a justice of peace. But let 's hear the bill of fare.

Marlow. (*Perusing.*) What 's here? For the first course; foı the second course; for the dessert. The devil, sir, do you think we have brought down the whole Joiners' Company, or the Corporation of Bedford, to eat up such a supper? Two or three little things, clean and comfortable, will do.

Hastings. But let 's hear it.

Marlow. (*Reading.*) For the first course at the top, a pig, and pruin sauce.

Hastings. Damn your pig, I say!

Marlow. And damn your pruin sauce, say I!

Hard. And yet, gentlemen, to men that are hungry, pig, with pruin sauce, is very good eating.

Marlow. At the bottom, a calf's tongue and brains.

Hastings. Let your brains be knocked out, my good sir; I don't like them.

Marlow. Or you may clap them on a plate by themselves, I do.

Hard. (*Aside.*) Their impudence confounds me. (*To them.*) Gentlemen, you are my guests, make what alterations you please. Is there anything else you wish to retrench or alter, gentlemen?

Marlow. Item. A pork pie, a boiled rab-

14 The first two were Hindoo potentates; the third, a popular Irish song.

15 In 1717.

bit and sausages, a florentine,[16] a shaking pudding, and a dish of tiff—taff—taffety cream!

Hastings. Confound your made dishes, I shall be as much at a loss in this house as at a green and yellow dinner at the French ambassador's table. I 'm for plain eating.

Hard. I 'm sorry, gentlemen, that I have nothing you like, but if there be anything you have a particular fancy to——

Marlow. Why, really, sir, your bill of fare is so exquisite, that any one part of it is full as good as another. Send us what you please. So much for supper. And now to see that our beds are aired, and properly taken care of.

Hard. I entreat you 'll leave all that to me. You shall not stir a step.

Marlow. Leave that to you! I protest, sir, you must excuse me, I always look to these things myself.

Hard. I must insist, sir, you 'll make yourself easy on that head.

Marlow. You see I 'm resolved on it.—(*Aside.*) A very troublesome fellow this, as ever I met with.

Hard. Well, sir, I 'm resolved at least to attend you.—(*Aside.*) This may be modern modesty, but I never saw anything look so like old-fashioned impudence.

(*Exeunt Marlow and Hardcastle.*)

(*Hastings solus.*)

Hastings. So I find this fellow's civilities begin to grow troublesome. But who can be angry at those assiduities which are meant to please him? Ha! what do I see! Miss Neville, by all that 's happy!

(*Enter Miss Neville.*)

Miss Neville. My dear Hastings! To what unexpected good fortune? to what accident am I to ascribe this happy meeting?

Hastings. Rather let me ask the same question, as I could never have hoped to meet my dearest Constance at an inn.

Miss Neville. An inn! sure you mistake! my aunt, my guardian, lives here. What could induce you to think this house an inn?

Hastings. My friend, Mr. Marlow, with whom I came down, and I, have been sent here as to an inn, I assure you. A young fellow whom we accidentally met at a house hard by directed us hither.

Miss Neville. Certainly it must be one of my hopeful cousin's tricks, of whom you have heard me talk so often, ha! ha! ha! ha!

Hastings. He whom your aunt intends for you? He of whom I have such just apprehensions?

Miss Neville. You have nothing to fear from him, I assure you. You 'd adore him if you knew how heartily he despises me. My aunt knows it too, and has undertaken to court me for him, and actually begins to think she has made a conquest.

Hastings. Thou dear dissembler! You must know, my Constance, I have just seized this happy opportunity of my friend's visit here to get admittance into the family. The horses that carried us down are now fatigued with their journey, but they 'll soon be refreshed; and then, if my dearest girl will trust in her faithful Hastings, we shall soon be landed in France, where even among slaves the laws of marriage are respected.

Miss Neville. I have often told you, that though ready to obey you, I yet should leave my little fortune behind with reluctance. The greatest part of it was left me by my uncle, the India Director, and chiefly consists in jewels. I have been for some time persuading my aunt to let me wear them. I fancy I 'm very near succeeding. The instant they are put into my possession you shall find me ready to make them and myself yours.

Hastings. Perish the baubles! Your person is all I desire. In the meantime, my friend Marlow must not be let into his mistake. I know the strange reserve of his temper is such, that if abruptly informed of it, he would instantly quit the house before our plan was ripe for execution.

Miss Neville. But how shall we keep him in the deception? Miss Hardcastle is just returned from walking; what if we still continue to deceive him?—This, this way——

(*They confer.*)

(*Enter Marlow.*)

Marlow. The assiduities of these good people tease me beyond bearing. My host seems to think it ill manners to leave me alone, and so he claps not only himself, but his old-fashioned wife on my back. They talk of coming to sup with us, too; and then, I suppose, we are to run the

16 A kind of pie.

gauntlet through all the rest of the family.—What have we got here?—

Hastings. My dear Charles! Let me congratulate you—The most fortunate accident!—Who do you think is just alighted?

Marlow. Cannot guess.

Hastings. Our mistresses, boy, Miss Hardcastle and Miss Neville. Give me leave to introduce Miss Constance Neville to your acquaintance. Happening to dine in the neighborhood, they called, on their return, to take fresh horses here. Miss Hardcastle has just stept into the next room, and will be back in an instant. Was n't it lucky? eh!

Marlow. (*Aside.*) I have just been mortified enough of all conscience, and here comes something to complete my embarrassment.

Hastings. Well! but wasn't it the most fortunate thing in the world?

Marlow. Oh! yes. Very fortunate—a most joyful encounter——But our dresses, George, you know, are in disorder——What if we should postpone the happiness till to-morrow?——To-morrow at her own house——It will be every bit as convenient——And rather more respectful——To-morrow let it be.

(*Offering to go.*)

Miss Neville. By no means, sir. Your ceremony will displease her. The disorder of your dress will show the ardor of your impatience. Besides, she knows you are in the house, and will permit you to see her.

Marlow. O! the devil! how shall I support it? Hem! hem! Hastings, you must not go. You are to assist me, you know. I shall be confoundedly ridiculous. Yet, hang it! I'll take courage. Hem!

Hastings. Pshaw, man! it 's but the first plunge, and all 's over. She 's but a woman, you know.

Marlow. And of all women, she that I dread most to encounter!

(*Enter Miss Hardcastle, as returned from walking, a bonnet, &c.*)

Hastings. (*Introducing them.*) Miss Hardcastle, Mr. Marlow, I 'm proud of bringing two persons of such merit together, that only want to know, to esteem each other.

Miss Hard. (*Aside.*) Now, for meeting my modest gentleman with a demure face, and quite in his own manner. (*After a pause, in which he appears very uneasy and disconcerted.*) I 'm glad of your safe arrival, sir——I 'm told you had some accidents by the way.

Marlow. Only a few, madam. Yes, we had some. Yes, madam, a good many accidents, but should be sorry—madam—or rather glad of any accidents—that are so agreeably concluded. Hem!

Hastings. (*To him.*) You never spoke better in your whole life. Keep it up, and I 'll insure you the victory.

Miss Hard. I 'm afraid you flatter, sir. You that have seen so much of the finest company can find little entertainment in an obscure corner of the country.

Marlow. (*Gathering courage.*) I have lived, indeed, in the world, madam; but I have kept very little company. I have been but an observer upon life, madam, while others were enjoying it.

Miss Neville. But that, I am told, is the way to enjoy it at last.

Hastings. (*To him.*) Cicero never spoke better. Once more, and you are confirmed in assurance for ever.

Marlow. (*To him.*) Hem! Stand by me, then, and when I 'm down, throw in a word or two to set me up again.

Miss Hard. An observer, like you, upon life, were, I fear, disagreeably employed, since you must have had much more to censure than to approve.

Marlow. Pardon me, madam. I was always willing to be amused. The folly of most people is rather an object of mirth than uneasiness.

Hastings. (*To him.*) Bravo, bravo. Never spoke so well in your whole life. Well, Miss Hardcastle, I see that you and Mr. Marlow are going to be very good company. I believe our being here will but embarrass the interview.

Marlow. Not in the least, Mr. Hastings. We like your company of all things. (*To him.*) Zounds! George, sure you won't go? How can you leave us?

Hastings. Our presence will but spoil conversation, so we 'll retire to the next room. (*To him.*) You don't consider, man, that we are to manage a little *tête-à-tête* of our own.

(*Exeunt.*)

Miss Hard. (*After a pause.*) But you have not been wholly an observer, I presume, sir. The ladies, I should hope, have employed some part of your addresses.

Marlow. (*Relapsing into timidity.*) Pardon me, madam, I—I—I—as yet have studied—only—to—deserve them.

Miss Hard. And that some say is the very worst way to obtain them.

Marlow. Perhaps so, madam. But I love to converse only with the more grave and sensible part of the sex.——But I 'm afraid I grow tiresome.

Miss Hard. Not at all, sir; there is nothing I like so much as grave conversation myself: I could hear it for ever. Indeed, I have often been surprised how a man of *sentiment* could ever admire those light airy pleasures, where nothing reaches the heart.

Marlow. It 's—a disease—of the mind, madam. In the variety of tastes there must be some who, wanting a relish for —um-a-um.

Miss Hard. I understand you, sir. There must be some, who, wanting a relish for refined pleasures, pretend to despise what they are incapable of tasting.

Marlow. My meaning, madam, but infinitely better expressed. And I can't help observing—a——

Miss Hard. (*Aside.*) Who could ever suppose this fellow impudent upon some occasions. (*To him.*) You were going to observe, sir——

Marlow. I was observing, madam——I protest, madam, I forget what I was going to observe.

Miss Hard. (*Aside.*) I vow and so do I. (*To him.*) You were observing, sir, that in this age of hypocrisy—something about hypocrisy, sir.

Marlow. Yes, madam. In this age of hypocrisy, there are few who upon strict enquiry do not—a—a—a——

Miss Hard. I understand you perfectly, sir.

Marlow. (*Aside.*) Egad! and that 's more than I do myself!

Miss Hard. You mean that in this hypocritical age there are few that do not condemn in public what they practise in private, and think they pay every debt to virtue when they praise it.

Marlow. True, madam; those who have most virtue in their mouths, have least of it in their bosoms. But I 'm sure I tire you, madam.

Miss Hard. Not in the least, sir; there 's something so agreeable and spirited in your manner, such life and force——pray, sir, go on.

Marlow. Yes, madam. I was saying——that there are some occasions——when a total want of courage, madam, destroys all the——and puts us——upon a——a——a——

Miss Hard. I agree with you entirely, a want of courage upon some occasions assumes the appearance of ignorance, and betrays us when we most want to excel. I beg you 'll proceed.

Marlow. Yes, madam. Morally speaking, madam——But I see Miss Neville expecting us in the next room. I would not intrude for the world.

Miss Hard. I protest, sir, I never was more agreeably entertained in all my life. Pray go on.

Marlow. Yes, madam. I was——But she beckons us to join her. Madam, shall I do myself the honor to attend you?

Miss Hard. Well then, I 'll follow.

Marlow. (*Aside.*) This pretty smooth dialogue has done for me.

(*Exit.*)

(*Miss Hardcastle sola.*)

Miss Hard. Ha! ha! ha! Was there ever such a sober sentimental interview? I 'm certain he scarce looked in my face the whole time. Yet the fellow, but for his unaccountable bashfulness, is pretty well, too. He has good sense, but then so buried in his fears, that it fatigues one more than ignorance. If I could teach him a little confidence, it would be doing somebody that I know of a piece of service. But who is that somebody?—that, faith, is a question I can scarce answer.

(*Exit.*)

(*Enter Tony and Miss Neville, followed by Mrs. Hardcastle and Hastings.*)

Tony. What do you follow me for, cousin Con? I wonder you 're not ashamed to be so very engaging.

Miss Neville. I hope, cousin, one may speak to one's own relations, and not be to blame.

Tony. Ay, but I know what sort of a relation you want to make me, though; but it won't do. I tell you, cousin Con, it won't do, so I beg you 'll keep your distance, I want no nearer relationship.

(*She follows coquetting him to the back scene.*)

Mrs. Hard. Well! I vow, Mr. Hastings, you are very entertaining. There 's nothing in the world I love to talk of so much as London, and the fashions, though I was never there myself.

Hastings. Never there! You amaze me! From your air and manner, I concluded you had been bred all your life either at

Ranelagh, St. James's or Tower Wharf.[17]

Mrs. Hard. O! sir, you 're only pleased to say so. We country persons can have no manner at all. I 'm in love with the town, and that serves to raise me above some of our neighboring rustics; but who can have a manner, that has never seen the Pantheon, the Grotto Gardens, the Borough,[18] and such places where the nobility chiefly resort? All I can do is to enjoy London at second-hand. I take care to know every *tête-à-tête* from the Scandalous Magazine, and have all the fashions as they come out, in a letter from the two Miss Rickets of Crooked Lane. Pray how do you like this head, Mr. Hastings?

Hastings. Extremely elegant and *dégagée,*[19] upon my word, madam. Your friseur is a Frenchman, I suppose?

Mrs. Hard. I protest, I dressed it myself from a print in the Ladies' Memorandum-book for the last year.

Hastings. Indeed. Such a head in a side-box, at the Play-house, would draw as many gazers as my Lady Mayoress at a City Ball.

Mrs. Hard. I vow, since inoculation[20] began, there is no such thing to be seen as a plain woman; so one must dress a little particular or one may escape in the crowd.

Hastings. But that can never be your case, madam, in any dress! (*Bowing.*)

Mrs. Hard. Yet, what signifies *my* dressing when I have such a piece of antiquity by my side as Mr. Hardcastle: all I can say will never argue down a single button from his clothes. I have often wanted him to throw off his great flaxen wig, and where he was bald, to plaster it over like my Lord Pately, with powder.

Hastings. You are right, madam; for, as among the ladies there are none ugly, so among the men there are none old.

Mrs. Hard. But what do you think his answer was? Why, with his usual Gothic[21] vivacity, he said I only wanted him to throw off his wig to convert it into a *tête* for my own wearing!

Hastings. Intolerable! At your age you may wear what you please, and it must become you.

Mrs. Hard. Pray, Mr. Hastings, what do you take to be the most fashionable age about town?

Hastings. Some time ago forty was all the mode; but I 'm told the ladies intend to bring up fifty for the ensuing winter.

Mrs. Hard. Seriously! Then I shall be too young for the fashion!

Hastings. No lady begins now to put on jewels till she 's past forty. For instance, miss there, in a polite circle, would be considered as a child, as a mere maker of samplers.

Mrs. Hard. And yet Mrs. Niece thinks herself as much a woman, and is as fond of jewels, as the oldest of us all.

Hastings. Your niece, is she? And that young gentleman, a brother of yours, I should presume?

Mrs. Hard. My son, sir. They are contracted to each other. Observe their little sports. They fall in and out ten times a day, as if they were man and wife already. (*To them.*) Well, Tony, child, what soft things are you saying to your cousin Constance, this evening?

Tony. I have been saying no soft things; but that it 's very hard to be followed about so! Ecod! I 've not a place in the house now that 's left to myself but the stable.

Mrs. Hard. Never mind him, Con, my dear. He 's in another story behind your back.

Miss Neville. There 's something generous in my cousin's manner. He falls out before faces to be forgiven in private.

Tony. That 's a damned confounded——crack.[22]

Mrs. Hard. Ah! he 's a sly one. Don't you think they 're like each other about the mouth, Mr. Hastings? The Blenkinsop mouth to a T. They 're of a size, too. Back to back, my pretties, that Mr. Hastings may see you. Come, Tony.

Tony. You had as good not make me, I tell you.

(*Measuring.*)

Miss Neville. O lud! he has almost cracked my head.

Mrs. Hard. O, the monster! For shame, Tony. You a man, and behave so!

Tony. If I 'm a man, let me have my fortin. Ecod! I 'll not be made a fool of no longer.

Mrs. Hard. Is this, ungrateful boy, all

17 The first two were fashionable places in the city, the third was just the reverse. Of course he is playing on her ignorance.

18 She betrays her ignorance; the Borough, in Southwark, was very unlike the fashionable Pantheon, a concert hall on Oxford St.

19 unconstrained, easy.

20 Which diminished small-pox.

21 barbarous.

22 lie.

that I'm to get for the pains I have taken in your education? I that have rocked you in your cradle, and fed that pretty mouth with a spoon! Did not I work that waistcoat to make you genteel? Did not I prescribe for you every day, and weep while the receipt was operating?

Tony. Ecod! you had reason to weep, for you have been dosing me ever since I was born. I have gone through every receipt in the *Complete Housewife* ten times over; and you have thoughts of coursing me through *Quincy* next spring. But, ecod! I tell you, I'll not be made a fool of no longer.

Mrs. Hard. Was n't it all for your good, viper? Was n't it all for your good?

Tony. I wish you'd let me and my good alone, then. Snubbing this way when I'm in spirits. If I'm to have any good, let it come of itself; not to keep dinging it, dinging it into one so.

Mrs. Hard. That's false; I never see you when you're in spirits. No, Tony, you then go to the ale-house or kennel. I'm never to be delighted with your agreeable, wild notes, unfeeling monster!

Tony. Ecod! Mamma, your own notes are the wildest of the two.

Mrs. Hard. Was ever the like? But I see he wants to break my heart, I see he does.

Hastings. Dear madam, permit me to lecture the young gentleman a little. I'm certain I can persuade him to his duty.

Mrs. Hard. Well! I must retire. Come, Constance, my love. You see, Mr. Hastings, the wretchedness of my situation. Was ever poor woman so plagued with a dear, sweet, pretty, provoking, undutiful boy?

(*Exeunt Mrs. Hardcastle and Miss Neville.*)

(*Hastings. Tony.*)

Tony. (*Singing.*) *There was a young man riding by, and fain would have his will. Rang do didlo dee.* Don't mind her. Let her cry. It's the comfort of her heart. I have seen her and sister cry over a book for an hour together, and they said, they liked the book the better the more it made them cry.

Hastings. Then you're no friend to the ladies, I find, my pretty young gentleman?

Tony. That's as I find 'um.

Hastings. Not to her of your mother's choosing, I dare answer! And yet she appears to me a pretty, well-tempered girl.

Tony. That's because you don't know her as well as I. Ecod! I know every inch about her; and there's not a more bitter cantankerous toad in all Christendom!

Hastings. (*Aside.*) Pretty encouragement, this, for a lover!

Tony. I have seen her since the height of that. She has as many tricks as a hare in a thicket, or a colt the first day's breaking.

Hastings. To me she appears sensible and silent!

Tony. Ay, before company. But when she's with her playmates, she's as loud as a hog in a gate.

Hastings. But there is a meek modesty about her that charms me.

Tony. Yes, but curb her never so little, she kicks up, and you're flung in a ditch.

Hastings. Well, but you must allow her a little beauty.—Yes, you must allow her some beauty.

Tony. Bandbox! She's all a made up thing, mun. Ah! could you but see Bet Bouncer of these parts, you might then talk of beauty. Ecod, she has two eyes as black as sloes, and cheeks as broad and red as a pulpit cushion. She'd make two of she.

Hastings. Well, what say you to a friend that would take this bitter bargain off your hands?

Tony. Anon.[23]

Hastings. Would you thank him that would take Miss Neville, and leave you to happiness and your dear Betsy?

Tony. Ay; but where is there such a friend, for who would take *her?*

Hastings. I am he. If you but assist me, I'll engage to whip her off to France, and you shall never hear more of her.

Tony. Assist you! Ecod, I will, to the last drop of my blood. I'll clap a pair of horses to your chaise that shall trundle you off in a twinkling, and maybe get you a part of her fortin beside, in jewels, that you little dream of.

Hastings. My dear 'Squire, this looks like a lad of spirit.

Tony. Come along then, and you shall see more of my spirit before you have done with me.

(*Singing.*)

We are the boys
That fears no noise

23 What do you mean?

Where the thundering cannons roar.
(*Exeunt.*)

ACT III.

Scene 1. *The House.*

(*Enter Hardcastle solus.*)

Hard. What could my old friend Sir Charles mean by recommending his son as the modestest young man in town? To me he appears the most impudent piece of brass that ever spoke with a tongue. He has taken possession of the easy chair by the fireside already. He took off his boots in the parlor, and desired me to see them taken care of. I'm desirous to know how his impudence affects my daughter.—She will certainly be shocked at it.

(*Enter Miss Hardcastle, plainly dressed.*)

Hard. Well, my Kate, I see you have changed your dress as I bid you; and yet, I believe, there was no great occasion.

Miss Hard. I find such a pleasure, sir, in obeying your commands, that I take care to observe them without ever debating their propriety.

Hard. And yet, Kate, I sometimes give you some cause, particularly when I recommended my *modest* gentleman to you as a lover to-day.

Miss Hard. You taught me to expect something extraordinary, and I find the original exceeds the description!

Hard. I was never so surprised in my life! He has quite confounded all my faculties!

Miss Hard. I never saw anything like it! And a man of the world, too!

Hard. Ay, he learned it all abroad,—what a fool was I, to think a young man could learn modesty by travelling. He might as soon learn wit at a masquerade.

Miss Hard. It seems all natural to him.

Hard. A good deal assisted by bad company and a French dancing-master.

Miss Hard. Sure, you mistake, papa! a French dancing-master could never have taught him that timid look,—that awkward address,—that bashful manner——

Hard. Whose look? whose manner, child?

Miss Hard. Mr. Marlow's: his *mauvaise honte,*[24] his timidity struck me at the first sight.

Hard. Then your first sight deceived you; for I think him one of the most brazen first sights that ever astonished my senses!

Miss Hard. Sure, sir, you rally! I never saw anyone so modest.

Hard. And can you be serious? I never saw such a bouncing swaggering puppy since I was born. Bully Dawson was but a fool to him.

Miss Hard. Surprising! He met me with a respectful bow, a stammering voice, and a look fixed on the ground.

Hard. He met me with a loud voice, a lordly air, and a familiarity that made my blood freeze again.

Miss Hard. He treated me with diffidence and respect; censured the manners of the age; admired the prudence of girls that never laughed; tired me with apologies for being tiresome; then left the room with a bow, and, "madam, I would not for the world detain you."

Hard. He spoke to me as if he knew me all his life before. Asked twenty questions, and never waited for an answer. Interrupted my best remarks with some silly pun, and when I was in my best story of the Duke of Marlborough and Prince Eugene, he asked if I had not a good hand at making punch. Yes, Kate, he asked your father if he was a maker of punch!

Miss Hard. One of us must certainly be mistaken.

Hard. If he be what he has shown himself, I'm determined he shall never have my consent.

Miss Hard. And if he be the sullen thing I take him, he shall never have mine.

Hard. In one thing then we are agreed—to reject him.

Miss Hard. Yes. But upon conditions. For if you should find him less impudent, and I more presuming; if you find him more respectful, and I more importunate—I don't know—the fellow is well enough for a man—Certainly we don't meet many such at a horse race in the country.

Hard. If we should find him so.—But that's impossible. The first appearance has done my business. I'm seldom deceived in that.

Miss Hard. And yet there may be many good qualities under that first appearance.

Hard. Ay, when a girl finds a fellow's outside to her taste, she then sets about guessing the rest of his furniture. With

24 embarrassment.

her, a smooth face stands for good sense, and a genteel figure for every virtue.

Miss Hard. I hope, sir, a conversation begun with a compliment to my good sense won't end with a sneer at my understanding?

Hard. Pardon me, Kate. But if young Mr. Brazen can find the art of reconciling contradictions, he may please us both, perhaps.

Miss Hard. And as one of us must be mistaken, what if we go to make further discoveries?

Hard. Agreed. But depend on 't I 'm in the right.

Miss Hard. And depend on 't I 'm not much in the wrong.

(*Exeunt.*)

(*Enter Tony, running in with a casket.*)

Tony. Ecod! I have got them. Here they are. My cousin Con's necklaces, bobs [25] and all. My mother shan't cheat the poor souls out of their fortune neither. O! my genius, is that you?

(*Enter Hastings.*)

Hastings. My dear friend, how have you managed with your mother? I hope you have amused her with pretending love for your cousin, and that you are willing to be reconciled at last? Our horses will be refreshed in a short time, and we shall soon be ready to set off.

Tony. And here 's something to bear your charges by the way. (*Giving the casket.*) Your sweetheart's jewels. Keep them, and hang those, I say, that would rob you of one of them!

Hastings. But how have you procured them from your mother?

Tony. Ask me no questions, and I 'll tell you no fibs. I procured them by the rule of thumb. If I had not a key to every drawer in mother's bureau, how could I go to the ale-house so often as I do? An honest man may rob himself of his own at any time.

Hastings. Thousands do it every day. But to be plain with you; Miss Neville is endeavoring to procure them from her aunt this very instant. If she succeeds, it will be the most delicate way at least of obtaining them.

Tony. Well, keep them, till you know how it will be. But I know how it will be well enough, she 'd as soon part with the only sound tooth in her head!

Hastings. But I dread the effects of her resentment, when she finds she has lost them.

Tony. Never you mind her resentment, leave *me* to manage that. I don't value her resentment the bounce of a cracker. Zounds! here they are! Morrice,[26] prance!

(*Exit Hastings.*)

(*Tony, Mrs. Hardcastle, Miss Neville.*)

Mrs. Hard. Indeed, Constance, you amaze me. Such a girl as you want jewels? It will be time enough for jewels, my dear, twenty years hence, when your beauty begins to want repairs.

Miss Neville. But what will repair beauty at forty, will certainly improve it at twenty, madam.

Mrs. Hard. Yours, my dear, can admit of none. That natural blush is beyond a thousand ornaments. Besides, child, jewels are quite out at present. Don't you see half the ladies of our acquaintance, my lady Kill-day-light, and Mrs. Crump, and the rest of them, carry their jewels to town, and bring nothing but paste and marcasites [27] back?

Miss Neville. But who knows, madam, but somebody that shall be nameless would like me best with all my little finery about me?

Mrs. Hard. Consult your glass, my dear, and then see, if with such a pair of eyes, you want any better sparklers. What do you think, Tony, my dear, does your cousin Con want any jewels, in your eyes, to set off her beauty?

Tony. That 's as thereafter may be.

Miss Neville. My dear aunt, if you knew how it would oblige me.

Mrs. Hard. A parcel of old-fashioned rose and table-cut [28] things. They would make you look like the court of king Solomon at a puppet-show. Besides, I believe I can't readily come at them. They may be missing, for aught I know to the contrary.

Tony. (*Apart to Mrs. Hard.*) Then why don't you tell her so at once, as she 's so longing for them. Tell her they 're lost. It 's the only way to quiet her. Say they 're lost, and call me to bear witness.

Mrs. Hard. (*Apart to Tony.*) You know, my dear, I 'm only keeping them for you. So if I say they 're gone, you 'll bear me witness, will you? He! he! he!

Tony. Never fear me. Ecod! I 'll say I

25 pendants.
26 Be off!
27 A cheap mineral used for ornaments.
28 Cut with a large flat surface.

saw them taken out with my own eyes.

Miss Neville. I desire them but for a day, madam. Just to be permitted to show them as relics, and then they may be locked up again.

Mrs. Hard. To be plain with you, my dear Constance, if I could find them, you should have them. They 're missing, I assure you. Lost, for aught I know; but we must have patience wherever they are.

Miss Neville. I 'll not believe it; this is but a shallow pretence to deny me. I know they 're too valuable to be so slightly kept, and as you are to answer for the loss.

Mrs. Hard. Don't be alarmed, Constance. If they be lost, I must restore an equivalent. But my son knows they are missing, and not to be found.

Tony. That I can bear witness to. They are missing, and not to be found, I 'll take my oath on 't!

Mrs. Hard. You must learn resignation, my dear; for though we lose our fortune, yet we should not lose our patience. See me, how calm I am!

Miss Neville. Ay, people are generally calm at the misfortunes of others.

Mrs. Hard. Now, I wonder a girl of your good sense should waste a thought upon such trumpery. We shall soon find them; and, in the meantime, you shall make use of my garnets till your jewels be found.

Miss Neville. I detest garnets!

Mrs. Hard. The most becoming things in the world to set off a clear complexion. You have often seen how well they look upon me. You *shall* have them.

(*Exit.*)

Miss Neville. I dislike them of all things. You shan't stir.—Was ever anything so provoking—to mislay my own jewels, and force me to wear her trumpery.

Tony. Don't be a fool. If she gives you the garnets, take what you can get. The jewels are your own already. I have stolen them out of her bureau, and she does not know it. Fly to your spark, he 'll tell you more of the matter. Leave me to manage *her*.

Miss Neville. My dear cousin!

Tony. Vanish. She 's here, and has missed them already. (*Exit Miss Neville.*) Zounds! how she fidgets and spits about like a Catharine wheel!

(*Enter Mrs. Hardcastle.*)

Mrs. Hard. Confusion! thieves! robbers! We are cheated, plundered, broke open, undone!

Tony. What 's the matter, what 's the matter, mamma? I hope nothing has happened to any of the good family!

Mrs. Hard. We are robbed. My bureau has been broke open, the jewels taken out, and I 'm undone!

Tony. Oh! is that all? Ha! ha! ha! By the laws, I never saw it better acted in my life. Ecod, I thought you was ruined in earnest, ha, ha, ha!

Mrs. Hard. Why, boy, I *am* ruined in earnest. My bureau has been broke open, and all taken away.

Tony. Stick to that; ha, ha, ha! stick to that. I 'll bear witness, you know, call me to bear witness.

Mrs. Hard. I tell you, Tony, by all that 's precious, the jewels are gone, and I shall be ruined for ever.

Tony. Sure I know they 're gone, and I am to say so.

Mrs. Hard. My dearest Tony, but hear me. They 're gone, I say.

Tony. By the laws, mamma, you make me for to laugh, ha! ha! I know who took them well enough, ha! ha! ha!

Mrs. Hard. Was there ever such a blockhead, that can't tell the difference between jest and earnest? I tell you I 'm not in jest, booby!

Tony. That 's right, that 's right: You must be in a bitter passion, and then nobody will suspect either of us. I 'll bear witness that they are gone.

Mrs. Hard. Was there ever such a cross-grained brute, that won't hear me! Can you bear witness that you 're no better than a fool? Was ever poor woman so beset with fools on one hand, and thieves on the other?

Tony. I can bear witness to that.

Mrs. Hard. Bear witness again, you blockhead, you, and I 'll turn you out of the room directly. My poor niece, what will become of *her?* Do you laugh, you unfeeling brute, as if you enjoyed my distress?

Tony. I can bear witness to that.

Mrs. Hard. Do you insult me, monster? I 'll teach you to vex your mother, I will!

Tony. I can bear witness to that.

(*He runs off, she follows him.*)

(*Enter Miss Hardcastle and Maid.*)

Miss Hard. What an unaccountable creature is that brother of mine, to send them to the house as an inn, ha! ha! I don't wonder at his impudence.

Maid. But what is more, madam, the young gentleman as you passed by in your present dress, asked me if you were the barmaid! He mistook you for the barmaid, madam.

Miss Hard. Did he? Then as I live I'm resolved to keep up the delusion. Tell me, Pimple, how do you like my present dress? Don't you think I look something like Cherry in the Beaux Stratagem? [29]

Maid. It's the dress, madam, that every lady wears in the country, but when she visits or receives company.

Miss Hard. And are you sure he does not remember my face or person?

Maid. Certain of it.

Miss Hard. I vow, I thought so; for though we spoke for some time together, yet his fears were such, that he never once looked up during the interview. Indeed, if he had, my bonnet would have kept him from seeing me.

Maid. But what do you hope from keeping him in his mistake?

Miss Hard. In the first place, I shall be *seen,* and that is no small advantage to a girl who brings her face to market. Then I shall perhaps make an acquaintance, and that's no small victory gained over one who never addresses any but the wildest of her sex. But my chief aim is to take my gentleman off his guard, and like an invisible champion of romance examine the giant's force before I offer to combat.

Maid. But you are sure you can act your part, and disguise your voice, so that he may mistake that, as he has already mistaken your person?

Miss Hard. Never fear me. I think I have got the true bar cant.—Did your honor call?——Attend the Lion there.——Pipes and tobacco for the Angel.—The Lamb [30] has been outrageous this half-hour!

Maid. It will do, madam. But he's here.

(*Exit Maid.*)

(*Enter Marlow.*)

Marlow. What a bawling in every part of the house; I have scarce a moment's repose. If I go to the best room, there I find my host and his story. If I fly to the gallery, there we have my hostess with her curtsey down to the ground. I have at last got a moment to myself, and now for recollection.

(*Walks and muses.*)

Miss Hard. Did you call, sir? did your honor call?

Marlow. (*Musing.*) As for Miss Hardcastle, she's too grave and sentimental for me.

Miss Hard. Did your honor call?

(*She still places herself before him, he turning away.*)

Marlow. No, child! (*Musing.*) Besides from the glimpse I had of her, I think she squints.

Miss Hard. I'm sure, sir, I heard the bell ring.

Marlow. No, no! (*Musing.*) I have pleased my father, however, by coming down, and I'll to-morrow please myself by returning.

(*Taking out his tablets, and perusing.*)

Miss Hard. Perhaps the other gentleman called, sir?

Marlow. I tell you, no.

Miss Hard. I should be glad to know, sir. We have such a parcel of servants.

Marlow. No, no, I tell you. (*Looks full in her face.*) Yes, child, I think I did call. I wanted——I wanted——I vow, child, you are vastly handsome!

Miss Hard. O la, sir, you'll make one ashamed.

Marlow. Never saw a more sprightly malicious eye. Yes, yes, my dear, I did call. Have you got any of your—a—what d'ye call it in the house?

Miss Hard. No, sir, we have been out of that these ten days.

Marlow. One may call in this house, I find, to very little purpose. Suppose I should call for a taste, just by way of trial, of the nectar of your lips; perhaps I might be disappointed in that, too!

Miss Hard. Nectar! nectar! that's a liquor there's no call for in these parts. French, I suppose. We keep no French wines here, sir.

Marlow. Of true English growth, I assure you.

Miss Hard. Then it's odd I should not know it. We brew all sorts of wines in this house, and I have lived here these eighteen years.

Marlow. Eighteen years! Why one would think, child, you kept the bar before you were born. How old are you?

Miss Hard. O! sir, I must not tell my

29 A play by Farquhar (1707).

30 The rooms in inns were often given such names.

age. They say women and music should never be dated.

Marlow. To guess at this distance, you can't be much above forty. (*Approaching.*) Yet nearer I don't think so much. (*Approaching.*) By coming close to some women they look younger still; but when we come very close indeed—(*Attempting to kiss her.*)

Miss Hard. Pray, sir, keep your distance. One would think you wanted to know one's age as they do horses, by mark of mouth.

Marlow. I protest, child, you use me extremely ill. If you keep me at this distance, how is it possible you and I can ever be acquainted?

Miss Hard. And who wants to be acquainted with you? I want no such acquaintance, not I. I 'm sure you did not treat Miss Hardcastle that was here awhile ago in this obstropalous manner. I'll warrant me, before her you looked dashed, and kept bowing to the ground, and talked, for all the world, as if you was before a justice of peace.

Marlow. (*Aside.*) Egad! she has hit it, sure enough. (*To her.*) In awe of her, child? Ha! ha! ha! A mere awkward, squinting thing, no, no! I find you don't know me. I laughed, and rallied her a little; but I was unwilling to be too severe. No, I could not be too severe, curse me!

Miss Hard. O! then, sir, you are a favorite, I find, among the ladies?

Marlow. Yes, my dear, a great favorite. And yet, hang me, I don't see what they find in me to follow. At the Ladies' Club in town I 'm called their agreeable Rattle. Rattle, child, is not my real name, but one I 'm known by. My name is Solomons. Mr. Solomons, my dear, at your service.

(*Offering to salute her.*)

Miss Hard. Hold, sir; you were introducing me to your club, not to yourself. And you 're so great a favorite there, you say?

Marlow. Yes, my dear. There 's Mrs. Mantrap, Lady Betty Blackleg, the Countess of Sligo, Mrs. Longhorns, old Miss Biddy Buckskin and your humble servant, keep up the spirit of the place.

Miss Hard. Then it 's a very merry place, I suppose.

Marlow. Yes, as merry as cards, suppers, wine, and old women can make us.

Miss Hard. And their agreeable Rattle, ha! ha! ha!

Marlow. (*Aside.*) Egad! I don't quite like this chit. She looks knowing, methinks. You laugh, child!

Miss Hard. I can't but laugh to think what time they all have for minding their work or their family.

Marlow. (*Aside.*) All 's well, she don't laugh at me. (*To her.*) Do *you* ever work, child?

Miss Hard. Ay, sure. There 's not a screen or a quilt in the whole house but what can bear witness to that.

Marlow. Odso! Then you must show me your embroidery. I embroider and draw patterns myself a little. If you want a judge of your work you must apply to me.

(*Seizing her hand.*)

Miss Hard. Ay, but the colors don't look well by candle light. You shall see all in the morning.

(*Struggling.*)

Marlow. And why not now, my angel? Such beauty fires beyond the power of resistance.——Pshaw! the father here! My old luck: I never nicked seven that I did not throw amesace [31] three times following.

(*Exit Marlow.*)

(*Enter Hardcastle, who stands in surprise.*)

Hard. So, madam! So I find *this* is your *modest* lover. This is your humble admirer that kept his eyes fixed on the ground, and only adored at humble distance. Kate, Kate, art thou not ashamed to deceive your father so?

Miss Hard. Never trust me, dear papa, but he 's still the modest man I first took him for, you 'll be convinced of it as well as I.

Hard. By the hand of my body, I believe his impudence is infectious! Did n't I see him seize your hand? Did n't I see him haul you about like a milkmaid? And now you talk of his respect and his modesty, forsooth!

Miss Hard. But if I shortly convince you of his modesty, that he has only the faults that will pass off with time, and the virtues that will improve with age, I hope you 'll forgive him.

Hard. The girl would actually make one run mad! I tell you I'll not be convinced. I am convinced. He has scarcely been three hours in the house,

31 Made a high throw without making a low throw (in dice).

and he has already encroached on all my prerogatives. You may like his impudence, and call it modesty. But my son-in-law, madam, must have very different qualifications.

Miss Hard. Sir, I ask but this night to convince you.

Hard. You shall not have half the time, for I have thoughts of turning him out this very hour.

Miss Hard. Give me that hour then, and I hope to satisfy you.

Hard. Well, an hour let it be then. But I'll have no trifling with your father. All fair and open, do you mind me?

Miss Hard. I hope, sir, you have ever found that I considered your commands as my pride; for your kindness is such, that my duty as yet has been inclination.

(*Exeunt.*)

ACT IV.

Scene 1. *The House.*

(*Enter Hastings and Miss Neville.*)

Hastings. You surprise me! Sir Charles Marlow expected here this night? Where have you had your information?

Miss Neville. You may depend upon it. I just saw his letter to Mr. Hardcastle, in which he tells him he intends setting out a few hours after his son.

Hastings. Then, my Constance, all must be completed before he arrives. He knows me; and should he find me here, would discover my name, and perhaps my designs, to the rest of the family.

Miss Neville. The jewels, I hope, are safe.

Hastings. Yes, yes. I have sent them to Marlow, who keeps the keys of our baggage. In the meantime, I'll go to prepare matters for our elopement. I have had the 'Squire's promise of a fresh pair of horses; and, if I should not see him again, will write him further directions.

(*Exit.*)

Miss Neville. Well! success attend you. In the meantime, I'll go amuse my aunt with the old pretence of a violent passion for my cousin.

(*Exit.*)

(*Enter Marlow, followed by a Servant.*)

Marlow. I wonder what Hastings could mean by sending me so valuable a thing as a casket to keep for him, when he knows the only place I have is the seat of a post-coach at an inn-door. Have you deposited the casket with the landlady, as I ordered you? Have you put it into her own hands?

Servant. Yes, your honor.

Marlow. She said she'd keep it safe, did she?

Servant. Yes, she said she'd keep it safe enough; she asked me how I came by it? and she said she had a great mind to make me give an account of myself.

(*Exit Servant.*)

Marlow. Ha! ha! ha! They're safe, however. What an unaccountable set of beings have we got amongst! This little barmaid though runs in my head most strangely, and drives out the absurdities of all the rest of the family. She's mine, she must be mine, or I'm greatly mistaken.

(*Enter Hastings.*)

Hastings. Bless me! I quite forgot to tell her that I intended to prepare at the bottom of the garden. Marlow here, and in spirits too!

Marlow. Give me joy, George! Crown me, shadow me with laurels! Well, George, after all, we modest fellows don't want for success among the women.

Hastings. Some women, you mean. But what success has your honor's modesty been crowned with now, that it grows so insolent upon us?

Marlow. Did n't you see the tempting, brisk, lovely little thing that runs about the house with a bunch of keys to its girdle?

Hastings. Well! and what then?

Marlow. She's mine, you rogue, you. Such fire, such motion, such eyes, such lips——but egad! she would not let me kiss them though.

Hastings. But are you so sure, so very sure of her?

Marlow. Why, man, she talked of showing me her work above-stairs, and I am to improve the pattern.

Hastings. But how can *you*, Charles, go about to rob a woman of her honor?

Marlow. Pshaw! pshaw! we all know the honor of the barmaid of an inn. I don't intend to *rob* her, take my word for it; there's nothing in this house I shan't honestly *pay* for!

Hastings. I believe the girl has virtue.

Marlow. And if she has, I should be the last man in the world that would attempt to corrupt it.

Hastings. You have taken care, I hope, of

the casket I sent you to lock up? It 's in safety?

Marlow. Yes, yes. It 's safe enough. I have taken care of it. But how could you think the seat of a post-coach at an inn-door a place of safety? Ah! numbskull! I have taken better precautions for you than you did for yourself.—— I have——

Hastings. What?

Marlow. I have sent it to the landlady to keep for you.

Hastings. To the landlady!

Marlow. The landlady.

Hastings. You did!

Marlow. I did. She 's to be answerable for its forth-coming, you know.

Hastings. Yes, she 'll bring it forth with a witness.

Marlow. Was n't I right? I believe you 'll allow that I acted prudently upon this occasion?

Hastings. (*Aside.*) He must not see my uneasiness.

Marlow. You seem a little disconcerted, though, methinks. Sure nothing has happened?

Hastings. No, nothing. Never was in better spirits in all my life. And so you left it with the landlady, who, no doubt, very readily undertook the charge?

Marlow. Rather too readily. For she not only kept the casket, but, through her great precaution, was going to keep the messenger too. Ha! ha! ha!

Hastings. He! he! he! They 're safe, however.

Marlow. As a guinea in a miser's purse.

Hastings. (*Aside.*) So now all hopes of fortune are at an end, and we must set off without it. (*To him.*) Well, Charles, I 'll leave you to your meditations on the pretty barmaid, and, he! he! he! may you be as successful for yourself as you have been for me.

(*Exit.*)

Marlow. Thank ye, George! I ask no more. Ha! ha! ha!

(*Enter Hardcastle.*)

Hard. I no longer know my own house. It 's turned all topsy-turvy. His servants have got drunk already. I 'll bear it no longer, and yet, from my respect for his father, I 'll be calm. (*To him.*) Mr. Marlow, your servant. I 'm your very humble servant.

(*Bowing low.*)

Marlow. Sir, your humble servant. (*Aside.*) What 's to be the wonder now?

Hard. I believe, sir, you must be sensible, sir, that no man alive ought to be more welcome than your father's son, sir. I hope you think so?

Marlow. I do, from my soul, sir. I don't want much entreaty. I generally make my father's son welcome wherever he goes.

Hard. I believe you do, from my soul, sir. But though I say nothing to your own conduct, that of your servants is insufferable. Their manner of drinking is setting a very bad example in this house, I assure you.

Marlow. I protest, my very good sir, that 's no fault of mine. If they don't drink as they ought, *they* are to blame. I ordered them not to spare the cellar, I did, I assure you. (*To the side scene.*) Here, let one of my servants come up. (*To him.*) My positive directions were, that as I did not drink myself, they should make up for my deficiencies below.

Hard. Then they had your orders for what they do! I 'm satisfied!

Marlow. They had, I assure you. You shall hear from one of themselves.

(*Enter Servant, drunk.*)

Marlow. You, Jeremy! Come forward, sirrah! What were my orders? Were you not told to drink freely, and call for what you thought fit, for the good of the house?

Hard. (*Aside.*) I begin to lose my patience.

Jeremy. Please your honor, liberty and Fleet Street for ever! Though I 'm but a servant, I 'm as good as another man. I 'll drink for no man before supper, sir, dammy! Good liquor will sit upon a good supper, but a good supper will not sit upon——hiccup——upon my conscience, sir.

Marlow. You see, my old friend, the fellow is as drunk as he can possibly be. I don't know what you 'd have more, unless you 'd have the poor devil soused in a beer-barrel.

Hard. Zounds! He 'll drive me distracted if I contain myself any longer. Mr. Marlow! Sir! I have submitted to your insolence for more than four hours, and I see no likelihood of its coming to an end. I 'm now resolved to be master here, sir, and I desire that you and your drunken pack may leave my house directly.

Marlow. Leave your house!—Sure, you jest, my good friend? What, when I 'm doing what I can to please you!

Hard. I tell you, sir, you don't please me; so I desire you 'll leave my house.

Marlow. Sure, you cannot be serious! At this time of night, and such a night! You only mean to banter me!

Hard. I tell you, sir, I 'm serious; and, now that my passions are roused, I say this house is mine, sir; this house is mine, and I command you to leave it directly.

Marlow. Ha! ha! ha! A puddle in a storm. I shan't stir a step, I assure you. (*In a serious tone.*) This your house, fellow! It 's my house. This is my house. Mine, while I choose to stay. What right have you to bid me leave this house, sir? I never met with such impudence, curse me, never in my whole life before!

Hard. Nor I, confound me if ever I did! To come to my house, to call for what he likes, to turn me out of my own chair, to insult the family, to order his servants to get drunk, and then to tell me,—*This house is mine, sir.* By all that 's impudent, it makes me laugh. Ha! ha! ha! Pray, sir (*Bantering*), as you take the house, what think you of taking the rest of the furniture? There 's a pair of silver candlesticks, and there 's a fire-screen, and here 's a pair of brazen-nosed bellows, perhaps you may take a fancy to them?

Marlow. Bring me your bill, sir, bring me your bill, and let 's make no more words about it.

Hard. There are a set of prints, too. What think you of the Rake's Progress [32] for your own apartment?

Marlow. Bring me your bill, I say; and I 'll leave you and your infernal house directly.

Hard. Then there 's a mahogany table, that you may see your own face in.

Marlow. My bill, I say.

Hard. I had forgot the great chair, for your own particular slumbers, after a hearty meal.

Marlow. Zounds! bring me my bill, I say, and let 's hear no more on 't.

Hard. Young man, young man, from your father's letter to me, I was taught to expect a well-bred modest man, as a visitor here, but now I find him no better than a coxcomb and a bully; but he will be down here presently, and shall hear more of it.

(*Exit.*)

Marlow. How 's this! Sure, I have not mistaken the house? Everything looks like an inn. The servants cry "coming." The attendance is awkward; the barmaid, too, to attend us. But she 's here, and will further inform me. Whither so fast, child? A word with you.

(*Enter Miss Hardcastle.*)

Miss Hard. Let it be short, then. I 'm in a hurry.—(*Aside.*) I believe he begins to find out his mistake, but it 's too soon quite to undeceive him.

Marlow. Pray, child, answer me one question. What are you, and what may your business in this house be?

Miss Hard. A relation of the family, sir.

Marlow. What? A poor relation?

Miss Hard. Yes, sir. A poor relation appointed to keep the keys, and to see that the guests want nothing in my power to give them.

Marlow. That is, you act as the barmaid of this inn.

Miss Hard. Inn! O law!—What brought that in your head? One of the best families in the county keep an inn! Ha, ha, ha, old Mr. Hardcastle's house an inn!

Marlow. Mr. Hardcastle's house! Is this house Mr. Hardcastle's house, child?

Miss Hard. Ay, sure. Whose else should it be?

Marlow. So then all 's out, and I have been damnably imposed on. O, confound my stupid head, I shall be laughed at over the whole town. I shall be stuck up in caricatura in all the print-shops,——The Dullissimo Maccaroni.[33] To mistake this house of all others for an inn, and my father's old friend for an inn-keeper! What a swaggering puppy must he take me for! What a silly puppy do I find myself! There again, may I be hanged, my dear, but I mistook you for the barmaid!

Miss Hard. Dear me! dear me! I 'm sure there 's nothing in my *behavour* to put me upon a level with one of that stamp.

Marlow. Nothing, my dear, nothing. But I was in for a list of blunders, and could not help making you a subscriber. My stupidity saw everything the wrong way. I mistook your assiduity for assurance,

32 A series of pictures by Hogarth.

33 A dandy; *Dullissimo*, a mock-Italian superlative.

and your simplicity for allurement. But it's over—this house I no more show *my* face in!

Miss Hard. I hope, sir, I have done nothing to disoblige you. I'm sure I should be sorry to affront any gentleman who has been so polite, and said so many civil things to me. I'm sure I should be sorry (*pretending to cry*) if he left the family upon my account. I'm sure I should be sorry people said anything amiss, since I have no fortune but my character.

Marlow. (*Aside.*) By heaven, she weeps. This is the first mark of tenderness I ever had from a modest woman, and it touches me. (*To her.*) Excuse me, my lovely girl, you are the only part of the family I leave with reluctance. But to be plain with you, the difference of our birth, fortune and education, make an honorable connexion impossible; and I can never harbor a thought of seducing simplicity that trusted in my honor, or bringing ruin upon one whose only fault was being too lovely.

Miss Hard. (*Aside.*) Generous man! I now begin to admire him. (*To him.*) But I'm sure my family is as good as Miss Hardcastle's, and though I'm poor, that's no great misfortune to a contented mind, and, until this moment, I never thought that it was bad to want fortune.

Marlow. And why now, my pretty simplicity?

Miss Hard. Because it puts me at a distance from one, that if I had a thousand pound I would give it all to.

Marlow. (*Aside.*) This simplicity bewitches me, so that if I stay I'm undone. I must make one bold effort, and leave her. (*To her.*) Your partiality in my favor, my dear, touches me most sensibly, and were I to live for myself alone, I could easily fix my choice. But I owe too much to the opinion of the world, too much to the authority of a father, so that—I can scarcely speak it—it affects me! Farewell!

(*Exit.*)

Miss Hard. I never knew half his merit till now. He shall not go, if I have power or art to detain him. I'll still preserve the character in which I stooped to conquer, but will undeceive my papa, who, perhaps, may laugh him out of his resolution. (*Exit.*)

(*Enter Tony, Miss Neville.*)

Tony. Ay, you may steal for yourselves the next time. I have done my duty. She has got the jewels again, that's a sure thing; but she believes it was all a mistake of the servants.

Miss Neville. But, my dear cousin, sure, you won't forsake us in this distress. If she in the least suspects that I am going off, I shall certainly be locked up, or sent to my aunt Pedigree's, which is ten times worse.

Tony. To be sure, aunts of all kinds are damned bad things. But what can I do? I have got you a pair of horses that will fly like Whistlejacket, and I'm sure you can't say but I have courted you nicely before her face. Here she comes, we must court a bit or two more, for fear she should suspect us.

(*They retire, and seem to fondle.*)

(*Enter Mrs. Hardcastle.*)

Mrs. Hard. Well, I was greatly fluttered, to be sure. But my son tells me it was all a mistake of the servants. I shan't be easy, however, till they are fairly married, and then let her keep her own fortune. But what do I see? Fondling together, as I'm alive! I never saw Tony so sprightly before. Ah! have I caught you, my pretty doves? What, billing, exchanging stolen glances, and broken murmurs! Ah!

Tony. As for murmurs, mother, we grumble a little now and then, to be sure. But there's no love lost between us.

Mrs. Hard. A mere sprinkling, Tony, upon the flame, only to make it burn brighter.

Miss Neville. Cousin Tony promises to give us more of his company at home. Indeed, he shan't leave us any more. It won't leave us, cousin Tony, will it?

Tony. O! it's a pretty creature. No, I'd sooner leave my horse in a pound, than leave you when you smile upon one so. Your laugh makes you so becoming.

Miss Neville. Agreeable cousin! Who can help admiring that natural humor, that pleasant, broad, red, thoughtless, (*Patting his cheek.*) ah! it's a bold face.

Mrs. Hard. Pretty innocence!

Tony. I'm sure I always loved cousin Con's hazel eyes, and her pretty long fingers, that she twists this way and that, over the haspicholls,[34] like a parcel of bobbins.

34 A corrupt form for *harpsichord.*

Mrs. Hard. Ah, he would charm the bird from the tree. I was never so happy before. My boy takes after his father, poor Mr. Lumpkin, exactly. The jewels, my dear Con, shall be yours incontinently. You shall have them. Is n't he a sweet boy, my dear? You shall be married to-morrow, and we 'll put off the rest of his education, like Dr. Drowsy's sermons, to a fitter opportunity.

(*Enter Diggory.*)

Diggory. Where 's the 'Squire? I have got a letter for your worship.

Tony. Give it to my mamma. She reads all my letters first.

Diggory. I had orders to deliver it into your own hands.

Tony. Who does it come from?

Diggory. Your worship mun ask that of the letter itself.

Tony. I could wish to know, though. (*Turning the letter, and gazing on it.*)

Miss Neville. (*Aside.*) Undone, undone! A letter to him from Hastings. I know the hand. If my aunt sees it, we are ruined for ever. I 'll keep her employed a little if I can. (*To Mrs. Hardcastle.*) But I have not told you, madam, of my cousin's smart answer just now to Mr. Marlow. We so laughed—you must know, madam—this way a little, for he must not hear us. (*They confer.*)

Tony. (*Still gazing.*) A damned cramp piece of penmanship, as ever I saw in my life. I can read your print-hand very well. But here there are such handles, and shanks, and dashes, that one can scarce tell the head from the tail. *To Anthony Lumpkin, Esquire.* It 's very odd, I can read the outside of my letters, where my own name is, well enough. But when I come to open it, it 's all—buzz. That 's hard, very hard; for the inside of the letter is always the cream of the correspondence.

Mrs. Hard. Ha! ha! ha! Very well, very well. And so my son was too hard for the philosopher!

Miss Neville. Yes, madam; but you must hear the rest, madam. A little more this way, or he may hear us. You 'll hear how he puzzled him again.

Mrs. Hard. He seems strangely puzzled now himself, methinks.

Tony. (*Still gazing.*) A damned up and down hand, as if it was disguised in liquor. (*Reading.*) *Dear Sir.* Ay, that 's that. Then there 's an *M,* and a *T,* and an *S,* but whether the next be an *izzard*[35] or an *R,* confound me, I cannot tell!

Mrs. Hard. What 's that, my dear? Can I give you any assistance?

Miss Neville. Pray, aunt, let me read it. Nobody reads a cramp hand better than I. (*Twitching the letter from her.*) Do you know who it is from?

Tony. Can't tell, except from Dick Ginger the feeder.

Miss Neville. Ay, so it is. (*Pretending to read.*) "Dear 'Squire, Hoping that you 're in health, as I am at this present. The gentlemen of the Shake-bag club has cut the gentlemen of the Goose-green quite out of feather. The odds—um—odd battle—um—long fighting—um, here, here, it 's all about cocks, and fighting; It 's of no consequence, here, put it up, put it up.

(*Thrusting the crumpled letter upon him.*)

Tony. But I tell you, miss, it 's of all the consequence in the world! I would not lose the rest of it for a guinea! Here, mother, do you make it out. Of no consequence!

(*Giving Mrs. Hardcastle the letter.*)

Mrs. Hard. How 's this! (*Reads.*) "Dear 'Squire, I 'm now waiting for Miss Neville, with a post-chaise and a pair, at the bottom of the garden, but I find my horses yet unable to perform the journey. I expect you 'll assist us with a pair of fresh horses, as you promised. Dispatch is necessary, as the *hag* (ay, the hag) your mother, will otherwise suspect us. Yours, Hastings." Grant me patience. I shall run distracted! My rage chokes me.

Miss Neville. I hope, madam, you 'll suspend your resentment for a few moments, and not impute to me any impertinence, or sinister design that belongs to another.

Mrs. Hard. (*Curtseying very low.*) Fine spoken, madam, you are most miraculously polite and engaging, and quite the very pink of courtesy and circumspection, madam. (*Changing her tone.*) And you, you great ill-fashioned oaf, with scarce sense enough to keep your mouth shut. Were you too joined against me? But I 'll defeat all your plots in a moment. As for you, madam, since you have got a pair of fresh horses ready, it would be cruel to disappoint them. So, if you please, instead of running away with your spark, prepare, this very mo-

35 Z.

ment to run off with *me*. Your old aunt Pedigree will keep you secure, I 'll warrant me. You, too, sir, may mount your horse, and guard us upon the way. Here, Thomas, Roger, Diggery! I 'll show you that I wish you better than you do yourselves.

(*Exit.*)

Miss Neville. So now I 'm completely ruined.

Tony. Ay, that 's a sure thing.

Miss Neville. What better could be expected from being connected with such a stupid fool, and after all the nods and signs I made him?

Tony. By the laws, miss, it was your own cleverness, and not my stupidity, that did your business. You were so nice and so busy with your Shake-bags and Goose-greens that I thought you could never be making believe.

(*Enter Hastings.*)

Hastings. So, sir, I find by my servant, that you have shown my letter, and betrayed us. Was this well done, young gentleman?

Tony. Here 's another. Ask miss there who betrayed you. Ecod, it was her doing, not mine.

(*Enter Marlow.*)

Marlow. So I have been finely used here among you. Rendered contemptible, driven into ill manners, despised, insulted, laughed at.

Tony. Here 's another. We shall have old Bedlam broke loose presently.

Miss Neville. And there, sir, is the gentleman to whom we all owe every obligation.

Marlow. What can I say to him? a mere boy, an idiot, whose ignorance and age are a protection.

Hastings. A poor contemptible booby, that would but disgrace correction.

Miss Neville. Yet with cunning and malice enough to make himself merry with all our embarrassments.

Hastings. An insensible cub.

Marlow. Replete with tricks and mischief.

Tony. Baw! damme, but I 'll fight you both one after the other,——with baskets.[36]

Marlow. As for him, he 's below resentment. But your conduct, Mr. Hastings, requires an explanation. You knew of my mistakes, yet would not undeceive me.

Hastings. Tortured as I am with my own disappointments, is this a time for explanations? It is not friendly, Mr. Marlow.

Marlow. But, sir——

Miss Neville. Mr. Marlow, we never kept on your mistake, till it was too late to undeceive you. Be pacified.

(*Enter Servant.*)

Servant. My mistress desires you 'll get ready immediately, madam. The horses are putting to. Your hat and things are in the next room. We are to go thirty miles before morning.

(*Exit Servant.*)

Miss Neville. Well, well; I 'll come presently.

Marlow. (*To Hastings.*) Was it well done, sir, to assist in rendering me ridiculous? To hang me out for the scorn of all my acquaintance? Depend upon it, sir, I shall expect an explanation.

Hastings. Was it well done, sir, if you 're upon that subject, to deliver what I entrusted to yourself, to the care of another, sir?

Miss Neville. Mr. Hastings. Mr. Marlow. Why will you increase my distress by this groundless dispute? I implore, I entreat you——

(*Enter Servant.*)

Servant. Your cloak, madam. My mistress is impatient.

(*Exit Servant.*)

Miss Neville. I come. Pray be pacified. If I leave you thus, I shall die with apprehension!

(*Enter Servant.*)

Servant. Your fan, muff, and gloves, madam. The horses are waiting.

Miss Neville. O, Mr. Marlow! if you knew what a scene of constraint and ill-nature lies before me, I 'm sure it would convert your resentment into pity.

Marlow. I 'm so distracted with a variety of passions, that I don't know what I do. Forgive me, madam. George, forgive me. You know my hasty temper, and should not exasperate it.

Hastings. The torture of my situation is my only excuse.

Miss Neville. Well, my dear Hastings, if you have that esteem for me that I think, that I am sure you have, your constancy for three years will but increase the happiness of our future connection. If——

36 Probably a stick with a hilt of basket-work.

Mrs. Hard. (*Within.*) Miss Neville. Constance, why, Constance, I say.

Miss Neville. I'm coming. Well, constancy. Remember, constancy is the word.

(*Exit.*)

Hastings. My heart! How can I support this? To be so near happiness, and such happiness!

Marlow. (*To Tony.*) You see now, young gentleman, the effects of your folly. What might be amusement to you, is here disappointment, and even distress.

Tony. (*From a reverie.*) Ecod, I have hit it. It's here. Your hands. Yours and yours, my poor Sulky. My boots there, ho! Meet me two hours hence at the bottom of the garden; and if you don't find Tony Lumpkin a more good-natured fellow than you thought for, I'll give you leave to take my best horse, and Bet Bouncer into the bargain! Come along. My boots, ho!

(*Exeunt.*)

ACT V.

SCENE 1. *Continues.*

(*Enter Hastings and Servant.*)

Hastings. You saw the old lady and Miss Neville drive off, you say?

Servant. Yes, your honor. They went off in a post-coach, and the young 'Squire went on horseback. They're thirty miles off by this time.

Hastings. Then all my hopes are over.

Servant. Yes, sir. Old Sir Charles is arrived. He and the old gentleman of the house have been laughing at Mr. Marlow's mistake this half-hour. They are coming this way.

Hastings. Then I must not be seen. So now to my fruitless appointment at the bottom of the garden. This is about the time.

(*Exit.*)

(*Enter Sir Charles and Hardcastle.*)

Hard. Ha! ha! ha! The peremptory tone in which he sent forth his sublime commands!

Sir Charles. And the reserve with which I suppose he treated all your advances.

Hard. And yet he might have seen something in me above a common innkeeper, too.

Sir Charles. Yes, Dick, but he mistook you for an uncommon innkeeper, ha! ha! ha!

Hard. Well, I'm in too good spirits to think of anything but joy. Yes, my dear friend, this union of our families will make our personal friendships hereditary: and though my daughter's fortune is but small——

Sir Charles. Why, Dick, will you talk of fortune to *me?* My son is possessed of more than a competence already, and can want nothing but a good and virtuous girl to share his happiness and increase it. If they like each other, as you say they do——

Hard. *If,* man! I tell you they *do* like each other. My daughter as good as told me so.

Sir Charles. But girls are apt to flatter themselves, you know.

Hard. I saw him grasp her hand in the warmest manner myself; and here he comes to put you out of your *ifs,* I warrant him.

(*Enter Marlow.*)

Marlow. I come, sir, once more, to ask pardon for my strange conduct. I can scarce reflect on my insolence without confusion.

Hard. Tut, boy, a trifle. You take it too gravely. An hour or two's laughing with my daughter will set all to rights again. She'll never like you the worse for it.

Marlow. Sir, I shall be always proud of her approbation.

Hard. Approbation is but a cold word, Mr. Marlow; if I am not deceived, you have something more than approbation thereabouts. You take me.

Marlow. Really, sir, I have not that happiness.

Hard. Come, boy, I'm an old fellow, and know what's what, as well as you that are younger. I know what has passed between you; but mum.

Marlow. Sure, sir, nothing has passed between us but the most profound respect on my side, and the most distant reserve on hers. You don't think, sir, that my impudence has been passed upon all the rest of the family.

Hard. Impudence! No, I don't say that—Not quite impudence—Though girls like to be played with, and rumpled a little too, sometimes. But she has told no tales, I assure you.

Marlow. I never gave her the slightest cause.

Hard. Well, well, I like modesty in its place well enough. But this is over-acting, young gentleman. You *may* be open. Your father and I will like you the better for it.

Marlow. May I die, sir, if I ever——

Hard. I tell you, she don't dislike you; and as I 'm sure you like her——

Marlow. Dear sir—I protest, sir——

Hard. I see no reason why you should not be joined as fast as the parson can tie you.

Marlow. But hear me, sir——

Hard. Your father approves the match, I admire it, every moment's delay will be doing mischief, so——

Marlow. But why won't you hear me? By all that 's just and true, I never gave Miss Hardcastle the slightest mark of my attachment, or even the most distant hint to suspect me of affection. We had but one interview, and that was formal, modest, and uninteresting.

Hard. (*Aside.*) This fellow's formal, modest impudence is beyond bearing.

Sir Charles. And you never grasped her hand, or made any protestations!

Marlow. As heaven is my witness, I came down in obedience to your commands, I saw the lady without emotion, and parted without reluctance. I hope you 'll exact no further proofs of my duty, nor prevent me from leaving a house in which I suffer so many mortifications.

(*Exit.*)

Sir Charles. I 'm astonished at the air of sincerity with which he parted.

Hard. And I 'm astonished at the deliberate intrepidity of his assurance.

Sir Charles. I dare pledge my life and honor upon his truth.

Hard. Here comes my daughter, and I would stake my happiness upon her veracity.

(*Enter Miss Hardcastle.*)

Hard. Kate, come hither, child. Answer us sincerely, and without reserve; has Mr. Marlow made you any professions of love and affection?

Miss Hard. The question is very abrupt, sir! But since you require unreserved sincerity, I think he has.

Hard. (*To Sir Charles.*) You see.

Sir Charles. And pray, madam, have you and my son had more than one interview?

Miss Hard. Yes, sir, several.

Hard. (*To Sir Charles.*) You see.

Sir Charles. But did he profess any attachment?

Miss Hard. A lasting one.

Sir Charles. Did he talk of love?

Miss Hard. Much, sir.

Sir Charles. Amazing! And all this formally?

Miss Hard. Formally.

Hard. Now, my friend, I hope you are satisfied.

Sir Charles. And how did he behave, madam?

Miss Hard. As most professed admirers do. Said some civil things of my face, talked much of his want of merit, and the greatness of mine; mentioned his heart, gave a short tragedy speech, and ended with pretended rapture.

Sir Charles. Now I 'm perfectly convinced, indeed. I know his conversation among women to be modest and submissive. This forward, canting,[37] ranting manner by no means describes him, and I am confident he never sat for the picture.

Miss Hard. Then what, sir, if I should convince you to your face of my sincerity? If you and my papa, in about half-an-hour, will place yourselves behind that screen, you shall hear him declare his passion to me in person.

Sir Charles. Agreed. And if I find him what you describe, all my happiness in him must have an end.

(*Exit.*)

Miss Hard. And if you don't find him what I describe—I fear my happiness must never have a beginning.

(*Exeunt.*)

Scene 2. *Changes to the Back of the Garden.*

(*Enter Hastings.*)

Hastings. What an idiot am I, to wait here for a fellow, who probably takes a delight in mortifying me! He never intended to be punctual, and I 'll wait no longer. What do I see? It is he, and perhaps with news of my Constance.

(*Enter Tony, booted and spattered.*)

Hastings. My honest 'Squire! I now find you a man of your word. This looks like friendship.

Tony. Ay, I 'm your friend, and the best friend you have in the world, if you knew but all. This riding by night, by-

37 Conventionally affected.

the-bye, is cursedly tiresome. It has shook me worse than the basket of a stage-coach.

Hastings. But how? Where did you leave your fellow-travellers? Are they in safety? Are they housed?

Tony. Five and twenty miles in two hours and a half is no such bad driving. The poor beasts have smoked for it: rabbit me, but I 'd rather ride forty miles after a fox, than ten with such *varment.*

Hastings. Well, but where have you left the ladies? I die with impatience.

Tony. Left them? Why, where should I leave them, but where I found them?

Hastings. This is a riddle.

Tony. Riddle me this, then. What 's that goes round the house, and round the house, and never touches the house?

Hastings. I 'm still astray.

Tony. Why, that 's it, mon. I have led them astray. By jingo, there 's not a pond or slough within five miles of the place but they can tell the taste of.

Hastings. Ha, ha, ha, I understand; you took them in a round, while they supposed themselves going forward. And so you have at last brought them home again?

Tony. You shall hear. I first took them down Feather-Bed Lane, where we stuck fast in the mud. I then rattled them crack over the stones of Up-and-down Hill—I then introduced them to the gibbet on Heavy-Tree Heath, and from that, with a circumbendibus, I fairly lodged them in the horse-pond at the bottom of the garden.

Hastings. But no accident, I hope.

Tony. No, no. Only mother is confoundedly frightened. She thinks herself forty miles off. She 's sick of the journey, and the cattle can scarce crawl. So, if your own horses be ready, you may whip off with cousin, and I 'll be bound that no soul here can budge afoot to follow you.

Hastings. My dear friend, how can I be grateful?

Tony. Ay, now it 's dear friend, noble 'Squire. Just now, it was all idiot, cub, and run me through the guts. Damn *your* way of fighting, I say. After we take a knock in this part of the country, we kiss and be friends. But if you had run me through the guts, then I should be dead, and you might go kiss the hangman.

Hastings. The rebuke is just. But I must hasten to relieve Miss Neville; if you keep the old lady employed, I promise to take care of the young one.

(*Exit Hastings.*)

Tony. Never fear me. Here she comes. Vanish. She 's got from the pond, and draggled up to the waist like a mermaid.

(*Enter Mrs. Hardcastle.*)

Mrs. Hard. Oh, Tony, I 'm killed. Shook. Battered to death. I shall never survive it. That last jolt that laid us against the quick-set hedge has done my business.

Tony. Alack, mamma, it was all your own fault. You would be for running away by night, without knowing one inch of the way.

Mrs. Hard. I wish we were at home again. I never met so many accidents in so short a journey. Drenched in the mud, overturned in a ditch, stuck fast in a slough, jolted to a jelly, and at last to lose our way! Whereabouts do you think we are, Tony?

Tony. By my guess we should be upon Crack-skull Common, about forty miles from home.

Mrs. Hard. O lud! O lud! the most notorious spot in all the country. We only want a robbery to make a complete night on 't.

Tony. Don't be afraid, mamma, don't be afraid. Two of the five that kept here are hanged, and the other three may not find us. Don't be afraid. Is that a man that 's galloping behind us? No; it 's only a tree. Don't be afraid.

Mrs. Hard. The fright will certainly kill me.

Tony. Do you see any thing like a black hat moving behind the thicket?

Mrs. Hard. O death!

Tony. No, it 's only a cow. Don't be afraid, mamma, don't be afraid.

Mrs. Hard. As I 'm alive, Tony, I see a man coming towards us. Ah! I 'm sure on 't. If he perceives us, we are undone.

Tony. (*Aside.*) Father-in-law, by all that 's unlucky, come to take one of his night walks. (*To her.*) Ah, it 's a highwayman, with pistols as long as my arm. A damned ill-looking fellow.

Mrs. Hard. Good heaven defend us! He approaches.

Tony. Do you hide yourself in that thicket, and leave me to manage him. If there be any danger I 'll cough and cry hem. When I cough be sure to keep close.

(*Mrs. Hardcastle hides behind a tree in the back scene.*)

(*Enter Hardcastle.*)

Hard. I 'm mistaken, or I heard voices of people in want of help. Oh, Tony, is that you? I did not expect you so soon back. Are your mother and her charge in safety?

Tony. Very safe, sir, at my aunt Pedigree's. Hem.

Mrs. Hard. (*From behind.*) Ah death! I find there 's danger.

Hard. Forty miles in three hours; sure, that 's too much, my youngster.

Tony. Stout horses and willing minds make short journeys, as they say. Hem.

Mrs. Hard. (*From behind.*) Sure he 'll do the dear boy no harm.

Hard. But I heard a voice here; I should be glad to know from whence it came?

Tony. It was I, sir, talking to myself, sir. I was saying that forty miles in four hours was very good going. Hem. As to be sure it was. Hem. I have got a sort of cold by being out in the air. We 'll go in if you please. Hem.

Hard. But if you talked to yourself, you did not answer yourself. I am certain I heard two voices, and am resolved (*Raising his voice.*) to find the other out.

Mrs. Hard. (*From behind.*) Oh! he 's coming to find me out. Oh!

Tony. What need you go, sir, if I tell you? Hem. I 'll lay down my life for the truth—hem—I 'll tell you all, sir.

(*Detaining him.*)

Hard. I tell you I will not be detained. I insist on seeing. It 's in vain to expect I 'll believe you.

Mrs. Hard. (*Running forward from behind.*) O lud, he 'll murder my poor boy, my darling. Here, good gentleman, whet your rage upon me. Take my money, my life, but spare that young gentleman, spare my child, if you have any mercy.

Hard. My wife! as I 'm a Christian. From whence can she come, or what does she mean?

Mrs. Hard. (*Kneeling.*) Take compassion on us, good Mr. Highwayman. Take our money, our watches, all we have, but spare our lives. We will never bring you to justice, indeed we won't, good Mr. Highwayman.

Hard. I believe the woman 's out of her senses. What, Dorothy, don't you know me?

Mrs. Hard. Mr. Hardcastle, as I 'm alive! My fears blinded me. But who, my dear, could have expected to meet you here, in this frightful place, so far from home? What has brought you to follow us?

Hard. Sure, Dorothy, you have not lost your wits! So far from home, when you are within forty yards of your own door! (*To him.*) This is one of your old tricks, you graceless rogue, you! (*To her.*) Don't you know the gate, and the mulberry-tree; and don't you remember the horsepond, my dear?

Mrs. Hard. Yes, I shall remember the horsepond as long as I live; I have caught my death in it. (*To Tony.*) And is it to you, you graceless varlet, I owe all this? I 'll teach you to abuse your mother, I will.

Tony. Ecod, mother, all the parish says you have spoiled me, and so you may take the fruits on 't.

Mrs. Hard. I 'll spoil you, I will.

(*Follows him off the stage. Exit.*)

Hard. There 's morality, however, in his reply.

(*Exit.*)

(*Enter Hastings and Miss Neville.*)

Hastings. My dear Constance, why will you deliberate thus? If we delay a moment, all is lost for ever. Pluck up a little resolution, and we shall soon be out of the reach of her malignity.

Miss Neville. I find it impossible. My spirits are so sunk with the agitations I have suffered, that I am unable to face any new danger. Two or three years' patience will at last crown us with happiness.

Hastings. Such a tedious delay is worse than inconstancy. Let us fly, my charmer. Let us date our happiness from this very moment. Perish fortune. Love and content will increase what we possess beyond a monarch's revenue. Let me prevail.

Miss Neville. No, Mr. Hastings, no. Prudence once more comes to my relief, and I will obey its dictates. In the moment of passion, fortune may be despised, but it ever produces a lasting repentance. I 'm resolved to apply to Mr. Hardcastle's compassion and justice for redress.

Hastings. But though he had the will, he has not the power to relieve you.

Miss Neville. But he has influence, and upon that I am resolved to rely.

Hastings. I have no hopes. But since you persist, I must reluctantly obey you.

(*Exeunt.*)

Scene 3. *Scene changes [to a Room at Mr. Hardcastle's.]*

(*Enter Sir Charles and Miss Hardcastle.*)

Sir Charles. What a situation am I in! If what you say appears, I shall then find a guilty son. If what he says be true, I shall then lose one that, of all others, I most wished for a daughter.

Miss Hard. I am proud of your approbation; and, to show I merit it, if you place yourselves as I directed, you shall hear his explicit declaration. But he comes.

Sir Charles. I'll to your father, and keep him to the appointment.

(*Exit Sir Charles.*)

(*Enter Marlow.*)

Marlow. Though prepared for setting out, I come once more to take leave, nor did I, till this moment, know the pain I feel in the separation.

Miss Hard. (*In her own natural manner.*) I believe these sufferings cannot be very great, sir, which you can so easily remove. A day or two longer, perhaps, might lessen your uneasiness, by showing the little value of what you now think proper to regret.

Marlow. (*Aside.*) This girl every moment improves upon me. (*To her.*) It must not be, madam. I have already trifled too long with my heart. My very pride begins to submit to my passion. The disparity of education and fortune, the anger of a parent, and the contempt of my equals, begin to lose their weight; and nothing can restore me to myself but this painful effort of resolution.

Miss Hard. Then go, sir. I'll urge nothing more to detain you. Though my family be as good as hers you came down to visit, and my education, I hope, not inferior, what are these advantages without equal affluence? I must remain contented with the slight approbation of imputed merit; I must have only the mockery of your addresses, while all your serious aims are fixed on fortune.

(*Enter Hardcastle and Sir Charles from behind.*)

Sir Charles. Here, behind this screen.

Hard. Ay, ay, make no noise. I'll engage my Kate covers him with confusion at last.

Marlow. By heavens, madam, fortune was ever my smallest consideration. Your beauty at first caught my eye; for who could see that without emotion? But every moment that I converse with you, steals in some new grace, heightens the picture, and gives it stronger expression. What at first seemed rustic plainness, now appears refined simplicity. What seemed forward assurance, now strikes me as the result of courageous innocence, and conscious virtue.

Sir Charles. What can it mean? He amazes me!

Hard. I told you how it would be. Hush!

Marlow. I am now determined to stay, madam, and I have too good an opinion of my father's discernment, when he sees you, to doubt his approbation.

Miss Hard. No, Mr. Marlow, I will not, cannot detain you. Do you think I could suffer a connexion, in which there is the smallest room for repentance? Do you think I would take the mean advantage of a transient passion, to load you with confusion? Do you think I could ever relish that happiness, which was acquired by lessening yours?

Marlow. By all that's good, I can have no happiness but what's in your power to grant me. Nor shall I ever feel repentance, but in not having seen your merits before. I will stay, even contrary to your wishes; and though you should persist to shun me, I will make my respectful assiduities atone for the levity of my past conduct.

Miss Hard. Sir, I must entreat you'll desist. As our acquaintance began, so let it end, in indifference. I might have given an hour or two to levity; but, seriously, Mr. Marlow, do you think I could ever submit to a connection where *I* must appear mercenary, and *you* imprudent? Do you think I could ever catch at the confident addresses of a secure admirer?

Marlow. (*Kneeling.*) Does this look like security? Does this look like confidence? No, madam, every moment that shows me your merit, only serves to increase my diffidence and confusion. Here let me continue——

Sir Charles. I can hold it no longer. Charles, Charles, how hast thou deceived me! Is this your indifference, your uninteresting conversation!

Hard. Your cold contempt! your formal interview! What have you to say now?

Marlow. That I'm all amazement! What can it mean?

Hard. It means that you can say and unsay things at pleasure. That you can address a lady in private, and deny it in public; that you have one story for us, and another for my daughter!

Marlow. Daughter!—this lady your daughter!

Hard. Yes, sir, my only daughter. My Kate, whose else should she be?

Marlow. Oh, the devil!

Miss Hard. Yes, sir, that very identical tall squinting lady you were pleased to take me for. (*Curtseying.*) She that you addressed as the mild, modest, sentimental man of gravity, and the bold, forward, agreeable Rattle of the Ladies' Club: ha, ha, ha!

Marlow. Zounds, there 's no bearing this; it 's worse than death!

Miss Hard. In which of your characters, sir, will you give us leave to address you? As the faltering gentleman, with looks on the ground, that speaks just to be heard, and hates hypocrisy: or the loud confident creature, that keeps it up with Mrs. Mantrap, and old Miss Biddy Buckskin, till three in the morning; ha, ha, ha!

Marlow. O, curse on my noisy head. I never attempted to be impudent yet, that I was not taken down. I must be gone.

Hard. By the hand of my body, but you shall not. I see it was all a mistake, and I am rejoiced to find it. You shall not, sir, I tell you. I know she 'll forgive you. Won't you forgive him, Kate? We 'll all forgive you. Take courage, man.

(*They retire, she tormenting him to the back scene.*)

(*Enter Mrs. Hardcastle, Tony.*)

Mrs. Hard. So, so, they 're gone off. Let them go, I care not.

Hard. Who gone?

Mrs. Hard. My dutiful niece and her gentleman, Mr. Hastings, from town. He who came down with our modest visitor here.

Sir Charles. Who, my honest George Hastings! As worthy a fellow as lives, and the girl could not have made a more prudent choice.

Hard. Then, by the hand of my body, I 'm proud of the connection.

Mrs. Hard. Well, if he has taken away the lady, he has not taken her fortune, that remains in this family to console us for her loss.

Hard. Sure, Dorothy, you would not be so mercenary?

Mrs. Hard. Ay, that 's my affair, not yours. But you know, if your son, when of age, refuses to marry his cousin, her whole fortune is then at her own disposal.

Hard. Ah, but he 's not of age, and she has not thought proper to wait for his refusal.

(*Enter Hastings and Miss Neville.*)

Mrs. Hard. (*Aside.*) What! returned so soon? I begin not to like it.

Hastings. (*To Hardcastle.*) For my late attempt to fly off with your niece, let my present confusion be my punishment. We are now come back, to appeal from your justice to your humanity. By her father's consent, I first paid her my addresses, and our passions were first founded in duty.

Miss Neville. Since his death, I have been obliged to stoop to dissimulation to avoid oppression. In an hour of levity, I was ready even to give up my fortune to secure my choice. But I 'm now recovered from the delusion, and hope from your tenderness what is denied me from a nearer connection.

Mrs. Hard. Pshaw, pshaw! this is all but the whining end of a modern novel.

Hard. Be it what it will, I 'm glad they 're come back to reclaim their due. Come hither, Tony, boy. Do you refuse this lady's hand whom I now offer you?

Tony. What signifies my refusing? You know I can't refuse her till I 'm of age, father.

Hard. While I thought concealing your age, boy, was likely to conduce to your improvement, I concurred with your mother's desire to keep it secret. But since I find she turns it to a wrong use, I must now declare, you have been of age these three months.

Tony. Of age! Am I of age, father?

Hard. Above three months.

Tony. Then you 'll see the first use I 'll make of my liberty. (*Taking Miss Neville's hand.*) Witness all men by these presents, that I, Anthony Lumpkin, Esquire, of blank place, refuse you, Constantia Neville, spinster, of no place at all, for my true and lawful wife. So Constance Neville may marry whom she pleases, and Tony Lumpkin is his own man again!

Sir Charles. O brave 'Squire!

Hastings. My worthy friend!

Mrs. Hard. My undutiful offspring!

Marlow. Joy, my dear George, I give you joy, sincerely. And could I prevail upon my little tyrant here to be less arbitrary, I should be the happiest man alive, if you would return me the favor.

Hastings. (*To Miss Hardcastle.*) Come, madam, you are now driven to the very last scene of all your contrivances. I know you like him, I 'm sure he loves you, and you must and shall have him.

Hard. (*Joining their hands.*) And I say so, too. And Mr. Marlow, if she makes as good a wife as she has a daughter, I don't believe you 'll ever repent your bargain. So now to supper, to-morrow we shall gather all the poor of the parish about us, and the Mistakes of the Night shall be crowned with a merry morning; so boy, take her; and as you have been mistaken in the mistress, my wish is, that you may never be mistaken in the wife.

EPILOGUE

By Dr. Goldsmith.

Well, having stooped to conquer with success,
And gained a husband without aid from dress,
Still as a barmaid, I could wish it too,
As I have conquered him to conquer you:
And let me say, for all your resolution,
That pretty barmaids have done execution.
Our life is all a play, composed to please,
"We have our exits and our entrances." [38]
The first act shows the simple country maid,
Harmless and young, of everything afraid;
Blushes when hired, and with unmeaning action,
I hopes as how to give you satisfaction.
Her second act displays a livelier scene,—
Th' unblushing barmaid of a country inn,
Who whisks about the house, at market caters,
Talks loud, coquets the guests, and scolds the waiters.
Next the scene shifts to town, and there she soars,
The chop-house toast of ogling connoisseurs.
On 'Squires and Cits [39] she there displays her arts,
And on the gridiron broils her lovers' hearts—
And as she smiles, her triumphs to complete,
Even Common Councilmen forget to eat.
The fourth act shows her wedded to the 'Squire,
And madam now begins to hold it higher;
Pretends to taste, at Operas cries *caro*,[40]
And quits her *Nancy Dawson*, for *Che Faro*.[41]
Doats upon dancing, and in all her pride,
Swims round the room, the *Heinel* [42] of Cheapside:
Ogles and leers with artificial skill,
Till having lost in age the power to kill,
She sits all night at cards, and ogles at spadille.[43]
Such, through our lives, the eventful history—
The fifth and last act still remains for me.
The barmaid now for your protection prays,
Turns female barrister, and pleads for Bayes.[44]

EPILOGUE

To be spoken in the character of Tony Lumpkin.

By J. Craddock, Esq.

Well—now all 's ended—and my comrades gone,
Pray what becomes of *mother's nonly son?*
A hopeful blade!—in town I 'll fix my station,
And try to make a bluster in the nation.
As for my cousin Neville, I renounce her,
Off—in a crack—I 'll carry big Bet Bouncer.
Why should not I in the great world appear?
I soon shall have a thousand pounds a year;
No matter what a man may here inherit,
In London—'gad, they 've some regard to spirit.
I see the horses prancing up the streets,
And big Bet Bouncer bobs to all she meets;
Then hoikes to jiggs and pastimes ev'ry night—
Not to the plays—they say it a'n't polite,
To Sadler's-Wells [45] perhaps, or Operas go,
And once by chance, to the roratorio.
Thus here and there, for ever up and down,
We 'll set the fashions too, to half the town;
And then at auctions—money ne'er regard,
Buy pictures like the great, ten pounds a yard:
Zounds, we shall make these London gentry say,
We know what 's damned genteel, as well as they.

38 This line and what follows are after the pattern of the "seven ages" in Shakespeare's *As You Like It*, II. vii.

39 Citizens, "bourgeois."

40 *I. e., bravo.*

41 The former is a popular song, the latter is an aria in Glück's opera *Orfeo*, 1764.—*Che farò senza Euridice?*

42 A Prussian dancer popular in London about this time.

43 The ace of spades in certain card-games.

44 *i. e.*, the dramatist (from the person who was a parody on Dryden in *The Rehearsal*). There is mock-modesty in using the word.

45 A pleasure-resort in the north of London.

RICHARD BRINSLEY SHERIDAN

THE SCHOOL FOR SCANDAL

Richard Brinsley Sheridan (1751–1816), like Goldsmith, was Irish in blood and somewhat in temperament; he was born in Dublin, though in boyhood he came to England, his home thereafter. Through his father, an actor and theater-manager, he was doubtless from the first thoroughly familiar with the stage. His six plays were all written in his youth; of the two best and most permanently popular, *The Rivals* was first acted in 1775 and *The School for Scandal* in 1777. His later eminence was political; he was in Parliament for many years, rose high in the government, and was celebrated as an eloquent and brilliant speaker.

The School for Scandal is the finest example in the eighteenth century of the comedy of manners. As usual with this type, the characters are many, the dialogue is sparkling, action abundant, and plot somewhat loose. It has often been noticed that the title of the play is derived from a very minor element in it, Lady Sneerwell and her sisterhood, and their irresponsible and venomous gossip. It is hardly true, however, that the scandal scenes are without function, for they give an extensive background, a sense that the action of the play is typical of a large society, which is essential to the comedy of manners. They also sharpen the satire; scandal half the time is mistaken, as the audience is shown in advance (Sheridan fully understood the advantage of flattering his audience); the tattlers make out Joseph Surface to be Lady Sneerwell's lover instead of Lady Teazle's, and him to be the saint and his brother Charles the sinner, instead of the nearly opposite truth; and no one will forget the immortal satire on scandal-mongering in act V. ii, where a purely imaginary bullet is said to have rebounded from the little bronze Pliny "and wounded the postman, who was just coming to the door with a double letter from Northamptonshire."

The essentials of the plot are neither especially original nor striking. Domestic quarrels and intrigues, the exposure of hypocrisy and the rewarding of generosity, are no more entertaining and pleasing than they are usual in comedy. Even the gossip-club is foreshadowed in Congreve's *The Way of the World* (I. i) and elsewhere. Much the same is true of the characters. The humor of the old man who marries a young wife, brags to her of the exploits of his youth, and is cajoled, managed, and deceived by her, is at least as old as Chaucer's *Merchant's Tale;* the two brothers, one plausible and unlovely, the other reckless but good-hearted, are familiar in Fielding's *Tom Jones* (not to mention the parable of the Prodigal Son). In this play, as often, the comedy of manners verges into the comedy of humors. That each character is intended to embody a single trait is announced in the names of most of them — Teazle, Surface, Crabtree, etc. The characterization is broad and simple, with little aim at subtlety. But it is endlessly diverting and vigorous; every stroke counts, and its force makes it seem more lifelike than it is. Nor is it wanting in original discernment, as in the person of Mrs. Candour, who gets a reputation for charity by professing disbelief in the malevolent gossip she spreads.

The vitality of the play consists chiefly in its situations and its dialogue. Every action and line show Sheridan's keen eye for the dramatically effective. Two scenes are especially celebrated. One (IV. i) is where Charles has his ancestors' portraits auctioned off, the other (IV. iii) where the screen is thrown down and Lady Teazle is disclosed. In each of them every speech makes the situation more tense. The comedy is made more piquant in each by the spectator being in the secret, which is not shared by the characters; he rejoices that Charles' loyalty to his uncle is serving him better than he knows, and that Joseph's agonized struggles (unseen by the other persons) are entangling him more and more. The scenes where Joseph rejects his disguised uncle's request (V. i), where Sir Peter walks in upon the gossips (V. ii), and the general clearing up at the end, are also admirable. It is perhaps chiefly the effectiveness on the stage of such scenes in this play and *The Rivals* that has enabled Sheridan to outlive all other men of the eighteenth century except Goldsmith as an acting dramatist; and that made Sir Henry Irving call this play the most popular comedy in the English language.

His popularity on the stage has been hardly less helped by his dialogue; which is the chief reason for his popularity among readers. He and Congreve are the most constantly brilliant of the older English dramatists, and even Congreve is less epigrammatic and quotable. Sheridan's dialogue resembles those fireworks which emit a steady shower of sparks, and now and then an exploding ball of fire. Its sheer cleverness cannot be surpassed, and justifies the sacrifices he makes to it. The chief of these is realism. It was said of Ben Jonson that he would rather lose his friend than his jest; Sheridan would rather lose his truth to nature than his jest. Snake declares that, since he lives by the badness of his character, "if it were once known that he had been betrayed into an honest action, he should lose every friend he has in the world." The cynical impudence is of the stage, not of life. It is acceptable because the play is a work of art, not a study of human character. Even the fop Sir Benjamin Backbite says clever things, and the clever Trip is rather the roguish servant of fiction than of life. The vigor of the play carries us over the obstructions of sober truth. Sheridan neglects no source of mirth; he is fond of leading his characters, especially Sir Peter Teazle, into verbal pitfalls whence they scramble out covered with ridicule. When Lady Teazle in her new station aspires to be thought a woman of taste, he sputters back, "Zounds, madam! You had no taste when you married me" (I. i).

No play better reflects the tastes of the age when it was written than *The School for Scandal.* Being a comedy of manners, it illustrates social life and conceptions; we are conscious of the dress and bearing of modish society, of its amusements, and its moral standards. The play vividly illustrates the differing moral standards for the two sexes, and the petty vices with which what used to be called the softer sex was allowed to solace itself for strictness in weightier matters. Maria, the model young woman, declares, "We have pride, envy, rivalship, and a thousand motives to depreciate each other; but the male slanderer must have the cowardice of a woman before he can traduce one" (I.i).

In a literary way, too, the play is of its time, just as Goldsmith's are. It embodies sentimentalism even more than *She Stoops to Conquer* does; but in the main satirizes it. It makes some concession to the popular taste in the complete poetic justice of the close, and in the ease with which the characters mend their ways. Lady Teazle is to settle down to rural domesticity (at least according to the epilogue). Charles is to illustrate the good old-fashioned theory that the reformed rake makes the best husband, though he is cautious enough to "make no promises" "as to reforming." He is the sentimental type of hero, almost to the present day beloved on the popular stage, and inherited by the nineteenth century from the eighteenth, the reckless dare-devil fellow, his own worst enemy, who rises to an occasion for loyalty and generosity where the plausible and well-behaved fails; a type more attractive than true to morals and life. Sentimental love appears but little; because, it is said, Sheridan doubted the success in a love-scene of the actor who was to play Charles. The play was called in its own day an "attempt to destroy the taste for sentimental comedy revived by Mr. Cumberland" (whose *West Indian* and other plays had met great success). Sheridan ridicules sentimentalism chiefly in the person of Joseph Surface, "a *man of sentiment.*" To the world he is a highly moral young man, who hardly opens his mouth without dropping edification. In reality he is a cynical hypocrite, who throws off his mask when he fancies it unnecessary. "O Lud," says Lady Sneerwell, "you are going to be moral, and forget that you are among friends." "Egad, that 's true," says he; "I 'll keep that sentiment till I see Sir Peter." He is a very difficult character to play. He must not seem shifty and unctuous, for he appears honest enough to deceive the world, and dashing enough to be the lover of the frivolous Lady Teazle, and to pass for the lover of the experienced Lady Sneerwell. Though heightened beyond ordinary reality, he is exceedingly effective dramatically.

The greatest charm of *The School for Scandal* is its combination of cleverness with geniality; in which it contrasts with Restoration comedy. We laugh with a clearer heart at the cynical wit of the scandalmongers because we are not expected to sympathize with them. Nothing is made ridiculous that does not deserve to be; the dramatist spares us the ordinary stage Jew, even Moses has his good points.[1] We accept characters on analysis somewhat conventional, situations a little forced, and poetic justice far more complete than squares with experience, because of the brilliant dash and good spirits with which it all goes through. It is all no more artificial than art has the right to be. It shows us something better than life, but with such originality and energy as insures sufficient illusion for supreme effectiveness.

1 Some seventeen years later the sentimental dramatist Cumberland produced a still more chivalrous picture in his play *The Jew.*

THE SCHOOL FOR SCANDAL

PROLOGUE

Written by Mr. Garrick.

A School for Scandal! tell me, I beseech you,
Needs there a school this modish art to teach you?
No need of lessons now, the knowing think;
We might as well be taught to eat and drink.
Caused by a dearth of scandal, should the vapors [1]
Distress our fair ones—let them read the papers;
Their powerful mixtures such disorders hit;
Crave what you will—there's *quantum sufficit.*[2]
"Lord!" cries my Lady Wormwood (who loves tattle,
And puts much salt and pepper in her prattle),
Just risen at noon, all night at cards when threshing
Strong tea and scandal—"Bless me, how refreshing!
Give me the papers, Lisp—how bold and free! (*Sips.*)
Last night Lord L. (*Sips*) *was caught with Lady D.*
For aching heads what charming sal volatile! (*Sips.*)
If Mrs. B. will still continue flirting,
We hope she'll draw, *or we'll* undraw *the curtain.*
Fine satire, poz [3]—in public all abuse it,
But, by ourselves (*Sips*), our praise we can't refuse it.
Now, Lisp, read you—there, at that dash and star:"
"Yes, ma'am—*A certain lord had best beware,*
Who lives not twenty miles from Grosvenor Square;
For, should he Lady W. find willing,
Wormwood is bitter"——"Oh, that's me! the villain!
Throw it behind the fire, and never more
Let that vile paper come within my door."
Thus at our friends we laugh, who feel the dart;
To reach our feelings, we ourselves must smart.
Is our young bard so young, to think that he
Can stop the full spring-tide of calumny?
Knows he the world so little, and its trade?
Alas! the devil's sooner raised than laid.
So strong, so swift, the monster there's no gagging:
Cut Scandal's head off, still the tongue is wagging.
Proud of your smiles once lavishly bestowed,
Again our young Don Quixote takes the road;
To show his gratitude he draws his pen,
And seeks his hydra, Scandal, in his den.
For your applause all perils he would through—
He'll fight—that's write—a cavalliero true,
Till every drop of blood—that's ink—is spilt for you.

DRAMATIS PERSONÆ

SIR PETER TEAZLE.
SIR OLIVER SURFACE.
YOUNG SURFACE.
CHARLES, *his Brother.*
CRABTREE.
SIR BENJAMIN BACKBITE.
ROWLEY.
SPUNGE.
MOSES.
SNAKE.
CARELESS — *and other companions to* CHARLES.
TRIP.

LADY TEAZLE.
MARIA.
LADY SNEERWELL.
MRS. CANDOUR.
MISS VERJUICE.

ACT I.

SCENE 1. *Lady Sneerwell's House.*

(*Lady Sneerwell at her dressing table with Lappet; Miss Verjuice drinking chocolate.*)

Lady Sneer. The paragraphs you say were all inserted?

Verj. They were, madam—and as I copied them myself in a feigned hand there can be no suspicion whence they came.

Lady Sneer. Did you circulate the report

[1] A fit of melancholy. [2] A sufficiency. [3] positively.

of Lady Brittle's intrigue with Captain Boastall?

Verj. Madam, by this time Lady Brittle is the talk of half the town—and I doubt not in a week the men will toast her as a demirep.

Lady Sneer. What have you done as to the insinuation as to a certain baronet's lady and a certain cook?

Verj. That is in as fine a train as your Ladyship could wish. I told the story yesterday to my own maid with directions to communicate it directly to my hair-dresser. He, I am informed, has a brother who courts a milliner's prentice in Pallmall, whose mistress has a first cousin whose sister is *femme de chambre* to Mrs. Clackit—so that in the common course of things it must reach Mrs. Clackit's ears within four-and-twenty hours, and then you know the business is as good as done.

Lady Sneer. Why, truly, Mrs. Clackit has a very pretty talent—a great deal of industry—yet—yes—been tolerably successful in her way. To my knowledge she has been the cause of breaking off six matches, of three sons being disinherited and four daughters being turned out of doors; of three several elopements, as many close confinements, nine separate maintenances, and two divorces.—Nay, I have more than once traced her causing a *tête-à-tête* in the Town and Country Magazine, when the parties perhaps had never seen each other's faces before in the course of their lives.

Verj. She certainly has talents.

Lady Sneer. But her manner is gross.

Verj. 'T is very true. She generally designs well, has a free tongue, and a bold invention; but her coloring is too dark and her outline often extravagant. She wants that delicacy of tint and mellowness of sneer which distinguish your Ladyship's scandal.

Lady Sneer. Ah, you are partial, Verjuice.

Verj. Not in the least; everybody allows that Lady Sneerwell can do more with a word or a look than many can with the most labored detail, even when they happen to have a little truth on their side to support it.

Lady Sneer. Yes, my dear Verjuice. I am no hypocrite to deny the satisfaction I reap from the success of my efforts. Wounded myself in the early part of my life by the envenomed tongue of slander, I confess I have since known no pleasure equal to the reducing others to the level of my own injured reputation.

Verj. Nothing can be more natural. But, my dear Lady Sneerwell, there is one affair in which you have lately employed me, wherein, I confess, I am at a loss to guess your motives.

Lady Sneer. I conceive you mean with respect to my neighbor, Sir Peter Teazle, and his family—Lappet.—And has my conduct in this matter really appeared to you so mysterious?

(*Exit Maid.*)

Verj. Entirely so. An old bachelor as Sir Peter was, having taken a young wife from out of the country—as Lady Teazle is—are certainly fair subjects for a little mischievous raillery; but here are two young men to whom Sir Peter has acted as a kind of guardian since their father's death, the eldest possessing the most amiable character and universally well spoken of, the youngest the most dissipated and extravagant young fellow in the kingdom, without friends or character; the former one an avowed admirer of yours and apparently your favorite, the latter attached to Maria, Sir Peter's ward, and confessedly beloved by her. Now on the face of these circumstances it is utterly unaccountable to me why you, a young widow with no great jointure, should not close with the passion of a man of such character and expectations as Mr. Surface, and more so why you should be so uncommonly earnest to destroy the mutual attachment subsisting between his brother Charles and Maria.

Lady Sneer. Then at once to unravel this mystery, I must inform you that love has no share whatever in the intercourse between Mr. Surface and me.

Verj. No!

Lady Sneer. His real attachment is to Maria or her fortune, but finding in his brother a favored rival, he has been obliged to mask his pretensions and profit by my assistance.

Verj. Yet still I am more puzzled why you should interest yourself in his success.

Lady Sneer. Heavens! how dull you are! cannot you surmise the weakness which I hitherto thro' shame have concealed even from you?—must I confess that Charles—that libertine, that extravagant, that bankrupt in fortune and reputation—that he it is for whom I am thus anxious and malicious and to gain whom I would sacrifice—everything?——

Verj. Now indeed, your conduct appears consistent and I no longer wonder at your enmity to Maria; but how came you and Surface so confidential?

Lady Sneer. For our mutual interest; but I have found out him a long time since, altho' he has contrived to deceive everybody beside. I know him to be artful, selfish, and malicious; while with Sir Peter, and indeed with all his acquaintance, he passes for a youthful miracle of prudence, good sense, and benevolence.

Verj. Yes, yes, I know Sir Peter vows he has not his equal in England; and, above all, he praises him as a *man of sentiment.*

Lady Sneer. True, and with the assistance of his sentiments and hypocrisy he has brought Sir Peter entirely in his interests with respect to Maria, and is now, I believe, attempting to flatter Lady Teazle into the same good opinion towards him, while poor Charles has no friend in the house; though I fear he has a powerful one in Maria's heart, against whom we must direct our schemes.

Serv. Mr. Surface.

Lady Sneer. Show him up. He generally calls about this time. I don't wonder at people's giving him to me for a lover.

(*Enter Surface.*)

Surf. My dear Lady Sneerwell, how do you do to-day—your most obedient.

Lady Sneer. Miss Verjuice has just been arraigning me on our mutual attachment now; but I have informed her of our real views and the purposes for which our geniuses at present co-operate. You know how useful she has been to us; and believe me, the confidence is not ill-placed.

Surf. Madam, it is impossible for me to suspect that a lady of Miss Verjuice's sensibility and discernment——

Lady Sneer. Well, well, no compliments now; but tell me when you saw your mistress or, what is more material to me, your brother.

Surf. I have not seen either since I saw you, but I can inform you that they are at present at variance; some of your stories have taken good effect on Maria.

Lady Sneer. Ah! my dear Verjuice, the merit of this belongs to you. But do your brother's distresses increase?

Surf. Every hour. I am told he had another execution in his house yesterday; in short, his dissipation and extravagance exceed anything I have ever heard of.

Lady Sneer. Poor Charles!

Surf. True, madam, notwithstanding his vices one can't help feeling for him; ah, poor Charles! I'm sure I wish it was in my power to be of any essential service to him, for the man who does not share in the distresses of a brother, even though merited by his own misconduct, deserves——

Lady Sneer. O Lud, you are going to be moral, and forget that you are among friends.

Surf. Egad, that's true—I'll keep that sentiment till I see Sir Peter. However, it is certainly a charity to rescue Maria from such a libertine, who, if he is to be reclaimed, can be so only by a person of your ladyship's superior accomplishments and understanding.

Verj. 'T would be a hazardous experiment.

Surf. But, madam, let me caution you to place no more confidence in our friend Snake the libeller; I have lately detected him in frequent conference with old [Rowley], who was formerly my father's steward and has never been a friend of mine.

Lady Sneer. I'm not disappointed in Snake; I never suspected the fellow to have virtue enough to be faithful even to his own villany.

(*Enter Maria.*)

Maria, my dear, how do you do? What's the matter?

Maria. O, there is that disagreeable lover of mine, Sir Benjamin Backbite, has just called at my guardian's with his odious Uncle Crabtree; so I slipt out and ran hither to avoid them.

Lady Sneer. Is that all?

Verj. Lady Sneerwell, I'll go and write the letter I mentioned to you.

(*Exit Verj.*)

Surf. If my brother Charles had been of the party, madam, perhaps you would not have been so much alarmed.

Lady Sneer. Nay, now, you are severe, for I dare swear the truth of the matter is Maria heard *you* were here; but, my dear, what has Sir Benjamin done that you should avoid him so?

Mar. Oh, he has done nothing; but his conversation is a perpetual libel on all his acquaintance.

Surf. Aye, and the worst of it is there is no advantage in not knowing [him], for he 'll abuse a stranger just as soon as his best friend; and Crabtree is as bad.

Lady Sneer. Nay, but we should make allowance—Sir Benjamin is a wit and a poet.

Mar. For my part, I own, madam, wit loses its respect with me, when I see it in company with malice.—What do you think, Mr. Surface?

Surf. Certainly, madam; to smile at the jest which plants a thorn on another's breast is to become a principal in the mischief.

Lady Sneer. Pshaw, there 's no possibility of being witty without a little [ill-]nature—the malice of a good thing is the barb that makes it stick.—What 's your opinion, Mr. Surface?

Surf. Certainly, madam; that conversation where the spirit of raillery is suppressed will ever appear tedious and insipid.

Mar. Well, I 'll not debate how far scandal may be allowable, but in a man I am sure it is always contemptible. We have pride, envy, rivalship, and a thousand motives to depreciate each other, but the male-slanderer must have the cowardice of a woman before he can traduce one.

Lady Sneer. I wish my cousin Verjuice hadn't left us—she should embrace you.

Surf. Ah! she 's an old maid, and is privileged, of course.

(*Enter Servant.*)

Serv. Madam, Mrs. Candour is below and if your Ladyship 's at leisure will leave her carriage.

Lady Sneer. Beg her to walk in. (*Exit Servant.*) Now, Maria, however, here is a character to your taste, for tho' Mrs. Candour is a little talkative, everybody allows her to be the best-natured and best sort of woman.

Mar. Yes, with a very gross affectation of good nature and benevolence, she does more mischief than the direct malice of old Crabtree.

Surf. I' faith, 't is very true, Lady Sneerwell. When ever I hear the current running again[st] the characters of my friends, I never think them in such danger as when Candour undertakes their defence.

Lady Sneer. Hush, here she is——

(*Enter Mrs. Candour.*)

Mrs. Can. My dear Lady Sneerwell, how have you been this century? I have never seen you tho' I have heard of you very often.—Mr. Surface, the world says scandalous things of you—but indeed it is no matter what the world says, for I think one hears nothing else but scandal.

Surf. Just so, indeed, ma'am.

Mrs. Can. Ah, Maria, child—what! is the whole affair off between you and Charles? His extravagance, I presume—the town talks of nothing else——

Mar. I am very sorry, ma'am, the town has so little to do.

Mrs. Can. True, true, child; but there 's no stopping people's tongues. I own I was hurt to hear it—as I indeed was to learn from the same quarter that your guardian, Sir Peter, and Lady Teazle have not agreed lately so well as could be wished.

Mar. 'T is strangely impertinent for people to busy themselves so.

Mrs. Can. Very true, child; but what 's to be done? People will talk—there 's no preventing it. Why, it was but yesterday I was told that Miss Gadabout had eloped with Sir Filagree Flirt. But, Lord! there is no minding what one hears; tho' to be sure I had this from very good authority.

Mar. Such reports are highly scandalous.

Mrs. Can. So they are, child—shameful! shameful! but the world is so censorious no character escapes. Lord, now! who would have suspected your friend, Miss Prim, of an indiscretion; yet such is the ill-nature of people that they say her uncle stopped her last week just as she was stepping into a postchaise with her dancing-master.

Mar. I 'll answer for 't there are no grounds for the report.

Mrs. Can. Oh, no foundation in the world, I dare swear; no more probably than for the story circulated last month, of Mrs. Festino's affair with Colonel Cassino—though to be sure that matter was never rightly cleared up.

Surf. The licence of invention some people take is monstrous indeed.

Mar. 'T is so; but in my opinion those who report such things are equally culpable.

Mrs. Can. To be sure they are; tale bearers are as bad as the tale makers—'t is an old observation and a very true one—but what 's to be done, as I said before? How will you prevent people from talking? To-day Mrs. Clackitt assured me Mr. and Mrs. Honeymoon were at last become mere man and wife—like [the rest of their] acquaintance; she likewise hinted that a certain widow in the next street had got rid of her dropsy and recovered her shape in a most surprising manner; at the same [time] Miss Tattle, who was by, affirmed that Lord Boffalo had discovered his Lady at a house of no extraordinary fame, and that Sir Harry Bouquet and Tom Saunter were to measure swords on a similar provocation. But, Lord! do you think I would report these things? No, no! tale bearers, as I said before, are just as bad as the tale makers.

Surf. Ah! Mrs. Candour, if everybody had your forbearance and good nature—

Mrs. Can. I confess, Mr. Surface, I cannot bear to hear people traduced behind their backs; and when ugly circumstances come out against our acquaintance, I own I always love to think the best.—By the bye, I hope 't is not true that your brother is absolutely ruined—

Surf. I am afraid his circumstances are very bad indeed, ma'am.

Mrs. Can. Ah! I heard so; but you must tell him to keep up his spirits; everybody almost is in the same way—Lord Spindle, Sir Thomas Splint, Captain Quinze, and Mr. Nickit—all up, I hear, within this week; so if Charles is undone, he 'll find half his acquaintance ruined too, and that, you know, is a consolation.

Surf. Doubtless, ma'am, a very great one.

(*Enter Servant.*)

Serv. Mr. Crabtree and Sir Benjamin Backbite.

Lady Sneer. Soh! Maria, you see your lover pursues you. Positively you shan't escape.

(*Enter Crabtree and Sir Benjamin Backbite.*)

Crab. Lady Sneerwell, I kiss your hand. Mrs. Candour, I don't believe you are acquainted with my nephew, Sir Benjamin Backbite. Egad, ma'am, he has a pretty wit, and is a pretty poet too, is n't he, Lady Sneerwell?

Sir Ben. O fie, uncle!

Crab. Nay, egad, it 's true. I back him at a rebus or a charade against the best rhymer in the kingdom. Has your Ladyship heard the epigram he wrote last week on Lady Frizzle's feather catching fire?—do, Benjamin, repeat it—or the charade you made last night extempore at Mrs. Drowzie's conversazione?[4] —Come now, your first is the name of a fish, your second a great naval commander—and—

Sir Ben. Dear uncle—now—prithee——

Crab. I' faith, ma'am, 't would surprise you to hear how ready he is at all these things.

Lady Sneer. I wonder, Sir Benjamin, you never publish anything.

Sir Ben. To say truth, ma'am, 't is very vulgar to print, and as my little productions are mostly satires and lampoons, I find they circulate more by giving copies in confidence to the friends of the parties; however, I have some love-elegies, which, when favored with this lady's smile, I mean to give to the public. (*Pointing to Maria.*)

Crab. 'Fore Heaven, ma'am, they 'll immortalize you—you 'll be handed down to posterity, like Petrarch's Laura, or Waller's Sacharissa.[5]

Sir Ben. Yes, madam, I think you will like them—when you shall see in a beautiful quarto page how a neat rivulet of text shall meander thro' a meadow of margin—'fore Gad, they will be the most elegant things of their kind.

Crab. But, ladies, have you heard the news?

Mrs. Can. What, sir, do you mean the report of——

Crab. No, ma'am, that 's not it.—Miss Nicely is going to be married to her own footman.

Mrs. Can. Impossible!

Crab. Ask Sir Benjamin.

Sir Ben. 'T is very true, ma'am; everything is fixed and the wedding livery bespoke.

Crab. Yes, and they say there were pressing reasons for 't.

Mrs. Can. It cannot be—and I wonder any one should believe such a story of so prudent a lady as Miss Nicely.

Sir Ben. O Lud! ma'am, that 's the very reason 't was believed at once. She has always been so cautious and so reserved that everybody was sure there was some reason for it at bottom.

Lady Sneer. Yes, a tale of scandal is as fatal to the reputation of a prudent lady of her stamp as a fever is generally to those of the strongest constitutions, but there is a sort of puny sickly reputation,

4 A sort of reception.

5 Petrarch (1304–1374) addressed his love-lyrics to Laura, and the English poet Waller (1606–1687) addressed his to Sacharissa (his name for Lady Dorothy Sidney).

that is always ailing yet will outlive the robuster characters of a hundred prudes.

Sir Ben. True, madam, there are valetudinarians in reputation as well as constitution, who being conscious of their weak part, avoid the least breath of air, and supply their want of stamina by care and circumspection.

Mrs. Can. Well, but this may be all mistake. You know, Sir Benjamin, very trifling circumstances often give rise to the most injurious tales.

Crab. That they do, I 'll be sworn, ma'am. Did you ever hear how Miss Shepherd came to lose her lover and her character last summer at Tunbridge?—Sir Benjamin, you remember it.

Sir Ben. O to be sure, the most whimsical circumstance—

Lady Sneer. How was it, pray?

Crab. Why, one evening at Mrs. Ponto's assembly, the conversation happened to turn on the difficulty of breeding Nova-Scotia sheep in this country. Says a young lady in company, "I have known instances of it, for Miss Letitia Shepherd, a first cousin of mine, had a Nova-Scotia sheep that produced her twins."—"What!" cries the old Dowager Lady Dundizzy (who you know is as deaf as a post), "has Miss Letitia Shepherd had twins?"—This mistake, as you may imagine, threw the whole company into a fit of laughing. However, 't was the next morning everywhere reported and in a few days believed by the whole town, that Miss Letitia Shepherd had actually been brought to bed by a fine boy and girl, and in less than a week there were people who could name the father, and the farm house where the babies were put out to nurse.

Lady Sneer. Strange indeed!

Crab. Matter of fact, I assure you. O Lud! Mr. Surface, pray, is it true that your uncle Sir Oliver is coming home?

Surf. Not that I know of indeed, sir.

Crab. He has been in the East Indies a long time; you can scarcely remember him, I believe. Sad comfort on his arrival to hear how your brother has gone on!

Surf. Charles has been imprudent, sir, to be sure; but I hope no busy people have already prejudiced Sir Oliver against him. He may reform.

Sir Ben. To be sure he may; for my part I never believed him to be so utterly void of principle as people say; and tho' he has lost all his friends, I am told nobody is better spoken of—by the Jews.

Crab. That 's true, egad, nephew; if the Old Jewry [6] was a ward I believe Charles would be an alderman—no man more popular there; 'fore Gad, I hear he pays as many annuities [7] as the Irish Tontine,[8] and that whenever he 's sick they have prayers for the recovery of his health in the synagogue.

Sir Ben. Yet no man lives in greater splendor:—they tell me when he entertains his friends, he can sit down to dinner with a dozen of his own securities, have a score of tradesmen waiting in the ante-chamber, and an officer behind every guest's chair.

Surf. This may be entertainment to you, gentlemen, but you pay very little regard to the feelings of a brother.

Mar. Their malice is intolerable. Lady Sneerwell, I must wish you a good morning—I 'm not very well.

(*Exit Mar.*)

Mrs. Can. O dear, she changed color very much!

Lady Sneer. Do, Mrs. Candour, follow her—she may want assistance.

Mrs. Can. That I will with all my soul, ma'am.—Poor, dear girl, who knows what her situation may be!

(*Exit Mrs. Can.*)

Lady Sneer. 'T was nothing but that she could not bear to hear Charles reflected on, notwithstanding their difference.

Sir Ben. The young lady's penchant is obvious.

Crab. But, Benjamin, you must n't give up the pursuit for that; follow her and put her into good humor—repeat her some of your verses; come, I 'll assist you—

Sir Ben. Mr. Surface, I did not mean to hurt you, but depend on 't your brother is utterly undone.

(*Going.*)

Crab. O Lud! aye—undone—as ever man was—can't raise a guinea.

6 A street in the center of London, named from a synagogue which stood there in the Middle Ages.

7 An annual payment made by a debtor.

8 A tontine is a kind of insurance scheme which sometimes paid annual dividends. Shortly before the date of this play the Irish government had undertaken to raise money by starting one.

Sir Ben. And everything sold, I'm told, that was movable.

(*Going.*)

Crab. I was at his house—not a thing left but some empty bottles that were overlooked and the family pictures, which I believe are framed in the wainscot.

(*Going.*)

Sir Ben. And I'm very sorry to hear also some bad stories against him.

(*Going.*)

Crab. O he has done many mean things, that's certain!

Sir Ben. But however, as he is your brother——

(*Going.*)

Crab. We'll tell you all another opportunity.

(*Exeunt.*)

Lady Sneer. Ha! ha! ha! 't is very hard for them to leave a subject they have not quite run down.

Surf. And I believe the abuse was no more acceptable to your ladyship than Maria.

Lady Sneer. I doubt her affections are farther engaged than we imagined; but the family are to be here this evening, so you may as well dine where you are and we shall have an opportunity of observing farther. In the meantime, I'll go and plot mischief and you shall study sentiments

(*Exeunt.*)

SCENE 2. *Sir Peter's House.*

(*Enter Sir Peter.*)

Sir Pet. When an old bachelor takes a young wife, what is he to expect? 'T is now six months since Lady Teazle made me the happiest of men—and I have been the most miserable dog ever since that ever committed wedlock. We tift a little going to church—and came to a quarrel before the bells had done ringing. I was more than once nearly choked with gall during the honeymoon, and had lost all comfort in life before my friends had done wishing me joy. Yet I chose with caution—a girl bred wholly in the country, who never knew luxury beyond one silk gown, nor dissipation above the annual gala of a race-ball. Yet she now plays her part in all the extravagant fopperies of the fashion and the town, with as ready a grace as if she had never seen a bush nor a grass plot out of Grosvenor-Square![9] I am sneered at by my old acquaintance—paragraphed in the newspapers. She dissipates my fortune, and contradicts all my humors. Yet the worst of it is I doubt[10] I love her or I should never bear all this. However, I'll never be weak enough to own it.

(*Enter Rowley.*)

Row. Sir Peter, your servant:—how is't with you, sir?

Sir Pet. Very bad, Master Rowley, very bad. I meet with nothing but crosses and vexations.

Row. What can have happened to trouble you since yesterday?

Sir Pet. A good question to a married man!

Row. Nay, I'm sure your lady, Sir Peter, can't be the cause of your uneasiness.

Sir Pet. Why, has anybody told you she was dead?

Row. Come, come, Sir Peter, you love her, notwithstanding your tempers do not exactly agree.

Sir Pet. But the fault is entirely hers, Master Rowley; I am myself the sweetest tempered man alive, and hate a teasing temper; and so I tell her a hundred times a day.

Row. Indeed!

Sir Pet. Aye, and what is very extraordinary in all our disputes, she is always in the wrong! But Lady Sneerwell and the set she meets at her house encourage the perverseness of her disposition. Then to complete my vexations, Maria, my ward, whom I ought to have the power of a father over, is determined to turn rebel too and absolutely refuses the man whom I have long resolved on for her husband—meaning, I suppose, to bestow herself on his profligate brother.

Row. You know, Sir Peter, I have always taken the liberty to differ with you on the subject of these two young gentlemen; I only wish you may not be deceived in your opinion of the elder. For Charles, my life on't! he will retrieve his errors yet; their worthy father, once my honored master, was at his years nearly as wild a spark.

Sir Pet. You are wrong, Master Rowley. On their father's death you know I acted as a kind of guardian to them both, till their uncle Sir Oliver's Eastern bounty

9 A fashionable district in the West End of London.

10 suspect. fear.

gave them an early independence. Of course no person could have more opportunities of judging of their hearts, and I was never mistaken in my life. Joseph is indeed a model for the young men of the age. He is a man of sentiment, and acts up to the sentiments he professes; but for the other, take my word for 't, if he had any grain of virtue by descent, he has dissipated it with the rest of his inheritance. Ah! my old friend, Sir Oliver, will be deeply mortified when he finds how part of his bounty has been misapplied.

Row. I am sorry to find you so violent against the young man, because this may be the most critical period of his fortune. I came hither with news that will surprise you.

Sir Pet. What! let me hear.

Row. Sir Oliver is arrived and at this moment in town.

Sir Pet. How!—you astonish me. I thought you did not expect him this month!

Row. I did not, but his passage has been remarkably quick.

Sir Pet. Egad, I shall rejoice to see my old friend. 'T is sixteen years since we met. We have had many a day together. But does he still enjoin us not to inform his nephews of his arrival?

Row. Most strictly. He means, before he makes it known, to make some trial of their dispositions, and we have already planned something for the purpose.

Sir Pet. Ah, there needs no art to discover their merits; however, he shall have his way. But pray does he know I am married?

Row. Yes, and will soon wish you joy.

Sir Pet. You may tell him 't is too late. Ah, Oliver will laugh at me—we used to rail at matrimony together, but he has been steady to his text. Well, he must be at my house tho'—I 'll instantly give orders for his reception. But, Master Rowley, don't drop a word that Lady Teazle and I ever disagree.

Row. By no means.

Sir Pet. For I should never be able to stand Noll's jokes; so I 'd have him think that we are a very happy couple.

Row. I understand you; but then you must be very careful not to differ while he 's in the house with you.

Sir Pet. Egad, and so we must—that 's impossible. Ah! Master Rowley, when an old bachelor marries a young wife, he deserves—no, the crime carries the punishment along with it.

(*Exeunt.*)

ACT II.

Scene 1. *At Sir Peter's.*

(*Sir Peter and Lady Teazle.*)

Sir Pet. Lady Teazle, Lady Teazle, I 'll not bear it.

Lady Teaz. Sir Peter, Sir Peter, you may scold or smile, according to your humor, but I ought to have my own way in everything, and what 's more I will too. What! tho' I was educated in the country, I know very well that women of fashion in London are accountable to nobody after they are married.

Sir Pet. Very well! ma'am, very well! so a husband is to have no influence, no authority?

Lady Teaz. Authority! no, to be sure—if you wanted authority over me, you should have adopted me and not married me: I am sure you were old enough.

Sir Pet. Old enough—aye, there it is! Well—well—Lady Teazle, tho' my life may be made unhappy by your temper, I 'll not be ruined by your extravagance.

Lady Teaz. My extravagance! I 'm sure I 'm not more extravagant than a woman of fashion ought to be.

Sir Pet. No, no, madam, you shall throw away no more sums on such unmeaning luxury. 'Slife,[11] to spend as much to furnish your dressing room with flowers in winter as would suffice to turn the Pantheon[12] into a greenhouse, and give a *fête champêtre* at Christmas.

Lady Teaz. Lord! Sir Peter, am I to blame because flowers are dear in cold weather? You should find fault with the climate, and not with me. For my part I 'm sure I wish it was spring all the year round, and that roses grew under one's feet!

Sir Pet. Oons![13] madam, if you had been born to those fopperies, I should n't wonder at your talking thus; but you forget what your situation was when I married you.

Lady Teaz. No, no, I don't; 't was a very disagreeable one or I should never have married you.

11 A disguised oath,—"by God's life!"
12 A large concert-hall in the West End.
13 Another disguised oath.

Sir Pet. Yes, yes, madam, you were then in somewhat a humbler style—the daughter of a plain country squire. Recollect, Lady Teazle, when I saw you first—sitting at your tambour [14] in a pretty figured linen gown—with a bunch of keys at your side, and your apartment hung round with fruits in worsted, of your own working.

Lady Teaz. O horrible! horrible!—don't put me in mind of it!

Sir Pet. Yes, yes, madam, and your daily occupation to inspect the dairy, superintend the poultry, make extracts from the family receipt-book, and comb your aunt Deborah's lap dog.

Lady Teaz. Abominable!

Sir Pet. Yes, madam, and what were your evening amusements? To draw patterns for ruffles, which you had n't the materials to make, play Pope Joan [15] with the curate, to read a sermon to your aunt, or be stuck down to an old spinet to strum your father to sleep after a fox chase.

Lady Teaz. Scandalous, Sir Peter—not a word of it true.

Sir Pet. Yes, madam, these were the recreations I took you from; and now—no one more extravagantly in the fashion—every foppery adopted—a head-dress to o'ertop Lady Pagoda with feathers pendant, horizontal, and perpendicular. You forget, Lady Teazle, when a little wired gauze with a few beads made you a fly cap not much bigger than a blue-bottle, and your hair was combed smooth over a roll.

Lady Teaz. Shocking! horrible roll!!

Sir Pet. But now—you must have your coach—*Vis-à-vis,*[16] and three powdered footmen before your chair,[17] and in the summer a pair of white cobs to draw you to Kensington Gardens [18]—no recollection when you were content to ride double, behind the butler, on a docked coach-horse!

Lady Teaz. Horrid!—I swear I never did.

Sir Pet. This, madam, was your situation; and what have I not done for you? I have made you woman of fashion, of fortune, of rank—in short I have made you my wife.

Lady Teaz. Well, then, and there is but one thing more you can make me to add to the obligation.

Sir Pet. What 's that, pray?

Lady Teaz. Your widow.

Sir Pet. Thank you, madam—but don't flatter yourself, for though your ill-conduct may disturb my peace, it shall never break my heart, I promise you. However I am equally obliged to you for the hint.

Lady Teaz. Then, why will you endeavor to make yourself so disagreeable to me and thwart me in every little elegant expense?

Sir Pet. 'Slife, madam, I pray, had you any of these elegant expenses when you married me?

Lady Teaz. Lud, Sir Peter, would you have me be out of the fashion?

Sir Pet. The fashion indeed!—what had you to do with the fashion before you married me?

Lady Teaz. For my part, I should think you would like to have your wife thought a woman of taste.

Sir Pet. Aye, there again—taste! Zounds, madam, you had no taste when you married me.

Lady Teaz. That 's very true indeed, Sir Peter! after having married you I should never pretend to taste again, I allow.

Sir Pet. So, so, then, madam, if these are your sentiments, pray how came I to be honored with your hand?

Lady Teaz. Shall I tell you the truth?

Sir Pet. If it 's not too great a favor.

Lady Teaz. Why, the fact is, I was tired of all those agreeable recreations which you have so good-naturedly described, and having a spirit to spend and enjoy a fortune, I determined to marry the first rich man that would have me.

Sir Pet. A very honest confession, truly—but pray, madam, was there no one else you might have tried to ensnare but me?

Lady Teaz. O lud—I drew my net at several but you were the only one I could catch.

Sir Pet. This is plain dealing indeed.

Lady Teaz. But now, Sir Peter, if we have finished our daily jangle, I presume I may go to my engagement at Lady Sneerwell's?

Sir Pet. Aye, there 's another precious circumstance—a charming set of acquaintance you have made there!

Lady Teaz. Nay, Sir Peter, they are people of rank and fortune, and remarkably tenacious of reputation.

Sir Pet. Yes, egad, they are tenacious of

14 An embroidery-frame.
15 A game of cards.
16 *I. e.*, a two-seated coach.
17 A sedan-chair.
18 A park at the West End.

reputation with a vengeance, for they don't choose anybody should have a character but themselves! Such a crew! Ah! many a wretch has rid on hurdles[19] who has done less mischief than these utterers of forged tales, coiners of scandal, and clippers of reputation.[20]

Lady Teaz. What! would you restrain the freedom of speech?

Sir Pet. Aye, they have made you just as bad as any one of the society.

Lady Teaz. Why, I believe I do bear a part with a tolerable grace. But I vow I bear no malice against the people I abuse; when I say an ill-natured thing, 't is out of pure good humor, and I take it for granted they deal exactly in the same manner with me. But, Sir Peter, you know you promised to come to Lady Sneerwell's too.

Sir Pet. Well, well, I 'll call in, just to look after my own character.

Lady Teaz. Then, indeed, you must make haste after me, or you 'll be too late; so good bye to ye.

Sir Pet. So—I have gained much by my intended expostulation. Yet with what a charming air she contradicts everything I say—and how pleasingly she shows her contempt of my authority. Well, tho' I can't make her love me, there is certainly a great satisfaction in quarrelling with her; and I think she never appears to such advantage as when she is doing everything in her power to plague me.

(*Exit.*)

Scene 2. *At Lady Sneerwell's.*

(*Lady Sneerwell, Mrs. Candour, Crabtree, Sir Benjamin Backbite, and Surface.*)

Lady Sneer. Nay, positively, we will hear it.

Surf. Yes, yes, the epigram, by all means.

Sir Ben. O plague on 't, uncle, 't is mere nonsense.

Crab. No, no; 'fore gad, very clever for an extempore!

Sir Ben. But, ladies, you should be acquainted with the circumstances. You must know that one day last week as Lady Betty Curricle was taking the dust in [Hyde] Park,[21] in a sort of duodecimo[22] phaeton, she desired me to write some verses on her ponies; upon which I took out my pocketbook, and in one moment produced—the following:—

Sure never were seen two such beautiful ponies;
Other horses are clowns—and these macaronies,[23]
Nay to give 'em this title, I 'm sure is n't wrong,
Their legs are so slim, and their tails are so long.

Crab. There, ladies—done in the smack of a whip and on horseback too.

Surf. A very Phœbus mounted, indeed, Sir Benjamin.

Sir Ben. Oh, dear sir—trifles—trifles.

(*Enter Lady Teazle and Maria.*)

Mrs. Can. I must have a copy.

Lady Sneer. Lady Teazle, I hope we shall see Sir Peter?

Lady Teaz. I believe he 'll wait on your Ladyship presently.

Lady Sneer. Maria, my love, you look grave. Come, you shall sit down to piquet with Mr. Surface.

Mar. I take very little pleasure in cards; however, I 'll do as you please.

Lady Teaz. I am surprised Mr. Surface should sit down with her; I thought he would have embraced this opportunity of speaking to me before Sir Peter came.

(*Aside.*)

Mrs. Can. Now, I 'll die but you are so scandalous I 'll forswear your society.

Lady Teaz. What 's the matter, Mrs. Candour?

Mrs. Can. They 'll not allow our friend Miss Vermillion to be handsome.

Lady Sneer. Oh, surely she is a pretty woman. . . .

Crab. I am very glad you think so, ma'am.

Mrs. Can. She has a charming fresh color.

Crab. Yes, when it is fresh put on.

Lady Teaz. O fie! I 'll swear her color is natural—I have seen it come and go.

Crab. I dare swear you have, ma'am: it goes of a night, and comes again in the morning.

Sir Ben. True, uncle, it not only comes and goes, but what 's more, egad, her maid can fetch and carry it.

Mrs. Can. Ha! ha! ha! how I hate to hear you talk so! But surely, now her sister is or was very handsome.

19 Light sledges on which great criminals used to be drawn to execution.

20 He alludes to the utterers (issuers) and coiners of counterfeit money, and to those who clipped bits off gold coins (a practice now prevented by milling the edge).

21 A variation on "taking the air": Hyde Park is in the West End.

22 *I. e.*, miniature.

23 Fashionables, dandies; cf. *Yankee Doodle* ("And called it macaroni").

Crab. Who? Mrs. Stucco? O lud! she 's six-and-fifty if she 's an hour!

Mrs. Can. Now positively you wrong her; fifty-two, or fifty-three is the utmost—and I don't think she looks more.

Sir Ben. Ah! there 's no judging by her looks, unless one was to see her face.

Lady Sneer. Well—well—if she does take some pains to repair the ravages of time, you must allow she effects it with great ingenuity—and surely that 's better than the careless manner in which the widow Ocre chalks her wrinkles.

Sir Ben. Nay, now, you are severe upon the widow; come, come, it is n't that she paints so ill—but when she has finished her face she joins it on so badly to her neck, that she looks like a mended statue, in which the connoisseur sees at once that the head 's modern though the trunk 's antique.

Crab. Ha! ha! ha! well said, nephew!

Mrs. Can. Ha! ha! ha! Well, you make me laugh but I vow I hate you for it. What do you think of Miss Simper?

Sir Ben. Why, she has very pretty teeth.

Lady Teaz. Yes, and on that account, when she is neither speaking nor laughing (which very seldom happens), she never absolutely shuts her mouth, but leaves it always on a-jar, as it were.

Mrs. Can. How can you be so ill-natured?

Lady Teaz. Nay, I allow even that 's better than the pains Mrs. Prim takes to conceal her losses in front—she draws her mouth till it resembles the aperture of a poor's-box, and all her words appear to slide out edgewise.

Lady Sneer. Very well, Lady Teazle, I see you can be a little severe.

Lady Teaz. In defence of a friend it is but justice, but here comes Sir Peter to spoil our pleasantry.

(*Enter Sir Peter.*)

Sir Pet. Ladies, your obedient—mercy on me, here is the whole set! a character 's dead at every word, I suppose.

Mrs. Can. I am rejoiced you are come, Sir Peter; they have been so censorious and Lady Teazle as bad as any one.

Sir Pet. That must be very distressing to you, Mrs. Candour, I dare swear.

Mrs. Can. O, they will allow good qualities to nobody—not even good nature to our friend, Mrs. Pursy.

Lady Teaz. What, the fat dowager who was at Mrs. Codrille's last night?

Lady Sneer. Nay, her bulk is her misfortune and when she takes such pains to get rid of it, you ought not to reflect on her.

Mrs. Can. 'T is very true, indeed.

Lady Teaz. Yes, I know she almost lives on acids and small whey, laces herself by pulleys, and often in the hottest noon of summer you may see her on a little squat pony, with her hair plaited up behind like a drummer's, and puffing round the Ring [24] on a full trot.

Mrs. Can. I thank you, Lady Teazle, for defending her.

Sir Pet. Yes, a good defence, truly!

Mrs. Can. But for Sir Benjamin, he is as censorious as Miss Sallow.

Crab. Yes, and she is a curious being to pretend to be censorious—an awkward gawky, without any one good point under Heaven!

Lady Sneer. Positively, you shall not be so very severe. Miss Sallow is a relation of mine by marriage, and, as for her person, great allowance is to be made; for, let me tell you, a woman labors under many disadvantages who tries to pass for a girl at six-and-thirty.

Mrs. Can. Though, surely she is handsome still—and for the weakness in her eyes, considering how much she reads by candle-light, it is not to be wondered at.

Lady Sneer. True, and then as to her manner—upon my word, I think it is particularly graceful considering she never had the least education: for you know her mother was a Welsh milliner, and her father a sugar-baker at Bristow.——

Sir Ben. Ah! You are both of you too good-natured!

Sir Pet. Yes, damned good-natured! Her own relation! mercy on me! (*Aside.*)

Mrs. Can. For my part I own I cannot bear to hear a friend ill-spoken of.

Sir Pet. No, to be sure!

Sir Ben. Ah, you are of a moral turn, Mrs. Candour, and can sit for an hour to hear Lady Stucco talk sentiments.

Lady Sneer. Nay, I vow Lady Stucco is very well with the dessert after dinner, for she 's just like the Spanish fruit one cracks for mottoes,—made up of paint and proverb.

Mrs Can. Well, I never will join in ridiculing a friend—and so I constantly tell my cousin Ogle—and you all know what

24 A circular road in Hyde Park.

pretensions she has to be critical in beauty.

Lady Teaz. O, to be sure, she has herself the oddest countenance that ever was seen —'t is a collection of features from all the different countries of the globe.

Sir Ben. So she has indeed—an Irish front——

Crab. Caledonian locks——

Sir Ben. Dutch nose——

Crab. Austrian lips——

Sir Ben. Complexion of a Spaniard——

Crab. And teeth *à la Chinoise*——

Sir Ben. In short, her face resembles a *table d'hôte* at Spa[25]—where no two guests are of a nation.

Crab. Or a congress at the close of a general war, wherein all the members even to her eyes appear to have a different interest, and her nose and chin are the only parties likely to join issue.

Mrs. Can. Ha! ha! ha!

Sir Pet. Mercy on my life! a person they dine with twice a week! (*Aside.*)

Lady Sneer. Go—go—you are a couple of provoking toads.

Mrs. Can. Nay, but I vow you shall not carry the laugh off so—for give me leave to say, that Mrs. Ogle——

Sir Pet. Madam, madam—I beg your pardon—there 's no stopping these good gentlemen's tongues; but when I tell you, Mrs. Candour, that the lady they are abusing is a particular friend of mine, I hope you 'll not take her part.

Lady Sneer. Ha! ha! ha! well said, Sir Peter; but you are a cruel creature—too phlegmatic yourself for a jest and too peevish[26] to allow wit in others.

Sir Pet. Ah, madam, true wit is more nearly [allied] to good nature than your ladyship is aware of.

Lady Sneer. True, Sir Peter—I believe they are so near akin that they can never be united.

Sir Ben. O rather, madam, suppose them man and wife, because one seldom sees them together.

Lady Teaz. But Sir Peter is such an enemy to scandal I believe he would have it put down by Parliament.

Sir Pet. 'Fore heaven! madam, if they were to consider the sporting with reputation of as much importance as poaching on manors, and pass an act for the preservation of fame, there are many would thank them for the bill.

Lady Sneer. O Lud! Sir Peter, would you deprive us of our privileges?

Sir Pet. Aye, madam, and then no person should be permitted to kill characters or run down reputations but qualified old maids and disappointed widows.

Lady Sneer. Go, you monster—

Mrs. Can. But sure you would not be quite so severe on those who only report what they hear?

Sir Pet. Yes, madam, I would have Law Merchant[27] for that too—and in all cases of slander currency, whenever the drawer of the lie was not to be found, the injured party should have a right to come on any of the indorsers.[28]

Crab. Well, for my part, I believe there never was a scandalous tale without some foundation.

Lady Sneer. Come, ladies, shall we sit down to cards in the next room?

(*Enter Servant, whispers Sir Peter.*)

Sir Pet. I 'll be with them directly.—(*Exit Servant.*) I 'll get away unperceived.

Lady Sneer. Sir Peter, you are not leaving us?

Sir Pet. Your ladyship must excuse me—I 'm called away by particular business—but I leave my character behind me. (*Exit.*)

Sir Ben. Well, certainly, Lady Teazle, that lord of yours is a strange being; I could tell you some stories of him would make you laugh heartily if he were n't your husband.

Lady Teaz. O, pray don't mind that—come, do let 's hear 'em. (*Join the rest of the company going into the next room.*)

Surf. Maria, I see you have no satisfaction in this society.

Mar. How is it possible I should? If to raise malicious smiles at the infirmities or misfortunes of those who have never injured us be the province of wit or humor, Heaven grant me a double portion of dullness.

Surf. Yet they appear more ill-natured than they are—they have no malice at heart.

Mar. Then is their conduct still more contemptible; for in my opinion, nothing

25 A watering-place in Belgium.

26 spiteful.

27 Law relating to business.

28 He is quibbling on a financial note or bill, for which the indorser is responsible after the drawer.

could excuse the intemperance of their tongues but a natural and ungovernable bitterness of mind.

Surf. Undoubtedly, madam; and it has always been a sentiment of mine that to propagate a malicious truth wantonly is more despicable than to falsify from revenge; but can you, Maria, feel thus for others and be unkind to me alone—nay, is hope to be denied the tenderest passion?

Mar. Why will you distress me by renewing this subject?

Surf. Ah! Maria! you would not treat me thus and oppose your guardian's, Sir Peter's, wishes—but that I see that my profligate brother is still a favored rival.

Mar. Ungenerously urged; but whatever my sentiments of that unfortunate young man are, be assured I shall not feel more bound to give him up because his distresses have sunk him so low as to deprive him of the regard even of a brother.

Surf. Nay but, Maria, do not leave me with a frown—by all that 's honest, I swear——Gad's life, here 's Lady Teazle—you must not—no, you shall—for though I have the greatest regard for Lady Teazle——

Mar. Lady Teazle!

Surf. Yet were Sir Peter to suspect——

(*Enter Lady Teazle, and comes forward.*)

Lady Teaz. What 's this, pray—do you take her for me?—Child, you are wanted in the next room.—What 's all this, pray—

[*Exit Maria.*]

Surf. O, the most unlucky circumstance in nature. Maria has somehow suspected the tender concern I have for your happiness, and threatened to acquaint Sir Peter with her suspicions, and I was just endeavoring to reason with her when you came.

Lady Teaz. Indeed, but you seemed to adopt—a very tender mode of reasoning. Do you usually argue on your knees?

Surf. O, she 's a child—and I thought a little bombast——but, Lady Teazle, when are you to give me your judgment on my library as you promised?

Lady Teaz. No—no, I begin to think it would be imprudent; and you know I admit you as a lover no farther than fashion requires.

Surf. True—a mere Platonic Cicisbeo,[29] what every London wife is entitled to.

Lady Teaz. Certainly one must not be out of the fashion—however, I have so much of my country prejudices left—that—though Sir Peter's ill humor may vex me ever so, it never shall provoke me to——

Surf. The only revenge in your power—well, I applaud your moderation.

Lady Teaz. Go—you are an insinuating hypocrite—but we shall be missed—let us join the company.

Surf. True, but we had best not return together.

Lady Teaz. Well, don't stay—for Maria shan't come to hear any more of your reasoning, I promise you.

(*Exit.*)

Surf. A curious dilemma, truly, my politics have run me into. I wanted at first only to ingratiate myself with Lady Teazle that she might not be my enemy with Maria; and I have, I don't know how, become her serious lover, so that I stand a chance of committing a crime I never meditated—and probably of losing Maria by the pursuit!—Sincerely I begin to wish I had never made such a point of gaining so very good a character, for it has led me into so many curst rogueries that I doubt I shall be exposed at last.

(*Exit.*)

Scene 3. *At Sir Peter's.*

(*Rowley and Sir Oliver.*)

Sir Oliv. Ha! ha! ha! and so my old friend is married, hey?—a young wife out of the country!—ha! ha! that he should have stood bluff to old bachelor so long and sink into a husband at last!

Row. But you must not rally him on the subject, Sir Oliver—'t is a tender point, I assure you, though he has been married only seven months.

Sir Oliv. Ah, then he has been just half a year on the stool of repentance—poor Peter! But you say he has entirely given up Charles—never sees him, hey?

Row. His prejudice against him is astonishing, and I am sure, greatly increased by a jealousy of him with Lady Teazle, which he has been industriously led into by a scandalous society in the neighborhood who have contributed not a little to Charles's ill name. Whereas the truth is, I believe, if the lady is par-

29 (Italian) **A trifling cavalier to a married woman.**

tial to either of them his brother is the favorite.

Sir Oliv. Aye—I know—there are a set of malicious, prating, prudent gossips both male and female, who murder characters to kill time, and will rob a young fellow of his good name before he has years to know the value of it . . . but I am not to be prejudiced against my nephew by such, I promise you! No, no! if Charles has done nothing false or mean, I shall compound [30] for his extravagance.

Row. Then, my life on 't, you will reclaim him. Ah, sir, it gives me new vigor to find that your heart is not turned against him, and that the son of my good old master has one friend, however, left.

Sir Oliv. What! shall I forget, Master Rowley, when I was at his house myself? —Egad, my brother and I were neither of us very prudent youths, and yet I believe you have not seen many better men than your old master was.

Row. 'T is this reflection gives me assurance that Charles may yet be a credit to his family—but here comes Sir Peter——

Sir Oliv. Egad, so he does. Mercy on me —he 's greatly altered—and seems to have a settled married look—one may read husband in his face at this distance.

(*Enter Sir Peter.*)

Sir Pet. Ha! Sir Oliver, my old friend—welcome to England—a thousand times!

Sir Oliv. Thank you—thank you—Sir Peter; and i' faith I am as glad to find you well, believe me.

Sir Pet. Ah! 't is a long time since we met —sixteen year, I doubt, Sir Oliver—and many a cross accident in the time.

Sir Oliv. Aye, I have had my share—but, what! I find you are married—hey, my old boy—well—well it can't be helped—and so I wish you joy with all my heart.

Sir Pet. Thank you—thanks, Sir Oliver. —Yes, I have entered into the happy state, but we 'll not talk of that now.

Sir Oliv. True, true, Sir Peter, old friends should n't begin on grievances at first meeting. No, no—

Row. Take care, pray, sir——

Sir Oliv. Well—so one of my nephews, I find, is a wild rogue—hey?

Sir Pet. Wild!—oh! my old friend—I grieve for your disappointment there. He 's a lost young man indeed; however his brother will make you amends; Joseph is indeed what a youth should be—everybody in the world speaks well of him.

Sir Oliv. I am sorry to hear it—he has too good a character to be an honest fellow. Everybody speaks well of him! Psha! then he has bowed as low to knaves and fools as to the honest dignity of virtue.

Sir Pet. What! Sir Oliver, do you blame him for not making enemies?

Sir Oliv. Yes—if he has merit enough to deserve them.

Sir Pet. Well—well—you 'll be convinced when you know him; 't is edification to hear him converse—he professes the noblest sentiments.

Sir Oliv. Ah, plague on his sentiments—if he salutes me with a scrap sentence of morality in his mouth, I shall be sick directly—but, however, don't mistake me, Sir Peter, I don't mean to defend Charles's errors; but before I form my judgment of either of them, I intend to make a trial of their hearts—and my friend Rowley and I have planned something for the purpose.

Row. And Sir Peter shall own he has been for once mistaken.

Sir Pet. My life on Joseph's honor——

Sir Oliv. Well, come, give us a bottle of good wine, and we 'll drink the lads' healths and tell you our scheme.

Sir Pet. *Allons,* then.

Sir Oliv. But don't, Sir Peter, be so severe against your old friend's son.

Sir Pet. 'T is his vices and follies have made me his enemy.

Row. Come—come—Sir Peter, consider how early he was left to his own guidance.

Sir Oliv. Odds my life [31]—I am not sorry that he has run out of the course a little; for my part, I hate to see dry prudence clinging to the green juices of youth—'t is like ivy round a sapling and spoils the growth of the tree.

ACT III.

Scene 1. *At Sir Peter's.*

(*Sir Peter, Sir Oliver, and Rowley.*)

Sir Pet. Well, then, we will see the fellows first and have our wine afterwards. But how is this, Master Rowley? I don't see the jet [32] of your scheme.

30 Settle, come to terms. 31 An almost meaningless exclamation; bless me! 32 Gist, main point.

Row. Why, sir, this Mr. Stanley whom I was speaking of is nearly related to them by their mother. He was once a merchant in Dublin, but has been ruined by a series of undeserved misfortunes, and now lately coming over to solicit the assistance of his friends here, has been flung into prison by some of his creditors, where he is now with two helpless boys.

Sir Oliv. Aye, and a worthy fellow, too, I remember him. But what is this to lead to?

Row. You shall hear. He has applied by letter both to Mr. Surface and Charles; from the former he has received nothing but evasive promises of future service, while Charles has done all that his extravagance has left him power to do, and he is at this time endeavoring to raise a sum of money, part of which, in the midst of his own distresses, I know he intends for the service of poor Stanley.

Sir Oliv. Ah! he is my brother's son.

Sir Pet. Well, but how is Sir Oliver personally to——

Row. Why, sir, I will inform Charles and his brother that Stanley has obtained permission to apply in person to his friends, and as they have neither of them ever seen him, let Sir Oliver assume his character, and he will have a fair opportunity of judging at least of the benevolence of their dispositions.

Sir Pet. Pshaw! this will prove nothing. I make no doubt Charles is coxcomb and thoughtless enough to give money to poor relations if he had it.

Sir Oliv. Then he shall never want it. I have brought a few rupees home with me, Sir Peter, and I only want to be sure of bestowing them rightly.

Row. Then, sir, believe me you will find in the youngest brother one who in the midst of folly and dissipation has still, as our immortal bard expresses it,—

"a tear for pity and a hand open as the day for melting charity." [33]

Sir Pet. Pish! What signifies his having an open hand or purse either when he has nothing left to give! But if you talk of humane sentiments, Joseph is the man. Well, well, make the trial, if you please. But where is the fellow whom you brought for Sir Oliver to examine, relative to Charles's affairs?

Row. Below, waiting his commands, and no one can give him better intelligence. This, Sir Oliver, is a friendly Jew, who to do him justice, has done everything in his power to bring your nephew to a proper sense of his extravagance.

Sir Pet. Pray, let us have him in.

Row. Desire Mr. Moses to walk upstairs. (*Calls to Servant.*)

Sir Pet. But, pray, why should you suppose he will speak the truth?

Row. Oh, I have convinced him that he has no chance of recovering certain sums advanced to Charles but through the bounty of Sir Oliver, who he knows is arrived; so that you may depend on his fidelity to his interest. I have also another evidence in my power, one Snake, whom I shall shortly produce to remove some of *your* prejudices, Sir Peter, relative to Charles and Lady Teazle.

Sir Pet. I have heard too much on that subject.

Row. Here comes the honest Israelite.

(*Enter Moses.*)

—This is Sir Oliver.

Sir Oliv. Sir, I understand you have lately had great dealings with my nephew Charles.

Mos. Yes, Sir Oliver, I have done all I could for him, but he was ruined before he came to me for assistance.

Sir Oliv. That was unlucky truly, for you have had no opportunity of showing your talents.

Mos. None at all—I had n't the pleasure of knowing his distresses till he was some thousands worse than nothing, till it was impossible to add to them.

Sir Oliv. Unfortunate indeed! but I suppose you have done all in your power for him, honest Moses?

Mos. Yes, he knows that. This very evening I was to have brought him a gentleman from the city who does not know him and will I believe advance some money.

Sir Pet. What! one Charles has never had money from before?

Mos. Yes, Mr. Premium, of Crutched Friars.[34]

Sir Pet. Egad, Sir Oliver, a thought strikes me!—Charles you say does n't know Mr. Premium?

Mos. Not at all.

Sir Pet. Now then, Sir Oliver, you may

33 Quoted (not quite accurately) from Shakespeare's II. *Henry IV.*, IV. iv.
34 A street in the financial district of London.

have a better opportunity of satisfying yourself than by an old romancing tale of a poor relation; go with my friend Moses and represent Mr. Premium, and then I 'll answer for 't you 'll see your nephew in all his glory.

Sir Oliv. Egad, I like this idea better than the other, and I may visit Joseph afterwards as old Stanley.

Sir Pet. True, so you may.

Row. Well, this is taking Charles rather at a disadvantage, to be sure! However, Moses, you understand Sir Peter and will be faithful.

Mos. You may depend upon me—and this is near the time I was to have gone.

Sir Oliv. I 'll accompany you as soon as you please, Moses. But hold—I have forgot one thing—how the plague shall I be able to pass for a Jew?

Mos. There 's no need; the principal[35] is Christian.

Sir Oliv. Is he? I 'm very sorry to hear it—but then again, an't I rather too smartly dressed to look like a money-lender?

Sir Pet. Not at all; 't would not be out of character, if you went in your own carriage, would it, Moses?

Mos. Not in the least.

Sir Oliv. Well—but—how must I talk? there 's certainly some cant of usury and mode of treating that I ought to know.

Sir. Pet. Oh, there 's not much to learn—the great point as I take it is to be exorbitant enough in your demands, hey, Moses?

Mos. Yes that 's very great point.

Sir Oliv. I 'll answer for 't I 'll not be wanting in that—I 'll ask him eight or ten per cent. on the loan—at least.

Mos. You 'll be found out directly; if you ask him no more than that, you 'll be discovered immediately.

Sir Oliv. Hey! what the plague!—how much then?

Mos. That depends upon the circumstances; if he appears not very anxious for the supply, you should require only forty or fifty per cent.—but if you find him in great distress, and want the monies very bad, you may ask double.

Sir Pet. A good, honest trade you 're learning, Sir Oliver—

Sir Oliv. Truly, I think so—and not unprofitable.

Mos. Then, you know, you have n't the monies yourself, but are forced to borrow them for him of a friend.

Sir Oliver. O, I borrow it of a friend, do I?

Mos. And your friend is an unconscioned dog—but you can't help it.

Sir Oliv. My friend 's an unconscionable dog, is he?

Mos. Yes—and he himself has n't the monies by him—but is forced to sell stock—at a great loss.

Sir Oliv. He is forced to sell stock, is he—at a great loss, is he? Well, that 's very kind of him.

Sir Pet. I' faith, Sir Oliver—Mr. Premium I mean—you 'll soon be master of the trade. But Moses would have him inquire if the borrower is a minor.

Mos. O yes.

Sir Pet. And in that case his conscience will direct him—

Mos. To have the bond in another name, to be sure.

Sir Oliv. Well—well, I shall be perfect.

Sir Pet. But, hearkee, would n't you have him also run out a little against the annuity bill?[36] That would be in character I should think.

Mos. Very much.

Row. And lament that a young man now must be at years of discretion before he is suffered to ruin himself!

Mos. Aye, great pity!

Sir Pet. And abuse the public for allowing merit to an act whose only object is to snatch misfortune and imprudence from the rapacious relief of usury! and give the minor a chance of inheriting his estate without being undone by coming into possession.

Sir Oliv. So—so—Moses shall give me further instructions as we go together.

Sir Pet. You will not have much time, for your nephew lives hard by.

Sir Oliv. Oh, never fear: my tutor appears so able that tho' Charles lived in the next street, it must be my own fault if I am not a complete rogue before I turn the corner.

(*Exeunt Sir Oliver and Moses.*)

Sir Pet. So, now I think Sir Oliver will be convinced—you shan't follow them, Rowley. You are partial and would have prepared Charles for t' other plot.

Row. No, upon my word, Sir Peter—

Sir Pet. Well, go bring me this Snake,

35 The person whose agent he is.

36 A recent parliamentary bill, partly for the protection of minors against usurers.

and I'll hear what he has to say presently. I see Maria, and want to speak with her. (*Exit Rowley.*) I should be glad to be convinced my suspicions of Lady Teazle and Charles were unjust; I have never yet opened my mind on this subject to my friend Joseph. . . . I am determined. I will do it—he will give me his opinion sincerely.—

(*Enter Maria.*)

So, child, has Mr. Surface returned with you?

Mar. No, sir, he was engaged.

Sir Pet. Well, Maria, do you not reflect, the more you converse with that amiable young man, what return his partiality for you deserves?

Mar. Indeed, Sir Peter, your frequent importunity on this subject distresses me extremely; you compel me to declare that I know no man who has ever paid me a particular attention whom I would not prefer to Mr. Surface.

Sir Pet. Soh! Here's perverseness; no, no, Maria, 't is Charles only whom you would prefer—'t is evident his vices and follies have won your heart.

Mar. This is unkind, sir. You know I have obeyed you in neither seeing nor corresponding with him—I have heard enough to convince me that he is unworthy my regard. Yet I cannot think it culpable, if while my understanding severely condemns his vices, my heart suggests some pity for his distresses.

Sir Pet. Well, well, pity him as much as you please, but give your heart and hand to a worthier object.

Mar. Never to his brother!

Sir Pet. Go—perverse and obstinate! but take care, madam, you have never yet known what the authority of a guardian is—don't compel me to inform you of it.

Mar. I can only say, you shall not have just reason. 'T is true, by my father's will I am for a short period bound to regard you as his substitute, but I must cease to think you so when you would compel me to be miserable.

(*Exit.*)

Sir Pet. Was ever man so crossed as I am, everything conspiring to fret me? I had not been involved in matrimony a fortnight, before her father, a hale and hearty man, died on purpose, I believe, for the pleasure of plaguing me with the care of his daughter. . . . But here comes my helpmate! She appears in great good humor; how happy I should be if I could teaze her into loving me tho' but a little!

(*Enter Lady Teazle.*)

Lady Teaz. Lud! Sir Peter, I hope you have n't been quarrelling with Maria? It is n't using me well to be ill-humored when I am not by!

Sir Pet. Ah! Lady Teazle, you might have the power to make me good-humored at all times.

Lady Teaz. I am sure, I wish I had—for I want you to be in a charming sweet temper at this moment—do be good-humored now—and let me have two hundred pounds, will you?

Sir Pet. Two hundred pounds! what, an't I to be in a good humor without paying for it? But speak to me thus—and i' faith there's nothing I could refuse you. You shall have it—but seal me a bond for the repayment.

Lady Teaz. O no—there—my note of hand will do as well.

Sir Pet. And you shall no longer reproach me with not giving you an independent settlement; I shall shortly surprise you, and you'll not call me ungenerous. But shall we always live thus—hey?

Lady Teaz. If you please; I'm sure I don't care how soon we leave off quarrelling provided you'll own you were tired first.

Sir Pet. Well—then let our future contest be who shall be most obliging.

Lady Teaz. I assure you, Sir Peter, good nature becomes you—you look now as you did before we were married—when you used to walk with me under the elms, and tell me stories of what a gallant you were in your youth—and chuck me under the chin, you would—and ask me if I thought I could love an old fellow who would deny me nothing—did n't you?

Sir Pet. Yes—yes—and you were as kind and attentive——

Lady Teaz. Aye, so I was—and would always take your part, when my acquaintance used to abuse you and turn you into ridicule.

Sir Pet. Indeed!

Lady Teaz. Aye—and when my cousin Sophy has called you a stiff, peevish, old bachelor and laughed at me for thinking of marrying one who might be my father—I have always defended you—and said I did n't think you so ugly by any means, and that you'd make a very good sort of a husband.

Sir Pet. And you prophesied right, and we shall certainly now be the happiest couple——

Lady Teaz. And never differ again.

Sir Pet. No, never—tho' at the same time indeed, my dear Lady Teazle, you must watch your temper very narrowly, for in all our little quarrels, my dear, if you recollect, my love, you always began first.

Lady Teaz. I beg your pardon—my dear Sir Peter—indeed—you always gave the provocation.

Sir Pet. Now—see, my love, take care—contradicting is n't the way to keep friends.

Lady Teaz. Then don't you begin it, my love!

Sir Pet. There now—you are going on: you don't perceive, my life, that you are just doing the very thing, my love, which you know always makes me angry.

Lady Teaz. Nay—you know if you will be angry without any reason—my dear—

Sir Pet. There now you want to quarrel again.

Lady Teaz. No, I am sure I don't, but if you will be so peevish——

Sir Pet. There, now who begins first?

Lady Teaz. Why, you, to be sure—I said nothing—but there's no bearing your temper.

Sir Pet. No, no, my dear—the fault's in your own temper.

Lady Teaz. Aye, you are just what my cousin Sophy said you would be—

Sir Pet. Your cousin Sophy—is a forward impertinent gipsey—

Lady Teaz. Go, you great bear—how dare you abuse my relations?

Sir Pet. Now may all the plagues of marriage be doubled on me, if ever I try to be friends with you any more!

Lady Teaz. So much the better.

Sir Pet. No, no, madam, 't is evident you never cared a pin for me; I was a madman to marry you.

Lady Teaz. And I am sure I was a fool to marry you—an old dangling bachelor, who was single at fifty, only because he never could meet with any one who would have him.

Sir Pet. Aye, aye, madam, but you were pleased enough to listen to me; you never had such an offer before—

Lady Teaz. No—did n't I refuse Sir Jeremy Terrier, who everybody said would have been a better match—for his estate is just as good as yours—and he has broke his neck since we have been married!

Sir Pet. I have done with you, madam! You are an unfeeling, ungrateful—but there's an end of everything—I believe you capable of anything that's bad; yes, madam—I now believe the reports relative to you and Charles,—madam—yes—madam—you and Charles are—not without grounds——

Lady Teaz. Take care, Sir Peter—you had better not insinuate any such thing! I'll not be suspected without cause, I promise you——

Sir Pet. Very—well—madam—very well! a separate maintenance, as soon as you please. Yes, madam, or a divorce—I'll make an example of myself for the benefit of all old bachelors. Let us separate, madam.

Lady Teaz. Agreed, agreed—and now—my dear Sir Peter, we are of a mind again, we may be the happiest couple—and never differ again, you know—ha! ha!—Well, you are going to be in a passion I see, and I shall only interrupt you—so, bye! bye! hey—young Jockey tried and countered.[37]

(*Exit.*)

Sir Pet. Plagues and tortures! She pretends to keep her temper; can't I make her angry neither! O! I am the miserable fellow! But I'll not bear her presuming to keep her temper—No, she may break my heart—but she shan't keep her temper.

(*Exit.*)

Scene 2. *At Charles's House.*

(*Enter Trip, Moses, and Sir Oliver.*)

Trip. Here, Master Moses—if you'll stay a moment—I'll try whether Mr.—what's the gentleman's name?

Sir Oliv. Mr.——Moses, what *is* my name——

Mos. Mr. Premium.

Trip. Premium—very well.

(*Exit Trip, taking snuff.*)

Sir Oliv. To judge by the servants—one would n't believe the master was ruined. But what—sure this was my brother's house—

Mos. Yes, sir, Mr. Charles bought it of Mr. Joseph with the furniture, pictures,

37 Apparently a cant phrase implying a taunt for failure.

etc.—just as the old gentleman left it. Sir Peter thought it a great piece of extravagance in him.

Sir Oliv. In my mind the other's economy in selling it to him was more reprehensible by half.——

(*Enter Trip.*)

Trip. My master, gentlemen, says you must wait, he has company, and can't speak with you yet.

Sir Oliv. If he knew who it was wanted to see him, perhaps he would n't have sent such a message.

Trip. Yes, yes, sir, he knows you are here—I did n't forget little Premium—no—no.

Sir Oliv. Very well—and pray, sir, what may be your name?

Trip. Trip, sir—my name is Trip, at your service.

Sir Oliv. Well, then, Mr. Trip—I presume your master is seldom without company——

Trip. Very seldom, sir—the world says ill-natured things of him but 't is all malice—no man was ever better beloved; sir, he seldom sits down to dinner without a dozen particular friends.

Sir Oliv. He 's very happy indeed—you have a pleasant sort of place here, I guess?

Trip. Why, yes, here are three or four of us pass our time agreeably enough; but then our wages are sometimes a little in arrear—and not very great either—but fifty pounds a year and find our own bags [38] and bouquets——

Sir Oliv. Bags and bouquets!—Halters and bastinadoes!

(*Aside.*)

Trip. But *à propos,* Moses—have you been able to get me that little bill discounted?

Sir Olive. Wants to raise money too!—mercy on me! has his distresses,[39] I warrant, like a lord—and affects creditors and duns!

(*Aside.*)

Mos. 'T was not to be done, indeed——

Trip. Good lack—you surprise me—my friend Brush has indorsed it and I thought when he put his name at the back of a bill, 't was as good as cash.

Mos. No, 't would n't do.

Trip. A small sum—but twenty pound—harkee, Moses, do you think you could get it me by way of annuity?

Sir Oliv. An annuity! ha! ha! a footman raise money by annuity! Well done, Luxury, egad!

(*Aside.*)

Mos. Who would you get to join with you?

Trip. You know my Lord Applice—you have seen him however——

Mos. Yes——

Trip. You must have observed what an appearance he makes—nobody dresses better, nobody throws off faster—very well, this gentleman will stand my security.

Mos. Well—but you must insure your place.

Trip. O with all my heart—I 'll insure my place, and my life too, if you please.

Sir Oliv. It 's more than I would your neck——

Mos. But is there nothing you could deposit?

Trip. Why nothing capital of my master's wardrobe has dropped lately—but I could give you a mortgage on some of his winter clothes with equity of redemption before November or—you shall have the reversion of the French velvet, or a post obit [40] on the blue and silver—these I should think, Moses, with a few pair of point ruffles as a collateral security—hey, my little fellow?

Mos. Well, well—we 'll talk presently—we detain the gentlemen.

Sir Oliv. O, pray, don't let me interrupt Mr. Trip's negotiation.

Trip. Harkee—I heard the bell—I believe, gentlemen, I can now introduce you—don't forget the annuity, little Moses.

Sir Oliv. If the man be a shadow of his master, this is the Temple of Dissipation indeed!

(*Exeunt.*)

SCENE 3. *Charles, Careless, Etc., Etc.*

(*At Table with Wine.*)

Chas. 'Fore Heaven, 't is true!—there is the great degeneracy of the age—many of our acquaintance have taste, spirit, and politeness—but plague on 't, they won't drink.

Care. It is so indeed, Charles; they give in to all the substantial luxuries of the

38 *I. e.,* provide the nets worn to hold the back-hair of wigs.

39 Legal seizures of goods not paid for. The word is sometimes punned on in this play.

40 A bond payable after the death of a specified person.

table—and abstain from nothing but wine and wit. Oh, certainly society suffers by it intolerably, for now instead of the social spirit of raillery that used to mantle over a glass of bright Burgundy their conversation is become just like the Spa water they drink which has all the pertness and flatulence of champagne without its spirit or flavor.

1st Gent. But what are they to do who love play better than wine?

Care. True—there 's Harry diets himself for gaming, and is now under a hazard regimen.

Chas. Then he 'll have the worst of it. What, you would n't train a horse for the course by keeping him from corn. For my part, egad, I am never so successful as when I 'm a little—merry;—let me throw on a bottle of champagne and I never lose—at least I never feel my losses, which is exactly the same thing.

2nd Gent. Aye, that may be—but it is as impossible to follow wine and play as to unite love and politics.

Chas. Pshaw! you may do both; Cæsar made love and laws in a breath—and was liked by the Senate as well as the ladies. But no man can pretend to be a believer in love, who is an abjurer of wine—'t is the test by which a lover knows his own heart. Fill a dozen bumpers to a dozen beauties, and she that floats atop is the maid that has bewitched you.

Care. Now then, Charles—be honest and give us yours.

Chas. Why, I have withheld her only in compassion to you—if I toast her you should give a round of her peers, which is impossible! on earth!

Care. O, then we 'll find some canonized vestals or heathen goddesses that will do, I warrant——

Chas. Here, then—bumpers—you rogues —bumpers! Maria—Maria—

1st Gent. Maria who?

Chas. Oh, damn the surname; 't is too formal to be registered in Love's calendar—but now, Careless, beware—beware —we must have Beauty's superlative.

1st Gent. Nay, never study, Careless—we 'll stand to the toast—tho' your mistress should want an eye—and you know you have a song will excuse you.

Care. Egad, so I have—and I 'll give him the song instead of the lady.

(*Song.—And Chorus—*)

Here 's to the maiden of bashful fifteen;
Here 's to the widow of fifty;
Here 's to the flaunting, extravagant quean,
And here 's to the housewife that 's thrifty.

(*Chorus.*)
Let the toast pass,—
Drink to the lass,
I 'll warrant she 'll prove an excuse for a glass.

Here 's to the charmer whose dimples we prize;
Now to the maid who has none, sir;
Here 's to the girl with a pair of blue eyes,
And here 's to the nymph with but one, sir.

(*Chorus.*)
Let the toast pass, &c.

Here 's to the maid with a bosom of snow:
Now to her that 's as brown as a berry:
Here 's to the wife with a face full of woe,
And now to the damsel that 's merry.

(*Chorus.*)
Let the toast pass, &c.

For let 'em be clumsy, or let 'em be slim,
Young or ancient, I care not a feather;
So fill a pint bumper quite up to the brim,
So fill up your glasses, nay, fill to the brim,
And let us e'en toast them together.

(*Chorus.*)
Let the toast pass, &c.

(*Enter Trip, whispers Charles.*)

2d Gent. Bravo, Careless. There 's toast and sentiment too.

1st Gent. I' faith, there 's infinite charity in that song.

Chas. Gentlemen, you must excuse me a little. Careless, take the chair, will you?

Care. Nay, prithee, Charles—what now—this is one of your peerless beauties, I suppose, has dropped in by chance?

Chas. No, faith, to tell you the truth, 't is a Jew and a broker who are come by appointment.

Care. O damn it, let 's have the Jew in.

1st Gent. Aye and the broker, too, by all means——

2d Gent. Yes, yes, the Jew and the broker.

Chas.—Egad, with all my heart. Trip, bid the gentlemen walk in—tho' there 's one of them a stranger I can tell you——

Trip. What, sir, would you chose Mr. Premium to come up with——

1st Gent. Yes, yes, Mr. Premium, certainly.

Care. To be sure, Mr. Premium, by all means, Charles; let us give them some generous Burgundy, and perhaps they 'll grow conscientious——

Chas. O, hang 'em, no; wine does but draw forth a man's natural qualities; and to make them drink would only be to whet their knavery.

(*Enter Trip, Sir Oliver, and Moses.*)

Chas. So—honest Moses, walk in, walk in, pray, Mr. Premium—that 's the gentleman's name, is n't it, Moses?

Mos. Yes, sir.

Chas. Set chairs, Tri[p].—Sit down, Mr. Premium. Glasses, Tri[p].—Sit down, Moses. Come, Mr. Premium, I 'll give you a sentiment. Here 's success to usury! Moses, fill the gentleman a bumper.

Mos. Success to usury!

Care. Right, Moses, usury is prudence and industry, and deserves to succeed.

Sir Oliv. Then, here is—all the success it deserves!

(*Drinks.*)

Chas. Mr. Premium, you and I are but strangers yet—but I hope we shall be better acquainted by and bye——

Sir Oliv. Yes, sir, hope we shall—more intimately perhaps than you 'll wish.

(*Aside.*)

Care. No, no, that won't do! Mr. Premium, you have demurred at the toast, and must drink it in a pint bumper.

1st Gent. A pint bumper, at least.

Mos. Oh, pray, sir, consider—Mr. Premium 's a gentleman.

Care. And therefore loves good wine.

2d Gent. Give Moses a quart glass—this is mutiny, and a high contempt for the chair.

Care. Here, now for 't! I 'll see justice done, to the last drop of my bottle.

Sir Oliv. Nay, pray, gentlemen, I did not expect this usage.

Chas. No, hang it, you shan't; Mr. Premium 's a stranger.

Sir Oliv. Odd! I wish I was well out of their company.

(*Aside.*)

Care. Plague on 'em then! if they won't drink, we 'll not sit down with them. Come, Harry, the dice are in the next room.—Charles, you 'll join us when you have finished your business with the gentlemen?

Chas. I will! I will!—(*Exeunt Sir Harry Bumper and Gentlemen; Careless following.*) Careless.

Care. (*Returning.*) Well!

Chas. Perhaps I may want you.

Care. Oh, you know I am always ready: word, note, or bond, 't is all the same to me.

(*Exit.*)

Mos. Sir, this is Mr. Premium, a gentleman of the strictest honor and secrecy; and always performs what he undertakes. Mr. Premium, this is——

Chas. Psha! have done. Sir, my friend Moses is a very honest fellow, but a little slow at expression: he 'll be an hour giving us our titles. Mr. Premium, the plain state of the matter is this: I am an extravagant young fellow who wants to borrow money; you I take to be a prudent old fellow, who have got money to lend. I am blockhead enough to give fifty per cent. sooner than not have it! and you, I presume, are rogue enough to take a hundred if you can get it. Now, sir, you see we are acquainted at once, and may proceed to business without further ceremony.

Sir Oliv. Exceeding frank, upon my word. I see, sir, you are not a man of many compliments.

Chas. Oh, no, sir! plain dealing in business I always think best.

Sir Oliv. Sir, I like you the better for it. However, you are mistaken in one thing; I have no money to lend, but I believe I could procure some of a friend; but then he 's an unconscionable dog. Is n't he, Moses? And must sell stock to accommodate you. Must n't he, Moses!

Mos. Yes, indeed! You know I always speak the truth, and scorn to tell a lie!

Chas. Right. People that speak truth generally do. But these are trifles, Mr. Premium. What! I know money is n't to be bought without paying for 't!

Sir Oliv. Well, but what security could you give? You have no land, I suppose?

Chas. Not a mole-hill, nor a twig, but

what 's in the bough-pots out of the window!

Sir Oliv. Nor any stock, I presume?

Chas. Nothing but live stock—and that 's only a few pointers and ponies. But pray, Mr. Premium, are you acquainted at all with any of my connections?

Sir Oliv. Why, to say the truth, I am.

Chas. Then you must know that I have a devilish rich uncle in the East Indies, Sir Oliver Surface, from whom I have the greatest expectations?

Sir Oliv. That you have a wealthy uncle, I have heard; but how your expectations will turn out is more, I believe, than you can tell.

Chas. Oh, no! there can be no doubt. They tell me I 'm a prodigious favorite, and that he talks of leaving me everything.

Sir Oliv. Indeed! this is the first I 've heard of it.

Chas. Yes, yes, 't is just so. Moses knows 't is true; don't you, Moses?

Mos. Oh, yes! I 'll swear to 't.

Sir Oliv. Egad, they 'll persuade me presently I 'm at Bengal. (*Aside.*)

Chas. Now I propose, Mr. Premium, if it 's agreeable to you, a post-obit on Sir Oliver's life: though at the same time the old fellow has been so liberal to me, that I give you my word, I should be very sorry to hear that anything had happened to him.

Sir Oliv. Not more than I should, I assure you. But the bond you mention happens to be just the worst security you could offer me—for I might live to a hundred and never see the principal.

Chas. Oh, yes, you would! the moment Sir Oliver dies, you know, you would come on me for the money.

Sir Oliv. Then I believe I should be the most unwelcome dun you ever had in your life.

Chas. What! I suppose you 're afraid that Sir Oliver is too good a life?

Sir Oliv. No, indeed I am not; though I have heard he is as hale and healthy as any man of his years in Christendom.

Chas. There again, now, you are misinformed. No, no, the climate has hurt him considerably, poor uncle Oliver. Yes, yes, he breaks apace, I 'm told—and is so much altered lately that his nearest relations would not know him.

Sir Oliv. No! Ha! ha! ha! so much altered lately that his nearest relations would not know him! Ha! ha! ha! egad—ha! ha! ha!

Chas. Ha! ha!—you 're glad to hear that, little Premium?

Sir Oliv. No, no, I 'm not.

Chas. Yes, yes, you are—ha! ha! ha!—you know that mends your chance.

Sir Oliv. But I 'm told Sir Oliver is coming over; nay, some say he is actually arrived.

Chas. Psha! sure I must know better than you whether he 's come or not. No, no, rely on 't he 's at this moment at Calcutta. Is n't he, Moses?

Mos. Oh, yes, certainly.

Sir Oliv. Very true, as you say, you must know better than I, though I have it from pretty good authority. Have n't I, Moses?

Mos. Yes, most undoubted!

Sir Oliv. But, sir, as I understand you want a few hundreds immediately, is there nothing you could dispose of?

Chas. How do you mean?

Sir Oliv. For instance, now, I have heard that your father left behind him a great quantity of massy old plate.

Chas. O Lud! that 's gone long ago. Moses can tell you how better than I can.

Sir Oliv. (*Aside.*) Good lack! all the family race-cups and corporation-bowls![41]—(*Aloud.*) Then it was also supposed that his library was one of the most valuable and compact.

Chas. Yes, yes, so it was—vastly too much so for a private gentleman. For my part, I was always of a communicative disposition, so I thought it a shame to keep so much knowledge to myself.

Sir Oliv. (*Aside.*) Mercy upon me! learning that had run in the family like an heirloom!—(*Aloud.*) Pray, what has become of the books?

Chas. You must inquire of the auctioneer, Master Premium, for I don't believe even Moses can direct you.

Mos. I know nothing of books.

Sir Oliv. So, so, nothing of the family property left, I suppose?

Chas. Not much, indeed; unless you have a mind to the family pictures. I have got a room full of ancestors above: and if you have a taste for old paintings, egad, you shall have 'em a bargain!

Sir Oliv. Hey! what the devil! sure, you

41 Cups or bowls received as prizes or presented by a city.

would n't sell your forefathers, would you?

Chas. Every man of them, to the best bidder.

Sir Oliv. What! your great-uncles and aunts?

Chas. Ay, and my great-grandfathers and grandmothers, too.

Sir Oliv. (*Aside.*) Now I give him up! —(*Aloud.*) What the plague, have you no bowels for your own kindred? Odd's life! do you take me for Shylock in the play, that you would raise money of me on your own flesh and blood?

Chas. Nay, my little broker, don't be angry: what need you care, if you have your money's worth?

Sir Oliv. Well, I'll be the purchaser: I think I can dispose of the family canvas. —(*Aside.*) Oh, I'll never forgive him this! never!

(*Re-enter Careless.*)

Care. Come, Charles, what keeps you?

Chas. I can't come yet. I' faith, we are going to have a sale above stairs; here 's little Premium will buy all my ancestors!

Care. Oh, burn your ancestors!

Chas. No, he may do that afterwards, if he pleases. Stay, Careless, we want you: egad, you shall be auctioneer—so come along with us.

Care. O, have with you, if that 's the case. I can handle a hammer as well as a dice box! Going! going!

Sir Oliv. Oh, the profligates! (*Aside.*)

Chas. Come, Moses, you shall be appraiser, if we want one. Gad's life, little Premium, you don't seem to like the business?

Sir Oliv. Oh, yes, I do vastly! Ha! ha! ha! yes, yes, I think it a rare joke to sell one's family by auction—ha! ha!—(*Aside.*) Oh, the prodigal!

Chas. To be sure! when a man wants money, where the plague should he get asistance if he can't make free with his own relations?

(*Exeunt.*)

Sir Oliv. I'll never forgive him; never! never!

ACT IV.

SCENE 1. *A Picture Room in Charles Surface's House.*

(*Enter Charles, Sir Oliver, Moses, and Careless.*)

Chas. Walk in, gentlemen, pray walk in; —here they are, the family of the Surfaces, up to the Conquest.

Sir Oliv. And, in my opinion, a goodly collection.

Chas. Ay, ay, these are done in the true spirit of portrait-painting; no *volontière grace*[42] or expression. Not like the works of your modern Raphaels, who give you the strongest resemblance, yet contrive to make your portrait independent of you; so that you may sink the original and not hurt the picture. No, no; the merit of these is the inveterate likeness—all stiff and awkward as the originals, and like nothing in human nature besides.

Sir Oliv. Ah! we shall never see such figures of men again.

Chas. I hope not. Well, you see, Master Premium, what a domestic character I am; here I sit of an evening surrounded by my family. But come, get to your pulpit, Mr. Auctioneer; here 's an old gouty chair of my grandfather's will answer the purpose.

Care. Ay, ay, this will do. But, Charles, I have n't a hammer; and what 's an auctioneer without his hammer?

Chas. Egad, that 's true. What parchment have we here? Oh, our genealogy in full. (*Taking pedigree down.*) Here, Careless, you shall have no common bit of mahogany, here 's the family tree for you, you rogue! This shall be your hammer, and now you may knock down my ancestors with their own pedigree.

Sir Oliv. What an unnatural rogue!—an *ex post facto* parricide! (*Aside.*)

Care. Yes, yes, here 's a list of your generation indeed;—faith, Charles, this is the most convenient thing you could have found for the business, for 't will not only serve as a hammer, but a catalogue into the bargain. Come, begin—A-going, a-going, a-going!

Chas. Bravo, Careless! Well, here 's my great uncle, Sir Richard Ravelin, a marvelous good general in his day, I assure you. He served in all the Duke of Marlborough's wars, and got that cut over his eye at the battle of Malplaquet. What say you, Mr. Premium? look at him—there 's a hero! not cut out of his feathers, as your modern clipped captains are, but enveloped in wig and regimentals,

42 Free artistic grace.

as a general should be. What do you bid?

Sir Oliv. (*Aside to Moses.*) Bid him speak.

Mos. Mr. Premium would have you speak.

Chas. Why, then, he shall have him for ten pounds, and I 'm sure that 's not dear for a staff-officer.

Sir Oliv. (*Aside.*) Heaven deliver me! his famous uncle Richard for ten pounds!—(*Aloud.*) Very well, sir, I take him at that.

Chas. Careless, knock down my uncle Richard.—Here, now, is a maiden sister of his, my great-aunt Deborah, done by Kneller,[43] in his best manner, and esteemed a very formidable likeness. There she is, you see, a shepherdess feeding her flock. You shall have her for five pounds ten—the sheep are worth the money.

Sir Oliv. (*Aside.*) Ah! poor Deborah! a woman who set such a value on herself!—(*Aloud.*) Five pounds ten—she 's mine.

Chas. Knock down my aunt Deborah! Here, now, are two that were a sort of cousins of theirs.—You see, Moses, these pictures were done some time ago, when beaux wore wigs, and the ladies their own hair.

Sir Oliv. Yes, truly, head-dresses appear to have been a little lower in those days.

Chas. Well, take that couple for the same.

Mos. 'T is a good bargain.

Chas. Careless!—This now, is a grandfather of my mother's, a learned judge, well known on the western circuit.—What do you rate him at, Moses?

Mos. Four guineas.

Chas. Four guineas! Gad's life, you don't bid me the price of his wig.—Mr. Premium, you have more respect for the woolsack;[44] do let us knock his lordship down at fifteen.

Sir Oliv. By all means.

Care. Gone!

Chas. And there are two brothers of his, William and Walter Blunt, Esquires, both members of Parliament, and noted speakers; and, what 's very extraordinary, I believe, this is the first time they were ever bought or sold.[45]

Sir Oliv. That is very extraordinary, indeed! I 'll take them at your own price, for the honor of Parliament.

Care. Well said, little Premium! I 'll knock them down at forty.

Chas. Here 's a jolly fellow—I don't know what relation, but he was mayor of Norwich: take him at eight pounds.

Sir Oliv. No, no; six will do for the mayor.

Chas. Come, make it guineas, and I 'll throw you the two aldermen here into the bargain.

Sir Oliv. They 're mine.

Chas. Careless, knock down the mayor and aldermen. But, plague on 't! we shall be all day retailing in this manner; do let us deal wholesale: what say you, little Premium? Give me three hundred pounds for the rest of the family in the lump.

Care. Ay, ay, that will be the best way.

Sir Oliv. Well, well, anything to accommodate you; they are mine. But there is one portrait which you have always passed over.

Care. What, that ill-looking little fellow over the settee?

Sir Oliv. Yes, sir, I mean that; though I don't think him so ill-looking a little fellow, by any means.

Chas. What, that? Oh; that 's my uncle Oliver. 'T was done before he went to India.

Care. Your uncle Oliver! Gad, then you 'll never be friends, Charles. That, now, to me, is as stern a looking rogue as ever I saw; an unforgiving eye, and a damned disinheriting countenance! an inveterate knave, depend on 't. Don't you think so, little Premium?

Sir Oliv. Upon my soul, sir, I do not; I think it is as honest a looking face as any in the room, dead or alive. But I suppose uncle Oliver goes with the rest of the lumber?

Chas. No, hang it! I 'll not part with poor Noll. The old fellow has been very good to me, and, egad, I 'll keep his picture while I 've a room to put it in.

Sir Oliv. (*Aside.*) The rogue 's my nephew after all!—(*Aloud.*) But, sir, I have somehow taken a fancy to that picture.

Chas. I 'm sorry for 't, for you certainly will not have it. Oons, have n't you got enough of them?

Sir Oliv. (*Aside.*) I forgive him everything!—(*Aloud.*) But, sir, when I take a whim in my head, I don't value money.

43 A very popular portrait-painter (1646–1723).

44 *I. e.*, for the legal profession (the head of which, the Lord Chancellor, sits on the woolsack in the House of Lords).

45 *I. e.*, of course, bribed.

I 'll give you as much for that as for all the rest.

Chas. Don't tease me, master broker; I tell you I 'll not part with it, and there 's an end of it.

Sir Oliv. (*Aside.*) How like his father the dog is.—(*Aloud.*) Well, well, I have done.—(*Aside.*) I did not perceive it before, but I think I never saw such a striking resemblance.—(*Aloud.*) Here is a draught for your sum.

Chas. Why, 't is for eight hundred pounds!

Sir Oliv. You will not let Sir Oliver go?

Chas. Zounds! no! I tell you, once more.

Sir Oliv. Then never mind the difference, we 'll balance that another time. But give me your hand on the bargain; you are an honest fellow, Charles—I beg pardon, sir, for being so free.—Come, Moses.

Chas. Egad, this is a whimsical old fellow!—But hark'ee, Premium, you 'll prepare lodgings for these gentlemen.

Sir Oliv. Yes, yes, I 'll send for them in a day or two.

Chas. But, hold; do now send a genteel conveyance for them, for, I assure you, they were most of them used to ride in their own carriages.

Sir Oliv. I will, I will—for all but Oliver.

Chas. Ay, all but the little nabob.

Sir Oliv. You 're fixed on that?

Chas. Peremptorily.

Sir Oliv. (*Aside.*) A dear extravagant rogue!—(*Aloud.*) Good day! Come, Moses.—(*Aside.*) Let me hear now who dares call him profligate!

(*Exit with Moses.*)

Care. Why, this is the oddest genius of the sort I ever met with!

Chas. Egad, he 's the prince of brokers, I think. I wonder how the devil Moses got acquainted with so honest a fellow.—Ha! here 's Rowley.—Do, Careless, say I 'll join the company in a few moments.

Care. I will—but don't let that old blockhead persuade you to squander any of that money on old musty debts, or any such nonsense; for tradesmen, Charles, are the most exorbitant fellows.

Chas. Very true, and paying them is only encouraging them.

Care. Nothing else.

Chas. Ay, ay, never fear.—(*Exit Careless.*) So! this was an odd old fellow, indeed. Let me see, two-thirds of these five hundred and thirty odd pounds are mine by right. Fore Heaven! I find one's ancestors are more valuable relations than I took them for!—Ladies and gentlemen, your most obedient and very grateful servant.

(*Bows ceremoniously to the pictures.*)

(*Enter Rowley.*)

Ha! old Rowley! egad, you are just come in time to take leave of your old acquaintance.

Row. Yes, I heard they were a-going. But I wonder you can have such spirits under so many distresses.

Chas. Why, there 's the point! my distresses [46] are so many, that I can't afford to part with my spirits; but I shall be rich and splenetic,[47] all in good time. However, I suppose you are surprised that I am not more sorrowful at parting with so many near relations; to be sure, 't is very affecting; but you see they never move a muscle, so why should I?

Row. There 's no making you serious a moment.

Chas. Yes, faith, I am so now. Here, my honest Rowley, here, get me this changed directly, and take a hundred pounds of it immediately to old Stanley.

Row. A hundred pounds! Consider only——

Chas. Gad's life, don't talk about it! poor Stanley's wants are pressing, and, if you don't make haste, we shall have some one call that has a better right to the money.

Row. Ah! there 's the point! I never will cease dunning you with the old proverb——

Chas. *Be just before you 're generous.*—Why, so I would if I could; but Justice is an old hobbling beldame, and I can't get her to keep pace with Generosity, for the soul of me.

Row. Yet, Charles, believe me, one hour's reflection——

Chas. Ay, ay, it 's very true; but, hark'ee, Rowley, while I have, by Heaven I 'll give; so, damn your economy! and now for hazard.[48]

(*Exeunt.*)

Scene 2. *The Parlor.*

(*Enter Sir Oliver and Moses.*)

Mos. Well sir, I think, as Sir Peter said, you have seen Mr. Charles in high glory—'t is great pity he 's so extravagant.

46 A pun, explained in an earlier note.

47 irritable.

48 *I. e.*, the dice.

Sir Oliv. True—but he would not sell my picture.

Mos. And loves wine and women so much—

Sir Oliv. But he would n't sell my picture.

Mos. And game so deep—

Sir Oliv. But he would n't sell my picture. O, here 's Rowley!

(*Enter Rowley.*)

Row. So, Sir Oliver. I find you have made a purchase——

Sir Oliv. Yes, yes, our young rake has parted with his ancestors, like old tapestry—sold judges and generals by the foot, and maiden aunts as cheap as broken china.

Row. And here has he commissioned me to re-deliver you part of the purchase-money—I mean, though, in your necessitous character of old Stanley.

Mos. Ah! there is the pity of all! He is so damned charitable.

Row. And I left a hosier and two tailors in the hall, who, I 'm sure, won't be paid, and this hundred would satisfy 'em.

Sir Oliv. Well—well—I 'll pay his debts and his benevolences too—I 'll take care of old Stanley, myself. But now I am no more a broker, and you shall introduce me to the elder brother as Stanley.

Row. Not yet a while; Sir Peter, I know, means to call there about this time.

(*Enter Trip.*)

Trip. O, gentlemen, I beg pardon for not showing you out. This way; Moses, a word.

(*Exit Trip with Moses.*)

Sir Oliv. There 's a fellow for you! Would you believe it, that puppy intercepted the Jew, on our coming, and wanted to raise money before he got to his master!

Row. Indeed!

Sir Oliv. Yes; they are now planning an annuity business. Ah, Master Rowley, in my day servants were content with the follies of their masters when they were worn a little threadbare, but now they have their vices like their birthday clothes, with the gloss on.

(*Exeunt.*)

Scene 3. *A Library.*

(*Surface and Servant.*)

Surf. No letter from Lady Teazle?

Serv. No, sir.

Surf. I am surprised she has n't sent if she is prevented from coming! Sir Peter certainly does not suspect me, yet I wish I may not lose the heiress, through the scrape I have drawn myself in with the wife. However, Charles's imprudence and bad character are great points in my favor.

Serv. Sir, I believe that must be Lady Teazle—

Surf. Hold! see whether it is or not before you go to the door; I have a particular message for you if it should be my brother.

Serv. 'T is her ladyship, sir. She always leaves her chair at the milliner's in the next street.

Surf. Stay, stay, draw that screen before the window—that will do; my opposite neighbor is a maiden lady of so curious a temper!—(*Servant draws the screen and exit.*) I have a difficult hand to play in this affair; Lady Teazle has lately suspected my views on Maria, but she must by no means be let into that secret, at least till I have her more in my power.

(*Enter Lady Teazle.*)

Lady Teaz. What! sentiment in soliloquy; have you been very impatient now? O Lud! don't pretend to look grave—I vow I could n't come before.

Surf. O madam, punctuality is a species of constancy, a very unfashionable quality in a lady.

Lady Teaz. Upon my word you ought to pity me; do you know Sir Peter is grown so ill-tempered to me of late; and so jealous! of Charles, too;—that 's the best of the story, is n't it?

Surf. I am glad my scandalous friends keep that up.

(*Aside.*)

Lady Teaz. I am sure I wish he would let Maria marry him, and then perhaps he would be convinced,—don't you, Mr. Surface?

Surf. Indeed I do not. (*Aside.*) O certainly I do, for then my dear Lady Teazle would also be convinced how wrong her suspicions were of my having any design on the silly girl.

Lady Teaz. Well, well, I 'm inclined to believe you; besides I really never could perceive why she should have so many admirers.

Surf. O for her fortune—nothing else.

Lady Teaz. I believe so, for tho' she is certainly very pretty, yet she has no conversation in the world, and is so grave and reserved that I declare I think she'd have made an excellent wife for Sir Peter.

Surf. So she would.

Lady Teaz. Then—one never hears her speak ill of anybody—which you know is mighty dull.

Surf. Yet she does n't want understanding.

Lady Teaz. No more she does—yet one is always disappointed when one hears her speak. For though her eyes have no kind of meaning in them, she very seldom talks nonsense.

Surf. Nay, nay, surely—she has very fine eyes.

Lady Teaz. Why, so she has—tho' sometimes one fancies there 's a little sort of a squint.

Surf. A squint—O fie, Lady Teazle.

Lady Teaz. Yes, yes, I vow now—come, there is a left-handed Cupid in one eye —that 's the truth on 't.

Surf. Well, his aim is very direct however,—but Lady Sneerwell has quite corrupted you.

Lady Teaz. No, indeed, I have not opinion enough of her to be taught by her, and I know that she has lately raised many scandalous hints of me; which you know one always hears from one common friend or other.

Surf. Why, to say truth, I believe you are not more obliged to her than others of her acquaintance.

Lady Teaz. But is n't it provoking to hear the most ill-natured things said to one, and there 's my friend Lady Sneerwell has circulated I don't know how many scandalous tales of me, and all without any foundation, too; that 's what vexes me.

Surf. Aye, madam, to be sure that is the provoking circumstance—without foundation—yes, yes—there 's the mortification indeed—for when a slanderous story is believed against one, there certainly is no comfort like the consciousness of having deserved it.

Lady Teaz. No, to be sure; then I'd forgive their malice—but to attack me, who am really so innocent and who never say an ill-natured thing of anybody—that is, of any friend—! and then Sir Peter too —to have him so peevish—and so suspicious—when I know the integrity of my own heart—indeed 't is monstrous.

Surf. But, my dear Lady Teazle, 't is your own fault if you suffer it—when a husband entertains a groundless suspicion of his wife and withdraws his confidence from her, the original compact is broke and she owes it to the honor of her sex to endeavor to outwit him.

Lady Teaz. Indeed! So that if he suspects me without cause, it follows that the best way of curing his jealousy is to give him reason for 't.

Surf. Undoubtedly, for your husband should never be deceived in you; and in that case it becomes you to be frail in compliment to his discernment.

Lady Teaz. To be sure what you say is very reasonable, and when the consciousness of my own innocence——

Surf. Ah, my dear—madam, there is the great mistake—'t is this very conscious innocence that is of the greatest prejudice to you. What is it makes you negligent of forms and careless of the world's opinion?—why, the consciousness of your innocence. What makes you thoughtless in your conduct and apt to run into a thousand little imprudences? —why, the consciousness of your innocence. What makes you impatient of Sir Peter's temper, and outrageous at his suspicions?—why, the consciousness of your own innocence.

Lady Teaz. 'T is very true.

Surf. Now, my dear Lady Teazle, if you but once make a trifling *faux pas,* you can't conceive how cautious you would grow, and how ready to humor and agree with your husband.

Lady Teaz. Do you think so?

Surf. O, I 'm sure on 't; and then you 'd find all scandal would cease at once, for in short your character at present is like a person in a plethora, absolutely dying of too much health.

Lady Teaz. So—so—then I perceive your prescription is that I must sin in my own defence, and part with my virtue to preserve my reputation.

Surf. Exactly so, upon my credit, ma'am.

Lady Teaz. Well, certainly this is the oddest doctrine, and the newest receipt for avoiding calumny.

Surf. An infallible one, believe me—prudence like experience must be paid for.

Lady Teaz. Why, if my understanding were once convinced——

Surf. Oh, certainly madam, your understanding *should* be convinced—yes—yes —Heaven forbid I should persuade you to do anything you *thought* wrong—no—

no—I have too much honor to desire it.

Lady Teaz. Don't—you think we may as well leave honor out of the argument? (*Rises.*)

Surf. Ah—the ill effects of your country education I see still remain with you.

Lady Teaz. I doubt they do indeed—and I will fairly own to you, that if I could be persuaded to do wrong it would be by Sir Peter's ill-usage, sooner than your honorable logic, after all.

Surf. Then by this hand, which he is unworthy of——

(*Enter Servant.*)

'Sdeath, you blockhead, what do you want?

Serv. I beg your pardon, sir, but I thought you would n't choose Sir Peter to come up without announcing him?

Surf. Sir Peter—Oons—the devil!

Lady Teaz. Sir Peter! O Lud! I 'm ruined! I 'm ruined!

Serv. Sir, 't was n't I let him in.

Lady Teaz. O, I 'm undone! what will become of me now, Mr. Logic?—Oh! mercy, he 's on the stairs—I 'll get behind here—and if ever I m so imprudent again——

(*Goes behind the screen.*)

Surf. Give me that—book!——

(*Sits down—Servant pretends to adjust his hair.*)

(*Enter Sir Peter.*)

Sir Pet. Aye—ever improving himself!—Mr. Surface—

Surf. Oh! my dear Sir Peter—I beg your pardon—(*Gaping and throws away the book.*) I have been dozing over a stupid book! well—I am much obliged to you for this call. You have n't been here, I believe, since I fitted up this room. Books you know are the only things I am a coxcomb in.

Sir Pet. 'T is very neat indeed; well, well, that 's proper—and you make even your screen a source of knowledge—hung I perceive with maps—

Surf. O yes—I find great use in that screen.

Sir Pet. I dare say you must; certainly, when you want to find out anything in a hurry.

Surf. Aye or to hide anything in a hurry either.

Sir Pet. Well, I have a little private business—if we were alone—

Surf. You need n't stay.

Serv. No, sir.

(*Exit Servant.*)

Surf. Here 's a chair, Sir Peter, I beg——

Sir Pet. Well, now we are alone, there *is* a subject, my dear friend, on which I wish to unburthen my mind to you—a point of the greatest moment to my peace; in short, my good friend—Lady Teazle's conduct of late has made me very unhappy.

Surf. Indeed, I 'm very sorry to hear it.

Sir Pet. Yes, 't is but too plain she has not the least regard for me, but what 's worse, I have pretty good authority to suspect that she must have formed an attachment to another.

Surf. Indeed! you astonish me.

Sir Pet. Yes—and between ourselves—I think I have discovered the person.

Surf. How—you alarm me exceedingly!

Sir Pet. Ah! my dear friend, I knew you would sympathize with me.

Surf. Yes—believe me, Sir Peter—such a discovery would hurt me just as much as it would you—

Sir Pet. I am convinced of it; ah, it is a happiness to have a friend whom one can trust even with one's family secrets. But have you no guess who I mean?

Surf. I have n't the most distant idea; it can't be Sir Benjamin Backbite.

Sir Pet. O, no. What say you to Charles?

Surf. My brother—impossible!—O no, Sir Peter, you must n't credit the scandalous insinuations you hear—no, no;—Charles to be sure has been charged with many things, but I can never think he would meditate so gross an injury.

Sir Pet. Ah! my dear friend, the goodness of your own heart misleads you—you judge of others by yourself.

Surf. Certainly, Sir Peter, the heart that is conscious of its own integrity is ever slowest to credit another's treachery.

Sir Pet. True—but your brother has no sentiment—you never hear him talk so.

Surf. Well, there certainly is no knowing what men are capable of—no—there is no knowing—yet I can't but think Lady Teazle herself has too much principle.

Sir Pet. Aye, but what 's principle against the flattery of a handsome, lively young fellow?

Surf. That 's very true.

Sir Pet. And then you know the difference of our ages makes it very improbable that she should have any great affection for me; and if she were to be frail and I were to make it public—why, the town would only laugh at the foolish old bachelor, who had married a girl.

Surf. That's true; to be sure people would laugh.

Sir Pet. Laugh—aye, and make ballads and paragraphs and the devil knows what of me.

Surf. No, you must never make it public.

Sir Pet. But then again that the nephew of my old friend, Sir Oliver, should be the person to attempt such an injury—hurts me more nearly.

Surf. Undoubtedly; when ingratitude barbs the dart of injury, the wound has double danger in it.

Sir Pet. Aye, I that was in a manner left his guardian—in [whose] house he had been so often entertained—who never in my life denied him my advice—

Surf. O, 't is not to be credited. There may be a man capable of such baseness, to be sure—but for my part till you can give me positive proofs you must excuse me withholding my belief. However, if this should be proved on him, he is no longer a brother of mine, I disclaim kindred with him—for the man who can break thro' the laws of hospitality and attempt the wife of his friend deserves to be branded as the pest of society.

Sir Pet. What a difference there is between you! what noble sentiments!

Surf. But I cannot suspect Lady Teazle's honor.

Sir Pet. I 'm sure I wish to think well of her and to remove all ground of quarrel between us. She has lately reproached me more than once with having made no settlement on her, and, in our last quarrel, she almost hinted that she should not break her heart if I was dead. Now as we seem to differ in our ideas of expense, I have resolved she shall be her own mistress in that respect for the future; and if I were to die, she shall find that I have not been inattentive to her interests while living. Here, my friend, are the draughts of two deeds which I wish to have your opinion on: by one she will enjoy eight hundred a year independent while I live, and by the other the bulk of my fortune after my death.

Surf. This conduct, Sir Peter, is indeed truly generous! I wish it may not corrupt my pupil.

(*Aside.*)

Sir Pet. Yes, I am determined she shall have no cause to complain, tho' I would not have her acquainted with the latter instance of my affection yet awhile.

Surf. Nor I—if I could help it.

Sir Pet. And now, my dear friend, if you please, we will talk over the situation of your hopes with Maria.

Surf. No, no, Sir Peter,—another time if you please—

(*Softly.*)

Sir Pet. I am sensibly chagrined at the little progress you seem to make in her affection.

Surf. I beg you will not mention it. What are my disappointments when your happiness is in debate. (*Softly.*) 'Sdeath, I shall be ruined every way.

Sir Pet. And tho' you are so averse to my acquainting Lady Teazle with *your* passion, I am sure she 's not your enemy in the affair.

Surf. Pray, Sir Peter, now oblige me. I am really too much affected by the subject we have been speaking of to bestow a thought on my own concerns. The man who is entrusted with his friend's distresses can never——

(*Enter Servant.*)

Well, sir?

Serv. Your brother, sir, is speaking to a gentleman in the street, and says he knows you 're within.

Surf. 'Sdeath, blockhead, I 'm *not* within,—I 'm out for the day.

Sir Pet. Stay—hold—a thought has struck me; you shall be at home.

Surf. Well—well—let him up.—(*Exit Serv.*) He 'll interrupt Sir Peter, however.

(*Aside.*)

Sir Pet. Now, my good friend, oblige me, I intreat you; before Charles comes let me conceal myself somewhere; then do you tax him on the point we have been talking on, and his answers may satisfy me at once.

Surf. O, fie, Sir Peter, would you have *me* join in so mean a trick? to trepan my brother too?

Sir Pet. Nay, you tell me you are *sure* he is innocent;—if so, you do him the greatest service in giving him an opportunity to clear himself, and you will set my heart at rest. Come, you shall not refuse me—here behind this screen will be—hey! what the devil—there seems to be one listener here already;—I 'll swear I saw a petticoat.—

Surf. Ha! ha! ha! Well, this is ridiculous enough! I'll tell you, Sir Peter—though I hold a man of intrigue to be a most despicable character, yet you know it does n't follow that a man is to be an absolute Joseph[49] either;—harkee, 't is a little French milliner—a silly rogue that plagues me—and having some character, on your coming she ran behind the screen.

Sir Pet. Ah, a rogue—but 'egad she has overheard all I have been saying of my wife.

Surf. O 't will never go any farther, you may depend on 't.

Sir Pet. No!—then i' faith, let her hear it out.—Here 's a closet will do as well.

Surf. Well, go in there.

Sir Pet. Sly rogue—sly rogue.

Surf. Gad 's my life, what an escape! and a curious situation I 'm in!—to part man and wife in this manner.

Lady Teaz. (*Peeps out.*) Could n't I steal off?

Surf. Keep close, my angel!

Sir Pet. (*Peeping out.*) Joseph, tax him home.

Surf. Back—my dear friend.

Lady Teaz. (*Peeping out.*) Could n't you lock Sir Peter in?—

Surf. Be still—my life!

Sir Pet. (*Peeping.*) You 're sure the little milliner won't blab?

Surf. In! in! my good Sir Peter—'Fore Gad, I wish I had a key to the door.

(*Enter Charles.*)

Chas. Hollo! brother—what has been the matter? your fellow would n't let me up at first—What! have you had a Jew or a wench with you?

Surf. Neither, brother, I assure you.

Chas. But—what has made Sir Peter steal off? I thought he had been with you—

Surf. He *was*, brother, but hearing you were coming he did n't choose to stay.

Chas. What! was the old gentleman afraid I wanted to borrow money of him?

Surf. No, sir, but I am sorry to find, Charles, you have lately given that worthy man grounds for great uneasiness.

Chas. Yes, they tell me I do that to a great many worthy men;—but how so, pray?

Surf. To be plain with you, brother, he thinks you are endeavoring to gain Lady Teazle's affections from him.

Chas. Who, I?—O Lud! not I, upon my word.—Ha! ha! ha! so the old fellow has found out that he has got a young wife, has he? or what 's worse she has discovered that she has an old husband?

Surf. This is no subject to jest on, brother. He who can laugh——

Chas. True, true, as you were going to say—then seriously I never had the least idea of what you charge me with, upon my honor.

Surf. Well, it will give Sir Peter great satisfaction to hear this.

Chas. (*Aloud.*) To be sure, I once thought the lady seemed to have taken a fancy—but upon my soul I never gave her the least encouragement.—Besides you know my attachment to Maria—

Surf. But sure, brother, even if Lady Teazle had betrayed the fondest partiality for you——

Chas. Why—look 'ee, Joseph—I hope I shall never deliberately do a dishonorable action; but if a pretty woman was purposely to throw herself in my way—and that pretty woman married to a man old enough to be her father——

Surf. Well?

Chas. Why I believe I should be obliged to borrow a little of your morality, that 's all. But, brother, do you know now that you surprise me exceeding[ly] by naming me with Lady Teazle—for faith I always understood *you* were her favorite—

Surf. O for shame! Charles. This retort is foolish.

Chas. Nay, I swear I have seen you exchange such significant glances——

Surf. Nay—nay—sir—this is no jest—

Chas. Egad, I 'm serious. Don't you remember one day, when I called here?——

Surf. Nay—prithee—Charles—

Chas. And found you together——

Surf. Zounds, sir, I insist——

Chas. And another time when your servant——

Surf. Brother, brother, a word with you—Gad, I must stop him— (*Aside.*)

Chas. Informed me that——

Surf. Hush!—I beg your pardon, but Sir Peter has overheard all we have been saying; I knew you would clear yourself, or I should n't have consented—

49 *I. e.*, a model of virtue (*Genesis*, xxxix).

Chas. How? Sir Peter?—Where is he?

Surf. Softly, there!

(*Points to the closet.*)

Chas. In the closet! O 'fore Heaven, I 'll have him out!—Sir Peter, come forth!

Surf. No—no——

Chas. I say, Sir Peter—come into court. (*Pulls in Sir Peter.*) What—my old guardian—what! turn inquisitor and take evidence incog.!—

Sir Pet. Give me your hand, Charles; I believe I have suspected you wrongfully; but you must n't be angry with Joseph—'t was my plan—

Chas. Indeed!

Sir Pet. But I acquit you; I promise you I don't think near so ill of you as I did. What I have heard has given me great satisfaction.

Chas. Egad, then 't was lucky you did n't hear any more, was n't it, Joseph?

Sir Pet. Ah! you would have retorted on him.

Chas. Aye—aye—that was a joke.

Sir Pet. Yes, yes, I know his honor too well.

Chas. Yet you might as well have suspected him as me in this matter, for all that, might n't he, Joseph?

Sir Pet. Well, well, I believe you.

Surf. Would they were both out of the room!

(*Enter Servant, whispers Surface.*)

Sir Pet. And in future perhaps we may not be such strangers.

Surf. Gentlemen—I beg pardon—I must wait on you downstairs,—here is a person come on particular business——

Chas. Well, you can see him in another room; Sir Peter and I have n't met a long time and I have something to say to him.

Surf. They must not be left together.—I 'll send this man away and return directly—

(*Surface goes out.*)

Sir Pet. Ah, Charles, if you associated more with your brother, one might indeed hope for your reformation. He is a man of sentiment. Well! there is nothing in the world so noble as a man of sentiment!

Chas. Pshaw! he is too moral by half, and so apprehensive of his good name, as he calls it, that I suppose he would as soon let a priest in his house as a girl.

Sir Pet. No, no, come, come, you wrong him. No, no, Joseph is no rake but he is no such saint in that respect either.—I have a great mind to tell him—we should have such a laugh! (*Aside.*)

Chas. Oh, hang him! He 's a very anchorite—a young hermit.

Sir Pet. Harkee, you must not abuse him, he may chance to hear of it again, I promise you.

Chas. Why, you won't tell him?

Sir Pet. No—but—this way.—Egad, I 'll tell him.—Harkee, have you a mind to have a good laugh against Joseph?

Chas. I should like it of all things.

Sir Pet. Then, i'faith, we will—I 'll be quit with him for discovering me.—He had a girl with him when I called.

(*Whispers.*)

Chas. What! Joseph! you jest.

Sir Pet. Hush!—a little French milliner—and the best of the jest is—she 's in the room now.

Chas. The devil she is!

Sir Pet. Hush! I tell you.

(*Points.*)

Chas. Behind the screen! Odds life, let 's unveil her!

Sir Pet. No—no! he 's coming—you shan't indeed!

Chas. Oh, egad, we 'll have a peep at the little milliner!

Sir Pet. Not for the world—Joseph will never forgive me.

Chas. I 'll stand by you——

Sir Pet. Odds life! Here he 's coming—

(*Surface enters just as Charles throws down the screen.*)

(*Re-enter Joseph Surface.*)

Chas. Lady Teazle! by all that 's wonderful!

Sir Pet. Lady Teazle! by all that 's horrible!

Chas. Sir Peter, this is one of the smartest French milliners I ever saw!—Egad, you seem all to have been diverting yourselves here at hide and seek—and I don't see who is out of the secret!—Shall I beg your ladyship to inform me?—Not a word!—Brother!—will you please to explain this matter? What! is Honesty dumb too?—Sir Peter, though I found you in the dark—perhaps you are not so now—all mute? Well tho' I can make nothing of the affair, I make no doubt but you perfectly understand one another,—so I 'll leave you to yourselves.—(*Going.*) Brother, I 'm sorry to find you have given that worthy man grounds for so much uneasiness!—Sir Peter—

there 's nothing in the world so noble as a man of sentiment!—

(*Stand for some time looking at one another. Exit Charles.*)

Surf. Sir Peter—notwithstanding I confess that appearances are against me, if you will afford me your patience, I make no doubt but I shall explain everything to your satisfaction.

Sir Pet. If you please—sir—

Surf. The fact is, sir—that Lady Teazle knowing my pretensions to your ward Maria—I say, sir, Lady Teazle—being apprehensive of the jealousy of your temper—and knowing my friendship to the family,—she, sir—I say called here —in order that I might explain those pretensions—but on your coming being apprehensive—as I said, of your jealousy—she withdrew—and this, you may depend on 't, is the whole truth of the matter.

Sir Pet. A very clear account, [upon] my word; and I dare swear the lady will vouch for every article of it.

Lady Teaz. For not one word of it, Sir Peter.

Sir Pet. How! don't you think it worth while to agree in the lie?

Lady Teaz. There is not one syllable of truth in what that gentleman has told you.

Sir Pet. I believe you upon my soul, ma'am.

Surf. 'Sdeath, madam, will you betray me!

(*Aside.*)

Lady Teaz. Good Mr. Hypocrite, by your leave I will speak for myself.

Sir Pet. Aye, let her alone, sir—you 'll find she 'll make out a better story than you without prompting.

Lady Teaz. Hear me, Sir Peter. I came hither on no matter relating to your ward and even ignorant of this gentleman's pretensions to her; but I came—seduced by his insidious arguments and pretended passion—at least to listen to his dishonorable love if not to sacrifice your honor to his baseness.

Sir Pet. Now, I believe, the truth is coming, indeed.

Surf. The woman 's mad—

Lady Teaz. No, sir, she has recovered her senses. Your own arts have furnished her with the means. Sir Peter—I do not expect you to credit me—but the tenderness you expressed for me, when I am sure you could not think I was a witness to it, has penetrated so to my heart that had I left the place without the shame of this discovery, my future life should have spoken the sincerity of my gratitude;—as for that smooth-tongued hypocrite, who would have seduced the wife of his too credulous friend while he pretended honorable addresses to his ward, I behold him now in a light so truly despicable that I shall never again respect myself for having listened to him.

(*Exit.*)

Surf. Notwithstanding all this, Sir Peter —Heaven knows—

Sir Pet. That you are a villain!—and so I leave you to your conscience.

Surf. You are too rash, Sir Peter—you *shall* hear me.—The man who shuts out conviction by refusing to——

(*Exeunt, Surface following and speaking.*)

ACT V.

Scene 1. *The Library.*

(*Enter Surface, Servant.*)

Surf. Mr. Stanley! and why should you think I would see him?—you must know he came to ask something!

Serv. Sir, I should n't have let him in but that Mr. Rowley came to the door with him.

Surf. Pshaw!—Blockhead to suppose that I should now be in a temper to receive visits from poor relations!—well, why don't you show the fellow up?

Serv. I will, sir! why, sir, it was not my fault that Sir Peter discovered my lady——

Surf. Go, fool! (*Exit Serv.*) Sure Fortune never play a man of my policy such a trick before—my character with Sir Peter!—my hopes with Maria!—destroyed in a moment! I 'm in a rare humor to listen to other people's distresses! I shan't be able to bestow even a benevolent sentiment on Stanley.—So! here he comes and Rowley with him—I *must* try to recover myself, and put a little charity into my face however.

(*Exit.*)

(*Enter Sir Oliver and Rowley.*)

Sir Oliv. What! does he avoid us? that was he, was it not?

Row. It was, sir, but I doubt you are come a little too abruptly—his nerves are so weak that the sight of a poor relation may be too much for him—I should have gone first to break you to him.

Sir Oliv. A plague of his nerves! yet this is he whom Sir Peter extols as a man of the most benevolent way of thinking!

Row. As to his way of thinking—I can't pretend to decide, for, to do him justice, he appears to have as much speculative benevolence as any private gentleman in the kingdom; though he is seldom so sensual as to indulge himself in the exercise of it.

Sir Oliv. Yet he has a string of charitable sentiments, I suppose, at his fingers' ends!

Row. Or rather at his tongue's end, Sir Oliver; for I believe there is no sentiment he has more faith in than that "charity begins at home."

Sir Oliv. And his I presume is of that domestic sort which never stirs abroad at all.

Row. I doubt you'll find it so—but he's coming—I must n't seem to interrupt you; and you know immediately, as you leave him, I come in to announce your arrival in your real character.

Sir Oliv. True, and afterwards you'll meet me at Sir Peter's—

Row. Without losing a moment.

(*Exit.*)

Sir Oliv. So—I see he has premeditated a denial by the complaisance of his features.

(*Enter Surface.*)

Surf. Sir, I beg you ten thousand pardons for keeping you a moment waiting—Mr. Stanley—I presume—

Sir Oliv. At your service.

Surf. Sir, I beg you will do me the honor to sit down—I entreat you, sir.

Sir Oliv. Dear sir, there's no occasion—too civil by half!

Surf. I have not the pleasure of knowing you, Mr. Stanley, but I am extremely happy to see you look so well; you were nearly related to my mother, I think, Mr. Stanley.

Sir Oliv. I was, sir, so nearly that my present poverty, I fear, may do discredit to her wealthy children, else I should not have presumed to trouble you.

Surf. Dear sir, there needs no apology; he that is in distress, tho' a stranger, has a right to claim kindred with the wealthy. I am sure I wish I was of that class, and had it in my power to offer you even a small relief.

Sir Oliv. If your uncle, Sir Oliver, were here, I should have a friend——

Surf. I wish he was, sir, with all my heart—you should not want an advocate with him, believe me, sir.

Sir Oliv. I should not need one—my distresses would recommend me. But I imagined his bounty had enabled you to become the agent of his charity.

Surf. My dear sir, you are strangely misinformed. Sir Oliver is a worthy man, a worthy man—a very worthy sort of man; but avarice, Mr. Stanley, is the vice of age—I will tell you, my good sir, in confidence:—what he has done for me has been a mere—nothing; tho' people, I know, have thought otherwise, and for my part I never chose to contradict the report.

Sir Oliv. What!—has he never transmitted you bullion—rupees—pagodas?[50]

Surf. O dear sir, nothing of the kind! no, no—a few presents now and then—china, shawls, congo tea, avadavats, and Indian crackers,[51] little more, believe me.

Sir Oliv. Here's gratitude for twelve thousand pounds!—avadavats and Indian crackers!

Surf. Then, my dear sir, you have heard, I doubt not, of the extravagance of my brother. Sir, there are very few would credit what I have done for that unfortunate young man.

Sir Oliv. Not I for one!

Surf. The sums I have lent him! Indeed, I have been exceedingly to blame—it was an amiable weakness! however, I don't pretend to defend it; and now I feel it doubly culpable, since it has deprived me of the power of serving *you,* Mr. Stanley, as my heart directs.

Sir Oliv. Dissembler!—Then, sir, you cannot assist me?

Surf. At present it grieves me to say I cannot—but whenever I have the ability, you may depend upon hearing from me.

Sir Oliv. I am extremely sorry——

Surf. Not more than I am, believe me; to pity without the power to relieve is still more painful than to ask and be denied.

Sir Oliv. Kind sir, your most obedient, humble servant.

50 East Indian coins (worth 7–8s.).

51 The last three mean respectively a black tea from China, small Indian song-birds, and fancy fire-crackers.

Surf. You leave me deeply affected, Mr. Stanley; William, be ready to open the door.

Sir Oliv. O, dear sir, no ceremony——

Surf. Your very obedient——

Sir Oliv. Your most obsequious——

Surf. You may depend on hearing from me whenever I can be of service——

Sir Oliv. Sweet sir, you are too good——

Surf. In the mean time I wish you health and spirits——

Sir Oliv. Your ever grateful and perpetual humble servant——

Surf. Sir, yours as sincerely——

Sir Oliv. Charles!—you are my heir.

(*Exit.*)

(*Surface, solus.*)

Soh!—This is one bad effect of a good character—it invites applications from the unfortunate and there needs no small degree of address to gain the reputation of benevolence without incurring the expense. The silver ore of pure charity is an expensive article in the catalogue of a man's good qualities, whereas the sentimental French plate I use instead of it makes just as good a show, and pays no tax.

(*Enter Rowley.*)

Row. Mr. Surface, your servant. I was apprehensive of interrupting you, though my business demands immediate attention, as this note will inform you.

Surf. Always happy to see Mr. Rowley. How—Oliver—Surface!—My uncle arrived!

Row. He is indeed—we have just parted—quite well—after a speedy voyage—and impatient to embrace his worthy nephew.

Surf. I am astonished!—William! stop Mr. Stanley, if he's not gone.

Row. O—he's out of reach, I believe.

Surf. Why did n't you let me know this when you came in together?

Row. I thought you had particular—business; but I must be gone to inform your brother, and appoint him here to meet his uncle. He will be with you in a quarter of an hour.

Surf. So he says. Well, I am strangely overjoyed at his coming!—Never to be sure was anything so damned unlucky!

Row. You will be delighted to see how well he looks.

Surf. O, I'm rejoiced to hear it—just at this time——

Row. I'll tell him how impatiently you expect him.

Surf. Do—do—pray—give my best duty and affection—indeed, I cannot express the sensations I feel at the thought of seeing him!—certainly his coming just at this time is the cruellest piece of ill fortune——

(*Exeunt.*)

Scene 2. *At Sir Peter's House.*

(*Enter Mrs. Candour and Servant.*)

Serv. Indeed, ma'am, my Lady will see nobody at present.

Mrs. Can. Did you tell her it was her friend, Mrs. Candour?

Serv. Yes, ma'am, but she begs you will excuse her.

Mrs. Can. Do go again—I shall be glad to see her if it be only for a moment, for I am sure she must be in great distress. (*Exit Maid.*)—Dear heart, how provoking!—I'm not mistress of half the circumstances!—We shall have the whole affair in the newspapers with the names of the parties at length before I have dropt the story at a dozen houses.

(*Enter Sir Benjamin.*)

Sir Benjamin, you have heard, I suppose——

Sir Ben. Of Lady Teazle and Mr. Surface——

Mrs. Can. And Sir Peter's discovery——

Sir Ben. O the strangest piece of business to be sure——

Mrs. Can. Well, I never was so surprised in my life!—I am so sorry for all parties—indeed.

Sir Ben. Now, I don't pity Sir Peter at all; he was so extravagant—partial to Mr. Surface——

Mrs. Can. Mr. Surface!—why, 't was with Charles Lady Teazle was detected.

Sir Ben. No such thing! Mr. Surface is the gallant.

Mrs. Can. No, no, Charles is the man; 't was Mr. Surface brought Sir Peter on purpose to discover them.

Sir Ben. I tell you I have it from one——

Mrs. Can. And I have it from one——

Sir Ben. Who had it from one who had it——

Mrs. Can. From one immediately—but here comes Lady Sneerwell—perhaps she knows the whole affair.

(*Enter Lady Sneerwell.*)

Lady Sneer. So, my dear Mrs. Candour, here 's a sad affair of our friend Teazle.

Mrs. Can. Aye, my dear friend, who could have thought it?

Lady Sneer. Well, there is no trusting to appearances; though, indeed, she was always too lively for me.

Mrs. Can. To be sure, her manners were a little too free—but she was very young——

Lady Sneer. And had indeed some good qualities.

Mrs. Can. So she had indeed—but have you heard the particulars?

Lady Sneer. No, but everybody says that Mr. Surface——

Sir Ben. Aye, there I told you—Mr. Surface was the man.

Mrs. Can. No, no, indeed the assignation was with Charles——

Lady Sneer. With Charles!—You alarm me, Mrs. Candour!

Mrs. Can. Yes, yes, he was the lover; Mr. Surface—do him justice—was only the informer.

Sir Ben. Well, I 'll not dispute with you, Mrs. Candour—but be it which it may, I hope that Sir Peter's wound will not——

Mrs. Can. Sir Peter's wound! O mercy! I did n't hear a word of their fighting——

Lady Sneer. Nor I a syllable!

Sir Ben. No! what, no mention of the duel?

Mrs. Can. Not a word—

Sir Ben. O, Lord, yes, yes, they fought before they left the room.

Lady Sneer. Pray, let us hear.

Mrs. Can. Aye—do oblige us with the duel——

Sir Ben. "Sir," says Sir Peter, immediately after the discovery, "you are a most ungrateful fellow."

Mrs. Can. Aye to Charles——

Sir Ben. No, no—to Mr. Surface—"a most ungrateful fellow; and old as I am, sir," says he, "I insist on immediate satisfaction."

Mrs. Can. Aye, that must have been to Charles, for 't is very unlikely Mr. Surface should go to fight in his own house.

Sir Ben. Gad's life, ma'am, not at all—"giving me immediate satisfaction"—on this, madam—Lady Teazle seeing Sir Peter in such danger—ran out of the room in strong hysterics—and Charles after her calling out for hartshorn and water! Then, madam, they began to fight with swords——

(*Enter Crabtree.*)

Crab. With pistols, nephew, I have it from undoubted authority.

Mrs. Can. Oh, Mr. Crabtree, then it is all true——

Crab. Too true indeed, ma'am, and Sir Peter dangerously wounded——

Sir Ben. By a thrust in second [52]—quite through his left side.

Crab. By a bullet lodged in the thorax——

Mrs. Can. Mercy on me! Poor Sir Peter——

Crab. Yes, ma'am, tho' Charles would have avoided the matter if he could——

Mrs. Can. I knew Charles was the person——

Sir Ben. O my uncle, I see, knows nothing of the matter——

Crab. But Sir Peter taxed him with the basest ingratitude——

Sir Ben. That I told you, you know——

Crab. Do, nephew, let me speak—and insisted on immediate——

Sir Ben. Just as I said——

Crab. Odd's life! Nephew, allow others to know something too—A pair of pistols lay on the bureau—for Mr. Surface, it seems, had come home the night before late from Salt-Hill where he had been to see the Montem [53] with a friend, who has a son at Eton—so unluckily the pistols were left charged——

Sir Ben. I heard nothing of this——

Crab. Sir Peter forced Charles to take one and they fired—it seems pretty nearly together—Charles's shot took place as I tell you, and Sir Peter's missed—but what is very extraordinary the ball struck against a little bronze Pliny that stood over the fire place—grazed out of the window at a right angle—and wounded the postman, who was just coming to the door with a double letter from Northamptonshire.

Sir Ben. My uncle's account is more circumstantial, I must confess,—but I believe mine is the true one for all that.

Lady Sneer. I am more interested in this affair than they imagine—and must have better information.—

(*Exit.*)

52 A position in fencing.

53 A festival formerly held at Eton College, in which the scholars marched to a mound (*ad montem*), called Salt Hill, near Slough.

Sir Ben. Ah! Lady Sneerwell's alarm is very easily accounted for.

Crab. Yes, yes, they certainly *do* say—but that 's neither here nor there.

Mrs. Can. But pray, where is Sir Peter at present?

Crab. Oh! they brought him home and he is now in the house, tho' the servants are ordered to deny it.

Mrs. Can. I believe so—and Lady Teazle, I suppose, attending him.

Crab. Yes, yes, and I saw one of the faculty [54] enter just before me.

Sir Ben. Hey, who comes here?

Crab. Oh, this is he, the physician, depend on 't.

Mrs. Can. O certainly, it must be the physician, and now we shall know——

(*Enter Sir Oliver.*)

Crab. Well, Doctor, what hopes?

Mrs. Can. Aye, Doctor, how 's your patient?

Sir Ben. Now, Doctor, is n't it a wound with a small sword——

Crab. A bullet lodged in the thorax—for a hundred!

Sir Oliv. Doctor!—a wound with a small sword! and a bullet in the thorax!—Oons! are you mad, good people?

Sir Ben. Perhaps, sir, you are not a doctor.

Sir Oliv. Truly, sir, I am to thank you for my degree if I am.

Crab. Only a friend of Sir Peter's, then, I presume; but, sir, you must have heard of his accident.

Sir Oliv. Not a word!

Crab. Not of his being dangerously wounded?

Sir Oliv. The devil he is!

Sir Ben. Run thro' the body——

Crab. Shot in the breast——

Sir Ben. By one Mr. Surface——

Crab. Aye, the younger.

Sir Oliv. Hey! what the plague! you seem to differ strangely in your accounts; however, you agree that Sir Peter is dangerously wounded.

Sir Ben. Oh yes, we agree in that.

Crab. Yes, yes, I believe there can be no doubt in that.

Sir Oliv. Then, upon my word, for a person in that situation, he is the most imprudent man alive, for here he comes walking as if nothing at all was the matter.

(*Enter Sir Peter.*)

Odd's heart, Sir Peter! you are come in good time I promise you, for we had just given you over!

Sir Ben. 'Egad, uncle, this is the most sudden recovery!

Sir Oliv. Why, man, what do you do out of bed with a small sword through your body, and a bullet lodged in your thorax?

Sir Pet. A small sword and a bullet—

Sir Oliv. Aye, these gentlemen would have killed you without law or physic, and wanted to dub me a doctor to make me an accomplice.

Sir Pet. Why! what is all this?

Sir Ben. We rejoice, Sir Peter, that the story of the duel is not true—and are sincerely sorry for your other misfortune.

Sir Pet. So, so,—all over the town already!

(*Aside.*)

Crab. Though, Sir Peter, you were certainly vastly to blame to marry at all at your years.

Sir Pet. Sir, what business is that of yours?

Mrs. Can. Though, indeed, as Sir Peter made so good a husband, he 's very much to be pitied.

Sir Pet. Plague on your pity, ma'am, I desire none of it.

Sir Ben. However, Sir Peter, you must not mind the laughing and jests you will meet with on the occasion.

Sir Pet. Sir, I desire to be master in my own house.

Crab. 'T is no uncommon case, that 's one comfort.

Sir Pet. I insist on being left to myself, without ceremony,—I insist on your leaving my house directly!

Mrs. Can. Well, well, we are going and depend on 't, we 'll make the best report of you we can.

Sir Pet. Leave my house!

Crab. And tell how hardly you have been treated.

Sir Pet. Leave my house—

Sir Ben. And how patiently you bear it.

Sir Pet. Friends! Vipers! Furies! Oh that their own venom would choke them!

Sir Oliver. They are very provoking indeed, Sir Peter.

(*Enter Rowley.*)

Row. I heard high words: what has ruffled you, Sir Peter.

54 *I. e.*, of the medical profession.

Sir Pet. Pshaw! what signifies asking—do I ever pass a day without my vexations?

Sir Oliv. Well, I 'm not inquisitive—I come only to tell you that I have seen both my nephews in the manner we proposed.

Sir Pet. A precious couple they are!

Row. Yes, and Sir Oliver is convinced that your judgment was right, Sir Peter.

Sir Oliv. Yes, I find Joseph is indeed the man after all.

Row. Aye, as Sir Peter says, he 's a man of sentiment.

Sir Oliv. And acts up to the sentiments he professes.

Row. It certainly is edification to hear him talk.

Sir Oliv. Oh, he 's a model for the young men of his age! But how 's this, Sir Peter? you don't join us in your friend Joseph's praise as I expected.

Sir Pet. Sir Oliver, we live in a damned wicked world, and the fewer we praise the better.

Row. What, do *you* say so, Sir Peter, who were never mistaken in your life?

Sir Pet. Pshaw! Plague on you both—I see by your sneering you have heard the whole affair—I shall go mad among you!

Row. Then to fret you no longer, Sir Peter, we are indeed acquainted with it all. I met Lady Teazle coming from Mr. Surface's so humbled that she deigned to request *me* to be her advocate with you.

Sir Pet. And does Sir Oliver know all too?

Sir Oliv. Every circumstance!

Sir Pet. What of the closet and the screen—hey?

Sir Oliv. Yes, yes—and the little French milliner. Oh, I have been vastly diverted with the story! ha! ha! ha!

Sir Pet. 'T was very pleasant!

Sir Oliv. I never laughed more in my life, I assure you; ha! ha!

Sir Pet. O vastly diverting! Ha! ha!

Row. To be sure, Joseph with his sentiments! ha! ha!

Sir Pet. Yes, his sentiments! ha! ha! a hypocritical villain!

Sir Oliv. Aye, and that rogue Charles—to pull Sir Peter out of the closet, ha! ha!

Sir Pet. Ha! ha! 't was devilish entertaining, to be sure.

Sir Oliv. Ha! ha! Egad, Sir Peter, I should like to have seen your face when the screen was thrown down—ha! ha!

Sir Pet. Yes, my face when the screen was thrown down: ha! ha! ha! O, I must never show my head again!

Sir Oliv. But come, come, it is n't fair to laugh at you neither, my old friend, tho' upon my soul I can't help it—

Sir Pet. O pray, don't restrain your mirth on my account: it does not hurt me at all—I laugh at the whole affair myself.—Yes—yes—I think being a standing jest for all one's acquaintance a very happy situation—O yes—and then of a morning to read the paragraphs about Mr. S——, Lady T——, and Sir P——, will be so entertaining!—I shall certainly leave town tomorrow and never look mankind in the face again!

Row. Without affectation, Sir Peter, you may despise the ridicule of fools. But I see Lady Teazle going towards the next room—I am sure you must desire a reconciliation as earnestly as she does.

Sir Oliv. Perhaps *my* being here prevents her coming to you; well, I 'll leave honest Rowley to mediate between you; but he must bring you all presently to Mr. Surface's—where I am now returning—if not to reclaim a libertine, at least to expose hypocrisy.

Sir Pet. Ah! I 'll be present at your discovering yourself there with all my heart; though 't is a vile unlucky place for discoveries.

Sir Oliv. However, it is very convenient to the carrying on of my plot that you all live so near one another!

(*Exit Sir Oliver.*)

Row. We 'll follow—

Sir Pet. She is not coming here, you see, Rowley—

Row. No, but she has left the door of that room open, you perceive.—See, she is in tears!

Sir Pet. She seems indeed to wish I should go to her. How dejected she appears!

Row. And will you refrain from comforting her?

Sir Pet. Certainly, a little mortification appears very becoming in a wife. Don't you think it will do her good to let her pine a little?

Row. O, this is ungenerous in you.

Sir Pet. Well, I know not what to think. You remember, Rowley, the letter I found of hers—evidently intended for Charles?

Row. A mere forgery, Sir Peter, laid in

your way on purpose. This is one of the points which I intend Snake shall give you conviction on.

Sir Pet. I wish I were once satisfied of that. She looks this way——what a remarkably elegant turn of the head she has! Rowley, I'll go to her.

Row. Certainly—

Sir Pet. Tho' when it is known that we are reconciled, people will laugh at me ten times more!

Row. Let them laugh—and retort their malice only by showing them you are happy in spite of it.

Sir Pet. I' faith, so I will—and if I'm not mistaken, we may yet be the happiest couple in the country.

Row. Nay, Sir Peter, he who once lays aside suspicion——

Sir Pet. Hold, Master Rowley, if you have any regard for me, never let me hear you utter anything like a sentiment. I have had enough of *them* to serve me the rest of my life.

(*Exeunt.*)

SCENE THE LAST. *The Library.*

(*Surface and Lady Sneerwell.*)

Lady Sneer. Impossible! will not Sir Peter immediately be reconciled to *Charles?* and of consequence no longer oppose his union with *Maria?* The thought is distraction to me!

Surf. Can passion furnish a remedy?

Lady Sneer. No, nor cunning either. O I was a fool, an idiot, to league with such a blunderer!

Surf. Surely, Lady Sneerwell, I am the greatest sufferer—yet you see I bear the accident with calmness.

Lady Sneer. Because the disappointment has n't reached your *heart;* your interest only attached you to Maria; had you felt for her what I have for that ungrateful libertine, neither your temper nor hypocrisy could prevent your showing the sharpness of your vexation.

Surf. But why should your reproaches fall on me for this disappointment?

Lady Sneer. Are not you the cause of it? what had you to bate in your pursuit of Maria to pervert Lady Teazle by the way?—had you not a sufficient field for your roguery in blinding Sir Peter and supplanting your brother? I hate such an avarice of crimes; 't is an unfair monopoly and never prospers.

Surf. Well, I admit I have been to blame. I confess I deviated from the direct road of wrong, but I don't think we're so totally defeated neither.

Lady Sneer. No!

Surf. You tell me you have made a trial of Snake since we met, and that you still believe him faithful to us.

Lady Sneer. I do believe so.

Surf. And that he has undertaken, should it be necessary, to swear and prove that Charles is at this time contracted by vows and honor to your ladyship, which some of his former letters to you will serve to support.

Lady Sneer. This, indeed, might have assisted—

Surf. Come, come, it is not too late yet; but hark! this is probably my uncle, Sir Oliver; retire to that room—we'll consult further when he's gone.

Lady Sneer. Well, but if *he* should find you out to[o]—

Surf. O, I have no fear of that—Sir Peter will hold his tongue for his own credit sake—and you may depend on 't, I shall soon discover Sir Oliver's weak side!—

Lady Sneer. I have no diffidence of your abilities—only be constant to one roguery at a time.

(*Exit.*)

Surf. I will, I will. So 't is confounded hard after such bad fortune, to be baited by one's confederate in evil. Well, at all events my character is so much better than Charles's, that I certainly—hey—what!—this is not Sir Oliver—but old Stanley again!—Plague on 't, that he should return to tease me just now;—I shall have Sir Oliver come and find him here—and—

(*Enter Sir Oliver.*)

Gad's life, Mr. Stanley, why have you come back to plague me at this time? you must not stay now, upon my word!

Sir Oliv. Sir, I hear your uncle Oliver is expected here, and tho' he has been so penurious to you, I'll try what he'll do for me.

Surf. Sir! 't is impossible for you to stay now; so I must beg——come any other time and I promise you, you shall be assisted.

Sir Oliv. No—Sir Oliver and I must be acquainted—

Surf. Zounds, sir, then I insist on your quitting the room directly—

Sir Oliver. Nay, sir——

Surf. Sir, I insist on 't. Here, William, show this gentleman out. Since you compel me, sir—not one moment—this is such insolence.

(*Going to push him out.*)

(*Enter Charles.*)

Chas. Heyday! what 's the matter now? what the devil, have you got hold of my little broker here! Zounds, brother, don't hurt little Premium. What 's the matter, my little fellow?

Surf. So! He has been with you, too, has he?

Chas. To be sure he has! Why, 't is as honest a little—— But sure, Joseph, you have not been borrowing money, too, have you?

Surf. Borrowing — no! — But, brother, you know sure we expect Sir Oliver every——

Chas. O Gad, that 's true—Noll must n't find the little broker here, to be sure—

Surf. Yet Mr. Stanley insists——

Chas. Stanley! why his name 's Premium—

Surf. No, no, Stanley.

Chas. No, no, Premium.

Surf. Well, no matter which—but——

Chas. Aye, aye, Stanley or Premium, 't is the same thing as you say—for I suppose he goes by half a hundred names, besides A. B's [55] at the coffee-house.

(*Knock.*)

Surf. 'Sdeath, here 's Sir Oliver at the door. Now, I beg, Mr. Stanley——

Chas. Aye, aye, and I beg, Mr. Premium——

Sir Oliv. Gentlemen——

Surf. Sir, by Heaven, you shall go—

Chas. Aye, out with him certainly——

Sir Oliv. This violence——

Surf. 'T is your own fault.

Chas. Out with him, to be sure.

(*Both forcing Sir Oliver out.*)

(*Enter Sir Peter Teazle, Lady Teazle, Maria, and Rowley.*)

Sir Pet. My old friend, Sir Oliver!—hey! what in the name of wonder!—Here are dutiful nephews!—assault their uncle at his first visit!

Lady Teaz. Indeed, Sir Oliver, 't was well we came in to rescue you.

Row. Truly it was, for I perceive, Sir Oliver, the character of old Stanley was no protection to you.

Sir Oliv. Nor of Premium, either. The necessities of the former could not extort a shilling from that benevolent gentleman; and with the other I stood a chance of faring worse than my ancestors, and being knocked down without being paid for.

Surf. Charles!

Chas. Joseph!

Surf. 'T is complete!

Chas. Very!

Sir Oliv. Sir Peter, my friend, and Rowley, too—look on that elder nephew of mine. You know what he has already received from my bounty and you know also how gladly I would have looked on half my fortune as held in trust for him. Judge then my disappointment in discovering him to be destitute of truth, charity, and gratitude.

Sir Pet. Sir Oliver, I should be more surprised at this declaration, if I had not myself found him to be selfish, treacherous, and hypocritical.

Lady Teaz. And if the gentleman pleads not guilty to these, pray let him call *me* to his character.

Sir Pet. Then I believe we need add no more. If he knows himself, he will consider it as the most perfect punishment that he is known to the world.

Chas. If they talk this way to Honesty, what will they say to *me* by and bye?

Sir Oliv. As for that prodigal, his brother there——

Chas. Aye, now comes my turn—the damned family pictures will ruin me.

Surf. Sir Oliver, uncle, will you honor me with a hearing?

Chas. I wish Joseph now would make one of his long speeches and I might recollect myself a little.

Sir Oliv. And I suppose you would undertake to vindicate yourself entirely—

Surf. I trust I could—

Sir Oliv. Nay, if you desert your roguery in its distress and try to be justified, you have even less principle than I thought you had.—(*To Charles Surface.*) Well, sir, and *you* could justify *yourself* too, I suppose?

Chas. Not that I know of, Sir Oliver.

Sir Oliv. What! little Premium has been let too much into the secret, I presume.

Chas. True, sir, but they were family secrets, and should not be mentioned again, you know.

Row. Come, Sir Oliver, I know you cannot speak of Charles's follies with anger.

55 An allusion to the practice of receiving at a coffee-house letters addressed with an assumed name or initials.

Sir Oliv. Odd's heart, no more I can—nor with gravity, either. Sir Peter, do you know the rogue bargained with me for all his ancestors—sold me judges and generals by the foot, and maiden aunts as cheap as broken china!

Chas. To be sure, Sir Oliver, I did make a little free with the family canvas, that's the truth on't:—my ancestors may certainly rise in judgment against me, there's no denying it;—but believe me sincere when I tell you, and upon my soul I would not say so if I was not, that if I do not appear mortified at the exposure of my follies, it is because I feel at this moment the warmest satisfaction in seeing you, my liberal benefactor.

Sir Oliv. Charles—I believe you—give me your hand again; the ill-looking little fellow over the couch has made your peace.

Chas. Then, sir, my gratitude to the original is still increased.

Lady Teaz. (*Advancing.*) Yet I believe, Sir Oliver, here is one whom Charles is still more anxious to be reconciled to.

Sir Oliv. O, I have heard of his attachment there—and with the young lady's pardon, if I construe right that blush——

Sir Pet. Well, child, speak your sentiments; you know, we are going to be reconciled to Charles.

Mar. Sir, I have little to say, but that I shall rejoice to hear that he is happy. For me, whatever claim I had to his affection I willing[ly] resign to one who has a better title.

Chas. How, Maria!

Sir Pet. Heyday, what's the mystery now? while he appeared an incorrigible rake, you would give your hand to no one else, and now that he's likely to reform I'll warrant you won't have him!

Mar. His own heart, and Lady Sneerwell, know the cause.

Chas. Lady Sneerwell!

Surf. Brother, it is with great concern—I am obliged to speak on this point, but my regard to justice obliges me—and Lady Sneerwell's injuries can no longer be concealed—

(*Goes to the door.*)

(*Enter Lady Sneerwell.*)

Sir Pet. Soh! another French milliner, egad! He has one in every room in the house, I suppose—

Lady Sneer. Ungrateful Charles! Well may you be surprised and feel for the indelicate situation which your perfidy has forced me into.

Chas. Pray, uncle, is this another plot of yours? for as I have life, I don't understand it.

Surf. I believe, sir, there is but the evidence of one person more necessary to make it extremely clear.

Sir Pet. And that person, I imagine, is Mr. Snake. Rowley, you were perfectly right to bring him with us, and pray let him appear.

Row. Walk in, Mr. Snake—

(*Enter Snake.*)

I thought his testimony might be wanted; however, it happens unluckily that he comes to confront Lady Sneerwell and not to support her.

Lady Sneer. A villain!—Treacherous to me at last! Speak, fellow, have you too conspired against me?

Snake. I beg your ladyship ten thousand pardons,—you paid me extremely liberally for the lie in question—but I unfortunately have been offered double to speak the truth.

Lady Sneer. The torments of shame and disappointment on you all!

Lady Teaz. Hold, Lady Sneerwell, before you go, let me thank you for the trouble you and that gentleman have taken in writing letters from me to Charles and answering them yourself; and let me also request you to make my respects to the Scandalous College, of which you are President, and inform them that Lady Teazle, Licentiate,[56] begs leave to return the diploma they granted her—as she leaves off practice and kills characters no longer.

Lady Sneer. Provoking — insolent!—may your husband live these fifty years!

(*Exit.*)

Sir Pet. Oons, what a fury!

Lady Teaz. A malicious creature indeed!

Sir Pet. Hey—not for the last wish?—

Lady Teaz. O, no—

Sir Oliv. Well, sir, and what have you to say now?

Surf. Sir, I am so confounded, to find that Lady Sneerwell could be guilty of suborning Mr. Snake in this manner to impose on us all, that I know not what to say.——However, lest her revengeful spirit should prompt her to injure my

56 graduate.

brother, I had certainly better follow her directly.

(*Exit.*)

Sir Pet. Moral to the last drop!

Sir Oliv. Aye, and marry her, Joseph, if you can.—Oil and vinegar, egad:—you 'll do very well together.

Row. I believe we have no more occasion for Mr. Snake at present.

Snake. Before I go, I beg pardon once for all for whatever uneasiness I have been the humble instrument of causing to the parties present.

Sir Pet. Well, well, you have made atonement by a good deed at last.

Snake. But I must request of the company that it shall never be known.

Sir Pet. Hey!—what the plague—are you ashamed of having done a right thing once in your life?

Snake. Ah, sir, consider I live by the badness of my character!—I have nothing but my infamy to depend on!—and, if it were once known that I had been betrayed into an honest action, I should lose every friend I have in the world.

Sir Oliv. Well, well, we 'll not traduce you by saying anything to your praise, never fear.

(*Exit Snake.*)

Sir Pet. There 's a precious rogue.—Yet that fellow is a writer and a critic.

Lady Teaz. See, Sir Oliver, there needs no persuasion now to reconcile your nephew and Maria.

Sir Oliv. Aye, aye, that 's as it should be, and egad, we 'll have the wedding tomorrow morning.

Chas. Thank you, dear uncle!

Sir Pet. What! you rogue, don't you ask the girl's consent first?

Chas. Oh, I have done that a long time—above a minute ago—and she has looked yes—

Mar. For shame, Charles! I protest, Sir Peter, there has not been a word——

Sir Oliv. Well, then, the fewer the better—may your love for each other never know abatement.

Sir Pet. And may you live as happily together as Lady Teazle and I—intend to do.

Chas. Rowley, my old friend, I am sure you congratulate me and I suspect too that I owe you much.

Sir Oliv. You do, indeed, Charles.

Row. If my efforts to serve you had not succeeded, you would have been in my debt for the attempt;—but deserve to be happy—and you over-repay me.

Sir Pet. Aye, honest Rowley always said you would reform.

Chas. Why, as to reforming, Sir Peter, I 'll make no promises—and that I take to be a proof that I intend to set about it.—But here shall be my monitor, my gentle guide.—Ah! can I leave the virtuous path those eyes illumine?

Tho' thou, dear maid, should'st waive thy beauty's sway,
—Thou still must rule—because I will obey:
An humbled fugitive from folly view,
No sanctuary near but love and *you:*
You can indeed each anxious fear remove,
For even scandal dies if you approve.

(*To the audience.*)

EPILOGUE.

By Mr. Colman.

Spoken by Lady Teazle.

I, who was late so volatile and gay,
Like a trade-wind must now blow all one way,
Bend all my cares, my studies, and my vows,
To one dull rusty weathercock—my spouse!
So wills our virtuous bard—the motley Bayes
Of crying epilogues and laughing plays!
Old bachelors, who marry smart young wives,
Learn from our play to regulate your lives:
Each bring his dear to town, all faults upon her—
London will prove the very source of honor.
Plunged fairly in, like a cold bath it serves,
When principles relax, to brace the nerves:
Such is my case; and yet I must deplore
That the gay dream of dissipation 's o'er.
And say, ye fair! was ever lively wife,
Born with the genius for the highest life,
Like me untimely blasted in her bloom,
Like me condemned to such a dismal doom?
Save money—when I just knew how to waste it!
Leave London—just as I began to taste it!
Must I then watch the early crowing cock,
The melancholy ticking of a clock;
In a lone rustic hall for ever pounded,
With dogs, cats, rats, and squalling brats surrounded?

With humble curate can I now retire,
(While good Sir Peter boozes with the squire,)
And at backgammon mortify my soul,
That pants for loo, or flutters at a vole?[57]
Seven 's the main! Dear sound that must expire,
Lost at hot cockles round a Christmas fire;
The transient hour of fashion too soon spent,
Farewell the tranquil mind, farewell content!
Farewell the plumèd head, the cushioned tête,
That takes the cushion from its proper seat!
That spirit-stirring drum!—card drums I mean,
Spadille—odd trick — pam — basto — king and queen!
And you, ye knockers, that, with brazen throat,
The welcome visitors' approach denote;
Farewell all quality of high renown,
Pride, pomp, and circumstance of glorious town!
Farewell! your revels I partake no more,
And Lady Teazle's occupation 's o'er!
All this I told our bard; he smiled, and said 't was clear,
I ought to play deep tragedy next year.
Meanwhile he drew wise morals from his play,
And in these solemn periods stalk'd away:—
"Blessed were the fair like you; her faults who stopped,
And closed her follies when the curtain dropped!
No more in vice or error to engage,
Or play the fool at large on life's great stage."

[57] Here and below are various terms used in card-games; much of the passage parodies Othello's farewell to war.

V. THE NINETEENTH CENTURY

PERCY BYSSHE SHELLEY

THE CENCI

Percy Bysshe Shelley (1792–1822), though the son of a conservative country gentleman, was at odds with English society most of his life; dividing his allegiance between poetry and the cause of liberty as he conceived it. His publication in 1811 of a pamphlet, *The Necessity of Atheism* (for which he was expelled from the University of Oxford), his irregular views and conduct as to marriage, his attempt in 1812 to rouse the Irish, his sympathy later for the Greek revolutionists, and much of his poetry, all show his liberalism. In 1813–4 he was intimate with such English radicals as Leigh Hunt and William Godwin, and after the suicide of his first wife he married Godwin's daughter. He was a somewhat unpractical enthusiast, who held ardent views, and acted on them, concerning many practical subjects. The latter part of his life especially he devoted to poetry, living in Italy from 1818 to 1822, when he was drowned.

In 1818, at the age of twenty-six, Shelley came upon a professedly historical manuscript account of the crimes and calamities of the Roman count Cenci and his family in the year 1598. Persecuted innocence, patience under affliction, like that of Beatrice in this story, always more than anything else moved his sympathy. Struck by the suitability of the story for drama, and more trusting his wife's abilities in that direction than his own, he urged her to write a play on it; but ended in writing it himself the following year. The fact that he turned from the vastness and abstractness of *Prometheus Unbound*, only semi-dramatic, to this intense, concrete and actable play is an example of versatility unusual in Shelley. While in general he took but little interest in the theater, he was most desirous and made every effort that *The Cenci* should be performed at Covent Garden in 1820, but the strange painfulness of the subject prevented, and the play has been performed but once, so far as is known, in London, 1886, under the auspices of the Shelley Society, before a huge and distinguished audience. With certain effective scenes, what gave the play its force on the stage was mainly the personalities of Count Cenci and especially Beatrice.

The Relation of the Death of the Family of the Cenci, the manuscript account mentioned above, is closely followed by the play and suggested all its essentials, and even such points as the abortive first plan for the murder, the hesitation of the murderers and Beatrice's firmness at the second attempt, and the gold-trimmed mantle given by her to one of them. Most of the characters are in both, Beatrice is the same in outline, and also Count Cenci. The *Relation* is naturally much more prosaically circumstantial, particularly as to what followed the murder, the successful concealment of it for a time, and the culprits' condemnation and execution. The narrative has a curiously popular and even *naïf* effect, with its particulars as to dress, personal appearance, pious last words, and the like; and though it shows sympathy chiefly toward Beatrice and her associates, it professes great horror at the parricide. The story is so hideous, and the guilt in it so one-sided, that we are not surprised to learn that legend has mingled with history; in real life heavenly innocents and devilish brutes rarely exist in the same family. There are even those who state that the harshness of the historic Cenci to his daughter was not without excuse, and that there was much more moral justification for her execution than for his murder. The family was one of criminals, the Count was better and less monstrous, and his family worse, than legend says. Thus another traditional story fades into the light of common day through historical criticism. Authenticity is also denied to the well-known supposed portrait of Beatrice Cenci attributed to Guido Reni.

But as with any creation of vital imagination, this matters little for the play; art deals rather with general than particular truth, and general truth is untouched by historical criticism. Unspeakable as the story is, it cannot be called impossible. Count Cenci may pass for one of the monsters of egotism, the combinations of uncontrolled crime and guile, of which we hear during the Italian Renascence; or, in more modern parlance, for a type of paranoia, of inversion and corruption of feeling and impulse. As we read we cannot but give the picture a horrified acceptance. He is so powerfully drawn that we accord him that willing suspension of disbelief which (as Coleridge says) constitutes poetic faith. His long course of crime is made the easier by contemporary conditions — the paternal authority which gave a father almost absolute power in his family and which would incline society to take his part, and (according to the play and the *Relation*) the corruption of the papal court, which preferred inflicting lucrative fines to more effective punishments. The poet draws more vividly Cenci's monstrous hate than his other sins; indeed hate is his motive throughout the play; but we are spared none of his hideous wickedness (some of it only hinted at), since only this could win our sympathy for such a crime as parricide. No play therefore could contain more violent conflicting emotions. Beatrice has her father's tendency to madness, a little of his shrewdness, and his powerful will, which overrides her associates and imposes on others her view of things. But the groundwork of her nature is not only normal and good; she is almost unique in the English drama for her combination of gentleness and energetic fortitude. As we read we can readily believe the *Relation*, that to her beauties she added "a spirit and a majestic vivacity that captivated every one." By her simple final words she leaves us with an impression of matchless self-command. To active evil in her father she at first opposes merely the passive resistance of goodness; to the active evil in society, at the end, which punishes those who are really victims, she opposes purely passive resistance; when she is goaded to active revenge, this constitutes in Shelley's view not a crime but only a "tragic error" (for the murder is at once seen to have been needless), which ends in the ruin of the family. Society in the person of the pope has refused to save her from irremediable degradation, and she takes the only way out. That this embodiment of Christian patience should first be left defenceless and then martyred by the church is one of the ironies of the play. To her, others of her family serve as foils — the weak Giacomo, who has not sufficient hold over his wife and children to neutralize his father's calumnies, and especially Lucretia, a lovable domestic soul, cruelly thrown into a situation too harsh for her, an Ophelia of fifty, we might say. Nothing could be more touching than the strong bond made between her and her step-children by their common misfortunes. According to the author of the *Relation*, who was sensible of the contrast, each on the way to her death carried a handkerchief, "with which Lucretia wiped her eyes, and Beatrice the perspiration from her forehead." With Shelley's dislike of ecclesiastics we should hardly expect from him a sympathetic portrait of pontiff or prelate; yet to offset the hard and mercenary pope (with the ironical name Clement) and the crafty, somewhat unreal Orsino, there is the humane cardinal Camillo. Indeed, it is with a realism and detachment unusual with Shelley, but more merciless than invective, that he is able to suggest the religious atmosphere in which his characters live, and in which the connection between religion and morality is a purely ceremonial one.

The structure of the play is symmetrical and simple, but somewhat wanting in incident and action, the interest being mainly psychological. Some of the most dramatic scenes are the poet's own invention, such as the banquet-scene, and the discovery (IV. iv) that the slayers were on the point of being relieved of their tyrant through the action of law. This superb and harrowing touch of pathos and dramatic irony is treated perhaps with excessive restraint, and serves chiefly to contrast Lucretia's repining with Beatrice's firmness. The simplicity of the plot and structure may reflect Shelley's admiration for Greek tragedy, for there are none of the comic elements which vary the tragedies of Shakespeare. His influence, however, on any English poetic drama is almost inevitable, and many reminiscences of his plays have been pointed out here; those of *Macbeth* in the murder and discovery scenes, and of *Lear* in Cenci's curse, are obvious.

In style the play is singularly unlike most of Shelley's poetry. Here is no "beautiful and ineffectual angel, beating in the void his luminous wings in vain," none of the melting imagery, full of beauty and transcendental feeling but intellectually baffling, which pervades his other work, and has had no very wholesome influence on later nineteenth-century poetry. Shelley realized that in an acting drama he must be

> Standing on earth, not rapt above the pole.

He avoided deliberately, he says in his Preface, "what is commonly called mere poetry, and I imagine there will scarcely be found a detached simile or a single isolated description." His style in the play is more austere than Shakespeare's; Keats was even minded to reproach him that he did not "load every rift of his subject with ore." His conscious endeavor was to let his characters express themselves, not him. The beautiful is subordinated to the significant.

When we look from this play back over the comedy and tragedy of the preceding century and more, the contrast is great and significant. The critical and satirical spirit which pervaded the greater literature of the earlier age had in the drama best expressed itself in comedy, the only form of drama in which the eighteenth century had excelled. Sentimental drama and tragedy had been hemmed in by rules, conventionality, and artificiality. Rarely had great emotion freely expressed itself. Shelley was filled with the grandeur and pathos of human character and fate as embodied in this story; he followed traditional forms of expression so far as suited him, but there is no longer any bondage to the three unities or to a definite moral lesson. The moral effect of the play stands in its exhibition of the human spirit rising superior to external torment and defilement; we are exalted by being shown the worth and dignity of man, and are more grateful for this than we should be for moral statements the truth of which we knew before. In literary style drama was freed from a somewhat artificial diction, and felt no other obligation than to express the thought and feeling of the moment as beautifully and fittingly as possible. In these various ways the freedom which was the moving spirit of the early nineteenth century, in literature as in life, was able occasionally to express itself in poetic tragedy. That it did not do so oftener and as worthily as in Shelley's play was due partly to the poets' desire for a more intimate self-expression than is possible in impersonal drama, and partly to the allurements of a newer literary form, the novel. As the century advanced, the spirit of realism more and more prevailed, which is hard to combine with poetic drama. The drama till near the end of the nineteenth century was even less notable than that of the eighteenth. That which was best as literature was not by professional dramatists, but by writers like Shelley, Byron, Browning, Tennyson, more distinguished in other fields; was of the nature of closet-drama, better to read than to act. The plays that year after year filled the theaters are mostly too poor as literature to be much read. But two not unworthy plays from the middle third of the century will be given after Shelley.

THE CENCI

DRAMATIS PERSONÆ

COUNT FRANCESCO CENCI.
GIACOMO, } *his Sons.*
BERNARDO, }
CARDINAL CAMILLO.
[PRINCE COLONNA.]
ORSINO, *a Prelate.*
SAVELLA, *the Pope's Legate.*
OLIMPIO, } *Assassins.*
MARZIO, }
ANDREA, *Servant to Cenci.*
Nobles, Judges, Guards, Servants.

LUCRETIA, *Wife of Cenci, and Step-mother of his Children.*
BEATRICE, *his Daughter.*

The Scene lies principally in Rome, but changes during the Fourth Act to Petrella, a castle among the Apulian Appennines.
Time. During the Pontificate of Clement VIII.

ACT I

SCENE 1. *An Apartment in the Cenci Palace. Enter Count Cenci, and Cardinal Camillo.*

Camillo. That matter of the murder is hushed up
If you consent to yield his Holiness
Your fief that lies beyond the Pincian gate.
It needed all my interest in the conclave
To bend him to this point: he said that you
Bought perilous impunity with your gold;
That crimes like yours if once or twice compounded
Enriched the Church, and respited from hell
An erring soul which might repent and live;
But that the glory and the interest
Of the high throne he fills, little consist
With making it a daily mart of guilt
As manifold and hideous as the deeds
Which you scarce hide from men's revolted eyes.

Cenci. The third of my possessions—let it go!
Ay, I once heard the nephew of the Pope
Had sent his architect to view the ground,
Meaning to build a villa on my vines
The next time I compounded with his uncle:
I little thought he should outwit me so!
Henceforth no witness—not the lamp—shall see
That which the vassal threatened to divulge,

Whose throat is choked with dust for his reward.
The deed he saw could not have rated higher
Than his most worthless life:[1]—it angers me!
Respited me from Hell!—So may the Devil
Respite their souls from Heaven. No doubt Pope Clement,
And his most charitable nephews, pray
That the Apostle Peter and the saints
Will grant for their sake that I long enjoy
Strength, wealth, and pride, and lust, and length of days
Wherein to act the deeds which are the stewards
Of their revenue.—But much yet remains
To which they show no title.

Cam. Oh, Count Cenci!
So much that thou mightst honorably live
And reconcile thyself with thine own heart
And with thy God, and with the offended world.
How hideously look deeds of lust and blood
Thro' those snow white and venerable hairs!
Your children should be sitting round you now,
But that you fear to read upon their looks
The shame and misery you have written there.
Where is your wife? Where is your gentle daughter?
Methinks her sweet looks, which make all things else
Beauteous and glad, might kill the fiend within you.
Why is she barred from all society
But her own strange and uncomplaining wrongs?
Talk with me, Count,—you know I mean you well.
I stood beside your dark and fiery youth
Watching its bold and bad career, as men
Watch meteors, but it vanished not: I marked
Your desperate and remorseless manhood; now
Do I behold you, in dishonored age,
Charged with a thousand unrepented crimes.
Yet I have ever hoped you would amend,
And in that hope have saved your life three times.

Cen. For which Aldobrandino owes you now
My fief beyond the Pincian. Cardinal,
One thing, I pray you, recollect henceforth,
And so we shall converse with less restraint.
A man you knew spoke of my wife and daughter:
He was accustomed to frequent my house;
So the next day *his* wife and daughter came
And asked if I had seen him; and I smiled:
I think they never saw him any more.

Cam. Thou execrable man, beware!—

Cen. Of thee?
Nay, this is idle: we should know each other.
As to my character for what men call crime,
Seeing I please my senses as I list,
And vindicate that right with force or guile,
It is a public matter, and I care not
If I discuss it with you. I may speak
Alike to you and my own conscious heart;
For you give out that you have half reformed me,
Therefore strong vanity will keep you silent
If fear should not; both will, I do not doubt.
All men delight in sensual luxury,
All men enjoy revenge; and most exult
Over the tortures they can never feel;
Flattering their secret peace with others' pain.
But I delight in nothing else. I love
The sight of agony, and the sense of joy,
When this shall be another's and that mine.
And I have no remorse and little fear,
Which are, I think, the checks of other men.
This mood has grown upon me, until now
Any design my captious fancy makes
The picture of its wish, and it forms none

1 The sense is a little obscure;—the fine for the crime which the man was killed to prevent his revealing would have been no higher than that for the murder.

But such as men like you would start to know,
Is as my natural food and rest debarred
Until it be accomplished.

Cam. Art thou not
Most miserable?

Cen. Why miserable?—
No. I am what your theologians call
Hardened; which they must be in impudence,
So to revile a man's peculiar taste.
True, I was happier than I am, while yet
Manhood remained to act the thing I thought;
While lust was sweeter than revenge; and now
Invention palls: ay, we must all grow old:
And but that there yet remains a deed to act
Whose horror might make sharp an appetite
Duller than mine—I 'd do,—I know not what.
When I was young I thought of nothing else
But pleasure; and I fed on honey sweets:
Men, by St. Thomas! cannot live like bees,
And I grew tired: yet, till I killed a foe,
And heard his groans, and heard his children's groans,
Knew I not what delight was else on earth,
Which now delights me little. I the rather
Look on such pangs as terror ill conceals:
The dry, fixed eyeball; the pale, quivering lip,
Which tell me that the spirit weeps within
Tears bitterer than the bloody sweat of Christ.
I rarely kill the body, which preserves,
Like a strong prison, the soul within my power,
Wherein I feed it with the breath of fear
For hourly pain.

Cam. Hell's most abandoned fiend
Did never, in the drunkenness of guilt,
Speak to his heart as now you speak to me;
I thank my God that I believe you not

(*Enter Andrea.*)

Andrea. My Lord, a gentleman from Salamanca
Would speak with you.

Cen. Bid him attend me
In the grand saloon.

(*Exit Andrea.*)

Cam. Farewell; and I will pray
Almighty God that thy false, impious words
Tempt not his spirit to abandon thee.

(*Exit Camillo.*)

Cen. The third of my possessions! I must use
Close husbandry, or gold, the old man's sword,
Falls from my withered hand. But yesterday
There came an order from the Pope to make
Fourfold provision for my cursed sons,
Whom I had sent from Rome to Salamanca,
Hoping some accident might cut them off:
And meaning if I could to starve them there.
I pray thee, God, send some quick death upon them!
Bernardo and my wife could not be worse
If dead and damned: then, as to Beatrice—
(*Looking around him suspiciously.*)
I think they cannot hear me at that door;
What if they should? And yet I need not speak,
Though the heart triumphs with itself in words.
O, thou most silent air, that shalt not hear
What now I think! Thou, pavement, which I tread
Towards her chamber,—let your echoes talk
Of my imperious step, scorning surprise,
But not of my intent! Andrea!

(*Enter Andrea.*)

Andr. My Lord!

Cen. Bid Beatrice attend me in her chamber
This evening:—no, at midnight, and alone.

(*Exeunt.*)

SCENE 2. *A Garden of the Cenci Palace. Enter Beatrice and Orsino, as in conversation.*

Beatrice. Pervert not truth,
Orsino. You remember where we held
That conversation;—nay, we see the spot
Even from this cypress;—two long years are past
Since, on an April midnight, underneath

The moonlight ruins of mount Palatine,
I did confess to you my secret mind.
Orsino. You said you loved me then.
Beatr. You are a priest,
Speak to me not of love.
Ors. I may obtain
The dispensation of the Pope to marry.
Because I am a priest do you believe
Your image, as the hunter some struck deer,
Follows me not whether I wake or sleep?
Beatr. As I have said, speak to me not of love;
Had you a dispensation, I have not;
Nor will I leave this home of misery
Whilst my poor Bernard, and that gentle lady
To whom I owe life and these virtuous thoughts,
Must suffer what I still have strength to share.
Alas, Orsino! All the love that once
I felt for you, is turned to bitter pain.
Ours was a youthful contract, which you first
Broke, by assuming vows no Pope will loose.
And thus I love you still, but holily,
Even as a sister or a spirit might;
And so I swear a cold fidelity.
And it is well perhaps we shall not marry.
You have a sly, equivocating vein
That suits me not. Ah, wretched that I am!
Where shall I turn? Even now you look on me
As you were not my friend, and as if you
Discovered that I thought so, with false smiles
Making my true suspicion seem your wrong.
Ah! No, forgive me; sorrow makes me seem
Sterner than else my nature might have been;
I have a weight of melancholy thoughts.
And they forebode,—but what can they forebode
Worse than I now endure?
Ors. All will be well.
Is the petition yet prepared? You know
My zeal for all you wish, sweet Beatrice;
Doubt not but I will use my utmost skill,
So that the Pope attend to your complaint.
Beatr. Your zeal for all I wish;—Ah me, you are cold!
Your utmost skill—speak but one word—
(*Aside.*) Alas!
Weak and deserted creature that I am,
Here I stand bickering with my only friend!
(*To Orsino.*) This night my father gives a sumptuous feast,
Orsino; he has heard some happy news
From Salamanca, from my brothers there,
And with this outward show of love he mocks
His inward hate. 'T is bold hypocrisy,
For he would gladlier celebrate their deaths,
Which I have heard him pray for on his knees:
Great God! that such a father should be mine!
But there is mighty preparation made,
And all our kin, the Cenci, will be there,
And all the chief nobility of Rome.
And he has bidden me and my pale mother
Attire ourselves in festival array.
Poor lady! She expects some happy change
In his dark spirit from this act; I none.
At supper I will give you the petition:
Till when—farewell.
Ors. Farewell. (*Exit Beatrice.*) I know the Pope
Will ne'er absolve me from my priestly vow
But by absolving me from the revenue
Of many a wealthy see; and, Beatrice,
I think to win thee at an easier rate.
Nor shall he read her eloquent petition:
He might bestow her on some poor relation
Of his sixth cousin, as he did her sister,
And I should be debarred from all access.
Then as to what she suffers from her father,
In all this there is much exaggeration:
Old men are testy and will have their way;
A man may stab his enemy, or his vassal,
And live a free life as to wine or women,
And with a peevish temper may return
To a dull home, and rate his wife and children;
Daughters and wives call this foul tyranny.
I shall be well content, if on my conscience
There rest no heavier sin than what they suffer
From the devices of my love—A net

From which she shall escape not. Yet I fear
Her subtle mind, her awe-inspiring gaze,
Whose beams anatomize me, nerve by nerve,
And lay me bare, and make me blush to see
My hidden thoughts.—Ah, no! A friendless girl
Who clings to me, as to her only hope:—
I were a fool, not less than if a panther
Were panic-stricken by the antelope's eye,
If she escape me.
(*Exit.*)

SCENE 3. *A magnificent Hall in the Cenci Palace. A Banquet. Enter Cenci, Lucretia, Beatrice, Orsino, Camillo, Nobles.*

Cenci. Welcome, my friends and kinsmen; welcome ye
Princes and Cardinals, pillars of the church,
Whose presence honors our festivity.
I have too long lived like an anchorite,
And, in my absence from your merry meetings,
An evil word is gone abroad of me:
But I do hope that you, my noble friends,
When you have shared the entertainment here,
And heard the pious cause for which 't is given,
And we have pledged a health or two together,
Will think me flesh and blood as well as you;
Sinful indeed, for Adam made all so,
But tender-hearted, meek and pitiful.
First Guest. In truth, my Lord, you seem too light of heart,
Too sprightly and companionable a man,
To act the deeds that rumor pins on you.
(*To his companion.*) I never saw such blithe and open cheer
In any eye!
Second Guest. Some most desired event,
In which we all demand a common joy,
Has brought us hither; let us hear it, Count.
Cen. It is indeed a most desired event.
If, when a parent, from a parent's heart,
Lifts from this earth to the great father of all
A prayer, both when he lays him down to sleep
And when he rises up from dreaming it;
One supplication, one desire, one hope,
That he would grant a wish for his two sons,
Even all that he demands in their regard—
And suddenly, beyond his dearest hope,
It is accomplished, he should then rejoice,
And call his friends and kinsmen to a feast,
And task their love to grace his merriment,
Then honor me thus far—for I am he.
Beatrice. (*To Lucretia.*) Great God! How horrible! Some dreadful ill
Must have befallen my brothers.
Lucretia. Fear not, child,
He speaks too frankly.
Beatr. Ah! My blood runs cold.
I fear that wicked laughter round his eye,
Which wrinkles up the skin even to the hair.
Cen. Here are the letters brought from Salamanca;
Beatrice, read them to your mother, God,
I thank thee! In one night didst thou perform,
By ways inscrutable, the thing I sought.
My disobedient and rebellious sons
Are dead!—Why, dead!—What means this change of cheer?
You hear me not, I tell you they are dead;
And they will need no food or raiment more:
The tapers that did light them the dark way
Are their last cost. The Pope, I think, will not
Expect I should maintain them in their coffins.
Rejoice with me, my heart is wondrous glad.
Beatr. (*Lucretia sinks, half fainting; Beatrice supports her.*) It is not true!—Dear lady, pray look up.
Had it been true, there is a God in Heaven,
He would not live to boast of such a boon.
Unnatural man, thou knowest that it is false.
Cen. Ay, as the word of God; whom here I call
To witness that I speak the sober truth;
And whose most favoring Providence was shown

Even in the manner of their deaths. For Rocco
Was kneeling at the mass, with sixteen others,
When the church fell and crushed him to a mummy;
The rest escaped unhurt. Cristofano
Was stabbed in error by a jealous man,
Whilst she he loved was sleeping with his rival;
All in the self-same hour of the same night;
Which shows that Heaven has special care of me.
I beg those friends who love me, that they mark
The day a feast upon their calendars.
It was the twenty-seventh of December:
Ay, read the letters if you doubt my oath.

(*The assembly appears confused; several of the guests rise.*)

First Guest. Oh, horrible! I will depart.
Second Guest. And I.
Third Guest. No, stay!
I do believe it is some jest; though faith,
'T is mocking us somewhat too solemnly.
I think his son has married the Infanta,
Or found a mine of gold in El Dorado;
'T is but to season some such news; stay, stay!
I see 't is only raillery by his smile.

Cen. (*Filling a bowl of wine, and lifting it up.*) Oh, thou bright wine, whose purple splendor leaps
And bubbles gaily in this golden bowl
Under the lamp-light, as my spirits do,
To hear the death of my accursed sons!
Could I believe thou wert their mingled blood,
Then would I taste thee like a sacrament.
And pledge with thee the mighty Devil in Hell;
Who, if a father's curses, as men say,
Climb with swift wings after their children's souls,
And drag them from the very throne of Heaven,
Now triumphs in my triumph!—But thou art
Superfluous; I have drunken deep of joy,
And I will taste no other wine to-night.
Here, Andrea! Bear the bowl around.

A Guest. (*Rising.*) Thou wretch!
Will none among this noble company
Check the abandoned villain?

Camillo. For God's sake,
Let me dismiss the guests! You are insane,
Some ill will come of this.

Second Guest. Seize, silence him!
First Guest. I will!
Third Guest. And I!

Cen. (*Addressing those who rise with a threatening gesture.*) Who moves? Who speaks?
(*Turning to the company.*) 'T is nothing,
Enjoy yourselves.—Beware! for my revenge
Is as the sealed commission of a king,
That kills, and none dare name the murderer.

(*The banquet is broken up; several of the guests are departing.*)

Beatr. I do entreat you, go not, noble guests;
What, although tyranny and impious hate
Stand sheltered by a father's hoary hair?
What, if 't is he who clothed us in these limbs
Who tortures them, and triumphs? What, if we,
The desolate and the dead, were his own flesh,
His children and his wife, whom he is bound
To love and shelter? Shall we therefore find
No refuge in this merciless wide world?
Oh, think what deep wrongs must have blotted out
First love, then reverence in a child's prone mind,
Till it thus vanquish shame and fear! O, think!
I have borne much, and kissed the sacred hand
Which crushed us to the earth, and thought its stroke
Was perhaps some paternal chastisement!
Have excused much, doubted; and when no doubt
Remained, have sought by patience, love and tears,
To soften him; and when this could not be,
I have knelt down through the long sleepless nights,
And lifted up to God, the father of all,
Passionate prayers: and when these were not heard
I have still borne;—until I meet you here,
Princes and kinsmen, at this hideous feast

Given at my brothers' deaths. Two yet remain,
His wife remains and I, whom if ye save not,
Ye may soon share such merriment again
As fathers make over their children's graves.
Oh! Prince Colonna, thou art our near kinsman;
Cardinal, thou art the Pope's chamberlain;
Camillo, thou art chief justiciary;
Take us away!

Cen. (*He has been conversing with Camillo during the first part of Beatrice's speech; he hears the conclusion, and now advances.*) I hope my good friends here
Will think of their own daughters—or perhaps
Of their own throats—before they lend an ear
To this wild girl.

Beatr. (*Not noticing the words of Cenci.*) Dare no one look on me?
None answer? Can one tyrant overbear
The sense of many best and wisest men?
Or is it that I sue not in some form
Of scrupulous law, that ye deny my suit?
Oh, God! That I were buried with my brothers!
And that the flowers of this departed spring
Were fading on my grave! And that my father
Were celebrating now one feast for all!

Cam. A bitter wish for one so young and gentle;
Can we do nothing?

Colonna. Nothing that I see.
Count Cenci were a dangerous enemy;
Yet I would second any one.

A Cardinal. And I.

Cen. Retire to your chamber, insolent girl!

Beatr. Retire thou, impious man! Ay, hide thyself
Where never eye can look upon thee more!
Wouldst thou have honor and obedience,
Who art a torturer? Father, never dream,
Though thou mayst overbear this company,
But ill must come of ill.—Frown not on me!
Haste, hide thyself, lest with avenging looks
My brothers' ghosts should hunt thee from thy seat!
Cover thy face from every living eye,
And start if thou but hear a human step:
Seek out some dark and silent corner, there
Bow thy white head before offended God,
And we will kneel around, and fervently
Pray that he pity both ourselves and thee.

Cen. My friends, I do lament this insane girl
Has spoiled the mirth of our festivity.
Good night, farewell; I will not make you longer
Spectators of our dull domestic quarrels.
Another time.—
(*Exeunt all but Cenci and Beatrice.*)
My brain is swimming round;
Give me a bowl of wine! (*To Beatrice.*)
Thou painted viper!
Beast that thou art! Fair and yet terrible!
I know a charm shall make thee meek and tame,
Now get thee from my sight!
(*Exit Beatrice.*)
Here, Andrea,
Fill up this goblet with Greek wine. I said
I would not drink this evening; but I must;
For, strange to say, I feel my spirits fail
With thinking what I have decreed to do.
(*Drinking the wine.*)
Be thou the resolution of quick youth
Within my veins, and manhood's purpose stern,
And age's firm, cold, subtle villainy;
As if thou wert indeed my children's blood
Which I did thirst to drink. The charm works well;
It must be done; it shall be done, I swear!
(*Exit.*)

ACT II.

Scene 1. *An Apartment in the Cenci Palace. Enter Lucretia and Bernardo.*

Lucretia. Weep not, my gentle boy; he struck but me,
Who have borne deeper wrongs. In truth, if he
Had killed me, he had done a kinder deed.
O, God Almighty, do thou look upon us,
We have no other friend but only thee!
Yet weep not; though I love you as my own.

I am not your true mother.

Bernardo. Oh, more, more
Than ever mother was to any child,
That have you been to me! Had he not been
My father, do you think that I should weep?

Lucr. Alas, poor boy, what else couldst thou have done?

(*Enter Beatrice.*)

Beatrice. (*In a hurried voice.*) Did he pass this way? Have you seen him, brother?
Ah! No, that is his step upon the stairs;
'T is nearer now; his hand is on the door;
Mother, if I to thee have ever been
A duteous child, now save me! Thou, great God,
Whose image upon earth a father is,
Dost thou indeed abandon me? He comes;
The door is opening now; I see his face;
He frowns on others, but he smiles on me,
Even as he did after the feast last night.

(*Enter a Servant.*)

Almighty God, how merciful thou art!
'T is but Orsino's servant.—Well, what news?

Servant. My master bids me say, the Holy Father
Has sent back your petition thus unopened.
(*Giving a paper.*)
And he demands at what hour 't were secure
To visit you again?

Lucr. At the Ave Mary.

(*Exit Servant.*)

So, daughter, our last hope has failed; Ah me,
How pale you look; you tremble, and you stand
Wrapped in some fixed and fearful meditation,
As if one thought were over strong for you:
Your eyes have a chill glare; O, dearest child!
Are you gone mad? If not, pray speak to me.

Beatr. You see I am not mad; I speak to you.

Lucr. You talked of something that your father did
After that dreadful feast? Could it be worse
Than when he smiled, and cried, My sons are dead!
And every one looked in his neighbor's face
To see if others were as white as he?
At the first word he spoke I felt the blood
Rush to my heart, and fell into a trance;
And when it past I sat all weak and wild;
Whilst you alone stood up, and with strong words
Checked his unnatural pride; and I could see
The devil was rebuked that lives in him.
Until this hour thus have you ever stood
Between us and your father's moody wrath
Like a protecting presence: your firm mind
Has been our only refuge and defence:
What can have thus subdued it? What can now
Have given you that cold melancholy look,
Succeeding to your unaccustomed fear?

Beatr. What is it that you say? I was just thinking
'T were better not to struggle any more.
Men, like my father, have been dark and bloody,
Yet never—O! before worse comes of it
'T were wise to die: it ends in that at last.

Lucr. Oh, talk not so, dear child! Tell me at once
What did your father do or say to you?
He stayed not after that accursed feast
One moment in your chamber.—Speak to me.

Ber. Oh, sister, sister, prithee, speak to us!

Beatr. (*Speaking very slowly with a forced calmness.*) It was one word, mother, one little word;
One look, one smile. (*Wildly.*) Oh! He has trampled me
Under his feet, and made the blood stream down
My pallid cheeks. And he has given us all
Ditch-water, and the fever-stricken flesh
Of buffaloes, and bade us eat or starve,
And we have eaten. He has made me look
On my beloved Bernardo, when the rust
Of heavy chains has gangrened his sweet limbs,

And I have never yet despaired—but now!
What would I say? (*Recovering herself.*) Ah! No, 't is nothing new.
The sufferings we all share have made me wild:
He only struck and cursed me as he passed;
He said, he looked, he did;—nothing at all
Beyond his wont, yet it disordered me.
Alas! I am forgetful of my duty,
I should preserve my senses for your sake.

Lucr. Nay, Beatrice; have courage, my sweet girl.
If any one despairs it should be I,
Who loved him once, and now must live with him
Till God in pity call for him or me.
For you may, like your sister, find some husband,
And smile, years hence, with children round your knees;
Whilst I, then dead, and all this hideous coil,
Shall be remembered only as a dream.

Beatr. Talk not to me, dear lady, of a husband.
Did you not nurse me when my mother died?
Did you not shield me and that dearest boy?
And had we any other friend but you
In infancy, with gentle words and looks,
To win our father not to murder us?
And shall I now desert you? May the ghost
Of my dead mother plead against my soul,
If I abandon her who filled the place
She left, with more, even, than a mother's love!

Ber. And I am of my sister's mind. Indeed
I would not leave you in this wretchedness,
Even though the Pope should make me free to live
In some blithe place, like others of my age,
With sports, and delicate food, and the fresh air.
Oh, never think that I will leave you, mother!

Lucr. My dear, dear children!

(*Enter Cenci, suddenly.*)

Cenci. What! Beatrice here!
Come hither! (*She shrinks back and covers her face.*) Nay, hide not your face, 't is fair;
Look up! Why, yesternight you dared to look
With disobedient insolence upon me,
Bending a stern and an inquiring brow
On what I meant; whilst I then sought to hide
That which I came to tell you—but in vain.

Beatr. (*Wildly, staggering towards the door.*) Oh, that the earth would gape! Hide me, oh God!

Cen. Then it was I whose inarticulate words
Fell from my lips, and who with tottering steps
Fled from your presence, as you now from mine.
Stay, I command you: from this day and hour
Never again, I think, with fearless eye,
And brow superior, and unaltered cheek,
And that lip made for tenderness or scorn,
Shalt thou strike dumb the meanest of mankind;
Me least of all. Now get thee to thy chamber!
Thou too, loathed image of thy cursed mother,
(*To Bernardo.*) Thy milky, meek face makes me sick with hate!

(*Exeunt Beatrice and Bernardo.*)

(*Aside.*) So much has past between us as must make
Me bold, her fearful. 'T is an awful thing
To touch such mischief as I now conceive:
So men sit shivering on the dewy bank
And try the chill stream with their feet; once in—
How the delighted spirit pants for joy!

Lucr. (*Advancing timidly towards him.*) Oh, husband! Pray forgive poor Beatrice,
She meant not any ill.

Cen. Nor you, perhaps?
Nor that young imp, whom you have taught by rote
Parricide with his alphabet? nor Giacomo
Nor those two most unnatural sons, who stirred
Enmity up against me with the Pope?
Whom in one night merciful God cut off:
Innocent lambs! They thought not any ill.

You were not here conspiring? You said nothing
Of how I might be dungeoned as a madman;
Or be condemned to death for some offence,
And you would be the witnesses?—This failing,
How just it were to hire assassins, or
Put sudden poison in my evening drink?
Or smother me when overcome by wine?
Seeing we had no other judge but God,
And he had sentenced me, and there were none
But you to be the executioners
Of his decree enregistered in heaven?
Oh, no! You said not this?

Lucr. So help me God,
I never thought the things you charge me with!

Cen. If you dare speak that wicked lie again,
I'll kill you. What! it was not by your counsel
That Beatrice disturbed the feast last night?
You did not hope to stir some enemies
Against me, and escape, and laugh to scorn
What every nerve of you now trembles at?
You judged that men were bolder than they are:
Few dare to stand between their grave and me.

Lucr. Look not so dreadfully! By my salvation
I knew not aught that Beatrice designed;
Nor do I think she designed anything
Until she heard you talk of her dead brothers.

Cen. Blaspheming liar! you are damned for this!
But I will take you where you may persuade
The stones you tread on to deliver you:
For men shall there be none but those who dare
All things; not question that which I command.
On Wednesday next I shall set out: you know
That savage rock, the Castle of Petrella:
'T is safely walled, and moated round about:
Its dungeons under-ground, and its thick towers,
Never told tales; though they have heard and seen
What might make dumb things speak.
Why do you linger?
Make speediest preparation for the journey!

(*Exit Lucretia.*)

The all-beholding sun yet shines; I hear
A busy stir of men about the streets;
I see the bright sky through the window panes:
It is a garish, broad and peering day;
Loud, light, suspicious, full of eyes and ears;
And every little corner, nook, and hole,
Is penetrated with the insolent light.
Come, darkness! Yet, what is the day to me?
And wherefore should I wish for night, who do
A deed which shall confound both night and day?
'T is she shall grope through a bewildering mist
Of horror: if there be a sun in heaven,
She shall not dare to look upon its beams,
Nor feel its warmth. Let her then wish for night;
The act I think shall soon extinguish all
For me: I bear a darker deadlier gloom
Than the earth's shade, or interlunar air,
Or constellations quenched in murkiest cloud,
In which I walk secure and unbeheld
Towards my purpose.—Would that it were done!

(*Exit.*)

SCENE 2. *A Chamber in the Vatican. Enter Camillo and Giacomo, in conversation.*

Camillo. There is an obsolete and doubtful law
By which you might obtain a bare provision
Of food and clothing—

Giacomo. Nothing more? Alas!
Bare must be the provision which strict law
Awards, and aged, sullen avarice pays.
Why did my father not apprentice me
To some mechanic trade? I should have then
Been trained in no high-born necessities
Which I could meet not by my daily toil.
The eldest son of a rich nobleman
Is heir to all his incapacities;
He has wide wants, and narrow powers. If you,

Cardinal Camillo, were reduced at once
From thrice-driven beds of down, and delicate food,
An hundred servants, and six palaces,
To that which nature doth indeed require?—

Cam. Nay, there is reason in your plea; 't were hard.

Giac. 'T is hard for a firm man to bear: but I
Have a dear wife, a lady of high birth,
Whose dowry in ill hour I lent my father,
Without a bond of witness to the deed:
And children, who inherit her fine senses,
The fairest creatures in this breathing world;
And she and they reproach me not. Cardinal,
Do you not think the Pope would interpose,
And stretch authority beyond the law?

Cam. Though your peculiar case is hard, I know
The Pope will not divert the course of law.
After that impious feast the other night
I spoke with him, and urged him then to check
Your father's cruel hand; he frowned and said,
"Children are disobedient, and they sting
Their fathers' hearts to madness and despair,
Requiting years of care with contumely.
I pity the Count Cenci from my heart;
His outraged love perhaps awakened hate,
And thus he is exasperated to ill.
In the great war between the old and young,
I, who have white hairs and a tottering body,
Will keep at least blameless neutrality."

(*Enter Orsino.*)

You, my good lord Orsino, heard those words.

Orsino. What words?

Giac. Alas, repeat them not again!
There then is no redress for me; at least
None but that which I may achieve myself,
Since I am driven to the brink. But, say,
My innocent sister and my only brother
Are dying underneath my father's eye.
The memorable torturers of this land,
Galeaz Visconti, Borgia, Ezzelin,
Never inflicted on the meanest slave
What these endure; shall they have no protection?

Cam. Why, if they would petition to the Pope,
I see not how he could refuse it—yet
He holds it of most dangerous example
In aught to weaken the paternal power,
Being, as 't were, the shadow of his own.
I pray you now excuse me. I have business
That will not bear delay.

(*Exit Camillo.*)

Giac. But you, Orsino,
Have the petition: wherefore not present it?

Ors. I have presented it, and backed it with
My earnest prayers, and urgent interest;
It was returned unanswered. I doubt not
But that the strange and execrable deeds
Alleged in it (in truth they might well baffle
Any belief) have turned the Pope's displeasure
Upon the accusers from the criminal:
So I should guess from what Camillo said.

Giac. My friend, that palace-walking devil, Gold,
Has whispered silence to his Holiness:
And we are left, as scorpions ringed with fire,
What should we do but strike ourselves to death?
For he who is our murderous persecutor
Is shielded by a father's holy name,
Or I would—

(*Stops abruptly.*)

Ors. What? Fear not to speak your thought.
Words are but holy as the deeds they cover:
A priest who has forsworn the God he serves;
A judge who makes truth weep at his decree;
A friend who should weave counsel, as I now,
But as the mantle of some selfish guile;
A father who is all a tyrant seems,
Were the profaner for his sacred name.

Giac. Ask me not what I think; the unwilling brain
Feigns often what it would not; and we trust
Imagination with such fantasies
As the tongue dares not fashion into words;

Which have no words, their horror makes them dim
To the mind's eye. My heart denies itself
To think what you demand.

Ors. But a friend's bosom
Is as the inmost cave of our own mind,
Where we sit shut from the wide gaze of day,
And from the all-communicating air.
You look what I suspected.

Giac. Spare me now!
I am as one lost in a midnight wood,
Who dares not ask some harmless passenger
The path across the wilderness, lest he,
As my thoughts are, should be—a murderer.
I know you are my friend, and all I dare
Speak to my soul, that will I trust with thee.
But now my heart is heavy, and would take
Lone counsel from a night of sleepless care.
Pardon me that I say farewell—farewell!
I would that to my own suspected self
I could address a word so full of peace.

Ors. Farewell!—Be your thoughts better or more bold.

(*Exit Giacomo.*)

I had disposed the Cardinal Camillo
To feed his hope with cold encouragement:
It fortunately serves my close designs
That 't is a trick of this same family
To analyze their own and other minds.
Such self-anatomy shall teach the will
Danderous secrets: for it tempts our powers,
Knowing what must be thought, and may be done,
Into the depth of darkest purposes:
So Cenci fell into the pit; even I,
Since Beatrice unveiled me to myself,
And made me shrink from what I cannot shun,
Show a poor figure to my own esteem,
To which I grow half reconciled. I'll do
As little mischief as I can; that thought
Shall fee the accuser conscience.

(*After a pause.*)

Now what harm
If Cenci should be murdered?—Yet, if murdered,
Wherefore by me? And what if I could take
The profit, yet omit the sin and peril
In such an action? Of all earthly things
I fear a man whose blows outspeed his words;
And such is Cenci: and while Cenci lives
His daughter's dowry were a secret grave,
If a priest wins her.—Oh, fair Beatrice!
Would that I loved thee not, or loving thee
Could but despise danger and gold, and all
That frowns between my wish and its effect,
O smiles beyond it! There is no escape:
Her bright form kneels beside me at the altar,
And follows me to the resort of men,
And fills my slumber with tumultuous dreams,
So, when I wake, my blood seems liquid fire;
And if I strike my damp and dizzy head,
My hot palm scorches it: her very name,
But spoken by a stranger, makes my heart
Sicken and pant; and thus unprofitably
I clasp the phantom of unfelt delights
Till weak imagination half possesses
The self-created shadow. Yet much longer
Will I not nurse this life of feverous hours:
From the unravelled hopes of Giacomo
I must work out my own dear purposes.
I see, as from a tower, the end of all:
Her father dead; her brother bound to me
By a dark secret, surer than the grave;
Her mother scared and unexpostulating
From the dread manner of her wish achieved:
And she!—Once more take courage, my faint heart;
What dares a friendless maiden matched with thee?
I have such foresight as assures success:
Some unbeheld divinity doth ever,
When dread events are near, stir up men's minds
To black suggestions; and he prospers best,
Not who becomes the instrument of ill,
But who can flatter the dark spirit, that makes
Its empire and its prey of other hearts,
Till it become his slave—as I will do.

(*Exit.*)

ACT III.

SCENE 1. *An Apartment in the Cenci Palace. Lucretia, to her enter Beatrice.*

Beatrice. (*She enters staggering, and speaks wildly.*) Reach me that handkerchief!—My brain is hurt;
My eyes are full of blood; just wipe them for me—
I see but indistinctly:—
Lucretia. My sweet child,
You have no wound; 't is only a cold dew
That starts from your dear brow—Alas! Alas!
What has befallen?
Beatr. How comes this hair undone?
Its wandering strings must be what blind me so,
And yet I tied it fast.—O, horrible!
The pavement sinks under my feet! The walls
Spin round! I see a woman weeping there,
And standing calm and motionless, whilst I
Slide giddily as the world reels—My God!
The beautiful blue heaven is flecked with blood!
The sunshine on the floor is black! The air
Is changed to vapors such as the dead breathe
In charnel-pits! Pah! I am choked! There creeps
A clinging, black, contaminating mist
About me—'t is substantial, heavy, thick,
I cannot pluck it from me, for it glues
My fingers and my limbs to one another,
And eats into my sinews, and dissolves
My flesh to a pollution, poisoning
The subtle, pure, and inmost spirit of life!
My God! I never knew what the mad felt
Before; for I am mad beyond all doubt!
(*More wildly.*) No, I am dead! These putrefying limbs
Shut round and sepulchre the panting soul,
Which would burst forth into the wandering air!
(*A pause.*) What hideous thought was that I had even now?
'T is gone; and yet its burthen remains here
O'er these dull eyes—upon this weary heart!
O, world! O, life! O, day! O, misery!
Lucr. What ails thee, my poor child? She answers not:
Her spirit apprehends the sense of pain,
But not its cause; suffering has dried away
The source from which it sprung.
Beatr. (*Frantically.*) Like parricide—
Misery has killed its father: yet its father
Never like mine—O, God! What thing am I?
Lucr. My dearest child, what has your father done?
Beatr. (*Doubtfully.*) Who art thou, questioner? I have no father.
(*Aside.*) She is the madhouse nurse who tends on me,
It is a piteous office. (*To Lucretia, in a slow, subdued voice.*) Do you know
I thought I was that wretched Beatrice
Men speak of, whom her father sometimes hales
From hall to hall by the entangled hair;
At others, pens up naked in damp cells
Where scaly reptiles crawl, and starves her there,
Till she will eat strange flesh. This woful story
So did I overact in my sick dreams,
That I imagined—no, it cannot be!
Horrible things have been in this wild world,
Prodigious mixtures, and confusions strange
Of good and ill; and worse have been conceived
Than ever there was found a heart to do.
But never fancy imaged such a deed
As—
(*Pauses, suddenly recollecting herself.*)
Who art thou? Swear to me, ere I die
With fearful expectation, that indeed
Thou art not what thou seemest—Mother!
Lucr. Oh!
My sweet child, know you—
Beatr. Yet speak it not:
For then if this be truth, that other too
Must be a truth, a firm enduring truth,
Linked with each lasting circumstance of life,
Never to change, never to pass away.
Why so it is. This is the Cenci Palace;
Thou art Lucretia; I am Beatrice.
I have talked some wild words, but will no more.
Mother, come near me: from this point of time,
I am—
(*Her voice dies away faintly.*)

Lucr. Alas! What has befallen thee, child?
What has thy father done?
Beatr. What have I done?
Am I not innocent? Is it my crime
That one with white hair, and imperious brow,
Who tortured me from my forgotten years,
As parents only dare, should call himself
My father, yet should be!—Oh, what am I?
What name, what place, what memory shall be mine?
What retrospects, outliving even despair?
Lucr. He is a violent tyrant, surely, child;
We know that death alone can make us free;
His death or ours. But what can he have done
Of deadlier outrage or worse injury?
Thou art unlike thyself; thine eyes shoot forth
A wandering and strange spirit. Speak to me,
Unlock those pallid hands whose fingers twine
With one another.
Beatr. 'T is the restless life
Tortured within them. If I try to speak,
I shall go mad. Ay, something must be done;
What, yet I know not—something which shall make
The thing that I have suffered but a shadow
In the dread lightning which avenges it;
Brief, rapid, irreversible, destroying
The consequence of what it cannot cure.
Some such thing is to be endured or done:
When I know what, I shall be still and calm,
And never any thing will move me more.
But now!—Oh blood, which art my father's blood,
Circling through these contaminated veins,
If thou, poured forth on the polluted earth,
Could wash away the crime, and punishment
By which I suffer—no, that cannot be!
Many might doubt there were a God above
Who sees and permits evil, and so die:
That faith no agony shall obscure in me.
Lucr. It must indeed have been some bitter wrong;
Yet what, I dare not guess. Oh, my lost child,
Hide not in proud impenetrable grief
Thy sufferings from my fear.
Beatr. I hide them not.
What are the words which you would have me speak?
I, who can feign no image in my mind
Of that which has transformed me: I, whose thought
Is like a ghost shrouded and folded up
In its own formless horror: of all words,
That minister to mortal intercourse,
Which wouldst thou hear? For there is none to tell
My misery; if another ever knew
Aught like to it, she died as I will die,
And left it, as I must, without a name.
Death! Death! Our law and our religion call thee
A punishment and a reward.—Oh, which
Have I deserved?
Lucr. The peace of innocence;
Till in your season you be called to heaven.
Whate'er you may have suffered, you have done
No evil. Death must be the punishment
Of crime, or the reward of trampling down
The thorns which God has strewed upon the path
Which leads to immortality.
Beatr. Ay, death—
The punishment of crime. I pray thee, God,
Let me not be bewildered while I judge.
If I must live day after day, and keep
These limbs, the unworthy temple of thy spirit,
As a foul den from which what thou abhorrest
May mock thee, unavenged—it shall not be!
Self-murder? no, that might be no escape,
For thy decree yawns like a Hell between
Our will and it. O! in this mortal world
There is no vindication and no law
Which can adjudge and execute the doom
Of that through which I suffer.

(*Enter Orsino.*)

(*She approaches him solemnly.*) Welcome, friend!
I have to tell you that, since last we met,
I have endured a wrong so great and strange,

That neither life nor death can give me rest.
Ask me not what it is, for there are deeds
Which have no form, sufferings which have no tongue.
Orsino. And what is he who has thus injured you?
Beatr. The man they call my father: a dread name
Ors. It cannot be—
Beatr. What it can be, or not,
Forbear to think. It is, and it has been;
Advise me how it shall not be again.
I thought to die, but a religious awe
Restrains me, and the dread lest death itself
Might be no refuge from the consciousness
Of what is yet unexpiated. Oh, speak!
Ors. Accuse him of the deed, and let the law
Avenge thee.
Beatr. Oh, ice-hearted counsellor!
If I could find a word that might make known
The crime of my destroyer; and that done,
My tongue should, like a knife, tear out the secret
Which cankers my heart's core; ay, lay all bare,
So that my unpolluted fame should be
With vilest gossips a stale mouthed story;
A mock, a bye-word, an astonishment:—
If this were done, which never shall be done,
Think of the offender's gold, his dreaded hate,
And the strange horror of the accuser's tale,
Baffling belief, and overpowering speech;
Scarce whispered, unimaginable, wrapt
In hideous hints—Oh, most assured redress!
Ors. You will endure it then?
Beatr. Endure! Orsino,
It seems your counsel is small profit.
(*Turns from him, and speaks half to herself.*) Ay,
All must be suddenly resolved and done
What is this undistinguishable mist
Of thoughts, which rise, like shadow after shadow,
Darkening each other?
Ors. Should the offender live?
Triumph in his misdeed? and make, by use,
His crime, whate'er it is, dreadful no doubt,
Thine element; until thou mayest become
Utterly lost; subdued even to the hue
Of that which thou permittest?
Beatr. (*To herself.*) Mighty death!
Thou double-visaged shadow! Only judge!
Rightfullest arbiter!
(*She retires absorbed in thought.*)
Lucr. If the lightning
Of God has e'er descended to avenge—
Ors. Blaspheme not! His high Providence commits
Its glory on this earth, and their own wrongs
Into the hands of men; if they neglect
To punish crime—
Lucr. But if one, like this wretch,
Should mock, with gold, opinion, law, and power?
If there be no appeal to that which makes
The guiltiest tremble? If, because our wrongs,
For that they are unnatural, strange, and monstrous,
Exceed all measure of belief? Oh, God!
If, for the very reasons which should make
Redress most swift and sure, our injurer triumphs?
And we, the victims, bear worse punishment
Than that appointed for their torturer?
Ors. Think not
But that there is redress where there is wrong,
So we be bold enough to seize it.
Lucr. How?
If there were any way to make all sure,
I know not—but I think it might be good
To—
Ors. Why, his late outrage to Beatrice;
For it is such, as I but faintly guess,
As makes remorse dishonor, and leaves her
Only one duty, how she may avenge:
You, but one refuge from ills ill endured;
Me, but one counsel—
Lucr. For we cannot hope
That aid, or retribution, or resource,
Will arise thence, where every other one
Might find them with less need.
(*Beatrice advances.*)
Ors. Then—
Beatr. Peace, Orsino!
And, honored Lady, while I speak, I pray
That you put off, as garments overworn,
Forbearance and respect, remorse and fear,

And all the fit restraints of daily life,
Which have been borne from childhood, but which now
Would be a mockery to my holier plea.
As I have said, I have endured a wrong,
Which, though it be expressionless, is such
As asks atonement, both for what is past,
And lest I be reserved, day after day,
To load with crimes an overburthened soul,
And be—what ye can dream not. I have prayed
To God, and I have talked with my own heart,
And have unravelled my entangled will,
And have at length determined what is right.
Art thou my friend, Orsino? False or true?
Pledge thy salvation ere I speak.

Ors. I swear
To dedicate my cunning, and my strength,
My silence, and whatever else is mine,
To thy commands.

Lucr. You think we should devise
His death?

Beatr. And execute what is devised,
And suddenly. We must be brief and bold.

Ors. And yet most cautious.

Lucr. For the jealous laws
Would punish us with death and infamy
For that which it became themselves to do.

Beatr. Be cautious as ye may, but prompt. Orsino,
What are the means?

Ors. I know two dull, fierce outlaws,
Who think man's spirit as a worm's, and they
Would trample out, for any slight caprice,
The meanest or the noblest life. This mood
Is marketable here in Rome. They sell
What we now want.

Lucr. To-morrow, before dawn,
Cenci will take us to that lonely rock,
Petrella, in the Apulian Apennines.
If he arrive there—

Beatr. He must not arrive.

Ors. Will it be dark before you reach the tower?

Lucr. The sun will scarce be set.

Beatr. But I remember
Two miles on this side of the fort, the road
Crosses a deep ravine; 't is rough and narrow,
And winds with short turns down the precipice;
And in its depth there is a mighty rock,
Which has, from unimaginable years,
Sustained itself with terror and with toil
Over a gulph, and with the agony
With which it clings seems slowly coming down;
Even as a wretched soul hour after hour,
Clings to the mass of life; yet clinging, leans;
And leaning, makes more dark the dread abyss
In which it fears to fall: beneath this crag,
Huge as despair, as if in weariness,
The melancholy mountain yawns; below,
You hear but see not an impetuous torrent
Raging among the caverns, and a bridge
Crosses the chasm; and high above there grow,
With intersecting trunks, from crag to crag,
Cedars, and yews, and pines; whose tangled hair
Is matted in one solid roof of shade
By the dark ivy's twine. At noon-day here
'T is twilight, and at sunset blackest night.

Ors. Before you reach that bridge make some excuse
For spurring on your mules, or loitering
Until—

Beatr. What sound is that?

Lucr. Hark! No, it cannot be a servant's step;
It must be Cenci, unexpectedly
Returned—Make some excuse for being here.

Beatr. (*To Orsino as she goes out.*) That step we hear approach must never pass
The bridge of which we spoke.

(*Exeunt Lucretia and Beatrice.*)

Ors. What shall I do?
Cenci must find me here, and I must bear
The imperious inquisition of his looks
As to what brought me hither: let me mask
Mine own in some inane and vacant smile.

(*Enter Giacomo, in a hurried manner.*)

How! Have you ventured hither? Know you then
That Cenci is from home?

Giacomo. I sought him here;
And now must wait till he returns.
Ors. Great God!
Weigh you the danger of this rashness?
Giac. Ay!
Does my destroyer know his danger? We
Are now no more, as once, parent and child,
But man to man; the oppressor to the oppressed;
The slanderer to the slandered; foe to foe.
He has cast Nature off, which was his shield,
And Nature casts him off, who is her shame;
And I spurn both. Is it a father's throat
Which I will shake, and say, I ask not gold;
I ask not happy years; nor memories
Of tranquil childhood; nor home-sheltered love;
Though all these hast thou torn from me, and more;
But only my fair fame; only one hoard
Of peace, which I thought hidden from thy hate,
Under the penury heaped on me by thee;
Or I will—God can understand and pardon,
Why should I speak with man?
Ors. Be calm, dear friend.
Giac. Well, I will calmly tell you what he did.
This old Francesco Cenci, as you know,
Borrowed the dowry of my wife from me,
And then denied the loan; and left me so
In poverty, the which I sought to mend
By holding a poor office in the state.
It had been promised to me, and already
I bought new clothing for my ragged babes,
And my wife smiled; and my heart knew repose;
When Cenci's intercession, as I found,
Conferred this office on a wretch, whom thus
He paid for vilest service. I returned
With this ill news, and we sate sad together
Solacing our despondency with tears
Of such affection and unbroken faith
As temper life's worst bitterness; when he,
As he is wont, came to upbraid and curse,
Mocking our poverty, and telling us
Such was God's scourge for disobedient sons.
And then, that I might strike him dumb with shame,
I spoke of my wife's dowry; but he coined
A brief yet specious tale, how I had wasted
The sum in secret riot; and he saw
My wife was touched, and he went smiling forth.
And when I knew the impression he had made,
And felt my wife insult with silent scorn
My ardent truth, and look averse and cold,
I went forth too: but soon returned again;
Yet not so soon but that my wife had taught
My children her harsh thoughts, and they all cried,
"Give us clothes, father! Give us better food!
What you in one night squander were enough
For months!" I looked, and saw that home was hell;
And to that hell will I return no more
Until mine enemy has rendered up
Atonement, or, as he gave life to me
I will, reversing nature's law—
Ors. Trust me,
The compensation which thou seekest here
Will be denied.
Giac. Then—Are you not my friend?
Did you not hint at the alternative,
Upon the brink of which you see I stand,
The other day when we conversed together?
My wrongs were then less. That word parricide,
Although I am resolved, haunts me like fear.
Ors. It must be fear itself, for the bare word
Is hollow mockery. Mark, how wisest God
Draws to one point the threads of a just doom,
So sanctifying it: what you devise
Is, as it were, accomplished.
Giac. Is he dead?
Ors. His grave is ready. Know that since we met
Cenci has done an outrage to his daughter.
Giac. What outrage?

Ors. That she speaks not, but you may
Conceive such half conjectures as I do,
From her fixed paleness, and the lofty grief
Of her stern brow, bent on the idle air,
And her severe unmodulated voice,
Drowning both tenderness and dread; and last
From this; that whilst her step-mother and I,
Bewildered in our horror, talked together
With obscure hints; both self-misunderstood,
And darkly guessing, stumbling, in our talk,
Over the truth, and yet to its revenge,
She interrupted us, and with a look
Which told before she spoke it, he must die:—

Giac. It is enough. My doubts are well appeased;
There is a higher reason for the act
Than mine; there is a holier judge than me,
A more unblamed avenger. Beatrice,
Who in the gentleness of thy sweet youth
Hast never trodden on a worm, or bruised
A living flower, but thou hast pitied it
With needless tears! Fair sister, thou in whom
Men wondered how such loveliness and wisdom
Did not destroy each other! Is there made
Ravage of thee? O, heart, I ask no more
Justification! Shall I wait, Orsino,
Till he return, and stab him at the door?

Ors. Not so; some accident might interpose
To rescue him from what is now most sure;
And you are unprovided where to fly,
How to excuse or to conceal. Nay, listen:
All is contrived; success is so assured
That—

(*Enter Beatrice.*)

Beatrice. 'T is my brother's voice! You know me not?

Giac. My sister, my lost sister!

Beatr. Lost indeed!
I see Orsino has talked with you, and
That you conjecture things too horrible
To speak, yet far less than the truth. Now, stay not,
He might return: yet kiss me; I shall know
That then thou hast consented to his death.
Farewell, farewell! Let piety to God,
Brotherly love, justice, and clemency,
And all things that make tender hardest hearts,
Make thine hard, brother. Answer not: farewell.

(*Exeunt severally.*)

SCENE II. *A mean Apartment in Giacomo's House. Giacomo alone.*

Giacomo. 'Tis midnight, and Orsino comes not yet. (*Thunder, and the sound of a storm.*)
What! can the everlasting elements
Feel with a worm like man? If so, the shaft
Of mercy-winged lightning would not fall
On stones and trees. My wife and children sleep:
They are now living in unmeaning dreams:
But I must wake, still doubting if that deed
Be just, which was most necessary. O,
Thou unreplenished lamp! whose narrow fire
Is shaken by the wind, and on whose edge
Devouring darkness hovers! Thou small flame,
Which, as a dying pulse rises and falls,
Still flickerest up and down, how very soon,
Did I not feed thee, wouldst thou fail and be
As thou hadst never been! So wastes and sinks
Even now, perhaps, the life that kindled mine:
But that no power can fill with vital oil
That broken lamp of flesh. Ha! 't is the blood
Which fed these veins, that ebbs till all is cold:
It is the form that moulded mine, that sinks
Into the white and yellow spasms of death:
It is the soul by which mine was arrayed
In God's immortal likeness, which now stands
Naked before Heaven's judgment seat!
(*A bell strikes.*) One! Two!
The hours crawl on; and, when my hairs are white,
My son will then perhaps be waiting thus,

Tortured between just hate and vain remorse;
Chiding the tardy messenger of news
Like those which I expect. I almost wish
He be not dead, although my wrongs are great;
Yet—'t is Orsino's step—

(*Enter Orsino.*)

Speak!
Orsino. I am come
To say he has escaped.
Giac. Escaped!
Ors. And safe
Within Petrella. He past by the spot
Appointed for the deed an hour too soon.
Giac. Are we the fools of such contingencies?
And do we waste in blind misgivings thus
The hours when we should act? Then wind and thunder,
Which seemed to howl his knell, is the loud laughter
With which Heaven mocks our weakness! I henceforth
Will ne'er repent of aught, designed or done,
But my repentance.
Ors. See, the lamp is out.
Giac. If no remorse is ours when the dim air
Has drank this innocent flame, why should we quail
When Cenci's life, that light by which ill spirits
See the worst deeds they prompt, shall sink forever?
No, I am hardened.
Ors. Why, what need of this?
Who feared the pale intrusion of remorse
In a just deed? Altho' our first plan failed,
Doubt not but he will soon be laid to rest.
But light the lamp; let us not talk i' the dark.
Giac. (*lighting the lamp*). And yet, once quenched, I cannot thus relume
My father's life: do you not think his ghost
Might plead that argument with God?
Ors. Once gone,
You cannot now recall your sister's peace;
Your own extinguished years of youth and hope;
Nor your wife's bitter words; nor all the taunts
Which, from the prosperous, weak misfortune takes;
Nor your dead mother; nor—
Giac. O, speak no more!
I am resolved, although this very hand
Must quench the life that animated it.
Ors. There is no need of that. Listen; you know,
Olimpio, the castellan of Petrella
In old Colonna's time; him whom your father
Degraded from his post? And Marzio,
That desperate wretch, whom he deprived last year
Of a reward of blood, well earned and due?
Giac. I knew Olimpio; and they say he hated
Old Cenci so, that in his silent rage
His lips grew white only to see him pass.
Of Marzio I know nothing.
Ors. Marzio's hate
Matches Olimpio's. I have sent these men,
But in your name, and as at your request,
To talk with Beatrice and Lucretia.
Giac. Only to talk?
Ors. The moments which even now
Pass onward to to-morrow's midnight hour
May memorize their flight with death: ere then
They must have talked, and may perhaps have done,
And made an end—
Giac. Listen! What sound is that?
Ors. The house-dog moans, and the beams crack: nought else.
Giac. It is my wife complaining in her sleep:
I doubt not she is saying bitter things
Of me; and all my children round her dreaming
That I deny them sustenance.
Ors. Whilst he
Who truly took it from them, and who fills
Their hungry rest with bitterness, now sleeps
Lapped in bad pleasures, and triumphantly
Mocks thee in visions of successful hate
Too like the truth of day.
Giac. If e'er he wakes
Again, I will not trust to hireling hands—

Ors. Why, that were well. I must be gone; good night!
When next we meet may all be done—
Giac. And all
Forgotten—Oh, that I had never been!
(*Exeunt.*)

ACT IV.

SCENE 1. *An Apartment in the Castle of Petrella. Enter Cenci.*

Cenci. She comes not; yet I left her even now
Vanquished and faint. She knows the penalty
Of her delay: yet what if threats are vain?
Am I not now within Petrella's moat?
Or fear I still the eyes and ears of Rome?
Might I not drag her by the golden hair?
Stamp on her? keep her sleepless till her brain
Be overworn? tame her with chains and famine?
Less would suffice. Yet so to leave undone
What I most seek! No, 't is her stubborn will,
Which, by its own consent, shall stoop as low
As that which drags it down.

(*Enter Lucretia.*)

Thou loathed wretch!
Hide thee from my abhorrence; fly, begone!
Yet stay! Bid Beatrice come hither.
Lucretia. Oh,
Husband! I pray, for thine own wretched sake,
Heed what thou dost. A man who walks like thee
Through crimes, and through the danger of his crimes,
Each hour may stumble o'er a sudden grave.
And thou art old; thy hairs are hoary grey;
As thou wouldst save thyself from death and hell,
Pity thy daughter; give her to some friend
In marriage: so that she may tempt thee not
To hatred, or worse thoughts, if worse there be.
Cen. What! like her sister who has found a home
To mock my hate from with prosperity?
Strange ruin shall destroy both her and thee
And all that yet remain. My death may be
Rapid, her destiny outspeeds it. Go,
Bid her come hither, and before my mood
Be changed, lest I should drag her by the hair.
Lucr. She sent me to thee, husband. At thy presence
She fell, as thou dost know, into a trance;
And in that trance she heard a voice which said,
"Cenci must die! Let him confess himself!
"Even now the accusing angel waits to hear
"If God, to punish his enormous crimes,
"Harden his dying heart!"
Cen. Why—such things are:
No doubt divine revealings may be made.
'T is plain I have been favored from above,
For when I cursed my sons they died—Ay—so—
As to the right or wrong that 's talk—repentance—
Repentance is an easy moment's work,
And more depends on God than me. Well—well—
I must give up the greater point, which was
To poison and corrupt her soul.
(*A pause; Lucretia approaches anxiously, and then shrinks back as he speaks.*)
One, two;
Ay—Rocco and Cristofano my curse
Strangled: and Giacomo, I think, will find
Life a worse Hell than that beyond the grave:
Beatrice shall, if there be skill in hate,
Die in despair, blaspheming: to Bernardo,
He is so innocent, I will bequeath
The memory of these deeds, and make his youth
The sepulchre of hope, where evil thoughts
Shall grow like weeds on a neglected tomb.
When all is done, out in the wide Campagna
I will pile up my silver and my gold;
My costly robes, paintings, and tapestries;

My parchments and all records of my wealth;
And make a bonfire in my joy, and leave
Of my possessions nothing but my name;
Which shall be an inheritance to strip
Its wearer bare as infamy. That done,
My soul, which is a scourge, will I resign
Into the hands of him who wielded it;
Be it for its own punishment or theirs,
He will not ask it of me till the lash
Be broken in its last and deepest wound;
Until its hate be all inflicted. Yet,
Lest death outspeed my purpose, let me make
Short work and sure— (*Going.*)

Lucr. (*stops him*). Oh, stay! It was a feint:
She had no vision, and she heard no voice.
I said it but to awe thee.

Cen. That is well.
Vile palterer with the sacred truth of God,
Be thy soul choked with that blaspheming lie!
For Beatrice, worse terrors are in store,
To bend her to my will.

Lucr. Oh, to what will?
What cruel sufferings, more than she has known,
Canst thou inflict?

Cen. Andrea! Go call my daughter,
And if she comes not tell her that I come.
What sufferings? I will drag her, step by step,
Through infamies unheard of among men:
She shall stand shelterless in the broad noon
Of public scorn, for acts blazoned abroad,
One among which shall be—What? Canst thou guess?
She shall become (for what she most abhors
Shall have a fascination to entrap
Her loathing will) to her own conscious self
All she appears to others; and when dead,
As she shall die unshrived and unforgiven,
A rebel to her father and her God.
Her corpse shall be abandoned to the hounds;
Her name shall be the terror of the earth;
Her spirit shall approach the throne of God
Plague-spotted with my curses. I will make
Body and soul a monstrous lump of ruin.

(*Enter Andrea.*)

Andrea. The lady Beatrice—

Cen. Speak, pale slave! What
Said she?

Andr. My Lord, 't was what she looked; she said:
"Go tell my father that I see the gulf
"Of Hell between us two, which he may pass,
"I will not."

(*Exit Andrea.*)

Cen. Go thou quick, Lucretia,
Tell her to come; yet let her understand
Her coming is consent; and say, moreover,
That if she come not I will curse her.

(*Exit Lucretia.*)

Ha!
With what but with a father's curse doth God
Panic-strike armed victory, and make pale
Cities in their prosperity? The world's Father
Must grant a parent's prayer against his child,
Be he who asks even what men call me.
Will not the deaths of her rebellious brothers
Awe her before I speak? for I on them
Did imprecate quick ruin, and it came.

(*Enter Lucretia.*)

Well; what? Speak, wretch!

Lucr. She said, "I cannot come;
"Go tell my father that I see a torrent
"Of his own blood raging between us."

Cen. (*kneeling*) God!
Hear me! If this most specious mass of flesh,
Which thou hast made my daughter; this my blood,
This particle of my divided being;
Or rather, this my bane and my disease,
Whose sight infects and poisons me; this devil,
Which sprung from me as from a hell, was meant
To aught good use; if her bright loveliness
Was kindled to illumine this dark world;
If, nursed by thy selectest dew of love

Such virtues blossom in her as should make
The peace of life, I pray thee, for my sake,
As thou the common God and Father art
Of her, and me, and all; reverse that doom!
Earth, in the name of God, let her food be
Poison, until she be encrusted round
With leprous stains! Heaven, rain upon her head
The blistering drops of the Maremma's dew,
Till she be speckled like a toad; parch up
Those love-enkindled lips, warp those fine limbs
To loathed lameness! All-beholding sun,
Strike in thine envy those life-darting eyes
With thine own blinding beams!

Lucr. Peace! Peace!
For thine own sake unsay those dreadful words.
When high God grants, he punishes such prayers.

Cen. (*leaping up, and throwing his right hand towards Heaven*). He does his will, I mine! This in addition,
That if she have a child —

Lucr. Horrible thought!

Cen. That if she ever have a child; and thou,
Quick Nature! I adjure thee by thy God,
That thou be fruitful in her, and encrease
And multiply, fulfilling his command,
And my deep imprecation! May it be
A hideous likeness of herself; that, as
From a distorting mirror, she may see
Her image mixed with what she most abhors,
Smiling upon her from her nursing breast.
And that the child may from its infancy
Grow, day by day, more wicked and deformed,
Turning her mother's love to misery:
And that both she and it may live, until
It shall repay her care and pain with hate,
Or what may else be more unnatural.
So he may hunt her through the clamorous scoffs
Of the loud world to a dishonored grave.
Shall I revoke this curse? Go, bid her come,
Before my words are chronicled in heaven.

(*Exit Lucretia.*)

I do not feel as if I were a man,
But like a fiend appointed to chastise
The offences of some unremembered world.
My blood is running up and down my veins;
A fearful pleasure makes it prick and tingle:
I feel a giddy sickness of strange awe;
My heart is beating with an expectation
Of horrid joy.

(*Enter Lucretia.*)

What? Speak!

Lucr. She bids thee curse;
And if thy curses, as they cannot do,
Could kill her soul —

Cen. She would not come. 'T is well,
I can do both: first take what I demand,
And then extort concession. To thy chamber!
Fly ere I spurn thee: and beware this night
That thou cross not my footsteps. It were safer
To come between the tiger and his prey.

(*Exit Lucretia.*)

It must be late; mine eyes grow weary dim
With unaccustomed heaviness of sleep.
Conscience! Oh, thou most insolent of lies!
They say that sleep, that healing dew of heaven,
Steeps not in balm the foldings of the brain
Which thinks thee an impostor. I will go,
First to belie thee with an hour of rest,
Which will be deep and calm, I feel: and then—
O, multitudinous Hell, the fiends will shake
Thine arches with the laughter of their joy!
There shall be lamentation heard in Heaven
As o'er an angel fallen; and upon Earth
All good shall droop and sicken, and ill things
Shall, with a spirit of unnatural life,
Stir and be quickened; even as I am now.

(***Exit.***)

SCENE 2. *Before the Castle of Petrella. Enter Beatrice and Lucretia above on the ramparts.*

Beatrice. They come not yet.
Lucretia. 'T is scarce midnight.
Beatr. How slow
Behind the course of thought, even sick with speed,
Lags leaden-footed time!
Lucr. The minutes pass—
If he should wake before the deed is done?
Beatr. O, mother! he must never wake again.
What thou hast said persuades me that our act
Will but dislodge a spirit of deep hell
Out of a human form.
Lucr. 'T is true he spoke
Of death and judgment with strange confidence
For one so wicked; as a man believing
In God, yet recking not of good or ill.
And yet to die without confession!
Beatr. Oh!
Believe that Heaven is merciful and just,
And will not add our dread necessity
To the amount of his offences.

(*Enter Olimpio and Marzio below.*)

Lucr. See,
They come.
Beatr. All mortal things must hasten thus
To their dark end. Let us go down.
(*Exeunt Lucretia and Beatrice from above.*)
Olimpio. How feel you to this work?
Marzio. As one who thinks
A thousand crowns excellent market price
For an old murderer's life. Your cheeks are pale.
Olim. It is the white reflection of your own,
Which you call pale.
Mar. Is that their natural hue?
Olim. Or 't is my hate, and the deferred desire
To wreak it, which extinguishes their blood.
Mar. You are inclined then to this business?
Olim. Ay,
If one should bribe me with a thousand crowns
To kill a serpent which had stung my child,
I could not be more willing.

(*Enter Beatrice and Lucretia below.*)

Noble ladies!
Beatr. Are ye resolved?
Olim. Is he asleep?
Mar. Is all
Quiet?
Lucr. I mixed an opiate with his drink:
He sleeps so soundly—
Beatr. That his death will be
But as a change of sin-chastising dreams,
A dark continuance of the Hell within him,
Which God extinguish! But ye are resolved?
Ye know it is a high and holy deed?
Olim. We are resolved.
Mar. As to the how this act
Be warranted, it rests with you.
Beatr. Well, follow!
Olim. Hush! Hark! What noise is that?
Mar. Ha! some one comes!
Beatr. Ye conscience-stricken cravens, rock to rest
Your baby hearts. It is the iron gate,
Which ye left open, swinging to the wind,
That enters whistling as in scorn. Come, follow!
And be your steps like mine, light, quick, and bold.
(*Exeunt.*)

SCENE 3. *An Apartment in the Castle. Enter Beatrice and Lucretia.*

Lucretia. They are about it now.
Beatrice. Nay, it is done.
Lucr. I have not heard him groan.
Beatr. He will not groan.
Lucr. What sound is that?
Beatr. List! 't is the tread of feet
About his bed.
Lucr. My God!
If he be now a cold, stiff corpse.
Beatr. O, fear not
What may be done, but what is left undone:
The act seals all.
(*Enter Olimpio and Marzio.*)
Is it accomplished?
Marzio. What?
Olimpio. Did you not call?
Beatr. When?
Olim. Now.
Beatr. I ask if all is over?
Olim. We dare not kill an old and sleeping man;
His thin grey hair, his stern and reverent brow,

His veined hands crossed on his heaving breast,
And the calm innocent sleep in which he lay,
Quelled me. Indeed, indeed, I cannot do it.

Mar. But I was bolder; for I chid Olimpio,
And bade him bear his wrongs to his own grave
And leave me the reward. And now my knife
Touched the loose wrinkled throat, when the old man
Stirred in his sleep, and said, "God! hear, O, hear
"A father's curse! What, art thou not our father?"
And then he laughed. I knew it was the ghost
Of my dead father speaking through his lips,
And could not kill him.

Beatr. Miserable slaves!
Where, if ye dare not kill a sleeping man,
Found ye the boldness to return to me
With such a deed undone? Base palterers!
Cowards and traitors! Why, the very conscience
Which ye would sell for gold and for revenge
Is an equivocation: it sleeps over
A thousand daily acts disgracing men;
And when a deed where mercy insults heaven—
Why do I talk? (*Snatching a dagger from one of them and raising it.*)
Hadst thou a tongue to say,
She murdered her own father, I must do it!
But never dream ye shall outlive him long!

Olim. Stop, for God's sake!

Mar. I will go back and kill him.

Olim. Give me the weapon, we must do thy will.

Beatr. Take it! Depart! Return!
(*Exeunt Olimpio and Marzio.*)
How pale thou art!
We do but that which 't were a deadly crime
To leave undone.

Lucr. Would it were done!

Beatr. Even whilst
That doubt is passing through your mind, the world
Is conscious of a change. Darkness and hell
Have swallowed up the vapor they sent forth
To blacken the sweet light of life. My breath
Comes, methinks, lighter, and the jellied blood
Runs freely through my veins. Hark!
(*Enter Olimpio and Marzio.*)
He is—

Olim. Dead!

Mar. We strangled him that there might be no blood;
And then we threw his heavy corpse i' the garden
Under the balcony; 't will seem it fell.

Beatr. (*giving them a bag of coin*). Here, take this gold, and hasten to your homes.
And, Marzio, because thou wast only awed
By that which made me tremble, wear thou this!
(*Clothes him in a rich mantle.*)
It was the mantle which my grandfather
Wore in his high prosperity, and men
Envied his state: so may they envy thine.
Thou wert a weapon in the hand of God
To a just use. Live long and thrive! And, mark,
If thou hast crimes, repent: this deed is none.
(*A horn is sounded.*)

Lucr. Hark! 't is the castle horn; my God! it sounds
Like the last trump.

Beatr. Some tedious guest is coming.

Lucr. The drawbridge is let down; there is a tramp
Of horses in the court; fly, hide yourselves!
(*Exeunt Olimpio and Marzio.*)

Beatr. Let us retire to counterfeit deep rest;
I scarcely need to counterfeit it now:
The spirit which doth reign within these limbs
Seems strangely undisturbed. I could even sleep
Fearless and calm: all ill is surely past.
(*Exeunt.*)

SCENE 4. *Another Apartment in the Castle. Enter on one side the Legate Savella, introduced by a Servant, and on the other Lucretia and Bernardo.*

Savella. Lady, my duty to his Holiness

Be my excuse that thus unseasonably
I break upon your rest. I must speak with
Count Cenci; doth he sleep?

Lucretia (*in a hurried and confused manner*). I think he sleeps;
Yet, wake him not, I pray, spare me awhile,
He is a wicked and a wrathful man;
Should he be roused out of his sleep to-night,
Which is, I know, a hell of angry dreams,
It were not well; indeed it were not well.
Wait till day break — (*aside*) O, I am deadly sick!

Sav. I grieve thus to distress you, but the Count
Must answer charges of the gravest import,
And suddenly; such my commission is.

Lucr. (*with increased agitation.*) I dare not rouse him: I know none who dare:
'T were perilous;—you might as safely waken
A serpent; or a corpse in which some fiend
Were laid to sleep.

Sav. Lady, my moments here
Are counted. I must rouse him from his sleep,
Since none else dare.

Lucr. (*aside*). O, terror! O, despair!
(*To Bernardo.*) Bernardo, conduct you the Lord Legate to
Your father's chamber.

(*Exeunt Savella and Bernardo.*)

Enter Beatrice.

Beatrice. 'T is a messenger
Come to arrest the culprit who now stands
Before the throne of unappealable God.
Both Earth and Heaven, consenting arbiters,
Acquit our deed.

Lucr. Oh, agony of fear!
Would that he yet might live! Even now I heard
The Legate's followers whisper, as they passed,
They had a warrant for his instant death.
All was prepared by unforbidden means,
Which we must pay so dearly, having done.
Even now they search the tower, and find the body;
Now they suspect the truth; now they consult
Before they come to tax us with the fact:
O, horrible, 't is all discovered!

Beatr. Mother,
What is done wisely, is done well. Be bold
As thou art just. 'T is like a truant child,
To fear that others know what thou hast done,
Even from thine own strong consciousness, and thus
Write on unsteady eyes and altered cheeks
All thou wouldst hide. Be faithful to thyself,
And fear no other witness but thy fear.
For if, as cannot be, some circumstance
Should rise in accusation, we can blind
Suspicion with such cheap astonishment,
Or overbear it with such guiltless pride,
As murderers cannot feign. The deed is done,
And what may follow now regards not me.
I am as universal as the light;
Free as the earth-surrounding air; as firm
As the world's centre. Consequence, to me,
Is as the wind which strikes the solid rock
But shakes it not.

(*A cry within and tumult.*)

Voices. Murder! Murder! Murder!

(*Enter Bernardo and Savella.*)

Sav. (*to his followers*). Go, search the castle round; sound the alarm;
Look to the gates that none escape!

Beatr. What now?

Bernardo. I know not what to say: my father 's dead!

Beatr. How? dead? he only sleeps: you mistake, brother.
His sleep is very calm, very like death;
'T is wonderful how well a tyrant sleeps.
He is not dead?

Ber. Dead! murdered!

Lucr. (*with extreme agitation*). Oh, no, no,
He is not murdered, though he may be dead;
I have alone the keys of those apartments.

Sav. Ha! Is it so?

Beatr. My Lord, I pray excuse us;
We will retire; my mother is not well:
She seems quite overcome with this strange horror.

(*Exeunt Lucretia and Beatrice.*)

Sav. Can you suspect who may have murdered him?

Ber. I know not what to think.

Sav. Can you name any
Who had an interest in his death?

Ber. Alas!
I can name none who had not, and those most
Who most lament that such a deed is done;
My mother, and my sister, and myself.

Sav. 'T is strange! There were clear marks of violence.
I found the old man's body in the moonlight
Hanging beneath the window of his chamber,
Among the branches of a pine: he could not
Have fallen there, for all his limbs lay heaped
And effortless; 't is true there was no blood.
Favor me, Sir (it much imports your house
That all should be made clear) to tell the ladies
That I request their presence.

(*Exit Bernardo.*)

(*Enter Guards, bringing in Marzio.*)

Guard. We have one.

Officer. My Lord, we found this ruffian and another
Lurking among the rocks; there is no doubt
But that they are the murderers of Count Cenci:
Each had a bag of coin; this fellow wore
A gold-inwoven robe, which, shining bright
Under the dark rocks to the glimmering moon,
Betrayed them to our notice: the other fell
Desperately fighting.

Sav. What does he confess?

Officer. He keeps firm silence; but these lines found on him
May speak.

Sav. Their language is at least sincere.

(*Reads.*)

"To the Lady Beatrice.

"That the atonement of what my nature sickens to conjecture may soon arrive, I send thee, at thy brother's desire, those who will speak and do more than I dare write—

"Thy devoted servant,

"Orsino."

(*Enter Lucretia, Beatrice, and Bernardo.*)

Knowest thou this writing, Lady?

Beatr. No.

Sav. Nor thou?

Lucr. (*Her conduct throughout the scene is marked by extreme agitation.*) Where was it found? What is it? It should be
Orsino's hand! It speaks of that strange horror
Which never yet found utterance, but which made
Between that hapless child and her dead father
A gulf of obscure hatred.

Sav. Is it so?
Is it true, Lady, that thy father did
Such outrages as to awaken in thee
Unfilial hate?

Beatr. Not hate, 't was more than hate:
This is most true, yet wherefore question me?

Sav. There is a deed demanding question done;
Thou hast a secret which will answer not.

Beatr. What sayest? My Lord, your words are bold and rash.

Sav. I do arrest all present in the name
Of the Pope's Holiness. You must to Rome.

Lucr. O, not to Rome! Indeed we are not guilty.

Beatr. Guilty! Who dares talk of guilt? My Lord,
I am more innocent of parricide
Than is a child born fatherless. Dear mother,
Your gentleness and patience are no shield
For this keen-judging world, this two-edged lie,
Which seems, but is not. What! will human laws,
Rather will ye who are their ministers,
Bar all access to retribution first,
And then, when heaven doth interpose to do
What ye neglect, arming familiar things
To the redress of an unwonted crime,
Make ye the victims who demanded it
Culprits? 'T is ye are culprits! That poor wretch
Who stands so pale, and trembling, and amazed,
If it be true he murdered Cenci, was

A sword in the right hand of justest God.
Wherefore should I have wielded it? Unless
The crimes which mortal tongue dare never name
God therefore scruples to avenge.

Sav. You own
That you desired his death?

Beatr. It would have been
A crime no less than his, if, for one moment,
That fierce desire had faded in my heart.
'T is true I did believe, and hope, and pray,
Ay, I even knew—for God is wise and just,
That some strange sudden death hung over him.
'T is true that this did happen, and most true
There was no other rest for me on earth,
No other hope in Heaven: now what of this?

Sav. Strange thoughts beget strange deeds; and here are both:
I judge thee not.

Beatr. And yet, if you arrest me,
You are the judge and executioner
Of that which is the life of life: the breath
Of accusation kills an innocent name,
And leaves for lame acquittal the poor life
Which is a mask without it. 'T is most false
That I am guilty of foul parricide;
Although I must rejoice, for justest cause,
That other hands have sent my father's soul
To ask the mercy he denied to me.
Now leave us free: stain not a noble house
With vague surmises of rejected crime;
Add to our sufferings and your own neglect
No heavier sum; let them have been enough;
Leave us the wreck we have.

Sav. I dare not, Lady.
I pray that you prepare yourselves for Rome:
There the Pope's further pleasure will be known.

Lucr. O, not to Rome! O, take us not to Rome!

Beatr. Why not to Rome, dear mother? There as here
Our innocence is as an armed heel
To trample accusation. God is there,
As here, and with his shadow ever clothes
The innocent, the injured, and the weak;
And such are we. Cheer up, dear Lady, lean
On me; collect your wandering thoughts. My Lord,
As soon as you have taken some refreshment,
And had all such examinations made
Upon the spot, as may be necessary
To the full understanding of this matter,
We shall be ready. Mother, will you come?

Lucr. Ha! they will bind us to the rack, and wrest
Self-accusation from our agony!
Will Giacomo be there? Orsino? Marzio?
All present; all confronted; all demanding
Each from the other's countenance the thing
Which is in every heart! O, misery!
(*She faints, and is borne out.*)

Sav. She faints: an ill appearance this.

Beatr. My Lord,
She knows not yet the uses of the world.
She fears that power is as a beast which grasps
And loosens not; a snake, whose look transmutes
All things to guilt which is its nutriment;
She cannot know how well the supine slaves
Of blind authority read the truth of things
When written on a brow of guilelessness:
She sees not yet triumphant Innocence
Stand at the judgment-seat of mortal man,
A judge and an accuser of the wrong
Which drags it there. Prepare yourself, my Lord;
Our suite will join yours in the court below.

(*Exeunt.*)

ACT V.

SCENE 1. *An Apartment in Orsino's Palace. Enter Orsino and Giacomo.*

Giacomo. Do evil deeds thus quickly come to end?
O, that the vain remorse which must chastise
Crimes done, had but as loud a voice to warn

As its keen sting is mortal to avenge!
O, that the hour when present had cast off
The mantle of its mystery, and shewn
The ghastly form with which it now returns
When its scared game is roused, cheering the hounds
Of conscience to their prey! Alas! Alas!
It was a wicked thought, a piteous deed,
To kill an old and hoary-headed father.

Orsino. It has turned out unluckily, in truth.

Giac. To violate the sacred doors of sleep;
To cheat kind nature of the placid death
Which she prepares for over-wearied age;
To drag from Heaven an unrepentant soul,
Which might have quenched in reconciling prayers
A life of burning crimes—

Ors. You cannot say
I urged you to the deed.

Giac. O, had I never
Found in thy smooth and ready countenance
The mirror of my darkest thoughts; hadst thou
Never with hints and questions made me look
Upon the monster of my thought, until
It grew familiar to desire—

Ors. 'T is thus
Men cast the blame of their unprosperous acts
Upon the abettors of their own resolve;
Or any thing but their weak, guilty selves.
And yet, confess the truth, it is the peril
In which you stand that gives you this pale sickness
Of penitence; confess 't is fear disguised
From its own shame that takes the mantle now
Of thin remorse. What if we yet were safe?

Giac. How can that be? Already Beatrice,
Lucretia, and the murderer, are in prison.
I doubt not officers are, whilst we speak,
Sent to arrest us.

Ors. I have all prepared
For instant flight. We can escape even now,
So we take fleet occasion by the hair.

Giac. Rather expire in tortures, as I may.
What! will you cast by self-accusing flight
Assured conviction upon Beatrice?
She, who alone in this unnatural work,
Stands like God's angel ministered upon
By fiends; avenging such a nameless wrong
As turns black parricide to piety;
Whilst we for basest ends—I fear, Orsino,
While I consider all your words and looks,
Comparing them with your proposal now,
That you must be a villain. For what end
Could you engage in such a perilous crime,
Training me on with hints, and signs, and smiles,
Even to this gulf? Thou art no liar? No,
Thou art a lie! Traitor and murderer!
Coward and slave! But, no, defend thyself;
(*Drawing.*) Let the sword speak what the indignant tongue
Disdains to brand thee with.

Ors. Put up your weapon.
Is it the desperation of your fear
Makes you thus rash and sudden with a friend,
Now ruined for your sake? If honest anger
Have moved you, know, that what I just proposed
Was but to try you. As for me, I think
Thankless affection led me to this point,
From which, if my firm temper could repent,
I cannot now recede. Even whilst we speak
The ministers of justice wait below:
They grant me these brief moments. Now if you
Have any words of melancholy comfort
To speak to your pale wife, 't were best to pass
Out at the postern, and avoid them so.

Giac. O, generous friend! how canst thou pardon me?
Would that my life could purchase thine!

Ors. That wish
Now comes a day too late. Haste; fare thee well!
Hear'st thou not steps along the corridor?

(*Exit Giacomo.*)

I'm sorry for it; but the guards are waiting
At his own gate, and such was my contrivance

That I might rid me both of him and them.
I thought to act a solemn comedy
Upon the painted scene of this new world,
And to attain my own peculiar ends
By some such plot of mingled good and ill
As others weave; but there arose a Power
Which grasped and snapped the threads of my device,
And turned it to a net of ruin—Ha!
(*A shout is heard.*)
Is that my name I hear proclaimed abroad?
But I will pass, wrapt in a vile disguise;
Rags on my back, and a false innocence
Upon my face, through the misdeeming crowd
Which judges by what seems. 'T is easy then
For a new name and for a country new,
And a new life, fashioned on old desires,
To change the honors of abandoned Rome.
And these must be the masks of that within,
Which must remain unaltered. Oh, I fear
That what is past will never let me rest!
Why, when none else is conscious but myself
Of my misdeeds, should my own heart's contempt
Trouble me? Have I not the power to fly
My own reproaches? Shall I be the slave
Of—what? A word? which those of this false world
Employ against each other, not themselves;
As men wear daggers not for self-offence.
But if I am mistaken, where shall I
Find the disguise to hide me from myself,
As now I skulk from every other eye?
(*Exit.*)

SCENE 2. *A Hall of Justice. Camillo, Judges, &c., are discovered seated. Marzio is led in.*

First Judge. Accused, do you persist in your denial?
I ask you, are you innocent, or guilty?
I demand who were the participators
In your offence? Speak truth and the whole truth.

Marzio. My God! I did not kill him; I know nothing;
Olimpio sold the robe to me from which
You would infer my guilt.
Second Judge. Away with him!
First Judge. Dare you, with lips yet white from the rack's kiss,
Speak false? Is it so soft a questioner
That you would bandy lover's talk with it
Till it wind out your life and soul? Away!
Mar. Spare me! O, spare! I will confess.
First Judge. Then speak.
Mar. I strangled him in his sleep.
First Judge. Who urged you to it?
Mar. His own son Giacomo, and the young prelate
Orsino sent me to Petrella; there
The ladies Beatrice and Lucretia
Tempted me with a thousand crowns, and I
And my companion forthwith murdered him.
Now let me die.
First Judge. This sounds as bad as truth.
Guards, there, lead forth the prisoners.

(*Enter Lucretia, Beatrice, and Giacomo, guarded.*)

Look upon this man;
When did you see him last?
Beatrice. We never saw him.
Mar. You know me too well, Lady Beatrice.
Beatr. I know thee! How? where? when?
Mar. You know 't was I
Whom you did urge with menaces and bribes
To kill your father. When the thing was done
You clothed me in a robe of woven gold
And bade me thrive: how I have thriven, you see.
You, my Lord Giacomo, Lady Lucretia,
You know that what I speak is true.
(*Beatrice advances towards him; he covers his face, and shrinks back.*)
O, dart
The terrible resentment of those eyes
On the dead earth! Turn them away from me!
They wound: 't was torture forced the truth. My Lords,
Having said this, let me be led to death.
Beatr. Poor wretch, I pity thee: yet stay awhile.

Camillo. Guards, lead him not away.
Beatr. Cardinal Camillo,
You have a good repute for gentleness
And wisdom: can it be that you sit here
To countenance a wicked farce like this?
When some obscure and trembling slave is dragged
From sufferings which might shake the sternest heart,
And bade to answer, not as he believes,
But as those may suspect or do desire,
Whose questions thence suggest their own reply;
And that in peril of such hideous torments
As merciful God spares even the damned. Speak now
The thing you surely know, which is, that you
If your fine frame were stretched upon that wheel,
And you were told: "Confess that you did poison
Your little nephew; that fair blue-eyed child
Who was the loadstar of your life:"—and though
All see, since his most swift and piteous death,
That day and night, and heaven and earth, and time,
And all the things hoped for or done therein
Are changed to you, through your exceeding grief,
Yet you would say, "I confess anything:"
And beg from your tormentors, like that slave,
The refuge of dishonorable death.
I pray thee, Cardinal, that thou assert
My innocence.
Cam. (*Much moved.*) What shall we think, my Lords?
Shame on these tears! I thought the heart was frozen
Which is their fountain. I would pledge my soul
That she is guiltless.
Judge. Yet she must be tortured.
Cam. I would as soon have tortured mine own nephew:
(If he now lived he would be just her age;
His hair, too, was her color, and his eyes
Like hers in shape, but blue and not so deep)
As that most perfect image of God's love
That ever came sorrowing upon the earth.
She is as pure as speechless infancy!
Judge. Well, be her purity on your head, my Lord,
If you forbid the rack. His Holiness
Enjoined us to pursue this monstrous crime
By the severest forms of law; nay, even
To stretch a point against the criminals.
The prisoners stand accused of parricide
Upon such evidence as justifies
Torture.
Beatr. What evidence? This man's?
Judge. Even so.
Beatr. (*To Marzio.*) Come near. And who art thou thus chosen forth
Out of the multitude of living men,
To kill the innocent?
Mar. I am Marzio,
Thy father's vassal.
Beatr. Fix thine eyes on mine;
Answer to what I ask. (*Turning to the Judges.*) I prithee mark
His countenance: unlike bold calumny
Which sometimes dares not speak the thing it looks,
He dares not look the thing he speaks, but bends
His gaze on the blind earth. (*To Marzio.*) What! wilt thou say
That I did murder my own father?
Mar. Oh!
Spare me! My brain swims round—I cannot speak—
It was that horrid torture forced the truth.
Take me away! Let her not look on me!
I am a guilty, miserable wretch;
I have said all I know; now, let me die!
Beatr. My Lords, if by my nature I had been
So stern, as to have planned the crime alleged,
Which your suspicions dictate to this slave,
And the rack makes him utter, do you think
I should have left this two-edged instrument
Of my misdeed; this man, this bloody knife
With my own name engraven on the heft
Lying unsheathed amid a world of foes,
For my own death? That with such horrible need
For deepest silence, I should have neglected
So trivial a precaution, as the making
His tomb the keeper of a secret written

On a thief's memory? What is his poor life?
What are a thousand lives? A parricide
Had trampled them like dust; and see, he lives!
(*Turning to Marzio.*) And thou—
Mar. Oh, spare me! Speak to me no more!
That stern yet piteous look, those solemn tones,
Wound worse than torture. (*To the Judges.*) I have told it all;
For pity's sake lead me away to death.
Cam. Guards, lead him nearer the Lady Beatrice,
He shrinks from her regard like autumn's leaf
From the keen breath of the serenest north.
Beatr. Oh, thou who tremblest on the giddy verge
Of life and death, pause ere thou answerest me;
So mayst thou answer God with less dismay:
What evil have we done thee? I, alas!
Have lived but on this earth a few sad years
And so my lot was ordered, that a father
First turned the moments of awakening life
To drops, each poisoning youth's sweet hope; and then
Stabbed with one blow my everlasting soul;
And my untainted fame; and even that peace
Which sleeps within the core of the heart's heart.
But the wound was not mortal; so my hate
Became the only worship I could lift
To our great father, who in pity and love,
Armed thee, as thou dost say, to cut him off;
And thus his wrong becomes my accusation;
And art thou the accuser? If thou hopest
Mercy in heaven, show justice upon earth:
Worse than a bloody hand is a hard heart.
If thou hast done murders, made thy life's path
Over the trampled laws of God and man,
Rush not before thy Judge, and say: "My Maker,
I have done this and more; for there was one
Who was most pure and innocent on earth;
And because she endured what never any,
Guilty or innocent, endured before;
Because her wrongs could not be told, not thought;
Because thy hand at length did rescue her;
I with my words killed her and all her kin."
Think, I adjure you, what it is to slay
The reverence living in the minds of men
Towards our ancient house, and stainless fame!
Think what it is to strangle infant pity,
Cradled in the belief of guileless looks,
Till it become a crime to suffer. Think
What 't is to blot with infamy and blood
All that which shows like innocence, and is,
Hear me, great God! I swear, most innocent,
So that the world lose all discrimination
Between the sly, fierce, wild regard of guilt,
And that which now compels thee to reply
To what I ask: Am I, or am I not
A parricide?
Mar. Thou art not!
Judge. What is this?
Mar. I here declare those whom I did accuse
Are innocent. 'T is I alone am guilty.
Judge. Drag him away to torments; let them be
Subtle and long drawn out, to tear the folds
Of the heart's inmost cell. Unbind him not
Till he confess.
Mar. Torture me as ye will:
A keener pain has wrung a higher truth
From my last breath. She is most innocent!
Bloodhounds, not men, glut yourselves well with me;
I will not give you that fine piece of nature
To rend and ruin.
(*Exit Marzio, guarded.*)
Cam. What say ye now, my Lords?
Judge. Let tortures strain the truth till it be white
As snow thrice sifted by the frozen wind.
Cam. Yet stained with blood.

Judge. (*To Beatrice.*) Know you this paper, Lady?
Beatr. Entrap me not with questions. Who stands here
As my accuser? Ha! wilt thou be he,
Who art my judge? Accuser, witness, judge,
What, all in one? Here is Orsino's name;
Where is Orsino? Let his eye meet mine.
What means this scrawl? Alas! ye know not what,
And therefore on the chance that it may be
Some evil, will ye kill us?

(*Enter an Officer.*)

Officer. Marzio's dead.
Judge. What did he say?
Officer. Nothing. As soon as we
Had bound him on the wheel, he smiled on us,
As one who baffles a deep adversary;
And holding his breath, died.
Judge. There remains nothing
But to apply the question to those prisoners,
Who yet remain stubborn.
Cam. I overrule
Further proceedings, and in the behalf
Of these most innocent and noble persons
Will use my interest with the Holy Father.
Judge. Let the Pope's pleasure then be done. Meanwhile
Conduct these culprits each to separate cells;
And be the engines ready: for this night,
If the Pope's resolution be as grave,
Pious, and just as once, I'll wring the truth
Out of those nerves and sinews, groan by groan.

(*Exeunt.*)

SCENE 3. *The Cell of a Prison. Beatrice is discovered asleep on a Couch. Enter Bernardo.*

Bernardo. How gently slumber rests upon her face,
Like the last thoughts of some day sweetly spent
Closing in night and dreams, and so prolonged.
After such torments as she bore last night.
How light and soft her breathing comes Ay, me!
Methinks that I shall never sleep again.
But I must shake the heavenly dew of rest
From this sweet folded flower, thus—wake! awake!
What, sister, canst thou sleep?
Beatrice. (*Awaking.*) I was just dreaming
That we were all in Paradise. Thou knowest
This cell seems like a kind of Paradise
After our father's presence.
Ber. Dear, dear sister,
Would that thy dream were not a dream! O, God!
How shall I tell?
Beatr. What wouldst thou tell, sweet brother?
Ber. Look not so calm and happy, or even whilst
I stand considering what I have to say
My heart will break.
Beatr. See now, thou mak'st me weep:
How very friendless thou wouldst be, dear child,
If I were dead. Say what thou hast to say.
Ber. They have confessed; they could endure no more
The tortures—
Beatr. Ha! What was there to confess?
They must have told some weak and wicked lie
To flatter their tormentors. Have they said
That they were guilty? O, white innocence,
That thou shouldst wear the mask of guilt to hide
Thine awful and serenest countenance
From those who know thee not!

(*Enter Judge, with Lucretia and Giacomo, guarded.*)

Ignoble hearts!
For some brief spasms of pain, which are at least
As mortal as the limbs through which they pass,
Are centuries of high splendor laid in dust?
And that eternal honor which should live
Sun-like, above the reek of mortal fame,
Changed to a mockery and a by-word? What!

Will you give up these bodies to be dragged
At horses' heels, so that our hair should sweep
The footsteps of the vain and senseless crowd,
Who, that they may make our calamity
Their worship and their spectacle, will leave
The churches and the theatres as void
As their own hearts? Shall the light multitude
Fling, at their choice, curses or faded pity,
Sad funeral flowers to deck a living corpse,
Upon us as we pass to pass away,
And leave—what memory of our having been?
Infamy, blood, terror, despair? O thou,
Who wert a mother to the parentless,
Kill not thy child! Let not her wrongs kill thee!
Brother, lie down with me upon the rack,
And let us each be silent as a corpse;
It soon will be as soft as any grave.
'T is but the falsehood it can wring from fear
Makes the rack cruel.

Giacomo. They will tear the truth
Even from thee at last, those cruel pains:
For pity's sake say thou art guilty now.

Lucr. O, speak the truth! Let us all quickly die;
And after death, God is our judge, not they;
He will have mercy on us.

Ber. If indeed
It can be true, say so, dear sister mine;
And then the Pope will surely pardon you,
And all be well.

Judge. Confess, or I will warp
Your limbs with such keen tortures—

Beatr. Tortures! Turn
The rack henceforth into a spinning-wheel!
Torture your dog, that he may tell when last
He lapped the blood his master shed—not me!
My pangs are of the mind, and of the heart,
And of the soul; ay, of the inmost soul,
Which weeps within tears as of burning gall
To see, in this ill world where none are true,
My kindred false to their deserted selves.
And with considering all the wretched life
Which I have lived, and its now wretched end,
And the small justice shown by Heaven and Earth
To me or mine; and what a tyrant thou art,
And what slaves these; and what a world we make,
The oppressor and the oppressed—such pangs compel
My answer. What is it thou wouldst with me?

Judge. Art thou not guilty of thy father's death?

Beatr. Or wilt thou rather tax high judging God
That he permitted such an act as that
Which I have suffered, and which he beheld;
Made it unutterable, and took from it
All refuge, all revenge, all consequence,
But that which thou hast called my father's death?
Which is or is not what men call a crime,
Which either I have done, or have not done;
Say what ye will. I shall deny no more.
If ye desire it thus, thus let it be.
And so an end of all. Now do your will;
No other pains shall force another word.

Judge. She is convicted, but has not confessed.
Be it enough. Until their final sentence
Let none have converse with them. You, young Lord,
Linger not here!

Beatr. O, tear him not away!

Judge. Guards! do your duty.

Ber. (*Embracing Beatrice.*) Oh! would ye divide
Body from soul?

Officer. That is the headsman's business.

(*Exeunt all but Lucretia, Beatrice, and Giacomo.*)

Giac. Have I confessed? Is it all over now?
No hope! No refuge! O weak, wicked tongue,
Which hast destroyed me, would that thou hadst been
Cut out and thrown to dogs first! To have killed
My father first, and then betrayed my sister;
Ay, thee! the one thing innocent and pure
In this black, guilty world, to that which I

So well deserve! My wife! my little ones!
Destitute, helpless, and I—Father! God!
Canst thou forgive even the unforgiving,
When their full hearts break thus, thus!
(*Covers his face, and weeps.*)

Lucr. O, my child!
To what a dreadful end are we all come!
Why did I yield? Why did I not sustain
Those torments? Oh, that I were all dissolved
Into these fast and unavailing tears,
Which flow and feel not!

Beatr. What 't was weak to do,
'T is weaker to lament, once being done;
Take cheer! The God who knew my wrong, and made
Our speedy act the angel of his wrath,
Seems, and but seems to have abandoned us.
Let us not think that we shall die for this.
Brother, sit near me; give me your firm hand,
You had a manly heart. Bear up! Bear up!
O, dearest Lady, put your gentle head
Upon my lap, and try to sleep awhile:
Your eyes look pale, hollow, and overworn,
With heaviness of watching and slow grief.
Come, I will sing you some low, sleepy tune,
Not cheerful, nor yet sad; some dull old thing,
Some outworn and unused monotony,
Such as our country gossips sing and spin,
Till they almost forget they live: lie down!
So, that will do. Have I forgot the words?
Faith! They are sadder than I thought they were.

SONG.

False friend, wilt thou smile or weep
When my life is laid asleep?
Little cares for a smile or a tear,
The clay-cold corpse upon the bier!
Farewell! Heighho!
What is this whispers low?
There is a snake in thy smile, my dear;
And bitter poison within thy tear.

Sweet sleep, were death like to thee,
Or if thou couldst mortal be,
I would close these eyes of pain;
When to wake? Never again.
O World! Farewell!
Listen to the passing bell!
It says, thou and I must part,
With a light and a heavy heart.

(*The scene closes.*)

SCENE 4. *A Hall of the Prison. Enter Camillo and Bernardo.*

Camillo. The Pope is stern; not to be moved or bent.
He looked as calm and keen as is the engine
Which tortures and which kills, exempt itself
From aught that it inflicts; a marble form,
A rite, a law, a custom: not a man.
He frowned, as if to frown had been the trick
Of his machinery, on the advocates
Presenting the defences, which he tore
And threw behind, muttering with hoarse, harsh voice:
"Which among ye defended their old father
Killed in his sleep?" Then to another: "Thou
Dost this in virtue of thy place; 't is well."
He turned to me then, looking deprecation,
And said these three words, coldly: "They must die."

Bernardo. And yet you left him not?

Cam. I urged him still;
Pleading, as I could guess, the devilish wrong
Which prompted your unnatural parent's death.
And he replied: "Paolo Santa Croce
Murdered his mother yester-evening,
And he is fled. Parricide grows so rife,
That soon, for some just cause no doubt, the young
Will strangle us all, dozing in our chairs.
Authority, and power, and hoary hair,
Are grown crimes capital. You are my nephew,
You come to ask their pardon; stay a moment;
Here is their sentence; never see me more
Till, to the letter, it be all fulfilled."

Ber. O, God, not so! I did believe indeed
That all you said was but sad preparation
For happy news. O, there are words and looks

To bend the sternest purpose! Once I knew them,
Now I forget them at my dearest need.
What think you if I seek him out and bathe
His feet and robe with hot and bitter tears?
Importune him with prayers, vexing his brain
With my perpetual cries, until in rage
He strike me with his pastoral cross, and trample
Upon my prostrate head, so that my blood
May stain the senseless dust on which he treads,
And remorse waken mercy? I will do it!
O, wait till I return!

(*Rushes out.*)

Cam. Alas! poor boy!
A wreck-devoted seaman thus might pray
To the deaf sea.

(*Enter Lucretia, Beatrice, and Giacomo, guarded.*)

Beatrice. I hardly dare to fear
That thou bring'st other news than a just pardon.

Cam. May God in heaven be less inexorable
To the Pope's prayers, than he has been to mine.
Here is the sentence and the warrant.

Beatr. (*Wildly.*) Oh,
My God! Can it be possible I have
To die so suddenly? So young to go
Under the obscure, cold, rotting, wormy ground!
To be nailed down into a narrow place;
To see no more sweet sunshine; hear no more
Blithe voice of living thing; muse not again
Upon familiar thoughts, sad, yet thus lost—
How fearful! To be nothing! Or to be—
What? O, where am I? Let me not go mad!
Sweet Heaven, forgive weak thoughts! If there should be
No God, no Heaven, no Earth in the void world;
The wide, grey, lampless, deep, unpeopled world!
If all things then should be—my father's spirit,
His eye, his voice, his touch, surrounding me;
The atmosphere and breath of my dead life!
If sometimes, as a shape more like himself,
Even the form which tortured me on earth,
Masked in grey hairs and wrinkles, he should come
And wind me in his hellish arms, and fix
His eyes on mine, and drag me down, down, down!
For was he not alone omnipotent
On Earth, and ever present? Even tho' dead,
Does not his spirit live in all that breathe,
And work for me and mine still the same ruin,
Scorn, pain, despair? Who ever yet returned
To teach the laws of death's untrodden realm?
Unjust perhaps as those which drive us now,
O, whither, whither?

Lucretia. Trust in God's sweet love,
The tender promises of Christ: ere night,
Think we shall be in Paradise.

Beatr. 'T is past!
Whatever comes, my heart shall sink no more.
And yet, I know not why, your words strike chill:
How tedious, false, and cold seem all things. I
Have met with much injustice in this world;
No difference has been made by God or man,
Or any power moulding my wretched lot,
'Twixt good or evil, as regarded me.
I am cut off from the only world I know,
From light, and life, and love, in youth's sweet prime.
You do well telling me to trust in God,
I hope I do trust in him. In whom else
Can any trust? And yet my heart is cold.

(*During the latter speeches Giacomo has retired conversing with Camillo, who now goes out. Giacomo advances.*)

Giacomo. Know you not, mother—sister, know you not?
Bernardo even now is gone to implore
The Pope to grant our pardon.

Lucr. Child, perhaps
It will be granted. We may all then live
To make these woes a tale for distant years:

O, what a thought! It gushes to my heart
Like the warm blood.

Beatr. Yet both will soon be cold.
O, trample out that thought! Worse than despair,
Worse than the bitterness of death, is hope:
It is the only ill which can find place
Upon the giddy, sharp and narrow hour
Tottering beneath us. Plead with the swift frost
That it should spare the eldest flower of spring:
Plead with awakening earthquake, o'er whose couch
Even now a city stands, strong, fair and free;
Now stench and blackness yawn, like death. O plead
With famine, or wind-walking pestilence,
Blind lightning, or the deaf sea, not with man!
Cruel, cold, formal man! righteous in words,
In deeds a Cain. No, mother, we must die:
Since such is the reward of innocent lives;
Such the alleviation of worst wrongs.
And whilst our murderers live, and hard, cold men,
Smiling and slow, walk thro' a world of tears
To death as to life's sleep; 't were just the grave
Were some strange joy for us. Come, obscure Death,
And wind me in thine all-embracing arms!
Like a fond mother hide me in thy bosom,
And rock me to the sleep from which none wake.
Live ye, who live, subject to one another
As we were once, who now—

(*Bernardo rushes in.*)

Ber. Oh, horrible!
That tears, that looks, that hope poured forth in prayer,
Even till the heart is vacant and despairs,
Should all be vain! The ministers of death
Are waiting round the doors. I thought I saw
Blood on the face of one—what if 't were fancy?
Soon the heart's blood of all I love on earth
Will sprinkle him, and he will wipe it off
As if 't were only rain. O, life! O, world!
Cover me! let me be no more! To see
That perfect mirror of pure innocence
Wherein I gazed, and grew happy and good,
Shivered to dust! To see thee, Beatrice,
Who made all lovely thou didst look upon—
Thee, light of life—dead, dark! while I say, sister,
To hear I have no sister; and thou, Mother,
Whose love was [as] a bond to all our loves—
Dead! The sweet bond broken!

(*Enter Camillo and Guards.*)

They come. Let me
Kiss those warm lips before their crimson leaves
Are blighted—white—cold. Say farewell, before
Death chokes that gentle voice! O, let me hear
You speak!

Beatr. Farewell, my tender brother. Think
Of our sad fate with gentleness, as now:
And let mild pitying thoughts lighten for thee
Thy sorrow's load. Err not in harsh despair,
But tears and patience. One thing more, my child,
For thine own sake be constant to the love
Thou bearest us; and to the faith that I,
Though wrapt in a strange cloud of crime and shame,
Lived ever holy and unstained. And though
Ill tongues shall wound me, and our common name
Be as a mark stamped on thine innocent brow
For men to point at as they pass, do thou
Forbear, and never think a thought unkind
Of those, who perhaps love thee in their graves.
So mayest thou die as I do; fear and pain
Being subdued. Farewell! farewell! farewell!

Ber. I cannot say, farewell!
Cam. O, Lady Beatrice!
Beatr. Give yourself no unnecessary pain,
My dear Lord Cardinal. Here, Mother, tie
My girdle for me, and bind up this hair
In any simple knot; ay, that does well.
And yours I see is coming down. How often
Have we done this for one another! now
We shall not do it any more. My Lord,
We are quite ready. Well, 't is very well.

EDWARD BULWER-LYTTON

THE LADY OF LYONS, OR, LOVE AND PRIDE

Edward Bulwer-Lytton, first Baron Lytton (1803–1873), of aristocratic birth, passed a youth of romantic emotion, precocious literary work, wide desultory study, and fashionable gaiety. Interested in political reform, he was in the House of Commons from 1831 most of the time till 1866, when he became a peer; and also held cabinet offices. His activity and versatility were great. His best-known literary works are his novels; his plays, notably *The Lady of Lyons* and *Richelieu*, have been among the most often acted of the century.

Bulwer-Lytton was rather a popular than a great writer, a man of much talent but not of genius. He seems to have taken to writing as a result of his ambition and desire for popularity and prominence, and of a mind which was restless and active rather than fine, penetrating, or imaginative. His earlier novels followed the prevalent romantic taste, being especially under the influence of Byron. Later, like Dickens, he combined realism with the spirit of reform; he also wrote some of the most popular of historical novels. In his style there is a grandiloquence, a flowery wordiness, that often seems insincere, and was made fun of by W. M. Thackeray in his *Burlesques.* From the first, the critics have had no very high praise for his novels, but their popular success was universal; which was due in large measure to active elaborate plots, and a profusion of "strong" dramatic situations. And much the same must be said of his plays. They follow instead of leading contemporary taste; their style is sometimes meretricious. Yet their popularity was and continued to be great. It shows how relatively low has been the literary quality of nineteenth-century acting drama that they are among the most favorable specimens of dramatic taste in the earlier Victorian period. Bulwer-Lytton was the only man, except perhaps Goldsmith, from Dryden to the present day, who was prominent in other literary work and greatly succeeded in the drama.

The Lady of Lyons was written in 1838, in little over two weeks. The author states in his Preface that the plot was suggested by a vague memory of a "very pretty little tale, called 'The Bellows-Mender'"; also that the play was written to help Macready in his newly assumed management of the Covent Garden theater, and to retrieve "the comparative failure on the stage of *The Duchess de la Vallière*," a play of his own which had appeared in 1836. When produced, *The Lady of Lyons* made an immediate success, and has held the stage intermittently till almost the present day. It was put on in elaborate and expensive style by so eminent an actor as Henry Irving in 1879, when it was already old and hackneyed, and played by him forty-five times, at a period when he was acting in such plays as *Faust* and *The Bells.* Irving used also to read it aloud publicly. For half a century, therefore, it was a representative play and pleased the best tastes.

A play like *The Lady of Lyons*, with its abundant action, its superficiality, its sensationalism, its emotionality, is properly to be classed as a melodrama; and it shows curiously a heritage from both sentimentalism and romanticism. It ends with a couple of maxims of the sort affected by the former, and such are to be found elsewhere in the play. Mme. Deschappelles is of a type of crudely worldly, designing woman often opposed to the celestial innocence of the eighteenth century heroine. The resemblance to sentimental drama is perhaps most important in the attempt to combine realism and humor with an all-pervading but shallow emotionality, and with an elaborate and not over-probable plot. A romantic element was inevitable in any play by Bulwer and written in the 30's. The lovers belong rather to romance than to sentimentalism. The eighteenth century liked to see a young man raise slighted and unfortunate merit to the honor of associating with county-families; what could give better opportunity for the mood of moral approbation in which sentimental drama basked? Sentimentalism was after all conventionality and worldliness on its good behavior; while romance hardly accepted the bonds even of possibility. Romance liked to hitch its wagon to a star, and eagerly granted a suspension of its disbelief to the gardener's son who learned painting, fencing, and deportment that he might woo the haughtiest beauty of Lyons. The romance was felt as the more delightful because the scene was in a neighboring country and the time within the memory of middle-aged people; those with an appetite for the strange and alluring were gratified at finding it so near their own lives. The setting had another advantage. A concession to common-sense was made by placing the action, as the author remarks in his Preface, at a time when the strata of society had just been shaken up by the Revolutionary earthquake, and an excess of mawkishness was avoided by treating Mme. Deschappelles (and her daughter at first) with satiric humor. The dramatist forgot his romance also in act IV, where, after being grossly tricked by him, Pauline betrays and finally confesses her continued desire for Claude. Such a strain on our credulity can be justified only by a physical passion such as crude realism may portray, a dash of cynicism, and the dramatist's desire to prepare for the happy outcome. Romance flourishes chiefly in the figure of Claude in act V, during most of which he is judiciously kept rather in the background, lest the beautifying glamour of fresh romance which now covers him should be dissipated. "This mysterious Morier," especially favored by Napoleon —" his constant melancholy, the loneliness of his habits — his daring valor, his brilliant rise in the profession, all tend to make him as much the matter of gossip as of admiration." This is a perfect description of the "Byronic hero," gloomy and piquing, who began his admired course in such poems as *The Giaour* and *Manfred*, and enthralled the world, not young ladies only, for a generation. Bulwer himself in his youth had been nicknamed "Childe Harold" by an Englishwoman in Paris. Claude Melnotte is a combination of romance and sheer improbability. In his Preface the author pleads the general ferment of the time as the excuse for Melnotte's "unsettled principles (the struggle between which makes the passion of this drama)"; but the most romantic spectator could hardly find here an excuse for his unmanly treachery. His ideal figure at the close was needed to restore him to the good graces of the audience. It must be remembered that in fiction of this type the barest minimum of psychological truth was all that was felt to be needed in the persons who acted out an interesting plot. Other traits characteristic of the age appear in the literary style, the composite style of the romanticists — not the language of life, but somewhat artificial and ornate and stiff, yet unlike the artificiality of the eighteenth century. With Shakespeare's example as a precedent, Bulwer puts the more high-emotional passages of this prose play into blank-verse.

In this play as in the romantic novel, such as Scott's, some solid mundane element was needed to hold the romance down from floating away into the palaces of the sunset clouds. Two of the characters especially fulfil this office, the two "character parts." Damas is the typical blunt soldier, affecting cynicism about women, but generous, good-hearted, and ready "to blubber" at an affecting scene. The other is Mme. Deschappelles, transparently silly and vain. This combination of the improbable-pleasing with the exaggerated-real may be regarded as inherited from sentimentalism, and makes a strong link between Bulwer-Lytton and Dickens. In life they were good friends, and both were equally interested in the novel and the drama, which have long been the most intimately connected of literary forms.

The success of the play was due first and foremost, no doubt, to its well-constructed plot, full of suspense, surprise, and variety. To it the author tells us he gave his chief attention. As in *The Alchemist*, *Venice Preserved* and *The Cenci*, the last act stands apart from the rest of the play; the main action being concluded, it seems as if all were over, yet a new interest is created as keen as the old, an admirable device. Bulwer himself attributed his success to the art "of creating agreeable emotions"; this amounts to saying that it was adapted to contemporary taste, which the author shared, but which, being somewhat crudely ambitious, he also studied. To us the play seems a somewhat unhappy combination of the romantic, the sentimental, the satiric, and the realistic. It seems to us lacking whether we compare it with the stalwart imagination of the Elizabethans, or the austere reality of Ibsen and his followers. It seems to us more old-fashioned, because it was more temporary, than the plays of Sheridan or Jonson. It is only the highest excellence that is timeless. But the qualities which won admiration for *The Lady of Lyons* in its day gain it tolerance now, and its suggestiveness as to early Victorian taste gives it considerable historical interest.

THE LADY OF LYONS, OR, LOVE AND PRIDE

DRAMATIS PERSONÆ

BEAUSEANT, *a rich gentleman of Lyons, in love with, and refused by, Pauline Deschappelles.*
GLAVIS, *his friend, also a rejected suitor to Pauline.*
COLONEL (afterwards General) DAMAS, *cousin to Mme. Deschappelles, and an officer in the French Army.*
MONSIEUR DESCHAPPELLES, *a Lyonnese merchant, father to Pauline.*
LANDLORD OF THE GOLDEN LION.
GASPAR.
CLAUDE MELNOTTE.
FIRST OFFICER, SECOND OFFICER, THIRD OFFICER.
Servants, Notary, &c.
MADAME DESCHAPPELLES.
PAULINE, *her daughter.*
THE WIDOW MELNOTTE, *mother to Claude.*
JANET, *the innkeeper's daughter.*
MARIAN, *maid to Pauline.*

SCENE—*Lyons and the neighborhood.*
TIME—1795–1798.

ACT I.

SCENE 1. *A room in the house of M. Deschappelles, at Lyons. Pauline reclining on a sofa; Marian, her maid fanning her.—Flowers and notes on a table beside the sofa.—Madame Deschappelles seated.—The gardens are seen from the open window.*

Mme. Deschap. Marian, put that rose a little more to the left.—(*Marian alters the position of a rose in Pauline's hair.*) —Ah, so!—that improves the air,—the *tournure*, the *je ne sais quoi!* [1]—You are certainly very handsome, child!—quite my style;—I don't wonder that you make such a sensation!—Old, young, rich, and poor, do homage to the Beauty of Lyons!—Ah, we live again in our children,—especially when they have our eyes and complexion!

Pauline. (*Languidly.*) Dear mother, you spoil your Pauline!—(*Aside.*) I wish I knew who sent me these flowers!

Mme. Deschap. No, child!—If I praise you, it is only to inspire you with a proper ambition.—You are born to make a great marriage.—Beauty is valuable or worthless according as you invest the property to the best advantage.—Marian, go and order the carriage!

(*Exit Marian.*)

Pauline. Who *can* it be that sends me, every day, these beautiful flowers?—how sweet they are!

(*Enter Servant.*)

Servant. Monsieur Beauseant, madam.

Mme. Deschap. Let him enter. Pauline, this is another offer!—I know it is!—Your father should engage an additional clerk to keep the account-book of your conquests.

(*Enter Beauseant.*)

Beau. Ah, ladies, how fortunate I am to find you at home!—(*Aside.*) How lovely she looks!—It is a great sacrifice I make in marrying into a family in trade!—they will be eternally grateful! —(*Aloud.*) Madame, you will permit me a word with your charming daughter. —(*Approaches Pauline, who rises disdainfully.*)—Mademoiselle, I have ventured to wait upon you, in a hope that you must long since have divined. Last night, when you outshone all the beauty of Lyons, you completed your conquest over me! You know that my fortune is not exceeded by any estate in the province,—you know that, but for the Revolution, which has defrauded me of my titles, I should be noble. May I, then, trust that you will not reject my alliance? I offer you my hand and heart.

Pauline. (*Aside.*) He has the air of a man who confers a favor!—(*Aloud.*) Sir, you are very condescending—I thank you humbly; but, being duly sensible of my own demerits, you must allow me to decline the honor you propose.

(*Curtsies, and turns away.*)

Beau. Decline! impossible!—you are not serious!—Madame, suffer me to appeal

[1] The general effect, the inexpressible something.

to *you.* I am a suitor for your daughter's hand—the settlements shall be worthy her beauty and my station. May I wait on M. Deschappelles?

Mme. Deschap. M. Deschappelles never interferes in the domestic arrangements, —you are very obliging. If you were still a marquis, or if my daughter were intended to marry a commoner,—why, perhaps, we might give you the preference.

Beau. A commoner!—we are all commoners in France now.

Mme. Deschap. In France, yes; but there is a nobility still left in the other countries in Europe. We are quite aware of your good qualities, and don't doubt that you will find some lady more suitable to your pretensions. We shall be always happy to see you as an acquaintance, M. Beauseant!—My dear child, the carriage will be here presently.

Beau. Say no more, madame!—say no more!—(*Aside*). Refused! and by a merchant's daughter!—refused! It will be all over Lyons before sunset!—I will go and bury myself in my château, study philosophy, and turn woman-hater. Refused! they ought to be sent to a madhouse!—Ladies, I have the honor to wish you a very good morning.

(*Exit.*)

Mme. Deschap. How forward these men are!—I think, child, we kept up our dignity. Any girl, however inexperienced, knows how to accept an offer, but it requires a vast deal of address to refuse one with proper condescension and disdain. I used to practise it at school with the dancing-master.

(*Enter Damas.*)

Damas. Good morning, cousin Deschappelles.—Well, Pauline, are you recovered from last night's ball?—So many triumphs must be very fatiguing. Even M. Glavis sighed most piteously when you departed; but that might be the effect of the supper.

Pauline. M. Glavis, indeed!

Mme. Deschap. M. Glavis?—as if my daughter would think of M. Glavis!

Damas. Hey-day!—why not?—His father left him a very pretty fortune, and his birth is higher than yours, cousin Deschappelles. But perhaps you are looking to M. Beauseant,—his father was a marquis before the Revolution.

Pauline. M. Beauseant!—Cousin, you delight in tormenting me!

Mme. Deschap. Don't mind him, Pauline! —Cousin Damas, you have no susceptibility of feeling,—there is a certain indelicacy in all your ideas.—M. Beauseant knows already that he is no match for my daughter!

Damas. Pooh! pooh! one would think you intended your daughter to marry a prince!

Mme. Deschap. Well, and if I did?—what then?—Many a foreign prince—

Damas. (*Interrupting her.*) Foreign prince!—foreign fiddlestick!—you ought to be ashamed of such nonsense at your time of life.

Mme. Deschap. My time of life!—That is an expression never applied to any lady till she is sixty-nine and three-quarters;—and only then by the clergyman of the parish.

(*Enter Servant.*)

Servant. Madame, the carriage is at the door.

(*Exit.*)

Mme. Deschap. Come, child, put on your bonnet—you really have a very thorough-bred air—not at all like your poor father.—(*Fondly.*) Ah, you little coquette! when a young lady is always making mischief, it is a sure sign that she takes after her mother!

Pauline. Good day, cousin Damas—and a better humor to you.—(*Going back to the table and taking the flowers.*) Who *could* have sent me these flowers?

(*Exeunt Pauline and Madame Deschappelles.*)

Damas. That would be an excellent girl if her head had not been turned. I fear she is now become incorrigible! Zounds, what a lucky fellow I am to be still a bachelor! They may talk of the devotion of the sex—but the most faithful attachment in life is that of a woman in love—with herself.

(*Exit.*)

SCENE 2. *The exterior of a small Village Inn—sign, the Golden Lion—a few leagues from Lyons, which is seen at a distance.*

Beau. (*Behind the scenes.*) Yes, you may bait the horses; we shall rest here an hour.

(*Enter Beauseant and Glavis.*)

Gla. Really, my dear Beauseant, consider that I have promised to spend a day or two with you at your château,—that I am quite at your mercy for my entertainment,—and yet you are as silent and as gloomy as a mute at a funeral, or an Englishman at a party of pleasure.

Beau. Bear with me;—the fact is that I am miserable.

Gla. You—the richest and gayest bachelor in Lyons?

Beau. It is because I am a bachelor that I am miserable.—Thou knowest Pauline—the only daughter of the rich merchant, Mons. Deschappelles?

Gla. Know her?—who does not?—as pretty as Venus, and as proud as Juno.

Beau. Her taste is worse than her pride.—(*Drawing himself up.*) Know, Glavis, she has actually refused *me!*

Gla. (*Aside.*) So she has me!—very consoling! In all cases of heart-ache, the application of another man's disappointment draws out the pain and allays the irritation.—(*Aloud.*) Refused you! and wherefore?

Beau. I know not, unless it be because the Revolution swept away my father's title of Marquis,—and she will not marry a commoner. Now, as we have no noblemen left in France,—as we are all citizens and equals, she can only hope that, in spite of the war, some English Milord or German Count will risk his life, by coming to Lyons and making her my Lady. Refused me, and with scorn!—By Heaven, I'll not submit to it tamely:—I'm in a perfect fever of mortification and rage.—Refuse me, indeed!

Gla. Be comforted, my dear fellow,—I will tell you a secret. For the same reason she refused ME!

Beau. You!—that's a very different matter! But give me your hand, Glavis,—we'll think of some plan to humble her. By Jove, I should like to see her married to a strolling player!

(*Enter Landlord and his Daughter from the Inn.*)

Land. Your servant, citizen Beauseant,—servant, sir. Perhaps you will take dinner before you proceed to your château; our larder is most plentifully supplied.

Beau. I have no appetite.

Gla. Nor I. Still it is bad travelling on an empty stomach. What have you got? (*Takes and looks over the bill of fare.*)

(*Shout without.*) "Long live the Prince!—Long live the Prince!"

Beau. The Prince!—what Prince is that? I thought we had no princes left in France.

Land. Ha, ha! the lads always call him Prince. He has just won the prize at the shooting-match, and they are taking him home in triumph.

Beau. Him! and who's Mr. Him?

Land. Who should he be but the pride of the village, Claude Melnotte?—Of course you have heard of Claude Melnotte?

Gla. (*Giving back the bill of fare.*) Never had that honor. Soup—ragout of hare—roast chicken, and, in short, all you have!

Beau. The son of old Melnotte, the gardener?

Land. Exactly so—a wonderful young man.

Beau. How, wonderful?—Are his cabbages better than other people's?

Land. Nay, he don't garden any more; his father left him well off. He's only a genus.

Gla. A what?

Land. A genus!—a man who can do everything in life except anything that's useful;—that's a genus.

Beau. You raise my curiosity;—proceed.

Land. Well, then, about four years ago, old Melnotte died, and left his son well to do in the world. We then all observed that a great change came over young Claude: he took to reading and Latin, and hired a professor from Lyons, who had so much in his head that he was forced to wear a great full-bottom wig to cover it. Then he took a fencing-master, and a dancing-master, and a music-master; and then he learned to paint; and at last it was said that young Claude was to go to Paris, and set up for a painter. The lads laughed at him at first; but he is a stout fellow, is Claude, and as brave as a lion, and soon taught them to laugh the wrong side of their mouths; and now all the boys swear by him, and all the girls pray for him.

Beau. A promising youth, certainly! And why do they call him Prince?

Land. Partly because he is at the head of them all, and partly because he has such a proud way with him, and wears such fine clothes—and, in short, looks like a prince.

Beau. And what could have turned the

foolish fellow's brain? The Revolution, I suppose?

Land. Yes—the revolution that turns us all topsy-turvy—the revolution of Love.

Beau. Romantic young Corydon! And with whom he is in love?

Land. Why—but it is a secret, gentlemen.

Beau. Oh! certainly.

Land. Why, then, I hear from his mother, good soul! that it is no less a person than the Beauty of Lyons, Pauline Deschappelles.

Beau. and Glavis. Ha, ha!—Capital!

Land. You may laugh, but it is as true as I stand here.

Beau. And what does the Beauty of Lyons say to his suit?

Land. Lord, sir, she never even condescended to look at him, though when he was a boy he worked in her father's garden.

Beau. Are you sure of that?

Land. His mother says that Mademoiselle does not know him by sight.

Beau. (*Taking Glavis aside.*) I have hit it,—I have it;—here is our revenge! Here is a prince for our haughty damsel! Do you take me?

Gla. Deuce take me if I do!

Beau. Blockhead!—it 's as clear as a map. What if we could make this elegant clown pass himself off as a foreign prince?—lend him money, clothes, equipage for the purpose?—make him propose to Pauline?—marry Pauline? Would it not be delicious?

Gla. Ha, ha!—excellent! But how shall we support the necessary expenses of his highness?

Beau. Pshaw! Revenge is worth a much larger sacrifice than a few hundred louis; —as for details, my valet is the trustiest fellow in the world, and shall have the appointment of his highness's establishment. Let 's go to him at once, and see if he be really this Admirable Crichton.[2]

Gla. With all my heart;—but the dinner?

Beau. Always thinking of dinner! Hark ye, landlord; how far is it to young Melnotte's cottage? I should like to see such a prodigy.

Land. Turn down the lane,—then strike across the common,—and you will see his mother's cottage.

Beau. True, he lives with his mother.—(*Aside.*) We will not trust to an old woman's discretion; better send for him hither. I 'll just step in and write him a note. Come, Glavis.

Gla. Yes,—Beauseant, Glavis, and Co., manufacturers of princes, wholesale and retail,—an uncommonly genteel line of business. But why so grave?

Beau. You think only of the sport,—I of the revenge.

(*Exeunt within the Inn.*)

SCENE 3. *The interior of Melnotte's cottage; flowers placed here and there; a guitar on an oaken table, with a portfolio, &c.; a picture on an easel, covered by a curtain; fencing-foils crossed over the mantelpiece; an attempt at refinement in spite of the homeliness of the furniture, &c.; a staircase to the right conducts to the upper story.*

(*Shout without.*) "Long live Claude Melnotte!" "Long live the Prince!"

The Widow Mel. Hark!—there 's my dear son;—carried off the prize, I 'm sure; and now he 'll want to treat them all.

Claude Mel. (*Opening the door.*) What! you won't come in, my friends! Well, well,—there 's a trifle to make merry elsewhere. Good day to you all,—good day!

(*Shout.*) "Hurrah! Long live Prince Claude!"

(*Enter Claude Melnotte, with a rifle in his hand.*)

Mel. Give me joy, dear mother!—I 've won the prize!—never missed one shot! Is it not handsome, this gun?

Widow. Humph!—Well, what is it worth, Claude?

Mel. Worth! What is a riband worth to a soldier? Worth! everything! Glory is priceless!

Widow. Leave glory to great folks. Ah! Claude, Claude, castles in the air cost a vast deal to keep up! How is all this to end? What good does it do thee to learn Latin, and sing songs, and play on the guitar, and fence, and dance, and paint pictures? All very fine; but what does it bring in?

Mel. Wealth! wealth, my mother! Wealth to the mind—wealth to the heart —high thoughts—bright dreams—the hope of fame—the ambition to be worthier to love Pauline.

Widow. My poor son!—The young lady will never think of thee.

2 James Crichton, 1560–1583 (?), was a Scotch adventurer noted for his versatility.

Mel. Do the stars think of us? Yet if the prisoner see them shine into his dungeon, wouldst thou bid him turn away from *their* lustre? Even so from this low cell, poverty, I lift my eyes to Pauline and forget my chains.—(*Goes to the picture and draws aside the curtain.*) See, this is her image—painted from memory. Oh, how the canvas wrongs her!—(*Takes up the brush and throws it aside.*) I shall never be a painter! I can paint no likeness but one, and that is above all art. I would turn soldier—France needs soldiers! But to leave the air that Pauline breathes! What is the hour?—so late? I will tell thee a secret, mother. Thou knowest that for the last six weeks I have sent every day the rarest flowers to Pauline?—she wears them. I have seen them on her breast. Ah, and then the whole universe seemed filled with odors! I have now grown more bold—I have poured my worship into poetry—I have sent the verses to Pauline—I have signed them with my own name. My messenger ought to be back by this time. I bade him wait for the answer.

Widow. And what answer do you expect, Claude?

Mel. That which the Queen of Navarre sent to the poor troubadour:—"Let me see the Oracle that can tell nations I am beautiful!" She will admit me. I shall hear her speak—I shall meet her eyes—I shall read upon her cheek the sweet thoughts that translate themselves into blushes. Then—then, oh, then—she may forget that I am the peasant's son!

Widow. Nay, if she will but hear thee talk, Claude?

Mel. I foresee it all. She will tell me that desert is the true rank. She will give me a badge—a flower—a glove! Oh rapture! I shall join the armies of the republic—I shall rise—I shall win a name that beauty will not blush to hear. I shall return with the right to say to her—"See, how love does not level the proud, but raise the humble!" Oh, how my heart swells within me!—Oh, what glorious prophets of the future are youth and hope!

(*Knock at the door.*)

Widow. Come in.

(*Enter Gaspar.*)

Mel. Welcome, Gaspar, welcome. Where is the letter? Why do you turn away, man? where is the letter? (*Gaspar gives him one.*) This! This is mine, the one I intrusted to thee. Didst thou not leave it?

Gaspar. Yes, I left it.

Mel. My own verses returned to me. Nothing else?

Gaspar. Thou wilt be proud to hear how thy messenger was honored. For thy sake, Melnotte, I have borne that which no Frenchman can bear without disgrace.

Mel. Disgrace, Gaspar! Disgrace?

Gaspar. I gave thy letter to the porter, who passed it from lackey to lackey till it reached the lady it was meant for.

Mel. It reached her, then;—you are sure of that? It reached her,—well, well!

Gaspar. It reached her, and was returned to me with blows. Dost hear, Melnotte? with blows! Death! are we slaves still, that we are to be thus dealt with, we peasants?

Mel. With blows? No, Gaspar, no; not blows!

Gaspar. I could show thee the marks if it were not so deep a shame to bear them. The lackey who tossed thy letter into the mire swore that his lady and her mother never were so insulted. What could thy letter contain, Claude?

Mel. (*Looking over the letter.*) Not a line that a serf might not have written to an empress. No, not one.

Gaspar. They promise thee the same greeting they gave me, if thou wilt pass that way. Shall we endure this, Claude?

Mel. (*Wringing Gaspar's hand.*) Forgive me, the fault was mine, I have brought this on thee; I will not forget it; thou shalt be avenged! The heartless insolence!

Gaspar. Thou are moved, Melnotte; think not of me; I would go through fire and water to serve thee; but,—a blow! It is not the *bruise* that galls,—it is the *blush*, Melnotte.

Mel. Say, what message?—How insulted!—Wherefore—What the offence?

Gaspar. Did you not write to Pauline Deschappelles, the daughter of the rich merchant?

Mel. Well?—

Gaspar. And are you not a peasant—a gardener's son?—that was the offence. Sleep on it, Melnotte. Blows to a French citizen, blows!

(*Exit.*)

Widow. Now you are cured, Claude!

Mel. (*Tearing the letter.*) So do I scatter her image to the winds—I will stop her in the open streets—I will insult her—I will beat her menial ruffians—I will—(*Turns suddenly to Widow.*) Mother, am I humpbacked—deformed—hideous?

Widow. You!

Mel. A coward—a thief—a liar?

Widow. You!

Mel. Or a dull fool—a vain, drivelling, brainless idiot?

Widow. No, no.

Mel. What am I then—worse than all these? Why, I am a peasant! What has a peasant to do with love? Vain revolutions, why lavish your cruelty on the great? Oh that we—we, the hewers of wood and drawers of water—had been swept away, so that the proud might learn what the world would be without us!—

(*Knock at the door.*)

(*Enter Servant from the Inn.*)

Servant. A letter for Citizen Melnotte.

Mel. A letter! from her perhaps—who sent thee?

Servant. Why, Monsieur—I mean Citizen—Beauseant, who stops to dine at the Golden Lion, on his way to his château.

Mel. Beauseant!—(*Reads.*) "Young man, I know thy secret—thou lovest above thy station: if thou hast wit, courage, and discretion, I can secure to thee the realization of thy most sanguine hopes; and the sole condition I ask in return is, that thou shalt be steadfast to thine own ends. I shall demand from thee a solemn oath to marry her whom thou lovest; to bear her to thine home on thy wedding night. I am serious—if thou wouldst learn more, lose not a moment, but follow the bearer of this letter to thy friend and patron,—Charles Beauseant."

Mel. Can I believe my eyes? Are our own passions the sorcerers that raise up for us spirits of good or evil? I will go instantly.

Widow. What is this, Claude?

Mel. "Marry her whom thou lovest"—"bear her to thine own home."—Oh, revenge and love; which of you is the stronger?—(*Gazing on the picture.*) Sweet face, thou smilest on me from the canvas: weak fool that I am, do I then love her still? No, it is the vision of my own romance that I have worshiped: it is the reality to which I bring scorn for scorn. Adieu, mother: I will return anon. My brain reels—the earth swims before me.—(*Looks again at the letter.*) No, it is *not* a mockery; I do *not* dream!

(*Exit.*)

ACT II.

Scene 1. *The gardens of M. Deschappelles' house at Lyons—the house seen at the back of the stage.*

(*Enter Beauseant and Glavis.*)

Beau. Well, what think you of my plot? Has it not succeeded to a miracle? The instant that I introduced his Highness the Prince of Como to the pompous mother and the scornful daughter, it was all over with them: he came—he saw—he conquered: and, though it is not many days since he arrived, they have already promised him the hand of Pauline.

Gla. It is lucky, though, that you told them his highness travelled *incognito,* for fear the Directory (who are not very fond of princes) should lay him by the heels; for he has a wonderful wish to keep up his rank, and scatters our gold about with as much coolness as if he were watering his own flower-pots.

Beau. True, he is damnably extravagant; I think the sly dog does it out of malice. However, it must be owned that he reflects credit on his loyal subjects, and makes a very pretty figure in his fine clothes, with my diamond snuff-box.

Gla. And my diamond ring! But do you think he will be firm to the last? I fancy I see symptoms of relenting: he will never keep up his rank, if he once let out his conscience.

Beau. His oath binds him! he cannot retract without being forsworn, and those low fellows are always superstitious! But, as it is, I tremble lest he be discovered: that bluff Colonel Damas (Madame Deschappelles' cousin) evidently suspects him: we must make haste and conclude the farce: I have thought of a plan to end it this very day.

Gla. This very day! Poor Pauline: her dream will be soon over.

Beau. Yes, this day they shall be married; this evening, according to his oath, he shall carry his bride to the Golden Lion, and then pomp, equipage, retinue, and title, all shall vanish at once; and her Highness the Princess shall find that she has refused the son of a Marquis, to marry the son of the gardener.—Oh, Pauline, once loved, now hated, yet still not relinquished, thou shalt drain the cup to the dregs,—thou shalt know what it is to be humbled!

(*Enter from the house, Melnotte, as the Prince of Como, leading in Pauline; Madame Deschappelles, fanning herself; and Colonel Damas.*)

(*Beauseant and Glavis bow respectfully. Pauline and Melnotte walk apart.*)

Mme. Deschap. Good morning, gentlemen; really I am so fatigued with laughter; the dear Prince is so entertaining. What wit he has! Any one may see that he has spent his whole life in courts.

Damas. And what the deuce do you know about courts, cousin Deschappelles? You women regard men just as you buy books—you never care about what is in them, but how they are bound and lettered. 'Sdeath, I don't think you would even look at your Bible if it had not a title to it.

Mrs. Deschap. How coarse you are, cousin Damas!—quite the manners of a barrack—you don't deserve to be one of our family; really we must drop your acquaintance when Pauline marries. I cannot patronize any relations that would discredit my future son-in-law, the Prince of Como.

Mel. (*Advancing.*) These are beautiful gardens, madame, (*Beauseant and Glavis retire.*)—who planned them?

Mme. Deschap. A gardener named Melnotte, your highness—an honest man who knew his station. I can't say as much for his son—a presuming fellow, who—ha! ha! actually wrote verses—such doggerel!—to my daughter.

Pauline. Yes, how you would have laughed at them, Prince!—*you*, who write such beautiful verses!

Mel. This Melnotte must be a monstrous impudent person!

Damas. Is he good-looking?

Mme. Deschap. I never notice such *canaille*—an ugly, mean-looking clown, if I remember right.

Damas. Yet I heard your porter say he was wonderfully like his highness.

Mel. (*Taking snuff.*) You are complimentary.

Mme. Deschap. For shame, cousin Damas!—like the Prince, indeed!

Pauline. Like you! Ah, mother, like our beautiful prince! I'll never speak to you again, cousin Damas.

Mel. (*Aside.*) Humph!—rank is a great beautifier! I never passed for an Apollo while I was a peasant; if I am so handsome as a prince, what should I be as an emperor! (*Aloud.*) Monsieur Beauseant, will you honor me?

(*Offers snuff.*)

Beau. No, your highness; I have no small vices.

Mel. Nay, if it were a vice, you 'd be sure to have it, Monsieur Beauseant.

Mme. Deschap. Ha! ha!—how very severe!—what wit!

Beau. (*In a rage and aside.*) Curse his impertinence!

Mme. Deschap. What a superb snuff-box!

Pauline. And what a beautiful ring!

Mel. You like the box—a trifle—interesting perhaps from associations—a present from Louis XIV. to my great-great-grandmother. Honor me by accepting it.

Beau. (*Plucking him by the sleeve.*) How!—what the devil! My box—are you mad? It is worth five hundred louis.

Mel. (*Unheeding him, and turning to Pauline.*) And you like this ring? Ah, it has, indeed, a lustre since your eyes have shone on it. (*Placing it on her finger.*) Henceforth hold me, sweet enchantress, the Slave of the Ring.

Gla. (*Pulling him.*) Stay, stay—what are you about? My maiden aunt's legacy—a diamond of the first water. You shall be hanged for swindling, sir.

Mel. (*Pretending not to hear.*) It is curious, this ring; it is the one with which my grandfather, the Doge of Venice, married the Adriatic!

(*Madame and Pauline examine the ring.*)

Mel. (*To Beauseant and Glavis.*) Fie, gentlemen! princes must be generous?—(*Turns to Damas, who watches them closely.*) These kind friends have my interest so much at heart, that they are as careful of my property as if it were their own!

Beau. and Gla. (*Confusedly.*) Ha! ha!—very good joke that!

(*Appear to remonstrate with Melnotte, in dumb show.*)

Damas. What 's all that whispering? I am sure there is some juggle here: hang me, if I think he is an Italian after all.

Gad, I 'll try him. Servitore umillissimo, Eccellenza.*

Mel. Hum—what does he mean, I wonder?

Damas. Godo di vedervi in buona salute.**

Mel. Hem—hem!

Damas. Fa bel tempo—che si dice di nuovo?***

Mel. Well, sir, what 's all that gibberish?

Damas. Oh, oh!—only Italian, your highness!—The Prince of Como does not understand his own language!

Mel. Not as you pronounce it; who the deuce could?

Mme. Deschap. Ha! ha! cousin Damas, never pretend to what you don't know.

Pauline. Ha! ha! cousin Damas; *you* speak Italian, indeed!

(*Makes a mocking gesture at him.*)

Beau. (*To Glavis.*) Clever dog!—how ready!

Gla. Ready, yes; with my diamond ring!—Damn his readiness!

Damas. Laugh at me!—laugh at a colonel in the French army!—the fellow 's an impostor; I know he is. I 'll see if he understands fighting as well as he does Italian.—(*Goes up to him, and aside.*) Sir, you are a jackanapes!—Can you construe that?

Mel. No, sir; I never construe affronts in the presence of ladies; by-and-by I shall be happy to take a lesson—or give one.

Damas. I 'll find the occasion, never fear!

Mme. Deschap. Where are you going, cousin?

Damas. To correct my Italian.

(*Exit.*)

Beau. (*To Glavis.*) Let us after, and pacify him; he evidently suspects something.

Gla. Yes!—but my diamond ring!

Beau. And my box!—We are overtaxed, fellow-subject!—we must stop the supplies and dethrone the prince.

Gla. Prince!—he ought to be heir-apparent to King Stork.[3]

(*Exeunt Beauseant and Glavis.*)

Mme. Deschap. Dare I ask your highness to forgive my cousin's insufferable vulgarity?

Pauline. Oh yes!—you will forgive his manner for the sake of his heart.

Mel. And the sake of his cousin.—Ah, madam, there is one comfort in rank,—we are so sure of our position that we are not easily affronted. Besides M. Damas has bought the right of indulgence from his friends, by never showing it to his enemies.

Pauline. Ah! he is, indeed, as brave in action as he is rude in speech. He rose from the ranks to his present grade, and in two years!

Mel. In two years!—two years, did you say?

Mme. Deschap. (*Aside.*) I don't like leaving girls alone with their lovers; but, with a prince, it would be so ill-bred to be prudish.

(*Exit.*)

Mel. You can be proud of your connection with one who owes his position to merit,—not birth.

Pauline. Why, yes; but still—

Mel. Still what, Pauline!

Pauline. There is something glorious in the heritage of command. A man who has ancestors is like a representative of the past.

Mel. True; but, like other representatives, nine times out of ten he is a silent member. Ah, Pauline! not to the past, but to the future, looks true nobility, and finds its blazon in posterity.

Pauline. You say this to please me, who have no ancestors; but you, prince, must be proud of so illustrious a race!

Mel. No, no! I would not, were I fifty times a prince, be a pensioner on the dead! I honor birth and ancestry when they are regarded as the incentives to exertion, not the title-deeds to sloth! I honor the laurels that overshadow the graves of our fathers;—it is our fathers I emulate, when I desire that beneath the evergreen I myself have planted my own ashes may repose! Dearest! couldst thou but see with my eyes!

Pauline. I cannot forego pride when I look on thee, and think that thou lovest me. Sweet Prince, tell me again of thy palace by the Lake of Como; it is so pleasant to hear of thy splendors since thou didst swear to me that they would be desolate without Pauline; and when thou describest them, it is with a mocking lip and a noble scorn, as if custom had made thee disdain greatness.

Mel. Nay, dearest, nay, if thou wouldst have me paint
The home to which, could love fulfil its prayers,

* Your Excellency's most humble servant [note in the original].
** I am glad to see you in good health.
*** Fine weather. What news is there?

3 A fabulous type of over-active ruler; as "King Log" is a type of inactivity.

This hand would lead thee, listen!—A deep vale
Shut out by Alpine hills from the rude world;
Near a clear lake, margin'd by fruits of gold
And whispering myrtles; glassing softest skies,
As cloudless, save with rare and roseate shadows,
As I would have thy fate!

Pauline. My own dear love!

Mel. A palace lifting to eternal summer
Its marble walls, from out a glossy bower
Of coolest foliage musical with birds,
Whose songs should syllable thy name! At noon
We'd sit beneath the arching vines, and wonder
Why Earth could be unhappy, while the Heavens
Still left us youth and love! We'd have no friends
That were not lovers; no ambition, save
To excel them all in love; we'd read no books
That were not tales of love—that we might smile
To think how poorly eloquence of words
Translates the poetry of hearts like ours!
And when night came, amidst the breathless Heavens
We'd guess what star should be our home when love
Becomes immortal; while the perfumed light
Stole through the mists of alabaster lamps,
And every air was heavy with the sighs
Of orange-groves and music from sweet lutes,
And murmurs of low fountains that gush forth
I' the midst of roses!—Dost thou like the picture?

Pauline. Oh, as the bee upon the flower, I hang
Upon the honey of thy eloquent tongue!
Am I not blest? And if I love too wildly,
Who would not love thee like Pauline?

Mel. (*Bitterly.*) Oh, false one!
It is the *prince* thou lovest, not the *man:*
If in the stead of luxury, pomp, and power,
I had painted poverty, and toil, and care,
Thou hadst found no honey on my tongue;—Pauline,
That is not love!

Pauline. Thou wrong'st me, cruel Prince!
[At first, in truth,] I might not [have] been won,
Save through the weakness of a flatter'd pride;
But *now,*—oh! trust me,—couldst thou fall from power
And sink—

Mel. As low as that poor gardener's son
Who dared to lift his eyes to thee?—

Pauline. Even then,
Methinks thou wouldst be only made more dear
By the sweet thought that I could prove how deep
Is woman's love! We are like the insects, caught
By the poor glittering of a garish flame;
But, oh, the wings once scorch'd, the brightest star
Lures us no more; and by the fatal light
We cling till death!

Mel. Angel!
(*Aside.*) O conscience! conscience!
It must not be;—her love hath grown a torture
Worse than her hate. I will at once to Beauseant,
And—ha! he comes. Sweet love, one moment leave me.
I have business with these gentlemen—I—I
Will forthwith join you.

Pauline. Do not tarry long!
(*Exit.*)

(*Enter Beauseant and Glavis.*)

Mel. Release me from my oath,—I will not marry her!

Beau. Then thou art perjured.

Mel. No, I was not in my senses when I swore to thee to marry her! I was blind to all but her scorn!—deaf to all but my passion and my rage! Give me back my poverty and my honor!

Beau. It is too late, you must marry her! and this day. I have a story already coined, and sure to pass current. This Damas suspects thee,—he will set the police to work;—thou wilt be detected—Pauline will despise and execrate thee. Thou wilt be sent to the common jail as a swindler.

Mel. Fiend!

Beau. And in the heat of the girl's resentment (you know of what resentment is capable), and the parents' shame, she will be induced to marry the first that offers—even perhaps your humble servant.

Mel. You! No; that were worse—for thou hast no mercy! I will marry her—I will keep my oath. Quick, then, with the damnable invention thou are hatching;—quick, if thou wouldst not have me strangle thee or myself.

Gla. What a tiger! Too fierce for a prince;—he ought to have been the Grand Turk.

Beau. Enough—I will despatch; be prepared.

(*Exeunt Beauseant and Glavis.*)

(*Enter Damas with two swords.*)

Damas. Now, then, sir, the ladies are no longer your excuse. I have brought you a couple of dictionaries; let us see if your Highness can find out the Latin for *bilbo.*

Mel. Away, sir! I am in no humor for jesting.

Damas. I see you understand something of the grammar; you decline the noun-substantive "small-sword" with great ease; but that won't do—you must take a lesson in *parsing.*[4]

Mel. Fool!

Damas. Sir, as sons take after their mother, so the man who calls me a fool insults the lady who bore me; there 's no escape for you—fight you shall, or—

Mel. Oh, enough! enough!—take your ground.

(*They fight; Damas is disarmed. Melnotte takes up the sword and returns it to Damas respectfully.*)

A just punishment to the brave soldier who robs the State of its best property—the sole right to his valor and his life.

Damas. Sir, you fence exceedingly well; you must be a man of honor—I don't care a jot whether you are a prince; but a man who has carte and tierce[5] at his fingers' ends must be a gentleman.

Mel. (*Aside.*) Gentleman! Ay, I was a gentleman before I turned conspirator; for honest men are the gentlemen of Nature!—Colonel, they tell me you rose from the ranks.

Damas. I did.

Mel. And in two years?

Damas. It is true; that 's no wonder in our army at present. Why the oldest general in the service is scarcely thirty, and we have some of two-and-twenty.

Mel. Two-and-twenty!

Damas. Yes; in the French army, now-a-days, promotion is not a matter of purchase. We are all heroes, because we may be all generals. We have no fear of the cypress, because we may all hope for the laurel.

Mel. A general at two-and-twenty! (*Turning away.*)—Sir, I may ask you a favor one of these days.

Damas. Sir, I shall be proud to grant it. It is astonishing how much I like a man after I 've fought with him.

(*Hides the swords.*)

(*Enter Madame Deschappelles and Beauseant.*)

Mme. Deschap. Oh, prince,—prince!—What do I hear? You must fly—you must quit us!

Mel. I—

Beau. Yes, prince: read this letter, just received from my friend at Paris, one of the Directory; they suspect you of designs against the Republic: they are very suspicious of princes, and your family take part with the Austrians. Knowing that I introduced your highness at Lyons, my friend writes to me to say that you must quit the town immediately, or you will be arrested,—thrown into prison, perhaps guillotined! Fly!—I will order horses to your carriage instantly. Fly to Marseilles; there you can take ship for Leghorn.

Mme. Deschap. And what 's to become of Pauline? Am I not to be mother to a princess, after all?

(*Enter Pauline and M. Deschappelles.*)

Pauline. (*Throwing herself into Melnotte's arms.*) You must leave us!—Leave Pauline!

Beau. Not a moment is to be wasted.

M. Deschap. I will go to the magistrates and inquire—

Beau. Then he is lost; the magistrates, hearing he is suspected, will order his arrest.

Mme. Deschap. And I shall not be a princess-dowager!

Beau. Why not? There is only one thing to be done:—send for the priest—let the marriage take place at once, and the prince carry home a bride!

Mel. Impossible!—(*Aside.*) Villain!

Mme. Deschap. What, lose my child?

Beau. And gain a princess!

Mme. Deschap. Oh, Monsieur Beauseant, you are so very kind, it must be so,—we

4 He means a pun on *passing* (a pass being a thrust).

5 Positions in fencing.

ought not to be selfish, my daughter's happiness at stake. She will go away, too, in a carriage and six!

Pauline. Thou art here still,—I cannot part from thee,—my heart will break.

Mel. But thou wilt not consent to this hasty union,—thou wilt not wed an outcast—a fugitive.

Pauline. Ah! if thou art in danger, who should share it but Pauline?

Mel. (*Aside.*) Distraction!—If the earth could swallow me!

M. Deschap. Gently! gently! The settlements—the contracts—my daughter's dowry!

Mel. The dowry!—I am not base enough for that; no, not one farthing!

Beau. (*To Madame.*) Noble fellow!—Really your good husband is too mercantile in these matters. Monsieur Deschappelles, you hear his Highness: we can arrange the settlements by proxy; 't is the way with people of quality.

M. Deschap. But—

Mme. Deschap. Hold your tongue!—Don't expose yourself!

Beau. I will bring the priest in a trice. Go in all of you and prepare; the carriage shall be at the door before the ceremony is over.

Mme. Deschap. Be sure there are six horses, Beauseant! You are very good to have forgiven us for refusing you; but you see—a prince!

Beau. And such a prince! Madame, I cannot blush at the success of so illustrious a rival.—(*Aside.*) Now will I follow them to the village, enjoy my triumph, and to-morrow, in the hour of thy shame and grief, I think, proud girl, thou wilt prefer even these arms to those of the gardener's son.

(*Exit.*)

Mme. Deschap. Come, Monsieur Deschappelles, give your arm to her highness that is to be.

M. Deschap. I don't like doing business in such a hurry; 't is not the way with the house of Deschappelles and Co.

Mme. Deschap. There, now, you fancy you are in the counting-house, don't you?

(*Pushes him to Pauline.*)

Mel. Stay, stay, Pauline—one word. Have you no scruple, no fear? Speak—it is not yet too late.

Pauline. When I loved thee, thy fate became mine. Triumph or danger—joy or sorrow—I am by thy side.

Damas. Well, well, prince, thou art a lucky man to be so loved. She is a good little girl in spite of her foibles—make her as happy as if she were not to be a princess. (*Slapping him on the shoulder.*) Come, sir, I wish you joy—young—tender—lovely;—zounds, I envy you!

Mel. (*Who has stood apart in gloomy abstraction.*) Do you?

ACT III.

Scene 1. *The exterior of the Golden Lion—time, twilight. The moon rises during the scene.*

(*Enter Landlord and his Daughter from the Inn.*)

Land. Ha—ha—ha! Well, I never shall get over it. Our Claude is a prince with a vengeance now. His carriage breaks down at my inn—ha—ha!

Janet. And what airs the young lady gives herself! "Is this the best room you have, young woman?" with such a toss of the head.

Land. Well, get in, Janet: get in and see to the supper: the servants must sup before they go back.

(*Exeunt.*)

(*Enter Beauseant and Glavis.*)

Beau. You see our princess is lodged at last—one stage more, and she 'll be at her journey's end—the beautiful palace at the foot of the Alps!—ha—ha!

Gla. Faith, I pity the poor Pauline—especially if she 's going to sup at the Golden Lion. (*Makes a wry face.*) I shall never forget that cursed ragout.

(*Enter Melnotte from the Inn.*)

Beau. Your servant, my prince; you reigned most worthily. I condole with you on your abdication. I am afraid that your highness's retinue are not very faithful servants. I think they will quit you in the moment of your fall—'t is the fate of greatness. But you are welcome to your fine clothes—also the diamond snuff-box, which Louis XIV. gave to your great-great-grandmother.

Gla. And the ring, with which your grandfather, the Doge of Venice, married the Adriatic.

Mel. I have kept my oath, gentlemen—say, have I kept my oath?

Beau. Most religiously.

Mel. Then you have done with me and mine—away with you!

Beau. How, knave?

Mel. Look you, our bond is over. Proud conquerors that we are, we have won the victory over a simple girl—compromised her honor—embittered her life—blasted, in their very blossoms, all the flowers of her youth. This is your triumph,—it is my shame! (*Turns to Beauseant.*) Enjoy thy triumph, but not in my sight. I *was* her betrayer—I *am* her protector! Cross but her path—one word of scorn, one look of insult—nay, but one quiver of that mocking lip, and I will teach thee that bitter word thou hast graven eternally in this heart—*Repentance!*

Beau. His highness is most grandiloquent.

Mel. Highness me no more! Beware! Remorse has made me a new being. Away with you! There is danger in me. Away!

Gla. (*Aside.*) He's an awkward fellow to deal with: come away, Beauseant.

Beau. I know the respect due to rank. Adieu, my prince. Any commands at Lyons? Yet hold—I promised you 200 louis on your wedding day; here they are.

Mel. (*Dashing the purse to the ground.*) I gave you revenge, I did not sell it. Take up your silver, Judas; take it.—Ay, it is fit you should learn to stoop.

Beau. You will beg my pardon for this some day. (*Aside to Glavis.*) Come to my château—I shall return hither tomorrow, to learn how Pauline likes her new dignity.

Mel. Are you not gone yet?

Beau. Your highness's most obedient, most faithful—

Gla. And most humble servants. Ha! ha!

(*Exeunt Beauseant and Glavis.*)

Mel. Thank heaven I had no weapon, or I should have slain them. Wretch! what can I say? Where turn? On all sides mockery—the very boors within.—(*Laughter from the Inn.*)—'Sdeath, if even in this short absence the exposure should have chanced. I will call her. We will go hence. I have already sent one I can trust to my mother's house. There, at least, none can insult her agony—gloat upon her shame! There alone must she learn what a villain she has sworn to love.

(*As he turns to the door enter Pauline from the Inn.*)

Pauline. Ah! my lord, what a place! I never saw such rude people. They stare and wink so. I think the very sight of a prince, though he travels *incognito*, turns their honest heads. What a pity the carriage should break down in such a spot! You are not well—the drops stand on your brow—your hand is feverish.

Mel. Nay, it is but a passing spasm; the air—

Pauline. Is not the soft air of your native south—
How pale he is!—indeed thou art not well.
Where are our people? I will call them.

Mel. Hold!
I—I am well.

Pauline. Thou art!—Ah! now I know it.
Thou fanciest, my kind lord—I know thou dost—
Thou fanciest these rude walls, these rustic gossips,
Brick'd floors, sour wine, coarse viands, vex Pauline;
And so they might, but thou art by my side,
And I forget all else.

(*Enter Landlord, the Servants peeping and laughing over his shoulder.*)

Land. My lord—your highness—
Will your most noble excellency choose—

Mel. Begone, sir!

(*Exit Landlord laughing.*)

Pauline. How could they have learn'd thy rank?
One's servants are so vain!—nay, let it not
Chafe thee, sweet prince!—a few short days and we
Shall see thy palace by its lake of silver,
And—nay, nay, spendthrift, is thy wealth of smiles
Already drain'd, or dost thou play the miser?

Mel. Thine eyes would call up smiles in deserts, fair one.
Let us escape these rustics: close at hand
There is a cot, where I have bid prepare
Our evening lodgment—a rude, homely roof,
But honest, where our welcome will not be
Made torture by the vulgar eyes and tongues
That are as death to Love! A heavenly night!
The wooing air and the soft moon invite us.
Wilt walk? I pray thee, now,—I know the path,
Ay, every inch of it!

Pauline. What, *thou!* methought

Thou wert a stranger in these parts? Ah, truant,
Some village beauty lured thee;—thou art now
Grown constant.

Mel. Trust me.

Pauline. Princes are so changeful.

Mel. Come, dearest, come.

Pauline. Shall I not call our people
To light us?

Mel. Heaven will lend its stars for torches!
It is not far.

Pauline. The night breeze chills me.

Mel. Nay,
Let me thus mantle thee;—it is not cold.

Pauline. Never beneath thy smile!

Mel. (*Aside.*) O Heaven! forgive me!
(*Exeunt.*)

SCENE 2. *Melnotte's cottage—Widow bustling about—a table spread for supper.*)

Widow. So, I think that looks very neat. He sent me a line, so blotted that I can scarcely read it, to say he would be here almost immediately. She must have loved him well indeed to have forgotten his birth; for though he was introduced to her in disguise, he is too honorable not to have revealed to her the artifice, which her love only could forgive. Well, I do not wonder at it; for though my son is not a prince, he ought to be one, and that 's almost as good. (*Knock at the door.*) Ah! here they are.

(*Enter Melnotte and Pauline.*)

Widow. Oh, my boy—the pride of my heart!—welcome, welcome! I beg pardon, ma'am, but I do love him so!

Pauline. Good woman, I really—why prince, what is this?—does the old lady know you? Oh, I guess, you have done her some service. Another proof of your kind heart; is it not?

Mel. Of my kind heart, ay!

Pauline. So you know the prince?

Widow. Know him, madam?—Ah, I begin to fear it is you who know him not!

Pauline. Do you think she is mad? Can we stay here, my lord? I think there 's something very wild about her.

Mel. Madam, I—no, I cannot tell her; my knees knock together: what a coward is a man who has lost his honor! Speak to her—speak to her (*To his mother.*)—tell her that—O Heaven, that I were dead!

Pauline. How confused he looks!—this strange place!—this woman—what can it mean?—I half suspect—Who are you, madam!—who are you? can't you speak? are you struck dumb?

Widow. Claude, you have not deceived her?—Ah, shame upon you! I thought that, before you went to the altar, she was to have known all.

Pauline. All! what?—My blood freezes in my veins!

Widow. Poor lady!—dare I tell her, Claude? (*Melnotte makes a sign of assent.*) Know you not then, madam, that this young man is of poor though honest parents? Know you not that you are wedded to my son, Claude Melnotte?

Pauline. Your son! hold—hold! do not speak to me.—(*Approaches Melnotte, and lays her hand on his arm.*) Is this a jest? is it? I know it is, only speak—one word—one look—one smile. I cannot believe—I who loved thee so—I cannot believe that thou art such a—No, I will not wrong thee by a harsh word—speak!

Mel. Leave us—have pity on her, on me: leave us.

Widow. Oh, Claude, that I should live to see thee bowed by shame! thee of whom I was so proud!
(*Exit by the staircase.*)

Pauline. Her son—her son!

Mel. Now, lady, hear me.

Pauline. Hear thee!
Ay, speak—her son! have fiends a parent? speak,
That thou mayst silence curses—speak!

Mel. No, curse me:
Thy curse would blast me less than thy forgiveness.

Pauline. (*Laughing wildly.*) "This is thy palace, where the perfumed light
Steals through the mist of alabaster lamps,
And every air is heavy with the sighs
Of orange-groves, and music from sweet lutes,
And murmurs of low fountains, that gush forth
I' the midst of roses! Dost thou like the picture?"
This is my bridal home, and *thou* my bridegroom.
O fool—O dupe—O wretch!—I see it all—
The by-word and the jeer of every tongue

In Lyons. Hast thou in thy heart one touch
Of human kindness? if thou hast, why, kill me,
And save thy wife from madness. No, it cannot—
It cannot be: this is some horrid dream:
I shall wake soon.—(*Touching him.*) Art flesh? art man? or but
The shadows seen in sleep? It is too real.
What have I done to thee? how sinn'd against thee,
That thou shouldst crush me thus?

Mel. Pauline, by pride
Angels have fallen ere thy time: by pride—
That sole alloy of thy most lovely mould—
The evil spirit of a bitter love,
And a revengeful heart, had power upon thee.
From my first years my soul was fill'd with thee:
I saw thee midst the flow'rs the lowly boy
Tended, unmark'd by thee—a spirit of bloom,
And joy, and freshness, as if Spring itself
Were made a living thing, and wore thy shape!
I saw thee, and the passionate heart of man
Enter'd the breast of the wild-dreaming boy.
And from that hour I grew—what to the last
I shall be—thine adorer! Well, this love
Vain, frantic, guilty, if thou wilt, became
A fountain of ambition and bright hope;
I thought of tales that by the winter hearth
Old gossips tell—how maidens sprung from kings
Have stoop'd from their high sphere; how love, like death,
Levels all ranks, and lays the shepherd's crook
Beside the sceptre. Thus I made my home
In the soft palace of a fairy Future!
My father died; and I, the peasant-born,
Was my own lord. Then did I seek to rise
Out of the prison of my mean estate;
And, with such jewels as the exploring mind
Brings from the caves of knowledge, buy my ransom
From those twin jailers of the daring heart—
Low birth and iron fortune. Thy bright image
Glass'd in my soul, took all the hues of glory,
And lured me on to those inspiring toils
By which man masters men! For thee I grew
A midnight student o'er the dreams of sages.
For thee I sought to borrow from each grace,
And every muse, such attributes as lend
Ideal charms to love. I thought of thee,
And passion taught me poesy—of thee,
And on the painter's canvas grew the life
Of beauty! Art became the shadow
Of the dear starlight of thy haunting eyes!
Men call'd me vain—some mad—I heeded not;
But still toil'd on—hoped on—for it was sweet,
If not to win, to feel more worthy thee!

Pauline. Has he a magic to exorcise hate!

Mel. At last, in one mad hour, I dared to pour
The thoughts that burst their channels into song,
And sent them to thee—such a tribute, lady,
As beauty rarely scorns, even from the meanest.
The name—appended by the burning heart
That long'd to show its idol what bright things
It had created—yea, the enthusiast's name,
That should have been thy triumph, was thy scorn!
That very hour—when passion, turn'd to wrath,
Resembled hatred most—when thy disdain
Made my whole soul a chaos—in that hour
The tempters found me a revengeful tool
For their revenge! Thou hadst trampled on the worm—
It turn'd and stung thee!

Pauline. Love, sir, hath no sting.
What was the slight of a poor powerless girl
To the deep wrong of this most vile revenge?

Oh, how I loved this man!—a serf!—a slave!

Mel. Hold, lady! No, not slave! Despair is free!
I will not tell thee of the throes—the struggles—
The anguish—the remorse! No, let it pass!
And let me come to such most poor atonement
Yet in my power. Pauline!—

(*Approaching her with great emotion, and about to take her hand.*)

Pauline. No, touch me not!
I know my fate. You are, by law, my tyrant;
And I—O Heaven! a peasant's wife! I'll work—
Toil—drudge—do what thou wilt—but touch me not;
Let my wrongs make me sacred!

Mel. Do not fear me.
Thou dost not know me, madam: at the altar
My vengeance ceased—my guilty oath expired!
Henceforth, no image of some marble saint,
Niched in cathedral aisles, is hallow'd more
From the rude hand of sacrilegious wrong.
I am thy husband—nay, thou need'st not shudder;—
Here, at thy feet, I lay a husband's rights.
A marriage thus unholy—unfulfill'd—
A bond of fraud—is, by the laws of France,
Made void and null. To-night sleep—sleep in peace.
To-morrow, pure and virgin as this morn
I bore thee, bathed in blushes, from the shrine,
Thy father's arms shall take thee to thy home.
The law shall do thee justice, and restore
Thy right to bless another with thy love.
And when thou art happy, and hast half forgot
Him who so loved—so wrong'd thee, think at least
Heaven left some remnant of the angel still
In that poor peasant's nature!
Ho! my mother!

(*Enter Widow.*)

Conduct this lady—(she is not my wife;
She is our guest,—our honor'd guest, my mother)—
To the poor chamber, where the sleep of virtue,
Never, beneath my father's honest roof,
Ev'n villains dared to mar! Now, lady, now,
I think thou wilt believe me. Go, my mother!

Widow. She is not thy wife!

Mel. Hush, hush! for mercy's sake!
Speak not, but go.

(*Widow ascends the stairs; Pauline follows, weeping—turns to look back.*)

Mel. (*Sinking down.*) All angels bless and guard her!

ACT IV.

SCENE 1. *The cottage as before—Melnotte seated before a table—writing implements, &c.—(Day breaking.)*

Mel. Hush, hush!—she sleeps at last!—thank Heaven, for a while she forgets even that I live! Her sobs, which have gone to my heart the whole, long, desolate night, have ceased!—all calm—all still! I will go now; I will send this letter to Pauline's father: when he arrives, I will place in his hands my own consent to the divorce, and then, O France! my country! accept among thy protectors, thy defenders—the Peasant's Son! Our country is less proud than custom, and does not refuse the blood, the heart, the right hand of the poor man.

(*Enter Widow.*)

Widow. My son, thou hast acted ill; but sin brings its own punishment. In the hour of thy remorse, it is not for a mother to reproach thee.

Mel. What is past is past. There is a future left to all men, who have the virtue to repent, and the energy to atone. Thou shalt be proud of thy son yet. Meanwhile, remember this poor lady has been grievously injured. For the sake of thy son's conscience, respect, honor, bear with her. If she weep, console—if she chide, be silent. 'T is but a little while more—I shall send an express fast as horse can speed to her father. Farewell! I shall return shortly.

Widow. It is the only course left to thee —thou wert led astray, but thou art not hardened. Thy heart is right still, as ever it was when, in thy most ambitious hopes, thou wert never ashamed of thy poor mother.

Mel. Ashamed of thee! No, if I yet endure, yet live, yet hope—it is only because I would not die till I have redeemed the noble heritage I have lost—the heritage I took unstained from thee and my dead father—a proud conscience and an honest name. I shall win them back yet—Heaven bless you!

(*Exit.*)

Widow. My dear Claude! How my heart bleeds for him.

(*Pauline looks down from above, and after a pause descends.*)

Pauline. Not here!—he spares me that pain at least: so far he is considerate—yet the place seems still more desolate without him. Oh, that I could hate him—the gardener's son!—and yet how nobly he—no—no—no, I will not be so mean a thing as to forgive him!

Widow. Good morning, madam; I would have waited on you if I had known you were stirring.

Pauline. It is no matter, ma'am—your son's wife ought to wait on herself.

Widow. My son's wife—let not that thought vex you, madam—he tells me that you will have your divorce. And I hope I shall live to see him smile again. There are maidens in this village, young and fair, madam, who may yet console him.

Pauline. I dare say—they are very welcome—and when the divorce is got, he will marry again. I am sure I hope so.

(*Weeps.*)

Widow. He could have married the richest girl in the province, if he had pleased it; but his head was turned, poor child! he could think of nothing but you.

(*Weeps.*)

Pauline. Don't weep, *mother.*

Widow. Ah, he has behaved very ill, I know, but love is so headstrong in the young. Don't weep, madam.

Pauline. So, as you were saying—go on.

Widow. Oh, I cannot excuse him, ma'am—he was not in his right senses.

Pauline. But he always—always (*Sobbing*) loved—loved me then?

Widow. He thought of nothing else. See here—he learnt to paint that he might take your likeness (*Uncovers the picture*). But that 's all over now—I trust you have cured him of his folly;—but, dear heart, you have had no breakfast!

Pauline. I can't take anything—don't trouble yourself.

Widow. Nay, madam, be persuaded; a little coffee will refresh you. Our milk and eggs are excellent. I will get out Claude's coffee-cup—it is of real Sèvres; he saved up all his money to buy it three years ago, because the name of *Pauline* was inscribed on it.

Pauline. Three years ago! Poor Claude!—Thank you; I think I will have some coffee. Oh! if he were but a poor gentleman, even a merchant: but a gardener's son—and what a home!—Oh no, it is too dreadful!

(*They seat themselves at the table, Beauseant opens the lattice and looks in.*)

Beau. So—so—the coast is clear! I saw Claude in the lane—I shall have an excellent opportunity.

(*Shuts the lattice and knocks at the door.*)

Pauline. (*Starting.*) Can it be my father?—he has not sent for him yet? No, he cannot be in such a hurry to get rid of me.

Widow. It is not time for your father to arrive yet; it must be some neighbor.

Pauline. Don't admit any one.

(*Widow opens the door, Beauseant pushes her aside and enters.*)

Ah! Heavens! that hateful Beauseant! This is indeed bitter!

Beau. Good morning, madam! O widow, your son begs you will have the goodness to go to him in the village—he wants to speak to you on particular business; you 'll find him at the inn, or the grocer's shop, or the baker's, or at some other friend's of your family—make haste.

Pauline. Don't leave me, mother!—don't leave me.

Beau. (*With great respect.*) Be not alarmed, madam. Believe me your friend—your servant.

Pauline. Sir, I have no fear of you, even in this house! Go, madam, if your son wishes it; I will not contradict his commands whilst, at least, he has still the right to be obeyed.

Widow. I don't understand this; however, I shan't be long gone.

(*Exit.*)

Pauline. Sir, I divine the object of your visit—you wish to exult in the humiliation of one who humbled you. Be it so; I am prepared to endure all—even your presence!

Beau. You mistake me, madam—Pauline,

you mistake me! I come to lay my fortune at your feet. You must already be disenchanted with this impostor; these walls are not worthy to be hallowed by your beauty! Shall that form be clasped in the arms of a base-born peasant? Beloved, beautiful Pauline! fly with me—my carriage waits without—I will bear you to a home more meet for your reception. Wealth, luxury, station—all shall yet be yours. I forget your past disdain—I remember only your beauty and my unconquerable love!

Pauline. Sir! leave this house—it is humble: but a husband's roof, however lowly, is, in the eyes of God and man, the temple of a wife's honor! Know that I would rather starve—yes—with him who has betrayed me, than accept your lawful hand, even were you the prince whose name he bore!—Go.

Beau. What, is not your pride humbled yet?

Pauline. Sir, what was pride in prosperity in affliction becomes virtue.

Beau. Look round: these rugged floors—these homely walls—this wretched struggle of poverty for comfort—think of this! and contrast with such a picture the refinement, the luxury, the pomp, that the wealthiest gentleman of Lyons offers to the loveliest lady. Ah, hear me!

Pauline. Oh! my father!—why did I leave you?—why am I thus friendless? Sir, you see before you a betrayed, injured, miserable woman!—respect her anguish!

(*Melnotte opens the door silently, and pauses at the threshold.*)

Beau. No! let me rather thus console it; let me snatch from those lips one breath of that fragrance which never should be wasted on the low churl thy husband.

Pauline. Help! Claude!—Claude!—Have I no protector?

Beau. Be silent! (*Showing a pistol.*) See, I do not come unprepared even for violence. I will brave all things—thy husband and all his race—for thy sake. Thus, then, I clasp thee!

Mel. (*Dashing him to the other end of the stage.*) Pauline—look up, Pauline! thou art safe.

Beau. (*Levelling his pistol.*) Dare you thus insult a man of my birth, ruffian?

Pauline. Oh, spare him—spare my husband!—Beauseant—Claude—no—no.

(*Faints.*)

Mel. Miserable trickster! shame upon you! brave devices to terrify a woman! Coward!—you tremble—you have outraged the laws—you know that your weapon is harmless—you have the courage of the mountebank, not the bravo!—Pauline, there is no danger.

Beau. I wish thou wert a gentleman—as it is, thou art beneath me.—Good day, and a happy honeymoon.—(*Aside.*) I will not die till I am avenged.

(*Exit.*)

Mel. I hold her in these arms—the last embrace!
Never, ah never more, shall this dear head
Be pillow'd on the heart that should have shelter'd
And has betray'd!—Soft—soft! one kiss—poor wretch!
No scorn on that pale lip forbids me now!
One kiss—so ends all record of my crime!
It is the seal upon the tomb of hope,
By which, like some lost, sorrowing angel, sits
Sad memory evermore;—she breathes—she moves—
She wakes to scorn, to hate, but not to shudder
Beneath the touch of my abhorred love.

(*Places her on a seat.*)

There—we are strangers now!

Pauline. All gone—all calm—
Is *every* thing a dream? thou art safe, unhurt—
I do not love thee; but—but I am woman,
And—and—no blood is spilt?

Mel. No, lady, no;
My guilt hath not deserved so rich a blessing
As even danger in thy cause.

(*Enter Widow.*)

Widow. My son, I have been everywhere in search of you; why did you send for me?

Mel. I did not send for you.

Widow. No! but I must tell you your express has returned.

Mel. So soon! impossible!

Widow. Yes, he met the lady's father and mother on the road; they were going into the country on a visit. Your messenger says that Monsieur Deschappelles turned almost white with anger when he read your letter. They will be here almost immediately. Oh, Claude, Claude! what will they do to you? How I tremble! Ah, madam! do not let them injure him —if you knew how he doated on you.

Pauline. Injure him! no, ma'am, be not afraid;—my father! how shall I meet him? how go back to Lyons? the scoff of the whole city! Cruel, cruel, Claude. (*In great agitation.*) Sir, you have acted most treacherously.

Mel. I know it, madam.

Pauline. (*Aside.*) If he would but ask me to forgive him!—I never can forgive you, sir.

Mel. I never dared to hope it.

Pauline. But you are my husband now, and I have sworn to—to love you, sir.

Mel. That was under a false belief, madam; Heaven and the laws will release you from your vow.

Pauline. He will drive me mad! if he were but less proud—if he would but ask me to remain—hark, hark—I hear the wheels of the carriage—Sir—Claude, they are coming; have you no word to say ere it is too late? Quick—speak.

Mel. I can only congratulate you on your release. Behold your parents!

(*Enter Monsieur and Madame Deschappelles and Colonel Damas.*)

M. Deschap. My child! my child!

Mme. Deschap. Oh, my poor Pauline!—what a villainous hovel this is! Old woman, get me a chair—I shall faint—I certainly shall. What will the world say? Child, you have been a fool. A mother's heart is easily broken.

Damas. Ha, ha! most noble Prince—I am sorry to see a man of your quality in such a condition; I am afraid your highness will go to the House of Correction.

Mel. Taunt on, sir; I spared *you* when you were unarmed—I am unarmed now. A man who has no excuse for crime is indeed defenceless!

Damas. There 's something fine in the rascal, after all!

M. Deschap. Where is the impostor?—Are you thus shameless, traitor? Can you brave the presence of that girl's father?

Mel. Strike me, if it please you—you *are* her father.

Pauline. Sir—sir, for my sake;—whatever his guilt, he has acted nobly in atonement.

Mme. Deschap. Nobly! Are you mad, girl? I have no patience with you—to disgrace all your family thus!—Nobly! Oh you abominable, hardened, pitiful, mean, ugly villain!

Damas. Ugly! Why he was beautiful yesterday!

Pauline. Madam, this is his roof, and he is my husband. Respect your daughter, or let blame fall alone on her.

Mme. Deschap. You—you—Oh, I 'm choking.

M. Deschap. Sir, it were idle to waste reproach upon a conscience like yours—you renounce all pretensions to the person of this lady?

Mel. I do. (*Gives a paper.*) Here is my consent to a divorce—my full confession of the fraud which annuls the marriage. Your daughter has been foully wronged—I grant it, sir; but her own lips will tell you that, from the hour in which she crossed this threshold, I returned to my own station, and respected hers. Pure and inviolate, as when yestermorn you laid your hand upon her head, and blessed her, I yield her back to you. For myself—I deliver you for ever from my presence. An outcast and a criminal, I seek some distant land, where I may mourn my sin, and pray for your daughter's peace. Farewell—farewell to you all, for ever!

Widow. Claude, Claude, you will not leave your poor old mother? *She* does not disown you in your sorrow—no, not even in your guilt. No divorce can separate a mother from her son.

Pauline. This poor widow teaches me my duty. No, mother,—no, for you are now *my* mother also!—nor should any law, human or divine, separate the wife from her husband's sorrows. Claude—Claude—all is forgotten—forgiven—I am thine for ever!

Mme. Deschap. What do I hear?—Come away, or never see my face again.

M. Deschap. Pauline, *we* never betrayed you!—do you forsake us for him?

Pauline. (*Going back to her father.*) Oh no—but you will forgive him too; we will live together—he shall be your son.

M. Deschap. Never! Cling to him and forsake your parents! His home shall be yours—his fortune yours—his fate yours: the wealth I have acquired by honest industry shall never enrich the dishonest man.

Pauline. And you would have a wife enjoy luxury while a husband toils! Claude, take me; thou canst not give me wealth, titles, station—but thou canst give me a true heart. I will work for thee, tend thee, bear with thee, and never, never shall these lips reproach thee for the past.

Damas. I 'll be hanged if I am not going to blubber!

Mel. This is the heaviest blow of all!—What a heart I have wronged!—Do not fear me, sir; I am not all hardened—I will not rob her of a holier love than mine. Pauline!—angel of love and mercy!—your memory shall lead me back to virtue!—The husband of a being so beautiful in her noble and sublime tenderness may be poor—may be low-born;—(there is no guilt in the decrees of Providence!—but he should be one who can look thee in the face without a blush,—to whom thy love does not bring remorse,—who can fold thee to his heart, and say,—"*Here* there is no deceit!"—I am not that man!

Damas. (*Aside to Melnotte.*) Thou art a noble fellow, notwithstanding; and wouldst make an excellent soldier. Serve in my regiment. I have had a letter from the Directory—our young general takes the command of the army in Italy,—I am to join him at Marseilles,—I will depart this day, if thou wilt go with me.

Mel. It is the favor I would have asked thee, if I dared. Place me wherever a foe is most dreaded,—wherever France most needs a life!

Damas. There shall not be a forlorn hope without thee!

Mel. There is my hand!—mother, your blessing. I shall see you again,—a better man than a prince,—a man who has bought the right to high thoughts by brave deeds. And thou!—thou! so wildly worshipped, so guiltily betrayed,—all is not yet lost!—for thy memory, at least, must be mine till death! If I live, the name of him thou hast once loved shall not rest dishonored;—if I fall, amidst the carnage and the roar of battle, my soul will fly back to thee, and love shall share with death my last sigh!—More—more would I speak to thee!—to pray!—to bless! But no!—when I am less unworthy I will utter it to Heaven!—I cannot trust myself to—(*Turning to Deschappelles.*) Your pardon, sir;—they are my last words—Farewell!

(*Exit.*)

Damas. I will go after him.—France will thank me for this.

(*Exit.*)

Pauline. (*Starting from her father's arms.*) Claude!—Claude!—my husband.

M. Deschap. You have a father still!

ACT V.

Two years and a half from the date of Act IV.

Scene 1. *The Streets of Lyons.*

(*Enter First, Second, and Third Officers.*)

First Officer. Well, here we are at Lyons, with gallant old Damas: it is his native place.

Second Officer. Yes; he has gained a step in the army since he was here last. The Lyonnese ought to be very proud of stout General Damas.

Third Officer. Promotion is quick in the French army. This mysterious Morier,—the hero of Lodi,[6] and the favorite of the commander-in-chief,—has risen to a colonel's rank in two years and a half.

(*Enter Damas, as a General.*)

Damas. Good morrow, gentlemen; I hope you will amuse yourselves during our short stay at Lyons. It is a fine city: improved since I left it. Ah! it is a pleasure to grow old,—when the years that bring decay to ourselves do but ripen the prosperity of our country. You have not met with Morier?

First Officer. No: we were just speaking of him.

Second Officer. Pray, general, can you tell us who this Morier really is?

Damas. Is!—why a colonel in the French army.

Third Officer. True. But what was he at first?

Damas. At first? Why a baby in long clothes, I suppose.

First Officer. Ha, ha! Ever facetious, general.

Second Officer. (*To Third.*) The general is sore upon this point; you will only chafe him.—Any commands, general?

Damas. None. Good day to you.

(*Exeunt Second and Third Officers.*)

6 At Lodi in Lombardy on the 10th May, 1796, Napoleon won a victory over the Austrians.

Damas. Our comrades are very inquisitive. Poor Morier is the subject of a vast deal of curiosity.

First Officer. Say interest, rather, general. His constant melancholy, the loneliness of his habits,—his daring valor, his brilliant rise in the profession,—your friendship, and the favors of the commander-in-chief,—all tend to make him as much the matter of gossip as of admiration. But where is he, general? I have missed him all the morning.

Damas. Why, captain, I 'll let you into a secret. My young friend has come with me to Lyons in hopes of finding a miracle.

First Officer. A miracle!

Damas. Yes, a miracle! in other words,—a constant woman.

First Officer. Oh! an affair of love!

Damas. Exactly so. No sooner did he enter Lyons than he waved his hand to me, threw himself from his horse, and is now, I warrant, asking every one who can know anything about the matter, whether a certain lady is still true to a certain gentleman!

First Officer. Success to him!—and of that success there can be no doubt. The gallant Colonel Morier, the hero of Lodi, might make his choice out of the proudest families in France.

Damas. Oh, if pride be a recommendation, the lady and her mother are most handsomely endowed. By the way, captain, if you should chance to meet with Morier, tell him he will find me at the hotel.

First Officer. I will, general.

(*Exit.*)

Damas. Now will I go to the Deschappelles, and make a report to my young Colonel. Ha! by Mars, Bacchus, Apollo, Virorum,—here comes Monsieur Beauseant!

(*Enter Beauseant.*)

Good morrow, Monsieur Beauseant! How fares it with you?

Beau. (*Aside.*) Damas! that is unfortunate;—if the Italian campaign should have filled his pockets, he may seek to baffle me in the moment of my victory. (*Aloud.*) Your servant, general,—for such, I think, is your new distinction! Just arrived in Lyons?

Damas. Not an hour ago. Well, how go on the Deschappelles? Have they forgiven you in that affair of young Melnotte? You had some hand in that notable device,—eh?

Beau. Why, less than you think for! The fellow imposed upon me. I have set it all right now. What has become of him? He could not have joined the army, after all. There is no such name in the books.

Damas. I know nothing about Melnotte. As you say, I never heard the name in the Grand Army.

Beau. Hem!—You are not married, general?

Damas. Do I look like a married man, sir?—No, thank Heaven! My profession is to make widows, not wives.

Beau. You must have gained much booty in Italy! Pauline will be your heiress—eh?

Damas. Booty! Not I! Heiress to what? Two trunks and a portmanteau,—four horses,—three swords,—two suits of regimentals, and six pair of white leather inexpressibles![7] A pretty fortune for a young lady!

Beau. (*Aside.*) Then all is safe. (*Aloud.*) Ha! ha! Is that really all your capital, General Damas? Why, I thought Italy had been a second Mexico to you soldiers.

Damas. All a toss-up, sir. I was not one of the lucky ones! My friend Morier, indeed, saved something handsome. But our commander-in-chief took care of him, and Morier is a thrifty, economical dog,—not like the rest of us soldiers, who spend our money as carelessly as if it were our blood.

Beau. Well, it is no matter! I do not want fortune with Pauline. And you must know, General Damas, that your fair cousin has at length consented to reward my long and ardent attachment.

Damas. You!—the devil! Why, she is already married! There is no divorce!

Beau. True; but this very day she is formally to authorize the necessary proceedings,—this very day she is to sign the contract that is to make her mine within one week from the day on which her present illegal marriage is annulled.

Damas. You tell me wonders!—Wonders! No; I believe anything of women!

Beau. I must wish you good morning.

(*As he is going, enter Deschappelles.*)

M. Deschap. Oh, Beauseant! well met. Let us come to the notary at once.

Damas. (*To Deschap.*) Why, cousin!

[7] Breeches.

M. Deschap. Damas, welcome to Lyons. Pray call on us; my wife will be delighted to see you.

Damas. Your wife be—blessed for her condescension! But (*taking him aside*) what do I hear? Is it possible that your daughter has consented to a divorce?—that she will marry Monsieur Beauseant?

M. Deschap. Certainly! What have you to say against it! A gentleman of birth, fortune, character. We are not so proud as we were; even my wife has had enough of nobility and princes!

Damas. But Pauline loved that young man so tenderly!

M. Deschap. (*Taking snuff.*) That was two years and a half ago!

Damas. Very true. Poor Melnotte!

M. Deschap. But do not talk of that impostor; I hope he is dead or has left the country. Nay, even were he in Lyons at this moment, he ought to rejoice that, in an honorable and suitable alliance, my daughter may forget her sufferings and his crime.

Damas. Nay, if it be all settled, I have no more to say. Monsieur Beauseant informs me that the contract is to be signed this very day.

M. Deschap. It is; at one o'clock precisely. Will you be one of the witnesses?

Damas. I?—No; that is to say—yes, certainly!—at one o'clock I will wait on you.

M. Deschap. Till then adieu—come, Beauseant.

(*Exeunt Beauseant and Deschappelles.*)

Damas. The man who sets his heart upon a woman
Is a chameleon, and doth feed on air;
From air he takes his colors—holds his life,—
Changes with every wind,—grows lean or fat,
Rosy with hope, or green with jealousy,
Or pallid with despair—just as the gale
Varies from north to south—from heat to cold!
Oh, woman! woman! thou shouldst have few sins
Of thine own to answer for! Thou art the author
Of such a book of follies in a man,
That it would need the tears of all the angels
To blot the record out!

(*Enter Melnotte, pale and agitated.*)

I need not tell thee! Thou hast heard—

Mel. The worst!
I have!

Damas. Be cheer'd; others are fair as she is!

Mel. Others!—The world is crumbled at my feet!
She *was* my world; fill'd up the whole of being—
Smiled in the sunshine—walk'd the glorious earth—
Sate in my heart—was the sweet life of life.
The Past was hers; I dreamt not of a Future
That did not wear her shape! Mem'ry and Hope
Alike are gone. Pauline is faithless! Henceforth
The universal space is desolate!

Damas. Hope yet.

Mel. Hope, yes!—one hope is left me still—
A soldier's grave! Glory has died with love.
I look into my heart, and, where I saw
Pauline, see Death!
(*After a pause.*)
—But am I not deceived?
I went but by the rumor of the town;
Rumor is false,—I was too hasty! Damas,
Whom hast thou seen?

Damas. Thy rival and her father.
Arm thyself for the truth.—He heeds not—

Mel. She
Will never know how deeply she was loved!
The charitable night, that wont to bring
Comfort to-day, in bright and eloquent dreams,
Is henceforth leagued with misery! Sleep, farewell,
Or else become eternal! Oh, the waking
From false oblivion, and to see the sun,
And know she is another's!

Damas. Be a man!

Mel. I am a man!—it is the sting of woe
Like mine that tells us we are men!

Damas. The false one
Did not deserve thee.

Mel. Hush—No word against her!
Why should she keep, through years and silent absence,
The holy tablets of her virgin faith
True to a traitor's name! Oh, blame her not;

It were a sharper grief to think her worthless
Than to be what I am! To-day,—to-day!
They said "To-day!" This day, so wildly welcomed—
This day, my soul had singled out of time
And mark'd for bliss! This day! oh, could I see her,
See her once more unknown; but hear her voice.
So that one echo of its music might
Make ruin less appalling in its silence.

Damas. Easily done! Come with me to her house;
Your dress—your cloak—moustache—the bronzed hues
Of time and toil—the name you bear—belief
In your absence, all will ward away suspicion.
Keep in the shade. Ay, I would have you come.
There may be hope! Pauline is yet so young,
They may have forced her to these second bridals
Out of mistaken love.

Mel. No, bid me hope not!
Bid me not hope! I could not bear again
To fall from such a heaven! One gleam of sunshine,
And the ice breaks and I am lost! Oh, Damas,
There 's no such thing as courage in a man;
The veriest slave that ever crawl'd from danger
Might spurn me now. When first I lost her, Damas,
I bore it, did I not? I still had hope,
And now I—I—

(*Bursts into an agony of grief.*)

Damas. What, comrade! all the women
That ever smiled destruction on brave hearts
Were not worth tears like these!

Mel. 'T is past—forget it.
I am prepared; life has no farther ills!
The cloud has broken in that stormy rain,
And on the waste I stand, alone with Heaven.

Damas. His very face is changed; a breaking heart
Does its work soon!—Come, Melnotte, rouse thyself:
One effort more. Again thou 'lt see her.

Mel. See her!
There is a passion in that simple sentence
That shivers all the pride and power of reason
Into a chaos!

Damas. Time wanes;—come, ere yet
It be too late.

Mel. Terrible words—*"Too late!"*
Lead on. One last look more, and then—

Damas. Forget her!

Mel. Forget her! yes.—For death remembers not.

(*Exeunt.*)

SCENE 2. *A room in the house of Monsieur Deschappelles; Pauline seated in great dejection.*)

Pauline. It is so, then. I must be false to Love,
Or sacrifice a father! Oh, my Claude,
My lover, and my husband! Have I lived
To pray that thou mayst find some fairer boon
Than the deep faith of this devoted heart,
Nourish'd till now—now broken?

(*Enter Monsieur Deschappelles.*)

M. Deschap. My dear child,
How shall I thank—how bless thee? Thou hast saved,
I will not say my fortune—I could bear
Reverse, and shrink not—but that prouder wealth
Which merchants value most—my name, my credit—
The hard-won honors of a toilsome life:—
These thou hast saved, my child!

Pauline. Is there no hope?
No hope but this?

M. Deschap. None. If, without the sum
Which Beauseant offers for thy hand, this day
Sinks to the west—to-morrow brings our ruin!
And hundreds, mingled in that ruin, curse
The bankrupt merchant! and the insolent herd
We feasted and made merry cry in scorn,
"How pride has fallen!—Lo, the bankrupt merchant!"

My daughter, thou hast saved us!
Pauline. And am lost!
M. Deschap. Come, let me hope that Beauseant's love—
Pauline. His love!
Talk not of love. Love has no thought of self!
Love buys not with the ruthless usurer's gold
The loathsome prostitution of a hand
Without a heart! Love sacrifices all things
To bless the thing it loves! *He* knows not love.
Father, his love is hate—his hope revenge!
My tears, my anguish, my remorse for falsehood—
These are the joys he wrings from our despair!
M. Deschap. If thou deem'st thus, reject him! Shame and ruin
Were better than thy misery;—think no more on 't.
My sand is wellnigh run—what boots it when
The glass is broken? We 'll annul the contract:
And if to-morrow in the prisoner's cell
These aged limbs are laid, why still, my child,
I 'll think thou art spared; and wait the liberal hour
That lays the beggar by the side of kings!
Pauline. No—no—forgive me! You, my honor'd father,—
You, who so loved, so cherish'd me, whose lips
Never knew one harsh word! I 'm not ungrateful;
I am but human!—hush! *Now,* call the bridegroom—
You see I am prepared—no tears—all calm;
But, father, *talk no more of love!*
M. Deschap. My child,
'T is but one struggle; he is young, rich, noble;
Thy state will rank first 'mid the dames of Lyons;
And when this heart can shelter thee no more,
Thy youth will not be guardianless.
Pauline. I have set
My foot upon the ploughshare—I will pass
The fiery ordeal. (*Aside.*) Merciful Heaven, support me!
And on the absent wanderer shed the light
Of happier stars—lost evermore to me.

(*Enter Madame Deschappelles, Beauseant, Glavis, and Notary.*)

Mme. Deschap. Why, Pauline, you are quite in *déshabille*—you ought to be more alive to the importance of this joyful occasion. We had once looked higher, it is true; but you see, after all, Monsieur Beauseant's father *was* a Marquis, and that 's a great comfort. Pedigree and jointure!—you have them both in Monsieur Beauseant. A young lady decorously brought up should only have two considerations in her choice of a husband: first, is his birth honorable? secondly, will his death be advantageous? All other trifling details should be left to parental anxiety.

Beau. (*Approaching and waving aside Madame.*) Ah, Pauline! let me hope that you are reconciled to an event which confers such rapture upon me.

Pauline. I am reconciled to my doom.

Beau. Doom is a harsh word, sweet lady.

Pauline. (*Aside.*) This man must have some mercy—his heart cannot be marble. (*Aloud.*) Oh, sir, be just—be generous! Seize a noble triumph—a great revenge. Save the father, and spare the child.

Beau. (*Aside.*) Joy—joy alike to my hatred and my passion! The haughty Pauline is at last my suppliant. (*Aloud.*) You ask from me what I have not the sublime virtue to grant—a virtue reserved only for the gardener's son! I cannot forego my hopes in the moment of their fulfilment! I adhere to the contract—your father's ruin or your hand.

Pauline. Then all is over. Sir, I have decided.

(*The clock strikes one.*)

(*Enter Damas and Melnotte.*)

Damas. Your servant, cousin Deschappelles. Let me introduce Colonel Morier.

Mme. Deschap. (*Curtsying very low.*) What, the celebrated hero? This is, indeed, an honor!

(*Melnotte bows, and remains in the background.*)

Damas. (*To Pauline.*) My little cousin, I congratulate you. What, no smile—no blush? You are going to be divorced from poor Melnotte, and marry this rich gentleman. You ought to be excessively happy!

Pauline. Happy!

Damas. Why, how pale you are, child!—Poor Pauline! Hist—confide in me! Do they force you to this?

Pauline. No!

Damas. You act with your own free consent?

Pauline. My own consent—yes.

Damas. Then you are the most—I will not say what you are.

Pauline. You think ill of me—be it so—yet if you knew all—

Damas. There is some mystery—speak out, Pauline.

Pauline. (*Suddenly.*) Oh, perhaps you can save me! you are our relation—our friend. My father is on the verge of bankruptcy—this day he requires a large sum to meet demands that cannot be denied; that sum Beauseant will advance—this hand the condition of the barter. Save me if you have the means—save me! You will be repaid above!

Damas. (*Aside.*) I recant—Women are not so bad after all! (*Aloud.*) Humph, child! I cannot help you—I am too poor.

Pauline. The last plank to which I clung is shivered!

Damas. Hold—you see my friend Morier: Melnotte is his most intimate friend—fought in the same fields—slept in the same tent. Have you any message to send to Melnotte? any word to soften this blow?

Pauline. He knows Melnotte—he will see him—he will bear to him my last farewell.—(*Approaches Melnotte.*)—He has a stern air—he turns away from me—he despises me!—Sir, one word I beseech you.

Mel. Her voice again! How the old time comes o'er me!

Damas. (*To Madame.*) Don't interrupt them. He is going to tell her what a rascal young Melnotte is; he knows him well, I promise you.

Mme. Deschap. So considerate in you, cousin Damas!

(*Damas approaches Deschappelles; converses apart with him in dumb show—Deschappelles shows him a paper, which he inspects and takes.*)

Pauline. Thrice have I sought to speak; my courage fails me.—
Sir, is it true that you have known—nay, are
The friend of—Melnotte?

Mel. Lady, yes!—Myself
And misery know the man!

Pauline. And you will see him,
And you will bear to him—ay—word for word,
All that this heart, which breaks in parting from him,
Would send, ere still for ever.

Mel. He hath told me
You have the right to choose from out the world
A worthier bridegroom;—he foregoes all claim,
Even to murmur at his doom. Speak on!

Pauline. Tell him, for years I never nursed a thought
That was not his;—that on his wandering way,
Daily and nightly, pour'd a mourner's prayers.
Tell him ev'n now that I would rather share
His lowliest lot,—walk by his side, an outcast,—
Work for him, beg with him,—live upon the light
Of one kind smile from him,—than wear the crown
The Bourbon lost!

Mel. (*Aside.*) Am I already mad?
And does delirium utter such sweet words
Into a dreamer's ear? (*Aloud.*) You love him thus,
And yet desert him?

Pauline. Say, that, if his eye
Could read this heart,—its struggles, its temptations,—
His love itself would pardon that desertion!
Look on that poor old man,—he is my father;
He stands upon the verge of an abyss!—
He calls his child to save him! Shall I shrink
From him who gave me birth?—withhold my hand,
And see a parent perish? Tell him this,
And say—that we shall meet again in Heaven!

Mel. (*Aside.*) The night is past—joy cometh with the morrow.
(*Aloud.*) Lady—I—I—what is this riddle?—what
The nature of this sacrifice?

Pauline. (*Pointing to Damas.*) Go, ask him!

Beau. (*From the table.*) The papers are prepared—we only need
Your hand and seal.

Mel. Stay, lady—one word more.
Were but your duty with your faith united,
Would you still share the low-born peasant's lot?

Pauline. Would I? Ah, better death with him I love
Than all the pomp—which is but as the flowers
That crown the victim!—(*Turning away.*) I am ready.

(*Melnotte rushes to Damas.*)

Damas. There—
This is the schedule—this the total.

Beau. (*To Deschappelles, showing notes.*) These
Are yours the instant she has sign'd; you are
Still the great House of Lyons!

(*The Notary is about to hand the contract to Pauline, when Melnotte seizes it and tears it.*)

Beau. Are you mad?

M. Deschap. How, sir! What means this insult?

Mel. Peace, old man!
I have a prior claim. Before the face
Of man and Heaven I urge it; I outbid
Yon sordid huckster for your priceless jewel.

(*Giving a pocket-book.*)

There is the sum twice told! Blush not to take it:
There's not a coin that is not bought and hallow'd
In the cause of nations with a soldier's blood!

Beau. Torments and death!

Pauline. That voice! Thou art—

Mel. Thy husband!

(*Pauline rushes into his arms.*)

Look up! Look up, Pauline!—for I can bear
Thine eyes! The stain is blotted from my name.
I have redeem'd mine honor. I can call
On France to sanction thy divine forgiveness!
Oh, joy!—Oh, rapture! By the midnight watchfires
Thus have I seen thee! thus foretold this hour!
And 'midst the roar of battle, thus have heard
The beating of thy heart against my own!

Beau. Fool'd, duped, and triumph'd over in the hour
Of mine own victory! Curses on ye both!
May thorns be planted in the marriage-bed!
And love grow sour'd and blacken'd into hate—
Such as the hate that gnaws me!

Damas. Curse away!
And let me tell thee, Beauseant, a wise proverb
The Arabs have,—"Curses are like young chickens,
(*Solemnly.*) And still come home to roost!"

Beau. Their happiness
Maddens my soul! I am powerless and revengeless!

(*To Madame.*)

I wish you joy! Ha! ha! the gardener's son!

(*Exit.*)

Damas. (*To Glavis.*) Your friend intends to hang himself! Methinks
You ought to be his travelling companion!

Gla. Sir, you are exceedingly obliging!

(*Exit.*)

Pauline. Oh!
My father, you are saved,—and by my husband!
Ah, blessed hour!

Mel. Yet you weep still, Pauline!

Pauline. But on thy breast—*these* tears are sweet and holy!

M. Deschap. You have won love and honor nobly, sir!
Take her;—be happy both!

Mme. Deschap. I'm all astonish'd!
Who, then, is Colonel Morier?

Damas. You behold him!

Mel. Morier no more after this happy day!
I would not bear again my father's name
Till I could deem it spotless! The hour's come!
Heaven smiled on conscience! As the soldier rose
From rank to rank, how sacred was the fame
That cancell'd crime, and raised him nearer thee!

Mme. Deschap. A colonel and a hero! Well, that 's something!
He 's wondrously improved! I wish you joy, sir!
Mel. Ah! the same love that tempts us into sin,
If it be true love, works out its redemption;
And he who seeks repentance for the Past
Should woo the Angel Virtue in the Future.

THOMAS WILLIAM ROBERTSON

CASTE

Thomas W. Robertson (1829–1871), son of an actor and actress, passed nearly all his life on the stage or writing for it. Completely immersed in the theatrical life of his time, he wrote scores of plays, largely adaptations from stories and from French plays, in the ephemeral contemporary style. But later in life he produced several of more worth and originality. *Society* appeared in 1865, *Caste* in 1867, the laconic titles of which are characteristic of him. His plays exemplify the close relation to each other of drama and prose fiction, especially at a time when the latter flourished as in the mid-nineteenth century; just as Dickens' novels were strongly influenced by his interest in acting, so Robertson's plays were influenced by Thackeray. Aside from the adaptations mentioned above, his plots were mostly invented, but made up out of the sort of characters, situations and other elements common in novels.

The originality of *Caste* is not easy to see for a reader unfamiliar with the theatrical world into which it came, and which Robertson's plays did a good deal to change. The enormous flood of plays of various types, mostly with short runs, were for the most part cheap, stagy, over-romantic, sensational, artificial, in short looking to other plays and other fiction for all their elements and not to life or even reasonable ideals; laying their stress on incident and plot (such as it was), and almost none on their characters and on fidelity to human nature. While some of all this may be detected in Robertson by a reader of to-day, used to still greater independence and reality in the drama, his comparative independence and reality made a deep impression. Indeed some critics of his time found in him even too much of trivial realism; but had his plays shown more, they might have had no audience.

The characters are simplified, and their peculiar traits heightened; though *Caste* was acted in a small theater, those subtleties had not yet returned to the drama which would have been wasted in the enormous theaters usual in mid-nineteenth century London. But the characters are not unreal. Upper-class people exist who are as arrogant and ill-mannered as the Marchioness and Hawtree, especially among the parvenus among whom one suspects both originated. The perpetual shop-talk of Sam, the blind indulgent loyalty of the warm-hearted daughters to their father, and his transparent pretenses and wiles are merely theatrical simplifying and heightening of ordinary human reality. The idle drunken father's feeble efforts to hide his vice are not only humorously lifelike but pathetic, and his addiction to what would now be called communist sentiments (act III), an attempt to retain some rag of self-respect, is a keenly ironical touch of nature, though likely to-day to irritate more earnest propagandists. Esther's very competence and dignity are just what may develop perforce in the daughter of such a father. The characters, though possibly more warm-hearted than the average of humanity, are all spirited and clean-cut, and they and their three love-affairs brightly contrasted. Some of the exaggeration in the talk is humorously intentional on the part of the characters; the dialogue is constantly brisk and lifelike, with much genuine though sometimes crude humor. Robertson did not, like earlier popular playwrights, represent all the rich as bad and all the poor as good; he assorted virtue as it is in life, creating here no wholly lost souls unless old Eccles, who jocosely hopes shortly to drink himself to death in Jersey. The very moral of the play, that there is something in "caste" but not everything, tame as it is, agrees with human facts. The skill in stagecraft must be evident to anyone; also the perpetual activity among the characters, the abundant opportunity for "stage business," and perhaps even more the perpetual and continually shifting emotions. The fainting women and sometimes tearful men partly belong to the sentimental literary tradition; but women still do faint and men weep, though seldomer in public. The emotionalism is one of the marked Victorian traits of the play.

Nothing seems more old-fashioned than a fashion which has gone out only rather recently; not so long ago plays following Robertson's example in feeling and composition were the usual thing, and indeed are still common enough in the moving-pictures. One trait in *Caste* in sharpest contrast with characteristic plays of our day is its geniality, cheerfulness, freedom from cynicism and despair. But the one kind of play is no more true to life than the other. The too-knowing person of our day is anxious above all things not to be fooled,—to cherish no illusions and to face grim facts. But any experienced observer has known family histories which worked out almost ideally, perhaps many more than those which ended in crime and madness. Robertson not only brought the English drama back to nature and truth, and created a new variety of drawing-room comedy. He was the ruling spirit of the stage for years in the later part of the century. Though his achievement was less than his influence, along with other influences he led on toward such men as Pinero, who is said to have called himself a disciple of Robertson.

CASTE

CAST OF CHARACTERS

Prince of Wales' Theatre, London,
April 6, 1867

HON. GEORGE D'ALROY	Mr. Frederick Younge	DIXON	
CAPTAIN HAWTREE	Mr. Bancroft	MARQUISE DE ST. MAUR	Miss Larkin
ECCLES	Mr. George Honey	ESTHER ECCLES	Miss Marie Wilton
SAM GERRIDGE	Mr. Hare	POLLY ECCLES	Miss Lydia Foote

ACT I. The Little House at Stangate.	COURTSHIP
ACT II. The Lodgings in Mayfair.	MATRIMONY
ACT III. The Little House in Stangate.	WIDOWHOOD

A lapse of eight months occurs between the first and the second Act, and a lapse of twelve months between the second and the third.

ACT I

SCENE I. *A plain set chamber, paper soiled. A window, with practicable* [1] *blind; street backing and iron railings. Door practicable, when opened showing street door (practicable). Fireplace; two-hinged gas-burners on each side of mantel-piece. Sideboard cupboard, cupboard in recess; tea-things, tea-pot, tea-caddy, tea-tray, etc., on it. Long table, before fire; old piece of carpet and rug down; plain chairs; book-shelf, back; a small table under it with ballet-shoe and skirt on it; bunch of benefit bills hanging under book-shelf. Theatrical printed portraits, framed, hanging about; chimney glass clock; box of lucifers and ornaments on mantel-shelf; kettle on hob, and fire laid; door-mats on the outside of door. Bureau in lower right-hand corner. Rapping heard at door, the handle is then shaken as curtain rises. The door is unlocked. Enter George D'Alroy.*

George D'Alroy. Told you so; the key was left under the mat in case I came. They 're not back from rehearsal. (*Hangs up hat on peg near door as Hawtree enters.*) Confound rehearsal!

(*Crosses to fireplace.*)

Hawtree. (*Back to audience, looking round.*) And this is the fairy's bower!

Geo. Yes; and this is the fairy's fireplace; the fire is laid. I 'll light it.

(*Lights fire with lucifer from mantel-piece.*)

Haw. (*Turning to George.*) And this is the abode rendered blessed by her abiding. It is here that she dwells, walks, talks,—eats and drinks. Does she eat and drink?

Geo. Yes, heartily. I 've seen her.

Haw. And you are really spoons!—case of true love—hit—dead.

Geo. Right through. Can't live away from her.

(*With elbow on end of mantel-piece, down stage.*)

Haw. Poor old Dal! and you 've brought me over the water to—

Geo. Stangate.

Haw. Stangate—to see her for the same sort of reason that when a patient is in a dangerous state one doctor calls in another—for a consultation.

Geo. Yes. Then the patient dies.

Haw. Tell us all about it—you know I 've been away.

(*Sits at table, leg on chair.*)

Geo. Well then, eighteen months ago—

Haw. Oh cut that! you told me all about that. You went to a theatre, and saw a girl in a ballet, and you fell in love.

Geo. Yes. I found out that she was an amiable, good girl.

Haw. Of course; cut that. We 'll credit her with all the virtues and accomplishments.

Geo. Who worked hard to support a drunken father.

Haw. Oh! the father 's a drunkard, is he? The father does not inherit the daughter's virtues?

[1] Which can be moved. (Robertson substituted realism for merely painted scenery.)

Geo. No. I hate him.

Haw. Naturally. Quite so! Quite so!

Geo. And she—that is, Esther—is very good to her younger sister.

Haw. Younger sister also angelic, amiable, accomplished, etc.

Geo. Um—good enough, but got a temper —large temper. Well, with some difficulty, I got to speak to her. I mean to Esther. Then I was allowed to see her to her door here.

Haw. I know—pastry-cooks—Richmond dinner—and all that.

Geo. You 're too fast. Pastry-cooks—yes. Richmond—no. Your knowledge of the world, fifty yards round barracks, misleads you. I saw her nearly every day, and I kept on falling in love—falling and falling, until I thought I should never reach the bottom; then I met you.

Haw. I remember the night when you told me; but I thought it was only an amourette. However, if the fire is a conflagration, subdue it; try dissipation.

Geo. I have.

Haw. What success?

Geo. None; dissipation brought me bad health and self-contempt, a sick head and a sore heart.

Haw. Foreign travel; absence makes the heart grow (*slight pause*)—stronger. Get leave and cut away.

Geo. I did get leave, and I did cut away; and while away I was miserable and a gone-er coon than ever.

Haw. What 's to be done?

(*Sits cross-legged on chair, facing George.*)

Geo. Don't know. That 's the reason I asked you to come over and see.

Haw. Of course, Dal, you 're not such a soft as to think of marriage. You know what your mother is. Either you are going to behave properly, with a proper regard for the world, and all that, you know; or you 're going to do the other thing. Now, the question is, what do you mean to do? The girl is a nice girl, no doubt; but as to your making her Mrs. D'Alroy, the thing is out of the question.

Geo. Why? What should prevent me?

Haw. Caste!—the inexorable law of caste. The social law, so becoming and so good, that commands like to mate with like, and forbids a giraffe to fall in love with a squirrel.

Geo. But my dear Bark—

Haw. My dear Dal, all those marriages of people with common people are all very well in novels and plays on the stage, because the real people don't exist, and have no relatives who exist, and no connections, and so no harm 's done, and it 's rather interesting to look at; but in real life with real relations, and real mothers and so forth, it 's absolute bosh; it 's worse, it 's utter social and personal annihilation and damnation.

Geo. As to my mother, I haven't thought about her.

(*Sits corner of table.*)

Haw. Of course not. Lovers are so damned selfish; they never think of anybody but themselves.

Geo. My father died when I was three years old, and she married again before I was six, and married a Frenchman.

Haw. A nobleman of the most ancient families of France, of equal blood to her own. She obeyed the duties imposed on her by her station and by caste.

Geo. Still, it caused a separation and a division between us, and I never see my brother, because he lives abroad. Of course the Marquise de St. Maur is my mother, and I look upon her with a sort of superstitious awe.

(*Moves chair with which he has been twisting about during speech from table to left corner.*)

Haw. She 's a grand Brahmin priestess.

Geo. Just so; and I know I'm a fool. Now you 're clever, Bark,—a little too clever, I think. You 're paying your devoirs—that 's the correct word, isn't it —to Lady Florence Carberry, the daughter of a countess. She 's above you—you 've no title. Is she to forget *her* caste?

Haw. That argument doesn't apply. A man can be no more than a gentleman.

Geo. "True hearts are more than coronets,
And simple faith than Norman blood."

Haw. Now, George, if you 're going to consider this question from the point of view of poetry, you 're off to No-Man's Land, where I won't follow you.

Geo. No gentleman can be ashamed of the woman he loves. No matter what her original station, once his wife he raises her to his rank.

Haw. Yes, he raises her;—*her;* but her connections—her relatives. How about them?

(*Eccles enters.*)

Eccles. (*Outside.*) Polly! Polly! Polly! (*Enters.*) Why the devil—

(*George crosses to Hawtree, who rises. Eccles sees them and assumes a deferential manner.*)

Eccles. Oh, Mr. De-Alroy! I didn't see you, sir. Good afternoon; the same to you, sir, and many on 'em.

(*Puts hat on bureau and comes down.*)

Haw. Who is this?

Geo. This is papa.

Haw. Ah!

(*Turns up to book-shelf, scanning Eccles through eye-glass.*)

Geo. Miss Eccles and her sister not returned from rehearsal yet?

Eccles. No, sir, they have not. I expect 'em in directly. I hope you've been quite well since I seen you last, sir?

Geo. Quite, thank you; and how have you been, Mr. Eccles?

Eccles. Well, sir, I have not been the thing at all. My 'ealth, sir, and my spirits is both broke. I'm not the man I used to be. I am not accustomed to this sort of thing. I've seen better days, but they are gone—most like for ever. It is a melancholy thing, sir, for a man of my time of life to look back on better days that are gone most like for ever.

Geo. I daresay.

Eccles. Once proud and prosperous, now poor and lowly. Once master of a shop, I am now, by the pressure of circumstances over which I have no control, driven to seek work and not to find it. Poverty is a dreadful thing, sir, for a man as has once been well off.

Geo. I daresay.

Eccles. (*Sighing.*) Ah, sir, the poor and lowly is often 'ardly used. What chance has the working-man?

Haw. None when he don't work.

Eccles. We are all equal in mind and feeling.

Geo. (*Aside.*) I hope not.

Eccles. I am sorry, gentlemen, that I cannot offer you any refreshment; but luxury and me has long been strangers.

Geo. I am very sorry for your misfortunes, Mr. Eccles. (*Looking round at Hawtree who turns away.*) May I hope that you will allow me to offer you this trifling loan?

(*Giving him half a sovereign.*)

Eccles. Sir, you're a gentleman. One can tell a real gentleman with half a sov—I mean half an eye—a real gentleman understands the natural emotions of the working-man. Pride, sir, is a thing as should be put down by the strong 'and of pecuniary necessity. There's a friend of mine round the corner as I promised to meet on a little matter of business; so if you will excuse me, sir—

Geo. With pleasure.

Eccles. (*Going up.*) Sorry to leave you, gentlemen, but—

Geo. Don't stay on my account.

Haw. Don't mention it.

Eccles. Business is business.

(*Goes up.*)

The girls will be in directly. Good afternoon, gentlemen,—good afternoon—(*Going out.*) Good afternoon. (*Exit.*)

(*George sits in chair, corner of table, right.*)

Haw. (*Coming down left of table.*) Papa is not nice, but— (*Sitting on corner of table down stage.*)

"True hearts are more than coronets,
And simple faith than Norman blood."

Poor George! I wonder what your mamma—the Most Noble the Marquise de St. Maur—would think of Papa Eccles. Come, Dal, allow that there *is something* in caste. Conceive that dirty ruffian—that rinsing of stale beer—that walking tap-room, for a father-in-law. Take a spin to Central America. Forget her.

Geo. Can't.

Haw. You'll be wretched and miserable with her.

Geo. I'd rather be wretched with her than miserable without her. (*Hawtree takes out cigar case.*) Don't smoke here!

Haw. Why not?

Geo. She'll be coming in directly.

Haw. I don't think she'd mind.

Geo. I should. Do you smoke before Lady Florence Carberry?

Haw. (*Closing case.*) Ha! You're suffering from a fit of the morals.

Geo. What's that?

Haw. The morals is a disease, like the measles, that attacks the young and innocent.

Geo. (*With temper.*) You talk like Mephistopheles, without the cleverness.

(*Goes up to window and looks at watch.*)

Haw. (*Arranging cravat at glass.*) I don't pretend to be a particularly good sort of fellow, nor a particularly bad sort of fellow. I suppose I'm about the average standard sort of thing, and I don't like to see a friend go down hill to the devil while I can put the drag on. (*Turning, with back to fire.*) Here is a girl of very humble station—poor, and all that, with a drunken father, who evidently doesn't care how he gets money so long as he don't work for it. Marriage! Pah! Couldn't the thing be arranged?

Geo. Hawtree, cut that! (*At window.*) She 's here!

(*Goes to door and opens it.*)

(*Enter Esther.*)

Geo. (*Flurried at sight of her.*) Good morning. I got here before you, you see.

Esther. Good morning.

(*Sees Hawtree—slight pause, in which Hawtree has removed his hat.*)

Geo. I 've taken the liberty—I hope you won't be angry—of asking you to let me present a friend of mine to you; Miss Eccles—Captain Hawtree.

(*Hawtree bows. George assists Esther in taking off bonnet and shawl.*)

Haw. (*Aside.*) Pretty.

Esther. (*Aside.*) Thinks too much of himself.

Geo. (*Hangs up bonnet and shawl on pegs.*) You 've had a late rehearsal. Where 's Polly?

Esther. She stayed behind to buy something.

(*Enter Polly.*)

Polly. (*Head through door.*) How de do, Mr. D'Alroy? Oh! I 'm tired to death. Kept at rehearsal by an old fool of a stage manager. But stage managers are always old fools,—except when they are young. We shan't have time for any dinner, so I 've brought something for tea.

Esther. What is it?

Polly. Ham. (*Showing ham in paper. Esther sits right, at window. Crossing. Seeing Hawtree.*) Oh! I beg your pardon, sir. I didn't see you.

Geo. A friend of mine, Mary. Captain Hawtree—Miss Mary Eccles.

(*George sits at window. Polly bows very low, to left, to right, and to front, half burlesquely, to Hawtree.*)

Haw. Charmed.

Polly. (*Aside.*) What a swell! Got nice teeth, and he knows it. How quiet we all are; let 's talk about something.

(*Hangs up her hat. She crosses to fire round table, front. Hawtree crosses and places hat on bureau.*)

Esther. What can we talk about?

Polly. Anything. Ham. Mr. D'Alroy, do you like ham?

Geo. I adore her—(*Polly titters.*)—I mean I adore it.

Polly. (*To Hawtree, who has crossed to table watching Polly undo paper containing ham. She turns the plate on top of the ham still in the paper, then throws the paper aside and triumphantly brings the plate under Hawtree's nose, Hawtree giving a little start back.*) Do you like ham, sir? (*Very tragically.*)

Haw. Yes.

Polly. Now that is very strange. I should have thought you 'd have been above ham.

(*Getting tea-tray.*)

Haw. May one ask why?

Polly. You look above it. You look quite equal to tongue—glazed. (*Laughing.*) Mr. D'Alroy is here so often that he knows our ways.

(*Getting tea-things from sideboard and placing them on table.*)

Haw. I like everything that is piquante and fresh, and pretty and agreeable.

Polly. (*Laying table all the time for tea.*) Ah! you mean that for me. (*Curtseying.*) Oh! (*Sings.*) Tra, la, la, la, la, la. (*Flourishes cup in his face; he retreats a step.*) Now I must put the kettle on. (*George and Esther are at window.*) Esther never does any work when Mr. D'Alroy is here. They're spooning; ugly word, spooning, isn't it?—reminds one of red-currant jam. By the bye, love *is* very like red-currant jam—at the first taste sweet, and afterwards shuddery. Do you ever spoon?

Haw. (*Leaning across table.*) I should like to do so at this moment.

Polly. I daresay you would. No, you 're too grand for me. You want taking down a peg—I mean a foot. Let 's see—what are you—a corporal?

Haw. Captain.

Polly. I prefer a corporal. See here. Let 's change about. You be corporal—it 'll do you good, and I 'll be "my lady."

Haw. Pleasure.

Polly. You must call me "my lady," though, or you shan't have any ham.

Haw. Certainly, "my lady"; but I cannot accept your hospitality, for I 'm engaged to dine.

Polly. At what time?

Haw. Seven.

Polly. Seven! Why, that 's half-past tea-time. Now, Corporal, you must wait on me.

Haw. As the pages did of old.

Polly. "My lady."

Haw. "My lady."

Polly. Here's the kettle, Corporal.

(*Holding out kettle at arm's length. Hawtree looks at it through eye-glass.*)

Haw. Very nice kettle.

Polly. Take it into the back kitchen.

Haw. Eh!

Polly. Oh, I 'm coming too.

Haw. Ah! that alters the case.

(*He takes out handkerchief and then takes hold of kettle—crosses as George rises and comes down, slapping Hawtree on back. Hawtree immediately places kettle on the floor. Polly throws herself into chair by fireside up stage, and roars with laughter. George and Esther laugh.*)

Geo. What are you about?

Haw. I 'm about to fill the kettle.

Esther. (*Going to Polly.*) Mind what you are doing, Polly. What will Sam say?

Polly. Whatever Sam chooses. What the sweetheart can't see the husband can't grieve at. Now then—Corporal!

Haw. "My lady!"

(*Takes up kettle.*)

Polly. Attention! Forward! March! and mind the soot don't drop upon your trousers.

(*Exeunt Polly and Hawtree, Hawtree first.*)

Esther. What a girl it is—all spirits! The worst is that it is so easy to mistake her.

Geo. And so easy to find out your mistake. (*They cross down stage, Esther first.*) But why won't you let me present you with a piano?

(*Following Esther.*)

Esther. I don't want one.

Geo. You said you were fond of playing.

Esther. We may be fond of many things without having them. (*Leaning against end of table. Taking out letter.*) Now here is a gentleman says he is attached to me.

Geo. (*Jealous.*) May I know his name?

Esther. What for? It would be useless, as his solicitations—

(*Throws letter into fire.*)

Geo. I lit that fire.

Esther. Then burn these, too. (*George crosses to fire.*) No, not that. (*Taking one back.*) I must keep that; burn the others.

(*George throws letters on fire, crosses back of table quickly takes hat from peg and goes to door as if leaving hurriedly. Esther takes chair from table and goes to centre of stage with it, noticing George's manner. George hesitates at door. Shuts it quickly, hangs his hat up again, and comes down to back of chair in which Esther has seated herself.*)

Geo. Who is that from?

Esther. Why do you wish to know?

Geo. Because I love you, and I don't think you love me, and I fear a rival.

Esther. You have none.

Geo. I know you have so many admirers.

Esther. They 're nothing to me.

Geo. Not one?

Esther. No. They 're admirers, but there 's not a husband among them.

Geo. Not the writer of that letter?

Esther. (*Coquettishly.*) Oh, I like him very much.

Geo. (*Sighing.*) Ah!

Esther. And I 'm very fond of this letter.

Geo. Then, Esther, you don't care for me.

Esther. Don't I? How do you know?

Geo. Because you won't let me read that letter.

Esther. It won't please you if you see it.

Geo. I daresay not. That 's just the reason that I want to. You won't?

Esther. (*Hesitates.*) I will. There!

(*Giving it to him.*)

Geo. (*Reads.*) "Dear Madam."

Esther. That 's tender, isn't it?

Geo. "The terms are four pounds—your dresses to be found. For eight weeks certain, and longer if you should suit. (*In astonishment.*) I cannot close the engagement until the return of my partner. I expect him back to-day, and I will write you as soon as I have seen him. Yours very," etc. Four pounds—find dresses. What does this mean?

Esther. It means that they want a Columbine for the Pantomime at Manchester, and I think I shall get the engagement.

Geo. Manchester; then you 'll leave London?

Esther. I must. (*Pathetically.*) You see this little house is on my shoulders. Polly only earns eighteen shillings a week, and father has been out of work a long, long time. I make the bread here, and it 's hard to make sometimes. I 've been mistress of this place, and forced to think ever since my mother died, and I was eight years old. Four pounds a week is a large sum, and I can save out of it.

(*This speech is not to be spoken in a tone implying hardship.*)

Geo. But you 'll go away, and I shan't see you.

Esther. P'raps it will be for the best. (*Rises and crosses.*) What future is there for us? You 're a man of rank, and I am a poor girl who gets her living by dancing. It would have been better that we had never met.

Geo. No.

Esther. Yes, it would, for I 'm afraid that—

Geo. You love me?

Esther. I don't know. I 'm not sure; but I think I do.

(*Stops and turns half-face to George.*)

Geo. (*Trying to seize her hand.*) Esther!

Esther. No. Think of the difference of our stations.

Geo. That 's what Hawtree says! Caste! caste! curse caste!

(*Goes up.*)

Esther. If I go to Manchester it will be for the best. We must both try to forget each other.

Geo. (*Comes down by table.*) Forget you! no, Esther; let me—

(*Seizing her hand.*)

Polly. (*Without.*) Mind what you 're about. Oh dear! oh dear!

(*George and Esther sit in window seat.*)

(*Enter Polly and Hawtree.*)

Polly. You nasty, great clumsy corporal, you 've spilt the water all over my frock. Oh dear! (*Coming down. Hawtree puts kettle on ham on table.*) Take it off the ham! (*Hawtree then places it on the mantel-piece.*) No, no! put it in the fireplace. (*Hawtree does so.*) You 've spoilt my frock.

(*Sitting.*)

Haw. Allow me to offer you a new one.

(*Crossing.*)

Polly. No, I won't. You 'll be calling to see how it looks when it 's on. Haven't you got a handkerchief?

Haw. Yes.

Polly. Then wipe it dry.

(*Hawtree bends almost on one knee, and wipes dress. Enter Sam, whistling. Throws cap into Hawtree's hat on drawers.*)

Sam. (*Sulkily.*) Arternoon—yer didn't hear me knock!—the door was open. I 'm afraid I intrude.

Polly. No, you don't. We 're glad to see you if you 've got a handkerchief. Help to wipe this dry.

(*Sam pulls out handkerchief from slop,*[2] *and dropping on one knee snatches skirt of dress from Hawtree, who looks up surprised.*)

Haw. I 'm very sorry. (*Rising.*) I beg your pardon.

(*Business; Sam stares Hawtree out.*)

Polly. It won't spoil it.

Sam. The stain won't come out.

(*Rising.*)

Polly. It 's only water.

Sam. (*To Esther.*) Arternoon, Miss Eccles. (*To George.*) Arternoon, sir! (*Polly rises. To Polly.*) Who 's the other swell?

Polly. I 'll introduce you. Captain Hawtree—Mr. Samuel Gerridge.

Haw. Charmed, I 'm sure. (*Staring at Sam through eye-glass. Sam acknowledges Hawtree's recognition by a "chuck" of the head over left shoulder; going up to George.*) Who 's this?

Geo. Polly's sweetheart.

Haw. Oh! Now if I can be of no further assistance, I 'll go.

(*Comes over back down to drawers.*)

Polly. Going, Corporal?

Haw. Yaas! (*Business; taking up hat and stick from bureau he sees Sam's cap. He picks it out carefully, and coming down stage examines it as a curiosity, drops it on the floor and pushes it away with his stick, at the same time moving backwards, causing him to bump against Sam, who turns round savagely.*) I beg your pardon. (*Crossing up stage.*) George, will you—(*George takes no notice.*) Will you—?

Geo. What?

Haw. Go with me?

Geo. Go? No!

Haw. (*Coming down to Polly.*) Then, Miss Eccles—I mean "my lady."

(*Shaking hands and going; as he backs*

2 Loose jacket.

away bumps against Sam, and business repeated, Hawtree close to door keeping his eye on Sam, who has shown signs of anger.)

Polly. Good-bye, Corporal!

Haw. (*At door.*) Good-bye! Good afternoon, Mr.—Mr.—er— Pardon me.

Sam. (*With constrained rage.*) Gerridge, sir—Gerridge.

Haw. (*As if remembering name.*) Ah! Gerridge. Good-day.

(*Exit.*)

Sam. (*Turning to Polly in awful rage.*) Who 's that fool? Who 's that long idiot?

Polly. I told you; Captain Hawtree.

Sam. What 's 'e want 'ere?

Polly. He 's a friend of Mr. D'Alroy's.

Sam. Ugh! Isn 't one of 'em enough!

Polly. What do you mean?

Sam. For the neighbors to talk about. Who 's he after?

Polly. What do you mean by after? You 're forgetting yourself, I think.

Sam. No, I 'm not forgetting myself—I 'm remembering you. What can a long fool of a swell dressed up to the nines within an inch of his life want with two girls of your class? Look at the difference of your stations! 'E don't come 'ere after any good.

(*During the speech, Esther crosses to fire and sits before it in a low chair. George follows her and sits on her left.*)

Polly. Samuel!

Sam. I mean what I say. People should stick to their own class. Life 's a railway journey, and Mankind 's a passenger—first class, second class, third class. Any person found riding in a superior class to that for which he has taken his ticket will be removed at the first station stopped at, according to the by-laws of the company.

Polly. You 're giving yourself nice airs! What business is it of yours who comes here? Who are you?

Sam. I 'm a mechanic.

Polly. That 's evident.

Sam. I ain't ashamed of it. I 'm not ashamed of my paper cap.

Polly. Why should you be? I daresay Captain Hawtree isn't ashamed of his fourteen-and-sixpenny gossamer.

Sam. You think a deal of him 'cos he 's a captain. Why did he call you "my lady"?

Polly. Because he treated me as one. I wish you 'd make the same mistake.

Sam. Ugh!

(*Sam goes angrily to bureau. Polly bounces up stage, and sits in window seat.*)

Esther. (*Sitting with George, tête-à-tête, by fire.*) But we must listen to reason.

Geo. I hate reason!

Esther. I wonder what it means?

Geo. Everything disagreeable. When people talk unpleasantly, they always say listen to reason.

Sam. (*Turning round.*) What will the neighbors say?

Polly. I don't care!

(*Coming down.*)

Sam. What will the neighbors *think?*

Polly. They can't think. They 're like you, they 've not been educated up to it.

Sam. It all comes of your being on the stage.

(*Going to Polly.*)

Polly. It all comes of your not understanding the stage or anything else—but putty. Now, if you were a gentleman—

Sam. Why then, of course, I should make up to a lady.

Polly. Ugh!

(*Polly flings herself into chair by table.*)

Geo. Reason 's an idiot. Two and two are four, and twelve are fifteen, and eight are twenty. That 's reason!

Sam. (*Turning to Polly.*) Painting your cheeks!

Polly. (*Rising.*) Better paint our *cheeks* than paint *nasty old doors* as you do. How can you understand art? You 're only a mechanic! You 're not a professional! You 're in trade. You are not of the same station as we are. When the manager speaks to you, you touch your hat, and say, "Yes, sir," because he 's your superior.

(*Snaps fingers under Sam's nose.*)

Geo. When people love there 's no such thing as money—it don't exist.

Esther. Yes, it does.

Geo. Then it oughtn't to.

Sam. The manager employs me same as he does you. Payment is good anywhere and everywhere. Whatever 's commercial, is right.

Polly. Actors are not like mechanics. They wear cloth coats, and not fustian jackets.

Sam. (*Sneeringly in Polly's face.*) I despise play actors.

Polly. I despise mechanics.

(*Polly slaps his face.*)

Geo. I never think of anything else but you.

Esther. Really?

Sam. (*Goes to bureau, misses cap, looks around, sees it on floor, picks it up angrily, and comes to Polly, who is sitting by the table.*) I won't stay here to be insulted.

(*Putting on cap.*)

Polly. Nobody wants you to stay. Go! Go! Go!

Sam. I will go. Good-bye, Miss Mary Eccles. (*Goes off and returns quickly.*) I shan't come here again!

(*At door half-open.*)

Polly. Don't! Good riddance to bad rubbish.

Sam. (*Rushing down stage to Polly.*) You can go to your *captain!*

Polly. And you to your *putty.*

(*Sam throws his cap down and kicks it—then goes up stage and picks it up. Polly turns and rises, leaning against table, facing him, crosses to door, and locks it. Sam, hearing click of lock, turns quickly.*)

Esther. And shall you always love me as you do now?

Geo. More.

Polly. Now you *shan't* go. (*Locking door, taking out key, which she pockets, and placing her back against door.*) Nyer![3] Now I'll just show you my power. Nyer!

Sam. *Miss Mary* Eccles, let me out!

(*Advancing to door.*)

Polly. *Mr.* Samuel Gerridge, I shan't!

(*Sam turns away.*)

Esther. Now you two. (*Postman's knock.*) The postman!

Sam. Now you must let me out. You must unlock the door.

Polly. No, I needn't. (*Opens window, looking out.*) Here—postman. (*Takes letter from postman at window.*) Thank you. (*Business; flicks Sam in the face with letter.*) For you, Esther!

Esther. (*Rising.*) For me?

Polly. Yes.

(*Gives it to her, and closes window, and returns to door triumphantly. Sam goes to window.*)

Esther. (*Going down.*) From Manchester!

Geo. Manchester?

(*Coming down back of Esther.*)

Esther. (*Reading.*) I've got the engagement—four pounds a week.

Geo. (*Placing his arm around her.*) You shan't go. Esther—stay—be my wife!

Esther. But the world—your world?

Geo. Hang the world! You're my world. Stay with your husband, *Mrs. George D'Alroy.*

(*During this Polly has been dancing up and down in front of the door.*)

Sam. I *will* go out!

(*Turning with sudden determination.*)

Polly. You can't, and you shan't!

Sam. I can—I will!

(*Opens window and jumps out.*)

Polly. (*Frightened.*) He's hurt himself. Sam—Sam,—dear Sam!

(*Running to window. Sam appears at window. Polly slaps his face and shuts window down violently.*)

Polly. Nyer!

(*During this George has kissed Esther.*)

Geo. My wife!

(*The handle of the door is heard to rattle, then the door is shaken violently. Esther crosses to door; finding it locked, turns to Polly sitting in window seat, who gives her the key. Esther then opens the door. Eccles reels in, very drunk, and clings to the corner of the bureau for support. George stands pulling his moustache. Esther, a little way up, looking with shame first at her father, then at George. Polly sitting in window recess.*)

ACT DROP

For call.—George, hat in hand, bidding Esther good-bye. Eccles sitting in chair, nodding before fire. Sam again looks in at window. Polly pulls the blind down violently.

ACT II

SCENE I. *D'Alroy's lodgings in Mayfair. A set chamber. Folding-doors opening on to drawing-room. Door on the right. Two windows, with muslin curtains. Loo-table.*[4] *Sofa above piano. Two easy-chairs, on each side of table. Dessert—claret in jug; two wine-glasses half full. Box of cigarettes, vase of flowers, embroidered slipper on canvas, and small*

[3] So there now! (pronounced *Nya'h*).

[4] Card-table.

basket of colored wools, all on table. Foot-stool by easy-chair. Ornamental gilt work-basket on stand in window. Easy-chair. Piano. Mahogany-stained easel with oil-painting of D'Alroy in full dragoon regimentals. Davenport[5] *with vase of flowers on it; a chair on each side; a water-color drawing over it, and on each side of room. Half moonlight through window. Esther and George discovered. Esther at window. When curtain has risen she comes down slowly to chair right of table, and George sitting in easy-chair left of table. George has his uniform trousers and spurs on.*

Esther. George, dear, you seem out of spirits.

George. (*Smoking cigarette.*) Not at all, dear, not at all.

(*Rallying.*)

Esther. Then why don't you talk?

Geo. I 've nothing to say.

Esther. That's no reason.

Geo. I can't talk about nothing.

Esther. Yes, you can; you often do. (*Crossing round back of table and caressing him.*) You used to do before we were married.

Geo. No, I didn't. I talked about you, and my love for you. D 'ye call that nothing?

Esther. (*Sitting on stool left of George.*) How long have we been married, dear? Let me see; six months yesterday. (*Dreamily.*) It hardly seems a week; it almost seems a dream.

Geo. (*Putting his arm around her.*) Awfully jolly dream. Don't let us wake up. (*Aside and recovering himself.*) How ever shall I tell her?

Esther. And when I married you I was twenty-two, wasn't I?

Geo. Yes, dear; but then, you know, you must have been some age or other.

Esther. No; but to think I lived two and twenty years without knowing you!

Geo. What of it, dear?

Esther. It seems such a dreadful waste of time.

Geo. So it was—awful.

Esther. Do you remember our first meeting? Then I was in the ballet.

Geo. Yes; now you 're in the heavies.[6]

Esther. Then I was in the front rank—now I am of high rank—the Honorable Mrs. George D'Alroy. You promoted me to be your wife.

Geo. No, dear, you promoted me to be your husband.

Esther. And now I 'm one of the aristocracy; ain't I?

Geo. Yes, dear; I suppose that we may consider ourselves—

Esther. Tell me, George; are you quite sure that you are proud of your poor little humble wife?

Geo. Proud of you! Proud as the winner of the Derby.

Esther. Wouldn't you have loved me better if I 'd been a lady?

Geo. You *are* a lady—you 're my wife.

Esther. What will your mamma say when she knows of our marriage? I quite tremble at the thought of meeting her.

Geo. So do I. Luckily she 's in Rome.

Esther. Do you know, George, I should like to be married all over again.

Geo. Not to anybody else, I hope?

Esther. My darling!

Geo. But why over again? Why?

Esther. Our courtship was so beautiful. It was like in a novel from the library, only better. You, a fine, rich, high-born gentleman, coming to our humble little house to court poor me. Do you remember the ballet you first saw me in? That was at Covent Garden. "Jeanne la Folle; or, the Return of the Soldier." (*Goes up to piano.*) Don't you remember the dance?

(*Plays a quick movement.*)

Geo. Esther, how came you to learn to play the piano? Did you teach yourself?

Esther. Yes. (*Turning on music-stool.*) So did Polly. We can only just touch the notes to amuse ourselves.

Geo. How was it?

Esther. I 've told you so often.

(*Rises and sits on stool at George's feet.*)

Geo. Tell me again. I 'm like the children—I like to hear what I know already.

Esther. Well, then, mother died when I was quite young. I can only just remember her. Polly was an infant; so I had to be Polly's mother. Father—who was a very eccentric man (*George sighs deeply—Esther notices it and goes on rapidly—all to be simultaneous in action.*) but a very good one when you know him—did not take much notice of us, and we got on as we could. We used to let the first floor, and a lodger took it—Herr Griffenhaagen. He was a ballet master

5 Writing-desk.

6 Heavy cavalry (alluding to himself), with a pun on heavy or serious theatrical parts.

at the Opera. He took a fancy to me, and asked me if I should like to learn to dance, and I told him father couldn't afford to pay for my tuition; and he said that (*Imitation.*) he did not vant bayment, but dat he would teach me for noding, for he had taken a fancy to me, because I was like a leetle lady he had known long years ago in de far off land he came from. Then he got us an engagement at the theatre. That was how we first were in the ballet.

Geo. (*Slapping his leg.*) That fellow was a great brick; I should like to ask him to dinner. What became of him?

Esther. I don't know. He left England.

(*George fidgets and looks at watch.*)

You are restless, George. What 's the matter?

Geo. Nothing.

Esther. Are you going out?

Geo. Yes. (*Looking at his boots and spurs.*) That 's the reason I dined in—

Esther. To the barracks?

Geo. Yes.

Esther. On duty?

Geo. (*Hesitatingly.*) On duty. (*Rising.*) And, of course, when a man is a soldier, he must go on duty when he 's ordered, and where he 's ordered—and—(*Aside*) —why did I ever enter the service?

(*Crosses.*)

Esther. (*Rises, crosses to George—and twining her arm round him.*) George, if you must go out to your club, go; don't mind leaving me. Somehow or other, George, these last few days everything seems to have changed with me—I don't know why. Sometimes my eyes fill with tears, for no reason, and sometimes I feel so happy, for no reason. I don't mind being left by myself as I used to do. When you are a few minutes behind time I don't run to the window and watch for you, and turn irritable. Not that I love you less—no, for I love you more; but often when you are away I don't feel that I am by myself. (*Dropping her head on his breast.*) I never feel alone.

(*Goes to piano and turns over music.*)

Geo. (*Watching Esther.*) What angels women are! At least, this one is. I forget all about the others. (*Carriage-wheels heard off.*) If I 'd known I could have been so happy, I 'd have sold out when I married.

(*Knock at street door.*)

Esther. (*Standing at table.*) That for us, dear?

Geo. (*At first window.*) Hawtree in a hansom. He 's come for—(*Aside*)—me. I *must* tell her sooner or later. (*At door.*) Come in, Hawtree.

(*Enter Hawtree, in regimentals.*)

Hawtree. How do? Hope you 're well, Mrs. D'Alroy? (*Coming down.*) George, are you coming to—

Geo. (*Coming down left of Hawtree.*) No, I 've dined—(*Gives a significant look.*)—we dined early.

(*Esther plays scraps of music at piano.*)

Haw. (*Sotto voce.*) Haven't you told her?

Geo. No, I daren't.

Haw. But you must.

Geo. You know what an awful coward I am. You do it for me.

Haw. Not for worlds. I 've just had my own adieux to make.

Geo. Ah, yes,—to Florence Carberry. How did she take it?

Haw. Oh, (*Slight pause.*) very well.

Geo. (*Earnestly.*) Did she cry?

Haw. No.

Geo. Nor exhibit any emotion whatever?

Haw. No, not particularly.

Geo. (*Surprisedly.*) Didn't you kiss her?

Haw. No; Lady Clardonax was in the room.

Geo. (*Wonderingly.*) Didn't she squeeze your hand?

Haw. No.

Geo. (*Impressively.*) Didn't she say anything?

Haw. No, except that she hoped to see me back again soon, and that India was a bad climate.

Geo. Umph! It seems to have been a tragic parting (*Serio-comically.*)—almost as tragic as parting—your back hair.

Haw. Lady Florence is not the sort of person to make a scene.

Geo. To be sure, she 's not your wife. I wish Esther would be as cool and comfortable. (*After a pause.*) No, I don't, —no, I don't.

(*A rap at door.*)

(*Enter Dixon.*)

Geo. (*Goes up to Dixon.*) Oh, Dixon, lay out my—

Dixon. I have laid them out, sir; everything is ready.

Geo. (*Going down to Hawtree—after a pause—irresolutely.*) I must tell her—mustn't I?

Haw. Better send for her sister. Let Dixon go for her in a cab.

Geo. Just so. I 'll send him at once. Dixon!

(*Goes up and talks to Dixon.*)

Esther. (*Rising and going to back of chair, left of table.*) Do you want to have a talk with my husband? Shall I go into the dining-room?

Haw. No, Mrs. D'Alroy.

(*Going to table and placing cap on it.*)

Geo. No, dear. At once, Dixon. Tell the cabman to drive like—(*Exit Dixon.*) —like a—cornet [7] just joined.

Esther. (*To Hawtree.*) Are you going to take him anywhere?

Haw. (*George comes down and touches Hawtree quickly on the shoulder before he can speak.*) No. (*Aside.*) Yes—to India. (*Crossing to George.*) Tell her now.

Geo. No, no. I 'll wait till I put on my uniform.

(*Going up.*)

(*Door opens and Polly peeps in.*)

Polly. How d 'ye do, good people,—quite well?

(*Polly gets back of table—kisses Esther.*)

Geo. Eh? Didn't you meet Dixon?

Polly. Who?

Geo. Dixon—my man.

Polly. No.

Geo. Confound it!—he 'll have his ride for nothing. How d 'ye do, Polly?

(*Shakes hands.*)

Polly. How d 'ye do, George.

(*Esther takes Polly's things and goes up stage with them.—Polly places parasol on table. Esther returns left of Polly.*)

Polly. Bless you, my turtles. (*Blessing them, ballet fashion.*) George, kiss your mother. (*He kisses her.*) That 's what I call an honorable brother-in-law's kiss. I 'm not in the way, am I?

Geo. (*Behind easy-chair right of table.*) Not at all. I 'm very glad you 've come.

(*Esther shows Polly the new music. Polly sits at piano and plays comic tune.*)

Haw. (*Back to audience, and elbow on easy-chair, aside to George.*) Under ordinary circumstances she 's not a very eligible visitor.

Geo. Caste again. (*Going up.*) I 'll be back directly.

(*Exit George.*)

Haw. (*Looking at watch and crossing.*) Mrs. D'Alroy, I—

Esther. (*Who is standing over Polly at piano.*) Going?

Polly. (*Rising.*) Do I drive you away, Captain?

(*Taking her parasol from table. Esther gets to back of chair left of table.*)

Haw. No.

Polly. Yes, I do. I frighten you, I 'm so ugly. I know I do. You frighten me.

Haw. How so?

Polly. You 're so handsome. (*Coming down.*) Particularly in those clothes, for all the world like an inspector of police.

Esther. (*Half aside.*) Polly!

Polly. I will! I like to take him down a bit.

Haw. (*Aside.*) This is rather a wild sort of thing in sisters-in-law.

Polly. Any news, Captain?

Haw. (*In a drawling tone.*) No. Is there any news with you?

Polly. (*Imitating him.*) Yaas; we 've got a new piece coming out at our theatre.

Haw. (*Interested.*) What 's it about?

Polly. (*Drawling.*) I don't know. (*To Esther.*) Had him there! (*Hawtree drops his sword from his arm; Polly turns round quickly, hearing the noise, and pretends to be frightened.*) Going to kill anybody to-day, that you 've got your sword on?

Haw. No.

Polly. I thought not.

(*Sings.*) "With a sabre on his brow,
And a helmet by his side,
The soldier sweethearts servant-maids,
And eats cold meat besides."

(*Laughs and walks about waving her parasol.*)

(*Enter George in uniform, carrying in his hand his sword, sword-belt, and cap. Esther takes them from him, and places them on sofa, then comes half down. George goes down by Hawtree.*)

Polly. (*Clapping her hands.*) Oh! here 's a beautiful brother-in-law! Why didn't you come in on horseback as they do at Astley's?—gallop in and say (*Imitating soldier on horseback and prancing up and down stage during the piece.*), Soldiers of France! the eyes of Europe are a-looking at you! The Empire has confidence in you, and France expects that every man

[7] Cavalry-officer who carried the colors.

this day will do his—little utmost! The foe is before you—more 's the pity—and you are before them—worse luck for you! Forward! Go and get killed; and to those who escape the Emperor will give a little bit of ribbon! Nineteens, about! Forward! Gallop! Charge!

(*Galloping to right, imitating bugle, and giving point with parasol. She nearly spears Hawtree's nose. Hawtree claps his hand upon his sword-hilt. She throws herself into chair, laughing, and clapping Hawtree's cap (from table) upon her head. All laugh and applaud. Carriage-wheels heard without.*)

Polly. Oh, what a funny little cap, it 's got no peak. (*A peal of knocks heard at street door.*) What 's that?

Geo. (*Who has hastened to window.*) A carriage! Good heavens—my mother!

Haw. (*At window.*) The Marchioness!

Esther. (*Crossing to George.*) Oh, George!

Polly. (*Crossing to window.*) A Marchioness! A real, live Marchioness! Let me look! I never saw a real live Marchioness in all my life.

Geo. (*Forcing her from window.*) No, no, no! She doesn't know I 'm married. I must break it to her by degrees. What shall I do?

(*By this time Hawtree is at door right. Esther at door left.*)

Esther. Let me go into the bedroom until—

Haw. Too late! She 's on the stairs.

Esther. Here, then!

(*At centre doors, opens them.*)

Polly. I want to see a real, live March—

(*George lifts her in his arms and places her within folding-doors with Esther—then shutting doors quickly, turns and faces Hawtree, who, gathering up his sword, faces George. They then exchange places much in the fashion of soldiers "mounting guard." As George opens door and admits Marchioness, Hawtree drops down to left.*)

Geo. (*With great ceremony.*) My dear mother, I saw you getting out of the carriage.

Marchioness. My dear boy. (*Kissing his forehead.*) I 'm so glad I got to London before you embarked. (*George nervous. Hawtree coming down.*) Captain Hawtree, I think. How do you do?

Haw. (*Coming forward a little.*) Quite well, I thank your ladyship. I trust you are—

Mar. (*Sitting in easy-chair.*) Oh, quite, thanks. (*Slight pause.*) Do you still see the Countess and Lady Florence?

(*Looking at him through her glasses.*)

Haw. Yes.

Mar. Please remember me to them—(*Hawtree takes cap from table, and places sword under his arm.*) Are you going?

Haw. Yaas— Compelled. (*Bows, crossing round back of table. To George who meets him.*) I 'll be at the door for you at seven. We must be at barracks by the quarter. (*George crosses back of table.*) Poor devil! This comes of a man marrying beneath him.

(*Exit Hawtree. George comes down left of table.*)

Mar. I 'm not sorry that he 's gone, for I wanted to talk to you alone. Strange that a woman of such good birth as the Countess should encourage the attention of Captain Hawtree for her daughter Florence. (*During these lines D'Alroy conceals Polly's hat and umbrella under table.*) Lady Clardonax was one of the old Carberrys of Hampshire—not the Norfolk Carberrys, but the direct line. And Mr. Hawtree's grandfather was in trade—something in the City—soap, I think. Stool, George! (*Points to stool. George brings it to her. She motions that he is to sit at her feet. George does so with a sigh.*) He 's a very nice person, but parvenu, as one may see by his languor and his swagger. My boy (*Kissing his forehead.*), I am sure, will never make a mésalliance. He is a D'Alroy, and by his mother's side Planta-genista. The source of our life stream is royal.

Geo. How is the Marquis?

Mar. Paralysed. I left him at Spa with three physicians. He is always paralysed at this time of the year; it is in the family. The paralysis is not personal, but hereditary. I came over to see my steward; got to town last night.

Geo. How did you find me out here?

Mar. I sent the footman to the barracks, and he saw your man Dixon in the street, and Dixon gave him this address. It 's so long since I 've seen you. (*Leans back in chair.*) You 're looking very well, and I daresay when mounted are quite a "beau cavalier." And so, my boy (*Playing with his hair.*), you are going abroad for the first time on active service.

Geo. (*Aside.*) Every word can be heard in the next room. If they 've only gone upstairs.

Mar. And now, my dear boy, before you go I want to give you some advice; and you mustn't despise it because I 'm an old woman. We old women know a great deal more than people give us credit for. You are a soldier—so was your father—so was his father—so was mine—so was our royal founder; we were born to lead! The common people expect it from us. It is our duty. Do you not remember in the Chronicles of Froissart? (*With great enjoyment.*) I think I can quote it word for word; I 've a wonderful memory for my age. (*With closed eyes.*) It was in the fifty-ninth chapter—"How Godefroy D'Alroy helde the towne of St. Amande duryng the siege before Tournay." It said "the towne was not closed but with pales, and captayne there was Sir Amory of Pauy—the Seneschall of Carcassoune—who had said it was not able to hold agaynste an hooste, when one Godefroy D'Alroy sayd that rather than he woulde depart, he woulde keepe it to the best of his power. Whereat the souldiers cheered and sayd, 'Lead us on, Sir Godefroy.' And then began a fierce assault; and they within were chased, and sought for shelter from street to street. But Godefroy stood at the gate so valyantly that the souldiers helde the towne until the commyng of the Earl of Haynault with twelve thousande men."

Geo. (*Aside.*) I wish she 'd go. If she once gets onto Froissart, she 'll never know when to stop.

Mar. When my boy fights—and you will fight—he is sure to distinguish himself. It is his nature to—(*Toys with his hair.*)—he cannot forget his birth. And when you meet these Asiatic ruffians, who have dared to revolt, and to outrage humanity, you will strike as your ancestor Sir Galtier of Chevrault struck at Poictiers. (*Changing tone of voice as if remembering.*) Froissart mentions it thus:—"Sir Galtier, with his four squires, was in the front, in that battell, and there did marvels in arms. And Sir Galtier rode up to the Prince, and sayd to him—'Sir, take your horse and ryde forth, this journey is yours. God is this daye in your handes. Gette us to the French Kynge's batayle. I think verily by his valyantnesse, he woll not fly. Advance banner in the name of God and of Saynt George!' And Sir Galtier galloped forward to see his Kynge's victory, and meet his own death."

Geo. (*Aside.*) If Esther hears all this!

Mar. There is another subject about which I should have spoken to you before this; but an absurd prudery forbade me. I may never see you more. I am old—and you—are going into battle—(*Kissing his forehead with emotion.*)—and this may be our last meeting. (*Noise heard within folding-doors.*) What 's that?

Geo. Nothing—my man Dixon in there.

Mar. We may not meet again on this earth. I do not fear your conduct, my George, with men; but I know the temptations that beset a youth who is well born. But a true soldier, a true gentleman, should not only be without fear, but without reproach. It is easier to fight a furious man than to forego the conquest of a love-sick girl. A thousand Sepoys slain in battle cannot redeem the honor of a man who has betrayed the confidence of a trusting woman. Think, George, what dishonor—what stain upon your manhood—to hurl a girl to shame and degradation! And what excuse for it? That she is plebeian? A man of real honor will spare the woman who has confessed her love for him as he would give quarter to an enemy he had disarmed. (*Taking his hands.*) Let my boy avoid the snares so artfully spread; and when he asks his mother to welcome the woman he has chosen for his wife, let me take her to my arms and plant a motherly kiss upon the white brow of a lady. (*Noise of a fall heard within folding-doors. Rising.*) What 's that?

Geo. (*Rising.*) Nothing.

Mar. I heard a cry.

(*Folding-doors open; discovering Esther with Polly, staggering in, fainting.*)

Polly. George! George!

(*George goes up and Esther falls in his arms. George places Esther on sofa. George on her right, Polly on her left.*)

Mar. (*Coming down.*) Who are these *women?*

Polly. Women!

Mar. George D'Alroy, these persons should have been sent away. How could you dare to risk your mother meeting women of their stamp?

Polly. (*Violently.*) What does she mean? How dare she call me a woman? What 's she, I 'd like to know?

Geo. Silence, Polly! You mustn't insult my mother.

Mar. The insult is from you. I leave you, and I hope that time may induce me to forget this scene of degradation.

(*Turning to go.*)

Geo. Stay, mother. (*Marchioness turns slightly away.*) Before you go (*George has raised Esther from sofa in his arms.*) let me present to you Mrs. George D'Alroy. *My wife!*

Mar. Married!

Geo. Married.

(*Marchioness sinks into easy-chair; George replaces Esther on sofa, but still retains her hand. Three hesitating taps at door heard. George crosses to door, opens it, discovers Eccles, who enters. George drops down back of Marchioness's chair.*)

Eccles. They told us to come up. When your man came Polly was out; so I thought I should do instead. (*Calling at door.*) Come up, Sam.

(*Enter Sam in his Sunday clothes, with short cane and smoking a cheroot. He nods and grins—Polly points to Marchioness—Sam takes cheroot from his mouth and quickly removes his hat.*)

Eccles. Sam had just called; so we three —Sam and I, and your man, all came in the 'ansom cab together. Didn't we, Sam?

(*Eccles and Sam go over to the girls, and Eccles drops down to front of table—smilingly.*)

Mar. (*With glasses up, to George.*) Who is this?

Geo. (*Coming left of Marchioness.*) My wife's father.

Mar. What is he?

Geo. A—nothing.

Eccles. I am one of nature's noblemen. Happy to see you, my lady—(*Turning to her.*)—now, my daughters have told me who you are—(*George turns his back in an agony as Eccles crosses to Marchioness.*)—we old folks, fathers and mothers of the young couples, ought to make friends.

(*Holding out his dirty hand.*)

Mar. (*Shrinking back.*) Go away! (*Eccles goes back to table again, disgusted.*) What 's his name?

Geo. Eccles.

Mar. Eccles! Eccles! There never was an Eccles. He don't exist.

Eccles. Don't he, though? What d 'ye call this?

(*Goes up again to back of table as Sam drops down. He is just going to take a decanter when Sam stops him.*)

Mar. No Eccles was ever born!

Geo. He takes the liberty of breathing notwithstanding. (*Aside.*) And I wish he wouldn't.

Mar. And who is the little man? Is he also Eccles?

(*Sam looks round. Polly gets close up to him, and looks with defiant glance at the Marchioness.*)

Geo. No.

Mar. Thank goodness! What then?

Geo. His name is Gerridge.

Mar. *Gerridge!* It breaks one's teeth. Why is he here?

Geo. He is making love to Polly, my wife's sister.

Mar. And what is he?

Geo. A gasman.

Mar. He looks it. (*George goes up to Esther.*) And what is she—the—the sister?

(*Eccles, who has been casting longing eyes at the decanter on table, edges towards it, and when he thinks no one is noticing, fills wine-glass.*)

Polly. (*Asserting herself indignantly.*) I 'm in the ballet at the Theatre Royal, Lambeth. So was Esther. We 're not ashamed of what we are! We have no cause to be.

Sam. That 's right, Polly! pitch into them swells!—who are they?

(*Eccles by this time has seized wine-glass, and turning his back, is about to drink, when Hawtree enters. Eccles hides glass under his coat, and pretends to be looking up at picture.*)

Haw. (*Entering.*) George! (*Stops suddenly, looking round.*) So, all 's known!

Mar. (*Rising.*) Captain Hawtree, see me to my carriage; I am broken-hearted.

(*Takes Hawtree's arm and is going up.*)

Eccles. (*Who has tasted the claret, spits it out with a grimace, exclaiming.*) Rot!

(*Polly goes to piano—sits on stool—Sam, back to audience, leaning on piano. Eccles exits through folding-doors.*)

Geo. (*To Marchioness.*) Don't go in anger. You may not see me again.

(*Esther rises in nervous excitement, clutch-

ing George's hand. Marchioness stops. Esther brings George down.)

Esther. (*With arm round his neck.*) Oh, George! must you go?

(*They come to front of table.*)

Geo. Yes.

Esther. I can't leave you. I'll go with you!

Geo. Impossible! The country is too unsettled.

Esther. May I come after you?

Geo. Yes.

Esther. (*With her head on his shoulder.*) I may.

Mar. (*Coming down, Hawtree at door.*) It is his duty to go. His honor calls him. The honor of his family—*our* honor.

Esther. But I love him so! Pray don't be angry with me!

Haw. (*Looking at watch and coming down.*) George!

Geo. I must go, love.

(*Hawtree goes up to door again.*)

Mar. (*Advancing.*) Let me arm you, George—let your mother, as in the days of old. There is blood—and blood, my son. See, your wife cries when she should be proud of you!

Geo. My Esther is all that is good and noble. No lady born to a coronet could be gentler or more true. Esther, my wife, fetch me my sword, and buckle my belt around me.

Esther. (*Clinging to him.*) No, no; I can't!

Geo. Try. (*Whispers to Esther.*) To please my mother. (*To Marchioness.*) You shall see. (*Esther totters up stage, Polly assisting her, and brings down his sword. As Esther is trying to buckle his belt, he whispers.*) I've left money for you, my darling. My lawyer will call on you to-morrow. Forgive me! I tried hard to tell you we were ordered for India; but when the time came, my heart failed me, and I—

(*Esther, before she can succeed in fastening his sword-belt, reels, and falls fainting in his arms. Polly hurries to her. Sam standing at piano, looking frightened; Hawtree with hand upon handle of door; Marchioness looking on, at right of George.*)

ACT DROP

For call—George and Hawtree gone. Esther in chair fainting; Polly and Sam each side of her, Polly holding her hands, and Sam fanning her with his red handkerchief. The folding-doors thrown open, and Eccles standing at back of table offering glass of claret.

ACT III

SCENE:—*The room in Stangate (as in Act I). Same furniture as in Act I, with exception of piano, with roll of music tied up on it, in place of bureau. Map of India over mantel-piece. Sword with crape knot, spurs, and cap, craped, hanging over chimney-piece. Portrait of D'Alroy (large) on mantel-piece. Berceaunette,*[8] *and child, with coral, in it. Polly's bonnet and shawl hanging on peg. Small tin saucepan in fender, fire alight, and kettle on it. Two candles (tallow) in sticks, one of which is broken about three inches from the top and hangs over. Slate and pencil on table. Jug on table, bandbox and ballet skirt on table. At rise of curtain Polly discovered at table, back of stage. Comes down and places skirt in bandbox. She is dressed in black.*

Polly. (*Placing skirt in box, and leaning her chin upon her hand.*) There—there's the dress for poor Esther in case she gets the engagement, which I don't suppose she will. It's too good luck, and good luck never comes to her, poor thing. (*Goes up to back of cradle.*) Baby's asleep still. How good he looks—as good as if he were dead, like his poor father; and alive too, at the same time, like his dear self. Ah! dear me; it's a strange world. (*Sits in chair right of table, feeling in pocket for money.*) Four and elevenpence. That must do for to-day and to-morrow. Esther is going to bring in the rusks for Georgey. (*Takes up slate.*) Three, five—eight, and four—twelve, one shilling—father can only have twopence. (*This all to be said in one breath.*) He must make do with that till Saturday, when I get my salary. If Esther gets the engagement, I shan't have many more salaries to take; I shall leave the stage and retire into private life. I wonder if I shall like private life, and if private life will like me. It will seem so strange being no longer Miss Mary Eccles—but Mrs. Samuel Gerridge. (*Writes it on slate.*) "Mrs. Samuel Ger-

[8] Kind of cradle.

ridge." (*Laughs bashfully.*) La! to think of my being Mrs. Anybody! How annoyed Susan Smith will be! (*Writing on slate.*) "Mrs. Samuel Gerridge presents her compliments to Miss Susan Smith, and Mrs. Samuel Gerridge requests the favor of Miss Susan Smith's company to tea, on Tuesday evening next, at Mrs. Samuel Gerridge's house." (*Pause.*) Poor Susan! (*Beginning again.*) "P.S.—Mrs. Samuel Gerridge—"

(*Knock heard at room door; Polly starts.*)

Sam. (*Without.*) Polly, open the door.

Polly. Sam! come in.

Sam. (*Without.*) I can't.

Polly. Why not?

Sam. I 've got somethin' on my 'ead.

(*Polly rises and opens door. Sam enters, carrying two rolls of wall-paper, one in each hand, and a small table on his head, which he deposits down stage, then puts roll of paper on piano, as also his cap. Sam has a rule-pocket in corduroys.*)

Polly. (*Shuts door.*) What 's that?

Sam. (*Pointing to table with pride.*) Furniture. How are you, my Polly? (*Kissing her.*) You look handsomer than ever this morning. (*Dances and sings.*) "Tid-dle-di-tum-ti-di-do."

Polly. What 's the matter, Sam? Are you mad?

Sam. No, 'appy—much the same thing.

Polly. Where have you been these two days?

Sam. (*All excitement.*) That 's just what I 'm goin' to tell yer. Polly, my pet, my brightest batswing and most brilliant burner, what do yer think?

Polly. Oh, do go on, Sam, or I 'll slap your face.

Sam. Well, then, you 've 'eard me speak of old Binks, the plumber, glazier, and gas-fitter, who died six months ago?

Polly. Yes.

Sam. (*Sternly and deliberately.*) I 've bought 'is business.

Polly. No!

Sam. (*Excitedly.*) Yes, of 'is widow, old Mrs. Binks—so much down, and so much more at the end of the year.

(*Dances and sings.*)

Ri-ti-toodle
Roodle-oodle
Ri-ti-tooral-lay.

Polly. La, Sam.

Sam. (*Pacing stage up and down.*) Yes; I 've bought the goodwill, fixtures, fittin's, stock, rolls of gas-pipe, and sheets of lead. (*Jumps on table, quickly facing Polly.*) Yes, Polly, I 'm a tradesman with a shop—a master tradesman. (*Coming to Polly seriously.*) All I want to complete the premises is a missus.

(*Tries to kiss her. She pushes him away.*)

Polly. Sam, don't be foolish.

Sam. (*Arm round her waist.*) Come and be Mrs. Sam Gerridge, Polly, my patent-safety-day-and-night-light. You 'll furnish me completely.

(*Polly goes up, Sam watching her admiringly; he then sees slate, snatches it up and looks at it. She snatches it from him with a shriek, and rubs out the writing, looking daggers at him, Sam laughing.*)

Sam. Only to think now.

(*Putting arm round her waist. Polly pouting.*)

Polly. Don't be a goose.

Sam. (*Going towards table.*) I spent the whole of yesterday lookin' up furniture. Now I bought that a bargain, and I brought it 'ere to show you for your approval. I 've bought lots of other things, and I 'll bring 'em all 'ere to show you for your approval.

Polly. I couldn't think what had become of you.

(*Seated right of table.*)

Sam. Couldn't yer? Oh, I say, I want yer to choose the new paper for the little back-parlor just behind the shop, you know. Now what d' yer think of this?

(*Fetching a pattern from piano and unrolling it.*)

Polly. No, I don't like that. (*Sam fetches the other, a flaming pattern.*) Ah! that 's neat.

Sam. Yes, that 's neat and quiet. I 'll new-paper it, and new-furnish it, and it shall all be bran-new.

(*Puts paper on top of piano.*)

Polly. But won't it cost a lot of money?

Sam. (*Bravely.*) I can work for it. With customers in the shop, and you in the back-parlor, I can work like fifty men. (*Sits on table, beckons Polly to him; she comes left of table, Sam puts his arm round Polly, sentimentally.*) Only fancy, at night, when the shop 's closed, and the shutters are up, counting out the till together! (*Changing his manner.*) Besides, that isn't all I 've been doin'.

I 've been writin', and what I 've written, I 've got printed.

Polly. No!

Sam. True.

Polly. You 've been writing—about me?

(*Delighted.*)

Sam. No—about the shop. (*Polly disgusted.*) Here it is. (*Takes roll of circulars from pocket of his canvas slop.*) Yer mustn't laugh—yer know—it 's my first attempt. I wrote it the night before last; and when I thought of you the words seemed to flow like—red-hot solder. (*Reads.*) Hem! "Samuel Gerridge takes this opportunity of informin' the nobility, gentry, and inhabitants of the Borough-road—"

Polly. The Borough-road?

Sam. Well, there ain't many of the nobility and gentry as lives in the Borough-road, but it pleases the inhabitants to make 'em believe yer think so (*Resuming.*)—"of informin' the nobility, gentry and inhabitants of the Borough-road, and its vicinity"—and "its vicinity." (*Looking at her.*) Now I think that 's rather good, eh?

Polly. Yes. (*Doubtfully.*) I 've heard worse.

Sam. I first thought of saying neighbor-'ood; but then vicinity sounds so much more genteel (*Resuming.*)—"*and* its vicinity, that 'e has entered upon the business of the late Mr. Binks, 'is relict, the present Mrs. B., 'avin' disposed to 'im of the same"—now listen, Polly, because it gets interestin'—"S. G.—"

Polly. S. G. Who 's he?

Sam. (*Looking at Polly with surprise.*) Why, me. S. G.—Samuel Gerridge—me, us. We 're S. G. Now don't interrupt me, or you 'll cool my metal, and then I can't work. "S. G. 'opes that, by a constant attention to business, and"—mark this—"by supplyin' the best articles at the most reasonable prices, to merit a continuance of those favors which it will ever be 'is constant study to deserve." There! (*Turning on table triumphantly.*) Stop a bit,—there 's a little bit more yet. "Bell-'angin', gas-fittin', plumbin', and glazin', as usual." There! and it 's all my own!

(*Puts circular on mantel-piece, and crossing contemplates it.*)

Polly. Beautiful, Sam. It looks very attractive from here, don't it?

Sam. (*Postman's knock.*) There 's the postman. I 'll go. I shall send some of these out by post.

(*Goes off and returns with letter.*)

Polly. (*Taking it.*) Oh, for Esther. I know who it 's from. (*Places letter on mantel-piece. At chair left of table. Sam sits corner of table, reading circular. Seriously.*) Sam, who do you think was here last night?

Sam. Who?

Polly. Captain Hawtree.

Sam. (*Deprecatingly.*) Oh, 'im!—Come back from India, I suppose.

Polly. Yes,—luckily Esther was out.

Sam. I never liked that long swell. He was a' uppish, conceited—

Polly. (*Sitting at end of table.*) Oh, he 's better than he used to be—he 's a major now. He 's only been in England a fortnight.

Sam. Did he tell yer anything about De Alroy?

Polly. (*Leaning against table end.*) Yes; he said he was riding out not far from the cantonment, and was surrounded by a troop of Sepoy cavalry, which took him prisoner, and galloped off with him.

Sam. But about 'is death?

Polly. Oh! (*Hiding her face.*) that he said was believed to be too terrible to mention.

Sam. (*Crossing to Polly at table.*) Did 'e tell yer anything else?

Polly. No; he asked a lot of questions, and I told him everything. How poor Esther had taken her widowhood and what a dear good baby the baby was, and what a comfort to us all, and how Esther had come back to live with us again.

Sam. (*Sharply.*) And the reason for it?

Polly. (*Looking down.*) Yes.

Sam. How your father got all the money that 'e 'd left for Esther?

Polly. (*Sharply.*) Don't say any more about that, Sam.

Sam. Oh! I only think Captain 'Awtree ought to know where the money *did* go to, and you shouldn't try and screen your father, and let 'im suppose that you and Esther spent it all.

Polly. I told him—I told him—I told him.

(*Angrily.*)

Sam. Did you tell 'im that your father was always at 'armonic meetin's at taverns, and 'ad 'arf cracked 'isself with drink, and was always singin' the songs and makin' the speeches 'e 'eard there, and was always goin' on about 'is wrongs as one of the workin' classes? 'E's a pretty one for one of the workin' classes, 'e is! 'Asn't done a stroke of work these twenty year. Now, I *am* one of the workin' classes, but I *don't* 'owl about it. I work, I don't spout.

Polly. Hold your tongue, Sam. I won't have you say any more against poor father. He has his faults, but he's a very clever man.

(*Sighing.*)

Sam. Ah! What else did Captain Hawtree say?

Polly. He advised us to apply to Mr. D'Alroy's mother.

Sam. What! the Marquissy? And what did you say to that?

Polly. I said that Esther wouldn't hear of it. And so the Major said that he'd write to Esther, and I suppose this is the letter.

Sam. Now, Polly, come along and choose the paper for the little back-parlor.

(*Going to table and taking it up to wall behind door.*)

Polly. (*Rising.*) Can't. Who's to mind baby?

Sam. The *baby?* Oh, I forgot all about 'im. (*Goes to cradle.*) I see yer! (*Goes to window casually.*) There's your father comin' down the street. Won't 'e mind 'im?

Polly. (*Going up.*) I daresay he will. If I promise him an extra sixpence on Saturday. (*Sam opens window.*) Hi! Father!

(*Polly goes to cradle.*)

Sam. (*Aside.*) 'E looks down in the mouth, 'e does. I suppose 'e's 'ad no drink this morning.

(*Goes to Polly.*)

Enter Eccles in shabby black. Pauses on entering, looks at Sam, turns away in disgust, takes off hat, places it on piano, and shambles across stage. Taking chair, places it, and sits before fire.)

Polly. (*Goes to Eccles.*) Come in to stop a bit, father?

Eccles. No; not for long. (*Sam comes down.*) Good morning, Samuel. Going back to work? that's right, my boy, —stick to it. (*Pokes fire.*) Stick to it —nothing like it.

Sam. (*Aside.*) Now, isn't that too bad? No, Mr. Eccles. I've knocked off for the day.

Eccles. (*Waving poker.*) That's bad,— that's very bad! Nothing like work— for the young. I don't work so much as I used to, myself, but I like to (*Polly sitting on corner of table up left.*) see the young 'uns at it. It does me good, and it does them good, too. What does the poet say?

(*Rising, impressively, and leaning on table.*)

"A carpenter said tho' that was well spoke,
It was better by far to defend it with hoak.
A currier, wiser than both put together,
Said say what you will, there is nothing
like *labor.*
For a' that, and a' that,
Your ribbon, gown and a' that,
The rank is but the guinea stamp,
The working man's the gold for a' that."

(*Sits again, triumphantly wagging his head.*)

Sam. (*Aside.*) This is one of the public-house loafers, that wants all the wages and none of the work, an idle old—

(*Goes in disgust to piano, puts on cap, and takes rolls of paper under his arm.*)

Polly. (*To Eccles.*) Esther will be in by-and-by. (*Persuasively.*) Do, father.

Eccles. No, no, I tell you I won't!

Polly. (*Whispering, arm round his neck.*) And I'll give you sixpence extra on Saturday.

(*Eccles's face relaxes into a broad grin. Polly gets hat and cloak.*)

Eccles. Ah! you sly little puss, you know how to get over your poor old father.

Sam. (*Aside.*) Yes, with sixpence.

Polly. (*Putting on bonnet and cloak at door.*) Give the cradle a rock if baby cries.

Sam. (*Crossing to Eccles.*) If you should 'appen to want employment or amusement, Mr. Eccles, just cast your eye over this. (*Puts circular on table, then joins Polly at door.*) Stop a bit, I've forgot to give the baby one.

(*Throws circular into cradle. Exeunt, Polly first. Eccles takes out pipe from pocket, looks into it, then blows through it making a squeaking noise, and finishes by tenderly placing it on table. He then hunts all his pockets for tobacco, finally finding a little paper packet containing a screw of tobacco in his waistcoat pocket, which he also places on table after turning up the corner of the tablecloth for the purpose of emptying the contents of his pocket of the few remnants of past screws *of tobacco on to the bare table and mixing a little out of the packet with it and filling pipe. He then brushes all that remains on the table into the paper packet, pinches it up, and carefully replaces it in waistcoat pocket. Having put the pipe into his mouth, he looks about for a light, across his shoulder and under table, though never rising from the chair; seeing nothing, his face assumes an expression of comic anguish. Turning to table he angrily replaces tablecloth and then notices Sam's circular. His face relaxes into a smile, and picking it up he tears the circular in half, makes a spill of it, and lighting it at fire, stands, with his back to fireplace, and smokes vigorously.)*

Eccles. Poor Esther! Nice market she 's brought her pigs to—ugh! Mind the baby indeed! What good is he to me? That fool of a girl to throw away all her chances!—a *honorable-hess*—and her father not to have on him the price of a pint of early beer or a quartern of cool, refreshing gin! Stopping in here to rock a young honorable! Cuss him! (*Business, puffs smoke in baby's face, rocking cradle.*) Are we slaves, we working men? (*Sings savagely.*) "Britons never, never, never shall be—" (*Nodding his head sagaciously, sits by table.*) I won't stand this, I 've writ to the old cat—I mean to the Marquissy—to tell her that her daughter-in-law and her grandson is almost starving. That fool Esther is too proud to write to her for money. I hate pride—it 's *beastly!* (*Rising.*) There 's no beastly pride about me. (*Goes up, smacking his lips.*) I 'm as dry as a lime-kiln. (*Takes up jug.*) Milk!—(*With disgust.*) for this young aristocratic pauper. Everybody in the house is sacrificed for him! (*At foot of cradle, with arms on chair back.*) And to think that a *working man*, and a member of the Committee of Banded Brothers for the Regeneration of Human Kind, by means of equal diffusion of intelligence and equal division of property, should be thusty, while this cub— (*Draws aside curtain, and looks at child. After a pause—*) That there coral he 's got round his neck is *gold*, real *gold!* (*With hand on knob at end of cradle.*) Oh, Society! Oh, Governments! Oh, Class Legislation!—*is this right?* Shall this mindless wretch enjoy himself, while sleeping, with a jewelled gawd, and his poor old grandfather want the price of half a pint? *No!* it shall not be! Rather than see it, I will myself resent this outrage on the rights of man! and in this holy crusade of class against class, of the weak and lowly against the *powerful and strong*—(*Pointing to child.*)—I will strike one blow for freedom! (*Goes to back of cradle.*) He 's asleep. It will fetch ten bob round the corner; and if the Marquissy gives us anything it can be got out with some o' that. (*Steals coral.*) Lie still, my darling!—it 's grandfather a-watchin' over you—

"Who ran to catch me when I fell,
And kicked the place to make it well?
My grandfather!"

(*Rocking cradle with one hand; leaves it quickly, and as he takes hat off piano Esther enters. She is dressed as a widow, her face pale, and her manner quick and imperious. She carries a parcel and paper bag of rusks in her hand; she puts parcel on table, goes to cradle, kneels down and kisses child.*)

Eccles. My lovey had a nice walk? You should wrap yourself up well,—you are so liable to catch cold.

Esther. My Georgey?—Where 's his coral? (*Eccles, going to door, fumbles with lock nervously, and is going out as Esther speaks.*) Gone!—Father! (*Rising—Eccles stops.*) The child's coral—where is it?

Eccles. (*Confused.*) Where 's what, duckey?

Esther. The coral! You 've got it,—I know it! Give it me! (*Quickly and imperiously.*) Give it me! (*Eccles takes coral from his pocket and gives it back.*) If you *dare* to touch *my* child—

(*Goes to cradle.*)

Eccles. Esther! (*Going quickly to piano and banging hat on it.*) Am I not your father?—

(*Esther gets round to front of table.*)

Esther. And I am his mother!

Eccles. (*Coming to her.*) Do you bandy words with me, you pauper, you pauper!!! to whom I have given shelter—shelter to you and your brat! I 've a good mind—

(*Raising his clenched fist.*)

Esther. (*Confronting him.*) If you dare! I am no longer your little drudge—your frightened servant. When mother died—(*Eccles changes countenance and cowers beneath her glance.*)—and I was so high, I tended you, and worked for you—and you beat me. That time is past. I am a woman—I am a wife—a widow—a *mother!* Do you think I will let you outrage *him?* Touch me if you dare!

(*Advancing a step.*)

Eccles. (*Bursting into tears and coming down.*) And this is my own child, which I nussed when a babby, and sang "Cootsicum Coo" to afore she could speak. (*Gets hat from piano, and returns a step or two.*) Hon. Mrs. De Alroy (*Esther drops down behind chair by table.*), I forgive you for all that you have said. I forgive you for all that you have done. In everything that I have done I have acted with the best intentions. May the babe in that cradle never treat you as you have this day *tret* a grey 'aired father. May he never cease to love and *h*onor you, as you have ceased to love and *h*onor me, after all that I have done for you, and the position to which I have raised you by my own *industry.* (*Goes to door.*) May he never behave to you like the bad daughters of King Lear; and may you never live to feel how much more sharper than a serpent's (*Slight pause as if remembering quotation.*) scale it is to have a thankless child!

(*Exit.*)

Esther. (*Kneeling back of cradle.*) My darling! (*Arranging bed and placing coral to baby's lips, then to her own.*) Mamma 's come back to her own. Did she stay away from him so long? (*Rises, and looks at sabre, etc.*) My George! to think that you can never look upon his face or hear his voice. My brave, gallant, handsome husband! My lion and my love! (*Comes down, pacing stage.*) Oh! to be a soldier, and to fight the wretches who destroyed him—who took my darling from me! (*Action of cutting with sabre.*) To gallop miles upon their upturned faces. (*Crossing with action, breaks down sobbing at mantelpiece; sees letter.*) What 's this? Captain Hawtree's hand. (*Sitting in chair, reads, at left hand of table.*) "My dear Mrs. D'Alroy,—I returned to England less than a fortnight ago. I have some papers and effects of my poor friend's, which I am anxious to deliver to you, and I beg of you to name a day when I can call with them and see you; at the same time let me express my deepest sympathy with your affliction. Your husband's loss was mourned by every man in the regiment. (*Esther lays the letter on her heart, and then resumes reading.*) I have heard with great pain of the pecuniary embarrassments into which accident and imprudence of others have placed you. I trust you will not consider me, one of poor George's oldest comrades and friends, either intrusive or impertinent in sending the enclosed (*She takes out a cheque.*), and in hoping that, should any further difficulties arise, you will inform me of them, and remember that I am, dear Mrs. D'Alroy, now, and always, your faithful and sincere friend, Arthur Hawtree." (*Esther goes to cradle and bends over it.*) Oh, *his* boy, if you could read it!

(*Sobs, with head on head of cradle.*)

(*Enter Polly.*)

Polly. Father gone!

Esther. Polly, you look quite flurried.

(*Polly laughs and whispers to Esther.*)

Esther. (*Near head of table, taking Polly in her arms and kissing her.*) So soon? Well, my darling, I hope you may be happy.

Polly. Yes. Sam 's going to speak to father about it this afternoon. (*Crosses round table, putting rusks in saucepan.*) Did you see the agent, dear?

Esther. (*Sits by table.*) Yes; the manager didn't come—he broke his appointment again.

Polly. (*Sits opposite at table.*) Nasty, rude fellow!

Esther. The agent said it didn't matter, he thought I should get the engagement. He 'll only give me thirty shillings a week, though.

Polly. But you said that two pounds was the regular salary.

Esther. Yes, but they know I 'm poor, and want the engagement, and so take advantage of me.

Polly. Never mind, Esther. I put the dress in that bandbox. It looks almost as good as new.

Esther. I 've had a letter from Captain Hawtree.

Polly. I know, dear; he came here last night.

Esther. A dear, good letter—speaking of George, and enclosing a cheque for thirty pounds.

Polly. Oh, how kind! Don't you tell father.

(*Noise of carriage-wheels without.*)

Esther. I shan't.

(*Eccles enters, breathless. Esther and Polly rise.*)

Eccles. It 's the Marquissy in her coach. (*Esther puts on the lid of bandbox.*) Now, girls, do be civil to her, and she may do something for us. (*Places hat on piano.*) I see the coach as I was coming out of the "Rainbow."

(*Hastily pulls an old comb out of his pocket, and puts his hair in order.*)

Esther. The Marquise!

(*Esther comes down to end of table, Polly holding her hand.*)

Eccles. (*At door.*) This way, my lady—up them steps. They 're rather awkward for the likes o' you; but them as is poor and lowly must do as best they can with steps and circumstances.

(*Enter Marquise. She surveys the place with aggressive astonishment.*)

Marquise. (*Going down, half aside.*) What a hole! And to think that my grandson should breathe such an atmosphere, and be contaminated by such associations! (*To Eccles, who is a little up.*) Which is the young woman who married my son?

Esther. I am Mrs. George D'Alroy, widow of George D'Alroy. Who are you?

Mar. I am his mother, the Marquise de St. Maur.

Esther. (*With the grand air.*) Be seated, I beg.

(*Eccles takes chair from right centre, which Esther immediately seizes as Sam enters with an easy-chair on his head, which he puts down, not seeing Marquise, who instantly sits down in it, concealing it completely.*)

Sam. (*Astonished.*) It 's the Marquissy! (*Looking at her.*) My eyes! These aristocrats are fine women—plenty of 'em —(*Describing circle.*) quality and quantity!

Polly. Go away, Sam; you 'd better come back.

(*Eccles nudges him and bustles him towards door. Exit Sam. Eccles shuts door on him.*)

Eccles. (*Coming down right of Marquise, rubbing his hands.*) If we 'd 'a' know'd your ladyship 'ad been a-coming we 'd 'a' 'ad the place cleaned up a bit.

(*With hands on chair back, in lower right corner of stage. He gets round to right, behind Marquise, who turns the chair slightly from him.*)

Polly. Hold your tongue, father!

(*Eccles crushed.*)

Mar. (*To Esther.*) You remember me, do you not?

Esther. Perfectly, though I only saw you once. (*Seating herself* en grande dame.) May I ask what has procured me the honor of this visit?

Mar. I was informed that you were in want, and I came to offer you assistance.

Esther. I thank you for your offer, and the delicate consideration for my feelings with which it is made. I need no assistance.

(*Eccles groans and leans on piano.*)

Mar. A letter that I received last night informed me that you did.

Esther. May I ask if that letter came from Captain Hawtree?

Mar. No—from this person—your father, I think.

Esther. (*To Eccles.*) How dare you interfere in my affairs?

Eccles. My lovey, I did it with the best intentions.

Mar. Then you will not accept assistance from me?

Esther. No.

Polly. (*Aside to Esther, holding her hand.*) Bless you, my darling.

(*Polly standing beside her.*)

Mar. But you have a child—a son—my grandson.

(*With emotion.*)

Esther. Master D'Alroy wants for nothing.

Polly. (*Aside.*) And never shall.

(*Eccles groans and turns on to piano.*)

Mar. I came here to propose that my grandson should go back with me.

(*Polly rushes up to cradle.*)

Esther. (*Rising defiantly.*) What! part with my boy! I 'd sooner die!

Mar. You can see him when you wish. As for money, I—

Esther. Not for ten thousand million worlds—not for ten thousand million marchionesses!

Eccles. Better do what the good lady asks you, my dear; she 's advising you for your own good, and for the child's likewise.

Mar. Surely you cannot intend to bring up my son's son in a place like this?

Esther. I do.

(*Goes up to cradle.*)

Eccles. It *is* a poor place, and we are poor people, sure enough. We ought not to fly in the faces of our pastors and masters—our pastresses and mistresses.

Polly. (*Aside.*) Oh, hold your tongue, do!

(*Up at cradle.*)

Esther. (*Before cradle.*) Master George D'Alroy will remain with his mother. The offer to take him from her is an insult to his dead father and to him.

Eccles. (*Aside.*) He don't seem to feel it, stuck-up little beast.

Mar. But you have no money—how can you rear him?—how can you educate him?—how can you live?

Esther. (*Tearing dress from bandbox.*) Turn columbine,—go on the stage again and dance.

Mar. (*Rising.*) You are insolent—you forget that I am a lady.

Esther. You forget that I am a mother. Do you dare to offer to buy my child—*his* breathing image, *his* living memory—with money? (*Crosses to door and throws it open.*) There is the door—go!

(*Picture.*)

Eccles. (*To Marquise, who has risen, aside.*) Very sorry, my lady, as you should be tret in this way, which was not my wishes.

Mar. Silence! (*Eccles retreats, putting back chair. Marquise goes up to door.*) Mrs. D'Alroy, if anything could have increased my sorrow for the wretched marriage my poor son was *decoyed* into, it would be your conduct this day to his mother.

(*Exit.*)

Esther. (*Falling into Polly's arms.*) Oh, Polly! Polly!

Eccles. (*Looking after her.*) To go away and not to leave a sov. behind her! (*Running up to open door.*) Cat! Cat! Stingy old cat!

(*Almost runs to fire, and pokes it violently; carriage-wheels heard without.*)

Esther. I'll go to my room and lie down. Let me have the baby, or that old woman may come back and steal him.

(*Exit Esther, and Polly follows with baby.*)

Eccles. Well, women is the obstinatest devils as never wore horse-shoes. Children? Beasts! Beasts!

(*Enter Sam and Polly.*)

Sam. Come along, Polly, and let's get it over at once. (*Sam places cap on piano, and goes to table. Polly takes bandbox from table, and places it up stage.*) Now, Mr. Eccles (*Eccles turns suddenly, facing Sam.*), since you've been talkin' on family matters, I'd like to 'ave a word with yer, so take this opportunity to—

Eccles. (*Waving his hand grandly.*) Take what you like, and then order more (*Rising and leaning over table.*), Samuel Gerridge. That hand is a hand that has never turned its back on a friend, or a bottle to give him.

(*Sings, front of table.*)

I'll stand by my friend,
I'll stand by my friend,
I'll stand by my friend,
If he'll stand to me [9]—me, gentlemen!

Sam. Well, Mr. Eccles, sir, it's this—

Polly. (*Aside, coming down to Sam.*) Don't tell him too sudden, Sam—it might shock his feelings.

Sam. It's this; yer know that for the last four years I've been keepin' company with Mary—Polly.

(*Turning to her and smiling. Eccles drops into chair as if shot.*)

Eccles. Go it! go it! strike home, young man! Strike on this grey head! (*Sings.*) "Britons, strike home!" Here (*Tapping his chest.*), to my heart! Don't spare me! Have a go at my grey hairs. Pull 'em—pull 'em out! A long pull, and a strong pull, and a pull all together!

(*Cries, and drops his face on arm on table.*)

Polly. Oh, father! I wouldn't hurt your feelings for the world.

(*Patting his head.*)

Sam. No, Mr. Eccles, I don't want to 'urt your feelin's, but I'm a-goin' to enter upon a business. Here's a circular.

(*Offering one.*)

Eccles. (*Indignantly.*) Circ'lars. What are circ'lars?—compared to a father's feelings?

Sam. And I want Polly to name the day, sir, and so I ask you—

Eccles. This is 'ard, this is 'ard. One of

9 I.e., pay for the drinks.

my daughters marries a soger. The other goes a-gasfitting.

Sam. (*Annoyed.*) The business which will enable me to maintain a wife is that of the late Mr. Binks, plumber, glazier, etc.

Eccles. (*Rising, sings. Air, "Lost Rosabelle."*) "They have given thee to a plumber,
They have broken every vow,
They have given thee to a plumber,
And my heart, my heart is breaking now."

(*Drops into chair again.*)

Now, gentlemen!

(*Sam thrusts circulars into his pocket, and turns away angrily.*)

Polly. You know, father, you can come and see me.

(*Leans over him.*)

Sam. (*Sotto voce.*) No, no.

(*Motions to Polly.*)

Eccles. (*Looking up.*) So I can, and that 's a comfort. (*Shaking her hand.*) And you can come and see me, and that 's a comfort. I 'll come and see you often —very often—every day (*Sam turns up stage in horror.*), and crack a fatherly bottle (*Rising.*), and shed a friendly tear.

(*Wipes eyes with dirty pocket-handkerchief, which he pulls from breast pocket.*)

Polly. Do, father, do.

(*Goes up and gets tea-tray.*)

Sam. (*With a gulp.*) Yes, Mr. Eccles, do.

(*Goes to Polly and gesticulates behind tray.*)

Eccles. I will. (*Goes to centre of stage.*) And this it is to be a father. I would part with any of my children for their own good, readily—if I was paid for it. (*Goes to right corner; sings.*) "For I know that the angels are whispering to me"—me, gentlemen!

(*Polly gets tea-things.*)

Sam. I 'll try and make Polly a good husband, and anything that I can do to prove it (*Lowering his voice.*), in the way of spirituous liquors and tobacco (*Slipping coin into his hand, unseen by Polly.*) shall be done.

Eccles. (*Lightening up and placing his left hand on Sam's head.*)
"Be kind to thy father,
Wherever you be,
For he is a blessing
And credit to thee"—thee, genlemen. (*Gets to centre of stage.*) Well, my children—bless you, take the blessing of a grey-'aired father. (*Polly looking from one to the other.*) Samuel Gerridge, she shall be thine. (*Mock heroically, looking at money.*) You shall be his wife (*Looking at Polly.*) and you (*Looking at Sam.*) shall be her husband—for a husband I know no fitter—no "gas-fitter" man. (*Runs to piano and takes hat; goes to door, looks comically pathetic at Sam and Polly, puts on hat and comes towards centre of stage.*) I 've a friend waiting for me round the corner, which I want to have a word with; and may you never know how much more sharper than a serpent's tooth it is to have a marriageable daughter.

(*Sings.*)

" When I heard she was married,
I breathed not a tone,
The heyes of all round me
Was fixed on my h'own;
I flew to my chamber
To hide my despair,
I tore the bright circlet
Of gems from my hair.
When I heard she was married,
When I heard she was married— "

(*Breaks down. Exit.*)

Polly. (*Drying her eyes.*) There, Sam. I always told you that though father had his faults, his heart was in the right place.

Sam. Poor Polly.

(*Crosses to fireplace. Knock at door.*)

Polly. (*Top of table.*) Come in.

(*Enter Hawtree.*)

Polly. Major Hawtree.

(*Sam turns away as they shake hands.*)

Hawtree. I met the Marquise's carriage on the bridge. Has she been here?

(*Sam at fire, with back to it.*)

Polly. Yes.

Haw. What happened?

Polly. Oh, she wanted to take away the child.

(*At head of table.*)

Sam. In the coach.

(*Polly sets tea-things.*)

Haw. And what did Mrs. D'Alroy say to that?

Sam. Mrs. D'Alroy said that she 'd see 'er blowed first! (*Polly pushes Sam.*)—or words to that effect.

Haw. I 'm sorry to hear this; I had hoped—however, that 's over.

Polly. (*Sitting at table.*) Yes, it 's over; and I hope we shall hear no more about it. Want to take away the child, indeed—like her impudence! What next! (*Getting ready tea-things.*) Esther 's gone to lie down. I shan't wake her up for tea, though she 's had nothing to eat all day.

Sam. (*Head of table.*) Shall I fetch some shrimps?

Polly. No. What made you think of shrimps?

Sam. They 're a relish, and consolin'—at least I always found 'em so.

(*Check lights, gradually.*)

Polly. I won't ask you to take tea with us, Major,—you 're too grand.

(*Sam motions approbation to Polly, not wanting Hawtree to remain.*)

Haw. (*Placing hat on piano.*) Not at all. I shall be most happy. (*Aside.*) 'Pon my word, these are very good sort of people. I 'd no idea—

Sam. (*Points to Hawtree.*) He 's a-goin' to stop to tea,—well, I ain't.

(*Goes up to window and sits. Hawtree crosses and sits opposite Polly at table.*)

Polly. Sam! Sam! (*Pause—he says* Eh?) Pull down the blind and light the gas.

Sam. No, don't light up; I like this sort of dusk. It 's unbusiness-like, but pleasant.

(*Sam cuts enormous slice of bread and hands it on point of knife to Hawtree. Cuts small lump of butter and hands it on point of knife to Hawtree, who looks at it through eye-glass, then takes it. Sam then helps himself. Polly meantime has poured out tea in two cups, and one saucer for Sam, sugars them, and then hands cup and saucer to Hawtree, who has both hands full. He takes it awkwardly and places it on table. Polly, having only one spoon, tastes Sam's tea, then stirs Hawtree's, attracting his attention by doing so. He looks into his teacup. Polly stirs her own tea, and drops spoon into Hawtree's cup, causing it to spurt in his eye. He drops eye-glass and wipes his eyes.*)

Polly. (*Making tea.*) Sugar, Sam! (*Sam takes tea and sits facing fire.*) Oh, there isn't any milk—it 'll be here directly, it 's just his time.

Voice. (*Outside; rattle of milk-pails.*) Mia-oow!

Polly. There he is. (*Knock at door.*) Oh, I know; I owe him fourpence. (*Feeling in her pocket.*) Sam, have you got fourpence?

(*Knock again, louder.*)

Sam. No (*His mouth full.*),—I ain't got no fourpence.

Polly. He 's very impatient. Come in!

(*Enter George, his face bronzed, and in full health. He carries a milk-can in his hand, which, after putting his hat on piano, he places on table.*)

George. A fellow hung this on the railings, so I brought it in.

(*Polly sees him, and gradually sinks down under table on one side. Then Sam, with his mouth full, and bread and butter in hand, does the same on the other. Hawtree pushes himself back a space, in chair; remains motionless. George astonished. Picture.*)

Geo. What 's the matter with you?

Haw. (*Rising.*) George!

Geo. Hawtree! You here?

Polly. (*Under table.*) O-o-o-h! the ghost! the ghost!

Sam. It shan't hurt you, Polly. Perhaps it 's only indigestion.

Haw. Then you are not dead?

Geo. Dead, no. Where 's my wife?

Haw. You were reported killed.

Geo. It wasn't true.

Haw. Alive! My old friend alive!

Geo. And well. (*Shakes hands.*) Landed this morning. Where 's my wife?

Sam. (*Who has popped his head from under the tablecloth.*) He ain't dead, Poll,—he 's alive.

(*Polly rises from under table slowly.*)

Polly. (*Pause; approaches him, touches him, retreats.*) George! (*He nods.*) George! George!

Geo. Yes! Yes!

Polly. Alive! My dear George! Oh, my brother! (*Looking at him intensely.*)

Alive! (*Going to him.*) Oh, my dear, dear brother! (*In his arms.*)—how could you go and do so? (*Laughs hysterically.*)

(*Sam goes to Polly. George places Polly in Sam's arms. Sam kisses Polly's hand violently. Hawtree comes up, stares—business. Sam with a stamp of his foot moves away.*)

Geo. Where 's Esther?
Haw. Here,—in this house.
Geo. Here!—doesn't she know I 'm back?
Polly. No,—how should she?
Geo. (*To Hawtree.*) Didn't you get my telegram?
Haw. No; where from?
Geo. Southampton! I sent it to the Club.
Haw. I haven't been there these three days.
Polly. (*Hysterically.*) Oh, my dear, dear, dear dead-and-gone, come-back-all-alive-oh, brother George!

(*George passes her.*)

Sam. Glad to see yer, sir.
Geo. Thank you, Gerridge. (*Shakes hands.*) Same to you—but Esther?
Polly. (*Back to audience, and 'kerchief to her eyes.*) She 's asleep in her room.

(*George is going; Polly stops him.*)

Polly. You mustn't see her.
Geo. Not see her!—after this long absence!—why not?
Haw. She 's ill to-day. She has been greatly excited. The news of your death, which we all mourned, has shaken her terribly.
Geo. Poor girl! Poor girl!
Polly. Oh, we all cried so when you died! —(*Crying.*)—and now you 're alive again, I want to cry ever so much more.

(*Crying.*)

Haw. We must break the news to her gently and by degrees.

(*Crosses behind, to fire, taking his tea with him.*)

Sam. Yes, if you turn the tap on to full pressure, she 'll explode.

(*Sam turns to Hawtree, who is just raising cup to his lips and brings it down on saucer with a bang; both annoyed.*)

Geo. To return, and not to be able to see her—to love her—to kiss her!

(*Stamps.*)

Polly. Hush!
Geo. I forgot—I shall wake her!
Polly. More than that,—you 'll wake the baby.
Geo. Baby!—what baby?
Polly. Yours.
Geo. Mine?—mine?
Polly. Yes,—yours and Esther's. Why, didn't you know there was a baby?
Geo. No!
Polly. La! the ignorance of these men!
Haw. Yes, George, you 're a father.

(*At fireplace.*)

Geo. Why wasn't I told of this? Why didn't you write?
Polly. How could we when you were dead?
Sam. And 'adn't left your address.

(*Looks at Hawtree, who turns away quickly.*)

Geo. If I can't see Esther, I will see the child. The sight of me won't be too much for its nerves. Where is it?
Polly. Sleeping in its mother's arms. (*George goes to door—she intercepts him.*) Please not! Please not!
Geo. I must! I will!
Polly. It might kill her, and you wouldn't like to do that. I 'll fetch the baby; but, oh, please don't make a noise. (*Going up.*) You won't make a noise—you 'll be as quiet as you can, won't you? Oh! I can't believe it!

(*Exit Polly. Sam dances break-down and finishes up by looking at Hawtree, who turns away astonished. Sam disconcerted; sits on chair by table; George at door.*)

Geo. My baby—my ba— It 's a dream! (*To Sam.*) You 've seen it— What 's it like?
Sam. Oh! it 's like a—like a sort of—infant—white and—milky, and all that.

(*Enter Polly with baby wrapped in shawls; George shuts door and meets her.*)

Polly. Gently! gently,—take care! Esther will hardly have it touched.

(*Sam rises and gets near to George.*)

Geo. But I 'm its father.
Polly. That don't matter. She 's very particular.
Geo. Boy or girl?
Polly. Guess.
Geo. Boy! (*Polly nods. George proud.*) What 's his name?
Polly. Guess.

Geo. George? (*Polly nods.*) Eustace? (*Polly nods.*) Fairfax? Algernon? (*Polly nods; pause.*) My names!

Sam. (*To George.*) You 'd 'ardly think there was room enough in 'im to 'old so many names, would yer?

(*Hawtree looks at him—turns to fire. Sam disconcerted again. Sits.*)

Geo. To come back all the way from India to find that I 'm dead, and that you 're alive. To find my wife a widow with a new love aged— How old are you? I 'll buy you a pony to-morrow, my brave little boy! What 's his weight? I should say two pound nothing. My—baby—my boy! (*Bends over him and kisses him.*) Take him away, Polly, for fear I should break him.

(*Polly takes child, and places it in cradle.*)

Haw. (*Crosses to piano. Passes Sam, front—stares—business. Sam goes round to fireplace, flings down bread and butter in a rage and drinks his tea out of saucer.*) But tell us how it is you 're back—how you escaped?

(*Hawtree leans against piano.*)

Geo. (*Coming down.*) By and by. Too long a story just now. Tell *me* all about it. (*Polly gives him chair.*) How is it Esther 's living here?

Polly. She came back after the baby was born, and the furniture was sold up.

Geo. Sold up? What furniture?

Polly. That you bought for her.

Haw. It couldn't be helped, George—Mrs. D'Alroy was so poor.

Geo. Poor! But I left her £600 to put in the bank!

Haw. We *must* tell you. She gave it to her father, who banked it in his own name.

Sam. And lost it in bettin'—every copper.

Geo. Then she 's been in want?

Polly. No—not in want. Friends lent her money.

Geo. (*Seated.*) What friends? (*Pause; he looks at Polly, who indicates Hawtree.*) You?

Polly. Yes.

Geo. (*Rising and shaking Hawtree's hand.*) Thank you, old fella.

(*Hawtree droops his head.*)

Sam. (*Aside.*) Now who 'd 'a' thought that long swell 'ad it in 'im? 'e never mentioned it.

Geo. So Papa Eccles had the money?

(*Sitting again.*)

Sam. And blued it.[10]

(*Sits on corner of table.*)

Polly. (*Pleadingly.*) You see father was very unlucky on the race-course. He told us that if it hadn't been that all his calculations were upset by a horse winning who had no business to, he should have made our fortunes. Father 's been unlucky, and he gets tipsy at times, but he 's a very clever man, if you only give him scope enough.

Sam. I 'd give 'im scope enough!

Geo. Where is he now?

Sam. Public-house.

Geo. And how is he?

Sam. Drunk!

(*Polly pushes him off table. Sam sits at fireplace up stage.*)

Geo. (*To Hawtree.*) You were right. There is *"something"* in caste. (*Aloud.*) But tell us all about it.

(*Sits.*)

Polly. Well, you know, you went away; and then the baby was born. Oh! he was such a sweet little thing, just like—your eyes—your hair.

(*Standing by George, who is sitting.*)

Geo. Cut that!

Polly. Well, baby came; and when baby was six days old, your letter came, Major (*To Hawtree.*). I saw that it was from India, and that it wasn't in your hand (*To George.*); I guessed what was inside it, so I opened it unknown to her, and I read there of your capture and death. I daren't tell her. I went to father to ask his advice, but he was too tipsy to understand me. Sam fetched the doctor. He told us that the news would kill her. When she woke up, she said she had dreamt there was a letter from you. I told her, No; and day after day she asked for a letter. So the doctor advised us to write one as if it came from you. So we did. Sam and I and the doctor told her—told Esther, I mean—that her eyes were bad and she mustn't read, and we read our letter to her; didn't we, Sam? But, bless you! she always knew it hadn't come from you! At last, when she was stronger, we told her all.

10 Wasted it.

Geo. (*After a pause.*) How did she take it?

Polly. She pressed the baby in her arms, and turned her face to the wall. (*A pause.*) Well, to make a long story short, when she got up, she found father had lost all the money you had left her. There was a dreadful scene between them. She told him he 'd robbed her and her child, and father left the house, and swore he 'd never come back again.

Sam. Don't be alarmed,—'e did come back.

(*Sitting by fire.*)

Polly. Oh, yes; he was too good-hearted to stop long from his children. He has his faults, but his good points, when you find 'em, are wonderful!

Sam. Yes, when you find 'em.

(*Rises, gets bread and butter from table, and sits at corner of table.*)

Polly. So she had to come back here to us, and that 's all.

Geo. Why didn't she write to my mother?

Polly. Father wanted her; but she was too proud—she said she 'd die first.

Geo. (*Rising, to Hawtree.*) There 's a woman! Caste 's all humbug. (*Sees sword over mantel-piece.*) That 's my sword (*Crossing round.*) and a map of India, and that 's the piano I bought her —I 'll swear to the silk.

Polly. Yes; that was bought in at the sale.

Geo. (*To Hawtree.*) Thank ye, old fella.

Haw. Not by me—I was in India at the time.

Geo. By whom, then?

Polly. By Sam. (*Sam winks to her to discontinue.*) I shall! He knew Esther was breaking her heart about anyone else having it, so he took the money he 'd saved up for our wedding, and we 're going to be married now—ain't we, Sam?

Sam. (*Rushing to George and pulling out circulars from his pocket.*) And hope by constant attention to business, to merit—

(*Polly pushes him away.*)

Polly. Since you died it hasn't been opened, but if I don't play it to-night, may I die an old maid!

(*Goes up. George crosses to Sam, and shakes his hand, then goes up stage, pulls up blind, and looks into street. Sam turns up and meets Polly by top of table.*)

Haw. (*Aside.*) Now who 'd have thought that little cad had it in him? He never mentioned it. (*Aloud.*) Apropos, George, your mother— I'll go to the Square, and tell her of—

(*Takes hat from piano.*)

Geo. Is she in town?

(*At cradle.*)

Haw. Yes. Will you come with me?

Geo. And leave my wife?—and such a wife!

Haw. I 'll go at once. I shall catch her before dinner. Good-bye, old fellow. Seeing you back again, alive and well, makes me feel quite—that I quite feel— (*Shakes George's hand. Goes to door, then crosses to Sam, who has turned Polly's tea into his saucer, and is just about to drink; seeing Hawtree, he puts it down quickly, and turns his back.*) Mr. Gerridge, I fear I have often made myself very offensive to you.

Sam. Well, sir, yer 'ave.

Haw. (*At bottom of table.*) I feared so. I didn't know you then. I beg your pardon. Let me ask you to shake hands—to forgive me, and forget it.

(*Offering his hand.*)

Sam. (*Taking it.*) Say no more, sir; and if ever I 've made myself offensive to you, I ask your pardon; forget it and forgive me. (*They shake hands warmly; as Hawtree crosses to door, recovering from Sam's hearty shake of the hand, Sam runs to him.*) Hi, sir! When yer marry that young lady as I know you 're engaged to, if you should furnish a house, and require anything in my way—

(*He brings out circular; begins to read it. Polly comes down and pushes Sam away, against Hawtree. Sam goes and sits on low chair by fireplace, down stage, disconcerted, cramming circulars into his pocket.*)

Haw. Good-bye, George, for the present. (*At door.*) Bye, Polly. (*Resumes his Pall Mall manner as he goes out.*) I 'm off to the Square.

(*Exit Hawtree.*)

Geo. (*At cradle.*) But Esther?

Polly. (*Meets George.*) Oh, I forgot all about Esther. I 'll tell her all about it.

Geo. How?

(*By door.*)

Polly. I don't know; but it will come. Providence will send it to me, as it has sent you, my dear brother. (*Embracing him.*) You don't know how glad I am to see you back again! You must go. (*Pushing him. George takes hat off piano.*) Esther will be getting up directly. (*At door with George, who looks through keyhole.*) It 's no use looking there; it 's dark.

Geo. (*At door.*) It isn't often a man can see his own widow.

Polly. And it isn't often that he wants to! Now, you must go.

(*Pushing him off.*)

Geo. I shall stop outside.

Sam. And I 'll whistle for you when you may come in.

Polly. Now—hush!

Geo. (*Opening door wide.*) Oh, my Esther, when you know I 'm alive! I 'll marry you all over again, and we 'll have a second honeymoon, my darling.

(*Exit.*)

Polly. Oh, Sam, Sam! (*Commencing to sing and dance. Sam also dances; they meet in centre of stage, join hands, and dance around two or three times, leaving Sam on the left of Polly, near table. Polly going down.*) Oh, Sam, I 'm so excited, I don't know what to do. What shall I do—what shall I do?

Sam. (*Taking up Hawtree's bread and butter.*) 'Ave a bit of bread and butter, Polly.

Polly. Now, Sam, light the gas; I 'm going to wake her up. (*Opening door.*) Oh, my darling, if I dare tell you! (*Whispering.*) He 's come back! He 's alive! He 's come back! He 's come back! Alive! Alive! Alive! Sam, kiss me!

(*Sam rushes to Polly, kisses her, and she jumps off, Sam shutting the door.*)

Sam. (*Dances shutter-dance.*) I 'm glad the swells are gone; now I can open my safety-valve, and let my feelings escape. To think of 'is comin' back alive from India just as I am goin' to open my shop. Perhaps he 'll get me the patronage of the Royal Family. It would look stunnin' over the door, a lion and a unicorn, a-standin' on their hind legs, doin' nothin' furiously, with a lozenge between 'em —thus. (*Seizes plate on table, puts his left foot on chair by table, and imitates the picture of the Royal arms.*) Polly said I was to light up, and whatever Polly says must be done. (*Lights brackets over mantel-piece, then candles; as he lights the broken one, says.*) Why this one is for all the world like old Eccles! (*Places candles on piano and sits on music-stool.*) Poor Esther! to think of my knowin' her when she was in the ballet line,—then in the 'onorable line; then a mother—no, *h*onorables is "mammas," —then a widow, and then in the ballet line again!—and 'im to come back (*Growing affected.*)—and find a baby, with all 'is furniture and fittin's ready for immediate use (*Crossing back of table during last few lines, sits in chair left of table.*)—and she, poor thing, lyin' asleep with 'er eye-lids 'ot and swollen, not knowin' that that great big, 'eavy, 'ulkin', overgrown dragoon is prowlin' outside, ready to fly at 'er lips, and strangle 'er in 'is strong, lovin' arms—it—it—it—

(*Breaks down and sobs, with his head on the table.*)

(*Enter Polly.*)

Polly. Why, Sam! What 's the matter?

Sam. (*Rises and crosses.*) I dunno. The water 's got into my meter.

Polly. Hush! Here 's Esther.

(*Enter Esther. They stop suddenly. Polly down stage.*)

Sam. (*Singing and dancing.*) "Tiddy-ti-tum," etc.

Esther. (*Sitting near fire, taking up costume and beginning to work.*) Sam, you seem in high spirits to-night!

Sam. Yes; yer see Polly and I are goin' to be married—and—and 'opes by bestowing a merit—to continue the favor—

Polly. (*Who has kissed Esther two or three times.*) What are you talking about?

Sam. I don't know,—I 'm off my burner.

(*Brings music-stool. Polly goes round to chair, facing Esther.*)

Esther. What 's the matter with you to-night, dear? (*To Polly.*) I can see something in your eyes.

Sam. P'raps it 's the new furniture!

(*Sits on music-stool.*)

Esther. Will you help me with the dress, Polly?

(*They sit, Esther upper end, back of table, Polly facing her, at lower end.*)

Polly. It was a pretty dress when it was new—not unlike the one Mdlle. Delphine used to wear. (*Suddenly clasping her hands.*) Oh!

Esther. What 's the matter?

Polly. A needle! (*Crosses to Sam, who examines finger.*) I 've got it!

Sam. What—the needle—in your finger?

Polly. No; an idea in my head!

Sam. (*Still looking at her finger.*) Does it 'urt?

Polly. Stupid! (*Sam still sitting on stool. Aloud.*) Do you recollect Mdlle. Delphine, Esther?

Esther. Yes.

Polly. Do you recollect her in that ballet that old Herr Griffenhaagen arranged?—"Jeanne la Folle, or, the Return of the Soldier?"

Esther. Yes; will you do the fresh hem?

Polly. What 's the use? Let me see—how did it go? How well I remember the scene!—the cottage was on that side, the bridge at the back—then ballet of villagers, and the entrance of Delphine as Jeanne, the bride—tra-lal-lala-lala-la-la. (*Sings and pantomimes, Sam imitating her.*) Then the entrance of Claude, the bridegroom— (*To Sam, imitating swell.*) How-de-do? how-de-do?

Sam. (*Rising.*) 'Ow are yer?

(*Imitating Polly, then sitting again.*)

Polly. Then there was the procession to church—the march of the soldiers over the bridge—(*Sings and pantomimes.*)—arrest of Claude, who is drawn for the conscription—(*Business; Esther looks dreamily.*), and is torn from the arms of his bride, at the church-porch. *Omnes* broken-hearted. *This* is *Omnes* broken-hearted.

(*Pantomimes.*)

Esther. Polly, I don't like this; it brings back memories.

Polly. (*Going to table and leaning her hands on it. Looks over at Esther.*) Oh, fuss about memories!—one can't mourn for ever. (*Esther surprised.*) Everything in this world isn't sad. There 's bad news—and there 's good news sometimes—when we least expect it.

Esther. Ah! not for me.

Polly. Why not?

Esther. (*Anxiously.*) Polly!

Polly. Second Act. (*This to be said quickly, startling Sam, who has been looking on the ground during last four or five lines.*) Winter—the Village Pump. This is the village pump. (*Pointing to Sam, seated by piano, on music-stool, Sam turns round on music-stool, disgusted.*) Entrance of Jeanne—now called Jeanne la Folle, because she has gone mad on account of the supposed loss of her husband.

Sam. The supposed loss?

Polly. The supposed loss!

Esther. (*Dropping costume.*) Polly!

Sam. (*Aside to Polly.*) Mind!

Polly. Can't stop now! Entrance of Claude, *who isn't dead,* in a captain's uniform—a cloak thrown over his shoulders.

Esther. Not dead!

Polly. Don't you remember the ballet? Jeanne is mad, and can't recognize her husband; and don't, till he shows her the ribbon she gave him when they were betrothed. A bit of ribbon! Sam, have you got a bit of ribbon? Oh, that crape sword-knot, that will do.

(*Crosses down. Sam astonished.*)

Esther. Touch that!

(*Rising, coming down.*)

Polly. Why not?—it 's no use *now.*

Esther. (*Slowly, looking into Polly's eyes.*) You have heard of George—I know you have—I see it in your eyes. You may tell me—I can bear it—I can indeed—indeed I can. Tell me—he is not dead?

(*Violently agitated.*)

Polly. No!

Esther. No?

Polly. No!

Esther. (*Whispers.*) Thank Heaven! (*Sam turns on stool, back to audience.*) You 've seen him,—I see you have!—I know it!—I feel it! I had a bright and happy dream—I saw him as I slept! Oh, let me know if he is near! Give me some sign—some sound—(*Polly opens piano.*)—some token of his life and presence!

(*Sam touches Polly on the shoulder, takes hat, and exit. All to be done very quickly. Polly sits immediately at piano and plays air softly—the same air played by Esther, Act II, on the treble only.*

Esther. (*In an ecstasy.*) Oh, my husband! come to me! for I know that you are near! Let me feel your arms clasp round me! Do not fear for me!—I can bear the sight of you!—(*Door opens showing Sam keeping George back.*)—it will not kill me!—George—love! husband—come, oh, come to me!

(*George breaks away from Sam, and coming down behind Esther places his hands over her eyes; she gives a faint scream, and turning, falls in his arms. Polly plays bass as well as treble of the air, forte, then fortissimo. She then plays at random, endeavoring to hide her tears. At last strikes piano wildly, and goes off into a fit of hysterical laughter, to the alarm of Sam, who, rushing down as Polly cries "Sam! Sam!" falls on his knees in front of her. They embrace, Polly pushing him contemptuously away afterwards. George gets chair, sits, and Esther kneels at his feet—he snatches off Esther's cap, and throws it up stage. Polly goes left of George, Sam brings music-stool, and she sits.*)

Esther. To see you here again—to feel your warm breath upon my cheek—is it real, or am I dreaming?

Sam. (*Rubbing his head.*) No; it 's real.

Esther. (*Embracing George.*) My darling!

Sam. My darling! (*Polly on music-stool, which Sam has placed for her. Sam, kneeling by her, imitates Esther— Polly scornfully pushes him away.*) But tell us—tell us how you escaped.

Geo. It 's a long story, but I 'll condense it. I was riding out, and suddenly found myself surrounded and taken prisoner. One of the troop that took me was a fella who had been my servant, and to whom I had done some little kindness. He helped me to escape, and hid me in a sort of cave, and for a long time used to bring me food. Unfortunately, he was ordered away; so he brought another Sepoy to look after me. I felt from the first this man meant to betray me, and I watched him like a lynx, during the one day he was with me. As evening drew on, a Sepoy picket was passing. I could tell by the look in the fella's eyes, he meant to call out as soon as they were near enough; so I seized him by the throat, and shook the life out of him.

Esther. You strangled him?

Geo. Yes.

Esther. Killed him—dead?

Geo. He didn't get up again.

(*Embraces Esther.*)

Polly. (*To Sam.*) You never go and kill Sepoys.

(*Pushes him over.*)

Sam. No! I pay rates and taxes.

Geo. The day after, Havelock and his Scotchmen marched through the village, and I turned out to meet them. I was too done up to join, so I was sent straight on to Calcutta. I got leave, took a berth on the P. & O. boat; the passage restored me. I landed this morning, came on here, and brought in the milk.

(*Enter the Marquise; she rushes to embrace George. All rise, Sam putting stool back.*)

Marquise. My dear boy,—my dear, dear boy!

Polly. Why, see, she 's crying! She 's glad to see him alive and back again.

Sam. (*Profoundly.*) Well! There 's always some good in women, even when they 're ladies.

(*Goes up to window. Polly puts dress in box, and goes to cradle; then beside Sam.*)

Mar. (*Crossing to Esther.*) My dear daughter, we must forget our little differences. (*Kissing her.*) Won't you? How history repeats itself! You will find a similar and as unexpected a return mentioned by Froissart in the chapter that treats of Philip Dartnell—

Geo. Yes, mother—I remember—

(*Kisses her.*)

Mar. (*To George, aside.*) We must take her abroad, and make a lady of her.

Geo. Can't, mamma;—she 's ready-made. Nature has done it to our hands.

Mar. (*Aside to George.*) But I won't have the man who smells of putty—(*Sam, business at back. He is listening, and at the word "putty" throws his cap irritably on table. Polly pacifies him, and makes him sit down beside her on window.*)—nor the man who smells of beer.

(*Goes to Esther, who offers her chair, and sits in chair opposite to her. Marquise back to audience, Esther facing audience.*)

(*Enter Hawtree, pale.*)

Haw. George! Oh, the Marchioness is here.

Geo. What 's the matter?

Haw. Oh, nothing. Yes, there is. I don't mind telling you. I 've been thrown. I called at my chambers as I came along and found this.

(*Gives George a note. Sits on music-stool.*)

Geo. From the Countess, Lady Florence's mother. (*Reads.*) "Dear Major Hawtree,—I hasten to inform you that my daughter Florence is about to enter into an alliance with Lord Saxeby, the eldest son of the Marquis of Loamshire. Under these circumstances, should you think fit to call here again, I feel assured—" Well, perhaps it 's for the best. (*Returning letter.*) Caste! you know. Caste! And a marquis is a bigger swell than a major.

Haw. Yes, best to marry in your own rank of life.

Geo. If you can find *the* girl. But if ever you find *the* girl, marry her. As to her station,—

"True hearts are more than coronets,
And simple faith than Norman blood."

Haw. Ya-as. But a gentleman should hardly ally himself to a nobody.

Geo. My dear fella, Nobody 's a mistake—he don't exist. Nobody 's nobody! Everybody 's somebody!

Haw. Yes. But still—Caste.

Geo. Oh, Caste 's all right. Caste is a good thing if it 's not carried too far. It shuts the door on the pretentious and the vulgar; but it should open the door very wide for exceptional merit. Let brains break through its barriers, and what brains can break through love may leap over.

Haw. Yes. Why, George, you 're quite inspired—quite an orator. What makes you so brilliant? Your captivity? The voyage? What then?

Geo. I 'm in love with my wife!

(*Enter Eccles, drunk, a bottle of gin in his hand.*)

Eccles. (*Crossing to centre of stage.*) Bless this 'appy company. May we 'ave in our arms what we love in our 'earts. (*Goes to head of table. Esther goes to cradle, back to audience. Polly and Sam, half amused, half angry. Marquise still sitting in chair, back to audience. Hawtree facing Eccles. George up stage, leaning on piano in disgust.*) Polly, fetch wine-glasses—a tumbler will do for me. Let us drink a toast. Mr. Chairman (*To Marquise.*), ladies and gentlemen,—I beg to propose the 'ealth of our newly returned warrior, *my son-in-law.* (*Marquise shivers.*) The Right Honorable George De Alroy. Get glasses, Polly, and send for a bottle of sherry wine for my ladyship. *My* ladyship! My ladyship! M'lad'ship! (*She half turns to him.*) You and me 'll have a drain together on the quiet. So delighted to see you under these altered circum—circum—circum—stangate.

(*Polly, who has shaken her head at him to desist, in vain, very distressed.*)

Sam. Shove 'is 'ead in a bucket!

(*Exit in disgust.*)

Haw. (*Aside to George.*) I think I can abate this nuisance—at least, I can remove it.

(*Rises and crosses to Eccles, who has got round to side of table, leaning on it. He taps Eccles with his stick, first on right shoulder, then on left, and finally sharply on right. Eccles turns round and falls on point of stick—Hawtree steadying him. George crosses behind, to Marquise, who has gone to cradle—puts his arm round Esther and takes her to mantel-piece.*)

Haw. Mr. Eccles, don't you think that, with your talent for liquor, if you had an allowance of about two pounds a week, and went to Jersey, where spirits are cheap, that you could drink yourself to death in a year?

Eccles. I think I could—I 'm sure I 'll try.

(*Goes up by table, steadying himself by it, and sits in chair by fire, with the bottle of gin. Hawtree standing by fire. Esther and Polly embracing. As they turn away from each other—*)

Geo. (*Coming across with Esther.*) Come and play me that air that used to ring in my ears as I lay awake, night after night, captive in the cave—you know.

(*He hands Esther to piano. She plays the air.*)

Mar. (*Bending over cradle, at end.*) My grandson!

(*Eccles falls off the chair in the last stage of drunkenness, bottle in hand. Hawtree, leaning one foot on chair from which Eccles has fallen, looks at him through eye-glass. Sam enters, and goes to Polly, behind cradle, and, producing wedding-ring from several papers, holds it up before her eyes. Esther plays until curtain drops.*)

OSCAR WILDE

LADY WINDERMERE'S FAN

Oscar Wilde (1854–1900), like so many writers of comedy during the last two centuries, was born in Ireland, the son of well-known and brilliant, but somewhat ill-balanced, parents. During the years 1874–8 he made his mark in scholarship and literary work at Oxford; and in the latter year began a career of artistic pose, social conspicuousness, and literary success in London. Besides his plays he wrote poems, novels, essays, and lectures; his first light comedy, the present one, came out with great success in 1892. He died in obscurity.

Wilde was a chief exponent of the so-called esthetic movement among certain clever young men in the eighties and nineties. It began under the influence of such men as Ruskin, William Morris, and Pater; but while their love of beauty broadened and deepened into something more manful and humane, high artistic creation and work toward social betterment, Wilde's was too shallow and unstable a nature to drive him to any more solid achievement than polished literary form and superficial brilliance. His plays are his best work, and are interesting for two reasons. They are admirable so far as they go, and indicate and helped on an important change in dramatic style.

Lady Windermere's Fan is a comedy of manners, brilliantly constructed and written, with much clever satire on social vapidity, some insight into human nature, and some appearance of depth, sympathy, and earnestness. When it appeared (1892), the influence on it of such earlier dramatists as Congreve and Sheridan was remarked at once, and also (less obvious to the general reader) that of nineteenth-century French comedy. The sparkling dialogue is what especially recalls Sheridan and Congreve. Airy unexpectedness and paradox are even more essential in Wilde, especially that which consists in contradicting or inverting a proverbial saying or a social commonplace —" the youth of the present have absolutely no respect for dyed hair," " he has one of these weak natures that are not susceptible to influence " (*An Ideal Husband*), " I can resist anything except temptation." Some of his agile twists passed from Wilde's plays into the common talk. Further, no one can fail to be reminded of the screen-scene in *The School for Scandal* by the third act in *Lady Windermere's Fan*, where Mrs. Erlynne and Lady Windermere are concealed in Lord Darlington's rooms. It cannot be said that in dramatic effectiveness Wilde has fallen behind his master. The situation is as probable, the final sensation as well led up to, the complication is greater yet as clear, the emotional state of things is more intricate and more serious — the conventionally good woman shows her real flimsy character, and the bad woman rises to the sort of self-sacrifice which meant most heroism for her. The scene is masterly. It is admirably planned, from the extraordinary meeting of the two women, and Dumby's unconscious dramatic irony (" The lively part of the evening is only just beginning "), to the device by which Lady Windermere escapes. The fine feeling which the scene shows is rare in Wilde, whose moral tone is not greatly different from Congreve's, and embodies that of the class of social life which he constantly satirizes, but really respected and chose to identify himself with. One feels dissatisfaction with the ending — that Lady Windermere's folly should be huddled up from her husband, so that, instead of facing it down, she may forget it, precisely as any worldly and superficial woman in the audience would have done. The decent and satisfying ending Wilde probably rejected as too " obvious." This last scene has the emotional complexity mentioned earlier, husband and wife each knowing something essential to the situation unknown to the other, and all the threads centering in Mrs. Erlynne's hand. Again she stands on a dramatic pedestal. She is the sort of person in portraying whom Wilde shows most insight and depth; the people in whom he is most fond of showing possibilities of goodness and sacrifice are women " with a past " and languid dandies. He makes a specialty of the heroism which may be latent behind the trivial-looking face, and in this he has been followed by many a later playwright; for nothing gains readier response from the moral feelings of the superficial, or excites more the genial mood of charity which is one of the pleasant results of seeing a play.

Wilde, along with the more important Pinero, Henry Arthur Jones and others, marks the rise of a prose drama of originality and high dramatic and literary worth, and with a realistic basis, — the emergence of the contemporary acting drama from the poverty in which it had lain throughout most of the century. The causes and the results of this poverty, as often with intangible conditions in social life, are sometimes hard to distinguish from each other. The drama in general had been for the uneducated masses, who desired mere romance and excitement, and were not critical as to originality, finesse and naturalness. The staging was bad, with shabby costumes, properties and scenery. There were few distinguished actors; the calling of the actor had scarcely ever sunk so low in merit, respectability and public esteem. Such good actors as there were preferred to play Shakespeare, and critical spectators to see Shakespeare, rather than new plays. Dramatists were ill-paid, and plays mostly had short runs. The government exercised an injurious control over the stage; during part of the period there were only two licensed theaters in London, the great size of which encouraged sensational effects and tended against the subtle and fine; the censorship checked and limited the dramatist's imagination. There still survived a good deal of puritanical prejudice, which tended not only to debase the theater but also to keep a high-minded and important class of people away from it. The copyright laws did not prevent the frequent pirating of plays from the French and other literatures, which was discouraging to native dramatists. The general low esteem for the drama is shown by the almost total ignoring of it by the newspapers. But for a variety of reasons—changes in some of these conditions, and the influence of certain actors—toward the end of the century there came a transformation; in part due also to a more general literary and ethical reaction against the sentimentalism, conventionalism, moral primness sometimes associated with the middle of Queen Victoria's reign. In the best of the latest nineteenth-century dramatists there is literary finish, a growth in reality and naturalness, more appearance of disillusionment, and a disposition to treat the sex-relation as freely as decorum would allow. All this is perceptible in Wilde.

LADY WINDERMERE'S FAN

DRAMATIS PERSONÆ

LORD WINDERMERE
LORD DARLINGTON
LORD AUGUSTUS LORTON
MR. CECIL GRAHAM
MR. DUMBY
MR. HOPPER
PARKER (*Butler*)
LADY WINDERMERE
THE DUCHESS OF BERWICK
LADY AGATHA CARLISLE
LADY PLYMDALE
LADY JEDBURGH
LADY STUTFIELD
MRS. COWPER-COWPER
MRS. ERLYNNE
ROSALIE (*Maid*)

THE SCENES OF THE PLAY

ACT I. Morning-room in Lord Windermere's House.
ACT II. Drawing-room in Lord Windermere's House.
ACT III. Lord Darlington's rooms.
ACT IV. Same as Act I.

Time—The Present.
Place—London.

The Action of the Play takes place within twenty-four hours, beginning on a Tuesday afternoon at five o'clock, and ending the next day at 1.30 p. m.

ACT I.

SCENE—*Morning-room of Lord Windermere's house in Carlton House Terrace. Doors c. and r. Bureau with books and papers r. Sofa with small tea-table l. Window opening on to terace l. Table r.*

(*Lady Windermere is at table r. Arranging roses in a blue bowl.*)

(*Enter Parker.*)

Parker. Is your ladyship at home this afternoon?

Lady W. Yes—who has called?

Parker. Lord Darlington, my lady.

Lady W. (*Hesitates for a moment.*) Show him up—and I'm at home to any one who calls.

Parker. Yes, my lady.

(*Exit c.*)

Lady W. It's best for me to see him before to-night. I'm glad he's come.

(*Enter Parker c.*)

Parker. Lord Darlington.

(*Enter Lord D. c. Exit Parker.*)

Lord D. How do you do, Lady Windermere?

Lady W. How do you do, Lord Darlington? No, I can't shake hands with you. My hands are all wet with these roses. Are n't they lovely? They came up from Selby this morning.

Lord D. They are quite perfect. (*Sees a fan lying on the table.*) And what a wonderful fan! May I look at it?

Lady W. Do. Pretty, is n't it! It 's got my name on it, and everything. I have only just seen it myself. It 's my husband's birthday present to me. You know to-day is my birthday?

Lord D. No? Is it really?

Lady W. Yes; I 'm of age to-day. Quite an important day in my life, is n't it? That is why I am giving this party to-night. Do sit down.

(*Still arranging flowers.*)

Lord D. (*Sitting down.*) I wish I had known it was your birthday, Lady Windermere. I would have covered the whole street in front of your house with flowers for you to walk on. They are made for you.

(*A short pause.*)

Lady W. Lord Darlington, you annoyed me last night at the Foreign Office. I am afraid you are going to annoy me again.

Lord D. I, Lady Windermere?

(*Enter Parker and Footman c. with tray and tea-things.*)

Lady W. Put it there, Parker. That will do. (*Wipes her hands with her pocket-handkerchief, goes to tea-table l. and sits down.*) Won't you come over, Lord Darlington?

(*Exit Parker c.*)

Lord D. (*Takes chair and goes across l. c.*) I am quite miserable, Lady Windermere. You must tell me what I did.

(*Sits down at table l.*)

Lady W. Well, you kept paying me elaborate compliments the whole evening.

Lord D. (*Smiling.*) Ah, now-a-days we are all of us so hard up, that the only pleasant things to pay *are* compliments. They 're the only thing we *can* pay.

Lady W. (*Shaking her head.*) No, I am talking very seriously. You must n't laugh, I am quite serious. I don't like compliments, and I don't see why a man should think he is pleasing a woman enormously when he says to her a whole heap of things that he does n't mean.

Lord D. Ah, but I did mean them.

(*Takes tea which she offers him.*)

Lady W. (*Gravely.*) I hope not. I should be sorry to have to quarrel with you, Lord Darlington. I like you very much, you know that. But I should n't like you at all if I thought you were what most other men are. Believe me, you are better than most other men, and I sometimes think you pretend to be worse.

Lord D. We all have our little vanities, Lady Windermere.

Lady W. Why do you make that your special one?

(*Still seated at table l.*)

Lord D. (*Still seated l. c.*) Oh, now-a-days so many conceited people go about Society pretending to be good, that I think it shows rather a sweet and modest disposition to pretend to be bad. Besides, there is this to be said. If you pretend to be good, the world takes you very seriously. If you pretend to be bad, it does n't. Such is the astounding stupidity of optimism.

Lady W. Don't you *want* the world to take you seriously then, Lord Darlington?

Lord D. No, not the world. Who are the people the world takes seriously? All the dull people one can think of, from the Bishops down to the bores. I should like *you* to take me very seriously, Lady Windermere, *you* more than any one else in life.

Lady W. Why—why me?

Lord D. (*After a slight hesitation.*) Because I think we might be great friends. Let us be great friends. You may want a friend some day.

Lady W. Why do you say that?

Lord D. Oh!—we all want friends at times.

Lady W. I think we 're very good friends already, Lord Darlington. We can always remain so as long as you don't——

Lord D. Don't what?

Lady W. Don't spoil it by saying extravagant, silly things to me. You think I am a Puritan, I suppose? Well, I have something of the Puritan in me. I was brought up like that. I am glad of it. My mother died when I was a mere child. I lived always with Lady Julia, my father's eldest sister, you know. She was stern to me, but she taught me, what the world is forgetting, the difference that there is between what is right and what is wrong. *She* allowed of no compromise. *I* allow of none.

Lord D. My dear Lady Windermere!

Lady W. (*Leaning back on the sofa.*) You look on me as being behind the age. —Well, I am! I should be sorry to be on the same level as an age like this.

Lord D. You think the age very bad?

Lady W. Yes, now-a-days people seem to look on life as a speculation. It is not a speculation. It is a sacrament. Its ideal is Love. Its purification is sacrifice.

Lord D. (*Smiling.*) Oh, anything is better than being sacrificed!

Lady W. (*Leaning forward.*) Don't say that.

Lord D. I do say it. I feel it—I know it.

(*Enter Parker c.*)

Parker. The men want to know if they are to put the carpets on the terrace for to-night, my lady?

Lady W. You don't think it will rain, Lord Darlington, do you?

Lord D. I won't hear of its raining on your birthday!

Lady W. Tell them to do it at once, Parker.

(*Exit Parker c.*)

Lord D. (*Still seated.*) Do you think then—of course I am only putting an imaginary instance—do you think, that in the case of a young married couple, say about two years married, if the husband suddenly becomes the intimate friend of a woman of—well, more than doubtful character, is always calling upon her, lunching with her, and probably paying her bills—do you think that the wife should not console herself?

Lady W. (*Frowning.*) Console herself?

Lord D. Yes, I think she should—I think she has the right.

Lady W. Because the husband is vile should the wife be vile also?

Lord D. Vileness is a terrible word, Lady Windermere.

Lady W. It is a terrible thing, Lord Darlington.

Lord D. Do you know I am afraid that good people do a great deal of harm in this world. Certainly the greatest harm they do is that they make badness of such extraordinary importance. It is absurd to divide people into good and bad. People are either charming or tedious. I take the side of the charming, and you, Lady Windermere, can't help belonging to them.

Lady W. Now, Lord Darlington. (*Rising and crossing r., front of him.*) Don't stir, I am merely going to finish my flowers.

(*Goes to table r. c.*)

Lord D. (*Rising and moving chair.*) And I must say I think you are very hard on modern life, Lady Windermere. Of course there is much against it, I admit. Most women, for instance, now-a-days, are rather mercenary.

Lady W. Don't talk about such people.

Lord D. Well, then, setting mercenary people aside, who, of course, are dreadful, do you think seriously that women who have committed what the world calls a fault should never be forgiven?

Lady W. (*Standing at table.*) I think they should never be forgiven.

Lord D. And me? Do you think that there should be the same laws for men as there are for women?

Lady W. Certainly!

Lord D. I think life too complex a thing to be settled by these hard and fast rules.

Lady W. If we had "these hard and fast rules," we should find life much more simple.

Lord D. You allow of no exceptions?

Lady W. None!

Lord D. Ah, what a fascinating Puritan you are, Lady Windermere!

Lady W. The adjective was unnecessary, Lord Darlington.

Lord D. I could n't help it. I can resist everything except temptation.

Lady W. You have the modern affectation of weakness.

Lord D. (*Looking at her.*) It 's only an affection, Lady Windermere.

(*Enter Parker c.*)

Parker. The Duchess of Berwick and Lady Agatha Carlisle.

(*Enter the Duchess of B. and Lady A. C. c.*)

(*Exit Parker c.*)

Duchess of B. (*Coming down c. and shaking hands.*) Dear Margaret, I am so pleased to see you. You remember Agatha, don't you? (*Crossing l. c.*) How do you do, Lord Darlington? I won't let you know my daughter, you are far too wicked.

Lord D. Don't say that, Duchess. As a wicked man I am a complete failure. Why, there are lots of people who say I have never really done anything wrong in the whole course of my life. Of course they only say it behind my back.

Duchess of B. Is n't he dreadful? Agatha, this is Lord Darlington. Mind you don't believe a word he says. (*Lord Darlington crosses r. c.*) No, no tea, thank you, dear. (*Crosses and sits on sofa.*) We have just had tea at Lady Markby's. Such bad tea, too. It was quite undrinkable. I was n't at all surprised. Her own son-in-law supplies it. Agatha is looking forward so much to your ball to-night, dear Margaret.

Lady W. (*Seated l. c.*) Oh, you must n't think it is going to be a ball, Duchess. It is only a dance in honor of my birthday. A small and early.

Lord D. (*Standing l. c.*) Very small, very early, and very select, Duchess.

Duchess of B. (*On sofa l.*) Of course it 's going to be select. But we know *that,* dear Margaret, about *your* house. It is really one of the few houses in London where I can take Agatha, and where I feel perfectly secure about poor Berwick. I don't know what Society is coming to. The most dreadful people seem to go everywhere. They certainly come to my parties—the men get quite furious if one does n't ask them. Really, some one should make a stand against it.

Lady W. *I* will, Duchess. I will have no one in my house about whom there is any scandal.

Lord D. (*r. c.*) Oh, don't say that, Lady Windermere. I should never be admitted!

(*Sitting.*)

Duchess of B. Oh, men don't matter. With women it is different. We 're good. Some of us are, at least. But we are positively getting elbowed into the corner. Our husbands would really forget our existence if we did n't nag at them from time to time, just to remind them that we have a perfect legal right to do so.

Lord D. It 's a curious thing, Duchess, about the game of marriage—a game, by the way, that is going out of fashion—the wives hold all the honors, and invariably lose the odd trick.

Duchess of B. The odd trick? Is that the husband, Lord Darlington?

Lord D. It would be rather a good name for the modern husband.

Duchess of B. Dear Lord Darlington, how thoroughly depraved you are!

Lady W. Lord Darlington is trivial.

Lord D. Ah, don't say that, Lady Windermere.

Lady W. Why do you *talk* so trivially about life, then?

Lord D. Because I think that life is far too important a thing ever to talk seriously about it.

(*Moves up c.*)

Duchess of B. What does he mean? Do, as a concession to my poor wits, Lord Darlington, just explain to me what you really mean?

Lord D. (*Coming down back of table.*) I think I had better not, Duchess. Now-a-days to be intelligible is to be found out. Good-bye! (*Shakes hands with Duchess.*) And now (*Goes up stage.*), Lady Windermere, good-bye. I may come to-night, may n't I? Do let me come.

Lady W. (*Standing up stage with Lord D.*) Yes, certainly. But you are not to say foolish, insincere things to people.

Lord D. (*Smiling.*) Ah, you are beginning to reform me. It is a dangerous thing to reform any one, Lady Windermere.

(*Bows, and exit c.*)

Duchess of B. (*Who has risen, goes c.*) What a charming, wicked creature! I like him so much. I 'm quite delighted he 's gone! How sweet you 're looking! Where *do* you get your gowns? And now I must tell you how sorry I am for you, dear Margaret. (*Crosses to sofa and sits with Lady W.*) Agatha, darling!

Lady A. Yes, mamma.

(*Rises.*)

Duchess of B. Will you go and look over the photograph album that I see there?

Lady A. Yes, mamma.

(*Goes to table L.*)

Duchess of B. Dear girl! She is so fond of photographs of Switzerland. Such a pure taste, I think. But I really am so sorry for you, Margaret.

Lady W. (*Smiling.*) Why, Duchess?

Duchess of B. Oh, on account of that horrid woman. She dresses so well, too, which makes it much worse, sets such a dreadful example. Augustus—you know my disreputable brother—such a trial to us all—well, Augustus is completely infatuated about her. It is quite scandalous, for she is absolutely inadmissible into society. Many a woman has a past, but I am told that she has at least a dozen, and that they all fit.

Lady W. Whom are you talking about, Duchess?

Duchess of B. About Mrs. Erlynne.

Lady W. Mrs. Erlynne? I never heard of her, Duchess. And what *has* she to do with me?

Duchess of B. My poor child. Agatha, darling!

Lady A. Yes, mamma.

Duchess of B. Will you go out on the terrace and look at the sunset?

Lady A. Yes, mamma.

(*Exit through window l.*)

Duchess of B. Sweet girl! So devoted to sunsets! Shows such refinement of feeling, does it not? After all, there is nothing like nature, is there?

Lady W. But what is it, Duchess? Why do you talk to me about this person?

Duchess of B. Don't you really know? I assure you we 're all so distressed about it. Only last night at dear Lady Fansen's every one was saying how extraordinary it was that, of all men in London, Windermere should behave in such a way.

Lady W. My husband—what has *he* got to do with any woman of that kind?

Duchess of B. Ah, what indeed, dear? That is the point. He goes to see her continually, and stops for hours at a time, and while he is there she is not at home to any one. Not that many ladies call on her, dear, but she has a great many disreputable men friends—my own brother in particular, as I told you—and that is what makes it so dreadful about Windermere. We looked upon *him* as being such a model husband, but I am afraid there is no doubt about it. My dear nieces—you know the Saville girls, don't you?—such nice domestic creatures—plain, dreadfully plain, but so good—well, they 're always at the window doing fancy work, and making ugly things for the poor, which I think so useful of them in these dreadful socialistic days, and this terrible woman has taken a house in Curzon Street, right opposite them—such a respectable street, too. I don't know what we 're coming to! And they tell me that Windermere goes there four and five times a week—they *see* him. They can't help it—and although they never talk scandal, they—well, of course—they remark on it to every one. And the worst of it all is, that I have been told that this woman has got a great deal of money out of somebody, for it seems that she came to London six months ago without anything at all to speak of, and now she has this charming house in Mayfair, drives her pony in the Park every afternoon, and all—well all—since she has known poor dear Windermere.

Lady W. Oh, I can't believe it!

Duchess of B. But it 's quite true, my dear. The whole of London knows it. That is why I felt it was better to come and talk to you, and advise you to take Windermere away at once to Homburg or to Aix, where he 'll have something to amuse him, and where you can watch him all day long. I assure you, my dear, that on several occasions after I was first married I had to pretend to be very ill, and was obliged to drink the most unpleasant mineral waters, merely to get Berwick out of town. He was so extremely susceptible. Though I am bound to say he never gave away any large sums of money to anybody. He is far too high-principled for that.

Lady W. (*Interrupting.*) Duchess, Duchess, it 's impossible! (*Rising and crossing stage c.*) We are only married two years. Our child is but six months old.

(*Sits in chair r. of l. table.*)

Duchess of B. Ah, the dear, pretty baby! How is the little darling? Is it a boy or a girl? I hope a girl—Ah, no, I remember it 's a boy! I 'm so sorry. Boys are so wicked. My boy is excessively immoral. You would n't believe at what hours he comes home. And he 's only left Oxford a few months—I really don't know what they teach them there.

Lady W. Are *all* men bad?

Duchess of B. Oh, all of them, my dear, all of them, without any exception. And they never grow any better. Men become old, but they never become good.

Lady W. Windermere and I married for love.

Duchess of B. Yes, we begin like that. It was only Berwick's brutal and incessant threats of suicide that made me accept him at all, and before the year was out he was running after all kinds of petticoats, every color, every shape, every material. In fact, before the honeymoon was over, I caught him winking at my maid, a most pretty, respectable girl. I dismissed her at once without a character.—No, I remember, I passed her on to my sister; poor dear Sir George is so short-sighted, I thought it would n't matter. But it did, though[—] it was most unfortunate. (*Rises.*) And now, my dear child, I must go, as we are dining out. And mind you don't take this little aberration of Windermere's too much to heart. Just take him abroad, and he'll come back to you all right.

Lady W. Come back to me? (*c.*)

Duchess of B. (*l. c.*) Yes, dear, these wicked women get our husbands away from us, but they always come back, slightly damaged, of course. And don't make scenes, men hate them!

Lady W. It is very kind of you Duchess, to come and tell me all this. But I can't believe that my husband is untrue to me.

Duchess of B. Pretty child! I was like that once. Now I know that all men are monsters. (*Lady W. rings bell.*) The only thing to do is to feed the wretches well. A good cook does wonders, and that I know you have. My dear Margaret, you are not going to cry?

Lady W. You need n't be afraid, Duchess, I never cry.

Duchess of B. That's quite right, dear. Crying is the refuge of plain women, but the ruin of pretty ones. Agatha, darling!

Lady A. (*Entering l.*) Yes, mamma.

(*Stands back of table l. c.*)

Duchess of B. Come and bid good-bye to Lady Windermere, and thank her for your charming visit. (*Coming down again.*) And by the way, I must thank you for sending a card to Mr. Hopper—he's that rich young Australian, people are taking such notice of just at present. His father made a great fortune by selling some kind of food in circular tins—most palatable, I believe—I fancy it is the thing the servants always refuse to eat. But the son is quite interesting. I think he's attracted by dear Agatha's clever talk. Of course, we should be very sorry to lose her, but I think that a mother who does n't part with a daughter every season has no real affection. We're coming to-night, dear. (*Parker opens c. doors.*) And remember my advice, take the poor fellow out of town at once, it is the only thing to do. Good-bye, once more; come, Agatha.

(*Exeunt Duchess and Lady A. c.*)

Lady W. How horrible! I understand now what Lord Darlington meant by the imaginary instance of the couple not two years married. Oh! it can't be true—she spoke of enormous sums of money paid to this woman. I know where Arthur keeps his bank-book—in one of the drawers of that desk. I might find out by that. I *will* find out. (*Opens drawer.*) No, it is some hideous mistake. (*Rises and goes c.*) Some silly scandal! He loves *me!* He loves *me!* But why should I not look? I am his wife, I have a right to look! (*Returns to bureau, takes out book and examines it, page by page, smiles and gives a sigh of relief.*) I knew it, there is not a word of truth in this stupid story. (*Puts book back in drawer. As she does so, starts and takes out another book.*) A second book—private—locked! (*Tries to open it, but fails. Sees paper knife on bureau, and with it cuts cover from book. Begins to start at the first page.*) Mrs. Erlynne—£600—Mrs. Erlynne—£700—Mrs. Erlynne—£400. Oh! it is true! it is true! How horrible!

(*Throws book on floor.*)

(*Enter Lord W. c.*)

Lord W. Well, dear, has the fan been sent home yet? (*Going r. c. sees book.*) Margaret, you have cut open my bank book. You have no right to do such a thing!

Lady W. You think it wrong that you are found out, don't you?

Lord W. I think it wrong that a wife should spy on her husband.

Lady W. I did not spy on you. I never knew of this woman's existence till half an hour ago. Some one who pitied me was kind enough to tell me what every one in London knows already—your daily visits to Curzon Street, your mad infatuation, the monstrous sums of money you squander on this infamous woman!

(*Crossing l.*)

Lord W. Margaret, don't talk like that of Mrs. Erlynne, you don't know how unjust it is!

Lady W. (*Turning to him.*) You are very jealous of Mrs. Erlynne's honor. I wish you had been as jealous of mine.

Lord W. Your honor is untouched, Margaret. You don't think for a moment that——

(*Puts book back into desk.*)

Lady W. I think that you spend your money strangely. That is all. Oh, don't imagine I mind about the money. As far as I am concerned, you may squander everything we have. But what

I *do* mind is that you who have loved me, you who have taught me to love you, should pass from the love that is given to the love that is bought. Oh, it 's horrible! (*Sits on sofa.*) And it is I who feel degraded. *You* don't feel anything. I feel stained, utterly stained. You can't realize how hideous the last six months seem to me now—every kiss you have given me is tainted in my memory.

Lord W. (*Crossing to her.*) Don't say that, Margaret, I never loved any one in the whole world but you.

Lady W. (*Rises.*) Who is this woman, then? Why do you take a house for her?

Lord W. I did not take a house for her.

Lady W. You gave her the money to do it, which is the same thing.

Lord W. Margaret, as far as I have known Mrs. Erlynne——

Lady W. Is there a Mr. Erlynne—or is he a myth?

Lord W. Her husband died many years ago. She is alone in the world.

Lady W. No relations?

(*A pause.*)

Lord W. None.

Lady W. Rather curious, is n't it? (*l.*)

Lord W. (*l. c.*) Margaret, I was saying to you—and I beg you to listen to me—that as far as I have known Mrs. Erlynne, she has conducted herself well. If years ago——

Lady W. Oh! (*Crossing r. c.*) I don't want details about her life.

Lord W. I am not going to give you any details about her life. I tell you simply this—Mrs. Erlynne was once honored, loved, respected. She was well born, she had a position—she lost everything—threw it away, if you like. That makes it all the more bitter. Misfortunes one can endure—they come from outside, they are accidents. But to suffer for one's own faults—ah! there is the sting of life. It was twenty years ago, too. She was little more than a girl then. She had been a wife for even less time than you have.

Lady W. I am not interested in her—and—you should not mention this woman and me in the same breath. It is an error of taste.

(*Sitting r. at desk.*)

Lord W. Margaret, you could save this woman. She wants to get back into society, and she wants you to help her.

(*Crossing to her.*)

Lady W. Me!

Lord W. Yes, you.

Lady W. How impertinent of her!

(*A pause.*)

Lord W. Margaret, I came to ask you a great favor, and I still ask it of you, though you have discovered what I had intended you should never have known, that I have given Mrs. Erlynne a large sum of money. I want you to send her an invitation for our party to-night.

(*Standing l. of her.*)

Lady W. You are mad.

(*Rises.*)

Lord W. I entreat you. People may chatter about her, do chatter about her, of course, but they don't know anything definite against her. She has been to several houses—not to houses where you would go, I admit, but still to houses where women who are in what is called Society now-a-days do go. That does not content her. She wants you to receive her once.

Lady W. As a triumph for her, I suppose?

Lord W. No; but because she knows that you are a good woman—and that if she comes here once she will have a chance of a happier, a surer life, than she has had. She will make no further effort to know you. Won't you help a woman who is trying to get back?

Lady W. No! If a woman really repents, she never wishes to return to the society that has made or seen her ruin.

Lord W. I beg of you.

Lady W. (*Crossing to door r.*) I am going to dress for dinner, and don't mention the subject again this evening. Arthur (*Going to him c.*), you fancy because I have no father or mother that I am alone in the world and that you can treat me as you choose. You are wrong, I have friends, many friends.

Lord W. (*l. c.*) Margaret, you are talking foolishly, recklessly. I won't argue with you, but I insist upon your asking Mrs. Erlynne to-night.

Lady W. (*r. c.*) I shall do nothing of the kind.

(*Crossing l. c.*)

Lord W. You refuse?

(*c.*)

Lady W. Absolutely!

Lord W. Ah, Margaret, do this for my sake; it is her last chance.

Lady W. What has that to do with me?

Lord W. How hard good women are!
Lady W. How weak bad men are!
Lord W. Margaret, none of us men may be good enough for the women we marry —that is quite true—but you don't imagine I would ever—oh, the suggestion is monstrous!
Lady W. Why should *you* be different from other men? I am told that there is hardly a husband in London who does not waste his life over *some* shameful passion.
Lord W. I am not one of them.
Lady W. I am not sure of that.
Lord W. You are sure in your heart. But don't make chasm after chasm between us. God knows the last few minutes have thrust us wide enough apart. Sit down and write the card.
Lady W. Nothing in the whole world would induce me.
Lord W. (*Crossing to the bureau.*) Then I will.
(*Rings electric bell, sits down and writes card.*)
Lady W. You are going to invite this woman?
(*Crossing to him.*)
Lord W. Yes.
(*Pause.*)

(*Enter Parker.*)

Lord W. Parker!
Parker. Yes, my lord.
(*Comes down l. c.*)
Lord W. Have this note sent to Mrs. Erlynne at No. 84A Curzon Street. (*Crossing to l. c. and giving note to Parker.*) There is no answer.

(*Enter Parker c.*)

Lady W. Arthur, if that woman comes here, I shall insult her.
Lord W. Margaret, don't say that.
Lady W. I mean it.
Lord W. Child, if you did such such a thing, there's not a woman in London who would n't pity you.
Lady W. There is not a *good* woman in London who would not applaud me. We have been too lax. We must make an example. I propose to begin tonight. (*Picking up fan.*) Yes, you gave me this fan to-day; it was your birthday present. If that woman crosses my threshold, I shall strike her across the face with it.
Lord W. Margaret, you could n't do such a thing.
Lady W. You don't know me!
(*Moves r.*)

(*Enter Parker.*)

Lady W. Parker!
Parker. Yes, my lady.
Lady W. I shall dine in my own room. I don't want dinner, in fact. See that everything is ready by half-past ten. And, Parker, be sure you pronounce the names of the guests very distinctly tonight. Sometimes you speak so fast that I miss them. I am particularly anxious to hear the names quite clearly, so as to make no mistake. You understand, Parker?
Parker. Yes, my lady.
Lady W. That will do! (*Exit Parker c.*) (*Speaking to Lord W.*) Arthur, if that woman comes here—I warn you—
Lord W. Margaret, you'll ruin us!
Lady W. Us! From this moment my life is separate from yours. But if you wish to avoid a public scandal, write at once to this woman, and tell her that I forbid her to come here!
Lord W. I will not—I cannot—she must come!
Lady W. Then I shall do exactly as I have said. (*Goes r.*) You leave me no choice.
(*Exit r.*)
Lord W. (*Calling after her.*) Margaret! Margaret! (*A pause.*) My God! What shall I do! I dare not tell her who this woman really is. The shame would kill her.
(*Sinks down into a chair and buries his face in his hands.*)
(*Act-drop.*)

ACT II.

SCENE—*Drawing-room in Lord W.'s house. Door r. u. opening into ball-room, where band is playing. Door l. through which guests are entering. Door l. u. opens on an illuminated terrace. Palms, flowers, and brilliant lights. Room crowded with guests. Lady W. is receiving them.*

Duchess of B. (*Up c.*) So strange Lord Windermere is n't here. Mr. Hopper is very late, too. You have kept those five dances for him, Agatha!
(*Comes down.*)
Lady A. Yes, mamma.
Duchess of B. (*Sitting on sofa.*) Just

let me see your card. I'm so glad Lady Windermere has revived cards.—They're a mother's only safeguard. You dear simple little thing! (*Scratches out two names.*) No nice girl should ever waltz with such particularly younger sons! It looks so fast! The last two dances you must pass on the terrace with Mr. Hopper.

(*Enter Mr. Dumby and Lady Plymdale from the ball-room.*)

Lady A. Yes, mamma.

Duchess of B. (*Fanning herself.*) The air is so pleasant there.

Parker. Mrs. Cowper-Cowper. Lady Stutfield. Sir James Royston. Mr. Guy Berkeley.

(*These people enter as announced.*)

Dumby. Good evening, Lady Stutfield. I suppose this will be the last ball of the season?

Lady S. I suppose so, Mr. Dumby. It's been a delightful season, hasn't it?

Dumby. Quite delightful! Good evening, Duchess. I suppose this will be the last ball of the season?

Duchess of B. I suppose so, Mr. Dumby. It has been a very dull season, hasn't it?

Dumby. Dreadfully dull! Dreadfully dull!

Mrs. C.-C. Good evening, Mr. Dumby. I suppose this will be the last ball of the season?

Dumby. Oh, I think not. There'll probably be two more. (*Wanders back to Lady P.*)

Parker. Mr. Rufford. Lady Jedburgh and Miss Graham. Mr. Hopper.

(*These people enter as announced.*)

Hopper. How do you do, Lady Windermere? How do you do, Duchess?

(*Bows to Lady A.*)

Duchess of B. Dear Mr. Hopper, how nice of you to come so early. We all know how you are run after in London.

Hopper. Capital place, London! They are not nearly so exclusive in London as they are in Sydney.

Duchess of B. Ah! we know your value, Mr. Hopper. We wish there were more like you. It would make life so much easier. Do you know, Mr. Hopper, dear Agatha and I are so much interested in Australia. It must be so pretty with all the dear little kangaroos flying about. Agatha has found it on the map. What a curious shape it is! Just like a large packing case. However, it is a very young country, isn't it?

Hopper. Wasn't it made at the same time as the others, Duchess?

Duchess of B. How clever you are, Mr. Hopper. You have a cleverness quite of your own. Now I mustn't keep you.

Hopper. But I should like to dance with Lady Agatha, Duchess.

Duchess of B. Well, I *hope* she has a dance left. Have you got a dance left, Agatha?

Lady A. Yes, mamma.

Duchess of B. The next one?

Lady Agatha. Yes, mamma.

Hopper. May I have the pleasure?

(*Lady Agatha bows.*)

Duchess of B. Mind you take great care of my little chatter-box, Mr. Hopper.

(*Lady A. and Mr. H. pass into ball-room.*)

(*Enter Lord W. l.*)

Lord W. Margaret, I want to speak to you.

Lady W. In a moment.

(*The music stops.*)

Parker. Lord Augustus Lorton.

(*Enter Lord A.*)

Lord A. Good evening, Lady Windermere.

Duchess of B. Sir James, will you take me into the ball-room? Augustus has been dining with us to-night. I really have had quite enough of dear Augustus for the moment.

(*Sir James r. gives the Duchess his arm and escorts her into the ball-room.*)

Parker. Mr. and Mrs. Arthur Bowden. Lord and Lady Paisley. Lord Darlington.

(*These people enter as announced.*)

Lord A. (*Coming up to Lord W.*) Want to speak to you particularly, dear boy. I'm worn to a shadow. Know I don't look it. None of us men do look what we really are. Demmed good thing, too. What I want to know is this. Who is she? Where does she come from? Why hasn't she got any demmed relations? Demmed nuisance, relations! But they make one so demmed respectable.

Lord W. You are talking of Mrs. Erlynne, I suppose? I only met her six months ago. Till then I never knew of her existence.

Lord A. You have seen a good deal of her since then.

Lord W. (*Coldly.*) Yes, I have seen a

good deal of her since then. I have just seen her.

Lord A. Egad! the women are very down on her. I have been dining with Arabella this evening! By Jove! you should have heard what she said about Mrs. Erlynne. She did n't leave a rag on her. . . . (*Aside.*) Berwick and I told her that did n't matter much, as the lady in question must have an extremely fine figure. You should have seen Arabella's expression! . . . But, look here, dear boy. I don't know what to do about Mrs. Erlynne. Egad! I might be married to her; she treats me with such demmed indifference. She 's deuced clever, too! She explains everything. Egad! She explains you. She has got any amount of explanations for you—and all of them different.

Lord W. No explanations are necessary about my friendship with Mrs. Erlynne.

Lord A. Hem! Well, look here, dear old fellow. Do you think she will ever get into this demmed thing called Society? Would you introduce her to your wife? No use beating about the confounded bush. Would you do that?

Lord W. Mrs. Erlynne is coming here to-night.

Lord A. Your wife has sent her a card?

Lord W. Mrs. Erlynne has received a card.

Lord A. Then she 's all right, dear boy. But why did n't you tell me that before? It would have saved me a heap of worry and demmed misunderstandings!

(*Lady A. and Mr. H. cross and exit on terrace l. u. e.*)

Parker. Mr. Cecil Graham!

(*Enter Mr. Cecil G.*)

Cecil G. (*Bows to Lady W., passes over and shakes hands with Lord W.*) Good evening, Arthur. Why don't you ask me how I am? I like people to ask me how I am. It shows a wide-spread interest in my health. Now to-night I am not at all well. Been dining with my people. Wonder why it is one's people are always so tedious? My father would talk morality after dinner. I told him he was old enough to know better. But my experience is that as soon as people are old enough to know better, they don't know anything at all. Hullo, Tuppy! Hear you 're going to be married again; thought you were tired of that game.

Lord A. You 're excessively trivial, my dear boy, excessively trivial!

Cecil G. By the way, Tuppy, which is it? Have you been twice married and once divorced, or twice divorced and once married? I say, you 've been twice divorced and once married. It seems so much more probable.

Lord A. I have a very bad memory. I really don't remember which.

(*Moves away r.*)

Lady P. Lord Windermere, I 've something most particular to ask you.

Lord W. I am afraid—if you will excuse me—I must join my wife.

Lady P. Oh, you must n't dream of such a thing. It 's most dangerous now-a-days for a husband to pay any attention to his wife in public. It always makes people think that he beats her when they 're alone. The world has grown so suspicious of anything that looks like a happy married life. But I 'll tell you what it is at supper.

(*Moves towards door of ball-room.*)

Lord W. (*c.*) Margaret, I *must* speak to you.

Lady W. Will you hold my fan for me, Lord Darlington? Thanks.

(*Comes down to him.*)

Lord W. (*Crossing to her.*) Margaret, what you said before dinner was, of course, impossible?

Lady W. That woman is not coming here to-night!

Lord W. (*r. c.*) Mrs. Erlynne is coming here, and if you in any way annoy or wound her, you will bring shame and sorrow on us both. Remember that! Ah, Margaret! only trust me! A wife should trust her husband!

Lady W. (*c.*) London is full of women who trust their husbands. One can always recognize them. They look so thoroughly unhappy. I am not going to be one of them. (*Moves up.*) Lord Darlington, will you give me back my fan, please? Thanks . . . A useful thing, a fan, is n't it? . . . I want a friend to-night, Lord Darlington. I did n't know I would want one so soon.

Lord D. Lady Windermere! I knew the time would come some day; but why to-night?

Lord W. I *will* tell her. I must. It would be terrible if there were any scene. Margaret . . .

Parker. Mrs. Erlynne.

(*Lord W. starts. Mrs. E. enters. very*

beautifully dressed and very dignified. Lady W. clutches at her fan, then lets it drop on the floor. She bows coldly to Mrs. E., who bows to her sweetly in turn, and sails into the room.)

Lord D. You have dropped your fan, Lady Windermere.

(*Picks it up and hands it to her.*)

Mrs. E. (*c.*) How do you do, again, Lord Windermere? How charming your sweet wife looks! Quite a picture!

Lord W. (*In a low voice.*) It was terribly rash of you to come!

Mrs. E. (*Smiling.*) The wisest thing I ever did in my life. And, by the way, you must pay me a good deal of attention this evening. I am afraid of the women. You must introduce me to some of them. The men I can always manage. How do you do, Lord Augustus? You have quite neglected me lately. I have not seen you since yesterday. I am afraid you 're faithless. Every one told me so.

Lord A. (*r.*) Now really, Mrs. Erlynne, allow me to explain.

Mrs. E. (*r. c.*) No, dear Lord Augustus, you can't explain anything. It is your chief charm.

Lord A. Ah! if you find charms in me, Mrs. Erlynne—

(*They converse together. Lord W. moves uneasily about the room watching Mrs. E.*)

Lord D. (*To Lady W.*) How pale you are!

Lady W. Cowards are always pale.

Lord D. You look faint. Come out on the terrace.

Lady W. Yes. (*To Parker.*) Parker, send my cloak out.

Mrs. E. (*Crossing to her.*) Lady Windermere, how beautifully your terrace is illuminated. Reminds me of Prince Doria's at Rome. (*Lady W. bows coldly, and goes off with Lord D.*) Oh, how do you do, Mr. Graham? Is n't that your aunt, Lady Jedburgh? I should so much like to know her.

Cecil G. (*After a moment's hesitation and embarrassment.*) Oh, certainly, if you wish it. Aunt Caroline, allow me to introduce Mrs. Erlynne.

Mrs. E. So pleased to meet you, Lady Jedburgh. (*Sits beside her on the sofa.*) Your nephew and I are great friends. I am so much interested in his political career. I think he 's sure to be a wonderful success. He thinks like a Tory, and talks like a Radical, and that 's so important now-a-days. He 's such a brilliant talker, too. But we all know from whom he inherits that. Lord Allendale was saying to me only yesterday in the Park, that Mr. Graham talks almost as well as his aunt.

Lady J. (*r.*) Most kind of you to say these charming things to me!

(*Mrs. E. smiles and continues conversation.*)

Dumby. (*To Cecil G.*) Did you introduce Mrs. Erlynne to Lady Jedburgh?

Cecil G. Had to, my dear fellow. Could n't help it. That woman can make one do anything she wants. How, I don't know.

Dumby. Hope to goodness she won't speak to me!

(*Saunters towards Lady P.*)

Mrs. E. (*c. To Lady J.*) On Thursday? With great pleasure. (*Rises and speaks to Lord W., laughing.*) What a bore it is to have to be civil to these old dowagers. But they always insist on it.

Lady P. (*To Mr. D.*) Who is that well-dressed woman talking to Windermere?

Dumby. Have n't got the slightest idea. Looks like an *edition de luxe* of a wicked French novel, meant specially for the English market.

Mrs. E. So that is poor Dumby with Lady Plymdale? I hear she is frightfully jealous of him. He does n't seem anxious to speak to me to-night. I suppose he is afraid of her. Those straw-colored women have dreadful tempers. Do you know, I think I 'll dance with you first, Windermere. (*Lord W. bites his lip and frowns.*) It will make Lord Augustus so jealous! Lord Augustus! (*Lord A. comes down.*) Lord Windermere insists on my dancing with him first, and, as it 's his own house, I can't well refuse. You know I would much sooner dance with you.

Lord A. (*With a low bow.*) I wish I could think so, Mrs. Erlynne.

Mrs. E. You know it far too well. I can fancy a person dancing through life with you and finding it charming.

Lord A. (*Placing his hand on his white waistcoat.*) Oh, thank you, thank you. You are the most adorable of all ladies!

Mrs. E. What a nice speech! So simple and so sincere! Just the sort of speech I like. Well, you shall hold my bouquet. (*Goes towards ball-room on Lord W.'s arm.*) Ah, Mr. Dumby, how are you?

I am so sorry I have been out the last three times you have called. Come and lunch on Friday.

Dumby. (*With perfect nonchalance.*) Delighted.

(*Lady P. glares with indignation at Mr. D. Lord A. follows Mrs. E. and Lord W. into the ball-room holding bouquet.*)

Lady P. (*To Mr. D.*) What an absolute brute you are! I never can believe a word you say! Why did you tell me you did n't know her? What do you mean by calling on her three times running? You are not to go to lunch there; of course you understand that?

Dumby. My dear Laura, I would n't dream of going!

Lady P. You have n't told me her name yet. Who is she?

Dumby. (*Coughs slightly and smooths his hair.*) She 's a Mrs. Erlynne.

Lady P. *That* woman!

Dumby. Yes, that is what every one calls her.

Lady P. How very interesting! How intensely interesting! I really must have a good stare at her. (*Goes to door of ball-room and looks in.*) I have heard the most shocking things about her. They say she is ruining poor Windermere. And Lady Windermere, who goes in for being so proper, invites her! How extremely amusing! It takes a thoroughly good woman to do a thoroughly stupid thing. You are to lunch there on Friday.

Dumby. Why?

Lady P. Because I want you to take my husband with you. He has been so attentive lately, that he has become a perfect nuisance. Now, this woman is just the thing for him. He 'll dance attendance upon her as long as she lets him, and won't bother me. I assure you, women of that kind are most useful. They form the basis of other people's marriages.

Dumby. What a mystery you are!

Lady P. (*Looking at him.*) I wish *you* were!

Dumby. I am—to myself. I am the only person in the world I should like to know thoroughly; but I don't see any chance of it just at present.

(*They pass into the ball-room, and Lady W. and Lord D. enter from the terrace.*)

Lady W. Yes. Her coming here is monstrous, unbearable. I know now what you meant to-day at tea time. Why did n't you tell me right out? You should have!

Lord D. I could n't! A man can't tell these things about another man! But if I had known he was going to make you ask her here to-night, I think I would have told you. That insult, at any rate, you would have been spared.

Lady W. I did not ask her. He insisted on her coming—against my entreaties—against my commands. Oh! the house is tainted for me. I feel that every woman here sneers at me as she dances by with my husband. What have I done to deserve this? I gave him all my life. He took it—used it—spoiled it! I am degraded in my own eyes; and I lack courage—I am a coward!

(*Sits down on sofa.*)

Lord D. If I know you at all, I know that you can't live with a man who treats you like this! What sort of life would you have with him? You would feel that he was lying to you every moment of the day. You would feel that the look in his eyes was false, his voice false, his touch false, his passion false. He would come to you when he was weary of others; you would have to comfort him. He would come to you when he was devoted to others; you would have to charm him. You would have to be to him the mask of his real life, the cloak to hide his secret.

Lady W. You are right—you are terribly right. But where am I to turn? You said you would be my friend, Lord Darlington.—Tell me, what am I to do? Be my friend now.

Lord D. Between men and women there is no friendship possible. There is passion, enmity, worship, love, but no friendship. I love you——

Lady W. No, no!

(*Rises.*)

Lord D. Yes, I love you! You are more to me than anything in the whole world. What does your husband give you? Nothing. Whatever is in him he gives to this wretched woman, whom he has thrust into your society, into your home, to shame you before every one. I offer you my life——

Lady W. Lord Darlington!

Lord D. My life—my whole life. Take it, and do with it what you will. . . . I love you—love you as I have never loved any living thing. From the moment I met you I loved you, loved you blindly, adoringly, madly! You did not know it then—you know it now! Leave this house to-night. I won't tell you that the world matters nothing, or the world's voice, or the voice of society. They matter a good deal. They matter far too much. But there are moments when one has to choose between living one's own life, fully, entirely, completely—or dragging out some false, shallow, degrading existence that the world in its hypocrisy demands. You have that moment now. Choose! O, my love, choose!

Lady W. (*Moving slowly away from him, and looking at him with startled eyes.*) I have not the courage.

Lord D. (*Following her.*) Yes; you have the courage. There may be six months of pain, of disgrace even, but when you no longer bear his name, when you bear mine, all will be well. Margaret, my love, my wife that shall be some day—yes, my wife! You know it! What are you now? This woman has the place that belongs by right to you. Oh! go—go out of this house, with head erect, with a smile upon your lips, with courage in your eyes. All London will know why you did it; and who will blame you? No one. If they do, what matter. Wrong? What is wrong? It 's wrong for a man to abandon his wife for a shameless woman. It is wrong for a wife to remain with a man who so dishonors her. You said once you would make no compromise with things. Make none now. Be brave! Be yourself!

Lady W. I am afraid of being myself. Let me think! Let me wait! My husband may return to me.

(*Sits down on sofa.*)

Lord D. And you would take him back! You are not what I thought you were. You are just the same as every other woman. You would stand anything rather than face the censure of a world whose praise you would despise. In a week you will be driving with this woman in the Park. She will be your constant guest—your dearest friend. You would endure anything rather than break with one blow this monstrous tie. You are right. You have no courage; none!

Lady W. Ah, give me time to think. I cannot answer you now.

(*Passes her hand nervously over her brow.*)

Lord D. It must be now or not at all.

Lady W. (*Rising from the sofa.*) Then not at all!

(*A pause.*)

Lord D. You break my heart!

Lady W. Mine is already broken.

(*A pause.*)

Lord D. To-morrow I leave England. This is the last time I shall ever look on you. You will never see me again. For one moment our lives met—our souls touched. They must never meet or touch again. Good-bye, Margaret.

(*Exit.*)

Lady W. How alone I am in life! How terribly alone!

(*The music stops. Enter the Duchess of B. and Lord P. laughing and talking. Other guests come on from ball-room.*)

Duchess of B. Dear Margaret, I 've just been having such a delightful chat with Mrs. Erlynne. I am so sorry for what I said to you this afternoon about her. Of course, she must be all right if *you* invite her. A most attractive woman, and has such sensible views on life. Told me she entirely disapproved of people marrying more than once, so I feel quite safe about poor Augustus. Can't imagine why people speak against her. It 's those horrid nieces of mine—the Saville girls—they 're always talking scandal. Still, I should go to Homburg, dear, I really should. She is just a little too attractive. But where is Agatha? Oh, there she is. (*Lady A. and Mr. H. enter from the terrace l. u. e.*) Mr. Hopper, I am very angry with you. You have taken Agatha out on the terrace, and she is so delicate.

Hopper. (*l. c.*) Awfully sorry, Duchess. We went out for a moment and then got chatting together.

Duchess of B. (*c.*) Ah, about dear Australia, I suppose?

Hopper. Yes.

Duchess of B. Agatha, darling!

(*Beckons her over.*)

Lady A. Yes, mamma!

Duchess of B. (*Aside.*) Did Mr. Hopper definitely——

Lady A. Yes, mamma.

Duchess of B. And what answer did you give him, dear child?

Lady A. Yes, mamma.

Duchess of B. (*Affectionately.*) My dear one! You always say the right thing. Mr. Hopper! James! Agatha has told me everything. How cleverly you have both kept your secret.

Hopper. You don't mind my taking Agatha off to Australia, then, Duchess?

Duchess of B. (*Indignantly.*) To Australia? Oh, don't mention that dreadful vulgar place.

Hopper. But she said she 'd like to come with me.

Duchess of B. (*Severely.*) Did you say that, Agatha?

Lady A. Yes, mamma.

Duchess of B. Agatha, you say the most silly things possible. I think on the whole that Grosvenor Square would be a more healthy place to reside in. There are lots of vulgar people live in Grosvenor Square, but at any rate there are no horrid kangaroos crawling about. But we 'll talk about that to-morrow. James, you can take Agatha down. You 'll come to lunch, of course, James. At half-past one instead of two. The Duke will wish to say a few words to you, I am sure.

Hopper. I should like to have a chat with the Duke, Duchess. He has not said a single word to me yet.

Duchess of B. I think you 'll find he will have a great deal to say to you to-morrow. (*Exit Lady A. with Mr. H.*) And now good-night, Margaret. I 'm afraid it 's the old, old story, dear. Love—well, not love at first sight, but love at the end of the season, which is so much more satisfactory.

Lady W. Good-night, Duchess.

(*Exit the Duchess of B. on Lord P.'s arm.*)

Lady P. My dear Margaret, what a handsome woman your husband has been dancing with! I should be quite jealous if I were you! Is she a great friend of yours?

Lady W. No!

Lady P. Really? Good-night, dear.

(*Looks at Mr. D. and exit.*)

Dumby. Awful manners young Hopper has!

Cecil G. Ah! Hopper is one of Nature's gentlemen, the worst type of gentlemen I know.

Dumby. Sensible woman, Lady Windermere. Lots of wives would have objected to Mrs. Erlynne coming. But Lady Windermere has that uncommon thing called common sense.

Cecil G. And Windermere knows that nothing looks so like innocence as an indiscretion.

Dumby. Yes; dear Windermere is becoming almost modern. Never thought he would.

(*Bows to Lady W. and exit.*)

Lady J. Good-night, Lady Windermere. What a fascinating woman Mrs. Erlynne is! She is coming to lunch on Thursday, won't you come too? I expect the Bishop and dear Lady Merton.

Lady W. I am afraid I am engaged, Lady Jedburgh.

Lady J. So sorry. Come, dear.

(*Exeunt Lady J. and Miss G.*)

(*Enter Mrs. E. and Lord W.*)

Mrs. E. Charming ball it has been! Quite reminds me of old days. (*Sits on the sofa.*) And I see that there are just as many fools in society as there used to be. So pleased to find that nothing has altered! Except Margaret. She 's grown quite pretty. The last time I saw her—twenty years ago, she was a fright in flannel. Positive fright, I assure you. The dear Duchess! and that sweet Lady Agatha! Just the type of girl I like! Well, really, Windermere, if I am to be the Duchess's sister-in-law——

Lord W. (*Sitting l. of her.*) But are you——?

(*Exit Mr. Cecil G. with rest of guests. Lady W. watches, with a look of scorn and pain, Mrs. E. and her husband. They are unconscious of her presence.*)

Mrs. E. Oh yes! He 's to call to-morrow at twelve o'clock. He wanted to propose to-night. In fact he did. He kept on proposing. Poor Augustus, you know how he repeats himself. Such a bad habit! But I told him I would n't give him an answer till to-morrow. Of course I am going to take him. And I dare say I 'll make him an admirable wife, as wives go. And there is a great deal of good in Lord Augustus. Fortunately it is all on the surface. Just where good qualities should be. Of course you must help me in this matter.

Lord W. I am not called on to encourage Lord Augustus, I suppose?

Mrs. E. Oh, no! I do the encouraging. But you will make me a handsome settlement, Windermere, won't you?

Lord W. (*Frowning.*) Is that what you want to talk to me about to-night?

Mrs. E. Yes.

Lord W. (*With a gesture of impatience.*) I will not talk of it here.

Mrs. E. (*Laughing.*) Then we will talk

of it on the terrace. Even business should have a picturesque background. Should it not, Windermere? With a proper background women can do anything.

Lord W. Won't to-morrow do as well?

Mrs. E. No; you see, to-morrow I am going to accept him. And I think it would be a good thing if I was able to tell him that—well, what shall I say—£2,000 a year left to me by a third cousin—or a second husband—or some distant relative of that kind. It would be an additional attraction, would n't it? You have a delightful opportunity now of paying me a compliment, Windermere. But you are not very clever at paying compliments. I am afraid Margaret does n't encourage you in that excellent habit. It 's a great mistake on her part. When men give up saying what is charming, they give up thinking what is charming. But seriously, what do you say to £2,000? £2,500, I think. In modern life margin is everything. Windermere, don't you think the world an intensely amusing place? I do!

(*Exit on terrace with Lord W. Music strikes up in ball-room.*)

Lady W. To stay in this house any longer is impossible. To-night a man who loves me offered me his whole life. I refused it. It was foolish of me. I will offer him mine now. I will give him mine. I will go to him! (*Puts on cloak and goes to door, then turns back. Sits down at table and writes a letter, puts it into an envelope, and leaves it on table.*) Arthur has never understood me. When he reads this, he will. He may do as he chooses now with his life. I have done with mine as I think best, as I think right. It is he who has broken the bond of marriage—not I. I only break its bondage.

(*Exit.*)

(*Parker enters l. and crosses towards the ball-room r. Enter Mrs. E.*)

Mrs. E. Is Lady Windermere in the ball-room?

Parker. Her ladyship has just gone out.

Mrs. E. Gone out? She 's not on the terrace?

Parker. No, madam. Her ladyship has just gone out of the house.

Mrs. E. (*Starts, and looks at the servant with a puzzled expression on her face.*) Out of the house?

Parker. Yes, madam—her ladyship told me she had left a letter for his lordship on the table.

Mrs. E. A letter for Lord Windermere?

Parker. Yes, madam.

Mrs. E. Thank you. (*Exit Parker. The music in the ball-room stops.*) Gone out of her house! A letter addressed to her husband! (*Goes over to bureau and looks at letter. Takes it up and lays it down again with a shudder of fear.*) No, no! It would be impossible! Life does n't repeat its tragedies like that! Oh, why does this horrible fancy come across me? Why do I remember now the one moment of my life I most wish to forget? Does life repeat its tragedies? (*Tears letter open and reads it, then sinks down into a chair with a gesture of anguish.*) Oh, how terrible! the same words that twenty years ago I wrote to her father! and how bitterly I have been punished for it! No; my punishment, my real punishment is to-night, is now!

(*Still seated r.*)

(*Enter Lord W. l. u. e.*)

Lord W. Have you said good-night to my wife?

(*Comes c.*)

Mrs. E. (*Crushing letter in her hand.*) Yes.

Lord W. Where is she?

Mrs. E. She is very tired. She has gone to bed. She said she had a headache.

Lord W. I must go to her. You 'll excuse me?

Mrs. E. (*Rising hurriedly.*) Oh, no! It 's nothing serious. She 's only very tired, that is all. Besides, there are people still in the supper-room. She wants you to make her apologies to them. She said she did n't wish to be disturbed. (*Drops letter.*) She asked me to tell you.

Lord W. (*Picks up letter.*) You have dropped something.

Mrs. E. Oh, yes, thank you, that is mine. (*Puts out her hand to take it.*)

Lord W. (*Still looking at letter.*) But it 's my wife's handwriting, is n't it?

Mrs. E. (*Takes the letter quickly.*) Yes, it 's—an address. Will you ask them to call my carriage, please?

Lord W. Certainly.

(*Goes l. and exit.*)

Mrs. E. Thanks. What can I do? What can I do? I feel a passion awakening within me that I never felt before. What can it mean? The daughter must not be like the mother—that would be terrible. How can I save her? How can I save my child? A moment may ruin a life. Who knows that better than I? Windermere must be got out of the house; that is absolutely necessary. (*Goes l.*) But how shall I do it? It must be done somehow. Ah!

(*Enter Lord A. r. u. e. carrying bouquet.*)

Lord A. Dear lady, I am in such suspense! May I not have an answer to my request?

Mrs. E. Lord Augustus, listen to me. You are to take Lord Windermere down to your club at once, and keep him there as long as possible. You understand?

Lord A. But you said you wished me to keep early hours!

Mrs. E. (*Nervously.*) Do what I tell you. Do what I tell you.

Lord A. And my reward?

Mrs. E. Your reward? Your reward? Oh! ask me that to-morrow. But don't let Windermere out of your sight to-night. If you do I will never forgive you. I will never speak to you again. I'll have nothing to do with you. Remember you are to keep Windermere at your club, and don't let him come back to-night.

(*Exit.*)

Lord A. Well, really, I might be her husband already. Positively I might.

(*Follows her in a bewildered manner.*)

Act-drop.

ACT III.

SCENE—*Lord Darlington's rooms. A large sofa is in front of fireplace r. At the back of the stage a curtain is drawn across the window. Doors l. and r. Table r. with writing materials. Table c. with syphons, glasses, and Tantalus frame. Table l. with cigar and cigarette box. Lamps lit.*

Lady W. (*Standing by the fireplace.*) Why does n't he come? This waiting is horrible. He should be here. Why is he not here, to wake by passionate words some fire within me? I am cold—cold as a loveless thing. Arthur must have read my letter by this time. If he cared for me, he would have come after me, would have taken me back by force. But he does n't care. He 's entrammelled by this woman—fascinated by her—dominated by her. If a woman wants to hold a man, she has merely to appeal to what is worst in him. We make gods of men, and they leave us. Others make brutes of them and they fawn and are faithful. How hideous life is! . . . Oh! it was mad of me to come here, horribly mad. And yet which is the worst, I wonder, to be at the mercy of a man who loves one, or the wife of a man who in one's own house dishonors one? What woman knows? What woman in the whole world? But will he love me always, this man to whom I am giving my life? What do I bring him? Lips that have lost the note of joy, eyes that are blighted by tears, chill hands and icy heart. I bring him nothing. I must go back—no; I can't go back, my letter has put me in their power—Arthur would not take me back! That fatal letter! No! Lord Darlington leaves England to-morrow. I will go with him—I have no choice. (*Sits down for a few moments. Then starts up and puts on her cloak.*) No, no! I will go back, let Arthur do with me what he pleases. I can't wait here. It has been madness my coming. I must go at once. As for Lord Darlington—Oh! here he is! What shall I do? What can I say to him? Will he let me go away at all? I have heard that men are brutal, horrible. . . .Oh!

(*Hides her face in her hands.*)

(*Enter Mrs. E. l.*)

Mrs. E. Lady Windermere! (*Lady W. starts and looks up. Then recoils in contempt.*) Thank Heaven I am in time. You must go back to your husband's house immediately.

Lady W. Must?

Mrs. E. (*Authoritatively.*) Yes, you must! There is not a second to be lost. Lord Darlington may return at any moment.

Lady W. Don't come near me!

Mrs. E. Oh! you are on the brink of ruin; you are on the brink of a hideous precipice. You must leave this place at once, my carriage is waiting at the corner of the street. You must come with me and drive straight home. (*Lady W. throws off her cloak and flings it on the sofa.*) What are you doing?

Lady W. Mrs. Erlynne—if you had not come here, I would have gone back. But now that I see you, I feel that nothing in the whole world would induce me to live under the same roof as Lord Windermere. You fill me with horror. There is something about you that stirs the wildest rage within me. And I know why you are here. My husband sent you to lure me back that I might serve as a blind to whatever relations exist between you and him.

Mrs. E. Oh! you don't think that—you can't.

Lady W. Go back to my husband, Mrs. Erlynne. He belongs to you and not to me. I suppose he is afraid of a scandal. Men are such cowards. They outrage every law of the world, and are afraid of the world's tongue. But he had better prepare himself. He shall have a scandal. He shall have the worst scandal there has been in London for years. He shall see his name in every vile paper, mine on every hideous placard.

Mrs. E. No—no——

Lady W. Yes! he shall. Had he come himself, I admit I would have gone back to the life of degradation you and he had prepared for me—I was going back—but to stay himself at home, and to send you as his messenger—oh! it was infamous—infamous.

Mrs. E. (*c.*) Lady Windermere, you wrong me horribly—you wrong your husband horribly. He does n't know you are here—he thinks you are safe in your own house. He thinks you are asleep in your own room. He never read the mad letter you wrote to him!

Lady W. (*r.*) Never read it!

Mrs. E. No—he knows nothing about it.

Lady W. How simple you think me! (*Going to her.*) You are lying to me!

Mrs. E. (*Restraining herself.*) I am not. I am telling you the truth.

Lady W. If my husband did n't read my letter, how is it that you are here? Who told you I had left the house you were shameless enough to enter? Who told you where I had gone to? My husband told you, and sent you to decoy me back.

(*Crosses l.*)

Mrs. E. (*r. c.*) Your husband has never seen the letter. I—saw it, I opened it. I—read it.

Lady W. (*Turning to her.*) You opened a letter of mine to my husband? You would n't dare!

Mrs. E. Dare! Oh! to save you from the abyss into which you are falling, there is nothing in the world I would not dare, nothing in the whole world. Here is the letter. Your husband has never read it. He never shall read it. (*Going to fire-place.*) It should never have been written. (*Tears it and throws it into the fire.*)

Lady W. (*With infinite contempt in her voice and look.*) How do I know that that was my letter after all? You seem to think the commonest device can take me in!

Mrs. E. Oh! why do you disbelieve everything I tell you! What object do you think I have in coming here, except to save you from utter ruin, to save you from the consequence of a hideous mistake? That letter that is burning now *was* your letter. I swear it to you!

Lady W. (*Slowly.*) You took good care to burn it before I had examined it. I cannot trust you. You, whose whole life is a lie, how could you speak the truth about anything?

(*Sits down.*)

Mrs. E. (*Hurriedly.*) Think as you like about me—say what you choose against me, but go back, go back to the husband you love.

Lady W. (*Sullenly.*) I do *not* love him!

Mrs. E. You do, and you know that he loves you.

Lady W. He does not understand what love is. He understands it as little as you do—but I see what you want. It would be a great advantage for you to get me back. Dear Heaven! what a life I would have then! Living at the mercy of a woman who has neither mercy nor pity in her, a woman whom it is an infamy to meet, a degradation to know, a vile woman, a woman who comes between husband and wife!

Mrs. E. (*With a gesture of despair.*) Lady Windermere, Lady Windermere, don't say such terrible things. You don't know how terrible they are, how terrible and how unjust. Listen, you must listen! Only go back to your husband, and I promise you never to communicate with him again on any pretext—never to see him—never to have anything to do with his life or yours. The money that he gave me, he gave me not through love, but through hatred, not in worship, but in contempt. The hold I have over him——

Lady W. (*Rising.*) Ah! you admit you have a hold!

Mrs. E. Yes, and I will tell you what it is. It is his love for you, Lady Windermere.

Lady W. You expect me to believe that?

Mrs. E. You must believe it! It is true. It is his love for you that has made him submit to—oh! call it what you like, tyranny, threats, anything you choose. But it is his love for you. His desire to spare you—shame, yes, shame and disgrace.

Lady W. What do you mean? You are insolent! What have I to do with you?

Mrs. E. (*Humbly.*) Nothing. I know it —but I tell you that your husband loves you—that you may never meet with such love again in your whole life—that such love you will never meet—and that if you throw it away, the day may come when you will starve for love and it will not be given to you, beg for love and it will be denied you—Oh! Arthur loves you!

Lady W. Arthur? And you tell me there is nothing between you?

Mrs. E. Lady Windermere, before Heaven your husband is guiltless of all offence towards you! And I—I tell you that had it ever occurred to me that such a monstrous suspicion would have entered your mind, I would have died rather than have crossed your life or his—oh! died, gladly died!

(*Moves away to sofa r.*)

Lady W. You talk as if you had a heart. Women like you have no hearts. Heart is not in you. You are bought and sold.

(*Sits l. c.*)

Mrs. E. (*Starts, with a gesture of pain. Then restrains herself, and comes over to where Lady W. is sitting. As she speaks, she stretches out her hands towards her, but does not dare to touch her.*) Believe what you choose about me. I am not worth a moment's sorrow. But don't spoil your beautiful young life on my account! You don't know what may be in store for you, unless you leave this house at once. You don't know what it is to fall into the pit, to be despised, mocked, abandoned, sneered at—to be an outcast! to find the door shut against one, to have to creep in by hideous byways, afraid every moment lest the mask should be stripped from one's face, and all the while to hear the laughter, the horrible laughter of the world, a thing more tragic than all the tears the world has ever shed. You don't know what it is. One pays for one's sin, and then one pays again, and all one's life one pays. You must never know that.—As for me, if suffering be an expiation, then at this moment I have expiated all my faults, whatever they have been; for to-night you have made a heart in one who had it not, made it and broken it.—But let that pass. I may have wrecked my own life, but I will not let you wreck yours. You—why, you are a mere girl, you would be lost. You have n't got the kind of brains that enables a woman to get back. You have neither the wit nor the courage. You could n't stand dishonor. No! Go back, Lady Windermere, to the husband who loves you, whom you love. You have a child, Lady Windermere. Go back to that child who even now, in pain or in joy, may be calling to you. (*Lady W. rises.*) God gave you that child. He will require from you that you make his life fine, that you watch over him. What answer will you make to God if his life is ruined through you? Back to your house, Lady Windermere—your husband loves you. He has never swerved for a moment from the love he bears you. But even if he had a thousand loves, you must stay with your child. If he was harsh to you, you must stay with your child. If he ill-treated you, you must stay with your child. If he abandoned you, your place is with your child. (*Lady W. bursts into tears and buries her face in her hands.*) (*Rushing to her.*) Lady Windermere!

Lady W. (*Holding out her hands to her, helplessly, as a child might do.*) Take me home. Take me home.

Mrs. E. (*Is about to embrace her. Then restrains herself. There is a look of wonderful joy in her face.*) Come! Where is your cloak? (*Getting it from sofa.*) Here. Put it on. Come at once! (*They go to the door.*)

Lady W. Stop! Don't you hear voices?

Mrs. E. No, no! There is no one!

Lady W. Yes, there is! Listen! Oh! that is my husband's voice! He is coming in! Save me! Oh, it 's some plot! You have sent for him!

(*Voices outside.*)

Mrs. E. Silence! I am here to save you if I can. But I fear it is too late! There! (*Points to the curtain across the window.*) The first chance you have, slip out, if you ever get a chance!

Lady W. But you!

Mrs. E. Oh! never mind me. I'll face them.

(*Lady W. hides herself behind the curtain.*)

Lord A. (*Outside.*) Nonsense, dear Windermere, you must not leave me!

Mrs. E. Lord Augustus! Then it is I who am lost!

(*Hesitates for a moment, then looks round and sees door r., and exit through it.*)

(*Enter Lord D., Mr. D., Lord W., Lord A. L., and Mr. Cecil G.*)

Dumby. What a nuisance their turning us out of the club at this hour! It 's only two o'clock. (*Sinks into a chair.*) The lively part of the evening is only just beginning.

(*Yawns and closes his eyes.*)

Lord W. It is very good of you, Lord Darlington, allowing Augustus to force our company on you, but I 'm afraid I can't stay long.

Lord D. Really! I am so sorry! You 'll take a cigar, won't you?

Lord W. Thanks!

(*Sits down.*)

Lord A. (*To Lord W.*) My dear boy, you must not dream of going. I have a great deal to talk to you about, of demmed importance, too.

(*Sits down with him at l. table.*)

Cecil G. Oh! we all know what that is! Tuppy can't talk about anything but Mrs. Erlynne!

Lord W. Well, that is no business of yours, is it, Cecil?

Cecil G. None! That is why it interests me. My own business always bores me to death. I prefer other people's.

Lord D. Have something to drink, you fellows. Cecil, you 'll have a whisky and soda?

Cecil G. Thanks. (*Goes to the table with Lord D.*) Mrs. Erlynne looked very handsome to-night, did n't she?

Lord D. I am not one of her admirers.

Cecil G. I use n't to be, but I am now. Why! she actually made me introduce her to poor dear Aunt Caroline. I believe she is going to lunch there.

Lord D. (*In surprise.*) No?

Cecil G. She is, really.

Lord D. Excuse me, you fellows. I 'm going away to-morrow. And I have to write a few letters.

(*Goes to writing table and sits down.*)

Dumby. Clever woman, Mrs. Erlynne.

Cecil G. Hallo, Dumby! I thought you were asleep.

Dumby. I am, I usually am!

Lord A. A very clever woman. Knows perfectly well what a demmed fool I am —knows it as well as I do myself. (*Cecil G. comes towards him laughing.*) Ah! you may laugh, my boy, but it is a great thing to come across a woman who thoroughly understands one.

Dumby. It is an awfully dangerous thing. They always end by marrying one.

Cecil G. But I thought, Tuppy, you were never going to see her again. Yes! you told me so yesterday evening at the club. You said you 'd heard—

(*Whispering to him.*)

Lord A. Oh, she 's explained that.

Cecil G. And the Wiesbaden affair?

Lord A. She 's explained that, too.

Dumby. And her income, Tuppy? Has she explained that?

Lord A. (*In a very serious voice.*) She 's going to explain that to-morrow.

(*Cecil G. goes back to c. table.*)

Dumby. Awfully commercial, women now-a-days. Our grandmothers threw their caps over the mills, of course, but, by Jove, their granddaughters only throw their caps over mills that can raise the wind for them.

Lord A. You want to make her out a wicked woman. She is not!

Cecil G. Oh! Wicked women bother one. Good women bore one. That is the only difference between them.

Lord D. (*Puffing a cigar.*) Mrs. Erlynne has a future before her.

Dumby. Mrs. Erlynne has a past before her.

Lord A. I prefer women with a past. They 're always so demmed amusing to talk to.

Cecil G. Well, you 'll have lots of topics of conversation with *her*, Tuppy.

(*Rising and going to him.*)

Lord A. You 're getting annoying, dear boy; you 're getting demmed annoying.

Cecil G. (*Puts his hands on his shoulders.*) Now, Tuppy, you 've lost your figure and you 've lost your character. Don't lose your temper; you have only got one.

Lord A. My dear boy, if I was n't the most good-natured man in London——

Cecil G. We 'd treat you with more respect, would n't we, Tuppy?

(*Strolls away.*)

Dumby. The youth of the present day are quite monstrous. They have absolutely no respect for dyed hair.

(*Lord A. looks round angrily.*)

Cecil G. Mrs. Erlynne has a very great respect for dear Tuppy.

Dumby. Then Mrs. Erlynne sets an admirable example for the rest of her sex.

It is perfectly brutal the way most women now-a-days behave to men who are not their husbands.

Lord W. Dumby, you are ridiculous, and Cecil, you let your tongue run away with you. You must leave Mrs. Erlynne alone. You don't really know anything about her, and you're always talking scandal against her.

Cecil G. (*Coming towards him l. c.*) My dear Arthur, *I* never talk scandal. *I* only talk gossip.

Lord W. What is the difference between scandal and gossip?

Cecil G. Oh! gossip is charming! History is merely gossip. But scandal is gossip made tedious by morality. Now I never moralize. A man who moralizes is usually a hypocrite, and a woman who moralizes is invariably plain. There is nothing in the whole world so unbecoming to a woman as a Non-conformist conscience. And most women know it, I'm glad to say.

Lord A. Just my sentiments, dear boy, just my sentiments.

Cecil G. Sorry to hear it, Tuppy; whenever people agree with me, I always feel I must be wrong.

Lord A. My dear boy, when I was your age——

Cecil G. But you never were, Tuppy, and you never will be. (*Goes up c.*) I say, Darlington, let us have some cards. You'll play, Arthur, won't you?

Lord W. No, thanks, Cecil.

Dumby. (*With a sigh.*) Good heavens! how marriage ruins a man! It's as demoralizing as cigarettes, and far more expensive.

Cecil G. You'll play, of course, Tuppy?

Lord A. (*Pouring himself out a brandy and soda at table.*) Can't, dear boy. Promised Mrs. Erlynne never to play or drink again.

Cecil G. Now, my dear Tuppy, don't be led astray into the paths of virtue. Reformed, you would be perfectly tedious. That is the worst of women. They always want one to be good. And if we are good, when they meet us, they don't love us at all. They like to find us quite irretrievably bad, and to leave us quite unattractively good.

Lord D. (*Rising from r. table, where he has been writing letters.*) They always do find us bad!

Dumby. I don't think we are bad. I think we are all good except Tuppy.

Lord D. No, we are all in the gutter, but some of us are looking at the stars.

(*Sits down at c. table.*)

Dumby. We are all in the gutter, but some of us are looking at the stars? Upon my word, you are very romantic to-night, Darlington.

Cecil G. Too romantic! You must be in love. Who is the girl?

Lord D. The woman I love is not free, or thinks she is n't.

(*Glances instinctively at Lord W. while he speaks.*)

Cecil G. A married woman, then! Well, there's nothing in the world like the devotion of a married woman. It's a thing no married man knows anything about.

Lord D. Oh! she does n't love me. She is a good woman. She is the only good woman I have ever met in my life.

Cecil G. The only good woman you have ever met in your life?

Lord D. Yes!

Cecil G. (*Lighting a cigarette.*) Well, you are a lucky fellow! Why, I have met hundreds of good women. I never seem to meet any but good women. The world is perfectly packed with good women. To know them is a middle-class education.

Lord D. This woman has purity and innocence. She has everything we men have lost.

Cecil G. My dear fellow, what on earth should we men do going about with purity and innocence? A carefully thought-out buttonhole is much more effective.

Dumby. She does n't really love you then?

Lord D. No, she does not!

Dumby. I congratulate you, my dear fellow. In this world there are only two tragedies. One is not getting what one wants, and the other is getting it. The last is much the worst, the last is a real tragedy! But I am interested to hear she does not love you. How long could you love a woman who did n't love you, Cecil?

Cecil G. A woman who did n't love me? Oh, all my life.

Dumby. So could I. But it's so difficult to meet one.

Lord D. How can you be so conceited, Dumby?

Dumby. I did n't say it as a matter of conceit. I said it as a matter of regret. I have been wildly, madly adored. I am sorry I have. It has been an immense nuisance. I should like to be allowed a little time to myself, now and then.

Lord A. (*Looking round.*) Time to educate yourself, I suppose.

Dumby. No, time to forget all I have learned. That is much more important, dear Tuppy.

(*Lord A. moves uneasily in his chair.*)

Lord D. What cynics you fellows are!

Cecil G. What is a cynic?

(*Sitting on the back of the sofa.*)

Lord D. A man who knows the price of everything, and the value of nothing.

Cecil G. And a sentimentalist, my dear Darlington, is a man who sees an absurd value in everything, and does n't know the market price of any single thing.

Lord D. You always amuse me, Cecil. You talk as if you were a man of experience.

Cecil G. I am.

(*Moves up to front of fireplace.*)

Lord D. You are far too young!

Cecil G. That is a great error. Experience is a question of instinct about life. I have got it. Tuppy has n't. Experience is the name Tuppy gives to his mistakes. That is all.

(*Lord A. looks round indignantly.*)

Dumby. Experience is the name every one gives to their mistakes.

Cecil G. (*Standing with his back to fireplace.*) One should n't commit any.

(*Sees Lady W.'s fan on sofa.*)

Dumby. Life would be very dull without them.

Cecil G. Of course you are quite faithful to this woman you are in love with, Darlington, to this good woman?

Lord D. Cecil, if one really loves a woman, all other women in the world become absolutely meaningless to one. Love changes one—I am changed.

Cecil G. Dear me! How very interesting! Tuppy, I want to talk to you.

(*Lord A. takes no notice.*)

Dumby. It 's no use talking to Tuppy. You might just as well talk to a brick wall.

Cecil G. But I like talking to a brick wall—it 's the only thing in the world that never contradicts me! Tuppy!

Lord A. Well, what is it? What is it?

(*Rising and going over to Cecil G.*)

Cecil G. Come over here. I want you particularly. (*Aside.*) Darlington has been moralizing and talking about the purity of love, and that sort of thing, and he has got some woman in his rooms all the time.

Lord A. No, really! really!

Cecil G. (*In a low voice.*) Yes, here is her fan.

(*Points to the fan.*)

Lord A. (*Chuckling.*) By Jove! By Jove!

Lord W. (*Up by door.*) I am really off now, Lord Darlington. I am sorry you are leaving England so soon. Pray call on us when you come back! My wife and I will be charmed to see you!

Lord D. (*Up stage with Lord W.*) I am afraid I shall be away for many years. Good-night!

Cecil G. Arthur!

Lord W. What?

Cecil G. I want to speak to you for a moment. No, do come!

Lord W. (*Putting on his coat.*) I can't—I 'm off!

Cecil G. It is something very particular. It will interest you enormously.

Lord W. (*Smiling.*) It is some of your nonsense, Cecil.

Cecil G. It is n't! It is n't really!

Lord A. (*Going to him.*) My dear fellow, you must n't go yet. I have a lot to talk to you about. And Cecil has something to show you.

Lord W. (*Walking over.*) Well, what is it?

Cecil G. Darlington has got a woman here in his rooms. Here is her fan. Amusing, is n't it?

(*A pause.*)

Lord W. Good God!

(*Seizes the fan—Dumby rises.*)

Cecil G. What is the matter?

Lord W. Lord Darlington!

Lord D. (*Turning round.*) Yes!

Lord W. What is my wife's fan doing here in your rooms? Hands off, Cecil. Don't touch me.

Lord D. Your wife's fan?

Lord W. Yes, here it is!

Lord D. (*Walking towards him.*) I don't know!

Lord W. You must know. I demand an explanation. Don't hold me, you fool.

(*To Cecil G.*)

Lord D. (*Aside.*) She is here after all!

Lord W. Speak, sir! Why is my wife's fan here? Answer me, by God! I 'll search your rooms, and if my wife 's here, I 'll——

(*Moves.*)

Lord D. You shall not search my rooms.

You have no right to do so. I forbid you!

Lord W. You scoundrel! I'll not leave your room till I have searched every corner of it! What moves behind that curtain?

(*Rushes towards the curtain c.*)

Mrs. E. (*Enters behind r.*) Lord Windermere!

Lord W. Mrs. Erlynne!

(*Every one starts and turns round. Lady W. slips out from behind the curtain and glides from the room l.*)

Mrs. E. I am afraid I took your wife's fan in mistake for my own, when I was leaving your house to-night. I am so sorry.

(*Takes fan from him. Lord W. looks at her in contempt. Lord D. in mingled astonishment and anger. Lord A. turns away. The other men smile at each other.*)

Act-drop.

ACT IV.

Scene—*Same as in Act I.*

Lady W. (*Lying on sofa.*) How can I tell him? I can't tell him. It would kill me. I wonder what happened after I escaped from that horrible room. Perhaps she told them the true reason of her being there, and the real meaning of that —fatal fan of mine. Oh, if he knows— how can I look him in the face again? He would never forgive me. (*Touches bell.*) How securely one thinks one lives —out of reach of temptation, sin, folly. And then suddenly—Oh! Life is terrible. It rules us, we do not rule it.

(*Enter Rosalie r.*)

Rosalie. Did your ladyship ring for me?

Lady W. Yes. Have you found out at what time Lord Windermere came in last night?

Rosalie. His lordship did not come in till five o'clock.

Lady W. Five o'clock! He knocked at my door this morning, did n't he?

Rosalie. Yes, my lady—at half-past nine. I told him your ladyship was not awake yet.

Lady W. Did he say anything?

Rosalie. Something about your ladyship's fan. I did n't quite catch what his lordship said. Has the fan been lost, my lady? I can't find it, and Parker says it was not left in any of the rooms. He has looked in all of them and on the terrace as well.

Lady W. It does n't matter. Tell Parker not to trouble. That will do.

(*Exit Rosalie.*)

Lady W. (*Rising.*) She is sure to tell him. I can fancy a person doing a wonderful act of self-sacrifice, doing it spontaneously, recklessly, nobly—and afterwards finding out that it costs too much. Why should she hesitate between her ruin and mine? . . . How strange! I would have publicly disgraced her in my own house. She accepts public disgrace in the house of another to save me. . . . There is a bitter irony in things, a bitter irony in the way we talk of good and bad women. . . . Oh, what a lesson! and what a pity that in life we only get our lessons when they are of no use to us! For even if she does n't tell, I must. Oh! the shame of it, the shame of it. To tell it is to live through it all again. Actions are the first tragedy in life, words are the second. Words are perhaps the worst. Words are merciless. . . . Oh!

(*Starts as Lord W. enters.*)

Lord W. (*Kisses her.*) Margaret—how pale you look!

Lady W. I slept very badly.

Lord W. (*Sitting on sofa with her.*) I am so sorry. I came in dreadfully late, and did n't like to wake you. You are crying, dear.

Lady W. Yes, I am crying, for I have something to tell you, Arthur.

Lord W. My dear child, you are not well. You 've been doing too much. Let us go away to the country. You 'll be all right at Selby. The season is almost over. There is no use staying on. Poor darling! We 'll go away to-day, if you like. (*Rises.*) We can easily catch the 4.30. I'll send a wire to Fannen.

(*Crosses and sits down at table to write a telegram.*)

Lady W. Yes; let us go away to-day. No; I can't go to-day, Arthur. There is some one I must see before I leave town —some one who has been kind to me.

Lord W. (*Rising and leaning over sofa.*) Kind to you?

Lady W. Far more than that. (*Rises and goes to him.*) I will tell you, Arthur, but only love me, love me as you used to love me.

Lord W. Used to? You are not thinking of that wretched woman who came here last night? (*Coming round and sitting r. of her.*) You don't still imagine ——no, you could n't.

Lady W. I don't. I know now I was wrong and foolish.

Lord W. It was very good of you to receive her last night—but you are never to see her again.

Lady W. Why do you say that?

(*A pause.*)

Lord W. (*Holding her hand.*) Margaret, I thought Mrs. Erlynne was a woman more sinned against than sinning, as the phrase goes. I thought she wanted to be good, to get back into a place that she had lost by a moment's folly, to lead again a decent life. I believed what she told me—I was mistaken in her. She is bad—as bad as a woman can be.

Lady W. Arthur, Arthur, don't talk so bitterly about any woman. I don't think now that people can be divided into the good and the bad, as though they were two separate races or creations. What are called good women may have terrible things in them, mad moods of recklessness, assertion, jealousy, sin. Bad women, as they are termed, may have in them sorrow, repentance, pity, sacrifice. And I don't think Mrs. Erlynne a bad woman—I know she 's not.

Lord W. My dear child, the woman 's impossible. No matter what harm she tries to do us, you must never see her again. She is inadmissible anywhere.

Lady W. But I want to see her. I want her to come here.

Lord W. Never!

Lady W. She came here once as *your* guest. She must come now as *mine*. That is but fair.

Lord W. She should never have come here.

Lady W. (*Rising.*) It is too late, Arthur, to say that now.

(*Moves away.*)

Lord W. (*Rising.*) Margaret, if you knew where Mrs. Erlynne went last night, after she left this house, you would not sit in the same room with her. It was absolutely shameless, the whole thing.

Lady W. Arthur, I can't bear it any longer. I must tell you. Last night——

(*Enter Parker with a tray on which lie Lady W.'s fan and a card.*)

Parker. Mrs. Erlynne has called to return your ladyship's fan which she took away by mistake last night. Mrs. Erlynne has written a message on the card.

Lady W. Oh, ask Mrs. Erlynne to be kind enough to come up. (*Reads card.*) Say I shall be very glad to see her. (*Exit Parker.*) She wants to see me, Arthur.

Lord W. (*Takes card and looks at it.*) Margaret, I *beg* you not to. Let me see her first, at any rate. She 's a very dangerous woman. She is the most dangerous woman I know. You don't realize what you 're doing.

Lady W. It is right that I should see her.

Lord W. My child, you may be on the brink of a great sorrow. Don't go to meet it. It is absolutely necessary that I should see her before you do.

Lady W. Why should it be necessary?

(*Enter Parker.*)

Parker. Mrs. Erlynne.

(*Enter Mrs. E. Exit Parker.*)

Mrs. E. How do you do, Lady Windermere? (*To Lord W.*) How do you do? Do you know, Lady Windermere, I am so sorry about your fan. I can't imagine how I made such a silly mistake. Most stupid of me. And as I was driving in your direction, I thought I would take the opportunity of returning your property in person, with many apologies for my carelessness, and of bidding you good-bye.

Lady W. Good-bye? (*Moves towards sofa with Mrs. E. and sits down beside her.*) Are you going away, then, Mrs. Erlynne?

Mrs. E. Yes; I am going to live abroad again. The English climate does n't suit me. My—heart is affected here, and that I don't like. I prefer living in the south. London is too full of fogs and—and serious people, Lord Windermere. Whether the fogs produce the serious people or whether the serious people produce the fogs, I don't know, but the whole thing rather gets on my nerves, and so I 'm leaving this afternoon by the Club Train.

Lady W. This afternoon? But I wanted so much to come and see you.

Mrs. E. How kind of you! But I am afraid I have to go.

Lady W. Shall I never see you again, Mrs. Erlynne?

Mrs. E. I am afraid not. Our lives lie

too far apart. But there is a little thing I would like you to do for me. I want a photograph of you, Lady Windermere—would you give me one? You don't know how gratified I should be.

Lady W. Oh, with pleasure. There is one on that table. I'll show it to you.

(*Goes across to the table.*)

Lord W. (*Coming up to Mrs. E. and speaking in a low voice.*) It is monstrous your intruding yourself here after your conduct last night.

Mrs. E. (*With an amused smile.*) My dear Windermere, manners before morals!

Lady W. (*Returning.*) I'm afraid it is very flattering—I am not so pretty as that.

(*Showing photograph.*)

Mrs. E. You are much prettier. But haven't you got one of yourself with your little boy?

Lady W. I *have.* Would you prefer one of those?

Mrs. E. Yes.

Lady W. I'll go and get it for you, if you'll excuse me for a moment. I have one upstairs.

Mrs. E. So sorry, Lady Windermere, to give you so much trouble.

Lady W. (*Moves to door r.*) No trouble at all, Mrs. Erlynne.

Mrs. E. Thanks so much. (*Exit Lady W. r.*) You seem rather out of temper this morning, Windermere. Why should you be? Margaret and I get on charmingly together.

Lord W. I can't bear to see you with her. Besides, you have not told me the truth, Mrs. Erlynne.

Mrs. E. I have not told *her* the truth, you mean.

Lord W. (*Standing c.*) I sometimes wish you had. I should have been spared then the misery, the anxiety, the annoyance of the last six months. But rather than my wife should know—that the mother whom she was taught to consider as dead, the mother whom she has mourned as dead, is living—a divorced woman going about under an assumed name, a bad woman preying upon life, as I know you now to be—rather than that, I was ready to supply you with money to pay bill after bill, extravagance after extravagance, to risk what occurred yesterday, the first quarrel I have ever had with my wife. You don't understand what that means to me. How could you? But I tell you that the only bitter words that ever came from those sweet lips of hers were on your account, and I hate to see you next her. You sully the innocence that is in her. (*Moves l. c.*) And then I used to think that with all your faults you were frank and honest. You are not.

Mrs. E. Why do you say that?

Lord W. You made me get you an invitation to my wife's ball.

Mrs. E. For my daughter's ball—yes.

Lord W. You came, and within an hour of your leaving the house, you are found in a man's rooms—you are disgraced before every one.

(*Goes up stage c.*)

Mrs. E. Yes.

Lord W. (*Turning round on her.*) Therefore I have a right to look upon you as what you are—a worthless, vicious woman. I have the right to tell you never to enter this house, never to attempt to come near my wife——

Mrs. E. (*Coldly.*) My daughter, you mean.

Lord W. You have no right to claim her as your daughter. You left her, abandoned her, when she was but a child in the cradle, abandoned her for your lover, who abandoned you in turn.

Mrs. E. (*Rising.*) Do you count that to his credit, Lord Windermere—or to mine?

Lord W. To his, now that I know you.

Mrs. E. Take care—you had better be careful.

Lord W. Oh, I am not going to mince words for you. I know you thoroughly.

Mrs. E. (*Looking steadily at him.*) I question that.

Lord W. I *do* know you. For twenty years of your life you lived without your child, without a thought of your child. One day you read in the papers that she had married a rich man. You saw your hideous chance. You knew that to spare her the ignominy of learning that a woman like you was her mother, I would endure anything. You began your blackmailing.

Mrs. E. (*Shrugging her shoulders.*) Don't use ugly words, Windermere. They are vulgar. I saw my chance, it is true, and took it.

Lord W. Yes, you took it—and spoiled it all last night by being found out.

Mrs. E. (*With a strange smile.*) You are quite right, I spoiled it all last night.

Lord W. And as for your blunder in taking my wife's fan from here, and then leaving it about in Darlington's rooms, it is unpardonable. I can't bear the sight of it now. I shall never let my wife use it again. The thing is soiled for me. You should have kept it, and not brought it back.

Mrs. E. I think I *shall* keep it. (*Goes up.*) It 's extremely pretty. (*Takes up fan.*) I shall ask Margaret to give it to me.

Lord W. I hope my wife will give it you.

Mrs. E. Oh, I 'm sure she will have no objection.

Lord W. I wish that at the same time she would give you a miniature she kisses every night before she prays—It 's the miniature of a young, innocent-looking girl with beautiful dark hair.

Mrs. E. Ah, yes, I remember. How long ago that seems! (*Goes to sofa and sits down.*) It was done before I was married. Dark hair and an innocent expression were the fashion then, Windermere!

(*A pause.*)

Lord W. What do you mean by coming here this morning? What is your object?

(*Crossing l. c. and sitting.*)

Mrs. E. (*With a note of irony in her voice.*) To bid good-bye to my dear daughter, of course. (*Lord W. bites his underlip in anger. Mrs. E. looks at him, and her voice and manner become serious. In her accents as she talks there is a note of deep tragedy. For a moment she reveals herself.*) Oh, don't imagine I am going to have a pathetic scene with her, weep on her neck and tell her who I am, and all that kind of thing. I have no ambition to play the part of a mother. Only once in my life have I known a mother's feelings. That was last night. They were terrible—they made me suffer—they made me suffer too much. For twenty years, as you say, I have lived childless—I want to live childless still. (*Hiding her feelings with a trivial laugh.*) Besides, my dear Windermere, how on earth could I pose as a mother with a grown-up daughter? Margaret is twenty-one, and I have never admitted that I am more than twenty-nine, or thirty at the most. Twenty-nine when there are pink shades, thirty when there are not. So you see what difficulties it would involve. No, as far as I am concerned, let your wife cherish the memory of this dead, stainless mother. Why should I interfere with her illusions? I find it hard enough to keep my own. I lost one illusion last night. I thought I had no heart. I find I have, and a heart does n't suit me, Windermere. Somehow it does n't go with modern dress. It makes one look old. (*Takes up hand-mirror from table and looks into it.*) And it spoils one's career at critical moments.

Lord W. You fill me with horror—with absolute horror.

Mrs. E. (*Rising.*) I suppose, Windermere, you would like me to retire into a convent or become a hospital nurse or something of that kind, as people do in silly modern novels. That is stupid of you, Arthur; in real life we don't do such things—not as long as we have any good looks left, at any rate. No—what consoles one now-a-days is not repentance, but pleasure. Repentance is quite out of date. And besides, if a woman really repents, she has to go to a bad dressmaker, otherwise no one believes in her. And nothing in the world would induce me to do that. No; I am going to pass entirely out of your two lives. My coming into them has been a mistake—I discovered that last night.

Lord W. A fatal mistake.

Mrs. E. (*Smiling.*) Almost fatal.

Lord W. I am sorry now I did not tell my wife the whole thing at once.

Mrs. E. I regret my bad actions. You regret your good ones—that is the difference between us.

Lord W. I don't trust you. I *will* tell my wife. It 's better for her to know, and from me. It will cause her infinite pain—it will humiliate her terribly, but it 's right that she should know.

Mrs. E. You propose to tell her?

Lord W. I am going to tell her.

Mrs. E. (*Going up to him.*) If you do, I will make my name so infamous that it will mar every moment of her life. It will ruin her and make her wretched. If you dare to tell her, there is no depth of degradation I will not sink to, no pit of shame I will not enter. You shall not tell her—I forbid you.

Lord W. Why?

Mrs. E. (*After a pause.*) If I said to you that I cared for her, perhaps loved her even—you would sneer at me, would n't you?

Lord W. I should feel it was not true. A mother's love means devotion, unselfishness, sacrifice. What could you know of such things?

Mrs. E. You are right. What could I know of such things? Don't let us talk any more about *it;* as for telling my daughter who I am, that I do not allow. It is my secret, it is not yours. If I make up my mind to tell her, and I think I will, I shall tell her before I leave this house—if not, I shall never tell her.

Lord W. (*Angrily.*) Then let me beg of you to leave our house at once. I will make your excuses to Margaret.

(*Enter Lady W. r. She goes over to Mrs. E. with the photograph in her hand. Lord W. moves to back of sofa, and anxiously watches Mrs. E. as the scene progresses.*)

Lady W. I am so sorry, Mrs. Erlynne, to have kept you waiting. I could n't find the photograph anywhere. At last I discovered it in my husband's dressing-room—he had stolen it.

Mrs. E. (*Takes the photograph from her and looks at it.*) I am not surprised—it is charming. (*Goes over to sofa with Lady W. and sits down beside her. Looks again at the photograph.*) And so that is your little boy! What is he called?

Lady W. Gerard, after my dear father.

Mrs. E. (*Laying the photograph down.*) Really?

Lady W. Yes. If it had been a girl, I would have called it after my mother. My mother had the same name as myself, Margaret.

Mrs. E. My name is Margaret, too.

Lady W. Indeed!

Mrs. E. Yes. (*Pause.*) You are devoted to your mother's memory, Lady Windermere, your husband tells me.

Lady W. We all have ideals in life. At least we all should have. Mine is my mother.

Mrs. E. Ideals are dangerous things. Realities are better. They wound, but they are better.

Lady W. (*Shaking her head.*) If I lost my ideals, I should lose everything.

Mrs. E. Everything?

Lady W. Yes.

(*Pause.*)

Mrs. E. Did your father often speak to you of your mother?

Lady W. No, it gave him too much pain. He told me how my mother had died a few months after I was born. His eyes filled with tears as he spoke. Then he begged me never to mention her name to him again. It made him suffer even to hear it. My father—my father really died of a broken heart. His was the most ruined life I know.

Mrs. E. (*Rising.*) I am afraid I must go now, Lady Windermere.

Lady W. (*Rising.*) Oh no, don't.

Mrs. E. I think I had better. My carriage must have come back by this time. I sent it to Lady Jedburgh's with a note.

Lady W. Arthur, would you mind seeing if Mrs. Erlynne's carriage has come back?

Mrs. E. Pray don't trouble Lord Windermere, Lady Windermere.

Lady W. Yes, Arthur, do go, please. (*Lord W. hesitates for a moment and looks at Mrs. E. She remains quite impassive. He leaves the room.*) (*To Mrs. E.*) Oh, what am I to say to you? You saved me last night!

(*Goes toward her.*)

Mrs. E. Hush—don't speak of it.

Lady W. I must speak of it. I can't let you think that I am going to accept this sacrifice. I am not. It is too great. I am going to tell my husband everything. It is my duty.

Mrs. E. It is not your duty—at least you have duties to others besides him. You say you owe me something?

Lady W. I owe you everything.

Mrs. E. Then pay your debt by silence. That is the only way in which it can be paid. Don't spoil the one good thing I have done in my life by telling it to any one. Promise me that what passed last night will remain a secret between us. You must not bring misery into your husband's life. Why spoil his love? You must not spoil it. Love is easily killed. Oh, how easily love is killed! Pledge me your word, Lady Windermere, that you will *never* tell him. I insist upon it.

Lady W. (*With bowed head.*) It is your will, not mine.

Mrs. E. Yes, it is my will. And never forget your child—I like to think of you as a mother. I like you to think of yourself as one.

Lady W. (*Looking up.*) I always will now. Only once in my life I have forgotten my own mother—that was last night. Oh, if I had remembered her, I should not have been so foolish, so wicked.

Mrs. E. (*With a slight shudder.*) Hush, last night is quite over.

(*Enter Lord W.*)

Lord W. Your carriage has not come back yet, Mrs. Erlynne.

Mrs. E. It makes no matter. I'll take a hansom. There is nothing in the world so respectable as a good Shrewsbury and Talbot. And now, dear Lady Windermere, I am afraid it is really good-bye. (*Moves up c.*) Oh, I remember. You'll think me absurd, but do you know, I've taken a great fancy to this fan that I was silly enough to run away with last night from your ball. Now, I wonder would you give it to me? Lord Windermere says you may. I know it is his present.

Lady W. Oh, certainly, if it will give you any pleasure. But it has my name on it. It has "Margaret" on it.

Mrs. E. But we have the same Christian name.

Lady W. Oh, I forgot. Of course, do have it. What a wonderful chance our names being the same!

Mrs. E. Quite wonderful. Thanks—it will always remind me of you.
(*Shakes hands with her.*)

(*Enter Parker.*)

Parker. Lord Augustus Lorton. Mrs. Erlynne's carriage has come.

(*Enter Lord A.*)

Lord A. Good-morning, dear boy. Good-morning, Lady Windermere. (*Sees Mrs. E.*) Mrs. Erlynne!

Mrs. E. How do you do, Lord Augustus? Are you quite well this morning?

Lord A. (*Coldly.*) Quite well, thank you, Mrs. Erlynne.

Mrs. E. You don't look at all well, Lord Augustus. You stop up too late—it is so bad for you. You really should take more care of yourself. Good-bye, Lord Windermere. (*Goes towards door with a bow to Lord A. Suddenly smiles, and looks back at him.*) Lord Augustus! Won't you see me to my carriage? You might carry the fan.

Lord W. Allow me!

Mrs. E. No, I want Lord Augustus. I have a special message for the dear Duchess. Won't you carry the fan, Lord Augustus?

Lord A. If you really desire it, Mrs. Erlynne.

Mrs. E. (*Laughing.*) Of course I do. You'll carry it so gracefully. You would carry off anything gracefully, dear Lord Augustus.

(*When she reaches the door she looks back for a moment at Lady W. Their eyes meet. Then she turns, and exit c., followed by Lord A.*)

Lady W. You will never speak against Mrs. Erlynne again, Arthur, will you?

Lord W. (*Gravely.*) She is better than one thought her.

Lady W. She is better than I am.

Lord W. (*Smiling as he strokes her hair.*) Child, you and she belong to different worlds. Into your world evil has never entered.

Lady W. Don't say that, Arthur. There is the same world for all of us, and good and evil, sin and innocence, go through it hand in hand. To shut one's eyes to half of life that one may live securely is as though one blinded oneself that one might walk with more safety in a land of pit and precipice.

Lord W. (*Moves down with her.*) Darling, why do you say that?

Lady W. (*Sits on sofa.*) Because I, who had shut my eyes to life, came to the brink. And one who had separated us——

Lord W. We were never parted.

Lady W. We never must be again. Oh, Arthur, don't love me less, and I will trust you more. I will trust you absolutely. Let us go to Selby. In the Rose Garden at Selby, the roses are white and red.

(*Enter Lord A. c.*)

Lord A. Arthur, she has explained everything! (*Lady W. looks horribly frightened. Lord W. starts. Lord A. takes Lord W. by the arm, and brings him to front of stage.*) My dear fellow, she has explained every demned thing. We all wronged her immensely. It was entirely for my sake she went to Darlington's rooms—called first at the club. Fact is, wanted to put me out of suspense, and being told I had gone on, followed—naturally—frightened when she heard a lot of men coming in—retired to another room—I assure you, most gratifying to me, the whole thing. We all behaved brutally to her. She is just the woman for me. Suits me down to the ground. All the condition she makes is that we live out of England—a very good thing, too!—Demmed clubs, demmed climate, demmed cooks, demmed everything! Sick of it all.

Lady W. (*Frightened.*) Has Mrs. Erlynne——?

Lord A. (*Advancing towards her with a bow.*) Yes; Lady Windermere, Mrs. Erlynne has done me the honor of accepting my hand.

Lord W. Well, you are certainly marrying a very clever woman.

Lady W. (*Taking her husband's hand.*) Ah! you're marrying a very good woman.

CURTAIN.

ARTHUR WING PINERO

THE SECOND MRS. TANQUERAY

Sir Arthur Wing Pinero (1855–1934), with a Portuguese name (the last two syllables like "Nero") and partly of Jewish descent, came of a family of lawyers and government employees settled in England for some generations. He learned the theater from front to back, at first as an actor, then at twenty-two beginning his life-long activity as a playwright, and regularly directing the production of his own plays. These he wrote by the score, of many kinds, plays of sentiment, comedies, farces, seriously and sometimes tragically realistic plays of contemporary English society. Among the most notable of such plays as these last are *The Notorious Mrs. Ebbsmith, Iris,* and *Mid-Channel;* but his fame had been already made by *The Second Mrs. Tanqueray.* This appeared in 1893, and has been credited with beginning the "modern" English drama, Wilde being more reminiscent of two centuries earlier. It was in these last plays that he was most interested; having become independent through his first great success in 1888, he then felt free "to write great plays regardless of the predilections of the public." But (whether they were "great" or not) the public followed him.

The chief influences behind *The Second Mrs. Tanqueray* (aside from that of the Robertson tradition) are foreign. On structure the influence is that of the French drama of Eugène Scribe, Alexandre Dumas the younger, and others,—the "well-made play" (*la pièce bien faite*), with its emphasis on close-knit, economical, clear and logical construction and motivation. The Norwegian Ibsen had for some time been ardently admired and fiercely attacked in England. Here we see followed his air of fatefulness, his seriousness, his everyday people, his inward rather than outward action.

An illusion of fatefulness in this play is secured partly by the abundant dramatic irony, in possible but not inevitable incidents giving the illusion of prearrangement by an ironic or warning destiny; to look merely at the first act, Drummle's censorious account of George Orreyed's marriage, Aubrey's quixotic burning of the letter which would have forewarned him against Ardale, his receipt too late of the news that his daughter was coming to remove his loneliness. The accumulation of such incidents, though perfectly possible, and undoubtedly impressive, may convey to the cool and critical observer an air of artificiality in plotting. The same illusion of fatefulness is produced by the fact that the people on the whole are the weak and foolish people who in life are at the mercy of circumstances. Without patience and good judgment, they can see no solution to their problems except that which leads straight to ruin. But fate is too majestic a word for what ruins these people. Ellean is not of this sort; the Ursuline nuns have done their work well; but she has been kept fresh only by a consistent policy of management and deception, of keeping her "ignorant of evil." This treatment of the one promising, intelligent and strong member of her family, and Aubrey's attempt in the fourth act to force her to relinquish her betrothed merely because he says she must, are among the reasons why a later generation does not gladly acquiesce in the story. Pinero avoids the error of showing any partizanship for her. Needless to analyze Paula; with all her courage and generous impulses, when after no long delay she is on the verge of securing some of the social recognition which is what she most desires, she pettishly throws away the chance. Aubrey, after every opportunity to know his world, attributes to Paula virtues of which she shows little sign, and underrates the difficulty of securing for her the recognition which to him also is the be-all and the end-all; he is fussy and obviously idle, and in an emergency his chief idea is to smooth things over on the surface by deception. The extreme contrast between his first wife and his second justifies the suspicion that he is deceiving himself as to his "temperate affection" for the second. The situation of his young daughter wishing to marry a man who had been his wife's lover is in good truth a difficult one; but he takes in haste the wrong turning, not recognizing that in fact his emotion is largely due to jealousy of his wife's past with her lover. Indeed jealousy is one of the chief moving forces of the whole play, with Ellean's natural jealousy of her lover's past with the wife, and with Paula's determination to force the girl's affections to herself and to keep her to herself. But these persons, if not admirable, are lifelike. The minor characters are sketched as firmly if more simply, and perform essential functions not only in the plot but to interpret the chief personages; Mrs. Cortelyon shows how far Paula has fallen, Lady Orreyed how much farther she might have fallen.

The fact is that the rock-bottom of reality on which the play rests is not the fundamental elements of human nature, but the sometimes temporary assumptions and standards of Society,—that English upper-class society late in Queen Victoria's reign which had little to do but amuse itself; and the treatment of these assumptions all through as if they were eternal throws at times an air of triviality and unreality over the play. The essential triviality of most of the people, also, keeps their mental agonies, genuine and intense though they are, from rising to high tragedy; we can watch them with no more than a sense of pathos and compassion. We could accept the play better had it an undercurrent of satire; but though no doubt Pinero realized what poor creatures the chief characters are (except Ellean), he gives no sign. All this is not to put him in the class of dramatists of snobbery, like Wilde; he wrote mostly of the upper class because he and his audience found them attractive and their life complex. Such people's problems of which he liked to write were the problems of sex; less as personal and affecting the depths of men's and women's nature than as the clash of moral and social convention with newer attitudes and individual desire for freedom. Pinero may be called the creator of the "problem play" in English, the problem being usually what to do in such trying situations. The solution or (as here) warning is always such as would be approved by such people.

The Second Mrs. Tanqueray must be regarded less as a "slice of life" than as a work of art. Pinero was not a preacher, and does not even disclose his own opinions; he presents problems, but no propaganda. As a work of art the play is almost beyond criticism. The people are drawn with the utmost consistency and firmness of outline. While we should not demand that every word and act shall be inevitable for such people, assuredly these are always probable and in character; we have already even paid the author the compliment of attributing to his people characteristic traits of which he himself may not have been entirely conscious. The dialogue is admirable,—lifelike (though, as it should be, more polished than in life), without wasted words, significant, often brilliant and witty, yet without visible artifice to admit the wit and brilliance. The dialogue never climbs out of its proper function as a means, not an end in itself. The best speeches, as usually in the greatest drama, are of simple words which owe their poignancy to the situation, like Ellean's heartrending "If I 'd only been merciful!" with which the play ends. Best of all is the structure, which gives keen pleasure to one who enjoys detecting a skilled writer at work. Especially admirable is the opening act, with its lucid but gradual exposition of the situation and its revelation of the characters through a series of completely natural conversations and unexpected significant incidents. Later the very disappearance of Jayne and Misquith from the play shows how complete is the Tanquerays' social exile. Every incident, almost every speech, telling in itself, contributes to the seemingly inexorable march of destiny, to the revelation of character and the closing in of disaster, down to the final almost unbearable accumulation, the sheltered Ellean's first hideous introduction to human evil and pain.

The Second Mrs. Tanqueray will serve as a favorable specimen of the rejuvenated modern prose drama, though in comparison with the enormous variety and far greater freedom and daring of its successors as to subjects and technique even this play may now seem confined. Fully to follow this newer drama, with its ablest representative George Bernard Shaw, and still later dramatists, would take us into the twentieth century and beyond the frontiers of this book.

THE SECOND MRS. TANQUERAY

PERSONS

Aubrey Tanqueray
Paula
Ellean
Cayley Drummle
Mrs. Cortelyon
Captain Hugh Ardale
Gordon Jayne, M.D.
Frank Misquith, Q.C., M.P.
Sir George Orreyed, Bart.
Lady Orreyed
Morse

The Present Day.

The Scene of the First Act is laid at Mr. Tanqueray's rooms, No. 2 x, The Albany, in the month of November; the occurrences of the succeeding acts take place at his house, "Highercoombe," near Willowmere, Surrey, during the early part of the following year.

THE FIRST ACT.

Aubrey Tanqueray's Chambers in the Albany—a richly and tastefully decorated room, elegantly and luxuriously furnished: on the right a large pair of doors opening into another room, on the left at the further end of the room a small door leading to a bed-chamber. A circular table is laid for a dinner for four persons, which has now reached the stage of dessert and coffee. Everything in the apartment suggests wealth and refinement. The fire is burning brightly.

Aubrey Tanqueray, Misquith, and Jayne are seated at the dinner-table. Aubrey is forty-two, handsome, winning in manner, his speech and bearing retaining some of the qualities of young-manhood. Misquith is about forty-seven, genial and portly. Jayne is a year or two Misquith's senior; soft-speaking and precise—in appearance a type of the prosperous town physician. Morse, Aubrey's servant, places a little cabinet of cigars and the spirit-lamp on the table beside Aubrey and goes out.

Misquith. Aubrey, it is a pleasant yet dreadful fact to contemplate, but it 's nearly fifteen years since I first dined with you. You lodged in Piccadilly in those days, over a hat-shop. Jayne, I met you at that dinner, and Cayley Drummle.

Jayne. Yes, yes. What a pity it is that Cayley isn't here to-night.

Aubrey. Confound the old gossip! His empty chair has been staring us in the face all through dinner. I ought to have told Morse to take it away.

Misquith. Odd, his sending no excuse.

Aubrey. I 'll walk round to his lodgings later on and ask after him.

Misquith. I 'll go with you.

Jayne. So will I.

Aubrey. (*Opening the cigar-cabinet.*) Doctor, it 's useless to tempt you, I know. Frank— (*Misquith and Aubrey smoke.*) I particularly wished Cayley Drummle to be one of us to-night. You two fellows and Cayley are my closest, my best friends—

Misquith. My dear Aubrey!

Jayne. I rejoice to hear you say so.

Aubrey. And I wanted to see the three of you round this table. You can't guess the reason.

Misquith. You desired to give us a most excellent dinner.

Jayne. Obviously.

Aubrey. (*Hesitatingly.*) Well—I— (*Glancing at the clock*)—Cayley won't turn up now.

Jayne. H'm, hardly.

Aubrey. Then you two shall hear it. Doctor, Frank, this is the last time we are to meet in these rooms.

Jayne. The last time?

Misquith. You 're going to leave the Albany?

Aubrey. Yes. You 've heard me speak of a house I built in the country years ago, haven't you?

Misquith. In Surrey.

Aubrey. Well, when my wife died I cleared out of that house and let it. I think of trying the place again.

Misquith. But you 'll go raving mad if ever you find yourself down there alone.

Aubrey. Ah, but I sha'n't be alone, and that 's what I wanted to tell you. I 'm going to be married.

Jayne. Going to be married?

Misquith. Married?

Aubrey. Yes—to-morrow.

Jayne. To-morrow?

Misquith. You take my breath away! My dear fellow, I—I—of course, I congratulate you.

Jayne. And—and—so do I—heartily.

Aubrey. Thanks—thanks.

(*There is a moment or two of embarrassment.*)

Misquith. Er—ah—this is an excellent cigar.

Jayne. Ah—um—your coffee is remarkable.

Aubrey. Look here; I dare say you two old friends think this treatment very strange, very unkind. So I want you to understand me. You know a marriage often cools friendships. What 's the usual course of things? A man's engagement is given out, he is congratulated, complimented upon his choice; the church is filled with troops of friends, and he goes away happily to a chorus of good wishes. He comes back, sets up house in town or country, and thinks to resume the old associations, the old companionships. My dear Frank, my dear good doctor, it 's very seldom that it can be done. Generally, a worm has begun to eat its way into those hearty, unreserved, pre-nuptial friendships; a damnable constraint sets in and acts like a wasting disease; and so, believe me, in nine cases out of ten a man's marriage severs for him more close ties than it forms.

Misquith. Well, my dear Aubrey, I earnestly hope—

Aubrey. I know what you 're going to say, Frank. I hope so, too. In the meantime let 's face dangers. I 've reminded you of the *usual* course of things, but my marriage isn't even the conventional sort of marriage likely to satisfy society. Now, Cayley 's a bachelor, but you two men have wives. By-the-by, my love to Mrs. Misquith and to Mrs. Jayne when you get home—don't forget that. Well, your wives may not—like—the lady I 'm going to marry.

Jayne. Aubrey, forgive me for suggesting that the lady you are going to marry may not like our wives—mine at least; I beg your pardon, Frank.

Aubrey. Quite so; then I must go the way my wife goes.

Misquith. Come, come, pray don't let us anticipate that either side will be called upon to make such a sacrifice.

Aubrey. Yes, yes, let us anticipate it. And let us make up our minds to have no slow bleeding-to-death of our friendship. We 'll end a pleasant chapter here to-night, and after to-night start afresh. When my wife and I settle down at Willowmere it 's possible that we shall all come together. But if this isn't to be, for Heaven's sake let us recognise that it is simply because it *can't* be, and not wear hypocritical faces and suffer and be wretched. Doctor, Frank—(*Holding out his hands, one to Misquith, the other to Jayne*)—good luck to all of us!

Misquith. But—but—do I understand we are to ask nothing? Not even the lady's name, Aubrey?

Aubrey. The lady, my dear Frank, belongs to the next chapter, and in that her name is Mrs. Aubrey Tanqueray.

Jayne. (*Raising his coffee-cup.*) Then, in an old-fashioned way, I propose a toast. Aubrey, Frank, I give you "The Next Chapter!"

(*They drink the toast, saying, "The Next Chapter!"*)

Aubrey. Doctor, find a comfortable chair; Frank, you too. As we 're going to turn out by-and-by, let me scribble a couple of notes now while I think of them.

Misquith and *Jayne.* Certainly—yes, yes.

Aubrey. It might slip my memory when I get back.

(*Aubrey sits at a writing-table at the other end of the room, and writes.*)

Jayne. (*To Misquith in a whisper.*) Frank— (*Misquith quietly leaves his chair, and sits nearer to Jayne.*) What is all this? Simply a morbid crank of Aubrey's with regard to ante-nuptial acquaintances?

Misquith. H'm! Did you notice *one* expression he used?

Jayne. Let me think—

Misquith. "My marriage is not even the conventional sort of marriage likely to satisfy society."

Jayne. Bless me, yes! What does that suggest?

Misquith. That he has a particular rather than a general reason for anticipating estrangement from his friends, I 'm afraid.

Jayne. A horrible *mésalliance!* A dairymaid who has given him a glass of milk during a day's hunting, or a little anæmic shopgirl! Frank, I 'm utterly wretched!

Misquith. My dear Jayne, speaking in absolute confidence, I have never been more profoundly depressed in my life.

(*Morse enters.*)

Morse. (*Announcing.*) Mr. Drummle.

(*Cayley Drummle enters briskly. He is a neat little man of about five-and-forty, in manner bright, airy, debonair, but with an undercurrent of seriousness.*)

(*Morse retires.*)

Drummle. I 'm in disgrace; nobody realises that more thoroughly than I do. Where 's my host?

Aubrey. (*Who has risen.*) Cayley.

Drummle. (*Shaking hands with him.*) Don't speak to me till I have tendered my explanation. A harsh word from anybody would unman me.

(*Misquith and Jayne shake hands with Drummle.*)

Aubrey. Have you dined?

Drummle. No—unless you call a bit of fish, a cutlet, and a pancake dining.

Aubrey. Cayley, this is disgraceful.

Jayne. Fish, a cutlet, and a pancake will require a great deal of explanation.

Misquith. Especially the pancake. My dear friend, your case looks miserably weak.

Drummle. Hear me! hear me!

Jayne. Now then!
Misquith. Come!
Aubrey. Well!
Drummle. It so happens that to-night I was exceptionally early in dressing for dinner.
Misquith. For which dinner—the fish and cutlet?
Drummle. For *this* dinner, of course—really, Frank! At a quarter to eight, in fact, I found myself trimming my nails, with ten minutes to spare. Just then enter my man with a note—would I hasten, as fast as cab could carry me, to old Lady Orreyed in Bruton Street?—"sad trouble." Now, recollect, please, I had ten minutes on my hands, old Lady Orreyed was a very dear friend of my mother's, and was in some distress.
Aubrey. Cayley, come to the fish and cutlet!
Misquith and *Jayne.* Yes, yes, and the pancake!
Drummle. Upon my word! Well, the scene in Bruton Street beggars description; the women servants looked scared, the men drunk; and there was poor old Lady Orreyed on the floor of her boudoir like Queen Bess among her pillows.
Aubrey. What 's the matter?
Drummle. (*To everybody.*) You know George Orreyed?
Misquith. Yes.
Jayne. I 've met him.
Drummle. Well, he 's a thing of the past.
Aubrey. Not dead!
Drummle. Certainly, in the worst sense. He 's married Mabel Hervey.
Misquith. What!
Drummle. It 's true—this morning. The poor mother showed me his letter—a dozen curt words, and some of those ill-spelt.
Misquith. (*Walking up to the fireplace.*) I 'm very sorry.
Jayne. Pardon my ignorance—who *was* Mabel Hervey?
Drummle. You don't—? Oh, of course not. Miss Hervey—Lady Orreyed, as she now is—was a lady who would have been, perhaps has been, described in the reports of the Police or the Divorce Court as an actress. Had she belonged to a lower stratum of our advanced civilisation she would, in the event of judicial inquiry, have defined her calling with equal justification as that of a dressmaker. To do her justice, she is a type of a class which is immortal. Physically, by the strange caprice of creation, curiously beautiful; mentally, she lacks even the strength of deliberate viciousness. Paint her portrait, it would symbolise a creature perfectly patrician; lance a vein of her superbly-modelled arm, you would get the poorest *vin ordinaire!* Her affections, emotions, impulses, her very existence—a burlesque! Flaxen, five-and-twenty, and feebly frolicsome; anybody's, in less gentle society I should say everybody's, property! That, doctor, was Miss Hervey who is the new Lady Orreyed. Dost thou like the picture?
Misquith. Very good, Cayley! Bravo!
Aubrey. (*Laying his hand on Drummle's shoulder.*) You 'd scarcely believe it, Jayne, but none of us really know anything about this lady, our gay young friend here, I suspect, least of all.
Drummle. Aubrey, I applaud your chivalry.
Aubrey. And perhaps you 'll let me finish a couple of letters which Frank and Jayne have given me leave to write. (*Returning to the writing-table.*) Ring for what you want, like a good fellow!

(*Aubrey resumes his writing.*)

Misquith. (*To Drummle.*) Still, the fish and cutlet remain unexplained.
Drummle. Oh, the poor old woman was so weak that I insisted upon her taking some food, and felt there was nothing for it but to sit down opposite her. The fool! the blackguard!
Misquith. Poor Orreyed! Well, he 's gone under for a time.
Drummle. For a time! My dear Frank, I tell you he has absolutely ceased to be. (*Aubrey, who has been writing busily, turns his head towards the speakers and listens. His lips are set, and there is a frown upon his face.*) For all practical purposes you may regard him as the late George Orreyed. To-morrow the very characteristics of his speech, as we remember them, will have become obsolete.
Jayne. But surely, in the course of years, he and his wife will outlive—
Drummle. No, no, doctor, don't try to upset one of my settled beliefs. You may dive into many waters, but there is *one* social Dead Sea—!
Jayne. Perhaps you 're right.
Drummle. Right! Good God! I wish you could prove me otherwise! Why, for years I 've been sitting, and watching and waiting.

Misquith. You 're in form to-night, Cayley. May we ask where you 've been in the habit of squandering your useful leisure?

Drummle. Where? On the shore of that same sea.

Misquith. And, pray, what have you been waiting for?

Drummle. For some of my best friends *to come up.* (*Aubrey utters a half-stifled exclamation of impatience; then he hurriedly gathers up his papers from the writing-table. The three men turn to him.*) Eh?

Aubrey. Oh, I—I 'll finish my letters in the other room if you 'll excuse me for five minutes. Tell Cayley the news.

(*He goes out.*)

Drummle. (*Hurrying to the door.*) My dear fellow, my jabbering has disturbed you! I 'll never talk again as long as I live!

Misquith. Close the door, Cayley.

(*Drummle shuts the door.*)

Jayne. Cayley—

Drummle. (*Advancing to the dinner table.*) A smoke, a smoke, or I perish!

(*Selects a cigar from the little cabinet.*)

Jayne. Cayley, marriages are in the air.

Drummle. Are they? Discover the bacillus, doctor, and destroy it.

Jayne. I mean, among our friends.

Drummle. Oh, Nugent Warrinder's engagement to Lady Alice Tring. I 've heard of that. They 're not to be married till the spring.

Jayne. Another marriage that concerns us a little takes place to-morrow.

Drummle. Whose marriage?

Jayne. Aubrey's.

Drummle. Aub—! (*Looking towards Misquith.*) Is it a joke?

Misquith. No.

Drummle. (*Looking from Misquith to Jayne.*) To whom?

Misquith. He doesn't tell us.

Jayne. We three were asked here to-night to receive the announcement. Aubrey has some theory that marriage is likely to alienate a man from his friends, and it seems to me he has taken the precaution to wish us good-bye.

Misquith. No, no.

Jayne. Practically, surely.

Drummle. (*Thoughtfully.*) Marriage in general, does he mean, or *this* marriage?

Jayne. That 's the point. Frank says—

Misquith. No, no, no; I feared it suggested—

Jayne. Well, well. (*To Drummle.*) What do you think of it?

Drummle. (*After a slight pause.*) Is there a light there? (*Lighting his cigar.*) He—wraps the lady—in mystery—you say?

Misquith. Most modestly.

Drummle. Aubrey 's—not—a very—young man.

Jayne. Forty-three.

Drummle. Ah! *L'âge critique!*

Misquith. A dangerous age—yes, yes.

Drummle. When you two fellows go home, do you mind leaving me behind here?

Misquith. Not at all.

Jayne. By all means.

Drummle. All right. (*Anxiously.*) Deuce take it, the man's second marriage mustn't be another mistake!

(*With his head bent he walks up to the fire-place.*)

Jayne. You knew him in his short married life, Cayley. Terribly unsatisfactory, wasn't it?

Drummle. Well—(*Looking at the door.*) I quite closed that door?

Misquith. Yes.

(*Settles himself on the sofa; Jayne is seated in an arm-chair.*)

Drummle. (*Smoking with his back to the fire.*) He married a Miss Herriott; that was in the year eighteen—confound dates—twenty years ago. She was a lovely creature—by Jove, she was; by religion a Roman Catholic. She was one of your cold sort, you know—all marble arms and black velvet. I remember her with painful distinctness as the only woman who ever made me nervous.

Misquith. Ha, ha!

Drummle. He loved her—to distraction, as they say. Jupiter, how fervently that poor devil courted her! But I don't believe she allowed him even to squeeze her fingers. She *was* an iceberg! As for kissing, the mere contact would have given him chapped lips. However, he married her and took her away, the latter greatly to my relief.

Jayne. Abroad, you mean?

Drummle. Eh? Yes. I imagine he gratified her by renting a villa in Lapland, but I don't know. After a while they returned, and then I saw how wofully Aubrey had miscalculated results.

Jayne. Miscalculated—?

Drummle. He had reckoned, poor wretch, that in the early days of marriage she would thaw. But she didn't. I used to picture him closing his doors and making up the fire in the hope of seeing her features relax. Bless her, the thaw never set in! I believe she kept a thermometer in her stays and always registered ten degrees below zero. However, in time a child came—a daughter.

Jayne. Didn't that—?

Drummle. Not a bit of it; it made matters worse. Frightened at her failure to stir up in him some sympathetic religious belief, she determined upon strong measures with regard to the child. He opposed her for a miserable year or so, but she wore him down, and the insensible little brat was placed in a convent, first in France, then in Ireland. Not long afterwards the mother died, strangely enough, of fever, the only warmth, I believe, that ever came to that woman's body.

Misquith. Don't, Cayley!

Jayne. The child is living, we know.

Drummle. Yes, if you choose to call it living. Miss Tanqueray—a young woman of nineteen now—is in the Loretto convent at Armagh. She professes to have found her true vocation in a religious life, and within a month or two will take final vows.

Misquith. He ought to have removed his daughter from the convent when the mother died.

Drummle. Yes, yes, but absolutely at the end there was reconciliation between husband and wife, and she won his promise that the child should complete her conventual education. He reaped his reward. When he attempted to gain his girl's confidence and affection he was too late; he found he was dealing with the spirit of the mother. You remember his visit to Ireland last month?

Jayne. Yes.

Drummle. That was to wish his girl good-bye.

Misquith. Poor fellow!

Drummle. He sent for me when he came back. I think he must have had a lingering hope that the girl would relent—would come to life, as it were—at the last moment, for, for an hour or so, in this room. he was terribly shaken. I'm sure he'd clung to that hope from the persistent way in which he kept breaking off in his talk to repeat one dismal word, as if he couldn't realise his position without dinning this damned word into his head.

Jayne. What word was that?

Drummle. Alone—alone.

(*Aubrey enters.*)

Aubrey. A thousand apologies!

Drummle. (*Gaily.*) We are talking about you, my dear Aubrey.

(*During the telling of the story, Misquith has risen and gone to the fire, and Drummle has thrown himself full-length on the sofa. Aubrey now joins Misquith and Jayne.*)

Aubrey. Well, Cayley, are you surprised?

Drummle. Surp—! I haven't been surprised for twenty years.

Aubrey. And you're not angry with me?

Drummle. Angry! (*Rising.*) Because you considerately withhold the name of a lady with whom it is now the object of my life to become acquainted? My dear fellow, you pique my curiosity, you give zest to my existence! And as for a wedding, who on earth wants to attend that familiar and probably draughty function? Ugh! My cigar's out.

Aubrey. Let's talk about something else.

Misquith. (*Looking at his watch.*) Not to-night, Aubrey.

Aubrey. My dear Frank!

Misquith. I go up to Scotland to-morrow, and there are some little matters—

Jayne. I am off too.

Aubrey. No, no.

Jayne. I must: I have to give a look to a case in Clifford Street on my way home.

Aubrey. (*Going to the door.*) Well! (*Misquith and Jayne exchange looks with Drummle. Opening the door and calling.*) Morse, hats and coats! I shall write to you all next week from Genoa or Florence. Now, doctor, Frank, remember, my love to Mrs. Misquith and to Mrs. Jayne!

(*Morse enters with hats and coats.*)

Misquith and *Jayne.* Yes, yes—yes, yes.

Aubrey. And your young people!

(*As Misquith and Jayne put on their coats there is the clatter of careless talk.*)

Jayne. Cayley, I meet you at dinner on Sunday.

Drummle. At the Stratfields'. That's very pleasant.

Misquith. (*Putting on his coat with Aubrey's aid.*) Ah-h!
Aubrey. What 's wrong?
Misquith. A twinge. Why didn't I go to Aix in August?
Jayne. (*Shaking hands with Drummle.*) Good-night, Cayley.
Drummle. Good-night, my dear doctor!
Misquith. (*Shaking hands with Drummle.*) Cayley, are you in town for long?
Drummle. Dear friend, I 'm nowhere for long. Good-night.
Misquith. Good-night.

(*Aubrey, Jayne, and Misquith go out, followed by Morse; the hum of talk is continued outside.*)

Aubrey. A cigar, Frank?
Misquith. No, thank you.
Aubrey. Going to walk, doctor?
Jayne. If Frank will.
Misquith. By all means.
Aubrey. It 's a cold night.

(*The door is closed. Drummle remains standing with his coat on his arm and his hat in his hand.*)

Drummle. (*To himself, thoughtfully.*) Now then! What the devil!—

(*Aubrey returns.*)

Aubrey. (*Eyeing Drummle a little awkwardly.*) Well, Cayley?
Drummle. Well, Aubrey?

(*Aubrey walks up to the fire and stands looking into it.*)

Aubrey. You 're not going, old chap?
Drummle. (*Sitting.*) No.
Aubrey. (*After a slight pause, with a forced laugh.*) Hah! Cayley, I never thought I should feel—shy—with you.
Drummle. Why do you?
Aubrey. Never mind.
Drummle. Now, I can quite understand a man wishing to be married in the dark, as it were.
Aubrey. You can?
Drummle. In your place I should very likely adopt the same course.
Aubrey. You think so?
Drummle. And if I intended marrying a lady not prominently in society, as I presume you do—as I presume you do—
Aubrey. Well?
Drummle. As I presume you do, I 'm not sure that *I* should tender her for preliminary dissection at afternoon tea-tables.
Aubrey. No?
Drummle. In fact, there is probably only one person—were I in your position tonight—with whom I should care to chat the matter over.
Aubrey. Who 's that?
Drummle. Yourself, of course. (*Going to Aubrey and standing beside him.*) Of course, yourself, old friend.
Aubrey. (*After a pause.*) I must seem a brute to you, Cayley. But there are some acts which are hard to explain, hard to defend—
Drummle. To defend—
Aubrey. Some acts which one must trust to time to put right.

(*Drummle watches him for a moment, then takes up his hat and coat.*)

Drummle. Well, I 'll be moving.
Aubrey. Cayley! Confound you and your old friendship! Do you think I forget it? Put your coat down! Why did you stay behind here? Cayley, the lady I am going to marry is the lady—who is known as—Mrs. Jarman.

(*There is a pause.*)

Drummle. (*In a low voice.*) Mrs. Jarman! are you serious?

(*He walks up to the fireplace, where he leans upon the mantelpiece uttering something like a groan.*)

Aubrey. As you 've got this out of me I give you leave to say all you care to say. Come, we 'll be plain with each other. You know Mrs. Jarman?
Drummle. I first met her at—what does it matter?
Aubrey. Yes, yes, everything! Come!
Drummle. I met her at Homburg, two—three seasons ago.
Aubrey. Not as Mrs. Jarman?
Drummle. No.
Aubrey. She was then—?
Drummle. Mrs. Dartry.
Aubrey. Yes. She has also seen you in London, she says.
Drummle. Certainly.
Aubrey. In Alford Street. Go on.
Drummle. Please!
Aubrey. I insist.
Drummle. (*With a slight shrug of the shoulders.*) Some time last year I was asked by a man to sup at his house, one night after the theatre.
Aubrey. Mr. Selwyn Ethurst—a bachelor.
Drummle. Yes.
Aubrey. You were surprised therefore to

find Mr. Ethurst aided in his cursed hospitality by a lady.

Drummle. I was unprepared.

Aubrey. The lady you had known as Mrs. Dartry? (*Drummle inclines his head silently.*) There is something of a yachting cruise in the Mediterranean too, is there not?

Drummle. I joined Peter Jarman's yacht at Marseilles, in the spring, a month before he died.

Aubrey. Mrs. Jarman was on board?

Drummle. She was a kind hostess.

Aubrey. And an old acquaintance?

Drummle. Yes.

Aubrey. You have told your story.

Drummle. With your assistance.

Aubrey. I have put you to the pain of telling it to show you that this is not the case of a blind man entrapped by an artful woman. Let me add that Mrs. Jarman has no legal right to that name; that she is simply Miss Ray—Miss Paula Ray.

Drummle. (*After a pause.*) I should like to express my regret, Aubrey, for the way in which I spoke of George Orreyed's marriage.

Aubrey. You mean you compare Lady Orreyed with Miss Ray? (*Drummle is silent.*) Oh, of course! To you, Cayley, all women who have been roughly treated, and who dare to survive by borrowing a little of our philosophy, are alike. You see in the crowd of the ill-used only one pattern; you can't detect the shades of goodness, intelligence, even nobility there. Well, how should you? The crowd is dimly lighted! And, besides, yours is the way of the world.

Drummle. My dear Aubrey, I *live* in the world.

Aubrey. The name we give our little parish of St. James's.

Drummle. (*Laying a hand on Aubrey's shoulder.*) And you are quite prepared, my friend, to forfeit the esteem of your little parish?

Aubrey. I avoid mortification by shifting from one parish to another. I give up Pall Mall for the Surrey hills; leave off varnishing my boots, and double the thickness of the soles.

Drummle. And your skin—do you double the thickness of that also?

Aubrey. I know you think me a fool, Cayley—you needn't infer that I'm a coward into the bargain. No! I know what I'm doing, and I do it deliberately, defiantly. I'm alone: I injure no living soul by the step I'm going to take; and so you can't urge the one argument which might restrain me. Of course, I don't expect you to think compassionately, fairly even, of the woman whom I—whom I am drawn to—

Drummle. My dear Aubrey, I assure you I consider Mrs.—Miss Jarman—Mrs. Ray—Miss Ray—delightful. But I confess there is a form of chivalry which I gravely distrust, especially in a man of —our age.

Aubrey. Thanks. I've heard you say that from forty till fifty a man is at heart either a stoic or a satyr.

Drummle. (*Protestingly.*) Ah! now—

Aubrey. I am neither. I have a temperate, honourable affection for Mrs. Jarman. She has never met a man who has treated her well— I intend to treat her well. That's all. And in a few years, Cayley, if you've not quite forsaken me, I'll prove to you that it's possible to rear a life of happiness, of good repute, on a—miserable foundation.

Drummle. (*Offering his hand.*) Do prove it!

Aubrey. (*Taking his hand.*) We have spoken too freely of—of Mrs. Jarman. I was excited—angry. Please forget it!

Drummle. My dear Aubrey, when we next meet I shall remember nothing but my respect for the lady who bears your name.

(*Morse enters, closing the door behind him carefully.*)

Aubrey What is it?

Morse. (*Hesitatingly.*) May I speak to you, sir? (*In an undertone.*) Mrs. Jarman, sir.

Aubrey. (*Softly to Morse.*) Mrs. Jarman! Do you mean she is at the lodge in her carriage?

Morse. No, sir—here. (*Aubrey looks towards Drummle, perplexed.*) There's a nice fire in your—in that room, sir.

(*Glancing in the direction of the door leading to the bedroom.*)

Aubrey. (*Between his teeth, angrily.*) Very well.

(*Morse retires.*)

Drummle. (*Looking at his watch.*) A quarter to eleven—horrible! (*Taking up his hat and coat.*) Must get to bed—up late every night this week. (*Aubrey assists Drummle with his coat.*) Thank you. Well, good-night, Aubrey. I feel

I 've been dooced serious, quite out of keeping with myself; pray overlook it.

Aubrey. (*Kindly.*) Ah, Cayley!

Drummle. (*Putting on a neck-handkerchief.*) And remember that, after all, I 'm merely a spectator in life; nothing more than a man at a play, in fact; only, like the old-fashioned playgoer, I love to see certain characters happy and comfortable at the finish. You understand?

Aubrey. I think I do.

Drummle. Then, for as long as you can, old friend, will you—keep a stall for me?

Aubrey. Yes, Cayley.

Drummle. (*Gaily.*) Ah, ha! Good-night! (*Bustling to the door.*) Don't bother! I 'll let myself out! Good-night! God bless yer!

(*He goes out; Aubrey follows him. Morse enters by the other door, carrying some unopened letters, which after a little consideration he places on the mantelpiece against the clock. Aubrey returns.*)

Aubrey. Yes?

Morse. You hadn't seen your letters that came by the nine o'clock post, sir; I 've put 'em where they 'll catch your eye by-and-by.

Aubrey. Thank you.

Morse. (*Hesitatingly.*) Gunter's cook and waiter have gone, sir. Would you prefer me to go to bed?

Aubrey. (*Frowning.*) Certainly not.

Morse. Very well, sir.

(*He goes out.*)

Aubrey. (*Opening the upper door.*) Paula! Paula!

(*Paula enters and throws her arms round his neck. She is a young woman of about twenty-seven: beautiful, fresh, innocent-looking. She is in superb evening dress.*)

Paula. Dearest!

Aubrey. Why have you come here?

Paula. Angry?

Aubrey. Yes—no. But it 's eleven o'clock.

Paula. (*Laughing.*) I know.

Aubrey. What on earth will Morse think?

Paula. Do you trouble yourself about what servants *think?*

Aubrey. Of course.

Paula. Goose! They 're only machines made to wait upon people—and to give evidence in the Divorce Court. (*Looking round.*) Oh, indeed! A snug little dinner!

Aubrey. Three men.

Paula. (*Suspiciously.*) Men?

Aubrey. Men.

Paula. (*Penitently.*) Ah! (*Sitting at the table.*) I 'm so hungry.

Aubrey. Let me get you some game pie, or some—

Paula. No, no, hungry for this. What beautiful fruit! I love fruit when it 's expensive. (*He clears a space on the table, places a plate before her, and helps her to fruit.*) I haven't dined, Aubrey dear.

Aubrey. My poor girl! Why?

Paula. In the first place, I forgot to order any dinner, and my cook, who has always loathed me, thought he 'd pay me out before he departed.

Aubrey. The beast!

Paula. That 's precisely what I—

Aubrey. No, Paula!

Paula. What I told my maid to call him. What next will you think of me?

Aubrey. Forgive me. You must be starved.

Paula. (*Eating fruit.*) I didn't care. As there was nothing to eat, I sat in my best frock, with my toes on the dining-room fender, and dreamt, oh, such a lovely dinner party.

Aubrey. Dear lonely little woman!

Paula. It was perfect. I saw you at the end of a very long table, opposite me, and we exchanged sly glances now and again over the flowers. We were host and hostess, Aubrey, and had been married about five years.

Aubrey. (*Kissing her hand.*) Five years.

Paula. And on each side of us was the nicest set imaginable—you know, dearest, the sort of men and women that can't be imitated.

Aubrey. Yes, yes. Eat some more fruit.

Paula. But I haven't told you the best part of my dream.

Aubrey. Tell me.

Paula. Well, although we had been married only such a few years, I seemed to know by the look on their faces that none of our guests had ever heard anything—anything—anything peculiar about the fascinating hostess.

Aubrey. That 's just how it will be, Paula. The world moves so quickly. That 's just how it will be.

Paula. (*With a little grimace.*) I wonder! (*Glancing at the fire.*) Ugh! Do throw another log on.

Aubrey. (*Mending the fire.*) There. But you mustn't be here long.

Paula. Hospitable wretch! I 've something important to tell you. No, stay where you are. (*Turning from him, her face averted.*) Look here, that was my dream, Aubrey; but the fire went out while I was dozing, and I woke up with a regular fit of the shivers. And the result of it all was that I ran upstairs and scribbled you a letter.

Aubrey. Dear baby!

Paula. Remain where you are. (*Taking a letter from her pocket.*) This is it. I 've given you an account of myself, furnished you with a list of my adventures since I—you know. (*Weighing the letter in her hand.*) I wonder if it would go for a penny. Most of it you 're acquainted with; *I 've* told you a good deal, haven't I?

Aubrey. Oh, Paula!

Paula. What I haven't told you I dare say you 've heard from others. But in case they 've omitted anything—the dears—it 's all here.

Aubrey. In Heaven's name, why must you talk like this to-night?

Paula. It may save discussion by-and-by, don't you think? (*Holding out the letter.*) There you are.

Aubrey. No, dear, no.

Paula. Take it. (*He takes the letter.*) Read it through after I 've gone, and then —read it again, and turn the matter over in your mind finally. And if, even at the very last moment, you feel you—oughtn't to go to church with me, send a messenger to Pont Street, any time before eleven to-morrow, telling me that you 're afraid, and I—I 'll take the blow.

Aubrey. Why, what—what do you think I am?

Paula. That 's it. It 's because I know you 're such a dear good fellow that I want to save you the chance of ever feeling sorry you married me. I really love you so much, Aubrey, that to save you that, I 'd rather you treated me as—as the others have done.

Aubrey. (*Turning from her with a cry.*) Oh!

Paula. (*After a slight pause.*) I suppose I 've shocked you. I can't help it if I have.

(*She sits, with assumed languor and indifference. He turns to her, advances, and kneels by her.*)

Aubrey. My dearest, you don't understand me I—I can't bear to hear you always talking about—what 's done with. I tell you I 'll never remember it; Paula, can't you dismiss it? Try. Darling, if we promise each other to forget, to forget, we 're bound to be happy. After all, it 's a mechanical matter; the moment a wretched thought enters your head, you quickly think of something bright—it depends on one's will. Shall I burn this, dear? (*Referring to the letter he holds in his hand.*) Let me, let me!

Paula. (*With a shrug of the shoulders.*) I don't suppose there 's much that 's new to you in it,—just as you like.

(*He goes to the fire and burns the letter.*)

Aubrey. There 's an end of it. (*Returning to her.*) What 's the matter?

Paula. (*Rising, coldly.*) Oh, nothing! I 'll go and put my cloak on.

Aubrey. (*Detaining her.*) What *is* the matter?

Paula. Well, I think you might have said, "You 're very generous, Paula," or at least, "Thank you, dear," when I offered to set you free.

Aubrey. (*Catching her in his arms.*) Ah!

Paula. Ah! ah! Ha! ha! It 's all very well, but you don't know what it cost me to make such an offer. I do so want to be married.

Aubrey. But you never imagined—?

Paula. Perhaps not. And yet I *did* think of what I 'd do at the end of our acquaintance if you had preferred to behave like the rest.

(*Taking a flower from her bodice.*)

Aubrey. Hush!

Paula. Oh, I forgot!

Aubrey. What would you have done when we parted?

Paula. Why, killed myself.

Aubrey. Paula, dear!

Paula. It 's true. (*Putting the flower in his buttonhole.*) Do you know, I feel certain I should make away with myself if anything serious happened to me.

Aubrey. Anything serious! What, has nothing ever been serious to you, Paula?

Paula. Not lately; not since a long while ago. I made up my mind then to have done with taking things seriously. If I hadn't, I— However, we won't talk about that.

Aubrey. But now, now, life will be different to you, won't it—quite different? Eh, dear?

Paula. Oh, yes, now. Only, Aubrey, mind you keep me always happy.
Aubrey. I will try to.
Paula. I know I couldn't swallow a second big dose of misery. I know that if ever I felt wretched again—truly wretched—I should take a leaf out of Connie Tirlemont's book. You remember? They found her—(*With a look of horror.*)
Aubrey. For God's sake, don't let your thoughts run on such things!
Paula. (*Laughing.*) Ha, ha, how scared you look! There, think of the time! Dearest, what will my coachman say? My cloak!

(*She runs off, gaily, by the upper door. Aubrey looks after her for a moment, then he walks up to the fire and stands warming his feet at the bars. As he does so he raises his head and observes the letters upon the mantelpiece. He takes one down quickly.*)

Aubrey. Ah! Ellean! (*Opening the letter and reading.*) "My dear father,—A great change has come over me. I believe my mother in Heaven has spoken to me, and counselled me to turn to you in your loneliness. At any rate, your words have reached my heart, and I no longer feel fitted for this solemn life. I am ready to take my place by you. Dear father, will you receive me?—Ellean."

(*Paula re-enters, dressed in a handsome cloak. He stares at her as if he hardly realises her presence.*)

Paula. What are you staring at? Don't you admire my cloak?
Aubrey. Yes.
Paula. Couldn't you wait till I 'd gone before reading your letters?
Aubrey. (*Putting the letter away.*) I beg your pardon.
Paula. Take me down-stairs to the carriage. (*Slipping her arm through his.*) How I tease you! To-morrow! I 'm so happy!

(*They go out.*)

THE SECOND ACT.

A morning-room in Aubrey Tanqueray's house, "Highercoombe," near Willowmere, Surrey—a bright and prettily furnished apartment of irregular shape, with double doors opening into a small hall at the back, another door on the left, and a large recessed window through which is obtained a view of extensive grounds. Everything about the room is charming and graceful. The fire is burning in the grate, and a small table is tastefully laid for breakfast. It is a morning in early spring, and the sun is streaming in through the window.

Aubrey and Paula are seated at breakfast, and Aubrey is silently reading his letters. Two servants, a man and a woman, hand dishes and then retire. After a little while Aubrey puts his letters aside and looks across to the window.

Aubrey. Sunshine! Spring!
Paula. (*Glancing at the clock.*) Exactly six minutes.
Aubrey. Six minutes?
Paula. Six minutes, Aubrey dear, since you made your last remark.
Aubrey. I beg your pardon: I was reading my letters. Have you seen Ellean this morning?
Paula. (*Coldly.*) Your last observation but one was about Ellean.
Aubrey. Dearest, what shall I talk about?
Paula. Ellean breakfasted two hours ago, Morgan tells me, and then went out walking with her dog.
Aubrey. She wraps up warmly, I hope; this sunshine is deceptive.
Paula. I ran about the lawn last night, after dinner, in satin shoes. Were you anxious about me?
Aubrey. Certainly.
Paula. (*Melting.*) Really?
Aubrey. You make me wretchedly anxious; you delight in doing incautious things. You are incurable.
Paula. Ah, what a beast I am! (*Going to him and kissing him, then glancing at the letters by his side.*) A letter from Cayley?
Aubrey. He is staying very near here, with Mrs.— Very near here.
Paula. With the lady whose chimneys we have the honour of contemplating from our windows?
Aubrey. With Mrs. Cortelyon—yes.
Paula. Mrs. Cortelyon! The woman who might have set the example of calling on me when we first threw out roots in this deadly-lively soil! Deuce take Mrs. Cortelyon!
Aubrey. Hush! my dear girl!
Paula. (*Returning to her seat.*) Oh, I know she 's an old acquaintance of yours

—and of the first Mrs. Tanqueray. And she joins the rest of 'em in slapping the second Mrs. Tanqueray in the face. However, I have my revenge—she 's six-and-forty, and I wish nothing worse to happen to any woman.

Aubrey. Well, she 's going to town, Cayley says here, and his visit 's at an end. He 's coming over this morning to call on you. Shall we ask him to transfer himself to us? Do say yes.

Paula. Yes.

Aubrey. (*Gladly.*) Ah, ha! old Cayley.

Paula. (*Coldly.*) He 'll amuse *you*.

Aubrey. And you too.

Paula. Because you find a companion, shall I be boisterously hilarious?

Aubrey. Come, come! He talks London, and you know you like that.

Paula. London! London or Heaven! which is farther from me!

Aubrey. Paula!

Paula. Oh! Oh, I am so bored, Aubrey!

Aubrey. (*Gathering up his letters and going to her, leaning over her shoulder.*) Baby, what can I do for you?

Paula. I suppose, nothing. You have done all you can for me.

Aubrey. What do you mean?

Paula. You have married me.

(*He walks away from her thoughtfully, to the writing table. As he places his letters on the table he sees an addressed letter, stamped for the post, lying on the blotting-book; he picks it up.*)

Aubrey. (*In an altered tone.*) You 've been writing this morning before breakfast?

Paula. (*Looking at him quickly, then away again.*) Er—that letter.

Aubrey. (*With the letter in his hand.*) To Lady Orreyed. Why?

Paula. Why not? Mabel 's an old friend of mine.

Aubrey. Are you—corresponding?

Paula. I heard from her yesterday. They 've just returned from the Riviera. She seems happy.

Aubrey. (*Sarcastically.*) That 's good news.

Paula. Why are you always so cutting about Mabel? She 's a kind-hearted girl. Everything 's altered; she even thinks of letting her hair go back to brown. She 's Lady Orreyed. She 's married to George. What 's the matter with her?

Aubrey. (*Turning away.*) Oh!

Paula. You drive me mad sometimes with the tone you take about things! Great goodness, if you come to that, George Orreyed's wife isn't a bit worse than yours! (*He faces her suddenly.*) I suppose I needn't have made that observation.

Aubrey. No, there was scarcely a necessity.

(*He throws the letter on to the table, and takes up the newspaper.*)

Paula. I am very sorry.

Aubrey. All right, dear.

Paula. (*Trifling with the letter.*) I—I 'd better tell you what I 've written. I meant to do so, of course. I—I 've asked the Orreyeds to come and stay with us. (*He looks at her, and lets the paper fall to the ground in a helpless way.*) George was a great friend of Cayley's; I 'm sure *he* would be delighted to meet them here.

Aubrey. (*Laughing mirthlessly.*) Ha, ha, ha! They say Orreyed has taken to tippling at dinner. Heavens above!

Paula. Oh! I 've no patience with you! You 'll kill me with this life! (*She selects some flowers from a vase on the table, cuts and arranges them, and fastens them in her bodice.*) What is my existence, Sunday to Saturday? In the morning, a drive down to the village, with the groom, to give my orders to the tradespeople. At lunch, you and Ellean. In the afternoon, a novel, the newspapers: if fine, another drive—*if* fine! Tea—you and Ellean. Then two hours of dusk; then dinner—you and Ellean. Then a game of Bésique, you and I, while Ellean reads a religious book in a dull corner. Then a yawn from me, another from you, a sigh from Ellean; three figures suddenly rise—"Good-night, good-night, good-night!" (*Imitating a kiss.*) "God bless you!" Ah!

Aubrey. Yes, yes, Paula—yes, dearest—that 's what it is *now*. But, by-and-by, if people begin to come round us—

Paula. Hah! That 's where we 've made the mistake, my friend Aubrey! (*Pointing to the window.*) Do you believe these people will *ever* come round us? Your former crony, Mrs. Cortelyon? Or the grim old vicar, or that wife of his whose huge nose is positively indecent? Or the Ullathornes, or the Gollans, or Lady William Petres? I know better! And when the young ones gradually take the place of the old, there will still remain the sacred tradition that the dreadful person who lives at the top of the hill is never, under any circumstances, to be called upon! And so we shall go on here, year in and year out, until the sap is run out of our lives, and we 're stale and dry and withered from sheer, solitary respectability. Upon my word, I wonder we didn't see that we should have been far happier if we 'd gone in for the devil-may-care, *café*-living sort of life in town! After all, *I* have a set, and you might have joined it. It 's true, I did want, dearly, dearly, to be a married woman, but where 's the pride in being a married woman among married women who are —married! If—(*Seeing that Aubrey's head has sunk into his hands.*) Aubrey! My dear boy! You 're not—crying?

(*He looks up, with a flushed face. Ellean enters, dressed very simply for walking. She is a low-voiced, grave girl of about nineteen, with a face somewhat resembling a Madonna. Towards Paula her manner is cold and distant.*)

Aubrey. (*In an undertone.*) Ellean!

Ellean. Good-morning, papa. Good-morning, Paula.

(*Paula puts her arms round Ellean and kisses her. Ellean makes little response.*)

Paula. Good-morning. (*Brightly.*) We've been breakfasting this side of the house, to get the sun.

(*She sits at the piano and rattles at a gay melody. Seeing that Paula's back is turned to them, Ellean goes to Aubrey and kisses him; he returns the kiss almost furtively. As they separate, the servants re-enter, and proceed to carry out the breakfast table.*)

Aubrey. (*To Ellean.*) I guess where you 've been: there 's some gorse clinging to your frock.

Ellean. (*Removing a sprig of gorse from her skirt.*) Rover and I walked nearly as far as Black Moor. The poor fellow has a thorn in his pad; I am going upstairs for my tweezers.

Aubrey. Ellean! (*She returns to him.*) Paula is a little depressed—out of sorts. She complains that she has no companion.

Ellean. I am with Paula nearly all the day, papa.

Aubrey. Ah, but you 're such a little mouse. Paula likes cheerful people about her.

Ellean. I 'm afraid I am naturally rather silent; and it 's so difficult to seem to be what one is not.

Aubrey. I don't wish that, Ellean.

Ellean. I will offer to go down to the village with Paula this morning—shall I?

Aubrey. (*Touching her hand gently.*) Thank you—do.

Ellean. When I 've looked after Rover, I 'll come back to her.

(*She goes out; Paula ceases playing, and turns on the music-stool, looking at Aubrey.*)

Paula. Well, have you and Ellean had your little confidence?

Aubrey. Confidence?

Paula. Do you think I couldn't feel it, like a pain between my shoulders?

Aubrey. Ellean is coming back in a few minutes to be with you. (*Bending over her.*) Paula, Paula dear, is this how you keep your promise?

Paula. Oh! (*Rising impatiently, and crossing swiftly to the settee, where she sits, moving restlessly.*) I *can't* keep my promise; I *am* jealous; it won't be smothered. I see you looking at her, watching her; your voice drops when you speak to her. I know how fond you are of that girl, Aubrey.

Aubrey. What would you have? I 've no other home for her. She is my daughter.

Paula. She is your saint. Saint Ellean!

Aubrey. You have often told me how good and sweet you think her.

Paula. Good!—yes! Do you imagine *that* makes me less jealous? (*Going to him and clinging to his arm.*) Aubrey, there are two sorts of affection—the love for a woman you respect, and the love for the woman you—love. She gets the first from you: I never can.

Aubrey. Hush, hush! you don't realise what you say.

Paula. If Ellean cared for me only a little, it would be different. I shouldn't be jealous then. Why doesn't she care for me?

Aubrey. She—she—she will, in time.

Paula. You can't say that without stuttering.

Aubrey. Her disposition seems a little unresponsive; she resembles her mother in many ways; I can see it every day.

Paula. She 's marble. It 's a shame. There 's not the slightest excuse; for all she knows, I 'm as much a saint as she—only married. Dearest, help me to win her over!

Aubrey. Help you?

Paula. You can. Teach her that it is her duty to love me; she hangs on to every word you speak. I 'm sure, Aubrey, that the love of a nice woman who believed me to be like herself would do me a world of good. You 'd get the benefit of it as well as I. It would soothe me; it would make me less horribly restless; it would take this—this—mischievous feeling from me. (*Coaxingly.*) Aubrey!

Aubrey. Have patience; everything will come right.

Paula. Yes, if you help me.

Aubrey. In the meantime you will tear up your letter to Lady Orreyed, won't you?

Paula. (*Kissing his hand.*) Of course I will—anything!

Aubrey. Ah, thank you, dearest! (*Laughing.*) Why, good gracious!—ha, ha!—just imagine "Saint Ellean" and that woman side by side!

Paula. (*Going back with a cry.*) Ah!

Aubrey. What?

Paula. (*Passionately.*) It 's Ellean you 're considering, not me? It 's all Ellean with you! Ellean! Ellean!

(*Ellean re-enters.*)

Ellean. Did you call me, Paula? (*Clenching his hands, Aubrey turns away and goes out.*) Is papa angry?

Paula. I drive him distracted sometimes. There, I confess it!

Ellean. Do you? Oh, why do you?

Paula. Because I—because I 'm jealous.

Ellean. Jealous?

Paula. Yes—of you. (*Ellean is silent.*) Well, what do you think of that?

Ellean. I knew it; I 've seen it. It hurts me dreadfully. What do you wish me to do? Go away?

Paula. Leave us! (*Beckoning her with a motion of the head.*) Look here! (*Ellean goes to Paula slowly and unresponsively.*) You could cure me of my jealousy very easily. Why don't you—like me?

Ellean. What do you mean by—like you? I don't understand.

Paula. Love me.

Ellean. Love is not a feeling that is under one's control. I shall alter as time goes on, perhaps. I didn't begin to love my father deeply till a few months ago, and then I obeyed my mother.

Paula. Ah, yes, you dream things, don't you—see them in your sleep? You fancy your mother speaks to you?

Ellean. When you have lost your mother it is a comfort to believe that she is dead only to this life, that she still watches over her child. I do believe that of my mother.

Paula. Well, and so you haven't been bidden to love *me?*

Ellean. (*After a pause, almost inaudibly.*) No.

Paula. Dreams are only a hash-up of one's day-thoughts, I suppose you know. Think intently of anything, and it 's bound to come back to you at night. I don't cultivate dreams myself.

Ellean. Ah, I knew you would only sneer!

Paula. I 'm not sneering; I 'm speaking the truth. I say that if you cared for me in the daytime I should soon make friends with those nightmares of yours. Ellean, why don't you try to look on me as your second mother? Of course there are not many years between us, but I 'm ever so much older than you—in experience. I shall have no children of my own, I know that; it would be a real comfort to me if you would make me feel we belonged to each other. Won't you? Perhaps you think I 'm odd—not nice. Well, the fact is I 've two sides to my nature, and I 've let the one almost smother the other. A few years ago I went through some trouble, and since then I haven't shed a tear. I believe if you put your arms round me just once I should run upstairs and have a good cry. There, I 've talked to you as I 've never talked to a woman in my life. Ellean, you seem to fear me. Don't! Kiss me!

(*With a cry, almost of despair, Ellean turns from Paula and sinks on to the settee, covering her face with her hands.*)

Paula. (*Indignantly.*) Oh! Why is it! How dare you treat me like this? What do you mean by it? What do you mean?

(*A servant enters.*)

Servant. Mr. Drummle, ma'am.

(*Cayley Drummle, in riding-dress, enters briskly. The servant retires.*)

Paula. (*Recovering herself.*) Well, Cayley!

Drummle. (*Shaking hands with her cordially.*) How are you? (*Shaking hands with Ellean, who rises.*) I saw you in the distance an hour ago, in the gorse near Stapleton's.

Ellean. I didn't see you, Mr. Drummle.

Drummle. My dear Ellean, it is my experience that no charming young lady of nineteen ever does see a man of forty-five. (*Laughing.*) Ha, ha!

Ellean. (*Going to the door.*) Paula, papa wishes me to drive down to the village with you this morning. Do you care to take me?

Paula. (*Coldly.*) Oh, by all means. Pray tell Watts to balance the cart for three.

(*Ellean goes out.*)

Drummle. How 's Aubrey?

Paula. Very well—when Ellean 's about the house.

Drummle. And you? I needn't ask.

Paula. (*Walking away to the window.*) Oh, a dog's life, my dear Cayley, mine.

Drummle. Eh?

Paula. Doesn't that define a happy marriage? I 'm sleek, well-kept, well-fed, never without a bone to gnaw and fresh straw to lie upon. (*Gazing out of the window.*) Oh, dear me!

Drummle. H'm! Well, I heartily congratulate you on your kennel. The view from the terrace here is superb.

Paula. Yes; I can see London.

Drummle. London! Not quite so far, surely?

Paula. *I* can. Also the Mediterranean, on a fine day. I wonder what Algiers looks like this morning from the sea! (*Impulsively.*) Oh, Cayley, do you remember those jolly times on board Peter Jarman's yacht when we lay off—? (*Stopping suddenly, seeing Drummle staring at her.*) Good gracious! What are we talking about!

(*Aubrey enters.*)

Aubrey. (*To Drummle.*) Dear old chap! Has Paula asked you?

Paula. Not yet.

Aubrey. We want you to come to us, now that you 're leaving Mrs. Cortelyon—at once, to-day. Stay a month, as long as you please—eh, Paula?

Paula. As long as you can possibly endure it—do, Cayley.

Drummle. (*Looking at Aubrey.*) Delighted. (*To Paula.*) Charming of you to have me.

Paula. My dear man, you 're a blessing. I must telegraph to London for more fish! A strange appetite to cater for! Something to do, to do, to do!

(*She goes out in a mood of almost childish delight.*)

Drummle. (*Eyeing Aubrey.*) Well?

Aubrey. (*With a wearied anxious look.*) Well, Cayley?

Drummle. How are you getting on?

Aubrey. My position doesn't grow less difficult. I told you, when I met you last week, of this feverish, jealous attachment of Paula's for Ellean?

Drummle. Yes. I hardly know why, but I came to the conclusion that you don't consider it an altogether fortunate attachment.

Aubrey. Ellean doesn't respond to it.

Drummle. These are early days. Ellean will warm towards your wife by-and-by.

Aubrey. Ah, but there 's the question, Cayley!

Drummle. What question?

Aubrey. The question which positively distracts me. Ellean is so different from —most women; I don't believe a purer creature exists out of heaven. And I—I ask myself, am I doing right in exposing her to the influence of poor Paula's light, careless nature?

Drummle. My dear Aubrey!

Aubrey. That shocks you! So it does me. I assure you I long to urge my girl to break down the reserve which keeps her apart from Paula, but somehow I can't do it—well, I don't do it. How can I make you understand? But when you come to us you 'll understand quickly enough. Cayley, there 's hardly a subject you can broach on which poor Paula hasn't some strange, out-of-the-way thought to give utterance to; some curious, warped notion. They are not mere worldly thoughts—unless, good God! they belong to the little hellish world which our blackguardism has created: no, her ideas have too little calculation in them to be called worldly. But it makes it the more dreadful that such thoughts should be ready, spontaneous; that expressing them has become a perfectly natural process; that her words, acts even, have almost lost their proper significance for her, and seem beyond her control. Ah, and the pain of listening to it all from the woman one loves, the woman one hoped to make happy and contented, who is really and truly a good woman, as it were, maimed! Well, this is my burden, and I shouldn't speak to you of it but for my anxiety about Ellean. Ellean! What is to be her future? It is in my hands; what am I to do? Cayley, when I remember how Ellean comes to me, from another world I always think,—when I realise the charge that 's laid on me, I find myself wishing, in a sort of terror, that my child were safe under the ground!

Drummle. My dear Aubrey, aren't you making a mistake?

Aubrey. Very likely. What is it?

Drummle. A mistake, not in regarding your Ellean as an angel, but in believing that, under any circumstances, it would be possible for her to go through life without getting her white robe—shall we say, a little dusty at the hem? Don't take me for a cynic. I am sure there are many women upon earth who are almost divinely innocent; but being on earth, they must send their robes to the laundry occasionally. Ah, and it 's right that they should have to do so, for what can they learn from the checking of their little washing-bills but lessons of charity? Now I see but two courses open to you for the disposal of your angel.

Aubrey. Yes?

Drummle. You must either restrict her to a paradise which is, like every earthly paradise, necessarily somewhat imperfect, or treat her as an ordinary flesh-and-blood young woman, and give her the advantages of that society to which she properly belongs.

Aubrey. Advantages?

Drummle. My dear Aubrey, of all forms of innocence mere ignorance is the least admirable. Take my advice, let her walk and talk and suffer and be healed with the great crowd. Do it, and hope that she 'll some day meet a good, honest fellow who 'll make her life complete, happy, secure. Now you see what I'm driving at.

Aubrey. A sanguine programme, my dear Cayley! Oh, I 'm not pooh-poohing it. Putting sentiment aside, of course I know that a fortunate marriage for Ellean would be the best—perhaps the only—solution of my difficulty. But you forget the danger of the course you suggest.

Drummle. Danger?

Aubrey. If Ellean goes among men and women, how can she escape from learning, sooner or later, the history of—poor Paula's—old life?

Drummle. H'm! You remember the episode of the Jeweller's Son in the Arabian Nights? Of course you don't. Well, if your daughter lives, she *can't* escape—what you 're afraid of. (*Aubrey gives a half-stifled exclamation of pain.*) And when she does hear the story, surely it would be better that she should have some knowledge of the world to help her to understand it.

Aubrey. To understand!

Drummle. To understand, to—philosophise.

Aubrey. To philosophise?

Drummle. Philosophy is toleration, and it is only one step from toleration to forgiveness.

Aubrey. You 're right, Cayley; I believe you always are. Yes, yes. But, even if I had the courage to attempt to solve the problem of Ellean's future in this way. I—I 'm helpless.

Drummle. How?

Aubrey. What means have I now of placing my daughter in the world I 've left?

Drummle. Oh, some friend—some woman friend.

Aubrey. I have none; they 're gone.

Drummle. You 're wrong there; I know one—

Aubrey. (*Listening.*) That 's Paula's cart. Let 's discuss this again.

Drummle. (*Going up to the window and looking out.*) It isn't the dog-cart. (*Turning to Aubrey.*) I hope you 'll forgive me, old chap.

Aubrey. What for?

Drummle. Whose wheels do you think have been cutting ruts in your immaculate drive?

(*A servant enters.*)

Servant. (*To Aubrey.*) Mrs. Cortelyon, sir.

Aubrey. Mrs. Cortelyon! (*After a short pause.*) Very well. (*The servant withdraws.*) What on earth is the meaning of this?

Drummle. Ahem! While I 've been our old friend's guest, Aubrey, we have very naturally talked a good deal about you and yours.

Aubrey. Indeed, have you?

Drummle. Yes; and Alice Cortelyon has arrived at the conclusion that it would have been far kinder had she called on Mrs. Tanqueray long ago. She 's going abroad for Easter before settling down in London for the season, and I believe she has come over this morning to ask for Ellean's companionship.

Aubrey. Oh, I see! (*Frowning.*) Quite a friendly little conspiracy, my dear Cayley!

Drummle. Conspiracy! Not at all, I assure you. (*Laughing.*) Ha, ha!

(*Ellean enters from the hall with Mrs. Cortelyon, a handsome, good-humoured, spirited woman of about forty-five.*)

Ellean. Papa—

Mrs. Cortelyon. (*To Aubrey, shaking hands with him heartily.*) Well, Aubrey, how are you? I 've just been telling this great girl of yours that I knew her when she was a sad-faced, pale baby. How is Mrs. Tanqueray? I have been a bad neighbour, and I 'm here to beg forgiveness. Is she indoors?

Aubrey. She 's up-stairs putting on a hat, I believe.

Mrs. Cortelyon. (*Sitting comfortably.*) Ah! (*She looks round: Drummle and Ellean are talking together in the hall.*) We used to be very frank with each other, Aubrey. I suppose the old footing is no longer possible, eh?

Aubrey. If so, I 'm not entirely to blame, Mrs. Cortelyon.

Mrs. Cortelyon. Mrs. Cortelyon? H'm! No, I admit it. But you must make some little allowance for me, *Mr. Tanqueray.* Your first wife and I, as girls, were like two cherries on one stalk, and then I was the confidential friend of your married life. That post, perhaps, wasn't altogether a sinecure. And now—well, when a woman gets to my age I suppose she 's a stupid, prejudiced, conventional creature. However, I 've got over it and—(*Giving him her hand*)—I hope you 'll be enormously happy and let me be a friend once more.

Aubrey. Thank you, Alice.

Mrs. Cortelyon. That 's right. I feel more cheerful than I 've done for weeks. But I suppose it would serve me right if the second Mrs. Tanqueray showed me the door. Do you think she will?

Aubrey. (*Listening.*) Here is my wife. (*Mrs. Cortelyon rises, and Paula enters, dressed for driving; she stops abruptly on seeing Mrs. Cortelyon.*) Paula, dear, Mrs. Cortelyon has called to see you.

(*Paula starts, looks at Mrs. Cortelyon irresolutely, then after a slight pause barely touches Mrs. Cortelyon's extended hand.*)

Paula. (*Whose manner now alternates between deliberate insolence and assumed sweetness.*) Mrs. ——? What name, Aubrey?

Aubrey. Mrs. Cortelyon.

Paula. Cortelyon? Oh, yes. Cortelyon.

Mrs. Cortelyon. (*Carefully guarding herself throughout against any expression of resentment.*) Aubrey ought to have told you that Alice Cortelyon and he are very old friends.

Paula. Oh, very likely he has mentioned the circumstance. I have quite a wretched memory.

Mrs. Cortelyon. You know we are neighbours, Mrs. Tanqueray.

Paula. Neighbours? Are we really? Won't you sit down? (*They both sit.*) Neighbours! That 's most interesting!

Mrs. Cortelyon. Very near neighbours. You can see my roof from your windows.

Paula. I fancy I *have* observed a roof. But you have been away from home; you have only just returned.

Mrs. Cortelyon. I? What makes you think that?

Paula. Why, because it is two months since we came to Highercoombe, and I don't remember your having called.

Mrs. Cortelyon. Your memory is now terribly accurate. No, I 've not been away from home, and it is to explain my neglect that I am here, rather unceremoniously, this morning.

Paula. Oh, to explain—quite so. (*With mock solicitude.*) Ah, you 've been very ill; I ought to have seen that before.

Mrs. Cortelyon. Ill!

Paula. You look dreadfully pulled down. We poor women show illness so plainly in our faces, don't we?

Aubrey. (*Anxiously.*) Paula dear, Mrs. Cortelyon is the picture of health.

Mrs. Cortelyon. (*With some asperity.*) I have never *felt* better in my life.

Paula. (*Looking round innocently.*) Have I said anything awkward? Aubrey, tell Mrs. Cortelyon how stupid and thoughtless I always am!

Mrs. Cortelyon. (*To Drummle, who is now standing close to her.*) Really, Cayley—! (*He soothes her with a nod and smile and a motion of his finger to his lip.*) Mrs. Tanqueray, I am afraid my explanation will not be quite so satisfactory as either of those you have just helped me to. You may have heard—but, if you have heard, you have doubtless forgotten—that twenty years ago, when your husband first lived here, I was a constant visitor at Highercoombe.

Paula. Twenty years ago—fancy! I was a naughty little child then.

Mrs. Cortelyon. Possibly. Well, at that time, and till the end of her life, my affections were centred upon the lady of this house.

Paula. Were they? That was very sweet of you.

(*Ellean approaches Mrs. Cortelyon, listening intently to her.*)

Mrs. Cortelyon. I will say no more on that score, but I must add this: when, two months ago, you came here, I realised, perhaps for the first time, that I was a middle-aged woman, and that it had become impossible for me to accept without some effort a breaking-in upon many tender associations. There, Mrs. Tanqueray, that is my confession. Will you try to understand it and pardon me?

Paula. (*Watching Ellean,—sneeringly.*) Ellean dear, you appear to be very interested in Mrs. Cortelyon's reminiscences; I don't think I can do better than make you my mouthpiece—there is such sympathy between us. What do you say—can we bring ourselves to forgive Mrs. Cortelyon for neglecting us for two weary months?

Mrs. Cortelyon. (*To Ellean, pleasantly.*) Well, Ellean? (*With a little cry of tenderness Ellean impulsively sits beside Mrs. Cortelyon and takes her hand.*) My dear child!

Paula. (*In an undertone to Aubrey.*) Ellean isn't so very slow in taking to Mrs. Cortelyon!

Mrs. Cortelyon. (*To Paula and Aubrey.*) Come, this encourages me to broach my scheme. Mrs. Tanqueray, it strikes me that you two good people are just now excellent company for each other, while Ellean would perhaps be glad of a little peep into the world you are anxious to avoid. Now, I'm going to Paris tomorrow for a week or two before settling down in Chester Square, so—don't gasp, both of you!—if this girl is willing, and you have made no other arrangements for her, will you let her come with me to Paris, and afterwards remain with me in town during the season? (*Ellean utters an exclamation of surprise. Paula is silent.*) What do you say?

Aubrey. Paula—Paula dear. (*Hesitatingly.*) My dear Mrs. Cortelyon, this is wonderfully kind of you; I am really at a loss to—eh, Cayley?

Drummle. (*Watching Paula apprehensively.*) Kind! Now I must say I don't think so! I begged Alice to take *me* to Paris, and she declined. I am thrown over for Ellean! Ha! ha!

Mrs. Cortelyon. (*Laughing.*) What nonsense you talk, Cayley!

(*The laughter dies out. Paula remains quite still.*)

Aubrey. Paula dear.

Paula. (*Slowly collecting herself.*) One moment. I—I don't quite— (*To Mrs. Cortelyon.*) You propose that Ellean leaves Highercoombe almost at once, and remains with you some months?

Mrs. Cortelyon. It would be a mercy to me. You can afford to be generous to a desolate old widow. Come, Mrs. Tanqueray, won't you spare her?

Paula. Won't *I* spare her. (*Suspiciously.*) Have you mentioned your plan to Aubrey—before I came in?

Mrs. Cortelyon. No; I had no opportunity.

Paula. Nor to Ellean?

Mrs. Cortelyon. Oh, no.

Paula. (*Looking about her in suppressed excitement.*) This hasn't been discussed at all, behind my back?

Mrs. Cortelyon. My dear Mrs. Tanqueray!

Paula. Ellean, let us hear your voice in the matter!

Ellean. I should like to go with Mrs. Cortelyon—

Paula. Ah!

Ellean. That is, if—if—

Paula. If—what?

Ellean. (*Looking towards Aubrey, appealingly.*) Papa!

Paula. (*In a hard voice.*) Oh, of course —I forgot. (*To Aubrey.*) My dear Aubrey, it rests with you, naturally, whether I am—to lose—Ellean.

Aubrey. Lose Ellean! (*Advancing to Paula.*) There is no question of losing Ellean. You would see Ellean in town constantly when she returned from Paris; isn't that so, Mrs. Cortelyon?

Mrs. Cortelyon. Certainly.

Paula. (*Laughing softly.*) Oh, I didn't know I should be allowed that privilege.

Mrs. Cortelyon. Privilege, my dear Mrs. Tanqueray!

Paula. Ha, ha! that makes all the difference, doesn't it?

Aubrey. (*With assumed gaiety.*) All the difference? I should think so! (*To Ellean, laying his hand upon her head tenderly.*) And you are quite certain you wish to see what the world is like on the other side of Black Moor!

Ellean. If you are willing, papa, I am quite certain.

Aubrey. (*Looking at Paula irresolutely, then speaking with an effort.*) Then I—I am willing.

Paula. (*Rising and striking the table lightly with her clenched hand.*) That decides it! (*There is a general movement. Excitedly to Mrs. Cortelyon, who advances towards her.*) When do you want her?

Mrs. Cortelyon. We go to town this afternoon at five o'clock, and sleep to-night at Bayliss's. There is barely time for her to make her preparations.

Paula. I will undertake that she is ready.

Mrs. Cortelyon. I've a great deal to scramble through at home too, as you may guess. Good-bye!

Paula. (*Turning away.*) Mrs. Cortelyon is going.

(*Paula stands looking out of the window, with her back to those in the room.*)

Mrs. Cortelyon. (*To Drummle.*) Cayley—

Drummle. (*To her.*) Eh?

Mrs. Cortelyon. I've gone through it, for the sake of Aubrey and his child, but I—I feel a hundred. Is that a madwoman?

Drummle. Of course; all jealous women are mad.

(*He goes out with Aubrey.*)

Mrs. Cortelyon. (*Hesitatingly, to Paula.*) Good-bye, Mrs. Tanqueray.

(*Paula inclines her head with the slightest possible movement, then resumes her former position. Ellean comes from the hall and takes Mrs. Cortelyon out of the room. After a brief silence, Paula turns with a fierce cry, and hurriedly takes off her coat and hat, and tosses them upon the settee.*)

Paula. Who's that? Oh! Oh! Oh!

(*She drops into the chair as Aubrey returns; he stands looking at her.*)

Aubrey. I—you have altered your mind about going out?

Paula. Yes. Please to ring the bell.

Aubrey. (*Touching the bell.*) You are angry about Mrs. Cortelyon and Ellean. Let me try to explain my reasons—

Paula. Be careful what you say to me just now! I have never felt like this—except once—in my life. Be careful what you say to me!

(*A servant enters.*)

Paula. (*Rising.*) Is Watts at the door with the cart?

Servant. Yes, ma'am.

Paula. Tell him to drive down to the post-office directly with this.

(*Picking up the letter which has been lying upon the table.*)

Aubrey. With that?

Paula. Yes. My letter to Lady Orreyed.

(*Giving the letter to the servant, who goes out.*)

Aubrey. Surely you don't wish me to countermand any order of yours to a servant? Call the man back—take the letter from him!

Paula. I have not the slightest intention of doing so.

Aubrey. I must, then. (*Going to the door. She snatches up her hat and coat and follows him.*) What are you going to do?

Paula. If you stop that letter, I walk out of the house.

(*He hesitates, then leaves the door.*)

Aubrey. I am right in believing that to be the letter inviting George Orreyed and his wife to stay here, am I not?

Paula. Oh, yes—quite right.

Aubrey. Let it go; I'll write to him by-and-by.

Paula. (*Facing him.*) You dare!

Aubrey. Hush, Paula!

Paula. Insult me again and, upon my word, I'll go straight out of the house!

Aubrey. Insult you?

Paula. Insult me! What else is it? My God! what else is it? What do you mean by taking Ellean from me?

Aubrey. Listen—!

Paula. Listen to *me!* And how do you take her? You pack her off in the care of a woman who has deliberately held aloof from me, who's thrown mud at me! Yet this Cortelyon creature has only to put foot here once to be entrusted with the charge of the girl you know I dearly want to keep near me!

Aubrey. Paula dear! hear me—!

Paula. Ah! of course, of course! I can't be so useful to your daughter as such people as this; and so I'm to be given the go-by for any town friend of yours who turns up and chooses to patronise us! Hah! Very well, at any rate, as you take Ellean from me you justify my looking for companions where I can most readily find 'em.

Aubrey. You wish me to fully appreciate your reason for sending that letter to Lady Orreyed?

Paula. Precisely—I do.

Aubrey. And could you, after all, go back to associates of that order? It 's not possible!

Paula. (*Mockingly.*) What, not after the refining influence of these intensely respectable surroundings? (*Going to the door.*) We 'll see!

Aubrey. Paula!

Paula. (*Violently.*) We 'll see!

(*She goes out. He stands still looking after her.*)

THE THIRD ACT.

The drawing-room at "Highercoombe." Facing the spectator are two large French windows, sheltered by a verandah, leading into the garden; on the right is a door opening into a small hall. The fireplace, with a large mirror above it, is on the left-hand side of the room, and higher up in the same wall are double doors recessed. The room is richly furnished, and everything betokens taste and luxury. The windows are open, and there is moonlight in the garden.

Lady Orreyed, a pretty, affected doll of a woman, with a mincing voice and flaxen hair, is sitting on the ottoman, her head resting against the drum, and her eyes closed. Paula, looking pale, worn, and thoroughly unhappy, is sitting at a table. Both are in sumptuous dinner-gowns.

Lady Orreyed. (*Opening her eyes.*) Well, I never! I dropped off! (*Feeling her hair.*) Just fancy! Where are the men?

Paula. (*Icily.*) Outside, smoking.

(*A servant enters with coffee, which he hands to Lady Orreyed. Sir George Orreyed comes in by the window. He is a man of about thirty-five, with a low forehead, a receding chin, a vacuous expression, and an ominous redness about the nose.*)

Lady Orreyed. (*Taking coffee.*) Here 's Dodo.

Sir George. I say, the flies under the verandah make you swear. (*The servant hands coffee to Paula, who declines it, then to Sir George, who takes a cup.*) Hi! wait a bit! (*He looks at the tray searchingly, then puts back his cup.*) Never mind. (*Quietly to Lady Orreyed.*) I say, they 're dooced sparin' with their liqueur, ain't they?

(*The servant goes out at window.*)

Paula. (*To Sir George.*) Won't you take coffee, George?

Sir George. No, thanks. It 's gettin' near time for a whiskey and potass. (*Approaching Paula, regarding Lady Orreyed admiringly.*) I say, Birdie looks rippin' to-night, don't she?

Paula. Your wife?

Sir George. Yaas—Birdie.

Paula. Rippin'?

Sir George. Yaas.

Paula. Quite—quite rippin'.

(*He moves round to the settee. Paula watches him with distaste, then rises and walks away. Sir George falls asleep on the settee.*)

Lady Orreyed. Paula love, I fancied you and Aubrey were a little more friendly at dinner. You haven't made it up, have you?

Paula. We? Oh, no. We speak before others, that 's all.

Lady Orreyed. And how long do you intend to carry on this game, dear?

Paula. (*Turning away impatiently.*) I really can't tell you.

Lady Orreyed. Sit down, old girl; don't be so fidgety. (*Paula sits on the upper seat of the ottoman, with her back to Lady Orreyed.*) Of course, it 's my duty, as an old friend, to give you a good talking-to—(*Paula glares at her suddenly and fiercely*)—but really I 've found one gets so many smacks in the face through interfering in matrimonial squabbles that I 've determined to drop it.

Paula. I think you 're wise.

Lady Orreyed. However, I must say that I do wish you 'd look at marriage in a more solemn light—just as I do, in fact. It is such a beautiful thing—marriage, and if people in our position don't respect it, and set a good example by living happily with their husbands, what can you expect from the middle classes? When did this sad state of affairs between you and Aubrey actually begin?

Paula. Actually, a fortnight and three days ago; I haven't calculated the minutes.

Lady Orreyed. A day or two before Dodo and I turned up—arrived.

Paula. Yes. One always remembers one

thing by another; we left off speaking to each other the morning I wrote asking you to visit us.

Lady Orreyed. Lucky for you I was able to pop down, wasn't it, dear?

Paula. (*Glaring at her again.*) Most fortunate.

Lady Orreyed. A serious split with your husband without a pal on the premises—I should say, without a friend in the house—would be most unpleasant.

Paula. (*Turning to her abruptly.*) This place must be horribly doleful for you and George just now. At least you ought to consider him before me. Why didn't you leave me to my difficulties?

Lady Orreyed. Oh, we 're quite comfortable, dear, thank you—both of us. George and me are so wrapped up in each other, it doesn't matter where we are. I don't want to crow over you, old girl, but I 've got a perfect husband.

(*Sir George is now fast asleep, his head thrown back and his mouth open, looking hideous.*)

Paula. (*Glancing at Sir George.*) So you 've given me to understand.

Lady Orreyed. Not that we don't have our little differences. Why, we fell out only this very morning. You remember the diamond and ruby tiara Charley Prestwick gave poor dear Connie Tirlemont years ago, don't you?

Paula. No, I do not.

Lady Orreyed. No? Well, it 's in the market. Benjamin of Piccadilly has got it in his shop window, and I 've set my heart on it.

Paula. You consider it quite necessary?

Lady Orreyed. Yes; because what I say to Dodo is this—a lady of my station must smother herself with hair ornaments. It 's different with you, love—people don't look for so much blaze from you, but I 've got rank to keep up; haven't I?

Paula. Yes.

Lady Orreyed. Well, that was the cause of the little set-to between I and Dodo this morning. He broke two chairs, he was in such a rage. I forgot they 're your chairs; do you mind?

Paula. No.

Lady Orreyed. You know, poor Dodo can't lose his temper without smashing something; if it isn't a chair, it 's a mirror; if it isn't that, it 's china—a bit of Dresden for choice. Dear old pet! he loves a bit of Dresden when he 's furious. He doesn't really throw things *at* me, dear; he simply lifts them up and drops them, like a gentleman. I expect our room upstairs will look rather wrecky before I get that tiara.

Paula. Excuse the suggestion; perhaps your husband can't afford it.

Lady Orreyed. Oh, how dreadfully changed you are, Paula! Dodo can always mortgage something, or borrow of his ma. What *is* coming to you!

Paula. Ah! (*She sits at the piano and touches the keys.*)

Lady Orreyed. Oh, yes, do play! That 's the one thing I envy you for.

Paula. What shall I play?

Lady Orreyed. What was that heavenly piece you gave us last night, dear?

Paula. A bit of Schubert. Would you like to hear it again?

Lady Orreyed. You don't know any comic songs, do you?

Paula. I 'm afraid not.

Lady Orreyed. I leave it to you.

(*Paula plays. Aubrey and Cayley Drummle appear outside the window; they look into the room.*)

Aubrey. (*To Drummle.*) You can see her face in that mirror. Poor girl, how ill and wretched she looks.

Drummle. When are the Orreyeds going?

Aubrey. Heaven knows!

(*Entering the room.*)

Drummle. But *you 're* entertaining them; what 's it to do with heaven?

(*Following Aubrey.*)

Aubrey. Do you know, Cayley, that even the Orreyeds serve a useful purpose? My wife actually speaks to me before our guests—think of that! I 've come to rejoice at the presence of the Orreyeds!

Drummle. I dare say; we 're taught that beetles are sent for a benign end.

Aubrey. Cayley, talk to Paula again tonight.

Drummle. Certainly, if I get the chance.

Aubrey. Let 's contrive it. George is asleep; perhaps I can get that doll out of the way. (*As they advance into the room, Paula abruptly ceases playing and finds interest in a volume of music. Sir George is now nodding and snoring apoplectically.*) Lady Orreyed, whenever you feel inclined for a game of billiards I 'm at your service.

Lady Orreyed. (*Jumping up.*) Charmed,

I'm sure! I really thought you'd forgotten poor little me. Oh, look at Dodo!

Aubrey. No, no, don't wake him; he's tired.

Lady Orreyed. I must, he looks so plain. (*Rousing Sir George.*) Dodo! Dodo!

Sir George. (*Stupidly.*) 'Ullo!

Lady Orreyed. Dodo dear, you were snoring.

Sir George. Oh, I say, you could 'a' told me that by-and-by.

Aubrey. You want a cigar, George; come into the billiard-room. (*Giving his arm to Lady Orreyed.*) Cayley, bring Paula.

(*Aubrey and Lady Orreyed go out.*)

Sir George. (*Rising.*) Hey, what! Billiard-room! (*Looking at his watch.*) How goes the—? Phew! 'Ullo, 'ullo! Whiskey and potass!

(*He goes rapidly after Aubrey and Lady Orreyed. Paula resumes playing.*)

Paula. (*After a pause.*) Don't moon about after me, Cayley; follow the others.

Drummle. Thanks, by-and-by. (*Sitting.*) That's pretty.

Paula. (*After another pause, still playing.*) I wish you wouldn't stare so.

Drummle. Was I staring? I'm sorry. (*She plays a little longer, then stops suddenly, rises, and goes to the window, where she stands looking out. Drummle moves from the ottoman to the settee.*) A lovely night.

Paula. (*Startled.*) Oh! (*Without turning to him.*) Why do you hop about like a monkey?

Drummle. Hot rooms play the deuce with the nerves. Now, it would have done you good to have walked in the garden with us after dinner and made merry. Why didn't you?

Paula. You know why.

Drummle. Ah, you're thinking of the—difference between you and Aubrey?

Paula. Yes, I *am* thinking of it.

Drummle. Well, so am I. How long—?

Paula. Getting on for three weeks.

Drummle. Bless me, it must be! And this would have been such a night to have healed it! Moonlight, the stars, the scent of flowers; and yet enough darkness to enable a kind woman to rest her hand for an instant on the arm of a good fellow who loves her. Ah, ha! It's a wonderful power, dear Mrs. Aubrey, the power of an offended woman! Only realise it! Just that one touch—the mere tips of her fingers—and, for herself and another, she changes the colour of the whole world.

Paula. (*Turning to him calmly.*) Cayley, my dear man, you talk exactly like a very romantic old lady.

(*She leaves the window and sits playing with the knick-knacks on the table.*)

Drummle. (*To himself.*) H'm, that hasn't done it! Well—ha, ha!—I accept the suggestion. An old woman, eh?

Paula. Oh, I didn't intend—

Drummle. But why not? I've every qualification—well, almost. And I confess it would have given this withered bosom a throb of grandmotherly satisfaction if I could have seen you and Aubrey at peace before I take my leave to-morrow.

Paula. To-morrow, Cayley!

Drummle. I must.

Paula. Oh, this house is becoming unendurable.

Drummle. You're very kind. But you've got the Orreyeds.

Paula. (*Fiercely.*) The Orreyeds! I—I hate the Orreyeds! I lie awake at night, hating them!

Drummle. Pardon me, I've understood that their visit is, in some degree, owing to—hem—your suggestion.

Paula. Heavens! that doesn't make me like them better. Somehow or another, I—I've outgrown these people. This woman—I used to think her "jolly"!—sickens me. I can't breathe when she's near me: the whiff of her handkerchief turns me faint! And she patronises me by the hour, until I—I feel my nails growing longer with every word she speaks!

Drummle. My dear lady, why on earth don't you say all this to Aubrey?

Paula. Oh, I've been such an utter fool, Cayley!

Drummle. (*Soothingly.*) Well, well, mention it to Aubrey!

Paula. No, no, you don't understand. What do you think I've done?

Drummle. Done! What, *since* you invited the Orreyeds?

Paula. Yes; I must tell you—

Drummle. Perhaps you'd better not.

Paula. Look here! I've intercepted some letters from Mrs. Cortelyon and Ellean to—him. (*Producing three unopened letters from the bodice of her dress.*) There are the accursed things! From

Paris—two from the Cortelyon woman, the other from Ellean!

Drummle. But why—why?

Paula. I don't know. Yes, I do! I saw letters coming from Ellean to her father; not a line to me—not a line. And one morning it happened I was downstairs before he was, and I spied this one lying with his heap on the breakfast-table, and I slipped it into my pocket—out of malice, Cayley, pure deviltry! And a day or two afterwards I met Elwes the postman at the Lodge, and took the letters from him, and found these others amongst 'em. I felt simply fiendish when I saw them—fiendish! (*Returning the letters to her bodice.*) And now I carry them about with me, and they 're scorching me like a mustard plaster!

Drummle. Oh, this accounts for Aubrey not hearing from Paris lately!

Paula. That 's an ingenious conclusion to arrive at! Of course it does! (*With an hysterical laugh.*) Ha, ha!

Drummle. Well, well! (*Laughing.*) Ha, ha, ha!

Paula. (*Turning upon him.*) I suppose it *is* amusing!

Drummle. I beg pardon.

Paula. Heaven knows I 've little enough to brag about! I 'm a bad lot, but not in mean tricks of this sort. In all my life this is the most caddish thing I 've done. How am I to get rid of these letters—that 's what I want to know? How am I to get rid of them?

Drummle. If I were you I should take Aubrey aside and put them into his hands as soon as possible.

Paula. What! and tell him to his face that I—! No, thank you. I suppose *you* wouldn't like to—

Drummle. No, no; I won't touch 'em!

Paula. And you call yourself my friend?

Drummle. (*Good-humouredly.*) No, I don't!

Paula. Perhaps I 'll tie them together and give them to his man in the morning.

Drummle. That won't avoid an explanation.

Paula. (*Recklessly.*) Oh, then he must miss them—

Drummle. And trace them.

Paula. (*Throwing herself upon the ottoman.*) I don't care!

Drummle. I know you don't; but let me send him to you now, may I?

Paula. Now! What do you think a woman 's made of? I couldn't stand it, Cayley. I haven't slept for nights; and last night there was thunder, too! I believe I 've got the horrors.

Drummle. (*Taking the little hand-mirror from the table.*) You 'll sleep well enough when you deliver those letters. Come, come, Mrs. Aubrey—a good night's rest! (*Holding the mirror before her face.*) It 's quite time.

(*She looks at herself for a moment, then snatches the mirror from him.*)

Paula. You brute, Cayley, to show me that!

Drummle. Then—may I? Be guided by a fr—a poor old woman! May I?

Paula. You 'll kill me, amongst you!

Drummle. What do you say?

Paula. (*After a pause.*) Very well. (*He nods his head and goes out rapidly. She looks after him for a moment, and calls "Cayley! Cayley!" Then she again produces the letters, deliberately, one by one, fingering them with aversion. Suddenly she starts, turning her head towards the door.*) Ah!

(*Aubrey enters quickly.*)

Aubrey. Paula!

Paula. (*Handing him the letters, her face averted.*) There! (*He examines the letters, puzzled, and looks at her enquiringly.*) They are many days old. I stole them, I suppose to make you anxious and unhappy.

(*He looks at the letters again, then lays them aside on the table.*)

Aubrey. (*Gently.*) Paula, dear, it doesn't matter.

Paula. (*After a short pause.*) Why—why do you take it like this?

Aubrey. What did you expect?

Paula. Oh, but I suppose silent reproaches are really the severest. And then, naturally, you are itching to open your letters. (*She crosses the room as if to go.*)

Aubrey. Paula! (*She pauses.*) Surely, surely, it 's all over now?

Paula. All over! (*Mockingly.*) Has my step-daughter returned then? When did she arrive? I haven't heard of it!

Aubrey. You can be very cruel.

Paula. That word 's always on a man's lips; he uses it if his soup 's cold. (*With another movement as if to go.*) Need we—

Aubrey. I know I 've wounded you, Paula. But isn't there any way out of this?

Paula. When does Ellean return? To-morrow? Next week?

Aubrey. (*Wearily.*) Oh! Why should we grudge Ellean the little pleasure she is likely to find in Paris and in London?

Paula. I grudge her nothing, if that 's a hit at me. But with that woman—?

Aubrey. It must be that woman or another. You know that at present we are unable to give Ellean the opportunity of —of—

Paula. Of mixing with respectable people.

Aubrey. The opportunity of gaining friends, experience, ordinary knowledge of the world. If you are interested in Ellean, can't you see how useful Mrs. Cortelyon's good offices are?

Paula. May I put one question? At the end of the London season, when Mrs. Cortelyon has done with Ellean, is it quite understood that the girl comes back to us? (*Aubrey is silent.*) Is it? Is it?

Aubrey. Let us wait till the end of the season—

Paula. Oh! I knew it. You 're only fooling me; you put me off with any trash. I believe you 've sent Ellean away, not for the reasons you give, but because you don't consider me a decent companion for her, because you 're afraid she might get a little of her innocence rubbed off in my company? Come, isn't that the truth? Be honest! Isn't that it?

Aubrey. Yes.

(*There is a moment's silence on both sides.*)

Paula. (*With uplifted hands as if to strike him.*) Oh!

Aubrey. (*Taking her by the wrists.*) Sit down. Sit down. (*He puts her into a chair; she shakes herself free with a cry.*) Now listen to me. Fond as you are, Paula, of harking back to your past, there 's one chapter of it you always let alone. I 've never asked you to speak of it; you 've never offered to speak of it. I mean the chapter that relates to the time when you were—like Ellean. (*She attempts to rise; he restrains her.*) No, no.

Paula. I don't choose to talk about that time. I won't satisfy your curiosity.

Aubrey. My dear Paula, I have no curiosity—I know what you were at Ellean's age. I 'll tell you. You hadn't a thought that wasn't a wholesome one, you hadn't an impulse that didn't tend towards good, you never harboured a notion you couldn't have gossiped about to a parcel of children. (*She makes another effort to rise: he lays his hand lightly on her shoulder.*) And this was a very few years back—there are days now when you look like a schoolgirl—but think of the difference between the two Paulas. You 'll have to think hard, because after a cruel life, one's perceptions grow a thick skin. But, for God's sake, do think till you get these two images clearly in your mind, and then ask yourself what sort of a friend such a woman as you are to-day would have been for the girl of seven or eight years ago.

Paula. (*Rising.*) How dare you? I could be almost as good a friend to Ellean as her own mother would have been had she lived. I know what you mean. How dare you?

Aubrey. You say that; very likely you believe it. But you 're blind, Paula; you 're blind. You! Every belief that a young, pure-minded girl holds sacred—that you once held sacred—you now make a target for a jest, a sneer, a paltry cynicism. I tell you, you 're not mistress any longer of your thoughts or your tongue. Why, how often, sitting between you and Ellean, have I seen her cheeks turn scarlet as you 've rattled off some tale that belongs by right to the club or the smoking-room! Have you noticed the blush? If you have, has the cause of it ever struck you? And this is the girl you say you love, I admit that you *do* love, whose love you expect in return! Oh, Paula, I make the best, the only, excuse for you when I tell you you 're blind!

Paula. Ellean—Ellean blushes easily.

Aubrey. You blushed as easily a few years ago.

Paula. (*After a short pause.*) Well! Have you finished your sermon?

Aubrey. (*With a gesture of despair.*) Oh, Paula!

(*Going up to the window, and standing with his back to the room.*)

Paula. (*To herself.*) A few—years ago! (*She walks slowly towards the door, then suddenly drops upon the ottoman in a paroxysm of weeping.*) O God! A few years ago!

Aubrey. (*Going to her.*) Paula!

Paula. (*Sobbing.*) Oh, don't touch me!

Aubrey. Paula!

Paula. Oh, go away from me! (*He goes back a few steps, and after a little while she becomes calmer and rises unsteadily;*

then in an altered tone.) Look here—! (*He advances a step; she checks him with a quick gesture.*) Look here! Get rid of these people—Mabel and her husband—as soon as possible! I—I 've done with them!

Aubrey. (*In a whisper.*) Paula!

Paula. And then—then—when the time comes for Ellean to leave Mrs. Cortelyon, give me—give me another chance! (*He advances again, but she shrinks away.*) No, no!

(*She goes out by the door on the right. He sinks on to the settee, covering his eyes with his hands. There is a brief silence, then a servant enters.*)

Servant. Mrs. Cortelyon, sir, with Miss Ellean.

(*Aubrey rises to meet Mrs. Cortelyon, who enters, followed by Ellean, both being in travelling dresses. The servant withdraws.*)

Mrs. Cortelyon. (*Shaking hands with Aubrey.*) Oh, my dear Aubrey!

Aubrey. Mrs. Cortelyon! (*Kissing Ellean.*) Ellean dear!

Ellean. Papa, is all well at home?

Mrs. Cortelyon. We 're shockingly anxious.

Aubrey. Yes, yes, all 's well. This is quite unexpected. (*To Mrs. Cortelyon.*) You 've found Paris insufferably hot?

Mrs. Cortelyon. Insufferably hot! Paris is pleasant enough. We 've had no letter from you!

Aubrey. I wrote to Ellean a week ago.

Mrs. Cortelyon. Without alluding to the subject I had written to you upon.

Aubrey. (*Thinking.*) Ah, of course—

Mrs. Cortelyon. And since then we 've both written, and you 've been absolutely silent. Oh, it 's too bad!

Aubrey. (*Picking up the letters from the table.*) It isn't altogether my fault. Here are the letters—

Ellean. Papa!

Mrs. Cortelyon. They 're unopened.

Aubrey. An accident delayed their reaching me till this evening. I 'm afraid this has upset you very much.

Mrs. Cortelyon. Upset me!

Ellean. (*In an undertone to Mrs. Cortelyon.*) Never mind. Not now, dear—not to-night.

Aubrey. Eh?

Mrs. Cortelyon. (*To Ellean, aloud.*) Child, run away and take your things off. She doesn't look as if she 'd journeyed from Paris to-day.

Aubrey. I 've never seen her with such a colour.

(*Taking Ellean's hands.*)

Ellean. (*To Aubrey, in a faint voice.*) Papa, Mrs. Cortelyon has been so very, very kind to me, but I—I have come home.

(*She goes out.*)

Aubrey. Come home! (*To Mrs. Cortelyon.*) Ellean returns to us then?

Mrs. Cortelyon. That 's the very point I put to you in my letters, and you oblige me to travel from Paris to Willowmere on a warm day to settle it. I think perhaps it 's right that Ellean should be with you just now, although I—. My dear friend, circumstances are a little altered.

Aubrey. Alice, you 're in some trouble.

Mrs. Cortelyon. Well—yes, I *am* in trouble. You remember pretty little Mrs. Brereton who was once Caroline Ardale?

Aubrey. Quite well.

Mrs. Cortelyon. She 's a widow now, poor thing. She has the *entresol* of the house where we 've been lodging in the Avenue de Friedland. Caroline 's a dear chum of mine; she formed a great liking for Ellean.

Aubrey. I 'm very glad.

Mrs. Cortelyon. Yes, it 's nice for her to meet her mother's friends. Er—that young Hugh Ardale the papers were full of some time ago—he 's Caroline Brereton's brother, you know.

Aubrey. No, I didn't know. What did he do? I forget.

Mrs. Cortelyon. Checked one of those horrid mutinies at some far-away station in India. Marched down with a handful of his men and a few faithful natives, and held the place until he was relieved. They gave him his company and a V.C. for it.

Aubrey. And he 's Mrs. Brereton's brother?

Mrs. Cortelyon. Yes. He 's with his sister—*was*, rather—in Paris. He 's home—invalided. Good gracious, Aubrey, why don't you help me out? Can't you guess what has occurred?

Aubrey. Alice!

Mrs. Cortelyon. Young Ardale—Ellean!

Aubrey. An attachment?

Mrs. Cortelyon. Yes, Aubrey. (*After a little pause.*) Well, I suppose I 've got myself into sad disgrace. But really I didn't foresee anything of this kind. A serious, reserved child like Ellean, and a boyish, high-spirited soldier—it never struck me as being likely. (*Aubrey paces to and fro thoughtfully.*) I did all I could directly Captain Ardale spoke—wrote to you at once. Why on earth don't you receive your letters promptly, and when you do get them why can't you open them? I endured the anxiety till last night, and then made up my mind—home! Of course, it has worried me terribly. My head 's bursting. Are there any salts about? (*Aubrey fetches a bottle from the cabinet and hands it to her.*) We 've had one of those hateful smooth crossings that won't let you be properly indisposed.

Aubrey. My dear Alice, I assure you I 've no thought of blaming you.

Mrs. Cortelyon. That statement always precedes a quarrel.

Aubrey. I don't know whether this is the worst or the best luck. How will my wife regard it? Is Captain Ardale a good fellow?

Mrs. Cortelyon. My dear Aubrey, you 'd better read up the accounts of his wonderful heroism. Face to face with death for a whole week; always with a smile and a cheering word for the poor helpless souls depending on him! Of course it 's that that has stirred the depths of your child's nature. I 've watched her while we 've been dragging the story out of him, and if angels look different from Ellean at that moment, I don't desire to meet any, that 's all!

Aubrey. If you were in my position—? But you can't judge.

Mrs. Cortelyon. Why, if I had a marriageable daughter of my own, and Captain Ardale proposed for her, naturally I should cry my eyes out all night—but I should thank Heaven in the morning.

Aubrey. You believe so thoroughly in him?

Mrs. Cortelyon. Do you think I should have only a headache at this minute if I didn't! Look here, you 've got to see me down the lane; that 's the least you can do, my friend. Come into my house for a moment and shake hands with Hugh.

Aubrey. What, is he here?

Mrs. Cortelyon. He came through with us, to present himself formally to-morrow. Where are my gloves? (*Aubrey fetches them from the ottoman.*) Make my apologies to Mrs. Tanqueray, please. She 's well, I hope? (*Going towards the door.*) I can't feel sorry she hasn't seen me in this condition.

(*Ellean enters.*)

Ellean. (*To Mrs. Cortelyon.*) I 've been waiting to wish you good-night. I was afraid I 'd missed you.

Mrs. Cortelyon. Good-night, Ellean.

Ellean. (*In a low voice, embracing Mrs. Cortelyon.*) I can't thank you. Dear Mrs. Cortelyon!

Mrs. Cortelyon. (*Her arms round Ellean, in a whisper to Aubrey.*) Speak a word to her.

(*Mrs. Cortelyon goes out.*)

Aubrey. (*To Ellean.*) Ellean, I 'm going to see Mrs. Cortelyon home. Tell Paula where I am; explain, dear.

(*Going to the door.*)

Ellean. (*Her head drooping.*) Yes. (*Quickly.*) Father! You are angry with me—disappointed?

Aubrey. Angry? No.

Ellean. Disappointed?

Aubrey. (*Smiling and going to her and and taking her hand.*) If so, it 's only because you 've shaken my belief in my discernment. I thought you took after your poor mother a little, Ellean; but there 's a look on your face to-night, dear, that I never saw on hers—never, never.

Ellean. (*Leaning her head on his shoulder.*) Perhaps I ought not to have gone away.

Aubrey. Hush! You 're quite happy?

Ellean. Yes.

Aubrey. That 's right. Then, as you are quite happy, there is something I particularly want you to do for me, Ellean.

Ellean. What is that?

Aubrey. Be very gentle with Paula. Will you?

Ellean. You think I have been unkind.

Aubrey. (*Kissing her upon the forehead.*) Be very gentle with Paula.

(*He goes out, and she stands looking after him; then, as she turns thoughtfully from the door, a rose is thrown through the window and falls at her feet. She picks up the flower wonderingly and goes to the window.*)

Ellean. (*Starting back.*) Hugh!

(*Hugh Ardale, a handsome young man of about seven-and-twenty, with a boyish face and manner, appears outside the window.*)

Hugh. Nelly! Nelly dear!

Ellean. What 's the matter?

Hugh. Hush! Nothing. It 's only fun. (*Laughing.*) Ha, ha, ha! I 've found out that Mrs. Cortelyon's meadow runs up to your father's plantation; I 've come through a gap in the hedge.

Ellean. Why, Hugh?

Hugh. I 'm miserable at The Warren: it 's so different from the Avenue de Friedland. Don't look like that! Upon my word I meant just to peep at your home and go back, but I saw figures moving about here, and came nearer, hoping to get a glimpse of you. Was that your father?

(*Entering the room.*)

Ellean. Yes.

Hugh. Isn't this fun! A rabbit ran across my foot while I was hiding behind that old yew.

Ellean. You must go away; it 's not right for you to be here like this.

Hugh. But it 's only fun, I tell you. You take everything so seriously. Do wish me good-night.

Ellean. We have said good-night.

Hugh. In the hall at The Warren, before Mrs. Cortelyon and a man-servant. Oh, it 's so different from the Avenue de Friedland!

Ellean. (*Giving him her hand hastily.*) Good-night, Hugh.

Hugh. Is that all? We might be the merest acquaintances.

(*He momentarily embraces her, but she releases herself.*)

Ellean. It 's when you 're like this that you make me feel utterly miserable. (*Throwing the rose from her angrily.*) Oh!

Hugh. I 've offended you now, I suppose?

Ellean. Yes.

Hugh. Forgive me, Nelly. Come into the garden for five minutes; we 'll stroll down to the plantation.

Ellean. No, no.

Hugh. For two minutes—to tell me you forgive me.

Ellean. I forgive you.

Hugh. Evidently. I sha'n't sleep a wink to-night after this. What a fool I am! Come down to the plantation. Make it up with me.

Ellean. There is somebody coming into this room. Do you wish to be seen here?

Hugh. I shall wait for you behind that yew-tree. You must speak to me. Nelly!

(*He disappears. Paula enters.*)

Paula. Ellean!

Ellean. You—you are very surprised to see me, Paula, of course.

Paula. Why are you here? Why aren't you with—your friend?

Ellean. I 've come home—if you 'll have me. We left Paris this morning; Mrs. Cortelyon brought me back. She was here a minute or two ago; papa has just gone with her to The Warren. He asked me to tell you.

Paula. There are some people staying with us that I 'd rather you didn't meet. It was hardly worth your while to return for a few hours.

Ellean. A few hours?

Paula. Well, when do you go to London?

Ellean. I don't think I go to London, after all.

Paula. (*Eagerly.*) You—you 've quarrelled with her?

Ellean. No, no, no, not that; but—Paula! (*In an altered tone.*) Paula!

Paula. (*Startled.*) Eh? (*Ellean goes deliberately to Paula and kisses her.*) Ellean!

Ellean. Kiss me.

Paula. What—what 's come to you?

Ellean. I want to behave differently to you in the future. Is it too late?

Paula. Too—late! (*Impulsively kissing Ellean and crying.*) No—no—no! No—no!

Ellean. Paula, don't cry.

Paula. (*Wiping her eyes.*) I 'm a little shaky; I haven't been sleeping. It 's all right,—talk to me.

Ellean. There is something I want to tell you—

Paula. Is there—is there?

(*They sit together on the ottoman, Paula taking Ellean's hand.*)

Ellean. Paula, in our house in the Avenue de Friedland, on the floor below us, there was a Mrs. Brereton. She used to be a friend of my mother's. Mrs. Cortelyon and I spent a great deal of our time with her.

Paula. (*Suspiciously.*) Oh! (*Letting Ellean's hand fall.*) Is this lady going to take you up in place of Mrs. Cortelyon?

Ellean. No, no. Her brother is staying

with her—*was* staying with her. Her brother—

(*Breaking off in confusion.*)

Paula. Well?

Ellean. (*Almost inaudibly.*) Paula—

(*She rises and walks away, Paula following her.*)

Paula. Ellean! (*Taking hold of her.*) You're not in love! (*Ellean looks at Paula appealingly.*) Oh, *you* in love! You! Oh, this is why you've come home! Of course, you can make friends with me now! You'll leave us for good soon, I suppose; so it doesn't much matter being civil to me for a little while!

Ellean. Oh, Paula!

Paula. Why, how you have deceived us—all of us! We've taken you for a cold-blooded little saint. The fools you've made of us! Saint Ellean, Saint Ellean!

Ellean. Ah, I might have known you'd only mock me!

Paula. (*Her tone changing.*) Eh?

Ellean. I—I can't talk to you. (*Sitting on the settee.*) You do nothing else but mock and sneer, nothing else.

Paula. Ellean dear! Ellean! I didn't mean it. I'm so horribly jealous, it's a sort of curse on me. (*Kneeling beside Ellean and embracing her.*) My tongue runs away with me. I'm going to alter, I swear I am. I've made some good resolutions, and as God's above me, I'll keep them! If you are in love, if you do ever marry, that's no reason why we shouldn't be fond of each other. Come, you've kissed me of your own accord—you can't take it back. Now we're friends again, aren't we? Ellean dear! I want to know everything, everything. Ellean dear, Ellean!

Ellean. Paula, Hugh has done something that makes me very angry. He came with us from Paris to-day, to see papa. He is staying with Mrs. Cortelyon and—I ought to tell you—

Paula. Yes, yes. What?

Ellean. He has found his way by The Warren meadow through the plantation up to this house. He is waiting to bid me good-night. (*Glancing towards the garden.*) He is—out there.

Paula. Oh!

Ellean. What shall I do?

Paula. Bring him in to see me! Will you?

Ellean. No, no.

Paula. But I'm dying to know him. Oh, yes, you must. I shall meet him before Aubrey does. (*Excitedly running her hands over her hair.*) I'm so glad. (*Ellean goes out by the window.*) The mirror—mirror. What a fright I must look! (*Not finding the hand-glass on the table, she jumps on to the settee, and surveys herself in the mirror over the mantelpiece, then sits quietly down and waits.*) Ellean! Just fancy! Ellean!

(*After a pause Ellean enters by the window with Hugh.*)

Ellean. Paula, this is Captain Ardale—Mrs. Tanqueray.

(*Paula rises and turns, and she and Hugh stand staring blankly at each other for a moment or two; then Paula advances and gives him her hand.*)

Paula. (*In a strange voice, but calmly.*) How do you do?

Hugh. How do you do?

Paula. (*To Ellean.*) Mr. Ardale and I have met in London, Ellean. Er—Captain Ardale now?

Hugh. Yes.

Ellean. In London?

Paula. They say the world's very small, don't they?

Hugh. Yes.

Paula. Ellean, dear, I want to have a little talk about you to Mr. Ardale—Captain Ardale—alone. (*Putting her arms round Ellean, and leading her to the door.*) Come back in a little while. (*Ellean nods to Paula with a smile and goes out, while Paula stands watching her at the open door.*) In a little while—in a little —(*Closing the door and then taking a seat facing Hugh.*) Be quick! Mr. Tanqueray has only gone down to The Warren with Mrs. Cortelyon. What is to be done?

Hugh. (*Blankly.*) Done?

Paula. Done—done. Something must be done.

Hugh. I understood that Mr. Tanqueray had married a Mrs.—Mrs.—

Paula. Jarman?

Hugh. Yes.

Paula. I'd been going by that name. You didn't follow my doings after we separated.

Hugh. No.

Paula. (*Sneeringly.*) No.

Hugh. I went out to India.

Paula. What's to be done?

Hugh. Damn this chance!
Paula. Oh, my God!
Hugh. Your husband doesn't know, does he?
Paula. That you and I—?
Hugh. Yes.
Paula. No. He knows about others.
Hugh. Not about me. How long were we—?
Paula. I don't remember, exactly.
Hugh. Do you—do you think it matters?
Paula. His—his daughter. (*With a muttered exclamation he turns away, and sits with his head in his hands.*) What 's to be done?
Hugh. I wish I could think.
Paula. Oh! Oh! What happened to that flat of ours in Ethelbert Street?
Hugh. I let it.
Paula. All that pretty furniture?
Hugh. Sold it.
Paula. I came across the key of the escritoire the other day in an old purse!

(*Suddenly realising the horror and hopelessness of her position, and starting to her feet with an hysterical cry of rage.*)

What am I maundering about?
Hugh. For God's sake, be quiet! Do let me think.
Paula. This will send me mad! (*Suddenly turning and standing over him.*) You—you beast, to crop up in my life again like this!
Hugh. I always treated you fairly.
Paula. (*Weakly.*) Oh! I beg your pardon—I know you did—I—

(*She sinks on to the settee crying hysterically.*)

Hugh. Hush!
Paula. She kissed me to-night! I'd won her over! I've had such a fight to make her love me! And now—just as she 's beginning to love me, to bring this on her!
Hugh. Hush, hush! Don't break down!
Paula. (*Sobbing.*) You don't know! I —I haven't been getting on well in my marriage. It 's been my fault. The life I used to lead spoilt me completely. But I 'd made up my mind to turn over a new leaf from to-night. From to-night!
Hugh. Paula—
Paula. Don't you call me that!
Hugh. Mrs. Tanqueray, there is no cause for you to despair in this way. It 's all right, I tell you—it *shall* be all right.
Paula. (*Shivering.*) What are we to do?
Hugh. Hold our tongues.
Paula. Eh?

(*Staring vacantly.*)

Hugh. The chances are a hundred to one against any one ever turning up who knew us when we were together. Besides, no one would be such a brute as to split on us. If anybody did do such a thing we should have to lie! What are we upsetting ourselves like this for, when we 've simply got to hold our tongues?
Paula. You 're as mad as I am!
Hugh. Can you think of a better plan?
Paula. There 's only one plan possible—let 's come to our senses!—Mr. Tanqueray must be told.
Hugh. Your husband! What, and I lose Ellean! I lose Ellean!
Paula. You 've got to lose her.
Hugh. I won't lose her; I can't lose her!
Paula. Didn't I read of your doing any number of brave things in India? Why, you seem to be an awful coward!
Hugh. That 's another sort of pluck altogether; I haven't this sort of pluck.
Paula. Oh, I don't ask *you* to tell Mr. Tanqueray. That 's my job.
Hugh. (*Standing over her.*) You—you —you 'd better! You—
Paula. (*Rising.*) Don't bully me! I intend to.
Hugh. (*Taking hold of her; she wrenches herself free.*) Look here, Paula, I never treated you badly—you 've owned it. Why should you want to pay me out like this? You don't know how I love Ellean!
Paula. Yes, that 's just what I *do* know.
Hugh. I say you don't! She 's as good as my own mother. I 've been downright honest with her, too. I told her, in Paris, that I 'd been a bit wild at one time, and, after a damned wretched day, she promised to forgive me because of what I 'd done since in India. She 's behaved like an angel to me! Surely I oughtn't to lose her, after all, just because I 've been like other fellows! No; I haven't been half as rackety as a hundred men we could think of. Paula, don't pay me out for nothing; be fair to me, there 's a good girl—be fair to me!
Paula. Oh, I 'm not considering you at all! I advise you not to stay here any longer: Mr. Tanqueray is sure to be back soon.
Hugh. (*Taking up his hat.*) What 's the understanding between us, then? What have we arranged to do?
Paula. I don't know what you 're going to do; I 've got to tell Mr. Tanqueray.

Hugh. By God, you shall do nothing of the sort!

(*Approaching her fiercely.*)

Paula. You shocking coward!

Hugh. If you dare! (*Going up to the window.*) Mind! If you dare!

Paula. (*Following him.*) Why, what would you do?

Hugh. (*After a short pause, sullenly.*) Nothing. I 'd shoot myself—that 's nothing. Good-night.

Paula. Good-night.

(*He disappears. She walks unsteadily to the ottoman, and sits; and as she does so her hand falls upon the little silver mirror, which she takes up, staring at her own reflection.*)

THE FOURTH ACT.

The drawing-room at "Highercoombe," the same evening.

Paula is still seated on the ottoman, looking vacantly before her, with the little mirror in her hand. Lady Orreyed enters.

Lady Orreyed. There you are! You never came into the billiard-room. Isn't it maddening—Cayley Drummle gives me sixty out of a hundred, and beats me. I must be out of form, because I know I play remarkably well for a lady. Only last month—. (*Paula rises.*) Whatever is the matter with you, old girl?

Paula. Why?

Lady Orreyed. (*Staring.*) It 's the light, I suppose. (*Paula replaces the mirror on the table.*) By Aubrey's bolting from the billiard-table in that fashion I thought perhaps—

Paula. Yes; it 's all right.

Lady Orreyed. You 've patched it up? (*Paula nods.*) Oh, I am jolly glad—! I mean—

Paula. Yes, I know what you mean. Thanks, Mabel.

Lady Orreyed. (*Kissing Paula.*) Now take my advice; for the future—

Paula. Mabel, if I 've been disagreeable to you while you 've been staying here, I—I beg your pardon.

(*Walking away and sitting down.*)

Lady Orreyed. You disagreeable, my dear? I haven't noticed it. Dodo and me both consider you make a first-class hostess; but then you 've had such practice, haven't you? (*Dropping on to the ottoman and gaping.*) Oh, talk about being sleepy—!

Paula. Why don't you—!

Lady Orreyed. Why, dear, I must hang about for Dodo. You may as well know it; he 's in one of his moods.

Paula. (*Under her breath.*) Oh—!

Lady Orreyed. Now, it 's not his fault; it was deadly dull for him while we were playing billiards. Cayley Drummle did ask him to mark, but I stopped that; it 's so easy to make a gentleman look like a billiard-marker. This is just how it always is; if poor old Dodo has nothing to do, he loses count, as you may say.

Paula. Hark!

(*Sir George Orreyed enters, walking slowly and deliberately; he looks pale and watery-eyed.*)

Sir George. (*With mournful distinctness.*) I 'm 'fraid we 've lef' you a grea' deal to yourself to-night, Mrs. Tanqueray. Attra'tions of billiards. I apol'gise. I say, where 's ol' Aubrey?

Paula. My husband has been obliged to go out to a neighbor's house.

Sir George. I want his advice on a rather pressing matter connected with my family—my family. (*Sitting.*) To-morrow will do just as well.

Lady Orreyed. (*To Paula.*) This is the mood I hate so—drivelling about his precious family.

Sir George. The fact is, Mrs. Tanqueray, I am not easy in my min' 'bout the way I am treatin' my poor ol' mother.

Lady Orreyed. (*To Paula.*) Do you hear that? That 's *his* mother, but *my* mother he won't so much as look at!

Sir George. I shall write to Bruton Street firs' thing in the morning.

Lady Orreyed. (*To Paula.*) Mamma has stuck to me through everything—well, you know!

Sir George. I 'll get ol' Aubrey to figure out a letter. I 'll drop line to Uncle Fitz too—dooced shame of the ol' feller to chuck me over in this manner. (*Wiping his eyes.*) All my family have chucked me over.

Lady Orreyed. (*Rising.*) Dodo!

Sir George. Jus' because I 've married beneath me, to be chucked over! Aunt Lydia, the General, Hooky Whitgrave, Lady Sugnall—my own dear sister!—all turn their backs on me. It 's more than I can stan'!

Lady Orreyed. (*Approaching him with dignity.*) Sir George, wish Mrs. Tanqueray good-night at once, and come upstairs. Do you hear me?
Sir George. (*Rising angrily.*) Wha—!
Lady Orreyed. Be quiet!
Sir George. You presoom to order me about!
Lady Orreyed. You 're making an exhibition of yourself!
Sir George. Look 'ere—!
Lady Orreyed. Come along, I tell you!

(*He hesitates, utters a few inarticulate sounds, then snatches up a fragile ornament from the table, and is about to dash it on the ground. Lady Orreyed retreats, and Paula goes to him.*)

Paula. George!

(*He replaces the ornament.*)

Sir George. (*Shaking Paula's hand.*) Good-ni', Mrs. Tanqueray.
Lady Orreyed. (*To Paula.*) Good-night, darling. Wish Aubrey good-night for me. Now Dodo?

(*She goes out.*)

Sir George. (*To Paula.*) I say, are you goin' to sit up for ol' Aubrey?
Paula. Yes.
Sir George. Shall I keep you comp'ny?
Paula. No, thank you, George.
Sir George. Sure?
Paula. Yes, sure.
Sir George. (*Shaking hands.*) Good-night again.
Paula. Good-night.

(*She turns away. He goes out, steadying himself carefully. Drummle appears outside the window, smoking.*)

Drummle. (*Looking into the room and seeing Paula.*) My last cigar. Where 's Aubrey?
Paula. Gone down to The Warren, to see Mrs. Cortelyon home.
Drummle. (*Entering the room.*) Eh? Did you say Mrs. Cortelyon?
Paula. Yes. She has brought Ellean back.
Drummle. Bless my soul! Why?
Paula. I—I 'm too tired to tell you, Cayley. If you stroll along the lane you 'll meet Aubrey. Get the news from him.
Drummle. (*Going up to the window.*) Yes, yes. (*Returning to Paula.*) I don't want to bother you, only—the anxious old woman, you know. Are you and Aubrey—?
Paula. Good friends again?
Drummle. (*Nodding.*) Um.
Paula. (*Giving him her hand.*) Quite, Cayley, quite.
Drummle. (*Retaining her hand.*) That 's capital. As I 'm off so early to-morrow morning, let me say now—thank you for your hospitality.

(*He bends over her hand gallantly, then goes out by the window.*)

Paula. (*To herself.*) "Are you and Aubrey—?" "Good friends again?" "Yes." "Quite, Cayley, quite."

(*There is a brief pause, then Aubrey enters hurriedly, wearing a light overcoat and carrying a cap.*)

Aubrey. Paula dear! Have you seen Ellean?
Paula. I found her here when I came down.
Aubrey. She—she 's told you?
Paula. Yes, Aubrey.
Aubrey. It 's extraordinary, isn't it! Not that somebody should fall in love with Ellean, or that Ellean herself should fall in love. All that 's natural enough and was bound to happen, I suppose, sooner or later. But this young fellow! You know his history?
Paula. His history?
Aubrey. You remember the papers were full of his name a few months ago?
Paula. Oh, yes.
Aubrey. The man 's as brave as a lion, there 's no doubt about that; and, at the same time, he 's like a big good-natured school-boy, Mrs. Cortelyon says. Have you ever pictured the kind of man Ellean would marry some day?
Paula. I can't say that I have.
Aubrey. A grave, sedate fellow I 've thought about—hah! She has fallen in love with the way in which Ardale practically laid down his life to save those poor people shut up in the Residency. (*Taking off his coat.*) Well, I suppose if a man can do that sort of thing, one ought to be content. And yet— (*Throwing his coat on the settee.*) I should have met him to-night, but he 'd gone out. Paula dear, tell me how you look upon this business.
Paula. Yes, I will—I must. To begin with, I—I 've seen Mr. Ardale.
Aubrey. Captain Ardale?
Paula. Captain Ardale.

Aubrey. Seen him?

Paula. While you were away he came up here, through our grounds, to try to get a word with Ellean. I made her fetch him in and present him to me.

Aubrey. (*Frowning.*) Doesn't Captain Ardale know there 's a lodge and a front door to this place? Never mind! What is your impression of him?

Paula. Aubrey, do you recollect my bringing you a letter—a letter giving you an account of myself—to the Albany late one night—the night before we got married?

Aubrey. A letter?

Paula. You burnt it; don't you know?

Aubrey. Yes; I know.

Paula. His name was in that letter.

Aubrey. (*Going back from her slowly, and staring at her.*) I don't understand.

Paula. Well—Ardale and I once kept house together. (*He remains silent, not moving.*) Why don't you strike me? Hit me in the face—I 'd rather you did! Hurt me! hurt me!

Aubrey. (*After a pause.*) What did you—and this man—say to each other—just now?

Paula. I—hardly—know.

Aubrey. Think!

Paula. The end of it all was that I—I told him I must inform you of—what had happened . . . he didn't want me to do that . . . I declared that I would . . . he dared me to. (*Breaking down.*) Let me alone!—oh!

Aubrey. Where was my daughter while this went on?

Paula. I—I had sent her out of the room . . . that is all right.

Aubrey. Yes, yes—yes, yes.

(*He turns his head towards the door.*)

Paula. Who 's that?

(*A servant enters with a letter.*)

Servant. The coachman has just run up with this from The Warren, sir. (*Aubrey takes the letter.*) It 's for Mrs. Tanqueray, sir; there 's no answer.

(*The servant withdraws. Aubrey goes to Paula and drops the letter into her lap; she opens it with uncertain hands.*)

Paula. (*Reading it to herself.*) It 's from—him. He 's going away—or gone—I think. (*Rising in a weak way.*) What does it say? I never could make out his writing.

(*She gives the letter to Aubrey, and stands near him, looking at the letter over his shoulder as he reads.*)

Aubrey. (*Reading.*) "I shall be in Paris by to-morrow evening. Shall wait there, at Meurice's, for a week, ready to receive any communication you or your husband may address to me. Please invent some explanation to Ellean. Mrs. Tanqueray, for God's sake, do what you can for me."

(*Paula and Aubrey speak in low voices, both still looking at the letter.*)

Paula. Has he left The Warren, I wonder, already?

Aubrey. That doesn't matter.

Paula. No; but I can picture him going quietly off. Very likely he 's walking on to Bridgeford or Cottering to-night, to get the first train in the morning. A pleasant stroll for him.

Aubrey. We 'll reckon he 's gone, that 's enough.

Paula. That isn't to be answered in any way?

Aubrey. Silence will answer that.

Paula. He 'll soon recover his spirits, I know.

Aubrey. You know. (*Offering her the letter.*) You don't want this, I suppose?

Paula. No.

Aubrey. It 's done with—done with.

(*He tears the letter into small pieces. She has dropped the envelope; she searches for it, finds it, and gives it to him.*)

Paula. Here!

Aubrey. (*Looking at the remnants of the letter.*) This is no good; I must burn it.

Paula. Burn it in your room.

Aubrey. Yes.

Paula. Put it in your pocket for now.

Aubrey. Yes.

(*He does so. Ellean enters, and they both turn, guiltily, and stare at her.*)

Ellean. (*After a short silence, wonderingly.*) Papa—

Aubrey. What do you want, Ellean?

Ellean. I heard from Willis that you had come in; I only want to wish you good-night. (*Paula steals away, without looking back.*) What 's the matter? Ah! Of course, Paula has told you about Captain Ardale?

Aubrey. Well?

Ellean. Have you and he met?

Aubrey. No.

Ellean. You are angry with him; so was

I. But to-morrow when he calls and expresses his regret—to-morrow—

Aubrey. Ellean—Ellean!

Ellean. Yes, papa?

Aubrey. I—I can't let you see this man again. (*He walks away from her in a paroxysm of distress, then, after a moment or two, he returns to her and takes her to his arms.*) Ellean! my child!

Ellean. (*Releasing herself.*) What has happened, papa? What is it?

Aubrey. (*Thinking out his words deliberately.*) Something has occurred, something has come to my knowledge, in relation to Captain Ardale, which puts any further acquaintanceship between you two out of the question.

Ellean. Any further acquaintanceship . . . out of the question?

Aubrey. Yes.

(*Advancing to her quickly, but she shrinks from him.*)

Ellean. No, no—I am quite well. (*After a short pause.*) It 's not an hour ago since Mrs. Cortelyon left you and me together here; you had nothing to urge against Captain Ardale then.

Aubrey. No.

Ellean. You don't know each other; you haven't even seen him this evening. Father!

Aubrey. I have told you he and I have not met.

Ellean. Mrs. Cortelyon couldn't have spoken against him to you just now. No, no, no; she 's too good a friend to both of us. Aren't you going to give me some explanation? You can't take this position towards me—towards Captain Ardale—without affording me the fullest explanation.

Aubrey. Ellean, there are circumstances connected with Captain Ardale's career which you had better remain ignorant of. It must be sufficient for you that I consider these circumstances render him unfit to be your husband.

Ellean. Father!

Aubrey. You must trust me, Ellean; you must try to understand the depth of my love for you and the—the agony it gives me to hurt you. You must trust me.

Ellean. I will, father; but you must trust me a little too. Circumstances connected with Captain Ardale's career?

Aubrey. Yes.

Ellean. When he presents himself here to-morrow of course you will see him and let him defend himself?

Aubrey. Captain Ardale will not be here to-morrow.

Ellean. Not! You have stopped his coming here?

Aubrey. Indirectly—yes.

Ellean. But just now he was talking to me at that window! Nothing had taken place then! And since then nothing can have—! Oh! Why—you have heard something against him from Paula.

Aubrey. From—Paula!

Ellean. She knows him.

Aubrey. She has told you so?

Ellean. When I introduced Captain Ardale to her she said she had met him in London. Of course! It is Paula who has done this!

Aubrey. (*In a hard voice.*) I—I hope you—you 'll refrain from rushing at conclusions. There 's nothing to be gained by trying to avoid the main point, which is that you must drive Captain Ardale out of your thoughts. Understand that! You 're able to obtain comfort from your religion, aren't you? I 'm glad to think that 's so. I talk to you in a harsh way, Ellean, but I feel your pain almost as acutely as you do. (*Going to the door.*) I—I can't say anything more to you to-night.

Ellean. Father! (*He pauses at the door.*) Father, I 'm obliged to ask you this; there 's no help for it—I 've no mother to go to. Does what you have heard about Captain Ardale concern the time when he led a wild, a dissolute life in London?

Aubrey. (*Returning to her slowly and staring at her.*) Explain yourself!

Ellean. He has been quite honest with me. One day—in Paris—he confessed to me—what a man's life is—what his life had been.

Aubrey. (*Under his breath.*) Oh!

Ellean. He offered to go away, not to approach me again.

Aubrey. And you—you accepted his view of what a man's life is?

Ellean. As far as *I* could forgive him, I forgave him.

Aubrey. (*With a groan.*) Why, when was it you left us? It hasn't taken you long to get your robe "just a little dusty at the hem"!

Ellean. What do you mean?

Aubrey. Hah! A few weeks ago my one

great desire was to keep you ignorant of evil.

Ellean. Father, it is impossible to be ignorant of evil. Instinct, common instinct, teaches us what is good and bad. Surely I am none the worse for knowing what is wicked and detesting it!

Aubrey. Detesting it! Why, you love this fellow!

Ellean. Ah, you don't understand! I have simply judged Captain Ardale as we all pray to be judged. I have lived in imagination through that one week in India when he deliberately offered his life back to God to save those wretched, desperate people. In his whole career I see now nothing but that one week; those few hours bring him nearer the saints, I believe, than fifty uneventful years of mere blamelessness would have done! And so, father, if Paula has reported anything to Captain Ardale's discredit—

Aubrey. Paula—!

Ellean. It must be Paula; it can't be anybody else.

Aubrey. You—you 'll please keep Paula out of the question. Finally, Ellean, understand me—I have made up my mind.

(*Again going to the door.*)

Ellean. But wait—listen! I have made up my mind also.

Aubrey. Ah! I recognise your mother in you now!

Ellean. You need not speak against my mother because you are angry with me!

Aubrey. I—I hardly know what I 'm saying to you. In the morning—in the morning—

(*He goes out. She remains standing, and turns her head to listen. Then, after a moment's hesitation she goes softly to the window, and looks out under the verandah.*)

Ellean. (*In a whisper.*) Paula! Paula!

(*Paula appears outside the window and steps into the room; her face is white and drawn, her hair is a little disordered.*)

Paula. (*Huskily.*) Well?

Ellean. Have you been under the verandah all the while—listening?

Paula. N—no.

Ellean. You *have* overheard us—I see you have. And it *is* you who have been speaking to my father against Captain Ardale. Isn't it? Paula, why don't you own it or deny it?

Paula. Oh, I—I don't mind owning it; why should I?

Ellean. Ah! You seem to have been very, very eager to tell your tale.

Paula. No, I wasn't eager, Ellean. I 'd have given something not to have had to do it. I wasn't eager.

Ellean. Not! Oh, I think you might safely have spared us all for a little while.

Paula. But, Ellean, you forget I—I am your stepmother. It was my—my duty—to tell your father what I—what I knew—

Ellean. What you knew! Why, after all, what can you know? You can only speak from gossip, report, hearsay! How is it possible that you—! (*She stops abruptly. The two women stand staring at each other for a moment; then Ellean backs away from Paula slowly.*) Paula!

Paula. What—what 's the matter?

Ellean. You—you knew Captain Ardale in London!

Paula. Why—what do you mean?

Ellean. Oh!

(*She makes for the door, but Paula catches her by the wrist.*)

Paula. You shall tell me what you mean!

Ellean. Ah! (*Suddenly, looking fixedly into Paula's face.*) You know what I mean.

Paula. You accuse me!

Ellean. It 's in your face!

Paula. (*Hoarsely.*) You—you think I 'm—that sort of creature, do you?

Ellean. Let me go!

Paula. Answer me! You 've always hated me! (*Shaking her.*) Out with it!

Ellean. You hurt me!

Paula. You 've always hated me! You shall answer me!

Ellean. Well, then, I have always—always—

Paula. What?

Ellean. I have always known what you were!

Paula. Ah! Who—who told you?

Ellean. Nobody but yourself. From the first moment I saw you I knew you were altogether unlike the good women I 'd left; directly I saw you I knew what my father had done. You 've wondered why I 've turned from you! There—that 's the reason! Oh, but this is a horrible way for the truth to come home to everyone! Oh!

Paula. It 's a lie! It 's all a lie! (*Forcing Ellean down upon her knees.*) You shall beg my pardon for it. (*Ellean utters a loud shriek of terror.*) Ellean, I 'm a good woman! I swear I am! I 've always been a good woman! You dare to say I 've ever been anything else! It 's a lie! (*Throwing her off violently.*)

(*Aubrey re-enters.*)

Aubrey. Paula! (*Paula staggers back as Aubrey advances. Raising Ellean.*) What 's this? What 's this?

Ellean. (*Faintly.*) Nothing. It—it 's my fault. Father, I—I don't wish to see Captain Ardale again.

(*She goes out, Aubrey slowly following her to the door.*)

Paula. Aubrey, she—she guesses.

Aubrey. Guesses?

Paula. About me—and Ardale.

Aubrey. About you—and Ardale?

Paula. She says she suspected my character from the beginning . . . that 's why she 's always kept me at a distance . . . and now she sees through—

(*She falters; he helps her to the ottoman, where she sits.*)

Aubrey. (*Bending over her.*) Paula, you must have said something—admitted something—

Paula. I don't think so. It—it 's in my face.

Aubrey. What?

Paula. She tells me so. She 's right! I 'm tainted through and through; anybody can see it, anybody can find it out. You said much the same to me to-night.

Aubrey. If she has got this idea into her head we must drive it out, that 's all. We must take steps to— What shall we do? We had better—better— What—what?

(*Sitting and staring before him.*)

Paula. Ellean! So meek, so demure! You 've often said she reminded you of her mother. Yes, I know now what your first marriage was like.

Aubrey We must drive this idea out of her head. We 'll do something. What shall we do?

Paula. She 's a regular woman too. She could forgive *him* easily enough—but *me!* That 's just a woman!

Aubrey. What *can* we do?

Paula. Why, nothing! She 'd have no difficulty in following up her suspicions. Suspicions! You should have seen how she looked at me! (*He buries his head in his hands. There is silence for a time, then she rises slowly, and goes and sits beside him.*) Aubrey.

Aubrey. Yes.

Paula. I 'm very sorry.

(*Without meeting her eyes, he lays his hand on her arm for a moment.*)

Aubrey. Well, we must look things straight in the face. (*Glancing around.*) At any rate, we 've done with this.

Paula. I suppose so. (*After a brief pause.*) Of course, she and I can't live under the same roof any more. You know she kissed me to-night, of her own accord.

Aubrey. I asked her to alter towards you.

Paula. That was it, then.

Aubrey. I—I'm sorry I sent her away.

Paula. It was my fault; I made it necessary.

Aubrey. Perhaps now she 'll propose to return to the convent,—well, she must.

Paula. Would you like to keep her with you and—and leave me?

Aubrey. Paula—!

Paula. You needn't be afraid I 'd go back to—what I was. I couldn't.

Aubrey. S-sh, for God's sake! We—you and I—we 'll get out of this place . . . what a fool I was to come here again!

Paula. You lived here with your first wife!

Aubrey. We 'll get out of this place and go abroad again, and begin afresh.

Paula. Begin afresh?

Aubrey. There 's no reason why the future shouldn't be happy for us—no reason that I can see—

Paula. Aubrey!

Aubrey. Yes?

Paula. You 'll never forget this, you know.

Aubrey. This?

Paula. To-night, and everything that 's led up to it. Our coming here, Ellean, our quarrels—cat and dog!—Mrs. Cortelyon, the Orreyeds, this man! What an everlasting nightmare for you!

Aubrey. Oh, we can forget it, if we choose.

Paula. That was always your cry. How *can* one do it!

Aubrey. We 'll make our calculations solely for the future, talk about the future, think about the future.

Paula. I believe the future is only the past again, entered through another gate.

Aubrey. That 's an awful belief.

Paula. To-night proves it. You must see now that, do what we will, go where we will, you 'll be continually reminded of—what I was. I see it.

Aubrey. You 're frightened to-night; meeting this man has frightened you. But that sort of thing isn't likely to recur. The world isn't quite so small as all that.

Paula. Isn't it! The only great distances it contains are those we carry within ourselves—the distances that separate husbands and wives, for instance. And so it 'll be with us. You 'll do your best—oh, I know that—you 're a good fellow. But circumstances will be too strong for you in the end, mark my words.

Aubrey. Paula—!

Paula. Of course I 'm pretty now—I 'm pretty still—and a pretty woman, whatever else she may be, is always—well, endurable. But even now I notice that the lines of my face are getting deeper; so are the hollows about my eyes. Yes, my face is covered with little shadows that usen't to be there. Oh, I know I 'm "going off." I hate paint and dye and those messes, but, by-and-by, I shall drift the way of the others; I sha'n't be able to help myself. And then, some day—perhaps very suddenly, under a queer, fantastic light at night or in the glare of the morning—that horrid, irresistible truth that physical repulsion forces on men and women will come to you, and you 'll sicken at me.

Aubrey. I—!

Paula. You 'll see me then, at last, with other people's eyes; you 'll see me just as your daughter does now, as all wholesome folks see women like me. And I shall have no weapon to fight with—not one serviceable little bit of prettiness left me to defend myself with! A worn-out creature—broken up, very likely, some time before I ought to be—my hair bright, my eyes dull, my body too thin or too stout, my cheeks raddled and ruddled—a ghost, a wreck, a caricature, a candle that gutters, call such an end what you like! Oh, Aubrey, what shall I be able to say to you then? And this is the future you talk about! I know it—I know it! (*He is still sitting staring forward; she rocks herself to and fro as if in pain.*) Oh, Aubrey! Oh! Oh!

Aubrey. Paula—!

(*Trying to comfort her.*)

Paula. Oh, and I wanted so much to sleep to-night! (*Laying her head upon his shoulder. From the distance, in the garden, there comes the sound of Drummle's voice; he is singing as he approaches the house.*) That 's Cayley, coming back from The Warren. (*Starting up.*) He doesn't know, evidently. I—I won't see him!

(*She goes out quickly. Drummle's voice comes nearer. Aubrey rouses himself and snatches up a book from the table, making a pretence of reading. After a moment or two, Drummle appears at the window and looks in.*)

Drummle. Aha! my dear chap!

Aubrey. Cayley?

Drummle. (*Coming into the room.*) I went down to The Warren after you.

Aubrey. Yes?

Drummle. Missed you. I 've been gossiping with Mrs. Cortelyon. Confound you, I 've heard the news!

Aubrey. What have you heard?

Drummle. What have I heard! Why—Ellean and young Ardale. (*Looking at Aubrey keenly.*) My dear Aubrey! Alice is under the impression that you are inclined to look on the affair favourably.

Aubrey. (*Rising and advancing to Drummle.*) You 've not—met—Captain Ardale?

Drummle. No. Why do you ask? By-the-by, I don't know that I need tell you—but it 's rather strange. He 's not at The Warren to-night.

Aubrey. No?

Drummle. He left the house half an hour ago, to stroll about the lanes; just now a note came from him, a scribble in pencil, simply telling Alice that she would receive a letter from him to-morrow. What 's the matter? There 's nothing very wrong, is there? My dear chap, pray forgive me if I 'm asking too much.

Aubrey. Cayley, you—you urged me to send her away!

Drummle. Ellean! Yes, yes. But—but—by all accounts this is quite an eligible young fellow. Alice has been giving me the history—

Aubrey. Curse him! (*Hurling his book to the floor.*) Curse him! Yes, I do curse him—him and his class! Perhaps I curse myself too in doing it. He has only led "a man's life"—just as I, how many of us, have done! The misery he has brought on me and mine it 's likely enough we, in our time, have helped to bring on others by this leading "a man's life!" But I do curse him for all that. My God, *I 've* nothing more to fear—I 've paid *my* fine! And so I can curse him in safety. Curse him! Curse him!

Drummle. In Heaven's name, tell me what 's happened.

Aubrey. (*Gripping Drummle's arm.*) Paula! Paula!

Drummle. What?

Aubrey. They met to-night here. They—they—they 're not strangers to each other.

Drummle. Aubrey!

Aubrey. Curse him! My poor, wretched wife! My poor, wretched wife!

(*The door opens and Ellean appears. The two men turn to her. There is a moment's silence.*)

Ellean. Father . . . father . . . !

Aubrey. Ellean?

Ellean. I—I want you. (*He goes to her.*) Father . . . go to Paula! (*He looks into her face, startled.*) Quickly—quickly! (*He passes her to go out; she seizes his arm, with a cry.*) No, no; don't go!

(*He shakes her off and goes. Ellean staggers back towards Drummle.*)

Drummle. (*To Ellean.*) What do you mean? What do you mean?

Ellean. I—I went to her room—to tell her I was sorry for something I had said to her. And I *was* sorry—I *was* sorry. I heard the fall. I—I 've seen her. It 's horrible.

Drummle. She—she has—!

Ellean. Killed—herself? Yes—yes. So everybody will say. But I know—I helped to kill her. If I 'd only been merciful!

(*She faints upon the ottoman. He pauses for a moment irresolutely—then he goes to the door, opens it, and stands looking out.*)

THE END.

BIBLIOGRAPHY

GENERAL WORKS

Bradbrook, M. C. *Elizabethan Stage Conditions.* 1931.
Cambridge History of English Literature. 1907–17.
Chambers, E. K. *Mediæval Stage.* 2 vols. 1903. *Elizabethan Stage.* 4 vols. 1923.
Clarence, R. *Stage Cyclopædia.* 1909 (on stage history and performances of plays).
Collier, J. P. *History of English Dramatic Poetry.* New ed. 3 vols. 1879.
Cunliffe, J. W. *Modern English Playwrights.* 1927.
Dickinson, T. H. *Contemporary Drama of England.* 1931.
Dictionary of National Biography (for biography and bibliography).
Dobrée, B. *Restoration Comedy.* 1924. *Restoration Tragedy.* 1929.
Fleay, F. G. *Biographical Chronicle of the English Drama, 1559–1642.* 2 vols. 1891. *Chronicle History of the English Stage, 1559–1642.* 1890.
Krutch, J. W. *Comedy and Conscience after the Restoration.* 1924.
Neilson, W. A. *Chief Elizabethan Dramatists.* 1911 (a collection).
Nettleton, G. H. *English Drama of the Restoration and Eighteenth Century.* 1914.
Nicoll, A. *History of Restoration Drama.* 1923. *History of Early Eighteenth Century Drama.* 1925. *History of Late Eighteenth Century Drama.* 1927. *History of Early Nineteenth Century Drama.* 2 vols. 1930.
Palmer, J. *Comedy of Manners.* 1913.
Schelling, F. E. *Elizabethan Drama.* 2 vols. 1908.
Spencer, H. *Elizabethan Plays* (a collection). 1933.
Swinburne, A. C. *Age of Shakespeare.* 1908.
Thaler, A. *Shakspere to Sheridan.* 1922.
Thorndike, A. H. *Shakespeare's Theatre.* 1916. *Tragedy.* 1908. *English Comedy.* 1929.
Tupper, F. and J. W. *Representative English Dramas from Dryden to Sheridan.* 1934 (a collection).

I

THE MIRACLE PLAY

Adams, J. Q. *Chief Pre-Shakespearean Dramas.* 1924.
Bates, K. L. *English Religious Drama.* 1893.
Deimling, G. *Chester Plays.* Early English Text Society. Ex. Ser. LXXII. 1893.
England, G. *Towneley Plays.* E. E. T. S. Ex. Ser. LXXI. 1897.
Gayley, C. M. *Plays of Our Forefathers.* 1907.
Halliwell-Phillipps, J. O. *Ludus Coventriæ.* Shakespeare Society Publications. 1841.
Manly, J. M. *Specimens of Pre-Shakespearean Drama.* 2 vols. 1897 (the source of the present texts).
Pollard, A. W. *English Miracle Plays, Moralities, and Interludes.* Fifth ed. 1909.
Smith, L. T. *York Mystery Plays.* 1885.
Wright, T. *Chester Plays,* Shakespeare Soc. Publ. 2 vols. 1843–7.

Examples of the miracle play, other than the three herein printed, may be found in Manly and in Adams. Modernized versions of various early plays, including most of those in this book, are in C. G. Child, *Second Shepherds' Play* (Riverside Literature Ser.) [1910].

THE MORALITY

Mackenzie, W. R. *English Moralities.* 1914. *Origin of the English Morality.* Washington Univ. Studies, vol. II. pt. ii. no. 2. 1915.
Everyman. Ed. W. W. Greg. Bang's *Materialen zur kunde des älteren englischen Dramas.* vol. IV. 1904 (the source of the present text). Ed. F. Sidgwick. 1902. Also in the *Everyman's Library,* vol. 381. Modernized by C. G. Child (see above).

For the relations between *Everyman* and the Dutch play *Elckerlijc,* see two articles by J. M. Manly and F. A. Wood on *Elckerlijc-Everyman: The Question of Priority,* in *Modern Philology,* Oct. 1900, vol. VIII. Other works are mentioned under the preceding heading.

Other moralities may be found in Manly and Adams; also other short early plays ("Interludes") of a more secular character.

II

JOHN LYLY

Bond, R. W. *Complete Works of John Lyly.* 3 vols. 1902 (the source of the present text).
Child, C. G. *John Lyly and Euphuism. Münchener Beiträge.* vol. VII. 1904.
Feuillerat, A. *John Lyly.* 1910.

Other plays of Lyly to be recommended are *Endymion* and *Sapho and Phao.*

Other plays showing the new classical influence are Sackville and Norton's *Gorboduc*, and Udall's *Ralph Roister Doister*.

CHRISTOPHER MARLOWE

Collected editions: R. H. Case, and others. *Works and Life of Christopher Marlowe.* 6 vols. 1930–3. C. F. T. Brooke. 1910. H. Ellis. *Mermaid* ed. 1887. W. L. Phelps. *Masterpieces of the English Drama.* 1912. *Plays and Poems* in the *Everyman's Library,* vol. 383.

Edward II. Ed. A. W. Verity. *Temple Dramatists.* 1896. W. D. Briggs. 1914.

Baker, G. P. *Dramatic Technique in Marlowe,* in *Essays and Studies by Members of the English Association,* vol. IV. 1913.

Boas, F. S. *Marlowe and his Circle,* 2nd ed. 1931.

Eccles, M. *Marlowe in London.* 1934.

Ellis-Fermor, U. M. *Christopher Marlowe.* 1927.

Hotson, J. L. *Death of Marlowe.* 1925.

Ingram, J. H. *Christopher Marlowe and his Associates.* 1904.

Schelling, F. E. *English Chronicle Play.* 1902.

(Present text based on Neilson's, collated with Brooke's.)

Other chronicle-plays are Bale's *Kyng Johan* and Sackville and Norton's *Gorboduc* (forerunners of the type), the anonymous *Troublesome Reign of King John,* Heywood's *Edward IV* and *If You Know not Me You Know Nobody,* Ford's *Perkin Warbeck.*

THOMAS DEKKER

Collected editions: J. Pearson, 4 vols. 1873. Rhys, E. *Mermaid* ed. 1895.

Shoemakers' Holiday. A. F. Lange (in Gayley's *Representative English Comedies.* vol. III. 1914).

Grosart, A. B. *The Non-Dramatic Works of Thomas Dekker.* 5 vols. 1884–6.

Hunt, Mary L. *Thomas Dekker: A Study.* 1911.

(Present text based on Neilson's, collated with Lange's.)

Other comedies of London life are *Eastward Ho!* by Jonson, Chapman and Marston, Middleton's *A Mad World My Masters, A Chaste Maid in Cheapside, A Trick to Catch the Old One,* Fletcher's *Monsieur Thomas* and *Wit Without Money.*

THOMAS HEYWOOD

Collected editions: J. Pearson. 6 vols. 1874. A. W. Verity. *Mermaid* ed. 1888.

The Captives. In Bullen's *Old Plays.* vol. IV. 1883.

Clark, A. M. *Thomas Heywood.* 1931.

A Woman Killed with Kindness. Ed. A. W. Ward. *Temple Dramatists.* 1897.

(Present text based on Neilson's, collated with Pearson's and Verity's.)

Other examples of domestic drama are: *Arden of Feversham, How a Man May Choose a Good Wife from a Bad,* Heywood's *The English Traveller* and *Fortune by Land and Sea,* Middleton and Rowley's *A Fair Quarrel.*

BEN JONSON

Collected editions: C. H. Herford and P. Simpson, 1925–. W. Gifford. 9 vols. 1816. F. Cunningham. 9 vols. 1871–5. B. Nicholson. *Mermaid* ed. 3 vols. 1893–4. E. Rhys. *Masterpieces of the English Drama. Everyman's Library,* vols. 489, 490. Several of the plays have been edited in *Yale Studies in English.*

The Alchemist. Ed. C. H. Hathaway. *Yale Studies in English.* 1903. Ed. with *Eastward Ho!* by F. E. Schelling. *Belles Lettres Ser.* 1903.

Castelain, M. *Ben Jonson: L'Homme et l'Œuvre.* 1907.

Koeppel, E. *Ben Jonson's Wirkung auf zeitgenössische Dramatiker. Anglistische Forschungen.* 1906. *Quellenstudien zu den Dramen Ben Jonson's.* 1895.

Palmer, J. *Ben Jonson.* 1934.

Swinburne, A. C. *A Study of Ben Jonson.* 1889.

Symonds, J. A. *Ben Jonson.* 1886.

Woodbridge, E. *Studies in Jonson's Comedy.* 1898.

(Present text based on Neilson's, collated with Schelling's.)

A reading of *The Alchemist* may be supplemented by that of others of Jonson's plays: *Every Man in His Humor, Sejanus, Volpone, Epicene, Bartholomew Fair.* Massinger's *A New Way to Pay Old Debts* shows his influence.

BEAUMONT AND FLETCHER

Collected editions: A. H. Bullen, Variorum ed. 1904, etc. A. Glover and A. R. Waller. 10 vols. 1905–12. F. E. Schelling. *Masterpieces of the English Drama.* 1912. *Select Plays,* in *Everyman's Library,* vol. 506. J. St. L. Strachey. *Mermaid* ed. 2 vols. 1887.

Philaster. Ed. F. S. Boas. *Temple Dramatists.* 1898. A. H. Thorndike. *Belles Lettres Ser.* 1906.

Gayley, C. M. *Beaumont the Dramatist.* 1914.

Hatcher, O. L. *John Fletcher, a Study in Dramatic Method.* 1905.

Macaulay, G. C. *Francis Beaumont, a Critical Study.* 1883.

Oliphant, E. H. C. *The Plays of Beaumont and Fletcher.* 1927.

Thorndike, A. H. *The Influence of Beaumont and Fletcher on Shakespeare.* 1901.

(Both present texts are based on Neilson's, collated with Thorndike's for *Philaster,* and Glover and Waller's for *Wild Goose Chase.*)

Other good examples of tragi-comedy are:

The Two Noble Kinsmen, attributed to Shakespeare and Fletcher, Beaumont and Fletcher's *King and No King*, Fletcher's *The Chances* and *The Loyal Subject*, Heywood's *A Challenge for Beauty*, Massinger's *The Maid of Honor* and *The Great Duke of Florence*, Middleton and Rowley's *The Spanish Gipsy*, Shirley's *The Coronation* and *The Royal Master*, D'Avenant's *Love and Honor*.

Other good examples of high comedy, pointing toward Restoration comedy, are Shirley's *Lady of Pleasure* and *Hyde Park*.

JOHN WEBSTER

Collected editions: F. L. Lucas. 4 vols. 1928. A. Dyce. 4 vols. 1830. W. Hazlitt. 4 vols. 1857.

The Duchess of Malfi and *The White Devil*. Ed. M. W. Sampson. *Belles Lettres Ser.* 1904. J. A. Symonds. *Mermaid* ed. 1888. A. H. Thorndike. *Masterpieces of the English Drama*. 1912.

Brooke, Rupert. *John Webster and the Elizabethan Drama*. 1917.

Gosse, E. *John Webster*, in *Seventeenth Century Studies*. 1883.

Stoll, E. E. *John Webster, the Periods of His Work*. 1905.

(Present text based on Neilson's, collated with Sampson's and Thorndike's.)

The most important early tragedy of blood or revenge is Kyd's *Spanish Tragedy*. Other examples of romantic tragedy are the following: Beaumont and Fletcher's *The Maid's Tragedy*, Fletcher's *Bonduca* and *Valentinian*, Marston's *The Insatiate Countess*, Tourneur's *The Revenger's Tragedy*, Middleton's *Women Beware Women*, Webster's *The White Devil*, Massinger's *The Virgin Martyr* and *The Bondman*, Ford's *The Broken Heart*, Shirley's *The Traitor* and *The Cardinal*.

MIDDLETON AND ROWLEY

Collected editions of Middleton: A. H. Bullen. 8 vols. 1885–6. H. Ellis. *Mermaid* ed. 2 vols. 1887. M. W. Sampson. *Masterpieces of the English Drama*.

Middleton and Rowley. *The Spanish Gipsy* and *All's Lost by Lust*. Ed. F. C. Morris. *Belles Lettres Ser.* 1908.

Rowley. *All's Lost by Lust*, and *A Shoemaker a Gentleman*. Ed. C. W. Stork. 1910.

Wiggin, P. G. *An Inquiry into the Authorship of the Middleton-Rowley Plays*. 1897.

(Present text based on Neilson's, collated with Ellis'.)

For similar plays see the list for Webster.

III

JOHN DRYDEN

Collected editions: W. Scott and G. Saintsbury. 18 vols. 1882–1893. *Selected Dramas*. Ed. G. R. Noyes, 1910 (the source of the present text). Ed. G. Saintsbury (*Mermaid* ed.), 2 vols.

Dryden's *Essay on Heroic Plays*, in Scott-Saintsbury, vol. IV. and in Noyes.

Chase, L. N. *The English Heroic Play*. 1903.

Eliot, T. S. *John Dryden, the Poet, the Dramatist, the Critic*. 1932.

Saintsbury, G. *Dryden* (*Engl. Men of Letters Ser.*), 1881.

Sherwood, M. *Dryden's Dramatic Theory and Practice* (*Yale Stud. in Engl.* no. 4).

Verrall, A. W. *Lectures on Dryden*. 1914.

The other play of Dryden's best to read is *All for Love*, "regularized" from Shakespeare's *Antony and Cleopatra*.

THOMAS OTWAY

Collected editions: J. C. Ghosh. 2 vols. 1932. M. Summers. 3 vols. 1926. T. Thornton, 3 vols., 1813. Roden Noel. *Mermaid* ed.

Venice Preserved. Ed. C. F. McClumpha (with *The Orphan* and the essential parts of St. Réal's narrative). *Belles Lettres Ser.* 1908 (the source of the present text). Ed. I. Gollancz, *Temple Dramatists*.

Brown, H. F. *Studies in Venetian History*, I. 245–295.

Gosse, E. W. *Seventeenth Century Studies*. 1883.

Otway's *The Orphan* is also characteristic.

WILLIAM CONGREVE

Collected editions: M. Summers. 4 vols. 1923. G. S. Street, 1895. W. Archer, 1912. A. C. Ewald (*Mermaid* ed.).

Gosse, E. W. *Life of Congreve*. 1888.

Lamb, Charles. Essay *On the Artificial Comedy of the Last Century*.

Macaulay, T. B. Essay on *Leigh Hunt's Comic Dramatists of the Restoration*.

Meredith, George. *Essay on Comedy*. 1897.

Thackeray, W. M. *English Humorists*.

The present text is founded on the first edition, 1700. Other similar comedies are Congreve's *Love for Love*, Wycherley's *Country Wife*, Farquhar's *Beaux Stratagem*, and *The Recruiting Officer*.

IV

JOSEPH ADDISON

Works. Ed. G. W. Greene, 6 vols., 1858.

Life, Lucy Aikin, 2 vols., 1843.

Life, W. J. Courthope (*English Men of Letters* Ser.). 1886.

Oliphant, M. *Historical Characters of the Reign of Queen Anne*. 1894.

The present text is founded on the edition of 1721. Another celebrated 18th-century tragedy, in verse, but romantic in character, is John Home's *Douglas*.

RICHARD STEELE

Plays. 4 vols. 1734–40. Ed. G. A. Aitken (*Mermaid* ed.).

Life. Aitken, G. A. 2 vols. 1889.
Life. Dobson, A. (*English Men of Letters* Ser.) 1888.
Bernbaum, E. *Drama of Sensibility.* 1915.
Waterhouse, O. *The Development of English Sentimental Comedy in the Eighteenth Century. Anglia,* XXX. (1907), 137–172, 269–305.

The present text is founded on Aitken's, but with collations (badly needed) from the edition of Edinburgh, 1755.

Later sentimental comedies are Richard Cumberland's *West Indian,* and Hugh Kelly's *False Delicacy.*

HENRY FIELDING

Works, 12 vols. Ed. W. E. Henley. 1902. Ed. G. H. Maynadier. 1903.
Tom Thumb, ed. by Felix Lindner (*Englische Textbibliothek*), 1899 (the source of the present text).
Cross, W. L. *History of Henry Fielding.* 3 vols. 1918.
Lindner, F. *Henry Fieldings dramatische Werke. Litterarische Studie.* 1895.
Godden, G. M. Memoir, 1910.
Dobson, A. Memoir, 1900.

Other burlesques are the Duke of Buckingham's *Rehearsal* (earlier) and Sheridan's *Critic* (later).

GEORGE LILLO

Ward, Sir A. W. *The London Merchant and Fatal Curiosity. Belles Lettres Ser.* 1906 (the source of the present text).
Hudson, W. H. *A Quiet Corner in a Library.* 1915.

OLIVER GOLDSMITH

Miscellaneous Works. Ed. David Masson (Globe edition). 1869.
Poems and Plays. *Everyman's Library,* vol. 415.
The Good Natur'd Man and *She Stoops to Conquer.* Ed. A. Dobson and G. P. Baker (*Belles Lettres Ser.*) 1903.
She Stoops to Conquer. Temple Dramatists.
Life and Adventures of Oliver Goldsmith, J. Forster. 1848.
Life. F. F. Moore. 1910.
Life. R. A. King. 1910.
Memoir. A. Dobson. 1899.
Buckland, E. S. L. (a short monograph) 1910.

The present text is founded on the fifth edition (1773), probably the most authentic. *The Good Natur'd Man* may also be mentioned.

R. B. SHERIDAN

Collected editions: R. C. Rhodes. 1928. *Sheridan's Plays now Printed as he Wrote them,* W. F. Rae, 1902 (the source of the present text). *The Major Dramas of Sheridan,* G. H. Nettleton, 1906. *Everyman's Library,* vol. 95.
The School for Scandal. Temple Dramatists.
Oliphant, M. Life (*English Men of Letters* Ser.). 1898.
Rae, W. F. Biography. 2 vols. 1896.
Rhodes, R. C. *Harlequin Sheridan.* 1933.
Sichel, W. S. *Sheridan, from New and Original Material.* 2 vols. 1909.

The Rivals may also be mentioned.

V

P. B. SHELLEY

Works. Ed. H. B. Forman. 8 vols. 1880. Ed. G. E. Woodberry, 1901. *Everyman's Library,* vols. 257, 258.
The Cenci. Ed. G. E. Woodberry (*Belles Lettres Ser.*). 1909.
Crawford, F. Marion. *Beatrice Cenci; the True Story of a Misunderstood Tragedy. The Century Magazine,* LXXV. 449–466 (Jan. 1908).
Bates, E. S. *A Study of The Cenci.* 1908.
Dowden, E. Life. 2 vols. 1886.

The present text is founded on A. and H. B. Forman's edition, published by the Shelley Society, 1886.

Other fine poetic tragedies of the early part of the century are Sir T. N. Talfourd's *Ion,* and J. S. Knowles' *Virginius.*

EDWARD BULWER-LYTTON

Works. 1840, 1848, 1850. *Dramatic Works, now First Collected,* 1841 (the source of the present text).
The Lady of Lyons. Ed. with others of Bulwer's plays, by R. F. Sharp. 1904.
Life. By his son, 2 vols. 1883. By his grandson, the Earl of Lytton. 2 vols. 1913.

Bulwer's best other play is *Richelieu.*

T. W. ROBERTSON

Principal Dramatic Works, with a Memoir by his Son. 2 vols. 1889.
Pemberton, T. E. *Society and Caste. Belles Lettres Ser.* 1905 (the source of the present text).
Pemberton, T. E. *Life and Writings.* 1893.
Scott, C. *Drama of Yesterday and To-day.* 1899.

OSCAR WILDE

Works (Sunflower ed.), 1909.
Life. R. H. Sherard. 1906.
Ingleby, L. C. *Oscar Wilde* (a study). 1907.
Ransome, A. *Oscar Wilde: A Critical Study.* 1912.

Others of Wilde's comedies are *The Importance of Being Earnest, A Woman of No Importance,* and *An Ideal Husband.*

SIR A. W. PINERO

Hamilton, C. *Social Plays of Arthur Wing Pinero,* ed. with introduction and critical prefaces. 4 vols. 1917–22.
Fyfe, H. H. *Arthur Wing Pinero. Playwright; a Study.* 1902. *Sir Arthur Pinero's Plays and Players.* 1930.